Handbook on the Law of Real Property

Earl P. Hopkins

Alpha Editions

This edition published in 2019

ISBN : 9789353976118

Design and Setting By
Alpha Editions
email - alphaedis@gmail.com

As per information held with us this book is in Public Domain.
This book is a reproduction of an important historical work. Alpha Editions uses the best technology to reproduce historical work in the same manner it was first published to preserve its original nature. Any marks or number seen are left intentionally to preserve its true form.

HANDBOOK

ON THE

LAW OF REAL PROPERTY

BY

EARL P. HOPKINS, A. B., LL. M.

Author of Problems and Quiz on Criminal Law, Contracts, Criminal Procedure, Constitutional Law, etc.

St. Paul, Minn.
WEST PUBLISHING CO.
1896

To

EMLIN McCLAIN, A. M., LL. D.,

Chancellor Law Department State University of Iowa,
this volume is affectionately inscribed.

PREFACE.

This volume is the result of an attempt to put the fundamental rules governing the law of real property into a form as easy of comprehension as possible, and so arranged that investigation of any part may be made with ease, promptness, and certainty. It will be found that many of the seeming technicalities of the subject disappear with the statement of the reasons on which they are based. These reasons are in many cases historical, and therefore as much of the history of the law of real property has been given as is necessary for an understanding of these reasons; but the mere curiosities of English law, and the interesting, but useless, legal antiquities sometimes found in books on this subject, have been excluded. The effort has been to present a clear-cut picture of the English system of real property law as introduced into this country, and, with this as a basis, to explain the effect of the statutory changes which have been made in many parts of that system. To do this, it is first shown to just what kinds of "things owned" the law of real property applies, and then the "equation of estates" is taken up, and carefully worked out. This is the backbone of our whole scheme of land ownership. The black-letter text shows the principles on which estates are classified, and the relation of the various possible interests in land to each other, and to the whole ownership. In following out the discussion under the several principles of classification,—for instance, in treating of future interests,—the essential facts which distinguish the various future estates have been emphasized, and then the incidents common to all future estates treated together, for the sake of clearness and ease of comprehension. So much of the law of persons as is peculiar to real property will be found collected in one chapter. In places where the law has become unsettled from confusion in the use of terms, as in the law of fixtures and the classification of trusts, the terminology adopted has been explained, and then followed throughout. While there has been no attempt to harmonize the cases on fixtures, a classification and working theory has been suggested which it is believed will prove useful. Special attention has been paid to the latest authorities as showing what parts of the law of real property are now in process of growth. The recent "Torren's Title Act," of Illinois, has been explained at some length, because it is in all probability the forerunner of the introduction into this country of some system of registration of title in place of our present system of the registration of conveyances.

E. P. H.

St. Paul, Minn., August 1, 1896.

TABLE OF CONTENTS.

CHAPTER I.

WHAT IS REAL PROPERTY.

Section		Page
1.	Real and Personal Property	1–3
2.	Real Property—Land	3–7
3.	Things Growing on Land	7–10
4.	Fixtures	10–11
5.	What Fixtures Removable	11–22
6.	Time of Removal	22–23
7.	Equitable Conversion	23–24
8.	Personal Interests in Land	24–25

CHAPTER II.

TENURE AND SEISIN.

9.	Tenure	26–31
10.	Seisin	31–32

CHAPTER III.

ESTATES AS TO QUANTITY—FEE SIMPLE.

11.	Estate Defined	33
12.	Classification of Estates	33
13.	Quantity of Estates	34
14–15.	Freehold—Estates of Inheritance	34–35
16.	Fee Simple	35–36
17.	Creation	36–39
18.	Right of User	39
19.	Alienation	39–41

REAL PROP. (vii)

CHAPTER IV.

ESTATES AS TO QUANTITY (Continued)—ESTATES TAIL.

Section		Page
20.	Estates Tail Defined	42–43
21–22.	Classes of Estates Tail	43–44
23.	Origin of Estates Tail	44–47
24–25.	Creation of Estates Tail	47–49
26.	Incidents of Estates Tail	49–50
27.	Duration of Estates Tail	50–52
28.	Tenant in Tail After Possibility of Issue Extinct	52
29–30.	Estates Tail in the United States	52–53
31.	Quasi Entail	53–54

CHAPTER V.

ESTATES AS TO QUANTITY (Continued)—CONVENTIONAL LIFE ESTATES.

32.	Life Estates Defined	55
33.	Creation of Life Estates	55–56
34–36.	Conventional Life Estates	56–58
37.	Incidents of Life Estates	58–67
38–39.	Estates per Autre Vie	67–68

CHAPTER VI.

ESTATES AS TO QUANTITY (Continued)—LEGAL LIFE ESTATES.

40–41.	Legal Life Estates—Estates by Marriage	69–70
42.	Estate during Coverture	70–73
43–44.	Curtesy	73–76
45.	In What Estates	76–79
46.	Incidents	79–80
47.	How Defeated	81–82
48.	Statutory Changes	82–83
49.	Dower—Definition	83–85
50.	In What Estates	86–93
51–52.	Quarantine	94–95
53.	Assignment	95–97
54.	When Value Estimated	97–98
55.	Method of Division	98–99

Section		Page
56.	By Whom Assigned	99–100
57.	Recovery by Action	100–101
58–59.	Incidents	101–102
60.	How Defeated	102–111
61.	Statutory Changes	112
62.	Homestead	112
63.	Who Entitled to Homestead	113–115
64.	Duration of Exemption	115
65.	In What Estates	116–117
66–67.	Amount of Exemption	117–118
68.	How Acquired	118–119
69.	Selection	120
70.	How Lost	120–124
71.	Privileged Debts	124–126
72.	Federal Homestead Act	126–127

CHAPTER VII.

ESTATES AS TO QUANTITY (Continued)—LESS THAN FREEHOLD.

Section		Page
73–75.	Estates for Years	128–129
76.	Creation of Estates for Years	130–134
77.	Rights and Liabilities of Landlord and Tenant	134
78–79.	Rights under Express Covenants	134–137
80–81.	Rights under Implied Covenants	138–141
82.	Rights Independent of Covenants	141–146
83.	Transfer of Estates for Years	147–150
84.	Termination of Estates for Years	150–153
85.	Letting Land on Shares	154–155
86.	Tenancies at Will	155
87.	Creation	155–156
88.	Incidents	156–157
89.	Termination	157–158
90.	Tenancies from Year to Year	158
91.	Creation	158–160
92.	Incidents	160
93.	Termination	161–162
94.	Letting of Lodgings	162–163
95.	Tenancies at Sufferance	163
96.	Creation	163–164
97.	Incidents	164
98.	Termination	165
99.	Licenses	165–167
100.	Revocation of Licenses	167–168

CHAPTER VIII.

ESTATES AS TO QUALITY—ON CONDITION—ON LIMITATION.

Section		Page
101.	Estates as to Quality.................................	169
102.	Estates on Condition.................................	169–170
103–104.	Conditions Precedent and Subsequent..................	170–172
105.	Void Conditions	172–173
106.	Termination of Estates on Condition..................	174–176
107.	Who can Enforce a Forfeiture........................	176–177
108.	Estates on Limitation................................	177–178
109.	Base or Determinable Fees...........................	178–179

CHAPTER IX.

ESTATES AS TO QUALITY (Continued)—MORTGAGES.

110.	Mortgage Defined	180–182
111.	Parties to a Mortgage...............................	182
112.	Nature of a Mortgage................................	182–184
113.	What may be Mortgaged...............................	184–185
114.	Form of a Mortgage..................................	186–194
115.	Rights and Liabilities of Mortgagor and Mortgagee......	194
116.	Nature of Mortgagor's Estate........................	195–196
117.	Possession of Mortgaged Premises....................	196–197
118.	Insurance on Mortgaged Premises.....................	197–199
119.	Accounting by the Mortgagee.........................	199
120.	Debits	199
121.	Credits	200
122.	Annual Rests	200–203
123–124.	Subrogation	203–205
125–126.	Assignment of the Equity of Redemption..............	205–209
127–129.	Assignment of the Mortgage..........................	209–212
130.	Priority of Mortgages and Other Conveyances.........	212–218
131.	Registration	218–227
132.	Discharge of a Mortgage.............................	227
133–134.	Performance	227–231
135.	Merger	231–233
136.	Redemption	233–238
137.	Form of Discharge...................................	238–239
138–139.	Foreclosure	239–242
140.	Kinds of Foreclosure................................	242–250

CHAPTER X.

EQUITABLE ESTATES.

Section		Page
141.	Legal and Equitable Estates	251–252
142.	Use or Trust Defined	252
143–144.	The Statute of Uses	253–254
145.	When the Statute does not Operate	254–257
146.	Classification of Trusts	257
147.	Express Trusts	258
148–149.	Executed and Executory Trusts	258–259
150–151.	Creation of Express Trusts	260–264
152.	Implied Trusts	264–265
153.	Resulting Trusts	265–268
154.	Constructive Trusts	269–271
155–156.	Incidents of Equitable Estates	271–274
157–158.	Charitable Trusts	274–277

CHAPTER XI.

ESTATES AS TO TIME OF ENJOYMENT—FUTURE ESTATES.

159.	Estates as to Time of Enjoyment	279
160.	Future Estates	279
161.	Future Estates at Common Law	279
162.	Reversions	280–281
163.	Possibilities of Reverter	281–282
164–165.	Remainders	282–286
166.	Successive Remainders	286
167.	Cross Remainders	286–287
168.	Alternate Remainders	287
169.	Vested Remainders	288–289
170–173.	Contingent Remainders	289–295
174.	Rule in Shelley's Case	295–298
175.	Future Estates under the Statute of Uses	298
176.	Future Uses	298–299
177.	Springing Uses	299
178.	Shifting Uses	300
179–180.	Future Estates under the Statute of Wills—Executory Devises	300–302
181.	Incidents of Future Estates	302–303
182.	Tenure of Future Estates	303–304
183.	Waste	304

Section		Page
184.	Alienation	305
185.	Descent of Future Estates	306
186–189.	Powers	306–309
190–191.	Creation	309–310
192.	Classes of Powers as to Donee	310
193.	Powers Appendant and in Gross	310–311
194.	Powers Collateral, or Naked Powers	311
195.	Classes of Powers as to Appointee	311
196.	General Powers	312
197.	Special Powers	312–313
198.	Execution	314–319
199–200.	Rights of Creditors	320
201.	Destruction	321–322
202.	Rule against Perpetuities	322–325
203.	Estates Subject to the Rule	325–329
204.	Rule against Perpetuities in the United States	330
205.	Rule against Accumulations	330–331

CHAPTER XII.

ESTATES AS TO NUMBER OF OWNERS—JOINT ESTATES.

206.	Estates as to Number of Owners	332
207.	Joint Estates	332
208.	Joint Tenancies	333–335
209.	Tenancies in Common	335–336
210.	Estates in Co-parcenary	336–337
211–212.	Estates in Entirety	337–339
213.	Estates in Partnership	339–340
214.	Incidents of Joint Estates	340–344
215–216.	Partition	344–347

CHAPTER XIII.

INCORPOREAL HEREDITAMENTS.

217.	Definition and Kinds	348–349
218.	Easements	349–350
219.	Creation	350
220.	By Grant	350–352
221.	By Prescription	352–354
222.	Classification	354–355

Section		Page
223.	Incidents	355–357
224.	Destruction	357–358
225.	Specific Easements	359
226.	Rights of Way	359–361
227.	Highways	361–363
228.	Light and Air	363–364
229–230.	Lateral and Subjacent Support	365–366
231.	Party Walls	366–368
232.	Easements in Water	368–373
233.	Profits à Prendre	373–375
234–235.	Rents	375–378
236.	Franchises	378–380

CHAPTER XIV.

LEGAL CAPACITY TO HOLD AND CONVEY REALTY.

237.	Personal Capacity	381
238.	Infants	382–383
239–240.	Persons of Unsound Mind	383–385
241–242.	Married Women	385–387
243–244.	Aliens	387–388
245.	Corporations	389

CHAPTER XV.

RESTRAINTS ON ALIENATION.

246.	Kinds of Restraints	390
247.	Restraints Imposed by Law	390–392
248.	Restraints in Favor of Creditors	392–394
249.	Restraints Imposed in Creation of Estate	394–397

CHAPTER XVI.

TITLE.

250.	Title Defined	399
251.	Acquisition of Title by State	399–401
252.	Acquisition by Private Persons	401
253.	Grant from the State	401–404
254.	Conveyances	405

TABLE OF CONTENTS.

Section		Page
255.	Common-Law Conveyances	405–409
256.	Conveyances under the Statute of Uses	409–411
257.	Modern Statutory Conveyances	411–412
258.	Registered Titles	412–414
259–260.	Requisites of Deeds	414–415
261.	Property to be Conveyed	415
262.	Words of Conveyance	416–419
263–264.	Description of the Property	419–426
265.	Execution of the Writing	426–432
266.	Delivery and Acceptance	433–436
267.	Acknowledgment	436–438
268.	Witnesses	439
269.	Registry	439–440
270.	Covenants for Title	440–442
271.	Covenant of Seisin	442
272.	When Broken	442
273.	How Broken	442–444
274.	Covenant against Incumbrances	444
275.	How Broken	444–446
276.	Covenant of Warranty	446
277.	How Broken	446
278.	Special Warranty	446–449
279.	Covenant for Further Assurance	449–450
280.	Estoppel	450–456
281.	Adverse Possession	456–470
282.	Accretion	470–472
283.	Devise	472–478
284.	Descent	478–486
285.	Judicial Process	486
286.	Conveyances under Licenses	486–488
287.	Conveyances under Decrees	488–490
288–290.	Tax Titles	490–494
291.	Eminent Domain	494–495

†

HANDBOOK

ON THE

LAW OF REAL PROPERTY.

CHAPTER I.

WHAT IS REAL PROPERTY.

1. Real and Personal Property.
2. Real Property—Land.
3. Things Growing on Land.
4. Fixtures.
5. What Fixtures Removable.
6. Time of Removal.
7. Equitable Conversion.
8. Personal Interests in Land.

REAL AND PERSONAL PROPERTY.

1. Property means things owned, and is divided into:
   (a) Real property, and
   (b) Personal property.

Real and Personal Actions.

For our present purposes, property is divided into two classes,—real property and personal property.[1] The terms come from the old division of the actions given a man deprived of his property into real actions and personal actions. All things which could be recovered in real actions were real property, and all other property

[1] This division, and similar ones in other systems of law, is historical, and not philosophical. See Maine Anc. Law (3d Am. Ed.) p. 266.

was personal.[2] In real actions there was an actual recovery of the land itself, but in personal actions there could be no recovery of the real thing, except in the action of replevin. The person detaining it could not be compelled to deliver the identical thing, but might elect to pay damages.[3] The action was accordingly in personam to obtain damages, and the property involved was called "personal property."

Importance of Distinction between Real and Personal Property.

The principal differences between real and personal property are as follows: On the death of the owner, realty passes at once to the heir or devisee,[4] while personalty goes to the personal representative, and through him to the distributee or legatee.[5] The personal property of a decedent is to be used in paying his debts before his realty.[6] The modes of transferring real and personal property are different. The ownership of realty is now transferred by means of a written instrument, executed with certain prescribed formalities,[7] while personalty passes generally by sale and delivery, without more.[8] So, also, there are different requirements as to the form and recording of mortgages affecting them.[9] Then, again, a transfer of real property is governed by the law of the place where the land is situated,[10] but of personal property by the law of the domicile of the owner.[11] There are differences in form and place of bringing action for damages to lands and to chattels.[12]

---

[2] Co. Litt. 121a, Butler & H. note 1; Bouv. Law Dict. tit. "Real Property." It has been suggested that the term "mixed" be added to cover those things which may be real or personal according to circumstances. Kelke, Real Prop. 4.

[3] Dig. Real Prop. (4th Ed.) 71, note 2.

[4] 1 Woerner, Adm'n, pp. 15, 408.

[5] 1 Woerner, Adm'n, p. 409.

[6] 2 Woerner, Adm'n, p. 1093.

[7] Post, p. 398.

[8] Tiff. Sales, p. 83.

[9] Stim. Am. St. Law, arts. 185–194, 453; post, p. 218; 1 Schouler, Pers. Prop. (2d Ed.) c. 6.

[10] Post, p. 474.

[11] Story, J., in Black v. Zacharie, 3 How. (U. S.) 483, 514; Woerner, Adm'n, p. 131.

[12] 1 Jag. Torts, p. 102 et seq.

There is also a difference as to taxation of the two kinds of property.[13]

Lands, Tenements, and Hereditaments.

At an early period in legal history the two classes of property were distinguished as "lands, tenements, and hereditaments," and "goods and chattels."[14] A tenement is anything which can be holden; that is, anything subject to tenure.[15] Hereditaments are things which can be inherited; that is, which, on the death of the owner intestate, descend to the heir. Personal as well as real property may be a hereditament; for instance, heirlooms, which, though personal property, descend with the inheritance.[16] Thus "tenement" is a broader term than "land," and "hereditament" broader than "tenement." The division of things into movables and immovables by the civil law is not the same as the common-law division of things into personalty and realty.[17]

REAL PROPERTY—LAND.

2. Land, meaning the soil and minerals of the earth, is real property, except:

EXCEPTION—Parts of the land actually severed with intent to make them personalty (p. 7).

Land.

The word "land" is often used as practically synonymous with "realty," and as such it includes not only the soil, but everything attached to it or growing or imbedded in it,[18] extending upward

---

[13] Cooley, Tax'n, pp. 270. 275; Stim. Am. St. Law, arts 33, 35.

[14] 2 Bl. Comm. 16.

[15] 2 Bl. Comm. 16; Potter, J., in Canfield v. Ford, 28 Barb. (N. Y.) 336; Hosmer, C. J., in Mitchell v. Warner, 5 Conn. 518. See post, p. 26.

[16] Id.

[17] Strong v. White, 19 Conn. 238; Dickey, J., in Ohio & M. R. Co. v. Weber, 96 Ill. 448; Penniman v. French, 17 Pick. (Mass.) 404. But see 2 Bl. Comm. 15.

[18] 2 Bl. Comm. 17; Barnett v. Johnson, 15 N. J. Eq. 481; Field v. Barling, 149 Ill. 556, 37 N. E. 850; Ruggles, J., in Mott v. Palmer, 1 N. Y. 564, 569; Isham v. Morgan, 9 Conn. 374. Cf. In re Department of Public Parks, 60 Hun, 576, 14 N. Y. Supp. 347.

indefinitely and downward to the center of the earth, as is expressed by the phrase "Cujus est solum ejus est usque ad cœlum usque ad orcum." [19] Therefore an owner of land may cut off the limbs of trees which hang over his boundary line without committing a tort.[20] (An exception to the rule is seen in the case of the ownership of realty by horizontal divisions, so that one person may own the surface and another have the right to the minerals which are under the surface.[21]) In a more limited sense, land means the soil of the earth, the water upon it, and the minerals, fossils, etc., imbedded in it.[22] Those things, like buildings, which are generally included in the meaning of the term "land," will be discussed separately.

Water.

Running waters are not owned by those who own the land over which they flow. These riparian owners, as they are called, have only an easement in such waters. These rights in water are treated as real property.[23] But standing water and percolations beneath the surface belong to the owner of the soil.[24] In any case a man

---

[19] Slosson, J., in Sherry v. Frecking, 4 Duer (N. Y.) 452, 457; Welles, J., in Aiken v. Benedict, 39 Barb. (N. Y.) 401.

[20] Grandona v. Lovdal, 70 Cal. 161, 11 Pac. 623; Smith, J., in Countryman v. Lighthill, 24 Hun, 406. But he has no right to the fruit on trees overhanging his land. Skinner v. Wilder, 38 Vt. 115; Lyman v. Hale, 11 Conn. 177. When a tree standing on one man's land sends roots into the soil of an adjoining proprietor, the one on whose land the trunk stands owns all the tree and its fruit. Masters v. Pollie, 2 Rolle, 141; Holder v. Coates, 1 Moody & M. 112; Lyman v. Hale, 11 Conn. 177; Hoffman v. Armstrong, 48 N. Y. 201; Skinner v. Wilder, 38 Vt. 115. But, as holding that they are tenants in common, see Waterman v. Soper, 1 Ld. Raym. 737. They are tenants in common when the tree stands on the line. Griffin v. Bixby, 12 N. H. 454; Dubois v. Beaver, 25 N. Y. 123.

[21] Lillibridge v. Coal Co., 143 Pa. St. 293, 22 Atl. 1035; Delaware, L. & W. R. Co. v. Sanderson, 109 Pa. St. 583, 1 Atl. 394; Lee v. Bumgardner, 86 Va. 315, 10 S. E. 3.

[22] 2 Bl. Comm. 17; Smith, C. J., in Johnson v. Richardson, 33 Miss. 462, 464; Ray, C. J., in State v. Pottmeyer, 33 Ind. 402, 403; Williamson v. Jones, 39 W. Va. 231, 19 S. E. 436.

[23] See post, p. 368.

[24] Ocean Grove v. Asbury Park, 40 N. J. Eq. 447, 3 Atl. 168; Village of Brooklyn v. Smith, 104 Ill. 429; Alexander v. U. S., 25 Ct. Cl. 87; Hills v.

has the exclusive right to sail, fish, etc., in water overlying his land.[25] But there are no such exclusive rights in connection with navigable waters,[26] because the title to the soil under them is in the state.[27] This is, however, denied by some cases, which hold the title to the bed of a navigable river to be in the riparian proprietor.[28] Navigable rivers are those which are navigable in fact.[29]

Bishop, 63 Hun, 624, 17 N. Y. Supp. 297; Walker v. Board, 16 Ohio, 540; People v. Platt, 17 Johns. 195.

[25] Shrunk v. Navigation Co., 14 Serg. & R. 70; Reece v. Miller, 8 Q. B. Div. 626; Waters v. Lilley, 4 Pick. 145; McFarlin v. Essex Co., 10 Cush. 304; Com. v. Chapin, 5 Pick. 199; Cobb v. Davenport, 32 N. J. Law, 369; Heckman v. Swett, 107 Cal. 276, 40 Pac. 420.

[26] Carson v. Blazer, 2 Bin. 475; Arnold v. Mundy, 6 N. J. Law, 1; Martin v. Waddell, 16 Pet. 367; McCready v. Virginia, 94 U. S 391, Weston v. Sampson, 8 Cush. 347; Chalker v. Dickinson, 1 Conn. 382; Attorney General v. Chambers, 4 De Gex, M. & G. 206; Sollers v. Sollers (Md.) 26 Atl. 188. And see Bagott v. Orr, 2 Bos. & P. 472; Packard v Ryder, 144 Mass. 440, 11 N. E. 578. But cf. Anon., 1 Camp. 517, note; Blundell v. Catterall, 5 Barn. & Ald. 268; Fleet v. Hegeman, 14 Wend. 42.

[27] Pacific Gas Imp. Co. v. Ellert, 64 Fed. 421; Shively v. Bowlby, 152 U. S. 1, 14 Sup. Ct. 548; Barney v. Keokuk, 94 U. S. 324; Poor v. McClure, 77 Pa. St. 214; Flannagan v. Philadelphia, 42 Pa. St. 219; McManus v. Carmichael, 3 Iowa, 1; Tomlin v. Railway Co., 32 Iowa, 106; Cooley v. Golden, 117 Mo. 33, 23 S. W. 100; Smith v. Levinus, 8 N. Y. 472; People v. Appraisers, 33 N. Y. 461; Rumsey v. Railway Co., 130 N. Y. 88, 28 N. E. 763; Saunders v. Railway Co., 144 N. Y. 75, 38 N. E. 992; State v. Pacific Guano Co., 22 S. C. 50; Bullock v. Wilson, 2 Port. 436; Goodwin v. Thompson, 83 Tenn. 209; Concord Manuf'g Co. v. Robertson, 66 N. H. 1, 25 Atl. 718; Illinois Cent. R. Co. v. Illinois, 146 U. S. 387, 13 Sup. Ct. 110; Wainwright v. McCullough, 63 Pa. St. 66. But cf. Wilson v. Welch, 12 Or. 353, 7 Pac. 341; Coxe v. State, 144 N. Y. 396, 39 N. E. 400. That the title to the bed of such streams is not in the United States, see Pollard v. Hagan, 3 How. 212. A riparian proprietor on a nonnavigable river owns the bed of the stream to the center. Ingraham v. Wilkinson, 4 Pick. (Mass.) 268; Wiggenhorn v. Kountz, 23 Neb. 690, 37 N. W. 603.

[28] Norcross v. Griffiths, 65 Wis. 599, 27 N. W. 606; Olson v. Merrill, 42 Wis. 203; Ensminger v. People, 47 Ill. 384; Middleton v. Pritchard, 4 Ill. 510; Houck v. Yates, 82 Ill. 179; Trustees of Schools v. Schroll, 120 Ill. 509, 12 N. E. 243; Gavit v. Chambers, 3 Ohio, 496; Blanchard v. Porter, 11 Ohio, 139; Commissioners of Canal Fund v. Kempshall, 26 Wend. (N. Y.) 404; Berry v.

[29] See note 29 on following page.

The English rule that only those in which the tide ebbs and flows are navigable does not apply in this country.[30]

Ice.

Ice belongs to the owner of the land over which it is formed,[31] but ice formed on public waters belongs to the one first appropriating it.[32]

Snyder, 3 Bush (Ky.) 266; Brown v. Chadbourne, 31 Me. 9; Keyport, etc., Steamboat Co. v. Farmers' Transp. Co., 18 N. J. Eq. 13; Morgan v. Reading, 3 Smedes & M. (Miss.) 366; Steamboat Magnolia v. Marshall, 39 Miss. 109; Cates v. Wadlington, 1 McCord (S. C.) 580; Mathis v. Board of Assessors, 46 La. Ann. 1570, 16 South. 454; Gibson v. Kelly (Mont.) 39 Pac. 517. Cf. Buttenuth v. Bridge Co., 123 Ill. 535, 17 N. E. 439; Ryan v. Brown, 18 Mich. 196; State v. Black River Phosphate Co., 32 Fla. 82, 13 South. 640; Wood v. Town of Edenton, 115 N. C. 10, 20 S. E. 165.

[29] Weise v. Smith, 3 Or. 445; Rhodes v. Otis, 33 Ala. 578; McManus v. Carmichael, 3 Iowa, 1; Morgan v. King, 35 N. Y. 454; Spring v. Russell, 7 Greenl. (Me.) 273; American River Water Co. v. Amsden, 6 Cal. 443; Jones v. Johnson (Tex. Civ. App.) 25 S. W. 650; Commissioners of Homochitto River v. Withers, 29 Miss. 21; Bayzer v. Mill Co. (Ala.) 16 South. 923; The Daniel Bell, 10 Wall. 557; The Montello, 20 Wall. 430; Chisolm v. Caines, 67 Fed. 285; Stover v. Jack, 60 Pa. St. 339; Heyward v. Mining Co., 42 S. C. 138, 19 S. E. 963, and 20 S. E. 64; Falls Manuf'g Co. v. Oconto River Imp. Co., 87 Wis. 134, 58 N. W. 257. And see Volk v. Eldred, 23 Wis. 410; Lewis v. Coffee Co., 77 Ala. 190; Rowe v. Bridge Corp., 21 Pick. 344; State v. Gilmanton, 14 N. H. 467; People v. Elk River Mill & Lumber Co. (Cal.) 40 Pac. 431; State v. Eason, 114 N. C. 787, 19 S. E. 88. That the stream must be navigable in its natural state, see Jeremy v. Elwell, 5 Ohio Cir. Ct. R. 379; Ten Eyck v. Town of Warwick, 75 Hun, 562, 27 N. Y. Supp. 536.

[30] Black, Const. Law, 124; Weise v. Smith, 3 Or. 445; Wilson v. Forbes, 2 Dev. (N. C.) 30; The Daniel Bell, 10 Wall. 557. Cf. Veazie v. Dwinel, 50 Me. 479; City of Chicago v. McGinn, 51 Ill. 266; People v. Tibbetts, 19 N. Y. 523; Glover v. Powell, 10 N. J. Eq. 211.

[31] State v. Pottmeyer, 33 Ind. 402; Washington Ice Co. v. Shortall, 101 Ill. 46; Brookville & Metamora Hydraulic Co. v. Butler, 91 Ind. 134; Stevens v. Kelley, 78 Me. 445, 6 Atl. 868; Village of Brooklyn v. Smith, 104 Ill. 429. And see Lorman v. Benson, 8 Mich. 18; People's Ice Co. v. The Excelsior, 44 Mich. 229, 6 N. W. 636; Howe v. Andrews, 62 Conn. 398, 26 Atl. 394.

[32] Wood v. Fowler, 26 Kan. 682; Inhabitants of West Roxbury v. Stoddard, 7 Allen, 158; Brastow v. Ice Co., 77 Me. 100; Woodman v. Pitman, 79 Me. 456, 10 Atl. 321; Barrett v. Ice Co., 84 Me. 155, 24 Atl. 802. But cf. McFadden v. Ice Co., 86 Me. 319, 29 Atl. 1068.

Minerals, Fossils, etc.

Unmined minerals, metals, and fossils are realty, and belong to the owner of the land as a part thereof,[33] as does also an aerolite which falls on the land.[34] In England the right to gold and silver mines is in the crown.[35] But the rule does not apply here. The United States and the states own mines as they own other property, —that is, the same as private individuals,—and not by reason of sovereignty.[36]

Exceptions—Things Severed from the Land.

Any of the things which have been enumerated as part of the land, and therefore realty, may become personalty by being severed from the land.[37] This is true of portions of the soil itself.[38]

SAME—THINGS GROWING ON LAND.

3. Everything growing on land is real property, except: EXCEPTIONS—(a) Things constructively severed. (b) Annual crops.

Things Growing on Land—Annual Crops—Trees.

Everything growing upon land, except annual crops [39] is realty [40] until it is made personalty by being severed.[41] The severance,

---

[33] Appeal of Stoughton, 88 Pa. St. 198; Dunham v. Kirkpatrick, 101 Pa. St. 36; Hartwell v. Camman, 10 N. J. Eq. 128.

[34] Goddard v. Winchell, 86 Iowa, 71, 52 N. W. 1124.

[35] If the gold or silver was found together with baser metals, they all belonged to the king if the value of the precious metals was greater than the value of the others. But if the baser metals were more valuable than the gold or silver, then the owner of the soil took both. Case of Mines, Plowd. 310; 3 Kent, Comm. 378, note; 1 Bl. Comm. 294.

[36] Boogs v. Mining Co., 14 Cal. 279; Moore v. Smaw, 17 Cal. 199; 1 Cooley, Bl. Comm. 294, note 4.

[37] Lykens Valley Coal Co. v. Dock, 62 Pa. St. 232; Higgins v. Kusterer, 41 Mich. 318, 2 N. W. 13; In re Clever's Estate, 23 Pittsb. Leg. J. (N. S.) 358; Kier v. Peterson, 41 Pa. St. 357.

[38] See Lacustrine Fertilizer Co. v. Lake Guano & Fertilizer Co., 82 N. Y. 476; Riley v. Water Power Co., 11 Cush. 11.

[39] Which are personalty. Robinson v. Ezzell, 72 N. C. 231; Crine v. Tifts, 65 Ga. 644; Bloom v. Welsh, 27 N. J. Law, 177; Pickens v. Webster, 31 La.

---

[40] See note 40 on following page.   [41] See note 41 on following page.

however, need not be an actual physical act, but may be constructive.[42] For instance, trees and the like can be made personal property by conveying the land and reserving the trees, or by the owner selling the trees as they stand on the land.[43]

Same—Emblements.

The term "emblements" denotes such annual products of the land as have resulted from a tenant's own care and labor, and which he is entitled to take away after his tenancy has ended.[44] Annual crops are all "vegetable products of the earth, as corn, etc.,"[45] which are produced annually [46] by labor, industry, and man-

---

Ann. 870; Brittain v. McKay, 1 Ired. (N. C.) 265; Polley v. Johnson, 52 Kan. 478, 35 Pac. 8; Mabry v. Harp, 53 Kan. 398, 36 Pac. 743. See, also, Wintermute v. Light, 46 Barb. 278; Miller v. Baker, 1 Metc. (Mass.) 27; Butterman v. Albright, 122 N. Y. 484, 25 N. E. 856. But they pass with a conveyance of the land. Backenstoss v. Stahler, 33 Pa. St. 251; Coman v. Thompson, 47 Mich. 22, 10 N. W. 62; Powell v. Rich, 41 Ill. 466; Smith v. Price, 39 Ill. 28; Terhune v. Elberson, 3 N. J. Law, 533; Tripp v. Hasceig, 20 Mich. 254. As to matured crops see 2 Jones, Real Prop. § 1621. And go to a devisee. Dennett v. Hopkinson, 63 Me. 350; Bradner v. Faulkner, 34 N. Y. 347; Mr. Spencer's Case, Winch. 51; Cooper v. Woolfitt, 2 Hurl. & N. 122. As to what are annual crops, see Latham v. Atwood, Cro. Car. 515.

[40] Maples v. Millon, 31 Conn. 598; Batterman v. Albright, 122 N. Y. 484, 25 N. E. 856; Adams v. Beadle, 47 Iowa, 439; Wescott v. Delano, 20 Wis. 514; Cockrill v. Downey, 4 Kan. 426; Brackett v. Goddard, 54 Me. 309.

[41] State v. Moore, 11 Ired. (N. C.) 70. Cf. State v. Stephenson, 2 Bailey (S. C.) 334. But see In re Mulholland's Estate, 154 Pa. St. 491, 26 Atl. 612.

[42] As when owned by one who does not own the land. Jencks v. Smith, 1 N. Y. 90; Dayton v. Vandoozer, 39 Mich. 749; Warren v. Leland, 2 Barb. 613.

[43] Yale v. Seely, 15 Vt. 221; Kingsley v. Holbrook, 45 N. H. 313. But cf. Brackett v. Goddard, 54 Me. 309. As to the requirements of the statute of frauds in relation to the sale of growing trees, see Clark, Cont. p. 106; Green v. Armstrong, 1 Denio, 550; Whitmarsh v. Walker, 1 Metc. (Mass.) 313; Harris v. Frink, 49 N. Y. 24.

[44] Black, Law Dict. "Emblements."

[45] This includes grain. Peacock v. Purvis, 2 Brod & B. 362; Cooper v. Woolfitt, 2 Hurl. & N. 122; Forsythe v. Price, 8 Watts, 282. And the straw. Craig v. Dale, 1 Watts & S. 509. Hemp. Co. Litt. 55a. Hops. Latham v. Atwood, Cro. Car. 515. Clover and artificial grasses. Graves v. Weld, 5

[46] As to teasels, see Graves v. Weld, 5 Barn. & Adol. 105; Kingsbury v. Collins, 4 Bing. 202.

§ 3) THINGS GROWING ON LAND. 9

urance, and are called 'fructus industriales,' " as distinguished from those spontaneous or natural products which are called "fructus naturales." Whenever such crops are planted [47] by one having an interest of uncertain duration in the land, and that interest terminates without his fault before the crops are harvested,[48] there is a right to enter to cultivate, harvest, and remove them.[49] This right is given on the principle that the crops are not planted with any intention to benefit the one next entitled to the land, but with the expectation of reaping them. No one is entitled to emblements who has terminated his estate by his own act.[50] The

---

Barn. & Adol. 105. Contra. Reiff v. Reiff, 64 Pa. St. 134; Evans v. Iglehart, 6 Gill & J. 171. But not growing grasses. Reiff v. Reiff, 64 Pa. St. 134. Nor young trees. Co. Litt. 55a. But turpentine "scrape" may be. Lewis v. McNatt, 65 N. C. 63. And nursery stock. Brooks v. Galster, 51 Barb. 196; King v. Howland, 7 Barb. 263. See, also, Brackett v. Goddard, 54 Me. 309.

[47] The seed must be sown. Mere preparation of the ground is not sufficient. Price v. Pickett, 21 Ala. 741.

[48] Harris v. Frink, 49 N. Y. 24. Therefore a tenant from year to year is entitled to emblements. Clark v. Harvey, 54 Pa. St. 142, Reeder v. Sayre, 70 N. Y. 180. A tenant at will. Davis v. Brocklebank, 9 N. H. 73; Davis v. Thompson, 13 Me. 209; Towne v. Bowers, 81 Mo. 491; Pfanner v. Sturmer, 40 How. Prac. 401; Sherburne v. Jones, 20 Me. 70. And a tenant for life. Poindexter v. Blackburn, 1 Ired. Eq. 286; Perry v. Terrel, 1 Dev. & B. Eq. 441; Hunt v. Watkins, 1 Humph. 497; Thornton v. Burch, 20 Ga. 791; Bradley v. Bailey, 56 Conn. 374, 15 Atl. 746. And his lessees. Bevans v. Briscoe, 4 Har. & J. (Md.) 139. But, when the interest is of definite duration, there is no right to emblements; for instance, under a tenancy for years. Whitmarsh v. Cutting, 10 Johns. 360; Sanders v. Ellington, 77 N. C. 255; Dircks v. Brant, 56 Md. 500; Hendrixson v. Cardwell, 68 Tenn. 389; Gossett v. Drydale, 48 Mo. App. 430. But a custom to the contrary will give the right. Stultz v. Dickey, 5 Bin. (Pa.) 285; Biggs v. Brown, 2 Serg. & R. 14; Templeman v. Biddle, 1 Har. (Del.) 522; Van Doren v. Everitt, 5 N. J. Law, 460; Foster v. Robinson, 6 Ohio St. 90; Clark v. Banks, 6 Houst. 584. Contra, Harris v. Carson, 7 Leigh, 632.

[49] Den v. Humphries, 3 Ired. (N. C.) 362.

[50] Debow v. Colfax, 10 N. J. Law, 128; Samson v. Rose, 65 N. Y. 411; Hawkins v. Skeggs, 10 Humph. (Tenn.) 30; Gregg v. Boyd, 69 Hun, 588, 23 N. Y. Supp. 918; Carney v. Mosher, 97 Mich. 554, 56 N. W. 935; Orland's Case, 5 Coke, 116a; Davis v. Eyton, 7 Bing. 154. Cf. Carpenter v. Jones, 63 Ill. 517. So the right is lost by the assertion of a title paramount. Howell v. Schenck, 24 N. J. Law, 89; King v. Fowler, 14 Pick. 238. As by foreclosure

right to remove crops may be given in any case by express contract.[51] In some states the subject is regulated by statute.[52]

SAME—FIXTURES.

4. Chattels which are annexed to land are called fixtures. Fixtures are either:
   (a) Real fixtures, or those which cannot be lawfully removed by the owner of a limited interest in the land. Real fixtures are real property.
   (b) Chattel fixtures, or those which can be lawfully removed by such an owner. Chattel fixtures are personal property.

Buildings erected upon land and chattels annexed to land or to buildings on the land are called "fixtures."[53] When the annexation is made by the owner in fee of the land, such fixtures become real property.[54] They may, of course, again become personalty by being actually severed from the land with that intent.[55] But, where the annexation is made by the tenant of a less estate than a fee, it is not always easy to determine whether such fixtures become realty or remain personalty. Things annexed by a tenant sometimes become realty, and sometimes do not. The question is of importance, because, if the chattels become realty, they cannot be lawfully severed or removed by the tenant, while if they remain personalty, notwithstanding their annexation, they may be removed by the tenant before or at the expiration of his term. There is great conflict in the cases. The confusion has

---

of a mortgage executed before the lease. Lane v. King, 8 Wend. 584; Downard v. Groff, 40 Iowa, 597; Gilman v. Wills, 66 Me. 273. But see Cassilly v. Rhodes, 12 Ohio, 88. Cf. Lewis v. Klotz, 39 La. Ann. 259, 1 South. 539.

[51] Van Doren v. Everitt, 5 N. J. Law, 460.

[52] 1 Stim. Am. St. Law, §§ 1334, 2064, 3233.

[53] Teaff v. Hewitt, 1 Ohio St. 511; Capen v. Peckham, 35 Conn. 88; Potter v. Cromwell, 40 N. Y. 287; Peirce v. Goddard, 22 Pick. 559.

[54] Harris v. Scovel, 85 Mich. 32, 48 N. W. 173; Dooley v. Crist, 25 Ill. 551; Sampson v. Cotton Mills, 64 Fed. 939. But see Jenkins v. McCurdy, 48 Wis. 630, 4 N. W. 807. And cf. Green, J., in Stevens v. Railway Co., 31 Barb. 597.

[55] Bostwick v. Leach, 3 Day (Conn.) 476; Lee v. Gaskell, 1 Q. B. Div. 700.

arisen largely from a loose use of the word "fixtures." The term has been used in three senses: First, as meaning simply chattels which are annexed to realty, irrespective of whether they may be removed or not; second, as meaning irremovable fixtures; and, third, as meaning removable fixtures.[56] The resulting confusion of the cases is natural. It is hoped to avoid this confusion by calling those fixtures which cannot be lawfully removed "real fixtures," because they have become realty. Fixtures which can be lawfully removed will be called "chattel fixtures," because they remain personal property.[57] They may be taken on execution against the tenant as long as the latter's right to remove them exists.[58]

5. **WHAT FIXTURES REMOVABLE**—Whether a fixture is a real or personal fixture, and lawfully removable, depends on the presumed intention with which it was annexed. This intention is determined with reference to:
(a) **Express contract of the parties** (p. 12).
(b) **Statutory regulation, which conclusively presumes intention** (p. 12).
(c) **Character of the annexation** (p. 13).
(d) **Adaptation of the fixture for use with the realty** (p. 15).
(e) **Nature of the chattels annexed, as:**
   (1) **Trade fixtures** (p. 16).
   (2) **Agricultural fixtures** (p. 17).
   (3) **Domestic fixtures** (p. 18).
(f) **Relation of the party making the annexation to the land, as:**
   (1) **Lessee** (p. 19).
   (2) **Tenant for life or in tail** (p. 19).
   (3) **Owner in fee** (p. 19).

[56] Ewell, Fixt. 1; Tyler, Fixt. 35.
[57] Voorhees v. McGinnis, 48 N. Y. 278; Teaff v. Hewitt, 1 Ohio St. 511.
[58] O'Donnell v. Hitchcock, 118 Mass. 401; Heffner v. Lewis, 73 Pa. St. 302; Fisher v. Saffer, 1 E. D. Smith, 611.

Intention.

The whole subject of fixtures is involved in difficulty, and the cases are in great conflict. The real or chattel character of a fixture is largely a question of fact, and few general rules can be laid down for determining what fixtures are removable.[60] But the tendency of modern cases is to make the intention with which a fixture is annexed the test of its character,[61] and to treat other things as evidence of that intention.[62] It is not, however, a secret intention which controls, but the intention which the law presumes from the acts and situation of the party at the time of making the annexation.[63]

Express Contract.

The parties between whom the question is likely to arise may settle all doubts in advance by express contract.[64] This is, of course, an instance of expressed intention.

Statutory Regulation.

In some states the question of fixtures has been made a matter of legislative enactment, and certain classes of annexations are

[60] Ewell, Fixt. 9.

[61] Farrar v. Chauffetete, 5 Denio (N. Y.) 527; Reynolds v. New York Security & Trust Co., 88 Hun. 569, 34 N. Y. Supp. 890; Hill v. Sewald, 53 Pa. St. 271; Seeger v. Pettit, 77 Pa. St. 437; Meig's Appeal, 62 Pa. St. 28; Hill v. Wentworth, 28 Vt. 428; Jones v. Ramsey, 3 Ill. App. 303; Kelly v. Austin, 46 Ill. 156; Congregational Society v. Fleming, 11 Iowa. 533; Copp v. Swift (Tex. Civ. App.) 26 S. W. 438; McDavid v. Wood, 5 Heisk. (Tenn.) 95; McFadden v. Crawford, 36 W. Va. 671, 15 S. E. 408; Strickland v. Parker, 54 Me. 263; Capen v. Peckham, 35 Conn. 88; Linahan v. Barr, 41 Conn. 471; Equitable Trust Co. v. Christ, 47 Fed. 756.

[62] Ottumwa Woolen Mill Co. v. Hawley, 44 Iowa, 57; Hutchins v. Masterson, 46 Tex. 551.

[63] Rogers v. Brokaw, 25 N. J. Eq. 496. Cf. Linahan v. Barr, 41 Conn. 471.

[64] Hines v. Ament, 43 Mo. 298; Tifft v. Horton, 53 N. Y. 377; Hendy v. Dinkerhoff, 57 Cal. 3; Mott v. Palmer, 1 N. Y. 564. See Ex parte Ames, 1 Low. 561, Fed. Cas. No. 323; Aldrich v. Husband, 131 Mass. 480; Taft v. Stetson, 117 Mass. 471; Hunt v. Iron Co., 97 Mass. 279; Lake Superior Ship Canal, Ry. & Iron Co. v. McCann, 86 Mich. 106, 48 N. W. 692; Lansing Iron & Engine Works v. Walker, 91 Mich. 409, 51 N. W. 1061; Holly Manuf'g Co. v. New Chester Water Co., 48 Fed. 879; Id., 3 C. C. A. 399, 53 Fed. 19; Advance Coal Co. v. Miller, 4 Pa. Dist. R. 352; White's Appeal, 10 Pa. St. 252; Blanchard v. Bowers, 67 Vt. 403, 31 Atl. 848.

§ 5) WHAT FIXTURES REMOVABLE. 13

by statute declared to be real fixtures, and others to be chattel fixtures.[65]

Character of Annexation.

The manner in which a fixture is attached or annexed to the realty is indicative of the intention with which it was placed there. It shows whether it was intended to be permanent or to be subsequently removed.[66] Some cases make the manner of fastening a thing the test of its character as a fixture.[67] By some of these courts a thing does not become a real fixture unless it is so annexed to the land that its severance would cause a considerable injury to the realty.[68] Although annexation is largely a question of fact in each case, it has been held that there may be an attachment of a thing to the land by its weight alone;[69] for instance, a heavy statue on a pedestal,[70] or a dry stone wall.[71]

[65] 1 Stim. Am. St. Law, §§ 2100–2102.

[66] Teaff v. Hewitt, 1 Ohio St. 511; Rogers v. Brokaw, 25 N. J. Eq. 496; Redlon v. Barker, 4 Kan. 445; O'Donnell v. Hitchcock, 118 Mass. 401; Pennybecker v. McDougal, 48 Cal. 160; Cook v. Whiting, 16 Ill. 480; Sayles v. Purifying Co. (Sup.) 16 N. Y. Supp. 555; Jones v. Bull (Tex. Sup.) 19 S. W. 1031; Kendall v. Hathaway, 67 Vt. 122, 30 Atl. 859; Chase v. Box Co., 11 Wash. 377, 39 Pac. 639; Roseville Alta Min. Co. v. Iowa Gulch Min. Co., 15 Colo. 29, 29 Pac. 920; Strickland v. Parker, 54 Me. 263.

[67] Rex v. Otley, 1 Barn. & Adol. 161; Wansbrough v. Maton, 4 Adol. & E. 884; Ex parte Astbury, 4 Ch. App. 630; Wadleigh v. Janvrin, 41 N. H. 503; Carpenter v. Walker, 140 Mass. 416, 5 N. E. 160. But see Landon v. Platt, 34 Conn. 517.

[68] Bewick v. Fletcher, 41 Mich. 625, 3 N. W. 162; Murdock v. Gifford, 18 N. Y. 28; Ford v. Cobb, 20 N. Y. 344; Vanderpoel v. Van Allen, 10 Barb. 157; Whiting v. Brastow, 4 Pick. 310; Swift v. Thompson, 9 Conn. 63; Hunt v. Mullanphy, 1 Mo. 361; Lanphere v. Lowe, 3 Neb. 131; Fullam v. Stearns, 30 Vt. 443; Bartlett v. Wood, 32 Vt. 372. But see Tifft v. Horton, 53 N. Y. 377; Morrison v. Berry, 42 Mich. 389, 4 N. W. 731; Quinby v. Paper Co., 24 N. J. Eq. 260; Degraffenreid v. Scruggs, 4 Humph. (Tenn.) 451; Thresher v. Water Works, 2 Barn. & C. 608.

[69] Smith v. Blake, 96 Mich. 542, 55 N. W. 978; Miller v. Waddingham (Cal.) 25 Pac. 688.

[70] Snedeker v. Warring, 12 N. Y. 170; Oakland Cemetery Co. v. Bancroft, 161 Pa. St. 197, 28 Atl. 1021.

[71] Ewell, Fixt. 31. Cf. Noble v. Sylvester, 42 Vt. 146.

Same—Severance.

Chattels which have become realty by a permanent annexation may nevertheless be converted into personalty again by being severed from the realty by the owner with an intent to produce that effect.[72] A mere intention to sever is not, however, sufficient.[73] This severance need not be actual, but may be constructive, as by the execution of a bill of sale or chattel mortgage.[74] A mere temporary severance, however, though actual, will not change the character of a real fixture.[75] For instance, when machinery is taken from a mill for repairs, it does not thereby become personal property.[76]

Same—Constructive Annexation.

Chattels may become realty by constructive annexation; for instance, keys to a house, storm windows, etc., though not at the time fastened to the house, will pass with a conveyance of the realty.[77] And the same has been held as to saws and belts in a factory,[78] and rolls in an iron mill, though detached.[79] As to whether railway cars are real or personal property the cases are conflicting,[80] but the tendency of late cases is to consider them

---

[72] Morgan v. Varick, 8 Wend. 587; Bliss v. Misner, 4 Thomp. & C. 633; Gardner v. Finley, 19 Barb. 317; Davis v. Emery, 61 Me. 140. See, also, Taylor v. Townsend, 8 Mass. 411.

[73] Bratton v. Clawson, 2 Strob. 478.

[74] Davis v. Emery, 61 Me. 140; Shaw v. Carbrey, 13 Allen (Mass.) 462. See, however, Richardson v. Copeland, 6 Gray (Mass.) 536; Dudley v. Foote, 63 N. H. 57.

[75] Rogers v. Gilinger, 30 Pa. St. 185; Wadleigh v. Janvrin, 41 N. H. 503; Davis v. Emery, 61 Me. 140. So fence boards, though temporarily removed, remain part of the realty, so as to pass to a vendee. Goodrich v. Jones, 2 Hill (N. Y.) 142; McLaughlin v. Johnson, 46 Ill. 163. But see Harris v. Scovel, 85 Mich. 32, 48 N. W. 173.

[76] Wadleigh v. Janvrin, 41 N. H. 503.

[77] Ewell, Fixt. 33. See, also, Wadleigh v. Janvrin, 41 N. H. 503.

[78] Burnside v. Twitchell, 43 N. H. 390; Farrar v. Stackpole, 6 Me. 154.

[79] Voorhis v. Freeman, 2 Watts & S. 116. And see Keating Implement Co. v. Marshall Electric Light & Power Co., 74 Tex. 605, 12 S. W. 489; McFadden v. Crawford, 36 W. Va. 671, 15 S. E. 408.

[80] For cases holding them realty, see Farmers' Loan & Trust Co. v. Hendrickson, 25 Barb. 484; Palmer v. Forbes, 23 Ill. 301; Titus v. Mabee, 25 Ill. 257; Farmers' Loan & Trust Co. v. St. Joseph & D. C. R. Co., 3 Dill. 412, Fed. Cas. No. 4,669; Baker v. Atherton, 15 Pa. Co. Ct. R. 471.

§ 5) WHAT FIXTURES REMOVABLE. 15

personalty,[81] and there are constitutional provisions to this effect in some states.[82]

Adaptation for Use with the Realty.

Another circumstance showing the intention with which a chattel is annexed is its adaptation for use with the realty.[83] Some cases even regard this as a decisive test.[84] The principal application of the rule is to machinery, engines, and boilers in mills and factories, without which the business could not be carried on.[85] The rule is not, however, extended to loose, movable machinery, no matter how complete its adaptation.[86] But such things as duplicate rolls in an iron rolling mill have been held real fixtures, because of their adaptation for use with the mill.[87] The same has been held of pans in salt works,[88] and of shelves, drawers, and

---

[81] See Williamson v. Railway Co., 25 N. J. Eq. 13; Stevens v. Railway Co., 31 Barb. 590; Beardsley v. Bank, 31 Barb. 619; Hoyle v. Railway Co., 54 N. Y. 314; Chicago & N. W. Ry. v. Ft. Howard, 21 Wis. 45; Coe v. Railway Co., 10 Ohio St. 372; Midland Ry. Co. v. State, 11 Ind. App. 433, 38 N. E. 57; Hoyle v. Railway Co., 54 N. Y. 314.

[82] 1 Stim. Am. St. Law, § 468. But there are provisions to the contrary in other states. Id. § 2100.

[83] Burnside v. Twitchell, 43 N. H. 394; Murdock v. Gifford, 18 N. Y. 28; Smith Paper Co. v. Servin, 130 Mass. 511; Ferris v. Quinby, 41 Mich. 202, 2 N. W. 9; Curran v. Smith, 37 Ill. App. 69; Wade v. Brewing Co., 10 Wash. 284, 38 Pac. 1009; Parsons v. Copeland, 38 Me. 537.

[84] Green v. Phillips, 26 Grat. 752; Morris' Appeal, 88 Pa. St. 368; Huston v. Clark, 162 Pa. St. 435, 29 Atl. 866, 868; Shelton v. Ficklin, 32 Grat. 727; Brennan v. Whitaker, 15 Ohio St. 446; Parsons v. Copeland, 38 Me. 537; Huston v. Clark, 3 Pa. Dist. R. 2.

[85] Walker v. Sherman, 20 Wend. 636; Winslow v. Insurance Co., 4 Metc. (Mass.) 306; Voorhees v. McGinnis, 48 N. Y. 278; Christian v. Dripps, 28 Pa. St. 271; Hill v. Hill, 43 Pa. St. 521; Laflin v. Griffiths, 35 Barb. 58; McConnell v. Blood, 123 Mass. 47; Winslow v. Insurance Co., 4 Metc. (Mass.) 306; Curran v. Smith, 37 Ill. App. 69; Keeler v. Keeler, 31 N. J. Eq. 181; Rice v. Adams, 4 Harr. (Del.) 332; Trull v. Fuller, 28 Me. 545; Davenport v. Shants, 43 Vt. 546; Case Manuf'g Co. v. Garven, 45 Ohio St. 289, 13 N. E. 493; Citizens' Bank v. Knapp, 22 La. Ann. 117.

[86] McKim v. Mason, 3 Md. Ch. 186; Cherry v. Arthur, 5 Wash. St. 787, 32 Pac. 744. See Burnside v. Twitchell, 43 N. H. 390.

[87] Voorhis v. Freeman, 2 Watts & S. 116; Pyle v. Pennock, 2 Watts & S. 390.

? Lawton v. Salmon, 1 H. Bl. 259, note.

counters in a retail store.[89] The test of adaptability has also been applied to the rolling stock of railroads, making such fixtures realty.[90]

Nature of the Fixtures—Trade Fixtures.

A valuable aid in determining the intention with which an annexation is made is found in the nature of the thing itself. It is not to be presumed that one engaged in trade or manufacture will attach valuable chattels to the realty, if his interest is of limited or uncertain duration, and intend that the things so annexed shall remain part of the realty. Annexations of this kind are called "trade fixtures," and their removal is permitted with considerable freedom,—in fact, is the rule rather than the exception. Show cases,[91] counters and shelves,[92] engines,[93] boilers,[94] machinery,[95] tanks in a distillery,[96] and even buildings [97] have been held removable as trade fixtures. Within the principle governing trade fixtures come also certain mixed cases where the annexation is

[89] Tabor v. Robinson, 36 Barb. 483. But see, as to an ice chest, Park v. Baker, 7 Allen, 78.

[90] Farmers' Loan & Trust Co. v. Hendrickson, 25 Barb. 484. And see cases cited ante, note 80.

[91] McCall v. Walter, 71 Ga. 287.

[92] Guthrie v. Jones, 108 Mass. 191. But see O'Brien v. Kusterer, 27 Mich. 289.

[93] Cook v. Transportation Co., 1 Denio (N. Y.) 91; Lemar v. Miles, 4 Watts, 330; Robertson v. Corsett, 39 Mich. 777; Crane v. Brigham, 11 N. J. Eq. 29.

[94] Cooper v. Johnson, 143 Mass. 108, 9 N. E. 33; Conrad v. Mining Co., 54 Mich. 249, 20 N. W. 39; Merritt v. Judd, 14 Cal. 60; Kelsey v. Durkee, 33 Barb. 410; Hayes v. Mining Co., 2 Colo. 273.

[95] Holbrook v. Chamberlain, 116 Mass. 155; Moore v. Smith, 24 Ill. 512.

[96] Chidley v. Churchwardens of West Ham, 32 Law T. (N. S.) 486. So vats of a soap boiler, but not partitions, etc., which were put up to complete the house, may be taken on execution. Poole's Case, 1 Salk. 368.

[97] Beers v. St. John, 16 Conn. 322; Walton v. Wray, 54 Iowa, 531, 6 N. W. 742; Kissam v. Barclay, 17 Abb. Prac. 360; Macdonough v. Starbird, 105 Cal. 15, 38 Pac. 510; West N. Car. Ry. v. Deal, 90 N. C. 110; Security Loan & Trust Co. v. Willamette Steam Mills Lumbering & Manuf'g Co., 99 Cal. 636, 34 Pac. 321. But buildings, though erected solely for purposes of trade, may be of so substantial a character that they are irremovable. Whitehead v. Bennett, 27 Law J. Ch. 474. And cf. Felcher v. McMillan, 103 Mich. 494, 61 N. W. 791.

§ 5) WHAT FIXTURES REMOVABLE. 17

made partly for purposes of trade and partly to secure the enjoyment of the demised estate, as in the case of engines erected in a colliery [98] or brickyard, or trees set out in a nursery; [99] or it may be that the fixtures are partly for domestic use and convenience and partly for purposes of trade.[100]

Same—Agricultural Fixtures.

Agricultural fixtures are, as the name shows, those which are used in farming, and consist principally of barns, sheds,[101] and farm machinery, such as cotton gins.[102] In England agricultural fixtures are for the most part irremovable,[103] but the rule is otherwise in many of the United States,[104] though it is not as liberal as in the case of trade fixtures.[105]

Manure made on a farm becomes part of the realty, and cannot be lawfully treated as personalty by one not the owner of the fee,[106] except when it is made from material not obtained on the premises, as in the case of a livery stable.[107] Manure passes with

[98] Lawton v. Lawton, 3 Atk. 12.

[99] King v. Wilcomb, 7 Barb. 263; Miller v. Baker, 1 Metc. (Mass.) 27.

[100] Van Ness v. Pacard, 2 Pet. 137, held that a dwelling house erected by a dairyman and used as accessory to that business was removable. See, also, Wall v. Hinds, 4 Gray, 256; Capehart v. Foster (Minn.) 63 N. W. 257.

[101] Elwes v. Maw, 3 East, 38.

[102] McJunkin v. Dupree, 44 Tex. 500. But see Bond v. Coke, 71 N. C. 97.

[103] See Elwes v. Maw, 3 East, 38, where an agricultural tenant erected several outbuildings of brick and mortar and let them into the ground, he was not permitted to remove them.

[104] Wing v. Gray, 36 Vt. 261; Harkness v. Sears, 26 Ala. 493; Dubois v. Kelly, 10 Barb. 496; Holmes v. Tremper, 20 Johns. 29.

[105] Tyler, Fixt. 271; Perkins v. Swank, 43 Miss. 349; Leland v. Gassett, 17 Vt. 403.

[106] Perry v. Carr, 44 N. H. 118; Hill v. De Rochemont, 48 N. H. 87; Daniels v. Pond, 21 Pick. 367; Middlebrook v. Corwin, 15 Wend. 169. Manure in a heap is personalty, but when scattered upon the ground it becomes part of the realty. Yearworth v. Pierce, Aleyn, 31; Ruckman v. Outwater, 28 N. J. Law, 581; Fay v. Muzzey, 13 Gray, 53; Collier v. Jenks (R. I.) 32 Atl. 208. And see Lassell v. Reed, 6 Greenl. (Me.) 222. It has been held that manure may be taken on execution against a tenant at will without incurring liability to the landlord. Staples v. Emery, 7 Greenl. (Me.) 201.

[107] Carroll v. Newton, 17 How. Prac. 189; Plumer v. Plumer, 30 N. H. 558; Gallagher v. Shipley, 24 Md. 418. So manure made after the sale of a

REAL PROP.—2

the freehold to a vendee of the land.[108] It cannot be taken on execution against the owner of the fee unless he has made it personal property by being severed.[109]

Same—Domestic Fixtures.

Certain annexations may be removed as domestic fixtures, which comprise such things as stoves,[110] wash tubs fastened to the house,[111] gas fixtures,[112] chimney-pieces,[113] marble shelves,[114] and sheds.[115] In the annexation of domestic fixtures, it is held that there is a stronger presumption of an intention to make them permanent additions to the realty than with either trade or agricultural fixtures, and consequently less freedom of removal.[116]

farm, where the vendor retains possession during the winter, but carries on no farming operations, may be sold by him. Needham v. Allison, 24 N. H. 355. But see Lassell v. Reed, 6 Greenl. (Me.) 222. Cf. Lewis v. Jones, 17 Pa. St. 262.

[108] Goodrich v. Jones, 2 Hill (N. Y.) 142; Daniels v. Pond, 21 Pick. (Mass.) 367; Kittredge v. Woods, 3 N. H. 503. Contra, Ruckman v. Outwater, 28 N. J. Law, 581. It may be reserved by a separate agreement. Strong v. Doyle, 110 Mass. 92.

[109] Sawyer v. Twiss, 26 N. H. 345.

[110] Towne v. Fiske, 127 Mass. 125; Gaffield v. Hapgood, 17 Pick. 192. Grates. Aldine Manuf'g Co. v. Barnard, 84 Mich. 632. 48 N. W. 280; Gaffield v. Hapgood, 17 Pick. 192. And steam valves and radiators. National Bank v. North, 160 Pa. St. 303, 28 Atl. 694.

[111] Wall v. Hinds, 4 Gray, 256. See, also, Kirchman v. Lapp (Super. Ct.) 19 N. Y. Supp. 831.

[112] Vaughen v. Haldeman, 33 Pa. St. 522; Kirchman v. Lapp (Super. Ct.) 19 N. Y. Supp. 831; Manning v. Ogden, 70 Hun, 399, 24 N. Y. Supp. 70. Contra, Johnson's Ex'r v. Wiseman's Ex'r, 4 Metc. (Ky.) 357.

[113] Winn v. Ingilby, 5 Barn. & Ald. 625. But see Spinney v. Barbe, 43 Ill. App. 585. So pictures and glasses put up instead of wainscot were given to the heir. Cave v. Cave, 2 Vern. 508. And see D'Eyncourt v. Gregory, L. R. 3 Eq. 382; Cahn v. Hewsey, 8 Misc. Rep. 384, 29 N. Y. Supp. 1107.

[114] Weston v. Weston, 102 Mass. 514. And see Sweet v. Myers, 3 S. D. 324, 53 N. W. 187.

[115] Krouse v. Ross, 1 Cranch, C. C. 368, Fed. Cas. No. 7,940.

[116] See Buckland v. Butterfield, 2 Brod. & B. 54 (where a conservatory and pinery, erected for ornament and attached to the dwelling house, were held part of the realty); Jenkins v. Gething, 2 Johns. & H. 520; State v. Elliot, 11 N. H. 540. But in Grymes v. Boweren, 6 Bing. 437, a tenant was permitted to remove a pump erected for domestic use, though quite firmly annexed to the freehold.

Party Making the Annexation.

The most important consideration of all in determining the probable intention with which an annexation is made is the relation of the person making the annexation to the land and the duration of his interest in it. The parties between whom the question arises may be put into three classes, as follows: (1) Lessor against lessee; (2) reversioner or remainder-man against tenant for life or in tail; (3) heir against personal representative of an owner in fee simple, vendee against vendor, and mortgagee against mortgagor. Any other persons between whom the question arises may easily be shown to stand in the same relation to each other as those in one of these three classes.[117] It is obvious that one having only a short term of years in certain land will be less likely to make erections thereon with the intention of having them become permanent than if his interest was that of an owner in fee simple. Therefore a tenant is accorded considerable freedom in removing fixtures, and the tendency of the modern cases seems to be towards a greater liberality in his favor, because the presumption is very strong that he made the annexation in order to secure more complete enjoyment during his term, and not with the intention of benefiting his landlord.[118] Persons having life estates are in many cases tenants in dower or by curtesy, and therefore often closely related to the one entitled to the next estate. It is accordingly not diffi-

[117] For other relations, equivalent to the first class, see Raymond v. White, 7 Cow. 319; Heffner v. Lewis, 73 Pa. St. 302; Havens v. Electric Light Co. (Sup.) 17 N. Y. Supp. 580. And for others, equivalent to the third class, see Parsons v. Copeland, 38 Me. 537; Bigler v. Bank, 26 Hun, 520; Cresson v. Stout, 17 Johns. 116; Gale v. Ward, 14 Mass. 352; Farrar v. Chauffetete, 5 Denio (N. Y.) 527; Goddard v. Chase, 7 Mass. 432; Tudor Iron Works v. Hitt, 49 Mo. App. 472.

[118] Youngblood v. Eubank, 68 Ga. 630; Thomas v. Crout, 5 Bush (Ky.) 37; Ambs v. Hill, 10 Mo. App. 108; Osgood v. Howard, 6 Greenl. (Me.) 452. Cf. Deane v. Hutchinson, 40 N. J. Eq. 83, 2 Atl. 292. For cases of trade fixtures, see Raymond v. White, 7 Cow. 319; Andrews v. Button Co., 132 N. Y. 348, 30 N. E. 831; Conrad v. Mining Co., 54 Mich. 249, 20 N. W. 39; Hayes v. Mining Co., 2 Colo. 273; Powell v. Bergner, 47 Ill. App. 33; Berger v. Hoerner, 36 Ill. App. 360; Lang v. Cox, 40 Ind. 142; Western N. C. Ry. Co. v. Deal, 90 N. C. 110; Cubbins v. Ayres, 4 Lea (Tenn.) 329; Brown v. Power Co., 55 Fed. 229. Domestic fixtures. Jenkins v. Gething, 2 Johns. & H. 520; Gaffield v. Hapgood, 17 Pick. 192.

cult to suppose an intention to make permanent annexations for the benefit of the estate.[119] And the same reasons hold good in the case of a tenant in tail. The assignees of life tenants and of tenants in tail are in the same situation, and are therefore accorded no greater freedom in removing fixtures.[120] On the same principle, when a question of fixtures arises between the heir and personal representative of an owner in fee, the presumptions are all in favor of the former,[121] and the same is true between vendee and vendor,[122] or mortgagee and mortgagor,[123] because a tenant

[119] D'Eyncourt v. Gregory, L. R. 3 Eq. 382; Cannon v. Hare, 1 Tenn. Ch. 22; Cave v. Cave, 2 Vern. 508; Lawton v. Salmon, 1 H. Bl. 260, note; McCullough v. Irvine's Ex'rs, 13 Pa. St. 438; Gledden v. Bennett, 43 N. H. 306; Demby v. Parse, 53 Ark. 526, 14 S. W. 899; Lord Ellenborough, C. J., in Elwes v. Maw, 3 East, 51. Some erections are, however, held removable. Lawton v. Lawton, 3 Atk. 12; Dudley v. Warde, Amb. 113; Overman v. Sasser, 107 N. C. 432, 12 S. E. 64; Clemence v Steere, 1 R. I. 272. So far as a tenant for life is individually concerned, "his estate lasts forever. It is only terminated by his death. He can have no personal interest in the removal of fixtures at the end of his term. The only interest he can possibly take in the matter is the welfare of his heirs. Whatever addition he makes to the permanent betterment of the estate, he will be permitted to enjoy all his life, and therefore there is the same reason for finding that he intended such betterment to last and continue through his term as there is in case of the owner in fee." Thomp. Fixt. & Easem. 31.

[120] White v. Arndt, 1 Whart. 91; Haflick v. Stober, 11 Ohio St. 482; Demby v. Parse, 53 Ark. 526, 14 S. W. 899; Elam v. Parkhill, 60 Tex. 581.

[121] Henry's Case, Y. B. 20 Hen. VII. p. 13, pl. 24; Anon., Y. B. 21 Hen. VII. p. 26, pl. 4; Lawton v. Salmon, 1 H. Bl. 259, note; Fisher v. Dixon, 12 Clark & F. 312; Bain v. Brand, 1 App. Cas. 762; Gibbs v. Estey, 15 Gray (Mass.) 587; Stillman v. Flenniken, 58 Iowa, 450, 10 N. W. 842; Kinsell v. Billings, 35 Iowa, 154; McDavid v. Wood, 5 Heisk. (Tenn.) 95. So of an annexation by a tenant in common. Baldwin v. Breed, 16 Conn. 60. Contra, Squier v. Mayer, Freem. Ch. 249. But see, as to trade fixtures, Murdock v. Gifford, 18 N. Y. 28.

[122] Noble v. Bosworth, 19 Pick. (Mass.) 314; Tabor v. Robinson, 36 Barb. 483; Voorhees v. McGinnis, 48 N. Y. 278; Miller v. Plumb, 6 Cow. 665; Leonard v. Clough, 133 N. Y. 292, 31 N. E. 93; Coher v. Kyler, 27 Mo. 122; Hutchins v. Masterson, 46 Tex. 551; Pea v. Pea, 35 Ind. 387. But see Leonard v. Clough, 59 Hun, 627, 14 N. Y. Supp. 339. So one making erections on land which he holds under contract to purchase cannot remove them if he fails to carry out the contract. McLaughlin v. Nash, 14 Allen,

[123] See note 123 on following page.

§ 5)   WHAT FIXTURES REMOVABLE.   21

in fee is not likely to make annexations with any intention of removing them, but rather for the benefit of his property. It is not true, however, that all chattels pass with the realty, although annexed by one owning the fee. For instance, carpets, pictures, and gas fixtures retain their character as personal property.[124] When chattels are annexed to the realty by a stranger without authority they become the property of the owner of the soil.[125] But, if put there in good faith, the enhanced value of the land may be set off in an action for rent.[126] The same rules apply to trees

136; Hinkley v. Black, 70 Me. 473; Ogden v. Stock, 34 Ill. 522; Michigan Mut. Life Ins. Co. v. Cronk, 93 Mich. 49, 52 N. W. 1035; Miller v. Waddingham (Cal.) 25 Pac. 688; Hemenway v. Cutler, 51 Me. 407.

[123] Winslow v. Insurance Co., 4 Metc. (Mass.) 306; Ex parte Astbury, 4 Ch. App. 630; Climie v. Wood, L. R. 4 Exch. 328; Clary v. Owen, 15 Gray (Mass.) 522; Brennan v. Whitaker, 15 Ohio St. 446; Davenport v. Shants, 43 Vt. 546; Burnside v. Twitchell, 43 N. H. 390; Tifft v. Horton, 53 N. Y. 377; McConnell v. Blood, 123 Mass. 47; Rogers v. Brokaw, 25 N. J. Eq. 496; Woodham v. Bank, 48 Minn. 67, 50 N. W. 1015. As to machinery annexed for trade purposes, see Helm v. Gilroy, 20 Or. 517, 26 Pac. 851; Hathaway v. Insurance Co., 58 Hun, 602, 11 N. Y. Supp. 413; Calumet Iron & Steel Co. v. Lathrop, 36 Ill. App. 249; Phelan v. Boyd (Tex. Sup.) 14 S. W. 290. But for trade fixtures held removable, see Rogers v. Brokaw, 25 N. J. Eq. 496; Johnson v. Mosher, 82 Iowa, 29, 47 N. W. 996. Cf. Padgett v. Cleveland, 33 S. C. 339, 11 S. E. 1069. The mortgagee is entitled to fixtures erected after the execution of the mortgage as against an assignee of the mortgagor. Walmsley v. Milne, 7 C. B. (N. S.) 115; Holland v. Hodgson, L. R. 7 C. P. 328; Winslow v. Insurance Co., 4 Metc. (Mass.) 306; Cooper v. Harvey, 62 Hun, 618, 16 N. Y. Supp. 660; Snedeker v. Warring, 12 N. Y. 170; Kloess v. Katt, 40 Ill. App. 99; Seedhouse v. Broward, 34 Fla. 509, 16 South. 425; Sands v. Pfeiffer, 10 Cal. 258.

[124] Jarechi v. Society, 79 Pa. St. 403; McKeage v. Insurance Co., 81 N. Y. 38; Towne v. Fiske, 127 Mass. 125. Cf., however, Central Trust & Safe Deposit Co. v. Cincinnati Grand Hotel Co., 26 Wkly. Law Bul. 149.

[125] Madigan v. McCarthy, 108 Mass. 376; Inhabitants of First Parish in Sudbury v. Jones, 8 Cush. 184; Huebschmann v. McHenry, 29 Wis. 655. Otherwise, when the owner consents. Fuller v. Tabor, 39 Me. 519; Gregg v. Railway Co., 48 Mo. App. 494; Merchants' Nat. Bank v Stanton (Minn.) 56 N. W. 821. But see Histe v. Buckley, 8 Ohio Cir. Ct. R. 470.

[126] Green v. Biddle, 8 Wheat. 1; Hylton v. Brown, 2 Wash. C. C. 165, Fed. Cas. No. 6,983; Jackson v. Loomis, 4 Cow. 168. And see Oregon Railway & Nav. Co. v. Mosier, 14 Or. 519, 13 Pac. 300.

set out and crops planted by one not the owner.[127] It is seen from the foregoing that the presumption of chattel character of a fixture is stronger in the first than in the second class, and in the second than in the third;[128] and consequently cases holding fixtures removable against a mortgagee or vendee in fee are authority to the same effect against a remainder-man or a lessor, and so in the other classes; and cases holding fixtures irremovable against a lessee are authority for holding them irremovable against any other person.

6. **TIME OF REMOVAL.**—Where the tenant's interest is of definite duration, the removal must be before its termination. Where the interest is of indefinite duration, the removal must be within a reasonable time after its termination.

Where the interest of the one making the annexation is of definite duration, the right to remove fixtures must be exercised before the termination of that interest or an abandonment of the right will be presumed;[129] and in cases of an interest of uncertain duration, the removal must be within a reasonable time after the interest comes to an end.[130] These rules do not apply when

[127] Simpkins v. Rogers, 15 Ill. 397; Mitchell v. Billingsley, 17 Ala. 391; Boyer v. Williams, 5 Mo. 335.
[128] Van Ness v. Pacard, 2 Pet. 137.
[129] Sampson v. Cotton Mills, 64 Fed. 939; White v. Arndt, 1 Whart. (Pa.) 91; Mackintosh v. Trotter, 3 Mees. & W. 184; Gibson v. Railway Co., 32 Law J. Ch. 337; Saint v. Pilley, L. R. 10 Exch. 137; Haflick v. Stober, 11 Ohio St. 482; Friedlander v. Ryder, 30 Neb. 783, 47 N. W. 83; Davis v. Buffum, 51 Me. 160; Josslyn v. McCabe, 46 Wis. 591, 1 N. W. 174; Thomas v. Crout, 5 Bush (Ky.) 37. Cf. Dubois v. Kelly, 10 Barb. 496. If a lessee mortgages tenant's fixtures, and afterwards surrenders his lease, the mortgagee has a right to enter and sever them. London & Westminster Loan & Discount Co. v. Drake, 6 C. B. (N. S.) 798. See, also, McKenzie v. City of Lexington, 4 Dana (Ky.) 130.
[130] Where a landlord enters on his tenant for breach of condition, and thereby puts an end to the tenancy, the right to remove fixtures is gone. Pugh v. Arton, L. R. 8 Eq. 626; Weeton v. Woodcock, 7 Mees. & W. 14; Ex parte Brook, 10 Ch. Div. 100; Morey v. Hoyt, 62 Conn. 542, 26 Atl. 127. Cf. Dunman v. Railway Co. (Tex. Civ. App.) 26 S. W. 304; Antoni v. Bel-

the removal of the fixtures is wrongfully prevented by injunction or otherwise.[131] And a tenant holding over with the consent of the landlord does not lose his right of removal.[132] Fixtures wrongfully removed may be recovered by the person entitled to them in the hands of any one [133] not a bona fide purchaser.[134]

SAME—EQUITABLE CONVERSION.

7. Equitable conversion is a notional change in the character of property, by means of which
  (a) Personal property is made real and
  (b) Real property is made personal.

"Money directed to be employed in the purchase of land,[135] and land directed to be sold and turned into money,[136] are to be con-

---

knap, 102 Mass. 193; Cooper v. Johnson, 143 Mass. 108, 9 N. E. 33; Berger v. Hoerner, 36 Ill. App. 360; Sullivan v. Carberry, 67 Me. 531; Turner v. Kennedy, 57 Minn. 104, 58 N. W. 823; Martin v. Roe, 7 El. & Bl. 237.

[131] Bircher v. Parker, 40 Mo. 118.

[132] Lewis v. Pier Co., 125 N. Y. 341, 26 N. E. 301; Torrey v. Burnett, 38 N. J. Law, 457; Fitzgerald v. Anderson, 81 Wis. 341, 51 N. W. 554; Brown v. Power Co., 55 Fed. 229. Cf. Free v. Stuart, 39 Neb. 220, 57 N. W. 991; Thorn v. Sutherland, 123 N. Y. 236, 25 N. E. 362. But by accepting a new lease, with different terms and covenants, he may lose the right. Watriss v. Bank, 124 Mass. 571; Loughran v. Ross, 45 N. Y. 792; Talbot v. Cruger, 81 Hun, 504, 30 N. Y. Supp. 1011; McIver v. Estabrook, 134 Mass. 550; Wright v. Macdonell (Tex. Civ. App.) 27 S. W. 1024; Merritt v. Judd, 14 Cal. 60. But see Kerr v. Kingsbury, 39 Mich. 150.

[133] Ogden v. Stock, 34 Ill. 522; Central Branch R. Co. v. Fritz, 20 Kan. 430; Huebschmann v. McHenry, 29 Wis. 655; Sands v. Pfeiffer, 10 Cal. 259. Cf. Salter v. Sample, 71 Ill. 430; Hartwell v. Kelly, 117 Mass. 235. But see 2 Jones, Real Prop. § 1760.

[134] Peirce v. Goddard, 22 Pick. 559.

[135] Kettleby v. Atwood, 1 Vern. 298; on rehearing, Id. 471; Chichester v. Bickerstaff, 2 Vern. 295; Sweetapple v. Bindon, Id. 526; Scudmore v. Scudmore, Prec. Ch. 544; Craig v. Leslie, 3 Wheat. 563; in re Becker's Estate, 150 Pa. St. 524, 24 Atl. 687.

[136] Fletcher v. Ashburner, 1 Brown, Ch. 497; Steed v. Preece, L. R. 18 Eq. 192; Evans v. Kingsberry, 2 Rand. (Va.) 120; Turner v. Davis, 41 Ark. 270; Fluke v. Fluke, 16 N. J. Eq. 478; Roy v. Monroe, 47 N. J. Eq. 356, 20

sidered as that species of property into which they are directed to be converted; and this in whatever manner the direction is given,—whether by will,[137] by way of contract, marriage articles, settlement, or otherwise;[138] and whether the money is actually deposited or only covenanted to be paid; whether the land is actually conveyed or only agreed to be conveyed."[139] This subject properly belongs however to works on equity.[140]

8. SAME—PERSONAL INTERESTS IN LAND.

There are also certain interests in land which are treated as personal property. For instance, chattels real,[141] which are estates less than freehold, or leaseholds.[142] Long terms of years are, however, in some states made real property by statute.[143] These and other personal interests in land, such as a mortgage debt, will be treated of in other connections. Corporate shares are not real property, even though the property which constitutes the capital of the corporation is realty. The ownership of this

Atl. 481; Crane v. Bolles, 49 N. J. Eq. 373, 24 Atl. 237; In re Blauvelt (Sup.) 15 N. Y. Supp. 586; Fraser v. Trustees, 124 N. Y. 479, 26 N. E. 1034; Bolton v. Myers, 146 N. Y. 257, 40 N. E. 737. But see In re Machemer's Estate, 140 Pa. St. 544, 21 Atl. 441.

[137] Fletcher v. Ashburner, 1 Brown, Ch. 497; Craig v. Leslie, 3 Wheat. 563; Jones' Ex'rs v. Jones, 13 N. J. Eq. 236; Hyman v. Devereux, 63 N. C. 624; Magruder v. Peter, 11 Gill & J. 217; Massey v. Modawell, 73 Ala. 421; Dodge v. Williams, 46 Wis. 70, 1 N. W. 92, and 50 N. W. 1103; Gould v. Orphan Asylum, 46 Wis. 106, 50 N. W. 422; Underwood v. Curtis, 127 N. Y. 523, 28 N. E. 585; Davenport v. Kirkland, 156 Ill. 169, 40 N. E. 304. The direction must be positive. Darlington v. Darlington, 160 Pa. St. 65, 28 Atl. 503; In re Ingersoll's Estate, 167 Pa. St. 536, 31 Atl. 858, 859.

[138] In re Hirst's Estate, 147 Pa. St. 319, 23 Atl. 455; Dobson's Estate, 11 Phila. 81; Evans v. Kingsberry, 2 Rand. (Va.) 120; Masterson v. Pullen, 62 Ala. 145; Turner v. Davis, 41 Ark. 270; Hunter v. Anderson, 152 Pa. St. 386, 25 Atl. 538; Williams v. Haddock, 145 N. Y. 144, 39 N. E. 825.

[139] Sewell, J., in Fletcher v. Ashburner, 1 Brown, Ch. 499.

[140] Fetter, Eq. p. 67; Bisp. Eq. (4th Ed.) 370; 3 Pom. Eq. (2d Ed.) p. 1765.

[141] As to other chattels real, see Schouler, Pers. Prop. (2d Ed.) 23.

[142] Keating v. Condon, 68 Pa. St. 75; Hellwig v. Bachman, 26 Ill. App. 165. And see post, p. 128.

[143] 1 Stim. Am. St. Law, § 1300.

realty is in the corporation and not in the individual stockholders. Therefore their interests are personalty only.[144]

[144] Bligh v. Brent, 2 Younge & C. Exch. 268; South Western Ry. v. Thomason, 40 Ga. 408; Arnold v. Ruggles, 1 R. I. 165; Mohawk & H. R. Co. v. Clute, 4 Paige, Ch. 384; Toll Bridge Co. v. Osborn, 35 Conn. 7. But shares in a turnpike company were held realty in Welles v. Cowles, 2 Conn. 567; and in a water company, in Drybutter v. Bartholomew, 2 P. Wms. 127. And see Price v. Price's Heirs, 6 Dana (Ky.) 107; Codman v. Winslow, 10 Mass. 146.

CHAPTER II.

TENURE AND SEISIN.

9. Tenure.
10. Seisin.

TENURE.

9. Tenure signifies the holding of lands or tenements in subordination to some superior, and the terms of the holding.[1]

The Feudal System.

The feudal system, which William the Conqueror introduced into England, was a system of military government, founded on the personal allegiance of the members of the organization to the leaders, and not a government resting on the obligations of citizenship. Under the feudal system, the king was surrounded by a body of men pledged to his support in war. The followers of the king likewise had their own followers, bound to them in the same way. This Norman military organization established itself in England, and the English lands were granted to the followers of William as a reward for past services and for services to be rendered in the future. That is, the lands were held on the condition that the grantees should perform the military and other obligations owed by them on account of their position as members of the feudal organization, and such additional obligations as might be imposed in connection with the grant. It was customary for each tenant of the king to subdivide his portion, distributing the greater part of it among subtenants on similar conditions of tenure to those which he himself was under obligation to perform to the sovereign. In this way a vast social structure was erected, with the king or prince at the apex, his immediate tenants directly beneath him, and so on down, through the various classes of subtenants, until we reach the class which actually cultivated the soil.

[1] 2 Bl. Comm. 59; Co. Litt. 1a.

Beneath these there were the serfs or slaves, consisting chiefly of the conquered race and their descendants. This was the typical social organization of the Middle Ages.

Thus the feudal system of property in land, as established in England, was based on the theory that all land held by a subject was derived originally by grant from the crown, as sovereign lord or owner; that land could not be held by a subject in absolute independent ownership, as personal property is owned, for such was the exclusive prerogative of the king, but that all land was held under obligation of duties and services, imposed either by force of law or by express terms of the grant, whereby a relation was constituted and permanently maintained, between the tenant and the crown, called the "tenure" of the land, characterized by the quality of the duties and services upon which the land was held. In like manner the tenants of the crown might grant out parts of their land to subtenants upon similar terms of rendering services, thereby creating a subtenure or relation of tenure between themselves, as mesne or intermediate lords, and their grantees, as tenants, but without affecting the ultimate tenure under the crown as lord paramount. A tenure without the interposition of any mesne lord was called a "tenure in capite" or "tenure in chief." [2] The estate of the tenant in the land was called a "feud," "fief," or "fee." The infeudation or grant was effected by the ceremony of feoffment, or delivery of the land by the lord to the tenant, to be held by him upon the terms then expressed or implied; and the tenant was thereby invested with the seisin or actual possession of the land.[3] Every acre of England was brought within the feudal principle, though the king did not grant all of the land, but retained part for his own use. This was called the "ancient demesne of the crown."[4]

Kinds of Tenure.

There were several kinds of tenure, dependent upon the nature of the services by which land was held. Originally most of the tenure was military, or "tenure by knight's service." One who

[2] Co. Litt. 108a.
[3] Leake, Land, 17.
[4] 1 Pol. & M. Hist. Eng. Law, 210, 366; Dig. Hist. Real Prop. (4th Ed.) 34; 2 Bl. Comm. 59; Co. Litt. 1a.

held by this tenure was bound to serve as a knight for 40 days a year in the king's army, and to provide himself with the equipment necessary for such service.[5] Serjeanty was another form of military tenure. The services in this case consisted in certain personal services rendered to the king or lord. "Tenure by grand serjeanty" was the term which designated the holdings of those who, in return for their lands, performed duties at the king's palace or in attendance on his person, such as to be a marshal, a chamberlain, or a butler.[6] There were also petty serjeanties, those who held by this tenure being bound to do acts of the same nature as in the case of grand serjeanties, but the duties were not connected with the king's person or his palace. Instances of these services are to carry his letters in a certain district, or to provide a given number of arrows or other military supplies each year.[7] Most of the lands owned by the church were held in "frankalmoigne," or free alms.. The only services connected with this tenure were of a spiritual kind, such as prayers for the soul of the donor.[8] Another kind of tenure was called "socage," or "free and common socage." Those who held in socage had to pay the lord a certain rent in the produce of the land, or to do certain defined work for him on his other lands, or both, as the case might be.[9] This is to be distinguished from the agricultural work required of those who held by villein tenure. Those holding in villeinage owed the lord a given number of days work each week, but what they were to do on those days the lord determined. The socage tenants, however, who owed services, owed so many days ploughing or reaping, and could not be made to do any other work. Those who held by villein tenure were for the most part serfs, or, at least, unfree men. Still, a free

[5] 1 Pol. & M. Hist. Eng. Law, 230; Dig. Hist. Real Prop. (4th Ed.) 39, 61n, 135; 2 Bl. Comm. 62; Co. Litt. 103.

[6] 1 Pol. & M. Hist. Eng. Law, 262; Dig. Hist. Real Prop. (4th Ed.) 39; 2 Bl. Comm. 73; Co. Litt. 105b.

[7] 1 Pol. & M. Hist. Eng. Law, 262; Dig. Hist. Real Prop. (4th Ed.) 49; 2 Bl. Comm. 74, 81; Co. Litt. 108a.

[8] 1 Pol. & M. Hist. Eng. Law, 218; Dig. Hist. Real Prop. (4th Ed.) 38; 2 Bl. Comm. 101; Co. Litt. 93b.

[9] 1 Pol. & M. Hist. Eng. Law, 271; Dig. Hist. Real Prop. (4th Ed.) 46; 2 Bl. Comm. 78; Co. Litt. 85a.

man might hold by this tenure and not lose his freedom.[10] It must not be thought that the men holding by the various kinds of tenure which have been enumerated constituted distinct classes, because it was often the case that one man held land by a number of different tenures,—for instance, one parcel by knight's service and another parcel by socage.[11] As time went on, the various kinds of services arising from tenure came to be regarded as due from the land, and not from the person holding the land. Thus, so many acres were bound to furnish one knight, or owed certain work to the lord; that is, tenure took on a real, rather than a personal, character.[12] A further development occurred when the various services were commuted for money payments, called "scutage." These finally took the form of a rent.[13] In later times socage tenures gained the ascendency, and military tenures were finally abolished in England.[14] Tenure in villeinage became copyhold tenure, but this form never existed in this country.[15]

Incidents of Tenure.

There were certain incidents, connected with military and with socage tenure, which constituted their chief importance, and continued to exist at a time when the services due on account of the tenure had fallen into disuse or had become unimportant. These incidents were aid, relief, wardship, and marriage. Aids were sums of money which the tenant was bound to pay the lord to secure the lord's release from prison, to help him knight his son, and to provide a marriage portion for his eldest daughter.[16] A relief was a sum which an heir must pay the lord on succeeding to the inheritance. In the case of socage tenements, this sum was

---

[10] 1 Pol. & M. Hist. Eng. Law, 337; Dig. Hist. Real Prop. (4th Ed.) 51; 2 Bl. Comm. 90; Co. Litt. 116a.

[11] 1 Pol. & M. Hist. Eng. Law, 276.

[12] 1 Pol. & M. Hist. Eng. Law, 235.

[13] 1 Pol. & M. Hist. Eng. Law, 245; Dig. Hist. Real Prop. (4th Ed.) 129; 2 Bl. Comm. 74.

[14] Dig. Hist. Real Prop. (4th Ed.) 392.

[15] 1 Pol. & M. Hist. Eng. Law, 351; Dig. Hist. Real Prop. (4th Ed.) 151; 2 Bl. Comm. 90; Co. Litt. 57b.

[16] 1 Pol. & M. Hist. Eng. Law, 330; Dig. Hist. Real Prop. (4th Ed.) 41, 48, 129; 2 Bl. Comm. 63, 87.

fixed at one year's rent.[17] When an heir holding by knight's service was under age, the lord possessed the right of wardship, and under this right he had the custody of the infant's person and of his lands, and the latter was a source of no small profit in the case of rich wards, because the lord was not required to account for the rents and profits of the estate.[18] But the wardship of an heir who held in socage belonged to the nearest relative to whom the inheritance of the ward's lands could not descend, and the guardian was accountable to the ward for the profits received by him.[19] To wardship was added the power to dispose of the ward in marriage, or, at least, to propose a match for the ward. If the ward refused the match, the guardian could claim a fine, as he could, also, if the ward married without his consent.[20]

Same—Escheat and Forfeiture.

On failure of the heirs of the tenant, or for his felony, the land escheated to the lord, and it was liable to forfeiture to the king for treason.[21]

Statute of Quia Emptores.

Prior to 1289 a tenant of lands could grant a part of them, to be held under him by feudal services. His tenant, thus created, could do the same. This process was called "subinfeudation." In the year mentioned the statute of quia emptores [22] was passed. It prohibited subinfeudation, and enacted that the grantee should hold immediately of the superior lord and not of the grantor. After this statute a conveyance passed all the grantor's interest to the grantee, and the grantor dropped out of the feudal chain between the tenant in possession of the land and the lord para-

[17] 1 Pol. & M. Hist. Eng. Law, 288; Dig. Hist. Real Prop. (4th Ed.) 40, 48, 80, 120; 2 Bl. Comm. 65, 87; Co. Litt. 76a, 83a.

[18] 1 Pol. & M. Hist. Eng. Law, 299; Dig. Hist. Real Prop. (4th Ed.) 41, 86, 136; 2 Bl. Comm. 67.

[19] 1 Pol. & M. Hist. Eng. Law, 303; Dig. Hist. Real Prop. (4th Ed.) 48; 2 Bl. Comm. 87.

[20] 1 Pol. & M. Hist. Eng. Law, 299; Dig. Hist. Real Prop. 41, 90, 123; 2 Bl. Comm. 70. Socage tenure gave no right to the ward's marriage. 2 Bl. Comm. 88; Dig. Hist. Real Prop. (4th Ed.) 48.

[21] 1 Pol. & M. Hist. Eng. Law, 332; 2 Pol. & M. Hist. Eng. Law, 22, 464, 498; Dig. Hist. Real Prop. (4th Ed.) 43, 61, 91, 422; 2 Bl. Comm. 72, 89.

[22] 18 Edw. I. c. 1.

mount, and had no further connection with the land granted. No new tenure in fee could be created.[23] This statute is in force in all the United States where tenure still exists,[24] except Pennsylvania and South Carolina.[25]

Tenure in the United States.

The feudal system never took root in the United States, and what tenures there were in the early holdings of land were by free and common socage, and not subject to the burdensome incidents of tenure which have been enumerated.[26] In many states feudal tenures are abolished.[27] Lands are in these states allodial; that is, held in absolute ownership, the same as personal property.[28] In other states where tenure still exists, lands cannot be holden in fee of another person, because of the statute of quia emptores, as was seen in the last paragraph. Other forms of tenure which do exist to-day, such as the tenure between landlord and tenant, or between tenant for life and reversioner or remainder-man, will be considered hereafter.[29]

SEISIN.

10. Seisin is the possession of land with an intent on the part of the one holding it to claim a freehold interest.[30] It may be either:

(a) Seisin in fact, or

(b) Seisin in law.

[23] Gray, Perp. 12; Dig. Hist. Real Prop. (4th Ed.) 232; Van Rensselaer v. Dennison, 35 N. Y. 393. Cf. Van Rensselaer v. Smith, 27 Barb. 104.

[24] Gray, Perp. 16; Denio, J., in Van Rensselaer v. Hays, 19 N. Y. 68, 75.

[25] Gray, Perp. pp. 17, 18; Ingersoll v. Sergeant, 1 Whart. 337. Cf. Wallace v. Harmstad, 44 Pa. St. 492. The charter of North Carolina permitted subinfeudation.

[26] Chisholm v. Georgia, 2 Dall. 419; Cornell v. Lamb, 2 Cow. 652; Combs v. Jackson, 2 Wend. 153; In re Desilver's Estate, 5 Rawle, 111. Cf. Martin v. Waddell, 16 Pet. 367; Johnson v. McIntosh, 8 Wheat. 543.

[27] 1 Stim. Am. St. Law, §§ 400, 401, 1100–1103; Gray, Perp. 13; Matthews v. Ward, 10 Gill & J. 443, 451.

[28] McLean, J., in Mayor, etc., of New Orleans v. U. S., 10 Pet. 716; Cook v. Hammond, 4 Mason, 467, 478, Fed. Cas. No. 3,159; Minneapolis Mill Co. v. Tiffany, 22 Minn. 463. Cf. Taylor v. Porter, 4 Hill, 140; Com. v. Tewksbury, 11 Metc. (Mass.) 55; Bancroft v. City of Cambridge, 126 Mass. 438.

[29] See post, pp. 142, 303.

[30] Towle v. Ayer, 8 N. H. 57.

By the early common law seisin signified the investing of a tenant with the legal right to his estate, and was properly used only in connection with freeholds.[31] Seisin is now often used as the equivalent of possession.[32] Seisin in fact is actual possession. Seisin in law is constructive possession.[33] The theory of the common law is that there must always be some one seised of the freehold. The early form of conveyance was by a transfer of the seisin.[34] Applications of the theory of seisin will be made in other places.

[31] Post, p. 34. Van Rensselaer v. Poucher, 5 Denio (N. Y.) 35; Sneed, J., in Upchurch v. Anderson, 3 Baxt. (Tenn.) 411; Peters, C. J., in Ford v. Garner's Adm'r, 49 Ala. 603.

[32] See Wilde, J., in Slater v. Rawson, 6 Metc. (Mass.) 439.

[33] Allen, J., in Jenkins v. Fahey, 73 N. Y. 362; Olin, J., in Hart v. Dean, 2 McArthur, 63.

[34] See post, p. 405.

CHAPTER III.

ESTATES AS TO QUANTITY—FEE SIMPLE.

    11. Estate Defined.
    12. Classification of Estates.
    13. Quantity of Estates.
4–15. Freehold—Estates of Inheritance.
    16. Fee Simple.
    17.   Creation.
    18.   Right of User.
    19.   Alienation.

ESTATE DEFINED.

11. The interest which a person has in real property is called an "estate."

The term "estate," in its technical sense, is used only in connection with real property. There can properly be no estates in personalty. "Estate" merely signifies the interest which the tenant has in the land he holds. This interest may be as absolute as the ownership of personalty, or it may be for a limited time, or qualified by conditions. Under the feudal system only the king could have absolute ownership of land, since all others held their land under him. The technical use of the word "estate" is to be distinguished from "estate" as meaning things owned,[1] or the aggregate of a man's property as an entity,—for example, a "decedent's estate."

CLASSIFICATION OF ESTATES.

12. Estates will be discussed:
  (a) **As to quantity** (p. 34).
  (b) **As to quality** (p. 169).
  (c) **As to legal or equitable character** (p. 251).
  (d) **As to time of enjoyment** (p. 278).
  (e) **As to number of owners** (p. 332).

---

[1] See Appleton, C. J., in Deering v. Tucker, 55 Me. 284.

QUANTITY OF ESTATES.

13. The quantity of an estate signifies its duration. As to quantity estates are:
(a) Freeholds, which are:
   (1) Of inheritance, comprising:
      I. Fee simple (p. 35).
      II. Fee tail (p. 42).
   (2) Not of inheritance, or life estates (p. 55).
(b) Less than freehold, which are:
   (1) For years (p. 128).
   (2) At will (p. 155).
   (3) From year to year (p. 158).
   (4) At sufferance (p. 163).

The quantity of an estate means almost the same thing as the length of time during which the owner of the estate is entitled to the use of the land.[2] For example, a life estate gives its owner an interest as long as he lives. The estate greatest in quantity is the fee simple. Quantity does not, however, mean the absolute number of years that an estate is to continue. A leasehold for 2 years is an estate of the same quantity as one for 15 years, to wit, an estate for years.

FREEHOLD—ESTATES OF INHERITANCE.

14. A freehold estate is one which may last during a life, and whose duration is uncertain, but is not dependent on the will of another.[3]

---

[2] See Sedgwick, J., in Cutts v. Com., 2 Mass. 284.

[3] 2 Bl. Comm. 704; Hanna, J., in Bradford v. State, 15 Ind. 353; People v. Board of Education of Grand Rapids, 38 Mich. 95; Wyatt v. Irrigation Co., 18 Colo. 298, 33 Pac. 144. For questions of freehold, as determining the jurisdiction of a court, see Wilson v. Dresser, 152 Ill. 387, 38 N. E. 888; Van Meter v. Thomas, 153 Ill. 65, 38 N. E. 1036; Hupp v. Hupp, 153 Ill. 490, 39 N. E. 124; Howe v. Warren, 154 Ill. 227, 40 N. E. 472; Moshier v. Reynolds, 155 Ill. 72, 39 N. E. 621.

15. An estate of inheritance is a freehold which, on the death of the owner intestate, descends to his heirs.[4]

In some states long terms of years are by statute declared to be freeholds,[5] and in others estates for the life of another[6] are declared to be estates of inheritance.[7] Estates less than freehold are chattel interests in lands, and go to the personal representative of the deceased owner, unless he has otherwise disposed of them by will.

FEE SIMPLE.

16. A fee simple is a freehold estate in perpetuity. It is an estate limited to a man and his heirs, and is the largest possible estate in land.

"The word 'fee' originally signified land holden of a superior, as distinguished from allodial land; 'fee' and 'feud' being synonymous. But 'fee' is now employed to denote the quantity of interest the tenant has in land, and is confined to estates of inheritance, i. e. those which may descend to a man's heirs. When the word 'fee' is used alone, it means 'fee simple.'"[*] A fee simple[8] is a freehold estate in perpetuity.[9] It may exist in incorporeal as well as in corporeal hereditaments.[10] A fee simple is practically equal to absolute ownership, if, indeed, it is not so, in theory, in most of the states. Under the feudal system, no one except the sovereign held a fee simple. Grants were made to tenants to hold in demesne as of a fee, but this was not the absolute fee simple of

---

[4] 2 Bl. Comm. 201.
[5] 1 Stim. Am. St. Law, § 1310.
[6] Post, p. 67.
[7] 1 Stim. Am. St. Law, § 1310.
[*] Graves, Real Prop. § 44.
[8] "Fee simple" means the same as "fee simple absolute," and generally "fee" alone is a sufficient designation. 2 Bl. Comm. 106; Co. Litt. 1b; Clark v. Baker, 14 Cal. 612, 631; Thompson, C. J., in Jackson v. Van Zandt, 12 Johns. (N. Y.) 169.
[9] 2 Bl. Comm. 106. An estate in fee simple may be subject to some condition or qualification which will put an end to it, in which case it is called a base or determinable fee. See post, p. 178.
[10] 2 Bl. Comm. 106.

to-day. An interest in the land still remained in the grantor or feudal lord, represented by his right to the feudal services due from the tenant. The fee simple might well be called our normal estate. It represents the whole ownership of the land. Out of the fee simple all other estates are carved. The powers incident to estates less than fee simple are in all cases less than those of the owner of that estate.

SAME—CREATION.

17. For the creation of a fee simple,
   (a) **By deed, the word "heirs" must be used, except,—**
EXCEPTIONS—(1) In quitclaim deeds.
                (2) In many states, by statute.
   (b) **By devise, the intention of the testator governs, and no technical words of limitation are necessary. In many states, by statute, a fee simple is presumed to be intended if not otherwise expressed.**

Creation by Deed.

In the creation of an estate in fee simple by deed [11] there is a technical rule of the common law that the limitation, as it is called, must be to one "and his heirs"; otherwise, the grantee will take only a life estate.[12] And no other words are sufficient, even though the meaning be the same and the intention clear.[13] In granting a fee simple to a corporation sole, "successors" is the

---

[11] For the limitation of a fee to a trustee, see North v. Philbrook, 34 Me. 532; Ewing v. Shannahan, 113 Mo. 188, 20 S. W. 1065.

[12] Adams v. Ross, 30 N. J. Law, 505; Edwardsville R. Co. v. Sawyer, 92 Ill. 377; Stell v. Barham, 87 N. C. 62; Batchelor v. Whitaker, 88 N. C. 350; Buffum v. Hutchinson, 1 Allen (Mass.) 58; Jordan v. McClure, 85 Pa. St. 495; Arms v. Burt, 1 Vt. 303. Contra, Cole v. Lake Co., 54 N. H. 242.

[13] For instance, a life estate only was held to pass by the words "successors and assigns forever," Sedgwick v. Laflin, 10 Allen (Mass.) 430; "executors, administrators, and assigns," Clearwater v. Rose, 1 Blackf. (Ind.) 137; "and his generation so long as the waters of the Delaware run," Foster v. Joice, 3 Wash. C. C. 498, Fed. Cas. No. 4,974. But see Evans v. Brady, 79 Md. 142, 28 Atl. 1061; Engel v. Ayer, 85 Me. 448, 27 Atl. 352; Adams v. Ross, 30 N. J. Law, 505.

proper word to use,[14] but in the case of a corporation aggregate no words of limitation are necessary.[15] The technical words are not required in a strict quitclaim deed. Thus, when one joint tenant or a co-parcener [16] releases his interest to his co-tenant, no words of inheritance, as it is called, are necessary to pass a fee.[17] But the rule is otherwise in the case of a conveyance by a tenant in common [18] to a co-tenant,[19] or where the reversion is released to the tenant for life.[20] In the case of a conveyance in which reference is made to another instrument, if the necessary words of inheritance are used in the instrument referred to, their absence from the other will not prevent a fee simple passing.[21] When a fee simple was intended to be conveyed, but adequate words were not employed, the deed may be reformed in equity, and made to express the intention of the parties.[22] This rule requiring the word "heirs" to be used has in many states been changed by statute, so that other expressions are adequate to convey a fee simple;

[14] Shaw, C. J., in Overseers of Poor of City of Boston v. Sears, 22 Pick. (Mass.) 126; Olcott v. Gabert, 86 Tex. 121, 23 S. W. 985.

[15] Congregational Soc. of Halifax v. Stark, 34 Vt. 243; Wilcox v. Wheeler, 47 N. H. 488. And see Beach v. Haynes, 12 Vt. 15; Wilkes-Barre v. Wyoming Historical & Geological Soc., 134 Pa. St. 616, 19 Atl. 809. Where land is settled upon or devised to a charity, it may happen that, when the corporation managing the charity comes to an end, and the charity itself becomes impracticable, the land will return to the donor's heirs. Stanley v. Colt, 5 Wall. 119. And see 1 Bl. Comm. 484. Rutherford v. Greene's Heirs, 2 Wheat. 196, and Proprietors of Enfield v. Permit, 5 N. H. 280, are often cit to the effect that technical words of limitation are not necessary to pass a fee in the case of legislative grants, but they do not support the proposition.

[16] See post, pp. 333, 336.

[17] Scott, J., in Rector v. Waugh, 17 Mo. 13, 28.

[18] See post, p. 335.

[19] Rector v. Waugh, 17 Mo. 13.

[20] 1 Washb. Real Prop. (5th Ed.) 90.

[21] Lemon v. Graham, 131 Pa. St. 447, 19 Atl. 48; Mercier v. Railway Co., 54 Mo. 506. But see Lytle v. Lytle, 10 Watts, 259; Reaume v. Chambers, 22 Mo. 36.

[22] See Fetter, Eq. p. 314; Vickers v. Leigh, 104 N. C. 248, 10 S. E. 308. Cf. Ewing v. Shannahan, 113 Mo. 188, 20 S. W. 1065; Defraunce v. Brooks, 8 Watts & S. (Pa.) 67.

and in some states it is to be presumed that a fee simple was intended unless the contrary appears.[23]

Creation by Devise.

The strictness of the common-law rule is relaxed in the case of limitations in wills, and the intention of the testator governs, so that he can devise a fee simple without using the word "heirs," if the expression employed shows that a fee simple is intended.[24] In many states there is now by statute a presumption that a fee simple is devised if no other intention appears.[25] That the testator meant to give a fee simple may be implied from a charge imposed on the devisee; for it is said, if he was required to pay out money, and received only a life estate, he might die before being reimbursed from the land.[26] If, however, the charge is imposed on the land, instead of on the devisee personally, the presumption

---

[23] 1 Stim. Am. St. Law, § 1474; 1 Shars. & B. Lead. Cas. Real Prop. 56. Pennsylvania, New Jersey, Delaware, South Carolina, Florida, Ohio, and Wyoming have not dispensed with words of inheritance in deeds. 1 Dembitz, Land Tit. 99.

[24] Ferguson v. Thomason, 87 Ky. 579, 9 S. W. 714; Lofton v. Murchison, 80 Ga. 391, 7 S. E. 322; Howze v. Barber, 29 S. C. 466, 7 S. E. 817; Webster's Trustee v. Webster (Ky.) 22 S. W. 920; Lockett v. Lockett, 94 Ky. 289, 22 S. W. 224; Mitchell v. Campbell, 94 Ky. 347, 22 S. W. 549; Thomson v. Peake, 38 S. C. 440, 17 S. E. 45, 725; Boutelle v. Bank, 17 R. I. 781, 24 Atl. 838; Campbell v. Carson, 12 Serg. & R. (Pa.) 54; In re Green's Estate, 140 Pa. St. 253, 21 Atl. 317; Armstrong v. Michener, 160 Pa. St. 21, 28 Atl. 447; Mills v. Franklin, 128 Ind. 444, 28 N. E. 60; Bridgewater v. Bolton, 6 Md. 106; Baker v. Bridge, 12 Pick. (Mass.) 27; Merritt v. Disney, 48 Md. 344; Dilworth v. Gusky, 131 Pa. St. 343, 18 Atl. 899; Doe d. Hitch v. Patten (Del. Err. & App.) 16 Atl. 558. In a devise it has been held that a fee simple passed by the words "all my right" or "property." Newkerk v. Newkerk, 2 Caines (N. Y.) 345; Jackson v. Housel, 17 Johns. (N. Y.) 281. Contra, Doe v. Allen, 8 Term. R. 497. "All my estate" (by one owning a fee simple), Godfrey v. Humphrey, 18 Pick. (Mass.) 537. To A. "or his heirs," Wright v. Wright, 1 Ves. Sr. 409. To A. "forever," Heath v. Heath, 1 Brown, Ch. 147. But see Vernon v. Wright, 28 Law J. Ch. 198, 204, 207; Davie v. Stevens, 1 Doug. 321. And cf. Clayton v. Clayton, 3 Bin. (Pa.) 476.

[25] 1 Stim. Am. St. Law, § 1474; 1 Shars. & B. Lead. Cas. Real Prop. 70.

[26] Doe v. Richards, 3 Term R. 356; Jackson v. Merrill, 6 Johns. (N. Y.) 185; Lithgow v. Kavenagh, 9 Mass. 161; Wait v. Belding, 24 Pick. (Mass.) 129; Blinston v. Warburton, 2 Kay & J. 400; Pickwell v. Spencer, L. R. 6 Exch. 190.

does not obtain.[27] A fee simple may be presumed from the nature of the land devised, if no other estate would be of any value to the devisee; for instance, in a devise of wild lands, which would be of no value unless the timber could be cut, and a tenant for life would have no such right.[28]

SAME—RIGHT OF USER.

18. The owner of a fee simple may use his land in any way he pleases, provided he does not cause injury to others.

One who has a fee simple estate in land possesses an indefinite right of user, so that he may commit unlimited waste, such as opening mines, cutting down trees, destroying buildings and other structures, or removing real fixtures.[29] This is not technical waste. In connection with other estates, it will be seen that these acts are wrongful, and are called "waste"; but when done by an owner in fee simple they are lawful. There is the one restriction on his right of user, namely, that he must not cause injury to others by the use to which he puts his land, or, in other words, he must not maintain a nuisance on his premises.[30]

SAME—ALIENATION.

19. A fee simple estate is subject to alienation, which may be:
  (a) Voluntary, which is:
    (1) Inter vivos, or
    (2) By will.
  (b) Involuntary, which is either:
    (1) For debts or taxes, or
    (2) Under the power of eminent domain.

[27] Jackson v. Bull, 10 Johns. (N. Y.) 148; McLellan v. Turner, 15 Me. 436; Doe v. Harter, 7 Blackf. (Ind.) 488; Funk v. Eggleston, 92 Ill. 515. And see Spraker v. Van Alstyne, 18 Wend. (N. Y.) 200.

[28] Sargent v. Towne, 10 Mass. 303.

[29] 2 Bl. Comm. 282. But see the Case of Mines, 1 Plow. 310, 336; Com. v. Tewksbury, 11 Metc. (Mass.) 55.

[30] 2 Jag. Torts, p. 748; 1 Wood, Nuis. (3d Ed.) 127.

Voluntary Alienation.

One of the principal incidents of a fee simple is the right of the owner to dispose of it, and in this way exert a control over his land even after death. Subject to certain disabilities of the person, to be noticed hereafter,[31] the owner of a fee simple can now[32] alien his estate by deed or by will very much as he pleases, provided he complies with the formalities of conveyancing required by law. There are, however, certain exceptions to this power. For instance, an owner of land, though he holds it in fee simple, cannot create estates and forms of tenure unknown to the law, or which are prohibited by law.[33] Within this principle comes the rule against perpetuities, to be discussed hereafter,[34] which prevents the creation of estates to take effect at a remote time in the future. Moreover, an owner of land is not permitted to convey to others, and at the same time forbid them to dispose of it, for the law allows only very limited restraints to be imposed on alienation.[35] In some states there is a limitation on the amount of land which a man can give by will for charitable purposes.[36] Furthermore, no one is allowed to dispose of his land in such a way that it is a fraud on his creditors;[37] and, when an action is pending which involves the title to lands, they cannot be conveyed away so as to prejudice the other party.[38] The most important exceptions, however, to the power of alienation, are those arising from the rights of dower, curtesy, and homestead, which will be explained in subsequent chapters.

Involuntary Alienation.

A fee simple is also subject to alienation without the owner's consent, for it may be taken for taxes, and, at the present time, to

---

[31] Post, p. 381, including the disabilities of aliens, corporations, etc.

[32] For the history of the right of alienation, see post, p. 390.

[33] See Doebler's Appeal, 64 Pa. St. 9.

[34] Post, p. 322.

[35] See post, p. 390; Blackstone Bank v. Davis, 21 Pick. (Mass.) 42; Langdon v. Ingram's Guardian, 28 Ind. 360. Restrictions as to use may be valid. Cowell v. Springs Co., 100 U. S. 55.

[36] 1 Stim. Am. St. Law, § 2618; Williams, Real Prop. (17th Am. Ed.) p. 95, note.

[37] See post, p. 392.

[38] See post, p. 218.

§ 19)　　　　　　　ALIENATION.　　　　　　　41

pay his debts.[39] Land may also be taken from the owner under the power of eminent domain, but this can only be done on making compensation for the land so taken.[40] Nor is there any way in which involuntary alienation may be avoided, except in a few states under the doctrine of spendthrift trusts.[41] But an estate may be so limited to a man that it shall determine on any attempt at alienation, voluntary or involuntary, and so it will not be available to creditors.[42] The restrictions on alienation by an owner in fee simple apply to lesser estates. If the owner of an estate in fee simple does not dispose of it during his life, it descends to his heirs, and vests in them without any act on their part.[43]

[39] Watkins v. Holman, 16 Pet. 25; Wyman v. Brigden, 4 Mass. 150; Nokes v. Smith, 1 Yeates (Pa.) 238. By different acts of congress a priority is given to the claims of the United States, and these acts are constitutional. U. S. v. Fisher, 2 Cranch, 358; Harrison v. Sterry, 5 Cranch, 289. Similar statutes exist in some states regulating the order of preference of claims. 2 Werner, Adm'n, 772.

[40] Taylor v. Porter, 4 Hill (N. Y.) 140. See post, p. 494.

[41] Post, p. 396. Keyser v. Mitchell, 67 Pa. St. 473; Ashhurst's Appeal, 77 Pa. St. 465; Hallett v. Thompson, 5 Paige (N. Y.) 583; McIlvaine v. Smith, 42 Mo. 45; Lampert v. Haydel, 96 Mo. 439, 9 S. W. 780; Johnston v. Zane, 11 Grat. (Va.) 552. Cf. Nichols v. Levy, 5 Wall. 433.

[42] Nichols v. Eaton, 91 U. S. 716; Bramhall v. Ferris, 14 N. Y. 41; Emery v. Van Syckel, 17 N. J. Eq. 564. And see post, p. 395.

[43] In re Estate of Donahue, 36 Cal. 329.

CHAPTER IV.

ESTATES AS TO QUANTITY (Continued)—ESTATES TAIL.

20. Estates Tail Defined.
21–22. Classes of Estates Tail.
23. Origin of Estates Tail.
24–25. Creation of Estates Tail.
26. Incidents of Estates Tail.
27. Duration of Estates Tail.
28. Tenant in Tail After Possibility of Issue Extinct.
29–30. Estates Tail in the United States.
31. Quasi Entail.

ESTATES TAIL DEFINED.

20. An estate tail is an estate of inheritance which descends only to the heirs of the body of the donee or to some special class of such heirs.

An estate tail is a freehold estate of inheritance, with the peculiarity that, on the death of the tenant, only the heirs of his body, or some particular description of them, can inherit. This limitation of the inheritance to the heirs of one's body, instead of to the general heirs, is the distinguishing feature of an estate tail.[1] Only heirs in the direct descending line can inherit. Thus, a brother of a tenant in tail cannot take.[2] The one who makes a "gift," as it is called, of an estate tail, is called the "donor," and the one to whom the estate is given is called the "donee."[3] An estate tail is a smaller interest in land than a fee simple. If the owner of a fee simple makes a grant of an estate tail, an estate still remains in him, called a "reversion."[4] If at any time

---

[1] Goodright v. Morningstar, 1 Yeates (Pa.) 313; Corbin v. Healy, 20 Pick. (Mass.) 514; Riggs v. Sally, 15 Me. 408. Cf. Reinhart v. Lantz, 37 Pa. St. 488.

[2] 2 Bl. Comm. 113.

[3] 2 Bl. Comm. 110.

[4] And therefore the statute of quia emptores does not apply to a fee tail, and tenure may exist between donor and donee. Dig. Hist. Real Prop. (4th Ed.) 248. And see post, p. 280.

there is a failure of heirs within the description of those entitled to take under the gift, the property reverts to the donor or his heirs. Where the donor of an estate tail, by the same instrument which creates it, gives the interest which remains in him to a third person, the estate of such third person is called a "remainder."[5]

CLASSES OF ESTATES TAIL.

21. Estates tail are divided into:
    (a) **Estates in general tail, the donee being the only parent named.**
    (b) **Estates in special tail, both parents being named.**
22. **Estates in general and special tail are further divided into:**
    (a) **Estates in tail male, descending only to male heirs.**
    (b) **Estates in tail female, descending only to female heirs.**

Where the estate is limited simply to the heirs of the donee's body, without further particularity of description, the estate is an estate in general tail. In such case, any of the issue of the donee's body can inherit.[6] The inheritance, however, may be restricted to the heirs of the body of the donee and another person named, as "to A. and his heirs begotten on the body of his wife, B."[7] Or the limitation may be to two donees and the heirs of their two bodies. These cases, where both parents of the heirs who are to take are named, are called estates in special tail.[8] Such limitations are valid if the persons named are husband and wife, or if there is a possibility of their becoming lawfully married,[9] no matter how improbable it is that they ever will be.[10] But, if the estate is given to a man and his heirs by a woman whom he cannot

[5] See post, p. 282.
[6] Co. Litt. §§ 14, 15; 2 Bl. Comm. 113.
[7] 2 Bl. Comm. 114.
[8] Co. Litt. § 16.
[9] Co. Litt. § 16.
[10] But a contrary presumption may arise, as in case of two donees who have already been married and divorced. Co. Litt. 25b, note 2.

marry because she is within a prohibited degree of consanguinity, the limitation to the heirs is void, and the donee will take only a life estate, the reversion remaining in the donor.[11] But a limitation in tail to two donees who are each married to other persons is good, since they may become free, by reason of death or divorce, to marry each other.[12] Whenever there can be no issue who can take the estate according to the form of the gift,—for example, because of the death of the wife named prior to the gift,—then the donee will take only a life estate.[13] The inheritance of an estate in general or special tail may be further restricted to the males or females of the class of heirs designated. Examples of such estates are "to A. and the heirs male of his body,"[14] and" to A. and his heirs male on the body of his wife, B., begotten.[15] Estates tail female are very rare. No one can inherit an estate in tail male who cannot trace his descent from the donee through males entirely. For this reason the son of a daughter of the donee cannot take the estate, because his mother could not have inherited. The same principle applies in estates tail female, so that only females and the female issue of females can take.[16]

ORIGIN OF ESTATES TAIL.

23. Estates tail were created by the operation of the statute de donis conditionalibus upon fees conditional at common law.

In early feudal times, when estates first became hereditary, and were given to a man and his heirs, the word "heirs" was considered to mean lineal heirs, or the descendants of the body of the first taker.[18] The collateral relations, such as brothers, sisters, and cousins, could not take. This was obviously to the advantage of the feudal lord or

---

[11] Co. Litt. § 283.

[12] Co. Litt. § 25.

[13] That is, the donee has an estate tail after possibility of issue extinct. Post, p. 52.

[14] Hulburt v. Emerson, 16 Mass. 241.

[15] Co. Litt. § 25.

[16] Co. Litt. §§ 23, 24.

[18] Dig. Hist. Real Prop. (4th Ed.) 220; Pol. & M. Hist. Eng. Law, 11.

grantor; for, by confining the inheritance to the issue of his tenant, he was more likely to have profitable wardships and escheats than if collateral kinsmen were admitted. At this time the heir derived his title to the estate from the grantor by designation in the grant per formam doni. But as the tenant acquired, in course of time, the power of alienating the fee, the interest of the heir became reduced to a mere expectation of succeeding, in the event of his ancestor not exercising that power. The additional grant to the heirs was then referred wholly to the estate of the ancestor, as importing merely an estate of inheritance, an essential incident of which was the power of transferring the land, and the heir no longer claimed as grantee by designation in the grant, but derived his title from the ancestor by descent.[19] The word "heirs" was also extended, so as to include collateral as well as lineal heirs.[20] When the grantor, therefore, wished to confine the estate to the lineal descendants of the tenant, it became necessary for him to expressly limit it to the heirs of the tenant's body. Estates so limited were called, indifferently, "conditional fees," "fees conditional," and "fees conditional at common law," because of the condition, implied in the grant, that if the grantee died without heirs of his body, or in case of a failure of such heirs at any future time, the land should revert to the grantor. The grantor had no reversion, but only a possibility of a reverter. The fee was still considered to be in the grantee, subject to be divested by the failure of the condition. The limitation to the heirs of his body did not otherwise affect the rights and powers of a tenant, and in respect of these it remained a fee simple. So long as the fee lasted, the tenant for the time being had all such powers, including the power of alienation, as were the inseparable incidents of an estate of inheritance. It was, however, a condition necessary to the full effect of his alienation, so as to bar, not only his issue, but also the possibility of reverting to the grantor, that he should have heritable issue.[21] The gift to one and to the heirs of his body was construed, for the purpose of alienation, to be the same as a gift to him and to his

[19] Leake, Prop. Land. 33.
[20] Williams, Real Prop. (17th Ed.) 101.
[21] 2 Bl. Comm. 110; 1 Spence, Eq. Jur. 141; Anon., Fitzh. Abr. "Formedon," 65.

heirs, if he had heirs of his body. By this construction the intention of the grantor in limiting the estate to the heirs of his tenant's body was again defeated.[22] The birth of issue was held to discharge the estate of the condition, and, like a fee simple, the tenant had power to alien or incumber it, and it was liable to forfeiture for treason. If the donee aliened the land before issue was born, the conveyance was effectual against both the donee and the donor during the donee's life. If issue was born to the donee subsequently to his conveyance, the grantee's estate became absolute, and cut off all rights of the issue and of the donor.*

The Statute de Donis Conditionalibus.

In 1285, the great landowners secured the passage of the famous statute "de donis conditionalibus," [23] or, as it is often called, the Statute of Westminster II. This act provided that, "where any giveth his land to any man and his wife and to the heirs begotten of the bodies, * * * the will of the giver according to the form in the deed of gift manifestly expressed shall be from henceforth observed, so that they to whom the land was given under such condition shall have no power to aliene the land so given, but it shall remain unto the issue of them to whom it was given after their death, or shall revert unto the giver or his heirs if issue fail," etc. No forfeiture was imposed on a tenant who should alien his estate, but his conveyance was of no effect, after his death, against his heirs or the donor. The statute, in taking away from the tenant the power to alien the land, deprived his estate of that incident which chiefly characterized it as a fee simple.[24] It was, therefore, no longer classed as a fee simple conditional, but it was recognized to be a new kind of fee or inheritance created by the statute, and thenceforth distinctively known as a "fee tail." "Where an estate to one and to the heirs of his body was a fee simple before the statute, now since the statute it is taken that he has but a fee tail, and this is included in the statute although it is not expressed; for when the statute restrained the donee from

---

[22] 2 Bl. Comm. 111.

* 1 Spence, Eq. Jur. p. 141. And see Nevil's Case, 7 Coke, 33a; Willion v. Berkley, Plow. 223; Buckworth v. Thirkell, 3 Bos. & P. 652, note.

[23] 13 Edw. I. St. 1, c. 1, § 2.

[24] Hill v. Hill, 74 Pa. St. 173.

aliening the fee simple, or from doing other acts which he that has a fee simple may do, it was presently taken that the fee was not in him, for it would be idle to adjudge it in him when he could not do anything with it, and therefore it was taken, by collection and implication of the act, that the fee simple continued in the donor. So that he has one inheritance, viz. a fee simple, and the donee has another inheritance of an inferior degree, viz. a fee tail. And immediately upon the making of the act it had this name given it." [25] It was so called from the inheritance being cut down —"talliatum"—to the line of heirs designated. The name was used for a restricted inheritance before the statute, but since the statute it is used distinctively for the new estate thereby created.[26] After the statute de donis the heirs of the donee again took per formam doni.

CREATION OF ESTATES TAIL.

24. For the creation of a fee tail there must be added to the words necessary to limit a fee simple, other words which restrict the inheritance to the heirs of the body of the first taker:

25. An estate tail cannot be created out of a chattel interest in lands.

Limitation of Estates Tail.

For the creation of an estate tail words of limitation and procreation are necessary; that is, not only is the word "heirs" required, as in the limitation of a fee simple, but there must also be some words which show that the heirs of the donee's body, or some class of them, are to inherit the estate. If the words of limitation are absent, the donee takes only a life estate,[27] while the omission of words of procreation gives the donee a fee simple.[26] As to what words are sufficient to create an estate tail, the same rules apply as to a fee simple, as far as words of limitation are concerned; so

[25] Willion v. Berkley, Plow. 251, per Dyer, C. J.

[26] Leake, Prop. Land, 37.

[27] Co. Litt. 20b; 2 Bl. Comm. 115; Ford v. Johnson, 41 Ohio St. 366. Cf. Lehndorf v. Cope, 122 Ill. 317, 13 N. E. 505.

[28] 2 Bl. Comm. 115; Co. Litt. 27a; Doe v. Smeddle, 2 Barn. & Ald. 126.

that the word "heirs" must be used in a deed, and "seed," "issue," or "children of the body" would be insufficient.[29] But any words which show that the word "heirs" is to be restricted to the heirs of the body will suffice to restrict the inheritance to a fee tail.[30] In wills there is the same relaxation as in the creation of a fee simple, and the intention of the testator governs, even though he does not use the technical words required in a deed.[31] So the word "issue,"[32] or "children"[33] may be sufficient to create an estate tail, without using the word "heirs," if it appears from the context that the devisor so intended.[34] And in a will the expression "heirs male" has been held to pass a fee tail, although it would create a fee simple if used in a deed. A limitation to A. and to his heirs male, or to A. and to his heirs female, creates an estate in fee simple, because it contains no restriction to a particular line of issue. It is not limited by the gift of what body the issue male or female shall be. Inheritance by heirs general cannot be restricted to one sex; therefore, the words "males" and "females," having here no legal import, are rejected, and all the heirs, female as well as male, may inherit. For no man can institute a new kind of inheritance not allowed by law.[35] The intention to give a

[29] Co. Litt. 20a; 2 Bl. Comm. 115.

[30] Hall v. Vandegrift, 3 Bin. (Pa.) 374; Corbin v. Healy, 20 Pick. (Mass.) 514; Pollock v. Speidel, 17 Ohio St. 439; Den v. Lake, 24 N. J. Law, 686; Morgan v. Morgan, L. R. 10 Eq. 99; Den v. Cox, 9 N. J. Law, 10; Buxton v. Inhabitants of Uxbridge, 10 Metc. (Mass.) 87; Brown v. Hospital, 155 Mass. 323, 29 N. E. 625; Holden v. Wells (R. I.) 31 Atl. 265.

[31] Reinoehl v. Shirk, 119 Pa. St. 108, 12 Atl. 806; Arnold v. Brown, 7 R. I. 189; Manwaring v. Tabor, 1 Root (Conn.) 79; Clark v. Baker, 3 Serg. & R. (Pa.) 470; Stone v. McMullen (May 3, 1881) 10 Wkly. Notes Cas. 541. But see Hill v. Hill, 74 Pa. St. 173. "Heirs lawfully begotten" has been held, in a will, to mean "begotten by him." Pratt's Lessee v. Flamer, 5 Har. & J. (Md.) 10.

[32] Clark v. Baker, 3 Serg. & R. (Pa.) 470; Taylor v. Taylor, 63 Pa. St. 481.

[33] Nightingale v. Burrell, 15 Pick. (Mass.) 104; Fletcher v. Fletcher, 88 Ind. 418.

[34] See, also, Braden v. Cannon, 24 Pa. St. 168; Gause v. Wiley, 4 Serg. & R. (Pa.) 509; Allen v. Markle, 36 Pa. St. 117; Wheatland v. Dodge, 10 Metc. (Mass.) 502.

[35] Co. Litt. 13a; Leake, Prop. Land, 171; Den v. Fogg, 3 N. J. Law, 598; Allin v. Bunce, 1 Root (Conn.) 96; Welles v. Olcott, Kirby (Conn.) 118;

§ 26)   INCIDENTS OF ESTATES TAIL.   49

fee tail may appear from a limitation over, if the donee "die without heirs of his body," or similar expressions. This is called an "estate tail by construction." [36]

Estates Tail—In Chattel Interests.

There can be no fee tail in personal property or in chattel interests, and an attempt to so limit an estate tail results in passing the donor's entire interest.*

INCIDENTS OF ESTATES TAIL.

26. The rights of the owner of a fee tail are the same as the rights of one owning a fee simple, except as to alienation.

As already seen, a tenant in tail can convey only an estate during his life; otherwise, the incidents of estates tail are the same as of those in fee simple.[37] The tenant in tail is not liable for waste,[38] and is not bound to pay off incumbrances or to keep down

---

Den v. Dubois, 16 N. J. Law, 285; Giddings v. Smith, 15 Vt. 344; Pollock v. Speidel, 17 Ohio St. 439; 4 Kent. Comm. 12; 1 Shars. & B. Lead. Cas. Real Prop. 94. See Jewell v. Warner, 35 N. H. 176. But not in South Carolina. Murrell v. Mathews, 2 Bay (S. C.) 397; Wright v. Herron, 5 Rich. Eq. (S. C.) 441.

[36] Allen v. Trustees, 102 Mass. 262; Potts' Appeal, 30 Pa. St. 168; Tate v. Tally, 3 Call (Va.) 354; Doe v. Craigen, 8 Leigh (Va.) 449; Den v. Hyatt, 1 Hawks (N. C.) 247; Covert v. Robinson, 46 Pa. St. 274; Smith's Appeal, 23 Pa. St. 9; Willis v. Bucher, 3 Wash. C. C. 369, Fed. Cas. No. 17,769; Albee v. Carpenter, 12 Cush. (Mass.) 382; Perry v. Kline, Id. 118; Parkman v. Bowdoin, 1 Sumn. 359, Fed. Cas. No. 10,763; Brown v. Weaver, 28 Ga. 377; Child v. Baylie, Cro. Jac. 459.

*Stockton v. Martin, 2 Bay (S. C.) 471; Albee v. Carpenter, 12 Cush. (Mass.) 382. But cf. Burkhart v. Bucher, 2 Bin. (Pa.) 455; Shoemaker v. Huffnagle, 4 Watts & S. (Pa.) 437; Duer v. Boyd, 1 Serg. & R. (Pa.) 203. And see post, p. 53.

[37] Buxton v. Inhabitants of Uxbridge, 10 Metc. (Mass.) 87; Partridge v. Dorsey, 3 Har. & J. 302.

[38] Hales v. Petit, Plow. 253; Secheverel v. Dale, Poph. 193; Liford's Case, 11 Coke, 46b; Attorney General v. Marlborough, 3 Madd. 498. But he cannot authorize it after his death. Liford's Case, supra. What is meant by "waste" will be treated of under "Life Estates," post, p. 62.

REAL PROP.—4

the interest on them.[39] An estate tail is subject to dower [40] and curtesy.[41] But the doctrine of merger does not apply to estates tail. By merger, when a greater and a lesser estate come together in one person, the latter is destroyed by the former, and the owner has only the one estate left, thus sometimes cutting out rights which came between the two estates. But, if the tenant in tail becomes the owner of the reversion or the remainder in fee, his estates do not consolidate and shut out the issue in tail, or other remainders, if there are such.[42]

DURATION OF ESTATES TAIL.

27. An estate tail endures until the particular heirs named in the gift are exhausted, and then reverts to the donor, unless it is sooner barred, which may be:
  (a) **By common recovery (obsolete).**
  (b) **By fine (obsolete).**
  (c) **By deed, in most estates.**

Barring Estates Tail—By Common Recovery.

After the statute de donis had been in force about 200 years,[43] a method of evading it and of barring the entail was devised, called a "common recovery." This consisted of a collusive suit, brought by the intended purchaser, called the "demandant," under a claim of paramount title against the tenant in tail. The latter did not defend, but claimed that his grantor had warranted the title to the lands, and asked that he be called upon to defend the suit. This was termed "vouching to warranty." [44] The vouchee, who

---

[39] Amesbury v. Brown, 1 Ves. Sr. 477; Chaplin v. Chaplin, 3 P. Wms. 235. But see Burgess v. Mawby, 1 Turn. & R. 176.

[40] Kennedy v. Kennedy, 29 N. J. Law, 185; Smith's Appeal, 23 Pa. St. 9. See post, p. 83.

[41] Voller v. Carter, 4 El. & Bl. 173. See post, p. 73. Before the statute the second husband could have curtesy. Anon., Fitzh. Abr. "Formedon," 66. But this was changed by the statute.

[42] Wiscot's Case, 2 Coke, 60a; Challis, Real Prop. c. 10.

[43] The house of lords had defeated all attempts to repeal the statute. See Mildmay's Case, 6 Coke, 40a; 2 Bl. Comm. 116.

[44] The proceeding was usually a more complicated one, called a "recovery

§ 27) DURATION OF ESTATES TAIL. 51

was a mere man of straw, suffered default to be entered against him, thus admitting the warranty. Then the lands were judged to belong to the demandant, and judgment was entered against the vouchee that he reimburse the tenant in tail with lands of equal value, according to the doctrine of warranty.[45] The entail was held to attach to this land, so the heirs and remainder-men would lose nothing; but in fact the vouchee was always a man of no means, and had not in fact warranted the estate to the defendant, but was a third person, called in to carry out the fiction, and the judgment against him was worthless. The efficacy of this proceeding to bar an estate tail was first recognized in the now famous Taltarum's Case.[46] A common recovery, being suffered, not only cut off the issue in tail, but destroyed all remainders or reversions as well, and thus effectually put an end to entailed estates.[47] That is, the tenant in tail, after Taltarum's Case, always had power to suffer a recovery, and no condition or restriction in the deed of gift could be devised which could prevent it.[48]

Same—By Fine.

Estates tail might also be barred by another kind of collusive action called a "fine."[49] Fines were actions for the recovery of lands on a claim of title, which were compromised by the parties with leave of the court, and the judgment record entered in the case became the record of title. The effect of a fine was to bar the issue in tail, but not the remainder-man or reversioner.[50]

---

with a double voucher." For further details as to recoveries, see 2 Bl. Comm. 357; Challis, Real Prop. 249.

[45] As to the origin of warranty, see Digby, Hist. Real Prop. 80, note 1.

[46] Y. B. 12 Edw. IV. 19.

[47] 2 Bl. Comm. 361. A recovery could be suffered only by one in possession as tenant in tail or with the consent of the person in possession. 1 Dembitz, Land Tit. 116.

[48] Mary Portington's Case, 10 Coke, 35b; Dewitt v. Eldred, 4 Watts & S. (Pa.) 415. And see Waters v. Margerum, 60 Pa. St. 39; Doyle v. Mullady, 33 Pa. St. 264; Elliott v. Pearsoll, 8 Watts & S. (Pa.) 38; Hall v. Thayer, 5 Gray, (Mass.) 523.

[49] The statute de donis declared that fines should have no effect on estates tail, but this was changed by the statutes of 4 Hen. VII. c. 24, and 32 Hen. VIII. c. 36.

[50] Seymor's Case, 10 Coke, 95b. They would also be barred unless they

Same—By Deed.

In many states it is now provided by statute that estates tail may be barred by deed.*

TENANT IN TAIL AFTER POSSIBILITY OF ISSUE EXTINCT.

28. When there is a tenant in special tail, and it has become impossible for him to have issue who can inherit under the entail, he is called "tenant in tail after possibility of issue extinct."

If one is tenant in tail, and it has become impossible that there shall be issue who can inherit, he is called "tenant in tail after possibility of issue extinct." This condition can only arise in estates in special tail, as where the limitation is to "A. and his heirs begotten on the body of his wife, B.," and B. dies without issue.[51] The presumption that the possibility of issue is extinct never arises from the great age of the parties, and so there can never be a tenant in tail after possibility of issue extinct in case of an estate in general tail.[52] The position of a tenant in tail after possibility of issue extinct is in some respects different from that of a tenant in tail. He cannot bar the entail, but the doctrine of merger applies.[53] Such a tenant is not punishable for waste.[54]

ESTATES TAIL IN THE UNITED STATES.

29. In many states estates tail have been abolished by statutes, which have turned them into either
  (a) Estates in fee simple, or
  (b) Life estates, with remainders to the donee's heirs who would take under the entail.

30. In some states estates tail still exist, but may be barred by deed.

made claim within a period fixed by statute. Further formalities were afterwards required called "proclamations." 2 Bl. Comm. 348; 1 Shep. Touch. c. 2.

* See post, § 30.

[51] Co. Litt. §§ 32–34; 2 Bl. Comm. 124.
[52] 2 Bl. Comm. 125.
[53] Co. Litt. 28a.
[54] Co. Litt. 27b.

Estates tail, as created by the statute de donis, were generally recognized in the original states of this country.[55] But great changes have been made by statute. In some of our states estates tail have been abolished, and a conveyance attempting to limit an estate tail would create a fee simple in the donee who would be first entitled to the estate under the form of the gift.[56] In others the first taker has a life estate, with remainder over in fee simple.[57] In still others estates tail may exist until barred, and this can be done by a simple deed or by one acknowledged in a manner provided by the statute.[58] Fines and recoveries are not now in use, though they were used somewhat in the early history of our country.[59] There are a number of states in which no statutory provisions as to estates tail exist. In these states, fees tail are as at common law unless, when the question comes before the courts, such estates are held not to be adapted to the genius of our institutions.[60]

QUASI ENTAIL.

31. A limitation to one and the heirs of his body out of a life estate is called a "quasi entail," and is not affected by the statute de donis conditionalibus.

[55] See Williams, Real Prop. (17th Am. Ed.) note 121.

[56] In re Robinson's Estate, 149 Pa. St. 418, 24 Atl. 297; Ray v. Alexander, 146 Pa. St. 242, 23 Atl. 383; Durant v. Muller, 88 Ga. 251, 14 S. E. 612; Burris v. Page, 12 Mo. 358; Pruitt v. Holland, 92 Ky. 641, 18 S. W. 852; Prichard v. James, 93 Ky. 306, 20 S. W. 216; Lanham v. Wilson (Ky.) 22 S. W. 438.

[57] Doty v. Teller, 54 N. J. Law, 163, 23 Atl. 944; Clarkson v. Clarkson, 125 Mo. 381, 28 S. W. 446; Brown v. Rogers, 125 Mo. 392, 28 S. W. 630. In some states remainders after estates tail are preserved if they take effect on the death of the first taker without issue, the entail being extinct by that event. 1 Dembitz, Land Tit. 117.

[58] 1 Stim. Am. St. Law, § 1313; Williams, Real Prop. (17th Am. Ed.) note 121; 1 Washb. Real Prop. (5th Ed.) 117, note 2; 1 Shars. & B. Lead. Cas. Real Prop. 109. As to barring the entail by deed, see Collamore v. Collamore, 158 Mass. 74, 32 N. E. 1034.

[59] Jewell v. Warner, 35 N. H. 176; Lyle v. Richards, 9 Serg. & R. (Pa.) 322; Carter v. McMichael, 10 Serg. & R. (Pa.) 429; Wood v. Bayard, 63 Pa. St. 320.

[60] Jordan v. Roach, 32 Miss. 481. In some states it has been held that the statute de donis conditionalibus is not in force, and that limitations to a man and the heirs of his body create fees conditional at common law. Pierson v.

An estate may be limited to one and the heirs of his body during the life of another person. The statute de donis does not apply to such an estate; so it is not a fee tail, but resembles more a fee conditional at common law.[61] This form of limitation is usually called a "quasi entail."

Lane, 60 Iowa, 60, 14 N. W. 90; Rowland v. Warren, 10 Or. 129; Izard v. Middleton, 1 Bailey, Eq. (S. C.) 227; Barksdale v. Gamage, 3 Rich. Eq. (S. C.) 279; Burnett v. Burnett, 17 S. C. 545.

[61] Further, as to quasi entail, see Grey v. Mannock, 2 Eden, 339; Dillon v. Dillon, 1 Ball. & B. 77; Allen v. Allen, 2 Dru. & War. 307; Campbell v. Sandys, 1 Schoales & L. 281.

CHAPTER V.

ESTATES AS TO QUANTITY (Continued)—CONVENTIONAL LIFE ESTATES.

  32. Life Estates Defined.
  33. Creation of Life Estate.
 34–36. Conventional Life Estates.
  37. Incidents of Life Estates.
 38–39. Estates per Autre Vie.

LIFE ESTATES DEFINED.

32. Life estates are freeholds not of inheritance. They include:

(a) **Estates for the tenant's own life.**

(b) **Estates for the life of another,—per autre vie.**

(c) **Estates for an uncertain period, which may continue during a life or lives.**

Life estates come next below estates tail in order of quantity of interest. They are freeholds, but not of inheritance.[1] In general terms, they are estates whose duration is limited by the length of a human life. Estates of uncertain duration, which may continue during a life or lives, are regarded as life estates.[2] It is immaterial how improbable it is that the estate will last during a life. It is sufficient if by possibility it may do so. An estate to a woman during widowhood is a life estate. It may last during her life, but it cannot last longer.[3]

CREATION OF LIFE ESTATES.

33. As to mode of creation, life estates are:

(a) **Conventional, created by act of the parties** (p. 56).

(b) **Legal, created by operation of law** (p. 69).

---

[1] 2 Bl. Comm. 120.

[2] Hurd v. Cushing, 7 Pick. (Mass.) 169; Warner v. Tanner, 38 Ohio St. 118; Beeson v. Burton, 12 C. B. 647. But cf. Gilmore v. Hamilton, 83 Ind. 198.

[3] Roseboom v. Van Vechten, 5 Denio (N. Y.) 414.

The main division of life estates is into conventional and legal life estates. The former are those which the parties create by their acts, having the creation of such estates in view as the result of the acts, as where the owner of a fee simple grants another the land for so long as he lives.[4] Legal life estates, on the other hand, result from the operation of law, without any acts by the parties looking to such result, but from acts done for other purposes. For example, marriage may give both husband and wife interests in the realty of the other, although nothing has been said, or no express contract made, in relation to such realty. These estates are created by operation of law, and are called life estates. Conventional life estates will be considered in the remainder of this chapter, and legal life estates in the succeeding chapter.

SAME—CONVENTIONAL LIFE ESTATES.

34. Conventional life estates may be measured by one or more lives.

35. At common law no words of limitation need be added to the grantee's name to create a life estate.

36. Estates per autre vie arise by express limitations to a grantee for the life of another person, or by the assignment of an existing life estate.

Conventional life estates are of two sorts, depending on the person whose life limits the duration of the estate. They are either for one's own life,[5] or during the life of another person, in which case they are called "estates per autre vie." [6] An estate for one's own life is regarded as of a higher nature than an estate per autre vie.[7] Estates during two lives, as "to A. and B., during their joint lives," or "to A., during the lives of B. and C.," are in

---

[4] 2 Bl. Comm. 120. By statute in several states, life estates "may be created in a term of years and a remainder limited thereon." 1 Stim. Am. St. Law, § 1427. A life estate cannot be created by parol. Stewart v. Clark, 13 Metc. (Mass.) 79; Garrett v. Clark, 5 Or. 464.

[5] Co. Litt. § 56.

[6] Co. Litt. § 56; 2 Bl. Comm. 120.

[7] 2 Bl. Comm. 121.

reality measured by a single life. A limitation during joint lives is in effect the same as during the life of the shortest liver of those named, and one during two or more lives is equivalent to an estate during the life of the one who lives longest.[8] An estate for joint lives must be expressly so limited.[9]

Words of Limitation.

According to common-law rules, if an estate is granted to a man without adding any words of limitation, he takes a life estate. Therefore, no special words need be used to create a life estate,[10] except where there is a statutory rule that a fee simple is presumed to be conveyed unless otherwise restricted.[11] Since an estate for one's own life is considered a higher interest than an estate per autre vie, where the conveyance does not specify for whose life the grantee is to hold, he takes it for his own life. But where the grantor can only give an estate for his own life, as where he is himself a tenant for life or a tenant in tail, then the grantee will take only what the grantor can lawfully give;[12] that is, an es-

[8] Brudnel's Case, 5 Coke, 9a. See Clark v. Owens, 18 N. Y. 434; Dale's Case, Cro. Eliz. 182.

[9] Brudnel's Case, 5 Coke, 9a.

[10] Jackson v. Embler, 14 Johns. (N. Y.) 198; Trusdell v. Lehman, 47 N. J. Eq. 218, 20 Atl. 391; Hunter v. Bryan, 5 Humph. (Tenn.) 47; Gray v. Packer, 4 Watts & S. (Pa.) 17; Jackson v. Van Hoesen, 4 Cow. (N. Y.) 325; Kearney v. Kearney, 17 N. J. Eq. 59; Wusthoff v. Dracourt, 3 Watts (Pa.) 240; Bozeman v. Bishop, 94 Ga. 459, 20 S. E. 11. So a life estate may be created by a reservation. Doe v. Grady, 2 Dev. (N. C.) 395; Hodges v. Spicer, 79 N. C. 223; Richardson v. York, 14 Me. 216. Or by a quitclaim to a co-tenant in common. McKinney v. Stacks, 6 Heisk. (Tenn.) 284.

[11] See ante, p. 37. As to what words will pass only a life estate, see Corby v. Corby, 85 Mo. 371; Leaper v. Neagle, 94 N. C. 338; Dew v. Kuehn, 64 Wis. 293, 25 N. W. 212; Lowrie v. Ryland, 65 Iowa, 584, 22 N. W. 686; Jones' Ex'rs v. Stills, 19 N. J. Eq. 324; Sheafe v. Cushing, 17 N. H. 508; Jossey v. White, 28 Ga. 265; Schaefer v. Schaefer, 147 Ill. 337, 31 N. E. 136; Robinson v. Robinson, 89 Va. 916, 14 S. E. 916. And cf. Beall's Lessee v. Holmes, 6 Har. & J. (Md.) 205; Jackson v. Wells, 9 Johns. (N. Y.) 222; Wheaton v. Andress, 23 Wend. (N. Y.) 452; Moore v. Dimond, 5 R. I. 121; In re Frothingham, 63 Hun, 430, 18 N. Y. Supp. 695; Allen v. Boomer, 82 Wis. 364, 52 N. W. 426; Kiene v. Gruehle, 85 Iowa, 312, 52 N. W. 232.

[12] Jackson v. Mancius, 2 Wend. (N. Y.) 357; Rogers v. Moore, 11 Conn. 553; Bell v. Twilight, 22 N. H. 500.

tate for the grantor's life. A man may take a life estate by implication, as by a devise of land to the testator's heirs after the death of B., from which it would be presumed that B. was to have the land during his life.[13] But, if the devise is to a stranger after B.'s death, no such presumption arises, and the estate goes to the heir during B.'s life.[14]

Estates per Autre Vie.

An estate for the life of another [15] usually arises by one who is tenant for life assigning his interest to another, who thereby becomes entitled to the land during the life of the grantor. It may, however, be expressly limited for the life of a third person. The one whose life limits the duration of the estate is called the "cestui qui vie." [16]

INCIDENTS OF LIFE ESTATES.

37. The principal incidents of life estates are the following:
  (a) Life estates are subject to alienation, voluntary and involuntary (p. 59).
  (b) The tenant must pay the interest on incumbrances (p. 60).
  (c) Rent due from a lessee of the tenant is apportionable on the death of the tenant (p. 60).
  (d) The tenant cannot recover compensation for improvements or repairs (p. 61).
  (e) The tenant is entitled to estovers (p. 61).
  (f) There is a right to emblements on the death of a tenant for life, but he cannot claim them when he forfeits his estate (p. 61).

[13] Barry v. Shelby, 4 Hayw. (Tenn.) 229; Haskins v. Tate, 25 Pa. St. 249; Nicholson v. Drennan, 35 S. C. 333, 14 S. E. 719.

[14] 1 Washb. Real Prop. (5th Ed.) p. 123.

[15] It may be for more than one life. Ante, p. 56. But, in four states, if more than two cestuis qui vie are named, the remainder nevertheless takes effect on the death of the two first named. 1 Stim. Am. St. Law, § 1422. Cf. Clark v. Owens, 18 N. Y. 434. By statute, 6 Anne, c. 18, if the one who claims an estate per autre vie cannot produce the cestui qui vie, it is presumed that he is dead, and the estate is terminated.

[16] 2 Bl. Comm. 258; Co. Litt. 41b.

(g) **A tenant must not commit waste,—that is, any permanent and material injury to the inheritance** (p. 62).

(h) **Life estates are subject to merger** (p. 66).

The following discussion of the incidents of life estates applies to legal as well as to conventional life estates.

Alienation.

A tenant for life has power to dispose of his interest in whole or in part, unless there is a condition in restraint, in the terms of his grant;[17] but he can give another no rights in the land which will extend beyond his life.[18] There was a common-law rule that a tenant for life forfeited his estate if he attempted to convey a greater interest than he owned, by a conveyance operating through transfer of possession, as by a feoffment in fee,[19] because such a feoffment was a renunciation of tenure, and worked a disseisin. But this is not now the rule.[20] Life estates are also subject to involuntary alienation, as for taxes and debts.[21]

[17] Criswell v. Grumbling, 107 Pa. St. 408; Hayward v. Kinney, 84 Mich. 591, 48 N. W. 170.

[18] Lehndorf v. Cope, 122 Ill. 317, 13 N. E. 505; McIntyre v. Clark, 6 Misc. Rep. 377, 26 N. Y. Supp. 744; McLendon v. Horton (Ga.) 22 S. E. 45; Fields v. Bush, 94 Ga. 664, 21 S. E. 827.

[19] 2 Bl. Comm. 274; French v. Rollins, 21 Me. 372. See, also, Stump v. Findlay. 2 Rawle (Pa.) 168. This did not apply to conveyances under the statute of uses. Jackson v. Mancius, 2 Wend. (N. Y.) 357; Pendleton v. Vandevier, 1 Wash. (Va.) 381; Stevens v. Winship, 1 Pick. (Mass.) 318. Nor to a quitclaim in fee. Bell v. Twilight, 22 N. H. 500. Nor to a lease for years. Locke v. Rowell, 47 N. H. 46.

[20] Stevens v. Winship, 1 Pick. (Mass.) 318; Rogers v. Moore, 11 Conn. 553; McCorry v. King's Heirs, 3 Humph. (Tenn.) 267; McKee's Lessee v. Pfout, 3 Dall. (Pa.) 486; McMichael v. Craig (Ala.) 16 South. 883. The conveyances which caused forfeitures were feoffment, fine, and recovery; but these are not now in use. 1 Dembitz, Land Tit. 108.

[21] Roberts v. Whiting, 16 Mass. 186; Wheeler v. Gorham, 2 Root (Conn.) 328; Ehrisman v. Sener, 162 Pa. St. 577, 29 Atl. 719; Thompson v. Murphy, 10 Ind. App. 464, 37 N. E. 1094; American Mortg. Co. of Scotland v. Hill, 92 Ga. 297, 18 S. E. 425. But see, as to the life tenant's liability for special assessments, Stilwell v. Doughty, 2 Bradf. Sur. (N. Y.) 311.

Interest on Incumbrances.

It is the duty of the tenant to keep down the interest on incumbrances, but he is not bound to pay off the principal;[22] and, if he does, he is entitled to contribution from the reversioner or remainder-man.[23]

Apportionment of Rent.

If the tenant for life makes a lease reserving rent and dies before the day the rent is due, the rent is apportioned, and his personal representative can recover the amount due when the lessor died.[24] The common-law rule was otherwise, however, until the statute of 11 Geo. II. c. 19, § 15.

[22] Thomas v. Thomas, 17 N. J. Eq. 356; Cogswell v. Cogswell, 2 Edw. Ch. (N. Y.) 231; Hunt v. Watkins, 1 Humph. (Tenn.) 498; McDonald v. Heylin, 4 Phila. (Pa.) 73; Barnum v. Barnum, 42 Md. 251. If he fails to pay the interest, he is liable to the remainder-man for any damage suffered. Wade v. Malloy, 16 Hun (N. Y.) 226. The life tenant must also pay taxes. Jenks v. Horton, 96 Mich. 13, 55 N. W. 372; Watkins v. Green, 101 Mich. 493, 60 N. W. 44; Bone v. Tyrrell, 113 Mo. 175, 20 S. W. 796; Disher v. Disher, 45 Neb. 100, 63 N. W. 368; Chaplin v. U. S., 29 Ct. Cl. 231; Varney v. Stevens, 22 Me. 331; Patrick v. Sherwood, 4 Blatchf. 112, Fed. Cas. No. 10,804; Fleet v. Dorland, 11 How. Prac. (N. Y.) 489; Johnson v. Smith, 5 Bush (Ky.) 102. But see Cochran v. Cochran, 2 Desaus. Eq. (S. C.) 521. But he is entitled to contribution on assessments for permanent improvements. Reyburn v. Wallace, 93 Mo. 326, 3 S. W. 482; In re Bradley's Estate, 3 Pa. Dist. R. 359; Bobb v. Wolff, 54 Mo. App. 515; Moore v. Simonson (Or.) 39 Pac. 1105. Cf. In re Wyatt's Estate, 9 Misc. Rep. 285, 30 N. Y. Supp. 275 (insurance premiums).

[23] Foster v. Hilliard, 1 Story, 77, Fed. Cas. No. 4,972; Hunt v. Watkins, 1 Humph. (Tenn.) 498; Daviess v. Myers, 13 B. Mon. (Ky.) 511. Cf. Stevens v. Melcher, 80 Hun, 514, 30 N. Y. Supp. 625. The tenant's share is found by computing the present worth of the interest payments which he would have to make during the probable existence of his life according to tables of mortality. The Carlisle tables are generally used. Abercrombie v. Riddle, 3 Md. Ch. 320; Bell v. Mayor, etc., 10 Paige (N. Y.) 49; Foster v. Hilliard, supra; Atkins v. Kron, 8 Ired. Eq. (N. C.) 1; Swaine v. Perine, 5 Johns. Ch. (N. Y.) 482; Cogswell v. Cogswell, 2 Edw. Ch. (N. Y.) 231. But see note to Estabrook v. Hapgood, 10 Mass. 313; Dorsey v. Smith, 7 Har. & J. (Md.) 345, 367. There was formerly an arbitrary rule that he should pay one-third, and this seems to still exist in South Carolina. Wright v. Jennings, 1 Bailey (S. C.) 277. Cf. Brand v. Rhodes' Adm'r (Ky.) 30 S. W. 597.

[24] Borie v. Crissman, 82 Pa. St. 125; Price v. Pickett, 21 Ala. 741. At common law there was no apportionment of rent. Clun v. Fisher, Cro. Jac. 309; Rockingham v. Penrice, 1 P. Wms. 177; Jenner v. Morgan, Id. 391; Norris v.

Improvements and Repairs.

The tenant for life can recover nothing for improvements which he makes on the estate;[25] but he may put buildings into tenantable condition at the expense of the estate, or complete a house begun by the testator under whom he holds.[26] He is, however, bound to make ordinary repairs at his own expense.[27]

Estovers.

A tenant for life has a right to cut timber growing on the land to use for certain purposes. This is called the right to estovers or botes, and comprises: (1) House bote, or the right to cut wood for repairing buildings and to use for fuel,[28] the latter sometimes being termed fire bote; (2) plough bote, or the right to cut wood for repairing farming implements;[29] and (3) hay bote, or the right to cut wood for repairing fences.[30]

Emblements.

The personal representative of a tenant for life is entitled to emblements,[31] since the tenant's estate is one of uncertain duration.[32] But the tenant himself cannot claim them if he forfeits his

---

Harrison, 2 Madd. 268. This was changed by the statute of 11 Geo. II. c. 19, § 15. The statute has been re-enacted in some states (1 Stim. Am. St. Law, § 2027), and followed in others.

[25] Hagan v. Varney, 147 Ill. 281, 35 N. E. 219; In re Rennie's Estate, 10 Misc. Rep. 638, 32 N. Y. Supp. 225; Thurston v. Dickinson, 2 Rich. Eq. (S. C.) 317; Merritt v. Scott, 81 N. C. 385; Corbett v. Laurens, 5 Rich. Eq. (S. C.) 301; Elam v. Parkhill, 60 Tex. 581; Wilson v. Parker (Miss.) 14 South. 264; Van Bibber v. Williamson, 37 Fed. 756. Cf. Austin v. Stevens, 24 Me. 520; Datesman's Appeal, 127 Pa. St. 348, 17 Atl. 1086, 1100; Caldwell v. Jacob (Ky.) 27 S. W. 86.

[26] Sohier v. Eldredge, 103 Mass. 345; Parsons v. Winslow, 16 Mass. 361. Cf. Brough v. Higgins, 2 Grat. (Va.) 408; In re Laytin (Surr.) 20 N. Y. Supp. 72.

[27] In re Steele, 19 N. J. Eq. 120; Kearney v. Kearney, 17 N. J. Eq. 59; Wilson v. Edmonds, 24 N. H. 517; Brooks v. Brooks, 12 S. C. 422.

[28] White v. Cutler, 17 Pick. (Mass.) 248; Webster v. Webster, 33 N. H. 18; Smith v. Jewett, 40 N. H. 530; Smith v. Poyas, 2 Desaus. Eq. (S. C.) 65. But see Padelford v. Padelford, 7 Pick. (Mass.) 152. Cf. Loomis v. Wilbur, 5 Mason, 13, Fed. Cas. No. 8,498.

[29] 2 Bl. Comm. 35, 122.

[30] Elliot v. Smith, 2 N. H. 430.

[31] See ante, p. 8.

[32] Perry v. Terrel, 1 Dev. & B. Eq. (N. C.) 441; Hunt v. Watkins, 1 Humph.

estate by not performing a condition,[33] though he can if his interest is terminated without his fault.[34] The lessee of a tenant for life is entitled to emblements;[35] and so, also, would the lessee of one who held during her widowhood, but terminated her estate by marriage.[36] If she was herself in possession, she could not claim emblements, because she terminated the estate by her own act.[37]

Waste.

Another important incident of an estate for life, and of all particular estates, is that the tenant must not commit waste;[38] that is, to cause or suffer any permanent and material injury to the inheritance. In other words, the one who is next entitled to the premises has a right to have them come to him without their value being impaired by any destruction of the corporeal thing.[39] It may be provided, at the creation of the estate, that the tenant shall not be liable for waste, or, that he shall hold "without impeachment for waste."[40] But even then wanton injury, or "equitable waste," will be restrained by a court of chancery.[41] Injury which occurs from positive acts of the tenant is "voluntary waste," and injury

(Tenn.) 498; Poindexter v. Blackburn, 1 Ired. Eq. (N. C.) 286; Spencer v. Lewis, 1 Houst. (Del.) 223. But cf. Reiff v. Reiff, 64 Pa. St. 134.

[33] 2 Bl. Comm. 123; Oland's Case, 5 Coke, 116a. Cf. Debow v. Colfax, 10 N. J. Law, 128; Bulwer v. Bulwer, 2 Barn. & Ald. 470.

[34] Price v. Pickett, 21 Ala. 741; King v. Whittle, 73 Ga. 482.

[35] King v. Foscue, 91 N. C. 116.

[36] 2 Bl. Comm. 124.

[37] Hawkins v. Skeggs' Adm'r, 10 Humph. (Tenn.) 31; Oland's Case, 5 Coke, 116a.

[38] The restriction applied only to a tenant in dower and curtesy until the statute of Marlebridge, 52 Hen. III. c. 23. But a tenant in tail after possibility of issue extinct is not liable for waste. Ante, p. 52.

[39] Proffitt v. Henderson, 29 Mo. 327; Sackett v. Sackett, 8 Pick. (Mass.) 309; Dejarnatte v. Allen, 5 Grat. (Va.) 499; Huntley v. Russell, 13 Q. B. Div. 572, 588.

[40] 2 Bl. Comm. 283; Pyne v. Dor, 1 Term R. 55; Bowles' Case, 11 Coke, 79b. See, also, Gent v. Harrison, 1 Johns. Eng. Ch. 517; Turner v. Wright, 2 De Gex, F. & J. 234.

[41] Vane v. Lord Barnard, 2 Vern. 738; Roet v. Somerville, 2 Eq. Cas. Abr. 759; Lushington v. Boldero, 15 Beav. 1. And see Marker v. Marker, 4 Eng. Law & Eq. 95.

resulting from his neglect of duty is "permissive waste,"—for example, permitting a building to fall down from want of repair, as distinguished from pulling it down, which would be permissive waste.[42]

The English rules as to waste are to a large extent inapplicable in this country, owing to the difference in circumstances, especially as to cutting down trees and the use of land;[43] and what would be waste in a thickly-settled Eastern state might not be in a new and undeveloped region.[44] In very many cases it is a question of fact for the jury whether the acts complained of are wrongful, as being injurious to the estate.[45]

Same—Husbandry.

If one holding farming lands as tenant for life cultivates in a way not sanctioned by the rules of good husbandry, he is guilty of waste.[46] For instance, he should not exhaust the land by constant tillage, without change of crop or the use of fertilizers,[47] nor should he permit brush to choke up meadow land.[48] But it would not, as in England,[49] be waste to change the character of the land, if no substantial injury results, as by plowing up pasture land.[50]

[42] 2 Bl. Comm. 281. As to permissive waste by a tenant at will, see Countess of Shrewsbury's Case, 5 Coke, 13. And see Herne v. Bembow, 4 Taunt. 764. Cf. Moore v. Townshend, 33 N. J. Law, 284.

[43] Keeler v. Eastman, 11 Vt. 293; Pynchon v. Stearns, 11 Metc. (Mass.) 304; Jackson v. Brownson, 7 Johns. (N. Y.) 227; Lynn's Appeal, 31 Pa. St. 44; Drown v. Smith, 52 Me. 141; Crockett v. Crockett, 2 Ohio St. 180; Kidd v. Dennison, 6 Barb. (N. Y.) 9; Findlay v. Smith, 6 Munf. (Va.) 134. And see Carpenter, J., in Morehouse v. Cotheal, 22 N. J. Law, 521.

[44] Morehouse v. Cotheal, 22 N. J. Law, 521; Webster v. Webster, 33 N. H. 18; Davis v. Gilliam, 5 Ired. Eq. (N. C.) 308.

[45] Webster v. Webster, 33 N. H. 18; King v. Miller, 99 N. C. 583, 6 S. E. 660.

[46] Sarles v. Sarles, 3 Sandf. Ch. (N. Y.) 601. Cf. Jackson v. Andrew, 18 Johns. (N. Y.) 431.

[47] Sarles v. Sarles, 3 Sandf. Ch. (N. Y.) 601.

[48] Clemence v. Steere, 1 R. I. 272.

[49] Keepers, etc., of Harrow School v. Alderton, 2 Bos. & P. 86.

[50] Pynchon v. Stearns, 11 Metc. (Mass.) 304; Clemence v. Steere, 1 R. I. 272; Alexander v. Fisher, 7 Ala. 514. Cf. Chase v. Hazelton, 7 N. H. 171.

Same—Trees.

We have seen that the tenant may take a reasonable amount of wood for estovers,[51] and the right may extend further as to the "clearing" of woodland for purposes of cultivation.[52] Whether this or any other cutting of timber is waste depends in each case on the customs of the locality and the condition of the estate.[53] A tenant for life cannot cut timber to sell,[54] except in cases where that has been the way of enjoying the land.[55]

Same—Mines and Quarries.

Whether or not it is waste to take minerals, stone, clay, or gravel depends on the previous use of the premises. If such has been the manner of enjoying the profits of the estate, the tenant may continue it;[56] but he must not open new mines or quarries.[57] Nor can the one entitled to the next estate work the mines and

---

[51] Ante, p. 61. Padelford v. Padelford, 7 Pick. (Mass.) 152; Calvert v. Rice, 91 Ky. 533, 16 S. W. 351; Gardiner v. Derring, 1 Paige (N. Y.) 573; Smith v. Jewett, 40 N. H. 530;) Miles v. Miles, 32 N. H. 147.

[52] Drown v. Smith, 52 Me. 141; Ward v. Sheppard, 2 Hayw. (Tenn.) 461; Owen v. Hyde, 6 Yerg. (Tenn.) 334; Disher v. Disher, 45 Neb. 100, 63 N. W. 368; Davis v. Clark, 40 Mo. App. 515. But cf. Chase v. Hazelton, 7 N. H. 171. And can sell the wood so cut. Wilkinson v. Wilkinson, 59 Wis. 557, 18 N. W. 527; Keeler v. Eastman, 11 Vt. 293; Crockett v. Crockett, 2 Ohio St. 180; Davis v. Gilliam, 5 Ired. Eq. (N. C.) 308.

[53] McCullough v. Irvine's Ex'rs, 13 Pa. St. 438; Keeler v. Eastman, 11 Vt. 293. Cf. Parkins v. Coxe, 2 Hayw. (N. C.) 339; Carr v. Carr, 4 Dev. & B. (N. C.) 179.

[54] Johnson v. Johnson, 18 N. H. 594; Davis v. Gilliam, 5 Ired. Eq. (N. C.) 308; Miller v. Shields, 55 Ind. 71; Parkins v. Coxe, Mart. & H. (N. C.) 517; Clemence v. Steere, 1 R. I. 272; Kidd v. Dennison, 6 Barb. (N. Y.) 9.

[55] Clemence v. Steere, 1 R. I. 272; Ballentine v. Poyner, Mart. & H. (N. C.) 268; Den v. Kinney, 5 N. J. Law, 552. And cf. Carr v. Carr, 4 Dev. & B. (N. C.) 179. See, also, the exception in note 44.

[56] Astry v. Ballard, 2 Mod. 193; Neel v. Neel, 19 Pa. St. 323; Sayers v. Hoskinson, 110 Pa. St. 473, 1 Atl. 308. Cf. Russell v. Bank, 47 Minn. 286, 50 N. W. 228; Billings v. Taylor, 10 Pick. (Mass.) 460; Reed's Ex'rs v. Reed, 16 N. J. Eq. 248; Lynn's Appeal, 31 Pa. St. 44. And see Irwin v. Covode, 24 Pa. St. 162. The life tenant is allowed new shafts into old veins. Crouch v. Puryear, 1 Rand. (Va.) 258; Clavering v. Clavering, 2 P. Wms. 388.

[57] Gaines v. Mining Co., 32 N. J. Eq. 86; Owings v. Emery, 6 Gill. (Md.) 260. Cf. Coates v. Cheever, 1 Cow. (N. Y.) 460; Williamson v. Jones, 39 W. Va. 231, 19 S. E. 436; Childs v. Railway Co., 117 Mo. 414, 23 S. W. 373.

quarries on the land during the continuation of the life tenant's interest without the consent of the latter.[56]

Same—Buildings and Fences.

Formerly there was a very strict rule that almost any alteration in a building would be waste;[59] but this is now relaxed, and the general test is applied as in other cases,—the question being, has the value of the reversion been impaired?[60] It would, of course, be waste for the tenant to remove things which he had made real fixtures by annexation.[61] But waste in respect to buildings may be committed by suffering them to become ruinous for want of repair.[62] This is almost the only case in which permissive waste occurs. As already stated,[63] wood may be cut to keep the buildings and fences in repair; but the duty to repair exists when there is no wood.[64] However, the tenant is not bound to put in repair buildings which are ruinous when he takes the premises.[65] The tenant is liable for negligent, but not for accidental, fires.[66]

Same—Liability for Waste by Strangers, etc.

The tenant is liable for waste committed by strangers,[67] but not for injury resulting from act of God or the law or the public enemy.[68]

---

[58] See Kier v. Peterson, 41 Pa. St. 357.

[59] This was on the ground that such change tended to destroy evidences of identity. Huntley v. Russell, 13 Q. B. Div. 572, 588. It made no difference that such changes increased the value of the building. City of London v. Greyme, Cro. Jac. 181. Cf. Douglass v. Wiggins, 1 Johns. Ch. 435.

[60] Agate v. Lowenbein, 57 N. Y. 604; Doe v. Earl of Burlington, 5 Barn. & Adol. 507; Young v. Spencer, 10 Barn. & C. 145; Hasty v. Wheeler, 12 Me. 434.

[61] McCullough v. Irvine, 13 Pa. St. 438; Dozier v. Gregory, 1 Jones (N. C.) 100. Cf. Clemence v. Steere, 1 R. I. 272.

[62] Abbot of Sherbourne's Case, Y. B. 12 Hen. IV. 5. Cf. Dozier v. Gregory, 1 Jones (N. C.) 100.

[63] Ante, p. 61.

[64] Co. Litt. 53a.

[65] Wilson v. Edmonds, 24 N. H. 517; Clemence v. Steere, 1 R. I. 272.

[66] Anon., Fitzh. Abr. "Waste," pl. 30; Cornish v. Strutton, 8 B. Mon. (Ky.) 586.

[67] Fay v. Brewer, 3 Pick. (Mass.) 203; Cook v. Transportation Co., 1 Denio (N. Y.) 91; Austin v. Railway Co., 25 N. Y. 334. Cf. Beers v. Beers, 21 Mich. 464.

[68] Co. Litt. 53a, 54a; 1 Washb. Real Prop. (5th Ed.) 156; Pollard v. Shaaffer,

Same—Remedies for Waste.

When waste has been committed, compensation may be recovered for the injury done; or, if it is threatened, it may be restrained by injunction.[69] When trees, ore, etc., have been wrongfully severed, they belong to the reversioner or remainder-man as personal property, and he can maintain appropriate actions therefor.[70] There were formerly many technical rules arising out of the common-law actions for waste, but the matter is now largely changed by statute.[71] By and against whom actions for waste lie is also a subject of statutory regulation.[72] By the statute of Gloucester[73] a penalty of treble damages and forfeiture of the place wasted was imposed, and forfeiture and double or treble damages are imposed by statute in many states.[74]

Merger.

Merger is the absorption of a less estate into a greater where two estates meet in the same person. Thus, where an estate in fee simple and an estate of less duration, such as a life estate or an estate for years, meet in the same person, the smaller interest is said to be "merged"—literally drowned—in the greater and all-com-

---

1 Dall. (Pa.) 210. Cf. Attersoll v. Stevens, 1 Taunt. 198; Huntley v. Russell, 13 Q. B. Div. 572.

[69] See Fetter, Eq. 299; Obrien v. Obrien, Amb. 107; Perrot v. Perrot, 3 Atk. 94. See, also, Smyth v. Carter, 18 Beav. 78; Cahn v. Hewsey, 8 Misc. Rep. 384, 29 N. Y. Supp. 1107; Arment v. Hensel, 5 Wash. 152, 31 Pac. 464; Webster v. Peet, 97 Mich. 326, 56 N. W. 558; Perry v. Hamilton, 138 Ind. 271, 35 N. E. 836. Cf. Jackson v. Andrew, 18 Johns. 431.

[70] Whitfield v. Bewit, 2 P. Wms. 240; Castlemain v. Craven, 22 Vin. Abr 523, pl. 11. And see Bewick v. Whitfield, 3 P. Wms. 267; Bateman v. Hotchkin, 31 Beav. 486; Honywood v. Honywood, L. R. 18 Eq. 306; Nicklase v. Morrison, 56 Ark. 553, 20 S. W. 414; Stowell v. Waddingham, 100 Cal. 7, 34 Pac. 436.

[71] See 1 Washb. Real Prop. (5th Ed.) p. 157; Smith v. Mattingly (Ky.) 28 S. W. 503.

[72] 1 Stim. Am. St. Law, § 1353. And see Dodge v. Davis, 85 Iowa, 77, 52 N. W. 2; Hatch v. Hatch, 31 Wkly. Law Bul. 57; Donald v. Elliott, 11 Misc. Rep. 120, 32 N. Y. Supp. 821.

[73] 6 Edw. I. c. 5.

[74] 1 Stim. Am. St. Law, § 1332; Smith v. Mattingly (Ky.) 28 S. W. 503. But cf. Danziger v. Silberthau (Super. Ct.) 18 N. Y. Supp. 350.

prising one.⁷⁵ When a life tenant becomes the heir of the one who has the reversion or remainder in fee, or if he conveys his life interest to the owner of such reversion, a merger takes place, and the smaller estate has lost its separate existence.⁷⁶ Where two estates meet in the same person and in the same right, it is immaterial, so far as merger is concerned, whether the union is produced by operation of law or by act of party. But where the two estates vest in the same person in different rights by operation of law, merger will not ensue. When the union occurred by act of party equity will not allow the estates to merge, though they would do so at common law.⁷⁷ There will be no merger unless the two estates are of the same character. Therefore, an equitable life estate will not merge in a legal fee simple.⁷⁸ A joint interest in a life estate will not merge in the reversion in severalty owned by one of the co-tenants.⁷⁹ If an estate per autre vie is assigned to one who is a tenant for his own life, it will merge, since, as has been seen, the estate for his own life is greater than the estate per autre vie.⁸⁰

SAME—ESTATES PER AUTRE VIE.

38. When a tenant per autre vie dies before the cestui que vie without having disposed of his estate, the residue of the estate goes to his heirs, if it was given to the tenant and his heirs; otherwise, the

---

[75] Bradford v. Griffin, 40 S. C. 468, 19 S. E. 76; Hovey v. Nellis, 98 Mich. 374, 57 N. W. 255.

[76] 2 Bl. Comm. 177; Co. Litt. 41b; Mudd v. Mullican (Ky.) 12 S. W. 263; Webster v. Gilman, 1 Story, 499, Fed. Cas. No. 17,335; Cary v. Warner, 63 Me. 571; Davis v. Townsend, 32 S. C. 112, 10 S. E. 837; Bennett v. Trustees of M. E. Church, 66 Md. 36, 5 Atl. 291; Shelton v. Hadlock, 62 Conn. 143; Harrison v. Moore, 64 Conn. 344, 30 Atl. 55. But see Browne v. Bockover, 84 Va. 424, 4 S. E. 745; In re Butler's Estate, 14 Pa. Co. Ct. R. 667.

[77] Edw. Prop. Land (2d Ed.) 130.

[78] Martin v. Pine (Sup.) 29 N. Y. Supp. 995. For equitable estates, see post, p. 251.

[79] See Jameson v. Hayward, 106 Cal. 682, 39 Pac. 1078. And see post, p. 332, for joint estates.

[80] Boykin v. Ancrum, 28 S. C. 486, 6 S. E. 305. But see Rosse's Case, 5 Coke, 13a; Snow v. Boycott [1892] 3 Ch. 110.

personal representative takes it. Before the statute of 29 Car. II., the residue of the estate belonged to the one first taking possession, who was called the "general occupant."

39. The incidents of life estates in general attach to estates per autre vie.

There was a common-law rule that, if the tenant of an estate per autre vie died before the cestui que vie, whoever first took possession of the land could hold it for the remainder of the term. Such a person was called a "general occupant." [81] If, however, the tenant had leased or assigned his estate,[82] or words of limitation, as heirs or executor, had been added in the creation of the estate, then these were entitled to the residue, and they were called "special occupants." [83] But, by the statute of 29 Car. II.,[84] general occupancy was abolished, and, when a tenant per autre vie died without having disposed of his estate, if the term was not limited to the heirs, then the executor took the residue, holding it as assets for the payment of debts.[85] This act also gave the owner power to dispose of it by will.[86] The usual incidents of a life estate attach to an estate per autre vie.[87] And in some states apportionment of rent is provided for by statute.[88]

[81] Co. Litt. 41b; 2 Bl. Comm. 258.

[82] Skelliton v. Hay, Cro. Jac. 554.

[83] Mosher v. Yost, 33 Barb. (N. Y.) 277; Salter v. Boteler, Moore, 664; Bowles v. Poore, Cro. Jac. 282; Low v. Burron, 3 P. Wms. 262; Doe v. Luxton, 6 Term R. 289; Atkinson v. Baker, 4 Term R. 229; Doe v. Robinson, 8 Barn. & C. 296.

[84] Chapter 3. And see 1 Stim. Am. St. Law, § 1310.

[85] Doe v. Lewis, 9 Mees. & W. 662. And the balance for the estate. Ripley v. Waterworth, 7 Ves. 425. But see Wall v. Byrne, 2 Jones & L. 118.

[86] See, also, 1 Stim. Am. St. Law, § 1335.

[87] Co. Litt. 41b.

[88] 1 Stim. Am. St. Law, § 2025.

CHAPTER VI.

ESTATES AS TO QUANTITY (Continued)—LEGAL LIFE ESTATES.

40–41. Legal Life Estates—Estates by Marriage.
42. Estate during Coverture.
43–44. Curtesy.
45. In What Estates.
46. Incidents.
47. How Defeated.
48. Statutory Changes.
49. Dower—Definition.
50. In What Estates.
51–52. Quarantine.
53. Assignment.
54. When Value Estimated.
55. Method of Division.
56. By Whom Assigned.
57. Recovery by Action.
58–59. Incidents.
60. How Defeated.
61. Statutory Changes.
62. Homestead.
63. Who Entitled to Homestead.
64. Duration of Exemption.
65. In What Estates.
66–67. Amount of Exemption.
68. How Acquired.
69. Selection.
70. How Lost.
71. Privileged Debts.
72. Federal Homestead Act.

LEGAL LIFE ESTATES—ESTATES BY MARRIAGE.

40. In American law all legal life estates are estates by marriage, except:

EXCEPTION—With the possible exception of estates tail after possibility of issue extinct.

41. The legal life estates are:
  (a) **Estates during coverture** (p. 70).
  (b) **Curtesy** (p. 73).
  (c) **Dower** (p. 83).
  (d) **Homestead** (p. 112).

Legal life estates have already been defined as those created by act of law, and in our system of law these estates all arise out of the marital relation, with the possible exception of an estate tail after possibility of issue extinct, which is by some classed as a legal life estate, though the correctness of such classification seems doubtful. The partnership ownership of real property by husband and wife, which exists under the community system, comes up for consideration more properly under joint estates,[1] and is only mentioned here because it is in a sense an estate by marriage.[2]

ESTATE DURING COVERTURE.

42. The estate during coverture is the right which the husband acquires at common law to the chattels real of his wife which he reduces to possession, and to the use and profits of her realty.
  QUALIFICATION—This right of the husband is qualified by:
  (a) **The doctrine of separate property.**
  (b) **By statutory changes in nearly all the states.**

By the rules of the common law, a husband acquired an interest in his wife's lands then owned or acquired during their joint lives, which was called an "estate during coverture." [3] This interest

---

[1] Post, p. 332. The joint interest of husband and wife, called an "estate in entirety," will be considered later, p. 337.

[2] Parties in contemplation of marriage may by contract fix the rights which each shall have in the property of the other during life, or which the survivor shall have in the property of the other after his or her decease. Desnoyer v. Jordan, 27 Minn. 295, 7 N. W. 140.

[3] His interest is a life estate, because it may last during his life; i. e. if he should die before his wife. Co. Litt. 351a (Butl. & H. Notes) note 1; Babb v.

§ 42) ESTATE DURING COVERTURE. 71

gave him complete ownership of her chattels real, provided he appropriated them to his use during his wife's life.[4] They were liable for his debts,[5] and he could sell, mortgage, or dispose of them without her consent;[6] but, if no such disposition of the chattels real was made, and she survived him, then they were hers absolutely.[7] As to her real estate proper, except future estates,[8] the husband had a right to the use and profits of it[9] until the marriage was terminated by death or divorce;[10] and this right excluded any control by the wife during his life. The husband could collect the rents and sue in his name for any injury to the profits,[11] but for injuries to the corpus of the estate it was necessary to join the wife.[12] He and his lessees were entitled to emblements.[13] At common law, although the husband, being a tenant for life, could not commit waste,[14] still the wife's remedy was imperfect,

[1] Perley, 1 Me. 6; Melvin v. Proprietors, 16 Pick. (Mass.) 161; Nunn's Adm'rs v. Givhan's Adm'r, 45 Ala. 370.

[4] Riley's Adm'r v. Riley, 19 N. J. Eq. 229; Packer v. Wyndham, Prec. Ch. 412; Sym's Case, Cro. Eliz. 33; Loftus' Case, Id. 279; Grute v. Locroft, Id. 287; Daniels v. Richardson, 22 Pick. (Mass.) 565.

[5] Mattocks v. Stearns, 9 Vt. 326.

[6] Meriwether v. Booker, 5 Litt. (Ky.) 254; Appleton, C. J., in Allen v. Hooper, 50 Me. 374; Robertson v. Norris, 11 Q. B. 916. But not by will, if he die first. Co. Litt. 351a.

[7] Co. Litt. 351a; Riley's Adm'r v. Riley, 19 N. J. Eq. 229.

[8] See post, p. 278.

[9] Chancey v. Strong, 2 Root (Conn.) 369; Burleigh v. Coffin, 22 N. H. 118; Lucas v. Rickerich, 1 Lea (Tenn.) 726; Royston v. Royston, 21 Ga. 161; Bishop v. Blair, 36 Ala. 80; Gray v. Mathis, 7 Jones (N. C.) 502; Meriwether v. Howe, 48 Mo. App. 148. And he may assign his right. Edrington v. Harper, 3 J. J. Marsh. (Ky.) 353; Bailey v. Duncan, 4 T. B. Mon. (Ky.) 256.

[10] Co. Litt. 351a; Burt v. Hurlburt, 16 Vt. 292; Barber v. Root, 10 Mass. 260. Separation does not terminate his right. Haralson v. Bridges, 14 Ill. 37; Van Note v. Downey, 28 N. J. Law, 219.

[11] Decker v. Livingston, 15 Johns. (N. Y.) 479; Mattocks v. Stearns, 9 Vt. 326; Fairchild v. Chastélleux, 1 Pa. St. 176; Fairchild v. Chaustelleux, 8 Watts (Pa.) 412; Dold v. Geiger's Adm'r, 2 Grat. (Va.) 98.

[12] 2 Kent, Comm. 131; Melvin v. Proprietors, 16 Pick. (Mass.) 161; Babb v. Perley, 1 Me. 6; Bratton v. Mitchell, 7 Watts (Pa.) 113.

[13] Bennett v. Bennett, 34 Ala. 53; Stroebe v. Fehl, 22 Wis. 337; Spencer v. Lewis, 1 Houst. (Del.) 223.

[14] Stroebe v. Fehl, 22 Wis. 337.

because she could not sue him.[15] But he might be restrained by injunction.[16] When waste was committed by the husband's assignee, this difficulty as to the remedy did not exist.[17] Full power of alienation, including liability for debts, resided in the husband to the extent of his life interest,[18] but he was not allowed to prejudice his wife's inheritance in any way.[19]

Equitable Doctrine—Separate Estate.

As to chattels real and personal property of the wife in general, courts of equity adopted a rule that, when a husband sought their aid in reducing such property to his possession, they might compel him to settle a reasonable amount for the support of the wife and her children. This was called her "equity to a settlement."[20] So courts of equity allow a wife to own and manage her land as if she were unmarried whenever it is settled on her in trust for her "sole and separate use."[21] Other expressions are also adequate to effect the purpose.[22]

---

[15] Davis v. Gilliam, 5 Ired. Eq. (N. C.) 308; Babb v. Perley, 1 Greenl. (Me.) 6. Cf. 1 Bish. Mar. Wom. 393.

[16] See Mellen, C. J., in Babb v. Perley, 1 Greenl. (Me.) 9. Cf. Stroebe v. Fehl, 22 Wis. 337.

[17] Stroebe v. Fehl, 22 Wis. 337; Davis v. Gilliam, 5 Ired. Eq. (N. C.) 308; Dejarnatte v. Allen, 5 Grat. (Va.) 499. Cf. Ware v. Ware, 6 N. J. Eq. 117.

[18] Trask v. Patterson, 29 Me. 499; Butterfield v. Beall, 3 Ind. 203; Coleman v. Satterfield, 2 Head (Tenn.) 259.

[19] Butterfield v. Beall, 3 Ind. 203; Coleman v. Satterfield, 2 Head (Tenn.) 259.

[20] Barron v. Barron, 24 Vt. 375; Hall v. Hall, 4 Md. Ch. 283; White v. Gouldin's Ex'rs, 27 Grat. (Va.) 491; Beeman v. Cowser, 22 Ark. 429; Kenny v. Udall, 5 Johns. Ch. (N. Y.) 464. Cf. Wiles v. Wiles, 3 Md. 1. See, further, Schouler, Husb. & W. §§ 160–162; Fetter, Eq. 37.

[21] Brandt v. Mickle, 28 Md. 436; Beeman v. Cowser, 22 Ark. 429; Pollard v. Merrill, 15 Ala. 169; Morrison v. Thistle, 67 Mo. 596; Porter v. Bank, 19 Vt. 410.

[22] Prout v. Roby, 15 Wall. 471; Brandt v. Mickle, 28 Md. 436; Stuart v. Kissam, 2 Barb. (N. Y.) 493; Flournoy v. Flournoy, 86 Cal. 286, 24 Pac. 1012; Atwood v. Dolan, 34 W. Va. 563, 12 S. E. 688. Cf. Buck v. Wroten, 24 Grat. (Va.) 250; In re Quinn's Estate, 144 Pa. St. 444, 22 Atl. 965. But for expressions which are not sufficient, see Scott v. Causey, 89 Ga. 749, 15 S. E. 650; Hart v. Leete, 104 Mo. 315, 15 S. W. 976; Warren v. Costello, 109 Mo.

Statutory Changes.

The importance of the equitable doctrine is, however, much lessened in this country by "Married Women's Acts" in all the states, which have made great changes in the law on this subject. In many states the husband's estate during coverture is abolished, and the wife holds her realty as if a feme sole, while in others the changes have not been so complete.[23] Reference must be made in each state to the statutes in force.

CURTESY.

43. By common law a husband is entitled to curtesy, which is an estate for the life of the husband in all the wife's realty, provided the following conditions concur:

(a) **Valid marriage.**
(b) **Issue born alive and capable of inheriting.**
(c) **Seisin in deed of the wife during coverture.**
(d) **Death of wife before husband.**

44. Curtesy is said to be initiate when issue is born alive, and consummate at the wife's death.

The estate in the wife's realty which the husband acquired by marriage was an estate for their joint lives,[24] and the death of either husband or wife terminated it, but the right of the husband in his wife's realty was enlarged, by the birth of issue capable of inheriting, into an estate for the husband's life.[25] This was called

---

338, 19 S. W. 29. And see Gaston v. Wright, 83 Tex. 282, 18 S. W. 576; Pickens' Ex'rs v. Kniseley, 36 W. Va. 794, 15 S. E. 997; Cliffton v. Anderson, 47 Mo. App. 35.

[23] 1 Stim. Am. St. Law, art. 642; Williams, Real Prop. (17th Ed.) Am. note, 373; 1 Washb. Real Prop. (5th Ed.) 346, note; Schouler, Husb. & W. 248; 2 Bish. Mar. Wom. 5.

[24] Melvin v. Proprietors, 16 Pick. (Mass.) 161; Polyblank v. Hawkins, 1 Doug. 329.

[25] Co. Litt. § 30a; Schermerhon v. Miller, 2 Cow. (N. Y.) 439; Adair v. Lott, 3 Hill (N. Y.) 182; Rawlings v. Adams, 7 Md. 26; Foster v. Marshall, 22 N. H. 491; Buckworth v. Thirkell, 3 Bos. & P. 652, note. The husband and wife are seised jointly. Guion v. Anderson, 8 Humph. (Tenn.) 298; Junction R. Co. v. Harris, 9 Ind. 184; Wass v. Bucknam, 38 Me. 356.

"curtesy," or, in the older books, "an estate by the curtesy of England." [26]

Marriage.

The first requisite of curtesy is lawful marriage. If the marriage was absolutely void, no curtesy will attach; but if it is only voidable, and is not annulled during the wife's life, then the husband will take his curtesy.[27]

Birth of Issue—Curtesy Initiate.

The husband's right to curtesy is said to be initiate as soon as there is issue of the marriage.[28] But such issue must be capable of inheriting the mother's estate. Thus the birth of a daughter would give the husband no curtesy in lands of which the wife was tenant in tail male, because the daughter could not inherit the estate.[29] And the issue must be born alive [30] and during the wife's life; that is, it will not be sufficient, to give curtesy, if the mother die in childbirth, and the child is afterwards taken from the womb by the Cæsarean operation.[31] It is immaterial whether the birth of issue is before or after the wife's estate is acquired.[32]

---

[26] 2 Bl. Comm. 126; Alexander v. Warrance, 17 Mo. 228. There is considerable difference of opinion as to the origin of curtesy. 1 Washb. Real Prop. (5th Ed.) p. 170; Wright, Ten. 192, 193; 2 Bl. Comm. 126. Many questions which might arise in connection with curtesy will be found discussed in treating of dower (post, p. 83). The rules stated there may be applied by analogy to the estate by curtesy if similar questions should arise.

[27] 2 Bl. Comm. 127; 1 Washb. Real Prop. (5th Ed.) 172; Wells v. Thompson, 13 Ala. 793.

[28] Schermerhorn v. Miller, 2 Cow. (N. Y.) 439; Comer v. Chamberlain, 6 Allen (Mass.) 166; Ryan v. Freeman, 36 Miss. 175. A child born out of wedlock, but made legitimate by a subsequent marriage, gives curtesy. Hunter v. Whitworth, 9 Ala. 965.

[29] Day v. Cochran, 24 Miss. 261; Heath v. White, 5 Conn. 228, 236; Barker v. Barker, 2 Sim. 249; Sumner v. Partridge, 2 Atk. 46.

[30] Brock v. Kellock, 30 Law J. Ch. 498; Goff v. Anderson, 91 Ky. 303, 15 S. W. 866; In re Winne, 1 Lans. (N. Y.) 508; Ryan v. Freeman, 36 Miss. 175; Doe v. Roe, 5 Houst. (Del.) 14; Goff v. Anderson, 91 Ky. 303, 15 S. W. 866.

[31] Co. Litt. 29b; Marsellis v. Thalhimer, 2 Paige (N. Y.) 42.

[32] Co. Litt. 29b; 2 Bl. Comm. 128; Jackson v. Johnson, 5 Cow. (N. Y.) 74; Comer v. Chamberlain, 6 Allen (Mass.) 166; Guion v. Anderson, 8 Humph. (Tenn.) 307; Heath v. White, 5 Conn. 236; Witham v. Perkins, 2 Me. 400. Cf. Hathon v. Lyon, 2 Mich. 93.

If curtesy has once become initiate, it will not be defeated by the subsequent death of the issue, either in the mother's lifetime or after her death.[33] In several states the birth of issue is made unnecessary by statute,[34] and in Pennsylvania the husband has curtesy if the issue, had any been born, could have inherited.[35]

Seisin of Wife.

By the common-law rule, in order that the husband might have curtesy, it was essential that the wife be seised in deed of fact,[36] or, less accurately, that she have actual seisin.[37] However, the rule as to seisin in deed has been relaxed,[38] and seisin in law is held sufficient to give curtesy in many states, particularly in the case of the wife's taking by descent,[39] and where the land is wild and unoccupied.[40] The seisin of a lessee is regarded as seisin of the wife.[41]

[33] Co. Litt. 29b; 2 Bl. Comm. 128; Jackson v. Johnson, 5 Cow. (N. Y.) 74; Heath v. White, 5 Conn. 235; Foster v. Marshall, 22 N. H. 491.

[34] 1 Stim. Am. St. Law, § 3301 B; Kingsley v. Smith, 14 Wis. 360.

[35] Brightly, Purd. Dig. Pa. "Intestates," 4.

[36] The reason assigned for this is that the husband can at any time perfect the wife's seisin by making an entry. 2 Ham. Bl. Comm. 233, note 32; Vanarsdall v. Fauntleroy's Heirs, 7 B. Mon. (Ky.) 401; Mercer v. Selden, 1 How. 37. For the difference between seisin in fact and in law, see ante, p. 31.

[37] Co. Litt. 29a; Stinebaugh v. Wisdom, 13 B. Mon. (Ky.) 467; Petty v. Molier, 15 B. Mon. (Ky.) 591; Mercer v. Selden, 1 How. 37; Den v. Demarest, 21 N. J. Law, 525; Parker v. Carter, 4 Hare, 400, 416; Davis v. Mason, 1 Pet. 507. Contra, Bush v. Bradley, 4 Day (Conn.) 298.

[38] Wass v. Bucknam, 38 Me. 356; Reaume v. Chambers, 22 Mo. 36, 54; Bush v. Bradley, 4 Day (Conn.) 298; Kline v. Beebe, 6 Conn. 494; Mitchell's Lessee v. Ryan, 3 Ohio St. 377; Powell v. Gossom, 18 B. Mon. (Ky.) 179; Ellsworth v. Cook, 8 Paige (N. Y.) 643; Mercer v. Selden, 1 How. 37; McCorry v. King's Heirs, 3 Humph. (Tenn.) 267; Adams v. Logan, 6 T. B. Mon. (Ky.) 175; Watkins v. Thornton, 11 Ohio St. 367; Rabb v. Griffin, 26 Miss. 579; Childers v. Bumgarner, 8 Jones (N. C.) 297.

[39] Borland v. Marshall, 2 Ohio St. 308; Day v. Cochran, 24 Miss. 261; Adair v. Lott, 3 Hill (N. Y.) 182; Jackson v. Johnson, 5 Cow. (N. Y.) 74; Chew v. Commissioners, 5 Rawle (Pa.) 160; Stephens v. Hume, 25 Mo. 349; Harvey v. Wickham, 23 Mo. 115; Carr v. Givens, 9 Bush (Ky.) 679; Enis v. Dittey (Ky.) 23 S. W. 366; Merritt's Lessee v. Horne, 5 Ohio St. 307; Eager v. Furnivall, 17 Ch. Div. 115; Withers v. Jenkins, 14 S. C. 597; McKee v. Cottle, 6 Mo. App. 416.

[40] Jackson v. Sellick, 8 Johns. (N. Y.) 262; Green v. Liter, 8 Cranch, 249; Davis v. Mason, 1 Pet. 503; Mettler v. Miller, 129 Ill. 630, 22 N. E. 529; Barr

[41] See note 41 on following page.

76   ESTATES AS TO QUANTITY—LEGAL LIFE ESTATES.   (Ch. 6

Possession by a grantee of the husband is sufficient to give curtesy.[42] The rule as stated above does not apply to incorporeal hereditaments, of which no actual possession is possible.[43]

Death of Wife—Curtesy Consummate.

If the wife dies before the husband, his right to curtesy is at once consummate, and his estate vests immediately, without any assignment or other formality.[44] Curtesy, having vested in the husband, cannot be defeated by a disclaimer.[45]

SAME—IN WHAT ESTATES.

45. The husband has curtesy in the following estates:
  (a) **In estates of inheritance.**
  (b) **In determinable estates, when they are determined by a shifting use or executory devise, and in all cases until they are defeated.**
  (c) **In equitable estates.**
  (d) **In estates in expectancy, when they vest in possession during the wife's life.**
  (e) **In joint estates, except joint tenancies.**

Estates of Inheritance.

A husband, as has been seen, has curtesy only in estates of which the wife is seised during the coverture. The estate of the wife

v. Galloway, 1 McLean, 476, Fed. Cas. No. 1,037; Den v. Wanett, 10 Ired. (N. C.) 446; McDaniel v. Grace, 15 Ark. 465; Day v. Cochran, 24 Miss. 261; Clay v. White, 1 Munf. (Va.) 162; De Grey v. Richardson, 3 Atk. 469; Lowry's Lessee v. Steele, 4 Ohio, 170; Wells v. Thompson, 13 Ala. 793; Malone v. McLaurin, 40 Miss. 161. Contra, Neely v. Butler, 10 B. Mon. (Ky.) 48.

[41] De Grey v. Richardson, 3 Atk. 469. Or of a tenant at sufferance. Tayloe v. Gould, 10 Barb. (N. Y.) 388; Jackson v. Johnson, 5 Cow. (N. Y.) 74; Lowry's Lessee v. Steele, 4 Ohio, 170; Green v. Liter, 8 Cranch, 245; Powell v. Gossom, 18 B. Mon. (Ky.) 179; Day v. Cochran, 24 Miss. 261; Carter v. Williams, 8 Ired. Eq. (N. C.) 177; Wells v. Thompson, 13 Ala. 793.

[42] Vanarsdall v. Fauntleroy's Heirs, 7 B. Mon. (Ky.) 401.

[43] Co. Litt. 29a; Davis v. Mason, 1 Pet. 507; Jackson v. Sellick, 8 Johns. (N. Y.) 262; Buckworth v. Thirkell, 3 Bos. & P. 652, note.

[44] Co. Litt. 30a; 2 Bl. Comm. 128. And a disclaimer by him will not divest his estate. Watson v. Watson, 13 Conn. 83.

[45] Watson v. Watson, 13 Conn. 83.

must also be one of inheritance.[46] Otherwise, it would be at an end with the death of the wife, and so there would be nothing left out of which the husband could have curtesy. That is, a fee simple or a fee tail in the wife gives the husband curtesy, but a life estate does not.

Determinable Estates.

There is considerable confusion in the cases as to whether there is curtesy in determinable estates, which, as will be seen,[47] are estates that may come to an end before their natural termination. As to such estates, it will be impossible to do more than to state the rule as it now seems to be recognized by the weight of authority. When the estate which arises and cuts off the wife's interest is a shifting use,[48] or executory devise,[49] the husband has curtesy. When the limitation over takes effect in some other way, there is no right to curtesy.[50] If the event which is to cut off the wife's estate has not happened at her death, the husband takes his curtesy until the happening of the event, no matter what the form of limitation of the estate may be.

Equitable Estates.

Curtesy attaches to the beneficial interest of the wife in equitable estates, as well as to legal interests.[51] But an equitable es-

[46] Barker v. Barker, 2 Sim. 249; Sumner v. Partridge, 2 Atk. 47; Janney v. Sprigg, 7 Gill (Md.) 197. If the wife was tenant in tail, and died without issue, still the husband would take curtesy, because the estate had been one of inheritance. Paine's Case, 8 Coke, 34; Buchannan's Lessee v. Sheffer, 2 Yeates (Pa.) 374; Hay v. Mayer, 8 Watts (Pa.) 203; Buckworth v. Thirkell, 3 Bos. & P. 652, note; Holden v. Wells (R. I.) 31 Atl. 265.

[47] Post, p. 169.

[48] Post, p. 300.

[49] Post, p. 300.

[50] 11 Am. Jur. 55; Grout v. Townsend, 2 Hill (N. Y.) 554; Wright v. Herron, 6 Rich. Eq. (S. C.) 406; Buckworth v. Thirkell, 3 Bos. & P. 652, note; Moody v. King, 2 Bing. 447; Hatfield v. Sneden, 54 N. Y. 285; Evans v. Evans, 9 Pa. St. 190; McMasters v. Negley, 152 Pa. St. 303, 25 Atl. 641; Webb v. Trustees, 90 Ky. 117, 13 S. W. 362; Withers v. Jenkins, 14 S. C. 597; Thornton's Ex'rs v. Krepps, 37 Pa. St. 391; Weller v. Weller, 28 Barb. (N. Y.) 588; Harvey v. Brisbin, 143 N. Y. 151, 38 N. E. 108. But see McMasters v. Negley, 152 Pa. St. 303, 25 Atl. 641.

[51] Davis v. Mason, 1 Pet. 503; Payne v. Payne, 11 B. Mon. (Ky.) 138; Young v. Langbein, 7 Hun (N. Y.) 151; Alexander v. Warrance, 17 Mo. 228;

tate may be so limited to the wife that the husband will not have curtesy.[52]

Dubs v. Dubs, 31 Pa. St. 149; Ege v. Medlar, 82 Pa. St. 86; Rawlings v. Adams, 7 Md. 26; Pierce v. Hakes, 23 Pa. St. 231; Baker v. Heiskell, 1 Cold. (Tenn.) 641; Norman's Ex'x v. Cunningham, 5 Grat. (Va.) 63; Tillinghast v. Coggeshall, 7 R. I. 383; Robie v. Chapman, 59 N. H. 41; Nightingale v. Hidden, 7 R. I. 115; Sentill v. Robeson, 2 Jones, Eq. (N. C.) 510; Cushing v. Blake, 30 N. J. Eq. 689; Carson v. Fuhs, 131 Pa. St. 256, 18 Atl. 1017; Gilmore v. Burch, 7 Or. 374; Ogden v. Ogden, 60 Ark. 70, 28 S. W. 796. Receipt by the wife of the rents and profits is a sufficient seisin. Hearle v. Greenbank, 3 Atk. 717; Withers v. Jenkins, 14 S. C. 597; Powell v. Gossom, 18 B. Mon. (Ky.) 179; Cushing v. Blake, 30 N. J. Eq. 689; Payne v. Payne, 11 B. Mon. (Ky.) 138; Taylor v. Smith. 54 Miss. 50; Sentill v. Robeson, 2 Jones, Eq. (N. C.) 510. So the husband may have curtesy in the proceeds of sale of the wife's land, Clepper v. Livergood, 5 Watts (Pa.) 113; Houghton v. Hapgood, 13 Pick. (Mass.) 154; Forbes v. Smith, 5 Ired. Eq. (N. C.) 369; Dunscomb v. Dunscomb, 1 Johns. Ch. (N. Y.) 508; Williams' Case, 3 Bland (Md.) 186; and in money directed to be laid out in land, Sweetapple v. Bindon, 2 Vern. 536; Dodson v. Hay, 3 Brown, Ch. 404; Cunningham v. Moody, 1 Ves. Sr. 174; Watts v. Ball, 1 P. Wms. 108; Chaplin v. Chaplin, 3 P. Wms. 229; Casborne v. Scarfe, 1 Atk. 603. By the weight of authority there is curtesy in estates held by the wife to her separate use. Winkler v. Winkler's Ex'rs, 18 W. Va. 455; Tillinghast v. Coggeshall, 7 R. I. 383; Nightingale v. Hidden, Id. 115; Sentill v. Robeson, 2 Jones, Eq. (N. C.) 510; Carter v. Dale, 3 Lea (Tenn.) 710; Chapman v. Price, 83 Va. 392, 11 S. E. 879; Rautenbusch v. Donaldson (Ky.) 18 S. W. 536; Nicrosi v. Phillippi, 91 Ala. 299, 8 South. 561; McTigue v. McTigue, 116 Mo. 138, 22 S. W. 501. Contra, Cochran v. O'Hern, 4 Watts & S. (Pa.) 95; Luntz v. Greve, 102 Ind. 173, 26 N. E. 128. And see Hutchings' Adm'r v. Bank (Va.) 17 S. E. 477. But there is no curtesy when the wife holds the bare legal title. Chew v. Commissioners, 5 Rawle (Pa.) 160; Welch's Heirs v. Chandler, 13 B. Mon. (Ky.) 431. Nor has the husband of a mortgagee curtesy, unless the mortgage has been foreclosed. Chaplin v. Chaplin, 7 Vin. Abr. 156, pl. 23.

[52] Pool v. Blakie, 53 Ill. 495; Stokes v. McKibbin, 13 Pa. St. 267; Payne v. Payne, 11 B. Mon. (Ky.) 138; Carter v. Dale, 3 Lea (Tenn.) 710; Cochran v. O'Hern, 4 Watts & S. (Pa.) 95; Rigler v. Cloud, 14 Pa. St. 361; Chapman v. Price, 83 Va. 392, 11 S. E. 879; Clark v. Clark, 24 Barb. (N. Y.) 582; Withers v. Jenkins, 14 S. C. 597; Cushing v. Blake, 30 N. J. Eq. 689; Ege v. Medlar, 82 Pa. St. 86; Waters v. Tazewell, 9 Md. 291. But see Dubs v. Dubs, 31 Pa. St. 149; Nightingale v. Hidden, 7 R. I. 115. If the husband conveys land to the wife, he has no curtesy in it. Sayers v. Wall, 26 Grat. (Va.) 374; Leake v. Benson, 29 Grat. (Va.) 153; Irvine v. Greever, 32 Grat. (Va.) 411; Dugger v. Dugger, 84 Va. 130, 4 S. E. 171. Contra, Frazer v. Hightower, 12 Heisk. (Tenn.) 94; Cushing v. Blake, 29 N. J. Eq. 399.

§ 46) CURTESY—INCIDENTS. 79

Estates in Expectancy.

The estate must have been one in possession during the wife's life. So there can be no curtesy in a reversion or a remainder,[53] unless the prior particular estate determined before her death, and the wife's estate thereby became vested in possession.[54] This will be clearer after estates in expectancy have been discussed.[55]

Joint Estates.

The husband has curtesy in estates held by his wife as a tenant in common or in coparcenary,[56] but not in her estates in joint tenancy.[57]

SAME—INCIDENTS.

46. Estates by curtesy have the usual incidents of life estates.

[53] Adair v. Lott, 3 Hill (N. Y.) 182; Adams v. Logan, 6 T. B. Mon. (Ky.) 175; Stoddard v. Gibbs, 1 Sumn. 263, Fed. Cas. No. 13,468; Lowry's Lessee v. Steele, 4 Ohio, 170; Watkins v. Thornton, 11 Ohio St. 367; Chew v. Commissioners, 5 Rawle (Pa.) 160; Hitner v. Ege, 23 Pa. St. 305; Orford v. Benton, 36 N. H. 395; Planters' Bank v. Davis, 31 Ala. 626; Malone v. McLaurin, 40 Miss. 161; Ferguson v. Tweedy, 43 N. Y. 543; Shores v. Carley, 8 Allen (Mass.) 425; Manning's Case, 8 Coke, 96; Robertson v. Stevens, 1 Ired. Eq. (N. C.) 247; Tayloe v. Gould, 10 Barb. (N. Y.) 388; Reed v. Reed, 3 Head (Tenn.) 491; Stewart v. Barclay, 2 Bush (Ky.) 550; De Grey v. Richardson, 3 Atk. 469. There is curtesy in a reversion after a term of years, because the seisin is then in the wife. Withers v. Jenkins, 14 S. C. 597.

[54] Kent v. Hartpoole, 3 Keb. 731; Doe v. Scudamore, 2 Bos. & P. 294; Boothby v. Vernon, 2 Eq. Cas. Abr. 728, 9 Mod. 147; Hooker v. Hooker, Cas. t. Hardw. 13; Todd v. Oviatt, 58 Conn. 174, 20 Atl. 440; Webster v. Ellsworth, 147 Mass. 602, 18 N. E. 569; Moore v. Calvert, 6 Bush (Ky.) 356; Hatfield v. Sneden, 54 N. Y. 280; Gentry v. Wagstaff, 3 Dev. (N. C.) 270; Hitner v. Ege, 23 Pa. St. 305; Keerl v. Fulton, 1 Md. Ch. 532; Mackey v. Proctor, 12 B. Mon. (Ky.) 433; Prater v. Hoover, 1 Cold. (Tenn.) 544; Watkins v. Thornton, 11 Ohio St. 367; Shores v. Carley, 8 Allén (Mass.) 425; Tayloe v. Gould, 10 Barb. (N. Y.) 388.

[55] Post, p. 278.

[56] Sterling v. Penlington, 2 Eq. Cas. Abr. 730; Wass v. Bucknam, 38 Me. 360; Vanarsdall v. Fauntleroy's Heirs, 7 B. Mon. (Ky.) 401; Carr v. Givens, 9 Bush (Ky.) 679.

[57] Co. Litt. § 45. As to what are joint estates, see post, p. 332.

80   ESTATES AS TO QUANTITY—LEGAL LIFE ESTATES.   (Ch. 6

The husband takes his curtesy subject, of course, to all existing incumbrances on the land.[56] And on the estate becoming initiate, the husband's interest is liable for his debts,[59] or he can sell and dispose of it, as he may see fit.[60] No alienation of the husband alone is effectual for a longer period than his life,[61] nor does the disseisin of the husband bar the rights of the wife's heirs or devisees.[62] The usual incidents of life estates attach to curtesy, such as liability for waste, and the right to emblements and estovers.[63] After the termination of the husband's estate by his death, the realty is disposed of according to the testamentary direction of the wife, where the wife has been given a power of testamentary disposition and has exercised it, or it is governed by the usual rules of descent.

[56] Barker v. Barker, 2 Sim. 249. But when incumbrances are paid off, they will be apportioned. In re Freeman, 116 N. C. 199, 21 S. E. 110.

[59] Burd v. Dansdale, 2 Bin. (Pa.) 80; Watson v. Watson, 13 Conn. 83; Rose v. Sanderson, 38 Ill. 247; Canby v. Porter, 12 Ohio, 79; Litchfield v. Cudworth, 15 Pick. (Mass.) 23; Roberts v. Whiting, 16 Mass. 186; Lancaster County Bank v. Stauffer, 10 Pa. St. 398; Wyatt v. Smith, 25 W. Va. 813; Hitz v. Bank, 111 U. S. 722, 4 Sup. Ct. 613; Jacobs v. Rice, 33 Ill. 369; Gardner v. Hooper, 3 Gray (Mass.) 398. But see Evans v. Lobdale, 6 Houst. (Del.) 212; Bruce v. Nicholson, 109 N. C. 202, 13 S. E. 790. But see Van Duzer v. Van Duzer, 6 Paige, Ch. (N. Y.) 366. This has been changed in some states by statute. Curry v. Bott, 53 Pa. St. 400; Staples v. Brown, 13 Allen (Mass.) 64; Welsh v. Solenberger, 85 Va. 441, 8 S. E. 91; Churchill v. Hudson, 34 Fed. 14

[60] Robertson v. Norris, 11 Q. B. 916; Shortall v. Hinckley, 31 Ill. 219; Central Bank v. Copeland, 18 Md. 305; Ward v. Thompson, 6 Gill & J. (Md.) 349; Hutchins v. Dixon, 11 Md. 29; Denton's Guardians v. Denton's Ex'rs, 17 Md. 403; Schermerhon v. Miller, 2 Cow. (N. Y.) 439; Kottenbrock v. Cracraft, 36 Ohio St. 584.

[61] Flagg v. Bean, 25 N. H. 49; Meraman's Heirs v. Caldwell's Heirs, 8 B. Mon. (Ky.) 32.

[62] Foster v. Marshall, 22 N. H. 491; Robertson v. Norris, 11 Q. B. 916; Miller v. Shackleford, 4 Dana (Ky.) 264; Lessee of Thompson's Heirs v. Green, 4 Ohio St. 216; Wass v. Bucknam, 38 Me. 356. But see Melvin v. Proprietors, 16 Pick. (Mass.) 161; Weisinger v. Murphy, 2 Head (Tenn.) 674; Coe v. Manufacturing Co., 35 Conn. 175; Watson v. Watson, 10 Conn. 75.

[63] Armstrong v. Wilson, 60 Ill. 226; Bates v. Shraeder, 13 Johns. (N. Y.) 260.

SAME—HOW DEFEATED.

47. Curtesy may be defeated by:
  (a) **Alienage of husband in some states.**
  (b) **Annulment of marriage, and, in some states, by divorce or desertion.**
  (c) **Termination of wife's estate.**
  (d) **Husband's joining in wife's conveyance, and, formerly, by husband's feoffment in fee.**
  (e) **The wife's conveyance of her estate, in some states.**

Alienage of the husband was formerly a bar to curtesy,[64] but the rule has been changed by statute in many states.[65] If the wife's estate is defeated by title paramount during her life, the husband, of course, loses his curtesy.[66] At common law, a feoffment in fee by the husband forfeited his curtesy,[67] but, as already seen, this is not now the rule in most states.[66] Annulment of the marriage or divorce,[69] especially for the husband's fault,[70] and in some states desertion of the wife, forfeits all rights to curtesy.[71] At common

---

[64] Foss v. Crisp, 20 Pick. (Mass.) 121; Reese v. Waters, 4 Watts & S. (Pa.) 145; Mussey v. Pierre, 24 Me. 559; Den v. Ward, 4 Dev. (N. C.) 247; Den v. Sauls, 1 Jones (N. C.) 70.

[65] 1 Stim. Am. St. Law, § 102; 1 Washb. Real Prop. (5th Ed.) p. 80, note; 1 Shars. & B. Lead. Cas. Real Prop. 276.

[66] Co. Litt. 241a (Butl. & H. Notes) note 4.

[67] 4 Kent, Comm. 83; French v. Rollins, 21 Me. 372; Wells v. Thompson, 13 Ala. 793. But not a bargain and sale deed. Meraman's Heirs v. Caldwell's Heirs, 8 B. Mon. (Ky.) 32; McKee's Lessee v. Pfout, 3 Dall. (Pa.) 486; a modern statutory deed, Miller v. Miller, Meigs, 484; nor a lease in fee, Grout v. Townsend, 2 Hill (N. Y.) 554.

[66] Ante, p. 59.

[69] Burgess v. Muldoon, 18 R. I. 607, 29 Atl. 298. But see Meacham v. Buntling, 156 Ill. 586, 41 N. E. 175.

[70] 1 Stim. Am. St. Law, §§ 3307, 6247, 6248, 6306; Wheeler v. Hotchkiss, 10 Conn. 225; Mattocks v. Stearns, 9 Vt. 326; Schuster v. Schuster, 93 Mo. 438, 6 S. W. 259. But not against prior assignees of the husband. Gillespie v. Worford, 2 Cold. (Tenn.) 632. But not divorce a mensa et thoro. Smoot v. Lecatt, 1 Stew. (Ala.) 590; Rochon v. Lecatt, 2 Stew. (Ala.) 429.

[71] 1 Stim. Am. St. Law, § 3307; Bealor v. Hahn (Pa. Sup.) 19 Atl. 74; Hart v. McGrew (Pa. Sup.) 11 Atl. 617.

REAL PROP.—6

law the wife cannot, by her conveyance, defeat the right of curtesy;[72] but the married women's acts in some cases give the wife power to dispose of her estate so as to cut off curtesy,[73] and in the other states the husband may do so by joining in his wife's conveyance.[74] He may be obliged to elect between curtesy and a devise by the wife,[75] or, where the husband is given dower by statute, it would be barred by jointure or antenuptial settlement or contract.[76]

SAME—STATUTORY CHANGES.

48. In some states curtesy exists as at common law, but in others it has been abolished or made the same as dower.

A number of statutory changes in the estate by curtesy have already been mentioned, but in some states there has been legislation which has made radical changes in the estate itself. In many states curtesy has been abolished by statute, in some the estate is made the same as dower, and in others a distributive share is given.[77] So, too, the changes effected by the married

---

[72] Mildmay's Case, 6 Coke, 41; Mullany v. Mullany, 4 N. J. Eq. 16; Pool v. Blakie, 53 Ill. 495; Cooper v. Macdonald, 7 Ch. Div. 288; Robinson v. Buck, 71 Pa. St. 386.

[73] Thurber v. Townsend, 22 N. Y. 517; Breeding v. Davis, 77 Va. 639; Browne v. Bockover, 84 Va. 424, 4 S. E. 745; Alexander v. Alexander, 85 Va. 353, 7 S. E. 335; Comer v. Chamberlain, 6 Allen (Mass.) 166; Silsby v. Bullock, 10 Allen (Mass.) 94. And see Burke v. Valentine, 52 Barb. (N. Y.) 412; Scott v. Guernsey, 60 Barb. (N. Y.) 163; Oatman v. Goodrich, 15 Wis. 589; Tyler v. Wheeler, 160 Mass. 206, 35 N. E. 666.

[74] Stewart v. Ross, 50 Miss. 776; Haines v. Ellis, 24 Pa. St. 253; Jackson v. Hodges, 2 Tenn. Ch. 276; Carpenter v. Davis, 72 Ill. 14. Or in her will. McBride's Estate, 81 Pa. St. 303.

[75] 1 Stim. Am. St. Law, §§ 3304–3306.

[76] 1 Stim. Am. St. Law, §§ 3303, 3304, 6440.

[77] 1 Stim. Am. St. Law, art. 330. In several states the husband has no curtesy in lands which descend to the issue of the wife by a former husband. Id. § 3302 B. Further, as to the statutory changes, see 1 Shars. & B. Lead. Cas. Real Prop. 286; 1 Washb. Real Prop. (5th Ed.) 170; Williams, Real Prop. (17th Am. Ed.) note 375; Smith v. Smith, 21 D. C. 289.

§ 49) DOWER—DEFINITION. 83

women's acts, already mentioned,[78] have nearly abolished curtesy initiate by giving wives extensive powers to control and dispose of their realty.[79]

DOWER—DEFINITION.

49. Dower is the provision which the law makes for a widow out of the lands or tenements of the husband for her support. In most states it is a life estate in one-third of the husband's realty. The requisites of dower are:

(a) **Marriage.**
(b) **Seisin of the husband during coverture.**
(c) **Death of the husband before the wife.**

Dower [80] is a legal life estate, and therefore a freehold. At common law it was one-third of all the realty of which the husband was seised at any time during coverture, but this amount has been changed to one-half in several of the states by statute.[81] The rights of a widow in her deceased husband's real property are in all cases governed by the law of the place where the land is situated. Thus, dower may have been abolished in the state of the residence of the husband and wife, and yet the widow would have dower in lands owned by him in a state where dower still existed.[82]

---

[78] Ante, p. 73.

[79] Hitz v. Bank, 111 U. S. 722, 4 Sup. Ct. 613; Breeding v. Davis, 77 Va. 639; Evans v. Lobdale, 6 Houst. (Del.) 212; Porch v. Fries, 18 N. J. Eq. 204; Thurber v. Townsend, 22 N. Y. 517; Walker v. Long, 109 N. C. 510, 14 S. E. 299; Beach v. Miller, 51 Ill. 206; McNeer v. McNeer, 142 Ill. 388, 32 N. E. 681; Jackson v. Jackson, 144 Ill. 274, 33 N. E. 51.

[80] For the distinction between dower and dowry, see 2 Bl. Comm. 129; Black, Law Dict. "Dower," "Dowry." For the history and origin of dower, see Digby, Hist. Real Prop. (4th Ed.) p. 126; 2 Bl. Comm. 129; 1 Washb. Real Prop. 147.

[81] 1 Stim. Am. St. Law, §§ 3105, 3202 F. And see Pearson v. Pearson, 135 Ind. 377, 35 N. E. 288; Zachry v. Lockard, 98 Ala. 371, 13 South. 514; Wadsworth v. Miller, 103 Ala. 130, 15 South. 520.

[82] Lamar v. Scott, 3 Strob. (S. C.) 562; Barnes v. Cunningham, 9 Rich. Eq. (S. C.) 475; Duncan v. Dick, Walk. (Miss.) 281; Jones v. Gerock, 6 Jones, Eq. (N. C.) 190.

Marriage—Dower Inchoate.

As in curtesy, there must be a lawful marriage in order to give dower.[83] No dower can be claimed if the marriage was void. But if merely voidable, and not avoided during coverture, the widow may have dower.[84] A marriage per verba de præsenti or per verba de futuro cum copula will give dower.[85] By marriage the right to dower attaches,[86] but remains inchoate until the death of the husband.[87]

Seisin of Husband—Transitory Seisin.

It is also required, to give the widow dower, that the husband be seised of the estate during coverture.[88] But a seisin in law is sufficient.[89] A mere right of entry, however, will not give dower at common law,[90] though this has been changed by the statutes of several states.[91]

[83] Jones v. Jones, 28 Ark. 19; Moore v. Mayor, etc., 8 N. Y. 110; Besson v. Gribble, 39 N. J. Eq. 111; De France v. Johnson, 26 Fed. 891.

[84] Higgins v. Breen, 9 Mo. 497; Jenkins v. Jenkins' Heirs, 2 Dana (Ky.) 102; Donnelly v. Donnelly's Heirs, 8 B. Mon. (Ky.) 113; Smith v. Smith, 5 Ohio St. 32; Smart v. Whaley, 6 Smedes & M. (Miss.) 308.

[85] 1 Scrib. Dower (2d Ed.) 71; Pearson v. Howey, 11 N. J. Law, 12; Fenton v. Reed, 4 Johns. (N. Y.) 52; Adams v. Adams, 57 Miss. 267. But the validity of such marriages is denied in some states. 1 Scrib. Dower (2d Ed.) 71, 99.

[86] Buzick v. Buzick, 44 Iowa, 259.

[87] Inchoate dower is not an estate in land, but only an interest. Blodget v. Brent, 3 Cranch, C. C. 394, Fed. Cas. No. 1,553; Moore v. Mayor, etc., 8 N. Y. 110; Howlett v. Dilts, 4 Ind. App. 23, 30 N. E. 313; McArthur v. Franklin, 16 Ohio St. 193; Gunnison v. Twitchel, 38 N. H. 62. And as holding that it is not even an interest, see 1 Washb. Real Prop. (5th Ed.) 312.

[88] Amcotts v. Catherich, Cro. Jac. 615; Price v. Hobbs, 47 Md. 359; Houston v. Smith, 88 N. C. 312; Butler v. Cheatham, 8 Bush (Ky.) 594; Poor v. Horton, 15 Barb. (N. Y.) 485; Grant v. Sutton (Va.) 22 S. E. 490; Kade v. Lauber, 48 How. Prac. (N. Y.) 382; Crabb v. Pratt, 15 Ala. 843; Blood v. Blood, 23 Pick. (Mass.) 80; Miller v. Wilson, 15 Ohio, 108; Rands v. Kendall, Id. 671; Grey v. McCune, 23 Pa. St. 447. In a few states she takes dower only in estates of which he died seised. 1 Stim. Am. St. Law, § 3202 E; 1 Washb. Real Prop. (5th Ed.) 196; 1 Williams, Real Prop. (17th Am. Ed.) note 377.

[89] Atwood v. Atwood, 22 Pick. (Mass.) 283; Apple v. Apple, 1 Head (Tenn.) 348; McIntyre v. Costello, 47 Hun (N. Y.) 289.

[90] 1 Scrib. Dower (2d Ed.) 255. Nor was the recovery of a judgment for the lands sufficient if no entry was made or execution served. Id. 257.

[91] 1 Stim. Am. St. Law, § 3211; 1 Scrib. Dower (2d Ed.) 258.

Although the rule is that the husband's seisin need be only for an instant of time,[92] still if he is a mere conduit for passing the seisin to another,[93] or if he acquires and parts with the seisin again by the same transaction, then no right of dower arises. This is the case when the husband buys land and gives a mortgage back for the purchase money. The wife in such case is entitled to dower in the equity of redemption alone.[94]

Death of the Husband—Dower Consummate.

The other requisites of dower being present, the right becomes consummate by the death of the husband. Until that occurs, the wife has only a contingent interest. This interest becomes vested if the husband dies before the wife.[95]

[92] Broughton v. Randall, Cro. Eliz. 503; Stanwood v. Dunning, 14 Me. 290; McCauley v. Grimes, 2 Gill & J. (Md.) 318; Sutherland v. Sutherland, 69 Ill. 481; Stanwood v. Dunning, 14 Me. 290; Smith v. McCarty, 119 Mass. 519; Douglass v. Dickson, 11 Rich. Law (S. C.) 417. Such seisin is good as against strangers, though it be tortious. Randolph v. Doss, 3 How. (Miss.) 205; Edmondson v. Welsh, 27 Ala. 578.

[93] Fontaine v. Savings Inst., 57 Mo. 552.

[94] Mayburry v. Brien, 15 Pet. 21; King v. Stetson, 11 Allen (Mass.) 407; Holbrook v. Finney, 4 Mass. 566; Stow v. Tifft, 15 Johns. (N. Y.) 458; Coates v. Cheever, 1 Cow. (N. Y.) 460; Wheatley's Heirs v. Calhoun, 12 Leigh (Va.) 264; Seekright v. Moore, 4 Leigh (Va.) 30; Ragsdale v. O'Day, 1 Mo. App. Rep'r, 363; Griggs v. Smith, 12 N. J. Law, 22; Crafts v. Crafts, 2 McCord (S. C.) 54; Ratcliffe v. Mason, 92 Ky. 190, 17 S. W. 438; Moore v. Esty, 5 N. H. 489. But see McClure v. Harris, 12 B. Mon. (Ky.) 261; Rawlings v. Lowndes, 34 Md. 639; Butler v. Thornburg, 131 Ind. 237, 30 N. E. 1073; Jefferies v. Fort, 43 S. C. 48, 20 S. E. 755. The mortgage may be to a third person. Glenn v. Clark, 53 Md. 580; Johnson v. Plume, 77 Ind. 166; Kittle v. Van Dyck, 1 Sandf. Ch. 76; Roush v. Miller, 39 W. Va. 638, 20 S. E. 663. And the mortgage may even be on another parcel of land which is acquired as a part of the same transaction. Adams v. Hill, 29 N. H. 202.

[95] Sutliff v. Forgey, 1 Cow. (N. Y.) 89; Truett v. Funderburk, 93 Ga. 686, 20 S. E. 260. There must be natural death; civil death will not give dower. Wooldridge v. Lucas, 7 B. Mon. (Ky.) 49; Platner v. Sherwood, 6 Johns. Ch. (N. Y.) 129. In a few states divorce makes the right to dower consummate. 1 Stim. Am. St. Law, § 6251 A (1). So an assignment for creditors. Wright v. Gelvin, 85 Ind. 128. And in two states judicial sale of the husband's lands. 1 Stim. Am. St. Law, § 3204. And see Kelley v. Canary, 129 Ind. 460, 29 N. E. 11; Whitney v. Marshall, 138 Ind. 472, 37 N. E. 964; Huffmaster v. Ogden, 135 Ind. 661, 35 N. E. 512. Contra, Gatewood v. Tomlinson, 113 N. C. 312, 18 S. E. 318.

SAME—IN WHAT ESTATES.

50. A widow has dower at common law in the husband's estates of inheritance, provided the following conditions concur:

(a) In many states the land must be capable of beneficial enjoyment as a life estate (p. 87).

(b) The estate must be one which issue of the wife could inherit (p. 88).

(c) The estate must not be terminated by the happening of a contingency (p. 88).

(d) At common law the husband must have the legal title; but there is dower in equities of redemption, and in many states in all equitable estates, by statute (p. 89).

(e) The husband must be seised in possession, not in expectancy (p. 91).

(f) The estate must not be one in joint tenancy (p. 92).

Estates of Inheritance.

Since dower is a continuation of the husband's estate, it is necessary that he have an estate of inheritance; that is, a fee simple or a fee tail.[96] There will be dower in a fee tail,[97] even though the estate be at an end, by failure of heirs, at the husband's death.[98] There is no dower, however, where an estate tail is by statute changed into a life estate and a remainder.[99] Nor is a widow dowable of her husband's life estates,[100] except where an

---

[96] Johnson v. Jacob, 11 Bush (Ky.) 646; Chew v. Chew, 1 Md. 163.

[97] But not in Kentucky. Gen. St. 1883, p. 527, c. 50, art. 4, § 2.

[98] Smith's Appeal, 23 Pa. St. 9; Moody v. King, 2 Bing. 447; Northcut v. Whipp, 12 B. Mon. (Ky.) 65.

[99] Trumbull v. Trumbull, 149 Mass. 200, 21 N. E. 366. And see Edwards v. Bibb, 54 Ala. 475.

[100] Gillis v. Brown, 5 Cow. (N. Y.) 388 (per autre vie); Knickerbacker v. Seymour, 46 Barb. (N. Y.) 198; In re Watson's Estate, 139 Pa. St. 461, 22 Atl. 638; Thompson v. Vance, 1 Metc. (Ky.) 669; Edwards v. Bibb, 54 Ala. 475; Alexander v. Cunningham, 5 Ired. (N. C.) 430; Kenyon v. Kenyon, 17 R. I. 539, 23 Atl. 101, and 24 Atl. 787.

§ 50)   DOWER—IN WHAT ESTATES.   87

estate per autre vie is made an estate of inheritance.[101] Where a long term of years is given the character of a fee simple, there is a right to dower,[102] but in no other case can there be dower in an estate for years.[103]

Same—Dower in Rents.

As will be seen in another place, the husband may have estates in the rents issuing out of land, the same as he may in the land itself; and the rule as to dower is the same. If the husband is owner of a rent in fee or in tail, the widow can have her dower in it;[104] but not if it is merely for life.[105] On the other hand, if the husband grants to another an interest in land, and reserves a rent, she will take her share of the rent as an incident of the dower which she takes in the land itself.[106]

Lands Capable of Enjoyment.

The dower right attaches only to real property,[107] and not to all kinds of realty even; for instance, in many states dower is not given in wild lands, because to clear them for cultivation would be waste,[108] and cause their forfeiture. For the same reason a widow

[101] See ante, pp. 35, 67. And see Stull v. Graham, 60 Ark. 461, 31 S. W. 46.
[102] 1 Stim. Am. St. Law, § 3218.
[103] Gaunt v. Wainman, 3 Bing. N. C. 69; Spangler v. Stanler, 1 Md. Ch. 36; Goodwin v. Goodwin, 33 Conn. 314; Whitmire v. Wright, 22 S. C. 446.
[104] 2 Bl. Comm. 132; 1 Scrib. Dower (2d Ed.) 373.
[105] 1 Scrib. Dower (2d Ed.) 374; Co. Litt. 32a.
[106] Co. Litt. 32a; Stoughton v. Leigh, 1 Taunt. 402; Bland, Ch., in Chase's Case, 1 Bland (Md.) 227; Weir v. Tate, 4 Ired. Eq. (N. C.) 264; Helbert v. Wren, 7 Cranch, 370.
[107] Hallett v. Hallett, 8 Ind. App. 305, 34 N. E. 740; Brackett v. Leighton, 7 Me. 383; Buckeridge v. Ingram, 2 Ves. Jr. 652. The term "widow's thirds," designating her share of the husband's personal estate, is sometimes applied to dower.
[108] Conner v. Shepherd, 15 Mass. 164; Webb v. Townsend, 1 Pick. (Mass.) 21; White v. Cutler, 17 Pick. (Mass.) 248; Johnson v. Perley, 2 N. H. 56; Kuhn v. Kaler, 14 Me. 409. But see Shattuck v. Gragg, 23 Pick. (Mass.) 88; White v. Willis, 7 Pick. (Mass.) 143; Mosher v. Mosher, 15 Me. 371; Stevens v. Owen, 25 Me. 94; Lothrop v. Foster, 51 Me. 367. This is not true where clearing wild lands is not waste. Allen v. McCoy, 8 Ohio, 418; Schnebly v. Schnebly, 26 Ill. 116; Brown v. Richards, 17 N. J. Eq. 32; Campbell's Case, 2 Doug. (Mich.) 141; Chapman v. Schroeder, 10 Ga. 321; Hickman v. Irvine's Heirs, 3 Dana (Ky.) 121.

is not dowable of mines, unless they are open, so that she can work them.[109]

Inheritance by Issue.

Dower attaches only to those estates of the husband which issue of the wife, if born, might inherit.[110] Thus, if an estate is given to a man and his heirs begotten on the body of his wife, B., a subsequent wife could not have dower, because her issue could in no case inherit the estate. But it is not necessary that the wife have issue born, nor need there be a physical ability to bear offspring.[111] Dower thus differs from curtesy, for which birth of issue is necessary.[112]

Determinable Estates.

Dower attaches to determinable estates,[113] but is defeated by the happening of the event which terminates the estate.[114] If this occurs before the husband's death, dower never becomes consummate; if after his death, the enjoyment of the land assigned as dower is cut off.

[109] Stoughton v. Leigh, 1 Taunt. 402; Lenfers v. Henke, 73 Ill. 405; Coates v. Cheever, 1 Cow. (N. Y.) 460; Billings v. Taylor, 10 Pick. (Mass.) 460; Moore v. Rollins, 45 Me. 493; Hendrix v. McBeth, 61 Ind. 473; cf. Black v. Mining Co., 49 Fed. 549. But see, as to mining leases, Seager v. McCabe, 92 Mich. 186, 52 N. W. 299; Priddy v. Griffith, 150 Ill. 560, 37 N. E. 999. There is no dower in a mining claim. Black v. Mining Co., 3 C. C. A. 312, 52 Fed. 859.

[110] Spangler v. Stanler, 1 Md. Ch. 36; Butler v. Cheatham, 8 Bush (Ky.) 594.

[111] Co. Litt. 40a; 1 Scrib. Dower (2d Ed.) 227. At common law the widow must be at least nine, as women have become mothers at that age, but a woman is never presumed to be too old to bear children. 2 Bl. Comm. 131; 1 Scrib. Dower (2d Ed.) 229.

[112] Ante, p. 73.

[113] Such as estates upon condition or limitation. See post, p. 169.

[114] Beardslee v. Beardslee, 5 Barb. (N. Y.) 324; Greene v. Reynolds, 72 Hun, 565, 25 N. Y. Supp. 625; Peay v. Peay, 2 Rich. Eq. (S. C.) 409; Moore v. Esty, 5 N. H. 469; Jackson v. Kip, 8 N. J. Law, 241; Northcut v. Whipp, 12 B. Mon. (Ky.) 65. That there is dower in a fee subject to an executory devise, see Moody v. King, 2 Bing. 447; Weller v. Weller, 28 Barb. (N. Y.) 588; Clark v. Clark, 84 Hun, 362, 32 N. Y. Supp. 325; Evans v. Evans, 9 Pa. St. 190. Pollard v. Slaughter, 92 N. C. 72; Milledge v. Lamar, 4 Desaus. Eq. (S. C.) 617; Jones v. Hughes, 27 Grat. (Va.) 560; Medley v. Medley, Id. 568. Contra, Edwards v. Bibb, 54 Ala. 475.

Equitable Estates.

At common law, equitable estates are not subject to dower;[115] but the rule has been changed in many states by statute.[116] Dower attaches to estates executed by the statute of uses.[117] In either case, the estate must be of the same quantity as required for legal estates;[118] and, if the husband is a bare trustee of the legal title, his wife has no dower.[119]

Same—Mortgages.

The widow of a mortgagee has no dower in the mortgaged premises unless the estate has become absolute by foreclosure.[120] Except as changed by statute,[121] the widow of one who has given a mortgage during coverture in which she has not joined has dower out of the whole estate;[122] but, when she has joined in the mortgage,[123] or it was executed by the husband before marriage,[124]

---

[115] Chaplin v. Chaplin, 3 P. Wms. 229; Blakeney v. Ferguson, 20 Ark. 547; Gully v. Ray, 18 B. Mon. (Ky.) 107; Steele v. Carroll, 12 Pet. 201; Williams v. Barrett, 2 Cranch, C. C. 673, Fed. Cas. No. 17,714; Hamlin v. Hamlin, 19 Me. 141; Bottomley v. Fairfax, Prec. Ch. 336; Mayburry v. Brien, 15 Pet. 21; Crawl v. Harrington, 33 Neb. 107, 49 N. W. 1118.

[116] 1 Stim. Am. St. Law, § 3212; 1 Shars. & B. Lead. Cas. Real Prop. 312; 1 Scrib. Dower (2d Ed.) 401; 5 Am. & Eng. Enc. Law, 895.

[117] See post, p. 253; 1 Scrib. Dower (2d Ed.) 385; Robison v. Codman, 1 Sumn. 121, Fed. Cas. No. 11,970.

[118] Davenport v. Farrar, 2 Ill. 314; Stroup v. Stroup, 140 Ind. 179, 39 N. E. 864. And see Tink v. Walker, 148 Ill. 234, 35 N. E. 765. Contra, Phelps v. Phelps, 143 N. Y. 197, 38 N. E. 280.

[119] Robison v. Codman, 1 Sumn. 121, Fed. Cas. 11,970; De Rush v. Brown, 8 Ohio, 412; Bartlett v. Gouge, 5 B. Mon. (Ky.) 152; Cowman v. Hall, 3 Gill & J. (Md.) 398; Cooper v. Whitney, 3 Hill (N. Y.) 95; Ragsdale v. O'Day, 1 Mo. App. Rep'r, 363; Noel v. Jevon, Freem. Ch. 43.

[120] Foster v. Dwinel, 49 Me. 44; Crittenden v. Johnson, 11 Ark. 94; Reed v. Shepley, 6 Vt. 602; Waller v. Waller's Adm'r, 33 Grat. (Va.) 83; Weir v. Tate, 4 Ired. Eq. (N. C.) 264; Cooper v. Whitney, 3 Hill (N. Y.) 95.

[121] 1 Stim. Am. St. Law, § 3213.

[122] Wedge v. Moore, 6 Cush. (Mass.) 8.

[123] Cox v. Garst, 105 Ill. 342; Smith v. Eustis, 7 Greenl. (Me.) 41; Mantz v. Buchanan, 1 Md. Ch. 202; Glenn v. Clark, 53 Md. 580; State Bank v. Hinton, 21 Ohio St. 509; Schweitzer v. Wagner (Ky.) 22 S. W. 883.

[124] Carll v. Butman, 7 Me. 102; Holbrook v. Finney, 4 Mass. 566; Denton v. Nanny, 8 Barb. (N. Y.) 618; Heth v. Cocke, 1 Rand. (Va.) 344. But see Shape v. Schaffner, 140 Ill. 470, 30 N. E. 872.

she takes her dower subject to the mortgage;[125] and if the mortgage is foreclosed either before or after the husband's death, she has dower in the surplus proceeds of the sale.[126] The widow has a right to have the mortgage paid off out of the husband's personal estate.[127] The common-law rule not allowing dower in equi-

---

[125] Mantz v. Buchanan, 1 Md. Ch. 202; Holmes v. Book, 1 Ohio N. P. 58. But not when a grantee has assumed the mortgage, she not joining in the conveyance to him. McCabe v. Swap, 14 Allen (Mass.) 188. Dower is also subject to a vendor's lien for the purchase price. Williams v. Woods, 1 Humph. (Tenn.) 408; Crane v. Palmer, 8 Blackf. (Ind.) 120; McClure v. Harris, 12 B. Mon. (Ky.) 261; Ellicott v. Welch, 2 Bland (Md.) 242; Warner v. Van Alstyne, 3 Paige (N. Y.) 513; Johnson v. Cautrell, 92 Ky. 59, 17 S. W. 206. Or a judgment recovered against the husband before marriage, where a judgment is a lien. Robbins v. Robbins, 8 Blackf. (Ind.) 174; Trustees, etc., of Queen Annes Co. v. Pratt, 10 Md. 5; Brown v. Williams, 31 Me. 403; Sandford v. McLean, 3 Paige (N. Y.) 117. But see Ingram v. Morris, 4 Har. (Del.) 111. Or a charge created by a testator on lands devised to the husband. Shiell v. Sloan, 22 S. C. 151. But dower is superior to a mechanic's lien for buildings on the husband's land. Bishop v. Boyle, 9 Ind. 169; Van Vronker v. Eastman, 7 Metc. (Mass.) 157; Shaeffer v. Weed, 3 Gilman (Ill.) 511; Pifer v. Ward, 8 Blackf. (Ind.) 252. Contra, Nazareth Literary & Benevolent Institute v. Lowe, 1 B. Mon. (Ky.) 257.

[126] Unger v. Leiter, 32 Ohio St. 210; Ketchum v. Shaw, 28 Ohio St. 503; Titus v. Neilson, 5 Johns. Ch. (N. Y.) 452; Hartshorne v. Hartshorne, 2 N. J. Eq. 349; Hawley v. Bradford, 9 Paige (N. Y.) 200; Thompson v. Cochran, 7 Humph. (Tenn.) 72; Mathews v. Duryee, 45 Barb. (N. Y.) 69; Culver v. Harper, 27 Ohio St. 464; Vreeland v. Jacobus, 19 N. J. Eq. 231; Jennison v. Hapgood, 14 Pick. (Mass.) 345. When foreclosure occurs before the death of the husband, the wife's right in the surplus will be secured to her by its investment. Denton v. Nanny, 8 Barb. (N. Y.) 618; Virtie v. Underwood, 18 Barb. (N. Y.) 561; De Wolf v. Murphy, 11 R. I. 630; Vreeland v. Jacobus, 19 N. J. Eq. 231. Contra, Newhall v. Bank, 101 Mass. 428. In certain states this right is given by statute. 1 Stim. Am. St. Law, § 3216.

[127] Hawley v. Bradford, 9 Paige (N. Y.) 200; Jennison v. Hapgood, 14 Pick. (Mass.) 345; Henagan v. Harllee, 10 Rich. Eq. (S. C.) 285; Caroon v. Cooper, 63 N. C. 386; Mantz v. Buchanan, 1 Md. Ch. 202. Contra, Peckham v. Hadwen, 8 R. I. 160. The right does not exist against creditors, Creecy v. Pearce, 69 N. C. 67; Rossiter v. Cossit, 15 N. H. 38; nor when the mortgage was assumed by the husband, Campbell v. Campbell, 30 N. J. Eq. 415. The right is given by statute in Vermont. R. L. 1880, § 2218; 1 Stim. Am. St. Law, § 3214. Where the husband dies seised of the equity of redemption, the widow may require redemption out of the assets. King v. King, 100 Mass. 224; Mathewson v. Smith, 1 R. I. 22; Henagan v. Harllee, 10 Rich. Eq. (S. C.) 285.

table estates does not hold in the United States as to equities of redemption.[128] Therefore the widow has a right to redeem [129] by contributing her share of the mortgage debt.[130] If the holder of the equity of redemption does not redeem, she can redeem from the mortgagee only by paying off the whole incumbrance.[131]

Estates in Expectancy[132]—*Dower out of Dower.*

When the husband has only a remainder or a reversion after an existing freehold estate, there is no dower, because he is not seised.[133] Of course, if the preceding estate determines during

---

[128] Manning v. Laboree, 33 Me. 343; Walker v. Griswold, 6 Pick. (Mass.) 416; Hinchman v. Stiles, 9 N. J. Eq. 361; Smith v. Eustis, 7 Me. 41; Eaton v. Simonds, 14 Pick. (Mass.) 98; Burrall v. Bender, 61 Mich. 608, 28 N. W. 731; Whitehead v. Middleton, 2 How. (Miss.) 692; Heth v. Cocke, 1 Rand. (Va.) 344; Woods v. Wallace, 30 N. H. 384; Swaine v. Perine, 5 Johns. Ch. (N. Y.) 482; Roan v. Holmes, 32 Fla. 295, 13 South. 339.

[129] Davis v. Wetherell, 13 Allen (Mass.) 60. The right extends to mortgages by the husband before marriage, Wheeler v. Morris, 2 Bosw. (N. Y.) 524; Coles v. Coles, 15 Johns. (N. Y.) 319; and to purchase-money mortgages, Mills v. Van Voorhies, 20 N. Y. 412.

[130] Noffts v. Koss, 29 Ill. App. 301; Swaine v. Perine, 5 Johns. Ch. (N. Y.) 482; Bell v. Mayor, etc., 10 Paige (N. Y.) 49; Cox v. Garst, 105 Ill. 342; Niles v. Nye, 13 Metc. (Mass.) 135; Gibson v. Crehore, 5 Pick. (Mass.) 146; Woods v. Wallace, 30 N. H. 384; Cass v. Martin, 6 N. H. 25; Richardson v. Skolfield, 45 Me. 386; Simonton v. Gray, 34 Me. 50. But see Shope v. Schaffner, 140 Ill. 470, 30 N. E. 872. For the method of computing his share, see Swaine v. Perine, 5 Johns. Ch. (N. Y.) 482; Gibson v. Crehore, 5 Pick. (Mass.) 146. When the mortgage is paid by the husband or by any other person in his place, the mortgage is extinguished, so that the widow is not required to contribute. Bolton v. Ballard, 13 Mass. 227; Snow v. Stevens, 15 Mass. 278; Barker v. Parker, 17 Mass. 564; Hildreth v. Jones, 13 Mass. 525; Jennison v. Hapgood, 14 Pick. (Mass.) 345; Hastings v. Stevens, 9 Fost. (N. H.) 564; Young v. Tarbell, 37 Me. 509; Mathewson v. Smith, 1 R. I. 22; Walker v. Griswold, 6 Pick. (Mass.) 416; Hobbs v. Harvey, 16 Me. 80; Smith v. Stanley, 37 Me. 11; Runyan v. Stewart, 12 Barb. (N. Y.) 537; Harrison v. Eldridge, 7 N. J. Law, 392. Cf. McArthur v. Porter, 1 Ohio, 99.

[131] Wheeler v. Morris, 2 Bosw. (N. Y.) 524; Peabody v. Patten, 2 Pick. (Mass.) 517; McCabe v. Bellows, 7 Gray (Mass.) 148; Van Duyne v. Thayre, 14 Wend. (N. Y.) 233.

[132] See post, p. 278.

[133] Durando v. Durando, 23 N. Y. 331; Green v. Putnam, 1 Barb. (N. Y.) 500; Apple v. Apple, 1 Head (Tenn.) 348; Cocke's Ex'r v. Philips, 12 Leigh (Va.) 248; Gardner v. Greene, 5 R. I. 104; Eldredge v. Forrestal, 7 Mass. 253;

coverture, and the husband is let into possession, dower attaches.[134] Where the intervening estate is a mere chattel interest, such as a term of years, dower attaches because the husband is seised.[135] The exclusion of dower from estates in expectancy gives rise to the rule that there can be no dower out of dower. For instance, lands descend or are devised [136] to a son, subject to a right of dower in his mother. If the son dies before the mother, his wife cannot have dower out of the lands assigned as the mother's dower.[137] If the junior widow's dower is first assigned, her right is only suspended by a subsequent assignment to the mother; and, if the mother dies first, the son's widow may re-enter upon the part taken from her.[138]

Joint Estates.

In a joint tenancy,[139] the possibility of survivorship in the cotenants prevents dower from attaching.[140] This, of course, does not apply when the husband has survived his co-tenants, or there has been partition of the estate.[141] In some states statutes have

Brooks v. Everett, 13 Allen (Mass.) 457; Otis v. Parshley, 10 N. H. 403; Fisk v. Eastman, 5 N. H. 240; Kellett v. Shepard, 139 Ill. 433, 28 N. E. 751, and 34 N. E. 254; Arnold's Heirs v. Arnold's Adm'r, 8 B. Mon. (Ky.) 202; Butler v. Cheatham, 8 Bush (Ky.) 594; Young v. Morehead, 94 Ky. 608, 23 S. W. 511. But, if the husband purchases the prior estate, the wife will have dower. House v. Jackson, 50 N. Y. 161. By statute, in Ohio, dower is given in reversions and remainders. 1 Stim. Am. St. Law, § 3211.

[134] 1 Scrib. Dower (2d Ed.) 321.

[135] Boyd v. Hunter, 44 Ala. 705; Sykes v. Sykes, 49 Miss. 190.

[136] Robinson v. Miller, 2 B. Mon. (Ky.) 284. If he take them by purchase, the rule is different. Co. Litt. 31a; In re Cregier, 1 Barb. (N. Y.) 598. But cf. Durando v. Durando, 23 N. Y. 331.

[137] Reynolds v. Reynolds, 5 Paige (N. Y.) 161; Safford v. Safford, 7 Paige (N. Y.) 259; Bear v. Snyder, 11 Wend. (N. Y.) 592; Geer v. Hamblin, 1 Greenl. (Me.) 54; Manning v. Laboree, 33 Me. 343; Reitzel v. Eckard, 65 N. C. 673; Carter v. McDaniel, 94 Ky. 564, 23 S. W. 507; Peckham v. Hadwen, 8 R. I. 160; Gardner v. Greene, 5 R. I. 104. But possession under a right of quarantine does not prevent the heir's widow taking dower. Null v. Howell, 111 Mo. 273, 20 S. W. 24.

[138] Steele v. La Frambois, 68 Ill. 456; In re Cregier, 1 Barb. Ch. (N. Y.) 598.

[139] See post, p. 333.

[140] Mayburry v. Brien, 15 Pet. 21; Cockrill v. Armstrong, 31 Ark. 580; Babbitt v. Day, 41 N. J. Eq. 392, 5 Atl. 275; Reed v. Kennedy, 2 Strob. (S. C.) 67.

[141] 1 Scrib. Dower (2d Ed.) 337. But a sale by one tenant of his interest is

abolished survivorship, and so given dower in joint tenancies; in others, it has been expressly granted.[142] Dower is, however, an incident of estates in co-parcenary [143] and in common.[144] If partition is made of such an estate, the right of dower no longer exists in the whole land, but merely in the portion set apart to the husband.[145]

Same—Partnership Lands.

Equity regards lands held by a partnership as personalty, and the widow of a deceased partner has dower only in his share of the firm realty which is left after the debts are paid.[146]

not such partition as gives his wife dower. Mayburry v. Brien, 15 Pet. 21; Cockrill v. Armstrong, 31 Ark. 580; Babbitt v. Day, 41 N. J. Eq. 392, 5 Atl. 275.

[142] 1 Stim. Am. St. Law, §§ 1371, 3211; 1 Scrib. Dower (2d Ed.) 338; Weir v. Tate, 4 Ired. Eq. (N. C.) 264; Davis v. Logan, 9 Dana (Ky.) 185.

[143] Jourdan v. Haran, 56 N. Y. Super. Ct. R. 185, 3 N. Y. Supp. 541; Baker v. Leibert, 125 Pa. St. 106, 17 Atl. 236; 1 Scrib. Dower (2d Ed.) 341.

[144] Harvill v. Holloway, 24 Ark. 19; Ross v. Wilson, 58 Ga. 249; French v. Lord, 69 Me. 537; Hill v. Gregory, 56 Miss. 341; Smith v. Smith, 6 Lans. (N. Y.) 313; Hudson v. Steere, 9 R. I. 106; Davis v. Bartholomew, 3 Ind. 485.

[145] Potter v. Wheeler, 13 Mass. 504; Wilkinson v. Parish, 3 Paige (N. Y.) 653; Totten v. Stuyvesant, 3 Edw. Ch. (N. Y.) 500; Lee v. Lindell, 22 Mo. 202; Mosher v. Mosher, 32 Me. 412; Lloyd v. Conover, 25 N. J. Law, 47; Docktermann v. Elder, 27 Wkly. Law Bul. 195; Holley v. Glover, 36 S. C. 404, 15 S. E. 605. So a sale in partition divests the wife's whole interest. Weaver v. Gregg, 6 Ohio St. 547. But see Coburn v. Herrington, 114 Ill. 104, 29 N. E. 478; Dehoney v. Bell (Ky.) 30 S. W. 400.

[146] Simpson v. Leech, 86 Ill. 286; Hale v. Plummer, 6 Ind. 121; Campbell v. Campbell, 30 N. J. Eq. 415; Dyer v. Clark, 5 Metc. (Mass.) 562; Mowry v. Bradley, 11 R. I. 370; Free v. Beatley, 95 Mich. 426, 54 N. W. 910; Dawson v. Parsons, 10 Misc. Rep. 428, 31 N. Y. Supp. 78; Riddell v. Riddell, 85 Hun, 482, 33 N. Y. Supp. 99; Parrish v. Parrish, 88 Va. 529, 14 S. E. 325; Deering v. Kerfoot's Ex'r, 89 Va. 491, 16 S. E. 671; Young v. Thrasher, 115 Mo. 222, 21 S. W. 1104; Woodward-Holmes Co. v. Nudd, 58 Minn. 236, 59 N. W. 1010; Holton v. Guinn, 65 Fed. 450. But see Ratcliffe v. Mason, 92 Ky. 190, 17 S. W. 438; Shipp v. Snyder, 121 Mo. 155, 25 S. W. 900; Hughes v. Allen, 66 Vt. 95, 28 Atl. 882.

SAME—QUARANTINE.

51. Quarantine is the right of a widow to remain in her husband's principal mansion house after his death for forty days.

52. The duration of quarantine has been extended in some states.

At common law a widow has a right, called her "quarantine," to remain 40 days in the mansion house [147] of the husband.[148] Statutes in some states give a longer time.[149] In several she can now remain until her dower is assigned.[150] The right can only be claimed as to property of which the widow is dowable.[151] She can lease [152] the premises, but her quarantine right is not subject to sale on execution.[153] By common law quarantine was for-

[147] In some states the right has been extended to other property besides the house. 1 Shars. & B. Lead. Cas. Real Prop. 403; 1 Washb. Real Prop. (5th Ed.) 282; Weaver v. Crenshaw, 6 Ala. 873; Stewart's Lessee v. Stewart, 3 J. J. Marsh. (Ky.) 49; Grimes v. Wilson, 4 Blackf. (Ind.) 331.

[148] Oakley v. Oakley, 30 Ala. 131. The right exists only against those claiming under the husband. Taylor v. McCrackin, 2 Blackf. (Ind.) 260.

[149] In several it is now one year. 1 Stim. Am. St. Law, § 3278; 1 Shars. & B. Lead. Cas. Real Prop. 403; 1 Washb. Real Prop. (5th Ed.) 282.

[150] 1 Stim. Am. St. Law, § 3278; 1 Shars. & B. Lead. Cas. Real Prop. 403; 1 Washb. Real Prop. (5th Ed.) 282; White v. Clarke, 7 T. B. Mon. (Ky.) 641; Pharis v. Leachman, 20 Ala. 662; Rambo v. Bell, 3 Ga. 207; Graham's Heirs v. Graham, 6 T. B. Mon. (Ky.) 561; Chaplin v. Simmons' Heirs, 7 T. B. Mon. (Ky.) 337; Stewart's Lessee v. Stewart, 3 J. J. Marsh. (Ky.) 48; Robinson v. Miller, 1 B. Mon. (Ky.) 88.

[151] Harrison v. Boyd, 36 Ala. 203. She cannot claim quarantine in the whole of a house held in common. Collins v. Warren, 29 Mo. 236. Except in states where such interests are made subject to dower, quarantine does not extend to leasehold estates. Voelckner v. Hudson, 1 Sandf. (N. Y.) 215; Pizzala v. Campbell, 46 Ala. 35.

[152] Wallace v. Hall's Heirs, 19 Ala. 367; White v. Clarke, 7 T. B. Mon. (Ky.) 641; Craige v. Morris, 25 N. J. Eq. 467. Cf. Doe d. Caillaret v. Bernard, 7 Smedes & M. (Miss.) 319. And see, contra, Stokes v. McAllister, 2 Mo. 163.

[153] Cook v. Webb, 18 Ala. 810. She need not pay the taxes on the premises. Branson v. Yancy, 1 Dev. Eq. (N. C.) 77. And see Roach v. Davidson, 3 Brev. (S. C.) 80; Bleecker v. Hennion, 23 N. J. Eq. 123.

feited by a second marriage,[154] but the rule is otherwise in this country.[155]

SAME—ASSIGNMENT.

53. Assignment is the setting out to the widow of her share in the husband's lands. It is:

(a) Of common right, which is an assignment of a life estate in one-third by metes and bounds.

(b) Against common right, which is an assignment in some other manner by consent of the parties.

Dower consummate before assignment is not an estate,[156] but only a chose in action.[157] At law it is not liable for the widow's debts,[158] nor can she transfer this right,[159] though a transfer may be enforced in equity.[160] She has no right of entry until assignment,[161] nor can she bring partition.[162]

[154] 2 Scrib. Dower (2d Ed.) 63.

[155] Shelton v. Carrol, 16 Ala. 148.

[156] Blodget v. Brent, 3 Cranch, C. C. 394, Fed. Cas. No. 1,553; Reynolds v. McCurry, 100 Ill. 356; Heisen v. Heisen, 145 Ill. 658, 34 N. E. 597; Scott v. Howard, 3 Barb. (N. Y.) 319.

[157] Rayner v. Lee, 20 Mich. 384; Summers v. Babb, 13 Ill. 483; Weaver v. Sturtevant, 12 R. I. 537; Downs v. Allen, 10 Lea (Tenn.) 652.

[158] Gooch v. Atkins, 14 Mass. 378; Petty v. Malier, 15 B. Mon. (Ky.) 591; Waller v. Mardus, 29 Mo. 25; Blain v. Harrison, 11 Ill. 384; Summers v. Babb, 13 Ill. 483; Nason v. Allen, 5 Greenl. (Me.) 479; Pennington's Ex'rs v. Yell, 11 Ark. 212. (But that it may be reached by creditors' bill, see Payne v. Becker, 87 N. Y. 153; Stewart v. McMartin, 5 Barb. (N. Y.) 438; Tompkins v. Fonda, 4 Paige (N. Y.) 448; Thomas v. Simpson, 3 Pa. St. 60; Shaupe v. Shaupe, 12 Serg. & R. (Pa.) 9; Boltz v. Stoltz, 41 Ohio St. 540; Davison v. Whittlesby, 1 McArthur, 163. Contra, Maxon v. Gray, 14 R. I. 641.

[159] Summers v. Babb, 13 Ill. 483; McDonald v. Hannah, 51 Fed. 73; Blain v. Harrison, 11 Ill. 384; Hoots v. Graham, 23 Ill. 81; Jackson v. Aspell, 20 Johns. (N. Y.) 411; Sutliff v. Forgey, 1 Cow. (N. Y.) 89; Cox v. Jagger, 2 Cow. (N. Y.) 638; Dillon, C. J., in Huston v. Seeley, 27 Iowa, 198; Parton v. Allison, 109 N. C. 674, 14 S. E. 107; Saltmarsh v. Smith, 32 Ala. 404. But she may mortgage it. Ferry v. Burnell, 14 Fed. 807; Pope v. Mead, 99 N. Y. 201, 1 N. E. 671; Herr v Herr, 90 Iowa, 538, 58 N. W. 897.

[160] Strong v. Clem, 12 Ind. 37; Parton v. Allison, 109 N. C. 674, 14 S. E. 107.

[161] Jackson v. O'Donaghy, 7 Johns. (N. Y.) 247; Sheafe v. O'Neil, 9 Mass. 13; Parsons, C. J., in Inhabitants of Windham v. Inhabitants of Portland, 4 Mass. 387.

[162] Reynolds v. McCurry, 100 Ill. 358; Coles v. Coles, 15 Johns. (N. Y.) 319;

Assignment of Common Right and against Common Right.

Assignment of dower of common right is where the widow's third is set out to her by metes and bounds.[163] She must be given an absolute and unconditional life estate in the premises assigned.[164] Assignment of common right is the method which must be adopted by the tenant when he makes the assignment without the widow's consent,[165] or by the sheriff or commissioners on the order of the court.[166] In assignment against common right the widow receives some other share in lieu of one-third by metes and bounds.[167] This kind of assignment is valid only by consent of the parties,[168] but they may agree upon a share in common, or any other method, so long as the provision for the widow is out of the lands of which she is dowable.[169] A parol assignment of dower by either method is good,[170] unless, as in some states, a writing or a sealed instrument is required by statute.[171] If the assignment has been of common right, and subsequently a superior title is enforced against the widow's share, so that she loses it, she can call upon the other party for a new assignment;[172]

Brown v. Adams, 2 Whart. (Pa.) 188. Cf. Jones v. Hollopeter, 10 Serg. & R. (Pa.) 326.

[163] 2 Scrib. Dower (2d Ed.) 80; Stevens' Heirs v. Stevens, 3 Dana (Ky.) 371; Schnebly v. Schnebly, 26 Ill. 116; Benner v. Evans, 3 Pen. & W. (Pa.) 454; French v. Pratt, 27 Me. 381.

[164] Wentworth v. Wentworth, Cro. Eliz. 452.

[165] 2 Scrib. Dower (2d Ed.) 80.

[166] 2 Scrib. Dower (2d Ed.) 582.

[167] French v. Peters, 33 Me. 396; French v. Pratt, 27 Me. 381; Marshall v. McPherson, 8 Gill & J. (Md.) 333; Welch v. Anderson, 28 Mo. 293; Hale v. James, 6 Johns. Ch. (N. Y.) 258.

[168] Jones v. Brewer, 1 Pick. (Mass.) 314; Welch v. Anderson, 28 Mo. 293.

[169] 2 Scrib. Dower (2d Ed.) 82; Hale v. James, 6 Johns. Ch. (N. Y.) 258; Marshall v. McPherson, 8 Gill & J. (Md.) 333; Fitzhugh v. Foote, 3 Call (Va.) 13.

[170] Johnson v. Neil, 4 Ala. 166; Curtis v. Hobart, 41 Me. 230; Meserve v. Meserve, 19 N. H. 240; Conant v. Little, 1 Pick. (Mass.) 189; Shattuck v. Gragg, 23 Pick. (Mass.) 88.

[171] 2 Scrib. Dower (2d Ed.) 74.

[172] But she gets only one-third of what remains. French v. Peters, 33 Me. 396; Mautz v. Buchanan, 1 Md. Ch. 202; Holloman v. Holloman, 5 Smedes & M. (Miss.) 559; St. Clair v. Williams, 7 Ohio, pt. 2, p. 110.

and the same right exists in favor of the heir against the widow.[173] But in an assignment against common right there is no such warranty, and each one must bear any subsequent loss alone.[174]

54. WHEN VALUE ESTIMATED—Against an heir, dower is estimated at the time of assignment; against a grantee of the husband, at the time of alienation in some states, in others at the time of assignment, not including improvements.

The widow's one-third or one-half is measured by the value of the husband's estates, not by the quantity of land. Against the husband's heirs, this value is estimated as of the time of assignment.[175] If the heir improves the land before assignment, the widow has dower in the increased value.[176] But in the United States improvements made by an alienee of the husband are not subject to dower.[177] In some states the widow is dowable, as against such alienee, of any increased value of the land,[178] while

[173] Singleton's Ex'r v. Singleton's Heirs, 5 Dana (Ky.) 87.

[174] French v. Pratt, 27 Me. 381.

[175] McGebee v. McGehee, 42 Miss. 747; McClanahan v. Porter, 10 Mo. 746. It is so provided in some states by statute. 1 Stim. Am. St. Law, § 3279; 2 Scrib. Dower (2d Ed.) 634; 1 Shars. & B. Lead. Cas. Real Prop. 401. And see Verlander v. Harvey, 36 W. Va. 374, 15 S. E. 54.

[176] Larrowe v. Beam, 10 Ohio, 498; Price v. Hobbs, 47 Md. 359. It is otherwise by statute in some states. 2 Scrib. Dower (2d Ed.) 597; 1 Shars. & B. Lead. Cas. Real Prop. 401.

[177] Summers v. Babb, 13 Ill. 483; Powell v. Manufacturing Co., 3 Mason, 347, Fed. Cas. No. 11,356; Barney v. Frowner, 9 Ala. 901; Stookey v. Stookey, 89 Ill. 40; Scammon v. Campbell, 75 Ill. 223; Wilson v. Oatman, 2 Blackf. (Ind.) 223; Dashiel v. Collier, 4 J. J. Marsh. (Ky.) 601; Price v. Hobbs, 47 Md. 359; Ayer v. Spring, 9 Mass. 8; Johnston v. Vandyke, 6 McLean, 422, Fed. Cas. No. 7,426; Catlin v. Ware, 9 Mass. 218; Humphrey v. Phinney, 2 Johns. (N. Y.) 484; Thompson v. Morrow, 5 Serg. & R. (Pa.) 289; Young v. Thrasher, 115 Mo. 222, 21 S. W. 1104; Morgan v. Hendrew, 102 Ala. 245, 14 South. 540.

[178] Thompson v. Morrow, 5 Serg. & R. (Pa.) 289; Fritz v. Tudor, 1 Bush (Ky.) 28; McClanahan v. Porter, 10 Mo. 746; Dunseth v. Bank, 6 Ohio, 76; Walker v. Schuyler, 10 Wend. (N. Y.) 480; Powell v. Manufacturing Co., 3 Mason, 347, Fed. Cas. No. 11,356. And conversely she must bear any depreciation in value. Westcott v. Campbell, 11 R. I. 378; McClanahan v. Porter,

in others she takes her share of the value at the time of alienation.[179]

55. METHOD OF DIVISION—Land subject to dower is divided by metes and bounds when practicable; otherwise, it is sold, and the proceeds divided.

Whenever possible, the widow's interest in the dower lands is set out to her by metes and bounds. In assigning dower the convenience and interests of all parties concerned should be considered. A widow may be given one of three parcels of land, instead of one-third of each.[180] But if the several parcels have been aliened to different persons by the husband, dower must be assigned in each one.[181] If only part of them have been sold, then dower is to be assigned in what remains, if sufficient, and the alienees exonerated.[182] In some states the dwelling house is to be included in the widow's share,[183] and, when her third does not entitle her to all of it, certain rooms may be assigned, with a right to use the halls and stairs.[184] Where lands are held by the husband as a co-tenant with others, dower may be assigned in com-

10 Mo. 746; Braxton v. Coleman, 5 Call (Va.) 433; Sanders v. McMillian, 98 Ala. 144, 11 South. 750.

[179] Hale v. James, 6 Johns. Ch. (N. Y.) 258; Walker v. Schuyler, 10 Wend. (N. Y.) 480; Guerin v. Moore, 25 Minn. 462; Tod v. Baylor, 4 Leigh (Va.) 498.

[180] Jones v. Jones, Busb. (N. C.) 177; Rowland v. Carroll, 81 Ill. 224; Alderson's Heirs v. Henderson, 5 W. Va. 182; 1 Stim. Am. St. Law, § 3277 B. Contra, Hardin v. Lawrence, 40 N. J. Eq. 154.

[181] Coulter v. Holland, 2 Har. (Del.) 330; Cook v. Fisk, 1 Walk. (Miss.) 423; Ellicott v. Mosier, 11 Barb. (N. Y.) 574; Thomas v. Hesse, 34 Mo. 13; Fosdick v. Gooding, 1 Greenl. (Me.) 30; Peyton v. Jeffries, 50 Ill. 143; Droste v. Hall (N. J. Ch.) 29 Atl. 437.

[182] 2 Scrib. Dower (2d Ed.) 637; Wood v. Keyes, 6 Paige (N. Y.) 478; Lawson v. Morton, 6 Dana (Ky.) 471; Morgan v. Conn, 3 Bush (Ky.) 58; Goodrum v. Goodrum, 56 Ark. 532, 20 S. W. 353.

[183] 1 Stim. Am. St. Law, § 3277 B; 1 Shars. & B. Lead. Cas. Real Prop. 398. And see Christopher v. Christopher, 92 Tenn. 408, 21 S. W. 890.

[184] White v. Story, 2 Hill (N. Y.) 543; Stewart v. Smith, 39 Barb. (N. Y.) 167; Patch v. Keeler, 27 Vt. 252; Symmes v. Drew, 21 Pick. (Mass.) 278; Parrish v. Parrish, 88 Va. 529, 14 S. E. 325.

§ 56) DOWER—BY WHOM ASSIGNED. 99

mon.[185] Sometimes, as in case of a mine, mill, or ferry, the only practical method of assigning dower is to give alternate enjoyment [186] or to divide the profits.[187] When a division is impossible, or would cause considerable loss, the land subject to dower is sold.[188] When there has been a sale, or when there is a sum of money in court subject to dower, there are two ways of making the assignment. In some jurisdictions one-third is invested and the proceeds paid to the widow during her life.[189] In others, she is given a gross sum at once, equal to the present worth of an annuity for the probable duration of her life.[190]

56. BY WHOM ASSIGNED—Dower can be assigned only by the tenant of the freehold, except in a few states, where the probate court is given the power.

Dower can be voluntarily assigned only by the tenant of the freehold,[191] and any one may assign dower who could be compelled to by suit.[192] So an assignment by an infant [193] or a guardian is

[185] Parrish v. Parrish, 88 Va. 529, 14 S. E. 325.

[186] Smith's Heirs v. Smith, 5 Dana (Ky.) 179; Stevens' Heirs v. Stevens, 3 Dana (Ky.) 371.

[187] Chase's Case, 1 Bland (Md.) 206; 1 Stim. Am. St. Law, § 3276; 1 Shars. & B. Lead. Cas. Real Prop. 396. And see Heisen v. Heisen, 145 Ill. 658, 34 N. E. 597.

[188] See 1 Stim. Am. St. Law, § 3276.

[189] Higbie v. Westlake, 14 N. Y. 281; Tabele v. Tabele, 1 Johns. Ch. (N. Y.) 45; Bonner v. Peterson, 44 Ill. 253.

[190] Williams' Case, 3 Bland (Md.) 186, 221; Eagle v. Emmet, 4 Bradf. Sur. (N. Y.) 117; Sherard v. Sherard's Adm'r, 33 Ala. 488. For the calculation of this (and the use of life tables), see 2 Scrib. Dower (2d Ed.) 678; Brown v. Bronson, 35 Mich. 415; 70 Ga. Append. pp. 843–848; Stein v. Stein, 80 Md. 306, 30 Atl. 703; and ante, p. 60.

[191] Hill's Adm'rs v. Mitchell, 5 Ark. 608; Drost v. Hall, 52 N. J. Eq. 68, 28 Atl. 81; Id. (N. J. Ch.) 29 Atl. 437 (a chattel interest gives no power to assign). But see 2 Scrib. Dower (2d Ed.) 76.

[192] Robinson v. Miller, 1 B. Mon. (Ky.) 88; Lenfers v. Henke, 73 Ill. 405; Meserve v. Meserve, 19 N. H. 240; Richardson v. Harms, 11 Misc. Rep. 254, 32 N. Y. Supp. 808. And see, as to parties to suit, Kenyon v. Kenyon (R. I.) 23 Atl. 101; Parton v. Allison, 111 N. C. 429, 16 S. E. 415; Coburn v. Herrington, 114 Ill. 104, 29 N. E. 478.

[193] 2 Scrib. Dower (2d Ed.) 78; Curtis v. Hobart, 41 Me. 230.

good.[194] Where a minor heir has made an excessive assignment, he may have a redistribution on reaching his majority.[195] In a number of states dower may be assigned by the probate court in which the husband's estate is being settled.[196]

57. RECOVERY BY ACTION—The procedure for the recovery of dower wrongfully detained varies greatly in the several states. In most states no demand is necessary before bringing suit.

Proceedings to Recover Dower.

If dower is not assigned by the one whose duty it is to do so, the widow can resort to the courts to compel assignment.[197] The procedure varies in the several states. It may be (1) by a proceeding at common law,[198] (2) in equity,[199] (3) by ejectment,[200] or (4) by a summary proceeding provided by statute.[201] It is not generally necessary to make a demand before bringing suit for dower,[202] except as to damages; but, in jurisdictions where it is

---

[194] Jones v. Brewer, 1 Pick. (Mass.) 314; Boyers v. Newbanks, 2 Ind. 388. But see Bonner v. Peterson, 44 Ill. 260. For assignment by a joint tenant, see 2 Scrib. Dower (2d Ed.) 79.

[195] McCormick v. Taylor, 2 Ind. 336.

[196] 1 Stim. Am. St. Law, § 3272.

[197] The action must be brought where the land is situated. Lamar v. Scott, 3 Strob. (S. C.) 562. The rule is not uniform as to when the action may be commenced. See 1 Stim. Am. St. Law, § 3271; 2 Scrib. Dower (2d Ed.) 109.

[198] See Ship. Com. Law Pl. (2d Ed.) p. 6; 2 Scrib. Dower (2d Ed.) 91; Williams, Real Prop. (17th Am. Ed.) p. 380, note. And see Hurd v. Grant, 3 Wend. (N. Y.) 340; Miller v. Beverly, 1 Hen. & M. (Va.) 368.

[199] 2 Scrib. Dower (2d Ed.) 145. The equitable remedy is sometimes exclusive. McMahan v. Kimball, 3 Blackf. (Ind.) 1; Chiswell v. Morris, 14 N. J. Eq. 101; Davis v. Davis, 5 Mo. 183; Smart v. Waterhouse, 10 Yerg. (Tenn.) 94.

[200] 2 Scrib. Dower (2d Ed.) 119; 1 Washb. Real Prop. (5th Ed.) 286; Ellicott v. Mosier, 11 Barb. (N. Y.) 574. But not in some states before assignment. 2 Scrib. Dower (2d Ed.) 115.

[201] 1 Stim. Am. St. Law, § 3274; 2 Scrib. Dower (2d Ed.) 175.

[202] Scrib. Dower, c. 6, § 1; Jackson v. Churchill, 7 Cow. (N. Y.) 287; Hopper v. Hopper, 22 N. J. Law, 715.

required,[203] it must be of the tenant of the freehold,[204] and should contain a general description of the premises out of which dower is demanded.[205]

SAME—INCIDENTS.

58. A dowress has, in the land assigned as her dower, the usual rights of a tenant for life.

59. On the death of the dowress, the owner of the land is entitled to possession at once.

When dower has been assigned, i. e. set apart to her, the widow has, in such realty, an estate subject to the usual incidents of life estates.[206] She may sell or lease the whole or any part of it.[207] She has not only the usual right to emblements,[208] but she has also the crops sown on the dower land by her husband,[209] or by the heir before assignment.[210] The dowress may take reasonable estovers,[211] and, when the land assigned consists of several parcels, she may take wood from one parcel for use on another.[212] The duty to repair is doubtful where not provided for by statute, as is the case in several states.[213] The tenant in dower must not commit waste,[214] and she must keep down the interest on incumbran-

---

[203] 2 Scrib. Dower (2d Ed.) 109.

[204] Id. 110. Cf. Young v. Tarbell, 37 Me. 509.

[205] Haynes v. Powers, 22 N. H. 590; Davis v. Walker, 42 N. H. 482; Ford v. Erskine, 45 Me. 484; Atwood v. Atwood, 22 Pick. (Mass.) 283. And see Falls v. Wright, 55 Ark. 562, 18 S. W. 1044.

[206] Whyte v. Mayor, etc., of Nashville, 2 Swan (Tenn.) 364.

[207] Summers v. Babb, 13 Ill. 483. Cf. Matlock v. Lee, 9 Ind. 298; Stockwell v. Sargent, 37 Vt. 16.

[208] See Talbot v. Hill, 68 Ill. 106. Any doubt as to this was removed by the statute of Merton (20 Hen. III. c. 2), which has been generally recognized or re-enacted in this country. 2 Scrib. Dower (2d Ed.) 779; 1 Stim. Am. St. Law, § 3233.

[209] Ralston v. Ralston, 3 G. Greene (Iowa) 533. Cf. Kain v. Fisher, 6 N. Y. 597; Street v. Saunders, 27 Ark. 554; Budd v. Hiler, 27 N. J. Law, 43.

[210] Parker v. Parker, 17 Pick. (Mass.) 236.

[211] White v. Cutler, 17 Pick. (Mass.) 248.

[212] Childs v. Smith, 1 Md. Ch. 483. But cf. Cook v. Cook, 11 Gray (Mass.) 123; Noyes v. Stone (Mass.) 40 N. E. 856.

[213] 1 Stim. Am. St. Law, § 3232; Beers v. Strong, Kirb. (Conn.) 19.

[214] See post, p. 111.

ces,[215] and pay the taxes.[216] There can be no claim for improvements made by the widow or her assignee.[217] If she has leased the premises, her personal representative is entitled to the rent due at her death.[218]

The reversion or remainder in fee simple after the life estate of the dowress descends to the husband's heirs, or goes to his devisees, as the case may be. If the land was aliened by the husband by a conveyance not good against the wife, the grantee's estate is by the assignment of dower defeated during the life of the dowress. On her death, the reversioner, remainder-man, or grantee is at once entitled to possession of the land, subject to any right to emblements that may exist.[219]

SAME—HOW DEFEATED.

60. The right to dower may be defeated by:
   (a) **Alienage of husband or wife, in some states** (p. 103).
   (b) **Elopement and living in adultery by the wife, in most states** (p. 103).
   (c) **Annulment of marriage** (p. 104).
   (d) **Divorce, in many states** (p. 104).
   (e) **Loss of husband's seisin** (p. 104).
   (f) **Conveyance by husband:**
      (1) **Before marriage** (p. 105).
      (2) **After marriage, in some states** (p. 105).
   (g) **Release by wife** (p. 106).
   (h) **Jointure, which is either:**
      (1) **Legal, or**
      (2) **Equitable** (p. 107).

---

[215] 2 Scrib. Dower (2d Ed.) 783.

[216] Graham v. Dunigan, 2 Bosw. (N. Y.) 516; Bidwell v. Greenshield, 2 Abb. N. C. (N. Y.) 427; Durkee v. Felton, 44 Wis. 467; Linden v. Graham, 34 Barb. (N. Y.) 316. So of assessments for street improvements. Whyte v. Mayor, etc., of Nashville, 2 Swan (Tenn.) 364.

[217] Maddocks v. Jellison, 11 Me. 482; Bent v. Weeks, 44 Me. 45; Cannon v. Hare, 1 Tenn. Ch. 22.

[218] 2 Scrib. Dower (2d Ed.) 781.

[219] 2 Scrib. Dower (2d Ed.) 785.

§ 60) DOWER—HOW DEFEATED. 103

(i) **Widow's election to take a testamentary or statutory provision in lieu of dower** (p. 109).

(j) **Estoppel** (p. 110).

(k) **Statute of limitations, in many states** (p. 111).

(l) **Laches in equity** (p. 111).

(m) **Waste after assignment which causes a forfeiture in several states** (p. 111).

Alienage.

At common law there was no dower when either husband or wife was an alien.[220] The statutes of many states have changed the rule,[221] but their effect is not retroactive, so as to give dower in lands sold before the enactment.[222]

Elopement and Adultery.

By the statute of Westminster II.,[223] which has been re-enacted [224] or recognized in most states, a wife forfeits her dower if she elope and live in adultery,[225] unless there be a subsequent

[220] 2 Bl. Comm. 131; Co. Litt. 31b; Calvin's Case, 7 Coke, 25a; Wightman v. Laborde, Speer (S. C.) 525.

[221] 1 Stim. Am. St. Law, §§ 102, 6013; 1 Scrib. Dower (2d Ed.) 156; 1 Washb. Real Prop. (5th Ed.) 80, note; 1 Shars. & B. Lead. Cas. Real Prop. 303, 515. In Michigan and Wisconsin, by statute, lands conveyed by a non-resident owner are not subject to dower. Ligare v. Semple, 32 Mich. 438. Cf. Bear v. Stahl, 61 Mich. 203, 28 N. W. 69; Bennett v. Harms, 51 Wis. 251, 8 N. W. 222.

[222] Priest v. Cummings, 20 Wend. (N. Y.) 338. Cf. White v. White, 2 Metc. (Ky.) 185.

[223] 13 Edw. I. c. 34.

[224] 1 Stim. Am. St. Law, § 3246 A (1); 2 Scrib. Dower (2d Ed.) 535; 1 Shars. & B. Lead. Cas. Real Prop. 384.

[225] Adultery without elopement does not bar. Cogswell v. Tibbetts, 3 N. H. 41; Reel v. Elder, 62 Pa. St. 308; Ondis v. Bates, 7 Kulp (Pa.) 309. If there has been a separation for any cause whatever, a subsequent adultery will be a bar. Woodward v. Dowse, 10 C. B. (N. S.) 722; Hethrington v. Graham, 6 Bing. 135. Cf. Goss v. Froman, 89 Ky. 318, 12 S. W. 387; Watters v. Jordan, 13 Ired. (N. C.) 361. But if the husband drives the wife away, or deserts her, dower is not lost by adultery committed afterwards. Heslop v. Heslop, 82 Pa. St. 537; Rawlins v. Buttel, 1 Houst. (Del.) 224. And see Reynolds v. Reynolds, 24 Wend. (N. Y.) 193.

reconciliation.[226] And in a few states an abandonment of the husband will cause a forfeiture of dower.[227]

Annulment of Marriage and Divorce.

When a marriage is terminated by a decree of nullity, dower is barred,[228] and an absolute divorce has the same effect in many states,[229] while in others divorce is no bar.[230]

Loss of Husband's Estate.

When the husband loses his estate by the enforcement of a paramount title or incumbrance, the wife has no dower.[231] Debts which had become charges on the land before marriage defeat dower when enforced.[232] So dower is barred if the husband's land is taken under the right of eminent domain.[233]

---

[226] See 2 Scrib. Dower (2d Ed.) 539.

[227] 1 Stim. Am. St. Law, § 3246 B.

[228] 2 Scrib. Dower (2d Ed.) 541.

[229] 1 Stim. Am. St. Law, §§ 3246 C, 6251 (1); 1 Sbars. & B. Lead. Cas. Real Prop. 386. And see Pullen v. Pullen, 52 N. J. Eq. 9, 28 Atl. 719; Thoms v. King, 95 Tenn. 60, 31 S. W. 983. As to the effect of limited divorce, see 1 Stim. Am. St. Law, § 6306. And see Van Cleaf v. Burns, 133 N. Y. 540, 30 N. E. 661; Chapman v. Chapman, 48 Kan. 636, 29 Pac. 1071.

[230] 1 Stim. Am. St. Law, §§ 3246 C, 6251.

[231] Toomey v. McLean, 105 Mass. 122; Stirbling v. Ross, 16 Ill. 122; McClure v. Fairfield, 153 Pa. St. 411, 26 Atl. 446; Vickers v. Henry, 110 N. C. 371, 15 S. E. 115; Waller v. Waller's Adm'r, 33 Grat. (Va.) 83. And see ante, p. 89.

[232] Trustees of Poor of Queen Anne's Co. v. Pratt, 10 Md. 5; Mantz v. Buchanan, 1 Md. Ch. 202; Holden v. Boggess, 20 W. Va. 62; Sandford v. McLean, 3 Paige (N. Y.) 117; Robbins v. Robbins, 8 Blackf. (Ind.) 174; Griffin v. Reece, 1 Har. (Del.) 508. But see House v. Fowle, 22 Or. 303, 29 Pac. 890; Whiteaker v. Belt, 25 Or. 490, 36 Pac. 534; Dayton v. Corser, 51 Minn. 406, 53 N. W. 717; Vinson v. Gentry (Ky.) 21 S. W. 578; Butler v. Fitzgerald, 43 Neb. 192, 61 N. W. 640. Bankruptcy of the husband during coverture is no bar. Porter v. Lazear, 109 U. S. 84, 3 Sup. Ct. 58; Id., 87 Pa. St. 513; In re Bartenbach, 11 N. B. R. 61, Fed. Cas. No. 1,068; In re Lawrence, 49 Conn. 411. Cf. Dudley v. Easton, 104 U. S. 99. The wife is, in some states, allowed dower on bankruptcy of husband as in case of death. Warford v. Noble, 9 Biss. 320, 2 Fed. 202; Rhea v. Meridith, 6 Lea (Tenn.) 605.

[233] Moore v. Mayor, etc., 8 N. Y. 110; Baker v. Railway Co., 122 Mo. 396, 30 S. W. 301; French v. Lord, 69 Me. 537. But see Nye v. Railroad Co., 113 Mass. 277. The dower right attaches to the proceeds. Bonner v. Peterson, 44 Ill. 253; In re New York & B. Bridge, 75 Hun, 558, 27 N. Y. Supp. 597;

§ 60) DOWER—HOW DEFEATED. 105

Devices to Bar Dower.

The husband may have estates conveyed to him under such limitations that dower will not attach. These are called "devices to bar dower." [234]

Conveyance by Husband.

Conveyances by the husband before marriage prevent dower attaching,[235] unless made to defraud the wife;[236] but no alienation or incumbrance by the husband alone during the coverture is good against the wife,[237] nor is a bona fide purchaser, ignorant of her dower right, protected.[238] But by statute in some states the husband's alienations are made effectual against the wife.[239] The

Wheeler v. Kirtland, 27 N. J. Eq. 534. A dedication of land to public uses bars dower. Gwynne v. City of Cincinnati, 3 Ohio, 24; Steel v. Board of Education, 31 Wkly. Cin. Law Bul. 84; Duncan v. City of Terre Haute, 85 Ind. 105; Venable v. Railway Co., 112 Mo. 103, 20 S. W. 493. And see Chouteau v. Railway Co., 122 Mo. 375, 22 S. W. 458, and 30 S. W. 299.

[234] For examples of these, see 2 Minor, Inst. 146; Ray v. Pung. 5 Barn. & Ald. 561.

[235] Oakley v. Oakley, 69 Hun, 121, 23 N. Y. Supp. 267; Rawlings v. Adams, 7 Md. 26; Richardson v. Skolfield, 45 Me. 386; Kintner v. McRae, 2 Ind. 453; Gaines v. Gaines' Ex'r, 9 B. Mon. (Ky.) 295; Firestone v. Firestone, 2 Ohio St. 415. But see In re Pulling's Estate, 97 Mich. 375, 56 N. W. 765.

[236] Such as a secret conveyance on the day before marriage. Stewart's Lessee v. Stewart, 3 J. J. Marsh. (Ky.) 48; Cranson v. Cranson, 4 Mich. 230; Pomeroy v. Pomeroy, 54 How. Prac. (N. Y.) 228; Brewer v. Connell, 11 Humph. (Tenn.) 500; Brooks v. McMeekin, 37 S. C. 285, 15 S. E. 1019.

[237] Rank v. Hanna, 6 Ind. 20; Thompson v. McCorkle, 136 Ind. 484, 34 N. E. 813; Graves v. Fligor, 140 Ind. 25, 38 N. E. 853; Chase v. Van Meter, 140 Ind. 321, 39 N. E. 455; Venable v. Railway Co. (Mo. Sup.) 19 S. W. 45; Deans v. Pate, 114 N. C. 194, 19 S. E. 146; Stein v. Stein, 80 Md. 306, 30 Atl. 703; 1 Stim. Am. St. Law, § 3249; 1 Shars. & B. Lead. Cas. Real Prop. 333. The grantee of the husband is estopped to deny the husband's title, Browne v. Potter, 17 Wend. (N. Y.) 164; but not when the conveyance is a quitclaim. Sparrow v. Kingman, 1 N. Y. 242. And see Coakley v. Perry, 3 Ohio St. 344; Gardner v. Greene, 5 R. I. 104.

[238] Dick v. Doughten, 1 Del. Ch. 320. The purchaser's estate is only defeated as to one-third during the life of the dowress. Id.

[239] As where she is dowable only of lands of which he died seised. 1 Stim. Am. St. Law, § 3202 E; 1 Shars. & B. Lead. Cas. Real Prop. 334. And see McRae v. McRae, 78 Md. 270, 27 Atl. 1038. But a voluntary conveyance for the purpose of defeating dower will be ineffectual. Jiggitts v. Jiggitts, 40 Miss. 718; McIntosh v. Ladd, 1 Humph. (Tenn.) 458; Thayer v. Thayer, 14 Vt. 107.

doctrine of conversion may operate in other cases to cut off dower, as when, before marriage, the husband has made a binding contract to sell.[240] On the other hand, the widow of the purchaser would be entitled to dower.[241] So, too, there would be dower in money directed to be laid out in land,[242] but not in land ordered to be turned into money.[243] In several states, if the husband make an exchange [244] during coverture of one tract of land for another, his widow cannot have dower in both tracts. She must elect out of which she will claim.[245]

Release by Wife.

The wife may, however, release her inchoate right of dower to her husband's alienee,[246] but not to the husband himself,[247] or to

Contra, Flowers v. Flowers, 89 Ga. 632, 15 S. E. 834. And see Patterson v. Patterson (Ky.) 24 S. W. 880; Brandon v. Dawson, 51 Mo. App. 237. And cf. Jenny v. Jenny, 24 Vt. 324; McGee v. McGee's Heirs, 4 Ired. (N. C.) 105.

[240] Rawlings v. Adams, 7 Md. 26; Hunkins v. Hunkins, 65 N. H. 95, 18 Atl. 655.

[241] 1 Stim. Am. St. Law, § 3212; Reed v. Whitney, 7 Gray (Mass.) 533; Church v. Church, 3 Sandf. Ch. (N. Y.) 434; Duke v. Brandt, 51 Mo. 221; Thompson v. Thompson, 1 Jones (N. C.) 430. But see Lobdell v. Hayes, 4 Allen (Mass.) 187. But the purchase money must have been paid. Taylor v. Kearn, 68 Ill. 339; Greenbaum v. Austrian, 70 Ill. 591; Crawl v. Harrington, 33 Neb. 107, 49 N. W. 1118; Pugh v. Bell, 2 T. B. Mon. (Ky.) 125.

[242] 1 Scrib. Dower (2d Ed.) 450.

[243] 1 Scrib. Dower (2d Ed.) 458.

[244] See post, p. 407.

[245] Stevens v. Smith, 4 J. J. Marsh. (Ky.) 64; Mahoney v. Young, 3 Dana (Ky.) 588. And so by statute. 1 Stim. Am. St. Law, § 3218; 1 Shars. & B. Lead. Cas. Real Prop. 346. But cf. Wilcox v. Randall, 7 Barb. (N. Y.) 633; Cass v. Thompson, 1 N. H. 65.

[246] Fowler v. Shearer, 7 Mass. 14; Kirk v. Dean, 2 Bin. (Pa.) 341; Chicago Dock Co. v. Kinzie, 49 Ill. 289; Howlett v. Dilts, 4 Ind. App. 23, 30 N. E. 313; Ortman v. Chute, 57 Minn. 452, 59 N. W. 533; Saunders v. Blythe, 112 Mo. 1, 20 S. W. 319; Shinkle's Assignees v. Bristow, 95 Ky. 84, 23 S. W. 670. Cf. Stull v. Graham, 60 Ark. 461, 31 S. W. 46. If the husband's deed is avoided, her dower is restored. Robinson v. Bates, 3 Metc. (Mass.) 40; Woodworth v. Paige, 5 Ohio St. 71; Malloney v. Horan, 49 N. Y. 111; Stinson v. Sumner, 9 Mass. 143; Blain v. Harrison, 11 Ill. 384; Morton v. Noble, 57 Ill. 176; Summers v. Babb, 13 Ill. 483. But see Den v. Johnson, 18 N. J. Law, 87.

[247] Carson v. Murray, 3 Paige (N. Y.) 483; Martin's Heirs v. Martin, 22 Ala. 86; Graham v. Van Wyck, 14 Barb. (N. Y.) 531; Wightman v. Schleifer,

§ 60) DOWER—HOW DEFEATED. 107

a stranger.[248] The release must be by deed, and the deed must contain words of grant or release,[249] although in a few states a mere signing of the husband's conveyance is sufficient.[250] The form of such deeds is in all cases governed by local statute.[251] In many states a separate examination of the wife is required.[252]

Jointure—Legal and Equitable.

Legal jointure [253] is a provision,[254] consisting of land exclusively,[255] made for the wife in lieu of dower. It must (1) take

---

63 Hun, 633, 18 N. Y. Supp. 551; In re Rausch, 35 Minn. 291, 28 N. W. 920; House v. Fowle, 22 Or. 303, 29 Pac. 890. See, however, Doremus v. Doremus, 66 Hun, 111, 21 N. Y. Supp. 13; Chittock v. Chittock, 101 Mich. 367, 59 N. W. 655. But the husband may be her attorney in fact to release. Andrews, J., in Wronkow v. Oakley, 133 N. Y. 505, 31 N. E. 521.

[248] Harriman v. Gray, 49 Me. 537; Reiff v. Horst, 55 Md. 42; Marvin v. Smith, 46 N. Y. 571; Bethune v. McDonald, 35 S. C. 88, 14 S. E. 674. But cf. Robbins v. Kinzie, 45 Ill. 354.

[249] Powell v. Manufacturing Co., 3 Mason, 347, 459, Fed. Cas. Nos. 11,356 and 11,357; Hall v. Savage, 4 Mason, 273, Fed. Cas. No. 5,944; Lufkin v. Curtis, 13 Mass. 223; McFarland v. Febiger's Heirs, 7 Ohio, 194; Carter v. Goodin, 3 Ohio St. 75; Stevens v. Owen, 25 Me. 94; Leavitt v. Lamprey, 13 Pick. (Mass.) 382. Cf. Gray v. McCune, 23 Pa. St. 447.

[250] Burge v. Smith, 7 Fost. (N. H.) 332; Dustin v. Steele, Id. 431; Smith v. Handy, 16 Ohio, 192; Daly v. Willis, 5 Lea (Tenn.) 100.

[251] For the statutory provisions in general, see 1 Stim. Am. St. Law, §§ 3245, 6504; 1 Shars. & B. Lead. Cas. Real Prop. 370. And see Coburn v. Herrington, 114 Ill. 104, 29 N. E. 478.

[252] 1 Stim. Am. St. Law, § 6501 (1); 1 Shars. & B. Lead. Cas. Real Prop. 372; 2 Scrib. Dower (2d Ed.) 321; Sibley v. Johnson, 1 Mich. 380.

[253] For the origin of jointure, see 2 Bl. Comm. 137; 2 Scrib. Dower, p. 367; 1 Washb. Real Prop. (2d Ed.) 325.

[254] Coke says it must be a competent livelihood, but the law gives no test. Co. Litt. 36b. M'Cartee v. Teller, 2 Paige (N. Y.) 511; Graham v. Graham, 67 Hun, 329, 22 N. Y. Supp. 299; Taylor v. Taylor, 144 Ill. 436, 33 N. E. 532. And see Brandon v. Dawson, 51 Mo. App. 237.

[255] So an annuity, unless charged on lands, would not be good as a jointure. Vance v. Vance, 21 Me. 364; Gibson v. Gibson, 15 Mass. 106; Caruthers v. Caruthers, 4 Brown, Ch. 500; Hastings v. Dickinson, 7 Mass. 153; M'Cartee v. Teller, 2 Paige (N. Y.) 511. But see Drury v. Drury, 2 Eden, 38; Earl of Buckinghamshire v. Drury, Id. 60 But by statute in many states a settlement of personalty is a good jointure. 1 Stim. Am. St. Law, § 3242. Williams, Real Prop. (17th Am. Ed.) note 378; 1 Shars. & B. Lead. Cas. Real Prop. 356.

effect immediately on the husband's death;[256] (2) be an estate for at least her own life;[257] (3) be to herself, and not in trust for her;[258] and (4) be expressed to be in satisfaction of dower.[259] But it need not be made by the husband.[260] Legal jointure is a bar to dower if made before marriage, whether the wife assent or not;[261] but if made during coverture she can elect to take the jointure or her dower.[262] In equity any reasonable provision[263] or contract for provision[264] is good as a jointure if the intended wife assents.[265] When made after marriage, there is the same right of election as in legal jointure.[266] If the widow be evicted from her jointure lands, she is let in to her dower in proportion to the amount lost.[267]

[256] Vance v. Vance, 21 Me. 364; Grogan v. Garrison, 27 Ohio St. 50; Caruthers v. Caruthers, 4 Brown, Ch. 500.

[257] Gelzer v. Gelzer, 1 Bailey, Eq. (S. C.) 387; Vernon's Case, 4 Coke, 1. A term of years, or an estate per autre vie, will not suffice. M'Cartee v. Teller, 8 Wend. (N. Y.) 267. And see 1 Stim. Am. St. Law, § 3241.

[258] Co. Litt. 36b; Hervey v. Hervey, 1 Atk. 561. But now otherwise by statute in many states. 1 Stim. Am. St. Law, § 3241; 1 Shars. & B. Lead. Cas. Real Prop. 356.

[259] 2 Bl. Comm. 138; Vernon's Case, 4 Coke, 1; Perry v. Perryman, 19 Mo. 469; Pepper v. Thomas (Ky.) 4 S. W. 297.

[260] 2 Scrib. Dower (2d Ed.) 404; Ashton's Case, Dyer, 228a. Contra in Maryland, by statute, 2 Code, Md. 1888, p. 1411, art. 93, § 296; 1 Stim. Am. St. Law, § 3241.

[261] 2 Scrib. Dower (2d Ed.) 403; M'Cartee v. Teller, 2 Paige (N. Y.) 511. Cf. Taft v. Taft, 163 Mass. 467, 40 N. E. 860. In some states her assent is made necessary by statute. 1 Stim. Am. St. Law, § 3241; 1 Shars. & B. Lead. Cas. Real Prop. 356.

[262] Bottomly v. Spencer, 36 Fed. 732; Vance v. Vance, 21 Me. 364; Townsend v. Townsend, 2 Sandf. (N. Y.) 711; Rowe v. Hamilton, 3 Greenl. (Me.) 63. For the general principle of equitable election, see Fetter, Eq. 50; Bisp. Eq. (4th Ed.) 361.

[263] Tinney v. Tinney, 3 Atk. 7; Andrews v. Andrews, 8 Conn. 79. But see Caruthers v. Caruthers, 4 Brown, Ch. 500; Blackmon v. Blackmon, 16 Ala. 633; Charles v. Andrews, 2 Eq. Cas. Abr. 388.

[264] Vincent v. Spooner, 2 Cush. (Miss.) 467; Dyke v. Rendall, 2 De Gex M. & G. 209.

[265] Tisdale v. Jones, 38 Barb. (N. Y.) 523; Worrell v. Forsyth, 141 Ill. 22, 30 N. E. 673; Logan v. Phillipps, 18 Mo. 22.

[266] Garrard v. Garrard, 7 Bush (Ky.) 436.

[267] 2 Scrib. Dower (2d Ed.) 432; Gervoyes' Case, Moore, 717. But see Beard

§ 60) DOWER—HOW DEFEATED. 109

Widow's Election—Testamentary Provision in Lieu of Dower.

In nearly all states, if the husband by his will make provision for his wife expressly in lieu of dower, she must elect which she will take.[268] So, too, if the devise is necessarily inconsistent with dower.[269] But if the testamentary provision does not show that

v. Nutthall, 1 Vern. 427. But not for elopement and adultery, except as changed by statute. Sidney v. Sidney, 3 P. Wms. 269; Buchanan v. Buchanan, 1 Ball & B. 203. Jointure is now rare. It is in some states forfeited for the same causes as dower. See 1 Stim. Am. St. Law, § 3247 A.

[268] In re Johnson's Estate, 10 Pa. Co. Ct. R. 461; Warren v. Warren, 148 Ill. 641, 36 N. E. 611; Pellizzarro v. Reppert, 83 Iowa, 497, 50 N. W. 19; Newman v. Newman, 1 Brown, Ch. 186. But see Bolling v. Bolling, 88 Va. 524, 14 S. E. 67. By some statutes she is presumed to elect dower; by others, the will. 1 Stim. Am. St. Law, § 3264. And see Doty v. Hendrix (Sup.) 16 N. Y. Supp. 284; Stone v. Vandermark, 146 Ill. 312, 34 N. E. 150. So there may be a presumption of election from lapse of time. In re Gunyon's Estate, 85 Wis. 122, 55 N. W. 152; Pratt v. Felton, 4 Cush. (Mass.) 174; Hastings v. Clifford, 32 Me. 132; Thompson v. Egbert, 17 N. J. Law, 459; Collins v. Carman, 5 Md. 503; Malone v. Majors, 8 Humph. (Tenn.) 577; Allen v. Hartnett, 116 Mo. 278, 22 S. W. 717. Cf. Stone v. Vandermark, 146 Ill. 312, 34 N. E. 150; Duffy v. Duffy, 70 Hun, 135, 24 N. Y. Supp. 408; Zimmerman v. Lebo, 151 Pa. St. 345, 24 Atl. 1082. Merrill v. Emery, 10 Pick. (Mass.) 507; Spruance v. Darlington (Del. Ch.) 30 Atl. 663. In order that her election be binding, she must have knowledge of the values of the two estates. Hender v. Rose, 3 P. Wms. 124, note; U. S. v. Duncan, 4 McLean 99, Fed. Cas. No. 15,002; Goodrum v. Goodrum, 56 Ark. 532, 20 S. W. 353. As to effect of election to take under the will, see Kuydendall v. Devecmon, 78 Mo. 537, 28 Atl. 412; Swihart v. Swihart, 7 Ohio Cir. Ct. R. 338; Schwatken v. Daudt, 53 Mo. App. 1; Truett v. Funderburk, 93 Ga. 686, 20 S. E. 260. The election must be by the widow herself, Boone's Representatives v. Boone, 3 Har. & McH. (Md.) 95; Sherman v. Newton, 6 Gray (Mass.) 307; Welch v. Anderson, 28 Mo. 293; unless she is insane, when her guardian may elect for her, Young v. Boardman, 97 Mo. 181, 10 S. W. 48. Contra, Lewis v. Lewis, 7 Ired. (N. C.) 72. If she elects to take under the will, lands aliened by the husband alone are freed from dower. Allen v. Pray, 12 Me. 138; Fairchild v. Marshall, 42 Minn. 14, 43 N. W. 563; In re Machemer's Estate, 140 Pa. St. 544, 21 Atl. 441; Spalding v. Hershfield, 15 Mont. 253, 39 Pac. 88; Stokes v. Norwood (S. C.) 22 S. E. 417. Cf. Chapin v. Hill, 1 R. I. 446.

[269] McCullough v. Allen, 3 Yeates (Pa.) 10; Hamilton v. Buckwalter, 2 Yeates (Pa.) 389; Turner v. Scheiber, 89 Wis. 1, 61 N. W. 280; Lewis v. Smith, 9 N. Y. 502; Church v. Bull, 2 Denio (N. Y.) 430; Jackson v. Churchill, 7 Cow. (N. Y.) 287; Savage v. Burnham, 17 N. Y. 561; Nelson v. Brown, 144 N. Y. 384, 39 N. E. 355; Ferris v. Ferris (Sup.) 30 N. Y. Supp. 982; Corriell v. Ham,

it was intended to be given in place of dower, the widow may take both.[270]

Same—Statutory Provision in Lieu of Dower.

In a few states a widow must elect between dower and an intestate share given her by statute,[271] or between dower and homestead.[272]

Estoppel.

A widow may be estopped to claim dower by covenants of warranty,[273] or by her conduct, as in inducing a purchaser to take the land, representing it free from dower.[274]

---

2 Iowa, 551; Cain v. Cain, 23 Iowa, 31; Tooke v. Hardeman, 7 Ga. 20; Helme v. Strater, 52 N. J. Eq. 591, 30 Atl. 333; Stewart v. Stewart, 31 N. J. Eq. 398; Bannister v. Bannister, 37 S. C. 529, 16 S. E. 612. In some states a devise is presumed to be in lieu of dower, unless the contrary appears. 1 Stim. Am. St. Law, § 3244.

[270] Stehlin v. Stehlin, 67 Hun, 110, 22 N. Y. Supp. 40; Sanford v. Jackson, 10 Paige (N. Y.) 266; Brown v. Caldwell, 1 Speers, Eq. (S. C.) 322; Cunningham v. Shannon, 4 Rich. Eq. (S. C.) 135; Tooke v. Hardeman, 7 Ga. 20; Lord v. Lord, 23 Conn. 327; Corriell v. Ham, 2 Iowa, 552; Tobias v. Ketchum, 32 N. J. 319; Lasher v. Lasher, 13 Barb. (N. Y.) 106; In re Blaney's Estate, 73 Iowa 113, 34 N. W. 768; McGowen v. Baldwin, 46 Minn. 477, 49 N. W. 251; Hall v. Smith, 103 Mo. 289, 15 S. W. 621; Sumerel v. Sumerel, 34 S. C. 85, 12 S. E. 932; Rivers v. Gooding (S. C.) 21 S. E. 310; Carper v. Crowl, 149 Ill. 465, 36 N. E. 1040; Kelley v. Ball (Ky.) 19 S. W. 581; Richards v. Richards, 90 Iowa, 606, 58 N. W. 926; Bare v. Bare (Iowa) 59 N. W. 20; Parker v. Hayden, 84 Iowa, 493, 51 N. W. 248; Nelson v. Pomeroy, 64 Conn. 257, 29 Atl. 534; Schorr v. Etling, 124 Mo. 42, 27 S. W. 395.

[271] 1 Stim. Am. St. Law. § 3264. Cf. Andrews v. Bassett, 92 Mich. 449, 52 N. W. 743; Payne v. Payne, 119 Mo. 174, 24 S. W. 781; Ford v. Ford, 88 Wis. 122, 59 N. W. 464; Draper v. Morris, 137 Ind. 169, 36 N. E. 714; Wilcox v. Wilcox. 89 Iowa, 388, 56 N. W. 517.

[272] Venable v. Railway Co. (Mo.) 19 S. W. 45. Cf. Whited v. Pearson, 90 Iowa, 488, 58 N. W. 32. But see Godwin v. King, 31 Fla. 525, 13 South. 108.

[273] This may be by her own covenants, 2 Scrib. Dower (2d Ed.) 261; Elmendorf v. Lockwood, 57 N. Y. 322; McKee v. Brown, 43 Ill. 130; Rosenthal v. Mayhugh, 33 Ohio St. 155; or by those of her ancestor, 2 Scrib. Dower (2d Ed.) 264; Torrey v. Minor, 1 Smedes & M. Ch. (Miss.) 489; Russ v. Perry, 49 N. H. 547.

[274] Desbler v. Beery, 4 Dall. (Pa.) 300; Dongrey v. Topping, 4 Paige (N. Y.) 94; Smiley v. Wright, 2 Ohio, 506; Sweaney v. Mallory, 62 Mo. 485; Magee v. Mellon, 23 Miss. 585; Cf. Heisen v. Heisen, 145 Ill. 658, 34 N. E. 597; Boorum v. Tucker, 51 N. J. Eq. 135, 26 Atl. 456; McCreary v. Lewis. 114 Mo.

§ 60) DOWER—HOW DEFEATED. 111

Statute of Limitations and Laches.

Adverse possession before the husband's death has no effect upon the dower right.[275] In several states it is provided by statute that the widow must bring action for her dower within a certain time, if at all.[276] In some states, too, the general statutes of limitation are held to apply to dower, though it is not expressly included.[277] In other states, the contrary is held.[278] But in equity the widow's laches will bar her right.[279]

Waste.

In several states dower is forfeited for waste.[280]

582, 21 S. W. 855; Whiteaker v. Belt, 25 Or. 490, 36 Pac. 534. But see McCreery v. Davis (S. C.) 22 S. E. 178.

[275] Durham v. Angier, 20 Me. 242; Hart v. McCollum, 28 Ga. 478; Moore v. Frost, 3 N. H. 126; Taylor v. Lawrence, 148 Ill. 388, 36 N. E. 74; Boling v. Clark, 83 Iowa, 481, 50 N. W. 57.

[276] 1 Stim. Am. St. Law, § 3271. And see Elyton Land Co. v. Denny, 96 Ala. 336, 11 South. 218; Hastings v. Mace, 157 Mass. 499, 32 N. E. 668; O'Gara v. Neylon, 161 Mass. 140, 36 N. E. 743.

[277] 2 Scrib. Dower (2d Ed.) 559; Owen v. Peacock, 38 Ill. 33; Whiting v. Nicholl, 46 Ill. 230; Proctor v. Bigelow, 38 Mich. 282; Care v. Keller, 77 Pa. St. 487; Tuttle v. Willson, 10 Ohio, 24; Moody v. Harper, 38 Miss. 599; Torrey v. Minor, 1 Smedes & M. Ch. (Miss.) 489; Carmichael v. Carmichael, 5 Humph. (Tenn.) 96; Kinsolving v. Pierce, 18 B. Mon. (Ky.) 782; Null v. Howell, 111 Mo. 273, 20 S. W. 24; Conover v. Wright, 6 N. J. Eq. 613; Berrien v. Conover, 16 N. J. Law, 107. But the statute is held not to begin to run until there is a denial of the widow's right. Rice v. Nelson, 27 Iowa, 148. And see Hart v. Randolph, 142 Ill. 521, 32 N. E. 517.

[278] Jones v. Powell, 6 Johns. Ch. (N. Y.) 194; Burt v. Sheep Co., 10 Mont. 571, 27 Pac. 399; Campbell v. Murphy, 2 Jones, Eq. (N. C.) 357; Spencer v. Weston, 1 Dev. & B. (N. C.) 213; Ralls v. Hughes, 1 Dana (Ky.) 407; Chapman v. Schroeder, 10 Ga. 321; Spencer v. Weston, 1 Dev. & B. (N. C.) 213; Chew v. Farmers' Bank, 2 Md. Ch. 231.

[279] Tuttle v. Willson, 10 Ohio, 24; Barksdale v. Garrett, 64 Ala. 277; Ralls v. Hughes, 1 Dana (Ky.) 407; Steiger's Adm'r v. Hillen, 5 Gill & J. (Md.) 121; Chew v. Farmers' Bank, 9 Gill (Md.) 361; Kiddall v. Trimble, 1 Md. Ch. 143.

[280] See 1 Stim. Am. St. Law, § 3231 B, C. But see Willey v. Laraway, 64 Vt. 559, 25 Atl. 436.

SAME—STATUTORY CHANGES.

61. Dower, as it existed at common law, has been abolished in some states, and in others largely modified by statute.

In some states, dower has been abolished by statute. In the others, the common-law estate has been modified in many particulars.[281] These statutory changes have been already considered in connection with the subjects to which they apply.

HOMESTEAD.

62. The homestead right is, in most states, an exemption to a debtor of a home free from liability for certain debts.

Homestead did not exist at common law, but is wholly a creation of statute, and is of comparatively recent origin.[282] The homestead laws of the several states, while agreeing somewhat in their general nature and plan, differ very much in wording and detail. Nor is there much harmony in the interpretations which have been given by the various courts to similar provisions of the acts. Therefore, all that can be done is to give a general outline of the subject. In every case the reader must consult the statutes and decisions of his own state.

---

[281] 1 Stim. Am. St. Law, § 3202, B; 1 Shars. & B. Lead. Cas. Real Prop. 299; Williams, Real Prop. (17th Ed. Am. note) 377; 1 Washb. Real Prop. (5th Ed.) 196, note 2. In three states the husband is endowed, curtesy being abolished. 1 Stim. Am. St. Law, § 3202 D. The community system is incompatible with dower and curtesy. See 1 Stim. Am. St. Law, §§ 6433, 3401–3404. For the constitutionality of laws changing the dower right, see Black, Const. Law, 431.

[282] Thomp. Homest. & Exemp. v.

SAME—WHO ENTITLED TO HOMESTEAD.

63. The homestead exemption can in most states be claimed only by the head of a family, but in a few states any resident of the state is entitled to the exemption.

Most of the homestead acts provide for the exemption to one who is the head of a family, or use words of equivalent meaning.[283] But in a few states all residents of the state are given the privilege, whether the head of a family or not.[284] The best test to determine whether one claiming a homestead is the head of a family seems to be the existence of a moral duty to support dependent persons living with him.[285] A husband and wife are such a family, though they have no children.[286] When a husband owning a homestead dies, the right survives to the widow for her life,[287]

---

[283] Thomp. Homest. & Exemp. 39. Alienage does not exclude one from the benefit of homestead exemptions. Cobbs v. Coleman, 14 Tex. 594; People v. McClay, 2 Neb. 7; Dawley v. Ayers, 23 Cal. 108; Sproul v. McCoy, 26 Ohio St. 577.

[284] Thomp. Homest. & Exemp. 52; Myers v. Ford, 22 Wis. 134; 1 Minn. St. at Large 1873, p. 630, § 165; Const. Ark. 1868, art. 12, § 3; Greenwood v. Maddox, 27 Ark. 649; Hesnard v. Plunkett (S. D.) 60 N. W. 159. And see Bank of Versailles v. Guthrey, 127 Mo. 189, 29 S. W. 1004.

[285] Thomp. Homest. & Exemp. 46; Connaughton v. Sands, 32 Wis. 387; Wade v. Jones, 20 Mo. 75; Blackwell v. Broughton, 56 Ga. 390; McMurray v. Shuck, 6 Bush (Ky.) 111; Mullins v. Looke, 8 Tex. Civ. App. 138, 27 S. W. 926. But see Powers v. Sample, 72 Miss. 187, 16 South. 293. In some cases a legal duty to support has been made the test. Whalen v. Cadman, 11 Iowa, 226; Marsh v. Lazenby, 41 Ga. 153; Sanderlin v. Sanderlin's Adm'r, 1 Swan (Tenn.) 441. Instances are: A single man supporting his mother and dependent brothers and sisters, Marsh v. Lazenby, 41 Ga. 153; or dependent minor brothers and sisters, Greenwood v. Maddox, 27 Ark. 649; McMurray v. Shuck, 6 Bush (Ky.) 111; or widowed sister, with her dependent children, Wade v. Jones, 20 Mo. 75; a widower supporting his widowed daughter and her children, Blackwell v. Broughton, 56 Ga. 390; or a grown-up daughter, Cox v. Stafford, 14 How. Prac. (N. Y.) 519; single woman supporting her illegitimate child, Ellis v. White, 47 Cal. 73.

[286] Kitchell v. Burgwin, 21 Ill. 40; Wilson v. Cochran, 31 Tex. 680.

[287] Thomp. Homest. & Exemp. 454; Fleetwood v. Lord, 87 Ga. 592, 13 S. E. 574; Fore v. Fore, 2 N. D. 260, 50 N. W. 712. But see Gowan v. Fountain, 50

though in some state she loses the homestead by a subsequent marriage.[288] On the other hand, where the wife was the owner of the homestead, the surviving husband is in some states entitled to a continuation of the exemption, although there are no minor children.[289] And a husband does not lose his homestead when his wife withdraws from the family under a decree of divorce.[290] But in several states it is held that a widow who is a nonresident is not entitled to the homestead.[291] Children, during the life of the parent who owns the homestead property, have no rights against such parent.[292] But, against a surviving parent who does not own the property, they have,[293] and in most states the minor children

---

Minn. 264, 52 N. W. 862; White's Adm'r v. White, 63 Vt. 577, 22 Atl. 602. But not in Georgia, unless there are minor children. Kidd v. Lesler, 46 Ga. 231. Some cases hold that the widow must elect between her dower and homestead, Butterfield v. Wicks, 44 Iowa, 310; or between her distributive share and homestead. Egbert v. Egbert, 85 Iowa, 525, 52 N. W. 478. And she may be compelled to choose between homestead and a devise, in a will which clearly requires such election. Meech v. Meech, 37 Vt. 414. And see Cowdrey v. Hitchcock, 103 Ill. 262.

[288] Dei v. Habel, 41 Mich. 88, 1 N. W. 964. And see Craddock v. Edwards, 81 Tex. 609, 17 S. W. 228. Contra, Fore v. Fore, 2 N. D. 260, 50 N. W. 712.

[289] In re Lamb's Estate, 95 Cal. 397, 30 Pac. 568; Stults v. Sale, 92 Ky. 5, 17 S. W. 148; Roberts v. Greer (Nev.) 40 Pac. 6.

[290] Doyle v. Coburn, 6 Allen (Mass.) 71; Hall v. Fields, 81 Tex. 553, 17 S. W. 82. But see Arp v. Jacobs, 3 Wyo. 489, 27 Pac. 800. See, however, Cooper v. Cooper, 24 Ohio St. 489. Where the wife withdraws from the family, she loses her homestead right, if her withdrawal was not justified, Trawick v. Harris, 8 Tex. 312; Cockrell v. Curtis, 83 Tex. 105, 18 S. W. 436; but not when the husband's conduct has forced her to withdraw, Meader v. Place, 43 N. H. 307; Atkinson v. Atkinson, 40 N. H. 249; Curtis v. Cockrell (Tex. Civ. App.) 28 S. W. 129. A divorced wife cannot claim her "widow's exemption." Dobson's Adm'r v. Butler's Adm'r, 17 Mo. 87. But see Alexander v. Alexander, 52 Ill. App. 195.

[291] Succession of Norton, 18 La. Ann. 36; Allen v. Manasse, 4 Ala. 554; Meyer v. Claus, 15 Tex. 516; Black v. Singley, 91 Mich. 50, 51 N. W. 704.

[292] Thomp. Homest. & Exemp. 476; Bateman v. Pool, 84 Tex. 405, 19 S. W. 552.

[293] Thomp. Homest. & Exemp. 475; Miller v. Marckle, 27 Ill. 405; Williams v. Whitaker, 110 N. C. 393, 14 S. E. 924; Hoppe v. Hoppe, 104 Cal. 94, 37 Pac. 894.

are entitled, after the death of both parents, to the homestead during their minority.[294]

SAME—DURATION OF EXEMPTION.

64. The homestead right is an exemption:
  (a) To the owner for life.
  (b) To the surviving spouse for life, in most states.
  (c) To the children during their minority, in some states.

The homestead interest or estate [295] is an exemption, on grounds of public policy, of a home to a debtor and his family.[296] The exemption continues in general for the life of the owner and of the surviving spouse, and until the minor children, if any, reach majority;[297] that is, during a life or lives, and the interest is therefore most closely allied to legal life estates, and possesses many of the incidents of such estates.[298]

[294] Thomp. Homest. & Exemp. 476; Hoppe v. Hoppe, 104 Cal. 94, 37 Pac. 894; Sparkman v. Roberts (Ark.) 31 S. W. 742; Fields v. Austin (Tex. Civ. App.) 30 S. W. 386; Hall v. Fields, 81 Tex. 553, 17 S. W. 82; Tate v. Goff, 89 Ga. 184, 15 S. E. 30; Vornberg v. Ewens, 88 Ga. 237, 14 S. E. 562; Lewis v. Lichty, 3 Wash. St. 213, 28 Pac. 356. But see Haynes v. Schaefer, 96 Ga. 743, 22 S. E. 327; Moore v. Peacock, 94 Ga. 523, 21 S. E. 144.

[295] In some states the homestead is not treated as an estate. McDonald v. Crandall, 43 Ill. 231; Black v. Curran, 14 Wall. 463; Atkinson v. Atkinson, 37 N. H. 434; Robinson v. Baker, 47 Mich. 619, 11 N. W. 410; Browning v. Harris, 99 Ill. 456. But see Helm v. Helm, 11 Kan. 21.

[296] Capek v. Kropik, 129 Ill. 509, 21 N. E. 836.

[297] See post, p. 382.

[298] Kerley v. Kerley, 13 Allen (Mass.) 286; Hunter's Adm'r v. Law, 68 Ala. 365; Jones v. Gilbert, 135 Ill. 27, 25 N. E. 566; Wilson v. Proctor, 28 Minn. 13, 8 N. W. 830. It is also an estate upon condition (see post, p. 169), namely, that it continue to be occupied as a homestead. Locke v. Rowell, 47 N. H. 46. Homestead also under some statutes resembles the common-law tenancy in entirety, since the estate goes to the survivor, and both husband and wife must join in a conveyance. See post, p. 337.

SAME—IN WHAT ESTATES.

65. Any estate in possession, legal or equitable, will support a homestead.

EXCEPTION — In some states homestead cannot be claimed in joint estates.

The interest which the debtor has in the land which he claims as a homestead can, it seems, make no difference to his creditors.[299] Accordingly, an equitable estate, such as an equity of redemption,[300] or a contract to purchase,[301] will support a claim of homestead.[302] So, also, will a life estate,[303] or a leasehold.[304] As to estates in common, the cases are conflicting.[305] Homestead rights in partnership realty are denied in most states.[306] So a

---

[299] Thomp. Homest. & Exemp. 144.

[300] Cheatham v. Jones, 68 N. C. 153; Doane v. Doane, 46 Vt. 485.

[301] McKee v. Wilcox, 11 Mich. 358; Fyffe v. Beers, 18 Iowa, 11; Bartholomew v. West, 2 Dill. 293, Fed. Cas. No. 1,071.

[302] Wilder v. Haughey, 21 Minn. 102; McKee v. Wilcox, 11 Mich. 358; Blue v. Blue, 38 Ill. 9; Allen v. Hawley, 66 Ill. 164; Bartholomew v. West, 2 Dill. 290, Fed. Cas. No. 1,071; McCabe v. Mazzuchelli, 13 Wis. 478; Orr v. Shraft, 22 Mich. 260; Alexander v. Jackson, 92 Cal. 514, 28 Pac. 593. Contra, Garaly v. Du Bose, 5 S. C. 493.

[303] Thomp. Homest. & Exemp. § 150; Deere v. Chapman, 25 Ill. 610; Potts v. Davenport, 79 Ill. 455. But that the widow cannot have a homestead in such estate, see Ogden v. Ogden, 60 Ark. 70, 28 S. W. 796.

[304] Thomp. Homest. & Exemp. § 152; Pelan v. De Bevard, 13 Iowa, 53; Conklin v. Foster, 57 Ill. 104; Johnson v. Richardson, 33 Miss. 462; Maatta v. Kippola, 102 Mich. 116, 60 N. W. 300; In re Emerson's Homestead, 58 Minn. 450, 60 N. W. 23. But a tenancy at will is not sufficient. Berry v. Dobson, 68 Miss. 483, 10 South. 45. And see Colwell v. Carper, 15 Ohio St. 279.

[305] Thomp. Homest. & Exemp. § 156. For cases holding the affirmative, see McClary v. Bixby, 36 Vt. 254; Horn v. Tufts, 39 N. H. 478; Hewitt v. Rankin, 41 Iowa, 35; Tarrant v. Swain, 15 Kan. 146; Smith v. Deschaumes, 37 Tex. 429; Williams v. Wethered, Id. 130. See, also, Greenwood v. Maddox, 27 Ark. 648. Contra, Thurston v. Maddocks, 6 Allen (Mass.) 427; Wolf v. Fleischacker, 5 Cal. 244; Ward v. Huhn, 16 Minn. 159 (Gil. 142); West v. Ward, 26 Wis. 579; Amphlett v. Hibbard, 29 Mich. 298; Ventress v. Collins, 28 La. Ann. 783; In re Carriger's Estate, 107 Cal. 618, 40 Pac. 1032. And see note to 12 Lawy. Rep. Ann. 519.

[306] Thomp. Homest. & Exemp. § 175; Kingsley v. Kingsley, 39 Cal. 665;

widow cannot have a homestead in lands to which the husband was entitled in remainder.[307] Title in the wife will give a homestead, though the husband be living;[308] but each cannot claim a homestead.[309]

SAME—AMOUNT OF EXEMPTION.

66. The homestead statutes limit the amount of exemption either:
  (a) **By the number of acres;**
  (b) **By the value of the premises; or**
  (c) **By both.**

67. The limitation is different in many states for:
  (a) **Urban homesteads, and**
  (b) **Rural homesteads.**

In all states the amount of which the homestead may consist is limited, either as to the number of acres, or the value of the premises, or both. Under limitations according to value, the value of improvements is added to the bare value of the land in estimating the exemption.[310] The amount of the homestead exemption depends, under most statutes, on whether the homestead is urban or rural,—the former meaning a home in a town or city, and the latter a home in the country, with land used in agricultural pursuits.[311] But the fact that the land is within the corporate limits

---

Rhodes v. Williams, 12 Nev. 20; Drake v. Moore, 66 Iowa, 58, 23 N. W. 263; Hoyt v. Hoyt, 69 Iowa, 174, 28 N. W. 500; Chalfant v. Grant, 3 Lea (Tenn.) 118. Contra, Hewitt v. Rankin, 41 Iowa, 35; West v. Ward, 26 Wis. 579; McMillan v. Parker, 109 N. C. 252, 13 S. E. 764.

[307] Howell v. Jones, 91 Tenn. 402, 19 S. W. 757. But see Stern v. Lee, 115 N. C. 426, 20 S. E. 736.

[308] Thomp. Homest. & Exemp. § 184; Orr v. Shraft, 22 Mich. 260; Crane v. Waggoner, 33 Ind. 83; Tourville v. Pierson, 39 Ill. 446; Partee v. Stewart, 50 Miss. 717; Murray v. Sells, 53 Ga. 257; Herdman v. Cooper, 39 Ill. App. 330.

[309] Tourville v. Pierson, 39 Ill. 447; Gambette v. Brock, 41 Cal. 84; McAdoo, J., in Holliman v. Smith, 39 Tex. 362.

[310] Thomp. Homest. & Exemp. 100; Williams v. Jenkins, 25 Tex. 306; Vanstory v. Thornton, 110 N. C. 10, 14 S. E. 637. Contra, Swayne v. Chase, (Tex. Sup.) 30 S. W. 1049.

[311] The husband cannot, without the wife's consent, change a rural into

of a town or city does not make it an urban homestead, if it is used for agricultural purposes.[312] Some cases hold that the homestead may consist of parcels of land not contiguous,[313] but this is denied in others.[314]

SAME—HOW ACQUIRED.

68. The homestead exemption is acquired by occupancy of the premises as a home. In some states there must also be a recorded notice that the premises are claimed as a homestead.

Occupancy.

In most of the states, the right to claim land exempt as a homestead is acquired by occupancy of the premises as a home.[315] To create a homestead by occupancy, the occupancy must be actual,[316]

---

an urban homestead by dividing it into town lots. Bassett v. Messner, 30 Tex. 604. Cf. Allen v. Whitaker (Tex. Sup.) 18 S. W. 160.

[312] Taylor v. Boulware, 17 Tex. 74; Frost v. Rainbow, 85 Iowa, 289, 52 N. W. 198. But see Heidel v. Benedict (Minn.) 63 N. W. 490.

[313] Mayho v. Cotton, 69 N. C. 289; Martin v. Hughes, 67 N. C. 293; Williams v. Hall, 33 Tex. 212; Perkins v. Quigley, 62 Mo. 498; West River Bank v. Gale, 42 Vt. 27; Shubert v. Winston, 95 Ala. 514, 11 South. 200; Webb v. Hayner, 49 Fed. 601, 605; Griswold v. Huffaker, 47 Kan. 690, 28 Pac. 696.

[314] Reynolds v. Hull, 36 Iowa, 394; Bunker v. Locke, 15 Wis. 635; Walters v. People, 18 Ill. 194; True v. Morrill, 28 Vt. 672; Adams v. Jenkins, 16 Gray (Mass.) 146; Linn Co. Bank v. Hopkins, 47 Kan. 580, 28 Pac. 606; McCrosky v. Walker, 55 Ark. 303, 18 S. W. 169; Williams v. Willis, 84 Tex. 398, 19 S. W. 683; Allen v. Whitaker (Tex. Sup.) 18 S. W. 160.

[315] Thomp. Homest. & Exemp. § 198.

[316] Thomp. Homest. & Exemp. 199; Gregg v. Bostwick, 33 Cal. 220; Kitchell v. Burgwin, 21 Ill. 40; Walters v. People, Id. 178; Tourville v. Pierson, 39 Ill. 446; True v. Morrill, 28 Vt. 672; McMonegle v. Wilson, 103 Mich. 264, 61 N. W. 495; Cahill v. Wilson, 62 Ill. 137; Campbell v. Ayres, 18 Iowa, 252; Coolidge v. Wells, 20 Mich. 79; Tillotson v. Millard, 7 Minn. 513 (Gil. 419); Petty v. Barrett, 37 Tex. 84; Campbell v. Adair, 45 Miss. 170. For cases where the facts did not show sufficient occupancy, see Evans v. Calman, 92 Mich. 427, 52 N. W. 787; Tromans v. Mahlman, 92 Cal. 1, 27 Pac. 1094, and 28 Pac. 579; Sharp v. Johnston (Tex. Sup.) 19 S. W. 259. The requirement of actual occupancy is relaxed in the case of a widow or minor children surviving the owner. Titman v. Moore, 43 Ill. 169; Locke

§ 68)　　　HOMESTEAD—HOW ACQUIRED.　　　119

and in many states must exist at the time the adverse right against which the exemption is claimed accrues.[317] Dedication by occupancy is based on the theory that the use of the premises as a home is notice to the world of the existence of the exemption.[318] Therefore the occupancy is required to be permanent,[319] and by the family as a home.[320] It must be personal, and not by a tenant.[321] But it is not required by the statutes that the occupancy be continued any stated length of time before the exemption is acquired. So, after premises have acquired a homestead character, that character is not lost by temporary interruptions in the occupancy.[322]

Recorded Notice.

In some states occupancy alone is not sufficient to create a homestead exemption. It is required, in addition, that there be a notice recorded that the premises are claimed as a homestead, or the word "homestead" must be entered in the margin of the record of the title to the premises.[323] It is, of course, necessary that the homestead continue to be occupied as such after the recording of the notice, or the exemption will be lost.[324]

---

v. Rowell, 47 N. H. 46; Phipps v. Acton, 12 Bush (Ky.) 375; Brettun v. Fox, 100 Mass. 234; Wright v. Dunning, 46 Ill. 271; Booth v. Goodwin, 29 Ark. 633; Johnston v. Turner, 29 Ark. 280.

[317] Villa v. Pico, 41 Cal. 469; Lee v. Miller, 11 Allen (Mass.) 37; Titman v. Moore, 43 Ill. 174; McCormick v. Wilcox, 25 Ill. 274; Reinback v. Walter, 27 Ill. 393.

[318] Christy v. Dyer, 14 Iowa, 438; Williams v. Dorris, 31 Ark. 466; Broome v. Davis, 87 Ga. 584, 13 S. E. 749. See, also, Grosholz v. Newman, 21 Wall. 481.

[319] Lee v. Miller, 11 Allen (Mass.) 37.

[320] Spaulding v. Crane, 46 Vt. 298; McClary v. Bixby, 36 Vt. 254; Dyson v. Sheley, 11 Mich. 527; Moerlein v. Investment Co. (Tex. Civ. App.) 29 S. W. 162; Bente v. Lange, Id. 813.

[321] Hoitt v. Webb, 36 N. H. 158; True v. Morrill, 28 Vt. 672. See, also, Kaster v. McWilliams, 41 Ala. 302; Elmore v. Elmore, 10 Cal. 224.

[322] Kitchell v. Burgwin, 21 Ill. 40, Walters v. People, Id. 178; Potts v. Davenport, 79 Ill. 455; Herrick v. Graves, 16 Wis. 157; Jarvais v. Moe, 38 Wis. 440; Wetz v. Beard, 12 Ohio St. 431; Bunker v. Paquette, 37 Mich. 79.

[323] Drake v. Root, 2 Colo. 685; Wright v. Westheimer, 2 Idaho, 962, 28 Pac. 430.

[324] Gregg v. Bostwick, 33 Cal. 220; Cole v. Gill, 14 Iowa, 527; Alley v. Bay, 9 Iowa, 509.

69. SELECTION—**The homestead may be selected by the one claiming the exemption, or set off for him by order of court.**

When the premises occupied as a home by a debtor exceed in area or value the exemption allowed by statute, the debtor may select the part which he will claim as his homestead. He may do so after an execution has been issued against him, provided he has not made a selection previously.[325] If the debtor fails to make a selection, the court will direct the sheriff or a board of appraisers to make one for him.[326] In case division of the premises is impossible or inexpedient,[327] in some states, the premises may be sold, and the amount which is exempt paid over to the debtor.[328] For the details of the procedure, the reader must consult the local statutes.

SAME—HOW LOST.

70. The homestead right may be lost:
  (a) **By abandonment.**
  (b) **By waiver.**
  (c) **By alienation of the premises, in some states.**

---

[325] Mackey v. Wallace, 26 Tex. 526; Davenport v. Alston, 14 Ga. 271; Kent v. Agard, 22 Wis. 145. Cf. Palmer v. Hawes, 80 Wis. 474, 50 N. W. 341. And see Thomp. Homest. & Exemp. 533. For the debtor's right to select in states where there is a limitation on area, but not on value, see Thomp. Homest. & Exemp. § 533; Tumlinson v. Swinney, 22 Ark. 400; Houston & G. N. R. Co. v. Winter, 44 Tex. 597; How v. Bank (Minn.) 63 N. W. 632.

[326] Holden v. Pinney, 6 Cal. 234; Fogg v. Fogg, 40 N. H. 282; Gary v. Eastabrook, 6 Cal. 457; Myers v. Ford, 22 Wis. 139; Hartwell v. McDonald, 69 Ill. 293; Lute v. Reilly, 65 N. C. 21; Anthony v. Rice, 110 Mo. 223, 19 S. W. 423. And see Pinkerton v. Tumlin, 22 Ga. 165. For procedure in such cases, see Dillman v. Bank, 139 Ill. 269, 28 N. E. 946; Ducote v. Rachal, 44 La. Ann. 580, 10 South. 933.

[327] Where the lower floor of a building occupied by a debtor as his home is rented for a store, partition may be made horizontally, and the part used for the store sold on execution. Amphlett v. Hibbard, 29 Mich. 298; Rhodes v. McCormick, 4 Iowa, 368; Mayfield v. Maasden, 59 Iowa, 517, 13 N. W. 652. But see Wright v. Ditzler, 54 Iowa, 620, 7 N. W. 98.

[328] Dearing v. Thomas, 25 Ga. 223; Miller's Appeal, 16 Pa. St. 300; Dodson's Appeal, 25 Pa. St. 232; Chaplin v. Sawyer, 35 Vt. 286.

Abandonment.

Like acquisition by occupancy, loss by abandonment is in all cases a question of fact,[329] and, in determining this, intention to return [330] and duration of absence are material points.[331] Leasing the homestead to a tenant is not conclusive evidence of an abandonment,[332] but acquisition of another homestead is.[333] Some statutes provide that only certain named acts or a written ac-

[329] Thomp. Homest. & Exemp. § 218; Feldes v. Duncan, 30 Ill. App. 469; Loveless v. Thomas, 152 Ill. 479, 38 N. E. 907; Stewart v. Brand, 23 Iowa, 477; Orman v. Orman, 26 Iowa, 361; Potts v. Davenport, 79 Ill. 459; Brennan v. Wallace, 25 Cal. 108; Shepherd v. Cassiday, 20 Tex. 24; Bradford v. Trust Co., 47 Kan. 587, 28 Pac. 702; Robinson v. Swearingen, 55 Ark. 55, 17 S. W. 365; Metcalf v. Smith (Ala.) 17 South. 537; Blackman v. Hardware Co. (Ala.) 17 South. 629. The removal must be voluntary, to constitute abandonment. So leaving the home for fear of Indian hostilities would not authorize the husband, before returning, to execute a mortgage without the wife joining. Moss v. Warner, 10 Cal. 296. Mere intention to abandon does not terminate the exemption. Dawley v. Ayers, 123 Cal. 108.

[330] Moore v. Smead, 89 Wis. 558, 62 N. W. 426; McMillan v. Warner, 38 Tex. 410; Shepherd v. Cassiday, 20 Tex. 24; Gouhenant v. Cockrell, Id. 97; Potts v. Davenport, 79 Ill. 455; Lazell v. Lazell, 8 Allen (Mass.) 575; Kitchell v. Burgwin, 21 Ill. 40; Buck v. Conlogue, 49 Ill. 391; Titman v. Moore, 43 Ill. 169; Cory v. Schuster, 44 Neb. 269, 62 N. W. 470; Cooper v. Basham (Tex. Sup.) 19 S. W. 704; Campbell v. Potter (Ky.) 29 S. W. 139; D. M. Osborne & Co. v. Schoonmaker, 47 Kan. 667, 28 Pac. 711; Gregory v. Oates, 92 Ky. 532, 18 S. W. 231.

[331] Fyffe v. Beers, 18 Iowa, 7; Dunton v. Woodbury, 24 Iowa, 74; Cabeen v. Mulligan, 37 Ill. 230; William Deering & Co. v. Beard, 48 Kan. 16, 28 Pac. 981.

[332] Herrick v. Graves, 16 Wis. 163; Austin v. Stanley, 46 N. H. 51; Campbell v. Adair, 45 Miss. 170; Wetz v. Beard, 12 Ohio St. 431; Pardo v. Bittorf, 48 Mich. 275, 12 N. W. 164; Wiggins v. Chance, 54 Ill. 175; Buck v. Conlogue, 49 Ill. 391; Myers v. Ford, 22 Wis. 139; Eckman v. Scott, 34 Neb. 817, 52 N. W. 822. But see In re Phelan's Estate, 16 Wis. 76; Fisher v. Cornell, 70 Ill. 216; Davis v. Andrews, 30 Vt. 678; Warren v. Peterson, 32 Neb. 727, 49 N. W. 703; Wynne v. Hudson, 66 Tex. 1, 17 S. W. 110; Malone v. Kornrumpf, 84 Tex. 454, 19 S. W. 607.

[333] Woodbury v. Luddy, 14 Allen (Mass.) 1; Cahill v. Wilson, 62 Ill. 137; Carr v. Rising, Id. 14; Drury v. Bachelder, 11 Gray (Mass.) 214; Blackburn v. Traffic Co., 90 Wis. 362, 63 N. W. 289; Wood v. Hawkins, 60 Ark. 262, 29 S. W. 892. Cf. Davis v. Kelley, 14 Iowa, 523; Brewer v. Wall, 23 Tex. 585; Titman v. Moore, 43 Ill. 169. But see Ross v. Porter, 72 Miss. 361, 16 South. 906; McMillan v. Warner, 38 Tex. 410.

knowledgment shall be evidence of abandonment.[334] No premises can be a homestead unless they are used as such.[335] A use of part of the premises for business purposes does not take away the exemption.[336] But in most states it is held that separate buildings rented to tenants will not be exempt, though they are on the homestead lot.[337]

Waiver.

The homestead may be made liable by an express waiver of the exemption at the time a debt is created, the waiver being made by the persons competent to sell the homestead.[338] The wife must, however, join in the waiver to make it effectual.[339]

Alienation.

A fraudulent conveyance of the homestead set aside by the husband's creditors does not estop the debtor or his wife, though she

[334] Dulanty v. Pynchon, 6 Allen (Mass.) 510; Doyle v. Coburn, Id. 71; Locke v. Rowell, 47 N. H. 46; Cross v. Everts, 28 Tex. 533; Jarvais v. Moe, 38 Wis. 445; Faivre v. Daley, 93 Cal. 664, 29 Pac. 256.

[335] Hoitt v. Webb, 36 N. H. 158; Stanley v. Greenwood, 24 Tex. 224; Philleo v. Smalley, 23 Tex. 499; Kelly v. Baker, 10 Minn. 154 (Gil. 124); Tillotson v. Millard, 7 Minn. 513 (Gil. 419); Grosholz v. Newman, 21 Wall. 481. A man can have only one homestead. Wright v. Dunning, 46 Ill. 271. In Texas there may be an exemption of a "business homestead," also. Leavell v. Lapowski, 85 Tex. 168, 19 S. W. 1004; Webb v. Hayner, 49 Fed. 601, 605. But see Houston v. Newsome, 82 Tex. 75, 17 S. W. 603.

[336] Kelly v. Baker, 10 Minn. 154 (Gil. 124); Phelps v. Rooney, 9 Wis. 70; Orr v. Shraft, 22 Mich. 260; Palmer v. Hawes, 80 Wis. 474, 50 N. W. 341; In re Ogburn's Estate, 105 Cal. 95, 38 Pac. 498; Groneweg v. Beck (Iowa) 62 N. W. 31. But see Rhodes v. McCormack, 4 Iowa, 368; Garrett v. Jones, 95 Ala. 96, 10 South. 702.

[337] Thomp. Homest. & Exemp. 113; Casselman v. Packard, 16 Wis. 114; McDonald v. Clark (Tex. Sup.) 19 S. W. 1023. Cf. Martin Clothing Co. v. Henly, 83 Tex. 592, 19 S. W. 167. But see Milford Sav. Bank v. Ayers, 48 Kan. 602, 29 Pac. 1149; Layson v. Grange, 48 Kan. 440, 29 Pac. 585; Burgher v. Henderson (Tex. Civ. App.) 29 S. W. 522.

[338] Thomp. Homest. & Exemp. 384; Beecher v. Baldy, 7 Mich. 488; Hutchings v. Huggins, 59 Ill. 29; Ayers v. Hawks, 1 Ill. App. 600; Ferguson v. Kumler, 25 Minn. 183; Moore v. Reaves, 15 Kan. 150; Webster v. Trust Co., 93 Ga. 278, 20 S. E. 310. The proceeds of sale are not exempt. Moursund v. Priess, 84 Tex. 554, 19 S. W. 775.

[339] Ayers v. Hawks, 1 Ill. App. 600; Beavan v. Speed, 74 N. C. 544; Beecher v. Baldy, 7 Mich. 488.

§ 70) HOMESTEAD—HOW LOST. 123

joined in the deed, to claim a homestead in the premises.[340] This is, however, denied by some courts.[341] The homestead right itself cannot be sold separately from the premises out of which the right is claimed.[342] But most cases hold that the homestead premises may be sold and the grantee hold them against the grantor's creditors.[343] In many states, however, the husband and wife must both execute the conveyance.[344] In these states the husband's sole deed is void, and estops neither to claim a homestead;[345] but

[340] Thomp. Homest. & Exemp. 352; Cox v. Wilder, 2 Dill. 45, Fed. Cas. No. 3,308; Sears v. Hanks, 14 Ohio St. 298; Castle v. Palmer, 6 Allen (Mass.) 401; Smith v. Rumsey, 33 Mich. 183; Murphy v. Crouch, 24 Wis. 365; Muller v. Inderreiden, 79 Ill. 382.

[341] Piper v. Johnston, 12 Minn. 60 (Gil. 27); Getzler v. Saroni, 18 Ill. 511; Huey's Appeal, 29 Pa. St. 219.

[342] McDonald v. Crandall, 43 Ill. 231; Chamberlain v. Lyell, 3 Mich. 458; Hewitt v. Templeton, 48 Ill. 367; Bowyer's Appeal, 21 Pa. St. 210.

[343] Green v. Marks, 25 Ill. 225; Fishback v. Lane, 36 Ill. 437; Lamb v. Shays, 14 Iowa, 567; Morris v. Ward, 5 Kan. 239; C. Aultman & Co. v. Salinas (S. C.) 22 S. E 465. This is the rule in states where judgments against the owner are not liens upon the homestead, but in other states such judgments are liens which remain in abeyance while the homestead right exists. The latter rule prevents a sale of the homestead, except subject to such judgment liens. Folsom v. Carli, 5 Minn. 333 (Gil. 264); Tillotson v. Millard, 7 Minn. 513 (Gil. 419); See, also, Hoyt v. Howe, 3 Wis. 752; Allen v. Cook, 26 Barb. (N. Y.) 374; Jackson v. Allen, 30 Ark. 110.

[344] Thomp. Homest. & Exemp. 401; Snyder v. People, 26 Mich. 106; Ring v. Burt, 17 Mich. 465; Wallace v. Insurance Co., 54 Kan. 442, 38 Pac. 489. So a contract to convey must be signed by the wife. Ring v. Burt, 17 Mich. 465. The rule does not apply to conveyances to the wife and children. Riehl v. Bingenheimer, 28 Wis. 84. See, also, Castle v. Palmer, 6 Allen (Mass.) 401; Malony v. Horan, 12 Abb. Prac. N. S. (N. Y.) 289; Turner v. Bernheimer, 95 Ala. 241, 10 South. 750. Cf., however, Barrows v. Barrows, 138 Ill. 649, 28 N. E. 983.

The statutes usually provide for acknowledgment by the wife separate and apart from the husband. Cross v. Everts, 28 Tex. 523–532; Lambert v. Kinnery, 74 N. C. 348.

[345] Dye v. Mann, 10 Mich. 291; Amphlett v. Hibbard, 29 Mich. 298; Richards v. Chace, 2 Gray (Mass.) 383; Williams v. Starr, 5 Wis. 534; Barton v. Drake, 21 Minn. 299; Wea Gas, Coal & Oil Co. v. Franklin Land Co., 54 Kan. 533, 38 Pac. 790. It is void even as to the husband. Beecher v. Baldy, 7 Mich. 488; Phillips v. Stauch, 20 Mich. 369; Myers v. Evans, 81 Tex. 317, 16 S. W. 1060. Such a conveyance is valid as to any excess over

where the conveyance is to secure a privileged debt,[346] or if the homestead has not been selected, the conveyance is good, because as to such debts there is no homestead exemption.[347] And some cases hold that the husband's deed becomes operative by a subsequent abandonment of the premises as a homestead.[348]

SAME—PRIVILEGED DEBTS.

71. The homestead is exempt from liability for all debts, except:
  (a) Public debts, in most cases.
  (b) Liabilities for torts, in some states.
  (c) Debts contracted before the passage of the homestead law.
  (d) Debts contracted and liens attaching before the acquisition of the homestead, in many states.
  (e) Debts contracted in removing incumbrances, in a few states.
  (f) Liens for the creation, improvement, or preservation of the property, in many states.

From most debts of the owner a homestead is exempt,[349] but some debts are privileged, and these are enforceable against the

---

the amount of the homestead. Hait v. Houle, 19 Wis. 472; Ring v. Burt, 17 Mich. 465; Wallace v. Harris, 32 Mich. 398; Boyd v. Cudderback, 31 Ill. 113; Smith v. Miller, Id. 157; Black v. Lusk, 69 Ill. 70. See, also, Smith v. Provin, 4 Allen (Mass.) 516.

[346] Burnside v. Terry, 51 Ga. 186. In some states, the husband may convey the reversionary interest in his homestead. Gilbert v. Cowan, 3 Lea (Tenn.) 203.

[347] People v. Plumsted, 2 Mich. 465; Homestead Ass'n v. Enslow, 7 S. C. 1. And see Wynne v. Hudson, 66 Tex. 1, 17 S. W. 110; Chicago, T. & M. C. Ry. Co. v. Titterington, 84 Tex. 218, 19 S. W. 472.

[348] Brown v. Coon, 36 Ill. 243; McDonald v. Crandall, 43 Ill. 231; Vasey v. Trustees, 59 Ill. 188; Jordan v. Godman, 19 Tex. 273.

[349] Ayres v. Grill, 85 Iowa, 720, 51 N. W. 14; Perry v. Ross, 104 Cal. 15, 37 Pac. 757; Anthony v. Rice, 110 Mo. 223, 19 S. W. 423; Webb v. Hayner, 49 Fed. 601, 605; Walters v. Association, 8 Tex. Civ. App. 500, 29 S. W. 51; Hofman v. Demple, 53 Kan. 792, 37 Pac. 976.

homestead.[350] Most cases hold that the land cannot be sold subject to the homestead during the time the homestead exists.[351] The homestead is not exempt from taxes;[352] but as to other public debts, such as fines for public offenses or liability on official bonds, the rule is not uniform.[353] The statutes of some states make the homestead subject to liability for torts and for the costs of such actions.[354] Debts contracted before the passage of a homestead act are privileged in all cases, since otherwise the constitutional prohibition against impairing the obligation of contracts would be infringed.[355] Debts contracted prior to the acquisition of the homestead and liens so attaching[356] are in most states enforceable against the homestead.[357] They include debts for unpaid purchase money,[358] and vendors' liens for the same.[359] A

[350] See Thomp. Homest. & Exemp. p. 246.

[351] Thomp. Homest. & Exemp. 511; Littell v. Jones, 56 Ark. 139, 19 S. W. 497; Cross v. Weare, 62 N. H. 125. In some states the homestead descends to the widow or children free from all claims of creditors, and so is not a life estate, but embraces the whole interest of the owner. Parker v. Dean, 45 Miss. 408; Fletcher v. Bank, 37 N. H. 369; Plate v. Koehler, 8 Mo. App. 396; Schneider v. Hoffmann, 9 Mo. App. 280; Lacy v. Lockett, 82 Tex. 190, 17 S. W. 916.

[352] Davis v. State, 60 Ga. 76; Hubbell v. Canady, 58 Ill. 426; Morris v. Ward, 5 Kan. 239; Com. v. Lay, 12 Bush (Ky.) 284. But see Higgins v. Bordages (Tex. Sup.) 31 S. W. 52.

[353] Thomp. Homest. & Exemp. p. 326.

[354] Thomp. Homest. & Exemp. 321; McLaren v. Anderson, 81 Ala. 106, 8 South. 188; Dunagan v. Webster, 93 Ga. 540, 21 S. E. 65.

[355] Gunn v. Barry, 15 Wall. 610; Talley v. Thompson, 20 Mo. 277.

[356] In some states a change of homestead is permitted, and the new homestead has the same exemption as the old. Mann v. Corrington (Iowa) 61 N. W. 409; White v. Kinley, Id. 176; Freiberg v. Walzem, 85 Tex. 264, 20 S. W. 60; Blum v. Light, 81 Tex. 414, 16 S. W. 1090; Broome v. Davis, 87 Ga. 584, 13 S. E. 749; Green v. Root, 62 Fed. 191. But see Peninsular Stove Co. v. Roark (Iowa) 63 N. W. 326. But existing liens are not prejudiced. Mabry v. Harrison, 44 Tex. 286. Cf. Dalton v. Webb, 83 Iowa, 478, 50 N. W. 58.

[357] Thomp. Homest. & Exemp. 253; Hensey v. Hensey's Adm'r, 92 Ky. 164, 17 S. W. 333; Titus v. Warren, 67 Vt. 242, 31 Atl. 297; Robinson v. Leach, 67 Vt. 128, 31 Atl. 32. But see Ontario State Bank v. Gerry, 91 Cal. 94, 27 Pac. 531; First Nat. Bank v. Bruce, 94 Cal. 77, 29 Pac. 488.

[358] Toole v. Dibrell (Tex. Civ. App.) 29 S. W. 387; Farmer v. Simpson, 6 Tex. 303; Stone v. Darnell, 20 Tex. 11; Barnes v. Gay, 7 Iowa, 26; Skinner

[359] Thomp. Homest. & Exemp. 281. And see post, p. 192.

statute giving a privilege to debts contracted in removing incumbrances means an incumbrance under which the homestead could be sold.[360] Debts privileged because contracted in creating, improving,[361] or preserving the homestead include, in general, the wages of clerks, servants, laborers, and mechanics.[362] Improvements, within the meaning of such statutes, include only real fixtures.[363]

FEDERAL HOMESTEAD ACT.

72. The federal homestead act provides for the acquisition of title to public lands by actual settlers, and exempts the land from liability for debts contracted before the patent is issued.

The federal homestead act is very different from the state homestead laws. It provides a method of acquiring title to public lands, and, incidentally, certain exemptions during the acquisition. Under statutes of congress,[364] the head of a family may acquire 160 acres of land by occupying and cultivating a certain portion of it for five years,[365] and lands so acquired are not liable for any debts

v. Beatty, 16 Cal. 156; Christy v. Dyer, 14 Iowa, 438. But see Loftis v. Loftis, 94 Tenn. 232, 28 S. W. 1091; Lone Star Brewing Co. v. Felder (Tex. Civ. App.) 31 S. W. 524. As to what is purchase money, see Thomp. Homest. & Exemp. § 285; Allen v. Howley, 66 Ill. 164; Eyster v. Hatheway, 50 Ill. 521; Austin v. Underwood, 37 Ill. 438; Magee v. Magee, 51 Ill. 500; Gruhn v. Richardson, 128 Ill. 178, 21 N. E. 18.

[360] Griffin v. Grentlen, 48 Ga. 148; Shroeder v. Bauer, 140 Ill. 135, 29 N. E. 560; Hensel v. Association, 85 Tex. 215, 20 S. W. 116; Watkins v. Spoull, 8 Tex. Civ. App. 427, 28 S. W. 356.

[361] United States Inv. Co. v. Phelps & Bigelow Windmill Co., 54 Kan. 144, 37 Pac. 982; Building & Loan Ass'n of Dakota v. Logan, 14 C. C. A. 133. 66 Fed. 827.

[362] Thomp. Homest. & Exemp. 314; Tyler v. Johnson, 47 Kan. 410, 28 Pac. 198; Farinholt v. Luckhard, 90 Va. 936, 21 S. E. 817.

[363] Greenwood v. Maddox, 27 Ark. 648, 660; Marshall v. Bacheldor, 47 Kan. 442, 28 Pac. 168.

[364] As to how far a state homestead is exempt from liability on judgments recovered in the federal courts, see Rev. St. U. S. 1878, § 916; Thomp. Homest. & Exemp. § 28.

[365] Seymour v. Sanders, 3 Dill. 437, Fed. Cas. No. 12,690. Or he may obtain title sooner by making certain payments. Clark v. Bayley, 5 Or. 343.

"contracted prior to the issuing of a patent therefor." [366] But such a homestead may be mortgaged as soon as the right to a patent is complete, though the patent has not been issued; and so exemption from state taxation terminates at the same time.[367]

In case of his death, the widow may thus commute. Perry v. Ashby, 5 Neb. 291; Jarvis v. Hoffman, 43 Cal. 314.

[366] Rev. St. U. S. 1878, § 2296. And see Dickerson v. Cuthburth, 56 Mo. App. 647; Miller v. Little, 47 Cal. 348. Both a state and a federal homestead cannot be held exempt at the same time. Hesnard v. Plunkett (S. D.) 60 N. W. 159.

[367] Thomp. Homest. & Exemp. 37d; Nycum v. McAllister, 33 Iowa, 374; Bellinger v. White, 5 Neb. 399; Axtell v. Warden, 7 Neb. 182; Carroll v. Safford, 3 How. 441. And see Weare v. Johnson, 20 Colo. 363, 38 Pac. 374.

CHAPTER VII.

ESTATES AS TO QUANTITY (Continued)—LESS THAN FREEHOLD.

73–75. Estates for Years.
  76.   Creation of Estates for Years.
  77.   Rights and Liabilities of Landlord and Tenant.
78–79.   Rights under Express Covenants.
80–81.   Rights under Implied Covenants.
  82.   Rights Independent of Covenants.
  83.   Transfer of Estates for Years.
  84.   Termination of Estates for Years.
  85. Letting Land on Shares.
  86. Tenancies at Will.
  87.   Creation.
  88.   Incidents.
  89.   Termination.
  90. Tenancies from Year to Year.
  91.   Creation.
  92.   Incidents.
  93.   Termination.
  94. Letting of Lodgings.
  95. Tenancies at Sufferance.
  96.   Creation.
  97.   Incidents.
  98.   Termination.
  99. Licenses.
100.   Revocation of Licenses.

ESTATES FOR YEARS.

73. **An estate for years is an estate created for a definite time, measured by years or fractions of a year.**

74. **The grantor of an estate for years is called the "lessor" or "landlord"; the grantee is called the "lessee" or "tenant."**

75. **A contract creating an estate for years is called a "lease."**

An estate for years is an estate less than freehold. As seen by the definition given in the black-letter text, the duration of the estate is measured by years, months, etc., and not by some uncertain measure, like the continuance of a life. Definitions of a lease, and the names of the parties to a lease, have been given. The term "lease," however, is often applied to instruments creating estates in fee or for life where a rent is reserved. By the creation of an estate for years, the modern relation of landlord and tenant is established between the creator of the estate or owner of the reversion and the grantee or owner of the estate for years.

Historical.

By the early common law a lessee had no interest which the law would protect against third persons, nor, indeed, against the lessor, unless the interest in the lands rested on a covenant by deed. It had been the practice from very early times to grant leases by deed, and in such a case, if the lessor wrongfully ejected the lessee, the lessee had his remedy by action on the covenant, as in the case of any other covenant under seal. A new writ was introduced, which afforded the lessee a remedy against his lord, whether the lease was by deed or not, and also gave him a right to protection against ejectment by a third person, and probably an additional remedy, by enabling the lessee to recover possession of the land, and not merely damages for breach of covenant. This was called the "writ of ejectio firmæ,"—a proceeding which, by a series of fictions, was extended till, in the form of the action of ejectment, it became the appropriate means of asserting the right to the possession of land, under whatever title, and took its place as the statutory substitute for all the forms of real actions. Thus the interest of the termor or lessee for years, instead of resting at best upon a covenant with his lessor, and therefore being enforceable only as against him, became a right of property, which could be enforced against any wrongdoer, by a remedy analogous to that provided for a wrongful ouster of a freeholder from his possession. Thus these interests became estates or rights of property in land.[1]

[1] Dig. Real Prop. (4th Ed.) 175.

REAL PROP.—9

SAME—CREATION OF ESTATES FOR YEARS.

76. The creation of estates for years is subject to the following rules:

(a) They can be created only by contract or devise (p. 130).

(b) The parties must be competent, and the lessor or testator must have an estate out of which an estate for years may be created (p. 131).

(c) There must be a writing, if the estate is for more than:

(1) One year in some states.

(2) Three years in other states (p. 132).

(d) They may begin in futuro (p. 133).

(e) They may be created to continue any number of years, except:

EXCEPTION—In some states, by statute, estates for years cannot be created for more than a limited number of years (p. 133).

Contract or Devise.

Estates for years can arise only by act of parties, not by operation of law.[2] After an estate for years is in existence, it may be transferred by operation of law, but it cannot come into existence in that way. Estates for years are usually created by contract,—that is, by lease,—though they may arise by devise. In the latter case no contractual obligations are imposed on the devisee, unless there are conditions contained in the devise which the devisee becomes bound to perform by accepting the devise.

Same—Lease and Agreement for a Lease.

The distinction between a lease and an agreement for a future lease should be noted. Where the point is in doubt, the test in

[2] Poppers v. Meagher, 148 Ill. 192, 35 N. E. 805; Board of Sup'rs of Cass Co. v. Cowgill, 97 Mich. 448, 56 N. W. 849; Sawyer v. Hanson, 24 Me. 542; Loring v. Taylor, 50 Mo. App. 80. But see Roe v. Ward, 1 H. Bl. 97; Bishop v. Howard, 2 Barn. & C. 100; Skinner v. Skinner, 38 Neb. 756, 57 N. W. 534.

§ 76) CREATION OF ESTATES FOR YEARS. 131

all cases in the intention of the parties.[3] The distinction is important, because a written lease, fully executed, cannot be varied by parol, while, if it is only a contract for a lease, omitted terms and conditions may be supplied according to the intention of the parties.[4]

Who may Create Estates for Years.

"Any person who by law may hold real estate, and who is under no legal disability, may make a lease of lands that accords with his estate or interest therein."[5] The qualifications required by law for parties to leases are the same as for parties to a contract. Therefore leases by and to infants,[6] lunatics, and intoxicated persons are voidable, rather than void.[7] But, except as now changed by statute, leases by a married woman of lands not part of her separate estate are void,[8] the husband having the sole power to lease such lands.[9] Leases may be made by agents,[10] guardians,[11] executors to whom land is devised,[12] and trustees. But, where the cestui que trust does not join, a lessee who has notice of the trust holds as trustee himself.[13]

No lease of land is valid where the lessor has been disseised,

---

[3] Goodtitle v. Way, 1 Term R. 735; Bacon v. Bowdoin, 22 Pick. (Mass.) 401; Western Boot & Shoe Co. v. Gannon, 50 Mo. App. 642; Poole v. Bentley, 12 East, 168.

[4] 1 Washb. Real Prop. (5th Ed.) 483; McFarlane v. Williams, 107 Ill. 33.

[5] 1 Wood, Landl. & Ten. (2d Ed.) § 80.

[6] Clark, Cont. 210; Field v. Herrick, 101 Ill. 110; Griffith v. Schwenderman, 27 Mo. 412.

[7] 1 Tayl. Landl. & Ten. (8th Ed.) 107; 1 Wood, Landl. & Ten. (2d Ed.) 228. Cf. Nichol v. Thomas, 53 Ind. 42. But when the lunatic is under guardianship his leases are void. See Elston v. Jasper, 45 Tex. 409. And see Van Deusen v. Sweet, 51 N. Y. 378.

[8] 1 Wood, Landl. & Ten. (2d Ed.) 216; 1 Tayl. Landl. & Ten. (8th Ed.) 111; Murray v. Emmons, 19 N. H. 483.

[9] See ante, p. 71.

[10] 1 Tayl. Landl. & Ten. (8th Ed.) 148; 1 Wood, Landl. & Ten. (2d Ed.) 267.

[11] Hughes' Minors' Appeal, 53 Pa. St. 500; Hicks v. Chapman, 10 Allen (Mass.) 463. Leases by guardians must not be for an unreasonable length of time, as beyond the minority of the ward. Ross v. Gill, 4 Call (Va.) 250; Van Doren v. Everitt, 5 N. J. Law, 460.

[12] 1 Wood, Landl. & Ten. (2d Ed.) 238; 1 Tayl. Landl. & Ten. (8th Ed.) 144.

[13] 1 Wood, Landl. & Ten. (2d Ed.) 312; 1 Tayl. Landl. & Ten. (8th Ed.) 141.

and the land is held adversely.[14] Tenants for life, as in dower, by curtesy, and per autre vie, can make demises of the land which are valid until the termination of the life estate.[15] Joint tenants,[16] tenants in common,[17] and co-parceners[18] can lease their undivided portions without the consent of the co-owners.[19] Leases by a mortgagor prior to the mortgage are valid against the mortgagee,[20] but not if subsequent to the execution of the mortgage, where the mortgagee does not join.[21]

Form.

By the statutes of frauds[22] of the several states, leases for longer than a year (or three years in some states) must be in writing,[23] and some statutes require a deed[24] for leases of more than a specified length.[25] The words generally used in granting an estate for years are "lease," "demise," and "farm let," signifying the creation of a present interest.[26] But other words will be sufficient if the meaning is clear.[27]

[14] 1 Tayl. Landl. & Ten. (8th Ed.) 96; 1 Wood, Landl. & Ten. (2d Ed.) 325.

[15] 1 Tayl. Landl. & Ten. (8th Ed.) 122; McIntyre v. Clark, 6 Misc. Rep. 377, 26 N. Y. Supp. 744; Sykes v. Benton, 90 Ga. 402, 17 S. E. 1002; Coakley v. Chamberlain, 1 Sweeny (N. Y.) 676.

[16] See post, p. 333.

[17] See post, p. 335.

[18] See post, p. 336.

[19] 1 Tayl. Landl. & Ten. (8th Ed.) 123. Cf. Tainter v. Cole, 120 Mass. 162. And see Grabfelder v. Gazetti (Tex. Civ. App.) 26 S. W. 436.

[20] 1 Tayl. Landl. & Ten. (8th Ed.) 129; Moss v. Gallimore, 1 Doug. 279; Rogers v. Humphreys, 4 Adol. & E. 299.

[21] 1 Tayl. Landl. & Ten. (8th Ed.) 128; 1 Wood, Landl. & Ten. (2d Ed.) 254. And see post, p. 196.

[22] For the memorandum, signing, etc., required by the statute of frauds, see Clark, Cont. p. 114.

[23] 1 Stim. Am. St. Law, § 4143; 2 Shars. & B. Lead. Cas. Real Prop. 54.

[24] See post, p. 415.

[25] See 1 Stim. Am. St. Law, §'1471; 2 Shars. & B. Lead. Cas. Real Prop. 55. And see Bratt v. Bratt, 21 Md. 578. But cf., as to the other terms, Doe v. Bell, 5 Term R. 471; Doe v. Stratton, 4 Bing. 446; Richardson v. Gifford, 1 Adol. & E. 52. In the absence of such a deed, the lessee is tenant from year to year. Clayton v. Blakey, 8 Term R. 3.

[26] Averill v. Taylor, 8 N. Y. 44; Wright v. Trevezant, 3 Car. & P. 441; Doe v. Benjamin, 9 Adol. & E. 644.

[27] Doe v. Ries, 8 Bing. 178; Roe v. Ashburner, 5 Term R. 163; Jackson v.

§ 76)　　　CREATION OF ESTATES FOR YEARS.　　　133

Commencement.

A term of years may be granted to begin in the future,[28] provided the time is not postponed beyond the period allowed by the rule against perpetuities.[29] An estate of freehold cannot be so limited at common law, because freehold estates were transferred by feoffment and livery of seisin; that is, by transfer of possession. This was a present act, and livery could not be made to operate at some future time. The creation of an estate for years, to begin in futuro, does not violate the common-law rule, since the only right the tenant has is a contract right to have the possession at a future time. The seisin remains in the landlord, and the tenant takes no present estate.

Same—Interesse Termini.

The interest which a lessee has between the making of the lease and his entry into possession is called an "interesse termini." This interest is assignable,[30] and as soon as, by the terms of the lease, the lessee is entitled to possession, he may maintain ejectment.[31] This right of entry is not destroyed by the death of the lessor or of the lessee.[32]

Duration.

In most states, estates for years may be created for any length of time, but in a few states there are statutes which forbid their creation for more than limited periods, ranging from 10 to 20 years.[33] Estates for years must be so limited that they will ter-

---

Delacroix, 2 Wend. (N. Y.) 433; Watson v. O'Hern, 6 Watts (Pa.) 362; Moore v. Miller, 8 Pa. St. 272; Moshier v. Reding, 12 Me. 478; Smith v. Hubert, 83 Hun, 503, 31 N. Y. Supp. 1076. A lease of "a building" is a lease of the land on which it stands. Lanpher v. Glenn, 37 Minn. 4, 33 N. W. 10.

[28] Colclough v. Carpeles, 89 Wis. 239, 61 N. W. 836; Cadell v. Palmer, 1 Clark & F. 372; Field v. Howell, 6 Ga. 423; Whitney v. Allaire, 1 N. Y. 305; Weld v. Traip, 14 Gray (Mass.) 330.

[29] See post, p. 322; Gomez v. Gomez, 81 Hun, 566, 31 N. Y. Supp. 206.

[30] 1 Wood, Landl. & Ten. (2d Ed.) 452; Soffyns' Case, 5 Coke, 123b; Wood v. Hubbell, 10 N. Y. 488.

[31] Doe v. Day, 2 Q. B. Div. 156; Gardner v. Keteltas, 3 Hill (N. Y.) 332; Trull v. Granger, 8 N. Y. 115; Whitney v. Allaire, 1 N. Y. 305, 311.

[32] 1 Wood, Landl. & Ten. (2d Ed.) 452; 1 Tayl. Landl. & Ten. (8th Ed.) 14; Co. Litt. 46b.

[33] 1 Stim. Am. St. Law, § 1341; 2 Shars. & B. Lead. Cas. Real Prop. 44.

minate at a definite time, or at a time which can be made certain.[34] However, a condition by which the estate may be determined before the expiration of the time for which it is limited does not make it invalid. For instance, a demise to a man for 99 years, if he live so long, is good.[35] Nor does an option residing in one party to put an end to the lease at any time make it invalid.[36]

SAME — RIGHTS AND LIABILITIES OF LANDLORD AND TENANT.

77. The rights and liabilities of landlord and tenant may, for convenience of treatment, be divided into three classes:
  (a) **Rights under express covenants** (p. 134).
  (b) **Rights under implied covenants** (p. 138).
  (c) **Rights independent of covenants** (p. 141).

78. RIGHTS UNDER EXPRESS COVENANTS—By express covenants the parties may vary their rights and liabilities almost at will.

79. Express covenants are either:
  (a) **Personal; or**
  (b) **Such as run with the land.**

In many states, leases for more than a certain number of years must be recorded. Post, p. 218; 1 Stim. Am. St. Law, § 1624; 1 Shars. & B. Lead. Cas. Real Prop. 56. And see Toupin v. Peabody, 162 Mass. 473, 39 N. E. 280. An estate for years may be for a single year, or even a less period. Brown v. Bragg, 22 Ind. 122.

[34] Murray v. Cherrington, 99 Mass. 229; Horner v. Leeds, 25 N. J. Law, 106; Cargar v. Fee, 140 Ind. 572, 39 N. E. 93; Goodright v. Richardson, 3 Term R. 462. For the method of computing time under a lease, see Atkins v. Sleeper, 7 Allen (Mass.) 487; Deyo v. Bleakley, 24 Barb. (N. Y.) 9; Sheets v. Selden's Lessee, 2 Wall. 177.

[35] 1 Tayl. Landl. & Ten. (8th Ed.) 86. And see Lacey v. Newcomb (Iowa) 63 N. W. 704.

[36] King v. Ransom, 86 Wis. 496; 56 N. W. 1084. Cf. Clifford v. Gressinger, 96 Ga. 789, 22 S. E. 399. And see, as to privilege of renewal, Pearce v. Turner, 150 Ill. 116, 36 N. E. 962; Robinson v. Beard, 140 N. Y. 107, 35 N. E. 441; Bullock v. Grinstead, 95 Ky. 261, 24 S. W. 867; Hughes v. Windpfennig (Ind. App.) 37 N. E. 432.

§§ 77-79) RIGHTS AND LIABILITIES OF LANDLORD AND TENANT.   135

The mutual obligations of lessor and lessee are fixed almost entirely by contract; that is, by the covenants of the lease. An express covenant is an agreement under seal,[37] though the same term is used in those states where seals are abolished. The most usual covenants by the lessor are for quiet enjoyment,[38] against incumbrances,[39] to repair,[40] and to renew the lease.[41] The lessee generally covenants to pay rent,[42] to insure,[43] and not to assign[44] or underlet.[45]

[37] 1 Tayl. Landl. & Ten. (8th Ed.) 2, 94; Clark, Cont. 72. No precise language is necessary to constitute a covenant. It may be in the form of a condition. Surplice v. Farnsworth, 7 Man. & G. 576. Or an exception. Russel v. Gulwel, Cro. Eliz. 657; Lowell South Congregational Meeting House v. Hilton, 11 Gray (Mass.) 407. Or a recital. Penn v. Preston, 2 Rawle (Pa.) 14; Vaughan v. Matlock, 23 Ark. 9.

[38] Shelton v. Codman, 3 Cush. (Mass.) 318; Markland v. Crump, 1 Dev. & B. (N. C.) 94; Suydam v. Jones, 10 Wend. (N. Y.) 180; Hunt v. Amidon, 4 Hill (N. Y.) 345; Friedland v. Myers, 139 N. Y. 432, 34 N. E. 1055; Campbell v. Lewis, 3 Barn. & Ald. 392. Cf. Hochenauer v. Hilderbrant (Colo. App.) 40 Pac. 470; Sheets v. Joyner, 11 Ind. App. 205, 38 N. E. 830.

[39] Ober v. Brooks, 162 Mass. 102, 38 N. E. 429; Sprague v. Baker, 17 Mass. 585; Gilbert v. Bulkley, 5 Conn. 262; Pillsbury v. Mitchell, 5 Wis. 17; Redwine v. Brown, 10 Ga. 311.

[40] John Morris Co. v. Southworth, 154 Ill. 118, 39 N. E. 1099; Thomson-Houston Electric Co. v. Durant Land-Imp. Co., 144 N. Y. 34, 39 N. E. 7; Clapper v. Kells, 78 Hun, 34, 28 N. Y. Supp. 1018; Dunn v. Robbins, 65 Hun, 625, 20 N. Y. Supp. 341; Clifton v. Montague (W. Va.) 21 S. E. 858; Mumford v. Brown, 6 Cow. (N. Y.) 475; Post v. Vetter, 2 E. D. Smith (N. Y.) 248; Benjamin v. Heeney, 51 Ill. 492. The landlord must be notified that repairs are needed. Ploen v. Staff, 9 Mo. App. 309; Walker v. Gilbert, 2 Rob. (N. Y.) 214; Wolcott v. Sullivan, 6 Paige (N. Y.) 117.

[41] Piggot v. Mason, 1 Paige (N. Y.) 412, Renoud v. Daskam, 34 Conn. 512; Blackmore v. Boardman, 28 Mo. 420; Kolasky v. Michels, 120 N. Y. 635, 24 N. E. 278. A covenant for perpetual renewal is good. Blackmore v. Boardman, 28 Mo. 420. But see Western Transp. Co. v. Lansing, 49 N. Y. 499.

[42] Hurst v. Rodney, 1 Wash. C. C. 375, Fed. Cas. No. 6,937; Main v. Feathers, 21 Barb. (N. Y.) 646; Jacques v. Short, 20 Barb. (N. Y.) 269; Demarest v. Willard, 8 Cow. (N. Y.) 206; Thomson-Houston Electric Co. v. Durant Land Imp. Co., 144 N. Y. 34, 39 N. E. 7. Further, as to rent, see post, p. 140.

[43] Vernon v. Smith, 5 Barn. & Ald. 1; Doe v. Peck, 1 Barn. & Adol. 428; Thomas' Adm'r v. Von Kapff's Ex'rs, 6 Gill & J. (Md.) 372.

[44] See note 44 on following page.   [45] See note 45 on following page.

Sometimes covenants are inserted binding him to repair,[46] to reside on the premises,[47] not to engage in certain trades,[48] to build in a prescribed manner,[49] or, if a farm lease, to cultivate in a certain way.[50] The parties may, of course, make such further special covenants as they see fit.[51]

Personal Covenants and Covenants Running with the Land.[52]

Covenants which may be enforced by the assignee[53] of the term or of the reversion[54] are said to run with the land. If a covenant touches or concerns the thing demised, and there is privity of estate between the parties, it runs with the land.[55] If it relates to something in existence when the lease was executed, the as-

---

[44] Williams v. Earle, 9 Best & S. 740; Matthews v. Whitaker (Tex. Civ. App.) 23 S. W. 538.

[45] Kew v. Trainor, 150 Ill. 150, 37 N. E. 223.

[46] Scott v. Brick Co., 135 N. Y. 141, 31 N. E. 1102. Cf. Standen v. Chrismas, 10 Q. B. Div. 135. But see 1 Stim. Am. St. Law, § 2045. The covenant to repair is always implied. See post, p. 139.

[47] Tatem v. Chaplin, 2 H. Bl. 133.

[48] Miller v. Prescott, 163 Mass. 12, 39 N. E. 409. And see Kugel v. Painter, 166 Pa. St. 592, 31 Atl. 338; Round Lake Ass'n v. Kellogg, 141 N. Y. 348, 36 N. E. 326.

[49] Mayor, etc., of New York v. Brooklyn Fire Ins. Co., 41 Barb. (N. Y.) 231; Mayor, etc., of New York v. Hamilton Fire Ins. Co., 10 Bosw. (N. Y.) 537.

[50] Cockson v. Cock, Cro. Jac. 125. See, also, Callan v. McDaniel, 72 Ala. 96.

[51] See Postal Tel. Cable Co. v. W. U. Tel. Co., 155 Ill. 335, 40 N. E. 587; Keating v. Springer, 146 Ill. 481, 34 N. E. 805; Pewaukee Milling Co. v. Howitt, 86 Wis. 270, 56 N. W. 784; Leydecker v. Brintnall, 158 Mass. 292, 33 N. E. 399; McManus v. Shoe, etc., Co., 1 Mo. App. Rep'r, 73; Cargill v. Thompson, 57 Minn. 534, 59 N. W. 638.

[52] See Clark, Cont. 545, for a discussion of this subject.

[53] The assignee is bound by privity of estate, while the personal representative is bound by privity of contract. 1 Tayl. Landl. & Ten. (8th Ed.) 308; Spencer's Case, 5 Coke, 16. See, also, Minshull v. Oakes, 2 Hurl. & N. 793; Martyn v. Clue, 18 Q. B. Div. 661; Hansen v. Meyer, 81 Ill. 321.

[54] Assignees of the lessor could not enforce covenants against the lessee or his assignees until the statute of 32 Hen. VIII. c. 34.

[55] 1 Tayl. Landl. & Ten. (8th Ed.) 308; Morse v. Aldrich, 19 Pick. (Mass.) 449; Piggot v. Mason, 1 Paige (N. Y.) 412; Norman v. Wells, 17 Wend. (N. Y.) 136; Wooliscroft v. Norton, 15 Wis. 198; Blackmore v. Boardman, 28 Mo. 420; Gordon v. George, 12 Ind. 408; Tatem v. Chaplin, 2 H. Bl. 133; Vernon v. Smith, 5 Barn. & Ald. 1; Vyvyan v. Arthur, 1 Barn. & C. 410; Williams v.

§§ 77-79) RIGHTS AND LIABILITIES OF LANDLORD AND TENANT.   137

signees may enforce it without being named in the lease.[56] But, if it relates to something not in existence at that time, the assignees must be named in the covenant, or they cannot enforce it.[57] In no case, however, are the lessee's assigns bound by personal covenants between the original parties.[58] Covenants to repair,[59] pay rent,[60] cultivate in a certain mode, for quiet enjoyment, etc., run with the land,[61] as do also all implied covenants,[62] while covenants purely personal, such as an agreement to pay the lessee for a building to be erected by him, do not run with the land.[63] So a covenant to build a wall in a certain place would not bind an assignee of the term.[64] A lessee is bound by an express covenant, even though he has assigned the term,[65] and so is the lessor.[66]

Earle, L. R. 3 Q. B. 739. Cf. Minshull v. Oakes, 2 Hurl. & N. 793. And see, for covenants running with the land, between parties not lessor and lessee, National Union Bank v. Segur, 39 N. J. Law, 173; Hurd v. Curtis, 19 Pick. (Mass.) 459; Lyon v. Parker, 45 Me. 474.

[56] Parkenham's Case, Y. B. 42 Edw. III. c. 3, pl. 14; Anon., Moore, 179, pl. 318.

[57] Spencer's Case, 5 Coke, 16; Hansen v. Meyer, 81 Ill. 321; Masury v. Southworth, 9 Ohio St. 340; Doe v. Seaton, 2 Cromp., M. & R. 730; Verplanck v. Wright, 23 Wend. (N. Y.) 506; Wakefield v. Brown, 9 Q. B. Div. 209.

[58] Mayor, etc., of Congleton v. Pattison, 10 East, 130; Dolph v. White, 12 N. Y. 296; Curtiss v. White, Clarke, Ch. (N. Y.) 389; Inhabitants of Plymouth v. Carver, 16 Pick. (Mass.) 183; Spencer's Case, supra; Gray v. Cuthbertson, 2 Chit. 482. Cf. Mayho v. Buckhurst, Cro. Jac. 438; Dolph v. White, 12 N. Y. 296.

[59] Congham v. King, Cro. Car. 221; Twynam v. Pickard, 2 Barn. & Ald. 105.

[60] Trask v. Graham, 47 Minn. 571, 50 N. W. 917. But see, as to a subtenant, Holford v. Hatch, 1 Doug. 183.

[61] 1 Tayl. Landl. & Ten. (8th Ed.) 313; 1 Wood, Landl. & Ten. (2d Ed.) 673.

[62] 1 Tayl. Landl. & Ten. (8th Ed.) 313.

[63] Thompson v. Rose, 8 Cow. (N. Y.) 266; Bream v. Dickerson, 2 Humph. (Tenn.) 126; Hansen v. Meyer, 81 Ill. 321; Mayor, etc., of Congleton v. Pattison, 10 East, 138; Sampson v. Easterby, 9 Barn. & C. 505. Cf. Thomas v. Hayward, L. R. 4 Exch. 311. Such a covenant may be enforced by an assignee of the lessee. Hunt v. Danforth, 2 Curt. 592, Fed. Cas. No. 6,887.

[64] Spencer's Case, 5 Coke, 16a. And see Norman v. Wells, 17 Wend. (N. Y.) 136; Masury v. Southworth, 9 Ohio St. 340.

[65] Barnard v. Godscall, Cro. Jac. 309. See post, p. 149.

[66] Jones v. Parker, 163 Mass. 564, 40 N. E. 1044.

80. RIGHTS UNDER IMPLIED COVENANTS—The principal implied covenants in a lease are:

(a) **By the lessor, for quiet enjoyment and to pay taxes.**

(b) **By the lessee, to repair, to cultivate in a husbandmanlike manner, and to pay rent.**

81. Implied covenants always run with the land.

Implied Covenants—By the Lessor.[67]

Besides express covenants, there are others which are implied by law from the execution of the lease.[68] It is held that the words "demise" or "grant" imply a covenant by the lessor for quiet enjoyment.[69] This covenant is broken only by an actual disturbance of possession or enjoyment.[70] A failure of title, unless followed by an ouster, would not constitute a breach.[71] And an eviction, to have that effect, must be under a legal title.[72] The lessor does not covenant against trespassing or other wrongful disturbance by strangers.[73] There is also an implied covenant by the lessor that

---

[67] For a discussion of implied contracts, see Clark, Cont. c. 13.

[68] 1 Tayl. Landl. & Ten. (8th Ed.) 301; 1 Wood, Landl. & Ten. (2d Ed.) 691.

[69] Duncklee v. Webber, 151 Mass. 408, 24 N. E. 1082; Grannis v. Clark, 8 Cow. (N. Y.) 36; Barney v. Keith, 4 Wend. (N. Y.) 502; Tone v. Brace, 8 Paige (N. Y.) 597; Stott v. Rutherford, 92 U. S. 107; Maule v. Ashmead, 20 Pa. St. 482; Hamilton v. Wright, 28 Mo. 199; Wade v. Halligan, 16 Ill. 507. But see Sedberry v. Verplanck (Tex. Civ. App.) 31 S. W. 242; Groome v. Ogden City Corp., 10 Utah, 54, 37 Pac. 90.

[70] Dexter v. Manley, 4 Cush. (Mass.) 14; Sherman v. Williams, 113 Mass. 481; International Trust Co. v. Schumann, 158 Mass. 287, 33 N. E. 509; Dyett v. Pendleton, 8 Cow. (N. Y.) 727; Edesheimer v. Quackenbush, 68 Hun, 427, 23 N. Y. Supp. 75; Lounsbery v. Snyder, 31 N. Y. 514; Schilling v. Holmes, 23 Cal. 227; Moore v. Weber, 71 Pa. St. 429. Cf. Cole's Case, 1 Salk. 196.

[71] 1 Tayl. Landl. & Ten. (8th Ed.) 355; 1 Wood, Landl. & Ten. (2d Ed.) 771; Sedgwick v. Hollenback, 7 Johns. (N. Y.) 376; Stanard v. Eldridge, 16 Johns. (N. Y.) 254; Mills v. Sampsel, 53 Mo. 360. Even a recovery in ejectment is no breach, unless it is followed by an ouster. Kerr v. Shaw, 13 Johns. (N. Y.) 236.

[72] Morse v. Goddard, 13 Metc. (Mass.) 177; Ross v. Dysart, 33 Pa. St. 452; Moore v. Weber, 71 Pa. St. 429; Mack v. Patchin, 42 N. Y. 167.

[73] A mere trespass by the lessor would not be a breach, as it is not an eviction. Mayor, etc., of New York v. Mabie, 13 N. Y. 151; Hayner v.

§§ 80-81)　RIGHTS AND LIABILITIES OF LANDLORD AND TENANT.　139

he will pay all taxes and assessments levied on the premises demised.[74] But there is no covenant implied that the premises are in a tenantable condition.[75]

Same—By the Lessee.

On the part of the lessee, there is an implied covenant to repair.[76] The duty extends, however, only to keeping a house wind and water tight,[77] and he is not liable for deteriorations resulting from ordinary wear and tear,[78] nor when the premises are accidentally burned down.[79] Failure to repair constitutes permissive waste.[80]

Smith, 63 Ill. 430; Avery v. Dougherty, 102 Ind. 443, 2 N. E. 123. But see Bennet v. Bittle, 4 Rawle (Pa.) 338.

[74] Stubbs v. Parsons, 3 Barn. & Ald. 516; Watson v. Atkins, Id. 647. If the lessor fails to do so, the lessee may pay them, to prevent the loss of his estate, and deduct the amount from the rent. McPherson v. Atlantic & P. R. Co., 66 Mo. 103.

[75] Reeves v. McComeskey, 168 Pa. St. 571, 32 Atl. 96; Blake v. Dick, 15 Mont. 236, 38 Pac. 1072; Doyle v. Railway Co., 147 U. S. 413, 13 Sup. Ct. 333; Jaffe v. Harteau, 56 N. Y. 398; Fisher v. Lighthall, 4 Mackey (D. C.) 82; Lucas v. Coulter, 104 Ind. 81, 3 N. E. 622; Blake v. Ranous, 25 Ill. App. 486; Stevens v. Pierce, 151 Mass. 207, 23 N. E. 1006. But the rule is otherwise when lodgings or furnished houses are let. Smith v. Marrable, 11 Mees. & W. 5. But see Fisher v. Lighthall, 4 Mackey (D. C.) 82.

[76] Demarest v. Willard, 8 Cow. (N. Y.) 206; Shelby v. Hearne, 6 Yerg. (Tenn.) 512; Pollard v. Shaffer, 1 Dall. 210; U. S. v. Bostwick, 94 U. S. 53; Miller v. Shields, 55 Ind. 71; Turner v. Townsend, 42 Neb. 376, 60 N. W. 587. The lessor is never bound to repair unless there is a stipulation to that effect. Nor must he rebuild a house, if it burns down, without a covenant to do so. Sheets v. Selden, 7 Wall. 423; Leavitt v. Fletcher, 10 Allen (Mass.) 121; Gill v. Middleton, 105 Mass. 478; Doupe v. Gerrin, 45 N. Y. 119; Little v. Macadaras, 29 Mo. App. 332, 38 Mo. App. 187; Heintze v. Bentley, 34 N. J. Eq. 562; Medary v. Cathers, 161 Pa. St. 87, 28 Atl. 1012; Cowell v. Lumley, 39 Cal. 151; Jones v. Millsaps, 71 Miss. 10, 14 South. 440. The duty is imposed by statute in several states. 1 Stim. Am. St. Law, § 2041; 2 Shars. & B. Lead. Cas. Real Prop. 94.

[77] Parrott v. Barney, Deady, 405, Fed. Cas. No. 10,773a; Kastor v. Newhouse, 4 E. D. Smith (N. Y.) 20; Auworth v. Johnson, 5 Car. & P. 239.

[78] Torriano v. Young, 6 Car. & P. 8.

[79] Eagle v. Swayze, 2 Daly (N. Y.) 140. And see Payne v. James, 45 La. Ann. 381, 12 South. 492. Cf., however, Peck v. Manufacturing Co., 43 Ill. App. 360.

[80] 1 Tayl. Landl. & Ten. (8th Ed.) 408; 1 Wood, Landl. & Ten. (2d Ed.) 980; Lothrop v. Thayer, 138 Mass. 466, and cases cited.

There is also an implied covenant to cultivate in a husbandmanlike manner.[81] But covenants to pay taxes,[82] to insure, or not to assign are never implied.[83]

Same—Rent.[84]

A valid term of years may be created without the reservation of a rent.[85] But whenever a rent is reserved there is an implied covenant on the part of the lessee to pay it whether he ever take possession or not.[86] And, where there is an express covenant to pay, a destruction of the demised premises will not relieve him.[87] But when the tenant is evicted from part or all of the premises by a title paramount, his liability for rent ceases in proportion.[88] And when he is evicted by the landlord even from a part, the whole lia-

---

[81] Walker v. Tucker, 70 Ill. 527; Aughinbaugh v. Coppenheffer, 55 Pa. St. 347; Powley v. Walker, 5 Term R. 373; Legh v. Hewitt, 4 East, 154; Dalby v. Hirst, 3 Moore, C. P. 536.

[82] Except by statute. 1 Stim. Am. St. Law, § 2042.

[83] 1 Wood, Landl. & Ten. (2d. Ed.) 701, 709; 2 Wood, Landl. & Ten. (2d Ed.) 954; 1 Tayl. Landl. & Ten. (8th Ed.) 398, 477, 479; Church v. Brown, 15 Ves. 258.

[84] For rent as an incorporeal hereditament, see post, p. 375.

[85] Sherwin v. Lasher, 9 Ill. App. 227; Hunt v. Comstock, 15 Wend. (N. Y.) 665. Cf. Hooton v. Holt, 139 Mass. 54, 22 N. E. 221; Osborne v. Humphrey, 7 Conn. 335. If no rent is reserved, there may be a recovery for use and occupation, according to the real value of the premises, unless a contrary intention of the parties is shown. 1 Tayl. Landl. & Ten. (8th Ed.) 434; 2 Wood, Landl. & Ten. (2d Ed.) 1328.

[86] McGlynn v. Brock, 111 Mass. 219; Mechanics' & Traders' Fire Ins. Co. v. Scott, 2 Hilt. (N. Y.) 550; McMurphy v. Minot, 4 N. H. 251.

[87] 1 Tayl. Landl. & Ten. (8th Ed.) 436; Peck v. Ledwidge, 25 Ill. 93; Hallett v. Wylie, 3 Johns. (N. Y.) 44; Fowler v. Bott, 6 Mass. 63; French v. Richards, 6 Phila. (Pa.) 547; Holtzapffel v. Baker, 18 Ves. 115.

[88] Frommer v. Roessler (Com. Pl.) 33 N. Y. Supp. 13; Lansing v. Van Alstyne, 2 Wend. (N. Y.) 561; Carter v. Burr, 39 Barb. (N. Y.) 59; Fillebrown v. Hoar, 124 Mass. 580; Stevenson v. Lambard, 2 East 575; Friend v. Supply Co., 165 Pa. St. 652, 30 Atl. 1134. Cf. M'Loughlin v. Craig, 7 Ir. Com. Law, 117; Folts v. Huntley, 7 Wend. (N. Y.) 210; Morse v. Goddard, 13 Metc. (Mass.) 177; Big Black Creek Imp. Co. v. Kemmerer, 162 Pa. St. 422, 29 Atl. 739; Sylvester v. Hall, 47 Ill. App. 304. But see Ray v. Johnson, 98 Mich. 34, 56 N. W. 1048; Miller v. Maguire, 18 R. I. 770, 30 Atl. 966.

bility for rent is at an end.[89] It is customary to reserve a right of re-entry for nonpayment of rent.[90]

82. RIGHTS INDEPENDENT OF COVENANTS—As incidents of the relation, and independent of any covenants, the parties have the following rights:

(a) **The landlord has a right to protect the reversion** (p. 141).
(b) **The tenant is entitled to exclusive possession** (p. 142).
(c) **He may take estovers** (p. 143).
(d) **He is entitled to emblements when his estate is cut off by some contingency, without his fault** (p. 143).
(e) **He is liable for waste** (p. 143).
(f) **The lessee, and all persons claiming under him, are estopped to deny the lessor's title** (p. 143).
(g) **The landlord may distrain for rent** (p. 145).

Although the rights and liabilities of the parties to a lease are fixed to a large extent by the terms thereof, there are some which exist by virtue of the relation of landlord and tenant. There is a

[89] Coulter v. Norton, 100 Mich. 389, 59 N. W. 163; Snow v. Pulitzer, 142 N. Y. 263, 36 N. E. 1059; Morris v. Kettle (N. J. Sup.) 30 Atl. 879; City Power Co. v. Fergus Falls Water Co., 55 Minn. 172, 56 N. W. 685, 1006; Leishman v. White, 1 Allen (Mass.) 489; Christopher v. Austin, 11 N. Y. 216; Graham v. Anderson, 3 Har. (Del.) 364; Bennet v. Bittle, 4 Rawle (Pa.) 339; Lewis v. Payn, 4 Wend. (N. Y.) 423; Colburn v. Morrill, 117 Mass. 262; Day v. Watson, 8 Mich. 535; Smith v. Stigleman, 58 Ill. 141; Pendleton v. Dyett, 4 Cow. (N. Y.) 581; Neale v. Mackenzie, 1 Mees. & W. 747; Cibel and Hill's Case, 1 Leon. 110; Burn v. Phelps, 1 Starkie, 94; Morrison v. Chadwick, 7 C. B. 266; McClurg v. Price, 59 Pa. St. 420. See, also, Grabenhorst v. Nicodemus, 42 Md. 236. See, also, Royce v. Guggenheim, 106 Mass. 201; Hoeveler v. Fleming, 91 Pa. St. 322. But cf. Smith v. Raleigh, 3 Camp. 513; Roper v. Lloyd, T. Jones, 148; Carrel v. Read, Cro. Eliz. 374; Dorrel v. Andrews, Hub. 190; Paradine v. Jane, Aleyn, 26; Ecclesiastical Com'rs v. O'Connor, 9 Ir. Com. Law, 242; Lawrence v. French, 25 Wend. (N. Y.) 443; McKenzie v. Hatton, 141 N. Y. 6, 35 N. E. 929; Ogilvie v. Hull, 5 Hill (N. Y.) 52; Edgerton v. Page, 20 N. Y. 281; De Witt v. Pierson, 112 Mass. 8; Townsend v. Wharf Co., 117 Mass. 501.

[90] When no right of re-entry is reserved, the landlord's only remedy for a breach of covenant is an action for damages. Brown v. Kite, 2 Overt. (Tenn.) 233; Den v. Post, 25 N. J. Law, 285. And see post, p. 150.

tenure existing between them, the tenant holding of the landlord, and paying rent in return for the use of the land. Of the rights growing out of this tenure, we need mention only the right of the landlord to protect the reversion by maintaining actions for acts which cause a permanent injury to the premises,[91] and that he may be liable to strangers for injuries resulting from the dangerous condition of the premises at the time the lease was executed.[92] The tenant has a right to exclusive possession,[93] which includes the right to enjoy all easements [94] servient to the demised

[91] Starr v. Jackson, 11 Mass. 519; French v. Fuller, 23 Pick. (Mass.) 104; Little v. Palister, 3 Greenl. (Me.) 6; Austin v. Railroad Co., 25 N. Y. 334; Aycock v. Railroad Co., 89 N. C. 321; Mayor, etc., of Cartersville v. Lyon, 69 Ga. 577; Jesser v. Gifford, 4 Burrows, 2141; Gulf, C. & S. F. Ry. Co. v. Smith, 3 Tex. Civ. App. 483, 23 S. W. 89; Missouri, K. & T. Ry. Co. v. Fulmore (Tex. Civ. App.) 26 S. W. 238. But see Anthony v. Railway Co., 162 Mass. 60, 37 N. E. 780.

[92] Bellows v. Sackett, 15 Barb. (N. Y.) 96; Moody v. Mayor, etc., 43 Barb. (N. Y.) 282; City of Peoria v. Simpson, 110 Ill. 294; Reichenbacher v. Pahmeyer, 8 Ill. App. 217; Marshall v. Heard, 59 Tex. 266; Todd v. Flight, 9 C. B. (N. S.) 377; City of Denver v. Soloman, 2 Colo. App. 534, 31 Pac. 507. So the landlord may be liable to the tenant for injuries, where the former retains control of part of the tenement. Elliott v. Pray, 10 Allen (Mass.) 378; Watkins v. Goodall, 138 Mass. 533; Alston v. Grant, 3 El. & Bl. 128; Phillips v. Ehrmaun (City Ct. Brook.) 28 N. Y. Supp. 519; Payne v. Irvin, 144 Ill. 482, 33 N. E. 756; Davis v. Power Co., 107 Cal. 563, 40 Pac. 950; Montieth v. Finkbeiner, 66 Hun, 633, 21 N. Y. Supp. 288; Phillips v. Library Co., 55 N. J. Law, 307, 27 Atl. 478; Brunker v. Cummins, 133 Ind. 443, 32 N. E. 732. But see Moynihan v. Allyn, 162 Mass. 276, 38 N. E. 497; Freeman v. Hunnewell, 163 Mass. 210, 39 N. E. 1012; McLean v. Warehouse Co., 158 Mass. 472, 33 N. E. 499; Daley v. Quick, 99 Cal. 179, 33 Pac. 859. The tenant, while he has control of the premises, is liable to strangers for negligence. Stickney v. Munroe, 44 Me. 195; Pickard v. Collins, 23 Barb. (N. Y.) 444; Payne v. Rogers, 2 H. Bl. 349; Anheuser-Busch Brewing Ass'n v. Peterson, 41 Neb. 897, 60 N. W. 373; Lee v. McLaughlin, 86 Me. 410, 30 Atl. 65. So he may be liable to the landlord for injury to the premises. Stevens v. Pantlind, 95 Mich. 145, 54 N. W. 716; Wilcox v. Cate, 65 Vt. 478, 26 Atl. 1105; Olsen v. Webb, 41 Neb. 147, 59 N. W. 520.

[93] Kansas Inv. Co. v. Carter, 160 Mass. 421, 36 N. E. 63; Phelps v. Randolph, 147 Ill. 335, 35 N. E. 243. And see Bentley v. City of Atlanta, 92 Ga. 623, 18 S. E. 1013. Any right of re-entry in the lessor is entirely a reserved right. Heermance v. Vernoy, 6 Johns. (N. Y.) 5; Dixon v. Clow, 24 Wend. (N. Y.) 188; Parker v. Griswold, 17 Conn. 288; State v. Piper, 89 N. C. 551.

[94] See post, p. 349.

premises.[95] He is entitled to estovers,[96] but not to emblements,[97] unless his interest is terminated, without his fault, by some contingency happening during the term.[98] If he causes a forfeiture, his subtenant is entitled to emblements.[99] A lessee is liable for waste committed either by himself [100] or another.[101] But he may remove his chattel fixtures without any express permission in the lease.[102]

Estoppel to Deny Lessor's Title.

A lessee is estopped to deny his lessor's title,[103] and the estoppel extends to all claiming under the lessee.[104] It can be set up by the

---

[95] Crook v. Hewitt, 4 Wash. 749, 31 Pac. 28. And see Marsh v. McNider, 88 Iowa, 390, 55 N. W. 469. The tenant is bound by any easements to which the land is subject. McDermott v. Railroad Co., 28 Hun (N. Y.) 325; Prescott v. White, 21 Pick. (Mass.) 342.

[96] Hubbard v. Shaw, 12 Allen (Mass.) 120; Walters v. Hutchins' Adm'x, 29 Ind. 136; Harris v. Goslin, 3 Har. (Del.) 340.

[97] Carney v. Mosher, 97 Mich. 554, 56 N. W. 935; Gossett v. Drydale, 48 Mo. App. 430; Baker v. McInturff, 49 Mo. App. 505; Maclary v. Turner, 9 Houst. (Del.) 281, 32 Atl. 325; Monig's Adm'x v. Phillips (Ky.) 29 S. W. 970. And see 1 Stim. Am. St. Law, § 2064.

[98] Gray v. Worst, 129 Mo. 122, 31 S. W. 585; Munday v. O'Neil (Neb.) 63 N. W. 32; Hubbard v. Berry, 10 Ind. App. 594, 38 N. E. 77.

[99] Bevans v. Briscoe, 4 Har. & J. (Md.) 139. But see Samson v. Rose, 65 N. Y. 411. They cannot be claimed by a mortgagee of the lessee. Gregg v. Boyd, 69 Hun, 588, 23 N. Y. Supp. 918. And one holding an estate for years as lessee of a tenant for life may claim emblements. Dorsett v. Gray, 98 Ind. 273; Bevans v. Briscoe, 4 Har. & J. (Md.) 139; Marshall, J., in Miller v. Shackleford, 4 Dana (Ky.) 277.

[100] Thorndike v. Burrage, 111 Mass. 531; Nave v. Berry, 22 Ala. 382; Fenton v. Montgomery, 19 Mo. App. 156; Brooks v. Rogers, 101 Ala. 111, 13 South. 386.

[101] Cook v. Transportation Co., 1 Denio (N. Y.) 91; Wood v. Griffin, 46 N. H. 230; Donald v. Elliott (Cir. Ct.) 32 N. Y. Supp. 821.

[102] Mason v. Fenn, 13 Ill. 525; Moore v. Wood, 12 Abb. Prac. (N. Y.) 393; Bircher v. Parker, 40 Mo. 118; Chandler v. Oldham, 55 Mo. App. 139; and ante, p. 19. Cf. Davidson v. Manufacturing Co., 99 Mich. 501, 58 N. W. 475; Pendill v. Maas, 97 Mich. 215, 56 N. W. 597; Wright v. Macdonnell, 88 Tex. 140, 30 S. W. 907; Goedeke v. Baker (Tex. Civ. App.) 28 S. W. 1039.

[103] Wolf v. Holton (Mich.) 62 N. W. 174; Gray v. Johnson, 14 N. H. 414; Pope v. Harkins, 16 Ala. 321; Hamilton v. Pittock, 158 Pa. St. 457, 27 Atl.

[104] See note 104 on following page.

heirs or assignees of the lessor,[105] but the lessee can controvert the fact of an assignment.[106] So, against the heir, he may show that the reversion was devised to a third person.[107] Against the lessor, he may show that the latter has parted with his interest since making the lease,[108] for the lessee may have purchased the reversion from the lessor,[109] or have paid the rent to the lessor's assignee.[110] But he cannot assert an outstanding title which he has bought in,[111] nor can he accept a lease from a stranger.[112] How-

1079; Sexton v. Carley, 147 Ill. 269, 35 N. E. 411; Knowles v. Murphy (Cal.) 40 Pac. 111; McKissick v. Ashby, 98 Cal. 422, 33 Pac. 729; Delaney v. Fox, 2 C. B. (N. S.) 768; Voss v. King, 38 W. Va. 607, 18 S. E. 762; Dixon v. Stewart, 113 N. C. 410, 18 S. E. 325; Hackett v. Marmet Co., 3 C. C. A. 76, 52 Fed. 268. But see Lakin v. Dolly, 53 Fed. 333; Chicago & A. R. Co. v. Keegan, 152 Ill. 413, 39 N. E. 33; Welder v. McComb (Tex. Civ. App.) 30 S. W. 822; McKinnis v. Mortgage Co., 55 Kan. 259, 39 Pac. 1018; Suddarth v. Robertson, 118 Mo. 286, 24 S. W. 151. The rule has been extended to adjoining lands gained by the tenant by disseisin. Doe v. Jones, 15 Mees. & W. 580; Doe v. Rees, 6 Car. & P. 610; Andrews v. Hailes, 2 El. & Bl. 349. The old common-law rule that a disclaimer of the landlord's title would cause a forfeiture is no longer the law. Fusselman v. Worthington, 14 Ill. 135; Newman v. Rutter, 8 Watts (Pa.) 51; Greeno v. Munson, 9 Vt. 37; Jackson v. Vincent, 4 Wend. (N. Y.) 633. But see Newman v. Rutter, 8 Watts (Pa.) 51. Refusal to pay rent will not cause a forfeiture. Doe v. Wells, 10 Adol. & E. 427; Kiernan v. Terry, 26 Or. 494, 38 Pac. 671.

[104] Rose v. Davis, 11 Cal. 133; Russell v. Erwin's Adm'r, 38 Ala. 44, 50; Derrick v. Luddy, 64 Vt. 462, 24 Atl. 1050; McLennan v. Grant, 8 Wash. 603, 36 Pac. 682. Cf. Swan v. Busby, 5 Tex. Civ. App. 63, 24 S. W. 303.

[105] Blantin v. Whitaker, 11 Humph. (Tenn.) 313; Russell v. Allard, 18 N. H. 225; State v. Votaw, 13 Mont. 403, 34 Pac. 315.

[106] Despard v. Walbridge, 15 N. Y. 377; Beall v. Davenport, 48 Ga. 165.

[107] Despard v. Walbridge, 15 N. Y. 377. And see Lane v. Young, 66 Hun, 563, 21 N. Y. Supp. 838.

[108] Wolf v. Johnson, 30 Miss. 513; Horner v. Leeds, 25 N. J. Law, 106; Robinson v. Mining Co., 55 Mo. App. 662; Winn v. Strickland, 34 Fla. 610, 16 South. 606; Robertson v. Biddell, 32 Fla. 304, 13 South. 358; West Shore Mills Co. v. Edwards, 24 Or. 475, 33 Pac. 987.

[109] Elliott v. Smith, 23 Pa. St. 131; George v. Putney, 4 Cush. (Mass.) 355; Camley v. Stanfield, 10 Tex. 546.

[110] Stedman v. Gassett, 18 Vt. 346; Welch v. Adams, 1 Metc. (Mass.) 494; Magill v. Hinsdale, 6 Conn. 464.

[111] Sharpe v. Kelley, 5 Denio (N. Y.) 431; Drane v. Gregory's Heirs, 3 B.

[112] See note 112 on following page.

§ 82)   RIGHTS AND LIABILITIES OF LANDLORD AND TENANT.   145

ever, if there is an eviction under a paramount title, the tenant may take a new lease from the holder of such title, and it is not necessary that he be actually expelled from the premises, to justify him in so doing. It is sufficient if the right to evict is asserted by one entitled to the possession, and the tenant in good faith accepts a new lease to avoid eviction.[113]

Distress for Rent.

At common law the landlord has a remedy, called "distress," [114] for enforcing the payment of rent, by seizing personal property

---

Mon. (Ky.) 619; Elliott v. Smith, 23 Pa. St. 131; Morley v. Rodgers, 5 Yerg. (Tenn.) 217; Anderson v. Anderson, 104 Ala. 428, 16 South. 14. And see Barlow v. Dahm, 97 Ala. 414, 12 South. 293.

[112] Doe v. Reynolds, 27 Ala. 364, 376; Russell v. Fabyan, 34 N. H. 223; Ragor v. McKay, 44 Ill. App. 79. But see Nash v. Springstead, 72 Hun, 474, 25 N. Y. Supp. 279.

[113] Morse v. Goddard, 13 Metc. (Mass.) 177; Simers v. Saltus, 3 Denio (N. Y.) 217. And see Delaney v. Fox, 2 C. B. (N. S.) 775.

[114] The other remedies of the lessor can only be enumerated. For rent, they are: Debt, Bordman v. Osborn, 23 Pick. (Mass.) 295; Allen v. Bryan, 5 Barn. & C. 512; assumpsit, Smith v. Stewart, 6 Johns. (N. Y.) 46; Chambers v. Ross, 25 N. J. Law, 293; Brolasky v. Ferguson, 48 Pa. St. 434; covenant, Gale v. Nixon, 6 Cow. (N. Y.) 445; Saltoun v. Houstoun, 1 Bing. 433; or bill in equity, Lawrence v. Hammett, 3 J. J. Marsh. (Ky.) 287; Livingston's Ex'rs v. Livingston, 4 Johns. Ch. (N. Y.) 287; North v. Strafford, 3 P. Wms. 148. For waste, are actions to prevent, Watson v. Hunter, 5 Johns. Ch. (N. Y.) 169; and for damages, Harder v. Harder, 26 Barb. (N. Y.) 409; Queen's College v. Hallett, 14 East, 489; Attersoll v. Stevens, 1 Taunt. 196. To recover possession, are ejectment, Jackson v. Brownson, 7 Johns. (N. Y.) 227; Penn v. Divellin, 2 Yeates (Pa.) 309; Cobb v. Lavalle, 89 Ill. 331; Colston v. McVay, 1 A. K. Marsh. (Ky.) 251; and summary proceeding given by statute in most states, Fratcher v. Smith (Mich.) 62 N. W. 832; Lewis v. Sheldon, 103 Mich. 102, 61 N. W. 269; Marsters v. Cling, 163 Mass. 477, 40 N. E. 763. The lessee's actions are: Replevin, for wrongful distress, Hunter v. Le Conte, 6 Cow. (N. Y.) 728; trespass, for interference with his possession, Taylor v. Cooper (Mich.) 62 N. W. 157; Hey v. Moorhouse, 8 Scott, 156; Van Brunt v. Schenck, 11 Johns. (N. Y.) 385; Lunt v. Brown, 13 Me. 236; case, for excessive distress, Hare v. Stegall, 60 Ill. 380 (and see Fishburne v. Engledove, 91 Va. 548, 22 S. E. 354); and covenant, 2 Taylor, Landl. & Ten. (8th Ed.) 260. For the action of forcible entry and detainer, see 2 Tayl. Landl. & Ten. (8th Ed.) 396; 2 Wood. Landl. & Ten. (2d Ed.) 1374; Willard v. Warren, 17 Wend. (N. Y.) 257; Toby v. Schultz, 51 Ill. App. 487; and post, p. 165.

REAL PROP.—10

found on the demised premises.[115] This remedy exists in some of our states,[116] while in many others it is incorporated into the law of attachments and liens.[117] It lies for all rents reserved which are certain.[118] The distraint may be made by the lessor, or the assignee of the reversion, for all the rent due.[119] It is now required, in most states, that the warrant be executed by a legal officer.[120] At common law, any chattels [121] found upon the premises could be distrained, whether belonging to the tenant, or to others,[122] though exception was made in favor of goods brought there in course of trade.[123] The tendency of modern decisions and statutes is to restrict the right of distraining to the property of the lessee.[124] There is a right to sell the goods taken, if they are not redeemed within the time fixed by the statutes.[125]

[115] 2 Tayl. Landl. & Ten. (8th Ed.) 168; 2 Wood, Landl. & Ten. (2d Ed.) 1305; Newman v. Anderton, 2 Bos. & P. (N. R.) 224. Cf. Beeszard v. Capel, 8 Barn. & C. 141; Prescott v. Boucher, 3 Barn. & Adol. 849.

[116] 2 Tayl. Landl. & Ten. (8th Ed.) 170.

[117] See 1 Stim. Am. St. Law, §§ 2031-2036. And see Willard v. Rogers, 54 Ill. App. 583; Rogers v. Grigg (Tex. Civ. App.) 29 S. W. 654; Belser v. Youngblood, 103 Ala. 545, 15 South. 863; Manhattan Trust Co. v. Sioux City & N. Ry. Co., 68 Fed. 72; Smith v. Dayton (Iowa) 62 N. W. 650; Toney v. Goodley, 57 Mo. App. 235; Ballard v. Johnson, 114 N. C. 141, 19 S. E. 98.

[118] Stewart v. Gregg, 42 S. C. 392, 20 S. E. 193. Cf. Tutter v. Fryer, Winch, 7; Paxton v. Kennedy, 70 Miss. 865, 12 South. 546.

[119] Slocum v. Clark, 2 Hill (N. Y.) 475; Lathrop v. Clewis, 63 Ga. 282. But not by executor for rent accruing in decedent's lifetime. Prescott v. Boucher, 3 Barn. & Adol. 849. Cf. — v. Cooper, 2 Wils. 375; Parmenter v. Webber, 8 Taunt. 593.

[120] For the details and procedure the student must consult the statutes of his state.

[121] Unless of a perishable nature. Morley v. Pincombe, 2 Exch. 101. And see Van Sickler v. Jacobs, 14 Johns. (N. Y.) 434.

[122] 2 Wood, Landl. & Ten. (2d Ed.) 1310; Blanche v. Bradford, 38 Pa. St. 344; Spencer v. McGowen, 13 Wend. (N. Y.) 256. And see Paine v. Lock Co., 64 Miss. 175, 1 South. 56; Davis v. Payne's Adm'r, 4 Rand. (Va.) 332.

[123] Brown v. Stackhouse, 155 Pa. St. 582, 26 Atl. 669; Cadwalader v. Tindall, 20 Pa. St. 422; Knowles v. Pierce, 5 Houst. (Del.) 178; Block v. Latham, 63 Tex. 414.

[124] 2 Tayl. Landl. & Ten. (8th Ed.) 197; Connah v. Hale, 23 Wend. (N. Y.) 475; Peacock v. Purvis, 2 Brod. & B. 362.

[125] 2 Wood, Landl. & Ten. (2d Ed.) 1322; 2 Tayl. Landl. & Ten. (8th Ed.) 214. The right to sell was first given by the statute of 2 W. & M. c. 5.

SAME—TRANSFER OF ESTATES FOR YEARS.

83. After an estate for years has been created, the intererests of the parties are transferable. The transfer may be:
 (a) By act of parties, as where:
   (1) The lessor assigns the rent or the reversion, or both (p. 147).
   (2) The lessee (p. 148)
     (I) Assigns his term, in which case the assignee is liable on all covenants running with the land.
     (II) Sublets his term, in which case the sublessee is liable only to the sublessor.
 (b) By operation of law, as where (p. 149):
   (1) The interest of either party is taken on execution.
   (2) On the lessor's death, his interest goes to his heirs or devisees.
   (3) On the lessee's death, his interest goes to his personal representative.

Transfer by Lessor.

Unless restrained by express covenants,[126] either the lessor or the lessee may transfer his interest under a lease.[127] The requirements of the statute of frauds are the same for an assignment or a subletting as for the original lease.[128] An assignee of the reversion is entitled to receive the rents from the tenant after giving notice of the assignment.[129] Such assignee can enforce, and

---

[126] Or by statute, as lessee is in a few states. 1 Stim. Am. St. Law, § 2043; 2 Shars. & B. Lead. Cas. Real Prop. 83.

[127] Dixon v. Buell, 21 Ill. 203; Webster v. Nichols, 104 Ill. 160; Crommelin v. Thiess, 31 Ala. 412, 421; Woodhull v. Rosenthal, 61 N. Y. 382; Gould v. School Dist., 8 Minn. 427 (Gil. 382); Indianapolis Manufacturing & Carpenters' Union v. Cleveland, C., C. & I. Ry. Co., 45 Ind. 281; Rex v. Inhabitants of Aldborough, 1 East, 597.

[128] Bedford v. Terhune, 30 N. Y. 453.

[129] Hunt v. Thompson, 2 Allen (Mass.) 341; O'Connor v. Kelly, 41 Cal. 432;

is liable on, covenants running with the land.[130] The lessor may assign the rent to one man, and the reversion to another, or he may assign one and keep the other.[131] So, too, he may split up the reversion into parcels, but the rent cannot be made payable to several without the consent of the tenant.[132]

Transfer by Lessee.

The lessee may either assign or sublet.[133] If the interest conveyed by him is for a shorter time than his own term, even by a day, it is a sublease;[134] and some cases hold that the reservation by the original lessee of a right of entry will have the same effect.[135] But there may be an assignment of part of the prem-

---

Moffatt v. Smith, 4 N. Y. 126; Childs v. Clark, 3 Barb. Ch. (N. Y.) 52; Watson v. Hunkins, 13 Iowa, 547; Page v. Culver, 55 Mo. App. 606. Prior to the statute of 4 Anne, c. 16, § 9 (which has been generally adopted in the United States), it was necessary that the tenant should agree to accept the assignee of the reversion as his landlord. This was called an "attornment." Fisher v. Deering, 60 Ill. 114; Burden v. Thayer, 3 Metc. (Mass.) 76; Tilford v. Fleming, 64 Pa. St. 300; Mortimer v. O'Reagan, 10 Phila. (Pa.) 500. But see Fox's Case, 8 Coke, 936. Attornment is not now necessary, in most states. 2 Tayl. Landl. & Ten. (8th Ed.) 224; 1 Stim. Am. St. Law, § 2009; Perrin v. Lepper, 34 Mich. 292. Contra, Fisher v. Deering, 60 Ill. 114; Duke v. Compton, 49 Mo. App. 304.

[130] Astor v. Miller, 2 Paige (N. Y.) 68; Stevenson v. Lambard, 2 East, 575; Burton v. Barclay, 7 Bing. 745; Van Horne v. Crain, 1 Paige (N. Y.) 455; Sutherland v. Goodnow, 108 Ill. 528; Campbell v. Lewis, 3 Barn. & Ald. 392; King v. Jones, 5 Taunt. 418.

[131] Co. Litt. 47a; McMurphy v. Minot, 4 N. H. 251; Crosby v. Loop, 13 Ill. 625; Dixon v. Niccolls, 39 Ill. 372, 384; Van Rensselaer v. Hays, 19 N. Y. 68, 99; Wineman v. Hughson, 44 Ill. App. 22.

[132] Ryerson v. Quackenbush, 26 N. J. Law, 254; Ards v. Watkin, Cro. Eliz. 637.

[133] So he may mortgage his interest. Menger v. Ward, 87 Tex. 622, 30 S. W. 853. And see Barrett v. Trainor, 50 Ill. App. 420; Drda v. Schmidt, 47 Ill. App. 267; Menger v. Ward (Tex. Civ. App.) 28 S. W. 821. Contra, as to a lease on shares. Lewis v. Sheldon, 103 Mich. 102, 61 N. W. 269. Assignment and subletting without lessor's consent may be restrained by covenant. Raymond v. Hodgson, 55 Ill. App. 423; Shannon v. Grindstaff, 11 Wash. 536, 40 Pac. 123.

[134] Post v. Kearney, 2 N. Y. 394; Collins v. Hasbrouck, 56 N. Y. 157.

[135] Linden v. Hepburn, 3 Sandf. (N. Y.) 668; People v. Robertson, 39 Barb. (N. Y.) 9; Doe v. Bateman, 2 Barn. & Ald. 168. And see 1 Wood, Landl. & Ten. (2d Ed.) 178.

ises.[136] In the case of a sublease, the subtenant is not liable for rent to the original lessor, or on the covenants of the original lease.[137] But an assignee is liable to the original lessor on all the covenants which run with the land.[138] The lessee continues liable after he has assigned, on express covenants.[139] But an assignee may avoid future obligation by assigning over, whether there is an express covenant or not.[140] The lessee and his assignee or sublessee may insert any covenants they choose in the instrument of transfer, and so regulate their obligations to each other.

Transfer by Operation of Law.

Both the reversion and the term are subject to involuntary alienation, such as sale on execution. A purchaser assumes the rights and liabilities of an assignee.[141] An assignee in bankruptcy or insolvency does not become liable as assignee of a term owned by his assignor until he has had a reasonable time to ascertain whether it is an available asset. Before then he is not presumed to accept.[142] A lessee may dispose of his estates for years by

---

[136] Cook v. Jones (Ky.) 28 S. W. 960. But see Shannon v. Grindstaff, 11 Wash. 536, 40 Pac. 123.

[137] 1 Tayl. Landl. & Ten. (8th Ed.) § 16; 1 Wood, Landl. & Ten. (2d Ed.) 181; Trustees of Dartmouth College v. Clough, 8 N. H. 22. But he may pay rent to avoid eviction. Peck v. Ingersoll, 7 N. Y. 528.

[138] Fennell v. Guffey, 155 Pa. St. 38, 25 Atl. 785; Sanders v. Partridge, 108 Mass. 556. But cf. Dey v. Greenebaum, 82 Hun, 533, 31 N. Y. Supp. 610.

[139] Grommes v. Trust Co., 147 Ill. 634, 35 N. E. 820; Wineman v. Phillips, 93 Mich. 223, 53 N. W. 168; Conrady v. Bywaters (Tex. Civ. App.) 24 S. W. 961; Bouscaren v. Brown, 40 Neb. 722, 59 N. W. 385; Charless v. Froebel, 47 Mo. App. 45; Pittsburg Consol. Coal Co. v. Greenlee, 164 Pa. St. 549, 30 Atl. 489; Bless v. Jenkins, 129 Mo. 647, 31 S. W. 938; Walker's Case, 3 Coke, 22a; Calborne v. Wright, 2 Lev. 239.

[140] McBee v. Sampson, 66 Fed. 416; Armstrong v. Wheeler, 9 Cow. (N. Y.) 88; Childs v. Clark, 3 Barb. Ch. (N. Y.) 52; Tibbals v. Iffland, 10 Wash. 451, 39 Pac. 102. But see Consolidated Coal Co. v. Peers, 150 Ill. 344, 37 N. E. 937; Drake v. Lacoe, 157 Pa. St. 17, 27 Atl. 538; Lindsley v. Brewing Co., 59 Mo. App. 271.

[141] McNeil v. Ames, 120 Mass. 481; Lancashire v. Mason, 75 N. C. 455.

[142] Pratt v. Levan, 1 Miles (Pa.) 358; Bagley v. Freeman, 1 Hilt. (N. Y.) 196; Copeland v. Stephens, 1 Barn. & Ald. 594; Carter v. Warne, 4 Car. & P. 191.

150   ESTATES AS TO QUANTITY—LESS THAN FREEHOLD.   (Ch. 7

will,[143] but if he fail to do so they pass on his death to his personal representative, who thus becomes an assignee.[144] The reversion, if not disposed of, is subject to the ordinary rules governing the descent of realty; and the rent follows the reversion, unless it has been separately assigned.[145]

SAME—TERMINATION OF ESTATES FOR YEARS.

84. An estate for years may be terminated:
   (a) **By lapse of time** (p. 150).
   (b) **By forfeiture** (p. 150).
   (c) **By merger** (p. 152).
   (d) **By surrender** (p. 152).
   (e) **By destruction of the premises, in some cases** (p. 153).
   (f) **By an exercise of the power of eminent domain** (p. 153).

Lapse of Time.

Estates for years in most cases determine by mere lapse of time; that is, the period for which the lease was made expires, and the term is thereby at an end, without any notice by either party.[146]

Forfeiture.

When the continuance of a term is made to depend on a condition, or there is a reservation of a right of re-entry for breach of

---

[143] They pass by a devise of "personal estate." Brewster v. Hill, 1 N. H. 350.

[144] Martin v. Tobin, 123 Mass. 85; Sutter v. Lackmann, 39 Mo. 91; Murdock v. Ratcliff, 7 Ohio, 119. But the rule is otherwise in a few states, by statute. 2 Shars. & B. Lead. Cas. Real Prop. 40. The lessee's estate continues liable for the rent. Hutchings v. Bank, 91 Va. 68, 20 S. E. 950.

[145] Lewis v. Wilkins, Phil. Eq. (N. C.) 303.

[146] Smith v. Snyder, 168 Pa. St. 541, 32 Atl. 64; Bedford v. M'Elherron, 2 Serg. & R. 49; Ackland v. Lutley, 9 Adol. & E. 879; Poppers v. Meagher, 148 Ill. 192, 35 N. E. 805; Dunphy v. Goodlander, 12 Ind. App. 609, 40 N. E. 924; Williams v. Mershon (N. J. Sup.) 30 Atl. 619; Montgomery v. Willis, 45 Neb. 434, 63 N. W. 794. And the tenant becomes a wrongdoer if he refuses to surrender possession. Frost v. Iron Co., 12 Misc. Rep. 348, 33 N. Y. Supp. 654; Jackson v. Parkhurst, 5 Johns. (N. Y.) 128; Ellis v. Palge, 1 Pick. (Mass.) 43; Bedford v. M'Elherron, 2 Serg. & R. (Pa.) 49.

§ 84)　　TERMINATION OF ESTATES FOR YEARS.　　151

the covenants of the lease, an entry in either instance puts an end to the term.[147] The courts are, however, rather averse to enforcing forfeitures;[148] and when the breach is due to accident or mistake, and can be compensated in damages, as it usually can be in the case of rent, relief will be granted the tenant.[149] The relief does not extend to cases where the damages are not a mere matter of computation, as where there is a breach of a covenant not to assign, or a covenant to repair.[150]

Re-entry for forfeiture is optional with the lessor.[151] The lessee cannot insist upon it, and so avail himself of his own breach.[152] Acceptance of rent accruing after a breach will be a waiver of the forfeiture,[153] but acceptance of rent due before the breach will not.[154] Other acts of the landlord may also constitute a waiver.[155]

---

[147] See Carnegie Nat. Gas Co. v. Philadelphia Co., 158 Pa. St. 317, 27 Atl. 951; Heinouer v. Jones, 159 Pa. St. 228, 28 Atl. 228. In a few states the statutes require a short notice. 1 Stim. Am. St. Law, §§ 2054, 2055.

[148] See Sommers v. Reynolds, 103 Mich. 307, 61 N. W. 501; Drake v. Lacoe, 157 Pa. St. 17, 27 Atl. 538. When there is a clause of forfeiture for nonpayment of rent a demand must be made therefor on the land, at the front door of the house, if there is a house, and at a convenient time before sunset of the very day the rent falls due, unless a demand is dispensed with by the terms of the lease. 2 Tayl. Landl. & Ten. § 493; Smith v. Whitbeck, 13 Ohio St. 471; Jackson v. Harrison, 17 Johns. (N. Y.) 66; Van Rensselaer v. Snyder, 9 Barb. (N. Y.) 302; Connor v. Bradley, 1 How. 211; Faylor v. Brice, 7 Ind. App. 551, 34 N. E. 833. Cf. Haynes v. Investment Co., 35 Neb. 766, 53 N. W. 979. But see Shanfelter v. Horner (Md.) 32 Atl. 184. Under the statutes of many states, the landlord may terminate the tenancy, for nonpayment of rent, without any agreement to that effect. 1 Stim. Am. St. Law, § 2054.

[149] Baxter v. Lansing, 7 Paige (N. Y.) 350; Gregory v. Wilson, 9 Hare. 683; Nokes v. Gibbon, 3 Drew. 681. But see Rolfe v. Harris, 2 Price, 206, note; Cage v. Russel, 2 Vent. 352.

[150] 2 Tayl. Landl. & Ten. (8th Ed.) 81.

[151] Cochran v. Pew. 159 Pa. St. 184, 28 Atl. 219. Or his assignee, who may also claim it. 2 Tayl. Landl. & Ten. (8th Ed.) 75. And see Wilson v. Goldstein, 152 Pa. St. 524, 25 Atl. 493.

[152] Gibson v. Oliver, 158 Pa. St. 277, 27 Atl. 961; Brady v. Nagle (Tex. Civ. App.) 29 S. W. 943; Arnsby v. Woodward, 6 Barn. & C. 519; Reid v. Parsons, 2 Chit. 247.

[153] Jackson v. Sheldon, 5 Cow. (N. Y.) 448; Bleecker v. Smith, 13 Wend.

---

[154] See note 154 on following page.　　[155] See note 155 on following page.

Merger.

An estate for years may be terminated by a merger, as where the fee is acquired by the tenant for years.[156]

An estate for years will merge in a life estate,[157] or in another term of years,[158] as well as in the fee.

Surrender.

A surrender [159] will terminate an estate for years,[160] but only when made to the holder of the next estate. Therefore an under-

---

(N. Y.) 530; Gomber v. Hackett, 6 Wis. 323; Newman v. Rutter, 8 Watts (Pa.) 51; Doe v. Rees, 4 Bing. N. C. 384; Doe v. Johnson, 1 Starkie, 411; Clark v. Greenfield (Com. Pl.) 34 N. Y. Supp. 1; Koehler v. Brady, 78 Hun, 443, 29 N. Y. Supp. 388; Michel v. O'Brien, 6 Misc. Rep. 408, 27 N. Y. Supp. 173; Brooks v. Rodgers, 99 Ala. 433, 12 South. 61. The landlord must have knowledge of the breach. Jackson v. Schutz, 18 Johns. (N. Y.) 174; Peop. s Bank v. Mitchell, 73 N. Y. 406; Garnhart v. Finney, 40 Mo. 449; Roe v. Harrison, 2 Term R. 425; Barber v. Stone (Mich.) 62 N. W. 139; Stover v. Hazelbaker, 42 Neb. 393, 60 N. W. 597; Bowling v. Crook, 104 Ala. 130, 16 South. 131. But see Miller v. Prescott, 163 Mass. 12, 39 N. E. 409.

[154] Jackson v. Allen, 3 Cow. (N. Y.) 220; Hunter v. Osterhoudt, 11 Barb. (N. Y.) 33; Conger v. Duryee, 24 Hun (N. Y.) 617; Frazier v. Caruthers, 44 Ill. App. 61; Carraher v. Bell, 7 Wash. 81, 34 Pac. 469.

[155] Lynch v. Gas Co., 165 Pa. St. 518, 30 Atl. 984; Nelson v. Enchel, 158 Pa. St. 372, 27 Atl. 1103; Frazier v. Caruthers, 44 Ill. App. 61; Deaton v. Taylor, 90 Va. 219, 17 S. E. 944; Little Rock Granite Co. v. Shall, 59 Ark. 405, 27 S. W. 562. But see Cleminger v. Gas Co., 159 Pa. St. 16, 28 Atl. 293; Williams v. Vanderbilt, 145 Ill. 238, 34 N. E. 476; Jones v. Durrer, 96 Cal. 95, 30 Pac. 1027; Moses v. Loomis, 156 Ill. 392, 40 N. E. 952; Doe v. Meux, 4 Barn. & C. 606; Balfour v. Russell, 167 Pa. St. 287, 31 Atl. 570. A notice to quit at the end of a certain time, given after the breach, may constitute a waiver. Doe v. Miller, 2 Car. & P. 348; Doe v. Allen, 3 Taunt. 78.

[156] Roberts v. Jackson, 1 Wend. (N. Y.) 478; Carroll v. Ballance, 26 Ill. 19; McMahan v. Jacoway (Ala.) 17 South. 39. Merger will also destroy covenants incident to the reversion. Webb v. Russel, 3 Term R. 393; Thorn v. Woollcombe, 3 Barn. & Adol. 586.

[157] Even though the term be longer than the life estate can possibly last. 1 Washb. Real Prop. (5th Ed.) 586.

[158] 4 Kent, Comm. (12th Ed.) 99. The second term need not be as long as the term to be merged. Stephens v. Bridges, 6 Madd. 66.

[159] For a definition of a surrender, and the requisites for, see post, p 408.

[160] Conway v. Carpenter, 80 Hun, 428, 30 N. Y. Supp. 315; Hooks v. Forst, 165 Pa. St. 238, 30 Atl. 846; Wolf v. Guffey, 161 Pa. St. 276, 28 Atl. 1117; Barnhart v. Lockwood, 152 Pa. St. 82, 25 Atl. 237; May v. Oil Co., 152 Pa. St. 518,

§ 84) TERMINATION OF ESTATES FOR YEARS. 153

lessee cannot surrender to the original lessor.[161] The making of a new lease may operate as a surrender of the old one.[162]

Destruction of Premises.

The destruction of the premises—for instance, where a room is leased, and the whole house is burned—puts an end to the tenancy, because the subject-matter of the lease has ceased to exist.[163] This is not true, of course, in the absence of an agreement, where the part destroyed is not the whole subject of the lease, as where a house and lot are leased, and the house is destroyed.[164]

Taking under Power of Eminent Domain.

If the demised premises are taken under the power of eminent domain, the relation of landlord and tenant comes to an end.[165] But, if only a part is taken, both lessor and lessee can claim compensation for the taking, and the tenancy continues.[166]

---

25 Atl. 564; Williams v. Vanderbilt, 145 Ill. 238, 34 N. E. 476; Smith v. Pendergast, 26 Minn. 318, 3 N. W. 978; Nelson v. Thompson, 23 Minn. 508. See Burnham v. O'Grady, 90 Wis. 461, 63 N. W. 1049; Hooks v. Forst, 165 Pa. St. 238, 30 Atl. 846; Aderhold v. Supply Co., 158 Pa. St. 401, 28 Atl. 22; Hough v. Brown (Mich.) 62 N. W. 143; National Union Bldg. Ass'n v. Brewer, 41 Ill. App. 223. The surrender must be accepted. Pendill v. Mining Co. (Mich.) 62 N. W. 1024; Joslin v. McLean, 99 Mich. 480, 58 N. W. 467; Stevens v. Pantlind, 95 Mich. 145, 54 N. W. 716; Lane v. Nelson, 167 Pa. St. 602, 31 Atl. 864; Reeves v. McComeskey, 168 Pa. St. 571, 32 Atl. 96; Rees v. Lowy, 57 Minn. 381, 59 N. W. 310; Stern v. Thayer, 56 Minn. 93, 57 N. W. 329.

[161] 2 Wood, Landl. & Ten. (2d Ed.) 1152; 2 Tayl. Landl. & Ten. (8th Ed.) 95.

[162] Walker v. Githens, 156 Pa. St. 178, 27 Atl. 36; Evans v. McKanna, 89 Iowa, 362, 56 N. W. 527. But see Witmark v. Railroad Co., 76 Hun, 302, 27 N. Y. Supp. 777. Cf. Beal v. Car-Spring Co., 125 Mass. 157.

[163] Hecht v. Herrwagen, 13 Misc. Rep. 316, 34 N. Y. Supp. 456; Graves v. Berdan, 26 N. Y. 498; Ainsworth v. Ritt, 38 Cal. 89; Buschman v. Wilson, 29 Md. 553. This is regulated by statute in some states. 1 Stim. Am. St. Law, § 2062. And see Craig v. Butler, 83 Hun, 286, 31 N. Y. Supp. 963; Fleischman v. Toplitz, 134 N. Y. 349, 31 N. E. 1089.

[164] Phillips v. Stevens, 16 Mass. 238; Davis' Adm'r v. Smith, 15 Mo. 467; Ross v. Overton, 3 Call (Va.) 309. But see New York Real-Estate & Bldg. Imp. Co. v. Motley, 143 N. Y. 156, 38 N. E. 103; Hunnewell v. Bangs, 161 Mass. 132, 36 N. E. 751; Meyer v. Henderson (La.) 16 South. 729.

[165] Barclay v. Picker, 38 Mo. 143.

[166] Parks v. City of Boston, 15 Pick. (Mass.) 198; Workman v. Mifflin, 30 Pa. St. 362; City of Chicago v. Garrity, 7 Ill. App. 474; Foote v. City of Cin-

LETTING LAND ON SHARES.

85. A letting of land on shares may make the cultivator:
  (a) **A servant.**
  (b) **A co-tenant.**
  (c) **A lessee.**

Land is often cultivated under an agreement by which both the owner and the cultivator are to share in the crop.[167] Such an agreement may establish the relation of employer and employé between the parties, a share of the crops being given in lieu of wages,[168] or they may be tenants in common of the crop,[169] or the transaction may constitute a leasing with a rent payable in crops, and the usual incidents of the relation of landlord and tenant exist.[170] Probably no rule can be laid down for determining the re-

cinnati, 11 Ohio, 408. And see Corrigan v. City of Chicago, 144 Ill. 537, 33 N. E. 746.

[167] Such holdings are now regulated by statute in some states. See 1 Stim. Am. St. Law, § 2037. The cropper, or one farming on shares, cannot assign his interest. McNeeley v. Hart, 10 Ired. (N. C.) 63.

[168] Tanner v. Hills, 48 N. Y. 662; Steel v. Frick, 56 Pa. St. 172; Chase v. McDonnell, 24 Ill. 236; Gray v. Robinson (Ariz.) 33 Pac. 712; Haywood v. Rogers, 73 N. C. 320; Neal v. Bellamy, Id. 384. But see Harrison v. Ricks, 71 N. C. 7; State v. Jones, 2 Dev. & B. (N. C.) 544. Possession and property in the crop remain in the owner of the land. Adams v. McKesson's Ex'x, 53 Pa. St. 81; Appling v. Odom, 46 Ga. 583.

[169] Walker v. Fitts, 24 Pick. (Mass.) 191; Creel v. Kirkham, 47 Ill. 344; De Mott v. Hagerman, 8 Cow. (N. Y.) 220; Dinehart v. Wilson, 15 Barb. (N. Y.) 595; Wilber v. Sisson, 53 Barb. (N. Y.) 258; Edgar v. Jewell, 34 N. J. Law, 259. And see Wood v. Noack, 84 Wis. 398, 54 N. W. 785; Caswell v. Districh, 15 Wend. (N. Y.) 379; Jones v. Durrer, 96 Cal. 95, 30 Pac. 1027; Lowe v. Miller, 3 Grat. (Va.) 205; Moser v. Lower, 48 Mo. App. 85. The usual incidents of a tenancy in common attach to such holdings. McLaughlin v. Salley, 46 Mich. 219, 9 N. W. 256; Otis v. Thompson, 1 Hill & D. (N. Y.) 131; Daniels v. Brown, 34 N. H. 454; Ferrall v. Kent, 4 Gill (Md.) 209; Hurd v. Darling, 14 Vt. 214. For tenancy in common, see post, p. 335.

[170] Walworth v. Jenness, 58 Vt. 670, 5 Atl. 887; Yates v. Kinney, 19 Neb. 275, 27 N. W. 132; Alwood v. Ruckman, 21 Ill. 200; Dixon v. Niccolls, 39 Ill. 372; Jackson v. Brownell, 1 Johns. (N. Y.) 267; Johnson v. Hoffman, 53 Mo. 504. Cf. Barry v. Smith, 69 Hun, 88, 23 N. Y. Supp. 261; Rich v. Hobson, 112 N. C. 79, 16 S. E. 931. The right of the landlord to the crop attaches only

sult of such an agreement which will hold good in all cases. The intention of the parties is in every instance to be given full effect.[171] But if the owner is to receive a definite amount of grain or other produce, not confined to crops grown on the premises, he receives it as lessor.[172]

TENANCIES AT WILL.

86. A tenancy at will is a letting of land to be held so long as neither party chooses to terminate it.

SAME—CREATION.

87. Tenancies at will are created:

(a) By a letting for an indefinite period, not in a form to pass a freehold, and without a reservation of rent.

(b) By express agreement.

(c) By implication of law.

A tenancy at will is where a person is in possession of land let to him to hold at the will of the lessor. The tenancy, however, is one at the will of either party. A general letting without limitation as to duration of a term (not being in a form to pass an estate of freehold), or a mere permission to enter and occupy, creates a tenancy at will, provided no rent is reserved. The reservation of a rent raises a presumption that the tenancy is from year to year.

---

on delivery. Burns v. Cooper, 31 Pa. St. 426; Caswell v. Districh, 15 Wend. (N. Y.) 379; Butterfield v. Baker, 5 Pick. (Mass.) 522; Alwood v. Ruckman, 21 Ill. 200; Dixon v. Niccolls, 39 Ill. 384; McLellan v. Whitney, 65 Vt. 510, 27 Atl. 117. But see Moulton v. Robinson, 27 N. H. 550; Horseley v. Moss, 5 Tex. Civ. App. 341, 23 S. W. 1115; Gray v. Robinson (Ariz.) 33 Pac. 712; Consolidated Land & Irrigation Co. v. Harvley (S. D.) 63 N. W. 904. The rent is only due at harvest time. Lamberton v. Stouffer, 55 Pa. St. 284; Cobel v. Cobel, 8 Pa. St. 342. But see Dixon v. Niccolls, 39 Ill. 372.

[171] Dixon v. Niccolls, 39 Ill. 384, 386; Lewis v. Lyman, 22 Pick. (Mass.) 437; Armstrong v. Bicknell, 2 Lans. (N. Y.) 216; Moulton v. Robinson, 27 N. H. 550. But see Birmingham v. Rogers, 46 Ark. 254.

[172] Hoskins v. Rhodes, 1 Gill & J. (Md.) 266; Newcomb v. Ramer, 2 Johns. (N. Y.) 421, note; Dockham v. Parker, 9 Greenl. (Me.) 137. And see Caruthers v. Williams, 58 Mo. App. 100.

A tenancy at will may, of course, be created by express agreement, even with a reservation of rent, if apt words are employed.[173] It also arises by implication of law. In such cases the entry is usually for some other purpose than to create a tenancy. Thus one who enters under a contract to purchase, and remains after the negotiation has fallen through, becomes a tenant at will.[174] So a vendor or lessor, by continuing in possession, may become a tenant at will.[175]

SAME—INCIDENTS.

88. The principal incidents of a tenancy at will are the following:

(a) The tenant is entitled to emblements, unless he terminates the tenancy himself.

(b) He must not commit waste.

(c) His interest cannot be sold on execution.

---

[173] Leake, Land. 208. Cf. Doe v. Cox, 11 Q. B. 122.

[174] Doe v. Chamberlaine, 5 Mees. & W. 14; Doe v. Miller, 5 Car. & P. 595; Gould v. Thompson, 4 Metc. (Mass.) 224; Manchester v. Doddridge, 3 Ind. 360. Entry under a parol contract to purchase creates a tenancy at will. Hall v. Wallace, 88 Cal. 434, 26 Pac. 360. But if the sale is not consummated, by fault of the vendee, he becomes a mere trespasser, and liable only in tort for the mesne profits. Prentice v. Wilson, 14 Ill. 91; Howard v. Shaw, 8 Mees. & W. 118; Smith v. Stewart, 6 Johns. (N. Y.) 46; Clough v. Hosford, 6 N. H. 231; Bell v. Ellis' Heirs, 1 Stew. & P. (Ala.) 294; Glascock v. Robards, 14 Mo. 350. A tenancy at will arises when possession is taken under an agreement for a lease, Childers v. Lee (N. M.) 25 Pac. 781; Weed v. Lindsay, 88 Ga. 686, 15 S. E. 836; Mayor, etc., of Thetford v. Tyler, 8 Q. B. 95; or under a parol lease for more than the time allowed by the statute of frauds, Jennings v. McComb, 112 Pa. St. 518, 4 Atl. 812; Talamo v. Spitzmiller, 120 N. Y. 37, 23 N. E. 980. But if rent is paid the holding is from year to year. Doe v. Amey, 12 Adol. & E. 476; Barlow v. Wainwright, 22 Vt. 88.

[175] Howard v. Merriam, 5 Cush. (Mass.) 563; Bennett v. Robinson, 27 Mich. 26; Tarlotting v. Bokern, 95 Mo. 541, 8 S. W. 547; Brooks v. Hyde, 37 Cal. 366; Sherburne v. Jones, 20 Me. 70; Currier v. Earl, 13 Me. 216. So of a debtor remaining in possession after execution sale. Nichols v. Williams, 8 Cow. (N. Y.) 13. But see Tucker v. Byers, 57 Ark. 215, 21 S. W. 227; Groome v. Almstead, 101 Cal. 425, 35 Pac. 1021.

§ 89)   TENANCIES AT WILL—TERMINATION.   157

If the tenant at will puts an end to the relation of lessor and lessee, he is not entitled to emblements,[176] but he is so entitled when the lessor causes the termination of the tenancy.[177] The tenant's interest is forfeited for waste.[178] Estates at will are chattel interests, but cannot be sold on execution.[179]

SAME—TERMINATION.

89. A tenancy at will may be terminated at any time by either party without notice, except:
EXCEPTIONS—(a) The parties may agree to give notice.
(b) In some states, notice is required by statute.

At common law, the parties to a tenancy at will terminate it at any time either one chooses to do so, and without giving any previous notice of such intention to the other party. The parties may, of course, by agreement, provide for any kind of a notice they choose, and for any length of time before terminating the tenancy. The statutes of many states now require a notice before a tenancy at will can be terminated.[180] Where such notice is not required, and the parties have not stipulated for one, either landlord or tenant may put an end to the tenancy by almost any act which shows such an intention.[181] Any assertion by the lessor of his right to possession terminates the tenancy.[182] An assignment by

---

[176] Carpenter v. Jones, 63 Ill. 517.

[177] Sherburne v. Jones, 20 Me. 70; Davis v. Thompson, 13 Me. 209; Simpkins v. Rogers, 15 Ill. 397; Harris v. Frink, 49 N. Y. 24.

[178] Daniels v. Bond, 21 Pick. (Mass.) 367; Phillips v. Covert, 7 Johns. (N. Y.) 1; Rapallo, J., in Harris v. Frink, 49 N. Y. 33. And see Perry v. Carr, 44 N. H. 118.

[179] 1 Stim. Am. St. Law, § 1344; 2 Shars. & B. Lead. Cas. Real Prop. 169.

[180] The length of notice required ranges from a few days to three months. 1 Stim. Am. St. Law, § 2051; 2 Shars. & B. Lead. Cas. Real Prop. 177. Cf. Morgan v. Powers, 83 Hun, 298, 31 N. Y. Supp. 954.

[181] 2 Tayl. Landl. & Ten. (8th Ed.) § 44; 1 Wood, Landl. & Ten. (2d Ed.) 67. But see Parker v. Constable, 3 Wils. 25; Jackson v. Bryan, 1 Johns. (N. Y.) 322. Death of either party terminates the tenancy. James v. Dean, 11 Ves. 383; Rising v. Stannard, 17 Mass. 282; Manchester v. Doddridge, 3 Ind. 360; Say v. Stoddard, 27 Ohio St. 478. But the tenant has a reasonable time to remove his property. Ellis v. Paige, 1 Pick. (Mass.) 43.

[182] Such as selling the premises, Howard v. Merriam, 5 Cush. (Mass.) 563;

the tenant of his interest destroys the tenancy, at the landlord's option.[183]

TENANCIES FROM YEAR TO YEAR.

90. A tenancy from year to year is a letting of land for an indefinite number of fixed periods.

SAME—CREATION.

91. A tenancy from year to year arises whenever there is a reservation of rent in a letting which would otherwise be a tenancy at will, except:

EXCEPTION—In a few states, by statute, a general letting creates a tenancy from year to year, unless a contrary intention is expressed.

Estates from year to year [184] include those from quarter to quarter,[185] month to month,[186] and so on; the length of the periods be-

---

Jackson v. Aldrich, 13 Johns. (N. Y.) 106; Curtis v. Galvin, 1 Allen (Mass.) 215; or leasing them, Clark v. Wheelock, 99 Mass. 14; Hildreth v. Conan, 10 Metc. (Mass.) 298; Kelly v. Waite, 12 Metc. (Mass.) 300; Groustra v. Bourges, 141 Mass. 7, 4 N. E. 623. So does a demand of possession, Doe v. M'Kaeg, 10 Barn. & C. 721; Den v. Howell, 7 Ired. (N. C.) 496; or acts which would otherwise be trespass, Turner v. Doe, 9 Mees. & W. 643; as an entry upon the land, Moore v. Boyd, 24 Me. 242.

[183] Cooper v. Adams, 6 Cush. (Mass.) 87; Packard v. Railway Co., 46 Ill. App. 244; Den v. Howell, 7 Ired. (N. C.) 496. And see Hersey v. Chapin, 162 Mass. 176, 38 N. E. 442. A denial of the landlord's title will, at his option, terminate the tenancy. Willison v. Watkins, 3 Pet. 43; Currier v. Earl, 13 Me. 216; Farrow's Heirs v. Edmundson, 4 B. Mon. (Ky.) 605; Harrison v. Middleton, 11 Grat. (Va.) 527; Fusselman v. Worthington, 14 Ill. 135.

[184] "From term to term" would be a more accurate designation of these tenancies, but the practice is otherwise. In many states there are statutes which raise presumptions as to the kind of a tenancy which arises in the absence of express contract, from a general occupancy. 1 Stim. Am. St. Law, § 2002.

[185] City of San Antonio v. French, 80 Tex. 575, 16 S. W. 440.

[186] Anderson v. Prindle, 23 Wend. (N. Y.) 616; Sebastian v. Hill, 51 Ill. App. 272; Lehman v. Nolting, 56 Mo. App. 549; Rogers v. Brown, 57 Minn. 223, 58 N. W. 981; Backus v. Sternberg, 59 Minn. 403, 61 N. W. 335. See, also, Cox v. Bent, 5 Bing. 185; Tress v. Savage, 4 El. & Bl. 36.

§ 91)   TENANCIES FROM YEAR TO YEAR—CREATION.   159

ing measured by the time for which rent is reserved.[187] They are, in effect, tenancies which continue until one of the parties takes the steps requisite to put an end to the relation.[188] By the early common law, all tenancies for an indefinite period were at will, but, to prevent the harsh effects often caused by their being terminable without notice, the rulings of the courts and statutory enactments have changed most of them into tenancies from year to year.[189] The principal distinction is that a reservation of rent makes a general letting a tenancy from year to year,[190] which, without a rent reserved, is at will;[191] that is, a tenancy from year to year arises from a general letting with a reservation of rent,[192] or when possession is taken under a void lease.[193] If no rent is

[187] In some states, tenancy from year to year does not exist. 1 Stim. Am. St. Law, § 2005.

[188] People v. Darling, 47 N. Y. 666; Lesley v. Randolph, 4 Rawle (Pa.) 123. A tenancy may be created to continue from year to year for two years. It may be determined at the end of a year by notice, and terminates at the end of two years without notice. Doe v. Smaridge, 7 Q. B. 957.

[189] 1 Wood, Landl. & Ten. (2d Ed.) 85; 1 Tayl. Landl. & Ten. (8th Ed.) 62.

[190] See ante, p. 155. But cf. Richardson v. Langridge, 4 Taunt. 128.

[191] Herrell v. Sizeland, 81 Ill. 457; Cheever v. Pearson, 16 Pick. (Mass.) 266; Burns v. Bryant, 31 N. Y. 453; Sarsfield v. Nealey, 50 Barb. (N. Y.) 245; Cross v. Upson, 17 Wis. 638; Amick v. Brubaker, 101 Mo. 473, 14 S. W. 627; Williams v. Deriar, 31 Mo. 13; Le Tourneau v. Smith, 53 Mich. 473, 19 N. W. 151; Blanchard v. Bowers, 67 Vt. 403, 31 Atl. 848; Den v. Humphries, 3 Ired. (N. C.) 362. And see Murray v. Cherrington, 99 Mass. 229; Sanford v. Johnson, 24 Minn. 172; Goodenow v. Allen, 68 Me. 308.

[192] Second Nat. Bank v. O. E. Merrill Co., 69 Wis. 501, 34 N. W. 514; Hunt v. Morton, 18 Ill. 75; Ganson v. Baldwin, 93 Mich. 217, 53 N. W. 171; Lesley v. Randolph, 4 Rawle (Pa.) 123. But see Union Depot Co. v. Chicago, K. & N. Ry. Co., 113 Mo. 213, 20 S. W. 792; Salomon v. O'Donnell (Colo. App.) 36 Pac. 893.

[193] Coudert v. Cohn, 118 N. Y. 309, 23 N. E. 298; Brant v. Vincent, 100 Mich. 426, 59 N. W. 169; Hosli v. Yokel, 58 Mo. App. 169; Koplitz v. Gustavus, 48 Wis. 48, 3 N. W. 754; Bateman v. Maddox, 86 Tex. 546, 26 S. W. 51; Rosenblat v. Perkins, 18 Or. 156, 22 Pac. 598. So, too, a tenancy from year to year may arise by holding over after the expiration of an estate for years. If the acts of the parties show an intention to continue the relation of landlord and tenant, the provisions of the old lease will govern, as far as they are applicable. Ashhurst v. Phonograph Co., 166 Pa. St. 357, 31 Atl. 116; Patterson v. Park, 166 Pa. St. 25, 30 Atl. 1041; Kleespies v. McKenzie, 12 Ind. App. 404, 40 N. E. 648; Johnson v. Doll, 11 Misc. Rep. 345, 32 N. Y. Supp. 132; Conway

reserved originally, the actual payment of rent will make the holding one from year to year.[194]

SAME—INCIDENTS.

92. The principal incidents of estates from year to year are the following:
  (a) The tenant may take estovers.
  (b) He is entitled to emblements when the landlord terminates the tenancy.
  (c) He must repair.
  (d) The interests of the parties are assignable.

The incidents of estates from year to year are for the most part the same as of estates for years.[195] The tenant is entitled to estovers, and to emblements, when the tenancy is terminated by the landlord,[196] but not when the tenant terminates it. The tenant's duty to repair extends to keeping the premises wind and water tight.[197] Either party may assign his interest,[198] and on the death of the tenant his interest goes to his personal representative.[199] After the termination of the tenancy has been fixed by notice, it becomes, in effect, equal to a term of years which has nearly expired.[200]

v. Starkweather, 1 Denio (N. Y.) 113; Hyatt v. Griffiths, 17 Q. B. 505; Amsden v. Atwood, 67 Vt. 289, 31 Atl. 448; Voss v. King, 38 W. Va. 607, 18 S. E. 762. But see Campau v. Michell (Mich.) 61 N. W. 890; Chicago & S. E. Ry. Co. v. Perkins, 12 Ind. App. 131, 38 N. E. 487; Montgomery v. Willis (Neb.) 63 N. W. 794; Goldsbrough v. Gable, 49 Ill. App. 554.

[194] Jackson v. Bradt, 2 Caines (N. Y.) 169; Lesley v. Randolph, 4 Rawle (Pa.) 123; Rich v. Bolton, 46 Vt. 84; Chamberlin v. Donahue, 45 Vt. 50; Roe v. Lees, 2 W. Bl. 1171; Richardson v. Langridge, 4 Taunt. 128. But see Brant v. Vincent, 100 Mich. 426, 59 N. W. 169.

[195] Washb. Real Prop. (5th Ed.) § 637.

[196] 2 Tayl. Landl. & Ten. (8th Ed.) § 134; Kingsbury v. Collins, 4 Bing. 202.

[197] 2 Wood. Landl. & Ten. (2d Ed.) 992; 1 Tayl. Landl. & Ten. (8th Ed.) 401. As to waste by a tenant from year to year, see 2 Wood, Landl. & Ten. (2d Ed.) 992; Torriano v. Young, 6 Car. & P. 8.

[198] Botting v. Martin, 1 Camp. 317; Cody v. Quarterman, 12 Ga. 386.

[199] Doe v. Porter, 3 Term R. 13; Cody v. Quarterman, 12 Ga. 386; Pugsley v. Aikin, 11 N. Y. 494.

[200] 1 Washb. Real Prop. (5th Ed.) 637.

SAME—TERMINATION.

93. A tenancy from year to year may be terminated by either party by a notice given six months before the end of any year, and by a notice equal to the length of the periods when the tenancy is for periods of six months or less. But these rules do not apply when a different notice has been provided for:

(a) By agreement of the parties.
(b) By statute, as is the case in some states.

By the common law, to terminate a tenancy from year to year there must be a six-months notice given by the party wishing to terminate the tenancy. This notice must be so given that the six months will expire at the end of a year.[201] Most cases hold that notice equal to the length of the periods is requisite in case of tenancies measured by shorter periods.[202] The time of notice is in many states regulated by statute,[203] and any time may be fixed by the agreement of the parties.[204] The time when the tenancy is to expire must be clearly indicated, and this must be at the end of one of the periods.[205] Unless otherwise provided by statute, or the

---

[201] Doe v. Watts, 7 Term R. 83; Jackson v. Bryan, 1 Johns. (N. Y.) 322; Den v. Drake, 14 N. J. Law, 523; Morehead v. Watkyns, 5 B. Mon. (Ky.) 228; Critchfield v. Remaley, 21 Neb. 178, 31 N. W. 687; Right v. Darby, 1 Term R. 159; Bessell v. Landsberg, 7 Q. B. 638. But see Logan v. Herrou, 8 Serg. & R. (Pa.) 459.

[202] Steffens v. Earl, 40 N. J. Law, 128; Sanford v. Harvey, 11 Cush. (Mass.) 93; Prescott v. Elm, 7 Cush. (Mass.) 346. And see Gruenewald v. Schaales, 17 Mo. App. 324; Doe v. Hazell, 1 Esp. 94.

[203] See 1 Stim. Am. St. Law, § 2052; 2 Shars. & B. Lead. Cas. Real Prop. 200.

[204] Woolsey v. Donnelly, 52 Hun, 614, 5 N. Y. Supp. 238.

[205] Brown v. Kayser, 60 Wis. 1, 18 N. W. 523; Hunter v. Frost, 47 Minn. 1, 49 N. W. 327; Finkelstein v. Herson, 55 N. J. Law, 217, 26 Atl. 688; Steffens v. Earl, 40 N. J. Law, 128; Logan v. Herron, 8 Serg. & R. (Pa.) 459; Prescott v. Elm, 7 Cush. (Mass.) 346; Baker v. Adams, 5 Cush. (Mass.) 99; Sanford v. Harvey, 11 Cush. (Mass.) 93. But see Currier v. Barker, 2 Gray (Mass.) 224.

agreement of the parties, the notice required to terminate an estate from year to year need not be in writing,[206] but it must be certain and definite.[207] The notice should be personally served.[208] Although the tenancy comes to an end at the expiration of the notice,[209] yet the parties may waive the effect, and continue the relation. This may be done by express agreement,[210] or by acts showing such intention;[211] for instance, acceptance by the landlord of rent accruing after the expiration of the notice.[212]

LETTING OF LODGINGS.

94. A letting of lodgings, where the owner of the house retains possession and control, creates only a contract relation.

The hiring of furnished apartments creates a tenancy from year to year; that is, the holding is from week to week, or from month to month, according to the periods at which rent is payable, when the terms of the demise are indefinite.[213] The relation of

[206] Timmins v. Rowlinson, 3 Burrows, 1603, 1 W. Bl. 533; Doe v. Crick, 5 Esp. 196; Eberlein v. Abel, 10 Ill. App. 626.

[207] Doe v. Morphett, 7 Q. B. Div. 577; Doe v. Smith, 5 Adol. & E. 350; Ayres v. Draper, 11 Mo. 548; Steward v. Harding, 2 Gray (Mass.) 335; Granger v. Brown, 11 Cush. (Mass.) 191; Hanchett v. Whitney, 1 Vt. 311; Huyser v. Chase, 13 Mich. 102.

[208] Doe v. Williams, 6 Barn. & C. 41; Jackson v. Baker, 10 Johns. (N. Y.) 270. But see Walker v. Sharpe, 103 Mass. 154; Bell v. Bruhn, 30 Ill. App. 300; Doe v. Dunbar, Moody & M. 10. Notice to a subtenant is not sufficient. Pleasant v. Benson, 14 East, 234. It is sufficient, however, if actual knowledge of the notice is shown, for the required length of time. Alford v. Vickery, Car. & M. 280.

[209] Hoske v. Gentzlinger, 87 Hun, 3, 33 N. Y. Supp. 747.

[210] Supplee v. Timothy, 124 Pa. St. 375, 16 Atl. 864.

[211] See Tuttle v. Bean, 13 Metc. (Mass.) 275; Doe v. Palmer, 16 East, 53.

[212] Goodright v. Cordwent, 6 Term R. 219; Collins v. Canty, 6 Cush. (Mass.) 415; Prindle v. Anderson, 19 Wend. (N. Y.) 391. Mere demand of rent so accruing will not necessarily be a waiver, Blyth v. Dennett, 13 C. B. 178; nor acceptance of rent due before the expiration of the notice, Kimball v. Rowland, 6 Gray (Mass.) 224; Norris v. Morrill, 43 N. H. 213. And see Graham v. Dempsey, 169 Pa. St. 460, 32 Atl. 408; Conner v. Jones, 28 Cal. 59.

[213] 1 Wood, Landl. & Ten. (2d Ed.) 132.

landlord and tenant does not arise, however, when there is merely a letting of lodgings.[214] The test of such a holding is the retention by the owner of full possession and control of the house. In such cases there is only a contract relation.[215] The letting of "French flats" does not come within this rule, however; for they are separate dwellings, and the hirer is a lessee, even though there is but a single outer door to the building.[216] Reasonable notice is all that is necessary to terminate the holding of a lodger.[217]

TENANCIES AT SUFFERANCE.

95. A tenancy at sufferance is a holding of lands after the expiration of a previous right to possession.

SAME—CREATION.

96. For the creation of a tenancy at sufferance, the tenant must have come in by agreement, and not as a trespasser, and he must hold without agreement.

Where there is a holding over by one whose right to occupy has expired, a tenancy at sufferance arises;[218] for instance, when a tenant for years continues in possession after the end of his term.[219] Such person must have come in originally by agreement,[220] and

---

[214] As to who are lodgers, see Morton v. Palmer, 51 Law J. Q. B. 7.

[215] Wilson v. Martin, 1 Denio (N. Y.) 602; White v. Maynard, 111 Mass. 250; Cochrane v. Tuttle, 75 Ill. 361.

[216] Musgrave v. Sherwood, 53 How. Prac. (N. Y.) 311; Young v. City of Boston, 104 Mass. 95; Porter v. Merrill, 124 Mass. 534; Swain v. Mizner, 8 Gray (Mass.) 182.

[217] 1 Tayl. Landl. & Ten. (8th Ed.) 78; 1 Wood, Landl. & Ten. (2d Ed.) 133. But see Huffell v. Armitstead, 7 Car. & P. 56.

[218] Doe v. Hull, 2 Dosol. & R. 38; Russell v. Fabyan, 34 N. H. 218; Eichengreen v. Appel, 44 Ill. App. 19; Uridias v. Morrell, 25 Cal. 31.

[219] Jackson v. Parkhurst, 5 Johns. (N. Y.) 128; Moore v. Smith (N. J. Sup.) 29 Atl. 159. So a subtenant, after the termination of the original lease, Simkin v. Ashurst, 1 Cromp., M. & R. 261; or a tenant at will, whose estate has been terminated, Co. Litt. 57b; Benedict v. Morse, 10 Metc. (Mass.) 223. And see Kinsley v. Ames, 2 Metc. (Mass.) 29.

[220] Cook v. Norton, 48 Ill. 20. So the entry must be lawful. Reckhow v. Schanck, 43 N. Y. 448; Cunningham v. Holton, 55 Me. 33.

not by operation of law, as a guardian, who becomes a trespasser by continuing to hold his ward's land after the ward is of age.[221] There is no tenancy at sufferance where the holding over is by agreement, express or implied.[222] And a tenant at sufferance may at any time become a tenant at will, or from year to year, by agreement with the landlord.[223] Payment of rent makes the holding a tenancy from year to year.[224]

SAME—INCIDENTS.

97. The principal incidents of a tenancy at sufferance are the following:
  (a) The tenant is estopped to deny the landlord's title.
  (b) He is not liable for rent.
  (c) He is not entitled to emblements.

The relation of landlord and tenant obtains in a tenancy at sufferance only to the extent that the tenant is not permitted to deny the landlord's title.[225] A tenant at sufferance is not liable for rent,[226] the landlord's remedy being an action for use and occupation.[227] The tenant cannot claim emblements, though the landlord terminates the tenancy before the tenant has harvested his crop.

---

[221] Johnson, J., in Livingston v. Tanner, 14 N. Y. 69.

[222] Johnson v. Carter, 16 Mass. 443. But see Landis' Appeal. 13 Wkly. Notes Cas. 226.

[223] Hoffman v. Clark, 63 Mich. 175, 29 N. W. 695; Emmons v. Scudder, 115 Mass. 367; Den v. Adams, 12 N. J. Law, 99.

[224] Schuyler v. Smith, 51 N. Y. 309.

[225] Griffin v. Sheffield, 38 Miss. 390; Jackson v. McLeod, 12 Johns. (N. Y.) 182.

[226] 2 Bl. Comm. 150; Flood v. Flood, 1 Allen (Mass.) 217; Delano v. Montague, 4 Cush. (Mass.) 42. In several states he is made liable for rent by statute. 1 Stim. Am. St. Law, § 2022. And see Cofran v. Shepard, 148 Mass. 582, 20 N. E. 181. In many states a tenant who holds over when his interest is ended, and after demand by the landlord, becomes liable for statutory penalties. 1 Stim. Am. St. Law, § 2060; 2 Shars. & B. Lead. Cas. Real Prop. 123.

[227] Ibbs v. Richardson, 9 Adol. & E. 849; National Oil-Refining Co. v. Bush, 88 Pa. St. 335; Hogsett v. Ellis, 17 Mich. 351. But see Merrill v. Bullock, 105 Mass. 486.

SAME—TERMINATION.

98. A tenancy at sufferance may be terminated at any time, by either party, without notice, except:

EXCEPTION—In some states a notice is required by statute.

A tenant at sufferance is entitled to no notice to quit,[228] except where statutes give the right.[229] The landlord can enter at any time, and thereafter treat him as a trespasser, though he cannot so treat him before entry or demand.[230] There is a conflict in the authorities as to whether the landlord may expel the tenant by force. This is because such an expulsion may be criminal.[231] The better opinion seems to be that the tenant may be expelled, notwithstanding the fact that the landlord may become criminally liable therefor.[232] But there will be no civil action for personal injuries suffered unless more force than necessary was used.[233]

LICENSES.

99. A license is an authority to do specified acts on the land of the licensor. A license is not an estate, and is not assignable.

Licenses are created either by express agreement, or by implication. An example of the latter is the implied license granted by

[228] Hooton v. Holt, 139 Mass. 54, 29 N. E. 221; Jackson v. Parkhurst, 5 Johns. (N. Y.) 128; Jackson v. McLeod, 12 Johns. (N. Y.) 182; Livingston v. Tanner, 14 N. Y. 64. And see Kinsley v. Ames, 2 Metc. (Mass.) 29; Benedict v. Morse, 10 Metc. (Mass.) 223.

[229] 1 Stim. Am. St. Law, § 2050; 2 Shars. & B. Lead. Cas. Real Prop. 146. And see Minard v. Burtis, 83 Wis. 267, 53 N. W. 509.

[230] 1 Wood, Landl. & Ten. (2d Ed.) 26; 1 Tayl. Landl. & Ten. (8th Ed.) 74.

[231] See Clark, Cr. Law, 345.

[232] Wilde v. Cantillon, 1 Johns. Cas. (N. Y.) 123; Overdeer v. Lewis, 1 Watts & S. (Pa.) 90; Allen v. Kelly, 17 R. I. 731, 24 Atl. 776; Stearns v. Sampson, 59 Me. 568; Todd v. Jackson, 26 N. J. Law, 525. Contra, Reeder v. Purdy, 41 Ill. 279; Wilder v. House, 48 Ill. 279; Dustin v. Cowdry, 23 Vt. 631.

[233] Sampson v. Henry, 13 Pick. (Mass.) 36; Adams v. Adams, 7 Phila. (Pa.) 160.

all business men to the public to enter their stores or offices during business hours.[234] So a license may be implied from other acts or representations of the owner of land.[235] A license gives no interest in the land, but is merely a personal right.[236] It differs from a lease of land chiefly in that the owner retains the possession of the land.[237] The effect of a license is to permit the licensee to do acts upon the land which would otherwise be trespass.[238] The grant of a license carries with it the right to use the necessary and proper means to accomplish the object.[259] The licensee is liable for all damages resulting from negligent or improper execution of the license,[240] but not for damages which are the natural result of the acts licensed.[241] A license is purely personal, and cannot be assigned by the licensee.[242] So a sale of the land by the

[234] Gibson, C. J., in Gowen v. Exchange Co., 5 Watts & S. (Pa.) 143. And see Kay v. Railroad Co., 65 Pa. St. 273; Cutler v. Smith, 57 Ill. 252; Sterling v. Warden, 51 N. H. 217; Heaney v. Heeney, 2 Denio (N. Y.) 625. So a sale of chattels gives an implied license to enter to remove them. Wood v. Manley, 11 Adol. & E. 34.

[235] So there is an implied license to go to a private residence to make social calls. Martin v. Houghton, 145 Barb. (N. Y.) 258; Adams v. Freeman, 12 Johns. (N. Y.) 408. And see Gibson v. Leonard, 143 Ill. 182, 32 N. E. 182.

[236] Mumford v. Whitney, 15 Wend. (N. Y.) 381; Dolittle v. Eddy, 7 Barb. (N. Y.) 74; Ex parte Coburn, 1 Cow. (N. Y.) 568; Blaisdell v. Railroad Co., 51 N. H. 483.

[237] Funk v. Haldeman, 53 Pa. St. 229. And see Holladay v. Power Co., 55 Ill. App. 463; Kabley v. Light Co., 102 Mass. 392; Smith v. Simons, 1 Root (Conn.) 318; Haywood v. Fulmer (Ind. Sup.) 32 N. E. 574. A license differs from an easement in not being created by deed. Morse v. Copeland, 2 Gray (Mass.) 302; Mumford v. Whitney, 15 Wend. (N. Y.) 381; Wiseman v. Lucksinger, 84 N. Y. 31; Wolfe v. Frost, 4 Sandf. Ch. (N. Y.) 72; Foot v. New Haven & Northampton Co., 23 Conn. 214. Cf. W. U. Tel. Co. v. Bullard, 67 Vt. 272, 31 Atl. 286.

[238] Blaisdell v. Railroad Co., 51 N. H. 483; Sterling v. Warden, Id. 217; Miller v. Railway Co., 6 Hill (N. Y.) 61.

[239] Com. v. Rigney, 4 Allen (Mass.) 316; Driscoll v. Marshall, 15 Gray (Mass.) 62. As to employ men to help remove a ponderous object from the licensor's land. Sterling v. Warden, 51 N. H. 217.

[240] Selden v. Canal Co., 29 N. Y. 634; Eaton v. Winnie, 20 Mich. 156; McKnight v. Ratcliff, 44 Pa. St. 156; Dean v. McLean, 48 Vt. 412.

[241] Selden v. Canal Co., 29 N. Y. 634.

[242] Mumford v. Whitney, 15 Wend. (N. Y.) 381; Mendenhall v. Klinck, 51

licensor puts an end to the authority.[243] A license is also terminated by the death of either party,[244] and by the expiration of the time for which it is given.[245]

SAME—REVOCATION OF LICENSES.

100. Licenses are revocable in all cases, except:
EXCEPTIONS—(a) **When coupled with an interest.**
(b) **When affecting only an easement of the licensor.**
(c) **In some states, when the licensee, relying on the license, has erected improvements on the licensor's land.**

The general rule is that licenses are revocable.[246] But a license coupled with an interest is not. For example, if personal property is sold, and a license given to go upon the land of the vendor to remove the goods, it cannot be revoked.[247] A license to do acts which obstruct or destroy an easement of the licensor cannot be revoked after it is executed.[248] There is great conflict in the cases as to the power to revoke a license after the licensee has expended money or erected improvements on the land of the licensor.[249]

N. Y. 246; Jackson v. Babcock, 4 Johns. (N. Y.) 418; De Haro v. U. S., 5 Wall. 599.

[243] Blaisdell v. Railroad Co., 51 N. H. 483.

[244] Prince v. Case, 10 Conn. 375; Blaisdell v. Railroad Co., 51 N. H. 483. Or by the insanity of the licensor. Berry v. Potter (N. J. Ch.) 29 Atl. 323.

[245] Detroit & B. Plank-Road Co. v. Detroit S. Ry. Co., 103 Mich. 585, 61 N. W. 880. A conveyance of the land by the licensor will be a revocation. Jackson v. Babcock, 4 Johns. (N. Y.) 418.

[246] Baldwin v. Taylor, 166 Pa. St. 507, 31 Atl. 250; Bass v. Power Co., 111 N. C. 439, 16 S. E. 402; Minneapolis W. Ry. v. Minneapolis & St. L. Ry. Co., 58 Minn. 128, 59 N. W. 983; Kremer v. Railway Co., 51 Minn. 15, 52 N. W. 977.

[247] Wood v. Manley, 11 Adol. & E. 34; Carter v. Wingard, 47 Ill. App. 296. But see Fish v. Capwell (R. I.) 29 Atl. 840. It may be lost by abandonment. Patterson v. Graham, 164 Pa. St. 234, 30 Atl. 247.

[248] Dyer v. Sanford, 9 Metc. (Mass.) 395; Morse v. Copeland, 2 Gray (Mass.) 302; Addison v. Hack, 2 Gill (Md.) 221.

[249] As holding such a license irrevocable, see Flickinger v. Shaw, 87 Cal. 126, 25 Pac. 268; Grimshaw v. Belcher, 88 Cal. 217, 26 Pac. 84; Nowlin v. Whipple, 120 Ind. 596, 22 N. E. 669; Saucer v. Keller, 129 Ind. 475, 28 N. E.

The difficulty is that if the license is held irrevocable the effect is to transfer an interest in realty by parol.[250] Some courts hold the licensor estopped to revoke.[251] Others require him to place the licensee in statu quo, by compensating him for his expenditures.[252] Where the license is in the nature of a contract for a definite time, the licensee is protected by awarding him specific performance.[253] In some states all licenses are held to be revocable,[254] and the licensee without remedy.[255]

1117; Messick v. Railway Co., 128 Ind. 81, 27 N. E. 419; McBroom v. Thompson, 25 Or. 559, 37 Pac. 57; Duke of Devonshire v. Eglin, 14 Beav. 530; Rerick v. Kern, 14 Serg. & R. 267; White v. Railway Co., 139 N. Y. 19, 34 N. E. 887. Cf. City Council of Augusta v. Burum, 93 Ga. 68, 19 S. E. 820. Contra, Village of Dwight v. Hayes, 150 Ill. 273, 37 N. E. 218; Crosdale v. Lanigan, 129 N. Y. 604, 29 N. E. 824; Lawrence v. Springer, 49 N. J. Eq. 289, 24 Atl. 933; Minneapolis Mill Co. v. Minneapolis & St. L. Ry. Co., 51 Minn. 304, 53 N. W. 639.

[250] Wood v. Leadbitter, 13 Mees. & W. 838; Bridges v. Purcell, 1 Dev. & B. (N. C.) 492.

[251] Risien v. Brown, 73 Tex. 135, 10 S. W. 661; School Dist. v. Lindsay, 47 Mo. App. 134; Rhodes v. Otis, 33 Ala. 578. But see Churchill v. Hulbert, 110 Mass. 42; Lake Erie & W. R. Co. v. Kennedy, 132 Ind. 274, 31 N. E. 943.

[252] Addison v. Hack, 2 Gill (Md.) 221; Woodbury v. Parshley, 7 N. H. 237. The licensee has in all cases a reasonable time to remove his property from the land after the revocation. Barnes v. Barnes, 6 Vt. 388.

[253] Williamston & T. Ry. Co. v. Battle, 66 N. C. 540; Veghte v. Power Co., 19 N. J. Eq. 142.

[254] Carley v. Gitchell (Mich.) 62 N. W. 1003; Shirley v. Crabb, 138 Ind. 200, 37 N. E. 130. A ticket to a theater is a license, and may be revoked, McCrea v. Marsh, 12 Gray (Mass.) 211; or to a horse race, Wood v. Leadbitter, 13 Mees. & W. 838.

[255] Pitzman v. Boyce, 111 Mo. 387, 19 S. W. 1104; Crockett v. Railway Co., 80 Tex. 292, 16 S. W. 38; Hodgkins v. Farrington, 150 Mass. 19, 22 N. E. 73; Shirley v. Crabb, 138 Ind. 200, 37 N. E. 130; Fentiman v. Smith, 4 East, 107.

CHAPTER VIII.

ESTATES AS TO QUALITY—ON CONDITION—ON LIMITATION.

  101. Estates as to Quality.
  102. Estates on Condition.
103–104. Conditions Precedent and Subsequent.
  105. Void Conditions.
  106. Termination of Estates on Condition.
  107. Who can Enforce a Forfeiture.
  108. Estates on Limitation.
  109. Base or Determinable Fees.

ESTATES AS TO QUALITY.

101. Estates as to quality are either absolute or qualified. Qualified estates will be treated under the following heads:
 (a) **Estates on condition** (p. 169).
 (b) **Estates on limitation** (p. 177).

ESTATES ON CONDITION.

102. An estate on condition is one which is created or defeated, enlarged or diminished, on the happening of a contingency.

102a. A mortgage is an estate on condition (p. 180).

Heretofore estates have been considered with reference to their quantity. The consideration of estates as to their quality introduces a new principle of classification. Estates may be absolute, as has been the case with the estates considered in the preceding chapters, or they may be qualified or defeasible; that is, any of the estates as to quantity, estates in fee simple, life estates, etc., may be held subject to a condition.[1] The owner of an estate in lands

---

[1] That the statute of quia emptores does not render conditions attached to fees invalid, see Gray, Perp. 19; Van Rensselaer v. Ball, 19 N. Y. 100; Van Rensselaer v. Dennison, 35 N. Y. 393. The words usually employed in an in-

may have his interest modified or destroyed by the happening of an event which may or may not occur.² So the vesting of an estate may depend on such a contingency. The existence of such a condition does not affect the owner's powers of dealing with his estate. He may use the land, sell or mortgage it, just as if his interest was absolute instead of qualified.³ But any alienation or incumbrance will be defeated if the estate is terminated by the happening of the contingency on which it depends.⁴

SAME—CONDITIONS PRECEDENT AND SUBSEQUENT.

103. Conditions are divided into two classes:
  (a) Conditions precedent.
  (b) Conditions subsequent.

strument of conveyance to create a condition are "on condition," "provided," "so that," and "if it so happen." Co. Litt. 203b, 204b; Stanley v. Colt, 5 Wall. 119; Bigelow, C. J., in Rawson v. School Dist., 7 Allen (Mass.) 125; Gray v. Blanchard, 8 Pick. (Mass.) 284; Warner v. Bennett, 31 Conn. 468; Hooper v. Cummings, 45 Me. 359. The use of these words is not essential, for a condition may be raised by any words which show such an intention. Hapgood v. Houghton, 22 Pick. (Mass.) 480; Attorney General v. Merrimack Manuf'g Co., 14 Gray (Mass.) 586; Watters v. Bredin, 70 Pa. St. 235; Underhill v. Railroad Co., 20 Barb. (N. Y.) 455; Gibert v. Peteler, 38 N. Y. 165; Worman v. Teagarden, 2 Ohio St. 380; Wheeler v. Walker, 2 Conn. 196; Bacon v. Huntington, 14 Conn. 92. But see Packard v. Ames, 16 Gray (Mass.) 327; Jennings v. O'Brien, 47 Iowa, 392; Gadberry v. Sheppard, 27 Miss. 203. Nor does the use of the words given in all cases raise a condition. Episcopal City Mission v. Appleton, 117 Mass. 326; Sohier v. Trinity Church, 109 Mass. 1; Chapin v. Harris, 8 Allen (Mass.) 594. Estates on condition may be created by will or deed. Wheeler v. Walker, 2 Conn. 196. In some states it is provided by statute that conditions merely nominal shall be disregarded. 1 Stim. Am. St. Law, § 1361; 1 Shars. & B. Lead. Cas. Real Prop. 136.

² Mr. Washburn treats in this connection the interest which is acquired in land by its sale for debts, and calls such an interest an "estate on execution." Where, as in most states, the debtor has a period within which he can redeem, the interest acquired by the execution purchaser is liable to be defeated by such a redemption. 2 Washb. Real Prop. (5th Ed.) 31.

³ Taylor v. Sutton, 15 Ga. 103; Shattuck v. Hastings, 99 Mass. 23; Chapman v. Pingree, 67 Me. 198. But see Siegel v. Lauer, 148 Pa. St. 236, 23 Atl. 996.

⁴ Gray v. Blanchard, 8 Pick. (Mass.) 284.

103a. Conditions precedent are conditions which must be fulfilled before the estate to which they are attached can vest.

104. Conditions subsequent are conditions upon the fulfillment or nonfulfillment of which an estate previously vested is defeated.

Conditions precedent are such as go before the estate to which they apply; that is, the happening of the event provided for in the condition creates an estate, or enlarges one already existing.[5] If the contingency does not occur, the conveyance containing the condition never becomes operative.[6] A condition subsequent diminishes or destroys the estate to which it is attached.[7] The distinc-

[5] Upington v. Corrigan, 69 Hun, 320, 23 N. Y. Supp. 451; In re Howard's Estate, 5 Misc. Rep. 295, 25 N. Y. Supp. 1111; Richards v. Richards, 90 Iowa, 606, 58 N. W. 926; Hurd v. Shelton, 64 Conn. 496, 30 Atl. 766; Moore v. Perry, 42 S. C. 369, 20 S. E. 200; City of Stockton v. Weber, 98 Cal. 433, 33 Pac. 332; Tilley v. King, 109 N. C. 461, 13 S. E. 936. Examples of conditions precedent are: That a devise shall not vest until the devisee's debts are paid. Nichol v. Levy, 5 Wall. 433. That a child shall be born to the grantees. Karchner v. Hoy, 151 Pa. St. 383, 25 Atl. 20. That a devisee shall abstain from the use of intoxicating liquors for five years. In re Steven's Estate, 164 Pa. St. 209, 30 Atl. 243. That the grantee support the grantors during their lives. Lashley v. Souder (N. J. Ch.) 24 Atl. 919.

[6] Donohue v. McNichol, 61 Pa. St. 73; Mizell v. Burnett, 4 Jones (N. C.) 249.

[7] Rice v. Railroad Corp., 12 Allen (Mass.) 141; Harrison v. Foote (Tex. Civ. App.) 30 S. W. 838; Mills v. Railway Co., 10 Wash. 520, 39 Pac. 246; Reichenbach v. Railway Co., 10 Wash. 357, 38 Pac. 1126; Bank of Suisun v. Stark, 106 Cal. 202, 39 Pac. 531; Ritchie v. Railway Co., 55 Kan. 36, 39 Pac. 718; McClure v. Cook, 39 W. Va. 579, 20 S. E. 612. But see Baker v. Mott, 78 Hun, 141, 28 N. Y. Supp. 968; Kilpatrick v. Baltimore, 81 Md. 179, 31 Atl. 805; Studdard v. Wells, 120 Mo. 25, 25 S. W. 201; Elyton Land Co. v. South & North Alabama R. Co., 100 Ala. 396, 14 South. 207. The following are conditions subsequent: Devise of real estate to a town for the purpose of building a school house, "provided it is built within 100 rods of the place where the meetinghouse now stands." Hayden v. Stoughton, 5 Pick. (Mass.) 528. Devise to A. and his heirs, if he live to 21. Edwards v. Hammond, 3 Lev. 132. Devise to one provided he supports the grantor for life. Spaulding v. Hallenbeck, 39 Barb. (N. Y.) 79. That the land conveyed shall not be used for certain purposes, Hayes v. Railway Co., 51 N. J. Eq. 345, 27 Atl. 648; Odessa Imp. & Irr. Co. v. Dawson, 5 Tex. Civ. App. 487, 24 S. W. 576;

tion between conditions precedent and subsequent depends on the intention of the parties, and the attendant circumstances.[8] The courts, however, construe conditions as subsequent, rather than as precedent.[9] Thus it is held, in cases of doubt, that an estate vests at once, subject to be defeated by nonperformance of conditions, rather than that the grantee must perform before he is entitled to the estate.[10] The time within which the condition must be performed is usually expressly stated, but, if it is not, the grantee has a reasonable time,[11] or his whole life, according to the circumstances of the case, and the probable intention of the parties.[12]

SAME—VOID CONDITIONS.

105. Conditions which are illegal or impossible of performance are void, and when precedent, prevent estates depending on them from vesting, but, when subsequent, are of no effect.

Not all conditions which may be imposed are valid. A condition may be invalid because its performance is impossible,[13] or because it is illegal. The illegal conditions most frequently imposed are those in restraint of alienation and of marriage. Conditions in restraint of alienation will be discussed in a subsequent chapter.[14]

Hopkins v. Smith, 162 Mass. 444, 38 N. E. 1122 (but see Jenks v. Pawlowski, 98 Mich. 110, 56 N. W. 1105); or shall be built upon only in a certain manner, Ogontz Land & Imp. Co. v. Johnson, 168 Pa. St. 178, 31 Atl. 1008; Reardon v. Murphy, 163 Mass. 501, 40 N. E. 854.

[8] Underhill v. Railway Co., 20 Barb. (N. Y.) 455; Burnett v. Strong, 26 Miss. 116; Jones v. Railway Co., 14 W. Va. 514.

[9] Martin v. Ballou, 13 Barb. (N. Y.) 119; Bell Co. v. Alexander, 22 Tex. 350. And see Webster v. Cooper, 14 How. 488; Taylor v. Mason, 9 Wheat. 325; Sackett v. Mallory, 1 Metc. (Mass.) 355; Tallman v. Snow, 35 Me. 342.

[10] Finlay v. Mitchell, 3 Pet. 346.

[11] Hamilton v. Elliott, 5 Serg. & R. 375; Allen v. Howe, 105 Mass. 241. As in a case where he is to pay off a mortgage, no time being expressed. Rowell v. Jewett, 69 Me. 293.

[12] Marshall, C. J., in Finlay v. King, 3 Pet. 346.

[13] A condition may become impossible by act of God, Thomas v. Howell, 1 Salk. 170; or by act of law, Board of Com'rs of Mahoning Co. v. Young, 8 C. C. A. 27, 59 Fed. 96; Scovill v. McMahon, 62 Conn. 378, 26 Atl. 479.

[14] See post, 394. Jenner v. Gurner, 16 Ch. Div. 188; Hodgson v. Halford,

§ 105) VOID CONDITIONS. 173

General conditions in restraint of marriage are void. Partial restrictions on marriage, such as not to marry a named person, or any one of a named family, are generally sustained, even without a limitation over, but are narrowly interpreted;[15] and so as to conditions against marrying without consent of parents, or of those who stand in loco parentis.[16]

Where a gift or devise is made to an unmarried woman, with a condition that the estate shall cease upon marriage, the condition, being in restraint of marriage, is said to be against the policy of the law; and it has generally been held that, unless the instrument imposing the condition says also to whom the estate shall go in case of disobedience, the condition is deemed to have been inserted in terrorem only, and may be disregarded. Here is a distinction against the heirs of the donor, and in favor of the strangers whom he may name by way of conditional limitation, for which no good reason can be given, but which seems to be well established, for the cases are very rare in which the condition without limitation over has been deemed valid.[17]

A void condition, if precedent, prevents the estate depending on it from vesting at all;[18] but, if subsequent, the condition is of no effect, and the estate becomes absolute.[19]

[11] Ch. Div. 959; Graydon's Ex'rs v. Graydon, 23 N. J. Eq. 229; Phillips v. Ferguson, 85 Va. 509, 8 S. E. 241; Hogan v. Curtin, 88 N. Y. 162; Kelly v. Monck, 3 Ridg. App. 205; Maddox v. Maddox's Adm'r, 11 Grat. (Va.) 804.

[15] Phillips v. Ferguson, 85 Va. 509, 8 S. E. 241.

[16] Denfield, Petitioner, 156 Mass. 265, 30 N. E. 1018.

[17] Otis v. Prince, 10 Gray (Mass.) 581. For other conditions which have been held illegal, see Newkerk v. Newkerk, 2 Caines (N. Y.) 345; Brown v. Peck, 1 Eden, 140; Wren v. Bradley, 2 De Gex & S. 49.

[18] Roundel v. Currer, 2 Brown, Ch. 67; Priestley v. Holgate, 3 Kay & J. 286. But see In re Moore, 39 Ch. Div. 116.

[19] Thomas v. Howell, 1 Salk. 170; Lowther v. Cavendish, 1 Eden, 99; Peyton v. Bury, 2 P. Wms. 626; Collett v. Collett, 35 Beav. 312; Booth v. Meyer, 38 Law T. (N. S.) 125; O'Brien v. Barkley, 78 Hun, 609, 28 N. Y. Supp. 1049; Hoss v. Hoss, 140 Ind. 551, 39 N. E. 255.

SAME—TERMINATION OF ESTATES ON CONDITION.

106. An estate on conditions subsequent is not determined by a breach of condition until there has been an entry, except:

EXCEPTIONS—(a) Commencing an action of ejectment is equivalent to an entry.

(b) If the grantor is in possession, the forfeiture is complete when a breach occurs.

106a. An estate on condition may come to a natural termination without a breach of the condition.

The breach of a condition gives the grantor an option to terminate the estate.[20] This he can do only by an entry,[21] but no previous demand of performance is necessary.[22] The technical action of ejectment has the same effect, because an entry is held to be confessed.[23] When, however, the grantor is in possession at the time a breach occurs, the forfeiture is complete without any act on his

---

[20] It is not necessary that any damage to the grantor has been caused by the breach. Sioux City & St. P. R. Co. v. Singer, 49 Minn. 301, 51 N. W. 905. The grantee cannot insist that he has forfeited his estate by a breach. Davenport v. Reg., 3 App. Cas. 115; Rede v. Farr, 6 Maule & S. 121. As to what constitutes a breach, see Razor v. Razor, 142 Ill. 375, 31 N. E. 678; Rose v. Hawley, 141 N. Y. 366, 36 N. E. 335; City of Quincy v. Attorney General, 160 Mass. 431, 35 N. E. 1066; Hurto v. Grant, 90 Iowa, 414, 57 N. W. 899; Crawford v. Wearn, 115 N. C. 540, 20 S. E. 724; Madigan v. Burns (N. H.) 29 Atl. 454.

[21] Warner v. Bennett, 31 Conn. 468; Bowen v. Bowen, 18 Conn. 535; Hubbard v. Hubbard, 97 Mass. 188; Guild v. Richards, 16 Gray (Mass.) 309; Adams v. Lindell, 5 Mo. App. 197; Kenner v. Contract Co., 9 Bush (Ky.) 202; Tallman v. Snow, 35 Me. 342; Sperry v. Sperry, 8 N. H. 477; Memphis & C. R. Co. v. Neighbors, 51 Miss. 412; Phelps v. Chesson, 12 Ired. (N. C.) 194. But see Schlesinger v. Railroad Co., 152 U. S. 444, 14 Sup. Ct. 647. A right of entry need not be expressly reserved. Gray v. Blanchard, 8 Pick. (Mass.) 284; Thomas v. Record, 47 Me. 500.

[22] Hamilton v. Elliott, 5 Serg. & R. (Pa.) 375.

[23] Ruch v. Rock Island, 97 U. S. 693; Jackson v. Crysler, 1 Johns. Cas. (N. Y.) 125; Cornelius v. Den, 26 N. J. Law, 376. After seeking to enforce a forfeiture by ejectment, the lessor cannot sue for rent subsequently accruing. Jones v. Carter, 15 Mees. & W. 718.

part,[24] unless he elects otherwise.[25] The performance of a condition may be waived, and a breach would then not work a forfeiture.[26] Or after a breach has occurred the forfeiture may be waived by express agreement, or by acts of the grantor having the same effect;[27] for instance, accepting performance of the condition at a subsequent time.[28] Such waiver cuts off the right to claim a forfeiture,[29] but not the right to an action for a breach of covenant in a proper case.[30] Mere delay to enforce the forfeiture will not constitute a waiver,[31] and acquiescence in a breach will not bar the right to a forfeiture for a subsequent breach.[32] Equity sometimes relieves from forfeitures for breach of conditions, where the breach is due to accident, and the grantor can be compensated by damages as by the payment of a sum of money with interest.[33] But other-

[24] Sheaffer v. Sheaffer, 37 Pa. St. 525; President, etc., of Lincoln & K. Bank v. Drummond, 5 Mass. 322; Collins v. Riley, 44 N. H. 9; Willard v. Olcott, 2 N. H. 120; Guffy v. Hukill, 34 W. Va. 49, 11 S. E. 754; Andrews v. Senter, 32 Me. 394. But see Stone v. Ellis, 9 Cush. (Mass.) 95.

[25] Andrews v. Senter, 32 Me. 394; Willard v. Olcott, 2 N. H. 120.

[26] Jones v. Doe, 2 Ill. 276; Lamb v. Miller, 18 Pa. St. 448; Petro v. Cassiday, 13 Ind. 289; Boone v. Tipton, 15 Ind. 270; Jones v. Railway Co., 14 W. Va. 514; Jones v. Walker, 13 B. Mon. (Ky.) 163. So a license excusing a breach as to part of the premises discharges the whole condition. Leede's & Crompton's Case, Godb. 93. But see 7 Am. Law Rev. 616, criticising Dumpor's Case, 4 Coke, 119b, and Brummell v. Macpherson, 14 Ves. 173.

[27] Barrie v. Smith, 47 Mich. 130, 10 N. W. 168; Sharon Iron Co. v. City of Erie, 41 Pa. St. 341; Hubbard v. Hubbard, 97 Mass. 188; Pennant's Case, 3 Coke, 64a.

[28] An acceptance of rent accruing after the breach is a waiver, Jackson v. Allen, 3 Cow. (N. Y.) 220; Goodright v. Davids, 2 Cowp. 803; or a demand for rent so accruing, Camp v. Scott, 47 Conn. 366; or bringing an action for it, Dendy v. Nicholl, 4 C. B. (N. S.) 376.

[29] Lehigh Coal & Nav. Co. v. Early, 162 Pa. St. 338, 29 Atl. 736.

[30] Dickey v. M'Cullough, 2 Watts & S. 88.

[31] But may be strong evidence of it. Ludlow v. Railway Co., 12 Barb. (N. Y.) 440; Hooper v. Cummings, 45 Me. 359.

[32] Doe v. Jones, 5 Exch. 498; Doe v. Bliss, 4 Taunt. 735; Ambler v. Woodbridge, 9 Barn. & C. 376; Flower v. Peck, 1 Barn. & Adol. 428; Bleeker v. Smith, 13 Wend. (N. Y.) 530; Price v. Norwood, 4 Hurl. & N. 512; Crocker v. Society, 106 Mass. 489; Gillis v. Bailey, 21 N. H. 149.

[33] Rogan v. Walker, 1 Wis. 527; Sanborn v. Woodman, 5 Cush. (Mass.) 36; Hancock v. Carlton, 6 Gray (Mass.) 39; Carpenter v. Westcott, 4 R. I. 225; Henry v. Tupper, 29 Vt. 358.

wise equity will not give relief. Therefore, for breaches of conditions to repair, to insure, etc., equity will leave the parties to their remedies at law.[34]

An estate on condition may expire under the form of the limitation, the same as an absolute estate. Thus, where a life estate is given on condition, the death of the life tenant puts an end to the estate, though the condition has not been broken.

SAME—WHO CAN ENFORCE A FORFEITURE.

107. An entry to enforce a forfeiture for a breach of condition can be made only by the grantor, or his heirs, except:

EXCEPTION—The assignee of a reversion after a leasehold estate can enforce covenants which run with the land.

The right of entry for breach of condition, to defeat an estate, cannot be reserved to a third person, but only to the grantor and his heirs.[35] Neither can it be assigned or transferred with a grant of the reversion.[36] As to whether a devisee of the grantor may enforce a forfeiture, the cases are conflicting.[37] But these rules do

[34] Dunklee v. Adams, 20 Vt. 415; Green v. Bridges, 4 Sim. 96; Hill v. Barclay, 18 Ves. 56. Equity, on the other hand, will not enforce a forfeiture. Fetter, Eq. 112.

[35] Fonda v. Sage, 46 Barb. (N. Y.) 109; Van Rensselaer v. Ball, 19 N. Y. 100; Marwick v. Andrews, 25 Me. 525. Contra, McKissick v. Pickle, 16 Pa. St. 140. And see Pinkum v. City of Eau Claire, 81 Wis. 301, 51 N. W. 550. Nor can a stranger raise the question of a forfeiture. Board of Education of Normal School Dist. v. Trustees of First Baptist Church of Normal, 63 Ill. 204; Schulenberg v. Harriman, 21 Wall. 44; Rector, etc., of King's Chapel v. Pelham, 9 Mass. 501; Smith v. Brannan, 13 Cal. 107; Dewey v. Williams, 40 N. H. 222; Norris v. Milner, 20 Ga. 563.

[36] Vermont v. Society for Propagation of Gospel, 2 Paine, 545, Fed. Cas. No. 16,920; Rice v. Railroad Co., 12 Allen (Mass.) 141; Nicoll v. Railroad Co., 12 N. Y. 121; Underhill v. Railroad Co., 20 Barb. (N. Y.) 455; Warner v. Bennett, 31 Conn. 468.

[37] As holding that he cannot, see Den v. Railroad Co., 26 N. J. Law, 13. Contra, Austin v. Cambridgeport Parish, 21 Pick. (Mass.) 215.

§ 108) ESTATES ON LIMITATION. 177

not apply to leasehold estates, for the assignee of the reversion can enforce covenants which run with the land.[38]

ESTATES ON LIMITATION.

108. An estate on limitation is one which is created to continue until the happening of a contingency upon which it comes to an end without an entry.

The phrase, "words of limitation," has already been used to designate the clause in a conveyance which determines the quantity of an estate. For instance, the use of the words "heirs of his body," in creating a fee tail. The meaning of the word "limitation" in estates on limitation is practically the same; that is, it defines the time at which an estate comes to an end.[39] An estate on limitation is therefore one which is determined, rather than defeated, by the happening of a contingency, "as when land is granted to a man so long as he is parson of Dale, or while he continues unmarried, or until out of the rents and profits he shall have made £500, and the like."[40] The words used to create an estate on limitation all refer to time; for example, "until," "while," "during," "as long as," etc.[41] But neither the use of these words, nor their absence, is conclusive.[42]

An estate on limitation differs from one on condition chiefly in that no entry is necessary to terminate the former; for it comes to

---

[38] See ante, p. 147.

[39] These are by some writers called "estates on conditional limitation." That term is also used to designate estates which vest on the happening of a contingency. As we shall see later, such estates can take effect only as springing uses, post, p. 299, or executory devises, post, p. 300. Still other writers use "conditional limitation" as meaning the event which terminates an estate, rather than the estate which is terminated, or the one coming into existence on the happening of the event. See Leake, Prop. Land, 214.

[40] 2 Bl. Comm. 155.

[41] Henderson v. Hunter, 59 Pa. St. 335; Bennett v. Robinson, 10 Watts (Pa.) 348; Vanatta v. Brewer, 32 N. J. Eq. 268.

[42] Chapin v. Harris, 8 Allen (Mass.) 594; Owen v. Field, 102 Mass. 90; Wheeler v. Walker, 2 Conn. 196; Camp v. Cleary, 76 Va. 140; Stearns v. Godfrey, 16 Me. 158.

REAL PROP.—12

an end absolutely by the happening of the contingency, because it was not created for any longer time. Conditions cut short an existing estate. Limitations do not, but mark its natural end. A third person may take advantage of the happening of the event on which the estate is limited to end.[43]

SAME—BASE OR DETERMINABLE FEES.

109. A base or determinable fee is a fee simple, which may be terminated by the happening of a contingency.

A fee which is liable to be terminated by a limitation is called a base or determinable fee. This is the kind of an estate which passed when a tenant in tail attempted to convey a fee simple by a conveyance which barred the issue under the entail, but not the remainder-men. The grantee took a fee determinable on the extinction of the issue who were entitled under the entail.[44] A base fee dependent on a collateral condition may also arise by express provision of the conveyance.[45] The most usual cases at the present time are where land is granted for a specified use, to revert to the grantor when that use ceases.[46] Mr. Gray, however, takes the position that a valid determinable fee cannot be created since the stat-

---

[43] Scheetz v. Fitzwater, 5 Pa. St. 126; Henderson v. Hunter, 59 Pa. St. 335; Ashley v. Warner, 11 Gray (Mass.) 43; Miller v. Levi, 44 N. Y. 489; Stearns v. Godfrey, 16 Me. 158. An example of the importance of this distinction arises in connection with conditions in restraint of marriage. Thus an estate to A. until she marries is valid as an estate on limitation. But an estate to A. provided she does not marry is void because it is an estate on condition, and the condition is in restraint of marriage. Bennett v. Robinson, 10 Watts (Pa.) 348; Mann v. Jackson, 84 Me. 400, 24 Atl. 886; Jones v. Jones, 1 Q. B. Div. 279.

[44] For a discussion of these base fees, see Challis, Real Prop. 264.

[45] Leonard v. Burr, 18 N. Y. 96.

[46] As for school purposes, Board of Education of Village of Van Wert v. Inhabitants of Village of Van Wert, 18 Ohio St. 221; or for public streets, Gebhardt v. Reeves, 75 Ill. 301; Helm v. Webster, 85 Ill. 116. And see People v. White, 11 Barb. (N. Y.) 26; Morris Canal & Banking Co. v. Brown, 27 N. J. Law, 13; Henderson v. Hunter, 59 Pa. St. 335; Bolling v. Mayor, etc., 8 Leigh (Va.) 224; Thayer v. McGee, 20 Mich. 195.

§ 109) BASE OR DETERMINABLE FEES. 179

ute of quia emptores.[47] The point has not, it seems, been raised in any reported case, but the validity of such limitation has been assumed without question.[48]

[47] Since the grantor has only a possibility of reverter. Gray, Perp. 19. Contra, Graves, Real Prop. 135.

[48] See cases cited in the preceding notes, and Siegel v. Lauer, 148 Pa. St. 236, 23 Atl. 996; Sheetz v. Fitzwater, 5 Pa. St. 126; Pennsylvania R. Co. v. Parke, 42 Pa. St. 31; Rowland v. Warren, 10 Or. 129.

CHAPTER IX.

ESTATES AS TO QUALITY (Continued)—MORTGAGES.

110. Mortgage Defined.
111. Parties to a Mortgage.
112. Nature of a Mortgage.
113. What may be Mortgaged.
114. Form of a Mortgage.
115. Rights and Liabilities of Mortgagor and Mortgagee.
116. Nature of Mortgagor's Estate.
117. Possession of Mortgaged Premises.
118. Insurance on Mortgaged Premises.
119. Accounting by the Mortgagee.
120. Debits.
121. Credits.
122. Annual Rests.
123–124. Subrogation.
125–126. Assignment of the Equity of Redemption.
127–129. Assignment of the Mortgage.
130. Priority of Mortgages and Other Conveyances.
131. Registration.
132. Discharge of a Mortgage.
133–134. Performance.
135. Merger.
136. Redemption.
137. Form of Discharge.
138–139. Foreclosure.
140. Kinds of Foreclosure.

MORTGAGE DEFINED.

110. A mortgage is a conveyance of land as security, and is usually in the form of an estate on condition subsequent.

The discussion of mortgages in this chapter includes only mortgages of real property. A more specific definition of a mortgage than a conveyance of land as a security would exclude some of the many forms which such a conveyance may assume.[1] A mortgage

[1] 1 Jones, Mortg. (5th Ed.) § 16. And see Draper v. Draper, 71 Hun, 349, 24 N. Y. Supp. 1127; Harriman v. Light Co., 163 Mass. 85, 39 N. E. 1004; Ander-

§ 110) MORTGAGE DEFINED. 181

is an estate on condition subsequent; that is, the mortgagee has an estate which is defeated by the performance of the condition by the mortgagor. The condition is usually for the payment of money, but it may be for the support of the mortgagee,[2] or for his indemnity against liability.[3] When a mortgage is given to secure a debt, it is usually accompanied by a note or other evidence of indebtedness, though this is not essential to the validity of the mortgage; for there may be a valid mortgage without any personal liability on the part of the mortgagor, for example, when the creditor's only right to payment is out of the mortgaged property,[4] or when the mortgage is given to secure a debt of another than the mortgagor.[5] It will not be presumed that the mortgagor is personally liable, from the mere execution of the mortgage.[*] The time when the debt is due should be fixed with certainty, so that it may be known when the mortgagor is in default.[6] A stipulation providing that,

---

son v. Smith, 103 Mich. 446, 61 N. W. 778; Baum v. Gaffy, 45 Ill. App. 138; Doescher v. Doescher (Minn.) 63 N. W. 736; Leiweke v. Jordan, 59 Mo. App. 619; Merrill v. Hurley (S. D.) 62 N. W. 958; Strouse v. Cohen, 113 N. C. 349, 18 S. E. 323.

[2] Soper v. Guernsey, 71 Pa. St. 219; Flanders v. Lamphear, 9 N. H. 201; Hoyt v. Bradley, 27 Me. 242; Austin v. Austin, 9 Vt. 420; Hiatt v. Parker, 29 Kan. 765. Unless otherwise provided, the obligation to support is a personal one, and cannot be assigned. Eastman v. Batchelder, 36 N. H. 141; Bethlehem v. Annis, 40 N. H. 34; Bryant v. Erskine, 55 Me. 153. But, contra, Joslyn v. Parlin, 54 Vt. 670. And see Bodwell Granite Co. v. Lane, 83 Me. 168, 21 Atl. 829.

[3] Lyle v. Ducomb, 5 Bin. (Pa.) 585; Gardner v. Webber, 17 Pick. (Mass.) 407; Commercial Bank v. Cunningham, 24 Pick. (Mass.) 270; Adams v. Niemann, 46 Mich. 135, 8 N. W. 719; Duncan v. Miller, 64 Iowa, 223, 20 N. W. 161.

[4] 1 Jones, Mortg. (5th Ed.) § 70; Hodgdon v. Shannon, 44 N. H. 572. As to description of the indebtedness, see Usher v. Skate Co., 163 Mass. 1, 39 N. E. 416; Merrill v. Elliott, 55 Ill. App. 34; Bowen v. Ratcliff, 140 Ind. 393, 39 N. E. 860; Harper v. Edwards, 115 N. C. 246, 20 S. E. 392.

[5] Chittenden v. Gossage, 18 Iowa, 157; New Orleans Canal & Banking Co. v. Hagan, 1 La. Ann. 62.

[*] 1 Jones, Mortg. (5th Ed.) § 678; Tusk v. Ridge, 41 N. Y. 201; Smith v. Rice, 12 Daly (N. Y.) 307; Coleman v. Van Rensselaer, 44 How. Prac. (N. Y.) 368.

[6] 1 Jones, Mortg. (5th Ed.) § 75. When the mortgage is to secure a note, the mortgagor is entitled to days of grace. Coffin v. Loring, 5 Allen (Mass.)

on default of payment of any installment of interest or principal, the whole debt shall become due, is valid.[7]

PARTIES TO A MORTGAGE.

111. The parties to a mortgage must be competent to convey and hold real property.

As to the parties who are competent to execute a mortgage,[8] it may be said that any one may be a mortgagor who has the capacity to transfer real property,[9] and any one may be a mortgagee who can hold real property.[10]

NATURE OF A MORTGAGE.

112. There are two theories as to the nature of a mortgage recognized in the different states:

(a) The common-law theory regards a mortgage as an estate in land, and the mortgagee as the owner of the land.

---

[153]. As to description of the mortgage debt, see Burt v. Gamble, 98 Mich. 402, 57 N. W. 261; Dunham v. Provision Co., 100 Mich. 75, 58 N. W. 627; Commercial Bank v. Weinberg, 70 Hun, 597, 25 N. Y. Supp. 235; Price v. Wood, 76 Hun, 318, 27 N. Y. Supp. 691; Snow v. Pressey, 85 Me. 408, 27 Atl. 272; Gleason v. Kinney's Adm'r, 65 Vt. 560, 27 Atl. 208; D'Oyly v. Capp, 99 Cal. 153, 33 Pac. 736.

[7] Grape Creek Coal Co. v. Farmers' Loan & Trust Co., 12 C. C. A. 350, 63 Fed. 891; Alabama & G. Manuf'g Co. v. Robinson, 6 C. C. A. 79, 56 Fed. 690; Owen v. Association, 55 Ill. App. 347; Dunn v. Sharpe, 9 Misc. Rep. 636, 30 N. Y. Supp. 353; New York Security & Trust Co. v. Saratoga Gas & Electric Light Co., 88 Hun, 569, 34 N. Y. Supp. 890; Osborne v. Ketcham, 76 Hun, 325, 27 N. Y. Supp. 694; Atkinson v. Walton, 162 Pa. St. 219, 29 Atl. 898; Morling v. Brownson, 37 Neb. 608, 56 N. W. 205; Swearingen v. Lahner (Iowa) 61 N. W. 431; Taylor v. Trust Co., 71 Miss. 694, 15 South. 121. And see Weber v. Huerstel, 11 Misc. Rep. 214, 32 N. Y. Supp. 1109. Cf., however, French v. Row, 77 Hun, 380, 28 N. Y. Supp. 849. No notice of election is necessary. Brown v. McKay, 151 Ill. 315, 37 N. E. 1037.

[8] As to personal capacity, see post, p. 381.

[9] 1 Jones, Mortg. (5th Ed.) § 102.

[10] 1 Jones, Mortg. (5th Ed.) § 131; Parker v. Lincoln, 12 Mass. 16. But see Thompson v. Holladay, 15 Or. 34, 14 Pac. 725.

(b) **The equitable or lien theory regards a mortgage as a mere security, and the mortgagee as having only a lien.**

The Common-Law Theory.

In the United States there are two theories as to the nature of a mortgage: One is that the mortgagee has an estate; the other, that he has only a lien. This difference is the result of the history of mortgage securities.[11] At common law the estate of the mortgagee became absolute on default of payment by the mortgagor.[12] This often resulted in injustice to both parties,—to the mortgagee, because he had no remedy to recover the balance of his debt, if the mortgaged property was inadequate; and to the mortgagor, because the value of the estate mortgaged was often greatly in excess of the amount of the debt secured. This inequality in the law was remedied by the courts of equity. They recognized a right in the mortgagor to redeem by paying the amount due, with interest; that is, the real intention of the parties to give a security was effectuated.[13] This right was termed an "equity of redemption." The mortgagee could cut off the mortgagor's right of redemption by appearing in court, and having a day set when the mortgagor must redeem, or lose the right to do so.[14]

The Equitable or Lien Theory.

In courts of equity the mortgagee's interest becomes absolute only after the foreclosure of the mortgagor's equity of redemption. The mortgagor's equity of redemption is recognized in all of the states: In some states the mortgagee is, as at common law, regarded as the owner,[15] while in others, either by statute or decisions of the courts,

---

[11] See Digby, Hist. Real Prop. (4th Ed.) 282, and 1 Jones, Mortg. (5th Ed.) § 1, for a description of the obsolete vivium vadium, and the Welsh mortgage.

[12] 1 Jones, Mortg. (5th Ed.) § 4.

[13] Id. § 10.

[14] Id. § 1538.

[15] Toomer v. Randolph, 60 Ala. 356; Welch v. Phillips, 54 Ala. 309; Knox v. Easton, 38 Ala. 345; Kannady v. McCarron, 18 Ark. 166; Chamberlain v. Thompson, 10 Conn. 243; Carroll v. Ballance, 26 Ill. 9; Nelson v. Pinegar, 30 Ill. 473 (but see Barrett v. Hinckley, 124 Ill. 32, 14 N. E. 863); M'Kim v. Mason, 3 Md. Ch. 186; Ewer v. Hobbs, 5 Metc. (Mass.) 1; Brown v. Cram,

it is held that the mortgagee has no estate in the mortgaged premises, but only a lien on them for the security of his debt.[16] In these states the mortgagor is considered the owner. Neither theory is entirely consistent, because both mortgagor and mortgagee are constantly recognized as having rights of ownership which they are permitted to defend in the courts.[17]

WHAT MAY BE MORTGAGED.

113. Any interest in realty which is subject to sale and assignment may be mortgaged.

As stated in the black-letter text, any interest in realty which is subject to sale or assignment may be mortgaged.[18] This interest may be either in possession or in expectancy.[19] So there may be

[1] N. H. 169; Kircher v. Schalk, 39 N. J. Law, 335; Hemphill v. Ross, 66 N. C. 477; State v. Ragland, 75 N. C. 12; Allen v. Everly, 24 Ohio St. 97; Rands v. Kendall, 15 Ohio, 671; Tryon v. Munson, 77 Pa. St. 250; Carpenter v. Carpenter, 6 R. I. 542; Henshaw v. Wells, 9 Humph. (Tenn.) 568; Hagar v. Brainerd, 44 Vt. 294; Lull v. Matthews, 19 Vt. 322; Faulkner's Adm'x v. Brockenbrough, 4 Rand. (Va.) 245. Modifications of the common-law theory, holding that the mortgagor is owner until breach, exist in some states. Doe v. Tunnell, 1 Houst. (Del.) 320; Hill v. Robertson, 24 Miss. 368; Johnson v. Houston, 47 Mo. 227; Woods v. Hilderbrand, 46 Mo. 284.

[16] McMillan v. Richards, 9 Cal. 365; Dutton v. Warschauer, 21 Cal. 609; McMahon v. Russell, 17 Fla. 698; Jordan v. Sayre, 29 Fla. 100, 10 South. 823; Vason v. Ball, 56 Ga. 268; Fletcher v. Holmes, 32 Ind. 497; Francis v. Porter, 7 Ind. 213; White v. Rittenmyer, 30 Iowa, 268; Chick v. Willetts, 2 Kan. 384; Woolley v. Holt, 14 Bush (Ky.) 788; Duclaud v. Rousseau, 2 La Ann. 168; Caruthers v. Humphrey, 12 Mich. 270; Adams v. Corriston, 7 Minn. 456 (Gil. 365); Gallatin Co. v. Beattie, 3 Mont. 173; Kyger v. Ryley, 2 Neb. 20; Hurley v. Estes, 6 Neb. 386; Hyman v. Kelly 1 Nev. 179; Jackson v. Willard, 4 Johns. (N. Y.) 41; Thompson v. Marshall, 21 Or. 171, 27 Pac. 957; Navassa Guano Co. v. Richardson, 26 S. C. 401. 2 S. E. 307; Wright v. Henderson, 12 Tex. 43; Wood v. Trask, 7 Wis. 566.

[17] 1 Jones, Mortg. (5th Ed.) § 14.

[18] Neligh v. Michenor, 11 N. J. Eq. 539; Miller v. Tipton, 6 Blackf. (Ind.) 238; Dorsey v. Hall, 7 Neb. 460. As to mortgages of homesteads, see ante, p. 124. That a pre-emption right, under the United States homestead laws, cannot be mortgaged, see Penn v. Ott, 12 La. Ann. 233; Gilbert v. Penn, Id. 235. Contra, Whitney v. Buckman, 13 Cal. 536.

[19] Wilson v. Wilson, 32 Barb. (N. Y.) 328; In re John and Cherry Sts., 19 Wend. (N. Y.) 659.

§ 113) WHAT MAY BE MORTGAGED. 185

a mortgage of a bond for title,[20] or of a right to possession under a contract for purchase,[21] or of an option to purchase.[22] A widow may mortgage her unassigned right of dower,[23] and a devisee may mortgage land devised to him in which he has a vested interest.[24] There may be a mortgage of a mortgage,[25] of an equitable right,[26] or of rents.[27] A mortgage of land covers the buildings and fixtures thereon, and a mortgage of a building includes the land on which it stands.[28] A mortgage may be made to cover subsequent improvements and future accessions,[29] such as crops to be planted.[30] So a mortgage may be given to cover after-acquired property,[31] subject, of course, to liens which may exist on the property at the time it is acquired.[32]

[20] Baker v. Colony, 45 Ill. 264; Crane v. Turner, 67 N. Y. 437.

[21] Bull v. Shepard, 7 Wis. 449; Sinclair v. Armitage, 12 N. J. Eq. 174.

[22] Bank of Louisville v. Baumeister, 87 Ky. 6, 7 S. W. 170.

[23] Mutual Life Ins. Co. of New York v. Shipman, 119 N. Y. 324, 24 N. E. 177.

[24] Drake v. Paige, 127 N. Y. 562, 28 N. E. 407. So an heir may mortgage his undivided interest. Carter v. McDaniel, 94 Ky. 564, 23 S. W. 507.

[25] Murdock v. Chapman, 9 Gray (Mass.) 156; Cutts v. Manufacturing Co., 18 Me. 190.

[26] Lincoln Bldg. & Sav. Ass'n v. Hass, 10 Neb. 581, 7 N. W. 327; Laughlin v. Braley, 25 Kan. 147; Wilson v. Wright, 91 Ga. 774, 18 S. E. 546.

[27] Van Rensselaer v. Dennison, 35 N. Y. 393.

[28] Wilson v. Hunter, 14 Wis. 683.

[29] Mitchell v. Winslow, 2 Story, 630, Fed. Cas. No. 9,673; Smithurst v. Edmunds, 14 N. J. Eq. 408.

[30] Van Hoozer v. Cory, 34 Barb. (N. Y.) 9; Arques v. Wasson, 51 Cal. 620; Jones v. Webster, 48 Ala. 109.

[31] Thompson v. Railroad Co., 132 U. S. 68, 10 Sup. Ct. 29; Central Trust Co. v. Kneeland, 138 U. S. 414, 11 Sup. Ct. 357; Parker v. Railroad Co., 33 Fed. 693; Omaha & St. L. Ry. Co. v. Wabash, St. L. & P. Ry. Co., 108 Mo. 298, 18 S. W. 1101; Frank v. Hicks (Wyo.) 35 Pac. 1025. But see Harriman v. Light Co., 163 Mass. 85, 39 N. E. 1004; Cook v. Prindle (Iowa) 63 N. W. 187; Paddock v. Potter, 67 Vt. 360, 31 Atl. 784; Grape Creek Coal Co. v. Farmers' Loan & Trust Co., 12 C. C. A. 350, 63 Fed. 891.

[32] Wood v. Manufacturing Co., 100 Ala. 326, 13 South. 948. And see Hobbs v. Trust Co., 15 C. C. A. 604, 68 Fed. 618; Patterson v. Trust Co. (Ky.) 30 S. W. 872.

FORM OF A MORTGAGE.

114. The ordinary form of a mortgage is that of an absolute conveyance with a defeasance clause. But a mortgage may be created:
- **(a) With a separate defeasance (p. 186).**
- **(b) With a parol defeasance (p. 187).**
- **(c) By a sale with an agreement to reconvey (p. 189).**
- **(d) By a deed of trust (p. 190).**
- **(e) By an instrument operating as an equitable mortgage, which may be:**
  - **(1) An agreement to give a mortgage (p. 190).**
  - **(2) An informal mortgage (p. 190).**
  - **(3) An assignment of a contract to purchase (p. 190).**
  - **(4) By deposit of title deeds, in a few states (p. 192).**
  - **(5) A vendor's lien (p. 192).**
  - **(6) A vendee's lien (p. 194).**

Under either theory as to the nature of a mortgage, the usual form is the same; that is, an absolute conveyance with a defeasance clause.[33] But no particular form is necessary. Whenever an instrument appears to have been intended for a mortgage, the courts will so construe it.[34] The defeasance clause may be in a separate instrument,[35] and this may be executed at a time subsequent to the execution of the conveyance.[36] Subsequent purchasers and grantees will be protected against such separate defeasance,

---

[33] As to execution of mortgages, see post, p. 414. For effect of alterations, see Clark, Cont. 686.

[34] Hughes v. Edwards, 9 Wheat. 489; Morris v. Nixon, 1 How. 118; Russell v. Southard, 12 How. 139; Gilson v. Gilson, 2 Allen (Mass.) 115; James v. Morey, 2 Cow. (N. Y.) 246; Clark v. Henry, Id. 324; Stoever v. Stoever, 9 Serg. & R. (Pa.) 434; Rogan v. Walker, 1 Wis. 527.

[35] Dubuque Nat. Bank v. Weed, 57 Fed. 513. Except in a few states where it is prohibited by statute, see 1 Stim. Am. St. Law, § 1856. And in some states the defeasance must be recorded, or the mortgagee takes nothing. See post, p. 218.

[36] Jeffery v. Hursh, 58 Mich. 246, 25 N. W. 176, and 27 N. W. 7; Waters v. Crabtree, 105 N. C. 394, 11 S. E. 240.

unless it is recorded, or they have notice thereof.[37] A separate defeasance may be canceled by a subsequent agreement to release, in which case the estate of the grantee becomes absolute.[38]

Parol Defeasance—Deed Absolute on Its Face.

In a court of law a grantor will not be permitted to show by parol evidence that his deed, absolute in form, was in fact a mortgage.[39] But courts of equity permit such parol defeasance to be established.[40] But a mortgage cannot be set up in this way against subsequent purchasers from the grantee, without notice,[41] though the mortgagee would be liable to account to the mortgagor either for the proceeds of the sale, or the value of the land.[42] Some courts say that the grantor will be permitted to establish a defeasance by parol only in cases of fraud, accident, or mistake.[43] But most courts grant this relief whenever necessary to effectuate the intention of the parties.[44] These cases are held not to be within the statute of

[37] Brown v. Dean, 3 Wend. (N. Y.) 208; Walton v. Cronly's Adm'r, 14 Wend. (N. Y.) 63; Dey v. Dunham, 2 Johns. Ch. (N. Y.) 182; Friedley v. Hamilton, 17 Serg. & R. (Pa.) 70.

[38] 1 Jones, Mortg. (5th Ed.) § 252.

[39] Webb v. Rice, 6 Hill (N. Y.) 219; Gates v. Sutherland, 76 Mich. 231, 42 N. W. 1112. Contra in some states. Tillson v. Moulton, 23 Ill. 648; Wilcox v. Bates, 26 Wis. 465; Plato v. Roe, 14 Wis. 453. And see Jones, Mortg. (5th Ed.) § 282, note 1.

[40] McArthur v. Robinson (Mich.) 62 N. W. 713; Morrow v. Jones, 41 Neb. 867, 60 N. W. 369; Dunton v. McCook (Iowa) 61 N. W. 977; Montgomery v. Beecher (N. J. Ch.) 31 Atl. 451; Ahern v. McCarthy, 107 Cal. 382, 40 Pac. 482. But see Fuller v. Trust Co., 157 Pa. St. 646, 28 Atl. 148. Contra, by statute, in some states. 1 Stim. Am. St. Law, § 1856; 1 Jones, Mortg. (5th Ed.) §§ 282, 312.

[41] Jackson v. Lawrence, 117 U. S. 679, 6 Sup. Ct. 915; Meehan v. Forrester, 52 N. Y. 277; Pancake v. Cauffman, 114 Pa. St. 113, 7 Atl. 67; Sweetzer v. Atterbury, 100 Pa. St. 22. But see Gibson v. Hutchins, 43 S. C. 287, 21 S. E. 250.

[42] Jackson v. Stevens, 108 Mass. 94; Heister v. Madeira, 3 Watts & S. (Pa.) 384; Boothe v. Fiest, 80 Tex. 141, 15 S. W. 799.

[43] Sprague v. Bond, 115 N. C. 530, 20 S. E. 709; Green v. Sherrod, 105 N. C. 197, 10 S. E. 986; Washburn v. Merrills, 1 Day (Conn.) 139; Brainerd v. Brainerd, 15 Conn. 575. And see Furguson v. Bond, 39 W. Va. 561, 20 S. E. 591.

[44] 1 Jones, Mortg. (5th Ed.) § 321; Sanborn v. Sanborn (Mich.) 62 N. W. 371; Emerson v. Atwater, 7 Mich. 12; Swetland v. Swetland, 3 Mich. 482; Klock v. Walter, 70 Ill. 416; Wynkoop v. Cowing, 21 Ill. 570; Workman v. Greening,

frauds, because that statute is never permitted to be made an instrument of fraud.[45] The test of the real character of the transaction is, in all cases, the intention of the parties.[46] This is shown by their acts. For instance, continued possession by the mortgagor,[47] and his payment of interest and taxes,[48] the continuance of the relation of debtor and creditor, and the retention of the evidence of debt by the grantee,[49] as well as inadequacy of price, all go to show that the conveyance was in fact a mortgage.[50] On the other hand, if the debt is canceled,[51] and the mortgagee takes possession and makes improvements, the presumption is almost conclusive that no mortgage was intended.* To permit the establishment of a parol defeasance, it is not necessary that the conveyance be made by the debtor,[52] since the grantee may have purchased at a foreclosure or execution sale on behalf of the one claiming to be mortgagor, and the purchaser have taken title in his own name for security.[53] It may also be shown by parol evidence that an assignment of a mortgage, or of a contract to purchase, absolute in

115 Ill. 477, 4 N. E. 385; Campbell v. Dearborn, 109 Mass. 130; Horn v. Keteltas, 46 N. Y. 605; Fiedler v. Darrin, 50 N. Y. 437; Rhines v. Baird, 41 Pa. St. 256; Plumer v. Guthrie, 76 Pa. St. 441; Rogan v. Walker, 1 Wis. 527; Wilcox v. Bates, 26 Wis. 465.

[45] Reigard v. McNeil, 38 Ill. 400; Landers v. Beck, 92 Ind. 49; Moore v. Wade, 8 Kan. 380; Klein v. McNamara, 54 Miss. 90; Sewell v. Price's Adm'r, 32 Ala. 97.

[46] Russell v. Southard, 12 How. 139; Darst v. Murphy, 119 Ill. 343, 9 N. E. 887; Workman v. Greening, 115 Ill. 477, 4 N. E. 385; Ingalls v. Atwood, 53 Iowa, 283, 5 N. W. 160; Lane v. Shears, 1 Wend. (N. Y.) 433; Cole v. Bolard, 22 Pa. St. 431.

[47] Campbell v. Dearborn, 109 Mass. 130.

[48] Boocock v. Phipard, 52 Hun, 614, 5 N. Y. Supp. 228.

[49] Ennor v. Thompson, 46 Ill. 214.

[50] Helm v. Boyd, 124 Ill. 370, 16 N. E. 85; Wilson v. Patrick, 34 Iowa, 362. But see Story v. Springer, 155 Ill. 25, 39 N. E. 570.

[51] Rue v. Dole, 107 Ill. 275; Ford v. Irwin, 18 Cal. 117.

*Woodworth v. Carman, 43 Iowa, 504.

[52] Jourdain v. Fox, 90 Wis. 99, 62 N. W. 936; Stoddard v. Whiting, 46 N. Y. 627; Carr v. Carr, 52 N. Y. 251.

[53] Ryan v. Dox, 34 N. Y. 307; Union Mut. Life Ins. Co. v. Slee, 123 Ill. 57, 12 N. E. 543; Phelan v. Fitzpatrick, 84 Wis. 240, 54 N. W. 614; Hoile v. Bailey, 58 Wis. 434, 17 N. W. 322.

§ 114)　　　FORM OF A MORTGAGE.　　　189

form, was intended as mere security.[54] But in all cases strict proof is required of the one who seeks to show that the transaction was a mortgage.[55] A judgment creditor, or other persons succeeding to the rights of the mortgagor, may show the true character of the transaction.[56] A parol defeasance may be extinguished by a subsequent agreement.[57]

Sale with Agreement to Reconvey.

A sale with an agreement to reconvey may be a mortgage,[58] or a conditional sale.[59] In a court of law it may be shown to be a mortgage, if the sale and the agreement are executed at the same time.[60] Courts of equity are more lenient, and sometimes permit it to be shown that the transaction was a mortgage, although the agreement to reconvey was executed subsequently.[61] Parol evidence is admissible to connect the two instruments.[62] The circumstances which tend to show that an absolute conveyance was in fact a mortgage would also show that a sale with an agreement to reconvey was a mortgage.[63] But such a transaction may be a condi-

[54] McClintock v. McClintock, 3 Brewst. (Pa.) 76; Briggs v. Rice, 130 Mass. 50; Smith v. Cremer, 71 Ill. 185.

[55] Magnusson v. Johnson, 73 Ill. 156; Case v. Peters, 20 Mich. 298; Tilden v. Streeter, 45 Mich. 533, 8 N. W. 502; Johnson v. Van Velsor, 43 Mich. 208, 5 N. W. 265; Pancake v. Cauffman, 114 Pa. St. 113, 7 Atl. 67; Lance's Appeal, 112 Pa. St. 456, 4 Atl. 375; Hartley's Appeal, 103 Pa. St. 23.

[56] Van Buren v. Olmstead, 5 Paige (N. Y.) 9; Judge v. Reese, 24 N. J. Eq. 387; Clark v. Condit, 18 N. J. Eq. 358.

[57] And this may be by parol. Jordan v. Katz, 89 Va. 628, 16 S. E. 866.

[58] Keithley v. Wood, 151 Ill. 566, 38 N. E. 149; Helbreg v. Schumann, 150 Ill. 12, 37 N. E. 99; Shields v. Russell, 142 N. Y. 290, 36 N. E. 1061; Rempt v. Geyer (N. J. Ch.) 32 Atl. 266; Eckford v. Berry, 87 Tex. 415, 28 S. W. 937; Williams v. Chambers-Roy Co. (Tex. Civ. App.) 26 S. W. 270; Alderson v. Caskey (Ky.) 24 S. W. 629; Nelson v. Atkinson, 37 Neb. 577, 56 N. W. 313.

[59] Blazy v. McLean, 77 Hun, 607, 28 N. Y. Supp. 286; Stowe v. Banks, 123 Mo. 672, 27 S. W. 347; Tygret v. Potter (Ky.) 29 S. W. 976.

[60] Murphy v. Calley, 1 Allen (Mass.) 107; Bennock v. Whipple, 12 Me. 346; McLaughlin v. Shepherd, 32 Me. 143. Delivery of the agreement to reconvey in escrow is not sufficient. Bodwell v. Webster, 13 Pick. (Mass.) 411.

[61] Walker v. Mining Co., 2 Colo. 89.

[62] Preschbaker v. Feaman, 32 Ill. 475; Umbenhower v. Miller, 101 Pa. St. 73; Gay v. Hamilton, 33 Cal. 686.

[63] 1 Jones, Mortg. (5th Ed.) §§ 274, 275.

tional sale, if the intention of the parties so appears, either by their express declaration, or by the circumstances of the case.[64] Such intention is shown by the fact that the debt previously due from the grantor is extinguished,[65] and that there is no agreement to pay,[66] and by an agreement that the grantee may buy the estate absolutely after a certain time.[67] Nor does the mere recording of the instrument as a mortgage prevent a showing that it was in fact a conditional sale.[68]

Deed of Trust.

A deed of trust in the nature of a mortgage—that is, a conveyance of realty to a trustee to secure the payment of a debt—is in many states treated as a mortgage.[69] The usual form of a deed of trust is a conveyance to the trustee to hold in trust to reconvey to the grantor if the debt secured is paid; otherwise, to sell the land and apply the proceeds to the payment of the debt, and pay the balance to the grantor.[70] Statutes which relate to mortgages are held to include deeds of trust, without express mention. Therefore they are subject to the same requirements as to execution and recording.[71]

Equitable Mortgage.

An equitable mortgage does not refer to the mortgage of an equitable interest, but to instruments having the effect of mortgages, which are recognized only in equity. An absolute deed with a parol

---

[64] Horbach v. Hill, 112 U. S. 144, 5 Sup. Ct. 81; Hughes v. Sheaff, 19 Iowa, 335; Davis v. Stonestreet, 4 Ind. 101; Smith v. Crosby, 47 Wis. 160, 2 N. W. 104; Henley v. Hotaling, 41 Cal. 22.

[65] Rue v. Dole, 107 Ill. 275; Kraemer v. Adelsberger, 122 N. Y. 467, 25 N. E. 859; Bridges v. Linder, 60 Iowa, 190, 14 N. W. 217.

[66] Bogk v. Gassert, 149 U. S. 17, 13 Sup. Ct. 738; Flagg v. Munn, 14 Pick. (Mass.) 467; Hanford v. Blessing, 80 Ill. 188.

[67] Baker v. Thrasher, 4 Denio (N. Y.) 493; Macauley v. Porter, 71 N. Y. 173.

[68] Morrison v. Brand, 5 Daly (N. Y.) 40.

[69] Shillaber v. Robinson, 97 U. S. 68; Southern Pac. R. Co. v. Doyle, 11 Fed. 253; McLane v. Paschal, 47 Tex. 366. The trustee is the agent of both parties, and so must be impartial. Peninsular Iron Co. v. Eells, 15 C. C. A. 189, 68 Fed. 24; Sherwood v. Saxton, 63 Mo. 78. Cf. Moran v. Hagerman, 12 C. C. A. 239, 64 Fed. 499.

[70] 2 Jones, Mortg. (5th Ed.) § 1770.

[71] Woodruff v. Robb, 19 Ohio, 212; Crosby v. Huston, 1 Tex. 203.

defeasance, which has been considered, is one of these.[72] Equitable mortgages must satisfy the same requisites as to execution and recording as other mortgages.[73] An agreement to mortgage is, in equity, treated as a mortgage, on the principle that equity treats that as done which ought to be done.[74] But, to have this effect, some specific property to be mortgaged must be designated.[75] The agreement, however, need not be in writing, if there is sufficient part performance to satisfy the statute of frauds.[76] It is not necessary that the estate conveyed by a mortgage be a legal one. A mere equitable interest may pass and be sufficient.[77]

An informal mortgage—that is, one invalid at law by reason of some defect in execution—is sometimes made effective as a mortgage in equity.[78] An assignment of rents as a security is regarded as an equitable mortgage, since a mortgage of such rents would in fact be an assignment of them.[79] The same is true of a power to collect rents.[80] Another form of equitable mortgage is an assignment of a contract to purchase,[81] or of a bond to convey.[82] Such assignment may be valid as a mortgage, even though the conveyance is dependent on the performance of a condition,[83] and the vendor and

[72] 1 Jones, Mortg. (5th Ed.) § 162.
[73] New Vienna Bank v. Johnson, 47 Ohio St. 306, 24 N. E. 503.
[74] See Fetter, Eq. 25; Ex parte Howe, 1 Paige (N. Y.) 125; Osgood v. Osgood, 78 Mich. 290, 44 N. W. 325; Ott's Ex'x v. King, 8 Grat. (Va.) 224.
[75] Langley v. Vaughn, 10 Heisk. (Tenn.) 553; Adams v. Johnson, 41 Miss. 258; Price v. Cutts, 29 Ga. 142.
[76] Baker v. Baker, 2 S. D. 261, 49 N. W. 1064; Burdick v. Jackson, 7 Hun (N. Y.) 488.
[77] Gale's Ex'rs v. Morris, 29 N. J. Eq. 222; New Vienna Bank v. Johnson, 47 Ohio St. 306, 24 N. E. 503.
[78] Central Trust Co. of New York v. Bridges, 6 C. C. A. 539, 57 Fed. 753; Gest v. Packwood, 39 Fed. 525; Abbott v. Godfroy's Heirs, 1 Mich. 179; Lake v. Doud, 10 Ohio, 415; McQuie v. Peay, 58 Mo. 56; Daggett v. Rankin, 31 Cal. 322; Atkinson v. Miller, 34 W. Va. 115, 11 S. E. 1007; Frank v. Hicks (Wyo.) 35 Pac. 475.
[79] Gest v. Packwood, 39 Fed. 525; Hulett v. Soullard, 26 Vt. 295.
[80] Joseph Smith Co. v. McGuinness, 14 R. I. 59.
[81] Shoecraft v. Bloxham, 124 U. S. 730, 8 Sup. Ct. 686; Fitzhugh v. Smith, 62 Ill. 486; Brockway v. Wells, 1 Paige (N. Y.) 617; Burrows v. Hovland, 40 Neb. 464, 58 N. W. 947.
[82] See Baker v. Colony, 45 Ill. 264; Sinclair v. Armitage, 12 N. J. Eq. 174.
[83] Curtis v. Buckley, 14 Kan. 449.

vendee cannot subsequently rescind the contract.[84] Every such assignment carries whatever interest the mortgagor has.[85]

Same—Deposit of Title Deeds.

At common law, and at present in England, a valid mortgage may be made by the deposit of title deeds; the absence of the deeds, or any of them, being considered notice to subsequent purchasers that the owner's title was not perfect.[86] This form of security, however, is recognized in only a few of our states,[87] and it is quite inconsistent with our registry system.[88] A deposit of title deeds, accompanied by a written memorandum, may, however, constitute an equitable mortgage.[89]

Same—Vendor's Lien.

At common law, whenever there is a conveyance of land, and the purchase price is not paid, a lien arises in favor of the grantor.[90] In some states it is held that such a lien does not exist,[91] and in some

[84] After notice to the vendor. 1 Jones, Mortg. (5th Ed.) § 172.

[85] Muehlberger v. Schilling (Sup.) 3 N. Y. Supp. 705.

[86] 1 Jones, Mortg. (5th Ed.) § 179.

[87] Rockwell v. Hobby, 2 Sandf. Ch. (N. Y.) 9; Jarvis v. Dutcher, 16 Wis. 307; Gale's Ex'rs v. Morris, 29 N. J. Eq. 222; Griffin v. Griffin, 18 N. J. Eq. 104; Hutzler v. Phillips, 26 S. C. 136, 1 S. E. 502; Hackett v. Reynolds, 4 R. I. 512; First Nat. Bank v. Caldwell, 4 Dill. 314, Fed. Cas. No. 4,798.

[88] 1 Jones, Mortg. (5th Ed.) § 185.

[89] Luch's Appeal, 44 Pa. St. 519; Edwards v. Trumbull, 50 Pa. St. 509.

[90] 2 Jones, Liens (2d Ed.) 1063; Shall v. Biscoe, 18 Ark. 142; Salmon v. Hoffman, 2 Cal. 138; Francis v. Wells, 2 Colo. 660; Wooten v. Bellinger, 17 Fla. 289; Moshier v. Meek, 80 Ill. 79; Keith v. Horner, 32 Ill. 524; Yaryan v. Shriner, 26 Ind. 364; Gropengether v. Fejervary, 9 Iowa, 163; Thornton v. Knox's Ex'r, 6 B. Mon. (Ky.) 74; Carr v. Hobbs, 11 Md. 285; Payne v. Avery, 21 Mich. 524; Duke v. Bulme, 16 Minn. 306 (Gil. 270); Dodge v. Evans, 43 Miss. 570; Bennett v. Shipley, 82 Mo. 448; Reese v. Kinkead, 18 Nev. 126, 1 Pac. 667; Herbert v. Scofield, 9 N. J. Eq. 492; Smith v. Smith, 9 Abb. Prac. (N. S.) 420; Stafford v. Van Rensselaer, 9 Cow. (N. Y.) 316; Pease v. Kelly, 3 Or. 417; Kent v. Gerhard, 12 R. I. 92; Ross v. Whitson, 6 Yerg. (Tenn.) 50; Pinchain v. Collard, 13 Tex. 333; Willard v. Reas, 26 Wis. 540.

[91] Godwin v. Collins, 3 Del. Ch. 189, affirmed 4 Houst. (Del.) 28; Simpson v. Mundee, 3 Kan. 172; Philbrook v. Delano, 29 Me. 410; Ahrend v. Odiorne, 118 Mass. 261; Edminster v. Higgins, 6 Neb. 265; Wamble v. Battle, 3 Ired. Eq. (N. C.) 182; Hiester v. Green, 48 Pa. St. 96; Wragg v. Comptroller General, 2 Desaus. Eq. (S. C.) 509. In some states the question is unsettled. Atwood v. Vincent, 17 Conn. 575; Arlin v. Brown, 44 N. H. 102.

§ 114) FORM OF A MORTGAGE. 193

it has been abolished by statute.[92] All subsequent purchasers through the grantee, who have notice of the lien, take the land subject thereto.[93] Recitals in the vendor's deed that the purchase money is unpaid,[94] and continued possession by the vendor, are held to be notice to such purchasers.[95] A vendor's lien is not good against judgment creditors of the vendee, without notice.[96] The vendor may waive his lien by acts which show an intention not to rely on it for security.[97] Taking the vendee's note will not constitute a waiver, unless the note is negotiated.[98] But it is waived by taking the note of the vendee with an indorser or guarantor,[99] or other collateral security.[100] So, too, it may be waived by express agreement.[101] A vendor's lien cannot be reserved in favor of a third person who has paid the purchase price,[102] nor in most states does it pass by assignment.[103]

[92] 1 Stim. Am. St. Law, § 1950.

[93] And those who are not purchasers for value. Beal v. Harrington, 116 Ill. 113, 4 N. E. 664; Petry v. Ambrosher, 100 Ind. 510; Strohm v. Good, 113 Ind. 93, 14 N. E. 901; Webster v. McCullough, 61 Iowa, 496, 16 N. W. 578; Thomas v. Bridges, 73 Mo. 530; Butterfield v. Okie, 36 N. J. Eq. 482.

[94] De Cordova v. Hood, 17 Wall. 1; Daughaday v. Paine, 6 Minn. 443 (Gil. 304); Willis v. Gay, 48 Tex. 463; McRimmon v. Martin, 14 Tex. 318.

[95] Melross v. Scott, 18 Ind. 250.

[96] Allen v. Loring, 34 Iowa, 499; Webb v. Robinson, 14 Ga. 216; Gann v. Chester, 5 Yerg. (Tenn.) 205; Adams v. Buchanan, 49 Mo. 64; Bayley v. Greenleaf, 7 Wheat. 46; Hulett v. Whipple, 58 Barb. (N. Y.) 224; Johnson v. Cawthorn, 1 Dev. & B. Eq. (N. C.) 32. But see Poe v. Paxton's Heirs, 26 W. Va. 607; Lissa v. Posey, 64 Miss. 352, 1 South. 500; Lewis v. Caperton's Ex'r, 8 Grat. (Va.) 148; Bowman v. Faw, 5 Lea (Tenn.) 472.

[97] Moshier v. Meek, 80 Ill. 79; Perry v. Grant, 10 R. I. 334.

[98] White v. Williams, 1 Paige (N. Y.) 502; Garson v. Green, 1 Johns. Ch. (N. Y.) 308; Warren v. Fenn, 28 Barb. (N. Y.) 333; Aldridge v. Dunn, 7 Blackf. (Ind.) 249; Baum v. Grigsby, 21 Cal. 173.

[99] Hazeltine v. Moore, 21 Hun (N. Y.) 355; Durette v. Briggs, 47 Mo. 356; Haskell v. Scott, 56 Ind. 564.

[100] Orrick v. Durham, 79 Mo. 174; Avery v. Clark, 87 Cal. 619, 25 Pac. 919; Hunt v. Waterman, 12 Cal. 301.

[101] Donovan v. Donovan, 85 Mich. 63, 48 N. W. 163; McCarty v. Williams, 69 Ala. 174; Williams v. McCarty, 74 Ala. 295.

[102] Crane v. Caldwell, 14 Ill. 468; Nottes' Appeal, 45 Pa. St. 361; Brown v. Budd, 2 Ind. 442. But see Nichols v. Glover, 41 Ind. 24; Hamilton v. Gilbert, 2 Heisk. (Tenn.) 680.

[103] Baum v. Grigsby, 21 Cal. 172; Webb v. Robinson, 14 Ga. 216; Keith v.

REAL PROP.—13

Same—Vendee's Lien.

A vendee also has a lien before he acquires possession for the amount he has advanced.[104] A subsequent grantee of the vendor takes the land subject to this lien, if he has notice of it.[105] The vendee, after notice of a conveyance by the vendor, must pay the balance of the purchase price to the second vendee, who is in fact an assignor of the vendor's rights; but if the vendee has no notice of such assignment, and pays the purchase price to the vendor, he is protected.[106] The other incidents of the vendee's lien are practically the same as of the vendor's lien.[107]

RIGHTS AND LIABILITIES OF MORTGAGOR AND MORTGAGEE.

115. The rights and liabilities of mortgagor and mortgagee will be considered under the following heads:
   (a) Nature of mortgagor's estates (p. 195).
   (b) Possession of mortgaged premises (p. 196).
   (c) Insurance on mortgaged premises (p. 197).
   (d) Accounting by the mortgagee (p. 199).
   (e) Subrogation (p. 203).

Horner, 32 Ill. 524; Carpenter v. Mitchell, 54 Ill. 126; Hammond v. Peyton, 34 Minn. 529, 27 N. W. 72; White v. Williams, 1 Paige (N. Y.) 502; First Nat. Bank of Salem v. Salem Capital Flour-Mills Co., 39 Fed. 89; Tharpe v. Dunlap, 4 Heisk. (Tenn.) 674. But see Carlton v. Buckner, 28 Ark. 66; Dixon v. Dixon, 1 Md. Ch. 220; and, contra, Weaver v. Brown, 87 Ala. 533, 6 South. 354; Honore's Ex'r v. Bakewell, 6 B. Mon. (Ky.) 67; Sloan v. Campbell, 71 Mo. 387; Cannon v. McDaniel, 46 Tex. 305; Board v. Wilson, 34 W. Va. 609, 12 S. E. 778.

[104] Lane v. Ludlow, 6 Paige (N. Y.) 316 note; Wickman v. Robinson, 14 Wis. 535; Small v. Small, 16 S. C. 64; Cooper v. Merritt, 30 Ark. 687; Stewart v. Wood, 63 Mo. 252; Galbraith v. Reeves, 82 Tex. 357, 18 S. W. 696.

[105] Clark v. Jacobs, 56 How. Prac. (N. Y.) 519; Shirley v. Shirley, 7 Blackf. (Ind.) 452; Stewart v. Wood, 63 Mo. 252.

[106] Rose v. Watson, 10 H. L. Cas. 672.

[107] Payne v. Atterbury, Har. (Mich.) 414; Anderson v. Spencer, 51 Miss. 869; Mackreth v. Symmons, 15 Ves. 345; Burgess v. Wheate, 1 W. Bl. 150.

SAME—NATURE OF MORTGAGOR'S ESTATE.

116. The mortgagor is owner of the mortgaged premises, as to all persons except the mortgagee.

As stated in the black-letter text, the mortgagor is owner of the estate, as to all persons except the mortgagee.[108] The mortgagor or his assignees do not hold adversely to the mortgagee,[109] and are estopped to deny the validity of the mortgage.[110] The mortgagor may disseise the mortgagee by repudiating the mortgage, and hold adversely from that time.[111] A disseisin of the mortgagor is a disseisin of the mortgagee also.[112] All improvements made by the mortgagor inure to the benefit of the mortgagee.[113] The mortgagor must pay taxes on the mortgaged land,[114] and he will be enjoined from committing any waste which would impair the mortgage security, such as cutting timber or removing buildings.[115] Such an injunction may be obtained by a surety of the mortgagor.[116] The same remedy is provided against the grantees of the mortgagor.[117] A mortgagor in possession is entitled to reasonable esto-

---

[108] Turner Coal Co. v. Glover, 101 Ala. 289, 13 South. 478. The mortgagor may sue for injuries to the mortgaged premises, whether in possession or not. Frankenthal v. Mayer, 54 Ill. App. 160; Heitkamp v. Granite Co., 59 Mo. App. 244; Atwood v. Pulp Co., 85 Me. 379, 27 Atl. 259.

[109] Wright v. Sperry, 25 Wis. 617; Seeley v. Manning, 37 Wis. 574; Doyle v. Mellen, 15 R. I. 523, 8 Atl. 709.

[110] Skelton v. Scott, 18 Hun (N. Y.) 375; Fisher v. Milmine, 94 Ill. 328; Kerngood v. Davis, 21 S. C. 183.

[111] Benton Co. v. Czarlinsky, 101 Mo. 275, 14 S. W. 114; Jamison v. Perry, 38 Iowa, 14. Contra, Hunt v. Hunt, 14 Pick. (Mass.) 374.

[112] Poignand v. Smith, 8 Pick. (Mass.) 272.

[113] Ivy v. Yancey, 129 Mo. 501, 31 S. W. 937. And see Malone v. Roy, 107 Cal. 518, 40 Pac. 1040.

[114] Mann v. Mann, 49 Ill. App. 472; Mutual Life Ins. Co. of New York v. Newell, 78 Hun, 293, 28 N. Y. Supp. 913. Cf. Wood v. Armour, 88 Wis. 488, 60 N. W. 791; Raymond v. Palmer, 47 La. Ann. 786, 17 South. 312.

[115] Fairbank v. Cudworth, 33 Wis. 358; Scott v. Webster, 50 Wis. 53, 6 N. W. 363; Dorr v. Dudderar, 88 Ill. 107; Verner v. Betz, 46 N. J. Eq. 256, 19 Atl. 206; Adams v. Corriston, 7 Minn. 456 (Gil. 365). And see, as to the abandonment of an easement, Duval v. Becker, 81 Md. 537, 32 Atl. 308.

[116] Johnson v. White, 11 Barb. (N. Y.) 194.

[117] Coker v. Whitlock, 54 Ala. 180.

vers,[118] and the mortgagee has no claim on the crops raised by him.[119] He is not, however, entitled to emblements, as when the mortgagee, being entitled to possession, enters on the mortgagor before harvest.[120] A tenant of the mortgagor under a lease executed subsequently to the mortgage is in the same position, and, when ejected by the mortgagee, is not entitled to the crops planted by him.[121]

SAME—POSSESSION OF MORTGAGED PREMISES.

117. The mortgagee is entitled to possession, unless it is otherwise provided:
  (a) By statute, as in many states.
  (b) By agreement of the parties, which may be either:
    (1) Express, or
    (2) Implied.

The mortgagor is entitled to possession against every one except the mortgagee and those claiming under him.[122] But at common law the mortgagee may take possession at any time.[123] Now, however, the mortgagor usually remains in possession; at least, until breach of condition. This is due to statutory enactments in many states.[124] And where there is no statute it is usually provided in

[118] Hapgood v. Blood, 11 Gray (Mass.) 400; Wright v. Lake, 30 Vt. 206; Judkins v. Woodman, 81 Me. 351, 17 Atl. 298.

[119] Woodward v. Pickett, 8 Gray (Mass.) 617; Allen v. Elderkin, 62 Wis. 627, 22 N. W. 842; Tobey v. Reed, 9 Conn. 216. But see Coor v. Smith, 101 N. C. 261, 7 S. E. 669.

[120] Downard v. Groff, 40 Iowa, 597; Gillett v. Balcom, 6 Barb. (N. Y.) 371; Gilman v. Wills, 66 Me. 273.

[121] Jones v. Thomas, 8 Blackf. (Ind.) 428.

[122] Huckins v. Straw, 34 Me. 166; Stinson v. Ross, 51 Me. 556; Ellison v. Daniels, 11 N. H. 274; Doe v. McLoskey, 1 Ala. 708; Bartlett v. Borden, 13 Bush (Ky.) 45.

[123] Smith v. Shuler, 12 Serg. & R. (Pa.) 240; Youngman v. Railroad Co., 65 Pa. St. 278; Barrett v. Hinckley, 124 Ill. 32, 14 N. E. 863; Mershon v. Castree (N. J. Sup.) 31 Atl. 602. And see Springer v. Lehman, 50 Ill. App. 139; Brundage v. Association, 11 Wash. St. 277, 39 Pac. 666. Cf., however, Armour Pack. Co. v. Wolff, 59 Mo. App. 665.

[124] See 1 Stim. Am. St. Law, §§ 1882, 1883. And see Michigan Trust Co. v. Lansing Lumber Co., 103 Mich. 392, 61 N. W. 668; Cullen v. Trust Co., 60 Minn. 6, 61 N. W. 818.

§ 118)   INSURANCE ON MORTGAGED PREMISES.   197

the mortgage that the mortgagor shall retain the possession. The agreement as to possession may be contained in a separate instrument. The intention of the parties that the mortgagor shall retain possession may often be implied from the terms of the mortgage; for instance, where there is provision that the mortgagor shall cultivate the farm mortgaged, and give one-half the crops to the mortgagee, to be applied in payment of the debt.[125] But by remaining in possession after the execution of the mortgage the mortgagor does not acquire a right to continue in possession.[126] When the mortgagor is rightfully in possession, he may bring any possessory action for the protection of the estate.[127] He need not pay rent to the mortgagee, even in states where the latter is considered the owner of the legal title.[128]

SAME—INSURANCE ON MORTGAGED PREMISES.

118. The mortgagor and the mortgagee each have an insurable interest in the mortgaged premises.

Both the mortgagor and the mortgagee have an insurable interest in the mortgaged premises. The mortgagor may insure them to their full value.[129] His insurable interest continues, after a sale of his equity of redemption on execution, until his right to redeem from such sale is barred.[130] If he has assigned the equity of redemption, and his grantee has assumed the mortgage note, he still has an insurable interest, since he remains liable on the mortgage note as a surety.[131] A covenant is usually inserted in the mortgage that the mortgagor shall keep the premises insured for the benefit

---

[125] Flagg v. Flagg, 11 Pick. (Mass.) 475. And see Hartshorn v. Hubbard, 2 N. H. 453; Flanders v. Lamphear, 9 N. H. 201; Lamb v. Foss, 21 Me. 240.

[126] Wakeman v. Banks, 2 Conn. 445.

[127] Morse v. Whitcher, 64 N. H. 590, 15 Atl. 217; Great Falls Co. v. Worster, 15 N. H. 412.

[128] 1 Jones, Mortg. (5th Ed.) § 670.

[129] Insurance Co. v. Stinson, 103 U. S. 25; Carpenter v. Insurance Co., 16 Pet. 495; Stephens v. Insurance Co., 43 Ill. 327; Illinois Fire Ins. Co. v. Stanton, 57 Ill. 354.

[130] Strong v. Insurance Co., 10 Pick. (Mass.) 40.

[131] Waring v. Loder, 53 N. Y. 581.

of the mortgagee. In such case, if the mortgagor should insure in his own name, the mortgagee has a lien on the insurance money,[132] but not unless there is such covenant.[133] When the mortgagor insures for the benefit of the mortgagee, anything which makes the policy void as to the mortgagor makes it void as to the mortgagee, unless there be a provision in the policy to the contrary.[134] The mortgagor cannot bind the mortgagee, for whose benefit he has taken insurance, by a release or adjustment.[135] In case of a loss under such a policy, the mortgagee must apply the insurance money to the mortgage debt, if it be due.[136] If it is not due, such application cannot be made without the consent of the mortgagor.[137] A provision in the policy of insurance forbidding alienation by the owner is not broken by a mortgage of the premises until the mortgage is foreclosed.[138] Such a mortgage is, however, a breach of a covenant against change of ownership.[139]

The mortgagee may also insure, and it will not constitute double insurance.[140] The mortgagee has an insurable interest equal to

[132] Wheeler v. Insurance Co., 101 U. S. 439; In re Sands Ale Brewing Co., 3 Biss. 175, Fed. Cas. No. 12,307; Cromwell v. Insurance Co., 44 N. Y. 42; Wattengel v. Schultz, 11 Misc. Rep. 165, 32 N. Y. Supp. 91; Carter v. Insurance Co., 8 Paige (N. Y.) 437; Miller v. Aldrich, 31 Mich. 408; Ames v. Richardson, 29 Minn. 330, 13 N. W. 137.

[133] Carter v. Insurance Co., 8 Paige (N. Y.) 437; Columbia Ins. Co. of Alexandria v. Lawrence, 10 Pet. 507; McDonald v. Black, 20 Ohio, 185; Ryan v. Adamson, 57 Iowa, 30, 10 N. W. 287; Plimpton v. Insurance Co., 43 Vt. 497; Nichols v. Baxter, 5 R. I. 491.

[134] Springfield Fire & Marine Ins. Co. v. Allen, 43 N. Y. 389.

[135] Hazard v. Draper, 7 Allen (Mass.) 267.

[136] Waring v. Loder, 53 N. Y. 581.

[137] Fergus v. Wilmarth, 117 Ill. 542, 7 N. E. 508; Gordon v. Bank, 115 Mass. 588.

[138] Powers v. Insurance Co., 136 Mass. 108; Judge v. Insurance Co., 132 Mass. 521; Conover v. Insurance Co., 3 Denio (N. Y.) 254; Aurora Fire Ins. Co. v. Eddy, 55 Ill. 213; Hartford Fire Ins. Co. v. Walsh, 54 Ill. 164; Loy v. Insurance Co., 24 Minn. 315. Otherwise in some states when the mortgage is by deed absolute. Western Massachusetts Ins. Co. v. Riker, 10 Mich. 279. And see Foote v. Insurance Co., 119 Mass. 259; Tomlinson v. Insurance Co., 47 Me. 232.

[139] Edmands v. Insurance Co., 1 Allen (Mass.) 311.

[140] Carpenter v. Insurance Co., 16 Pet. 495; Westchester Fire Ins. Co. v. Foster, 90 Ill. 121; Aetna Fire Ins. Co. v. Tyler, 16 Wend. (N. Y.) 385. So a

the amount of his lien, if that does not exceed the value of the mortgaged property.[141] This interest continues after an assignment of the mortgage and the mortgage debt, if he is liable to the assignee, as by an indorsement of the note.[142] If the mortgagee insures, he cannot charge the premiums paid to the mortgagor,[143] unless the latter has covenanted to insure, and has failed to do so;[144] nor can he charge the premiums to the mortgagor, when he insures only his own interest.[145] When the insurance is of the mortgagee's interest, the loss is payable, whether the property remaining is sufficient security for the mortgage debt or not.[146] But the insurer is subrogated to the rights of the mortgagee, to the amount of the loss.[147] In such case the insurance, of course, is of no benefit to the mortgagor.[148] When the insurance is in the name of the mortgagor, or is taken out by him for the benefit of the mortgagee, the insurer has no right to subrogation.[149]

SAME—ACCOUNTING BY THE MORTGAGEE.

119. **A mortgagee, or his assignee, in possession, must account to the mortgagor.**
120. **DEBITS—He is liable for the rents and profits of the land, and for damages caused by waste** (p. 200).

trustee under a deed of trust has an insurable interest. Dick v. Insurance Co., 81 Mo. 103.

[141] Excelsior Fire Ins. Co. v. Royal Ins. Co., 55 N. Y. 343; Sussex Co. Mut. Ins. Co. v. Woodruff, 26 N. J. Law, 541.

[142] Williams v. Insurance Co., 107 Mass. 377.

[143] Faure v. Winans, Hopk. Ch. (N. Y.) 283.

[144] Fowley v. Palmer, 5 Gray (Mass.) 549; Garza v. Investment Co. (Tex. Civ. App.) 27 S. W. 1090.

[145] 1 Jones, Mortg. (5th Ed.) § 414.

[146] Kernochan v. Insurance Co., 17 N. Y. 428, 435; Excelsior Fire Ins. Co. v. Royal Ins. Co., 55 N. Y. 343.

[147] Norwich Fire Ins. Co. v. Boomer, 52 Ill. 442; Foster v. Van Reed, 70 N. Y. 20; Bound Brook Mut. Fire Ins. Ass'n v. Nelson, 41 N. J. Eq. 485, 5 Atl. 590; Concord Union Mut. Fire Ins. Co. v. Woodbury, 45 Me. 447.

[148] White v. Brown, 2 Cush. (Mass.) 412; Ely v. Ely, 80 Ill. 532; Stinchfield v. Milliken, 71 Me. 567.

[149] Cone v. Insurance Co., 60 N. Y. 619.

121. CREDITS—He is to be credited with amounts paid for repairs and reasonable improvements, the expense of collecting the rents, taxes paid, and sums expended in removing incumbrances and in protecting the property (p. 201).

122. ANNUAL RESTS—In computing the account, rests are made whenever, at the end of an interest period, the net debits exceed the interest due (p. 202).

When the mortgagee is in possession, he must account for the rents and profits received, and apply them to the reduction of the mortgage debt.[150] The remedy of accounting can be had only in equity.[151] The mortgagor is not entitled to an accounting unless he redeems the mortgage, or on foreclosure.[152] A junior mortgagee who redeems a prior mortgage is entitled to an accounting from the prior mortgagee, if he has been in possession.[153] An assignee of the mortgagee, who takes possession, must account,[154] and an accounting can be compelled by the assignee of the mortgagor.[155]

Debits.

The mortgagee is chargeable with whatever he has collected as rents and profits of the mortgaged premises,[156] or what he should have received if he had managed the estate as a prudent owner.[157]

[150] Reitenbaugh v. Ludwick, 31 Pa. St. 131; Chapman v. Porter, 69 N. Y. 276; Dawson v. Drake, 30 N. J. Eq. 601; Rooney v. Crary, 11 Ill. App. 213; Wood v. Whelen, 93 Ill. 153; Byers v. Byers, 65 Mich. 598, 32 N. W. 831. But he must hold as mortgagee. Daniel v. Coker, 70 Ala. 260; Young v. Omohundro, 69 Md. 424, 16 Atl. 120; Ayers v. Staley (N. J. Ch.) 18 Atl. 1046.

[151] Hubbell v. Moulson, 53 N. Y. 225; Dailey v. Abbott, 40 Ark. 275; Farris v. Houston, 78 Ala. 250.

[152] Weeks v. Thomas, 21 Me. 465; Farris v. Houston, 78 Ala. 250.

[153] Gaskell v. Viquesney, 122 Ind. 244, 23 N. E. 791.

[154] Strang v. Allen, 44 Ill. 438.

[155] Ruckman v. Astor, 9 Paige (N. Y.) 517; Gelston v. Thompson, 29 Md. 595.

[156] Peugh v. Davis, 113 U. S. 542, 5 Sup. Ct. 622; Strang v. Allen, 44 Ill. 428; Donohue v. Chase, 139 Mass. 407, 2 N. E. 84; Brown v. Bank, 148 Mass. 300, 19 N. E. 382; Van Buren v. Olmstead, 5 Paige (N. Y.) 9; Walsh v. Insurance Co., 13 Abb. Prac. (N. Y.) 33.

[157] Harper v. Ely, 70 Ill. 581; Engleman Transp. Co. v. Longwell, 48 Fed. 129; Montague v. Railroad, 124 Mass. 242.

He may be liable for rents which he has not actually received, by reason of his negligence in leasing to an insolvent tenant, or by employing an incompetent agent.[158] A grantee under an absolute deed which is shown to be a mortgage is chargeable only with the reasonable value of the use of the property.[159] If the mortgagee himself occupies the premises, he must credit the mortgagor with an amount equal to their fair rental value.[160] The damages for any waste committed while the mortgagee is in possession will be credited on the mortgage debt.[161] The mortgagee may cut wood or work a mine on the mortgaged premises, if such is a proper mode of enjoying the profits of the estate.[162] If he does so, the profits must be accounted for.

Credits.

A mortgagee in possession must make necessary repairs,[163] and he will be allowed, in his accounting, to charge for any repairs made by him which are reasonable.[164] He is also allowed the expense of any improvements which are proper for the enjoyment of the premises, but not for mere ornamental improvements.[165] On the other hand, he is not chargeable with an increased rental value due to improvements made by him with which he is not credited.[166]

[158] Miller v. Lincoln, 6 Gray (Mass.) 556; Greer v. Turner, 36 Ark. 17.

[159] Harper's Appeal, 64 Pa. St. 315; Morrow v. Jones, 41 Neb. 867, 60 N. W. 369. Or with what he has actually received, if he has not occupied personally. Morris v. Budlong, 78 N. Y. 543.

[160] Montgomery v. Chadwick, 7 Iowa, 114; Holabird v. Burr, 17 Conn. 556; Sanders v. Wilson, 34 Vt. 318.

[161] Onderdonk v. Gray, 19 N. J. Eq. 65; Daniel v. Coker, 70 Ala. 260. Cf. Whiting v. Adams, 66 Vt. 679, 30 Atl. 32.

[162] Irwin v. Davidson, 3 Ired. Eq. (N. C.) 311; Millett v. Davey, 31 Beav. 470.

[163] Barnett v. Nelson, 54 Iowa, 41, 6 N. W. 49; Dozier v. Mitchell, 65 Ala. 511.

[164] Miller v. Curry, 124 Ind. 48, 24 N. E. 219, 374; Hicklin v. Marco, 46 Fed. 424; Sparhawk v. Wills, 5 Gray (Mass.) 423; Woodward v. Phillips, 14 Gray (Mass.) 132; Malone v. Roy, 107 Cal. 518, 40 Pac. 1040.

[165] Harper's Appeal, 64 Pa. St. 315; Rowell v. Jewett, 73 Me. 365. And see American Button-Hole, Overseaming & Sewing-Mach. Co. v. Burlington Mut. Loan Ass'n, 68 Iowa, 326, 27 N. W. 271; Mickles v. Dillaye, 17 N. Y. 80.

[166] Hagthorp v. Hook's Adm'rs, 1 Gill & J. (Md.) 270; Bell v. Mayor, etc., 10 Paige (N. Y.) 49.

When a mortgagee is in possession under a mistaken belief that he has absolute title, he will be allowed compensation for all improvements erected.[167] The general rule is that the mortgagee can claim no compensation for his own services in the management of the estate.[168] But in some states he is now allowed a commission for collecting the rents.[169] He may employ an agent to manage the property, when necessary.[170] The principal disbursements for which he may be credited are taxes and assessments;[171] money paid in discharging a prior incumbrance,[172] or otherwise protecting the title;[173] and expenses in preserving the property, such as employing a watchman.[174] He may charge for counsel fees necessarily expended in collecting the rents.[175]

Annual Rests.

Whenever the rents and profits are more than the annual interest, a rest is made; that is, the net amount of rents and profits in excess of the interest is deducted from the mortgage debt, and from that time interest is computed only upon the balance.[176] If, at the end of any interest period, the rents and profits are less than the

---

[167] Miner v. Beekman, 50 N. Y. 337; Roberts v. Fleming, 53 Ill. 196; Millard v. Truax, 73 Mich. 381, 41 N. W. 328; Hadley v. Stewart, 65 Wis. 481, 27 N. W. 340; Bacon v. Cottrell, 13 Minn. 194 (Gil. 183); Troost v. Davis, 31 Ind. 34.

[168] Eaton v. Simonds, 14 Pick. (Mass.) 98; Clark v. Smith, 1 N. J. Eq. 121; Elmer v. Loper, 25 N. J. Eq. 475.

[169] 2 Jones, Mortg. (5th Ed.) § 1133.

[170] Davis v. Dendy, 3 Madd. 170; Harper v. Ely, 70 Ill. 581.

[171] Harper v. Ely, 70 Ill. 581; Dooley v. Potter, 146 Mass. 148, 15 N. E. 499; Sidenberg v. Ely, 90 N. Y. 257; Gooch v. Botts, 110 Mo. 419, 20 S. W. 192; Savings & Loan Soc. v. Burnett, 106 Cal. 514, 39 Pac. 922.

[172] McCormick v. Knox, 105 U. S. 122; Davis v. Bean, 114 Mass. 360; Comstock v. Michael, 17 Neb. 288, 22 N. W. 549; Fitch v. Stallings, 5 Colo. App. 106, 38 Pac. 393.

[173] Hughes v. Johnson, 38 Ark. 285.

[174] Johnson v. Hosford, 110 Ind. 572, 10 N. E. 407.

[175] Hubbard v. Shaw, 12 Allen (Mass.) 120.

[176] Van Vronker v. Eastman, 7 Metc. (Mass.) 157; Reed v. Reed, 10 Pick. (Mass.) 398; Gladding v. Warner, 36 Vt. 54; Blum v. Mitchell, 59 Ala. 535; Jencks v. Alexander, 11 Paige (N. Y.) 619. And see Adams v. Sayre, 76 Ala. 509.

interest charged, no rest is made, but the account continues until the rents and profits due exceed the interest.[177]

SAME—SUBROGATION.

123. Whenever one not primarily liable for the mortgage debt pays it to protect his own rights, he is substituted in equity in place of the mortgagee, and may enforce against the person primarily liable all the securities held by the mortgagee. This is called "subrogation."

124. The persons entitled to a deceased mortgagor's realty can compel the mortgage debt to be paid out of his personal property (p. 204).

Subrogation.

Subrogation is a method of enforcing payment against one ultimately liable on a mortgage debt.[178] In effect, it is an assignment of the creditor's mortgage and other securities to the one paying the debt.[179] Subrogation does not arise when part only of the mortgage debt is paid.[180] It can be claimed only in favor of one who has paid a mortgage debt not his duty to pay.[181] A mere volunteer cannot invoke the aid of subrogation. He must have paid under some compulsion made necessary for the protection of his rights; otherwise payment extinguishes the debt.* A mortgagor who has conveyed subject to the mortgage, and who has been proceeded against personally for the mortgage debt, is entitled to subrogation

---

[177] Bennett v. Cook, 2 Hun (N. Y.) 526; French v. Kennedy, 7 Barb. (N. Y.) 452; Moshier v. Norton, 100 Ill. 63; Snavely v. Pickle, 29 Grat. (Va.) 27.

[178] See Fetter, Eq. p. 254; Matthews v. Trust Co., 52 Fed. 687; McCormick v. Irwin, 35 Pa. St. 111.

[179] Barnes v. Mott, 64 N. Y. 397; Ellsworth v. Lockwood, 42 N. Y. 89; Laylin v. Knox, 41 Mich. 40, 1 N. W. 913; Levy v. Martin, 48 Wis. 198, 4 N. W. 35; Muir v. Berkshire, 52 Ind. 149; Sessions v. Kent, 75 Iowa, 601, 39 N. W. 914.

[180] In re Graff's Estate, 139 Pa. St. 69, 21 Atl. 233.

[181] Arnold v. Green, 116 N. Y. 566, 23 N. E. 1; Pease v. Egan, 131 N. Y. 262, 30 N. E. 102; Young v. Morgan, 89 Ill. 199.

* See Fetter, Eq. 254.

against his grantee.[182] But one loaning money to the mortgagor to pay the mortgage debt is not subrogated unless there be a special agreement to that effect.[183] An indorser of a note, or a surety of the mortgage debt, are subrogated to the rights of the mortgagee, when compelled to discharge the indebtedness.[184] And the principal creditor is subrogated to any securities held by the surety.[185]

Marshaling.

By the doctrine of marshaling,[186] where a prior mortgagee is entitled to satisfaction of his debt out of two parcels of land, a junior mortgagee, who has a lien on only one of these parcels, may be subrogated to the rights of the prior mortgagee;[187] and some cases hold that the prior mortgagor may be compelled to enforce payment as far as possible out of the land which the subsequent mortgage does not cover.[188]

Relief of the Real by the Personal Estate.

The personal estate of a decedent is the primary fund for the payment of his debts, and therefore the deceased owner's personal property is to be applied to the payment of mortgages on his realty,[189]

---

[182] Johnson v. Zink, 51 N. Y. 333; Stillman's Ex'rs v. Stillman, 21 N. J. Eq. 126; Greenwell v. Heritage, 71 Mo. 459.

[183] Wilton v. Mayberry, 75 Wis. 191, 43 N. W. 901; Downer v. Miller, 15 Wis. 612; Kitchell v. Mudgett, 37 Mich. 81; Bolman v. Lohman, 74 Ala. 507.

[184] Gossin v. Brown, 11 Pa. St. 527; Richeson v. Crawford, 94 Ill. 165; Dick v. Moon, 26 Minn. 309, 4 N. W. 39; Motley v. Harris, 1 Lea (Tenn.) 577.

[185] Demott v. Manufacturing Co., 32 N. J. Eq. 124.

[186] See Fetter, Eq. p. 256.

[187] Detroit Sav. Bank v. Truesdail, 38 Mich. 430; Alexander v. Welch, 10 Ill. App. 181; Washington Bldg. & Loan Ass'n v. Beaghen, 27 N. J. Eq. 98; Herbert v. Association, 17 N. J. Eq. 497.

[188] Ball v. Setzer, 33 W. Va. 444, 10 S. E. 798; Sherron v. Acton (N. J. Ch.) 18 Atl. 978; Abbott v. Powell, 6 Sawy. 91, Fed. Cas. No. 13. And see, for other applications, Brown v. McKay, 151 Ill. 315, 37 N. E. 1037; Cullen v. Trust Co., 6 Minn. 6, 61 N. W. 818; Witt v. Rice, 90 Iowa, 451, 57 N. W. 951; Henkel v. Bohnke, 7 Tex. Civ. App. 16, 26 S. W. 645; Hanes v. Denby (N. J. Ch.) 28 Atl. 798; Black v. Reno, 59 Fed. 917.

[189] Hoff's Appeal, 24 Pa. St. 200; Lupton v. Lupton, 2 Johns. Ch. (N. Y.) 614; Parsons v. Freeman, Amb. 115; Woods v. Huntingford, 3 Ves. 128. But see Tweddell v. Tweddell, 2 Brown, Ch. 101; Scott v. Beecher, 5 Madd. 96; Loosemore v. Knapman, Kay, 123.

unless he has expressed a contrary intention.[190] This right can, however, be claimed only by the widow, heirs, or devisees.[191] Nor can it be enforced against any others than the personal representative, next of kin, or residuary legatee.[192] It is not available against creditors, or when the personal estate is insolvent,[193] nor against a specific legatee.[194]

ASSIGNMENT OF THE EQUITY OF REDEMPTION.

125. A mortgagor may assign his equity of redemption, but the assignment is subject to the following conditions, among others:
  (a) The equity of redemption cannot be assigned to the mortgagee at the time the mortgage is executed.
  (b) An assignee takes the land subject to the mortgage.
  (c) He does not become personally liable for the mortgage debt unless he expressly assumes it.
  (d) In some states, when he does assume it, he may be sued personally by the mortgagee.

126. An equity of redemption may be transferred by operation of law, as:
  (a) By descent.
  (b) By sale on execution.

No Mortgage without an Equity of Redemption.

The mortgagor's equity of redemption is an inseparable incident of a mortgage. A mortgage cannot be created without an equity of redemption. An instrument having that effect would not be a mortgage, but an absolute conveyance, or a sale with a right to re-

---

[190] As by specific bequests of his personal property. Hoff's Appeal, 24 Pa. St. 200. See Serle v. St. Elvy, 2 P. Wms. 386.

[191] Haven v. Foster, 9 Pick. (Mass.) 112; Lockhart v. Hardy, 9 Beav. 379. And see Duke of Cumberland v. Codrington, 3 Johns. Ch. (N. Y.) 229.

[192] Hocker's Appeal, 4 Pa. St. 497; Gibson v. McCormick, 10 Gill & J. (Md.) 65; Cope v. Cope, 2 Salk. 449.

[193] Hocker's Appeal, 4 Pa. St. 497; Duke of Cumberland v. Codrington, 3 Johns. Ch. (N. Y.) 229.

[194] Oneal v. Mead, 1 P. Wms. 693; Lutkins v. Leigh, Cas. t. Talb. 53. See also, Evelyn v. Evelyn, 2 P. Wms. 659; Middleton v. Middleton, 15 Beav. 450.

purchase. Nor can the equity of redemption be assigned to the mortgagee at the time the mortgage is executed.[195] The mortgagee may purchase the equity of redemption at a subsequent time,[196] but such transactions are carefully scrutinized by the courts.[197]

Rights of an Assignee.

After the execution of a mortgage the mortgagor may sell his equity of redemption as a whole or in parcels. So he may make successive mortgages.[198] But in each case the transfer is subject to the previous mortgage.[199] The mortgagee is a purchaser, to the extent of his claim, and as such is protected under the recording laws.[200] He is entitled to have the whole of the mortgaged premises as security for his debt, and cannot be made to accept part of them as payment. Nor can a purchaser of the equity of redemption compel him to make partition.[201]

A purchaser of the mortgagor's rights, or, as he is usually called, an "assignee of the equity of redemption," though he takes the land subject to the mortgage, may acquire a paramount title, and set it up against the mortgagee,[202] unless he is estopped by recitals in his deed.[203] He may, however, in such case, show that the mortgage

[195] Peugh v. Davis, 96 U. S. 332; Willets v. Burgess, 34 Ill. 494; Bayley v. Bailey, 5 Gray (Mass.) 505.

[196] Ten Eyck v. Craig, 62 N. Y. 406; Phelan v. De Martin, 85 Cal. 365, 24 Pac. 725.

[197] Phelan v. De Martin, 85 Cal. 365, 24 Pac. 725; Hinkley v. Wheelwright, 29 Md. 341; Peugh v. Davis, 96 U. S. 332; Oliver v. Cunningham, 7 Fed. 689.

[198] Hodson v. Treat, 7 Wis. 263; Buchanan v. Monroe, 22 Tex. 537.

[199] Kruse v. Scripps, 11 Ill. 98; Hartley v. Harrison, 24 N. Y. 170. As to leases of the mortgaged premises, see ante, p. 132.

[200] Rowell v. Williams, 54 Wis. 636, 12 N. W. 86; Bass v. Wheless, 2 Tenn. Ch. 531; Moore v. Walker, 3 Lea (Tenn.) 656; Patton v. Eberhart, 52 Iowa, 67, 2 N. W. 954; Herff v. Griggs, 121 Ind. 471, 23 N. E. 279.

[201] Spencer v. Waterman, 36 Conn. 342; McConihe v. Fales, 107 N. Y. 404, 14 N. E. 285; Carpenter v. Koons, 20 Pa. St. 222; Gerdine v. Menage, 41 Minn. 417, 43 N. W. 91; Daniel v. Wilson, 91 Ga. 238, 18 S. E. 134.

[202] Knox v. Easton, 38 Ala. 345.

[203] Such as, that he takes subject to the mortgage, or assumes the mortgage. Kennedy v. Borie, 166 Pa. St. 360, 31 Atl. 98. But see Robinson Bank v. Miller, 153 Ill. 244, 38 N. E. 1078. Nor can the assignee deny its validity for failure of consideration, Crawford v. Edwards, 33 Mich. 354; Miller v. Thompson, 34 Mich. 10; Haile v. Nichols, 16 Hun (N. Y.) 37; or for

§§ 125-126) ASSIGNMENT OF THE EQUITY OF REDEMPTION.   207

has been paid by the mortgagor, or other matter in discharge.[204] The mortgagor may covenant to pay the mortgage, but otherwise his assignee is not entitled to compensation from the mortgagor if the mortgage is enforced against the land.[205] Nor is a purchaser from the mortgagor entitled to collateral security held by the mortgagee.[206] An assignee of the equity of redemption does not become personally liable for the mortgage debt unless he expressly assumes its payment.[207] When the grantee assumes the mortgage debt, the mortgagor becomes merely a surety for him, and, if he is forced to pay the debt, may collect it from his grantee.[208] The mortgagee

---

usury, Hartley v. Harrison, 24 N. Y. 170; De Wolf v. Johnson, 10 Wheat. 367; Cleaver v. Burcky, 17 Ill. App. 92; Frost v. Shaw, 10 Iowa, 491. But the mortgagor may confer on his grantee a right to contest the validity of the mortgage. Bennett v. Bates, 94 N. Y. 354; Magie v. Reynolds (N. J. Ch.) 26 Atl. 150.

[204] Hartley v. Tatham, 2 Abb. Dec. (N. Y.) 333; Williams v. Thurlow, 31 Me. 392; Bennett v. Keehn, 57 Wis. 582, 15 N. W. 776.

[205] Gerdine v. Menage, 41 Minn. 417, 43 N. W. 91; Gayle v. Wilson, 30 Grat. (Va.) 166.

[206] Brewer v. Staples, 3 Sandf. Ch. (N. Y.) 579.

[207] Strong v. Converse, 8 Allen (Mass.) 557; Middaugh v. Bachelder, 33 Fed. 706; Comstock v. Hitt, 37 Ill. 542; Trotter v. Hughes, 12 N. Y. 74; Stebbins v. Hall, 29 Barb. (N. Y.) 524; Metzger v. Huntington, 139 Ind. 501, 37 N. E. 1084; Offut v. Cooper, 136 Ind. 701, 36 N. E. 273; Green v. Hall, 45 Neb. 89, 63 N. W. 119; Granger v. Roll (S. D.) 62 N. W. 970. Such is the effect of a clause providing that "the mortgagee assumes a mortgage," etc. Corning v. Burton, 102 Mich. 86, 62 N. W. 1040; Stephenson v. Elliott, 53 Kan. 550, 36 Pac. 980; Burbank v. Roots (Colo. App.) 35 Pac. 275; Grand Island Sav. & Loan Ass'n v. Moore, 40 Neb. 686, 59 N. W. 115; Wayman v. Jones, 58 Mo. App. 313; Williams v. Everham, 90 Iowa, 420, 57 N. W. 901. And see Lennox v. Brower, 160 Pa. St. 191, 28 Atl. 839; Williams v. Moody, 95 Ga. 8, 22 S. E. 30. But cf. Carrier v. Paper Co., 73 Hun, 287, 26 N. Y. Supp. 414; Hopper v. Calhoun, 52 Kan. 703, 35 Pac. 816. But not a provision that he takes "subject to the mortgage." Tanguay v. Felthousen, 45 Wis. 30; Moore's Appeal, 88 Pa. St. 450; Walker v. Goodsill, 54 Mo. App. 631; Lang v. Cadwell, 13 Mont. 458, 34 Pac. 957. He may assume the debt by a parol agreement. Merriman v. Moore, 90 Pa. St. 78; Lamb v. Tucker, 42 Iowa, 118.

[208] Flagg v. Geltmacher, 98 Ill. 293; Calvo v. Davies, 73 N. Y. 211; Alt v. Banholzer, 36 Minn. 57, 29 N. W. 674; Williams v. Moody, 95 Ga. 8, 22 S. E. 30. The mortgagor may take an assignment of the mortgage, and foreclose it against his grantee. 1 Jones, Mortg. (5th Ed.) § 768. He may do this without a formal assignment. Baker v. Terrell, 8 Minn. 195 (Gil. 165); Risk v. Hoff-

need not accept such an agreement between a mortgagor and his grantee;[209] but, if he does accept, it constitutes a novation, and an extension of time given by the mortgagee to the grantee will discharge the mortgagor from personal liability, since he is merely a surety.[210] When, however, it is expressed in a subsequent mortgage that the prior mortgage is assumed, the subsequent mortgagee does not become personally liable for the prior mortgage debt.[211] In some states the mortgagee may enforce an assumption of the mortgage debt by an assignee of the equity of redemption.[212]

Assignment by Operation of Law.

On the death of the mortgagor the equity of redemption passes to his heirs according to the rules of descent of realty.[213] If the mortgage is foreclosed in his lifetime, any surplus proceeds is personalty, and, on his death, goes to his personal representative. But, if the foreclosure is not until after his death, the heirs are entitled

---

man, 69 Ind. 137. The mortgagor may bring an action against his assignee to enforce the promise before he has himself paid the debt. Rubens v. Prindle, 44 Barb. (N. Y.) 336.

[209] Fish v. Glover, 154 Ill. 86, 39 N. E. 1081; Connecticut Mut. Life Ins. Co. v. Tyler, 8 Biss. 369, Fed. Cas. No. 3,109.

[210] Spencer v. Spencer, 95 N. Y. 353; Murray v. Marshall, 94 N. Y. 611; Calvo v. Davies, 73 N. Y. 211; Union Mut. Life Ins. Co. v. Hanford, 27 Fed. 588; George v. Andrews, 60 Md. 26; Travers v. Dorr, 60 Minn. 173, 62 N. W. 269. Cf., however, Cook v. Prindle (Iowa) 63 N. W. 187.

[211] Garnsey v. Rogers, 47 N. Y. 233; Bassett v. Bradley, 48 Conn. 224. Even if the mortgage be in form an absolute deed. Pardee v. Treat, 82 N. Y. 385; Cole v. Cole, 110 N. Y. 630, 17 N. E. 682; Gaffney v. Hicks, 131 Mass. 124.

[212] 1 Jones, Mortg. (5th Ed.) § 755; Clark, Cont. p. 513; Winters v. Mining Co., 57 Fed. 287; Trotter v. Hughes, 12 N. Y. 74; Osborne v. Cabell, 77 Va. 462. In some states the mortgagee can proceed only in equity. Willard v. Worsham, 76 Va. 392. In these states the mortgagor cannot release the grantee from liability without the mortgagee's consent. Gifford v. Corrigan, 117 N. Y. 257, 22 N. E. 756; Douglass v. Wells, 18 Hun (N. Y.) 88. But see Gold v. Ogden (Minn.) 63 N. W. 266. In other states the mortgagee is treated as merely subrogated to the mortgagor's security, and cannot sue the assignee directly at law. Keller v. Ashford, 133 U. S. 610, 10 Sup. Ct. 494; Booth v. Insurance Co., 43 Mich. 299, 5 N. W. 381; Crowell v. Currier, 27 N. J. Eq. 152; Biddel v. Brizzolara, 64 Cal. 354, 30 Pac. 609. In these states the mortgagor may release his grantee without the assent of the mortgagee. O'Neill v. Clark, 33 N. J. Eq. 444.

[213] See post, p. 478.

to the surplus.[214] An equity of redemption may be sold on execution,[215] even by the mortgagee,[216] but, in most states, not under an execution issuing on the mortgage debt.[217] The same rules apply to equitable mortgages.[218]

ASSIGNMENT OF THE MORTGAGE.

127. A mortgagee may assign his interest, or part of it, on the following conditions:
  (a) It must be by deed.
  (b) The mortgage debt must accompany the mortgage.
  (c) The assignee takes the mortgage subject to the same equities as he takes the mortgage debt, and no other.

128. On the death of the mortgagee before foreclosure, his interest goes to his personal representative.

129. Before foreclosure the mortgagee's interest is not subject to attachment or sale on execution.

The mortgagee may assign the mortgage,[219] and so may his executor or administrator.[220] An assignment must be by deed,[221]

---

[214] Dunning v. Bank, 61 N. Y. 497; Fliess v. Buckley, 22 Hun (N. Y.) 551.

[215] Atkins v. Sawyer, 1 Pick. (Mass.) 351; Fitch v. Pinckard, 5 Ill. 69. And see Bernstein v. Humes, 71 Ala. 260.

[216] Cushing v. Hurd, 4 Pick. (Mass.) 253; Seaman v. Hax, 14 Colo. 536, 24 Pac. 461.

[217] Young v. Ruth, 55 Mo. 515; Goring's Ex'x v. Shreve, 7 Dana (Ky.) 64; Tice v. Annin, 2 Johns. Ch. (N. Y.) 125; Washburn v. Goodwin, 17 Pick. (Mass.) 137. Contra, Cottingham v. Springer, 88 Ill. 90.

[218] Clinton Nat. Bank v. Manwarring, 39 Iowa, 281; Turner v. Watkins, 31 Ark. 429. But see Gibson v. Hough, 60 Ga. 588; Phinizy v. Clark, 62 Ga. 623.

[219] A mortgage of indemnity cannot be assigned until the mortgagee has paid the debt. Abbott v. Upton, 19 Pick. (Mass.) 434; Wallace v. Goodall, 18 N. H. 439; Jones v. Bank, 29 Conn. 25. Contra, Carper v. Munger 62 Ind. 481; Murray v. Porter, 26 Neb. 288, 41 N. W. 1111.

[220] Ex parte Blair, 13 Metc. (Mass.) 126; Ladd v. Wiggin, 35 N. H. 421; Crooker v. Jewell, 31 Me. 306.

[221] Warden v. Adams, 15 Mass. 233; Torrey v. Deavitt, 53 Vt. 331. But see Kinna v. Smith, 3 N. J. Eq. 14.

and an assignment indorsed on the mortgage deed would not be operative at law.[222] An assignee of the mortgage takes the mortgagee's interest,[223] and he can foreclose in his own name.[224] After an assignment, an agreement by the mortgagor and mortgagee cannot affect the assignee's rights, provided the mortgagor has had notice of the assignment.[225] There may be an assignment of part of a mortgage.[226] If the mortgage is assigned without a transfer of the mortgage debt, the assignee takes only the legal title. He holds as a trustee for the protection of the mortgage debt, when that is held by another than the mortgagee.[227] But, if the mortgage debt has not been transferred by the mortgagee, some courts hold that it passes to the assignee by the transfer of the mortgage.[228]

An assignment of the mortgage debt carries with it the benefit

[222] Adams v. Parker, 12 Gray (Mass.) 53. A mere delivery of the mortgage deed, unaccompanied by the note secured, is not an assignment. Bowers v. Johnson, 49 N. Y. 432; Merritt v. Bartholick, 36 N. Y. 44.

[223] Anderson v. Bank, 98 Mich. 543, 57 N. W. 808; Harrison v. Yerby (Ala.) 14 South. 321; Hunt v. Mortgage Security Co., 92 Ga. 720, 19 S. E. 27. Cf. Gray v. Waldron, 101 Mich. 612, 60 N. W. 288; Geiger v. Peterson, 164 Pa. St. 352, 30 Atl. 262.

[224] Irish v. Sharp, 89 Ill. 261.

[225] Black v. Reno, 59 Fed. 917; Whipple v. Fowler, 41 Neb. 675, 60 N. W. 15; Parker v. Randolph, 5 S. D. 549, 59 N. W. 722. And see Cutler v. Clementson, 67 Fed. 409.

[226] Union Mut. Life Ins. Co. v. Slee, 123 Ill. 57, 12 N. E. 543; McSorley v. Larissa, 100 Mass. 270; Wyman v. Hooper, 2 Gray (Mass.) 141. So part of the mortgage debt may be assigned, and with it all of the mortgage. Langdon v. Keith, 9 Vt. 299. In several states where notes secured by a mortgage are assigned successively, the one first due has the first right to the mortgage security. Horn v. Bennett, 135 Ind. 158, 34 N. E. 956; Stanley v. Beatty, 4 Ind. 134; Grapengether v. Fejervary, 9 Iowa, 163; Wood v. Trask, 7 Wis. 566. Contra, Cullum v. Erwin, 4 Ala. 452; State Bank v. Mathews. 45 Neb. 659, 63 N. W. 930; Bartlett v. Wade, 66 Vt. 629, 30 Atl. 4; First Nat. Bank v. Andrews, 7 Wash. 261, 34 Pac. 913.

[227] Bailey v. Gould, Walk. (Mich.) 478; Merritt v. Bartholick, 36 N. Y. 44; Aymar v. Bill, 5 Johns. Ch. (N. Y.) 570; Swan v. Yaple, 35 Iowa, 248; Peters v. Bridge Co., 5 Cal. 335; Johnson v. Cornett, 29 Ind. 59; Thayer v. Campbell, 9 Mo. 280.

[228] Philips v. Bank, 18 Pa. St. 394. But see Fletcher v. Carpenter, 37 Mich. 412. And cf. Johnson v. Clarke (N. J. Ch.) 28 Atl. 558; State Bank v. Mathews, 45 Neb. 659, 63 N. W. 930.

of the mortgage,[229] and, when a debt secured by a trust deed is assigned, the trustee holds for the benefit of the assignee.[230] A mortgagee may set up an after-acquired title against his assignee, unless his assignment was with covenants of warranty.[231] And he may show that his assignment, though absolute in form, was for security only.[232] An assignment of the mortgage carries with it all other securities which the mortgagee has for the same debt.[233] An assignment raises no implied warranty as to the solvency of the mortgagor, but it does create a warranty that the mortgage debt has not been paid.[234] An assignee of a mortgage and the note which it secures takes the mortgage free from all equities of which he has no notice, because the note itself, which is the principal thing, is free from such equities.[235] But when the note is overdue, or is nonnegotiable, the mortgage is subject, in the hands of the assignee, to all the equities which existed between the original parties before notice of assignment to the mortgagor,[236] and the rule is the same when the mortgage is given without a mortgage note.[237]

If the mortgagee dies before foreclosure, his interest goes to his

[229] Larned v. Donovan, 31 Abb. N. C. 308, 29 N. Y. Supp. 825; Jenkins v. Wilkinson, 113 N. C. 532, 18 S. E. 696; Gumbel v. Boyer, 46 La. Ann. 762, 15 South. 84; Longfellow v. McGregor (Minn.) 63 N. W. 1032. But see Fitch v. McDowell, 145 N. Y. 498, 40 N. E. 205.

[230] Thomas v. Linn (W. Va.) 20 S. E. 878; Clark v. Jones, 93 Tenn. 639, 27 S. W. 1009.

[231] Weed Sewing Mach. Co. v. Emerson, 115 Mass. 554.

[232] Pond v. Eddy, 113 Mass. 149.

[233] Philips v. Bank, 18 Pa. St. 394. But see Smith v. Starr, 4 Hun (N. Y.) 123.

[234] 1 Jones, Mortg. (5th Ed.) § 831; French v. Turner, 15 Ind. 59.

[235] Dutton v. Ives, 5 Mich. 515; Jones v. Smith, 22 Mich. 360; Taylor v. Page, 6 Allen (Mass.) 86; Kenicott v. Supervisors, 16 Wall. 452; Preston v. Case, 42 Iowa, 549; Farmers' Nat. Bank v. Fletcher, 44 Iowa, 252; Swett v. Stark, 31 Fed. 858; Barnum v. Phenix, 60 Mich. 388, 27 N. W. 577; Helmer v. Krolick, 36 Mich. 371; Gould v. Marsh, 1 Hun (N. Y.) 566; Lewis v. Kirk, 28 Kan. 497. Contra, Scott v. Magloughlin, 133 Ill. 33, 24 N. E. 1030.

[236] McKenna v. Kirkwood, 50 Mich. 544, 15 N. W. 898; Fish v. French, 15 Gray (Mass.) 520; Owen v. Evans, 134 N. Y. 514, 31 N. E. 999. That in New York he takes it subject also to latent equities in favor of third persons, see Bush v. Lathrop, 22 N. Y. 535.

[237] Corbett v. Woodward, 5 Sawy. 403, Fed. Cas. No. 3,223.

personal representative, and it may be assigned or otherwise disposed of by the latter without an order of the court.[238] The heirs of the mortgagee cannot sell the mortgage, nor can they foreclose it.[239] Unless the mortgagee has acquired the mortgaged premises under a strict foreclosure, or has bid them in at a foreclosure sale, he has no interest which is subject to attachment, or to a sale on execution. The same is true of a beneficiary under a deed of trust.[240] This is because the mortgage is a mere incident to the mortgage debt. The creditor's remedy is against the mortgage debt, which is the principal thing.

PRIORITY OF MORTGAGES AND OTHER CONVEYANCES.

130. No subsequent purchaser or incumbrancer can take priority over a conveyance of which he has notice. Such notice may be:
  (a) **Actual** (p. 213).
  (b) **Implied** (p. 215).
  (c) **Constructive, which includes notice:**
     (1) **By recitals in title deeds** (p. 216).
     (2) **By possession** (p. 216).
     (3) **By lis pendens** (p. 218).
     (4) **By registration** (p. 218).

The priority of mortgages and other conveyances of realty depends almost entirely on the doctrine of notice.[241] There is a maxim of equity, that, between equal equities, priority of time prevails;[242] but in dealing with conveyances of realty the question usually is whether the equities are equal, and they are not if the subsequent purchaser has notice of the prior conveyance. How-

---

[238] Baldwin v. Hatchett, 56 Ala. 461; Collamer v. Langdon, 29 Vt. 32; Douglass v. Durin, 51 Me. 121.

[239] Collamer v. Langdon, 29 Vt. 32; Webster v. Calden, 56 Me. 204.

[240] Marsh v. Austin, 1 Allen (Mass.) 235; Jackson v. Willard, 4 Johns. (N. Y.) 41; Rickert v. Madeira, 1 Rawle (Pa.) 325; Nicholson v. Walker, 4 Ill. App. 404; Scott v. Mewhirter, 49 Iowa, 487; Buck v. Sanders, 1 Dana (Ky.) 187.

[241] See Fetter, Eq. c. 5.

[242] Fetter, Eq. p. 36.

§ 130)   PRIORITY OF MORTGAGES AND OTHER CONVEYANCES.   213

ever, a purchaser with notice may acquire a good title from one who purchased without notice, because otherwise the latter's free right of disposal would be abridged.[243] On the other hand, a purchaser without notice can take a good title from one who had notice.[244] The question of priority is in many cases affected by fraud of the prior grantee; as, where a prior mortgagee conceals the existence of his mortgage from one about to take a mortgage on the same premises,[245] or, on inquiry being made, states that nothing is due on his mortgage, he is estopped to set up the mortgage against the subsequent mortgagee.[246] But a mortgagor is not bound to disclose his mortgage if it is on record.[247]

Actual Notice.

Whenever a subsequent mortgagee or grantee has actual notice of a prior conveyance, he can acquire no priority over such conveyance.[248] When the unrecorded conveyance has actually been seen by, or read before, the purchaser, but under circumstances where he could not well suspect the identity of the land, nor remember its description,—as where lots are sold by number from a plat, and he comes himself to buy what he naturally thinks are other lots,—the purchaser is not charged with notice.[249] Actual notice does not

[243] Alexander v. Pendleton, 8 Cranch, 462; Boone v. Chiles, 10 Pet. 177; Morse v. Curtis, 140 Mass. 112, 2 N. E. 929; Boynton v. Rees, 8 Pick. (Mass.) 329; Webster v. Van Steenbergh, 46 Barb. (N. Y.) 211; Bracken v. Miller, 4 Watts & S. (Pa.) 102; Day v. Clark, 25 Vt. 397; Pringle v. Dunn, 37 Wis. 449. Contra, Sims v. Hammond, 33 Iowa, 368. But see, contra, where the deed is recorded in the meantime. Van Rensselaer v. Clark, 17 Wend. (N. Y.) 25; Bayles v. Young, 51 Ill. 127. But one who has taken a title, with notice, and transferred it, cannot acquire a good title by subsequently repurchasing from one who had no notice. Schutt v. Large, 6 Barb. (N. Y.) 373.

[244] Wood v. Mann, 1 Sumn. 506, Fed. Cas. No. 17,951; Choteau v. Jones, 11 Ill. 300; Trull v. Bigelow, 16 Mass. 406; Somes v. Brewer, 2 Pick. (Mass.) 184; Glidden v. Hunt, 24 Pick. (Mass.) 221; Fallass v. Pierce, 30 Wis. 443.

[245] L'Amoureux v. Vandenburgh, 7 Paige (N. Y.) 316.

[246] Platt v. Squire, 12 Metc. (Mass.) 494; Miller v. Bingham, 29 Vt. 82. And see Fay v. Valentine, 12 Pick. (Mass.) 40; Chester v. Greer, 5 Humph. (Tenn.) 25.

[247] Brinckerhoff v. Lansing, 4 Johns. Ch. (N. Y.) 65; Paine v. French, 4 Ohio, 318; Palmer v. Palmer, 48 Vt. 69.

[248] Fetter, Eq. 102. And see Wallace v. McKenzie, 104 Cal. 130, 37 Pac. 859.

[249] Armstrong v. Abbott, 11 Colo. 220, 17 Pac. 517; Vest v. Michie, 31 Grat. (Va.) 149.

necessitate actual knowledge.[250] It may be shown by circumstantial evidence. Whether there was such notice depends in each instance upon the facts of the case.[251] The test is whether the circumstances were such as to cause a reasonably prudent man to make inquiry.[252] But the notice must afford sufficient information to make a reasonable inquiry on, and not merely to put him on inquiry.[253] For instance, a mere rumor is not notice.[254] A purchaser who is put on inquiry must make a reasonable investigation of the title,[255] and he cannot rely on statements of his grantor, or one who is interested in concealing the prior incumbrance.[256] He is presumed to have notice of facts which due inquiry would have shown him.[257] The burden of proof, however, is on the one who seeks to establish the existence of notice.[258] Notice, to affect a subsequent purchaser, must be received before the transaction is completed and the price

[250] Fetter, Eq. 81. See, however, Lamb v. Pierce, 113 Mass. 72.

[251] Lamb v. Pierce, 113 Mass. 72; White v. Foster, 102 Mass. 375; Sibley v. Leffingwell, 8 Allen (Mass.) 584; Michigan Mut. Life Ins. Co. v. Conant, 40 Mich. 530; Vest v. Michie, 31 Grat. (Va.) 149; Vaughn v. Tracy, 22 Mo. 415; Speck v. Riggin, 40 Mo. 405.

[252] Fassett v. Smith, 23 N. Y. 252; Williamson v. Brown, 15 N. Y. 354; Baker v. Bliss, 39 N. Y. 70; Maupin v. Emmons, 47 Mo. 304; Wilcox v. Hill, 11 Mich. 256; Helms v. Chadbourne, 45 Wis. 60; Brinkman v. Jones, 44 Wis. 498; Heaton v. Prather, 84 Ill. 330; Curtis v. Mundy, 3 Metc. (Mass.) 405; Wilson v. Hunter, 30 Ind. 466.

[253] Dey v. Dunham, 2 Johns. Ch. (N. Y.) 182; Jackson v. Van Valkenburgh, 8 Cow. (N. Y.) 260; City of Chicago v. Witt, 75 Ill. 211; Maul v. Rider, 59 Pa. St. 167.

[254] Parkhurst v. Hosford, 21 Fed. 827; Pittman v. Sofley, 64 Ill. 155; Otis v. Spencer, 102 Ill. 622; Buttrick v. Holden, 13 Metc. (Mass.) 355; Shepard v. Shepard, 36 Mich. 173; Appeal of Bugbee, 110 Pa. St. 331, 1 Atl. 273; Kerns v. Swope, 2 Watts (Pa.) 75; Lamont v. Stimson, 5 Wis. 443.

[255] Schweiss v. Woodruff, 73 Mich. 473, 41 N. W. 511; Oliver v. Sanborn, 60 Mich. 346, 27 N. W. 527; Cambridge Valley Bank v. Delano, 48 N. Y. 326; Maul v. Rider, 59 Pa. St. 167; Wilson v. Miller, 16 Iowa, 111. But, if inquiry fails to disclose the prior conveyance, he is protected. Williamson v. Brown, 15 N. Y. 354.

[256] Blatchley v. Osborn, 33 Conn. 226; Russell v. Petree, 10 B. Mon. (Ky.) 184; Littleton v. Giddings, 47 Tex. 109.

[257] Passumpsic Sav. Bank v. First Nat. Bank, 53 Vt. 82; Austin v. Pulschen (Cal.) 39 Pac. 799. Notice of an unrecorded deed is notice of all its contents. Martin v. Cauble, 72 Ind. 67; Hill v. Murray, 56 Vt. 177.

[258] Ryder v. Rush, 102 Ill. 338; McCormick v. Leonard, 38 Iowa, 272.

§ 130) PRIORITY OF MORTGAGES AND OTHER CONVEYANCES.   215

paid.[259] If notice is received after part of the money has been paid over, the protection extends to that part, but not to money subsequently paid.[260]

Implied Notice.

By the doctrine of implied notice, one who has no notice himself is presumed to have notice because of his legal relations with one who has notice. This arises most often from the relation of principal and agent,[261] which includes attorney and client.[262] One who deals with real property through an agent is bound by any notice which may come to the agent in the scope of his employment.[263] In the same way, a cestui que trust is bound by notice to his trustee.[264] But notice to a husband is not notice to his wife.[265] Notice to a corporation can be given only by notice to an officer who has the matter in charge. Notice to the agent of a corporation is not notice to the corporation, unless it touches matters in the line of the agent's business.[266] The implication of notice in any case may be rebutted by showing facts which raise a presumption that the agent did not communicate his knowledge to his principal. This is the case where the agent has been guilty of fraud, or where the knowledge comes to the agent in another transaction, or under such circumstances that he will not be presumed to have remembered it.[267]

[259] Brown v. Welch, 18 Ill. 343; Schultze v. Houfes, 96 Ill. 335; Palmer v. Williams, 24 Mich. 328; Dixon v. Hill, 5 Mich. 404; Everts v. Agnes, 4 Wis 343.

[260] Baldwin v. Sager, 70 Ill. 503; Redden v. Miller, 95 Ill. 336.

[261] Jackson v. Van Valkenburgh, 8 Cow. (N. Y.) 260; Bigley v. Jones, 114 Pa. St. 510, 7 Atl. 54; Sowler v. Day, 58 Iowa, 252, 12 N. W. 297. But see Reynolds v. Black (Iowa) 58 N. W. 922.

[262] May v. Le Claire, 11 Wall. 217; Josephthal v. Heyman, 2 Abb. N. C. (N. Y.) 22; Walker v. Schreiber, 47 Iowa, 529.

[263] Hoppock v. Johnson, 14 Wis. 303; Tucker v. Tilton, 55 N. H. 223.

[264] Pope v. Pope, 40 Miss. 516.

[265] Pringle v. Dunn, 37 Wis. 449; Satterfield v. Malone, 35 Fed. 445.

[266] Wilson v. McCullough, 23 Pa. St. 440.

[267] Armstrong v. Abbott, 11 Colo. 220, 17 Pac. 517; 1 Jones, Mortg. (5th Ed.) § 560.

Constructive Notice—Recitals in Title Deeds.

Constructive notice is notice implied by operation of law, and cannot be controverted by extraneous evidence.[268] One who takes a conveyance of realty is bound by the recitals in all the instruments in his chain of title,[269] such as a recital in a deed that the premises are conveyed subject to a mortgage. This is binding on a subsequent purchaser, even though the mortgage is not recorded.[270] And so he is bound by notice of facts of which he is put on inquiry by recitals in his title deeds.[271] And, when one has actual notice of an unrecorded conveyance, he is bound by all the facts of which such conveyance is notice.[272] But, when a reference in one of the deeds making up the chain of title to other deeds or writings is only incidental (for instance, if it is in a part of the deed in which other lands are granted), the purchaser is not bound to pursue the inquiry; and he has no actual, and, it seems, not even constructive, notice of the matter which may be found in those deeds.[273]

Same—Possession.

In most states it is held that possession by one not the owner of record is notice of the rights of the occupant,[274] as when one is

[268] Rogers v. Jones, 8 N. H. 264.

[269] George v. Kent, 7 Allen (Mass.) 16; United States Mortg. Co. v. Gross, 93 Ill. 483; Dean v. Long, 122 Ill. 447, 14 N. E. 34; Baker v. Mather, 25 Mich. 51; Cambridge Valley Bank v. Delano, 48 N. Y. 326; Parke v. Neeley, 90 Pa. St. 52; Kerr v. Kitchen, 17 Pa. St. 433; Dailey v. Kastell, 56 Wis. 444, 14 N. W. 635; Clark v. Holland, 72 Iowa, 34, 33 N. W. 350.

[270] Kitchell v. Mudgett, 37 Mich. 81; Baker v. Mather, 25 Mich. 51; Garrett v. Puckett, 15 Ind. 485.

[271] Cordova v. Hood, 17 Wall. 1; Lytle v. Turner, 12 Lea (Tenn.) 641.

[272] Howard Ins. Co. v. Halsey, 8 N. Y. 271; Green v. Slayter, 4 Johns. Ch. 38; Bent v. Coleman, 89 Ill. 364.

[273] See Kansas City Land Co. v. Hill, 87 Tenn. 589, 11 S. W. 797.

[274] Phillips v. Costley, 40 Ala. 486; Byers v. Engles, 16 Ark. 543; Smith v. Yule, 31 Cal. 180; Massey v. Hubbard, 18 Fla. 688; Sewell v. Holland, 61 Ga. 608; Brainard v. Hudson, 103 Ill. 218; Sutton v. Jervis, 31 Ind. 265; Moore v. Pierson, 6 Iowa, 279; Lyons v. Bodenhamer, 7 Kan. 455; Hackwith v. Damron, 1 T. B. Mon. (Ky.) 235, Ringgold v. Bryan, 3 Md. Ch. 488; Allen v. Cadwell, 55 Mich. 8, 20 N. W. 692; New v. Wheaton, 24 Minn. 406; Vaughn v. Tracy, 22 Mo. 415; Phelan v. Brady, 119 N. Y. 587, 23 N. W. 1109; Appeal of Bugbee, 110 Pa. St. 331, 1 Atl. 273. But other courts hold the contrary. Harral v. Leverty, 50 Conn. 46; Pomroy v. Stevens, 11 Metc. (Mass.) 244; Brinkman v. Jones, 44 Wis. 498.

§ 130) PRIORITY OF MORTGAGES AND OTHER CONVEYANCES.   217

in possession as vendee under an executory contract to purchase,[275] or when one holds as lessee.[276] And most cases hold that possession by a tenant is notice, not only of his own rights, but of the rights of his landlord as well.[277] It is held by many courts that possession is notice, although the possession is not actually known to the subsequent purchaser.[278] But possession is notice only during its continuance,[279] and it must be visible, notorious, and exclusive.[280] Possession of part may operate as notice of a title to the whole of the premises.[281] In order that possession may constitute notice, it must be inconsistent with the title on which the purchaser relies.[282] Therefore possession by a grantor is not notice to a subsequent purchaser of any right reserved,[283] though it may be notice of rights subsequently acquired.[284] On the other hand, long-continued possession by the grantor is held to be notice of any right claimed by him,[285] as where he holds as mortgagor after giving a deed absolute in form.[286] Possession by the mortgagor or his grantee is not notice of an unrecorded release.[287]

[275] Bank of Orleans v. Flagg, 3 Barb. Ch. (N. Y.) 316.

[276] Kerr v. Day, 14 Pa. St. 112.

[277] U. S. v. Sliney, 21 Fed. 894; Haworth v. Taylor, 108 Ill. 275; Whitaker v. Miller, 83 Ill. 381; Hood v. Fahnestock, 1 Pa. St. 470; Dickey v. Lyon, 19 Iowa, 544; But see Beatie v. Butler, 21 Mo. 313; Flagg v. Mann, 2 Sumn. 486, Fed. Cas. No. 4,847.

[278] Ranney v. Hardy, 43 Ohio St. 157; Hodge v. Amerman, 40 N. J. Eq. 99, 2 Atl. 257; Edwards v. Thompson, 71 N. C. 177.

[279] Ehle v. Brown, 31 Wis. 405; Meehan v. Williams, 48 Pa. St. 238.

[280] Morrison v. Kelly, 22 Ill. 610; Bogue v. Williams, 48 Ill. 371; Kendall v. Lawrence, 22 Pick. (Mass.) 540; M'Mechan v. Griffing, 3 Pick. (Mass.) 149; Webster v. Van Steenbergh, 46 Barb. (N. Y.) 211; Page v. Waring, 76 N. Y. 463; Ely v. Wilcox, 20 Wis. 523; Meehan v. Williams, 48 Pa. St. 238.

[281] Nolan v. Grant, 51 Iowa, 519, 1 N. W. 709; Watkins v. Edwards, 23 Tex. 443.

[282] Staples v. Fenton, 5 Hun (N. Y.) 172; Plumer v. Robertson, 6 Serg. & R. (Pa.) 177; Smith v. Yule, 31 Cal. 180.

[283] Newhall v. Pierce, 5 Pick. (Mass.) 450; Dawson v. Danbury Bank, 15 Mich. 489; Koon v. Tramel, 71 Iowa, 132, 32 N. W. 243.

[284] 1 Jones, Mortg. (5th Ed.) § 597.

[285] White v. White, 89 Ill. 460; Ford v. Marcall, 107 Ill. 136; Illinois Cent. R. Co. v. McCullough, 59 Ill. 166; Hopkins v. Garrard, 7 B. Mon. (Ky.) 312.

[286] New v. Wheaton, 24 Minn. 406.

[287] Briggs v. Thompson, 86 Hun, 607, 33 N. Y. Supp. 765.

Same—Lis Pendens.

By the doctrine of lis pendens,[288] one who purchases realty from a party to a suit which involves the title thereto takes it subject to the rights of the litigants, as they may be determined by the action; that is, the pendency of the suit affecting the title to realty is constructive notice to purchasers who acquire interests in the property after the commencement of the action.[289]

SAME—REGISTRATION.

131. By recording instruments affecting real property in the manner provided by statute, constructive notice of the contents of such instruments is given to subsequent purchasers and incumbrancers.

In all states there are statutes which make it possible to give constructive notice of any conveyance affecting realty by recording the instrument in an office designated by the statute.[290] These statutes will be treated of in this place in their application to other kinds of instruments besides mortgages. The theory of the registry acts is that, by the record of a conveyance, constructive notice is given of its existence and provisions, because every one can examine the record. If a man does not record his deed or mortgage, he is negligent, and should suffer, rather than an innocent purchaser.[291] There is a difference between the effect of notice (actual or constructive), and that of recording, upon the action of a subsequent purchaser. While, under the laws of many states, such a purchaser is protected against a prior, unrecorded convey-

---

[288] See Fetter, Eq. p. 93.

[289] Haven v. Adams, 8 Allen (Mass.) 363; Jackson v. Andrews, 7 Wend. (N. Y.) 152; Bolling v. Carter, 9 Ala. 921; Blanchard v. Ware, 37 Iowa, 305; Hersey v. Turbett, 27 Pa. St. 418; Youngman v. Railroad Co., 65 Pa. St. 278; Edwards v. Banksmith, 35 Ga. 213; Grant v. Bennett, 96 Ill. 513; Smith v. Hodsdon, 78 Me. 180, 3 Atl. 276. But see Newman v. Chapman, 2 Rand. (Va.) 93; Douglass v. McCrackin, 52 Ga. 596; M'Cutchen v. Miller, 31 Miss. 65; Wyatt v. Barwell, 19 Ves. 435.

[290] 1 Stim. Am. St. Law, art. 161.

[291] In some states a mortgage is of no validity unless recorded within a certain time. 1 Stim. Am. St. Law, § 1615; 1 Jones, Mortg. (5th Ed.) § 458. And see Truman v. Weed, 14 C. C. A. 595, 67 Fed. 645.

ance only if he has first put his own deed on record, and thus the recording of the first deed would defeat him, though he has laid out his money and received his deed, it is otherwise with notice in pais, which comes too late when the price or consideration has been paid, and the deed delivered to the later purchaser.

What Instruments Recorded.

The registry acts generally require the recording of all instruments affecting real estate, except short leases, in a number of states.[292] The laws in most of the states provide, also, for the recording of plats and subdivisions, for the double purpose—First, of enabling the grantor and others in subsequent deeds to refer in their deeds to the blocks and lots of the plat as matters of public record; secondly, of dedicating to the public the streets, wharves, alleys, and open places laid down on the plat.[293] But the record of an instrument which is not required by the statute to be recorded does not give notice of its existence.[294] Nor are purchasers affected by the registry of a forged deed.[295] No constructive notice is raised by the record of an instrument defectively executed,[296] though it would be otherwise if there was an actual examination of the record.[297] However, in Illinois and Kansas the recording of deeds defectively executed is notice of the equities arising under them.[298]

As previously stated, equitable mortgages come within the provisions of the recording acts,[299] as do also mortgages affecting lease-

[292] 1 Stim. Am. St. Law, § 1624; 2 Dembitz, Land Tit. 948, 955.

[293] Satchell v. Doram, 4 Ohio St. 542; Williams v. Smith, 22 Wis. 598; Maywood Co. v. Village of Maywood, 118 Ill. 65, 6 N. E. 866.

[294] Moore v. Hunter, 6 Ill. 317; Pringle v. Dunn, 37 Wis. 449; Parret v. Shaubhut, 5 Minn. 323 (Gil. 258).

[295] Pry v. Pry, 109 Ill. 466.

[296] Heister's Lessee v. Fortner, 2 Bin. (Pa.) 40; Graves v. Graves, 6 Gray (Mass.) 391; Blood v. Blood, 23 Pick. (Mass.) 80; St. Louis Iron & Mach. Works v. Kimball, 53 Ill. App. 636; Carter v. Champion, 8 Conn. 549.

[297] Bass v. Estill, 50 Miss. 300; Pringle v. Dunn, 37 Wis. 449.

[298] Morrison v. Brown, 83 Ill. 562; Reed v. Kemp, 16 Ill. 445; Gillespie v. Reed, 3 McLean, 377, Fed. Cas. No. 5,436; Simpson v. Mundee, 3 Kan. 172; Brown v. Simpson, 4 Kan. 76. And see Healey v. Worth, 35 Mich. 166.

[299] Hunt v. Johnson, 19 N. Y. 279; Parkist v. Alexander, 1 Johns. Ch. (N. Y.) 394; Smith v. Nellson, 13 Lea (Tenn.) 461; Russell's Appeal, 15 Pa. St. 319.

hold estates.[300] Assignments of mortgages are to be recorded the same as mortgages.[301]

Manner of Recording.

To entitle a mortgage or other conveyance to be admitted to record, the requirements of the statutes as to execution [302] and delivery must be complied with.[303] But a conveyance may be recorded after the death of the grantor, if made effectual by delivery before his death.[304] In most of the states before a conveyance can be recorded it must be acknowledged by the maker before an officer designated by statute.[305] A conveyance must be recorded within the county where the land is situated.[306] A power of attorney to

[300] Although leasehold estates are treated as chattel interests, mortgages affecting them are recorded with mortgages of real property. Berry v. Insurance Co., 2 Johns. Ch. (N. Y.) 603; Breese v. Bange, 2 E. D. Smith (N. Y.) 474; Paine v. Mason, 7 Ohio St. 198. Mortgages of growing crops and of trees, as long as they are realty, are to be recorded with mortgages of real property. Jones v. Chamberlin, 5 Heisk. (Tenn.) 210. Powers of attorney are sometimes required to be recorded. 1 Stim. Am. St. Law, § 1624 (10).

[301] See 1 Stim. Am. St. Law, § 1624; Howard v. Shaw, 10 Wash. 151, 38 Pac. 746; Larned v. Donovan, 84 Hun, 533, 32 N. Y. Supp. 731; Murphy v. Barnard, 162 Mass. 72, 38 N. E. 29; Bowling v. Cook, 39 Iowa, 200; Merrill v. Luce (S. D.) 61 N. W. 43; Stein v. Sullivan, 31 N. J. Eq. 409; Turpin v. Ogle, 4 Ill. App. 611. But see James v. Morey, 2 Cow. (N. Y.) 246. Question of priority of assignments of the same mortgage seldom arises, because the mortgage note and mortgage are usually delivered to the first assignee. 1 Jones, Mortg. (5th Ed.) § 483.

[302] As to description of the property, and the requirements for signing, sealing, witnessing, etc., see post, pp. 419, 426.

[303] Sigourney v. Larned, 10 Pick. (Mass.) 72; Galpin v. Abbott, 6 Mich. 17; Fryer v. Rockefeller, 63 N. Y. 268; Green v. Drinker, 7 Watts & S. (Pa.) 440; McKean & Elk Land Imp. Co. v. Mitchell, 35 Pa. St. 269; Ely v. Wilcox, 20 Wis. 551; White v. Denman, 1 Ohio St. 110.

[304] Gill v. Pinney's Adm'r, 12 Ohio St. 38; Haskell v. Bissell, 11 Conn. 174.

[305] 1 Stim. Am. St. Law, § 1570.

[306] 1 Stim. Am. St. Law, § 1614; Lewis v. Baird, 3 McLean, 56, Fed. Cas. No. 8,316; St. John v. Conger, 40 Ill. 535; Stewart v. McSweeney, 14 Wis. 468. In New Hampshire, Rhode Island, and Connecticut, the town is the unit instead of the county. 2 Dembitz, Land Tit. 941. Where an instrument affects land lying in two or more counties, it must be recorded in each. Oberholtzer's Appeal, 124 Pa. St. 583, 17 Atl. 143, 144; 1 Stim. Am. St. Law, §§ 1614, 1627. But see, as to change of boundaries, Koerper v. Railway

convey land may be recorded in any county in which the grantor may at the time or thereafter have land to convey (unless it is restricted to particular tracts); that is, in any county of the state. But it does not follow that, when recorded in one county, it will make a deed as to land in another county recordable; nor will it, at least in some states, and where the statute does not expressly authorize the recording of such instruments in every county, make a deed as to land in another county recordable, or even prove itself by the record.[307] The notice takes effect from the time the instrument is filed for record,[308] and the certificate of the recording officer is conclusive as to the time of such filing.[309] If the instrument is erroneously recorded, it is, in some states, notice only of what appears on the record.[310] But in other states the first grantee, having done all he could to secure a proper record, is not made to suffer by the recording officer's mistake.[311] The officer is liable for damages suffered by the one or the other through negligence in recording.[312] He may, however, correct errors in the record at a time,[313] but notice of the instrument as corrected begins only from the time such corrections are made.[314]

When an instrument has been properly recorded, its priority is nowise affected by a destruction of the records.[315]

Co., 40 Minn. 132, 41 N. W. 656; Milton v. Turner, 38 Tex. 81; Garrison v. Haydon, 1 J. J. Marsh. (Ky.) 222.

[307] Muldrow v. Robison, 58 Mo. 331.

[308] Haworth v. Taylor, 108 Ill. 275; Sinclair v. Slawson, 44 Mich. 123, 6 N. W. 207; Mutual Life Ins. Co. v. Dake, 87 N. Y. 257; Brooke's Appeal, 64 Pa. St. 127; Woodward v. Boro, 16 Lea (Tenn.) 678.

[309] Tracy v. Jenks, 15 Pick. (Mass.) 465; Hatch v. Haskins, 17 Me. 391.

[310] Frost v. Beekman, 1 Johns. Ch. (N. Y.) 288; s. c., appeal, 18 Johns. (N. Y.) 544; Miller v. Bradford, 12 Iowa, 14; Brydon v. Campbell, 40 Md. 331. Contra, Mims v. Mims, 35 Ala. 23, under a statute making conveyances "operative as a record" from the time of delivery to the officer.

[311] Merreck v. Wallace, 19 Ill. 486; Tousley v. Tousley, 5 Ohio St. 78. And see Sinclair v. Slawson, 44 Mich. 123, 6 N. W. 207.

[312] 1 Jones, Mortg. (5th Ed.) § 579.

[313] Sellers v. Sellers, 98 N. C. 13, 3 S. E. 917.

[314] Chamberlain v. Bell, 7 Cal. 292.

[315] Shannon v. Hall, 72 Ill. 354; Heaton v. Prather, 84 Ill. 330. See 1 Stim. Am. St. Law, § 1620. But some statutes require a re-recording within a given time. Tolle v. Alley (Ky.) 24 S. W. 113. And see Hyatt v. Cochran, 69 Ind. 436.

In a few states, the index is made a part of the record, so that an instrument recorded, but not indexed, is not notice.[316] In others the index is no part of the record.[317]

Of What Facts Record is Notice.

When an instrument is properly recorded, it is constructive notice of everything which could be learned by an actual examination of the record. Therefore purchasers are bound by recitals in the recorded deed,[318] and a reference to a prior, unrecorded instrument gives notice of that instrument.[319] There is notice, also, of anything as to which the record would put one on inquiry.[320]

To Whom Record is Notice.

Most of the recording laws provide that unrecorded instruments shall be void against subsequent purchasers and incumbrancers without notice, and for value, whose deeds or mortgages are recorded first.[321] The effect of these statutes is that priority of record gives priority of title,[322] and, when both instruments are unrecorded, priority is according to the time of execution.[323] In a few states the subsequent conveyance has priority, although it is not first recorded,[324] and in some states actual notice of a deed or mortgage does not make it valid against subsequent purchasers unless it has been recorded.[325] In several states the statutes provide

---

[316] Barney v. McCarty, 15 Iowa, 510; Lombard v. Culbertson, 59 Wis. 433, 18 N. W. 399. But see Lane v. Duchac, 73 Wis. 646, 41 N. W. 962.

[317] Mutual Life Ins. Co. v. Dake, 87 N. Y. 257; Curtis v. Lyman, 24 Vt. 338; Stockwell v. McHenry, 107 Pa. St. 237; Green v. Garrington, 16 Ohio St. 548.

[318] McPherson v. Rollins, 107 N. Y. 316, 14 N. E. 411; Dexter v. Harris, 2 Mason, 531, Fed. Cas. No. 3,862.

[319] White v. Foster, 102 Mass. 375.

[320] Heaton v. Prather, 84 Ill. 330. But see Interstate Bldg. & Loan Ass'n v. McCartha, 43 S. C. 72, 20 S. E. 807. Record of an incumbrance on land given prior to the acquisition of the title, is not notice. Calder v. Chapman, 52 Pa. St. 359; Oliphant v. Burns, 146 N. Y. 218, 40 N. E. 980.

[321] See 1 Stim. Am. St. Law, § 1611.

[322] Ely v. Wilcox, 20 Wis. 523; Lacustrine Fertilizer Co. v. Lake Guano & Fertilizer Co., 82 N. Y. 476; Burrows v. Hovland, 40 Neb. 464, 58 N. W. 947.

[323] 1 Stim. Am. St. Law, § 1611 A (1).

[324] 1 Stim. Am. St. Law, § 1611 A (2).

[325] Mayham v. Coombs, 14 Ohio, 428; Doe v. Allsop, 5 Barn. & Ald. 142; Bostic v. Young, 116 N. C. 766, 21 S. E. 552; Quinnerly v. Quinnerly, 114 N.

that a conveyance shall be constructive notice from the time of its execution, if it is recorded within a certain time.[326] Such a provision seems most pernicious, and certainly is productive of the very frauds which registry acts are designed to prevent.[327] In some, at least, of these states, if the instrument is not recorded within the time allowed by the statute, it is then notice only from the time it is actually recorded.[328]

The record of an instrument is notice only to those who are bound to search the records. Consequently no one is affected with notice who does not claim through the same chain of title.[329] Nor is the record of a deed of any effect against a prior grantee whose deed is already recorded.[330] A subsequent conveyance does not become effectual by record against a prior unrecorded instrument, unless the subsequent conveyance was for value, and without notice in any way.[331] In some states a purchaser by a quitclaim deed is held to take subject to prior unrecorded instruments.[332] But in most states the cases hold the contrary.[333] A purchaser from an

C. 145, 19 S. E. 99. To the contrary, see Blades v. Blades, 1 Eq. Cas. Abr. 358, pl. 12; Stroud v. Lockart, 4 Dall. 153; Britton's Appeal, 45 Pa. St. 172.

[326] 1 Stim. Am. St. Law, § 1615 B.

[327] See Clarke v. White, 12 Pet. 178; Phifer v. Barnhart, 88 N. C. 333.

[328] 1 Stim. Am. St. Law, § 1615 B; Northrup's Lessee v. Brehmer, 8 Ohio, 392; Pollard v. Cocke, 19 Ala. 188; Harding v. Allen, 70 Md. 395, 17 Atl. 377; Sanborn v. Adair, 29 N. J. Eq. 338; Anderson v. Dugas, 29 Ga. 440.

[329] Webber v. Ramsey, 100 Mich. 58, 58 N. W. 625; Long v. Dollarhide, 24 Cal. 218; Tilton v. Hunter, 24 Me. 29; Crockett v. Maguire, 10 Mo. 34; Losey v. Simpson, 11 N. J. Eq. 246; Rodgers v. Burchard, 34 Tex. 441; Rankin v. Miller, 43 Iowa, 11.

[330] George v. Wood, 9 Allen (Mass.) 80; Bell v. Fleming's Ex'rs, 12 N. J. Eq. 13.

[331] Adams v. Cuddy, 13 Pick. (Mass.) 460; Jackson v. Page, 4 Wend. (N. Y.) 585; Jackson v. Elston, 12 Johns. (N. Y.) 452; Mills v. Smith, 8 Wall. 27; Goodenough v. Warren, 5 Sawy. 494, Fed. Cas. No. 5,534.

[332] Marshall v. Roberts, 18 Minn. 405 (Gil. 365). See, also, Fitzgerald v. Libby, 142 Mass. 235, 7 N. E. 917; De Veaux v. Fosbender, 57 Mich. 579, 24 N. W. 790.

[333] Dow v. Whitney, 147 Mass. 1, 16 N. E. 722; Doe v. Reed, 5 Ill. 117; Pettingill v. Devin, 35 Iowa, 344; Cutler v. James, 64 Wis. 173, 24 N. W. 874; Willingham v. Hardin, 75 Mo. 429; Graff v. Middleton, 43 Cal. 341; Johnson v. Williams, 37 Kan. 179, 14 Pac. 537. But see Stivers v. Horne, 62 Mo. 473.

heir takes land free from the unrecorded conveyances of the ancestor, of which he has no notice.[334]

Unrecorded deeds and mortgages are, of course, valid against the grantor or mortgagor, his heirs and devisees.[335] And they are valid also against his assignee in bankruptcy,[336] but not against a bona fide purchaser from such assignee.[337] A mortgagee and a trustee under a deed of trust are purchasers within the meaning of the recording laws.[338] But in some states one who takes a mortgage to secure a pre-existing debt is not a purchaser, and takes only the mortgagor's equitable interest.[339] For example, in these states, if the mortgagor had made a valid contract for the sale of the mortgaged premises, a mortgage, to secure a pre-existing debt, though to one having no notice of the contract, would create a lien only on the part of the purchase price still unpaid.[340]

Mortgages to secure future advances by the mortgagee are valid,[341] and, if properly recorded, have priority over subsequent conveyances and incumbrances, up to the amount expressed in the

[334] Earle v. Fiske, 103 Mass. 491; Powers v. McFerran, 2 Serg. & R. (Pa.) 44; Kennedy v. Northup, 15 Ill. 148; Vaughan v. Greer, 38 Tex. 530; Youngblood v. Vastine, 46 Mo. 239; McCulloch's Lessee v. Endaly, 3 Yerg. (Tenn.) 346; Hill v. Meeker, 24 Conn. 211. Contra, Harlan's Heirs v. Seaton's Heirs, 18 B. Mon. (Ky.) 312; Hancock v. Beverly's Heirs, 6 B. Mon. (Ky.) 531; Rodgers v. Burchard, 34 Tex. 441.

[335] 1 Stim. Am. St. Law, § 1611 B; Secard's Lessee v. Davis, 6 Pet. 124; Burns v. Berry, 42 Mich. 176, 3 N. W. 924.

[336] Stewart v. Platt, 101 U. S. 731; Mellon's Appeal, 32 Pa. St. 121.

[337] Holbrook v. Dickenson, 56 Ill. 497. As to who are bona fide purchasers, see Fetter, Eq. 95.

[338] Martin v. Jackson, 27 Pa. St. 504; Hulett v. Insurance Co., 114 Pa. St. 142, 6 Atl. 554; Porter v. Greene, 4 Iowa, 571; Kesner v. Trigg, 98 U. S. 50; Sheffey v. Bank, 33 Fed. 315.

[339] Boxheimer v. Gunn, 24 Mich. 372. But he is a purchaser if he releases some valuable right, such as a vendor's lien, Lane v. Logue, 12 Lea (Tenn.) 681; or gives an extension of time, Koon v. Tramel, 71 Iowa, 132, 32 N. W. 243; Cary v. White, 52 N. Y. 138; Gilchrist v. Gough, 63 Ind. 576.

[340] Young v. Guy, 87 N. Y. 457.

[341] Campbell v. Freeman, 99 Cal. 546, 34 Pac. 113; Merchants' & Farmers' Bank v. Hervey Plow Co., 45 La. Ann. 1214, 14 South. 139. Cf. Bowen v. Ratcliff, 140 Ind. 393, 39 N. E. 860. But see Fuller v. Griffith (Iowa) 60 N. W. 247; Savings & Loan Soc. v. Burnett (Cal.) 37 Pac. 180.

§ 131) REGISTRATION. 225

mortgage.[342] The mortgagee is a purchaser from the time the advances are made, if without actual notice of the subsequent conveyance.[343] If one who has a mortgage for future advances acquires actual notice of a subsequent mortgage, he is not protected as to advances made after that time,[344] unless, by the terms of his contract with the mortgagor, he is bound to make such advances.[345] The recording of the subsequent mortgage is not, however, notice to the first mortgagee.[346]

A judgment creditor is not a purchaser, under the registry acts,[347] unless the statute expressly so provides.[348] When there is no such provision, a judgment, as against a prior unrecorded mortgage, will bind only the equity of redemption.[349] A purchaser at an execution sale, without notice of a prior mortgage, takes the land free from such mortgage.[350] In most states a purchase-money mortgage [351] takes priority over all previous conveyances and judgment liens.[352] But, to have this effect, it must be part of the same trans-

[342] Reynolds v. Webster, 71 Hun, 378, 24 N. Y. Supp. 1133; Bank of Oroville v. Lawrence (Cal.) 37 Pac. 936.

[343] Simons v. Bank, 93 N. Y. 269.

[344] Frye v. President, etc., 11 Ill. 367; Hall v. Crouse, 13 Hun (N. Y.) 557; Todd v. Outlaw, 79 N. C. 235; Savings & Loan Soc. v. Burnett, 106 Cal. 514, 39 Pac. 922.

[345] Brinkmeyer v. Helbling, 57 Ind. 435; Moroney's Appeal, 24 Pa. St. 372.

[346] Nelson's Heirs v. Boyce, 7 J. J. Marsh. (Ky.) 401; Bedford v. Backhouse, 2 Eq. Cas. Abr. 615, pl. 12; Morecock v. Dickins, 1 Amb. 678.

[347] Jackson v. Dubois, 4 Johns. (N. Y.) 216; Cover v. Black, 1 Pa. St. 493; Pixley v. Huggins, 15 Cal. 128; Bell v. Evans, 10 Iowa, 353; Righter v. Forrester, 1 Bush (Ky.) 278. Contra, Dutton v. McReynolds, 31 Minn. 66, 16 N. W. 468. And see Van Thorniley v. Peters, 26 Ohio St. 471.

[348] 1 Stim. Am. St. Law, § 1611 A (2). Where a mistake in omitting property from a mortgage is reformed, the lien of a mortgage on the omitted property is superior to that of a judgment obtained after the execution of the mortgage, and before its reformation. Phillips v. Roquemore, 96 Ga. 719, 23 S. E. 855.

[349] And the rule is the same when the judgment is against an heir to whom the land has descended. Voorhis v. Westervelt, 43 N. J. Eq. 642, 12 Atl. 533.

[350] McFadden v. Worthington, 45 Ill. 362; Jackson v. Chamberlain, 8 Wend. (N. Y.) 620; Morrison v. Funk, 23 Pa. St. 421; Ehle v. Brown, 31 Wis. 405. But see, for some limitations on this rule, a full discussion of creditors' rights under the registry laws in 2 Dembitz, Land Tit. 992.

[351] See ante, p. 85.

[352] By statute in some states, 1 Stim. Am. St. Law, § 1864; and without statute in others, Roane v. Baker, 120 Ill. 308, 11 N. E. 246; Curtis v. Root, 20 Ill.

action as the deed of conveyance.[353] Such a mortgage must be recorded, the same as any other, in order to have priority over subsequent conveyances. A mortgagee under an absolute deed, with a separate defeasance, is protected by the record of the deed, without a record of the defeasance.[354] An assignee of a mortgage is protected as a purchaser.[355] The record of the assignment of a mortgage is not constructive notice to the mortgagor, and payments made by him to the mortgagee, without actual notice, are protected.[356] It is otherwise when the mortgage is to secure a negotiable note.[357] And the record of an assignment of a mortgage is notice to subsequent purchasers of the equity of redemption.[358]

When the mortgagee has assigned the mortgage, and then wrongfully discharges it of record, the cases are conflicting as to whether subsequent purchasers from the mortgagor are protected against the assignee of the mortgage.[359] But they are in states where the

54; Phelps v. Fockler, 61 Iowa, 340, 14 N. W. 729, 16 N. W. 210; Rogers v. Tucker, 94 Mo. 346, 7 S. W. 414. Such mortgage may be to a third person who advances the purchase money. Jackson v. Austin, 15 Johns. (N. Y.) 477; Laidley v. Aiken, 80 Iowa, 112, 45 N. W. 384; Jones v. Tainter, 15 Minn. 512 (Gil. 423). But see Stansell v. Roberts, 13 Ohio, 149; Heuisler v. Nickum, 38 Md. 270.

[353] Foster's Appeal, 3 Pa. St. 79; Cake's Appeal, 23 Pa. St. 186; Banning v. Edes, 6 Minn. 402 (Gil. 270).

[354] Short v. Caldwell, 155 Mass. 57, 28 N. E. 1124; Jackson v. Ford, 40 Me. 381. But in some states, by statute, the defeasance must be recorded, or the mortgagee takes no interest under the mortgage. 1 Stim. Am. St. Law, § 1860 A.

[355] Bank of Ukiah v. Petaluma Sav. Bank, 100 Cal. 590, 35 Pac. 170.

[356] Foster v. Carson, 159 Pa. St. 477, 28 Atl. 356; Ely v. Scofield, 35 Barb. (N. Y.) 330; Hubbard v. Turner, 2 McLean, 519, Fed. Cas. No. 6,819. It is so by statute in some states. 1 Stim. Am. St. Law, § 1870; 1 Jones, Mortg. (5th Ed.) § 480.

[357] Murphy v. Barnard, 162 Mass. 72, 38 N. E. 29; Mulcahy v. Fenwick, 161 Mass. 164, 36 N. E. 689; Biggerstaff v. Marston, 161 Mass. 101, 36 N. E. 785; Baumgartner v. Peterson (Iowa) 62 N. W. 27; Eggert v. Beyer, 43 Neb. 711, 62 N. W. 57; Stark v. Olsen, 44 Neb. 646, 63 N. W. 37. But see Vann v. Marbury, 100 Ala. 438, 14 South. 273.

[358] Brewster v. Carnes, 103 N. Y. 556, 9 N. E. 323; Eggert v. Beyer, 43 Neb. 711, 62 N. W. 57.

[359] The weight of authority holds that they are. Ogle v. Turpin, 102 Ill. 148; Lewis v. Kirk, 28 Kan. 497. But see, contra, Lee v. Clark, 89 Mo. 553,

assignment of a mortgage must be recorded.[360] And such a discharge is not good, in favor of one who took his interest before the discharge was entered of record.[361] When the holder of the mortgage is dead, payment must be made to his personal representative, who is the proper one to enter satisfaction.[362]

DISCHARGE OF A MORTGAGE.

132. A mortgage may be discharged:
  (a) **By performance** (p. 227).
  (b) **By merger** (p. 231).
  (c) **By redemption** (p. 233).

SAME—PERFORMANCE.

133. Performance of the condition in the defeasance discharges a mortgage. Performance may be:
  (1) **On the day named in the defeasance.**
  (2) **Before the day named, if accepted by the mortgagee.**
  (3) **After the day named, if accepted by the mortgagee.**

134. Tender of performance by one entitled to perform will discharge the mortgage.

Performance or Payment.

A mortgage being an estate on condition subsequent, the mortgagee's estate is defeated by the performance of the condition named in the defeasance. Performance usually requires the payment of money, but the condition may require other acts as the support of the mortgage. Payment[363] at the time mentioned in the defeasance dis-

---

1 S. W. 142; Bamberger v. Geiser, 24 Or. 203, 33 Pac. 609. And cf. Roberts v. Halstead, 9 Pa. St. 32.

[360] Ferguson v. Glassford, 68 Mich. 36, 35 N. W. 820; Girardin v. Lampe, 58 Wis. 267, 16 N. W. 614; Van Keuren v. Corkins, 66 N. Y. 77; Bacon v. Van Schoonhoven, 87 N. Y. 446; Connecticut Mut. Life Ins. Co. v. Talbot, 113 Ind. 373, 14 N. E. 586.

[361] Crumlish v. Railroad Co., 32 W. Va. 244, 9 S. E. 180.

[362] Crawford v. Simon, 159 Pa. St. 585, 28 Atl. 491; Woodruff v. Mutschler, 34 N. J. Eq. 33.

[363] For payment as a discharge, see Clark, Cont. p. 629.

charges the mortgage;[364] that is, the mortgagor defeats the mortgagee's estate on condition by performance of the condition, and the title to the mortgaged premises revests in the mortgagor without a reconveyance.[365] Payment before the day on which the debt falls due cannot be enforced by either party,[366] but, if the mortgagee accepts such payment, it will operate as a discharge of the mortgage.[367] Payment after the day mentioned in the condition—that is, after the breach of condition—does not divest the estate of the mortgagee, and, if the mortgagee will not reconvey voluntarily, the mortgagor must resort to equity to secure a reconveyance.[368] But, in those states where the lien theory prevails, if the mortgagee accept payment after breach of condition, he is held to waive breach of performance, and the title revests in the mortgagor without a reconveyance.[369] A discharge of the mortgage debt discharges the mortgage,[370] but a discharge by bankruptcy, or by the statute of limitations, does not.[371]

When the mortgagor is holder of the mortgage as administrator of the mortgagee, he may discharge the mortgage at any time by

[364] McCarn v. Wilcox (Mich.) 63 N. W. 978; Gage v. McDermid, 150 Ill. 598, 37 N. E. 1026; Kingsley v. Purdom, 53 Kan. 56, 35 Pac. 811. Cf. Greensburg Fuel Co. v. Irwin Nat. Gas Co., 162 Pa. St. 78, 29 Atl. 274; Bartlett v. Wade, 66 Vt. 629, 30 Atl. 4. But see Sturges v. Hart, 84 Hun, 409, 32 N. Y. Supp. 422; Herber v. Thompson, 47 La. Ann. 800, 17 South. 318. As to application of payments, see Clark, Cont. p. 634; Fetter, Eq. p. 249.

[365] Holman v. Bailey, 3 Metc. (Mass.) 55; Crain v. McGoon, 86 Ill. 431. So, in a mortgage for support, if the condition is performed up to the death of the mortgagee the title revests in the mortgagor. Munson v. Munson, 30 Conn. 425.

[366] Weldon v. Tollman, 15 C. C. A. 138, 67 Fed. 986; Bowen v. Julius, 141 Ind. 310, 40 N. E. 700; Moore v. Kime, 43 Neb. 517, 61 N. W. 736.

[367] 1 Jones, Mortg. (5th Ed.) § 888.

[368] Currier v. Gale, 9 Allen (Mass.) 522; Doton v. Russell, 17 Conn. 146.

[369] Caruthers v. Humphrey, 12 Mich. 270; McNair v. Picotte, 33 Mo. 57; Kortright v. Cady, 21 N. Y. 343; Shields v. Lozear, 34 N. J. Law, 496.

[370] Sherman v. Sherman, 3 Ind. 337; Shields v. Lozear, 34 N. J. Law, 496.

[371] Chamberlain v. Meeder, 16 N. H. 381; Bush v. Cooper, 26 Miss. 599. Foreclosure is not payment, and does not discharge the mortgage debt. See post, p. 241. But the parties may agree that it shall constitute a discharge. Shepherd v. May, 115 U. S. 505, 6 Sup. Ct. 119; Renwick v. Wheeler, 48 Fed. 431; Vansant v. Allmon, 23 Ill. 30; Germania Bldg. Ass'n v. Neill, 93 Pa. St. 322.

charging the amount thereof to himself on his probate account,[872] and a subsequent assignment would transfer no title to the assignee.[373] A change in the form of a mortgage debt, such as the substitution of a new note in the place of the original note, does not effect a discharge.[874] Nor does the merger of the mortgage note in a judgment produce that result.[375] So there is no discharge by taking further security for the mortgage debt.[876] Extending the time of payment does not discharge the mortgage as to subsequent mortgagees.[377] But it is otherwise where the mortgage is to secure the debt of another, unless the mortgagor consents to the extension.[378] A release of part of the mortgaged premises does not discharge the mortgage as to the other parts,[379] unless it would injuriously affect subsequent mortgages, of which the first mortgagee had notice.[380] On the other hand, the personal liability of the mortgagor may be released without discharging the mortgage, if there is no intention to discharge the debt.[381] After a mortgage has been discharged, it cannot be revived so as to take precedence over intervening incumbrances;[382] that is, the mortgage cannot

[872] Martin v. Smith, 124 Mass. 111. But see Soverhill v. Suydam, 59 N. Y. 140; Kinney v. Ensign, 18 Pick. (Mass.) 232; Crow v. Conant, 90 Mich. 247, 51 N. W. 450.

[373] Ipswich Manuf'g Co. v. Story, 5 Metc. (Mass.) 310.

[374] Flower v. Elwood, 66 Ill. 438; Watkins v. Hill, 8 Pick. (Mass.) 522; Williams v. Starr, 5 Wis. 534; Gregory v. Thomas, 20 Wend. (N. Y.) 17; Geib v. Reynolds, 35 Minn. 321, 28 N. W. 923; Swan v. Yaple, 35 Iowa, 248; Walters v. Walters, 73 Ind. 425.

[375] Priest v. Wheelock, 58 Ill. 114; Torrey v. Cook, 116 Mass. 163; Ely v. Ely, 6 Gray (Mass.) 439; Morrison v. Morrison, 38 Iowa, 73.

[376] Gregory v. Thomas, 20 Wend. (N. Y.) 17; Flower v. Elwood, 66 Ill. 438; Cissna v. Haines, 18 Ind. 496; Hutchinson v. Swartsweller, 31 N. J. Eq. 205.

[377] Bank of Utica v. Finch, 3 Barb. Ch. (N. Y.) 293; Whittacre v. Fuller, 5 Minn. 508 (Gil. 401); Cleveland v. Martin, 2 Head (Tenn.) 128; Naltner v. Tappey, 55 Ind. 107.

[378] Smith v. Townsend, 25 N. Y. 479; Metz v. Todd, 36 Mich. 473; Christner v. Brown, 16 Iowa, 130.

[379] Patty v. Pease, 8 Paige (N. Y.) 277.

[380] Stewart v. McMahan, 94 Ind. 389.

[381] Hayden v. Smith, 12 Metc. (Mass.) 511; Donnelly v. Simonton, 13 Minn. 301 (Gil. 278); Walls v. Baird, 91 Ind. 429.

[382] Bogert v. Striker, 11 Misc. Rep. 88, 32 N. Y. Supp. 815; Mitchell v. Coombs, 96 Pa. St. 430; Lindsay v. Garvin, 31 S. C. 259, 9 S. E. 862.

be continued as security for another debt, to the detriment of subsequent creditors or purchasers.[383] But when the discharge of a mortgage has been obtained by fraud or mistake, it may be set aside unless third persons, without notice, whose rights have intervened since the discharge, would be injuriously affected.[384]

Tender.

Whenever payment would discharge a mortgage, tender of payment[385] will have the same effect.[386] To have this effect, however, tender must be absolute and unconditional,[387] and it must be for the whole amount of the mortgage debt.[388] Tender of the whole amount is required, though the mortgagee has received rents and profits for which there has been no accounting.[389] Tender will be effectual only when made by one entitled to make payment, such as the mortgagor,[390] a grantee who has assumed the mortgage,[391] or a junior mortgagee.[392] Payment or tender, to operate as a discharge, must be to one authorized to receive payment, and having a right to enter satisfaction.[393] If the mortgage has been assign-

[383] Marvin v. Vedder, 5 Cow. (N. Y.) 671; Bogert v. Bliss, 13 Misc. Rep. 72, 34 N. Y. Supp. 147; Carlton v. Jackson, 121 Mass. 592; Blake v. Broughton, 107 N. C. 220, 12 S. E. 127.

[384] Willcox v. Foster, 132 Mass. 320; Grimes v. Kimball, 3 Allen (Mass.) 518; Weir v. Mosher, 19 Wis. 311; West's Appeal, 88 Pa. St. 341; Henschel v. Mamero, 120 Ill. 660, 12 N. E. 203; Ferguson v Glassford, 68 Mich. 36, 35 N. W. 820; Kern v. A. P. Hotaling (Or.) 40 Pac. 168. Cf. Cambreleng v. Graham, 84 Hun, 550, 32 N. Y. Supp. 843.

[385] As to what constitutes tender, see Clark, Cont. p. 639.

[386] Maynard v. Hunt, 5 Pick. (Mass.) 240; Willard v. Harvey, 5 N. H. 252; Schearff v. Dodge, 33 Ark. 340. But that tender only stops interest, see Parker v. Beasley, 116 N. C. 1, 21 S. E. 955.

[387] Potts v. Plaisted, 30 Mich. 149; Engle v. Hall, 45 Mich. 57, 7 N. W. 239; Roosevelt v. Bank, 45 Barb. (N. Y.) 579.

[388] Graham v. Linden, 50 N. Y. 547; Sager v. Tupper, 35 Mich. 134; Cupples v. Galligan, 6 Mo. App. 62.

[389] Bailey v. Metcalf, 6 N. H. 156.

[390] Blim v. Wilson, 5 Phila. (Pa.) 78.

[391] Harris v. Jex, 66 Barb. (N. Y.) 232.

[392] Frost v. Bank, 70 N. Y. 553; Sayer v. Tupper, 35 Mich. 134.

[393] Grussy v. Schneider, 50 How. Prac. (N. Y.) 134; Dorkray v. Noble, 8 Me. 278; U. S. Bank v. Burson, 90 Iowa, 191, 57 N. W. 705; Lawson v. Nicholson (N. J. Err. & App.) 31 Atl. 386; Mulford v. Brown (N. J. Ch.) 28 Atl. 513.

ed, payment or tender is to be made to the assignee, if the mortgagor has notice of the assignment.[394]

SAME—MERGER.

135. A mortgage is discharged by merger whenever the mortgage and the equity of redemption are owned by the same person in the same right, except:

EXCEPTIONS—(a) When there is an intervening right in a third person.

(b) When there is an intention of the parties to the contrary, unless preventing a merger would injure some third person.

The general doctrine of merger has already been explained, and examples of it noticed in connection with several different estates. Merger generally takes place whenever the mortgage and the equity of redemption come into the same hands.[395] But it does not occur when the owner has an interest in keeping the mortgage alive,[396] as where the owner of the equity of redemption is not the original mortgagor, and has not assumed the mortgage debt.[397] Nor is there any merger when there is an intervening right between the mortgage and the equity of redemption.[398] For example, when

---

[394] Kennedy v. Moore (Iowa) 58 N. W. 1066; Dorkray v. Noble, 8 Me. 278. And see Hetzell v. Barber, 6 Hun (N. Y.) 534.

[395] Gibson v. Crehore, 3 Pick. (Mass.) 475; Ann Arbor Sav. Bank v. Webb, 56 Mich. 377, 23 N. W. 51; Judd v. Seekins, 62 N. Y. 266; McGale v. McGale (R. I.) 29 Atl. 967. But see Burt v. Gamble, 98 Mich. 402, 57 N. W. 261; Cook v. Foster, 96 Mich. 610, 55 N. W. 1019.

[396] Edgerton v. Young, 43 Ill. 464; Richardson v. Hockenhall, 85 Ill. 124; Tuttle v. Brown, 14 Pick. (Mass.) 514; Snyder v. Snyder, 6 Mich. 470; Spencer v. Ayrault, 10 N. Y. 202; Duncan v. Drury, 9 Pa. St. 332; Davis v. Pierce, 10 Minn. 376 (Gil. 302); McCrory v. Little, 136 Ind. 86, 35 N. E. 836; White v. Hampton, 13 Iowa, 259; Lyon v. McIlvaine, 24 Iowa, 9.

[397] Grover v. Thatcher, 4 Gray (Mass.) 526; Evans v. Kimball, 1 Allen (Mass.) 240. But see Byington v. Fountain, 61 Iowa, 512, 14 N. W. 220, and 16 N. W. 534.

[398] Grover v. Thatcher, 4 Gray (Mass.) 526; New England Jewelry Co. v. Merriam, 2 Allen (Mass.) 390; Coburn v. Stephens, 137 Ind. 683, 36 N. E. 132; Jewett v. Tomlinson, 137 Ind. 326, 36 N. E. 1106; Shaffer v. McCloskey, 101 Cal. 576, 36 Pac. 196.

a first mortgagee purchases the equity of redemption, there will be no merger if there are subsequent mortgages.[399] In order that merger may take place, the mortgage and the equity of redemption must be held by the same person, and in the same right.[400] In determining whether a merger takes place, the intention of the parties is the chief test;[401] and, as to such intention, their relation to each other and to the mortgage debt is material, when they have not shown their intention by express words.[402] However, a merger will never be prevented by the intention of the parties, where it will work wrong or injury to others.[403] When one who has warranted against incumbrances pays a mortgage, the mortgage is discharged.[404] And so when payment is by the mortgagor, except under special circumstances, such as when the mortgagor has conveyed the equity of redemption to one who has assumed the mortgage debt.[405] When the mortgagee acquires the right of redemption, there is no merger, if there are intervening incumbrances or liens,[406] nor when the mortgagee has assigned the mortgage before he ac-

[399] Gibbs v. Johnson (Mich.) 62 N. W. 145; Dutton v. Ives, 5 Mich. 515; Hooper v. Henry, 31 Minn. 264, 17 N. W. 476; Bell v. Woodward, 34 N. H. 90; Swatts v. Bowen, 141 Ind. 322, 40 N. E. 1057.

[400] Mann v. Mann, 49 Ill. App. 472; Sprague v. Beamer, 45 Ill. App. 17; Souther v. Pearson (N. J. Ch.) 28 Atl. 450. At common law an assignment of the mortgage to the wife of the mortgagor discharged it by merger. 1 Jones, Mortg. (5th Ed.) § 850. But such is not now the rule. Model Lodging House Ass'n v. Boston, 114 Mass. 133; Newton v. Manwarring, 56 Hun, 645, 10 N. Y. Supp. 347; McCrory v. Little, 136 Ind. 86, 35 N. E. 836; Bean v. Boothby, 57 Me. 295. And see Bemis v. Call, 10 Allen (Mass.) 512.

[401] Lynch v. Pfeiffer, 110 N. Y. 33, 17 N. E. 402; Loomer v. Wheelwright, 3 Sandf. Ch. (N. Y.) 135; Aetna Life Ins. Co. v. Corn, 89 Ill. 170; Jarvis v. Frink, 14 Ill. 396; Loverin v. Trust Co., 113 Pa. St. 6, 4 Atl. 191; Aiken v. Railway Co., 37 Wis. 469; Walker v. Goodsill, 54 Mo. App. 631.

[402] Smith v. Roberts, 91 N. Y. 470; James v. Morey, 2 Cow. (N. Y.) 246; Chase v. Van Meter, 140 Ind. 321, 39 N. E. 455.

[403] McGiven v. Wheelock, 7 Barb. (N. Y.) 22; First Nat. Bank of Lebanon v. Essex, 84 Ind. 144.

[404] 1 Jones, Mortg. (5th Ed.) § 854; Hancock v. Fleming, 103 Ind. 533, 3 N. E. 254.

[405] And see Abbott v. Kasson, 72 Pa. St. 183.

[406] Smith v. Swan, 69 Iowa, 412, 29 N. W. 402; Pike v. Gleason, 60 Iowa, 150, 14 N. W. 210; Hanlon v. Doherty, 109 Ind. 37, 9 N. E. 782. But see Temple v. Whittier, 117 Ill. 282, 7 N. E. 642.

§ 136) DISCHARGE OF A MORTGAGE—REDEMPTION. 233

quires the equity of redemption.[407] Whether or not a merger has taken place cannot be determined by an inspection of the record, because, as we have seen, a merger may be prevented by the intention of the parties.[408]

SAME—REDEMPTION.

136. A mortgage may be discharged by being redeemed by any one who has an interest in the equity of redemption paying the whole amount due on the mortgage, before the right to redeem is barred by foreclosure or lapse of time.

At common law, after breach of condition, the estate of the mortgagor was absolutely determined. But courts of equity subsequently granted relief from the harshness of this rule, by giving the mortgagor, or those succeeding to his interests, a right of redemption.[409] This constitutes the chief difference between mortgages at common law and in equity. It has already been said that a mortgage may be discharged by performance after breach of the condition, if the mortgagee accepts the performance. If the mortgagee refuses to accept, the mortgagor must resort to a court of equity to enforce his right of redemption, and secure a discharge of the mortgage. A bill in equity is the only method of enforcing a right of redemption.[410] To such a bill all persons having an interest in the mortgaged premises should be made parties.[411] The decree in such case fixes the time within which redemption must be made.[412]

[407] International Bank of Chicago v. Wilshire, 108 Ill. 143.

[408] Morgan v. Hammett, 34 Wis. 512; Worcester Nat. Bank v. Cheney, 87 Ill. 602; Purdy v. Huntington, 42 N. Y. 334.

[409] 2 Jones, Mortg. (5th Ed.) § 1038; Digby, Hist. Real Prop. (4th Ed.) 283.

[410] 2 Jones, Mortg. (5th Ed.) § 1093; Chase v. Peck, 21 N. Y. 581; Hill v. Payson, 3 Mass. 559; Parsons v. Welles, 17 Mass. 419; Woods v. Woods, 66 Me. 206.

[411] Posten v. Miller, 60 Wis. 494, 19 N. W. 540; Sutherland v. Rose, 47 Barb. (N. Y.) 144; Chase v. Bank, 1 Tex. Civ. App. 595, 20 S. W. 1027; Stillwell v. Hamm, 97 Mo. 579, 11 S. W. 252; Marco v. Hicklin, 6 C. C. A. 10, 56 Fed. 549.

[412] Chicago & C. Rolling-Mill Co. v. Scully, 141 Ill. 408, 30 N. E. 1062;

Who may Redeem.

Any one having an interest in the mortgaged premises may redeem, if he would be a loser by foreclosure.[413] But the interest must come through the mortgagor, and therefore one holding a tax title has no right to redeem.[414] An interest in part of the mortgaged premises is sufficient to give the right.[415] Nor need the interest be one in fee. A tenant for life or years may exercise the right.[416] A mortgagor who has conveyed the premises with covenants of warranty cannot redeem.[417] If a second mortgage has been foreclosed, the mortgagor has no right to redeem from the first mortgage.[418] But if a first mortgage is foreclosed a junior mortgagee may redeem, if not made a party to the foreclosure of the first mortgage.[419] An assignee of the equity of redemption may redeem, whether he is an assignee by act of parties,[420] or by operation of law.[421] The heirs of the mortgagor or of the owner of the equity of redemption may redeem, unless the equity has been devised to another.[422] So the guardian of an infant heir may exercise the right.[423] A joint owner may redeem by paying the whole debt,[424]

Bremer v. Dock Co., 127 Ill. 464, 18 N. E. 321; Dennett v. Codman, 158 Mass. 371, 33 N. E. 574; McKenna v. Kirkwood, 50 Mich. 544, 15 N. W. 898.

[413] Campbell v. Ellwanger, 81 Hun, 259, 30 N. Y. Supp. 792; Grant v. Duane, 9 Johns. (N. Y.) 591; Powers v. Lumber Co., 43 Mich. 468, 5 N. W. 656; Platt v. Squire, 12 Metc. (Mass.) 494; Farnum v. Metcalf, 8 Cush. (Mass.) 46. As a mortgagor under a deed absolute in form. McArthur v. Robinson (Mich.) 62 N. W. 713.

[414] Sinclair v. Learned, 51 Mich. 335, 16 N. W. 672.

[415] In re Willard, 5 Wend. (N. Y.) 94; Boqut v. Coburn, 27 Barb. (N. Y.) 230.

[416] Averill v. Taylor, 8 N. Y. 44; Lamson v. Drake, 105 Mass. 564.

[417] Phillips v. Leavitt, 54 Me. 405; True v. Haley, 24 Me. 297.

[418] Calwell v. Warner, 36 Conn. 224.

[419] Jackson v. Weaver, 138 Ind. 539, 38 N. E. 166; Thompson v. Chandler, 7 Me. 377; Loomis v. Knox, 60 Conn. 343, 22 Atl. 771.

[420] Scott v. Henry, 13 Ark. 112; Gordon v. Smith, 10 C. C. A. 516, 62 Fed. 503. And on seeking redemption he need not prove a valuable consideration. Barnard v. Cushman, 35 Ill. 451.

[421] White v. Bond, 16 Mass. 400.

[422] Zaegel v. Kuster, 51 Wis. 31, 7 N. W. 781; Chew v. Hyman, 10 Biss. 240, 7 Fed. 7; Lewis v. Nangle, 2 Ves. Sr. 431.

[423] Pardee v. Van Anken, 3 Barb. (N. Y.) 534.

[424] Taylor v. Porter, 7 Mass. 355; Calkins v. Munsel, 2 Root (Conn.) 333; Lyon v. Robbins, 45 Conn. 513.

and can hold the land to secure contribution from his co-owners.[425] A junior mortgagee may, of course, redeem;[426] but he must have given a valuable consideration for his mortgage, so that it is a valid security.[427] And he may redeem, although a prior mortgagee holds the equity of redemption.[428] A widow of the mortgagor, who has released her dower, may redeem from the mortgage;[429] but, to do so, she is required to pay the whole amount, and not merely one-third.[430] So also a tenant by the curtesy has a right of redemption. A judgment creditor of the mortgagor may redeem without the land being first sold on execution.[431] On the other hand, a general creditor of a mortgagor, who has no specific lien on the lands mortgaged, cannot exercise a right of redemption.[432] But an assignee in bankruptcy may.[433]

Amount Payable.

The sum which must be paid in order to redeem from a mortgage is the amount of the mortgage debt and interest still due.[434] But money paid by the mortgagee in discharging a prior incumbrance, together with the costs thereby incurred, may be added to the

---

[425] Taylor v. Porter, 7 Mass. 355.

[426] Frost v. Bank, 70 N. Y. 553; Sager v. Tupper, 35 Mich. 134; Lamb v. Jeffrey, 41 Mich. 719, 3 N. W. 204; Morse v. Smith, 83 Ill. 396.

[427] Skinner v. Young, 80 Iowa, 234, 45 N. W. 889.

[428] Rogers v. Herron, 92 Ill. 583.

[429] Phelan v. Fitzpatrick, 84 Wis. 240, 54 N. W. 614; Posten v. Miller, 60 Wis. 494, 19 N. W. 540; Denton v. Nanny, 8 Barb. (N. Y.) 618; McCabe v. Bellows, 1 Allen (Mass.) 269, 7 Gray (Mass.) 148; McArthur v. Franklin, 16 Ohio St. 193. And see Campbell v. Ellwanger, 81 Hun, 259, 30 N. Y. Supp. 792.

[430] McCabe v. Bellows, 7 Gray (Mass.) 148.

[431] Boynton v. Pierce, 151 Ill. 197, 37 N. E. 1024; Whitehead v. Hall, 148 Ill. 253, 35 N. E. 871; Todd v. Johnson, 56 Minn. 60, 57 N. W. 320. But he cannot redeem a mortgage on a homestead when he has no lien thereon. Spurgin v. Adamson, 62 Iowa, 661, 18 N. W. 293.

[432] Long v. Mellet (Iowa) 63 N. W. 190; McNiece v. Eliason, 78 Md. 168, 27 Atl. 940.

[433] Lloyd v. Hoo Sue, 5 Sawy. 74, Fed. Cas. No. 8,432.

[434] Cowles v. Marble, 37 Mich. 158; Childs v. Childs, 10 Ohio St. 339. And see Shearer v. Field, 6 Misc. Rep. 189, 27 N. Y. Supp. 29; Gleason v. Kinney, 65 Vt. 560, 27 Atl. 208.

amount of the mortgage,[435] as may be also attorney's fees provided for in the mortgage,[436] and insurance premiums.[437] The mortgagee cannot be compelled to release a portion of the premises by payment of part of the sum due.[438] When one who has not been made a party redeems, the entire amount of the mortgage debt must be paid, though the land has sold for less.[439] By agreement of the parties, there may be a redemption of part of the premises only.[440]

Same—Contribution to Redeem.

One who redeems by paying the whole of a debt, for which he is liable for a part only, is entitled to contribution from those who are liable for the balance.[441] Contribution is never enforced, except between those whose equities are equal.[442] Therefore purchasers subsequent to a second mortgage cannot compel contribution against the second mortgagee, when the first mortgage is enforced against them.[443] And a mortgagor who has conveyed with covenants of warranty, after he has paid the mortgage, cannot en-

[435] Long v. Long, 111 Mo. 12, 19 S. W. 537.

[436] Hosford v. Johnson, 74 Ind. 479.

[437] Id.

[438] Boqut v. Coburn, 27 Barb. (N. Y.) 230; Merritt v. Hosmer, 11 Gray (Mass.) 276; Meacham v. Steele, 93 Ill. 135; Knowles v. Rablin, 20 Iowa, 101. And see Commercial Bank v. Hiller (Mich.) 63 N. W. 1012; Norton v. Henry, 67 Vt. 308, 31 Atl. 787. So as to redemption by joint owners. Ward v. Green (Tex. Civ. App.) 28 S. W. 574.

[439] Bradley v. Snyder, 14 Ill. 263; Martin v. Fridley, 23 Minn. 13; Hosford v. Johnson, 74 Ind. 479; Johnson v. Harmon, 19 Iowa, 56.

[440] Union Mut. Life Ins. Co. v. Kirchoff, 133 Ill. 368, 27 N. E. 91. In England, by what is called the "doctrine of consolidation," one who owns several mortgages, though on different lands, and executed at different times, may compel a redemption of all of them by one seeking to redeem any one of them. This doctrine has been recognized in only a few American cases. 2 Jones, Mortg. (5th Ed.) § 1082. See Scripture v. Johnson, 3 Conn. 211; Bank of South Carolina v. Rose, 1 Strob. Eq. (S. C.) 257. The English doctrine of tacking, by which the holder of a first and subsequent mortgage may cut out the rights of intervening mortgagees, is inconsistent with our registry system, and does not prevail in this country. 2 Jones, Mortg. (5th Ed.) § 1082.

[441] Coffin v. Parker, 127 N. Y. 117, 27 N. E. 814; Stevens v. Cooper, 1 Johns. Ch. (N. Y.) 425; Damm v. Damm, 91 Mich. 424, 51 N. W. 1069. But see Chase v. Woodbury, 6 Cush. (Mass.) 143.

[442] Sanford v. Hill, 46 Conn. 42; Henderson v. Truitt, 95 Ind. 309.

[443] Henderson v. Truitt, 95 Ind. 309.

force contribution against his grantee.[444] Where the mortgaged premises have been conveyed in separate parcels, the parcels are liable in the inverse order of their alienation.[445] Between those who hold separate parts of mortgaged land by simultaneous conveyances, contribution is to be enforced according to the present value of the parcels, exclusive of the improvements placed thereon by the purchasers.[446]

When Redemption is Barred.

The right of redemption is barred by foreclosure, and by lapse of time.[447] Foreclosure, however, does not have this effect if the mortgagee subsequently recognizes the mortgage as still existing.[448] Nor does foreclosure bar a right to redeem against one not made a party to the foreclosure suit.[449] In several states, by statute, redemption may be made for a certain period after a foreclosure sale, the same as after a sale on execution.[450]

By analogy to the statute of limitations, the courts of most states hold that the right of redemption is barred when the mortgagee is in possession after the lapse of a time sufficient to give title to realty by prescription.[451] Some states have express statutory enactments as to when the right of redemption is barred.[452] The

[444] Sargeant v. Rowsey, 89 Mo. 617, 1 S. W. 823.

[445] Gill v. Lyon, 1 Johns. Ch. (N. Y.) 447; Clowes v. Dickenson, 5 Johns. Ch. (N. Y.) 235, affirmed 9 Cow. (N. Y.) 403; Bates v. Ruddick, 2 Iowa, 423; Deavitt v. Judevine, 60 Vt. 695, 17 Atl. 410; Solicitors' Loan & Trust Co. v. Washington & I. Ry. Co., 11 Wash. 684, 40 Pac. 344. But that the parcels are proportionately liable, see Huff v. Farwell, 67 Iowa, 298, 25 N. W. 252; Dickey v. Thompson, 8 B. Mon. (Ky.) 312. And cf. Turner v. Flenniken, 164 Pa. St. 469, 30 Atl. 486; Dates v. Winstanley, 53 Ill. App. 623.

[446] Bates v. Ruddick, 2 Iowa, 423.

[447] Weiner v. Heintz, 17 Ill. 259; Stoddard v. Forbes, 13 Iowa, 296.

[448] Lounsbury v. Norton, 59 Conn. 170, 22 Atl. 153.

[449] Farwell v. Antis, 2 Wis. 533; Murphy v. Farwell, 9 Wis. 102; Hodgen v. Guttery, 58 Ill. 431; Strang v. Allen, 44 Ill. 428; American Buttonhole, etc., Co. v. Burlington Mut. L. Ass'n, 61 Iowa, 464, 16 N. W. 527.

[450] 1 Stim. Am. St. Law, § 1944 A, B; 2 Jones, Mortg. (5th Ed.) § 1051; Gates v. Ege, 57 Minn. 465, 59 N. W. 495.

[451] Harter v. Twohig, 158 U. S. 448, 15 Sup. Ct. 883; Robinson v. Fife, 3 Ohio St. 551; Jarvis v. Woodruff, 22 Conn. 548; Fox v. Blossom, 17 Blatchf. 352, Fed. Cas. No. 5,008. As to prescription, see post, p. 456.

[452] 1 Stim. Am. St. Law, § 1944 C.

courts of some states hold that the right to redeem is barred at the same time as the right to foreclose.[453] In order that possession by the mortgagee may bar the right of redemption, it is necessary that the possession be adverse during the whole period of limitation.[454] The right to redeem is lost by limitation only when the mortgagee is in possession.[455] The bar of the right of redemption by lapse of time is removed by anything which shows the mortgage as still continuing, such as by the rendering of an account,[456] the assignment of the mortgage,[457] recitals by the mortgagee in a deed or will,[458] or by proceedings to foreclose.[459]

SAME—FORM OF DISCHARGE.

137. The formal discharge of a mortgage may be by:
  (a) **A reconveyance.**
  (b) **An entry of satisfaction on the record.**

It has been seen that, in the states where the lien theory of mortgages prevails, the mortgage is discharged merely by performance, but the mortgage still remains a cloud upon the mortgagor's title, so that some formal discharge is necessary. The discharge of a mortgage may take the form of a reconveyance,[460] as by a quitclaim deed from the mortgagee to the mortgagor.[461] It is gener-

---

[453] Green v. Cross, 45 N. H. 574; King v. Meighen, 20 Minn. 264 (Gil. 237); Koch v. Briggs, 14 Cal. 256.

[454] Simmons v. Ballard, 102 N. C. 105, 9 S. E. 495; McPherson v. Hayward, 81 Me. 329, 17 Atl. 164; Frisbee v. Frisbee, 86 Me. 444, 29 Atl. 1115.

[455] Maurhoffer v. Mittnacht, 12 Misc. Rep. 585, 34 N. Y. Supp. 439; Bird v. Keller, 77 Me. 270. And see Frink v. Le Roy, 49 Cal. 314; Anding v. Davis, 38 Miss. 574.

[456] Edsell v. Buchanan, 2 Ves. Jr. 83.

[457] Borst v. Boyd, 3 Sandf. Ch. (N. Y.) 501.

[458] Hansard v. Hardy, 18 Ves. 455.

[459] Calkins v. Calkins, 3 Barb. (N. Y.) 305; Robinson v. Fife, 3 Ohio St. 551.

[460] 1 Jones, Mortg. (5th Ed.) § 972; Mutual Building & Loan Ass'n v. Wyeth (Ala.) 17 South. 45.

[461] Donlin v. Bradley, 119 Ill. 412, 10 N. E. 11; Woodbury v. Aikin, 13 Ill. 639; Barnstable Sav. Bank v. Barrett, 122 Mass. 172. But see Weldon v. Tollman, 15 C. C. A. 138, 67 Fed. 986. As to what is a quitclaim deed, see post, p. 412.

ally provided by statute that a mortgage may be discharged by putting on record a satisfaction; that is, a certificate by the mortgagee that the mortgage has been satisfied. In many states an entry of satisfaction on the margin of the record of the mortgage is sufficient.[462] Discharge of a mortgage may be compelled by a bill in equity,[463] but in many states a penalty is provided by statute, which the mortgagor may collect of the owner of the mortgage for failure to enter satisfaction of record.[464]

FORECLOSURE.

138. Foreclosure is the proceeding by which the mortgaged premises are applied to the payment of the mortgage debt, and the right of redemption barred.

139. Foreclosure will be treated under the following heads:
   (a) **When the right to foreclose accrues** (p. 239).
   (b) **When the right to foreclose is barred** (p. 240).
   (c) **Decree for deficiency** (p. 241).
   (d) **Personal remedies** (p. 241).
   (e) **Receivers** (p. 241).
   (f) **Kinds of foreclosure** (p. 242).

When the Right to Foreclose Accrues.

By the early common law, a mortgagee's interest became absolute by breach of the condition in the defeasance; but, after the right to an equity of redemption became established,[465] some proceeding had to be taken before the mortgagee could make the land available for the satisfaction of the mortgage debt.

---

[462] 1 Stim. Am. St. Law, § 1905.

[463] Remington Paper Co. v. O'Dougherty, 81 N. Y. 474.

[464] 1 Stim. Am. St. Law, § 1902; Crawford v. Simon, 159 Pa. St. 585, 28 Atl. 491; Spaulding v. Sones (Ind. App.) 39 N. E. 526; Jones v. Trust Co. (S. D.) 63 N. W. 553; Walker v. English (Ala.) 17 South. 715. There are in some states similar provisions as to the entry of credits. Loeb v. Huddleston (Ala.) 16 South. 714.

[465] See ante, p. 183.

The right to enforce a mortgage exists as soon as there is a breach by nonpayment at the time fixed, or by failure of performance of the condition of the mortgage, whatever it may be.[466] But a surety or indorser of the mortgage note cannot foreclose a mortgage given to indemnify him, until he has actually paid the note.[467] When, however, the condition of the mortgage is to save harmless, foreclosure proceedings may be begun on the failure of the mortgagor to pay the note when due.[468]

When the Right to Foreclose is Barred.

The courts have applied the statute of limitations, by analogy, to proceedings for the foreclosure of mortgages.[469] And in some states there are special statutory provisions on the subject.[470] The right to foreclose is never barred by lapse of time, unless the mortgagor has been in possession without the payment of principal or interest.[471] Such a bar to foreclosure may be waived by recognition of the mortgage as still existing.[472] Discharge of the debt by the statute of limitations does not discharge the mortgage lien,[473] except in a few states.[474] A decree for deficiency cannot be had in a foreclosure suit after the debt is barred,[475] nor can an equitable lien for purchase money be enforced after the debt itself is bar-

---

[466] Harding v. Manufacturing Co., 34 Conn. 458; Trayser v. Trustees of Asbury University, 39 Ind. 556; Gladwyn v. Hitchman, 2 Vern. 135.

[467] Burt v. Gamble, 98 Mich. 402, 57 N. W. 261; Lewis v. Richey, 5 Ind. 152; Francis v. Porter, 7 Ind. 213; Dye v. Mann, 10 Mich. 291. Cf. Kramer v. Bank, 15 Ohio, 253.

[468] Thurston v. Prentiss, 1 Mich. 193.

[469] Ray v. Pearce, 84 N. C. 485; Cleveland Ins. Co. v. Reed, 1 Biss. 180, Fed. Cas. No. 2,889.

[470] See 1 Stim. Am. St. Law, § 1928; 2 Jones, Mortg. (5th Ed.) § 1193. And see In re Tarbell, 160 Mass. 407, 36 N. E. 55.

[471] Locke v. Caldwell, 91 Ill. 417; Chouteau's Ex'r v. Burlando, 20 Mo. 482.

[472] Schifferstein v. Allison, 123 Ill. 662, 15 N. E. 275; Blair v. Carpenter, 75 Mich. 167, 42 N. W. 790; Carson v. Cochran, 52 Minn. 67, 53 N. W. 1130.

[473] Thayer v. Mann, 19 Pick. (Mass.) 535; Michigan Ins. Co. v. Brown, 11 Mich. 265; Mott v. Maris (Tex. Civ. App.) 29 S. W. 825.

[474] Pollock v. Maison, 41 Ill. 516; Duty v. Graham, 12 Tex. 427; City of Ft. Scott v. Schulenberg, 22 Kan. 648; Lord v. Morris, 18 Cal. 482.

[475] Hulbert v. Clark, 57 Hun, 558, 11 N. Y. Supp. 417; Slingerland v. Sherer, 46 Minn. 422, 49 N. W. 237.

red.[476] The statute begins to run from the time the condition is broken.[477]

Decree for Deficiency.

In almost all the states, and in the federal courts, a decree for a deficiency of the mortgage debt may be rendered in the foreclosure suit.[478] And for this purpose, in most states, third persons liable for the debt may be joined as defendants.[479] But such a judgment cannot be rendered against one who has not been made a party.[480] When the mortgagor or principal debtor is dead, no judgment for the deficiency can be rendered against his personal representative. The deficiency must be proved against his estate.[481]

Personal Remedies—Receivers.

The proceedings for enforcing a mortgage, and the personal remedies against the debtor, are concurrent.[482] But, in most states where judgment for the deficiency may be given on foreclosure, a personal action for the debt cannot be maintained against the debtor while foreclosure proceedings are pending,[483] and in some states

---

[476] Borst v. Corey, 15 N. Y. 505; Littlejohn v. Gordon, 32 Miss. 235.

[477] The mortgagor, or the one holding under him, being in possession. Nevitt v. Bacon, 32 Miss. 212. See Coyle v. Wilkins, 57 Ala. 108.

[478] Grand Island Savings & Loan Ass'n v. Moore, 40 Neb. 686, 59 N. W. 115; Flentham v. Steward, 45 Neb. 640, 63 N. W. 924; Shumway v. Orchard (Wash.) 40 Pac. 634. To authorize such a judgment against a grantee, he must have assumed the mortgage. Blass v. Terry, 87 Hun, 563, 34 N. Y. Supp. 475; Williams v. Maftzger, 103 Cal. 438, 37 Pac. 411; Green v. Hall, 45 Neb. 89, 63 N. W. 119. Cf. Farmers' Loan & Trust Co. v. Grape Creek Coal Co., 13 C. C. A. 87, 65 Fed. 717.

[479] Palmeter v. Carey, 63 Wis. 426, 21 N. W. 793, and 23 N. W. 586; 2 Jones, Mortg. (5th Ed.) § 1710. But not in the absence of a statute permitting it. Id. But see Hilton v. Bank, 26 Fed. 202.

[480] Williams v. Follett, 17 Colo. 51, 28 Pac. 330. Such as a nonresident who has not appeared. Schwinger v. Hickok, 53 N. Y. 280 (a mortgagor); Blumberg v. Birch, 99 Cal. 416, 34 Pac. 102.

[481] Leonard v. Morris, 9 Paige (N. Y.) 90; Pechaud v. Rinquet, 21 Cal. 76. And see Mutual Ben. Life Ins. Co. v. Howell, 32 N. J. Eq. 146; Null v. Jones, 5 Neb. 500.

[482] Rothschild v. Railway Co., 84 Hun, 103, 32 N. Y. Supp. 37; Jackson v. Hull, 10 Johns. (N. Y.) 481; Hughes v. Edwards, 9 Wheat. 489; Torrey v. Cook, 116 Mass. 163. But see Felton v. West, 102 Cal. 266, 36 Pac. 676.

[483] Holmes v. Railway Co. (N. J. Sup.) 29 Atl. 419; Hargreaves v. Men-

such a proceeding cannot be maintained while foreclosure is pending without consent of the court.[484] After foreclosure sale the creditor may sue on the mortgage debt for any deficiency which may remain unsatisfied.[485] As an auxiliary remedy, the mortgagee may obtain the appointment of a receiver to take charge of the mortgaged premises whenever the mortgage is insufficient and the mortgagor is insolvent,[486] and in some cases when the mortgagor is impairing the security by committing waste.[487] And the mortgagor may secure the appointment of a receiver when the mortgagee in possession is insolvent, and is committing waste.[488]

SAME—KINDS OF FORECLOSURE.

140. The principal forms of foreclosure employed in the several states are:
  (a) **By entry and possession** (p. 243).
  (b) **By writ of entry** (p. 244).
  (c) **By an equitable proceeding, under which there may be**
    (1) **A strict foreclosure, or**
    (2) **A decree of sale** (p. 248).
  (d) **By a power of sale in the mortgage or deed of trust** (p. 248).

There is great variety in the modes of foreclosure in use in the several states, and but little uniformity in detail in the states where the same method is used. Jurisdiction to foreclose mortgages was

ken, 45 Neb. 668, 63 N. W. 951; Powell v. Patison, 100 Cal. 236, 34 Pac. 677; Winters v. Mining Co., 57 Fed. 287.

[484] In re Moore, 81 Hun, 389, 31 N. Y. Supp. 110; Meehan v. Bank, 44 Neb. 213, 62 N. W. 490.

[485] Globe Ins. Co. v. Lansing, 5 Cow. (N. Y.) 380; Lansing v. Goelet, 9 Cow. (N. Y.) 346; Hunt v. Stiles, 10 N. H. 466. But see Bassett v. Mason, 18 Conn. 131.

[486] Rider v. Bagley, 84 N. Y. 461; Douglass v. Cline, 12 Bush (Ky.) 608; Ogden v. Chalfant, 32 W. Va. 559, 9 S. E. 879.

[487] Cortleyeu v. Hathaway, 11 N. J. Eq. 39; Stockman v. Wallis, 30 N. J. Eq. 449.

[488] 2 Jones, Mortg. (5th Ed.) § 1517. And see Boston & P. R. Corp. v. New York & N. E. R. Co., 12 R. I. 220.

originally in courts of equity, and this jurisdiction is very generally retained.[489] In a number of states the subject is fully covered by statutory provisions,[490] while in others the proceedings are left to the inherent powers of the court. Equitable mortgages are foreclosed in the same way as mortgages in the usual form.[491]

Foreclosure by Entry and Possession.

In some of the New England states,[492] foreclosure is effected by an entry on the mortgaged premises, and the holding possession for a limited time, after which all right of redemption is barred.[493] After the expiration of this time the mortgagee takes an absolute estate, and becomes entitled to all the rents and profits. The entry must be peaceable, and in the presence of two witnesses, who are to make a certificate of the fact, and the certificate is to be recorded. But a certificate of the mortgagor who consents to the entry, if duly recorded, has the same effect.[495] An entry on part of the land is good,[496] and, when several parcels are covered by the same mortgage, an entry on one is sufficient.[497] Possession under the entry may be constructive.[498] Although the estate of the mortgagee becomes absolute by the failure of the mortgagor to redeem within the time allowed, this effect may be waived by the acceptance of payment after the time for redemption has passed.[499] The rights acquired by the entry may be assigned before the time for redemption has expired.[500] Foreclosure by this method, when complete,

[489] 2 Jones, Mortg. (5th Ed.) § 1443.

[490] 1 Stim. Am. St. Law, art. 192; 2 Jones, Mortg. (5th Ed.) c. 30.

[491] Sprague v. Cochran, 144 N. Y. 104, 38 N. E. 1000.

[492] These are Maine, New Hampshire, Massachusetts, and Rhode Island.

[493] This is three years in all the states except New Hampshire, where only one year is allowed for redemption. 2 Jones, Mortg. (5th Ed.) § 1239; 1 Stim. Am. St. Law, § 1921.

[495] 1 Stim. Am. St. Law, § 1921; 2 Jones, Mortg. (5th Ed.) §§ 1259, 1261.

[496] Lennon v. Porter, 5 Gray (Mass.) 318; Colby v. Poor, 15 N. H. 198. But see Spring v. Haines, 21 Me. 126.

[497] Bennett v. Conant, 10 Cush. (Mass.) 163; Green v. Pettingill, 47 N. H. 375; Shapley v. Rangeley, 1 Woodb. & M. 213, Fed. Cas. No. 12,707.

[498] Ellis v. Drake, 8 Allen (Mass.) 161; Fletcher v. Cary, 103 Mass. 475; Deming v. Comings, 11 N. H. 474.

[499] Joslin v. Wyman, 9 Gray (Mass.) 63; McNeil v. Call, 19 N. H. 403; Chase v. McLellan, 49 Me. 375.

[500] Deming v. Comings, 11 N. H. 474.

operates as a discharge of the mortgage debt, to the amount of the value of the land.[501]

Foreclosure by Writ of Entry.

In the same states a mortgage may also be foreclosed by a writ of entry.[502] The proceeding is essentially the same as that by entry and possession, except a writ of entry is brought to secure the possession. This must always be the method where a peaceable entry is impossible. A legal interest in the land is necessary to sustain the action, and the writ must be brought against the tenant of the freehold.[503] But the mortgagor may always be joined as defendant, though he has assigned all his interest.[504] If the plaintiff is successful, a conditional judgment is rendered,—that, unless defendant pays the amount due within two months, the plaintiff shall have possession; and this possession, when acquired, has the same effect as possession acquired by peaceable entry,—that is, the mortgagor has still three years within which to redeem.[505]

Foreclosure in Equity—Parties Plaintiff.

As before stated, the most usual method of foreclosure is by a proceeding in equity. In such an action the rights of all parties in the mortgaged premises are to be determined. Therefore all persons interested in the mortgage debt should join as plaintiffs.[506] However, a mortgagee who has assigned all his interest is not a proper party plaintiff,[507] unless the assignment was only for secur-

[501] Smith v. Packard, 19 N. H. 575. And see Ray v. Scripture (N. H.) 29 Atl. 454.

[502] 2 Jones, Mortg. (5th Ed.) § 1276. In Rhode Island possession is obtained by an action of ejectment. Id. § 1279.

[503] Somes v. Skinner, 16 Mass. 348; Wheelwright v. Freeman, 12 Metc. (Mass.) 154; Young v. Miller, 6 Gray (Mass.) 152; Johnson v. Brown, 31 N. H. 405.

[504] Straw v. Greene, 14 Allen (Mass.) 206; Hunt v. Hunt, 17 Pick. (Mass.) 118.

[505] 2 Jones, Mortg. (5th Ed.) § 1306. Except in New Hampshire, where it is one year.

[506] Mangels v. Brewing Co., 53 Fed. 513; Pogue v. Clark, 25 Ill. 351; Shirkey v. Hanna, 3 Blackf. (Ind.) 403.

[507] Cutler v. Clementson, 67 Fed. 409; Whitney v. McKinney, 2 Johns. Ch. (N. Y.) 144; McGuffey v. Finley, 20 Ohio, 474; Garrett v. Puckett, 15 Ind. 485. But see Saenger v. Nightingale, 48 Fed. 708.

ity.[508] An assignee of the mortgage, to whom the bond or note sesured thereby has not been transferred, cannot foreclose the mortgage.[509] But, in states where an assignment of the note carries the mortgage with it, an assignee of the note without the mortgage may bring foreclosure without joining the mortgagee with him.[510] When several notes are secured by the same mortgage, the holder of one note can file a bill to foreclose, making the holders of the other notes defendants.[511] A trustee may foreclose in his own name without joining the beneficiaries, when their number is very large.[512] But a beneficiary who seeks to foreclose must always join his trustee.[513] On the death of the mortgagee, his personal representative is the proper party to bring foreclosure.[514] Mortgages given to persons in their official capacity may be foreclosed by their successors in office.[515]

Same—Parties Defendant.

Of parties defendant there are two kinds,—necessary and proper parties.[516] But the distinction is not of much importance, because all who are proper parties should be joined as defendants,

[508] Kittle v. Van Dyck, 1 Sandf. Ch. (N. Y.) 76; Cerf v. Ashley, 68 Cal. 419, 9 Pac. 658. Or where he has guarantied payment. Burnett v. Hoffman, 40 Neb. 569, 58 N. W. 1134.

[509] Cooper v. Newland, 17 Abb. Prac. (N. Y.) 342; Merritt v. Bartholick, 47 Barb. (N. Y.) 253.

[510] Briggs v. Hannowald, 35 Mich. 474; Gower v. Howe, 20 Ind. 396; Swett v. Stark, 31 Fed. 858.

[511] Pettibone v. Edwards, 15 Wis. 95; Myers v. Wright, 33 Ill. 284; Godall v. Mopley, 45 Ind. 355. That the holders of the notes cannot be joined as plaintiffs, see Swenson v. Plow Co., 14 Kan. 387. Contra, Pogue v. Clark, 25 Ill. 351. Joint mortgagees may join, though the debts secured are several. Shirkey v. Hanna, 3 Blackf. (Ind.) 403.

[512] Chicago & G. W. Railroad Land Co. v. Peck, 112 Ill. 408; Lambertville Nat. Bank v. McCready Bag & Paper Co. (N. J. Ch.) 15 Atl. 388.

[513] Martin v. McReynolds, 6 Mich. 70; Hambrick v. Russell, 86 Ala. 199, 5 South. 298. But see Ettlinger v. Carpet Co., 142 N. Y. 189, 36 N. E. 1055.

[514] Dayton v. Dayton, 7 Ill. App. 136.

[515] Iglehart v. Bierce, 36 Ill. 133.

[516] See Tyler v. Hamilton, 62 Fed. 187; Galford v. Gillett, 55 Ill. App. 576; Pettingill v. Hubbell (N. J. Ch.) 32 Atl. 76; London, Paris & American Bank v. Smith, 101 Cal. 415, 35 Pac. 1027.

in order that all rights of redemption may be cut off.[517] In general, all parties may be joined who have any interest in the mortgaged premises. And, when such persons are not joined, they may redeem from the mortgage.[518] A trustee in a deed of trust is a necessary party, since he holds the legal title.[519] But, when the beneficiaries under a trust deed are very numerous, it is not necessary to make them defendants.[520] The holder of an equitable estate or lien should be made a defendant.[521] The mortgagor, while holding the equity of redemption, is a necessary party.[522] And so he must be joined whenever a personal judgment is sought against him.[523] But when no personal judgment against the mortgagor is asked, and he has no interest in the mortgaged premises, he is not a proper party.[524] An assignee of the equity of redemption is a necessary party,[525] but, if he has transferred the equity, he cannot be joined.[526] A purchaser pendente lite need not be made a defendant.[527] The

[517] 2 Jones, Mortg. (5th Ed.) § 1394.

[518] Chase v. Abbott, 20 Iowa, 154; Gaines v. Walker, 16 Ind. 361; Bradley v. Snyder, 14 Ill. 263; Brainard v. Cooper, 10 N. Y. 356; Kennedy v. Moore (Iowa) 58 N. W. 1066; Hunt v. Nolen, 40 S. C. 284, 18 S. E. 798. But see Eschmann v. Alt, 4 Misc. Rep. 305, 24 N. Y. Supp. 763.

[519] Gardner v. Brown, 21 Wall. 36.

[520] Van Vechten v. Terry, 2 Johns. Ch. (N. Y.) 197; Willis v. Henderson, 5 Ill. 13.

[521] Noyes v. Hall, 97 U. S. 34; De Ruyter v. St. Peter's Church, 2 Barb. Ch. (N. Y.) 555. As to joining as defendants persons entitled in remainder or reversion, see Nodine v. Greenfield, 7 Paige (N. Y.) 544; Eagle Fire Ins. Co. v. Cammet, 2 Edw. Ch. (N. Y.) 127; 2 Jones, Mortg. (5th Ed.) § 1401.

[522] Kay v. Whitaker, 44 N. Y. 565; Michigan Ins. Co. of Detroit v. Brown, 11 Mich. 265; Moore v. Starks, 1 Ohio St. 369.

[523] Miller v. Thompson, 34 Mich. 10; Jones v. Lapham, 15 Kan. 540; Stevens v. Campbell, 21 Ind. 471.

[524] Swift v. Edson, 5 Conn. 532; Craig v. Miller, 41 S. C. 37, 19 S. E. 192; Baker v. Collins, 4 Tex. Civ. App. 520, 23 S. W. 493.

[525] Watson v. Spence, 20 Wend. (N. Y.) 260; Cord v. Hirsch, 17 Wis. 415; Travellers' Ins. Co. v. Patten, 98 Ind. 209; Clark v. Gregory, 87 Tex. 189, 27 S. W. 56. But not when the deed is not recorded. Connely v. Rue, 148 Ill. 207, 35 N. E. 824; Oakford v. Robinson, 48 Ill. App. 270; Hatfield v. Malcolm, 71 Hun, 51, 24 N. Y. Supp. 596.

[526] Lockwood v. Benedict, 3 Edw. Ch. (N. Y.) 472; Scarry v. Eldridge, 63 Ind. 44.

[527] Stout v. Lye, 103 U. S. 66; McPherson v. Housel, 13 N. J. Eq. 299.

§ 140)   KINDS OF FORECLOSURE.   247

heirs or devisees of the owner of an equity of redemption, who has died seised, must be made defendants;[528] and so must legatees whose legacies are charges on the mortgaged premises.[529] The wife of the mortgagor must be made a defendant, to cut off her dower;[530] but, when she did not join in the mortgage, she is not a proper party, unless some defense as to her dower has arisen subsequently to the mortgage.[531]   But the wife must be joined where the mortgage is on the homestead,[532] unless it be for purchase money.[533] Subsequent mortgagees are proper, though not necessary, parties, since they may redeem.[534]   And so a subsequent mortgagee who has assigned his mortgage for security is a proper party.[535] Where an assignment of the mortgage note carries the mortgage with it, the assignee of the note may be made defendant.[536]   On the death of a junior mortgagee, his personal representative is the proper party to make defendant.[537]   Judgment creditors having a lien are proper parties, because they may redeem if not joined,[538] but a general creditor without any lien cannot be joined.[539]   Prior mortgagees need not be made defendants, though they may be.[540]   Ad-

[528] Stark v. Brown, 12 Wis. 638; Abbott v. Godfroy, 1 Mich. 178; Richards v. Thompson, 43 Kan. 209, 23 Pac. 106; Hill v. Townley, 45 Minn. 167, 47 N. W. 653. But see Wood v. Morehouse, 1 Lans. (N. Y.) 405.

[529] McGown v. Yerks, 6 Johns. Ch. (N. Y.) 450.

[530] Foster v. Hickox, 38 Wis. 408; Wright v. Langley, 36 Ill. 381; Mills v. Van Voorhies, 20 N. Y. 412; Gibson v. Crehore, 5 Pick. (Mass.) 146. And see Moomey v. Maas, 22 Iowa, 380.

[531] Barr v. Vanalstine, 120 Ind. 590, 22 N. E. 965.

[532] Sargent v. Wilson, 5 Cal. 504.

[533] Amphlett v. Hibbard, 29 Mich. 298.

[534] Kenyon v. Shreck, 52 Ill. 382; Gower v. Winchester, 33 Iowa, 303; Pattison v. Shaw, 6 Ind. 377; Jewett v. Tomlinson, 137 Ind. 326, 36 N. E. 1106; Williams v. Kerr, 113 N. C. 306, 18 S. E. 501. And see Rose v. Chandler, 50 Ill. App. 421.

[535] Dalton v. Smith, 86 N. Y. 176; Bard v. Poole, 12 N. Y. 495.

[536] Burton v. Baxter, 7 Blackf. (Ind.) 297.

[537] Citizens' Nat. Bank v. Dayton, 116 Ill. 257, 4 N. E. 492; Lockman v. Reilly, 95 N. Y. 64.

[538] Brainard v. Cooper, 10 N. Y. 356; Com. v. Robinson (Ky.) 29 S. W. 306.

[539] Gardner v. Lansing, 28 Hun (N. Y.) 413; Sumner v. Skinner, 80 Hun, 201, 30 N. Y. Supp. 4.

[540] Jerome v. McCarter, 94 U. S. 734; Strobe v. Downer, 13 Wis. 11; Frost

verse claimants of the mortgaged land cannot be made parties, because their claims to title cannot be litigated in the foreclosure suit.[541]

Same—Strict Foreclosure and Decree of Sale.

In a few states the original form of decree in foreclosure is still used; that is, unless the mortgagor redeems within a limited time after the decree, the estate becomes absolute in the mortgagee.[542] The time allowed for such redemption is within the discretion of the court.[543]

But in most states, instead of a strict foreclosure, a sale of the mortgaged land is decreed,[545] and the amount due the mortgagee is paid him, while any surplus is applied for the benefit of the mortgagor, in paying off other incumbrances according to their priority.[546] Such a sale is made by an officer of the court, and the manner of conducting it is prescribed by statute.[547] However, before such a sale becomes effective, it must be confirmed by the court.[548]

Power of Sale.

It is usually provided in a mortgage or deed of trust that the mortgagee or trustee, respectively, shall, on default of payment, have power to sell the mortgaged premises without going into court.[549]

v. Koon, 30 N. Y. 428; Bexar Bldg. & Loan Ass'n v. Newman (Tex. Civ. App.) 25 S. W. 461.

[541] Summers v. Bromley, 28 Mich. 125; Pelton v. Farmin, 18 Wis. 222; Banning v. Bradford, 21 Minn. 308.

[542] 2 Jones, Mortg. (5th Ed.) §§ 1538, 1542; Hitchcock v. Bank, 7 Ala. 386; Sheldon v. Patterson, 55 Ill. 507; Caufman v. Sayre, 2 B. Mon. (Ky.) 202; Shaw v. Railroad Co., 5 Gray (Mass.) 162; Heyward v. Judd, 4 Minn. 483 (Gil. 375); Woods v. Shields, 1 Neb. 453; Bolles v. Duff, 43 N. Y. 469; Higgins v. West, 5 Ohio, 554. But not in others. Goodenow v. Ewer, 16 Cal. 461; Smith v. Brand, 64 Ind. 427; Gamut v. Gregg, 37 Iowa, 573; Jackson v. Weaver, 138 Ind. 539, 38 N. E. 166; Davis v. Holmes, 55 Mo. 349; Winton's Appeal, 87 Pa. St. 77; Hord v. James, 1 Overt. (Tenn.) 201.

[543] Chicago, D. & V. R. Co. v. Fosdick, 106 U. S. 47, 1 Sup. Ct. 10; Ellis v. Leek, 127 Ill. 60, 20 N. E. 218.

[545] 1 Stim. Am. St. Law, § 1925 C.

[546] 1 Stim. Am. St. Law, § 1926; 2 Jones, Mortg. (5th Ed.) § 1684.

[547] 1 Stim. Am. St. Law, § 1925 I–O; 2 Jones, Mortg. (5th Ed.) § 1608.

[548] 2 Jones, Mortg. (5th Ed.) § 1637.

[549] 1 Stim. Am. St. Law, § 1924 A.

§ 140) KINDS OF FORECLOSURE. 249

In some states, however, such provisions are not valid.[550] The existence of a power of sale does not take away the right to foreclose.[551] Such a power passes with an assignment of the mortgage,[552] but not to an assignee of the beneficiary under the deed of trust. In the latter case it remains in the trustee, who must execute it for the benefit of the assignee.[553] The one holding the legal title under the mortgage is the one who should sell under the power.[554] The manner of conducting the sale is usually provided for in the instrument creating the power, and is in many states regulated by statute.[555] In the absence of a statutory provision, or direction in the power, the sale need not be in parcels.[556] A mortgagor cannot revoke a power of sale, nor does his death have that effect.[557] The power of sale is suspended by a bill to redeem brought by the mortgagor,[558] but not when filed by a subsequent mortgagee.[559] The surplus is distributed in the same way as when a sale is by decree of court.[560]

Same—Purchase by the Mortgagee at the Sale.

At a sale under a power, the mortgagee is not usually allowed to become the purchaser, unless permission is given in the mortgage.[561] Nor can he become a purchaser through an agent, or by

[550] 1 Stim. Am. St. Law, § 1924 D.
[551] Morrison v. Bean, 15 Tex. 267; Utermehle v. McGreal, 1 App. D. C. 359.
[552] Bush v. Sherman, 80 Ill. 160.
[553] Whittelsey v. Hughes, 39 Mo. 13; Johnson v. Johnson, 27 S. C. 309, 3 S. E. 606; Western Maryland Railroad Land & Imp. Co. v. Goodwin, 77 Md. 271, 26 Atl. 319; Banick v. Horner, 78 Md. 253, 27 Atl. 1111.
[554] Miller v. Clark, 56 Mich. 337, 23 N. W. 35; Backus v. Burke, 48 Minn. 260, 51 N. W. 284.
[555] Notice to the mortgagor and the public is nearly always provided for. 1 Stim. Am. St. Law, § 1924 E.
[556] Loveland v. Clark, 11 Colo. 265, 18 Pac. 544; Singleton v. Scott, 11 Iowa, 589; Gray v. Shaw, 14 Mo. 341.
[557] Reilly v. Phillips, 4 S. D. 604, 57 N. W. 780; Schwab Clothing Co. v. Claunch (Tex. Civ. App.) 29 S. W. 922. Contra in Illinois by statute. 1 Stim. Am. St. Law, § 1924 C. And see Williams v. Washington, 40 S. C. 457, 19 S. E. 1.
[558] 2 Jones, Mortg. (5th Ed.) § 1797.
[559] Holland v. Bank, 16 R. I. 734, 19 Atl. 654.
[560] 1 Stim. Am. St. Law, § 1924 E; 2 Jones, Mortg. (5th Ed.) § 1927.
[561] Griffin v. Marine Co., 52 Ill. 130; Jones v. Pullen, 115 N. C. 465, 20 S. E.

other indirect means.[562] A purchase by the mortgagee, however, is only voidable, and not void.[563] Nor can a trustee who sells the premises under a power of sale in a deed of trust become the purchaser,[564] but the beneficiary—that is, the mortgagee—may purchase.[565] The mortgagee is allowed to purchase at foreclosure sale under decree of court.[566]

624; Garland v. Watson, 74 Ala. 323; Lovelace v. Hutchinson (Ala.) 17 South. 623. But see Hambrick v. Security Co., 100 Ala. 551, 13 South. 778.

[562] Nichols v. Otto, 132 Ill. 91, 23 N. E. 411; Harper v. Ely, 56 Ill. 179; Tipton v. Wortham, 93 Ala. 321, 9 South. 596; Joyner v. Farmer, 78 N. C. 196.

[563] Cunningham v. Railroad Co., 156 U. S. 400, 15 Sup. Ct. 361; Burns v. Thayer, 115 Mass. 89; Mulvey v. Gibbons, 87 Ill. 367; Connolly v. Hammond, 51 Tex. 635; Averitt v. Elliot, 109 N. C. 560, 13 S. E. 785.

[564] Lass v. Sternberg, 50 Mo. 124. Cf. Stephen v. Beall, 22 Wall. 329; Felton v. Le Breton, 92 Cal. 457, 28 Pac. 490.

[565] Easton v. Bank, 127 U. S. 532, 8 Sup. Ct. 1297.

[566] Maxwell v. Newton, 65 Wis. 261, 27 N. W. 31; Ramsey v. Merriam, 6 Minn. 168 (Gil. 104).

CHAPTER X.

EQUITABLE ESTATES.

141. Legal and Equitable Estates.
142. Use or Trust Defined.
143–144. The Statute of Uses.
145. When the Statute does not Operate.
146. Classification of Trusts.
147. Express Trusts.
148–149. Executed and Executory Trusts.
150–151. Creation of Express Trusts.
152. Implied Trusts.
153. Resulting Trusts.
154. Constructive Trusts.
155–156. Incidents of Equitable Estates.
157–158. Charitable Trusts.

LEGAL AND EQUITABLE ESTATES.

141. The various kinds of estates as to quantity and quality may be either
  (a) Legal, or
  (b) Equitable.

We now come to a new principle upon which to classify estates, namely, their legal or equitable character. So far our attention has been occupied with legal interests, though equitable estates have been mentioned in treating of curtesy,[1] dower,[2] homestead,[3] and mortgages.[4] It will now be seen that the different estates, as to quantity and quality, may any of them be held by a title which is recognized only in courts of equity.[5] And some estates are possible under equitable limitations which cannot be created at common law; these are estates which defeat a preceding estate, or spring into existence without a preceding freehold to support them.[6] Estates

---

[1] Ante, p. 73.   [2] Ante, p. 83.   [3] Ante, p. 112.   [4] Ante, p. 180.
[5] On the whole subject of this chapter, see Fetter, Eq. c. 8.
[6] See ante, p. 177, note 39, and post, pp. 284, 299.

which are recognized by the common law are called "legal estates." Estates which owe their existence to courts of equity are called "equitable estates."

USE OR TRUST DEFINED.

142. A use or trust is an equitable right to the beneficial enjoyment of an estate, the legal title to which is held by another person.

At common law there were many restraints on the alienation of real property which impeded its full enjoyment. Estates were subject to escheat and forfeiture for treason. Statutes of mortmain had been passed, which prevented lands from being conveyed to religious corporations, and other restraints existed which prevented land becoming an article of commerce. In order that these burdens might be avoided, the practice of conveying lands to uses was introduced; that is, land would be conveyed to a person in whom the grantor had confidence, for the use of the grantor or another, and would by such grantee be disposed of or used according to the wishes of the grantor. The clergy were probably the first to employ this method of transferring and holding land. At first there were no means by which the grantor could compel the execution of the confidence thus imposed, but later the chancellors, who were ecclesiastics, gave a subpœna in chancery by which such confidences were enforced.[7] Although in courts of law only the legal estate and title were recognized, yet in equity the person entitled to the beneficial interest was, for all purposes, recognized as owner.[8] In this way a dual system of ownership arose, by the legal title to the land being held by one person, and all of the beneficial rights arising out of it belonging to another. These equitable interests were held free from most of the burdens attached to common-law estates. For example, they could be conveyed without a feoffment, or could be disposed of by will, which was not true of a legal estate.[9]

---

[7] See Dig. Hist. Real Prop. (4th Ed.) 313; Anon., Y. B. 14 Hen. VIII. 4 pl. 5.
[8] 2 Washb. Real Prop. (5th Ed.) 409.
[9] 2 Pol. & M. Hist. Eng. Law, 226; Burgess v. Wheate, 1 W. Bl. 123; Chudleigh's Case, 1 Coke, 120a.

THE STATUTE OF USES.

143. The statute of uses enacted that whenever any person should be seised of any lands to the use, confidence, or trust of another, the latter should be deemed in lawful seisin of a legal estate of a like quantity and quality as he had in the use.

144. The statute of uses is in force in many of the United States (p. 254).

Although many convenient purposes were served by the practice of conveying lands to uses, on the other hand it had a tendency to make titles uncertain, and was very unpopular with the great landowners of England, because they were deprived of many of the incidents attached to feudal estates.[10] A number of statutes were passed, attempting to prevent these results, but they proved ineffectual. Finally the famous statute of uses [11] was enacted, which provided "that where any person or persons stand, or be seized, or at any time hereafter shall happen to be seized of and in any honours, castles, manors, lands, tenements, rents, services, reversions, remainders, or other hereditaments to the use, confidence, or trust of any other person or persons or of any body politick by reason of any bargain, sale, feoffment, fine, recovery, covenant, contract, agreement, will or otherwise, by any manner means whatsoever it be, that in every such case, all and every such person and persons * * * shall from henceforth stand and be seized, deemed, and adjudged in lawful seisin, estate, and possession of and in the same honours, castles, manors," etc., "* * * to all intents, constructions and purposes in the law, of and in such like estates as they had or shall have and in use, trust or confidence of or in the same."[12] The statute contained other provisions, all intended to produce the effect that, whenever a person was entitled to the beneficial interest

---

[10] The inconveniences arising from lands being conveyed to uses are recited in the preamble of the statute of uses. See, also, Lloyd v. Spillet, 2 Atk. 148.

[11] 27 Hen. VIII. c. 10.

[12] Broughton v. Langley, 2 Salk. 679; Lord Altham v. Earl of Anglesey, Gilb. Cas. 16. The possession passes immediately. Anon., Cro. Eliz. 46. Heelis v. Blain, 18 C. B. (N. S.) 90. But see Orme's Case, L. R. 8 C. P. 281.

in land, the legal title should be vested in him. An exception was made, however, so that wives on whom a jointure had been settled would not be entitled to dower in the equitable estates of their husbands which should be executed by the statute.[13] The statute of uses had a very important effect on conveyancing, because, as we shall see later,[14] it became possible to convey the legal title to lands by methods unknown to the common law.[15]

Statute of Uses in the United States.

The statute of uses has been re-enacted in a number of our states, either in terms or in substance, and in some others it is held to exist as part of the common law.[16] Other states, however, following the lead of New York, have abolished all uses and trusts, except in certain specified cases permitted by the statutes.[17] These are: (1) Trusts implied by law, for the prevention of fraud; (2) active trusts, where the trustee is clothed with some actual power of disposition or management, which cannot be properly exercised without giving him the legal estate and actual possession.

SAME—WHEN THE STATUTE DOES NOT OPERATE.

145. The statute of uses was held not to apply to,—
  (a) **Chattel interests.**
  (b) **Future uses.**
  (c) **Active uses.**
  (d) **Estates for the separate use of married women.**
  (e) **A use upon a use.**
  (f) **Trusts created by operation of law.**

According to the wording of the statute of uses, it was held that three things were necessary for its operation: There must be (1) a

---

[13] 27 Hen. VIII. c. 10, § 6.

[14] Post, p. 409.

[15] Lutwich v. Milton, Cro. Jac. 604; Roe v. Tranmer, 2 Wils. 75. See, also, Sammes' Case, 13 Coke, 54.

[16] 2 Washb. Real Prop. (5th Ed.) p. 465. The statute of uses is not in force in Ohio. Gray, Perp. p. 45, § 68.

[17] 1 Stim. Am. St. Law, § 1703. For trusts not within the statute, see Cowen v. Rinaldo, 82 Hun, 479, 31 N. Y. Supp. 554.

§ 145)   WHEN THE STATUTE OF USES DOES NOT OPERATE.   255

person seised to a use; (2) a cestui que use in esse; (3) a use in esse.[18] The use, however, might be either in possession or in expectancy.[19] The cases in which the statute of uses was held not to operate to vest the legal title in the beneficiary, enumerated in the black-letter text, rendered the statute practically inoperative. It was held that chattel interests were not within the statute, because there could be no seisin of such interests, and the provision of the statute was "that where any person or persons stand or be seized."[20] Nor did the statute operate upon future uses,[21] but such uses would be executed by the statute as soon as they became vested.[22] A distinction was made by the courts between active and passive uses; that is, where the trustee had no duties to perform, but merely held the legal title for the benefit of the cestui que use, the statute was permitted to operate.[23] But when anything was to be done by the trustee in relation to the trust property, such as collecting the rents and profits, or selling the property, the statute did not operate, because the trustee could not perform these duties unless he held the title to the land.[24] The former was called a passive, and the latter an active, use. Very slight duties imposed on the trustee were sufficient to prevent the operation of the statute.[25] Lands conveyed to the separate use of a married woman are not within the scope of the statute, because, if the legal title should vest in her, her husband would become entitled to the control of the estate, thus producing an effect contrary to the intention with which such uses are created.[26] Under statutes

[18] Witham v. Brooner, 63 Ill. 344; Brent's Case, 2 Leon. 14.

[19] 2 Washb. Real Prop. (5th Ed.) 434.

[20] Merrill v. Brown, 12 Pick. (Mass.) 216; Galliers v. Moss, 9 Barn. & C. 267; Hopkins v. Hopkins, 1 Atk. 581.

[21] Wyman v. Brown, 50 Me. 139; Proprietors of Town of Shapleigh v. Pilsbury, 1 Me. 271; Savage v. Lee, 90 N. C. 320.

[22] See Chudleigh's Case, 1 Coke, 120a, and cases in note 21 supra.

[23] Posey v. Cook, 1 Hill (S. C.) 413; Ware v. Richardson, 3 Md. 505; Sullivan v. Chambers, 18 R. I. 799, 31 Atl. 167.

[24] Fay v. Taft, 12 Cush. (Mass.) 448; Barnett's Appeal, 46 Pa. St. 392; Gott v. Cook, 7 Paige (N. Y.) 521; Morton v. Barrett, 22 Me. 257; Posey v. Cook, 1 Hill (S. C.) 413; Schley v. Lyon, 6 Ga. 530.

[25] Morton v. Barrett, 22 Me. 257. As soon as the active duties of the trustee are performed, the statute vests the legal estate in the cestui que trust. Felgner v. Hooper, 80 Md. 262, 30 Atl. 911.

[26] Steacy v. Rice, 27 Pa. St. 75; Pullen v. Rianhard, 1 Whart. (Pa.) 514;

which give a married woman the same right of disposition over her property as a feme sole, the reason for this rule would not obtain, and the legal estate would vest in her.[27] And without such statutes, if a married woman conveyed her equitable estate, the statute would execute the legal title in her assignee.[28]

The most important ruling of the courts on the statute of uses, however, was in Tyrrell's Case,[29] about 20 years after the statute was passed, in which it was held that a use upon a use was not within the terms of the statute; that is, where an estate was conveyed to A. for the use of B. for the use of C. Before the enactment of the statute, under such a conveyance, the use to C. would be void. A use could not be engendered of a use, it was said. And after the statute it was held that the legal title would be executed in B., but that then the force of the statute would be exhausted, and B. would hold the estate for the benefit of C.[30] In this way the necessity arose again for the protection of the beneficiary by the court of chancery. In other words, the courts of law treated the first use as executed by the statute, and the second as void. Such a construction evidently defeated the intention of the grantor, and consequently equity interposed, and gave effect to the second use. Therefore all that was necessary to avoid the effect of the statute was to add the words, "to the use of."[31] The statute of uses does not operate upon beneficial interests created by operation of law.[32] The equitable estates upon which the statute of uses was held not to operate are called "trusts,"[33] and their incidents are the same as those of

Bush's Appeal, 33 Pa. St. 85; Nevil v. Saunders, 1 Vern. 415; Harton v. Harton, 7 Term R. 653. But see Ware v. Richardson, 3 Md. 504.

[27] Bratton v. Massey, 15 S. C. 277; Sutton v. Aiken, 62 Ga. 733; Bayer v. Cockrill, 3 Kan. 282.

[28] Leaycraft v. Hedden, 4 N. J. Eq. 512; Imlay v. Huntington, 20 Conn. 146; Cooke v. Husbands, 11 Md. 492.

[29] Dyer, 155a.

[30] And see Doe v. Passingham, 6 Barn. & C. 305. But see Peacock v. Eastland, L. R. 10 Eq. 17.

[31] Croxall v. Shererd, 5 Wall. 268; Jackson v. Cary, 16 Johns. (N. Y.) 302; Jackson v. Myers, 3 Johns. (N. Y.) 388; Guest v. Farley, 19 Mo. 147. This rule has been abolished by statute in Georgia, and the use is executed to the last beneficiary. See 1 Stim. Am. St. Law, § 1701; Code, Ga. 1882, § 2315.

[32] See post, p. 265.

[33] Before the statute of uses the term "trust" was applied to equitable es-

uses before the enactment of the statute, and the rights and duties of the owners of the two classes of estates will be treated of together in this chapter.

CLASSIFICATION OF TRUSTS.

146. Trusts, according to the method of their creation, are divided into
  (a) **Express trusts** (p. 258).
  (b) **Implied trusts** (p. 264).

A great deal of confusion exists in the books and cases on the subject of the classification of trusts. This has arisen principally from a loose and incorrect use of the word "implied." Some courts, as well as text writers, use the words "implied," "resulting," and "constructive," indifferently, while in fact both resulting and constructive trusts are implied trusts; that is, they are implied or created by operation of law. On the other hand, all trusts which can properly be called implied are either constructive or resulting. The term "implied," however, has often been used to designate certain express trusts, in the creation of which the language of the settlor is obscure, and his intention has to be inferred by the courts from the words used. These trusts can in no proper sense be termed implied, because the only question that arises is one of construction. It is sufficient to call attention at this point to the confusion which has arisen from the improper use of the words. The definitions and distinctions between the different kinds of trusts will appear as they are treated of separately. In examining the cases it must be borne in mind that the language of the courts in many cases cannot be relied upon in determining the kind of trust in question.

tates created for a limited period, while those of indefinite duration were called "uses." 2 Washb. Real Prop. (5th Ed.) 414.

EXPRESS TRUSTS.

147. Express trusts are those which are created by act of the parties. They are either
  (a) Executed, or
  (b) Executory.

SAME—EXECUTED AND EXECUTORY TRUSTS.

148. An executed trust is one in which the terms and limitations are definitely and completely declared by the instrument creating it.

149. An executory trust is one in which the limitations are not completely declared, but only an outline given, by which the trustee is to declare the final limitations of the trust estates.

Under an executed trust, the intention of the settlor must be taken from the instrument creating the trust,[34] while in the case of an executory trust the terms and limitations of the trust, as they are finally declared, are to be determined, not only by the words used, but by the circumstances surrounding the parties.[35] A trust is executed when the instrument creating it contains all the terms of the trust, and is in its final form,—nothing remaining to be done but to carry out the terms as therein declared. But in an executory trust it is intended that there shall be a further and more definite declaration of the terms and limitations of the trust, and the instrument creating an executory trust is more in the nature of a memorandum containing directions according to which the trust is to be completely declared.[36]

---

[34] Wright v. Pearson, 1 Eden, 125; Austen v. Taylor, Id. 361; Jervoise v. Duke of Northumberland, 1 Jac. & W. 559.

[35] Austen v. Taylor, 1 Eden, 361; Neves v. Scott, 9 How. 196; Cushing v. Blake, 30 N. J. Eq. 689; Tallman v. Wood, 26 Wend. (N. Y.) 9.

[36] Wright v. Pearson, 1 Eden, 125; Jervoise v. Duke of Northumberland, 1 Jac. & W. 559. Executory trusts are closely applied to powers. See post, p. 306.

Executory trusts are special or active trusts directing the trustee to settle or dispose of the land for the estates and interests required by the trust. They are so called because they have to be executed by a deed conveying the land for the estates and limitations intended, as distinguished from trusts directing the trustee to hold the property upon trusts then executed, in the sense of being then perfectly limited and defined. Executory trusts are fulfilled and discharged by the execution of a deed in conformity with the directions of the trust. Executory trusts are here distinguished, as regards the limitation of estates, by admitting of an exceptional construction of the limitations expressed. They are often expressed in compendious terms by way of instructions for the limitations directed to be made, without setting out the limitations at length, as by directing or agreeing that property shall be settled "in strict settlement," "entailed," settled "with usual and proper powers," or the like; in which cases the construction consists in developing the limitations involved in such expressions in the form best suited to carry out the general intention of the trust. And, even where an executory trust is expressed in technical terms of limitation, the terms are not necessarily construed with the same strictness as is applied to ordinary legal limitations; but, having regard to the directory character of the trust, the technical meaning is held subordinate to the general object required to be carried out.[37]

The two principal classes of executory trusts are those arising under contracts for marriage settlements, and under trusts declared in wills. In the former the courts presume that the intention in creating the trust was to provide for the offspring of the marriage, and construe the terms accordingly; but in trusts arising under wills no such intention can be presumed.[38] Most of the cases of executory trusts arise under limitations calling for a consideration of the rule in Shelley's Case, which will be considered in another place.[39]

---

[37] Tallman v. Wood, 26 Wend. (N. Y.) 9. McElroy v. McElroy, 113 Mass. 509; Cushing v. Blake, 30 N. J. Eq. 689; Wight v. Leigh, 15 Ves. 564.

[38] Neves v. Scott, 9 How. 196; Gause v. Hale, 2 Ired. Eq. (N. C.) 241; Smith v. Maxwell, 1 Hill (S. C.) 101; Green v. Rumph, 2 Hill (S. C.) 1; Carroll v. Renich, 7 Smedes & M. (Miss.) 798.

[39] See post, p. 295.

SAME—CREATION OF EXPRESS TRUSTS.

150. An express trust may be created by any language which shows an intention to create a trust, and which sufficiently designates the property, the beneficiary, and the terms of the trust. Under the statute of frauds, an express trust cannot be created by parol.

151. The parties to the creation of a trust are,—
  (a) The feoffor, or creator.
  (b) The feoffee, or trustee, who holds the legal title.
  (c) The cestui que trust, or beneficiary.

The creation of an express trust is a mere matter of conveyancing. And being a conveyance, rather than a contract, no consideration is necessary to support an express trust.[40] A mere contract to create a trust will not be enforced, in the absence of a consideration. Some cases, however, hold that such an agreement will be enforced in favor of a wife or child, though not for other relatives.[41]

The presence or absence of consideration, however, plays an important part, as will be seen when resulting trusts are considered. For, if the legal title is conveyed to one who pays no consideration, a presumption may arise that such grantee was not intended to take the beneficial interest.[42]

Any real property may be held in trust.[43] The requirements as to

---

[40] Bunn v. Winthrop, 1 Johns. Ch. (N. Y.) 329; Ownes v. Ownes, 23 N. J. Eq. 60; Massey v. Huntington, 118 Ill. 80, 7 N. E. 269; Brunson v. Henry, 140 Ind. 455, 39 N. E. 256; Anon., Brooke, 89. But see Beeman v. Beeman, 88 Hun, 14, 34 N. Y. Supp. 484; Hamilton v. Downer, 152 Ill. 651, 38 N. E. 733. The instrument of creation must be executed and delivered. Govin v. De Miranda, 9 Misc. Rep. 684, 30 N. Y. Supp. 550.

[41] Hayes v. Kershow, 1 Sandf. Ch. (N. Y.) 258; Bunn v. Winthrop, 1 Johns. Ch. (N. Y.) 329; Buford v. McKee, 1 Dana (Ky.) 107.

[42] See post, p. 267.

[43] 1 Perry, Trusts (4th Ed.) §§ 67–69; 2 Washb. Real Prop. (5th Ed.) p. 416. But a trust cannot be created in a mortgage, where it is only a lien, though there may be a trust in the mortgage debt. Merrill v. Brown, 12 Pick. (Mass.) 216.

description of the property conveyed, the designation of the feoffee and of the cestui que trust, etc., are matters of conveyancing, and will be discussed in a subsequent chapter.

Limitation of Trustee's Estate.

In limiting the legal estate to a trustee, the strict requirements as to the use of technical words in conveying legal estates are relaxed, and the trustee is held to take an estate sufficient to carry out the purposes of the trust.[44] For example, if the cestui que trust is given the beneficial interest in fee, and only a life estate is given to the trustee, the latter's estate will be enlarged to a fee, if it is necessary to carry out the settlor's intention.[45] On the other hand, the estate of the trustee will be cut down to what is necessary to enable him to carry out the trust. In most cases this would be accomplished by the statute of uses executing the legal estate in the beneficiary as soon as the trustee's active duties were completed.[46]

Precatory Words.

In the creation of an express trust, it is not necessary to use the words "use, confidence, or trust," or in fact any technical expression.[47] It is sufficient if from the whole instrument an intention appears to create a trust.[48] In fact, the intention of the settlor may be shown by what are called "precatory words"; that is, by such expressions as "desire," "request," "entreat," "trust and confide." [49]

[44] Neilson v. Lagow, 12 How. 98; Fisher v. Fields, 10 Johns. (N. Y.) 495; Gould v. Lamb, 11 Metc. (Mass.) 84; Newhall v. Wheeler, 7 Mass. 189; Angell v. Rosenbury, 12 Mich. 241. But see Cooper v. Franklin, Cro. Jac. 400.

[45] Newhall v. Wheeler, 7 Mass. 189.

[46] Norton v. Norton, 2 Sandf. (N. Y.) 296; Bush's Appeal, 33 Pa. St. 85; Renziehausen v. Keyser, 48 Pa. St. 351. But see Lewis v. Rees, 3 Kay & J. 132.

[47] Wright v. Douglass, 7 N. Y. 564; Raybold v. Raybold, 20 Pa. St. 308; Ready v. Kearsley, 14 Mich. 215; White v. Fitzgerald, 19 Wis. 480; Zuver v. Lyons, 40 Iowa, 510.

[48] Toms v. Williams, 41 Mich. 552, 2 N. W. 814; Taft v. Taft, 130 Mass. 461; McElroy v. McElroy, 113 Mass. 509; Kintner v. Jones, 122 Ind. 148, 23 N. E. 701.

[49] Warner v. Bates, 98 Mass. 274; Knox v. Knox, 59 Wis. 172, 18 N. W. 155; Webster v. Morris, 66 Wis. 366, 28 N. W. 353; McRee v. Means, 34 Ala. 349; Erickson v. Willard, 1 N. H. 217; Collins v. Carlisle's Heirs, 7 B. Mon. (Ky.) 13; Bull v. Bull, 8 Conn. 47; Hunter v. Stembridge, 12 Ga. 192. But see,

No definite rule can be laid down as to when the use of such words will be sufficient to create a trust, but it will depend in each case on the construction of the whole instrument, and the intention of the settlor appearing therefrom.[50] In limiting equitable estates, it is not necessary to use the same technical words as are required in the limitation of estates at common law. All that is necessary is sufficient words to show the intention.[51]

Statute of Frauds.

At common law an express trust could be created by parol,[52] but under the statute of frauds it must be evidenced in writing.[53] But for this purpose any writing signed by the person against whom the trust is so to be enforced will be sufficient, if it show the existence of the trust.[54] And if the statute of frauds is not set up, and the trust is admitted, it can be enforced, although created by parol, since no evidence of its existence is necessary in such case.[55] In some states

for expressions held not to raise a trust, Hopkins v. Glunt, 111 Pa. St. 287, 2 Atl. 183; Burt v. Herron's Ex'rs, 66 Pa. St. 400; Bowlby v. Thunder, 105 Pa. St. 173; Colton v. Colton, 10 Sawy. 325, 21 Fed. 594; Sears v. Cunningham, 122 Mass. 538.

[50] 1 Perry, Trusts (4th Ed.) § 114. See cases cited in last note. Of this same nature are "trusts for maintenance." When property is given to a parent, or to one standing in that relation, and expressions as to support and education of the grantee's children are used, the property will be impressed with a trust, if it appears that such was the grantor's or testator's intention. Whiting v. Whiting, 4 Gray (Mass.) 240; Andrews v. President, etc., 3 Allen (Mass.) 313; Rittgers v. Rittgers, 56 Iowa, 218, 9 N. W. 188; Babbitt v. Babbitt, 26 N. J. Eq. 44. But there will be no trust if the expressions as to maintenance were used merely to show the motive. Rhett v. Mason's Ex'r, 18 Grat. (Va.) 541.

[51] Stanley v. Colt, 5 Wall. 119; Neilson v. Lagow, 12 How. 98; Fisher v. Fields, 10 Johns. (N. Y.) 495; Welch v. Allen, 21 Wend. (N. Y.) 147; Gould v. Lamb, 11 Metc. (Mass.) 84; Newhall v. Wheeler, 7 Mass. 189; Angell v. Rosenbury, 12 Mich. 241; Meredith v. Joans, Cro. Car. 244; Egerton's Case, Cro. Jac. 525.

[52] 1 Perry, Trusts (4th Ed.) § 75.

[53] 29 Car. II. c. 3, § 7; Moore v. Horsley, 156 Ill. 36, 40 N. E. 323; Callard v. Callard, Moore, 687; Movan v. Hays, 1 Johns. Ch. (N. Y.) 339; Sherley v. Sherley (Ky.) 31 S. W. 275; Acker v. Priest (Iowa) 61 N. W. 235.

[54] Steere v. Steere, 5 Johns. Ch. (N. Y.) 1; Barrell v. Joy, 16 Mass. 221; McClellan v. McClellan, 65 Me. 500; Dyer's Appeal, 107 Pa. St. 446.

[55] Whiting v. Gould, 2 Wis. 552; Thornton v. Vaughan, 2 Scam. (Ill.) 219; Trustees of Schools v. Wright, 12 Ill. 432; Woods v. Dille, 11 Ohio, 455.

it is provided by statute that trusts must be created and declared in writing.[56] When a trust is created by will, the same formalities in the execution of the will are required as for a valid devise of lands.[57] The statute of frauds applies to public or charitable trusts as well as to private.[58]

Parties.

The person creating a use or trust is called the "feoffor." Any one owning land who has capacity to make a contract or a will can create a trust.[59] For instance, a state [60] or a corporation, if the latter is permitted by its charter, may be a feoffor.[61] The capacity of married women, infants, aliens, etc., to create trusts, is the same as their capacity to deal with real property.[62]

Any one may be a trustee who is capable of taking the legal title to realty.[63] The United States and the states may, of course, be trustees, although they cannot be sued, without their consent, for the enforcement of the trust.[64] Corporations may hold lands as trustees, and many trust companies now do so.[65] A married woman may be a trustee, and cannot plead her incapacity to deal with the title to

[56] 1 Stim. Am. St. Law, § 1710; Whiting v. Gould, 2 Wis. 552; Bibb v. Hunter, 79 Ala. 351; Dunn v. Zwilling (Iowa) 62 N. W. 746. But see Pinnock v. Clough, 16 Vt. 508; Jenkins v. Eldridge, 3 Story, 181, Fed. Cas. No. 7,266; McClellan v. McClellan, 65 Me. 500.

[57] 1 Perry, Trusts (4th Ed.) §§ 90–94; Thayer v. Wellington, 9 Allen (Mass.) 283.

[58] Thayer v. Wellington, 9 Allen (Mass.) 283.

[59] 1 Perry, Trusts (4th Ed.) § 28.

[60] Commissioners of Sinking Fund v. Walker, 6 How. (Miss.) 143; Buchanan v. Hamilton, 5 Ves. 722.

[61] Dana v. Bank, 5 Watts & S. (Pa.) 223; Barry v. Exchange Co., 1 Sandf. Ch. (N. Y.) 280; Hopkins v. Turnpike Co., 4 Humph. (Tenn.) 403; State v. President, etc., of Bank of Maryland, 6 Gill & J. (Md.) 205.

[62] See post, p. 381.

[63] Commissioners of Sinking Fund v. Walker, 6 How. (Miss.) 143; 1 Perry, Trusts (4th Ed.) § 39.

[64] 1 Perry, Trusts (4th Ed.) § 41; McDonogh's Ex'rs v. Murdock, 15 How. 367; Shoemaker v. Commissioners, 36 Ind. 175.

[65] Trustees of Phillips Academy v. King, 12 Mass. 546. So municipal corporations may be trustees. Vidal v. Girard's Ex'rs, 2 How. 127, 187. It was formerly held that a corporation could not be a trustee, because the subpœna of the chancellor operates only upon the conscience of the trustee, and corporations were said to have no souls. 1 Perry, Trusts (4th Ed.) § 42.

land when a trust is sought to be enforced against her.[66] The appointment of a married woman as trustee, however, is often attended with many inconveniences, owing to her limited power of dealing with property. For similar reasons, an infant cannot act effectively as a trustee, though, of course, a trust may be enforced against him, and his infancy will not furnish a means of defrauding his beneficiary.[67] An alien may act as a trustee in jurisdiction where he is permitted to hold realty, and where he is not he may act until "office found," upon which the legal title would escheat to the state, but would still be held for the benefit of the cestui que trust.[68] A bankrupt or insolvent person may be a trustee,[69] and, if he became such before his insolvency, an assignment by him of his property for the benefit of creditors would not carry with it any right to the enjoyment of the property, unless the assignor had also some beneficial interest in it.[70] A feoffor may make himself a trustee.[71]

Any one who has capacity to take the legal title to lands may be a beneficiary.[72]

IMPLIED TRUSTS.

152. Implied trusts are those created by operation of law in order to do justice between the parties. They are either

  (a) Resulting trusts (p. 265), or

  (b) Constructive trusts (p. 269).

Some of the cases which are treated as trusts are not properly called trusts. They are such only because the person wronged is given some of the remedies which a cestui que trust has.[73] As to

---

[66] Livingston v. Livingston, 2 Johns. Ch. (N. Y.) 537; Clarke v. Saxton, 1 Hill, Eq. (S. C.) 69; Berry v. Norris, 1 Duv. (Ky.) 302.

[67] Jevon v. Bush, 1 Vern. 342.

[68] 1 Perry, Trusts (4th Ed.) § 55.

[69] Shryock v. Waggoner, 28 Pa. St. 430.

[70] Carpenter v. Marnell, 3 Bos. & P. 40; Kip v. Bank, 10 Johns. (N. Y.) 63; Ontario Bank v. Mumford, 2 Barb. Ch. (N. Y.) 596.

[71] Emery v. Chase, 5 Me. 232; Brewer v. Hardy, 22 Pick. (Mass.) 376; Hayes v. Kershow, 1 Sandf. Ch. (N. Y.) 258.

[72] 1 Perry, Trusts (4th Ed.) § 60; Neilson v. Lagow, 12 How. 107.

[73] 1 Perry, Trusts (4th Ed.) § 166; 2 Pom. Eq. Jur. (2d Ed.) § 1058; Green-

§ 153)   IMPLIED TRUSTS—RESULTING TRUSTS.   265

the division of implied trusts into resulting and constructive, a good deal of confusion exists; and, while the mere matter of classification may not be attended with any important legal consequences, it seems well to make the distinction clear, and treat as constructive trusts only those into which an element of fraud enters.[74]

Trusts created by operation of law, as already stated, are not executed by the statute of uses, nor are they within the statute of frauds; for, in the nature of things, they must be established by evidence outside of the instrument by which the legal title is transferred.[75]

SAME—RESULTING TRUSTS.

153. Resulting trusts are those in which the court seeks to carry out the presumed intention of the parties. The principal classes of resulting trusts are:

(a) **Those where the grantor disposes of only the legal title** (p. 266).

(b) **Those where the object of the trust fails in whole or in part** (p. 267).

(c) **Those where the conveyance is taken in the name of another than the one paying the consideration** (p. 267).

The ruling element in a resulting trust is the probable intention of the parties.[76] In every case in which a resulting trust arises,

---

wood's Appeal, 92 Pa. St. 181; Lathrop v. Bampton, 31 Cal. 17; Hammond v. Pennock, 61 N. Y. 145; Johnson v. Johnson, 51 Ohio, 446, 38 N. E. 61.

[74] 2 Pom. Eq. Jur. (2d Ed.) § 1053; Moore v. Crawford, 130 U. S. 122, 9 Sup. Ct. 447; Dewey v. Moyer, 72 N. Y. 70; Huxley v. Rice, 40 Mich. 73; Kayser v. Maugham, 8 Colo. 232, 6 Pac. 803.

[75] Kayser v. Maugham, 8 Colo. 232, 6 Pac. 803; Bohm v. Bohm, 9 Colo. 100, 10 Pac. 790; Kennedy v. Kennedy, 2 Ala. 571; Connolly v. Keating, 102 Mich. 1, 60 N. W. 289; Cooksey v. Bryan, 2 App. D. C. 557; Rozell v. Vansyckle, 11 Wash. 79, 39 Pac. 270.

[76] 2 Pom. Eq. Jur. (2d Ed.) § 1031. Fraud is not a necessary element. Talbott v. Barber, 11 Ind. App. 1, 38 N. E. 487. And see Thompson v. Marley, 102 Mich. 476, 60 N. W. 976.

there is the transfer of the legal title to land to one who is not intended to hold the beneficial interest, or at least not all of it.[77]

Legal Title Only Conveyed.

In the first class of resulting trusts mentioned in the black-letter text, there is a transfer of the legal title only, without any intention to convey the beneficial interest.[78] If a man transfers the legal title to land to one who is not entitled to the beneficial interest, the equitable title remains in the grantor, and the grantee is a mere trustee for him.[79] Such cases were frequent even before the statute of uses, and were called "resulting uses."[80] The reason for the rule is that a court of equity will not presume an intention to convey the beneficial interest in lands to a stranger without any consideration. If, however, there is any consideration,[81] or in the conveyance the use is declared to be to the grantee, as is the case in modern conveyances operating under the statute of uses, the beneficial interest passes to the grantee.[82] A use is held to result only in cases where the fee is conveyed to the stranger. If any less estate is transferred, the presumption that the grantor did not intend to benefit the stranger is rebutted, and the grantee takes the beneficial interest.[83]

[77] Lloyd v. Spillet, 2 Atk. 150; 1 Perry, Trusts (4th Ed.) § 125; 2 Pom. Eq. Jur. (2d Ed.) § 1031.

[78] Hogan v. Strayhorn, 65 N. C. 279; Paice v. Archbishop of Canterbury, 14 Ves. 364; Levet v. Needham, 2 Vern. 138; Cooke v. Dealey, 22 Beav. 196.

[79] 1 Perry, Trusts (4th Ed.) § 150; Armstrong v. Wolsey, 2 Wils. 19. And see Burt v. Wilson, 28 Cal. 632.

[80] Farrington v. Barr, 36 N. H. 86; Philbrook v. Delano, 29 Me. 410.

[81] An actual consideration will prevent a trust resulting. Hogan v. Jaques, 19 N. J. Eq. 123. The consideration need not be expressed in the instrument of conveyance. Bank of U. S. v. Housman, 6 Paige (N. Y.) 526; Miller v. Wilson, 15 Ohio, 108. A good consideration is sufficient. Groff v. Rohrer, 35 Md. 327; Sharington v. Strotton, 1 Plow. 298. Cf. Mildmay's Case, 1 Coke, 175. But not friendship. Warde v. Tuddingham, 2 Rolle, Abr. 783, pl. 5. The earlier cases hold a mere nominal consideration sufficient to rebut the presumption. Barker v. Keete, Freem. 249. And see Sandes' Case, 2 Rolle, Abr. 791.

[82] See post, p. 409, and cf. Dillaye v. Greenough, 45 N. Y. 438; Squire v. Harder, 1 Paige (N. Y.) 494; Jackson v. Cleveland, 15 Mich. 94. Cf. Blodgett v. Hildreth, 103 Mass. 484; Stevenson v. Crapnell, 114 Ill. 19, 28 N. E. 379; McKinney v. Burns, 31 Ga. 295.

[83] Shortridge v. Lamplugh, 2 Salk. 678; Anon., Brooke, 89.

Failure of Object of Trust.

When lands are conveyed to a trustee, and the trust fails either in whole or in part, because of illegality, or of some defect in the instrument declaring it, as much of the trust as fails results back to the grantor, his heirs, or residuary devisee.[84] The result is the same where the instrument conveying the legal title shows that the grantee is to hold it in trust, as, for instance, by the use of the words "in trust," or "upon the trusts hereafter to be declared," and no trusts are declared, or trusts are declared as to part of the estate only. In such case the grantor holds the beneficial interest under the trust which results.[85]

Consideration Paid by Another.

The third class of resulting trusts is where the purchase price is paid by one person, and the conveyance taken in the name of another. In these cases equity presumes that it was the intention that the one who paid the money should hold the beneficial estate.[86] In order that this presumption may arise, however, the payment must be actually made,[87] or a present obligation to pay incurred, at the time of the conveyance,[88] and the payment must be made as a

---

[84] Gumbert's Appeal, 110 Pa. St. 496, 1 Atl. 437; Stevens v. Ely, 1 Dev. Eq. (N. C.) 493; Hawley v. James, 5 Paige (N. Y.) 318; Russell v. Jackson, 10 Hare, 204; Pilkington v. Boughey, 12 Sim. 114; Williams v. Coade, 10 Ves. 500.

[85] Sturtevant v. Jaques, 14 Allen (Mass.) 523; Morice v. Bishop of Durham, 10 Ves. 521; Dawson v. Clarke, 18 Ves. 247.

[86] Sayre v. Townsend, 15 Wend. (N. Y.) 647; Kendall v. Mann, 11 Allen (Mass.) 15; Latham v. Henderson, 47 Ill. 185; Mathis v. Stufflebeam, 94 Ill. 481; Moss v. Moss, 95 Ill. 449; McLenan v. Sullivan, 13 Iowa, 521; Rogan v. Walker, 1 Wis. 527; Collins v. Corson (N. J. Ch.) 30 Atl. 862; Gashe v. Young (Ohio Sup.) 38 N. E. 20; Lee v. Patten, 34 Fla. 149, 15 South. 775; Hews v. Kenney, 43 Neb. 815, 62 N. W. 204. When a co-tenant takes the legal title to the whole tract, a resulting trust arises. Rogers v. Donnellan (Utah) 39 Pac. 494. For evidence held insufficient to establish this form of trust, see Throckmorton v. Throckmorton (Va.) 22 S. E. 162.

[87] Barnet v. Dougherty, 32 Pa. St. 371; Perkins v. Nichols, 11 Allen (Mass.) 542; Alexander v. Tams, 13 Ill. 221; Whiting v. Gould, 2 Wis. 552; Sullivan v. McLenans, 2 Iowa, 442; Howell v. Howell, 15 N. J. Eq. 75.

[88] Gilchrist v. Brown, 165 Pa. St. 275, 30 Atl. 839; Whaley v. Whaley, 71 Ala. 159.

purchase, and not as a loan.[89] A payment of part of the purchase price will raise a resulting trust, in proportion to the amount paid.[90] Trusts of this kind often arise in cases of joint purchase, where the title is taken in the name of one only.[91] These resulting trusts are abolished by statute in several states, except where the title is taken in the name of another person without the consent of the person paying the purchase price.[92] It is provided in each of these states, however, that these trusts may be enforced in favor of creditors of the one paying the money.[93]

Same—Deed to Wife or Child.

Where the legal title is taken in the name of the wife or a child of the one paying the purchase price, the usual presumption does not obtain, and no trust results; for it is considered that, when the one advancing the money takes the title in the name of one whom he is under a legal or moral obligation to support, the transaction is intended as an advancement or gift.[94] Parol evidence, however, is admissible to show that no such intention existed, and in this way to establish a resulting trust;[96] and the transferee may, on the other hand, introduce evidence to show that an advancement was intended.[97] Here, as in all other cases where a trust is sought to be established by parol evidence, the proof must be clear.[98]

---

[89] Francestown v. Deering, 41 N. H. 438. Cf. McGowan v. McGowan, 14 Gray (Mass.) 119; Cramer v. Hoose, 93 Ill. 503; Berry v. Wiedman (W. Va.) 20 S. E. 817.

[90] Smith v. Smith, 85 Ill. 189; Botsford v. Burr, 2 Johns. Ch. (N. Y.) 405; Sayre v. Townsend, 15 Wend. (N. Y.) 647; Latham v. Henderson, 47 Ill. 185.

[91] Robarts v. Haley, 65 Cal. 397, 4 Pac. 385; Paige v. Paige, 71 Iowa, 318, 32 N. W. 360. And see cases in the last note.

[92] 1 Stim. Am. St. Law, § 1706; Haaven v. Hoaas, 60 Minn. 313, 62 N. W. 110.

[93] 1 Stim. Am. St. Law, § 1706. But see McCahill v. McCahill, 11 Misc. Rep. 258, 32 N. Y. Supp. 836; Gage v. Gage, 83 Hun, 362, 31 N. Y. Supp. 903.

[94] Cartwright v. Wise, 14 Ill. 417; Guthrie v. Gardner, 19 Wend. (N. Y.) 414; Seibold v. Christman, 75 Mo. 308.

[96] Guthrie v. Gardner, 19 Wend. (N. Y.) 414; Jackson v. Matsdorf, 11 Johns. (N. Y.) 91; Persons v. Persons, 25 N. J. Eq. 250; Taylor v. Taylor, 4 Gilm. (Ill.) 303; Butler v. Insurance Co., 14 Ala. 777; Dudley v. Bosworth, 10 Humph. (Tenn.) 8.

[97] Sidmouth v. Sidmouth, 2 Beav. 455.

[98] Cartwright v. Wise, 14 Ill. 417; Cairns v. Coleburn, 104 Mass. 274.

SAME—CONSTRUCTIVE TRUSTS.

154. Where the title to real property is acquired by fraud, the law to do justice treats the wrongdoer as a trustee for the one defrauded. Trusts so established are called constructive.

Constructive trusts are raised in order to do justice between the parties, without any reference to the probable intention, and in most cases contrary to the intention, of the trustee. Constructive trusts, in all cases, arise out of fraud.[99] The fraud, however, need not be actual, but may be implied,—such as fraud which is presumed from the relation of the parties.[100] The kinds of constructive trusts which may arise are as numerous as the frauds by which property may be obtained. Only the principal types of such trusts which arise in relation to realty can be mentioned. Where property which is held in trust is acquired by a purchaser who has notice of the trust,[101] or by one who pays no consideration for the transfer, the transferee will hold the property subject to a constructive trust in favor of the one beneficially entitled.[102] This same result obtains where the title is transferred by operation of law; for instance, when it descends to the heirs of the trustee.[103] In this class of constructive trust no actual fraud is necessary, and in fact it might be said that a trust already existing is continued against the transferee

---

[99] 1 Perry, Trusts (4th Ed.) § 166. See Frick Co. v. Taylor, 94 Ga. 683, 21 S. E. 713; Farris v. Farris (Ky.) 29 S. W. 618; Lawson v. Hunt, 153 Ill. 232, 38 N. E. 629; Goldsmith v. Goldsmith, 145 N. Y. 313, 39 N. E. 1067.

[100] See Fetter, Eq. p. 142; 1 Perry, Trusts (4th Ed.) § 194; Roggenkamp v. Roggenkamp, 15 C. C. A. 600, 68 Fed. 605; Cobb v. Trammell (Tex. Civ. App.) 30 S. W. 482; Haight v. Pearson, 11 Utah, 51, 39 Pac. 479. But see Brown v. Brown, 154 Ill. 35, 39 N. E. 983.

[101] Wormley v. Wormley, 8 Wheat. 421; Oliver v. Piatt, 3 How. 333; Caldwell v. Carington's Heirs, 9 Pet. 86; James v. Cowing, 17 Hun (N. Y.) 256; Ryan v. Doyle, 31 Iowa, 53; Smith v. Walser, 49 Mo. 250; Smith v. Jeffreys, (Miss.) 16 South. 377.

[102] Caldwell v. Carington's Heirs, 9 Pet. 86.

[103] Randall v. Phillips, 3 Mason, 378, Fed. Cas. No. 11,555; Caines v. Grant's Lessee, 5 Bin. (Pa.) 119.

of the property, rather than that a new one is created.[104] Another class of cases in which constructive trusts are raised is where a trustee or other fiduciary person purchases property with trust funds, and takes the title in his own name. In such case he holds the property so purchased in trust for the one entitled to the money with which the property was purchased.[105] From the principle that a trustee will not be permitted to make any profit for himself out of transactions connected with the trust property,[106] if one holding a fiduciary position renews a lease to lands held by the beneficiary the renewal will operate to the benefit of the latter. These cases arise principally where leases are renewed by a partner or by a trustee.[107] Whenever a man appropriates another's property, or wrongfully converts it into a changed form, the person wronged may treat the other as holding the property in trust for him. This is the case where an agent embezzles money and invests it in land. So long as the money can be traced, a trust may be established in favor of the one defrauded.[108] Another class of cases where constructive trusts are raised is where the trustee acquires the trust property by a purchase at his own sale of the property,[109] or by purchase or gift from the cestui que trust.[110] Where a transfer of property is procured by fraud or misrepresentations, a constructive trust is said to arise ex maleficio.[111] An instance of this is where a devise is pro-

[104] Gardner v. Ogden, 22 N. Y. 327; Swinburne v. Swinburne, 28 N. Y. 568; Hubbell v. Medbury, 53 N. Y. 98; Baldwin v. Allison, 4 Minn. 25 (Gil. 11).

[105] Rice v. Rice, 108 Ill. 199; Weaver v. Fisher, 110 Ill. 146; Murphy v. Murphy, 80 Iowa, 740, 45 N. W. 914; Everly v. Harrison, 167 Pa. St. 355, 31 Atl. 668; Morgan v. Fisher, 82 Va. 417; Pillars v. McConnell, 141 Ind. 670, 40 N. E. 689; Merket v. Smith, 33 Kan. 66, 5 Pac. 394; Thompson v. Hartline (Ala.) 16 South. 711.

[106] 1 Perry, Trusts (4th Ed.) § 129.

[107] Featherstonhaugh v. Fenwick, 17 Ves. 298; Ex parte Grace, 1 Bos. & P. 376.

[108] Foote v. Colvin, 3 Johns. (N. Y.) 216; Oliver v. Piatt, 3 How. 333; Grouch v. Lumber Co. (Miss.) 16 South. 496.

[109] Sypher v. McHenry, 18 Iowa, 232; Bush v. Sherman, 80 Ill. 160. Cf. Hawley v. Cramer, 4 Cow. (N. Y.) 717.

[110] Berkmeyer v. Kellerman, 32 Ohio St. 239; Johnson v. Bennett, 39 Barb. (N. Y.) 237; Kern v. Chalfant, 7 Minn. 487 (Gil. 393); 2 Pom. Eq. Jur. (2d Ed.) § 1053.

[111] Hoge v. Hoge, 1 Watts (Pa.) 163.

cured by a false promise to hold the property for the benefit of another person. The courts will enforce such a promise by making the devisee a trustee of the property for such person.[112] So, if one purchases property upon a fraudulent verbal promise to hold it for another, he will be treated as trustee for such person, as where he claims to be purchasing for the mortgagor at a foreclosure sale.[113]

It is often said that a trust arises in favor of creditors where there has been a fraudulent transfer of a debtor's property; but this is a misuse of the term, because the creditors are only entitled to some of the remedies given against a trustee, and no real trust in fact exists.[114] The same objection exists to treating a vendor under a contract of sale as a trustee for the vendee, or a surviving partner as a trustee of the partnership funds.

INCIDENTS OF EQUITABLE ESTATES.

155. A trustee is the holder of the legal title. The cestui que trust is the beneficial owner.

156. The rights and duties of trustee and cestui que trust depend, in each case, upon the nature and terms of the trust.

Few general principles of value can be given with reference to the rights and duties of trustees and their beneficiaries, beyond the fact that each trust contains special terms and provisions which affect the rights of the parties. In passive trusts, which are infrequent from the fact of their being executed by the statute of uses in most cases, except in trusts of chattel interests,[115] the beneficiary is entitled to the possession of the premises, and the exercise of all rights of an actual owner.[116] The trustee merely holds the legal title subject to the rights of the cestui que trust.[117]

[112] Williams v. Vreeland, 29 N. J. Eq. 417; Dowd v. Tucker, 41 Conn. 197. And see Trustees of Amherst College v. Ritch, 10 Misc. Rep. 503, 31 N. Y. Supp. 885.

[113] Sheriff v. Neal, 6 Watts (Pa.) 534; Ryan v. Dox, 34 N. Y. 307; Dennis v. McCagg, 32 Ill. 429; Vanbever v. Vanbever (Ky.) 30 S. W. 983.

[114] 2 Pom. Eq. Jur. (2d Ed.) § 1057.

[115] See ante, p. 255.

[116] Campbell v. Prestons, 22 Grat. (Va.) 396; Harris v. McElroy, 45 Pa. St.

[117] Stewart v. Chadwick, 8 Iowa, 463; Bowditch v. Andrew, 8 Allen (Mass.) 339; Matthews v. McPherson, 65 N. C. 189.

In active or special trusts, on the other hand, it is often necessary that the trustee retain the possession in order that he may perform the duties connected with the carrying out of the trust.[116] The principal cases of active trusts are those to convey the lands held in trust to a certain person or persons, to sell the lands, to invest the trust funds, and to hold the property and receive the rents and profits for the benefit of the cestuis que trustent.[119]

Interest of the Trustee.

Trust estates are generally given to two or more trustees jointly. When the instrument creating the trust is obscure, such a construction would be favored.[120] Joint trustees, however, cannot have partition.[121] A trust will never be allowed to fail for want of a trustee, for the court will appoint one to carry out the trust.[122] The questions relating to appointment and removal of trustees, their duties, etc., relate more properly to treatises on equity, and will not be considered here.[123]

The incidents of a legal estate in lands attach to the title held by a trustee.[124] For instance, he may sell and convey[125] or devise it by his will.[126] In New York, Michigan, and some other states, property held by a trustee cannot be devised by him, but vests in the

---

216; Stevenson v. Lesley, 70 N. Y. 512. Retention of possession by the grantor does not invalidate the trust. Williams v. Evans, 154 Ill. 98, 39 N. E. 698.

[118] Matthews v. McPherson, 65 N. C. 189; Young v. Miles' Ex'rs, 10 B. Mon. (Ky.) 290; Shankland's Appeal, 47 Pa. St. 113; Barnett's Appeal, 46 Pa. St. 392; McCosker v. Brady, 1 Barb. Ch. (N. Y.) 329.

[119] See cases last cited, and Blake v. Bumbury, 1 Ves. Jr. 514; Tidd v. Lister, 5 Madd. 429; Stanley v. Colt, 5 Wall. 119.

[120] Saunders v. Schmaelzle, 49 Cal. 59.

[121] See post, p. 344. Baldwin v. Humphrey, 44 N. Y. 609.

[122] Adams v. Adams, 21 Wall. 185; Tainter v. Clark, 5 Allen (Mass.) 66; Shepherd v. McEvers, 4 Johns. Ch. (N. Y.) 136.

[123] See Fetter, Eq. p. 200; 1 Perry, Trusts, § 259; 2 Pom. Eq. Jur. § 1059.

[124] Devin v. Hendershott, 32 Iowa, 192; 1 Perry, Trusts (4th Ed.) § 321.

[125] Shortz v. Unangst, 3 Watts & S. (Pa.) 45; Den v. Troutman, 7 Ired. (N. C.) 155.

[126] As to the words which, in a general devise, will carry estates of which the testator holds the legal title as trustee, see Taylor v. Benham, 5 How. 233; Jackson v. De Lancy, 13 Johns. (N. Y.) 537; Merritt v. Loan Co., 2 Edw. Ch. (N. Y.) 547; Ballard v. Carter, 5 Pick. (Mass.) 112.

court.[127] The trustee's estate on his death descends the same as legal estates held by him.[128] All assignees of the trustee's title, however, take it subject to the rights of the beneficiary, if they have notice of the trust, or do not pay a valuable consideration.[129]

The trustee, being in law the legal owner, must bring and defend all actions affecting the legal title.[130] If the cestui que trust is in possession, he may maintain trespass.[131]

Whenever the legal and equitable titles are united in the same person, there is a merger, if the estates are of the same quantity.[132] No merger takes place, however, if it is contrary to the intention of the parties, or would work a wrong.[133]

Interest of the Cestui Que Trust.

When equitable estates were introduced, the feudal incidents attaching to legal titles were discarded, and with them the restraints on alienation which existed at common law.[134] Under a passive trust the beneficiary is, in equity, treated as an absolute owner.[135] Except under the statutes of New York and a few other states,[136] he may assign his equitable interest, and compel a conveyance by the trustees.[137] Rights of curtesy and dower in equitable estates

---

[127] 1 Perry, Trusts (4th Ed.) § 341.

[128] Zabriskie v. Railroad Co., 33 N. J. Eq. 22.

[129] Cruger v. Jones, 18 Barb. (N. Y.) 468; Lahens v. Dupasseur, 56 Barb. (N. Y.) 266. See ante, notes 101, 102.

[130] Mackey's Adm'r v. Coates, 70 Pa. St. 350; Warland v. Colwell, 10 R. I. 369; Stearns v. Palmer, 10 Metc. (Mass.) 32; Second Congregational Soc. v. Waring, 24 Pick. (Mass.) 309.

[131] Cox v. Walker, 26 Me. 504.

[132] James v. Morey, 2 Cow. (N. Y.) 246; Mason v. Mason's Ex'rs, 2 Sandf. Ch. (N. Y.) 432; Healey v. Alston, 25 Miss. 190; Den v. Cooper, 25 N. J. Law, 137. But see, where the estates are not equal, Donalds v. Plumb, 8 Conn. 446.

[133] Gardner v. Astor, 3 Johns. Ch. (N. Y.) 53. Star v. Ellis, 6 Johns. Ch. (N. Y.) 393; Hunt v. Hunt, 14 Pick. (Mass.) 374; Lewis v. Starke, 10 Smedes & M. (Miss.) 120.

[134] Dig. Hist. Real Prop. (4th Ed.) 317.

[135] Bowditch v. Andrew, 8 Allen (Mass.) 339.

[136] 1 Stim. Am. St. Law, § 1720.

[137] Sherman v. Dodge, 28 Vt. 26; Waring's Ex'r v. Waring, 10 B. Mon. (Ky.) 331; Winona & St. P. R. Co. v. St. Paul & S. C. R. Co., 26 Minn. 179, 2 N. W. 489. Where it was the duty of the trustee to convey at the request of his cestui, a conveyance may be presumed, in order to give security to titles,

have already been considered.[138] Under a special or active trust, the rights of the beneficiary consist principally in his power to compel the trustee to perform the trust. Equitable estates are subject to payment of the owner's debts,[139] though this was not the rule at common law.[140] An equitable estate may be lost by disseisin, if not recovered within the time prescribed by the statute of limitations.[141] Possession by the trustee, however, is regarded as the possession of the cestui que trust, and so is not adverse, unless the trustee repudiates the trust.[142]

CHARITABLE TRUSTS.

157. **Charitable trusts are those created for the benefit of the public at large, or of some portion of it, and include benevolent, religious, and educational objects.**

158. **Charitable trusts differ from private trusts principally in that**
   (a) **Less certainty of description in designating the object and beneficiaries is required.**
   (b) **A gift from one charity to another may be valid, though on a contingency which is remote, under the rule against perpetuities.**
   (c) **The rule against accumulations probably does not apply to charitable trusts.**
   (d) **By the cy-pres doctrine, the trust funds may be applied to some other object than the one designated by the creator of the trust.**

although in fact none has ever been made. Moore v. Jackson, 4 Wend. (N. Y.) 58.

[138] Ante, pp. 77, 89.

[139] Jackson v. Walker, 4 Wend. (N. Y.) 462; Hutchins v. Heywood, 50 N. H. 491.

[140] Pratt v. Colt, Freem. Ch. 139; Forth v. Duke of Norfolk, 4 Madd. 503.

[141] Kane v. Bloodgood, 7 Johns. Ch. (N. Y.) 90; Hubbell v. Medbury, 53 N. Y. 98; Halsey v. Tate, 52 Pa. St. 311; Neel v. McElbenny, 69 Pa. St. 300; Robertson v. Wood, 15 Tex. 1.

[142] Zacharias v. Zacharias, 23 Pa. St. 452; Seymour v. Freer, 8 Wall. 203;

The terms "public trust" and "charitable trust" are practically synonymous in their use, as is shown by the following definition: "A charity, in a legal sense, may be more fully defined as a gift to be applied, consistently with existing laws, for the benefit of an indefinite number of persons,—either by bringing their hearts under the influence of education or religion; by relieving their bodies from disease, suffering, or constraint; by assisting them to establish themselves for life; or by erecting or maintaining public buildings or works, or otherwise lessening the burdens of government." * The most usual objects for which public trusts are created are for the founding and maintaining of schools and hospitals;[143] the establishment of funds and homes for the poor, and other dependent classes;[144] the building and repair of churches; and the propagation of religious doctrines in other ways.[145] After considerable conflict of opinion, it has been decided that the "statute of charitable uses,"[146] so called, was not the origin of charitable trusts, but that they existed prior to the enactment of that statute, and that courts of equity have jurisdiction over them even in states where that statute has not been recognized nor re-enacted.[147]

Public trusts are created in the same way as private trusts.[148]

Boone v. Chiles, 10 Pet. 177; Oliver v. Piatt, 3 How. 333; Davis v. Coburn, 128 Mass. 377. But see Halsey v. Tate, 52 Pa. St. 311; Neel v. McElhenny, 69 Pa. St. 300.

* Gray, C. J., in Jackson v. Phillips, 14 Allen (Mass.) 556.

[143] Tainter v. Clark, 5 Allen (Mass.) 66; Andrews v. Andrews, 110 Ill. 223; Board of Education v. Bakewell, 122 Ill. 339, 10 N. E. 378. Or a library. Cottman v. Grace, 41 Hun (N. Y.) 345.

[144] Attorney General v. Old South Soc., 13 Allen (Mass.) 474; Shotwell v. Mott, 2 Sandf. Ch. (N. Y.) 46; Chambers v. St. Louis, 29 Mo. 543.

[145] Andrews v. Andrews, 110 Ill. 223; Bridges v. Pleasants, 4 Ired. Eq. (N. C.) 26; Attorney General v. Wallace's Devisees, 7 B. Mon. (Ky.) 611.

[146] 43 Eliz. c. 4.

[147] Vidal v. Girard, 2 How. 127; Going v. Emery, 16 Pick. (Mass.) 107; Gilman v. Hamilton, 16 Ill. 225. But see Trustees of Philadelphia Baptist Ass'n v. Hart's Ex'rs, 4 Wheat. 1.

[148] Olliffe v. Wells, 130 Mass. 221. They are not executed by the statute of uses, because the trustees generally have actual duties to perform, and the beneficiaries are uncertain. Beckwith v. Rector, etc., 69 Ga. 564.

Beneficiary Indefinite.

Charitable trusts differ from private trusts, in the first place, in the fact that they are favored by the courts in the construction of instruments creating them, and less certainty of description in designating the purpose of the trust and the persons intended to be benefited is permitted.[149] This must necessarily be the case, for those who are to be the cestuis que trustent are generally unknown, and incapable of being pointed out specifically;[150] for instance, in a trust for the benefit of the "poor" of a certain county.[151]

Perpetuities and Accumulations.

Although it is often said that charitable trusts are not within the rule against perpetuities, this is true, however, only in the case stated in the black letter.[152] The subject will be discussed later, in considering perpetuities,[153] as will also the application of the rule against accumulations.[154]

Doctrine of Cy-Pres.

There is some confusion as to the real meaning of the doctrine of cy-pres. In many cases nothing more is meant than that courts are favorable to the establishment of charitable trusts, and will construe instruments creating them liberally in order to carry out the intention of the one creating the trust.[155] The true doctrine of cy-pres, however, is that when, for any reason, the original intention of the settlor cannot be carried out,[156] or where, under the provisions of the trust, funds accrue for which no disposition has been provided,[157] the court will carry out the intention of the testator as near as possible (cy-pres); that is to say, the trust funds will be administered according to what would probably have been the intention

[149] Jackson v. Phillips, 14 Allen (Mass.) 539; Bartlet v. King, 12 Mass. 536; Saltonstall v. Sanders, 11 Allen (Mass.) 446; Inglis v. Trustees, 3 Pet. 99.

[150] Burke v. Roper, 79 Ala. 142; Holland v. Alcock, 108 N. Y. 312, 16 N. E. 305.

[151] State v. Gerard, 2 Ired. Eq. (N. C.) 210.

[152] Grey, Perp. § 592.

[153] Post, p. 322.

[154] Post, p. 330.

[155] 2 Perry, Trusts (4th Ed.) § 727.

[156] Jackson v. Phillips, 14 Allen (Mass.) 539.

[157] Attorney General v. Rector, etc., 9 Allen (Mass.) 422; Glasgow College v. Attorney General, 1 H. L. Cas. 800. Cf. Marsh v. Renton, 99 Mass. 132.

of the settlor under the circumstances then existing. An example of this is where a trust was created, having for its object the creating of a public sentiment that would lead to the abolition of negro slavery. After slavery was abolished, the income from the trust property was applied to the education of the freed slaves, as carrying out the testator's general intention.[158]

The doctrine of cy-pres is recognized in the federal courts,[159] and in Massachusetts,[160] Kentucky,[161] and Rhode Island.[162] In some states it is recognized in a modified form,[163] and in the rest the doctrine does not exist,[164] except, as previously mentioned, the term is sometimes applied to the favorable rules of construction which exist in the case of charitable trusts.

[158] Jackson v. Phillips, 14 Allen (Mass.) 539

[159] Trustees of Philadelphia Baptist Ass'n v. Hart's Ex'rs, 4 Wheat. 1; Perrin v. Carey, 24 How. 465. Cf. Wheeler v. Smith, 9 How. 55.

[160] Marsh v. Renton, 99 Mass. 132; Attorney General v. Rector, etc., 9 Allen (Mass.) 422; Jackson v. Phillips, 14 Allen (Mass.) 539.

[161] Moore's Heirs v. Moore's Devisees, 4 Dana (Ky.) 354; Gass v. Wilhite, 2 Dana (Ky.) 170; Curling's Adm'rs v. Curling's Heirs, 8 Dana (Ky.) 38.

[162] Derby v. Derby, 4 R. I. 414.

[163] See Second Congregational Soc. v. First Congregational Soc., 14 N. H. 315; Tappan v. Deblois, 45 Me. 122; Howard v. Peace Soc., 49 Me. 288; McCord v. Ochiltree, 8 Blackf. (Ind.) 15; Beall v. Fox's Ex'rs, 4 Ga. 404; Chambers v. St. Louis, 29 Mo. 592; Lepage v. McNamara, 5 Iowa, 124.

[164] Bascom v. Albertson, 34 N. Y. 584; White v. Howard, 46 N. Y. 144; Methodist Episcopal Church v. Clark, 41 Mich. 730, 3 N. W. 207; Little v. Willford, 31 Minn. 173, 17 N. W. 282; Grimes' Ex'rs v. Harmon, 35 Ind. 198.

CHAPTER XI.

ESTATES AS TO TIME OF ENJOYMENT—FUTURE ESTATES.

- 159. Estates as to Time of Enjoyment.
- 160. Future Estates.
- 161. Future Estates at Common Law.
- 162.   Reversions.
- 163.   Possibilities of Reverter.
- 164–165.   Remainders.
- 166.   Successive Remainders.
- 167.   Cross Remainders.
- 168.   Alternate Remainders.
- 169.   Vested Remainders.
- 170–173.   Contingent Remainders.
- 174.   Rule in Shelley's Case.
- 175. Future Estates under the Statute of Uses.
- 176.   Future Uses.
- 177.   Springing Uses.
- 178.   Shifting Uses.
- 179–180. Future Estates under the Statute of Wills—Executory Devises.
- 181. Incidents of Future Estates.
- 182.   Tenure of Future Estates.
- 183.   Waste.
- 184.   Alienation.
- 185.   Descent of Future Estates.
- 186–189. Powers.
- 190–191.   Creation.
- 192.   Classes of Powers as to Donee.
- 193.   Powers Appendant and in Gross.
- 194.   Powers Collateral, or Naked Powers.
- 195.   Classes of Powers as to Appointee.
- 196.   General Powers.
- 197.   Special Powers.
- 198.   Execution.
- 199–200.   Rights of Creditors.
- 201.   Destruction.
- 202. Rule against Perpetuities.
- 203.   Estates Subject to the Rule.
- 204.   Rule against Perpetuities in the United States.
- 205. Rule against Accumulations.

ESTATES AS TO TIME OF ENJOYMENT.

159. **Estates classified with reference to the time at which the owner is entitled to enjoyment in possession are either**
    (a) **Present, or**
    (b) **Future.**

FUTURE ESTATES.

160. **A future estate is one which does not entitle its owner to the possession of the land until some time in the future. Future estates, according to the source to which they are to be referred, are:**
    (a) **Those possible at common law** (p. 279).
    (b) **Those arising under the statute of uses** (p. 298).
    (c) **Those arising under the statute of wills** (p. 300).

The estates which have been considered so far have been, for the most part, estates which entitle their owners to the immediate possession of the land in which the estate exists; that is, they have been present estates. However, mention has been made incidentally, in several places, of future estates, or estates which do not entitle their owners to immediate possession. A future estate is what remains of a fee simple after some present estate of a less quantity has been carved out of it. It is the difference between a fee simple and a fee tail, or a fee simple and a life estate, etc. When the present estate comes to an end, the future estate takes effect in possession, and becomes a present estate.

FUTURE ESTATES AT COMMON LAW.

161. **The future estates or interests possible under the common law are:**
    (a) **Reversions** (p. 280).
    (b) **Possibilities of reverter** (p. 281).
    (c) **Remainders** (p. 282).

SAME—REVERSIONS.

162. A reversion is the estate which remains in an owner after he has granted away part of his estate. The estate granted is called the particular estate. There may be a reversion after any estate except a fee.

"An estate in reversion is the residue of an estate left in the grantor to commence in possession after the determination of some particular estate granted out by him."[1] A reversion can be created out of any estate except an estate at will or at sufferance. Out of the latter estates there can be no reversion, because in creating a reversion the grant of a particular estate is necessary, and no alienation is possible of the whole or of part of an estate at will or at sufferance.[2] Any number of particular estates may be created by one owning a fee-simple, and still a reversion may remain, so long as the fee itself is not disposed of. For example, the owner of a fee may grant a fee tail, and on failure of the specified heirs the estate will revert to the grantor or his heirs. So out of a fee tail a life estate might be granted, and there would be a reversion, or out of a life estate there might be a reversion after an estate for years. The owner of an estate for years may grant to another a term for a shorter time than his own, and the balance may revert to him; but, if he grants an estate of as long duration as his own, it will be an assignment, and there will be nothing to revert.[3] Reversions may exist, also, after estates created by operation of law; for instance, after an estate of dower.[4] So, too, there are reversionary interests in equitable estates, as where there is a resulting trust to the grantor after an equitable life estate in another person.[5] In each case the estate which precedes the reversion is called a particular estate.

---

[1] 2 Bl. Comm. 175.

[2] See ante, pp. 157, 164.

[3] See ante, p. 148. And see, as to reversions generally, Cook v. Hammond, 4 Mason, 467, Fed. Cas. No. 3,159; State v. Brown, 27 N. J. Law, 13; McKelway v. Seymour, 29 N. J. Law, 321.

[4] See ante, p. 102.

[5] Loring v. Eliot, 16 Gray (Mass.) 568; Read v. Stedman, 26 Beav. 495.

§ 163)   POSSIBILITIES OF REVERTER.   281

The nature of a reversion after an estate less than a freehold has already been considered, and in that connection the right of a reversioner to rents, and the rights and liabilities of the parties on covenants contained in the lease, have been treated of.[6] The rights of reversioners will be considered in connection with the incidents of future estates in general.[7] When both the particular estate and the reversion are united in the same person, they will merge.[8] This is true whether the estates are freehold or leasehold.[9] And, if the latter, a particular estate consisting of a longer term of years will merge in a shorter reversion, and the former estate will be destroyed, leaving only the shorter term.[10] Disseisin of the tenant of the particular estate does not affect the reversioner, because he has no immediate right of entry. And the statute of limitation under such disseisin does not begin to run before the time at which the reversioner becomes entitled to the possession.[11]

SAME—POSSIBILITIES OF REVERTER.

163. After a fee on condition or on limitation, the interest remaining in the grantor is called a possibility of reverter.

As has been stated, a reversion may exist after any particular estate less than a fee. Where a fee is granted, and a right of entry reserved for the breach of a condition, no reversion exists. There is only what is called a possibility of reverter.[12] The same was true of a fee conditional at common law before the statute de donis, though there was a possibility that the estate might revert to the grantor for the failure of heirs of the body of the grantee; yet, this possibility not being an estate, there was no reversion,

[6] Ante, p. 134.
[7] Post, p. 302.
[8] 2 Washb. Real Prop. (5th Ed.) 806.
[9] See Martin v. Tobin, 123 Mass. 85.
[10] Hughes v. Robotham, Cro. Eliz. 302; Stephens v. Bridges, 6 Madd. 66.
[11] Jackson v. Schoonmaker, 4 Johns. (N. Y.) 390.
[12] Slegel v. Lauer, 148 Pa. St. 236, 23 Atl. 996; Nicoll v. Railroad Co., 12 N. Y. 121.

but only a possibility of reverter.[13] In such case, however, after the statute de donis had changed the fee conditional into an estate tail, there was a reversion.[14] A possibility of reverter may be transferred.[15] "In Gray's rule against perpetuities,[16] it is contended that since quia emptores, abolishing tenure between feoffor and feoffee on a grant of the fee simple, possibilities of reverter are not valid interests in land, and that by virtue of that statute base fees have ceased to exist. But in the United States base fees are not considered as dependent on the existence of tenure, and are still recognized as valid estates, as Prof. Gray concedes and laments."*

SAME—REMAINDERS.

164. A remainder is an estate depending on a preceding particular estate, created by the same instrument, and limited to arise on the termination of the preceding estate, but not in derogation of it.

165. Remainders are either
  (a) **Vested** (p. 288), **or**
  (b) **Contingent** (p. 289).

It will be seen from the above definition of a remainder that it differs from a reversion principally in that the residue of the estate remaining after the particular estate in the case of a reversion goes back to the grantor or his heirs, but in a remainder this residue is limited over to a third person.[17] Remainders are always created by express limitation, and can never arise by operation of law.[18] A remainder must always be created by the same instru-

---

[13] See ante, p. 45.

[14] 2 Washb. Real Prop. (5th Ed.) 801.

[15] Slegel v. Lauer, 148 Pa. St. 236, 23 Atl. 996; Scheetz v. Fitzwater, 5 Pa. St. 126. Contra, Nicoll v. Railroad Co., 12 N. Y. 126.

[16] Sections 31–42.

*Graves, Real Prop. 135, citing Bolling v. Mayor, etc., of Petersburg, 8 Leigh (Va.) 229; Leonard v. Burr, 18 N. Y. 96.

[17] Booth v. Terrell, 16 Ga. 20; Phelps v. Phelps, 17 Md. 120.

[18] See Dennett v. Dennett, 40 N. H. 498. As to the difference between purchase and descent, see post, p. 399.

ment as the particular estate which precedes it.[19] This is, in effect, an assignment of the reversion at the time of the creation of the particular estate. But, if the reversion is assigned at a subsequent time, it is still called a reversion, and not a remainder. A remainder must always be so limited as to take effect at once on the termination of the particular estate on which it depends.[20] But it is held that a child in ventre sa mere at the termination of the preceding estate is capable of taking a remainder which vests then.[21] The rule that remainders must take effect immediately on the termination of the preceding estate has been changed in some states by statute.[22] A remainder must not take effect in derogation of the particular estate on which it depends; that is, the vesting of the remainder must not cut short the preceding estate.[23] Such a limitation can take effect only as a shifting use or a shifting devise.[24] There may, however, be a remainder after an estate on limitation.[25] That is, when an estate is given to determine absolutely on the happening of an event, a valid remainder may be limited to begin on the termination of that estate. For example, an estate may be given to A. and his heirs until B. returns from Rome, and then the remainder given to C. This would be valid, since the remainder does not cut short the prior estate. But if the limitation was to A. and his heirs, but, if B. returns from Rome, then to C., the estate could not take effect as a remainder. The preceding estate, being one on condition, is cut short by the event on which it is attempted to cause the remainder to vest.[27] A remainder may be created out of an equitable estate.[28] Any estate as to quantity may be created in remainder; that is, a fee, fee tail,

[19] 2 Washb. Real Prop.
[20] Hennessy v. Patterson, 85 N. Y. 91; Doe v. Considine, 6 Wall. 458, 474.
[21] See Burdet v. Hopegood, 1 P. Wms. 486.
[22] 1 Stim. Am. St. Law, §§ 1421, 1426.
[23] 2 Washb. Real Prop. (5th Ed.) 601. In New York, Michigan, and some other states contingent remainders are not bad because they may defeat the preceding estate. 1 Stim. Am. St. Law, § 1426 C. And see Gillespie v. Allison, 115 N. C. 542, 20 S. E. 627.
[24] See post, pp. 299, 300.
[25] See ante, p. 177.
[27] See Proprietors of Church in Brattle Square v. Grant, 3 Gray (Mass.) 142.
[28] Scofield v. Alcott, 120 Ill. 362, 11 N. E. 351.

life estate, etc., may be created to take effect in futuro as remainders. In limiting such estates the technical words to be used are the same as when creating estates in possession.[29]

The Particular Estate.

As already seen, there can be no remainder without a preceding particular estate; that is, a remainder cannot be limited after an estate reserved to the grantor. The particular estate must be a freehold.[30] And the particular estate which is required to support a remainder cannot be created by operation of law. For instance, an heir, in assigning dower, cannot limit a remainder to begin on the termination of the widow's life estate.[31] As a general rule, there can be no remainder where there can be no reversion,[32] though there may be a reversion where there can be no remainder. So there can be no remainder after a fee, except in a few states where the rule has been changed by statute,[33] nor after a qualified fee;[34] but, as already stated, there may be one after a fee tail.[35] If the particular estate on which a remainder depends never takes effect, as where the tenant of the first estate refuses or is not qualified to take, the remainder, if vested, takes effect at once. This is called acceleration of remainders.[36]

Freehold in Futuro.

At common law there was a rule that no limitation of an estate was valid which would put the freehold in abeyance; or, as it was otherwise expressed, a freehold could not be created to commence in futuro.[37] This is but another form of the rule that the particular estate which precedes and supports a remainder must be a

---

[29] Phelps v. Phelps, 17 Md. 120, 134; Nelson v. Russell, 135 N. Y. 137, 31 N. E. 1008; Livingston v. Greene, 52 N. Y. 118; Jones v. Swearingen, 42 S. C. 58, 19 S. E. 947; Doren v. Gillum, 136 Ind. 134, 35 N. E. 1101.

[30] See ante, p. 34.

[31] Cook v. Hammond, 4 Mason, 467, Fed. Cas. No. 3,159.

[32] See 2 Washb. Real Prop. (5th Ed.) 586.

[33] 1 Stim. Am. St. Law, § 1424d.

[34] Proprietors of Church in Brattle Square v. Grant, 3 Gray (Mass.) 142.

[35] Driver v. Edgar, 1 Comp. 379.

[36] Dareus v. Crump, 6 B. Mon. (Ky.) 363; Macknet's Ex'rs v. Macknet, 24 N. J. Eq. 277; Yeaton v. Roberts, 28 N. H. 459. But see Blatchford v. Newberry, 99 Ill. 11.

[37] Buckler v. Hardy, Cro. Eliz. 585.

freehold. This was due to the technical doctrine that there must always be some one seised of the inheritance.[38] This rule did not apply, as has been seen,[39] to the creation of chattel interests, because for them no seisin was required, the only thing transferred to the tenant being the possession. And there is the further reason that a leasehold to begin in the future is a contract to create an estate for years, which is executed by the lessee taking possession. It was possible, however, at common law, to create reversions and remainders, because, though they were future estates, their creation did not place the freehold in abeyance, the tenant of the particular estate having the seisin of a freehold. Remainders cannot be created to begin in futuro.[40] By statute, in many states, freeholds may now be limited to commence in futuro, with or without a preceding estate,[41] and freeholds in futuro may be created by conveyances not operating at common law; that is, by conveyances operating under the statute of uses or the statute of wills. These are springing and shifting uses and executory devises. They take effect without a particular estate to support them or in derogation of such an estate. Remainders cannot be valid in either of these cases. Limitations of future estates must not be good as remainders, or they will be so construed.* If a limitation takes effect as a remainder, it cannot subsequently operate as a springing or shifting use or an executory devise when it has failed as a remainder.†

But a limitation in a will which would be good as a remainder at the time the will was executed, but, on account of an event occurring before the death of the testator, becomes impossible as a remainder, may take effect as an executory devise.‡ But an estate which has

[38] See ante, p. 32.

[39] See ante, p. 133.

[40] Doe v. Considine, 6 Wall. 458, 474; Brown v. Lawrence, 3 Cush. (Mass.) 390, 398; Wilkes v. Lion, 2 Cow. (N. Y.) 333.

[41] 1 Stim. Am. St. Law, § 1421.

*Sawley v. Northampton, 8 Mass. 3; Parker v. Parker, 5 Metc. (Mass.) 134; Stehman v. Stehman, 1 Watts (Pa.) 466; Manderson v. Lukens, 23 Pa. St. 31; Doe v. Selby, 2 Barn. & C. 926; Hasker v. Sutton, 1 Bing. 500.

†Manderson v. Lukens, 23 Pa. St. 31; Crozier v. Bray, 39 Hun, 121; Doe v. Howell, 10 Barn. & C. 191; Purefoy v. Rogers, 2 Saund. 380. But see Doe v. Roach, 5 Maule & S. 482.

‡Hopkins v. Hopkins, Cas. t. Talb. 44; Doe v. Howell, 10 Barn. & C. 191.

become operative as springing or shifting use or executory devise will be turned into a remainder at any time when that becomes possible.**

166. SUCCESSIVE REMAINDERS — One remainder may be limited to take effect after another, until the fee is exhausted. Such limitations are called successive remainders.

One remainder may be limited to take effect after another, and so on until the fee is exhausted.[42] For example, there may be an estate given to A. for life, with remainder to B. for life, with remainder to C. for life; and, if no further disposition of the estate was made on the death of C., the estate would revert to the grantor or his heirs. These successive remainders must, like other remainders, take effect immediately after each other.[43]

167. CROSS REMAINDERS — Remainders after two or more particular estates which all go over to the last survivor of the particular tenants are called cross remainders.

Where two or more have particular estates, the remainders of which are so limited that on the death of any one his share goes over to the others, and so on until all the shares are vested in the last survivor,[44] the estates which are limited over in this way are

---

**Thompson v. Hoop, 6 Ohio St. 480; Wells v. Ritter, 3 Whart. (Pa.) 208. At common law, future estates cannot be created out of chattel interests. A life estate and a remainder cannot be limited out of a term of years, though the duration of the term be greater than the possible duration of the life of the first taker. Maulding v. Scott, 13 Ark. 88; Merrill v. Emery, 10 Pick. (Mass.) 507. But such limitations may be made either as future uses or executory devises. Smith v. Bell, 6 Pet. 68; Gillespie v. Miller, 5 Johns. Ch. (N. Y.) 21; Maulding v. Scott, 13 Ark. 88; Wright v. Cartwright. 1 Burrows, 282; Lampet's Case, 10 Coke, 46.

[42] 2 Washb. Real Prop. (5th Ed.) 589.
[43] Whitcomb v. Taylor, 122 Mass. 243.
[44] Hawley v. Northampton, 8 Mass. 3; Seabrook v. Mikell, 1 Cheves (S. C.) 80. But see, for cases where the whole does not go to the last survivor,

called cross remainders. The term applies only to the limitation over after the particular estates, and not to those estates themselves. The limitation may be either by deed [45] or by will.[46] Those in whom cross remainders are vested in some respects resemble joint tenants.[47]

168. ALTERNATE REMAINDERS—When remainders are so limited after a particular estate that only one of them can ever take effect they are called alternate remainders.

Two or more remainders in fee may be so limited that one of them only can take effect. For example, land may be given to A. for life, and, if he have issue male, then to such issue male and his heirs forever, but, if he die without issue male, then to B. and his heirs forever.[48] In this case only one remainder could take effect, and the other would be absolutely void; or, in other words, an alternate remainder in fee can be limited to take effect in place of another, but not subsequently to it, for there can be no remainder after a fee.[49] Limitations of this character are called alternate remainders in fee, substitutional fees, and fees with a double aspect.[50]

McGee v. Hall, 26 S. C. 179, 1 S. E. 711; Reynolds v. Crispin (Pa. Sup.) 11 Atl. 236.

[45] Bohon v. Bohon, 78 Ky. 408. But they will not be raised in a deed by implication. Doe v. Worsley, 1 East, 416; Doe v. Dorvell, 5 Term R. 518.

[46] Atberton v. Pye, 4 Term R. 710. Cf. Doe v. Cooper, 1 East, 229. In a will they may arise by implication. Watson v. Foxon, 2 East, 36; Doe v. Webb, 1 Taunt. 234; Ashley v. Ashley, 6 Sim. 358.

[47] See post, p. 333. But it is not necessary that the four unities which are required for joint tenants be present in the case of cross remainders.

[48] Terrell v. Reeves, 103 Ala. 264, 16 South. 54; Loddington v. Kime, 1 Salk. 224; Goodright v. Dunham, Doug. 264; Smith v. Horlock, 7 Taunt. 129.

[49] See Demill v. Reid, 71 Md. 175, 17 Atl. 1014; Taylor v. Taylor, 63 Pa. St. 481; Beckley v. Leffingwell, 57 Conn. 163, 17 Atl. 766; Bank v. Ballard's Assignee, 83 Ky. 481.

[50] See Whitesides v. Cooper, 115 N. C. 570, 20 S. E. 295.

169. VESTED REMAINDERS—A vested remainder is one where neither the right to the estate nor the person entitled is uncertain. The only uncertainty is as to the enjoyment.

It will be seen from this definition that in a vested remainder only the possession is postponed; that is, a vested remainder is a present right to the future enjoyment of an estate, and will vest in possession as soon as the particular estate determines.[51] No amount of uncertainty as to enjoyment makes a remainder contingent. For instance, a vested remainder may be given to A. for life, to take effect after an estate tail in B. In this case, if A. is a person in being, the remainder is vested, although he will probably never enjoy his estate.[52] In doubtful cases remainders are construed as vested, rather than as contingent.[53] A contingent remainder becomes vested upon the happening of the event which makes it contingent, and is then in all respects like other vested remainders.[54]

Remainders to a Class.

Where a remainder is given to a class of persons, as "to the children of A.," as soon as A. has children the remainder becomes vested; but, if other children are born before the particular estate determines, it will open to admit them.[55] A conveyance by the children in whom

---

[51] Croxall v. Shererd, 5 Wall. 268, 288; Haward v. Peavey, 128 Ill. 430, 21 N. E. 503; Marvin v. Ledwith, 111 Ill. 144; Hill v. Bacon, 106 Mass. 578; In re Young, 145 N. Y. 535, 40 N. E. 226; Crews' Adm'r v. Hatcher, 91 Va. 378, 21 S. E. 811.

[52] Kemp v. Bradford, 61 Md. 330; Gourley v. Woodbury, 42 Vt. 395.

[53] Scofield v. Olcott, 120 Ill. 362, 11 N. E. 351; Wedekind v. Hallenberg, 88 Ky. 114, 10 S. W. 368; Anthony v. Anthony, 55 Conn. 256, 11 Atl. 45; Weatherhead v. Stoddard, 58 Vt. 623, 5 Atl. 517; Dingley v. Dingley, 5 Mass. 535.

[54] Doe v. Considine, 6 Wall. 458; Wendell v. Crandall, 1 N. Y. 491; Van Giesen v. White (N. J. Ch.) 30 Atl. 331; Doe v. Perryn, 3 Term R. 484.

[55] Rudebaugh v. Rudebaugh, 72 Pa. St. 271; Minnig v. Batdorff, 5 Pa. St. 503; Ross v. Drake, 37 Pa. St. 373; Doe v. Provoost, 4 Johns. (N. Y.) 61; In re Young, 145 N. Y. 535, 40 N. E. 226; Haggerty v. Hockenberry (N. J. Ch.) 30 Atl. 88; Downes v. Long, 79 Md. 382, 29 Atl. 827; Security Co. v. Cone, 64 Conn. 579, 31 Atl. 7; Parker v. Leach (N. H.) 31 Atl. 19; In re

the remainder had vested would not bar the rights of others subsequently born, not even if the conveyance was made by a guardian of the children under an order of court.[56] Limitations of this kind, however, are to be distinguished from those which are not to take effect until the death of the parent; for instance, where a remainder is given "to the children of A. living at his death." In this case the remainder is contingent, and does not vest until A.'s death, because up to that time the persons who are to take cannot be ascertained.[57]

Destruction of Vested Remainders.

There may be a vested remainder subject to be defeated by a contingency; that is, a vested remainder may be limited as an estate on condition or on limitation.[58] Vested remainders are destroyed by merger,[59] and, when limited after estates tail, may be barred in the same way as the entail.[60] But in no other case will acts of the tenant of the particular estate defeat a vested remainder.[61]

170. CONTINGENT REMAINDERS — A contingent remainder is one where there is an uncertainty as to either the right to the estate, or the person entitled, or as to both. A contingent remainder depends on an event which may never happen, or which may not happen until after the termination of the particular estate.

Lechmere & Lloyd, 18 Ch. Div. 524. See, also, Ayton v. Ayton, 1 Cox, Ch. 327; Gilmore v. Severn, 1 Brown, Ch. 582. No one born after the particular estate determines can take. Ayton v. Ayton, 1 Cox, Ch. 327; Demill v. Reid, 71 Md. 175, 17 Atl. 1014.

[56] Graham v. Houghtalin, 30 N. J. Law, 552.

[57] Dwight v. Eastman, 62 Vt. 398, 20 Atl. 594; Kansas City Land Co. v. Hill, 87 Tenn. 589, 11 S. W. 797; Chambers v. Chambers, 139 Ind. 111, 38 N. E. 334; Crews' Adm'r v. Hatcher, 91 Va. 378, 21 S. E. 811.

[58] Roome v. Phillips, 24 N. Y. 463; Doe v. Moore, 14 East, 601.

[59] See ante, p. 51.

[60] Gray, Perp. § 111.

[61] Rohn v. Harris, 130 Ill. 525, 22 N. E. 587; Whitney v. Salter, 36 Minn. 103, 30 N. W. 755; Allen v. De Groodt, 98 Mo. 159, 11 S. W. 240; Varney v. Stevens, 22 Me. 331; Wilson v. Parker (Miss.) 14 South. 264. But see

An example of a contingent remainder is where an estate is given to A. for life, and, if B. die before C., then to C. in fee. This is contingent, because, if A. die before B., the remainder will not be ready to vest, and will be defeated.[62] Before the vesting of a contingent remainder, the fee continues in the grantor, and, on the failure of the remainder, reverts to him, unless otherwise disposed of.[63] A contingent remainder must vest at or before the termination of the particular estate which precedes it; but, as already said, a child in ventre sa mere is regarded as in being, so that a remainder may vest in it.[64]

Distinguished from Vested.

In contingent remainders, as distinguished from vested,[65] there is an uncertainty as to vesting of the right or title, as well as to the vesting of the possession.[66] For a vested remainder there must be some certain, defined person, in esse and ascertained, who answers the description of remainder-man at some time during the continuance of the particular estate, and not merely at its termination; and the remainder must, of course, be capable of taking effect in possession immediately on the termination of the preceding particular estate.[67] For example, a limitation to A. for life, with re-

Fidelity Insurance, Trust & Safe-Deposit Co. v. Dietz, 132 Pa. St. 36, 18 Atl. 1090.

[62] See McCampbell v. Mason, 151 Ill. 500, 38 N. E. 672; Cheney v. Teese, 108 Ill. 473; McCartney v. Osburn, 118 Ill. 403, 9 N. E. 210; Kingman v. Harmon, 131 Ill. 171, 23 N. E. 430; Waddell v. Ratlew, 5 Rawle (Pa.) 231; Richardson v. Wheatland, 7 Metc. (Mass.) 169. Alternate remainders are necessarily both contingent. Luddington v. Kime, 1 Ld. Raym. 203.

[63] Shapleigh v. Pilsbury, 1 Me. 271. Cf. Wilson v. Denig, 166 Pa. St. 29, 30 Atl. 1025.

[64] Reeve v. Long, 3 Lev. 408; Doe v. Clarke, 2 H. Bl. 399; Blasson v. Blasson, 2 De Gex, J. & S. 665. So by statute in some states. 1 Stim. Am. St. Law, § 1413.

[65] See Napper v. Sanders, Hut. 118.

[66] Temple v. Scott, 143 Ill. 290, 32 N. E. 366; L'Etourneau v. Henquenet, 89 Mich. 428, 50 N. W. 1077; Loddington v. Kime, 1 Salk. 224; Goodright v. Dunham, Doug. 264. Where a devise is made to a woman, and, if she "die childless," remainder over, the remainder is contingent until her death. Furnish v. Rogers, 154 Ill. 569, 39 N. E. 989.

[67] Blanchard v. Blanchard, 1 Allen (Mass.) 223. And see Thompson v. Hill (Sup.) 33 N. Y. Supp. 810.

mainder to the eldest son of B., becomes vested as soon as B. has a son; but, if the remainder had been to the eldest son of B. living at A.'s death, the remainder would have been contingent, and could not possibly vest until A.'s death, which in this case is also a termination of a particular estate. This remainder will be contingent, because the person who is to take can only be ascertained at the termination of the particular estate; yet, if B. has a son, the remainder is capable of vesting in possession at any time the particular estate may be determined.[68]

A remainder is defined by the New York Code [69] as vested "when there is a person in being who would have an immediate right to the possession of the land upon the ceasing of the intermediate or precedent estate." This definition has been followed by the courts of New York and of other states as a correct definition of a vested remainder at common law, and has introduced great confusion into American law on the distinction between vested and contingent remainders.[70] Its defect lies in the fact that it embraces such remainders as the one we were discussing in the preceding paragraph. Mr. Tiedeman suggests as "a reliable test" between vested and contingent remainders "the present capacity to convey an absolute title to the remainder." [71] This criterion might be valuable, were it not for the fact that it is necessary to know whether or not a remainder is vested, before the capacity of the remainder-man to convey an absolute title can be determined.

In determining whether a remainder is vested or contingent, it should be borne in mind that limitations of remainders are sometimes in such form that the contingency refers to the enjoyment of the estate, rather than to the vesting of the title.

Estates Which will Support a Contingent Remainder.

A contingent remainder, if of an estate of freehold, must have a particular estate of freehold to support it. There must be some

[68] And see Richardson v. Wheatland, 7 Metc. (Mass.) 169; Olney v. Hull, 21 Pick. (Mass.) 311; Thomson v. Ludington, 104 Mass. 193; Colby v. Duncan, 139 Mass. 398, 1 N. E. 744; In re Callahan's Estate, 13 Phila. (Pa.) 230; Craige's Appeal, 126 Pa. St. 223, 17 Atl. 585. But see Smith v. West, 103 Ill. 332.

[69] Rev. St. (8th Ed.) pt. 2, c. 1, tit. 2, § 13.

[70] Croxall v. Shererd, 5 Wall. 268. See Chapl. Suspen. § 28.

[71] Tied. Real Prop. (Enl. Ed.) 389, note 2.

one to take the seisin, and for this a freehold is necessary.[72] For example, if land be given to A. for 25 years, if he lives so long, with remainder after his death to B., the remainder to B. is contingent, since A. may not die until after the expiration of the 25 years, and therefore is invalid, because there is no freehold to support it. But, if the term of years given to A. was so long—for instance, 80 or 100 years—that there is no probability of A.'s living until the expiration of the time, it is held that remainder is good, because A. really has an estate for life. But no length of time which is not sufficient to raise a strong presumption that the first taker will die before its expiration, and so give him, in effect, a life estate, is sufficient to change the rule, and to make the contingent remainder valid.[73]

Contingency on Which Remainder may Depend.

From the definition of a remainder, the contingency on which a remainder is to vest must in no case be in derogation of the preceding estate.[74] And so a contingent remainder will be void if it is made to depend on an unlawful condition, or one against public policy.[75] For example, a remainder to illegitimate children, to be subsequently conceived, is void.[76] With these exceptions, a remainder may be made to depend on any contingency which the ingenuity of the person creating the remainder may devise. Elaborate schemes of classifying remainders according to the contingencies on which they depend have been devised,[77] but such refinements serve no useful purpose.

[72] See ante, p. 32; Doe v. Considine, 6 Wall. 458, 474. In some states this has been changed by statute. 1 Stim. Am. St. Law, § 1424.

[73] 2 Washb. Real Prop. (5th Ed.) 615; Weale v. Lower, Poll. 55, 67; Napper v. Sanders, Hut. 118.

[74] Proprietors of Brattle Square Church v. Grant, 3 Gray (Mass.) 142, 149; Green v. Hewitt, 97 Ill. 113. But see Goodtitle v. Billington, 1 Doug. 753.

[75] 2 Washb. Real Prop. (5th Ed.) 629. A contingent remainder may be void for remoteness, as will be seen when the rule against perpetuities is discussed, post, p. 322.

[76] Blodwell v. Edwards, Cro. Eliz. 509; Lomas v. Wright, 2 Mylne & K. 769.

[77] Fearne's classification is as follows: First class: Where the remainder depends entirely on the contingent determination of the preceding estate

171. At common law, contingent remainders may be destroyed
  (a) By the expiration of the particular estate before the remainder vests.
  (b) By the destruction of the particular estate.
  (c) By merger of the particular estate and the next vested remainder.
  (d) By forfeiture of the particular estate.

172. In many states the liability of contingent remainders to destruction has been removed by statute (p. 294).

173. In any state the destruction of contingent remainders may be prevented by limitations "to trustees to preserve contingent remainders" being added in the creation of the estates (p. 295).

As has already been said,[78] if the particular estate should terminate by its natural limitation, any contingent remainders, dependent thereon, which are not then capable of taking possession, will be destroyed, because, from the nature of a remainder, it must take effect immediately after the expiration of the preceding estate.[79] In general, it may be said that a contingent remainder is destroyed by any means arising after the limitation of the estate

itself. Second class: Where some uncertain event, unconnected with and collateral to the determination of the preceding estate, is, by the nature of the limitation, to precede the remainder. Third class: Where a remainder is limited to take effect upon an event which, though it certainly must happen some time or other, yet may not happen until after the determination of the particular estate. Fourth class: Where a remainder is limited to a person not ascertained or not in being at the time when such limitation is made. Contingent Remainders, 5-9. Blackstone divides contingent remainders into two classes, where the limitation is, first, "to a dubious and uncertain person"; or, second, "upon a dubious and uncertain event." 2 Comm. 169.

[78] Ante, p. 283.
[79] Doe v. Considine, 6 Wall. 458; Irvine v. Newlin, 63 Miss. 192; Festing v. Allen, 12 Mees. & W. 279; Price v. Hall, L. R. 5 Eq. 399; Astley v. Micklethwait, 15 Ch. Div. 59; Holmes v. Prescott, 33 Law J. Ch. 264; Rhodes v. Whitehead, 2 Drew. & S. 532.

by which the particular estate is defeated.[80] This is not the case, however, when the legal fee is outstanding, and the particular estate and remainder are both equitable.[81] So, at common law, the tenant of the particular estate, by surrendering his title to the one having the next vested remainder, could cause his particular estate to be merged, and thus cut out all contingent remainders intervening between his estate and the vested remainder.[82] Merger occurs, and thus destroys intervening contingent remainders, whenever the particular estate and the next vested remainder are united in the same person by act of law or of the parties.[83] This is not the case, however, when the two estates are so limited by the instrument creating them.[84] At common law if the tenant of the particular estate asserted a greater right or title than he had, as by making a tortious feoffment, it caused a forfeiture of his estate, and thus destroyed any contingent remainders depending thereon.[85] But, to have this effect, there must have been an entry by the one entitled to the next vested remainder, or by the reversioner.[86] But, as already stated, the tortious effect of a feoffment no longer obtains.[87]

Destruction Prevented by Statute.

By statutes in many states it is now provided that a contingent remainder shall not be destroyed by acts of the tenant of the particular estate, nor by the termination of the particular estate before the remainder vests.[88]

---

[80] Doe v. Gatacre, 5 Bing. N. C. 609; Archer's Case, 1 Coke, 66b. As to the effect of a disseisin of the tenant of the particular estate, see 1 Stim. Am. St. Law, § 1403b.

[81] Abbiss v. Burney, 17 Ch. Div. 211; Berry v. Berry, 7 Ch. Div. 657; Marshall v. Gingell, 21 Ch. Div. 790; Astley v. Micklethwait, 15 Ch. Div. 59.

[82] See Fisher v. Edington, 12 Lea (Tenn.) 189.

[83] Jordan v. McClure, 85 Pa. St. 495; Craig v. Warner, 5 Mackey (D. C.) 460.

[84] Dennett v. Dennett, 40 N. H. 498. See, however, Egerton v. Massey, 3 C. B. (N. S.) 338; Bennett v. Morris, 5 Rawle (Pa.) 8.

[85] Archer's Case, 1 Coke, 66b; Doe v. Howell, 10 Barn. & C. 191.

[86] Williams v. Angell, 7 R. I. 145.

[87] Ante, p. 59.

[88] 1 Stim. Am. St. Law, §§ 1403, 1426; 2 Snars. & B. Lead. Cas. Real Prop. 368.

§ 174)　　　RULE IN SHELLEY'S CASE.　　　295

Trustees to Preserve Contingent Remainders.

On account of the liability of contingent remainders to destruction by the determination of the preceding estate, a device was introduced to prevent this result, as follows: After the limitation of a particular estate,—for instance, an estate to A. for life,—the remainder was given to trustees to preserve contingent remainders during the life of A., and then other remainders over as in the usual limitations. In these cases, if by any means A.'s life estate was determined before his death, the trustees would hold the estate until his death, when the other remainders would take effect as though A. had not lost his estate. The trustees were held to take vested remainders under these limitations; otherwise their estates would be destroyed like other contingent remainders.[89] The statute of uses does not execute the estate of the trustees.[90] If the trustees should do anything to destroy their own estate, and thereby defeat the contingent remainders depending thereon, they would be guilty of a breach of trust, and liable for the damages suffered by the remainder-men.[91]

SAME—RULE IN SHELLEY'S CASE.

174. If an estate of freehold be limited to a person, and by the same instrument an estate be limited in the form of a remainder, whether immediately after the estate, or after other estates interposed, to the heirs, or to the heirs of the body, of the same person, the words "heirs," or "heirs of the body," are words of limitation of an estate of inheritance in the ancestor, and the heirs can take only by descent, and not as purchasers.[92]

A grant "to A. and to his heirs," and a grant "to A. for life, and after his decease to his heirs," according to the primitive force

[89] Smith v. Packhurst, 3 Atk. 135.
[90] Vanderheyden v. Crandall, 2 Denio (N. Y.) 9.
[91] 2 Bl. Comm. 171. For a full account of trustees to preserve contingent remainders, see Webster v. Cooper, 14 How. 488.
[92] Leake, Land, 343.

and effect of the expressions, were manifestly identical, inasmuch as they both conferred life estates upon A., and upon the persons designated as his heirs in succession. They were still construed as identical, notwithstanding the change in the position and interest of the heir consequent upon the enlarged power of alienation in the ancestor. The limitation "to the heirs," in both cases, ceased to confer directly any estate upon the persons answering to that designation, and was referred to the estate of the ancestor, which, though expressed to be, in the first place, for life, it enlarged to an estate of inheritance, so that the heir took only by descent. This is the origin and simplest form of the rule in Shelley's Case.

The limitations with which we have to do in considering this rule are not, as is seen from the definition, remainders, but they are remainders in form. The rule above stated is called the rule in Shelley's Case because it was applied in an early case by that name,[93] though the rule did not originate in that case. As indicated by the statement of the rule given in the black letter, where a remainder is given to the heirs, or the heirs of the body, of the one who by the same instrument is given the particular estate, the word "heirs" is a word of limitation, and not of purchase; and the first taker has a fee simple, or a fee tail, as the case may be, instead of a life estate followed by a remainder, as the form of limitation would indicate.[94] The rule in Shelley's Case applies to leaseholds as well as to freeholds.[95] The limitations must be all in one instrument,[96] but for this purpose a resulting use in the first taker

[93] Shelley's Case, 1 Coke, 88b, 93b; Moore, 136. A good discussion of the case will be found in Challis, Real Prop. 123.

[94] Kleppner v. Laverty, 70 Pa. St. 70; Carson v. Fuhs, 131 Pa. St. 256, 18 Atl. 1017; Butler v. Huestis, 68 Ill. 594; Hageman v. Hageman, 129 Ill. 164, 21 N. E. 814; Leathers v. Gray, 101 N. C. 162, 7 S. E. 657; Waters v. Lyon, 141 Ind. 170, 40 N. E. 662; Taney v. Fahnley, 126 Ind. 88, 25 N. E. 882; Langley v. Baldwin, 1 Eq. Cas. Abr. 185. Cf. Turman v. White, 14 B. Mon. (Ky.) 560; Pratt v. Leadbetter, 38 Me. 9; Hamilton v. Wentworth, 58 Me. 101; Perrin v. Blake, 1 W. Bl. 672. But see note on this case in 5 Gray, Cas. Real Prop. 99.

[95] Ogden's Appeal, 70 Pa. St. 501; Hughes v. Nicklas, 70 Md. 484, 17 Atl. 398; Seeger v. Leakin, 76 Md. 500, 25 Atl. 862; Horne v. Lyeth, 4 Har. & J. (Md.) 431.

[96] Adams v. Guerard, 29 Ga. 651; Moor v. Parker, 4 Mod. 316.

is sufficient.[97] But if one limitation is in a will, and the other in a codicil to the will, the rule applies.[98] If the word "heirs" is added to the first word "heirs," as where the limitation is to A. for life, remainder to his heirs and their heirs forever, the second word "heirs" is of no effect, and A. takes a fee simple.[99] The rule operates upon limitations of equitable estates as well as of legal, but both the remainder and the particular estate must be of the same kind.[100] In a devise, the word "children," "sons," or "issue" may be equivalent to the word "heirs"; and, if such appears to be the intention of the testator, the rule will operate the same as if the word "heirs" had been used.[101] On the other hand, the word "heirs" may be used as a word of purchase, where it designates certain ascertained persons, as children. In these cases the rule does not apply, and the person designated as heir takes a remainder.[102] Nor is the rule applicable when the remainder is limited to the heirs of another than the person who takes the particular estate; for instance, where a life estate is given to A., with a remainder to the heirs of A. and B., his wife.[103] An express direction, in the deed or will containing a limitation of a form within the rule in Shelley's Case, that the rule shall not operate, will be ineffectual. And the one who takes the preceding estate may convey a fee simple, or a fee tail, as the case may be, without regard to the heirs.[104] And

[97] Pibus v. Mitford, 1 Vent. 372.
[98] Hayes v. Foorde, 2 W. Bl. 698.
[99] Mills v. Seward, 1 Johns. & H. 733.
[100] Croxall v. Shererd, 5 Wall. 268; Ward v. Amory, 1 Curt. 419, Fed. Cas. No. 17,146; Baile v. Coleman, 2 Vern. 670; Garth v. Baldwin, 2 Ves. Sr. 646.
[101] Jackson v. Jackson, 127 Ind. 346, 26 N. E. 897; Roe v. Grew, 2 Wils. 322; Doe v. Cooper, 1 East, 229. But see Adams v. Ross, 30 N. J. Law, 505; Henderson v. Henderson, 64 Md. 185, 1 Atl. 72.
[102] Righter v. Forrester, 1 Bush (Ky.) 278; Mitchell v. Simpson, 88 Ky. 125, 10 S. W. 372; Papillon v. Voice, 2 P. Wms. 471; Jordan v. Adams, 9 C. B. (N. S.) 483; Cowell v. Hicks (N. J. Ch.) 30 Atl. 1091. But see Jesson v. Wright, 2 Bligh, 1.
[103] Shaw v. Robinson, 42 S. C. 342, 20 S. E. 161; Frogmorton v. Wharrey, 2 W. Bl. 728. Cf. Archer's Case, 1 Coke, 66b.
[104] Cf. Thong v. Bedford, 4 Maule & S. 362. But see Jenkins v. Jenkins, 96 N. C. 254, 2 S. E. 522; Fields v. Watson, 23 S. C. 42; Earnhart v. Earnhart, 127 Ind. 397, 26 N. E. 895.

the heirs will take the estate by inheritance only in case he does not dispose of it in his lifetime, or by will. In some states the rule in Shelley's Case has been abolished by statute,[105] and the heirs take a contingent remainder, according to the form of the limitation.[106]

FUTURE ESTATES UNDER THE STATUTE OF USES.

175. Future estates created under the statute of uses are,—
  (a) **Future uses** (p. 298).
  (b) **Springing uses** (p. 299).
  (c) **Shifting uses** (p. 300).

As has already been seen, after the introduction of uses it became possible to create estates in land which could not be raised at common law.[107] Before the statute of uses, the owner of land could enfeoff another in fee to hold for the use of the feoffor for life, and after his death to the use of a third person, etc. After the passage of the statute of uses, the legal title in such cases was executed in the beneficiaries,—that is, if the estate was vested,— and contingent estates were executed as soon as they became vested, and in this way legal estates could be created which were impossible before the statute. Although freeholds could not be made to commence in future at common law, future uses were recognized before the statute of uses, and continued to be after its passage.[108] In some of the books there is a great deal of discussion as to where the seisin was in case of future uses, but this refinement is now of no value.[109]

SAME—FUTURE USES.

176. Future uses are uses which take effect as remainders.

Uses which take effect as remainders are most properly called future uses, though the term "contingent uses" is often applied

[105] 1 Stim. Am. St. Law, § 1406.
[106] Richardson v. Wheatland, 7 Metc. (Mass.) 169; Moore v. Littel, 41 N. Y. 66.
[107] Ante, p. 254.
[108] Welsh v. Foster, 12 Mass. 93; Wyman v. Brown, 50 Me. 139.
[109] See Brent's Case, 3 Dyer, 340a; Chudleigh's Case, 1 Coke, 120.

to them. This is incorrect, however, since such uses may take effect as vested remainders as well as contingent.[110] Remainders arising under the statute of uses have the same incidents as those at common law.[111] A future use must have a preceding particular estate to support it, and must not take effect in derogation of that estate. If these requisites fail, the limitation will take effect as a springing or shifting use.[112] Contingent uses may be defeated the same as contingent remainders.[113]

SAME—SPRINGING USES.

177. Springing uses are uses which take effect without any preceding estate to support them.

"A springing use is a use, either vested or contingent, limited to arise without any preceding limitation."[114] Springing uses do not defeat a preceding particular estate.[115] When there is a limitation of a springing use, there is also a resulting use in fee in the grantor, until the springing use takes effect, so that in reality the springing use operates on the preceding resulting use in the grantor in the same way that a shifting use does upon the particular estate which precedes it.[116] An example of a springing use is a limitation to the use of B. and his heirs after the death of A.[117] A springing use may be contingent as well as vested.[118]

[110] Adams v. Terre-Tenants of Savage, 2 Salk. 679; Davies v. Speed, Id. 675; Southcote v. Stowell, 1 Mod. 238; Cole v. Sewell, 4 Dru. & War. 1; Gore v. Gore, 2 P. Wms. 28.

[111] 2 Washb. Real Prop. (5th Ed.) 663; Rogers v. Fire Co., 9 Wend. (N. Y.) 611; State v. Trask, 6 Vt. 355. So they cannot be limited after an estate for years. Adams v. Savage, 2 Ld. Raym. 854; Rawley v. Holland, 22 Vin. Abr. 189, pl. 11.

[112] Gore v. Gore, 2 P. Wms. 28; Davies v Speed, 2 Salk. 675.

[113] See Davies v. Speed, 2 Salk. 675.

[114] Cornish, Uses, 91.

[115] McKee v. Marshall (Ky.) 5 S. W. 415. Wyman v. Brown, 50 Me. 139; Egerton v. Brownlow, 4 H. L. Cas. 1, 205.

[116] Shapleigh v. Pilsbury, 1 Me. 139; Nicolls v. Sheffield, 2 Brown, Ch. 215.

[117] Jackson v. Dunsbach, 1 Johns. Cas. (N. Y.) 92; Mutton's Case, 3 Dyer, 274.

[118] Shapleigh v. Pilsbury, 1 Me. 271.

SAME—SHIFTING USES.

178. Shifting uses are uses which take effect in derogation of a preceding estate.

Shifting uses are also called secondary uses, and are future limitations which cut short a preceding estate;[119] for example, a limitation to A. and his heirs, and after B. returns from Rome to C. The estate which C. takes when B. returns from Rome cuts off the preceding estate in A. By means of a shifting use, it is possible to limit a fee after a fee.[120]

FUTURE ESTATES UNDER THE STATUTE OF WILLS— EXECUTORY DEVISES.

179. Executory devises are future estates created by devise under the statute of wills, which cannot take effect as remainders.

180. Executory devises may be either springing or shifting.

The statute of uses prohibited the alienation of real property by will, which had been possible before the statute by means of uses.[121] The inconvenience produced, however, was so great that it led to the enactment of the statute of wills [122] before those decisions which, as was seen, virtually repealed the statute of uses.[123] By the very liberal provisions of the statute of wills, it was possible to create any future interest in realty which could be created by means of uses before the statute of uses; and the construction placed on such limitation by the courts is more

---

[119] Fogarty v. Stack, 86 Tenn. 610, 8 S. W. 846; Battey v. Hopkins, 6 R. I. 443; Buckworth v. Thirkell, 3 Bos. & P. 652, note; Mutton's Case, 3 Dyer, 274; Carwardine v. Carwardine, 1 Eden, 28, 34; Egerton v. Brownlow, 4 H. L. Cas. 1.

[120] Battey v. Hopkins, 6 R. I. 443. And see cases in last note.

[121] See Dig. Hist. Real Prop. (4th Ed.) 375.

[122] 32 Hen. VIII. c. 1.

[123] Ante, p. 254.

liberal than the construction of future uses, owing to the attempts of the courts to carry out the intentions of the testators.[124] These executory limitations arising under wills are called executory devises. An executory devise may be by direct gift to the devisee, or it may be through the medium of a declaration of uses.[125] So, too, remainders may be limited by devise.[126] One or more remainders may be followed by an executory devise, but there cannot be a remainder after an executory devise, all such limitations being construed as executory devises also. These are in fact successive executory devises, like successive remainders. When, however, the first devise vests, all the others will vest as remainders that can.[127] Executory devises are presumed to be devises in præsenti, rather than limitations of future estates, whenever it is possible to so construe them, so that if they do not take effect at the death of the testator they will lapse.[128] But slight circumstances are in the later cases held sufficient to rebut this presumption.[129] Like other executory limitations, executory devises may be either vested or contingent, and a destruction of the first devise does not defeat subsequent ones.[130] It is not necessary to state the distinctions between executory devises and remainders, as they have already been considered,[131] but it should be borne in

[124] Annable v. Patch, 3 Pick. (Mass.) 360; Scott v. West, 63 Wis. 529, 24 N. W. 161, and 25 N. W. 18; Smith v. Kimbell, 153 Ill. 368, 38 N. E. 1029; Rupp v. Eberly, 79 Pa. St. 141; Wood v. Wood, 5 Paige (N. Y.) 596; Smith v. Bell, 6 Pet. 68.

[125] Crerar v. Williams, 145 Ill. 625, 34 N. E. 467.

[126] Watson v. Smith, 110 N. C. 6, 14 S. E. 640; Nightingale v. Burrell, 15 Pick. (Mass.) 104; Hall v. Priest, 6 Gray (Mass.) 18; Manderson v. Lukens, 23 Pa. St. 31.

[127] Brownsword v. Edwards, 2 Ves. Sr. 243; Doe v. Howell, 10 Barn. & C. 191; Pay's Case, Cro. Eliz. 878.

[128] Scott v. West, 63 Wis. 529, 24 N. W. 161, and 25 N. W. 18; Kouvalinka v. Geibel, 40 N. J. Eq. 443, 3 Atl. 260; Jones v. Webb, 5 Del. Ch. 132.

[129] Annable v. Patch, 3 Pick. (Mass.) 360; Rupp v. Eberly, 79 Pa. St. 141; Darcus v. Crump, 6 B. Mon. (Ky.) 363; Napier v. Howard, 3 Ga. 192.

[130] Moffat's Ex'rs v. Strong, 10 Johns. (N. Y.) 12; Ford v. Ford, 70 Wis. 19, 33 N. W. 188; Smith v. Hunter, 23 Ind. 580; Randall v. Josselyn, 59 Vt. 557, 10 Atl. 577; Den v. Hance, 11 N. J. Law, 244; Mathis v. Hammond, 6 Rich. Eq. (S. C.) 121.

[131] Ante, p. 285. Cf. Plunket v. Holmes, 1 Lev. 11; Doe v. Scudamore, 2 Bos. & P. 289.

mind that there may be alternate remainders in fee which in form are much like executory devises.[132] An estate limited to take effect after a fee tail is always construed as a remainder, if possible, rather than as an executory devise.[133]

It has already been stated that executory devises may be either springing or shifting, but the distinction is seldom used in the books. A shifting devise may divest the preceding estate in part only, and in cases where the first taker is given a fee, with a shifting devise to another of a life estate, the question often arises whether the devise will defeat the prior estate altogether, or only to the extent of the life estate. The decision in all of these cases must depend upon the intention of the testator.[134]

Executory devises cannot be defeated by the tenant of the prior estate.[135] Where an estate is divested by a devise over on a contingency, if the contingency happens the first estate is divested, though the devise over be void.[136]

INCIDENTS OF FUTURE ESTATES.

181. The rights of the owners of future estates are correlatives of the duties of the tenants of the preceding estates.

---

[132] See Wilson v. White, 109 N. Y. 59, 15 N. E. 749; Taylor v. Taylor, 63 Pa. St. 481; Dunwoodie v. Reed, 3 Serg. & R. (Pa.) 435.

[133] Allen v. Trustees, 102 Mass. 262; Parker v. Parker, 5 Metc. (Mass.) 134; Hawley v. Northampton, 8 Mass. 3; Wolfe v. Van Nostrand, 2 N. Y. 436; Reinoehl v. Shirk, 119 Pa. St. 108, 12 Atl. 806; Titzell v. Cochran (Pa. Sup.) 10 Atl. 9; Richardson v. Richardson, 80 Me. 585, 16 Atl. 250. But see, for limitations which have been held to create executory devises, Jackson v. Chew, 12 Wheat. 153; Richardson v. Noyes, 2 Mass. 56; Lion v. Burtiss, 20 Johns. (N. Y.) 483; Jackson v. Thompson, 6 Cow. (N. Y.) 178; Nicholson v. Bettle, 57 Pa. St. 384.

[134] Gatenby v. Morgan, 1 Q. B. Div. 685; Jackson v. Noble, 2 Keen, 590.

[135] Moffat's Ex'rs v. Strong, 10 Johns. (N. Y.) 12; Doe v. Craig, Busb. (N. C.) 169; Pells v. Brown, Cro. Jac. 590. But see Gray, Perp. §§ 142, 147.

[136] Doe v. Eyre, 5 C. B. 713; Robinson v. Wood, 27 Law J. Ch. 726. See, also, Murray v. Jones, 2 Ves. & B. 313; Avelyn v. Ward, 1 Ves. Sr. 420; Lomas v. Wright, 2 Mylne & K. 769; Tarbuck v. Tarbuck, 4 Law J. Ch. 129.

The rights and duties of the owners of future estates are the correlatives of the rights and duties of the owners of the estates which precede them, and these have already been considered in treating of the different estates in possession.[137] So, too, the right to dower and curtesy in future estates has been treated of in the chapters on those subjects.[138] And in other connections it has been seen that the tenant of an estate which precedes a future estate has no claim on the owner of the latter for improvements.[139] The methods by which the different future estates may be destroyed have been touched upon briefly in connection with reversions[140] and remainders,[141] and as to the other it may be said that no act of the tenant of the particular estate can destroy the future estate.[142]

SAME—TENURE OF FUTURE ESTATES.

182. There is a relation of tenure between the owner of a future estate and the tenant of the preceding estate only in the case of a reversion.

Possession by the tenant of the particular estate is in no case adverse to the owner of the future estate, and so the former cannot disseise the latter.[143] In reversions, tenure exists between the tenant of the particular estate and the reversioner.[144] In case the particular estate is a freehold, the tenant of the particular estate has the seisin, but, when the particular estate is less than a freehold, the actual seisin is in the reversioner.[145] In remain-

[137] Ante, pp. 49, 58, 134.
[138] Ante, pp. 79, 91.
[139] Ante, p. 61.
[140] Ante, p. 281.
[141] Ante, pp. 289, 293.
[142] Archer's Case, 1 Coke, 66b; Chudleigh's Case, Id. 120. And as to executory devises, see ante, p. 302.
[143] Jackson v. Schoonmaker, 4 Johns. (N. Y.) 390; Jackson v. Sellick, 8 Johns. (N. Y.) 262; Jackson v. Johnson, 5 Cow. (N. Y.) 74; Davis v. Dickson, 92 Pa. St. 365; Miller v. Shackleford, 3 Dana (Ky.) 289; Meraman's Heirs v. Caldwell's Heirs, 8 B. Mon. (Ky.) 32; Stubblefield v. Menzies, 8 Sawy. 41, 11 Fed. 268.
[144] 2 Washb. Real Prop. (5th Ed.) 803.
[145] 2 Washb. Real Prop. (5th Ed.) 804; Williams, Real Prop. (17th Ed.) 387.

ders there is no tenure between the tenant of the particular estate and the remainder-man, because both hold under the same person.[146] In future uses and devises, no relation of tenure exists.

SAME—WASTE.

183. Waste by the tenant in possession will be restrained in favor of the owner of a future estate, unless that is a contingent remainder, which may be defeated by the tenant of the preceding estate.

Subject to the following exceptions, waste by the tenant of the particular estate will be restrained in favor of the owner of the future estate.[147] And, for injuries to the corpus of the estate committed by strangers, both the owner of the particular estate and of the future estate may have actions according to their interests.[148] At common law, while waste would be restrained in favor of the owner of a vested remainder, it would not be for the owner of a contingent remainder, because the tenant of the particular estate could defeat the contingent remainder absolutely.[149] This was not the case, however, when there was immediate limitation to trustees to preserve the contingent remainders, because the tenant then had no power to destroy the remainders.[150] As soon as a contingent remainder becomes vested, waste would be restrained; and it will now, in these jurisdictions where the power to destroy contingent remainders has been abolished. Springing and shifting uses and executory devises are indestructible by the tenant in possession, and so he will be enjoined from committing waste; but, when the limitation is after a fee, ordinary waste by the owner of the fee will not be restrained, but equitable waste will be.[151]

[146] Van Deusen v. Young, 29 N. Y. 9; Hill v. Roderick, 4 Watts & S. (Pa.) 221.

[147] See ante, p. 66. Livingston v. Reynolds, 2 Hill (N. Y.) 157.

[148] Foot v. Dickinson, 2 Metc. (Mass.) 611; Bates v. Shraeder, 13 Johns. (N. Y.) 260; Elliot v. Smith, 2 N. H. 430; Chase v. Hazelton, 7 N. H. 171. But see Peterson v. Clark, 15 Johns. (N. Y.) 205.

[149] Hunt v. Hall, 37 Me. 363; Bacon v. Smith, 1 Q. B. 345.

[150] See ante, p. 293.

[151] Matthews v. Hudson, 81 Ga. 120. 7 S. E. 286; Robinson v. Litton, 3 Atk. 209. As to what constitutes equitable waste, see ante, p. 62.

SAME—ALIENATION.

184. Any future estate may be transferred, if the person who is to take is ascertained.

The transfer of a reversion after a term of years has already been considered.[152] Estates in reversion may be conveyed by deed or by devise, and the transfer may be of part of the reversion only.[153] At common law, however, a reversion could not be conveyed by feoffment, unless the particular estate was less than a freehold.[154] Reversions may be conveyed by any form of deed operating under the statute of uses.

A vested remainder may be transferred by the owner in the same way, and under the same conditions as to the kind of conveyance, as a reversion.[155] But a contingent remainder at common law could only be released or conveyed by will, though transfers of contingent remainders are now upheld.[156] A contingent remainder, however, in which the contingency consists in the uncertainty of the person who is to take, can in no case be transferred until such person is ascertained.[157] The same rule applies, also, to springing and shifting uses and executory devises.[158] At common law, executory devises are not subject to alienation.[159] In equity, however, these interests may be devised or assigned if the person entitled is in being and ascertained.[160]

---

[152] See ante, p. 147.
[153] Doe v. Cole, 7 Barn. & C. 243.
[154] Co. Litt. 48b.
[155] Stewart v. Neely, 139 Pa. St. 309, 20 Atl. 1002; Robertson v. Wilson, 38 N. H. 48; Brown v. Fulkerson, 125 Mo. 400, 28 S. W. 632.
[156] Kenyon v. Lee, 94 N. Y. 563; Ackerman's Adm'rs v. Vreeland's Ex'r, 14 N. J. Eq. 23, 29; Godman v. Simmons, 113 Mo. 122, 20 S. W. 972; Hall v. Chaffee, 14 N. H. 216.
[157] Havens v. Land Co., 47 N. J. Eq. 365, 20 Atl. 497.
[158] Young v. Young, 89 Va. 675, 17 S. E. 470; Nutter v. Russell, 3 Metc. (Ky.) 163; Jacob v. Howard (Ky.) 22 S. W. 332; Hall v. Chaffee, 14 N. H. 216.
[159] Hall v. Chaffee, 14 N. H. 215; Lampet's Case, 10 Coke, 46b.
[160] Bayler v. Com., 40 Pa. St. 37; Wright v. Wright, 1 Ves. Sr. 409; Crofts v. Middleton, 8 De Gex, M. & G. 192.

SAME—DESCENT OF FUTURE ESTATES.

185. When the person who is to take a future estate is ascertained, it descends, on his death intestate, to his heirs, except:

EXCEPTION—In states where the rule has not been changed by statute, a reversion descends only to those who can trace their descent from the one last seised.

A reversion descends to the heirs of the reversioner, but at common law it was subject to the rule that no one could take a reversion as heir unless he could trace his descent as heir of the one last actually seised of the reversion.[161] If the reversion is transferred the transferee becomes a new stock, from whom subsequent persons claiming the reversion as heirs must trace their descent.[162] This rule has been abolished in many states by statute.[163] Remainders, future estates under the statute of uses, and executory devises descend to the heirs of their owners, except in cases where the person who is to take is not ascertained.[164] The owner may dispose of his estate by will, and cut off any chance of his heirs inheriting. The future estate, in order that it may descend, must in any case be of sufficient quantity; that is, it must be an estate of inheritance.

POWERS.

186. A power is an authority to create some estate in lands, or a charge thereon, or to revoke an existing estate in the same way that the owner, granting the power, might himself do.

---

[161] 2 Bl. Comm. 209; Miller v. Miller, 10 Metc. (Mass.) 393; Cook v. Hammond, 4 Mason, 467, Fed. Cas. No. 3,159.

[162] 2 Washb. Real Prop. (5th Ed.) 803; West v. Williams, 15 Ark. 682.

[163] Preston v. Carr, 29 N. H. 453; Doe v. Roe, 2 Har. (Del.) 103; Cook v. Hammond, 4 Mason, 467, Fed. Cas. No. 3,159.

[164] Barnitz's Lessee v. Casey, 7 Cranch, 456; Ackless v. Seekright, 1 Ill. 76; Medley v. Medley, 81 Va. 265.

187. The one who creates a power is called the donor.

188. The one to whom a power is given is called the donee.

189. The one for whose benefit the power is exercised is called the appointee.

In addition to the powers above defined, which are usually called simply powers, we have "common-law powers," such as powers given by a will to executors to sell land; "statutory powers," which are authorities conferred by legislative act; and "powers of attorney," to be subsequently considered.[165] Simple powers over real estate are used principally in limiting family settlements, and are seldom employed in the United States. In New York, Michigan, and some other states, powers, as they exist at common law, have been abolished by statute, and another system, in many respects practically the same, has been established.[166] And in these states, though trusts have been abolished, limitations in the form of trusts may take effect as powers.[167]

A power is simply a right to create or change an estate in lands.[168] Before the statute of uses, lands could be conveyed to be held to such uses as the grantor might declare; and, after the statute, such a right to declare the uses of land was called a power,[169] and the uses so declared were executed by the statute, and took effect as if they had been limited in the original instrument creating the power.[170] But if a limitation is in the form, "to and to the use of A., to such uses as he may appoint," or "to A., to the use of A.," etc., the uses which he may appoint will not be executed by the statute, on the principle that the statute will not execute a use upon a use.[171] The instrument creating the power

---

[165] See post, p. 431.

[166] 1 Stim. Am. St. Law, §§ 1650–1659.

[167] 1 Stim. Am. St. Law, § 1703(8).

[168] Burleigh v. Clough, 52 N. H. 267; Rodgers v. Wallace, 5 Jones (N. C.) 181.

[169] Harrison v. Battle, 1 Dev. & B. Eq. (N. C.) 213.

[170] Rodgers v. Wallace, 5 Jones (N. C.) 181; Smith v. Garey, 2 Dev. & B. Eq. (N. C.) 42; Leggett v. Doremus, 25 N. J. Eq. 122.

[171] See ante, p. 254.

does not generally limit the uses, but merely gives an authority to create them.

Common-Law Powers.

The only instances of powers over land that have effect by the common law, or "common-law powers," are powers given by will to the testator's executors to sell his real estate in order to raise money for the payment of his debts, or of legacies given by the will; the land not being devised for the purpose to the executors, but devolving, until the power is exercised, upon the testator's heir at law. Such directions to executors were recognized in the early law as valid in wills of lands, which, by custom, were devisable at common law; and after the extension of the testamentary power by statute, in the reign of King Henry VIII., their validity in wills generally was established. Upon an alienation in pursuance of such a power, the estate passes to the alienee by force of the will, as if he had been named therein as devisee, the exercise of the power being merely the nomination of the person who is to take the estate under the will. In this respect a mere power of sale given to executors differs from a devise of land to the executors in trust for sale; for under such a devise the testator's estate in the land vests in the executors as trustees, and the purchaser takes by the conveyance from them.[172]

Powers Distinguished from Estates.

Powers are distinguished from estates, in that the former are mere rights over land, and not interests in it.[173] A power may, however, be coupled with an interest in the land.[174] The owner of an estate has power to alienate it, in connection with the other incidents of the estate; but the owner of a power has merely a right to alienate, without any other right. A power and an estate in the same land may co-exist. For example, a man may be given an estate for life, with a general power of alienation, and in default of appointment a remainder in fee. In such case he could transfer a fee simple in the lands, either by the exercise of the power, or

---

[172] Edw. Prop. in Land (2d Ed.) 203.

[173] Eaton v. Straw, 18 N. H. 320; Sewall v. Wilmer, 132 Mass. 131.

[174] Peter v. Beverly, 10 Pet. 532; Osgood v. Franklin, 2 Johns. Ch. (N. Y.) 1; Shearman v. Hicks, 14 Grat. (Va.) 96.

out of the estate which he owns, in default of appointment.[175] In wills it is many times difficult to ascertain whether a testator meant to dispose of his estate, or to exercise a power which he had in the lands. In such cases the testator's intention governs, as far as it can be ascertained.[176] Under deeds the same difficulty seldom arises, because technical words are used in limiting the estates. These are, however, questions of construction of instruments, and are not properly part of the law of real property.

Powers of Revocation and Appointment.

Powers are generally divided into powers of appointment, by which estates may be created; powers of revocation, by which estates may be terminated or reduced; and powers of appointment and revocation, which include both rights. But the distinction is hardly of much value, since a power to limit new uses implies the power to revoke the old ones, and powers of revocation, unless a contrary intention expressly appears, include by implication powers to create new estates in place of those defeated.[177] A power of revocation may be reserved, in limiting estates, to revoke the estates created either wholly or in part, or part at one time and part at another.[178] Limiting new uses under a power of revocation or appointment is a revocation of the old estates, without any special words to that effect. When uses are revoked, and new ones appointed, there cannot be another revocation, unless a power to do so is reserved in the instrument limiting the uses.[179]

SAME—CREATION.

190. **Powers may be created**
 (a) **By deed under the statute of uses.**
 (b) **By devise under the statute of wills.**

191. **Technical words of limitation are not required.**

[175] Phillips v. Brown, 16 R. I. 279, 15 Atl. 90; Brown v. Phillips, 16 R. I. 612, 18 Atl. 249; Lee v. Simpson, 34 U. S. 572, 10 Sup. Ct. 631; Funk v. Eggleston, 92 Ill. 515; Logan v. Bell, 1 C. B. 872.

[176] See cases cited in note 175.

[177] 2 Washb. Real Prop. (5th Ed.) 694; Wright v. Tallmadge, 15 N. Y. 307.

[178] Ricketts v. Railroad Co., 91 Ky. 221, 15 S. W. 182. See, also, Willis v. Martin, 4 Term R. 39.

[179] 1 Sugd. Powers, 243.

A power of appointment over land is created by a limitation, either inter vivos or by will, of the legal estate in the land, as an executory interest,—or by a corresponding limitation of the equitable estate,—to take effect in possession through the exercise of an authority or power given to some person by the instrument containing the limitation, or thereby reserved to the grantor or his successors.

Where land is limited by will, subject to a power of this class, an appointment under the power takes effect as an executory devise. But, as executory devises do not depend for their operation on the statute of uses, a power of appointment may be created by will, as well by a devise simply to the persons or for the purposes to be specified by the appointment as by a devise to uses to be declared by the appointment.[180]

Powers may be created by will or by deed, and any words which show an intention of the donor are sufficient, technical words as to the estates to be created by the power not being required.[181] For example, a power to sell in general would give a power to sell a fee, if the donor had a fee.[182]

SAME—CLASSES OF POWERS AS TO DONEE.

192. Powers are divided, with reference to the donee's relation to the land affected by the power, into—

(a) **Powers appendant and in gross** (p. 310).

(b) **Powers collateral, or naked powers** (p. 311).

193. POWERS APPENDANT AND IN GROSS—A power may be given to a donee who has some estate in the land in addition to the power. Such powers are

(a) **Appendant when the power is to be executed wholly or in part out of the estate of the donee.**

(b) **In gross when the execution of the power does not affect the donee's estate.**

---

[180] Leake, Prop. in Land, 377.

[181] Harris v. Knapp, 21 Pick. (Mass.) 412; Cherry v. Greene, 115 Ill. 591, 4 N. E. 257; Brant v. Iron Co., 93 U. S. 326.

[182] North v. Philbrook. 34 Me. 532; Benesch v. Clark, 49 Md. 497; **Liefe** v. Saltingstone, 1 Mod. 189.

It is not necessary that the donee of a power have also an estate in the land on which the power is to operate, but he may have, and in such case the power is said to be connected or coupled with an interest. Unless he has some estate, he will not have a power coupled with an interest, although he does have an interest in the execution of the power.[183] When the estates to be created by the execution of power must take effect out of the interest in the lands held by the donee, the power is said to be appendant or appurtenant; for example, where one having a life estate is given a power to make leases which must take effect wholly or in part out of his own estate.[184] But, when the execution of the power will not affect the donee's estate in the lands, the power is said to be in gross, as when the owner of a life estate has a power to create estates to begin after the termination of his estate.[185]

194. POWERS COLLATERAL, OR NAKED POWERS—A power may be given to a donee who has no interest in the land apart from the power. Such powers are called powers collateral, or naked powers.

A power collateral, or a naked power, or a power unconnected with an interest, is a power given to a person who had no interest in the land at the time of the execution of the instrument creating the power, and to whom no estate is limited by that instrument.[186]

SAME—CLASSES OF POWERS AS TO APPOINTEES.

195. Powers are divided, with reference to the persons who may be appointees, into
   (a) **General powers** (p. 312).
   (b) **Special powers** (p. 312).

[183] Hunt v. Rousmanier's Adm'rs, 8 Wheat. 174; Osgood v. Franklin, 2 Johns. Ch. (N. Y.) 1; Coney v. Sanders, 28 Ga. 511.

[184] Wilson v. Troup, 2 Cow. (N. Y.) 195; Maundrell v. Maundrell, 10 Ves. 246.

[185] Wilson v. Troup, 2 Cow. (N. Y.) 195; Thorington v. Thorington, 82 Ala. 489, 1 South. 716.

[186] Taylor v. Eatman, 92 N. C. 601; Potter v. Couch, 141 U. S. 296, 11 Sup. Ct. 1005.

196. GENERAL POWERS—Under a general power, the donee can make any one he chooses an appointee.

A general power is one in which the donee is given a right to appoint the estates to any one he may choose. Such power is equal to the ownership of the fee, because the donee can convey a fee simple.[187] It should be noted, however, that a general power may be held in trust; that is, the donee may have the power of conveying a fee simple, but the conveyance will be for the benefit of other persons.[188] These are not called general powers, but powers in trust. Under a general power, any person may be an appointee. For instance, the donee may appoint himself, a husband may appoint his wife, and so on.[189]

197. SPECIAL POWERS—Under a special power, the donee can make only certain designated persons appointees. Special powers are

(a) **Exclusive** when the donee must select one out of a class, and appoint to him.

(b) **Nonexclusive** when the donee can appoint to all of the class of persons designated.

A special or particular power is one in which the appointment can be made to only certain specified persons or classes of persons.[190] Under a particular power, the appointment may be to a trustee for the benefit of the appointee, but otherwise the donee is limited, in his appointment under such a power, to the persons or class designated.[191] In such an instrument an authority to

---

[187] Wright v. Wright, 41 N. J. Eq. 382, 4 Atl. 855; Com. v. Williams' Ex'rs, 13 Pa. St. 29; Roach v. Wadham, 6 East, 289.

[188] Howell v. Tyler, 91 N. C. 207; Blanchard v. Blanchard, 4 Hun, 287.

[189] 2 Washb. Real Prop. (5th Ed.) 714; New v. Potts, 55 Ga. 420. But see Shank v. Dewitt, 44 Ohio St. 237, 6 N. E. 255.

[190] Wright v. Wright, 41 N. J. Eq. 382, 4 Atl. 855. And see, as to powers under the New York statute, which establishes a new classification, Jennings v. Conboy, 73 N. Y. 230; Coleman v. Beach, 97 N. Y. 545.

[191] Hood v. Haden, 82 Va. 588; Varrell v. Wendell, 20 N. H. 431; Stuyvesant v. Neil, 67 How. Prac. (N. Y.) 16; In re Farncombe's Trusts, 9 Ch. Div. 652.

appoint to the children of the donor does not include the grandchildren,[192] unless some special circumstances show that such must have been the intention; as, for instance, where there are no children living.[193] A power to appoint "to relations" would include only those relatives who could take under the statute of distributions, but the word "issue" would include all descendants of the donor.[194]

If the power is to select one or more of certain designated persons, and to appoint the whole estate to him, the power is said to be exclusive. But if part of the estate may be given to each of the persons named, or the power is only to determine the amount which each shall receive, the power is nonexclusive. For example, a power to appoint "amongst the testator's children" would be a nonexclusive power, and the donee would only have a discretion as to the amount which each should receive.[195] Under a nonexclusive power, where a number of persons or a class are named as donees, if no appointment is made the court will give the estate to all the donees, in equal shares, according to the maxim that equality is equity.[196] Until appointment, the uses revert to the grantor, unless otherwise provided,[197] as would be the case when the estate is given to the donee for life, with a power of appointing the remainder.[198]

[192] Horwitz v. Norris, 49 Pa. St. 213; Carson v. Carson, Phil. Eq. (N. C.) 57; Little v. Bennett, 5 Jones, Eq. (N. C.) 156.

[193] Ingraham v. Meade, 3 Wall. Jr. 32, Fed. Cas. No. 7,045.

[194] Drake v. Drake, 56 Hun. 590, 10 N. Y. Supp. 183; Glenn v. Glenn, 21 S. C. 308; Varrell v. Wendell, 20 N. H. 431.

[195] Walsh v. Wallinger, 2 Russ. & M. 78; Gainsford v. Dunn, L. R. 17 Eq. 405. See for applications, Wilson v. Piggott, 2 Ves. Jr. 351; Ricketts v. Loftus, 4 Younge & C. 519; Paske v. Haselfoot, 33 Beav. 125. If only one child, the whole could be appointed to that child. Bray v. Bree, 2 Clark & F. 453. As to illusory appointments, see Burrell v. Burrell, Amb. 660; Butcher v. Butcher, 1 Ves. & B. 79.

[196] Withers v. Yeadon, 1 Rich. Eq. Cas. (S. C.) 324; Harding v. Glyn, 1 Atk. 469; In re Phene's Trusts, L. R. 5 Eq. 346; Casterton v. Sutherland, 9 Ves. 445; Wilson v. Duguid, 24 Ch. Div. 244. See, also, Faulkner v. Wynford, 15 Law J. Ch. 8.

[197] Ante, p. 266. See Lambert v. Thwaites, L. R. 2 Eq. 151.

[198] Ward v. Amory, 1 Curt. 419, Fed. Cas. No. 17,146; Burleigh v. Clough, 52 N. H. 267.

SAME—EXECUTION.

198. The execution of a power is subject to the following conditions:
   (a) It must be by the donee or donees named (p. 314).
   (b) It must be in the form provided (p. 315).
   (c) It must be at the time required (p. 317).
   (d) The defective execution of a special power will be aided in equity (p. 318).
   (e) The execution of a power in trust may be compelled (p. 318).
   (f) When the execution of a power is excessive, the excess will be void (p. 318).

Who may Execute a Power.

In general, no one can execute a power as donee unless he has capacity to transfer real estate; but it is held that an infant may execute a naked power in which he has no beneficial interest; that is, one which is to be exercised for the benefit of another.[199] Such powers are called powers simply collateral. And a married woman may execute any power as to real estate without the consent of her husband; and, before the married woman's property acts, this was the usual mode of conferring upon a married woman a right to deal with her separate estate.[200] Under a will creating powers, if no donees are named, the executors may execute the power.[201] If two or more donees are named in the instrument creating the power, all must join in the execution,[202] unless otherwise provided.

---

[199] Thompson v. Lyon, 20 Mo. 155. But cf. In re Cardross' Settlement, 7 Ch. Div. 728.

[200] Claflin v. Van Wagoner, 32 Mo. 252; Rush v. Lewis, 21 Pa. St. 72; Ladd v. Ladd, 8 How. 10.

[201] Mandlebaum v. McDonell, 29 Mich. 78; Silverthorne v. McKinster, 12 Pa. St. 67. Cf. Doyley v. Attorney General, 4 Vin. Abr. 485, pl. 16, where a power was executed by the court.

[202] Shelton v. Homer, 5 Metc. (Mass.) 462; Wilder v. Ranney, 95 N. Y. 7; Hertell v. Van Buren, 3 Edw. Ch. (N. Y.) 20. Where executors are donees, less than all may execute if one or more refuse to act. Bonifaut v. Greenfield, Cro. Eliz. 80; Zebach v. Smith, 3 Bin. (Pa.) 69.

But such powers survive, and, after the death of one of the donees, may be executed by the survivor,[203] unless the power is given to the several donees by name, showing that personal trust and confidence is imposed in them,[204] and even in these cases the power may be exercised by the survivors, if coupled with an interest.[205]

If a power is given to executors nominatim, they may appoint under the power, though they have resigned as executors.[206] Where no personal trust or confidence is imposed on the donee of a power, it may be executed by attorney;[207] otherwise the donee must use his own discretion in making the appointment.[208] The mere execution of an instrument may in all cases be by attorney.[209] A general power may be transferred, and, when a power is given to a person and his assigns, it may be executed by his assigns in fact or in law.[210]

Form of Execution.

At common law no particular form of execution of a power was required. It might be by a simple writing.[211] This, however, is now changed by statute in several states, and the execution must be by deed or will, according to the provisions of the instrument creating the power, and accompanied by the same formalities as are required for a conveyance of realty.[212] The form prescribed

[203] Philadelphia Trust, etc., Co. v. Lippincott, 106 Pa. St. 295; Franklin v. Osgood, 14 Johns. (N. Y.) 527; Lee v. Vincent, Cro. Eliz. 26; Houell v. Barnes, Cro. Car. 382; Lane v. Debenham, 11 Hare, 188.

[204] Peter v. Beverley, 10 Pet. 532, 563; Franklin v. Osgood, 14 Johns. (N. Y.) 527; Tainter v. Clark, 13 Metc. (Mass.) 220; Anon., 2 Dyer, 177a, pl. 32.

[205] Franklin v. Osgood, 14 Johns. (N. Y.) 527; Gutman v. Buckler, 69 Md. 7, 13 Atl. 635; Parrott v. Edmondson, 64 Ga. 332.

[206] Clark v. Tainter, 7 Cush. (Mass.) 567; Tainter v. Clark, 13 Metc. (Mass.) 222.

[207] Howard v. Thornton, 50 Mo. 291; Bales v. Perry, 51 Mo. 449.

[208] Graham v. King, 50 Mo. 22; Hood v. Haden, 82 Va. 588.

[209] Singleton v. Scott, 11 Iowa, 589; Bales v. Perry, 51 Mo. 449.

[210] Pardee v. Lindley, 31 Ill. 174; Strother v. Law, 54 Ill. 413; Druid Park Heights Co. of Baltimore City v. Oettinger, 53 Md. 46; Collins v. Hopkins, 7 Iowa, 463.

[211] Ladd v. Ladd, 8 How. 10, 30; Christy v. Pulliam, 17 Ill. 59.

[212] 4 Shars. & B. Lead. Cas. Real Prop. 46; 1 Stim. Am. St. Law, § 1659.

by the instrument creating the power must be strictly observed.[213] For instance, a power to be executed by deed cannot be appointed by will, nor one to be executed by will be appointed by deed during the donee's lifetime.[214] The execution of a power by will is revocable at any time during the donee's life.[215] If the first execution of a power is void, it may be disregarded, and there can be another execution.[216]

In an instrument appointing an estate under a power an intention to execute the power must appear,[217] but the power need not be recited or referred to.[218] Many questions arise in considering wills, whether the testator has exercised powers of which he was the donee, or has merely disposed of his estates. For example, a devise of "all the estate which the testator has power to dispose of" would operate as an exercise of powers held by the testator.[219] The question, however, being one of construction, cannot be gone into in detail, but a number of the cases will be found in the notes.[220] A power will be held to be executed in any case where the instrument can operate in no other way; as where a testator has a power

[213] Hacker's Appeal (Pa. Sup.) 15 Atl. 500. Cf. Morse v. Martin, 34 Beav. 500.

[214] Moore v. Dimond, 5 R. I. 121; Weir v. Smith, 62 Tex. 1; Porter v. Thomas, 23 Ga. 467.

[215] 1 Sugd. Powers, 461.

[216] 1 Sugd. Powers, 355.

[217] Blake v. Hawkins, 98 U. S. 315; Blagge v. Miles, 1 Story, 426, Fed. Cas. No. 1,479; Hutton v. Bankard, 92 N. Y. 295; South v. South, 91 Ind. 221.

[218] Warner v. Insurance Co., 109 U. S. 357, 3 Sup. Ct. 221; White v. Hicks, 33 N. Y. 383; Munson v. Berdan, 35 N. J. Eq. 376; Roach v. Wadham, 6 East, 289.

[219] Lee v. Simpson, 134 U. S. 572, 10 Sup. Ct. 631; Cowx v. Foster, 1 Johns. & H. 30; Ferrier v. Jay, L. R. 10 Eq. 550; Bruce v. Bruce, L. R. 11 Eq. 371. See, also, Walker v. Mackie, 4 Russ. 76; Blagge v. Miles, 1 Story, 426, Fed. Cas. No. 1,479.

[220] Funk v. Eggleston, 92 Ill. 515; Amory v. Meredith, 7 Allen (Mass.) 397; Williard v. Ware, 10 Allen (Mass.) 263; Bangs v. Smith, 98 Mass. 270; Cumston v. Bartlett, 149 Mass. 243, 21 N. E. 373; Bingham's Appeal, 64 Pa. St. 345; Burleigh v. Clough, 52 N. H. 267; Maryland Mut. Ben. Soc. v. Clendinen, 44 Md. 429; Hollister v. Shaw, 46 Conn. 248; Bilderback v. Boyce, 14 S. C. 528; Andrews v. Emmot, 2 Brown, Ch. 297; Lewis v. Lewellyn, Turn. & R. 104; Grant v. Lynam, 4 Russ. 292; Denn v. Roake, 6 Bing. 475;

over certain land, but no estate therein, a devise of the land will be treated as an appointment under the power.[221] Where another estate is limited until the power is executed, an appointment will put an end to such prior estate.[222]

Time of Execution.

When, from the object for which a power is created, or from express direction in the instrument creating the power, it must be exercised within a certain time, any execution after that time will be void.[223] While this is the rule, there are broad exceptions. The courts look for the main purpose of the donor, and when they conclude that the sale or other appointment directed by him was his main purpose, and that the time was inserted only as a matter of choice or preference, they have sustained an execution of the power at some other time than the one directed.[224] When no time is prescribed for the execution of the power, it may be executed at any time which falls within the general purpose.[225] Thus an execution at any time during the donee's life has been held good.[226]

Pomfret v. Perring, 5 De Gex, M. & G. 775; Thornton v. Thornton, L. R. 20 Eq. 599; Ames v. Cadogan, 12 Ch. Div. 868; Nannock v. Horton, 7 Ves. 392; Napier v. Napier, 1 Sim. 28; Webb v. Honnor, 1 Jac. & W. 352; In re Goods of Merritt, Swab. & T. 112; In re Teape's Trusts, L. R. 16 Eq. 442.

[221] Sir Edward Clere's Case, 6 Coke, 17b; Standen v. Standen, 2 Ves. Jr. 589; Maundrell v. Maundrell, 10 Ves. 246.

[222] Hollman v. Tigges, 42 N. J. Eq. 127, 7 Atl. 347; Shearman's Adm'r v. Hicks, 14 Grat. (Va.) 96; Doe v. Jones, 10 Barn. & C. 459; Jones v. Winwood, 3 Mees. & W. 653. For cases of lapse, see In re Harries' Trust, 1 Johns. Eng. Ch. 199; Chamberlain v. Hutchinson, 22 Beav. 444; In re Davies' Trusts. L. R. 13 Eq. 163; Eales v. Drake, 1 Ch. Div. 217.

[223] Wilkinson v. Buist, 124 Pa. St. 253, 16 Atl. 856; Fidler v. Lash, 125 Pa. St. 87, 17 Atl. 240; Harvey v. Brisbin, 50 Hun, 376, 3 N. Y. Supp. 676; Harmon v. Smith, 38 Fed. 482. So the power must not be exercised before the time directed. Booraem v. Wells, 19 N. J. Eq. 87; Henry v. Simpson, 19 Grant (N. C.) 522; Jackson v. Ligon, 3 Leigh (Va.) 161.

[224] Snell's Ex'rs v. Snell, 38 N. J. Eq. 119; Shalter's Appeal, 43 Pa. St. 83; Hale v. Hale, 137 Mass. 168; Hallum v. Silliman, 78 Tex. 347, 14 S. W. 797.

[225] Moores v. Moores, 41 N. J. Law, 440; Cotton v. Burkelman, 142 N. Y. 160, 36 N. E. 890.

[226] 1 Sugd. Powers, 330; Richardson v. Sharpe, 29 Barb. (N. Y.) 222; Bakewell v. Ogden, 2 Bush (Ky.) 265.

Defective Execution.

When a general power is defectively executed, equity will not aid the appointee, unless a valuable consideration has been paid,[227] but, where there are defects in the execution of a special power, the aid of a court of equity will be given,[228] if there has been a substantial compliance, and such defects as the omission of the requisite number of witnesses will be supplied;[229] and so, where the execution has been by will instead of by deed, it will be held good.[230]

Compelling Execution.

The execution of a power can be compelled only where the power is mandatory, or is a power in trust;[231] that is, a power held in trust, without any discretion as to its exercise, and in which the donee has no beneficial interest, will be enforced in equity in conformity with the trust, although not executed by the donee of the power. Thus where there is a power given to trustees to sell property and apply the proceeds upon trusts, and the trustees die without executing the power, the court will order a sale, and compel the heirs to join in the conveyance.[232] A court of equity will not execute or control a discretionary power.[233]

Excessive Execution.

The execution of a power may be excessive as to the object, as when, under a special power, estates are given to some who cannot

---

[227] Schenck v. Ellingwood, 3 Edw. Ch. (N. Y.) 175; Bradish v. Gibbs, 3 Johns. Ch. (N. Y.) 523; Beatty v. Clark, 20 Cal. 11; Morgan v. Milman, 3 De Gex, M. & G. 24. See, however, Blove v. Sutton, 3 Mer. 237; Sayer v. Sayer, 7 Hare, 377, affirmed Innes v. Sayer, 3 Macn. & G. 606; Pepper's Will, 1 Pars. Eq. Cas. 436.

[228] Barr v. Hatch, 3 Ohio, 527; Mutual Life Ins. Co. v. Everett, 40 N. J. Eq. 345, 3 Atl. 126; Clifford v. Clifford, 2 Vern. 379; Fothergil v. Fothergil, 1 Eq. Cas. Abr. 222, pl. 9; Jackson v. Jackson, 4 Brown, Ch. 462; Moodie v. Reid, 1 Madd. 516. See, also, Johnson v. Touchet, 37 Law J. Ch. 25.

[229] Wilkes v. Holmes, 9 Mod. 485; Sergeson v. Sealey, 2 Atk. 412. Or want of a seal. Smith v. Ashton, Ch. Cas. 263. See, also, Piggot v. Penrice, Prec. Ch. 471.

[230] Tollet v. Tollet, 2 P. Wms. 489; Sneed v. Sneed, Amb. 64.

[231] Smith v. Kearney, 2 Barb. Ch. (N. Y.) 533; Doe v. Ladd, 77 Ala. 223.

[232] Sugd. Powers, 588.

[233] Sugd. Powers, 258, 659.

§ 198) EXECUTION OF POWERS. 319

be donees;[234] or it may be excessive as to amount of subject-matter, when more is given than the donee had power to appoint.[235] A power to sell does not authorize the donee to mortgage, in the absence of expressions showing such intention.[236] And a power to mortgage does not authorize a sale,[237] but the mortgage may be in the usual form, and might be by a trust deed or a mortgage with a power of sale, if that was the usual mode of effecting a mortgage.[238] A power to appoint a fee includes power to create lesser estates, because such a power is equal to ownership in fee, and the owner of a fee simple may create any estate he chooses.[239] When the excess can be separated, the execution as to the remainder will be valid. For instance, in case of excessive execution as to the objects of the power, the estates appointed to those who could not take as donees would be void, and the others good.[240] So a lease for 40 years under a power to lease for 21 would be good as a lease for 21 years, the excess only being void.[241] If conditions are improperly annexed to the appointment, the conditions will be treated as void, and the appointment freed from them.[242]

[234] Alexander v. Alexander, 2 Ves. Sr. 640; Sadler v. Pratt, 5 Sim. 632.

[235] Commissioners of Knox Co. v. Nichols, 14 Ohio St. 260. See for executions held good, Whitlock's Case, 8 Coke, 69b; Trollope v. Linton, 1 Sim. & S. 477; Talbot v. Tipper, Skin. 427; Thwayles v. Dye, 2 Vern. 80.

[236] Green v. Claiborne, 83 Va. 386, 5 S. E. 376; Norris v. Woods, 89 Va. 873, 17 S. E. 552; Smith v. Morse, 2 Cal. 524. But see Lancaster v. Dolan, 1 Rawle (Pa.) 231; Zane v. Kennedy, 73 Pa. St. 182.

[237] 1 Sugd. Powers, 514.

[238] Wilson v. Troup, 7 Johns. Ch. (N. Y.) 25; Jesup v. Bank, 14 Wis. 331; Bolles v. Munnerlyn, 83 Ga. 727, 10 S. E. 365. A power to mortgage will authorize a renewal of a previous mortgage. Warner v. Insurance Co., 109 U. S. 357, 3 Sup. Ct. 221.

[239] Williams v. Woodard, 2 Wend. (N. Y.) 487; Hedges v. Riker, 5 Johns. Ch. (N. Y.) 163. But see Seymour v. Bull, 3 Day (Conn.) 388; Hubbard v. Elmer, 7 Wend. (N. Y.) 446.

[240] 2 Sugd. Powers, 66. Proper appointees will take the whole. Alexander v. Alexander, 2 Ves. Sr. 640; Sadler v. Pratt, 5 Sim. 632; In re Kerr's Trusts, 4 Ch. Div. 600.

[241] Sinclair v. Jackson, 8 Cow. (N. Y.) 543; Powcey v. Bowen, 1 Ch. Cas. 23; Campbell v. Leach, Amb. 740.

[242] 2 Sugd. Powers (Ed. 1856) 84; Blomfield v. Eyre, 5 C. B. 713. See, however, In re Brown's Trust, L. R. 1 Eq. 74.

SAME—RIGHTS OF CREDITORS.

199. Creditors of the donee of a power have no rights in the power, except:
  EXCEPTION—When the power is general, creditors may enforce their claims against a voluntary appointee.

200. Creditors of the appointee may enforce their claims against his estate after appointment to him, but cannot compel the execution of the power, except:
  EXCEPTION—In some states, by statute, creditors may compel the execution of a beneficial power.

The donee of a power has no estate in the lands subject thereto, and his interest can be reached by his creditors only in equity.[243] Under a special power in which the donee has no beneficial interest, his creditors have no rights.[244] Most cases hold that creditors of the donee may levy on lands in the hands of a voluntary appointee under a general power,[245] though the correctness of the rulings has been doubted.[246] Creditors of the appointee under a power may levy on the lands after the power is executed, but they cannot compel an execution, even in cases of special powers.[247] But in several states, including New York, Michigan, Wisconsin, and Minnesota, it is provided by statute that the execution of a beneficial power—that is, a special power under which the debtor could compel an appointment in his favor—may be compelled by the creditors of the one entitled to the appointment.[248]

---

[243] Holmes v. Coghill, 12 Ves. 206.

[244] Johnson v. Cushing, 15 N. H. 298.

[245] Clapp v. Ingraham, 126 Mass. 200; Knowles v. Dodge, 1 Mackey (D. C.) 66; Wales' Adm'r v. Bowdish's Ex'r, 61 Vt. 23, 17 Atl. 1000; Lassells v. Cornwallis, 2 Vern. 465; Holmes v. Coghill, 12 Ves. 206.

[246] Com. v. Duffield, 12 Pa. St. 277; Thorpe v. Goodall, 17 Ves. 388.

[247] 2 Sugd. Powers, 102.

[248] Schars. & B. Lead. Cas. Real Prop. 28; 1 Stim. Am. St. Law, § 1657.

SAME—DESTRUCTION.

201. **Powers may be destroyed**
  (a) **By execution.**
  (b) **By death of one whose consent to the execution is required.**
  (c) **By alienation of the estate to which the power is appendant.**
  (d) **By release, unless the power is simply collateral.**
  (e) **By cesser.**

A power is like a conveyance of land, and cannot be revoked by the donor after it has been created, nor will his death put an end to the right to exercise it.[249] A power is, of course, extinguished by its execution, and any further power reserved in the instrument of execution would not be the same, but a new power.[250] The death of one whose consent to the execution of the power is required destroys the power.[251] Where a power is appendant, the alienation of the estate to which the power is annexed destroys the power, in whole or in part, because the donee will not be permitted to execute the power in derogation of his conveyance of the estate.[252] So a partial alienation of the estate might suspend or qualify the power; as, where the donee has made a lease, an estate created by a subsequent execution of the power would be postponed until the termination of the lease.[253] A power in gross,

---

[249] Wilburn v. Spofford, 4 Sneed (Tenn.) 698; Armstrong v. Moore, 59 Tex. 646.

[250] Hele v. Bond, Prec. Ch. 474; Hatcher v. Curtis, Freem. Ch. 61.

[251] Kissam v. Dierkes, 49 N. Y. 602; Powles v. Jordan, 62 Md. 499. But see Leeds v. Wakefield, 10 Gray (Mass.) 514; Sohier v. Williams, 1 Curt. 479, Fed. Cas. No. 13,159.

[252] Wilson v. Troup, 2 Cow. (N. Y.) 195; Parkes v. White, 11 Ves. 209; Bringloe v. Goodson, 4 Bing. N. C. 726. So a recovery extinguishes, Smith v. Death, 5 Madd. 371; Savile v. Blacket, 1 P. Wms. 777; or a fine, Bickley v. Guest, 1 Russ. & M. 440; Walmsley v. Jowett, 23 Eng. Law & Eq. 353. And see Hole v. Escott, 2 Keen, 444.

[253] Noel v. Henley, McClel. & Y. 302.

however, is not affected by an alienation of the donee's estate.[254] And a power simply collateral cannot be destroyed by the donee.[255] All other powers may be released to one having a freehold in possession, reversion, or remainder, and so destroyed.[256] The doctrine of merger, however, does not apply to powers, because the donee may have both an estate and a power.[257] When the object for which a special power is created has failed, the power is said to be destroyed by cesser.[258]

RULE AGAINST PERPETUITIES.

202. "No interest subject to a condition precedent is good, unless the condition must be fulfilled, if at all, within 21 years after some life in being at the creation of the interest."[259]

It has already been stated that at common law freeholds could not be created to commence in futuro, and the exceptions to this rule which have grown up have been discussed;[260] but some forms of such limitations are invalid if made to commence at a too remote period. This is called the rule against perpetuities, but unfortunately so, for a better designation would be the rule "against remoteness." The misnomer has in all probability given rise to much of the confusion which exists in relation to the rule. What is known as

---

[254] 1 Sugd. Powers, 85; Maundrell v. Maundrell, 10 Ves. 246b. But see Doe v. Britain, 2 Barn. & Ald. 93.

[255] A power simply collateral is "a power to a person not having any interest in the land, and to whom no estate is given, to dispose of, or charge the estate in favor of some other person." 1 Sudg. Powers, 45. See West v. Berney, 1 Russ. & M. 431.

[256] D'Wolf v. Gardiner, 9 R. I. 145; Grosvenor v. Bowen, 15 R. I. 549, 10 Atl. 589; Albany's Case, 1 Coke, 110b.

[257] Benesch v. Clark, 49 Md. 497; Henderson v. Vaulx, 10 Yerk. (Tenn.) 30.

[258] Hetzel v. Barber, 69 N. Y. 1; Sharpsteen v. Tillou, 3 Cow. (N. Y.) 651; Smith's Lessee v. Folwell, 1 Bin. (Pa.) 546; Bates v. Bates, 134 Mass. 110. But see Ely v. Dix, 118 Ill. 477, 9 N. E. 62 (a partial failure).

[259] Gray, Perp. 144; Paxson, J., in Smith's Appeal, 88 Pa. St. 493. For the origin and history of the rule against perpetuities, see Gray, Perp. c. 5.

[260] See ante, pp. 133, 284.

the rule against perpetuities has nothing to do with restraints on alienation, as might be supposed, though many statutes and cases have so treated it. It is based entirely on public policy, and its only object is to prevent the creation of estates which are to vest in interest at a remote time. That this is true will be seen from the fact that interests may be too remote, though they are capable of a present alenation.[261]

The rule against perpetuities applies only to estates which are limited to vest on the happening of a contingency. This contingency must happen, if at all, within the prescribed period, or the estate so limited is void.[262] The fact that it may and does happen within such time is not sufficient to make the limitation valid, if it might have happened beyond the prescribed time.[263] An estate may be limited, according to this rule, after any number of lives in being.[264] The only restriction suggested is that the number must not be so great that evidence of the termination of the lives cannot be obtained.[265] In the usual form in which the rule is stated, the period of gestation is added to 21 years, but this is not strictly accurate. The same effect is reached by holding that a child in ventre sa mere is in being, so as that an estate can vest in it.[266] In this way it is possible that three periods of gestation may occur in a limitation which does not violate the rule.[267] The term of 21 years after the dropping of a life which is allowed by the rule may be in gross without reference to the

---

[261] Gray, Perp. § 140.

[262] Jee v. Audley, 1 Cox, Ch. 324; Abbiss v. Burney, 17 Ch. Div. 211; In re Frost, 43 Ch. Div. 246; In re Hargreaves, Id. 401; Porter v. Fox, 6 Sim. 485; Doe v. Challis, 18 Q. B. 224, 231. See Sawyer v. Cubby, 146 N. Y. 192, 40 N. E. 869; Lloyd v. Carew, Show. Parl. Cas. 137. For a longer period made possible under statutes affecting estates tail, see 1 Dembitz, Land Tit. 118.

[263] Stephens v. Evans' Adm'x, 30 Ind. 39; Jee v. Audley, 1 Cox, Ch. 324; Lett v. Randall, 3 Smale & G. 83. Contra, Longhead v. Phelps, 2 W. Bl. 704.

[264] Or after the lives of unborn persons, if the vesting is during the lives of persons in being. Evans v. Walker, 3 Ch. Div. 211.

[265] Thellusson v. Woodford, 11 Ves. 112; Low v. Burron, 3 P. Wms. 262. See Scatterwood v. Edge, 1 Salk. 229.

[266] Gray, Perp. § 220; Storrs v. Benbow, 3 De Gex, M. & G. 390; Long v. Blackall, 7 Term R. 100.

[267] "Suppose, for instance, a devise to testator's children for life, on their death to be accumulated till the youngest grandchild reaches twenty-one,

minority of any person.[268] Therefore a limitation of an estate after a term of 21 years is good.[269] In cases of contingent remainders, however, the time within which they must vest is limited to the duration of lives in being, and the period of 21 years additional is not allowed.[270] The time within which an estate limited must vest under the rule is computed from the death of the testator, when the limitation is by will,[271] and, when by deed, from the execution of the deed.[272] The rule is satisfied if the estate vests within this time, though the interest so created does not terminate until a later time.[273]

The rule against perpetuities is not one of construction, but it is applied to a devise or a deed after the instrument limiting the estates is construed, and is applied regardless of the intention; for the rule is not intended to effect the intention, but more often defeats it.[274] It is only in cases of ambiguous construction that it is presumed that the intention was to limit an estate which would not be void as contravening the rule.[275]

---

and then to be divided among all the grandchildren then living, and the issue then living of any deceased grandchild. The testator leaves a posthumous child, who dies, leaving one child, A., born, and another, B., en ventre sa mere. B. is born, and reaches twenty-one, but before he does so A. dies, leaving his wife enceinte, who gives birth to a child after B. reaches twenty-one. Here we have (1) the period until the testator's child is born; (2) the life of such child; (3) the period after the death of such child until B. is born; (4) the minority of B.; (5) the period from the time when B. reaches twenty-one until A.'s child is born. Here we have a life, a minority of twenty-one years, and three periods of gestation." Gray, Perp. § 222. And compare Long v. Blackall, 7 Term R. 100; Thellusson v. Woodford, 11 Ves. 112.

[268] Beard v. Westcott, 5 Taunt. 393; Cadell v. Palmer, 1 Clark & F. 372. But see Mayor, etc., of New York v. Stuyvesant's Heirs, 17 N. Y. 34.

[269] Gray, Perp. § 225; Low v. Burron, 3 P. Wms. 262. See Stephens v. Stephens, Cas. t. Talb. 228; Avern v. Lloyd, L. R. 5 Eq. 383.

[270] Gray, Perp. § 294; Cattlin v. Brown, 11 Hare, 372.

[271] Southern v. Wollaston, 16 Beav. 276.

[272] McArthur v. Scott, 113 U. S. 340, 5 Sup. Ct. 652.

[273] Otis v. McLellan, 13 Allen (Mass.) 339; Minot v. Taylor, 129 Mass. 160; Heald v. Heald, 56 Md. 300. But see Slade v. Patten, 68 Me. 380.

[274] Gray, Perp. § 629; Maule, J., in Dungannon v. Smith, 12 Clark & F. 546; James, L. J., in Heasman v. Pearse, 7 Ch. App. 275.

[275] Post v. Hover, 33 N. Y. 593; Du Bois v. Ray, 35 N. Y. 162.

Effect of Limitations too Remote.

When the limitation of a future estate is void on account of the rule against perpetuities, the prior estates take effect, as if there had been no subsequent limitations.[276] But estates which are to take effect after limitations that are too remote, if vested, or if they become vested within the time prescribed by the rule, will not be affected by the void limitations.[277] In cases where a good limitation of an estate is made, and a subsequent modification is added which would make the estate void for remoteness, the modification will be rejected, and the estate will stand as under the original limitation.[278] When there is no disposition in a will, except the void limitation, the heirs take.[279]

SAME—ESTATES SUBJECT TO THE RULE.

203. The rule against perpetuities applies to all estates and interests in land, legal or equitable, but does not include
- **(a) Vested interests.**
- **(b) Present interests.**
- **(c) Powers which cannot be exercised beyond the time allowed by the rule.**

EXCEPTIONS—The following cases are recognized exceptions to the rule:
- **(a) Rights of entry for condition broken.**
- **(b) Gifts to a charity, with a remote gift over to another charity.**

---

[276] Proprietors of Church in Brattle Square v. Grant, 3 Gray (Mass.) 142.

[277] Gray, Perp. § 251. But see Proctor v. Bishop of Bath & Wells, 2 H. Bl. 358. So some of the limitations may vest in time, and be valid though others fail. Wilkinson v. Duncan, 30 Beav. 111; Cattlin v. Brown, 11 Hare, 372; Picken v. Matthews, 10 Ch. Div. 264; Hills v. Simonds, 125 Mass. 53 ;. But see Pearks v. Moseley, 5 App. Cas. 714.

[278] Slade v. Patten, 68 Me. 380; Ring v. Hardwick, 2 Beav. 352; Gove v. Gove, 2 P. Wms. 28. Otherwise when the first limitation is not absolute. Whitehead v. Rennett, 22 Law J. Ch. 1020.

[279] Fosdick v. Fosdick, 6 Allen (Mass.) 41; Wainman v. Field, Kay, 507.

The rule against perpetuities does not apply to vested interests, but only to those which are contingent.[280] Covenants running with the land are present interests, and therefore do not violate the rule.[281] If property is vested absolutely in a person, and a condition is added postponing his enjoyment, such condition will be void for repugnancy if for a longer period than the minority of the person entitled to the property. Such cases have nothing to do with the rule against perpetuities.[282] We have already seen that reversions and vested remainders are vested interests, and therefore they are not within the rule against perpetuities.[283] There is considerable conflict as to whether contingent remainders are within the rule. It is argued that they are not within the rule, because they may be destroyed by the tenant of the preceding estate. But the better opinion is that they are subject to the rule. This is the case under statutes which prevent the destruction of such remainders by acts of the tenant of the particular estate.[284] Remainders after estates tail are not too remote, because they may be barred by the tenant in tail at any time.[285]

A great many cases have arisen where there were limitations over "on failure of issue." At common law the words are held to mean an indefinite failure of issue, and not a failure at the death of the person named.[286] The tendency of the later cases is away from this rule,[287] and in some states it has been changed by stat-

---

[280] Gray, Perp. § 205.

[281] Tobey v. Moore, 130 Mass. 448; Ex parte Ralph, 1 De Gex, 219.

[282] Daniels v. Eldredge, 125 Mass. 356; Josselyn v. Josselyn, 9 Sim. 63; Saunders v. Vautier, 4 Beav. 115. In re Ridley, 11 Ch. Div. 645. But see Herbert v. Webster, 15 Ch. Div. 610. See Leake v. Robinson, 2 Mer. 363.

[283] Gray, Perp. § 205.

[284] Gray, Perp. §§ 284–286, and see ante, p. 294.

[285] Goodwin v. Clark, 1 Lev. 35; Nicolls v. Sheffield, 2 Brown, Ch. 215. See Duke of Norfolk's Case, 3 Ch. Cas. 1. And cf. Bristow v. Boothby, 2 Sim. & S. 465.

[286] Chadock v. Cowley, Cro. Jac. 695; Burrough v. Foster, 6 R. I. 534; Cf. Ashley v. Ashley, 6 Sim. 358. But otherwise as to leaseholds, Forth v. Chapman, 1 P. Wms. 663; or legacies, Nichols v. Hooper, 1d. 1.8. And see Hughes v. Sayer, Id. 534.

[287] Anderson v. Jackson, 16 Johns. (N. Y.) 382; Benson v. Corbin, 145 N. Y. 351, 40 N. E. 11; Abbott v. Essex Co., 18 How. 202; Greenwood v. Verdon,

ute.[288] When the failure is of the issue of some other person than the holder of the estate, the limitation over is an executory devise, and so void in cases of indefinite failure.[289] But, if the remainder is given to another on the failure of issue of the first taker, a limitation after an indefinite failure is construed to give him an estate tail, and the remainder after it therefore does not violate the rule against perpetuities.[290] In any case where a definite failure of issue of a living person is meant, limitations over are not within the rule, because they must take effect at the end of a life in being.[291]

When a remainder limited in a will is void on account of this rule, it will, if possible, be construed to give an estate tail in the first taker, as being as near the testator's real intention as possible. This is called the cy-pres doctrine of construction.[292]

It is often stated that a contingent remainder cannot be limited to an unborn child of an unborn person. But this is believed to be inaccurate. It was founded on the exploded notion that there could not be a "possibility on a possibility."[293] In the United States, rights of entry for condition broken are probably an exception to the rule against perpetuities, though no sufficient reason can be given for making the difference.[294] The rule against perpetuities applies to equitable as well as to legal estates. If they

---

1 Kay & J. 74; Trotter v. Oswald, 1 Cox, Ch. 317; Ex parte Davies, 2 Sim. (N. S.) 114; Roe v. Jeffery, 7 Term R. 589; Barlow v. Salter, 17 Ves. 479.

[288] 1 Stim. Am. St. Law, § 1415.

[289] Sanders v. Cornish, Cro. Car. 230; Love v. Wyndham, 1 Mod. 50.

[290] Tatton v. Mollineux, Moore, 809; Retherick v. Chappel, 2 Bulst. 28.

[291] Gray, Perp. §§ 155-158; Davenport v. Kirkland, 156 Ill. 169, 40 N. E. 304; Terrell v. Reeves, 103 Ala. 264, 16 South. 54. But, contra, Child v. Baylie, Cro. Jac. 459.

[292] Allyn v. Mather, 9 Conn. 114; Vanderplank v. King, 3 Hare, 1; Parfitt v. Hember, L. R. 4 Eq. 443; Humberston v. Humberston, 1 P. Wms. 332; Elliott v. Elliott, 12 Sim. 276; Kevern v. Williams, 5 Sim. 171. Cf. Hampton v. Holman, 5 Ch. Div. 183; Routledge v. Dorril, 2 Ves. Jr. 358; Hale v. Pew, 25 Beav. 335. But see St. Amour v. Rivard, 2 Mich. 294.

[293] See Gray, Perp. §§ 287-294. Contra, that they are void, Whitby v. Mitchell, 44 Ch. Div. 85.

[294] Brattle Square Church v. Grant, 3 Gray (Mass.) 142; Hunt v. Wright, 47 N. H. 396. Contra, Dunn v. Flood, 25 Ch. Div. 629. See, however, London & S. W. Ry. Co. v. Gomm, 20 Ch. Div. 562.

are vested they are not subject to the rule; otherwise they are.[295] The rule in fact has principally to do with cases of future uses and executory devises. A trust does not violate the rule against perpetuities because it is to continue indefinitely, if it vests within the time required, because, as has been seen, the rule against perpetuities is concerned with the vesting of estates, not with their duration.[296] The question of remoteness in connection with mortgages does not seem to have been raised, but Mr. Gray thinks that no good reason can be assigned why it should not apply.[297]

Under limitations to a class which are void because some of the persons who are to take cannot be ascertained within the time required by the rule against perpetuities, the limitations are void as to all of the class, unless so made that the amount one is to receive is not affected by the existence of the other limitations. In the latter case those limitations will be good which can vest within the required time, and the others will be bad.[298] Under limitations to a series of persons, the limitation to the first one of the series will not be rendered void by the fact that the limitations to the others are too remote.[299]

Powers.

The application of the rule against perpetuities to powers is stated by Mr. Gray as follows: "(1) If a power can be exercised at a time beyond the limits of the rule against perpetuities it is bad. (2) A power which cannot be exercised beyond the limits of the rule against perpetuities is not rendered bad by the fact that within its terms an appointment could be made which would be too remote. (3) The remoteness of an appointment depends upon its distance from its creation, and not from the exercise of the

---

[295] See Abbiss v. Burney, 17 Ch. Div. 211; Bull v. Pritchard, 5 Hare, 567; Blagrove v. Hancock, 16 Sim. 371.

[296] Philadelphia v. Girard's Heirs, 45 Pa. St. 9; Yard's Appeal, 64 Pa. St. 95. Contra, Slade v. Patten, 68 Me. 380.

[297] Gray, Perp. §§ 562-571.

[298] Lowry v. Muldrow, 8 Rich. Eq. (S. C.) 241; Hills v. Simonds, 125 Mass. 536; Boughton v. Boughton, 1 H. L. Cas. 406; Storrs v. Benbow, 3 De Gex, M. & G. 390; Wilkinson v. Duncan, 30 Beav. 111; Elliott v. Elliott, 12 Sim. 276.

[299] Goldsborough v. Martin, 41 Md. 488; Caldwell v. Willis, 57 Miss. 555; Dillon v. Reilly, Ir. R. 10 Eq. 152; Liley v. Hey, 1 Hare, 580; Wainman v. Field, Kay, 507.

§ 203) RULE AGAINST PERPETUITIES. 329

power."[300] The effect of appointments under powers which are too remote is the same as for estates limited in violation of the rule.[301]

Gifts to Charities.

The rule against perpetuities also applies to gifts to charities in nearly all their forms. For instance, where there is a gift to a charity with a gift over to an individual, whether in trust for him or not, the gift over is void if it violates the rule.[302] So with a gift to an individual followed by a remote gift over to a charity.[303] Again, property may be held in trust for an individual, to be held, on the happening of a contingency, for a charity. If the contingency is too remote, the gift to the charity is void.[304] In the case, however, of a gift to one charity, with a gift over to another, the rule against perpetuities has been held not to apply.[305] But Mr. Gray doubts the correctness of such a holding.[306] It has also been held that a gift which could not take effect at the testator's death would be held by the court a reasonable time, at least, for the benefit of the charity.[307]

[300] Gray, Perp. § 473; Hillen v. Iselin, 144 N. Y. 365, 39 N. E. 368; In re Powell's Trusts, 39 Law J. Ch. 188. Contra, Rous v. Jackson, 29 Ch. Div. 521.

[301] Morgan v. Gronon. L. R. 16 Eq. 1. The appointment is bad if it might vest at a too remote period, though it does not. Smith's Appeal, 88 Pa. St. 492. An appointment over on a contingency after an appointment which violates the rule is void also. Routledge v. Dorril, 2 Ves. Jr. 357. A power collateral to an estate tail is not void, since the tenant in tail may bar it at any time. Lantsbery v. Collier, 2 Kay & J. 709. A void clause may be rejected, and the rest of the appointment stand. In re Teague's Settlement, L. R. 10 Eq. 564.

[302] Gray, Perp. § 593; Brattle Square Church v. Grant, 3 Gray (Mass.) 142; Wells v. Heath, 10 Gray (Mass.) 17; Society for Promoting Theological Education v. Attorney General, 135 Mass. 285; Palmer v. Bank, 17 R. I. 627, 24 Atl. 109.

[303] Gray, Perp. § 594; Leonard v. Burr, 18 N. Y. 96; Smith v. Townsend, 32 Pa. St. 434; Commissioners of Charitable Donations & Bequests v. De Clifford, 1 Dru. & War. 245; Attorney General v. Gill, 2 P. Wms. 369; In re Johnson's Trusts, L. R. 2 Eq. 716.

[304] Gray, Perp. §§ 595, 596.

[305] Christ's Hospital v. Grainger, 16 Sim. 83, 1 McN. & G. 460, approved Odell v. Odell, 10 Allen (Mass.) 1, 9; Jones v. Habersham, 107 U. S. 174, 185, 2 Sup. Ct. 336; Chamberlayne v. Brockett, 8 Ch. App. 206.

[306] Gray, Perp. §§ 597-603.

[307] Sinnett v. Herbert, 7 Ch. App. 232.

SAME—RULE AGAINST PERPETUITIES IN THE UNITED STATES.

204. In the United States the rule against perpetuities exists as at common law, except:

EXCEPTION—In some states it is provided by statute that all future estates must vest within two lives in being.

As has been stated, the rule against perpetuities was established by construction of the courts. In most American states the rule has been adopted as part of the common law. In some there are statutes which are merely declaratory of the common-law rule. In others a different rule has been provided,—notably, in New York, Michigan, Wisconsin, and Minnesota,—and the time is limited to the duration of two lives in being.[308]

RULE AGAINST ACCUMULATIONS.

205. At common law the rents and profits of land could be directed to be accumulated for the period allowed by the rule against perpetuities for the vesting of estates, but in a number of states statutes have prescribed a different period.

At common law, rents and profits of an estate can be directed to be accumulated during the time allowed by the rule against perpetuities.[309] This, however, has been restricted to a shorter time, in many states, by statute. In some states these periods are measured by minorities; in others, a definite number of years, as 10 or 21, is prescribed, regardless of lives or minorities.[310] This rule

---

[308] 1 Stim. Am. St. Law, §§ 1440, 1442. The rule in these states has been discussed at length in Chapl. Suspen. Power. And see Dean v. Mumford, 102 Mich. 510, 61 N. W. 7; Morris v. Bolles, 65 Conn. 45, 31 Atl. 538; Ketchum v. Corse, 65 Conn. 85, 31 Atl. 486.

[309] Thellusson v. Woodford, 11 Ves. 112.

[310] 1 Stim. Am. St. Law, § 1443; Brandt v. Brandt, 13 Misc. Rep. 431, 34 N. Y. Supp. 684. The English statute on this subject is called the "Thellusson Act" (39 & 40 Geo. III. c. 98). And see In re Woods [1894] 3 Ch. 381.

differs, however, from the rule against perpetuities, in that directions for accumulations are void only as to the excess after the time permitted.[311] There is some doubt as to whether the rule against accumulations applies to gifts to charities. Where there is a present gift to a charity, with directions to accumulate the profits, if the directions are void the property will be applied to the use of the charity at once.[312]

[311] 1 Stim. Am. St. Law, § 1444; Odell v. Odell, 10 Allen (Mass.) 1; Martin v. Maugham, 14 Sim. 230. But compare Southampton v. Hertford, 2 Ves. & B. 54; Curtis v. Lukin, 5 Beav. 147. The right to the income may be vested and only the enjoyment postponed. Smith v. Parsons, 146 N. Y. 116, 40 N. E. 736.

[312] Gray, Perp. § 678.

CHAPTER XII.

ESTATES AS TO NUMBER OF OWNERS—JOINT ESTATES.

> 206. Estates as to Number of Owners.
> 207. Joint Estates.
> 208. Joint Tenancies.
> 209. Tenancies in Common.
> 210. Estates in Co-parcenary.
> 211–212. Estates in Entirety.
> 213. Estates in Partnership.
> 214. Incidents of Joint Estates.
> 215–216. Partition.

ESTATES AS TO NUMBER OF OWNERS.

206. Estates are divided according to the number of owners who are entitled to possession at the same time into,—

(a) **Estates in severalty, and**
(b) **Joint estates.**

JOINT ESTATES.

207. Joint estates are those which are owned by two or more persons. The joint estates at common law are,—

(a) **Joint tenancies** (p. 333).
(b) **Tenancies in common** (p. 335).
(c) **Estates in co-parcenary** (p. 336).
(d) **Estates in entirety** (p. 337).
(e) **Estates in partnership** (p. 339).

The interests so far considered have been those in which the right to possession is in one person at a time. Such interests are called estates in severalty. But these same estates, as to quantity, quality, time of enjoyment, etc., may be held by two or more persons in an undivided ownership, and when so held they are called joint estates.

SAME—JOINT TENANCIES.

208. A joint tenancy is an ownership of land in community in equal undivided shares by virtue of a conveyance which imports an intention that the tenants shall hold one and the same estate. The interests of all the tenants go to the last survivor. For the existence of a joint tenancy the following unities are necessary:
  (a) **Unity of interest.**
  (b) **Unity of title.**
  (c) **Unity of time.**
  (d) **Unity of possession.**

At common law all joint estates were presumed to be joint tenancies unless there was a contrary provision in the instrument creating them,[1] but this presumption does not now obtain in many states.[2] Joint estates held by trustees or mortgagees continue, however, in many of these states, to be joint tenancies.[3] The chief incident of a joint tenancy is the right of survivorship by which the interest of a tenant does not pass to his heirs, but vests, after his death, in his co-tenant, or, if there be more than one, it vests in all of them. The doctrine of survivorship is applied until only one tenant remains, who then holds in severalty, and the land will go to his heirs.[4] A joint tenancy is said to be held "per my et per tout." This is translated by Blackstone as meaning by the half or moiety and by the whole,[5] while others translate it as meaning by nothing and by the whole.[6] For the existence of a joint tenancy it is necessary that there be present the four unities as they are called.[7]

---

[1] Martin v. Smith, 5 Bin. (Pa.) 16. Cf. Caines v. Grant, Id. 119.

[2] See post, p. 335. On the difference between tenancies in common and joint tenancies, see Doe v. Abey, 1 Maule & S. 428.

[3] 1 Stim. Am. St. Law, § 1371, 3, 5.

[4] Overton v. Lacy, 6 T. B. Mon. (Ky.) 13; Spencer v. Austin, 38 Vt. 258; Herbemont's Ex'rs v. Thomas, 1 Cheves, Eq. (S. C.) 21.

[5] 2 Bl. Comm. 182.

[6] Murray v. Hall, 7 Man., G. & S. 440, note, 445.

[7] De Witt v. San Francisco, 2 Cal. 289.

These are interest,[8] title,[9] time,[10] and possession.[11] By unity of interest, in reference to joint tenancy, is meant a similarity of estate, as regards its extent or duration, in each joint tenant. Since joint tenants hold under a grant of a single estate, their interests are necessarily the same in extent. Thus one cannot be tenant in fee simple and the others in tail, or for life, or for a term of years. But where two or more are joint tenants for life, one of them may have the inheritance in severalty, subject to the joint estate; as where land is granted to A. and B. for their lives, and to the heirs or heirs of the body of A. By unity of the title of joint tenants is meant the creation of their interests by one and the same act; that is, by the same grant or devise. Joint tenants cannot be acquired under different titles. And, at common law, unity of time of commencement of the title was requisite; that is, the interests of the tenants must have vested at one and the same time. Thus, if the fee simple in remainder after a life estate were limited to the heirs of A. and the heirs of B., A. and B. being alive at the time of the limitation, but subsequently dying at different times, their respective heirs would not be joint tenants, but tenants in common; since their interests would not have arisen at the same moment. But by means of limitations operating by way of springing or shifting use, or executory devise, the interests of joint tenants may be made to arise at different times. Unity of possession means only a joint right to possession, which is essential to all joint estates. A joint tenancy can be created only by purchase. It cannot arise by descent.[12] One joint tenant cannot convey the whole estate or any part by metes and bounds,[13] but he may convey his share, and such a conveyance causes a severance of the tenancy.[14] That is, when a joint tenant mortgages or conveys his share to a stranger, it

[8] Wiscot's Case, 2 Coke, 60b; Putney v. Dresser, 2 Metc. (Mass.) 583; Jones v. Jones, 1 Call (Va.) 458.

[9] De Witt v. San Francisco, 2 Cal. 289.

[10] Strattan v. Best, 2 Brown, Ch. 233; Sammes' Case, 13 Coke, 54.

[11] Thornton v. Thornton, 3 Rand. (Va.) 179.

[12] 1 Washb. Real Prop. (5th Ed.) 676. Cf. Putney v. Dresser, 2 Metc. (Mass.) 583. But see Rev. St. Ind. 1894, §§ 2624, 2625.

[13] Porter v. Hill, 9 Mass. 34; Hanks v. Enloe, 33 Tex. 624.

[14] Robison v. Codman, 1 Sumn. 121, Fed. Cas. No. 11,970; Davidson v. Heydom, 2 Yeates (Pa.) 459.

turns the joint tenancy into a tenancy in common so far as that share is concerned, though the other owners continue to hold as joint tenants between themselves with all the incidents of joint tenancy.[15] In many states joint tenancies have been turned into tenancies in common by statute, or the right of survivorship has been abolished, or a power to devise has been given.[16]

SAME—TENANCIES IN COMMON.

209. A tenancy in common is a joint ownership of lands, to which the principle of survivorship does not apply. The only unity necessary for a tenancy in common is that of possession.

A tenancy in common is where two or more hold the same land with interests accruing under different titles, or accruing under the same title, but at different periods, or conferred by words of limitation importing that the grantees are to take in distinct shares.[17] Unity of possession is necessary for a tenancy in common. A joint tenancy differs from a tenancy in common in being subject to the right of survivorship, and in requiring the four unities, while for a tenancy in common only unity of possession is necessary. Though the other unities may exist, their presence is immaterial. The interests may be held by several and distinct titles.[18] These titles may be acquired in different ways.[19] In many of the United States all joint estates are presumed to be tenancies in common, unless the contrary appears.[20] Tenancies in common may be created by

---

[15] Simpson's Lessee v. Ammons, 1 Bin. (Pa.) 175; Brown v. Raindle, 3 Ves. 256.

[16] 1 Stim. Am. St. Law, §§ 1371, 2630; 3 Shars. & B. Lead. Cas. Real Prop. 15. For exceptions to the operation of these statutes, see 2 Jones, Real Prop. §§ 1783, 1788, 1789.

[17] 1 Steph. Comm. 323.

[18] Mittel v. Karl, 133 Ill. 65, 24 N. E. 553; Spencer v. Austin, 38 Vt. 258; Griswold v. Johnson, Conn. 363. They may arise by descent, but not at common law. Fenton v. Miller, 94 Mich. 204, 53 N. W. 957.

[19] 2 Bl. Comm. 192. And see Putnam v. Ritchie, 6 Paige (N. Y.) 390.

[20] 1 Stim. Am. St. Law, § 1371 B; 3 Shars. & B. Lead. Cas. Real Prop. 20. See Case v. Owen, 139 Ind. 22, 38 N. E. 395.

conveyances expressly providing for such estates,[21] or they may arise by implication; as where one-half of a parcel of land is conveyed without metes and bounds, or where a certain number of acres out of a larger tract are conveyed without the particular part being designated.[22] In all cases of tenancies in common the share of each tenant, whatever the number of tenants may be, is presumed to be equal to the shares of the others,[23] unless it is otherwise expressly provided, or circumstances, such as unequal contributions to the purchase price, rebut such a presumption.[24]

Joint Mortgagees.

Many of the rules governing joint estates apply to those who hold land in the capacity of joint mortgagees. Under the common-law theory of mortgages, joint mortgagees are, after a strict foreclosure, tenants in common.[25] Before the foreclosure of a mortgage given to two or more jointly, the doctrine of survivorship applies, and the survivor may foreclose the mortgage without making the heirs or the personal representative of the deceased mortgagee parties to the action.[26] If the mortgage is given to secure debts which are several, the joint mortgagees hold as tenants in common.[27]

SAME—ESTATES IN CO-PARCENARY.

210. An estate in co-parcenary is an ownership of land in community in undivided shares by co-heirs. Unities of interest, title, and possession are necessary for estates in co-parcenary. Estates in co-parcenary exist in only a few states.

---

[21] See Emerson v. Cutler, 14 Pick. (Mass.) 108; Martin v. Smith, 5 Bin. (Pa.) 16.

[22] Preston v. Robinson, 24 Vt. 583; Seckel v. Engle, 2 Rawle (Pa.) 68; Wallace v. Miller, 52 Cal. 655.

[23] See Campau v. Campau, 44 Mich. 31, 5 N. W. 1062; Gregg v. Patterson, 9 Watts & S. (Pa.) 197.

[24] Rankin v. Black, 1 Head (Tenn.) 650.

[25] Goodwin v. Richardson, 11 Mass. 469.

[26] Appleton v. Boyd, 7 Mass. 131. For the application of the principle of survivorship to the mortgage debt, see 2 Jones, Mortg. (5th Ed.) § 1382.

[27] Burnett v. Pratt, 22 Pick. (Mass.) 556; Brown v. Bates, 55 Me. 520.

Under the American rules of descent both male and female heirs may hold as co-parceners,[28] but under rules of primogeniture only co-heiresses could be co-parceners.[29] An estate in co-parcenary arises only by descent. Co-parceners may hold unequal interests because some of them may be children and others grandchildren. The doctrine of survivorship does not apply to estates held in co-parcenary.[30] In an estate in co-parcenary the unities discussed under joint tenancies are necessary, except the unity of time.[*] Estates in co-parcenary differ from joint tenancies in that the doctrine of survivorship does not apply, and that they arise by descent, while joint tenancies arise only by purchase. In some states this estate has been abolished, and co-heirs take as tenants in common, though in a few the tenancy still exists.[31]

SAME—ESTATES IN ENTIRETY.

211. An estate in entirety is one conveyed to a man and his wife to hold jointly. The doctrine of survivorship applies to these estates.

212. Estates in entirety have been abolished in many states.

When at common law a joint estate was conveyed to a man and his wife, the effect was not the same as if the conveyance had been to two persons not married, but the peculiar joint holding known as a tenancy in entirety arose.[32] It is, of course, possible to convey to a man and his wife land to be held as a tenancy in common or a joint tenancy by the use of words indicating such an intention.[33] When an estate was conveyed to a man and his wife and

---

[28] 1 Stim. Am. St. Law, § 1375; Hoffar v. Dement, 5 Gill (Md.) 132; Gilpin v. Hollingsworth, 3 Md. 190.

[29] Co. Litt. §§ 241, 242, 254.

[30] 2 Bl. Comm. 188.

[*] Id.

[31] 1 Stim. Am. St. Law, § 1375 A.

[32] Thornton v. Thornton, 3 Rand. (Va.) 179; Hunt v. Blackburn, 128 U. S. 464, 9 Sup. Ct. 125.

[33] Hicks v. Cochran, 4 Edw. Ch. (N. Y.) 107; McDermott v. French, 15 N. J. Eq. 78; Hoffman v. Stigers, 28 Iowa, 302; Fladung v. Rose, 58 Md. 13;

a third person, the husband and wife took only one-half, which they held as tenants in entirety, while the third person took the other half, holding it in common, or as a joint tenancy, as the case might be, with the husband and wife. So, if there were more than three persons to whom the conveyance was made, the husband and wife would together take only one share.[34] The doctrine of survivorship applies to estates in entirety, and they go to the heirs of the survivor only, the heirs of the first deceased taking nothing.[35] During the joint lives of the husband and wife the husband has the control of the joint estate, and a conveyance made by him will be effectual during his life;[36] but if he die first she may avoid the conveyance.[37] So land held by this tenancy may be levied on by the husband's creditors, but such a conveyance will be no more effectual against a surviving wife than a voluntary alienation.[38]

Estates in Entirety in the United States—Community System.

In some of our states estates in entirety still exist. In some states the married women's acts are held to have abolished them,[39] though in other states the contrary is held.[40] In some jurisdictions they are treated as tenancies in common,[41] in others as joint tenancies.[42]

Thornburg v. Wiggins, 135 Ind. 178, 34 N. E. 999. But see, contra, Stuckey v. Keefe's Ex'rs, 26 Pa. St. 397.

[34] Barber v. Harris, 15 Wend. (N. Y.) 616; Johnson v. Hart, 6 Watts & S. (Pa.) 319.

[35] Stuckey v. Keefe's Ex'rs, 26 Pa. St. 397. Cf. Thornton v. Thornton, 3 Rand. (Va.) 179.

[36] Barber v. Harris, 15 Wend. (N. Y.) 616; Bennett v. Child, 19 Wis. 362; Ames v. Norman, 4 Sneed (Tenn.) 683.

[37] Pierce v. Chace, 108 Mass. 254; McCurdy v. Canning, 64 Pa. St. 39; Chandler v. Cheney, 37 Ind. 391; Washburn v. Burns, 34 N. J. Law, 18.

[38] Farmers' & Mechanics' Bank v. Gregory, 49 Barb. (N. Y.) 155. And see McCurdy v. Canning, 64 Pa. St. 39.

[39] Cooper v. Cooper, 76 Ill. 57.

[40] Bennett v. Child, 19 Wis. 362; Lewis' Appeal, 85 Mich. 340, 48 N. W. 580; Carver v. Smith, 90 Ind. 222; Zorntlein v. Bram, 100 N. Y. 13, 2 N. E. 388; Diver v. Diver, 56 Pa. St. 106.

[41] Hoffman v. Stigers, 28 Iowa, 302; Farmers' & Merchants' Nat. Bank v. Ohio St. 152, 12 N. E. 439.

[42] Whittlesey v. Fuller, 11 Conn. 337. Land may be conveyed to husband and wife as joint tenants. Wilken v. Young (Ind. Sup.) 41 N. E. 68. And see Hiles v. Fisher, 144 N. Y. 306, 39 N. E. 337.

In a number of our Southern and Western states, owing to the influence of French and Spanish law, a system of property ownership by married persons has been adopted, called the community system. This regards the relation of husband and wife, as far as their property rights are concerned, as a kind of partnership, and as such the property is primarily liable for the debts of the community.[43] The community doctrine, however, applies only to property acquired by the spouses during the marriage,[44] and even as to this property there is merely a presumption that it is held in community. The presumption may be rebutted, and it may be shown that the property belongs individually to the husband or to the wife.[45] The husband, under the community system, has the right to control the common property.[46] On the death of either spouse the common property goes one-half to the survivor and one-half to the heirs of the deceased. If there are no heirs, then the survivor takes it all.[47]

SAME—ESTATES IN PARTNERSHIP.

213. An estate in partnership is one where land purchased with partnership funds is held by the members of a partnership for partnership purposes.

In order that land may be held as an estate in partnership, it must be purchased with partnership funds, and for partnership purposes.[48] The equitable title to such property belongs to the partnership as an entity in severalty, the legal title being held in trust

---

[43] Jones v. Jones, 15 Tex. 143; Carter v. Conner, 60 Tex. 52. But see Chaffe v. McIntosh, 36 La. Ann. 824. It is also liable for any debts of the husband. Adams v. Knowlton, 22 Cal. 283; Forbes v. Dunham, 24 Tex. 611. And for the wife's antenuptial debts. Vlautin v. Bumpus, 35 Cal. 214; Taylor v. Murphy, 50 Tex. 291.

[44] Pancoast v. Pancoast, 57 Cal. 320; Althof v. Conheim, 38 Cal. 230; Burns v. Thompson, 39 La. 377, 1 South. 913.

[45] Cooke v. Bremond, 27 Tex. 457; McDonald v. Badger, 23 Cal. 393; Higgins v. Higgins, 46 Cal. 259; Schuyler v. Broughton, 70 Cal. 282, 11 Pac. 719.

[46] 1 Stim. Am. St. Law, § 6433.

[47] 1 Stim. Am. St. Law, art. 340.

[48] Hoxie v. Carr, 1 Sumn. 173, Fed. Cas. No. 6,802; Alkire v. Kahle, 123 Ill. 496, 17 N. E. 693; Buchan v. Sumner, 2 Barb. Ch. (N. Y.) 165.

for the firm.[49] The legal title may be in one partner[50] or in all the partners. In the latter case they hold as tenants in common.[51] The firm's interest in the land is personalty,[52] and is primarily liable for partnership debts.[53] The surplus, if any, goes to the partners as tenants in common.[54]

INCIDENTS OF JOINT ESTATES.

214. The rights of tenants of joint estates will be treated under the following heads:
  (a) **Possession and disseisin** (p. 340).
  (b) **Accounting between co-tenants** (p. 341).
  (c) **Repairs and waste** (p. 342).
  (d) **Transfer of joint estates** (p. 343).
  (e) **Actions affecting joint estates** (p. 343).

Possession and Disseisin.

The owners of joint estates have in general all the rights of owners in severalty except the right to sole possession.[55] Therefore the possession of one tenant of a joint estate is not adverse to his co-tenants,[56] but it may be made so by an actual disseisin of the other tenants, such as a known denial of their rights, or a long exclusive possession without accounting for the rents and profits.[57]

---

[49] Fairchild v. Fairchild, 64 N. Y. 471; Dyer v. Clark, 5 Metc. (Mass.) 562; Paige v. Paige, 71 Iowa, 318, 32 N. W. 360.

[50] Williams v. Shelden, 61 Mich. 311, 28 N. W. 115; Fairchild v. Fairchild, 64 N. Y. 471.

[51] Pepper v. Pepper, 24 Ill. App. 316; Dyer v. Clark, 5 Metc. (Mass.) 562; Howard v. Priest, Id. 582.

[52] Arnold v. Wainwright, 6 Minn. 358 (Gil. 241). And see ante, p. 24.

[53] Buchan v. Sumner, 2 Barb. Ch. (N. Y.) 165; Galbraith v. Gedge, 16 B. Mon. (Ky.) 631.

[54] Strong v. Lord, 107 Ill. 25; Buchan v. Sumner, 2 Barb. Ch. (N. Y.) 165.

[55] Wood v. Phillips, 43 N. Y. 152; Erwin v. Olmsted, 7 Cow. (N. Y.) 229; Gower v. Quinlan, 40 Mich. 572.

[56] Clapp v. Bromagham, 9 Cow. (N. Y.) 530; Challefoux v. Ducharme, 4 Wis. 554.

[57] M'Clung v. Ross, 5 Wheat. 116; Puckett v. McDaniel, 8 Tex. Civ. App. 630, 28 S. W. 360; Cameron v. Railway Co., 60 Minn. 100, 61 N. W. 814; Liscomb v. Root, 8 Pick. (Mass.) 376; Cummings v. Wyman, 10 Mass. 464;

So one co-tenant may disseise the others by conveying the whole of the estate to a stranger, if the conveyance is followed by possession by the grantee.[58] One co-tenant cannot let the joint property be sold for taxes, and purchase it himself; if he does so, his title will not be good against his co-tenants.[59] Nor can a co-tenant set up any other adverse title in himself or in another.[60]

Accounting between Co-Tenants.

Trespass quare clausum does not lie against a co-tenant for taking the crops nor for cutting trees,[61] though one tenant may recover his proportion if the whole has been sold by the other tenant.[62] So one tenant cannot recover rent from his co-tenant when the latter has been occupying the joint premises,[63] though the rule is otherwise in

Blackmore v. Gregg, 2 Watts & S. (Pa.) 182; Feliz v. Feliz, 105 Cal. 1, 38 Pac. 521. There must be an actual ouster. Mansfield v. McGinnis, 86 Me. 118, 29 Atl. 956.

[58] Clapp v. Bromagham, 9 Cow. (N. Y.) 530; Kinney v. Slattery, 51 Iowa, 353, 1 N. W. 626. But see Noble v. Hill, 8 Tex. Civ. App. 171, 27 S. W. 756; Caldwell v. Neely, 81 N. C. 114; Price v. Hall, 140 Ind. 314, 39 N. E. 941. Such a conveyance must be followed by possession, or there will be no ouster of the other tenants. New York & T. Land Co. v. Hyland, 8 Tex. Civ. App. 601, 28 S. W. 206. Such a purchaser from one co-tenant is not estopped to set up a title adverse to that of the joint owners. Watkins v. Green, 101 Mich. 493, 60 N. W. 44.

[59] Dubois v. Campau, 24 Mich. 360; Page v. Webster, 8 Mich. 263; Conn v. Conn, 58 Iowa, 747, 13 N. W. 51; Clark v. Rainey, 72 Miss. 151, 16 South. 499. And see Bracken v. Cooper, 80 Ill. 221; Montague v. Selb, 106 Ill. 49.

[60] Rothwell v. Dewees, 2 Black, 613; Van Horne v. Fonda, 5 Johns. Ch. (N. Y.) 388; Davis v. Givens, 71 Mo. 94. An adverse title purchased by one tenant inures to the benefit of the others only when they pay their proportion of the cost. McFarlin v. Leaman (Tex. Civ. App.) 29 S. W. 44. When the co-tenants hold in remainder, the purchase of the preceding life estate by one tenant does not inure to the benefit of the others. McLaughlin v. McLaughlin, 80 Md. 115, 30 Atl. 607. Cf. Roberts v. Thorn, 25 Tex. 728; Kirkpatrick v. Mathiot, 4 Watts & S. (Pa.) 251. See, also, Palmer v. Young, 1 Vern. 276; Hamilton v. Denny, 1 Ball & B. 199.

[61] Filbert v. Hoff, 42 Pa. St. 97.

[62] Abbey v. Wheeler, 85 Hun, 226, 32 N. Y. Supp. 1069; McGahan v. Bank, 156 U. S. 218, 15 Sup. Ct. 347; Hayden v. Merrill, 44 Vt. 336; Richardson v. Richardson, 72 Me. 403. But see Calhoun v. Curtis, 4 Metc. (Mass.) 413.

[63] McLaughlin v. McLaughlin, 80 Md. 115, 30 Atl. 607; Sargent v. Parsons, 12 Mass. 149; Woolever v. Knapp, 18 Barb. (N. Y.) 265; Valentine v. Healey, 86 Hun, 259, 33 N. Y. Supp. 246; Thomas v. Thomas, 5 Exch. 28; Henderson

some states by statute,[64] and there may be such a recovery if the land has been leased, and the whole of the rent collected by one tenant.[65] A co-tenant has no claim for improvements which he has made on the common property,[66] though he may be given the benefit of them in a partition of the land.[67]

Repairs and Waste.

One co-tenant may make necessary repairs, and enforce contribution therefor against the other tenants.[68] One tenant in possession of the joint property may become liable to his co-tenants for waste if he does acts which amount to a destruction of the property.[69] The technical rules of waste, however, do not apply. There must be some actual injury to the estate, or the liability is not incurred.[70] A tenant in possession may be restrained by injunction from malicious injury to the property.[71]

---

v. Eason, 17 Q. B. 701. One tenant may take a lease from his co-tenants. Valentine v. Healey, 86 Hun, 259, 33 N. Y. Supp. 246.

[64] 1 Stim. Am. St. Law, § 1378; 3 Shars. & B. Lead. Cas. Real Prop. 98. And see McParland v. Larkin, 155 Ill. 84, 39 N. E. 609.

[65] Miner v. Lorman, 70 Mich. 173, 38 N. W. 18; Reynolds v. Wilmeth, 45 Iowa, 693.

[66] Rico Reduction & Mining Co. v. Musgrave, 14 Colo. 79, 23 Pac. 458; Scott v. Guernsey, 48 N. Y. 106.

[67] Kurtz v. Hibner, 55 Ill. 514; Alleman v. Hawley, 117 Ind. 532, 20 N. E. 441.

[68] Stewart v. Stewart (Wis.) 63 N. W. 886; Leigh v. Dickeson, 12 Q. B. Div. 194; Ward v. Ward's Heirs (W. Va.) 21 S. E. 746; Pickering v. Pickering, 63 N. H. 468, 3 Atl. 744; Dech's Appeal, 57 Pa. St. 467; Beaty v. Bordwell, 91 Pa. St. 438; Alexander v. Ellison, 79 Ky. 148; Fowler v. Fowler, 50 Conn. 256; Haven v. Mehlgarten, 19 Ill. 91. But see Calvert v. Aldrich, 99 Mass. 74. But there is no lien on the land to secure such expenditures. Branch v. Makeig (Tex. Civ. App.) 28 S. W. 1050. But see, as to improvements by a co-parcener, Ward v. Ward's Heirs (W. Va.) 21 S. E. 746. Co-tenants must contribute for expenses incurred in defending the common title. Gosselin v. Smith, 154 Ill. 74, 39 N. E. 980.

[69] Dodge v. Davis, 85 Iowa, 77, 52 N. W. 2; Childs v. Railroad Co., 117 Mo. 414, 23 S. W. 373; Wilkinson v. Haygarth, 12 Q. B. 837. But see Wait v. Richardson, 33 Vt. 190. The amount of recovery is apportioned according to the interests of the several owners. McDodrill v. Lumber Co. (W. Va.) 21 S. E. 878.

[70] Martyn v. Knowllys, 8 Term R. 145.

[71] Ballou v. Wood, 8 Cush. (Mass.) 48. But see Hihn v. Peck, 18 Cal. 640; Obert v. Obert, 5 N. J. Eq. 397.

Transfer of Joint Estates.

All tenants of joint estates except those holding in entirety [72] may convey all or part of their interests to a stranger without the consent of their co-tenants.[73] But they cannot, by such conveyance, pass a valid title to any separate part of the common property.[74] So a tenant of a joint estate cannot dedicate land to the public for a street.[75] It has already been said that one joint tenant, by conveying to a stranger, severs the joint tenancy,[76] but such a tenant cannot devise his share, unless he be the last survivor.[77] A co-parcener may pass his interests by devise.[78]

Actions Affecting Joint Estates.

For injuries to the possession of a joint estate or to rights growing out of possession, the co-tenants should sue jointly.[79] Joint tenants at common law must join in an action affecting the title,[80]

[72] McCurdy v. Canning, 64 Pa. St. 39; Ames v. Norman, 4 Sneed (Tenn.) 683; Arnold v. Arnold, 30 Ind. 305.

[73] Peabody v. Minot, 24 Pick. (Mass.) 329; Barnes v. Lynch, 151 Mass. 510, 24 N. E. 783; Butler v. Roys, 25 Mich. 53; Rector v. Waugh, 17 Mo. 13; Simpson's Lessee v. Ammons, 1 Bin. (Pa.) 175. Rights of curtesy and dower in joint estates have already been considered, ante, pp. 79, 92. For the words of limitation necessary to pass a fee in conveyances by joint owners, see ante, p. 37.

[74] Porter v. Hill, 9 Mass. 34; Varnum v. Abbot, 12 Mass. 474. So, also, as to levy of execution, Bartlet v. Harlow, 12 Mass. 348; Starr v. Leavitt, 2 Conn. 243; Butler v. Roys, 25 Mich. 53; Peabody v. Minot, 24 Pick. (Mass.) 329; Thompson v. Barber, 12 N. H. 563.

[75] Scott v. State, 1 Sneed (Tenn.) 629. Cf. Stevens v. Town of Norfolk, 46 Conn. 227, and Stevens v. Battell, 49 Conn. 156.

[76] Ante, p. 334.

[77] Wilken v. Young (Ind. Sup.) 41 N. E. 68; Duncan v. Forrer, 6 Bin. (Pa.) 193. But see Nichols v. Denny, 37 Miss. 59. The interest of a joint tenant may be sold on execution. Midgley v. Walker, 101 Mich. 583, 60 N. W. 296.

[78] 1 Washb. Real Prop. (5th Ed.) 684.

[79] Decker v. Livingston, 15 Johns. (N. Y.) 479; De Puy v. Strong, 37 N. Y. 372; Daniels v. Daniels, 7 Mass. 135; Gilmore v. Wilbur, 12 Pick. (Mass.) 120. As on a joint lease for the recovery of rent. Sherman v. Ballou, 8 Cow. (N. Y.) 304; Wall v. Hinds, 4 Gray (Mass.) 256. But see Hayden v. Paterson, 51 Pa. St. 261.

[80] Wheat v. Morris, 21 D. C. 11; Marshall v. Palmer, 91 Va. 344, 21 S. E. 672; Webster v. Vandeventer, 6 Gray (Mass.) 428; Dewey v. Lambier, 7 Cal. 347. But see Lowery v. Rowland, 104 Ala. 420, 16 So. 88; Morgan v. Hudnell (Ohio Sup.) 40 N. E. 716.

but by statute in some states tenants of joint estates may join or not, as they choose.[81] Tenants in common and co-parceners cannot bring joint action when the title is involved.[82]

PARTITION.

215. Partition is the dividing of land held by the owners of joint estates into distinct portions, so that each may hold his share in severalty.

216. There may be a partition of all kinds of joint estates except tenancies in entirety.

Partition may be either voluntary [83] or compulsory. Voluntary partition cannot be by parol [84] except for tenancies in co-parcenary,[85] though many cases give effect to a parol partition when followed by possession of the shares in severalty.[86] Rights may be acquired under such partition by long possession.[87] Voluntary partition should be made by mutual deeds. Joint estates may be so created that partition of them cannot be had,[88] but, in the absence of such

---

[81] 3 Shars. & B. Lead. Cas. Real Prop. 29.

[82] Inhabitants of Rehoboth v. Hunt, 1 Pick. (Mass.) 224; Hill v. Gibbs, 5 Hill (N. Y.) 56. And see Mooers v. Bunker, 29 N. H. 420.

[83] But see as to rights of third persons, Emson v. Polhemus, 28 N. J. Eq. 439.

[84] Duncan v. Sylvester, 16 Me. 388; Dan v. Longstreet, 18 N. J. Law, 405. But see Ebert v. Wood, 1 Bin. (Pa.) 216; Wood v. Fleet, 36 N. Y. 499.

[85] 2 Bl. Comm. 324; Wildey v. Bonney's Lessee, 31 Miss. 644; Bolling v. Teel, 76 Va. 487.

[86] Wolf v. Wolf, 158 Pa. St. 621, 28 Atl. 164; Jackson v. Harder, 4 Johns. (N. Y.) 202; Shepard v. Rinks, 78 Ill. 188; Buzzell v. Gallagher, 28 Wis. 678.

[87] Manly v. Pettee, 38 Ill. 128; Taylor v. Millard, 118 N. Y. 244, 23 N. E. 376; Mellon v. Reed, 114 Pa. St. 647, 8 Atl. 227; McMahan v. McMahan, 13 Pa. St. 376. See further, as to parol partition, 2 Jones, Real Prop. §§ 1940–1950.

[88] Winthrop v. Minot, 9 Cush. (Mass.) 405; Hunt v. Wright, 47 N. H. 396. So there may be a valid agreement not to partition. Coleman v. Coleman, 19 Pa. St. 100; Eberts v. Fisher, 54 Mich. 294, 20 N. W. 80; Avery v. Payne, 12 Mich. 540. But see Mitchell v. Starbuck, 10 Mass. 5; Kean v. Tilford, 81 Ky. 600.

a provision, any joint estate except estates in entirety may be divided at the suit of one of the tenants without the consent of the others.[89] But when compulsory partition is sought it must be for the whole estate, and not for part of it.[90] At common law, partition could be compelled against the consent of the co-tenants only in the case of co-parcenary.[91] The right to compel partition by an action at law was first given by the statutes of 31 Hen. VIII. c. 1, and 32 Hen. VIII. c. 32. These statutes have been re-enacted in most of the United States.[92] The remedy is now, however, almost exclusively in courts of chancery, or is by a special form of action provided by statute.[93] Partition can be had only by those having seisin and possession; therefore there can be no partition of joint estates in reversion or remainder.[94] In New York and a few other states vested remainders are excepted from this rule.[95] In an action for partition all the co-tenants must be made parties,[96] as well as all other persons interested in the lands, such as lienholders, or they will not be bound by the action.[97] The action of partition is a local action in rem.[98] Questions of title cannot be settled in an action for partition.[99] The actual division of the land in partition

---

[89] Willard v. Willard, 145 U. S. 116, 12 Sup. Ct. 818; Rohn v. Harris, 130 Ill. 525, 22 N. E. 587; Danville Seminary v. Mott, 136 Ill. 289, 28 N. E. 54; Smith v. Smith, 10 Paige (N. Y.) 470.

[90] Duncan v. Sylvester, 16 Me. 388.

[91] 1 Washb. Real Prop. (5th Ed.) 710.

[92] 1 Washb. Real Prop. (5th Ed.) 711. And see Hall v. Piddock, 21 N. J. Eq. 311; Ford v. Knapp, 102 N. Y. 135, 6 N. E. 283.

[93] 1 Washb. Real Prop. (5th Ed.) 723, note; Buckley v. Superior Court, 102 Cal. 6, 36 Pac. 360; Bailey v. Sisson, 1 R. I. 233.

[94] Hodgkinson, Petitioner, 12 Pick. (Mass.) 374; Bragg v. Lyon, 93 N. C. 151. And see as to disseisees, Rickard v. Rickard, 13 Pick. 251.

[95] Hilliard v. Scoville, 52 Ill. 449; Howell v. Mills, 56 N. Y. 226; Jenkins v. Fahey, 73 N. Y. 355; Smalley v. Isaacson, 40 Minn. 450, 42 N. W. 352.

[96] Holman v. Gill, 107 Ill. 467.

[97] De Uprey v. De Uprey, 27 Cal. 330; Bogert v. Bogert, 53 Hun, 629, 5 N. Y. Supp. 893; Cornish v. Gest, 2 Cox, Ch. 27. But cf. Sebring v. Mersereau, 9 Cow. (N. Y.) 344; Stewart v. Bank, 101 Pa. St. 342.

[98] Bonner, Petitioner, 4 Mass. 122; Corwithe v. Griffing, 21 Barb. (N. Y.) 9.

[99] Fenton v. Circuit Judge, 76 Mich. 405, 43 N. W. 437; Fuller v. Montague, 8 C. C. A. 100, 59 Fed. 212. Cf., however, Welch's Appeal, 126 Pa. St. 297, 17 Atl. 623; Hayes' Appeal, 123 Pa. St. 110, 16 Atl. 600.

is made by commissioners appointed by the court.[100] If an equitable division cannot be made, one of the co-tenants may be given a larger share than the other, and he be decreed to pay the other a sum of money called the owelty of partition.[101] This cannot be done, however, without his consent.[102] When one co-tenant has made improvements on the joint property, for which the others have not contributed, the court may, in its discretion, give him the land on which those improvements stand.[103] Two or more co-tenants may have their interests set off to them to be held in severalty as regards the other tenants, but jointly between themselves.[104] If the estate to be partitioned consists of a number of parcels, each parcel need not be divided, but the partition may be made by assigning the separate parcels to different tenants.[105] Some kinds of property, such as mills and factories, cannot be divided, in which case either an owelty of partition must be paid by the one who takes the whole property, or the property must be sold, and the money divided.[106] Probate courts in many states have power to make partition of estates over which they have acquired jurisdiction.[107] After voluntary partition, if the title to the part which one co-tenant has received fails, such tenant has no remedy against his former co-tenants.[108] But, if the partition was compulsory, each co-tenant is in the position of a warrantor of the title of the shares

[100] Enyard v. Nevins (N. J. Ch.) 18 Atl. 192; Dondero v. Vansickle, 11 Nev. 389.

[101] Green v. Arnold, 11 R. I. 364; Dobbin v. Rex, 106 N. C. 444, 11 S. E. 260. And see Marks v. Sewall, 120 Mass. 174; Stewart v. Bank, 101 Pa. St. 342.

[102] Whitney v. Parker, 63 N. H. 416. And see Corrothers v. Jolliffe, 32 W. Va. 562, 9 S. E. 889.

[103] Town v. Needham, 3 Paige (N. Y.) 545; St. Felix v. Rankin, 3 Edw. Ch. (N. Y.) 323; Brookfield v. Williams, 2 N. J. Eq. 341.

[104] Abbott v. Berry, 46 N. H. 369. And see Colton v. Smith, 11 Pick. (Mass.) 311.

[105] Hagar v. Wiswall, 10 Pick. (Mass.) 152.

[106] King v. Reed, 11 Gray (Mass.) 490; Higginbottom v. Short, 25 Miss. 160; Crowell v. Woodbury, 52 N. H. 613. But see Hills v. Day, 14 Wend. (N. Y.) 204; Miller v. Miller, 13 Pick. (Mass.) 237.

[107] Appeal of Wistar, 115 Pa. St. 241, 8 Atl. 797; Hurley v. Hamilton, 37 Minn. 160, 33 N. W. 912.

[108] Weiser v. Weiser, 5 Watts (Pa.) 279; Beardsley v. Knight, 10 Vt. 185; Morrice's Case, 6 Coke, 12b.

of the others, and, in the event of a failure of title, a new partition may be compelled, or there may be a reliance on the warranty.[109] Therefore, one co-tenant cannot set up an adverse title against the others after partition.[110]

[109] But that a new partition cannot be compelled against an allenee after partition, see 1 Washb. Real Prop. (5th Ed.) 723.

[110] Venable v. Beauchamp, 3 Dana (Ky.) 321. But cf. Coleman v. Coleman, 3 Dana (Ky.) 398.

CHAPTER XIII.

INCORPOREAL HEREDITAMENTS.

217. Definition and Kinds.
218. Easements.
219.   Creation.
220.   By Grant.
221.   By Prescription.
222.   Classification.
223.   Incidents.
224.   Destruction.
225. Specific Easements.
226.   Rights of Way.
227.   Highways.
228.   Light and Air.
229–230.   Lateral and Subjacent Support.
231.   Party Walls.
232.   Easements in Water.
233. Profits à Prendre.
234–235. Rents.
236. Franchises.

DEFINITION AND KINDS.

217. An incorporeal hereditament is anything, the subject of property, which is inheritable, and not tangible or visible.

217a. Incorporeal hereditaments in the United States are
 (a) **Easements** (p. 349).
 (b) **Commons, or profits a prendre** (p. 373).
 (c) **Rents** (p. 375).
 (d) **Franchises** (p. 378).

Hereditaments are said to be either corporeal or incorporeal. A corporeal hereditament is any right of property which entitles the person in whom it is vested to the possession of the land. An incorporeal hereditament is any right of property which is not a right to the possession of land. Incorporeal hereditaments differ from corporeal hereditaments chiefly in that they are rights issuing out of land, rather than rights to land. The term "incorporeal hereditaments" is used by some writers to include future estates, and the interests in realty which we are considering are distinguished as "hereditaments purely incorporeal." The distinction between corporeal and incorporeal hereditaments was, in the early law, of some importance; since rights to the possession of land were transferable only by delivery of such possession, while rights not involving possession of land were transferable by deed of grant. Corporeal hereditaments were therefore said to "lie in livery,"[1] while incorporeal hereditaments were said to "lie in grant."[2] This distinction, however, is not now of practical importance; for in modern law corporeal as well as incorporeal hereditaments are transferable without actual delivery of possession. Other differences between the two kinds of property will be noticed as we proceed with the discussion of the various kinds of incorporeal hereditaments. As enumerated by Blackstone:[3] "Incorporeal hereditaments are principally of ten sorts: Advowsons, tithes, commons, ways, offices, dignities, franchises, corodies or pensions, annuities, and rents." However, only a few of these are now of any importance in this country, and of the others no further mention will be made.

EASEMENTS.

218. An easement is a right in the owner of one parcel of land, by reason of such ownership, to use the land of another for a special purpose not inconsistent with the general property in the latter.[4]

Easements are rights which one man may exercise over the land of another.[5] These rights can exist only in connection with some other land called the dominant estate, while the land over which the right is exercised is called the servient estate. Looked at from

---

[1] Drake v. Wells, 11 Allen (Mass.) 141; Huff v. McCauley, 53 Pa. St. 206.
[2] 1 Washb. Real Prop. (5th Ed.) 37.
[3] 2 Comm. 21.
[4] 2 Washb. Real Prop. 25.
[5] Wolfe v. Frost, 4 Sandf. Ch. (N. Y.) 72; Wagner v. Hanna, 38 Cal. 111; Harrison v. Boring, 44 Tex. 255; Perrin v. Garfield, 37 Vt. 304.

the standpoint of the owner of the dominant estate, the right is an easement, but from the standpoint of the servient estate it is a servitude. According to Mr. Washburn:[6] "The essential qualities of easements are: (1) They are incorporeal; (2) they are imposed on corporeal property, and not upon the owner thereof; (3) they confer no right to a participation in the profits arising from such property; (4) they are imposed for the benefit of corporeal property; (5) there must be two tenements,—the dominant, to which the right belongs; and the servient, upon which the obligation rests."

It is thus seen that easements differ from licenses principally in their duration, for licenses are generally only to do a number of specific acts on the land of the licensor. So, too, licenses are, as we have seen,[7] for the most part, revocable, while easements are not.[8] Easements differ also from commons or profits à prendre, which will be discussed later in this chapter,[9] in that an easement never gives the right to take anything from the corpus of the servient estate.[10]

SAME—CREATION.

219. Easements are created
  (a) **By grant** (p. 350).
  (b) **By prescription** (p. 352).

220. BY GRANT—Easements may be created by grant, which includes easements arising under covenants and by implied grants. The grant of an easement must be in writing.

Easements may be created by grants, like other interests in land.[11] They need not be created in fee, but may be for a limited term.[12]

---

[6] Washb. Easem. (4th Ed.) 3.

[7] Ante, p. 167.

[8] Hills v. Miller, 3 Paige (N. Y.) 254; Ex parte Coburn, 1 Cow. (N. Y.) 568; Foster v. Browning, 4 R. I. 47; Wallis v. Harrison, 4 Mees. & W. 538.

[9] Post, p. 373.

[10] Huntington v. Asher, 96 N. Y. 604; Post v. Pearsall, 22 Wend. (N. Y.) 425; Huff v. McCauley, 53 Pa. St. 206.

[11] Cronkhite v. Cronkhite, 94 N. Y. 323; Wiseman v. Lueksinger, 84 N. Y. 314; Forbes v. Balenseifer, 74 Ill. 183; Duinneen v. Rich, 22 Wis. 550.

[12] Curtis v. Gardner, 13 Metc. (Mass.) 457; Jamaica Pond Aqueduct Corp. v. Chandler, 9 Allen (Mass.) 159.

They cannot be created by parol, and an attempt to do so would give only a license, which would be revocable.[13] Easements may, however, be either granted or reserved.[14] When an easement is appurtenant to an estate, it passes by a grant of the dominant estate, without express mention.[15] Easements are sometimes conveyed by implication. These are called easements of necessity, and exist whenever they are necessary to the enjoyment of the estate conveyed.[16]

Easements are often raised by covenants. A number of lots are sometimes conveyed with covenants by the grantee of each lot that he will not build within a certain distance of the street. Such covenants are held to impose a servitude on each lot in favor of the others.[17] In equity, also, there may be easements between two parcels of land owned by the same person, although this is not possible at law.[18] For instance, an owner of two lots may construct a drain for one of them across the other, and then sell either of them. In

[13] Taylor v. Millard, 118 N. Y. 244, 23 N. E. 376; Wiseman v. Lucksinger, 84 N. Y. 31; Cronkhite v. Cronkhite, 94 N. Y. 323; Tinker v. Forbes, 136 Ill. 221, 26 N. E. 503; Minneapolis W. Ry. Co. v. Minneapolis & St. L. Ry. Co., 58 Minn. 128, 59 N. W. 983. But see Wilkinson v. Suplee, 166 Pa. St. 315, 31 Atl. 36.

[14] Bowen v. Conner, 6 Cush. (Mass.) 132; Inhabitants of Winthrop v. Fairbanks, 41 Me. 307; Emerson v. Mooney, 50 N. H. 315; Ashcroft v. Railroad Co., 126 Mass. 196; Jones v. Adams, 162 Mass. 224, 38 N. E. 437; Sullivan v. Eddy, 154 Ill. 199, 40 N. E. 482. There must be a sufficient description of the easement. Wells v. Tolman, 88 Hun, 438, 34 N. Y. Supp. 840; Nunnelly v. Iron Co., 94 Tenn. 397, 29 S. W. 361. Cf. Borst v. Empie, 5 N. Y. 33.

[15] Underwood v. Carney, 1 Cush. (Mass.) 285; Morgan v. Mason, 20 Ohio, 402. Cf. Grant v. Chase, 17 Mass. 443.

[16] Boland v. St. John's Schools, 163 Mass. 229, 39 N. E. 1035; Atkins v. Bordman, 2 Metc. (Mass.) 457; Nichols v. Luce, 24 Pick (Mass.) 102; Weynand v. Lutz (Tex. Civ. App.) 29 S. W. 1097. See post, p. 359.

[17] Tulk v. Moxhay, 2 Phil. Ch. 774; Tallmadge v. Bank, 26 N. Y. 105; Winfield v. Henning, 21 N. J. Eq. 188; Peck v. Conway, 119 Mass. 546. So an agreement to clean and repair a water course which has been granted through covenantor's land was held to run with the land. Holmes v. Buckley, Prec. Ch. 39. But see Keates v. Lyon, 4 Ch. App. 218; Renals v. Cowlishaw, 11 Ch. Div. 866; Haywood v. Building Soc., 8 Q. B. Div. 403; Sharp v. Ropes, 110 Mass. 381; Norcross v. James, 140 Mass. 188, 2 N. E. 946.

[18] Johnson v. Jordan, 2 Metc. (Mass.) 234; Lampman v. Milks, 21 N. Y. 505; Watts v. Kelson, 6 Ch. App. 166. But see Suffield v. Brown, 4 De Gex, J. & S. 185; Thomson v. Waterlow, L. R. 6 Eq. 36.

such case, if he transfer the dominant estate, the right to drain across the remaining lot will continue, and the same result may obtain if he transfers the servient estate to one who has knowledge of the existence of the drain, and the easement is necessary to the enjoyment of the other lot.[19] Easements of this character and those created by covenants are often called equitable easements.

221. BY PRESCRIPTION—Easements may be acquired by prescription by adverse user continued for the time required by the statute of limitations.

At common law many easements were acquired by prescription,[20] but it was held that prescription presumed a grant.[21] The acquirement of easements by prescription is now superseded by the doctrine of the statute of limitations.[22] To acquire an easement by prescription, it must have been exercised from time immemorial,[23] but by the statute of limitations, 20 years is the time required, and in some states even a less period is provided by the statute.[24] The character of the acts necessary for gaining an easement under the statute of limitations and by the doctrine of prescription are the same, and the term "prescription" is generally used to denote the former. The user must be uninterrupted[25] and continuous, according to the nature

[19] Thayer v. Payne, 2 Cush. (Mass.) 327; Pyer v. Carter, 1 Hurl. & N. 916; Dunklee v. Railroad Co., 24 N. H. 489; Seymour v. Lewis, 13 N. J. Eq. 439. But see Nicholas v. Chamberlain, Cro. Jac. 121; Johnson v. Jordan, 2 Metc. (Mass.) 234; Collier v. Pierce, 7 Gray (Mass.) 18; Carbrey v. Willis, 7 Allen (Mass.) 364; Randall v. McLaughlin, 10 Allen (Mass.) 366; Buss v. Dyer, 125 Mass. 287; Butterworth v. Crawford, 46 N. Y. 349.

[20] Cross v. Lewis, 2 Barn. & C. 686; Mayor of Kingston v. Horner, Cowp. 102.

[21] Webb v. Bird, 13 C. B. (N. S.) 841; Mayor of Kingston v. Horner, Cowp. 102.

[22] Claflin v. Railroad Co., 157 Mass. 489, 32 N. E. 659; Jones v. Crow, 32 Pa. St. 398; Ricard v. Williams, 7 Wheat. 59.

[23] Melvin v. Whiting, 10 Pick. (Mass.) 295. See Mayor of Kingston v. Horner, Cowp. 102. And see Kent v. Waite, 10 Pick. (Mass.) 138. The term "prescription" is, however, often used when the statute of limitations is meant.

[24] Sibley v. Ellis, 11 Gray (Mass.) 417; Carger v. Fee, 140 Ind. 572, 39 N. E. 93; Boyd v. Woolwine (W. Va.) 21 S. E. 1020; 1 Stim. Am. St. Law, § 2281.

[25] Pollard v. Barnes, 2 Cush. (Mass.) 191; Livett v. Wilson, 3 Bing. 115. A

§ 221)　　　CREATION OF EASEMENTS.　　　353

of the easement.[26] The statute does not begin to run while the owner of the servient estate is under disability.[27] So the period of limitation does not begin against a reversioner or remainder-man until he is entitled to possession of the estate.[28] The use of the easement must be under an adverse claim of right, though color of title is not necessary.[29] Such use cannot be adverse if it is begun with the permission of the owner of the servient estate,[30] or by his license.[31] User will not be sufficient to establish the right if it is secret.[32] The period of adverse occupancy required by the statute need not be all by one person, but may be by a number if they are in privity.[33] It should be observed that the public cannot acquire an easement by

right of flowage may be acquired by prescription. Williams v. Barber (Mich.) 62 N. W. 155.

[26] Bodfish v. Bodfish, 105 Mass. 317; Cox v. Forrest, 60 Md. 74; Iselin v. Starin, 144 N. Y. 453, 39 N. E. 488; Humphreys v. Blasingame, 104 Cal. 40, 37 Pac. 804; Dalton v. Angus, 6 App. Cas. 740, affirming Angus v. Dalton, 4 Q. B. Div. 162; Dare v. Heathcote, 25 Law J. Exch. 245. For user held insufficient to establish an easement across a railroad company's right of way, see Andries v. Railway Co. (Mich.) 63 N. W. 526. And for acts held insufficient to create easements in water by prescription, see Green Bay & M. Canal Co. v. Kaukauna Water Power Co., 90 Wis. 370, 61 N. W. 1121; Mason v. Horton, 67 Vt. 266, 31 Atl. 291.

[27] Reimer v. Stuber, 20 Pa. St. 458. Disability arising after the user is begun does not interrupt the acquisition of the right. Tracy v. Atherton, 36 Vt. 503; Wallace v. Fletcher, 30 N. H. 434. Contra, Lamb v. Crosland, 4 Rich. Law (S. C.) 536.

[28] Schenley v. Com., 36 Pa. St. 29; Pentland v. Keep, 41 Wis. 490.

[29] Burbank v. Fay, 65 N. Y. 57; Bachelder v. Wakefield, 8 Cush. (Mass.) 243; Blanchard v. Moulton, 63 Me. 434; Richard v. Hupp (Cal.) 37 Pac. 920. And see post, p. 460.

[30] Smith v. Miller, 11 Gray (Mass.) 145; Perrin v. Garfield, 37 Vt. 304; Caiger v. Fee (Ind. Sup.) 39 N. E. 93. See Atkins v. Bordman, 2 Metc. (Mass.) 457. That no easement is acquired by the use of a way maintained by the owner of the land for his own convenience, see Wood v. Reed (Sup.) 30 N. Y. Supp. 112.

[31] Wiseman v. Lucksinger, 84 N. Y. 31; Cronkhite v. Cronkhite, 94 N. Y. 323; Johnson v. Skillman, 29 Minn. 95, 12 N. W. 149; Colchester v. Roberts, 4 Mees. & W. 769.

[32] Cook v. Gammon, 93 Ga. 298, 20 S. E. 332; Daniel v. North, 11 East, 372. But when the user is open and uninterrupted, the servient owner is charged with notice. Bushey v. Santiff, 86 Hun, 384, 33 N. Y. Supp. 473.

[33] Melvin v. Whiting, 13 Pick. (Mass.) 184; Hill v. Crosby, 2 Pick. (Mass.) 466.

REAL PROP.—23

prescription,[34] though a dedication may be presumed from use by the public.[35]

SAME—CLASSIFICATION.

222. The principal classifications of easements are the following:
  (a) Continuous and discontinuous.
  (b) Appendant or appurtenant and in gross.
  (c) Negative and affirmative.
  (d) Natural and conventional.

There are a number of classifications of easements, which, though they have no great value in law, are often met with in the books, and therefore will be briefly mentioned here. The first of these is the distinction between continuous and discontinuous easements, which arises from the nature of the use of the easement.[36] An example of the former is a right to lateral or subjacent support,[37] while a right of way is an instance of a discontinuous easement, since the right is only exercised at intervals.[38] Another classification of easements is that which divides them into easements appendant or appurtenant and easements in gross.[39] The former class comprise easements proper, which cannot be severed from the tenement with which they are connected; that is, an easement belongs to an estate and not to a person. But easements in gross are not connected with any parcel of land, and exist in a person or in the public.[40] Highways are easements of this kind, and there may be

---

[34] Pearsall v. Post, 20 Wend. (N. Y.) 111; Ackerman v. Shelp, 8 N. J. Law, 125.

[35] Verona Borough v. Allegheny Val. R. R., 152 Pa. St. 368, 25 Atl. 518; Kelenk v. Town of Walnut Lake, 51 Minn. 381, 53 N. W. 703.

[36] Larsen v. Peterson (N. J. Ch.) 30 Atl. 1094; Fetters v. Humphreys, 18 N. J. Eq. 260.

[37] See post, p. 365.

[38] See post, p. 359.

[39] Dennis v. Wilson, 107 Mass. 591; Spensley v. Valentine, 34 Wis. 154; McMahon v. Williams, 79 Ala. 288.

[40] See Abbot v. Weekly, 1 Lev. 176; Fitch v. Rawling, 2 H. Bl. 393; Mounsey v. Ismay, 1 Hurl. & C. 729, 3 Hurl. & C. 486; Hall v. Nottingham, 1 Exch. Div. 1; Tyson v. Smith, 9 Adol. & E. 406; Nudd v. Hobbs, 17 N. H. 524;

easements in gross in respect to the flowage of water.[41] Easements are also divided, with respect to the obligation imposed on the owner of the servient estate, into negative easements and affirmative easements. Under the former the owner of the servient estate is prohibited from doing some acts of ownership on his own property, as an easement that land shall not be built upon,[42] while in the case of an affirmative easement the owner of the servient estate is merely required to permit something to be done on his land, such as piling materials on it.[43] Easements are also divided into natural and conventional. The former exist as the outgrowth of natural rights, and are necessary, as a matter of course, for the enjoyment of the dominant estate. Instances of natural easements are rights to support of land and to the flowage of water.[44] Conventional easements, on the other hand, are those which are created by the agreements of the parties, and add rights to the dominant estate, which, though not strictly necessary, add to its enjoyment, such as rights of way or to light and air.[45]

SAME—INCIDENTS.

223. The principal rights and incidents growing out of easements are the following:

  (a) The dominant owner must use his easement, and the servient owner his estate, in a reasonable manner.
  (b) The dominant owner must repair the easement.
  (c) The servient owner must not obstruct the easement.

Knowles v. Dow, 22 N. H. 387. Such rights do not exist in some states. Ackerman v. Shelp, 8 N. J. Law, 125. An easement cannot be granted in gross so that it will be assignable. Ackroyd v. Smith, 10 C. B. 164; Boatman v. Lasley, 23 Ohio St. 614. See Garrison v. Rudd, 19 Ill. 558, and, contra, Goodrich v. Burbank, 12 Allen (Mass.) 459; Amidon v. Harris, 113 Mass. 59. Nor to give a right of action against a third person. Hill v. Tupper, 2 Hurl. & C. 121.

[41] De Witt v. Harvey, 4 Gray (Mass.) 486; Bissell v. Grant, 35 Conn. 288; Pouli v. Mockley, 33 Wis. 482.

[42] Hills v. Miller, 3 Paige (N. Y.) 254.

[43] Voorhees v. Burchard, 55 N. Y. 98; Big Mountain Imp. Co.'s Appeal, 54 Pa. St. 361. And see Melvin v. Whiting, 13 Pick. (Mass.) 184.

[44] Laumier v. Francis, 23 Mo. 181.

[45] Stokoe v. Singers, 8 El. & Bl. 31.

Use of the Easement.

The owner of the dominant estate must make his use of the easement reasonable, so as to interfere as little as possible with the servient owner's enjoyment of his land.[46] On the other hand, the latter must not use his estate in such a way as to obstruct the easement or unreasonably interfere with its enjoyment.[47] The grant of an easement includes a grant of all rights necessary for its use. But the use of an easement must be confined to the object for which it is granted.[48]

Repairs of the Easement.

In the absence of a contract providing otherwise, the owner of the dominant estate—that is, the one who has the benefit of the easement—must keep it in repair and condition for use.[49] The easement carries with it the right to do anything necessary to make repairs.[50]

Obstruction of the Easement.

The owner of the dominant estate may have an action for the obstruction of his easement by the servient owner, though no actual damage has been caused.[51] The owner of the dominant estate may

[46] Kaler v. Beaman, 49 Me. 207.

[47] Wells v. Tolman, 88 Hun, 438, 34 N. Y. Supp. 840; Bakeman v. Talbot, 31 N. Y. 366; Gerrish v. Shattuck, 132 Mass. 235; Welch v. Wilcox, 101 Mass. 162; Williams v. Clark, 140 Mass. 238, 5 N. E. 802; Connery v. Brooke, 73 Pa. St. 80. Cf. Baker v. Frick, 45 Md. 337; Attorney General v. Williams, 140 Mass. 329, 2 N. E. 80, and 3 N. E. 214. Plowing part of land over which there is a right of way is not necessarily an interference with the easement. Moffitt v. Lytle, 165 Pa. St. 173, 30 Atl. 922. A contract to permit the use of a wall for a sign space is an easement, and implies the right of such access to the wall as is necessary for the purpose indicated. Gunning v. Cusack, 50 Ill. App. 290.

[48] Shaughnessey v. Leary, 162 Mass. 108, 38 N. E. 197; Waters v. Lumber Co., 115 N. C. 648, 20 S. E. 718. And see post, p. 360. Nor can the use of the dominant tenement be changed so as to increase the burden. Wood v. Saunders, 10 Ch. App. 582.

[49] Washb. Easem. & Serv. (4th Ed.) 730; Doane v. Badger, 12 Mass. 65. But cf. Pomfret v. Ricroft, 1 Saund. 321; Morrison v. Marquardt, 24 Iowa, 35.

[50] Thayer v. Payne, 2 Cush. (Mass.) 327; Prescott v. White, 21 Pick. (Mass.) 341; Williams v. Safford, 7 Barb. (N. Y.) 309; Hamilton v. White, 5 N. Y. 9.

[51] Joyce v. Conlin, 72 Wis. 607, 40 N. W. 212; McCord v. High, 24 Iowa, 336; Amoskeag Manuf'g Co. v. Goodale, 46 N. H. 53. For acts held not to constitute

also remove obstructions to his easement, and may enter upon the servient estate for that purpose.[52] In cases where the title to the easement is clear, the owner of the servient estate may be restrained by injunction from obstructing it.[53]

SAME—DESTRUCTION.

224. Easements may be destroyed
 (a) **By release.**
 (b) **By abandonment.**
 (c) **By license to the servient owner.**
 (d) **By misuser.**
 (e) **By merger.**

An easement may be released to the owner of the servient estate, but such release is not good if by parol, unless it be executed.[54] Easements may also be lost by abandonment,[55] but this does not apply where the easement has been granted, unless there has been claim of adverse right.[56] Easements are lost by abandonment only when they have been acquired by prescription.[57] An easement may also

---

an obstruction, see Green v. Goff, 153 Ill. 534, 39 N. E. 975. That a gate is not an obstruction of a right of way, see Hartman v. Fick, 167 Pa. St. 18, 31 Atl. 342. But see Rowe v. Nally, 81 Md. 367, 32 Atl. 198.

[52] Joyce v. Conlin, 72 Wis. 607, 40 N. W. 212; McCord v. High, 24 Iowa, 336.

[53] Herman v. Roberts, 119 N. Y. 37, 23 N. E. 442; Frey v. Lowden, 70 Cal. 550, 11 Pac. 838; Stallard v. Cushing, 76 Cal. 472, 18 Pac. 427; Schnitzius v. Bailey (N. J. Err. & App.) 32 Atl. 219; Martin v. Price [1894] 1 Ch. 276.

[54] Dyer v. Sanford, 9 Metc. (Mass.) 395; Comstock v. Sharp (Mich.) 64 N. W. 22. A right to use a stairway in a building may be destroyed by the destruction of the building. Douglas v. Coonley, 84 Hun, 158, 32 N. Y. Supp. 444.

[55] Snell v. Levitt, 110 N. Y. 595, 18 N. E. 370; Canny v. Andrews, 123 Mass. 155; Hickox v. Railroad Co., 78 Mich. 615, 44 N. W. 143; Town of Freedom v. Norris, 128 Ind. 377, 27 N. E. 869; Steere v. Tiffany, 13 R. I. 568; Richard v. Hupp (Cal.) 37 Pac. 920. But see Jones v. Van Bochove, 103 Mich. 98, 61 N. W. 342; Pratt v. Sweetser, 68 Me. 344; Duncan v. Rodecker (Wis.) 62 N. W. 533; Suydam v. Dunton, 84 Hun, 506, 32 N. Y. Supp. 338.

[56] Butterfield v. Reed, 160 Mass. 361, 35 N. E. 1128; Barnes v. Lloyd, 112 Mass. 224; Riehle v. Heulings, 38 N. J. Eq. 20; Ford v. Harris (Ga.) 22 S. E. 144; Edgerton v. McMullan, 55 Kan. 90, 39 Pac. 1021; Lovell v. Smith, 3 C. B. (N. S.) 120. See, also, Ward v. Ward, 7 Exch. 838.

[57] Bannon v. Angier, 2 Allen (Mass.) 128; Barnes v. Lloyd, 112 Mass. 224;

be destroyed by a license to the owner of the servient estate to do acts upon his land which interfere with the exercise of the easement;[58] for instance, an easement of light and air may be lost by a permission given the servient owner to erect a wall on his land which would obstruct the light.[59] If the owner of the dominant estate does anything which increases the burden of the easement, he thereby destroys his easement, unless the increase of burden can be separated from the original.[60] Easements are also destroyed by merger; that is, by a union of the dominant and servient estates in the same person.[61] But if the dominant estate is of greater duration than the servient, the easement will only be suspended during the continuance of the servient estate.[62] And if the title to the latter estate is subsequently defeated, the result is the same,—a mere suspension of the easement.[63] When there is a merger, the easement is extinguished, and is not renewed by a subsequent grant of the dominant estate, though the same or a similar easement may be implied, or may arise by necessity.[64]

Smyles v. Hastings, 22 N. Y. 217; Wiggins v. McCleary, 49 N. Y. 346; Nitzell v. Paschall, 3 Rawle (Pa.) 76; Lindeman v. Lindsey, 69 Pa. St. 93; Erb v. Brown, Id. 216; Bombaugh v. Miller, 82 Pa. St. 203. But see Owen v. Field, 102 Mass. 90.

[58] Morse v. Copeland, 2 Gray (Mass.) 302; Addison v. Hack, 2 Gill (Md.) 221; Liggins v. Inge, 7 Bing. 682.

[59] Winter v. Brockwell, 8 East, 308. See, also, Morse v. Copeland, 2 Gray (Mass.) 302.

[60] Washb. Easem. & Serv. (4th Ed.) 704; Jones v. Tapling, 11 C. B. (N. S.) 283. Cf. Harvey v. Walters, L. R. 8 C. P. 162.

[61] McAllister v. Devane, 76 N. C. 57; Ritger v. Parker, 8 Cush. (Mass.) 145.

[62] Thomas v. Thomas, 2 Cromp., M. & R. 34.

[63] Tyler v. Hammond, 11 Pick. (Mass.) 193; Dewal v. Becker, 81 Md. 537, 32 Atl. 308.

[64] Hurlburt v. Firth, 10 Phila. (Pa.) 135; Kieffer v. Imhoff, 26 Pa. St. 438; Miller v. Lapham, 44 Vt. 416; Hazard v. Robinson, 3 Mason, 272, Fed. Cas. No. 6,281.

SPECIFIC EASEMENTS.

225. The following specific easements will be considered:
(a) **Rights of way** (p. 359).
(b) **Highways** (p. 361).
(c) **Light and air** (p. 363).
(d) **Lateral and subjacent support** (p. 365).
(e) **Party walls** (p. 366).
(f) **Easements in water** (p. 368).

SAME—RIGHTS OF WAY.

226. A right of way is an easement in favor of an individual or class of individuals to have a passage on an established line over land of the servient owner to and from land of the dominant owner.

Rights of way are created by the various methods mentioned in discussing easements in general. They, however, frequently arise by implication, as where land granted is represented as bounded or reached by a street.[65] This is the case where a map showing such a street is referred to in the deed.[66] Ways of necessity are also said to arise by implication.[66] They can exist only over land of the grantor, not over that of a stranger.[69] Though the necessity need not be absolute, yet great inconvenience or expense will not be sufficient.[70] Ways of necessity arise chiefly through grants of parcels

---

[65] Tobey v. Taunton, 119 Mass. 404; Franklin Ins. Co. v. Cousens, 127 Mass. 258; Crow v. Wolbert, 7 Phila. (Pa.) 178; Ford v. Harris (Ga.) 22 S. E. 144.

[66] Taylor v. Hopper, 62 N. Y. 649; Regan v. Light Co., 137 Mass. 37; Chapin v. Brown, 15 R. I. 579, 10 Atl. 639.

[66] Holmes v. Seeley, 19 Wend. (N. Y.) 507; Kripp v. Curtis, 71 Cal. 62, 11 Pac. 879; Pernam v. Wead, 2 Mass. 203.

[69] Bass v. Edwards, 126 Mass. 445; Kuhlman v. Hecht, 77 Ill. 570; Taylor v. Warnaky, 55 Cal. 350; Tracy v. Asherton, 35 Vt. 52; Bullard v. Harrison, 4 Maule & S. 387.

[70] Nichols v. Luce, 24 Pick. (Mass.) 102; Oliver v. Pitman, 98 Mass. 46; Francis' Appeal, 96 Pa. St. 200; Parsons v. Johnson, 68 N. Y. 62; Pentland v. Keep, 41 Wis. 490; Field v. Mark, 125 Mo. 502, 28 S. W. 1004.

of land to which there is no access. It is held that the grantor must have intended to give a right to pass over his land to enable the granted estate to be enjoyed.[71] Where such right of way exists, the owner of the servient estate has the first right to select the way.[72] If he neglects to do so, the owner of the dominant estate may locate the way, doing as little damage as possible.[73] The rule is the same as to the location of ways created by express agreement if it is not otherwise provided for.[74] After a right of way has once been located, it cannot be changed without the consent of both parties.[75] Ways of necessity may be used for all purposes necessary for the enjoyment of the dominant estate;[76] but other ways can be used only for the purposes for which they were created.[77] Therefore one who has the right of way to drive beasts to one lot

[71] Nichols v. Luce, 24 Pick. (Mass.) 102; Holmes v. Seely, 19 Wend. (N. Y.) 507; Wissler v. Hershey, 23 Pa. St. 333; Miller v. Richards (Ind. Sup.) 38 N. E. 854; Boyd v. Woolwine (W. Va.) 21 S. E. 1020; Clark v. Cogge, Cro. Jac. 170; Parker v. Welsted, 2 Sid. 39, 111; Pinnington v. Galland, 9 Exch. 1. But see Kingsley v. Improvement Co., 86 Me. 279, 29 Atl. 1074. Cf. Worthington v. Gimson, 2 El. & El. 618; Dodd v. Burchell, 1 Hurl. & C. 113; Wheeldon v. Burrows, 12 Ch. Div. 31. Where one conveys to a railroad company a right of way through his land, so as to cut off access to a part thereof, he has a way of necessity over the land conveyed. New York & N. E. R. Co. v. Board of Railroad Com'rs, 162 Mass. 81, 38 N. E. 27. And see Morris v. Edgington, 3 Taunt. 24.

[72] Schmidt v. Quinn, 136 Mass. 575; Russell v. Jackson, 2 Pick. (Mass.) 574.

[73] Powers v. Harlow, 53 Mich. 507, 19 N. W. 257.

[74] Hart v. Connor, 25 Conn. 331.

[75] Wynkoop v. Burger, 12 Johns. (N. Y.) 222; Smith v. Lee, 14 Gray (Mass.) 473; Kraut's Appeal, 71 Pa. St. 64; Karmuiler v. Krotz, 18 Iowa, 352. When rights of way are acquired by prescription, the user must be of some definite track. Bushey v. Santiff, 86 Hun, 384, 33 N. Y. Supp. 473; Garnett v. City of Slater, 56 Mo. App. 207; Follendore v. Thomas. 93 Ga. 300, 20 S. E. 329.

[76] Gunson v. Healy, 100 Pa. St. 42. A way of necessity ceases as soon as there is another way which the dominant owner can use. Holmes v. Goring, 2 Bing. 76. But see Proctor v. Hodgson, 10 Exch. 824.

[77] Atwater v. Bodfish, 11 Gray (Mass.) 150; French v. Marstin, 24 N. H. 440; Allan v. Gomme, 11 Adol. & E. 759; Wimbledon and Putney Commons Conservators v. Dixon, 1 Ch. Div. 362; Henning v. Burnet, 8 Exch. 187; Corporation of London v. Riggs, 13 Ch. Div. 798. But see Newcomen v. Coulson, 5 Ch. Div. 133; Cannon v. Villars, 8 Ch. Div. 415; Abbott v. Butler, 59 N. H. 317.

cannot drive beasts, over that way, to another lot also.[78] Where there is such an excessive use of a right of way, it will give the servient owner a right of action, but will not justify him in closing the way.[79] A right of way may include the right to erect and maintain a bridge.[80] In the absence of other arrangement, the owner of the dominant estate is required to keep the way in repair.[81] If the owner of the servient estate has agreed to repair, and fails to do so, those entitled to the use of the way may go upon other land of the servient owner, when necessary, to pass around obstructions.[82] Rights of way may be for footpath merely or for carriages, or they may be for both foot and horse.[83] Easements of this kind may be created in such form and with such conditions as the parties choose to impose, by their express contracts.[84]

SAME—HIGHWAYS.

227. Highways are rights of way in the public in general. They may be either
   (a) Easements, or
   (b) Estates in fee simple.

With highways owned in fee simple we have nothing to do in this connection. The ownership in such case is in the public,—the state

---

[78] Howell v. Rex, 1 Mod. 190. And see Skull v. Glenister, 16 C. B. (N. S.) 81; Davenport v. Lampson, 21 Pick. (Mass.) 72; French v. Marstin, 32 N. H. 316; Kirkham v. Sharp, 1 Whart. (Pa.) 323; Lewis v. Carstairs, 6 Whart. (Pa.) 193. Cf. Williams v. James, L. R. 2 C. P. 577; Parks v. Bishop, 120 Mass. 340.

[79] Walker v. Gerhard, 9 Phila. (Pa.) 116; Hayes v. Di Vito, 141 Mass. 233, 4 N. E. 828.

[80] See Schuylkill Nav. Co. v. Stoever, 2 Grant, Cas. (Pa.) 462.

[81] Wynkoop v. Burger, 12 Johns. (N. Y.) 222; Taylor v. Whitehead, 2 Doug. 745. See Gerrard v. Cooke, 2 Bos. & P. N. R. 109.

[82] So when the servient owner has obstructed. Farnum v. Platt, 8 Pick. (Mass.) 339; Leonard v. Leonard, 2 Allen (Mass.) 543; Kent v. Judkins, 53 Me. 160; Haley v. Colcord, 59 N. H. 7. But cf. Taylor v. Whitehead, 2 Doug. 745; Williams v. Safford, 7 Barb. (N. Y.) 309.

[83] Ballard v. Dyson, 1 Taunt. 279; Cowling v. Higginson, 4 Mees. & W. 245.

[84] Whether a way has been created or granted is in each case a matter of construction. Espley v. Wilkes, L. R. 7 Exch. 298; Kay v. Oxley, L. R. 10 Q. B. 360.

or the municipality.[85] It has already been said that highways are not easements proper, because they are held in gross, and not appendant to any dominant estate.[86] When a highway is only an easement, the owners on each side of the road hold the fee to the middle, subject to the right of the public to pass over it.[87] The adjoining owners, therefore, are entitled to the trees, minerals, etc.[88] Highways are usually acquired by dedication, either express[89] or implied by user by the public.[90] Highways may also be acquired by the exercise of the right of eminent domain, in which case compensation must be made for the land taken.[91] No deed or other formal act is necessary for the dedication of a highway to the public. The dedication is complete when made and accepted by the public,[92] and use as a highway may be sufficient to constitute an acceptance.[93] Until there is an acceptance by the public, it does not become bound to keep the road in repair, or liable for injuries caused by its being out of repair.[94] Dedication of a highway may be for special pur-

[85] Washb. Easm. & Serv. (4th Ed.) 252.

[86] See Deerfield v. Railroad Co., 144 Mass. 325, 11 N. E. 105; Com. v. Low, 3 Pick. (Mass.) 408; Nudd v. Hobbs, 17 N. H. 524.

[87] Adams v. Rivers, 11 Barb. (N. Y.) 390.

[88] Makepeace v. Worden, 1 N. H. 16; Tucker v. Eldred, 6 R. I. 404; Daily v. State, 51 Ohio, 348, 37 N. E. 710. And see Lade v. Shepherd, 2 Strange, 1004; Reg. v. Pratt, 4 El. & Bl. 860; Perley v. Chandler, 6 Mass. 454; Codman v. Evans, 5 Allen (Mass.) 308; State v. Davis, 80 N. C. 351.

[89] Com. v. Inhabitants of Newbury, 2 Pick. (Mass.) 51; Warren v. President, etc., of Town of Jacksonville, 15 Ill. 236.

[90] James v. Sammis, 132 N. Y. 239, 30 N. E. 502; Buchanan v. Curtis, 25 Wis. 99.

[91] And the owner is entitled to further compensation for an additional burden, such as a railroad, Williams v. Railroad Co., 16 N. Y. 97; or street railway, Craig v. Railway Co., 39 N. Y. 404; or pipes for natural gas, Bloomfield & R. N. Gaslight Co. v. Calkins, 62 N. Y. 386. But otherwise as to sewers and reservoirs, Stoudinger v. Newark, 28 N. J. Eq. 187; West v. Bancroft, 32 Vt. 367; or telegraph lines, Pierce v. Drew, 136 Mass. 75.

[92] Bangor House Proprietary v. Brown, 33 Me. 309. Repairing may not show acceptance. State v. Bradbury, 40 Me. 154.

[93] Buchanan v. Curtis, 25 Wis. 99; Witter v. Damitz, 81 Wis. 385, 51 N. W. 575; Brakken v. Railroad Co., 29 Minn. 41, 11 N. W. 124; Rex v. Inhabitants of Leake, 5 Barn. & Adol. 469.

[94] Reed v. Inhabitants of Northfield, 13 Pick. (Mass.) 94.

poses only.[95] In any case a dedication can be made only by the owner of the fee.[96] A dedication of streets to a city is implied by the owner of land platting it for city lots with streets between them.[97] For injuries to highways and obstructions of them the right of action is in the public. But if any person is specially damaged, he may have an individual action.[98]

SAME—LIGHT AND AIR.

223. An easement of light and air is a right to the uninterrupted flow of light, and possibly air, to the windows of a building over an adjoining lot. This right can be acquired by prescription in only a few of the United States.

At common law, when one had a building near the boundary line of his land, with windows opening on the adjoining lot, and had enjoyed the access of light over such lot during the period required by the statute of limitations for the acquisition of an easement, he was held to have a right not to have the light obstructed.[99] This right would be infringed by the erection of a wall or building which would shut out the light from the windows of the building of the dominant estate.[100] The power to acquire this easement by prescription has

[95] Ayres v. Railroad Co., 52 N. J. Law, 405, 20 Atl. 54; Mercer v. Woodgate, L. R. 5 Q. B. 26; Arnold v. Holbrook, L. R. 8 Q. B. 96.

[96] Baugan v. Mann, 59 Ill. 492; Lee v. Lake, 14 Mich. 12; Warren v. Brown, 31 Neb. 8, 47 N. W. 633.

[97] Taylor v. Hopper, 62 N. Y. 649; Chapin v. Brown, 15 R. I. 579, 10 Atl. 639. Land may be dedicated for public parks in the same manner as for streets. President, etc., of City of Cincinnati v. White, 6 Pet. 431. So as to a burial place. Beatty v. Kurtz, 2 Pet. 566; Hunter v. Trustees of Sandy Hill, 6 Hill (N. Y.) 407.

[98] Ft. Plain Bridge Co. v. Smith, 30 N. Y. 44; Rogers v. Rogers, 14 Wend. (N. Y.) 131; State v. Parrott, 71 N. C. 311. And see Bateman v. Bluck, 18 Q. B. Div. 870; McKee v. Perchment, 69 Pa. St. 342. For the right to go on adjoining land when a highway is impassable, see Absor v. French, 2 Show. 28; Campbell v. Race, 7 Cush. (Mass.) 408.

[99] Cross v. Lewis, 2 Barn. & C. 686; Compton v. Richards, 1 Price, 27; Renshaw v. Bean, 18 Q. B. 112. Cf. White v. Bass, 7 Hurl. & N. 722; Haynes v. King [1893] 3 Ch. 439; Callis v. Laugher [1894] 3 Ch. 659.

[100] The inconvenience caused must be appreciable. Back v. Stacey, 2 Car. & P. 465; Wells v. Ody, 7 Car. & P. 410; Arcedeckne v. Kelk, 2 Giff. 683.

been recognized in only a few states.[101] It may, however, be acquired by express grant, and in some states it is held that it may be raised by implied grant, as when there is a conveyance of land with buildings on it which overlook a vacant lot of the grantor.[102] Where the easement may be acquired by prescription, its acquisition may be prevented by the erection of any structure which shuts off the light before the full period has elapsed which is required by the statute of limitations.[103] When the right exists, the burden on the servient estate must not be increased by the opening of new windows or the enlargement of old ones.[104] If the old building is destroyed or pulled down, the easement can be claimed for a new structure erected in its place only when the windows are substantially the same as before.[105] A change in the use of the building, however, does not destroy nor enlarge the right.[106] In speaking of this easement, the word "air" is usually added to the word "light," though it seems that this is incorrect, and that the easement is only for the passage of light.[107] No easement in a view or prospect can be acquired by prescription.[108]

[101] Gerber v. Grabel, 16 Ill. 217 (but contra, Guest v. Reynolds, 68 Ill. 478); Robeson v. Pittenger, 2 N. J. Eq. 57; Sutphen v. Therkelson, 38 N. J. Eq. 318; Durel v. Boisblanc, 1 La. Ann. 407; Clawson v. Primrose, 4 Del. Ch. 643. It is denied in the following: Parker v. Foote, 19 Wend. (N. Y.) 309; Keats v. Hugo, 115 Mass. 204; Mullen v. Stricker, 19 Ohio St. 135; Haverstick v. Sipe, 33 Pa. St. 368. So, by statute, in some states. 1 Stim. Am. St. Law, § 2254; 4 Shars. & B. Lead. Cas. Real Prop. 246.

[102] Palmer v. Fletcher, 1 Lev. 122; U. S. v. Appleton, 1 Sumn. 492, Fed. Cas. No. 14,463; Sutphen v. Therkelson, 38 N. J. Eq. 318. But see Maynard v. Esher, 17 Pa. St. 222; Doyle v. Lord, 64 N. Y. 432; Rennyson's Appeal, 94 Pa. St. 147.

[103] Bury v. Pope, Cro. Eliz. 118. And see, Pearson, P. J., in Shell v. Kemmerer, 13 Phila. 502. And the easement may be lost by abandonment. Moore v. Rawson, 3 Barn. & C. 332. But cf. Stokoe v. Singers, 8 El. & Bl. 31; Ecclesiastical Com'rs v. Kino, 14 Ch. Div. 213.

[104] Blanchard v. Bridges, 4 Adol. & E. 176.

[105] Cherrington v. Abney Mil, 2 Vern. 646.

[106] Martin v. Goble, 1 Camp. 320.

[107] But see American Bank-Note Co. v. New York El. R. Co., 129 N. Y. 252, 29 N. E. 302; Field v. Barling, 149 Ill. 556, 37 N. E. 850; Barnett v. Johnson, 15 N. J. Eq. 481. As to windmills, see Washb. Easem. (4th Ed.) 669.

[108] Butt v. Gas Co., 2 Ch. App. 158. But see Kirkwood v. Finegan, 95 Mich. 543, 55 N. W. 457; Kessler v. Letts, 7 Ohio Cir. Ct. R. 108.

SAME—LATERAL AND SUBJACENT SUPPORT.

229. The easement of lateral support is the right to have one's ground supported so that it will not cave in when an adjoining owner makes an excavation. It exists only for the land itself, and not for erections on the land.

230. The easement of subjacent support is a similar right between the owners of land which has been partitioned horizontally.

The right to lateral support is, as already said, a right to have land supported by the adjoining land.[109] It is a natural, rather than a conventional, easement. The right exists only for the land itself, and not when the burden has been increased by greater weight placed upon the land through the erection of buildings or other structures.[110] The right to the support of land with the buildings on it may, however, be acquired by prescription.[111] When such easement does not exist, the adjoining owner must, nevertheless, make excavation in a reasonable manner, and give notice to the other party of his intention to excavate, so that the latter may take the necessary steps to prevent his buildings from falling in.[112]

The right to subjacent support is also a natural right, but exists only where land has been partitioned horizontally. This is the case when the surface belongs to one owner and the right to the minerals imbedded in the soil to another. The latter must not so

---

[109] Gilmore v. Driscoll, 122 Mass. 199; Tunstall v. Christian, 80 Va. 1; Transportation Co. v. Chicago, 99 U. S. 635. Cf. Corporation of Birmingham v. Allen, 6 Ch. Div. 284. As to support of a house by a house, see Solomon v. Master, etc., of Mystery of Vintners, 4 Hurl. & N. 585; Richards v. Rose, 9 Exch. 218.

[110] Thurston v. Hancock, 12 Mass. 220; Gilmore v. Driscoll, 122 Mass. 199; Panton v. Holland, 17 Johns. (N. Y.) 92; Smith v. Thackerah, L. R. 1 C. P. 564. But see Brown v. Robins, 4 Hurl. & N. 186.

[111] Hunt v. Peake, Johns. Eng. Ch. 705; Partridge v. Scott, 3 Mees. & W. 220.

[112] Lasala v. Halbrook, 4 Paige (N. Y.) 169; Moody v. McClelland, 39 Ala. 45; Austin v. Railroad Co., 25 N. Y. 334; Shafer v. Wilson, 44 Md. 268; Dodd v. Holme, 1 Adol. & E. 493; Chadwick v. Trower, 6 Bing. N. C. 1.

operate his mine as to cause the surface to fall in.[113] The person working the mines, however, is not required to furnish support for buildings which have been placed upon the land after the severance of the ownership of the mines and the surface, unless such increased easement has been acquired by lapse of time. But, even when buildings have been thus placed upon the surface, there would be a liability for negligent excavations.[114]

Horizontal Ownership of Buildings.

The same principles apply to the horizontal ownership of buildings. The owner of the upper stories of a house has a right to support from the owner of the lower portion, and an easement in the use of the halls and stairs.[115] The owner of the lower floors has an easement of protection by the roof.[116] The two owners must so use their property as not to injure each other. But the law as to their rights is still very unsettled. Some cases hold that the upper owner must keep the roof in repair;[117] others say that if he fails to do so the lower owner may enter to make the necessary repairs; while still other cases tend towards the French rule, which holds that the expenses are to be borne equally.[118]

SAME—PARTY WALLS.

231. Party walls are walls used to support contiguous structures which belong to different proprietors.

A party wall does not necessarily have any connection with easements, for it may "(1) belong to the adjoining proprietors as tenants in common;[119] (2) it may be divided longitudinally into two

---

[113] Jones v. Wagner, 66 Pa. St. 429; Humphries v. Brogden, 12 Q. B. Div. 739.

[114] Marvin v. Mining Co., 55 N. Y. 538; Bonomi v. Backhouse, El., Bl. & El. 622; Rowbotham v. Wilson, 8 H. L. Cas. 348.

[115] Mayo v. Newhoff, 47 N. J. Eq. 31, 19 Atl. 837; Rhodes v. McCormack, 4 Iowa, 368; Humphries v. Brogden, 12 Q. B. Div. 739; Harris v. Ryding, 5 Mees. & W. 60.

[116] Wright, C. J., in Rhodes v. McCormack, 4 Iowa, 368, 376.

[117] Loring v. Bacon, 4 Mass. 575; Ottumwa Lodge, etc., v. Lewis, 34 Iowa, 67; Cheeseborough v. Green, 10 Conn. 318; Keilw. 98b, pl. 4; Anon., 11 Mod. 7.

[118] Pierce v. Dyer, 109 Mass. 374; Loring v. Bacon, 4 Mass. 575.

[119] Cubitt v. Porter, 8 Barn. & C. 257; Watson v. Gray, 14 Ch. Div. 192.

strips, each strip belonging to the adjoining owner in severalty;[120] (3) it may belong wholly to one proprietor, subject to a right held by the other to have it maintained as a party wall; (4) it may be divided longitudinally into two moieties, each moiety subject to a cross easement, a right of support in favor of the other."[121] Party walls are, however, usually built one-half on the land of each proprietor. If a wall is so built by one party, the other need not pay one-half its cost without an express agreement.[122] It is usual for one of the adjoining proprietors to build the wall and the other to pay his half when he has occasion to use the wall. In some states, by statute, one owner is permitted to build one-half of a wall on the land of an adjoining proprietor, whether the latter consents or not.[123] Such a statute has been held unconstitutional in Massachusetts.[124] An agreement to pay for one-half of a party wall when used does not bind assignees unless recorded, or there is notice.[125] When walls are constructed one-half on the land of each, each owner has an easement in the land of the other for the support of the wall.[126] But this easement in the other's land is lost by the destruction of the wall.[127] When the wall becomes ruinous, either may repair and compel contribution by the other;[128] but

[120] Matts v. Hawkins, 5 Taunt. 20. Where one intending to construct a wall within the line of his lot by mistake extends his foundation slightly onto an adjoining lot, the wall does not thereby become a party wall. Pile v. Pedrick, 167 Pa. St. 296, 31 Atl. 646, 647.

[121] Thomp. Fixt. & Easem. 93; Burton v. Moffitt, 3 Or. 29.

[122] Walker v. Stetson, 162 Mass. 86, 38 N. E. 18; Wilkins v. Jewett, 139 Mass. 29, 29 N. E. 214; McCord v. Herrick, 18 Ill. App. 423; Preiss v. Parker, 67 Ala. 500.

[123] 1 Stim. Am. St. Law, § 2170.

[124] Wilkins v. Jewett, 139 Mass. 29, 29 N. E. 214.

[125] Sebald v. Mulholland, 11 Misc. Rep. 714, 31 N. Y. Supp. 863; Sherred v. Cisco, 4 Sandf. (N. Y.) 480; Joy v. Bank, 115 Mass. 60; Cole v. Hughes, 54 N. Y. 444; Conduitt v. Ross, 102 Ind. 166, 26 N. E. 198. Cf. Frohman v. Dickinson, 11 Misc. Rep. 9, 31 N. Y. Supp. 851. But cf. Savage v. Mason, 3 Cush. (Mass.) 500; Maine v. Cumston, 98 Mass. 317; Standish v. Lawrence, 111 Mass. 111.

[126] Brooks v. Curtis, 50 N. Y. 639; Ingals v. Plamondon, 75 Ill. 118; Andrae v. Haseltine, 58 Wis. 395, 17 N. W. 18.

[127] Partridge v. Gilbert, 15 N. Y. 601; Sherred v. Cisco, 4 Sandf. (N. Y.) 480; Hoffman v. Kuhn, 57 Miss. 746.

[128] Campbell v. Mesier, 4 Johns. Ch. (N. Y.) 334. Cf., however, Pierce v. Dyer, 109 Mass. 374.

if the wall has been destroyed there is no right to compel the other party to stand half of the expense of rebuilding.[129] Each owner, in using the wall, must do nothing to weaken it or otherwise to injure the adjoining proprietor.[130]

Partition Fences.

Partition fences are in many respects like party walls. They are usually erected one-half on the land of each, and the obligation to repair is the same as in the case of party walls.[131] The duty to maintain such fences may exist by reason of a statute,[132] or it may arise from agreement or prescription.[133] Such fences are usually divided into halves, each owner being required to maintain his half.

SAME—EASEMENTS IN WATER.

232. The owner of land fronting on a natural water course has the right to have it maintained in its natural condition; that is, the water must not be prevented from coming to him or from flowing away, or be polluted.

Water, as a subject of ownership, was discussed somewhat in our first chapter. Rights in water depend largely on whether the water is naturally on the land or has been brought there by artificial means.[134] Rights in water in its natural state consist almost entirely in a right to use it as contrasted with ownership of it. When there is a defined water course, one who owns the land over which it flows, or who owns land on one bank of the stream, has a

---

[129] Sherred v. Cisco, 4 Sandf. (N. Y.) 480; Partridge v. Gilbert, 15 N. Y. 601.

[130] Dowling v. Hemings, 20 Md. 179; Brodbee v. Mayor, etc., of London, 4 Man. & G. 714.

[131] 1 Stim. Am. St. Law, § 2185. One may be bound to repair the whole by prescription, Binney v. Proprietors, 5 Pick. (Mass.) 503; Anon., Y. B. 19 Hen. VI. p. 33, pl. 68; Star v. Rookesby, 1 Salk. 335; Lawrence v. Jenkins, L. R. 8 Q. B. 274; or by contract, Bronson v. Coffin, 108 Mass. 175, reversed as to measure of damages, 118 Mass. 156.

[132] 1 Stim. Am. St. Law, art. 218.

[133] Cowles v. Balzer, 47 Barb. (N. Y.) 562.

[134] See ante, p. 4; Earl v. De Hart, 12 N. J. Eq. 280.

§ 232)   EASEMENTS IN WATER.   369

right to have the flow continue without unreasonable interference by the riparian owners, either above or below him.[135] In order that there may be such a water course, a continuous flow is not necessary. It is sufficient if water flows in the channels at certain seasons of the year.[136] A riparian owner [137] has a right to use the water in a reasonable way, but he must not divert it from its course,* or detain it more than a reasonable time.[138] So he has no right to corrupt the water which flows over his land, unless such right is acquired by prescription or otherwise.[139] Furthermore, he must not dam up the water, and cause it to flow back on the lands of the owners above,[140] though, of course, an easement of this kind may

[135] Darlington v. Painter, 7 Pa. St. 473; Prescott v. White, 21 Pick. (Mass.) 341; Omelvany v. Jaggers, 2 Hill (S. C.) 634; Tyler v. Wilkinson, 4 Mason, 397, Fed. Cas. No. 14,312; Embrey v. Owen, 6 Exch. 353; Williams v. Morland, 2 Barn. & C. 910; Miner v. Gilmour, 12 Moore, P. C. 131; Wood v. Waud, 3 Exch. 748; Earl of Sandwich v. Railway Co., 10 Ch. Div. 707; Sampson v. Hoddinott, 1 C. B. (N. S.) 590.

[136] Shields v. Arndt, 4 N. J. Eq. 234; Eulrich v. Richter, 41 Wis. 318; New York, C. & St. L. R. Co. v. Speelman, 12 Ind. App. 372, 40 N. E. 541; R'gney v. Water Co., 9 Wash. 576, 38 Pac. 147.

[137] As to easements in persons not riparian owners, see Stockport Waterworks Co. v. Potter, 3 Hurl. & C. 300; Ormerod v. Mill Co., 11 Q. B. Div. 155; Nuttall v. Bracewell, L. R. 2 Exch. 1; Bristol Hydraulic Co. v. Boyer, 67 Ind. 236.

* Hogg v. Water Co., 168 Pa. St. 456, 31 Atl. 1010; Green Bay & M. Canal Co. v. Kaukauna Water Power Co., 90 Wis. 370, 61 N. W. 1121, and 63 N. W. 1019; Southern Marble Co. v. Darnell, 94 Ga. 231, 21 S. E. 531; Vernon Irrigation Co. v. City of Los Angeles, 106 Cal. 237, 39 Pac. 762. But a stream may be diverted if it is returned to the established channels before passing off the land of the one diverting it. Missouri Pac. Ry. Co. v. Keys, 55 Kan. 205, 40 Pac. 275.

[138] Pitts v. Lancaster Mills, 13 Metc. (Mass.) 156; Elliot v. Railway Co., 10 Cush. (Mass.) 191; Garwood v. Railroad Co., 83 N. Y. 400; Snow v. Parsons, 28 Vt. 459; Canfield v. Andrew, 54 Vt. 1; Gillis v. Chase (N. H.) 31 Atl. 18; Blodgett v. Stone, 60 N. H. 167; Vernon Irrigation Co. v. City of Los Angeles, 106 Cal. 237, 39 Pac. 762. Cf. Wheatley v. Chrisman, 24 Pa. St. 298. As to custom to show reasonable use, see Canfield v. Andrew, 54 Vt. 1.

[139] Jackman v. Arlington Mills, 137 Mass. 277; Smith v. Cranford, 84 Hun, 318, 32 N. Y. Supp. 375; Lewis v. Stein, 16 Ala. 214; Hayes v. Waldron, 44 N. H. 580; People v. Elk River Mill & Lumber Co., 107 Cal. 214, 40 Pac. 486.

[140] McCoy v. Danley, 20 Pa. St. 85; Sprague v. Worcester, 13 Gray (Mass.) 193; Railroad Co. v. Carr, 38 Ohio St. 448.

REAL PROP.—24

be acquired,[141] and in some states a mill owner may exercise the power of eminent domain in order to acquire such right.[142] Rights to change the natural uses of water are easements, and must be acquired in the same ways as other conventional easements.[143] In some states, the one first appropriating a stream of water especially for use in irrigation obtains the first right to the water [144] to the extent of his appropriation.[145] The rights of owners whose lands border on navigable streams are the same, so far as the law of easements is concerned, as the rights of other riparian owners; but they must not obstruct navigation.[146] Where rivers are used by boom companies for the transportation of logs, the rule is that the first in has the first right to the use of the current; but they must not cause unnecessary obstruction.[147]

---

[141] But long user will not give a right to prevent the erection of a mill above. Thurber v. Martin, 2 Gray (Mass.) 394.

[142] Washb. Easem. (4th Ed.) 445.

[143] Russell v. Scott, 9 Cow. (N. Y.) 279; Postlethwaite v. Payne, 8 Ind. 104; Smith v. Russ, 17 Wis. 234. Cf. Shury v. Piggot, 3 Bulst. 339.

[144] Smith v. O'Hara, 43 Cal. 371; Schilling v. Rommger, 4 Colo. 100; Barnes v. Sabron, 10 Nev. 217; Wimer v. Simmons (Or.) 39 Pac. 6. Such appropriation on public lands is authorized by congress. Rev. St. U. S. §§ 2339, 2340. The right may be lost by abandonment. Vernon Irrigation Co. v. City of Los Angeles, 106 Cal. 237, 39 Pac. 762; Beaver Brook Reservoir & Canal Co. v. St. Vrain Reservoir & Fish Co. (Colo. App.) 40 Pac. 1066. See, also, Sampson v. Hoddinott, 1 C. B. (N. S.) 590; Embrey v. Owen, 6 Exch. 353.

[145] Creek v. Waterworks Co., 15 Mont. 121, 38 Pac. 459.

[146] Ensminger v. People, 47 Ill. 384; Gifford v. McArthur, 55 Mich. 535, 22 N. W. 28; Bainbridge v. Sherlock, 29 Ind. 364; Fulmer v. Williams, 122 Pa. St. 191, 15 Atl. 726; Field v. Driving Co., 67 Wis. 569, 31 N. W. 17. And see Original Hartlepool Collieries Co. v. Gibb, 5 Ch. Div. 713. The public are not entitled to a tow path along a navigable river. Ball v. Herbert, 3 Term R. 253. Contra, Reg. v. Inhabitants of Cluworth, 6 Mod. 163; Young v. ———, 1 Ld. Raym. 725.

[147] Butterfield v. Gilchrist, 53 Mich. 22, 18 N. W. 542; Sullivan v. Jernigan, 21 Fla. 264. Cf. Brown v. Chadbourne, 31 Me. 9; Gwaltney v. Land Co., 115 N. C. 579, 20 S. E. 465. As to what streams are "floatable," see Commissioners of Burke Co. v. Catawha Lumber Co., 116 N. C. 731, 21 S. E. 941.

Subterranean Waters.

Underground waters, when not flowing in a defined course,[148] but existing merely as percolations, may be diverted,[149] although by so doing the wells of adjoining landowners may be injured.[150] Upon the same principle, in working a mine, subterranean waters may be drawn off from the surrounding land without incurring liability.[151] But underground percolations must not be fouled by the introduction of foreign substances.[152] No easements can be acquired by prescription in subterranean waters, because the user necessary to acquire such rights would be unknown, and therefore not adverse.[153]

Surface Waters.

Surface waters are such as do not flow in a regular channel.[154] The cases are conflicting as to the duty of a lower owner to receive such waters onto his land,[155] but it certainly does not exist in the

[148] See Grand Junction Canal Co. v. Shugar, 6 Ch. App. 483. Dudden v. Guardians of Poor of the Clutton Union, 1 Hurl. & N. 627; West Cumberland Iron & Steel Co. v. Kenyon, 6 Ch. Div. 773; Burroughs v. Saterlee, 67 Iowa, 396, 25 N. W. 808.

[149] Chatfield v. Wilson, 28 Vt. 49; Phelps v. Nowlen, 72 N. Y. 39. But see Pixley v. Clark, 35 N. Y. 520. Under Rev. St. U. S. § 2339. Rights in percolating waters may be acquired by prior appropriation. Sullivan v. Mining Co. (Utah) 40 Pac. 709.

[150] Bloodgood v. Ayres, 108 N. Y. 400, 15 N. E. 433; Chasemore v. Richards, 7 H. L. Cas. 349; and ante, p. 5. But see Chesley v. King, 74 Me. 164; Hollingsworth & Vose Co. v. Foxborough Water-Supply Dist. (Mass.) 42 N. E. 574.

[151] Acton v. Blundell, 12 Mees. & W. 324; Popplewell v. Hodkinson, L. R. 4 Exch. 248. The use must not be malicious or extravagant. Willis v. City of Perry (Iowa) 60 N. W. 727. Cf. Horner v. Watson, 79 Pa. St. 242.

[152] Ball v. Nye, 99 Mass. 582; Wahle v. Reinbach, 76 Ill. 322; Pottstown Gas Co. v. Murphy, 39 Pa. St. 257. But see Upjohn v. Board, 46 Mich. 542, 9 N. W. 845.

[153] Lybe's Appeal, 106 Pa. St. 626; Haldeman v. Bruckhart, 45 Pa. St. 514. Cf. Davis v. Spaulding, 157 Mass. 431, 32 N. E. 650; Acton v. Blundell, 12 Mees. & W. 324. But see Smith v. Adams, 6 Paige (N. Y.) 435; Balston v. Bensted, 1 Camp. 463.

[154] Gibbs v. Williams, 25 Kan. 214; Eulrich v. Richter, 37 Wis. 226, 41 Wis. 318; Hebron Gravel Road Co. v. Harvey, 90 Ind. 192; Earl v. De Hart, 12 N. J. Eq. 280; Bowlsby v. Speer, 31 N. J. Law, 351.

[155] That he must receive surface water, see Adams v. Walker, 34 Conn. 466. Contra, Gannon v. Hargadon, 10 Allen (Mass.) 106; Barkley v. Wilcox, 86

case of city property.[156] Surface waters must not be collected by one proprietor and discharged upon the land of his neighbor in any increased quantity in one place,[157] unless the discharge be into a regular water course.[158] Surface water may be appropriated, and prevented from reaching the natural water courses, without incurring liability.[159]

Eaves' Drip.

The right to have water fall from the roof of one's building onto the land of another is an easement, and is called the right of "eaves' drip."[160] This right may be acquired by prescription.[161]

Artificial Water Courses.

As already stated, rights in water which has been brought upon land by artificial means differ in many respects from the rights which we have been discussing.[162] For instance, an artificial water course cannot be established without the consent of the lower proprietor.[163] But when such a water course has been established, no right is acquired to have it continued,[164] though it must not be

---

N. Y. 140; Lessard v. Stram, 62 Wis. 112, 22 N. W. 284; Abbott v. Railway Co., 83 Mo. 271; Hill v. Railroad Co., 109 Ind. 511, 10 N. E. 410.

[156] Parks v. Newburyport, 10 Gray (Mass.) 28; Barkley v. Wilcox, 86 N. Y. 140.

[157] Noonan v. Albany, 79 N. Y. 470; Curtis v. Railroad Co., 98 Mass. 428; Hogenson v. Railway Co., 31 Minn. 224, 17 N. W. 374; Hurdman v. Railway Co., 3 C. P. Div. 168. When by the operation of pumps more water is discharged upon the land of a lower proprietor than would flow there naturally, the upper proprietor is liable for any damage which he could have prevented at a reasonable cost. Pfeiffer v. Brown, 165 Pa. St. 267, 30 Atl. 844.

[158] McCormick v. Horan, 81 N. Y. 86; Waffle v. Railroad Co., 53 N. Y. 11; Peck v. Herrington, 109 Ill. 611; Jackman v. Arlington Mills, 137 Mass. 277.

[159] Bowlsby v. Speer, 31 N. J. Law, 351; Broadbent v. Ramsbotham, 11 Exch. 602.

[160] Neale v. Seeley, 47 Barb. (N. Y.) 314. Cf. Billows v. Sackett, 15 Barb. (N. Y.) 96; Harvey v. Walters, L. R. 8 C. P. 162.

[161] Neale v. Seeley, 47 Barb. (N. Y.) 314.

[162] Ante, p. 368.

[163] Norton v. Volentine, 14 Vt. 239.

[164] Norton v. Volentine, 14 Vt. 239; Wood v. Waud, 3 Exch. 748; Greatrex v. Hayward, 8 Exch. 291; Arkwright v. Gell, 5 Mees. & W. 203; Brymbo Water Co. v. Lesters Lime Co., 8 Reports, 329. But such a right may be acquired by prescription. Cole v. Bradbury, 86 Me. 380, 29 Atl. 1097.

maliciously fouled by the one establishing it.[165] The right to lay water pipes across another's land is an easement,[166] and carries with it the right to enter on such land to repair the pipes.[167]

PROFITS A PRENDRE.

233. A profit a prendre is a right exercised by one man in the land of another, accompanied by a participation in the profits of that land.

Profits à prendre have already been distinguished from easements as being a right to take a profit out of another man's land.[168] These rights may be as various as the nature of the soil and the things which grow thereon or are imbedded in it will permit.[169] For instance, there may be a right to mine for metals or for coal, a right to take wood or turf, or any other product of the land.[170] Profits à prendre have to do with our system of law chiefly as rights of common. These rights of common were privileges which the lord of an English manor granted to his tenants to take certain profits from his waste land. The principal rights of common were (1) common of pasture, (2) common of turbary, (3) common of estovers, (4) common of piscary. The first, or common of pasture, was a right in the tenants to turn their cattle out to graze on the lord's waste. The number of cattle which each tenant had a right to depasture was strictly regulated by the local customs.[171] Commons of pasture are either appurtenant or appendant.[172] The latter ex-

[165] Magor v. Chadwick, 11 Adol. & E. 571.
[166] Goodrich v. Burbank, 12 Allen (Mass.) 459; Bissell v. Grant, 35 Conn. 288. Cf. Amidon v. Harris, 113 Mass. 59.
[167] See Goodrich v. Burbank, 12 Allen (Mass.) 459. So to enter and clean a railway for a mill. Prescott v. White, 21 Pick. (Mass.) 341.
[168] Ante, p. 350. See, also, Race v. Ward, 4 El. & Bl. 702; Wickham v. Hawker, 7 Mees. & W. 63.
[169] A right to take water from a spring is not a profit à prendre. Race v. Ward, 4 El. & Bl. 702.
[170] Waters v. Lilley, 4 Pick. (Mass.) 145; Tinicum Fishing Co. v. Carter, 61 Pa. St. 21; Hill v. Lord, 48 Me. 83.
[171] Whitelock v. Hutchinson, 2 Moody & R. 205; Carr v. Lambert, L. R. 1 Exch. 168.
[172] 2 Bl. Comm. 33.

ist only in connection with arable land,[173] and give a right to pasture no other beasts than those of the plow; that is, those beasts which are necessary to the cultivation of the land to which the common is appendant. Commons of pasture appendant do not exist in the United States. Commons of pasture appurtenant may exist in connection with any kind of land, and give a right to pasture other beasts than those of the plow.[174] Common of turbary is the right to take turf or peat for fuel to burn in the tenant's house. The same term would apply to the right to take coal.[175] Common of estovers corresponded to the right of estovers, which has already been defined,[176] and the kinds are the same. Common of piscary is a right to fish in the lord's waters.[177] It has been seen that the owner of land has the exclusive right to fish in waters thereon, except in the case of navigable rivers.[178] Such an owner must not, however, obstruct the passage of fish up and down.[179] The right to fish in another man's waters may be created by express grant or acquired by prescription.[180] The right to take fish is now very largely regulated by statute in the various states. With rights of common, or any other profits à prendre, there is no obligation to maintain a supply of the things to which the right exist.[181] Commons are the same as easements in their method of creation [182] and

[173] Anon., Y. B. 26 Hen. VIII., p. 4. pl. 15.

[174] Cowlam v. Slack, 15 East, 108; Commissioners of Sewers v. Glasse, L. R. 19 Eq. 134; Baylis v. Tyssen-Amhurst, 6 Ch. Div. 500.

[175] 2 Bl. Comm. 34. See Wilkinson v. Proud, 11 Mees. & W. 33; Caldwell v. Fulton, 31 Pa. St. 475; Massot v. Moses, 3 S. C. 168.

[176] Ante, p. 81.

[177] 2 Bl. Comm. 34.

[178] Ante, p. 5.

[179] Parker v. People, 111 Ill. 581; Boatwright v. Bookman, 1 Rice (S. C.) 447. And see Case v. Weber, 2 Cart. (Ind.) 108.

[180] Treary v. Cooke, 14 Mass. 488; Melvin v. Whiting, 7 Pick. (Mass.) 79; Smith v. Kemp, 2 Salk. 637; Benett v. Costar, 8 Taunt. 183; Seymour v. Courtenay, 5 Burrows, 2814.

[181] See Rivers v. Adams, 3 Exch. Div. 361; Chilton v. Corporation of London, 7 Ch. Div. 735.

[182] Tottel v. Howell, Noy, 54; Duke of Somerset v. Fogwell, 5 Barn. & C. 875; Bailey v. Stephens, 12 C. B. (N. S.) 91; Pitt v. Chick, Hut. 45; Huntington v. Asher, 96 N. Y. 604. Common appendant can be acquired only by prescription. 2 Bl. Comm. 33. And see Smith v. Floyd, 18 Barb. (N. Y.) 522; Smith v. Gatewood, Cro. Jac. 152.

destruction.[183] They are subject to merger,[184] and common appurtenant is extinguished by an alienation of a part of the land to which the right is attached.[185] They descend with the land, but cannot be devised separate from the land.[186] Rights of common are rare in the United States, but a number of cases have come before the courts, in which these rights have been considered. For any more than this brief outline of rights of common the reader is referred to those cases which will be found in the notes.[187] Profits à prendre other than rights of common are merely matters of contract rights between the owner of the land and the grantee of the profit.[188] They are closely allied to licenses, which have already been considered.[189]

RENTS.

234. Rent is a profit issuing out of land, which is to be rendered or paid periodically by the tenant. Rents are of the following kinds:

(a) **Rent service.**

(b) **Rent charge.**

(c) **Rent seck.**

235. Rents charge and seck are called "fee farm rents."

[183] Van Rensselaer v. Radcliff, 10 Wend. (N. Y.) 639. See Drury v. Kent, Cro. Jac. 14.

[184] Bradshaw v. Eyre, Cro. Eliz. 570; Saundeys v. Oliff, Moore, 467.

[185] Tyrringham's Case, 4 Coke, 36b; Van Rensselaer v. Radcliff, 10 Wend. (N. Y.) 639; Watts v. Coffin, 11 Johns. (N. Y.) 495; Leyman v. Abeel, 16 Johns. (N. Y.) 30; Livingston v. Ketcham, 1 Barb. (N. Y.) 592; Livingston v. Ten Broeck, 16 Johns. (N. Y.) 14; Bell v. Railroad Co., 25 Pa. St. 161. But see Hall v. Lawrence, 2 R. I. 218.

[186] Livingston v. Ketcham, 1 Barb. (N. Y.) 592. But see Welcome v. Upton, 6 Mees. & W. 536; Leyman v. Abeel, 16 Johns. (N. Y.) 30. As to apportionment of commons, see Van Rensselaer v. Radcliff, 10 Wend. (N. Y.) 639; Livingston v. Ten Broeck, 16 Johns. (N. Y.) 14.

[187] Van Rensselaer v. Radcliff, 10 Wend. (N. Y.) 639; Livingston v. Ten Broeck, 16 Johns. (N. Y.) 14; Leyman v. Abeel, Id. 30; Smith v. Floyd, 18 Barb. (N. Y.) 522; Livingston v. Ketcham, 1 Barb. (N. Y.) 592; Inhabitants of

[188] Anon., Dyer, 285, pl. 40. See Wilson v. Mackreth, 3 Burrows, 1824; Cox v. Glue, 5 C. B. 533.

[189] Ante, p. 165.

Rents have already been considered in treating of landlord and tenant,[191] but they will here be discussed as incorporeal hereditaments. As such they are rights to receive money out of the profits of land. Estates may be created in rents, and for such purpose the same words of limitation are to be used as in creating estates in corporeal property.[192] Estates so created are good only to the extent of the grantor's interest in the rent or in the land out of which the rent issues. Estates in rent are subject to dower and curtesy, like corresponding corporeal estates;[193] and when the estate in the rent is one of inheritance it descends to the heirs.[194] The classes of rents have been named in the black letter. Rent service was the only kind of rent originally known to the common law. It was accompanied by tenure and was given as a compensation for the services for which the land originally was liable. Distress was always an incident of rent service.[195] The statute of quia emptores, by abolishing subinfeudation, prevented the creation of a rent service in fee;[196] but such rents may exist in those states in which the statute of quia emptores has not been adopted,[197] and they may exist in all states when the rent is less than a fee simple.[198] A rent seck is one which is created by agreement of the parties, but no relation of tenure exists, and there was no right of distress at common law for the recovery of the rent,[199] though the right was given by the statute of 4 George II. c. 28, § 5. Rent charge is the

Worcester v. Green, 2 Pick. (Mass.) 425; Bell v. Railroad Co., 25 Pa. St. 161; Trustees of Western University v. Robinson, 12 Serg. & R. 29; Carr v. Wallace, 7 Watts (Pa.) 394; Hall v. Lawrence, 2 R. I. 218; Peck v. Lockwood, 5 Day (Conn.) 22.

[191] Ante, p. 134.

[192] Van Rensselaer v. Hays, 19 N. Y. 68; Van Rensselaer v. Read, 26 N. Y. 558.

[193] 2 Washb. Real Prop. (5th Ed.) 288; ante, p. 87.

[194] See Sacheverel v. Frogate, 1 Vent. 161. But it may be a chattel only, as when reserved on a lease for years. Knolles' Case, Dyer, 5b.

[195] Kenege v. Elliot, 9 Watts (Pa.) 258.

[196] Van Rensselaer v. Read, 26 N. Y. 563; Van Rensselaer v. Hays, 19 N. Y. 68.

[197] Wallace v. Harmstad, 44 Pa. St. 492; Ingersoll v. Sergeant, 1 Whart (Pa.) 337. See ante, p. 30.

[198] 2 Washb. Real Prop. (5th Ed.) 286.

[199] 2 Bl. Comm. 42; Cornell v. Lamb, 2 Cow. (N. Y.) 652.

§§ 234-235) RENTS. 877

same thing as rent seck, except that a right of distress is given by the original agreement of the parties.[200] These two forms of rent are called collectively "fee farm rents," and differ only in the matter of the right of distress. Fee farm rents seldom occur in the United States. They may be used for the same purpose as a mortgage. Fee farm rents are often used in England to raise portions for heirs and jointures for married women.[201] Rents may be created either by deed[202] or by prescription.[203] When created by deed, it may be by a grant of a rent to a person to whom no estate in the land is conveyed, or by a reservation of a rent out of land granted.[204] Rents may be created by any form of conveyance which is sufficient to transfer other incorporeal hereditaments, and also they may be granted in trust, or conveyed by way of uses. After a rent has been created, it may be transferred like any other estate.[205] The rules governing assignments of rent of the land out of which they issue, and of the reversion, if there be one, have already been considered.[206] Although the rule was otherwise at common law, the owner of a rent may now divide it up, or it may descend to several heirs.[207] When the owner of a rent service purchases part of the land out of which the rent issues, or releases a part of the rent to the owner of that land, the rent is apportioned pro rata.[208] With a rent charge, however, it is otherwise, and the same acts would cause an extinguishment of the rent, because no apportionment is possible except by a new agreement of the parties.[209] It is otherwise,

---

[200] Van Rensselaer v. Read, 26 N. Y. 558; Hosford v. Ballard, 39 N. Y. 147; Van Rensselaer v. Hays, 19 N. Y. 68. But cf. Turner v. Lee, Cro. Car. 471. And see contra, Hool v. Bell, 1 Ld. Raym. 172.

[201] And see Scott v. Lunt, 7 Pet. 596; Foltz v. Huntley, 7 Wend. (N. Y.) 210; Adams v. Bucklin, 7 Pick. (Mass.) 121; Williams's Appeal, 47 Pa. St. 283.

[202] Ingersoll v. Sergeant, 1 Whart. (Pa.) 337; Taylor v. Vale, Cro. Eliz. 166. Cf. Williams v. Hayward, 1 El. & El. 1040.

[203] Wallace v. Presbyterian Church, 111 Pa. St. 164, 2 Atl. 347.

[204] Scott v. Lunt, 7 Pet. 596; Folts v. Huntley, 7 Wend. (N. Y.) 210.

[205] Van Rensselaer v. Read, 26 N. Y. 558; Van Rensselaer v. Hays, 19 N. Y. 68. Cf. Trulock v. Donahue, 76 Iowa, 758, 40 N. W. 696.

[206] Ante, p. 147.

[207] Cook v. Brightly, 46 Pa. St. 439; Farley v. Craig, 11 N. J. Law, 262. But see Ryerson v. Quackenbush, 26 N. J. Law, 236.

[208] Co. Litt. § 222; Ingersoll v. Sergeant, 1 Whart. (Pa.) 337.

[209] Dennett v. Pass, 1 Bing. N. C. 388. But see Farley v. Craig, 11 N. J. Law, 262.

however, when part of the land has come to the owner of the land by descent, instead of by his own act.[210] An eviction of the tenant from the land out of which the rent is reserved will extinguish the rent, but, if the eviction is from part of the land only, the rent will be apportioned. But if the eviction is by the owner of the rent, though it be from only part of the land, the rent is extinguished.[211] Apportionment of rent as to time has been considered in another place.[212] The doctrine of merger applies to rents.[213] Distress, as a remedy for rent, we have already considered,[214] as well as covenants for the payment of rent,[215] and conditions of re-entry for its nonpayment.[216] The remedy by which rent may be recovered by action is governed by the form of instrument creating the rent. Thus, if the rent is created by indenture, covenant is the proper form of action;[217] while, if the creation was by a deed poll, assumpsit would be the remedy.[218] Debt for rent lies in nearly all cases.[219]

FRANCHISES.

236. "A franchise is a privilege or immunity of a public nature, which cannot be legally exercised without legislative grant." At common law, franchises are hereditaments.

[210] Cruger v. McLaury, 41 N. Y. 219, 223.
[211] 2 Washb. Real Prop. (5th Ed.) 289.
[212] Ante, p. 60.
[213] Cook v. Brightly, 46 Pa. St. 439.
[214] Ante, p. 145.
[215] Ante, p. 140.
[216] Ante, p. 150.
[217] Finley v. Simpson, 22 N. J. Law, 311. And see Thursby v. Plant, 1 Lev. 259; Stevenson v. Lambard, 2 East, 575. But cf. Milnes v. Branch, 5 Maule & S. 411.
[218] Goodwin v. Gilbert, 9 Mass. 510; Johnson v. Muzzy, 45 Vt. 419; Hinsdale v. Humphrey, 15 Conn. 431. And cf. Falhers v. Corbret, 2 Barnard, 386; Johnson v. May, 3 Lev. 150.
[219] Farewell v. Dickenson, 6 Barn. & C. 251; Reade v. Johnson, Cro. Eliz. 242; Newcomb v. Harvey, Carth. 161; Stroud v. Rogers, 6 Term. R. 63, note; Case of Loringe's Ex'rs, Y. B. 26 Edw. III., p. 10, pl. 5; Gibson v. Kirk, 1 Q. B. 850; Thomas v. Sylvester, L. R. 8 Q. B. 368. But see Marsh v. Brace, Cro. Jac. 334; Bord v. Cudmore, Cro. Car. 183; Pine v. Leicester, Hob. 37; Humble v. Glover, Cro. Eliz. 328; Webb v. Jiggs, 4 Maule & S. 113.

§ 236) FRANCHISES. 379

At common law, franchises are heritable; but now they are usually held by corporations, and corporations can have no heirs. So, too, franchises are now usually granted for a term of years, and not in fee.[220] The law of franchises now pertains more properly to the law of corporations, and we will give only a brief account of some of the common-law rules. A franchise need not necessarily be a monopoly, but may be nonexclusive. Franchises are alienable, and are liable for the debts of their owners.[221] A franchise is in the nature of a contract, being, on the one hand, a grant by the state or a municipality of certain rights and privileges which could not be otherwise exercised, in consideration for certain benefits to the public, to be supplied by the grantee. A failure of the grantees to carry out the purposes for which the franchise was granted gives cause for forfeiture of the franchise. But forfeiture is had only at the suit of the government.[222] Where an exclusive franchise has been granted, it assumes the character of a contract which is protected by the constitutional provisions against impairing the obligation of the contract, and therefore no conflicting franchises can be granted.[223] An exclusive franchise, however, like other property, may be taken under the right of eminent domain.[224] One of the most usual franchises at common law was the right to maintain and operate a ferry.[225] A right of this kind is personal property in Iowa.[226] A riparian owner has no right to set up a ferry on a nav-

[220] Stark v. M'Gowen, 1 Nott & McC. (S. C.) 387; Clark v. White, 5 Bush. (Ky.) 353; Conway v. Taylor, 1 Black, 603.

[221] 2 Washb. Real Prop. (5th Ed.) 310; Greer v. Haugabook, 47 Ga. 282. But see Foster v. Fowler, 60 Pa. St. 27; Yellow River Imp. Co. v. Wood Co., 81 Wis. 554, 51 N. W. 1004.

[222] Chicago City Ry. Co. v. People, 73 Ill. 541; Jeffersonville v. The John Shallcross, 35 Ind. 19; Greer v. Haugabook, 47 Ga. 282.

[223] Milhan v. Sharp, 27 N. Y. 611; Newburgh & C. Turnpike Road Co. v. Miller, 5 Johns. Ch. (N. Y.) 101; Boston & L. R. Corp. v. Salem & L. R. Co., 2 Gray (Mass.) 1; McRoberts v. Washburne, 10 Minn. 23 (Gil. 8). But see Hopkins v. Railroad Co., 2 Q. B. Div. 224; Ft. Plain Bridge Co. v. Smith, 30 N. Y. 44.

[224] West River Bridge Co. v. Dix, 6 How. 507; In re Towanda Bridge Co., 91 Pa. St. 216.

[225] Ipswich v. Browne, Sav. 11; Peter v. Kendal, 6 Barn. & C. 703, 711; Mabury v. Ferry Co., 9 C. C. A. 174, 60 Fed. 645.

[226] Lippencott v. Allander, 27 Iowa, 460.

igable river without authority from the state.[227] When a franchise for a ferry has been accepted by the grantees, they are bound to provide accommodation for the public, and are liable for injuries caused by defect in their boats and other appliances. On the other hand, they become entitled to take toll.[228] If an exclusive franchise has been granted for maintaining a ferry, it includes the right to enjoy it, free from interference by contiguous and injurious competition.[229] If another ferry was established so near as to produce such effect, it would constitute a nuisance.[230] Franchises for bridges and turnpike roads are subject to the same rules as those for ferries.[231]

[227] Mills v. Learn, 2 Or. 215; Prosser v. Wapello Co., 18 Iowa, 327. But see Chenango Bridge Co. v. Paige, 83 N. Y. 178; Cooper v. Smith, 9 Serg. & R. (Pa.) 26.

[228] Ferrel v. Woodward, 20 Wis. 458; Willoughby v. Horridge, 12 C. B. 742.

[229] Huzzey v. Field, 2 Cromp., M. & R. 432; Long v. Beard, 3 Murphy (N. C.) 57; Aikin v. Railway Corp., 20 N. Y. 370. So building a bridge may interfere with a ferry. Gates v. M'Daniel, 2 Stew. (Ala.) 211; Smith v. Haskins, 3 Ired. Eq. (N. C.) 613. Cf. Newton v. Cubitt, 12 C. B. (N. S.) 32, affirmed 13 C. B. (N. S.) 864.

[230] Midland Terminal & Ferry Co. v. Wilson, 28 N. J. Eq. 537; Collins v. Ewing, 51 Ala. 101; Walker v. Armstrong, 2 Kan. 198.

[231] Ft. Plain Bridge Co. v. Smith, 30 N. Y. 44; President, etc., of Newburgh & Cochecton Turnpike Road v. Miller, 5 Johns. Ch. (N. Y.) 101; Norris v. Teamsters' Co., 6 Cal. 590; Proprietors of Charles River Bridge v. Proprietors of Warren Bridge, 11 Pet. 420.

CHAPTER XIV.

LEGAL CAPACITY TO HOLD AND CONVEY REALTY.

    237. Personal Capacity.
    238. Infants.
    239-240. Persons of Unsound Mind.
    241-242. Married Women.
    243-244. Aliens.
    245. Corporations.

PERSONAL CAPACITY.

237. Personal capacity to convey real estate is, in general, the same as capacity to contract. The power to take and hold real estate is greater in some instances than the power to convey it.

Personal capacity in connection with power to take, hold, and convey real estate has already been mentioned in connection with the various subjects of which we have treated. In the main, however, the topics which have already been considered have been treated of only in connection with normal persons. Power to convey real property is, in general, the same as the power to make contracts.[1] Disabilities connected with personal capacity are of two kinds,—natural, such as that of insanity, and legal, as in case of married women and corporations. Some disabilities, such as infancy, may be both natural and legal. The degree of disability varies in each case. It has already been said that some persons have power to hold land, but cannot convey it. For instance, persons under disability may take land by descent, though by reason of insanity or some other cause they might have no power to make a binding contract to sell it. Certain disabilities which arise from the relation of mortgagor and mortgagee, trustee and cestui que trust, have been treated of heretofore.[2]

[1] See Clark, Cont. 211.
[2] Ante, pp. 182, 263.

INFANTS.

238. An infant's conveyances of his real property are voidable, not void. They may be ratified or disaffirmed by him after he reaches majority.

At common law all persons were infants who had not reached the age of 21 years, but this has been changed in many states, and females reach their majority at 18 or at marriage.[3] An infant, of course, has power to take real estate either by descent or by conveyance to him.[4] His transfers of his real property are not void, but only voidable,[5] and the privilege of avoiding them is personal with him, and cannot be taken advantage of by a stranger,[6] although it may be by his representatives after his death.[7] An infant who has made a conveyance of his real property has no power to disaffirm the conveyance during his infancy; nor, of course, would a ratification by him during that time be of any validity.[8] In the event of the infant's death before reaching majority, his heirs may affirm or disaffirm the conveyance without waiting until the time has elapsed which would have made him of age had he lived. Ratification or disaffirmance by one who has reached majority, of a conveyance made during infancy, need not be by express acts, but may be by implication. Thus a conveyance of the property to another person is a disaffirmance of a deed made during minority.[9] A ratification need not be by deed.[10] The cases are conflicting as to whether acquiescence after reaching majority is an affirmance. The best rule

[3] 1 Stim. Am. St. Law, § 6601.
[4] 1 Devl. Deeds, § 116.
[5] Kendall v. Lawrence, 22 Pick. (Mass.) 540; Jenkins v. Jenkins, 12 Iowa, 195; Shipley v. Bunn, 125 Mo. 445, 28 S. W. 754; Tucker v. Moreland, 10 Pet. 58. As to the appointment of an attorney in fact by an infant, see 1 Jones, Real Prop. § 4.
[6] Brown v. Caldwell, 10 Serg. & R. (Pa.) 114.
[7] Veal v. Fortson, 57 Tex. 482; Bozeman v. Browning, 31 Ark. 364.
[8] See Bool v. Mix, 17 Wend. (N. Y.) 119.
[9] Jackson v. Carpenter, 11 Johns. (N. Y.) 539; Chapin v. Shafer, 49 N. Y. 407; Cresinger v. Welch, 15 Ohio, 156.
[10] Barnaby v. Barnaby, 1 Pick. (Mass.) 221; Phillips v. Green, 5 T. B. Mon. (Ky.) 344; Robbins v. Eaton, 10 N. H. 561.

seems to be that an infant shall have a reasonable time after coming of age in which to affirm or disaffirm.[11] A second deed executed during minority is no disaffirmance of a prior one.[12] Bringing suit for the land conveyed during infancy is, of course, a disaffirmance of such conveyance. On disaffirming a conveyance, there must be a restoration of the consideration received for the land, if the money is still in the grantor's hands.[13] The lands of an infant may be conveyed by his guardian by order of court.[14]

PERSONS OF UNSOUND MIND.

239. Conveyances by insane persons who are under guardianship are void, but, if not under guardianship, their conveyances are voidable only.

240. The same rules govern conveyances by intoxicated persons and habitual drunkards.

The disabilities of persons of nonsane mind to convey their real property are much the same as disabilities of infants. Their incapacity is a question of fact in each case. The test which is generally applied is the grantor's capacity to comprehend the business which he is transacting.[15] Nonsoundness of mind may arise from age, sickness, accident, or other cause, but the legal consequences are the same in each case. Mere weakness of mind does not incapacitate a

[11] Jones v. Butler, 30 Barb. (N. Y.) 641; Goodnow v. Lumber Co., 31 Minn. 468, 18 N. W. 283. So by statute in some states. 1 Stim. Am. St. Law, § 6602; Wright v. Germain, 21 Iowa, 585; Green v. Wilding, 59 Iowa, 679, 13 N. W. 761. Contra, Tucker v. Moreland, 10 Pet. 58; Irvine v. Irvine, 9 Wall. 617; Prout v. Wiley, 28 Mich. 164; Huth v. Dock Co., 56 Mo. 202.

[12] Bool v. Mix, 17 Wend. (N. Y.) 119; McCormic v. Leggett, 8 Jones (N. C.) 425.

[13] Brandon v. Brown, 106 Ill. 519. Where the consideration received has been wasted by the infant, no offer to restore it is necessary. Chandler v. Simmonds, 97 Mass. 508; Green v. Green, 7 Hun (N. Y.) 492. But contra, Stout v. Merrill, 35 Iowa, 47; Kerr v. Bell, 44 Mo. 120.

[14] Battell v. Torrey, 65 N. Y. 294; Wood v. Truax, 39 Mich. 628. Cf. Merritt v. Simpson, 41 Ill. 391.

[15] Odell v. Buck, 21 Wend. (N. Y.) 142; Titcomb v. Vantyle, 84 Ill. 371; Corbit v. Smith, 7 Iowa, 60.

person to convey his property.[16] But when such weakness of mind is shown, less proof of duress or fraud is required to have his conveyance set aside.[17] If the person is so insane that he has been placed under guardianship, any conveyances made by him are absolutely void, and not merely voidable;[18] otherwise they are voidable only,[19] but in some states the courts hold that conveyances by insane persons, though not under guardianship, are void.[20] When the unsoundness of mind is only in the form of a monomania, power to transact business is affected only in case the transaction in question is connected with the subject on which the person is insane.[21] Insanity arising after a valid contract of sale or purchase has been made does not affect the validity of the contract.[22] On the other hand, conveyances made during the insanity of the grantor may be ratified by him after he has recovered.[23] The voidable conveyance of an insane person may be set aside at the suggestion of his guardian during his life or after his death on the application of his heirs or personal representatives.[24] The cases are conflicting as to the necessity for the restoration of the purchase money when deeds of

[16] Alman v. Stout, 42 Pa. St. 114; Taylor v. Cox, 153 Ill. 220, 38 N. E. 656; Miller v. Craig, 36 Ill. 109; Odell v. Buck, 21 Wend. (N. Y.) 142; In re Pike's Will, 83 Hun, 327, 31 N. Y. Supp. 689.

[17] Allore v. Jewell, 94 U. S. 506; Harding v. Handy, 11 Wheat. 103.

[18] Corbit v. Smith, 7 Iowa, 60; Mohr v. Tullp, 40 Wis. 66; Rogers v. Walker, 6 Pa. St. 371. A deed of his homestead is void though his wife joins. New England Loan & Trust Co. v. Spitler, 54 Kan. 560, 38 Pac. 799.

[19] Bunham v. Kidwell, 113 Ill. 425; Allis v. Billings, 6 Metc. (Mass.) 415; Breckenridge v. Ormsby, 1 J. J. Marsh. (Ky.) 236.

[20] Evans v. Horan, 52 Md. 602; Van Deusen v. Sweet, 51 N. Y. 378; Farley v. Parker, 6 Or. 105; German Sav. & Loan Soc. v. De Lashmutt, 67 Fed. 399. See, as to the theory of lucid intervals, Whart. & S. Med. Jur. §§ 61, 62; 2 Hamilton, Leg. Med. 113, 222.

[21] Trich's Ex'r v. Trich, 165 Pa. St. 586, 30 Atl. 1053; Ekin v. McCracken, 11 Phila. (Pa.) 534; Turner v. Rusk, 53 Md. 65; Farmer v. Farmer, 129 Mo. 530, 31 S. W. 926; Blough v. Parry (Ind. Sup.) 40 N. E. 70; McClary v. Stull, 44 Neb. 175, 62 N. W. 501.

[22] Ekin v. McCracken, 11 Phila. (Pa.) 534.

[23] Arnold v. Iron Works, 1 Gray (Mass.) 434; Eaton v. Eaton, 37 N. J. Law, 108.

[24] Campbell v. Kuhn, 45 Mich. 513, 8 N. W. 523; Arnold v. Townsend, 14 Phila. (Pa.) 216. But see Key's Lessee v. Davis, 1 Md. 32. The wife and children of the grantor cannot, during his lifetime, question his mental capacity

insane persons are set aside. But it seems that there should be a restoration when the grantee was ignorant of his grantor's incapacity, or when there was no fraud present.[25] As in the case of infants, the lands of insane persons may be conveyed by order of court.

Drunkards.

The disability of persons who are incapacitated to deal with their real property by reason of intoxication is much the same as that of insane persons. In fact, the rules to be applied are those which determine the soundness of the understanding of the person. Unsoundness of mind may as well result from intoxication as from insanity, and, indeed, in many cases habitual drunkenness leads to insanity. Conveyances by such persons are voidable,[26] though it might be that in states where a drunkard may be placed under guardianship deeds made by him after that time would be void.[27]

MARRIED WOMEN.

241. At common law a married woman could not take land without her husband's consent, and her conveyances, except of her separate property, were absolutely void.

242. These disabilities have been more or less removed in all states by statute.

Under the disabilities of which we have heretofore treated there has been no loss of power to take lands, the disabilities being merely as to conveyances. But at common law a husband could disaffirm a conveyance made to his wife.[28] If the husband did con-

---

to convey land, Baldwin v. Golde, 88 Hun, 115, 34 N. Y. Supp. 587; nor can a remainder-man, McMillan v. William Deering & Co., 139 Ind. 70, 38 N. E. 398.

[25] Davis Sewing-Mach. Co. v. Barnard, 43 Mich. 379, 5 N. W. 411; Scanlan v. Cobb, 85 Ill. 296; Rusk v. Fenton, 14 Bush (Ky.) 490. Contra, Gibson v. Sopher, 6 Gray (Mass.) 279; Crawford v. Scoville, 94 Pa. St. 48; Flanders v. Davis, 19 N. H. 139.

[26] Mansfield v. Watson, 2 Iowa, 111; Wilson v. Bigger, 7 Watts & S. (Pa.) 111; Wiley v. Ewalt, 66 Ill. 26; Warnock v. Campbell, 25 N. J. Eq. 485.

[27] See Clark, Cont. 275.

[28] Baxter v. Smith 6 Bin. (Pa.) 427.

sent to such a conveyance, the wife did not have power to avoid the conveyance.[29] On the other hand, a married woman's deeds, at common law, were absolutely void.[30] The statute of 3 & 4 Wm. IV. c. 75, gave a married woman power to sell her lands if her husband joined in the conveyance, though it required that she be examined separate and apart from her husband, by an officer, as to whether her consent to the conveyance was voluntary. Any land, however, which constituted part of the wife's separate estate, she could deal with as if unmarried.[31] In some states the deed of a married woman who is also an infant is void;[32] in others it is voidable only.[33] Conveyances at common law of a wife's lands could be made only by a fine or recovery.[34] The disabilities of married women to take and deal with real estate have been very largely removed by statute.[35] In some states they have as much power in this respect as if unmarried, though the statutes in many states provide that the husband must join in the conveyance, and the provision for a separate examination of the wife has been re-enacted in many states. The cases under these married women's acts, as they are called, are conflicting on many points, but it is held that the statutes must be strictly followed.[36] At common law a wife could not take a conveyance of real property directly from the husband.[37] In order to make such a conveyance of land, it was necessary for the husband to first transfer to a trustee, who would convey back to the wife.[38] Relief was, however, granted

[29] 2 Bl. Comm. 293; Scanlan v. Wright, 13 Pick. (Mass.) 523.

[30] 2 Bl. Comm. 293. But see, as to her separate estate, ante, p. 72.

[31] See ante, p. 72. She cannot avoid a conveyance of such land. McAnally v. Heflin (Ala.) 17 South. 87.

[32] Hoyt v. Swar, 53 Ill. 134; Youse v. Norcum, 12 Mo. 549.

[33] Bool v. Mix, 17 Wend. (N. Y.) 119; Wilson v. Branch, 77 Va. 65; Losey v. Bond, 94 Ind. 67; Richardson v. Pate, 93 Ind. 423. See Ellis v. Alford, 64 Miss. 8, 1 South. 155.

[34] 2 Bl. Comm. 293.

[35] 1 Stim. Am. St. Law, art. 650. An attempted conveyance may operate as a contract to convey. Brown v. Dressler (Mo. Sup.) 29 S. W. 13.

[36] Garrett v. Moss, 22 Ill. 363; Rumfelt v. Clemens, 46 Pa. St. 455; Glidden v. Strupler, 52 Pa. St. 400; Elwood v. Klock, 13 Barb. (N. Y.) 50.

[37] Shepard v. Shepard, 7 Johns. Ch. (N. Y.) 57.

[38] Jewell v. Porter, 31 N. H. 34; Bancroft v. Curtis, 108 Mass. 47.

in equity when such a precaution had not been taken.[39] The rule is now different in most states, and the husband may convey to the wife and the wife to the husband directly.[40] In some states it is held that a wife cannot give a power of attorney to convey her lands;[41] but where her disabilities have been removed there seems to be no good reason for this rule.[42] Even at common law, when the disability of coverture was removed by death or divorce, the power to convey was restored. The power of a married woman to act as trustee has already been considered.[44]

Wills.

By the common law a married woman has no power to dispose of her lands by will,[45] but in equity such a power is recognized as to all property coming under the jurisdiction of the court.[46] In many states the statutes now give married women the same testamentary power as though unmarried,[47] and in some states married women have greater power to devise their lands than if unmarried, since marriage removes the disability of infancy.[48]

ALIENS.

243. At common law, aliens could take real property, but their title could be divested by proceedings instituted by the officers of the government, called "office found."

244. This disability has been removed in many states by statute.

[39] Loomis v. Brush, 36 Mich. 40.

[40] Burdeno v. Amperse, 14 Mich. 91; Allen v. Hopper, 50 Me. 371. But see Winans v. Peebles, 32 N. Y. 423; 1 Stim. Am. St. Law, § 6471.

[41] Snyder v. Sponable, 1 Hill (N. Y.) 567; Oulds v. Sansom, 3 Taunt. 261.

[42] See 1 Stim. Am. St. Law, § 6506.

[44] Ante, p. 363.

[45] In re Steinmetz's Estate, 168 Pa. St. 175, 31 Atl. 1092. The power of a married woman to devise land held by her in right of another—for instance, as executrix—is an apparent, rather than a real, exception to the common-law disability. Scammell v. Wilkinson, 2 East, 552. And see Rich v. Cockell, 9 Ves. 369.

[46] 1 Jarm. Wills, 39; 1 Woerner, Adm. 27.

[47] 1 Stim. Am. St. Law, § 6460. And see Dillard v. Dillard's Ex'rs (Va.) 21 S. E. 669.

[48] 1 Stim. Am. St. Law, § 2602.

Disabilities of aliens consist principally in their incapacity to hold real property after the title has been passed to them, for it is held that the title passes out of the grantor and is held by the alien until the state institutes proceedings to divest it.[49] This is called "office found." Before office found the alien can sell and convey the land as if not under disability.[50] While the power of aliens to hold land is a matter for state regulation, any state laws are subject to treaties which may be made by the United States.[51] In many states the disabilities of alienage have been removed, while in others they are removed only as to resident aliens. In some states aliens may buy and hold land, but are not permitted to take it by descent.[52]

Inheritance by Aliens.

At common law, aliens could not inherit, nor could the inheritance be transmitted through them. The rules, however, have been largely changed by statute. In some states the disabilities are entirely removed; in others they exist except as to alien friends or residents; and now in all states, probably, the alienage of an ancestor would not prevent the inheritance passing to naturalized citizens.[53]

---

[49] Doe v. Robertson, 11 Wheat. 332; Sheaffe v. O'Neil, 1 Mass. 256; Wadsworth v. Wadsworth, 12 N. Y. 376.

[50] Sheaffe v. O'Neil, 1 Mass. 256; Marshall v. Conrad, 5 Call (Va.) 364; Halstead v. Lake Co., 56 Ind. 363; Montgomery v. Dorion, 7 N. H. 475. But that the estate so conveyed will be subject to forfeiture in the hands of the grantee, see Scanlan v. Wright, 13 Pick. (Mass.) 523; People v. Conklin, 2 Hill (N. Y.) 67.

[51] Schultze v. Schultze, 144 Ill. 290, 33 N. E. 201; Hauenstein v. Lynham, 100 U. S. 483; Carneal v. Banks, 10 Wheat. 181; Chirac v. Chirac, 2 Wheat. 259. For restrictions imposed by congress on the capacity of aliens to hold real property, see 24 Stat. 476.

[52] 1 Stim. Am. St. Law, § 6013; 1 Shars. & B. Lead. Cas. Real Prop. 515. See Bennett v. Hibbert, 88 Iowa, 154, 55 N. W. 93; Wunderle v. Wunderle, 144 Ill. 40, 33 N. E. 195. A citizen cannot inherit in some states through an alien ancestor. Furenes v. Michelson, 86 Iowa, 508, 53 N. W. 416; Beavan v. Went, 155 Ill. 592, 41 N. E. 91.

[53] 1 Stim. Am. St. Law, §§ 6013–6017; 1 Dembitz, Land Tit. 302.

CORPORATIONS.

245. The power of corporations to take and convey real property is regulated by their charters.

The buying and selling of real property by corporations is a matter of corporate power, which in each case is regulated by the rights and privileges conferred on the corporation by its charter.[54] It is usual to limit the amount of real property which certain corporations may own. These restrictions apply, however, to the value of the land at the time it is purchased, and a subsequent rise in value will not require the corporation to dispose of a part of it.[55] At common law, statutes of mortmain existed, which prevented the acquisition of lands by the church. No such statutes exist in this country,[56] except in Pennsylvania, where the English statutes are held to apply as far as applicable.[57] At common law, corporations could not take land in trust, though they have this power now.[58] Any fuller discussion of the powers of corporations in respect to real property belongs more particularly to a treatise on corporations.

[54] Barry v. Exchange Co., 1 Sandf. Ch. (N. Y.) 280; Coggeshall v. Home for Friendless Children (R. I.) 31 Atl. 694.

[55] Bogardus v. Trinity Church, 4 Sandf. Ch. (N. Y.) 633. The right to question the capacity of a corporation to hold land held to belong exclusively to the state. Schwab Clothing Co. v. Claunch (Tex. Civ. App.) 29 S. W. 922.

[56] McCartee v. Asylum, 9 Cow. (N. Y.) 437; Lathrop v. Bank, 8 Dana (Ky.) 114; Potter v. Thornton, 7 R. I. 252. But see Carroll v. City of East St. Louis, 67 Ill. 568.

[57] Methodist Church v. Remington, 1 Watts (Pa.) 218.

[58] See ante, p. 263.

CHAPTER XV.

RESTRAINTS ON ALIENATION.

246. Kinds of Restraints.
247. Restraints Imposed by Law.
248. Restraints in Favor of Creditors.
249. Restraints Imposed in Creation of Estate.

KINDS OF RESTRAINTS.

246. Restraints on the power to alienate real property are of the following kinds:
 (a) **Restraints imposed by law** (p. 390).
 (b) **Restraints imposed in favor of creditors** (p. 392).
 (c) **Restraints imposed in the creation of the estate** (p. 394).

SAME—RESTRAINTS IMPOSED BY LAW.

247. By the early common law, restraints independent of the personal capacity of the grantor or the form of his estate were imposed on the owner of lands
 (a) **In favor of his heirs.**
 (b) **In favor of his lord.**

History of the Right of Alienation.

At first estates were given for life only, no larger interests being conveyed when the feudal system was at its height. By custom, or by the construction of the courts, these estates were enlarged into estates to a man and his heirs. By such limitations at first only the issue of the first taker were meant. Afterwards heirs came to include collaterals, so that the estates were about the same in quantity as a fee simple at present.[1] To avoid this result, estates were limited to the heirs of the body of the first tenant; that is, they were fees conditional at common law.

---

[1] See ante, p. 44.

§ 247)   RESTRAINTS IMPOSED BY LAW.   391

These were changed into estates in fee tail by the statute de donis. The tenants were thereby prevented from aliening their estates, as against their heirs or the lord, until Taltarum's Case, which, as we have seen, took away all restraints on the alienation of estates in fee tail.[2] As to the general power of a man to alienate his estate as against his heirs or the lord of whom he held it, the authorities offer two theories.[3] One is that we are to begin with an almost unlimited power of alienation, which is gradually restricted, and at a later time the restrictions are removed. The other is that there was at first little or no power to alienate real property, and that the history of the subject of alienation has been a history of restrictions removed. It is probable, however, that neither theory is correct, but that the law in early times was unsettled,[4] and remained so from the fact that there were but few sales of land for cash, but that all transfers took the form of subinfeudations, in which, from the services and rent reserved, the heirs or the lord would receive as much benefit as from the land, so would not be inclined to question the validity of the conveyance. There are some statements in the books that a man had greater power to dispose of lands which he had acquired by purchase than those which came to him by descent.[5] In other places it is intimated that a man could only dispose of a reasonable portion of his lands, unless the alienation was confirmed by his heir; though he always had power to give a portion of his lands to his daughter on her marriage, to be held by a tenure, which was called frank marriage.[6] Questions as to the power of an owner of lands to alienate them did not begin to arise until after the passage of the statute of quia emptores, which prevented subinfeudation in fee. As to the power of a lord to object to a conveyance by his tenants, there seems to be little evidence, though it was provided in Magna Charta[7] that a tenant could not dispose of so much of his land that he would not have enough left to perform the services due his lord. The churches and other ecclesiastical bodies began to secure so much of the land in England that statutes were passed, called statutes

[2] See ante, p. 51.
[3] 1 Pol. & M. Hist. Eng. Law, 310.
[4] 1 Pol. & M. Hist. Eng. Law, 326.
[5] Dig. Hist. Real Prop. (4th Ed.) 11.
[6] Dig. Hist. Real Prop. 101.
[7] Chapter 39.

of mortmain, which made conveyances to them void.[8] These statutes have already been mentioned in another connection.[9] By the early common law a man's land was not liable to be taken for his debts, but this was changed by the statute of Westminster,[10] the statute of Merchants,[11] and the statute of 27 Edw. III. c. 9.[12]

Personal Capacity and Form of Estate.

In the last chapter it was seen that certain disabilities of the person restrict the power of an owner of lands to convey it. Other restrictions on the power of alienation due to the nature of the owner's interest have been considered in connection with the various estates; for instance, the restrictions imposed by rights of dower and curtesy, or restraints imposed by covenant on the power of a tenant for years to assign or sublet.

SAME—RESTRAINTS IN FAVOR OF CREDITORS—FRAUDULENT CONVEYANCES.

248. An owner of land must not so dispose of it that his creditors will be delayed or defrauded.

Another form of restriction on alienation is that imposed by the law when it prevents a man from conveying his lands in such a manner as to delay or defraud his creditors in the collection of their debts.[13] Conveyances for such a purpose are, however, valid between the parties,[14] and in other cases it is a question of consideration and intent.[15] Deeds fraudulent as to creditors are not void, but only voidable, and an innocent purchaser from the grantee

---

[8] Magna Charta, c. 43; 1 Pol. & M. Hist. Eng. Law, 314.

[9] Ante, p. 252.

[10] 13 Edw. I. c. 18.

[11] 13 Edw. I.

[12] Called "statute staple." See 2 Bl. Comm. 161.

[13] Strauss v. Abrahams, 32 Fed. 310; Spencer v. Slater, 4 Q. B. Div. 13. See as to frauds on purchasers, Gooch's Case, 5 Coke, 60a; Colville v. Parker, Cro. Jac. 158; Doe v. Manning, 9 East, 59.

[14] Campbell v. Whitson, 68 Ill. 240; Harmon v. Harmon, 63 Ill. 512; Welsh v. Welsh, 105 Mass. 229.

[15] Chandler v. Von Roeder, 24 How. 224; Bunn v. Ahl, 29 Pa. St. 387.

§ 248)   RESTRAINTS IN FAVOR OF CREDITORS.   393

takes a good title.[16] Conveyances of a homestead do not come within the rules against fraudulent conveyances, because a homestead is not subject to levy and sale for debts, except privileged debts.[17] As to what conveyances are regarded as fraudulent, the rule is that, if the grantee does not know of the fraudulent purpose of his grantor, he takes a good title,[18] though if he does not pay a valuable consideration, he cannot hold the land against the creditors.[19] In some cases a sale for an insufficient consideration may be enough to put the grantee on inquiry, and thus affect him with notice.[20] On the other hand, though the grantee pays a valuable consideration, if he knows of the fraudulent purpose of the grantor, he cannot hold the land against the grantor's creditors.[21] Though a person be actually insolvent, he still may sell his lands for a valuable consideration, inasmuch as this may be the best way of providing funds for the benefit of his creditors.[22] But when a man is in embarrassed financial circumstances, any conveyance made by him upon a merely good consideration will not stand,—such as transfers to a wife or children.[23] Marriage, however, is

[16] Anderson v. Roberts, 18 Johns. (N. Y.) 515; Campbell v. Whitson, 68 Ill. 240. But cf. Doe v. Rusham, 17 Q. B. 723; Beal v. Warren, 2 Gray (Mass.) 447; Fleming v. Townsend, 6 Ga. 103; Prodgers v. Langham, 1 S.d. 133; Manhattan Co. v. Evertson, 6 Paige (N. Y.) 457.

[17] Dreutzer v. Bell, 11 Wis. 114; Wood v. Chambers, 20 Tex. 247. And see Gassett v. Grout, 4 Metc. (Mass.) 490.

[18] Gridley v. Bingham, 51 Ill. 153; Waterbury v. Sturtevant, 18 Wend. (N. Y.) 353.

[19] Van Wyck v. Seward, 18 Wend. (N. Y.) 375; Potter v. McDowell, 31 Mo. 62; Hunters v. Waite, 3 Grat. (Va.) 26.

[20] Kaine v. Weigley, 22 Pa. St. 179; State v. Evans, 38 Mo. 150.

[21] Wadsworth v. Williams, 100 Mass. 126; Williamson v. Wachenheim, 58 Iowa, 277, 12 N. W. 302. Twyne's Case, 3 Coke, 80b. Cf. Tibbals v. Jacobs, 31 Conn. 428.

[22] State Bank v. Whittle, 48 Mich. 1, 11 N. W. 756; Wood v. Clark, 121 Ill. 359, 12 N. E. 271; Kellog v. Richardson, 19 Fed. 70.

[23] Boyd v. De La Montagnie, 73 N. Y. 498; Pratt v. Curtis, 2 Lowell, 87, Fed. Cas. No. 11,375; Gridley v. Watson, 53 Ill. 193; Baldwin v. Tuttle, 23 Iowa, 74; Hinde's Lessee v. Longworth, 11 Wheat. 199; Reade v. Livingstone, 3 Johns. Ch. (N. Y.) 481; In re Ridler, 22 Ch. Div 74. Cf. Freeman v. Pope, 5 Ch. App. 538; Kent v. Riley, L. R. 14 Eq. 190; Salmon v. Bennett, 1 Conn. 525; Winchester v. Charter, 12 Allen (Mass.) 606; Newstead v. Searles, 1 Atk. 265.

regarded as a valuable consideration.[24] Conveyances of the kind we are discussing are voidable only as to existing creditors in most states, though in some other states subsequent creditors are permitted to assail the transaction,[25] especially if the conveyance is made on the eve of incurring large obligations, or before embarking on financial risks.[26] As to bankrupt and insolvent laws, it can only be said here that any preference attempted to be given one creditor over the others is void,[27] but the debtor may convey all of his property to one creditor, instead of making an assignment.[28]

SAME—RESTRAINTS IMPOSED IN CREATION OF ESTATE.

249. Restraints on alienation of real property imposed in the creation of the estate are either
  (a) Clauses of forfeiture for alienation, or
  (b) Clauses forbidding alienation.

Mr. Gray, in his work Restraints on Alienation, divides the subject as we have indicated in the black letter; that is, into convey-

---

[24] Prewit v. Wilson, 103 U. S. 22; Otis v. Spencer, 102 Ill. 622; Clayton v. Earl of Wilton, 6 Maule & S. 67, note; Clarke v. Wright, 6 Hurl. & N. 849, affirming s. c. sub. nom. Dickenson v. Wright, 5 Hurl. & N. 401; Price v. Jenkins, 5 Ch. Div. 619, reversing 4 Ch. Div. 483. Cf. Townsend v. Westacott, 2 Beav. 340; Jenkins v. Keymes, 1 Lev. 237; Warden v. Jones, 2 De Gex & J. 76.

[25] Dodd v. Adams, 125 Mass. 398; Tunison v. Chamblin, 88 Ill. 378; Morrill v. Kilner, 113 Ill. 318; Buckley v. Duff, 114 Pa. St. 596, 8 Atl. 188; Shand v. Hanley, 71 N. Y. 319; Sexton v. Wheaton, 8 Wheat. 229. See Jenkyn v. Vaughan, 3 Drew. 419.

[26] Case v. Phelps, 39 N. Y. 164; Tunison v. Chamblin, 88 Ill. 378; Mackay v. Douglas, L. R. 14 Eq. 106; Ex parte Russell, 19 Ch. Div. 588. But see Todd v. Nelson, 109 N. Y. 316, 16 N. E. 360.

[27] Penniman v. Cole, 8 Metc. (Mass.) 500; Mackie v. Cairns, 5 Cow. (N. Y.) 547. Any reservation to the debtor is void. Harris v. Sumner, 2 Pick. (Mass.) 129.

[28] Giddings v. Sears, 115 Mass. 505; Holbird v. Anderson, 5 Term R. 235; Livingston v. Bell, 3 Watts (Pa.) 198; McFarland v. Birdsall, 14 Ind. 126. But see Harris v. Sumner, 2 Pick (Mass.) 129; Grover v. Wakeman, 11 Wend. (N. Y.) 187; Thomas v. Jenks, 5 Rawle (Pa.) 221; Barney v. Griffin, 2 N. Y. 365; Collomb v. Caldwell, 16 N. Y. 484.

§ 249)   RESTRAINTS IMPOSED IN CREATION OF ESTATE.   395

ances in which there is a clause of forfeiture on attempted alienation, and cases in which there is a clause attempting to make any alienation by the grantee of no effect. When a fee-simple estate is conveyed an unqualified condition against alienation is wholly void.[29] But clauses providing for a forfeiture on alienation to certain persons are valid,[30] though it is doubtful how far such provisions for imposing a forfeiture for alienation except to certain persons would hold good.[31] By the weight of authority, conditions against alienation for a limited time are void.[32] Conditions of forfeiture may be attached to estates in fee simple while they are contingent.[33] As to estates in fee tail, a condition imposing a forfeiture for alienation is good,[34] but such a condition may be destroyed by a barring of the entail,[35] which we have seen cannot be prevented.[36] As to life estates, conditions against alienation

[29] Potter v. Couch, 141 U. S. 296, 11 Sup. Ct. 1005; Walker v. Vincent, 19 Pa. St. 369; Schermerhorn v. Negus, 1 Denio (N. Y.) 448; Ware v. Cann, 10 Barn. & C. 433; Hood v. Oglander, 34 Beav. 513; In re Rosher, 26 Ch. Div. 801. A condition against alienation in a certain manner is bad. Joslin v. Rhoades, 150 Mass. 301, 23 N. E. 42; Campbell v. Beaumont, 91 N. Y. 464; Van Horne v. Campbell, 100 N. Y. 287, 3 N. E. 316; Bills v. Bills, 80 Iowa, 269, 45 N. W. 748; Holmes v. Godson, 8 De Gex, M. & G. 152. See Doe v. Glover, 1 C. B. 448. See, also, Shaw v. Ford, 7 Ch. Div. 669; Jackson v. Robins, 16 Johns. (N. Y.) 537.

[30] Gray, Restr. Alien (2d Ed.) § 31; Winsor v. Mills, 157 Mass. 362, 32 N. E. 352; Jackson v. Schutz, 18 Johns. (N. Y.) 174.

[31] Doe v. Pearson, 6 East, 173, held a restriction of alienation, except to sisters or their children, good. But see Attwater v. Attwater, 18 Beav. 330; Schermerhorn v. Negus, 1 Denio (N. Y.) 448. And see for other valid conditions In re Macleay, L. R. 20 Eq. 186.

[32] Potter v. Couch, 141 U. S. 296, 315, 11 Sup. Ct. 1005; Mandlebaum v. McDonell, 29 Mich. 78; Bennett v. Chapin, 77 Mich. 526, 43 N. W. 893; Roosevelt v. Thurman, 1 Johns. Ch. (N. Y.) 220; Kepple's Appeal, 53 Pa. St. 211; Jauretche v. Proctor, 48 Pa. St. 466; Anderson v. Cary, 36 Ohio St. 506; In re Rosher, 26 Ch. Div. 801. Contra, In re Dugdale, 38 Ch. Div. 176. See Large's Case, 2 Leon. 82.

[33] Bank of State v. Forney, 2 Ired. Eq. (N. C.) 181; Large's Case, 2 Leon. 82, 3 Leon. 182.

[34] Croker v. Trevithin, Cro. Eliz. 35; Anon., 1 Leon. 292; Newis v. Lark, Plowd. 403.

[35] Stansbury v. Hubner, 73 Md. 228, 20 Atl. 904; Rex v. Burchell, Amb. 379; Dawkins v. Penrhyn, 4 App. Cas. 51. And see Bradley v. Peixoto, 3 Ves. 324.

[36] Ante, p. 51.

are good,[37] except when the settlor attempts to make the estate forfeitable for involuntary alienation.[38] So, too, estates for years may be granted with the condition that they shall be forfeited on alienation, and such a condition will be good.[39]

As to the other form of restraints on alienation,—that is, by the clause providing that the alienation itself shall be void,—it may be said that such conditions are valid in no case,[40] except: (1) That of a fee tail, though this may be destroyed by barring the entail.[41] (2) In many states an equitable life interest may be so limited that it may be held without power of voluntary or involuntary alienation.[42] (3) The separate estates of married women may be limited with valid conditions restraining their alienation.[43]

---

[37] Waldo v. Cummings, 45 Ill. 421; Camp v. Cleary, 76 Va. 140; Dommett v. Bedford, 6 Term R. 684; Shee v. Hale, 13 Ves. 404; Hurst v. Hurst, 21 Ch. Div. 278. See, also, Rochford v. Hackman, 9 Hare, 475.

[38] In re Pearson, 3 Ch. Div. 807; Higinbotham v. Holme, 19 Ves. 88; Ex parte Oxley, 1 Ball & B. 257. See, also, Phipps v. Ennismore, 4 Russ. 131; Lester v. Garland, 5 Sim. 205; Synge v. Synge, 4 Ir. Ch. 337. But see Brooke v. Pearson, 27 Beav. 181; Knight v. Browne, 30 Law J. Ch. 649; In re Detmold, 40 Ch. Div. 585.

[39] Doe v. Hawke, 2 East, 481; Roe v. Harrison, 2 Term R. 425; Roe v. Galliers, Id. 133. And see ante, p. 135.

[40] As to a fee simple, Blackstone Bank v. Davis, 21 Pick. (Mass.) 42; Todd v. Sawyer, 147 Mass. 570, 17 N. E. 527; McIntyre v. McIntyre, 123 Pa. St. 329, 16 Atl. 783; Bouldin v. Miller, 87 Tex. 359, 28 S. W. 940; as to life estates, Bridge v. Ward, 35 Wis. 687; Butterfield v. Reed, 160 Mass. 361, 35 N. E. 1128; McCormick Harvesting Mach. Co. v. Gates, 75 Iowa, 343, 39 N. W. 657.

[41] Cooper v. Macdonald, 7 Ch. Div. 288.

[42] Fisher v. Taylor, 2 Rawle (Pa.) 33; Eyrick v. Hetrick, 13 Pa. St. 488; Overman's Appeal, 88 Pa. St. 276; Thackara v. Mintzer, 100 Pa. St. 151; Claflin v. Claflin, 149 Mass. 19, 20 N. E. 454; Broadway Nat. Bank v. Adams, 133 Mass. 170; Billings v. Marsh, 153 Mass. 311, 26 N. E. 1000; Steib v. Whitehead, 111 Ill. 247; Roberts v. Stevens, 84 Me. 325, 24 Atl. 873; Smith v. Towers, 69 Md. 77, 14 Atl. 497, and 15 Atl. 92; Barnes v. Dow, 59 Vt.

[43] Moses v. Micou, 79 Ala. 564; Monroe v. Trenholm, 114 N. C. 590, 19 S. E. 377; Baggett v. Meux, 1 Phil. 627; Tullett v. Armstrong, 4 Mylne & C. 377; Cooper v. Macdonald, 7 Ch. Div. 288. Cf. Barton v. Briscoe, Jac. 603. But see Pacific Nat. Bank v. Windram, 133 Mass. 175; Jackson v. Von Zedlitz, 136 Mass. 342; Holmes v. Penney, 3 Kay & J. 90. And cf. Harland v. Binks, 15 Q. B. 713; Russell v. Woodward, 10 Pick. (Mass.) 408.

§ 249)   RESTRAINTS IMPOSED IN CREATION OF ESTATE.   397

In a number of states statutes forbid the suspension of the power of alienation beyond two lives in being at the creation of the estate [44] or of persons in being.[45]

530, 10 Atl. 258; Partridge v. Cavender, 96 Mo. 452, 9 S. W. 785. Cf. Sanford v. Lackland, 2 Dill. 6, Fed. Cas. No. 12,312; In re Coleman, 39 Ch. Div. 443; Lord v. Bunn, 2 Younge & C. Ch. 98. A limitation over on bankruptcy is good. Nichols v. Eaton, 91 U. S. 716. Contra, in other states. Bryan v. Knickerbocker, 1 Barb. Ch. (N. Y.) 409; Mebane v. Mebane, 4 Ired. Eq. (N. C.) 131; Tillinghast v. Bradford, 5 R. I. 205; Heath v. Bishop, 4 Rich. Eq. (S. C.) 46; Graves v. Dolphin, 1 Sim. 66; Green v. Spicer, 1 Russ. & M. 395; Younghusband v. Gisborne, 1 Colly. 400. And see Gray, Restr. Alien. (2d Ed.) preface.

[44] Galway v. Bryce (Sup.) 30 N. Y. Supp. 985; Rausch v. Rausch (Sup.) 31 N. Y. Supp. 786; In re Corlies' Will, 11 Misc. Rep. 670, 33 N. Y. Supp. 572; Sanford v. Goodell, 82 Hun, 369, 31 N. Y. Supp. 490. See, generally, Chapl. Suspen. Power, c. 2.

[45] Jordan v. Woodin (Iowa) 61 N. W. 948. And see Phillips v. Harrow (Iowa) 61 N. W. 434.

CHAPTER XVI.

TITLE.

250. Title Defined.
251. Acquisition of Title by State.
252. Acquisition by Private Persons.
253. Grant from the State.
254. Conveyances.
255.   Common-Law Conveyances.
256.   Conveyances under the Statute of Uses.
257.   Modern Statutory Conveyances.
258.   Registered Titles.
259–260.   Requisites of Deeds.
261.   Property to be Conveyed.
262.   Words of Conveyance.
263–264.   Description of the Property.
265.   Execution of the Writing.
266.   Delivery and Acceptance.
267.   Acknowledgment.
268.   Witnesses.
269.   Registry.
270.   Covenants for Title.
271.   Covenant of Seisin.
272.   When Broken.
273.   How Broken.
274.   Covenant against Incumbrances.
275.   How Broken.
276.   Covenant of Warranty.
277.   How Broken.
278.   Special Warranty.
279.   Covenant for Further Assurance.
280. Estoppel.
281. Adverse Possession.
282. Accretion.
283. Devise.
284. Descent.
285. Judicial Process.
286.   Conveyances under Licenses.
287.   Conveyances under Decrees.
288–290. Tax Titles.
291. Eminent Domain.

TITLE DEFINED.

250. Title is the means by which the ownership of real property is acquired and held. This is either
(a) By descent, or
(b) By purchase.

The fact which in any case gives or creates ownership over real property is called title. Title signifies the manner in which estates and interests in land are acquired. At the beginning of real-property law in any country there must be an original acquisition of title to land. After title has been thus acquired all subsequent acquisitions of title to the same land must be by transfer of the title.

Descent and Purchase.

All titles are said to be acquired by descent or by purchase. Purchase means more than mere buying, it includes the acquisition of title by devise or by gift. In short title by purchase means title acquired in all ways except by descent.

ACQUISITION OF TITLE BY STATE.

251. Title is acquired by the state
(a) By discovery, conquest, and treaty.
(b) By confiscation and escheat.
(c) By exercise of the right of eminent domain.
(d) By ordinary transfer from individuals.

Discovery, Conquest, and Treaty.

In the United States the title to the land was acquired by European governments by discovery. The rights so gained were claimed to be exclusive against other nations, though certain rights were recognized in the Indians as occupants.[1] Great Britain acquired title to the land within the limits of the original colonies partly by discovery and partly by conquests and treaties. Rights so acquired were granted to proprietors and corporations, and these

[1] Martin v. Waddell's Lessee, 16 Pet. 367; Fletcher v. Peck, 6 Cranch, 87. See, as to Indian titles, 1 Dembitz, Land Tit. § 65.

in turn purchased the rights of the Indians. These conveyances by the Indians were held not to convey the freehold, but merely to release the rights of the grantors.[2] Private persons were, in the main, prohibited from buying lands from the Indians without authority from the government of the colony in which the lands were situated.[3] The rights of the crown of Great Britain passed as a result of the Revolutionary War to the states and to the United States.[4] The rights of the states in land thus acquired, which had not been disposed of to actual settlers, were nearly all conveyed at a later time to the general government. The lands held by the United States as public domain have been increased since that time by various treaties and purchases, the treatment of which pertains rather to history than to law.

Confiscation and Escheat.

In some states the lands of persons convicted of treason or felony are confiscated by the state,[5] and in nearly all of the states, if a person dies intestate, leaving no heirs, his real property escheats to the state.[6] This kind of escheat is not the same as the feudal escheat which a lord could claim on the death of his tenant without heirs.[7]

Eminent Domain.

The acquisition of land by the state under the power of eminent domain is subject to the same rules as acquisition in this way by

---

[2] Johnson v. McIntosh, 8 Wheat. 543; Cherokee Nation v. Georgia, 5 Pet. 1, 17; U. S. v. Cook, 19 Wall. 591.

[3] Goodell v. Jackson, 20 Johns. (N. Y.) 693. And see Marshall, C. J., in Johnson v. McIntosh, 8 Wheat. 543.

[4] Martin v. Waddell's Lessee, 16 Pet. 367; Com. v. Roxbury, 9 Gray (Mass.) 451; People v. Ferry Co., 68 N. Y. 71, 78.

[5] 1 Stim. Am. St. Law, § 1162. The United States constitution forbids forfeiture beyond the life of the offender. Under the act of July 17, 1862, confiscating the property of persons in rebellion, the offender had no estate remaining in him which he could convey. Wallach v. Van Riswick, 92 U. S. 202. When a forfeiture is enforced, the United States or state takes only the title of the offender. Borland v. Dean, 4 Mason, 174, Fed. Cas. No. 1,660; Shields v. Schiff, 124 U. S. 351, 8 Sup. Ct. 510.

[6] 1 Stim. Am. St. Law, art. 115. As to escheat of land held by an alien on office found, see ante, p. 388.

[7] See ante, p. 30.

§ 253) GRANT FROM THE STATE. 401

private persons and corporations, and will be treated of in that connection.[8]

Transfer from Private Persons.

And for the same reason acquisition of land by the state from private persons by any of the modes of conveyance which operate between individuals will not be considered here. The states may convey land to the United States, or vice versa, by ordinary forms of conveyance.

ACQUISITION BY PRIVATE PERSONS.

252. Title is acquired by private persons
 (a) **By grant from the state** (p. 401).
 (b) **By conveyance from individuals** (p. 405).
 (c) **By estoppel** (p. 450).
 (d) **By adverse possession** (p. 456).
 (e) **By accretion** (p. 470).
 (f) **By devise** (p. 472).
 (g) **By descent** (p. 478).
 (h) **By judicial process** (p. 486).

GRANT FROM THE STATE.

253. **Land owned by the United States and the states is conveyed to individuals by instruments of conveyance called patents.**

Titles held by private persons are, of course, originally derived from the state. In construing grants from the state the cases say the presumption is always in favor of the state, thus varying from the usual rule, which is that in conveyances all presumptions are in favor of the grantee and against the grantor.[9] It is doubted, however, whether the rule as to the presumption being in favor of the state obtains in cases where the grantee has paid a valuable

---

[8] Post, p. 494.

[9] Mayor, etc., of Allegheny v. Ohio & P. R. Co., 26 Pa. St. 355; Townsend v. Brown, 24 N. J. Law, 80; Dubuque & P. R. Co. v. Litchfield, 23 How. 66, 88.

consideration.[10] The rule is never applied unless there is an actual ambiguity.[11] When an estate on condition is granted by the state, no entry is necessary to revest the title in the state on breach of the condition.[12]

Public Land System.

The lands owned by the United States are surveyed and sold according to the following plan, and states which own public lands follow the plan of the federal government very closely:[13] The lands are divided, by lines running to the cardinal points of the compass, into ranges, townships, and sections; the ranges being numbered east or west from a principal meridian. Each township contains 23,040 acres, being 6 miles square. The sections contain 640 acres, and are divided in halves, quarters, eighths, etc.[14] By this system any portion of land may be located with certainty and accuracy by means of section, township, etc. Descriptions of this kind are sufficient in deeds.[15] The public domain can be sold only by authority of congress. This authority is exercised by either general or special acts.[16] The first sales of the public domain were made in large tracts. But since this congressional survey was adopted the public land has been sold through local land offices established in the Western states; the land is first put up at auction to be sold to the highest bidder at not less than a minimum price, and, if not disposed of at that price, it is left to be sold by the land office.[17]

Certificate and Patent.

One who wishes to acquire public land must make an entry on the land selected, and, after making the required payment, or

[10] Proprietors of Charles River Bridge v. Proprietors of Warren Bridge, 11 Pet. 420, 589; Hyman v. Read, 13 Cal. 444.

[11] Martin v. Waddell's Lessee, 16 Pet. 367, 411; Com. v. Roxbury, 9 Gray (Mass.) 492; Proprietors of Charles River Bridge v. Proprietors of Warren Bridge, 11 Pet. 420, 589.

[12] Kennedy v. McCartney's Heirs, 4 Port. (Ala.) 141.

[13] See 1 Dembitz, Land Tit. 18, 513.

[14] Rev. St. U. S. 1878, § 2395 et seq.

[15] Bowen v. Prout, 52 Ill. 354.

[16] Irvine v. Marshall, 20 How. 558; Bagnell v. Broderick, 13 Pet. 436.

[17] Rev. St. U. S. 1878, § 2357.

§ 253)　　　GRANT FROM THE STATE.　　　403

becoming entitled to the land under the provisions of the federal homestead law,[18] a certificate of entry is issued by the register of the land office, which entitles the claimant to a patent. The patent is the formal conveyance. It is signed by the president of the United States, or by some authorized person for him, and sealed with the seal of the United States. The cases as to the effect of a certificate of entry and a patent are somewhat confused, and there is in particular some conflict between the decisions of the federal and the state courts. A patent is the highest evidence of title.[19] Between two patents, the first issued is superior, and the second conveys nothing.[20] A patent can be assailed only for fraud or mistake, and can be avoided only by the government, or by suit in its name.[21] A patent cannot be attacked in a collateral proceeding.[22] Until the patent is issued, the legal title remains in the United States.[23] The equitable title, however, is in the holder of the certificate of entry.[24] This equitable title he may sell or devise, and it descends to his heirs.[25] His heir, devisee, or assignee may claim the patent by virtue of the certificate.[26] If the claimant dies before the patent is issued, it is issued to his heir or devisee, as the case may be.[27] If it is issued in the name of the holder of the certificate after his death, it takes effect for the benefit of the heirs.[28]

[18] See ante, p. 126.
[19] Irvine v. Tarbat, 105 Cal. 237, 38 Pac. 896; Bagnell v. Broderick, 13 Pet. 436. And see Maxey v. O'Connor, 23 Tex. 238.
[20] Stockton v. Williams, 1 Doug. (Mich.) 546, 560.
[21] Carter v. Thompson, 65 Fed. 329; San Pedro & Canon del Agua Co. v. U. S., 146 U. S. 120, 13 Sup. Ct. 94; U. S. v. Minor, 114 U. S. 233, 5 Sup. Ct. 836; U. S. v. Iron Silver Min. Co., 128 U. S. 673, 9 Sup. Ct. 195. But see Tameling v. Emmigration Co., 93 U. S. 644.
[22] Knight v. Land Ass'n, 142 U. S. 161, 12 Sup. Ct. 258. But see Minter v. Crommelin, 18 How. 87.
[23] U. S. v. Steenerson, 1 C. C. A. 552, 50 Fed. 504.
[24] American Mortg. Co. v. Hopper, 56 Fed. 67.
[25] Brill v. Stiles, 35 Ill. 305.
[26] Brush v. Ware, 15 Pet. 93; Forsythe v. Ballance, 6 McLean, 562, Fed. Cas. No. 4,951.
[27] Galt v. Galloway, 4 Pet. 332; Reeder v. Barr, 4 Ohio, 458; Shanks v. Lucas, 4 Blackf. (Ind.) 476.
[28] Schedda v. Sawyer, 4 McLean, 181, Fed. Cas. No. 12,443; Stubblefield v.

Pre-Emption.

Under the pre-emption laws, which are enacted for the purpose of encouraging actual settlement of the public lands, a right is acquired by entry and settlement to claim a certificate of entry at the minimum price fixed for the land in preference to any other person. The right can be claimed only for 160 acres,[29] and this must not be lands which have been reserved, or which are within any city or town. Nor can lands on which there are known salt or other mines or lands which are occupied for the purpose of trade or manufacture be pre-empted.[30] One claiming the pre-emption right must not own more than 320 acres in any state or territory, and must not have abandoned, in order to make the pre-emption, a home within the state or territory wherein the pre-empted land lies.[31] The right of pre-emption is assignable only against the assignor,[32] and not against the government.[33] Nor is it subject to levy for the debts of the pre-emptor.[34] The pre-emption laws were repealed by the act of March 3, 1891,[35] and therefore land can no longer be acquired in this way.[36]

Boggs, 2 Ohio St. 216; Phillips v. Sherman, 36 Ala. 189. But see Galt v. Galloway, 4 Pet. 332; Galloway v. Findley, 12 Pet. 264; Blankenpickler v. Anderson's Heirs, 16 Grat. (Va.) 59.

[29] Rev. St. U. S. § 2259.

[30] Rev. St. U. S. § 2258.

[31] Rev. St. U. S. § 2260. And see Bogan v. Mortgage Co., 11 C. C. A. 128, 63 Fed. 192.

[32] Delaunay v. Burnett, 9 Ill. 454; Camp v. Smith, 2 Minn. 155 (Gil. 131). The pre-emptor's rights descend to his heirs. Bernier v. Bernier, 147 U. S. 243, 13 Sup. Ct. 244.

[33] Rev. St. U. S. § 2263.

[34] Rogers v. Rawlings, 8 Port. (Ala.) 326.

[35] 26 Stat. 1097.

[36] See 1 Dembitz, Land Tit. 524.

CONVEYANCES.

254. The instruments by which title is conveyed are of four kinds:
  (a) **Common-law conveyances** (p. 405).
  (b) **Conveyances operating under the statute of uses** (p. 409).
  (c) **Modern statutory conveyances** (p. 411).
  (d) **Conveyances of registered titles** (p. 412).

SAME—COMMON-LAW CONVEYANCES.

255. The common-law conveyances are divided into
  (a) **Primary, which include**
    (1) **Feoffment** (p. 405).
    (2) **Gift** (p. 406).
    (3) **Grant** (p. 407).
    (4) **Lease** (p. 407).
    (5) **Exchange** (p. 407).
    (6) **Partition** (p. 408).
  (b) **Secondary, which include**
    (1) **Release** (p. 408).
    (2) **Confirmation** (p. 408).
    (3) **Surrender** (p. 408).
    (4) **Assignment** (p. 409).
    (5) **Defeasance** (p. 409).

Primary and Secondary Conveyances.

By primary conveyances are meant those which are original, and create estates in land. Secondary conveyances are those which enlarge, restrain, extinguish, or transfer estates already existing.[37] These distinctions are not now much used.

Feoffment.

Feoffments, though little used in modern times, were at common law, in early times, almost the only form of conveyance used for

[37] 2 Bl. Comm. 310, 324.

the transfer of estates in possession. Feoffment signifies the granting of a feud, and the word "feoffment" was used at common law as meaning the conveyance of a fee simple. Feoffment as a conveyance consists of a symbolical delivery of the land by the grantor or feoffor, as he was called, to the grantee or feoffee. This was done by the persons going upon the land, and the feoffor giving to the feoffee a twig or turf taken from the land, at the same time using words which showed that he intended to transfer the land to him. This ceremony was called livery of seisin.[38] There was a distinction made between seisin in deed and seisin in law. The former was when the livery of seisin took place on the land itself; the latter when the parties were not actually on the land,— as when the transfer was made in sight of the premises, but without an actual entry on them.[39] In later times livery of seisin was usually accompanied by a written deed, especially when the limitations of the estate granted were numerous. But this deed was only evidence of title, and not a conveyance itself.[40] As has already been said, a feoffment might have a tortious operation, as when a person attempted to convey by feoffment a greater estate than he himself possessed. The effect of such a feoffment was to destroy the estate which the feoffor did possess, and entitle the remainder-man to enter at once. The tortious operation of these conveyances is now abolished in the United States.[41]

Gift.

"Gift" was the term applied to a conveyance creating an estate in fee tail. The only difference between a gift and a feoffment was that the former, while accompanied by the same ceremony as a feoffment, had limitations to the heirs of the body of the first donee; that is, an estate tail was created.[42]

---

[38] See 2 Bl. Comm. 310, 313; Perry v. Price, 1 Mo. 553; Bryan v. Bradley, 16 Com. 474.

[39] Digby, Hist. Real Prop. (4th Ed.) 145.

[40] French v. French, 3 N. H. 234; Smith v. Lawrence, 12 Mich. 431. Livery might be made by the delivery of the deed. Thoroughgood's Case, 9 Coke, 136a.

[41] See ante, p. 59.

[42] 2 Bl. Comm. 316; Pierson v. Armstrong, 1 Iowa, 282, 292.

Grant.

"Grant" was the name of the conveyances which were proper for the transfer of incorporeal interests in land,[43] which were said "to lie in grant," and not "in livery," the latter being the term used to designate conveyances of corporeal interests by feoffment. The term "grant" is now used to designate all kinds of conveyances.[44] A grant did not have any tortious operation.

Lease.

A lease is the instrument used to create estates less than freehold, and usually contains a reservation of rent. At common law, however, the term was applied to conveyances of particular estates as for life as well as estates in fee simple in which a rent was reserved.[45] By the early common law no writing was necessary for a lease, though an entry was.[46] Now, however, by the statute of frauds, there must be a writing when the lease is for more than a short period, which differs in the various states.[47] Leases have already been considered more fully in treating of estates less than freehold.[48]

Exchange.

An exchange is a "mutual grant of equal interests," the transfer of one estate being the consideration for the transfer of the other. Exchange applies to transfers of estates in expectancy as well as of those in possession.[49] But estates which are exchanged must be of the same kind, as a fee simple for a fee simple, and not a fee simple for a life estate. The estates, however, need not be of the same value.[50] To make an exchange effectual, there must be an entry, though no livery of seisin is necessary. If the estates are not in possession, a deed is required, and in the deed the word

---

[43] 2 Bl. Comm. 317; Huff v. McCauley, 53 Pa. St. 206; Drake v. Wells, 11 Allen (Mass.) 141. As to a reversion, see Doe v. Cole, 7 Barn. & C. 243.

[44] Ross v. Adams, 28 N. J. Law, 160; Peck v. Walton, 26 Vt. 85.

[45] 2 Bl. Comm. 317.

[46] Williams v. Downing, 18 Pa. St. 60.

[47] 1 Stim. Am. St. Law, § 4143.

[48] Ante, p. 128.

[49] 2 Bl. Comm. 323. And see Long v. Fuller, 21 Wis. 123.

[50] Wilcox v. Randall, 7 Barb. (N. Y.) 633.

"escambium" had to be used at common law, and no equivalent expression was sufficient.[51]

Partition.

Partition has already been treated of as the method of dividing joint estates so that the owners would hold in severalty,[52] and needs no further consideration here.

Release.

We now come to the secondary conveyances, the first of which is release. A release technically is the conveyance of a future estate to one having an estate in possession, though, if the grantee has a constructive possession, it is sufficient. For a release no livery of seisin is necessary, but the future estate must be an immediate one; that is, with no intervening estate between the one in possession and the estate which is released.[53] A release is like our modern quitclaim deed, except that in the quitclaim possession in the grantee is not necessary.[54] And, further, in the release, privity of estate between the parties was required.[55] The usual words in the release are "demise, release, and forever quitclaim."

Confirmation.

A confirmation is a conveyance used to make good a former voidable conveyance.[56] It cannot be used if the conveyance which it is attempted to validate was originally void,[57] though such an instrument would now by many courts be made operative as some other form of conveyance; for instance, as a bargain and sale.[58] The operative words used in a confirmation are "given, granted, ratified, approved, and confirmed."

Surrender.

A surrender is the converse of a release,—that is, it is a conveyance by one in possession of a present vested estate of his in-

[51] 2 Bl. Comm. 323.
[52] Ante, p. 344.
[53] 2 Bl. Comm. 324.
[54] Doe v. Reed, 5 Ill. 117; Kerr v. Freeman, 33 Miss. 292.
[55] Smith's Heirs v. Bank, 21 Ala. 125.
[56] Adlum v. Yard, 1 Rawle (Pa.) 171, 177; Ing v. Brown, 3 Md. Ch. 521; English v. Young, 10 B. Mon. (Ky.) 141.
[57] Branham v. Mayor, etc., 24 Cal. 585; Barr v. Schroeder, 32 Cal. 609.
[58] Fauntleroy's Heirs v. Dunn, 3 B. Mon. (Ky.) 594.

terest to one entitled to the next estate in the remainder or reversion,[59] as in a release, privity of estate between the parties is necessary, and the surrender can be only to one who holds the next immediate estate.[60] No deed, however, is necessary to the validity of a surrender.[61] The technical words used for a conveyance operating as a surrender are "surrendered, granted, and yielded up." Quitclaim deeds are now used in place of surrenders.

Assignment.

An assignment is, as we already know, the term applied to a conveyance of a leasehold which is already in existence.[62] So, too, there may be an assignment of a mortgage.[63]

Defeasance.

A defeasance has been treated of in connection with mortgages. it being a condition, either in the mortgage or in the separate instrument, which makes the mortgage void on the performance of the condition.[64]

SAME—CONVEYANCES UNDER THE STATUTE OF USES.

256. The conveyances operating under the statute of uses are
- (a) **Covenant to stand seised** (p. 410).
- (b) **Bargain and sale** (p. 410).
- (c) **Lease and release** (p. 411).

[59] Martin v. Stearns, 52 Iowa, 345, 3 N. W. 92; Scott's Ex'r v. Scott, 18 Grat. (Va.) 159.

[60] 2 Bl. Comm. 326.

[61] Milling v. Becker, 96 Pa. St. 182; Whitley v. Gough, Dyer, 140b; Thomas v. Cook, 2 Barn. & Ald. 119; Nickells v. Atherstone, 10 Q. B. 944. Cf. Dodd v. Acklom, 6 Mon. & G. 672; Phené v. Popplewell, 12 C. B. (N. S.) 334. But see Auer v. Penn, 99 Pa. St. 370; Magennis v. MacCullogh, Gilb. Ch. 235; Roe v. Archbishop of York, 6 East, 86. And see Hamerton v. Stead, 3 Barn. & C. 478. A surrender may be implied by the acceptance of another lease, Ive v. Sams, Cro. Eliz. 521; Lyon v. Reed, 13 Mees. & W. 285; but not if the second lease is void, Davison v. Stanley, 4 Burrows, 2210; Doe v. Courtenay, 11 Q. B. 702; Doe v. Poole, 11 Q. B. 713. And see Schieffelin v. Carpenter, 15 Wend. (N. Y.) 400; Coe v. Hobby, 72 N. Y. 141.

[62] See ante, p. 147.

[63] See ante, p. 205. And see Cowles v. Ricketts, 1 Iowa, 582.

[64] See ante, p. 183, and 2 Bl. Comm. 327.

In treating of equitable estates it was seen that the statute of uses made it possible to convey lands by instruments which would have no effect at common law.[65] Three conveyances operating under this statute came into general use. They were covenants to stand seised, bargain and sale, and lease and release. These conveyances are used to create legal estates. The conveyance itself transfers an equitable estate,—that is, a use,—and the statute executes the legal estate in the cestui que use, by transferring the seisin to him.[66]

Covenant to Stand Seised.

A covenant to stand seised is a conveyance operating under the statute of uses, in which the consideration is either blood or marriage; that is, only a good consideration is required.[67] In Massachusetts no consideration whatever is required for the validity of a covenant to stand seised.[68] This form of conveyance is practically obsolete in the United States, though the courts, in order to give effect to the intention of the parties, will sometimes construe a conveyance to be a covenant to stand seised.[69] From the nature of the consideration it could be used only to convey land to a husband or wife, children, or other kinsmen.

Bargain and Sale.

The conveyance called a bargain and sale was the same as a covenant to stand seised, except that a valuable consideration was required for its validity.[70] Many of the cases hold that a recital in the deed of the consideration is sufficient evidence of its having been received, and the requirement for a valuable consideration has become a mere form.[71] The operation of a deed of bargain and

---

[65] Ante, p. 254.

[66] 2 Bl. Comm. 327; Chenery v. Stevens, 97 Mass. 77.

[67] Jackson v. Sebring, 16 Johns. (N. Y.) 515; Jackson v. Delancey, 4 Cow. (N. Y.) 427; Bell v. Scammon, 15 N. H. 381.

[68] Trafton v. Hawes, 102 Mass. 533.

[69] Eckman v. Eckman, 68 Pa. St. 460; Fisher v. Strickler, 10 Pa. St. 348; Jackson v. McKenny, 3 Wend. (N. Y.) 233; Jackson v. Swart, 20 Johns. (N. Y.) 85; Wallis v. Wallis, 4 Mass. 135.

[70] Wood v. Chapin, 13 N. Y. 509; Jackson v. Alexander, 3 Johns. (N. Y.) 484; Wood v. Beach, 7 Vt. 522; Busey v. Reese, 38 Md. 264.

[71] Fetrow v. Merriwether, 53 Ill. 278; Jackson v. Fish, 10 Johns. (N. Y.)

sale is as follows: The conveyance which is in the form of a contract to sell raises a use in the feoffee which the statute of uses executes, and thereby conveys the legal estate to the bargainee.[72] In order to give notoriety to conveyances by bargain and sale, which became the usual form for transfer of lands, the statute of enrollments provides that such deeds must be enrolled within six months after their execution, or be of no validity.[73]

Lease and Release.

To evade the requirements of the statute of enrollments the expedient called a lease and a release was devised, and soon became the most usual form for a conveyance for lands. Its operation was as follows. A lease, usually for one year, was given to the intended grantee. This was not required to be enrolled, because the statute did not make any provision for chattel interests. By a release dated the next day after the lease the reversion of the estate was conveyed to the lessee, who in this way acquired the full interest in the land without the use of any conveyance which had to be enrolled.[74]

SAME—MODERN STATUTORY CONVEYANCES.

257. Statutes in many states provide short forms of conveyances, which are either
  (a) Warranty deeds, or
  (b) Quitclaim deeds.

In a number of states short forms have been prescribed by the statutes, which are declared sufficient to convey various estates in land.[75] Except where superseded by these statutory conveyances, conveyances operating under the statute of uses may still be employed. The common-law conveyances are, however, still sufficient to transfer lands, though their use is unusual,[76] with the exception that feoff-

---

456; Jackson v. Dillon's Lessee, 2 Overt. (Tenn.) 261. But see Perry v. Price, 1 Mo. 553.

[72] Chenery v. Stevens, 97 Mass. 77.

[73] 27 Hen. VIII. c. 16.

[74] 2 Bl. Comm. 339; Lewis' Lessee v. Beall, 4 Har. & McH. (Md.) 488.

[75] 1 Stim. Am. St. Law, art. 148.

[76] Funk v. Creswell, 5 Iowa, 68; Brewer v. Hardy, 22 Pick. (Mass.) 376; Rogers v. Fire Co., 9 Wend. (N. Y.) 611.

ments have been abolished in some states.[77] Where statutory forms have been provided, their exclusive use is not required. Many of the deeds now in use have a dual character from the operative words used, which frequently are "give, grant, bargain, and sell." When such words are used, courts will construe them in the way most fitted to give effect to the intention of the parties,[78] but they will be held to convey legal, rather than equitable, estates, when such construction is possible.[79]

Warranty and Quitclaim Deeds.

Our most usual form of modern conveyance is called a warranty deed. Its distinguishing characteristic is that it contains, besides the words of conveyance, covenants of warranty, the meaning and effect of which will be explained subsequently.[80] Quitclaim deeds differ from warranty deeds in that they contain no such covenants, and are much like a common-law release, except, as has already been stated, they need not be to one in possession.[81] A quitclaim deed transfers only the title which the grantor has,[82] and does not prevent the grantor from setting up a future acquired title.[83]

SAME—REGISTERED TITLES.

258. Illinois has provided by statute an optional system of title registration, the principal features of which are:

  (a) Certificates of title are issued to the owner of each estate in registered land for his interest (p. 413).

  (b) Transfers of title can be made only on the public register (p. 413).

[77] 1 Stim. Am. St. Law, § 1470.
[78] Russell v. Coffin, 8 Pick. (Mass.) 143; Trafton v. Hawes, 102 Mass. 533.
[79] Sprague v. Woods, 4 Watts & S. (Pa.) 194.
[80] Post, p. 446.
[81] Kyle v. Kavanagh, 103 Mass. 356; Rowe v. Beckett, 30 Ind. 154.
[82] Gage v. Sanborn (Mich.) 64 N. W. 32; McInerney v. Beck, 10 Wash. 515, 39 Pac. 130.
[83] Frost v. Society, 56 Mich. 62, 22 N. W. 189; City and County of San Francisco v. Lawton, 18 Cal. 465. But see Welch v. Dutton, 79 Ill. 465; Green Bay & M. Canal Co. v. Hewitt, 55 Wis. 96, 12 N. W. 382.

(c) **Acquisition of title by adverse possession is abolished as to registered land** (p. 414).

(d) **An indemnity fund is provided to reimburse any persons who may be injured by the operation of the act** (p. 414).

By an act approved June 13, 1895,[84] the legislature of Illinois inaugurated a system of registration of titles following in its main lines the German Grundbuch and the Australian system of registry of titles, or the so-called Torrens title system.* The act does not become operative in any county until adopted by the voters of the county.[85] After the act has been adopted by a county, the registration of the title of any owner is optional with him.[86]

Certificates of Title.

When a tract of land is registered, a certificate of title is made out and kept in the office of the registrar, and a duplicate given the owner. Each estate in the land is represented by a separate certificate, on which are indorsed "the particulars of all estates, mortgages, incumbrances, liens, and charges to which the owner's title is subject."[87] Joint owners may each take separate certificates for their individual interests, or may have all the interests embraced in a single certificate.[88]

Same—Mortgages, Leases, and Other Charges.

Mortgages and other incumbrances, contracts to sell, and leases for not more than 10 years, are not represented by separate certificates, but the instrument creating the mortgage, etc., is filed in the registrar's office, and a duplicate retained by the mortgagee or lessee, a "memorial" of the incumbrance being entered on the certificate.[89]

Transfers of Registered Land.

After land has been registered, any of the ordinary forms of conveyance purporting to transfer the title operate only as contracts to convey, and as authority to the registrar to transfer the title.[90] The transfer itself is effected by the surrender of the duplicate

---

* Since the text was written a similar act has been passed in Ohio. 35 Wkly. Law Bul. Append.

[84] Laws Ill. 1895, p. 107.
[85] Laws Ill. 1895, § 94.
[86] Laws Ill. 1895, § 7.
[87] Laws Ill. 1895, § 20.
[88] Laws Ill. 1895, § 22.
[89] Laws Ill. 1895, §§ 48–55.
[90] Laws Ill. 1895, § 45.

certificate of title and the issuing of a new certificate to the transferee.[91] If only part of the owner's interest is transferred, another certificate is issued to him for the interest remaining in him.[92] Transfers by descent, devise, or by judicial process are made by the registrar in accordance with the orders and decrees of the court.[93]

No Title by Adverse Possession.

Section 30 of the act provides: "After land has been registered, no title thereto, adverse or in derogation to the title of the registered owner, shall be acquired by any length of possession merely."

Indemnity Fund.

When land is first registered, one-tenth of one per cent. of its value must be paid to the registrar, to provide an indemnity fund, out of which the county is to reimburse any person sustaining "damage through any omission, mistake, or misfeasance of the registrar." [94]

SAME—REQUISITES OF DEEDS.

259. For a valid deed or other conveyance of land the following are requisites:
  (a) **Property to be conveyed** (p. 415).
  (b) **Words of conveyance** (p. 416).
  (c) **A description of the property** (p. 419).
  (d) **A writing, executed by signing, and in some states by sealing** (p. 426).
  (e) **Delivery and acceptance** (p. 433).
  (f) **Acknowledgment, in some states** (p. 436).
  (g) **Witnesses, in some states** (p. 439).
  (h) **Registry, in some states** (p. 439).

260. Acknowledgment, witnesses, and registry are not, in some states, essential to the validity of a deed, but are necessary to give priority.

By the early common law, feoffments were sufficient to convey title by the mere transfer of possession, but now a writing is required by the statute of frauds for the transfer of any estate,

---

[91] Laws Ill. 1895, § 39.
[92] Laws Ill. 1895, § 40.
[93] Laws Ill. 1895, §§ 59–82.
[94] Laws Ill. 1895, §§ 90–93.

§ 261)　　　REQUISITES OF DEEDS.　　　415

except, as already seen,[95] tenancies for short terms. Conveyances in writing are called deeds. The definition of a deed in real property law is, "a sealed writing conveying real estate." But in those states where seals have been abolished, written instruments which convey real estate are still termed deeds. And hereafter the term deed must be taken to mean, unless otherwise specified, a written instrument conveying the title to lands with or without a seal, according to the local laws. Deeds, however, are to be distinguished from mere agreements to convey lands, which belong to the law of contracts.[96] Instruments of conveyance, such as mortgages and leases, are properly included under the term "deed."

261. PROPERTY TO BE CONVEYED—For a valid deed there must be some real property to be conveyed.

In order that a deed may operate, there must be something to be conveyed. What can be conveyed by deed will be seen by referring to the discussion of what is real property, given in our first chapter; and the converse is also true,—that anything which is real property can only be conveyed by deed.[97] On the other hand, at common law it was held that a mere possibility of having an estate in land at a future time could not be conveyed,[98] but this rule has been somewhat relaxed. For instance, an heir has been permitted to make a deed of lands which he expected to inherit, and when the title came to him by descent his grantee was given the benefit thereof.[99] But the contrary has also been held.[100]

[95] Ante, p. 132.

[96] See Clark, Cont. 103.

[97] A deed is necessary for the conveyance of an incorporeal hereditament. Duke of Somerset v. Fogwell, 5 Barn. & C. 875; Bird v. Higginson, 2 Adol. & E. 696; Tottel v. Howell, Noy, 54. And see ante, p. 351. A parol license to a tenant from year to year to quit in the middle of a quarter is bad. Mollett v. Brayne, 2 Camp. 103. A written instrument is, of course, necessary for the conveyance of a freehold interest in lands. Jackson v. Wood, 12 Johns. (N. Y.) 73. But see Neale v. Neale, 9 Wall. 1; Syler v. Eckhart, 1 Bin. (Pa.) 378.

[98] Dart v. Dart, 7 Conn. 255.

[99] Trull v. Eastman, 3 Metc. (Mass.) 121; Stover v. Eycleshimer, 46 Barb. (N. Y.) 84.

[100] Davis v. Hayden, 9 Mass. 519. The conveyance of an expectancy can-

262. WORDS OF CONVEYANCE—A valid deed must contain sufficient words of conveyance to transfer an estate in the land from the grantor to the grantee. This will be treated under the following heads:

(a) **Names of parties** (p. 416).
(b) **Granting clause** (p. 417).
(c) **Exceptions** (p. 417).
(d) **Reservations** (p. 418).
(e) **Habendum** (p. 418).

Names of Parties.

The name of the grantor should be stated in the deed, though some cases hold that the mere signing of the grantor's name is sufficient.[101] If the grantor's name is mentioned in the deed, his signing the deed by a wrong name will not invalidate it.[102] The grantee in a deed must be made certain, and therefore it is generally necessary to name him, though a description of the person will be sufficient if it clearly designates who is to take; as, for instance, where the grantee is named by his office.[103] A deed of land to a "neighborhood" is not sufficiently certain.[104] The grantee may, however, be designated by an assumed name, though a deed to a fictitious

---

not be given effect as an executory contract to convey unless there is a sufficient consideration. Bayler v. Com., 40 Pa. St. 37. And cf. Gardner v. Pace (Ky.) 11 S. W. 779.

[101] Burge v. Smith, 27 N. H. 332; Elliott v. Sleeper, 2 N. H. 525; Catlin v. Ware, 9 Mass. 218; Lord Say & Seal's Case, 10 Mod. 40. And see Mardes v. Meyers, 8 Tex. Civ. App. 542, 28 S. W. 693. A deed signed, "A. B., Executor," shows sufficiently that it is made in a representative capacity. Babcock v. Collins, 60 Minn. 73, 61 N. W. 1020. But see Agricultural Bank of Mississippi v. Rice, 4 How. 225; Peabody v. Hewett, 52 Me. 33; Harrison v. Simons, 55 Ala. 510; Adams v. Medsker, 25 W. Va. 127. When a husband conveys his life estate in his wife's lands, the fee will not pass by the wife signing the deed. Flagg v. Bean, 25 N. H. 49, 62, 63.

[102] Middleton v. Findla, 25 Cal. 76. But cf. Boothroyd v. Engles, 23 Mich. 19.

[103] Lawrence v. Fletcher, 8 Metc. (Mass.) 153. And see American Emigrant Co. v. Clark, 62 Iowa, 182, 17 N. W. 483.

[104] Thomas v. Inhabitants of Marshfield, 10 Pick. (Mass.) 364. A deed to "A. B. Deceased Estate" is void for want of a grantee. McInerney v. Beck, 10 Wash. 515, 39 Pac. 130.

§ 262)   REQUISITES OF DEEDS.   417

person will not be good.[105] A mistake in the name of a corporation which is to take as grantee will not make the conveyance void if the intended grantee can be ascertained.[106] And where the grantee is uncertain, evidence is admissible to show which of several persons was intended to take,[107] and parties to the deed are sufficiently designated by their first and last names without the use of a middle name;[108] and so the addition of the word "junior" and "senior" are not necessary.[109] It is usual to make some "addition" to the names of the parties in the deed, as by giving the residence. And in the case of a married woman the name of her husband is frequently added.

Granting Clause.

In order that any deed may be operative, it must contain words of conveyance sufficient to transfer an estate from the grantor to the grantee.[110] The technical words which are used in connection with the various forms of conveyances have already been mentioned,[111] and these words, or some equivalent of them, must be used. Therefore a deed which contains no other words of conveyance than "sign over" will not pass a title.[112]

Exceptions.

An exception is something reserved from the operation of the deed; that is, it is something which would otherwise pass by the description of the lands to be conveyed.[113] For a valid exception,

[105] Thomas v. Wyatt, 31 Mo. 188.
[106] Ashville Division No. 15 v. Aston, 92 N. C. 578.
[107] Webb v. Den, 17 How. 579; Aultman & Taylor Manuf'g Co. v. Richardson, 7 Neb. 1.
[108] Games v. Stiles, 14 Pet. 322; Dunn v. Games, 1 McLean, 321, Fed. Cas. No. 4,176; Erskine v. Davis, 25 Ill. 251; Franklin v. Talmadge, 5 Johns. (N. Y.) 84. A middle initial may be important when used. See Ambs v. Railway Co., 44 Minn. 266, 46 N. W. 321.
[109] Kincaid v. Howe, 10 Mass. 203; Cobb v. Lucas, 15 Pick. (Mass.) 7.
[110] Hummelman v. Mounts, 87 Ind. 178; Webb v. Mullins, 78 Ala. 111.
[111] Ante, pp. 36, 47, 56.
[112] McKinney v. Settles, 31 Mo. 541.
[113] Craig v. Wells, 11 N. Y. 315; Thompson v. Gregory, 4 Johns. (N. Y.) 81; Whitaker v. Brown, 46 Pa. St. 197; Ashcroft v. Railroad Co., 126 Mass. 197; Stockbridge Iron Co. v. Hudson Iron Co., 107 Mass. 290; Wiley v. Sirdorus, 41 Iowa, 224; Sloan v. Furniture Co., 29 Ohio St. 568.

REAL PROP.—27

the thing excepted must be described with as much particularity as is required in the description of the land conveyed.[114] All rights in the land excepted from the operation of the deed remain in the grantor as they were before the conveyance.[115]

Reservations.

A reservation is a right created out of the land granted, such as the reservation of a rent. The word "reservation," however, need not be used if the intention is otherwise clear.[116] An exception, so called, in the deed, will be construed to be a reservation if such was the intention of the parties; and a reservation will be held an exception if that was the purpose.[117] A reservation can be made only in favor of the grantor; not for a stranger.[118] In creating a reservation the same words of limitation are necessary as in the creation of an estate.[119] Reservations are used generally for the creation of rents,[120] but may be for other purposes, such as an easement reserved to the grantor out of the land granted.[121] A reservation is the same as a reddendum.

Habendum.

The habendum of a deed is merely formal, and is that part of the conveyance which commences with the words "to have and to hold."

[114] Thompson v. Gregory, 4 Johns. (N. Y.) 81; Thayer v. Torrey, 37 N. J. Law, 339. But see Wells v. Dillard, 93 Ga. 682, 20 S. E. 263. No words of limitation are necessary. Winthrop v. Fairbanks, 41 Me. 307. Cf. Achorn v. Jackson, 86 Me. 215, 29 Atl. 989.

[115] Munn v. Worrall, 53 N. Y. 44; Whitaker v. Brown, 46 Pa. St. 197.

[116] Hornbeck v. Westbrook, 9 Johns. (N. Y.) 73; Rich v. Zeilsdorff, 22 Wis. 544; Barnes v. Burl, 38 Conn. 541.

[117] Winthrop v. Fairbanks, 41 Me. 307.

[118] Illinois Cent. R. Co. v. Indiana & I. C. R. Co., 85 Ill. 211; Hornbeck v. Westbrook, 9 Johns. (N. Y.) 74. But see West Point Iron Co. v. Raymert, 45 N. Y. 703. A reservation to the grantor and a stranger to the deed for the lives of both has been upheld. Martin v. Cook, 102 Mich. 267, 60 N. W. 679.

[119] Ashcroft v. Railroad Co., 126 Mass. 198. But see Dennis v. Wilson, 107 Mass. 591.

[120] See ante, p. 376.

[121] Pettee v. Hawes, 13 Pick (Mass.) 323; Hurd v. Curtis, 7 Metc. (Mass.) 94; Choate v. Burnham, 7 Pick. (Mass.) 274; Bates v. Swiger (W. Va.) 21 S. E. 874; Lacy v. Comstock, 55 Kan. 86, 39 Pac. 1024. When a right of way is reserved, the fee in the whole land passes subject to the easement. Moffitt v. Lytle, 165 Pa. St. 173, 30 Atl. 922.

§§ 263-264)   REQUISITES OF DEEDS.   419

The object of the habendum is to designate what estate is to pass, and contains the words of limitation.[122] If the habendum is repugnant to the granting clause, the habendum is void.[123] Nor can the habendum be made to include lands which are not in the description.[124] The habendum usually repeats the names of the grantees, and one may be named in the habendum who is not in the granting clause; for instance, a remainder-man.[125] The habendum may enlarge the estate given in the granting clause,[126] or restrict it.[127] The habendum will not be permitted to change the nature of the ownership, as by making owners in severalty joint owners.[128] The uses and trusts accompanying an estate are usually limited in the habendum.

263. **DESCRIPTION OF THE PROPERTY**—A valid deed must contain a sufficient description of the property to be conveyed to identify it. This may be by reference to
   (a) **Plats and maps** (p. 421).
   (b) **Monuments** (p. 422).
   (c) **Courses and distances** (p. 424).
   (d) **Quantity** (p. 425).

264. All things which are appurtenant to the property described pass with it (p. 425).

[122] Wager v. Wager, 1 Serg. & R. (Pa.) 374; Mitchell v. Wilson, 3 Cranch, C. C. 242, Fed. Cas. No. 9,672.

[123] Major v. Bukley, 51 Mo. 227; Ratcliffe v. Marrs, 87 Ky. 26, 7 S. W. 395, and 8 S. W. 876; Flagg v. Eames, 40 Vt. 16; Budd v. Brooke, 3 Gill (Md.) 198.

[124] Manning v. Smith, 6 Conn. 289.

[125] Riggin v. Love, 72 Ill. 553; Tyler v. Moore, 42 Pa. St. 374; Irwin's Heirs v. Longworth, 20 Ohio, 581.

[126] Moss v. Sheldon, 3 Watts & S. (Pa.) 160; Jackson v. Ireland, 3 Wend. (N. Y.) 99.

[127] Watters v. Bredin, 70 Pa. St. 237; Whitby v. Duffy, 135 Pa. St. 620, 19 Atl. 1065. As where, by the granting clause, a fee simple absolute would pass, the habendum may show an intention to convey a less estate. Jamaica Pond Aqueduct v. Chandler, 9 Allen (Mass.) 159, 168; Riggin v. Love, 72 Ill. 553; Montgomery v. Sturdivant, 41 Cal. 290.

[128] Greenwood v. Tyler, Hob. 314. In ascertaining the intention of the

The object of the description in a deed is to identify the land to be conveyed, and no conveyance can be operative without a description which is sufficient for such purpose of identification.[129] The description, however, need not be technically accurate, or even clear. It will be sufficient if a surveyor can locate the land by the description given, and therefore a mere error will be disregarded.[130] Where there are material errors in a description, which are so gross that the deed cannot take effect, the instrument may be reformed in equity.[131] Latent ambiguities in the description may always be explained by parol.[132] Where such ambiguities exist, or the description is conflicting, the question for the courts is one of construction. To give effect to the deed, the situation of the parties at the time of its execution is to be considered, and their intention at that time is the test.[133] For the purpose of showing such intentions, contemporaneous writings by the parties may be used.[134] Where the terms of the description are clear, however, no question of construction arises, and the intention of the parties will not be allowed to control, though it is shown to be different from that expressed in the deed.[135] In construing a deed, grammatical construction and punctuation are given little effect, though they may be of value, in connection with other things.[136] All parts of the deed are to be construed together, and that description will be adopted which will give effect to the deed, rather than one which

parties, "the entire instrument, the habendum as well as the premises, is to be considered." Barnett v. Barnett, 104 Cal. 298, 37 Pac. 1049.

[129] George v. Bates, 90 Va. 839, 20 S. E. 828; Wilson v. Johnson (Ind. Sup.) 38 N. E. 38; Campbell v. Johnson, 44 Mo. 247; Wofford v. McKinna, 23 Tex. 44; Dwyre v. Speer, 8 Tex. Civ. App. 88, 27 S. W. 585.

[130] Mason v. White, 11 Barb. (N. Y.) 173; Bosworth v. Sturtevant, 2 Cush. (Mass.) 392; Hoban v. Cable, 102 Mich. 206, 60 N. W. 466; Eggleston v. Bradford, 10 Ohio, 312; Travellers Ins. Co. v. Yount, 98 Ind. 454; Wells v. Heddenberg (Tex. Civ. App.) 30 S. W. 702; Gress Lumber Co. v. Coody, 94 Ga. 519, 21 S. E. 217; Denver, M. & A. Ry. Co. v. Lockwood, 54 Kan. 586, 38 Pac. 794.

[131] See Canedy v. Marcy, 13 Gray (Mass.) 373.

[132] Bybee v. Hageman, 66 Ill. 519; Clark v. Powers, 45 Ill. 283.

[133] Long v. Wagoner, 47 Mo. 178; Stanley v. Green, 12 Cal. 148.

[134] Putzel v. Van Brunt, 40 N. Y. Super. Ct. 501.

[135] Kimball v. Semple, 25 Cal. 449.

[136] Martind. Conv. (2d Ed.) § 98.

would make it void for uncertainty.[137] General expressions in the deed are controlled by more specific ones,[138] and surplusage is to be rejected.[139] All presumptions are taken most strongly against the grantor,[140] and where the deed contains two conflicting descriptions the grantee will, on this principle, be permitted to elect under which he will hold.[141]

Plats and Maps.

The principal means employed to describe land in conveyances are reference to maps and plats, description by means of monuments, or courses and distances, and description by the amount of land to be conveyed. Where land is described by means of reference to a map or a plat, the map or plat referred to becomes a part of the deed for the purpose of that conveyance, and anything which appears thereon may affect the terms of the grant;[142] as, where land is conveyed by means of reference to a plat which shows streets as in existence at certain places, the grantor may be estopped by such fact, and the grantee would have a right to have a street as located on the plat.[143] So, also, if the land is described by a mere reference to another deed in which the land is conveyed, the effect is the same as when the reference is to the map.[144] When maps or deeds are referred to for purposes of description, they may be identified by parol evidence.[145] The loss of the map or deed would not make the conveyance in which they are referred to void, but the

[137] Anderson v. Baughman, 7 Mich. 69; City of Alton v. Illinois Transp. Co., 12 Ill. 38; Gano v. Aldridge, 27 Ind. 294.

[138] Hannibal & St. J. R. Co. v. Green, 68 Mo. 169; Wade v. Deray, 50 Cal. 376.

[139] Jackson v. Clark, 7 Johns. (N. Y.) 223; Kruse v. Wilson, 79 Ill. 235.

[140] Charles River Bridge v. Warren Bridge, 11 Pet. 420, 589; Cocheco Manuf'g Co. v. Whittier, 10 N. H. 305.

[141] Armstrong v. Mudd, 10 B. Mon. (Ky.) 144.

[142] Dolde v. Vodicka, 49 Mo. 100; Masterson v. Munro, 105 Cal. 431, 38 Pac. 1106.

[143] See ante, p. 359.

[144] Mardis v. Meyers, 8 Tex. Civ. App. 542, 28 S. W. 693; Wuestcott v. Seymour, 22 N. J. Eq. 66; Deacons of Cong. Church in Auburn v. Walker, 124 Mass. 69. But see Lovejoy v. Lovett, Id. 270. Land may be described as bounded by land conveyed in another deed. Probett v. Jenkinson (Mich.) 63 N. W. 648.

[145] McCullough v. Wall, 4 Rich. (S. C.) 68; Penry v. Richards, 52 Cal. 496.

contents of the lost instrument could be established by other evidence.[146]

Monuments.

Monuments are permanent landmarks, established for the purpose of indicating boundaries.[147] They may be either natural or artificial.[148] Examples of natural monuments are trees, rocks, rivers, etc. Artificial monuments are anything which may be treated by the parties as such. In describing lands by means of monuments, the monuments themselves must be identified, and it is not sufficient to refer to them as "a certain tree" or "stake."[149] Where land is conveyed by descriptions referring to highways or nonnavigable rivers for boundaries, it is taken that the center of the highway or the river is intended.[150] When points on the bank of the river or side of the road are named in describing the land conveyed, the cases are in conflict as to whether the boundary is in the center or at the side of the highway or river.[151] An intention may, in any case, be expressed that the grantee shall not take to the center, as where the land is described as bounding on "the side or banks" of the highway or river. In such case the line would not be in the center, but on the edge.[152] Where no such intention is

[146] New Hampshire Land Co. v. Tilton, 19 Fed. 73.

[147] Black, Law Dict. "Monuments."

[148] The monuments may he erected by the parties after the conveyance is executed. Makepeace v. Bancroft, 12 Mass. 469; Lerned v. Morrill, 2 N. H. 197.

[149] Drew v. Swift, 46 N. Y. 204; Bagley v. Morrill, 46 Vt. 94.

[150] Boston v. Richardson, 13 Allen (Mass.) 146; Highways Berridge v. Ward, 10 C. B. (N. S.) 400; Champlin v. Pendleton, 13 Conn. 23; Paul v. Carver, 26 Pa. St. 223; Fisher v. Smith, 9 Gray (Mass.) 441; Cox v. Freedley, 33 Pa. St. 124; Bissell v. Railroad Co., 23 N. Y. 61; White v. Godfrey, 97 Mass. 472; Dodd v. Witt, 139 Mass. 63, 29 N. E. 475. But see Leigh v. Jack, 5 Exch. Div. 264; Sibley v. Holden, 10 Pick. (Mass.) 249; White's Bank of Buffalo v. Nichols, 64 N. Y. 65; Kings Co. Fire Ins. Co. v. Stevens, 87 N. Y. 287; In re Robbins, 34 Minn. 99, 24 N. W. 356.

[151] 1 Dembitz, Land Tit. 72. And see Luce v. Carley, 24 Wend. (N. Y.) 451; Sleeper v. Laconia, 60 N. H. 201; Arnold v. Elmore, 16 Wis. 509; Watson v. Peters, 26 Mich. 508. And, as to artificial streams, see Warner v. Southworth, 6 Conn. 471; Agawam Canal Co. v. Edwards, 36 Conn. 476. Cf. Buck v. Squiers, 22 Vt. 484.

[152] Halsey v. McCormick, 13 N. Y. 296; Child v. Stair, 4 Hill (N. Y.) 369,

§§ 263-264)   REQUISITES OF DEEDS.   423

expressed, but the usual case of the boundary line being in the middle of the road or stream exists, the grantee of the land owns to the boundary line in the center, subject to the easement of the highway or stream.[153] The cases are in great confusion on the question of where the boundary line is when the land conveyed is bounded by a navigable river. Three different rules exist in the different states. In some states the land of the riparian proprietor is bounded by high-water mark,[154] in other states by low-water mark,[155] and in still others he owns to the center of the stream.[156] While the body of the Great Lakes is never subjected to riparian ownership, the ponds and smaller lakes from half a mile to three miles in width which are found in the Northwest have caused much difficulty. The same conflict exists as in the case of navigable rivers.[157] In any case, if a natural body of water has been raised by artificial means, the boundary lines continue as before the change.[158]

---

reversing 20 Wend. (N. Y.) 149; Murphy v. Copeland, 58 Iowa, 409, 10 N. W. 786; Dunlap v. Stetson, 4 Mason, 349, Fed. Cas. No. 4,164. See Lowell v. Robinson, 16 Me. 357.

[153] Town of Old Town v. Dooley, 81 Ill. 255; Fisher v. Rochester, 6 Lans. (N. Y.) 225; West Covington v. Freking, 8 Bush (Ky.) 121. And see ante, pp. 361, 368.

[154] Barney v. Keokuk, 94 U. S. 324; McManus v. Carmichael, 3 Iowa, 1; Wood v. Fowler, 26 Kan. 682; Mayor, etc., of City of Mobile v. Eslava, 16 Pet. 234.

[155] Union Depot Street-Railway & Transfer Co. of Stillwater v. Brunswick, 31 Minn. 297, 17 N. W. 626; People v. Canal Appraisers, 33 N. Y. 461; Monongahela Bridge Co. v. Kirk, 46 Pa. St. 112; Wood v. Appal, 63 Pa. St. 210; Lux v. Haggin, 69 Cal. 255, 10 Pac. 674. And see Handly's Lessee v. Anthony, 5 Wheat. 375; Booth v. Shepherd, 8 Ohio St. 247.

[156] Arnold v. Elmore, 16 Wis. 509; Jones v. Pettibone, 2 Wis. 308; Fuller v. Dauphin, 124 Ill. 542, 16 N. E. 917; Fletcher v. Boom Co., 51 Mich. 277, 16 N. W. 645; Webber v. Boom Co., 62 Mich. 626, 30 N. W. 469; Morgan v. Reading, 3 Smedes & M. (Miss.) 366; Gavit's Adm'rs v. Chambers, 3 Ohio, 496.

[157] 1 Dembitz, Land Tit. 67; Jefferis v. Land Co., 134 U. S. 178, 10 Sup. Ct. 518; Hardin v. Jordan, 140 U. S. 371, 11 Sup. Ct. 808, 838; Clute v. Fisher, 65 Mich. 48, 31 N. W. 614; Lamprey v. State, 52 Minn. 181, 53 N. W. 1130; Trustees of Schools v. Schroll, 120 Ill. 509, 12 N. E. 243; Cortelyou v. Van Brundt, 2 Johns. (N. Y.) 357.

[158] Paine v. Woods, 108 Mass. 160. But see Bradley v. Rice, 13 Me. 198.

Courses and Distances.

Land is said to be described by courses and distances when an identified starting point is given, and the boundaries are traced from that point as so many rods or feet in a certain direction, etc.[159] When such descriptions are given, the lines are always to be taken as straight lines,[160] and directions expressed as "northward," "eastward," etc., mean due north and due east.[161] When monuments and courses and distances are both given, the monuments control, and the distances must be lengthened or shortened,[162] though the courses and distances will control where such an intention clearly appears in the deed.[163] When lands are described according to the congressional survey, and the corners—that is, the monuments—have been lost, the courses and distances, as they appear on the maps and field notes of the surveyor general, will control. But a difficulty arises from the fact that the chains used in making the surveys were often stretched by use, and so more land will be included in the description than would be indicated by the courses and distances. In the federal courts, and in some of the states, it is held, in conformity with the United States statutes,[164] that the lost corner shall be established by locating it a proportionate distance from the nearest known corners. In this way the surplus land is divided among the several owners.[165] In some states, however, a different rule prevails, and the lost corner is located by measuring the distance which it ought, by an accurate survey, to be from the eastern corner of the township. By this rule the surplus land all goes to the owners on the western side.[166]

---

[159] As to the use of the words "more or less" in giving courses and distances, see Blaney v. Rice, 20 Pick. (Mass.) 62; Howell v. Merrill, 30 Mich. 283; Williamson v. Hall, 62 Mo. 405.

[160] Campbell v. Branch, 4 Jones (N. C.) 313.

[161] Jackson v. Reeves, 3 Caines (N. Y.) 295.

[162] Preston v. Bowmar, 6 Wheat. 580; Bowman v. Farmer, 8 N. H. 402; Knowles v. Toothaker, 58 Me. 172; White v. Williams, 48 N. Y. 344; Miles v. Barrows, 122 Mass. 579. Cf. Hall v. Eaton, 139 Mass. 217, 29 N. E. 660.

[163] Higinbotham v. Stoddard, 72 N. Y. 94; Buffalo, N. Y. & E. R. Co. v. Stigeler, 61 N. Y. 348. And see Hall v. Eaton, 139 Mass. 217, 29 N. E. 600.

[164] Rev. St. U. S. § 2396.

[165] Jones v. Kimble, 19 Wis. 429; Moreland v. Page, 2 Iowa, 139.

[166] Major v. Watson, 73 Mo. 665; Vaughn v. Tate, 64 Mo. 491; Knight v. Elliott, 57 Mo. 317.

Quantity.

When the quantity of land to be conveyed is given in the deed, it will not control either monuments or courses or distances,[167] though it may aid a description otherwise defective, and quantity may be made to control by express words.[168] In the absence of such words, the quantity given in a deed will have no effect unless there is a covenant as to the amount. When the quantity is given, and the words "more or less" are added, no more is meant than what the law would imply, namely, that the grantee takes the risk as to the amount.[169] The addition of the words "more or less" will not prevent an action for fraud when there has been a misrepresentation as to the amount.[170]

Appurtenances.

The old form of a deed adds, after the description of the lands or tenements conveyed, words like the following: "With all the privileges and appurtenances thereto belonging or in any way appertaining," or, simply, "With the appurtenances." It is doubtful whether these general words in any case enlarge the effect of the deeds.[171] The primary meaning of "appurtenances" is the easements and other incorporeal hereditaments enjoyed with the land, such as rights of way, water courses, rights to light and air, etc. But it seems that whatever easements or hereditaments will pass under the general description of "privileges and appurtenances" will pass without them as mere incidents to the land, unless the intention to reserve such right, and to detach it from the land, is apparent.[172] But it is a general principle that "land cannot pass as an appurtenance to land," and it has been said that even the necessity of enjoyment cannot make one parcel of land pass as an ap-

---

[167] Mann v. Pearson, 2 Johns. (N. Y.) 37; Pernam v. Wead, 6 Mass. 131; Emery v. Fowler, 38 Me. 99.

[168] Moran v. Lezotte, 54 Mich. 83, 19 N. W. 757; Davis v. Hess, 103 Mo. 31, 15 S. W. 324.

[169] Williamson v. Hall, 62 Mo. 405.

[170] McConn v. Delany, 3 Bibb (Ky.) 46.

[171] See Crosby v. Parker, 4 Mass. 110; Nicholas v. Chamberlain, Cro. Jac. 121.

[172] 1 Dembitz, Land Tit. 55.

purtenance to another.[173] But the sale of a house, mill, factory, barn, etc., will carry with it not only the soil actually covered by the building, but the "curtilage"; that is, the yard and garden that are habitually occupied with a dwelling house, and certain small parcels, with or without outbuildings, without which the mill, factory, barn, etc., cannot be enjoyed, or which are left open between it and the highway.[174] And where the word "appurtenances" is added to the designation of a dwelling house or other building, it is not a mere empty phrase, but means what is habitually occupied with it even though it be an unfenced lot.[175]

265. EXECUTION OF THE WRITING—A valid deed must be executed in writing, subject to the following rules:

(a) **No consideration is necessary except for bargain and sale deeds and covenants to stand seised** (p. 427).

(b) **No date is necessary** (p. 428).

(c) **All blanks must be filled before delivery, except where the law implies what is to be inserted, or, in some states, where parol authority has been given to fill them** (p. 428).

(d) **No alterations can be made after delivery** (p. 428).

(e) **The grantor is presumed to know the contents of his deed** (p. 429).

(f) **The deed must be sealed, in some states** (p. 429).

(g) **The deed must be signed by the grantor, or by some one authorized to sign for him. Indentures are signed by the grantee also** (p. 430).

[173] Armstrong v. Dubois, 90 N. Y. 95; Ogden v. Jennings, 62 N. Y. 526; Humphreys v. McKissock, 140 U. S. 304, 11 Sup. Ct. 779; Wilson v. Beckwith, 117 Mo. 61, 22 S. W. 639. A tree in the adjoining street will pass as an appurtenance. Gorham v. Electric Co. (Co. Ct.) 29 N. Y. Supp. 1094.

[174] Allen v. Scott, 21 Pick. (Mass.) 25; Whitney v. Olney, 3 Mason, 280, Fed. Cas. No. 17,595. For the right to use a drain as appurtenant to a house, see Thayer v. Payne, 2 Cush. (Mass.) 327; Johnson v. Jordan, 2 Metc. (Mass.) 234.

[175] Ammidown v. Ball, 8 Allen (Mass.) 293; Cunningham v. Webb, 69 Me. 92. But see Leonard v. White, 7 Mass. 6; Archer v. Bennett, 1 Lev. 131.

What Writing Necessary.

Deeds are to be written on paper or parchment,[176] and should be written with ink, though possibly a deed written with a pencil would be valid.[177] The chief desideratum is durability. Part of the deed may be written and part printed. When there is any conflict between the written and the printed parts, the written words will control.[178]

Consideration.

No consideration is necessary for modern statutory conveyances.[179] Bargain and sale deeds, however, require, as we have seen,[180] a consideration to make them valid, though the requirement has been greatly relaxed in modern times. For a covenant to stand seised a good consideration is sufficient.[181] Between the parties to a deed it is valid without the payment of any consideration,[182] but it may not be so as to purchasers and creditors of the grantor who attack its validity, claiming that it is in fraud of their rights.[183] Where the receipt of a consideration is acknowledged in a deed, this may be rebutted so far as it operates as a receipt;[184] though the amount so stated is prima facie the amount paid for the conveyance of the land.[185] When the receipt of consideration is thus acknowledged, it may operate as a waiver of the vendor's lien as to subsequent purchasers.[186]

---

[176] 2 Bl. Comm. 297.

[177] 1 Devl. Deeds, § 136. See Merritt v. Clason, 12 Johns. (N. Y.) 102.

[178] Martind. Conv. (2d Ed.) § 15.

[179] Cunningham v. Freeborn, 11 Wend. (N. Y.) 241, 248; Rogers v. Hillhouse, 3 Conn. 398.

[180] Ante, p. 410.

[181] Ante, p. 411.

[182] Brown v. Brown (S. C.) 22 S. E. 412.

[183] De Lancey v Stearns, 66 N. Y. 157; Keys v. Test, 33 Ill. 317; Palmer v. Williams, 24 Mich. 328; Glidden v. Hunt, 24 Pick. (Mass.) 221.

[184] McCrea v. Purmort, 16 Wend. (N. Y.) 460; Bullard v. Briggs, 7 Pick. (Mass.) 537; Wilkinson v. Scott, 17 Mass. 257; Goodspeed v. Fuller, 46 Me. 141. And see Mildmay's Case, 1 Coke, 175; Gale v. Williamson, 8 Mees. & W. 405.

[185] Clements v. Landrum, 26 Ga. 401. And cf. Wilkes v. Leuson, Dyer, 169a; Frafton v. Hawes, 102 Mass. 533.

[186] Jackson v. M'Chesney, 7 Cow. (N. Y.) 360; per Sutherland, J.

Date.

A date is not strictly necessary for the validity of a deed,[187] and, when used, may be placed in any part of the instrument. A deed takes effect from the time of delivery, and prima facie the date given in the instrument is the date of delivery,[188] though this presumption may be rebutted.[189]

Filling Blanks.

When blanks are left in the deed, the deed is of no effect, unless it can be operative without the omitted words; and if the blanks are filled after delivery the deed is void.[190] There is an exception to this, however, in the case where the blanks which are filled are only such as would be implied by law.[191] Some cases hold that the grantee's name which has been omitted may be inserted according to the intention of the parties.[192] So, also, a deed may be delivered accompanied by a parol power to fill blanks,[193] though the contrary is held by some courts.[194]

Alterations.

A deed must be completely written when it is delivered, and for this reason any alterations or interlineations in the instrument must be made before delivery,[195] though they may be added after the deed has been signed.[196] An alteration by a stranger to the instrument does not affect the validity of a deed,[197] and as to the

---

[187] Thompson v. Thompson, 9 Ind. 323.

[188] Lake Erie & W. R. Co. v. Whitham, 155 Ill. 514, 40 N. E. 1014; Ellsworth v. Railroad Co., 34 N. J. Law, 93; Ford v. Gregory's Heirs, 10 B. Mon. (Ky.) 175.

[189] Fash v. Blake, 44 Ill. 302; Blanchard v. Tyler, 12 Mich. 339; Henderson v. Baltimore, 8 Md. 353; Flynn v. Flynn (N. J. Ch.) 31 Atl. 30.

[190] Ingram v. Little, 14 Ga. 172.

[191] U. S. v. Nelson, 2 Brock. 64, Fed. Cas. No. 15,862, per Marshal, C. J.

[192] Duncan v. Hodges, 4 McCord (S. C.) 239; Devin v. Himer, 29 Iowa, 300. But see Chauncey v. Arnold, 24 N. Y. 330; Drury v. Foster, 2 Wall. 24.

[193] Schintz v. McManamy, 33 Wis. 299; Clark v. Allen, 34 Iowa, 190; Pence v. Arbuckle, 22 Minn. 417; Otis v. Browning, 59 Mo. App. 326 (grantee's name).

[194] Though an element of fraud is generally present. Upton v. Archer, 41 Cal. 85; Cooper v. Page, 62 Me. 192.

[195] People v. Organ, 27 Ill. 26; Wallace v. Harmstad, 15 Pa. St. 462.

[196] Stiles v. Probst, 69 Ill. 382; Penny v. Corwithe, 18 Johns. (N. Y.) 499.

[197] Robertson v. Hay, 91 Pa. St. 242.

§ 265) REQUISITES OF DEEDS. 429

effect of such alterations by the grantee the cases are conflicting. Some courts hold that the only effect is on the remedy,—that is, that the grantee cannot bring suit on the deed;[198] while other courts hold that the validity of the deed is affected only as far as it is to be used in evidence.[199] Where alterations or interlineations are present in a deed, the presumption is that they were made before the deed was delivered,[200] though there are cases holding the contrary.[201]

Reading.

A party to a deed, who can read, is conclusively presumed to know the contents of the instrument, though he did not actually read it before it was executed.[202] If the grantor is blind, illiterate, or for any other reason unable to read, the deed must be read to him, if he requests it, and an incorrect reading will invalidate the deed.[203]

Sealing.

At common law a seal was necessary in the execution of a valid deed,[204] but in many states this requirement has been abolished.[205] A seal is defined to be "an impression on wax or wafer or some other tenacious substance capable of being impressed."[206] But a seal stamped on paper has been held good.[207] In many states a seal

[198] Herrick v. Malin, 22 Wend. (N. Y.) 388; Waring v. Smyth, 2 Barb. Ch. (N. Y.) 133; Johnson v. Moore, 33 Kan. 90, 5 Pac. 406.

[199] Hatch v. Hatch, 9 Mass. 307.

[200] Herrick v. Malin, 22 Wend. (N. Y.) 388; Holton v. Kemp, 81 Mo. 661; Van Horn v. Bell, 11 Iowa, 465.

[201] Montag v. Linn, 23 Ill. 503.

[202] School Committee v. Kesler, 67 N. C. 443; Kimball v. Eaton, 8 N. H. 391.

[203] Jackson v. Hayner, 12 Johns. (N. Y.) 469; Morrison v. Morrison, 27 Grat. (Va.) 190; Lyons v. Van Riper, 26 N. J. Eq. 337.

[204] Davis v. Brandon, 1 How. (Miss.) 154; Grandin v. Hernandez, 29 Hun, 399; Le Franc v. Richmond, 5 Sawy. 603, Fed. Cas. No. 8,209. But see Moss v. Anderson, 7 Mo. 337.

[205] 1 Stim. Am. St. Law, §§ 421, 1564. Such statutes are not retroactive. Wisdom v. Reeves (Ala.) 18 South. 13.

[206] Warren v. Lynch, 5 Johns. (N. Y.) 239; Tasker v. Bartlett, 5 Cush. (Mass.) 359, 364; Bradford v. Randall, 5 Pick. (Mass.) 496.

[207] Pierce v. Indseth, 106 U. S. 546, 1 Sup. Ct. 418; Pillow v. Roberts, 13 How. 473. But see Farmers' & Manufacturers' Bank v. Haight, 3 Hill (N. Y.) 493. . The printed device "[L. S.]" has been held sufficient. Williams v. Starr, 5 Wis. 534, 549.

may be supplied by a mere scroll, made with the pen.[209] In such case the instrument must declare that a seal is attached.[210] Corporations usually have seals of their own, though they may adopt any other in executing a deed.[211] The seal of a corporation can only be attached by some one having authority.[212] Where several persons execute the same deed, they may all use one seal.[213]

Signing.

At common law it was not necessary that a deed be signed, though this is now required by the statute of frauds.[214] Where the statute requires the deed to be subscribed, the signature must be written at the end; but, in the absence of such provision, the signing may be at any other place.[215] If the party signing the deed is unable to write, he may sign it by a mark, and this would probably be true even though he could write.[216] The name of the grantor may be written by another for him, in his presence;[217] though, if the grantor is absent, the power to sign his name must be in writing.[218] Where a deed is signed by another for the grantor without his authority, he may adopt the signature as his own, and ratify the execution.[219] A deed by a corporation is to be signed in the corporate name.[220]

---

[209] 1 Stim. Am. St. Law, § 1565; Cosner v. McCrum (W. Va.) 21 S. E. 739. But see Warren v. Lynch, 5 Johns. (N. Y.) 239; Perrine v. Cheeseman, 11 N. J. Law, 174.

[210] Jenkins v. Hurt's Com'rs, 2 Rand. (Va.) 446. An instrument containing the words "sealed with my seal," but having no seal on it, is not a technical deed. Deming v. Bullitt, 1 Blackf. (Ind.) 241.

[211] Proprietors of Mill Dam Foundry v. Hovey, 21 Pick. (Mass.) 417, 428; Stebbins v. Merritt, 10 Cush. (Mass.) 27, 34.

[212] See Jackson v. Campbell, 5 Wend. (N. Y.) 572.

[213] Yale v. Flanders, 4 Wis. 96. But see note on seals, 3 Gray, Cas. Prop. 624.

[214] 1 Devl. Deeds, § 231.

[215] 1 Dembitz, Land Tit. 345.

[216] Devereux v. McMahon, 108 N. C. 134, 12 S. E. 902; Baker v. Dening, 8 Adol. & E. 94.

[217] Conlan v. Grace, 36 Minn. 276, 30 N. W. 880; Schmitt v. Schmitt, 31 Minn. 106, 16 N. W. 543.

[218] McMurtry v. Brown, 6 Neb. 368.

[219] Bartlett v. Drake, 100 Mass. 174; Mutual Benefit Life Ins. Co. v. Brown, 30 N. J. Eq. 193.

[220] Hatch v. Barr, 1 Ohio, 390; Zoller v. Ide, 1 Neb. 439. But see Bason v. Mining Co., 90 N. C. 417.

Same—Power of Attorney.

A power of attorney to execute a deed is an authority given a person to act in behalf of the grantor in making a conveyance of land. Such a person is an attorney in fact. For the execution of a valid power of attorney the same solemnities are required as for the execution of a deed.[221] The power of attorney must contain a description of the premises to be conveyed,[222] and in many states it must be recorded.[223] Powers of attorney can be created only by persons who are sui juris.[224] In some states, by statute, a married woman may release her dower by power of attorney. In other states it is held that a married woman cannot give a power of attorney, even though her husband joins with her.[225] One member of a firm cannot convey partnership lands without a power of attorney from the other members.[226] A power of attorney may be revoked at any time, unless a consideration has been paid for it;[227] but not if it is coupled with an interest, in which case the power to revoke must be expressly reserved, or none exists.[228] Death of the one executing a power of attorney revokes it if it is a mere naked power. That is, one not coupled with an interest, and powers of attorney to convey land are generally of this kind.[229] The revocation of a power of attorney should be recorded if the power itself has been.[230] Where a power of attorney has been given, the authority cannot be delegated unless such delegation is authorized by the power.[231] A power to several cannot be executed by less than all, in the absence of a provision to that effect.[232] Powers

---

[221] Van Ostrand v. Reed, 1 Wend. (N. Y.) 424; Goree v. Wadsworth, 91 Ala. 416, 8 South. 712.

[222] Stafford v. Lick, 13 Cal. 240.

[223] 1 Stim. Am. St. Law, § 1624 (10).

[224] Dexter v. Hall, 15 Wall. 9.

[225] 1 Dembitz, Land Tit. 403.

[226] Frost v. Cattle Co., 81 Tex. 505, 17 S. W. 52.

[227] MacGregor v. Gardner, 14 Iowa, 326.

[228] Martind. Conv. (2d Ed.) § 241; Mansfield v. Mansfield, 6 Conn. 559.

[229] Jenkins v. Atkins, 1 Humph. (Tenn.) 294

[230] Morgan v. Stell, 5 Bin. (Pa.) 305.

[231] Loeb v. Drakeford, 75 Ala. 464. And see Rogers v. Cruger, 7 Johns. (N. Y.) 557.

[232] Cedar Rapids & St. P. R. Co. v. Stewart, 25 Iowa, 115; White v. Davidson, 8 Md. 169.

of attorney are strictly construed,[233] and a power to "sell" does not give authority to "convey."[234] A power to sell implies a sale for cash.[235] Where a deed is executed by one who has a power of attorney, it must be in the name of the grantor, and not of the agent, and the agent himself must show that he executes it for his principal, as by signing "A. [principal] by B. [agent]."[236] Some cases, however, are less exacting. A deed executed, "A. B., Agt. of C. D.," has been held a good execution of a deed in which C. D. was the grantor.[237] In executing a deed by virtue of a power of attorney, the attorney must purport to bind the grantor, and not himself.[238]

Indentures and Deeds Poll.

Conveyances are either indentures or deeds poll. The former is an instrument executed and signed by both the grantor and the grantee. In its usual form, it is executed in duplicate. Originally the two pieces were cut apart by an irregular line, which gave the name to this form of deed. One part was given to each party, and when the deeds were produced in court the irregular margins, if they fitted, were evidence that the instruments before the court were genuine. This cutting of the margin is no longer usual, and an indenture means only a deed executed by both parties. Conveyances of this kind usually begin with the words "This indenture."[239] A deed poll on the other hand is one executed by the grantor only, and binds the grantee by its provisions only by reason of his acceptance of it. A deed poll usually commences with the words, "Know ye all men by these presents."[240]

---

[233] Geiger v. Bolles, 1 Thomp. & C. (N. Y.) 129; Brantley v. Insurance Co., 53 Ala. 554.

[234] Tharp v. Brenneman, 41 Iowa, 251; Force v. Dutcher, 18 N. J. Eq. 401.

[235] Lumpkin v. Wilson, 5 Heisk. (Tenn.) 555; Coulter v. Trust Co., 20 Or. 469, 26 Pac. 565, and 27 Pac. 266.

[236] Townsend v. Hubbard, 4 Hill (N. Y.) 351; Clarke's Lessee v. Courtney, 5 Pet. 349.

[237] Wilks v. Back, 2 East, 142. And see Devinney v. Reynolds, 1 Watts & S. (Pa.) 328.

[238] Echols v. Cheney, 28 Cal. 157; Fowler v. Shearer, 7 Mass. 14; Bassett v. Hawk, 114 Pa. St. 502, 8 Atl. 18.

[239] Martind. Conv. (2d Ed.) § 61; Finley v. Simpson, 22 N. J. Law, 311; Atlantic Dock Co. v. Leavitt, 54 N. Y. 35; Currie v. Donald, 2 Wash. (Va.) 58; Maule v. Weaver, 7 Pa. St. 329.

[240] Goodwin v. Gilbert, 9 Mass. 510.

266. DELIVERY AND ACCEPTANCE—A deed does not become operative until it is delivered and accepted, but the delivery may be in escrow.

The delivery which is essential to the validity of a deed is the same as that required for the completion of a contract.[241] A deed does not become effective until delivered,[242] though an actual delivery of the paper is not necessary.[243] The instrument must pass out of the control of the grantor,[244] and, as to the effect of the acts of the parties, the intention governs in all cases.[245] If the deed is taken by the grantee without the consent of the grantor, there is no delivery,—as where it is stolen; and the grantee cannot pass title to a subsequent purchaser[246] unless the grantor is estopped by his negligence from setting up his title against an innocent third person.[247] Delivery may be made to a third person for the grantee.[248] This is the case where future estates are created in the same instrument with those vesting in possession at once. The deed is

---

[241] See Clark, Cont. 73. A delivery obtained by fraud is ineffectual. Golden v. Hardesty (Iowa) 61 N. W. 913. And see Raymond v. Glover (Cal.) 37 Pac. 772.

[242] Mills v. Gore, 20 Pick. (Mass.) 28; Prutsman v. Baker, 30 Wis. 644; Johnson v. Farley, 45 N. H. 505; Paddock v. Potter, 67 Vt. 360, 31 Atl. 784; Boyd v. Slayback, 63 Cal. 493. Cf. Exton v. Scott, 6 Sim. 31.

[243] Walker v. Walker, 42 Ill. 311; Dayton v. Newman, 19 Pa. St. 194; Farrar v. Bridges, 5 Humph. (Tenn.) 411; Doe v. Knight, 5 Barn. & C. 671.

[244] Fisher v. Hall, 41 N. Y. 416; Bank of Healdsburg v. Bailhacke, 65 Cal. 327, 4 Pac. 106.

[245] Conlan v. Grace, 36 Minn. 276, 30 N. W. 880; Hill v. McNichol, 80 Me. 209, 13 Atl. 883. But see Hinchliff v. Hinman, 18 Wis. 139.

[246] Tisher v. Beckwith, 30 Wis. 55.

[247] Id. And see Gage v. Gage, 36 Mich. 229.

[248] Winterbottom v. Pattison, 152 Ill. 334, 38 N. E. 1050; Stephens v. Hussk, 54 Pa. St. 20. A deed may become operative by being delivered to the recording officer, if so intended by the parties. Davis v. Davis (Iowa) 60 N. W. 507; Cooper v. Jackson, 4 Wis. 537; Stevenson v. Kaiser (Super. N. Y.) 29 N. Y. Supp. 1122; Kemp v. Walker, 16 Ohio, 118; Laughlin v. Dock Co., 13 C. C. A. 1, 65 Fed. 441. The presumption that a deed which has been recorded was delivered may be rebutted, for instance, by showing that the grantee had no knowledge of the existence of the deed. Union Mut. Life Ins. Co. v. Campbell, 95 Ill. 268; Sullivan v. Eddy, 154 Ill. 199, 40 N. E. 482; Russ v. Stratton, 11 Misc. Rep. 565, 32 N. Y. Supp. 767.

given to the owner of the particular estate, and he accepts it for the grantees of the future estates.[249] Where there are several grantees in a deed delivery to one is sufficient,[250] and delivery of a deed in which a corporation is grantee must be made to some one authorized to accept it for the corporation.[251] A deed retained for security is not delivered so as to become effectual.[252] So there can be no delivery of a deed after the death of the grantor.[253] A delivery to a third person, to be delivered to the grantee on the death of the grantor, is good.[254] Where there is a delivery to a third person for the grantee, the grantor must not retain power to recall the deed.[255] Not only is delivery necessary to the validity of a deed, but there must also be an acceptance by the grantee,[256] though acceptance will sometimes be presumed from the grantee

[249] Folk v. Varn, 9 Rich. Eq. (S. C.) 303.

[250] Shelden v. Erskine, 78 Mich. 627, 44 N. W. 146. But see Hannah v. Swarner, 8 Watts (Pa.) 9.

[251] Western R. Corp. v. Babcock, 6 Metc. (Mass.) 346.

[252] Gudgen v. Besset, 6 El. & Bl. 986.

[253] Jackson v. Leek, 12 Wend. (N. Y.) 107. A deed found among the grantor's papers after his death is of no effect, though it is fully executed and acknowledged, since there must be a delivery in the grantor's lifetime. Wiggins v. Lusk, 12 Ill. 132; Miller v. Lullman, 81 Mo. 311. But see Cummings v. Glass, 162 Pa. St. 241, 29 Atl. 848.

[254] Ruggles v. Lawson, 13 Johns. (N. Y.) 285; Foster v. Mansfield, 3 Metc. (Mass.) 412; Miller v. Meers, 155 Ill. 284, 40 N. E. 577; Belden v. Carter, 4 Day (Conn.) 66; Wheelwright v. Wheelwright, 2 Mass. 447; Hathaway v. Payne, 34 N. Y. 92; Latham v. Udell, 38 Mich. 238; Stephens v. Rinehart, 72 Pa. St. 434; Squires v. Summers, 85 Ind. 252; Dinwiddie v. Smith, 141 Ind. 318, 40 N. E. 748. The grantor must not reserve power to recall the deed, or the delivery is ineffectual. Cook v. Brown, 34 N. H. 460; Baker v. Haskell, 47 N. H. 479; Prutsman v. Baker, 30 Wis. 644.

[255] Maynard v. Maynard, 10 Mass. 456. The return or cancellation of a deed after it has become operative by execution and delivery will not divest the estate conveyed, or restore the grantor to his former position. Furguson v. Bond, 39 W. Va. 561, 20 S. E. 591; National Union Bldg. Ass'n v. Brewer, 41 Ill. App. 223; Jackson v. Chase, 2 Johns. (N. Y.) 84; Raynor v. Wilson, 6 Hill (N. Y.) 469; Botsford v. Morehouse, 4 Conn. 550; 1 Dembitz, Land Tit. 325. But see Albright v. Albright, 70 Wis. 532, 36 N. W. 254; Com. v. Dudley, 10 Mass. 403; Holbrook v. Tirrell, 9 Pick. (Mass.) 105; Hopp v. Hopp, 156 Ill. 183, 41 N. E. 39; Cadwallader v. Lovece (Tex. Civ. App.) 29 S. W. 666.

[256] Jackson v. Phipps, 12 Johns. (N. Y.) 418; Thompson v. Leach, 3 Lev. 284; Beardsley v. Hilson, 94 Ga. 50, 20 S. E. 272; Derry Bank v. Webster,

having possession of the deed.[257] And also there may be a presumption of acceptance from the beneficial character of the instrument,[258] though this presumption does not obtain unless the grantee has knowledge of the existence of the deed.[259] The presumption of acceptance may be rebutted.[260] When the actual delivery and acceptance of the deed consists of a number of connected acts, these acts may all be taken as having occurred together, and the date of the first of them is treated as the time when the deed takes effect and the title passes.[261] This is known as the doctrine of relation. When a conveyance is beneficial to the grantee, it is held that a father may accept for an infant child, or a husband for a wife.[262] Until a deed has been accepted by the grantee, it may be recalled, though there has been a delivery by the grantor. But this is not possible after there has been an acceptance.[263] Delivery and acceptance are in each case matters to be proved by parol evidence.[264]

Delivery in Escrow.

A deed may be delivered in escrow; that is, into the keeping of a third person to be delivered to the grantee on the performance of some condition.[265] When there is a delivery in escrow, and the

44 N. H. 264; Johnson v. Farley, 45 N. H. 505; Hibberd v. Smith, 67 Cal. 547, 4 Pac. 473, and 8 Pac. 46. But see Wilt v. Franklin, 1 Bin. (Pa.) 502; Merrills v. Swift, 18 Conn. 257. And cf. Moore v. Hazleton, 9 Allen (Mass.) 102.

[257] Tunison v. Chamblin, 88 Ill. 379; Tuttle v. Turner, 28 Tex. 759.

[258] Church v. Gilman, 15 Wend. (N. Y.) 656; Jones v. Swayze, 42 N. J. Law, 279; Stewart v. Weed, 11 Ind. 92.

[259] Jackson v. Phipps, 12 Johns. (N. Y.) 418; Younge v. Guilbeau, 3 Wall. 636; Fisher v. Hall, 41 N. Y. 416. But see Mitchell v. Ryan, 3 Ohio St. 377; Myrover v. French, 73 N. C. 609.

[260] Hulick v. Scovil, 4 Gilman (Ill.) 159; Stewart v. Weed, 11 Ind. 92.

[261] Johnson v. Stagg, 2 Johns. (N. Y.) 520. But the application of this doctrine will not be permitted to work an injury to third persons. Jackson v. Bard, 4 Johns. (N. Y.) 230.

[262] Cowell v. Daggett, 97 Mass. 434; Bryan v. Wash, 7 Ill. 557. And see Douglas v. West, 140 Ill. 455, 31 N. E. 403.

[263] Warren v. Tobey, 32 Mich. 45; Souverbye v. Arden, 1 Johns. Ch. (N. Y.) 240; Albert v. Burbank, 25 N. J. Eq. 404.

[264] Roberts v. Jackson, 1 Wend. (N. Y.) 478; Earle's Adm'rs v. Earle, 20 N. J. Law, 347.

[265] Arnold v. Patrick, 6 Paige (N. Y.) 310; Johnson v. Branch, 11 Humph. (Tenn.) 521; Loubat v. Kipp, 9 Fla. 60. And see Blight v. Schenck, 10 Pa. St. 285; Wallace v. Butts (Tex. Civ. App.) 31 S. W. 687.

condition is performed,[266] the deed becomes effectual from the time of the first delivery, unless intervening rights have attached.[267] There can be no delivery in escrow to the grantee himself,[268] nor to his agent or attorney, unless the agent or attorney agrees to hold in that way;[269] otherwise, the deed would take effect as if no condition had been attached.[270] The deed, however, may be passed through the grantee to another person to hold in escrow.[271] A deed delivered in escrow is of no effect until the condition accompanying is performed, even though it is actually delivered to the grantee without the performance of the condition through the wrongful act of the depositary.[272] For a valid delivery in escrow there must be no power in the grantor to recall the deed.[273] The death of the grantor before the second delivery does not prevent the deed becoming effectual by the performance of the condition and a second delivery.[274]

267. ACKNOWLEDGMENT—A deed must be acknowledged by the grantor to be his voluntary act, before some officer designated by the statute,
  (a) To entitle it to record.
  (b) To give it validity, in some states.

To make an acknowledgment the grantor goes before an officer, designated by statute, and declares that the deed is a genuine one,

---

[266] See Johnson v. Baker, 4 Barn. & Ald. 440.

[267] Hall v. Harris, 5 Ired. Eq. (N. C.) 303; Price v. Railroad Co., 34 Ill. 13; Foster v. Mansfield, 3 Metc. (Mass.) 414; Ruggles v. Lawson, 13 Johns. (N. Y.) 285; Stephens v. Rinehart, 72 Pa. St. 434; Lindley v. Groff, 37 Minn. 338, 34 N. W. 26.

[268] Whyddon's Case, Cro. Eliz. 520; Williams v. Green, Id. 884. See Degory v. Roe, 1 Leon. 152. Contra, Hawksland v. Gatchel, Cro. Eliz. 835.

[269] Cincinnati, W. & Z. R. Co. v. Iliff, 13 Ohio St. 235; Southern Life Ins. & Trust Co. v. Cole, 4 Fla. 359; Watkins v. Nash, L. R. 20 Eq. 262.

[270] Stevenson v. Crapnell, 114 Ill. 19, 28 N. E. 379; Miller v. Fletcher, 27 Grat. 403.

[271] Gilbert v. Insurance Co., 23 Wend. (N. Y.) 43.

[272] Everts v. Agnes, 6 Wis. 453; Illinois Cent. R. Co. v. McCullough, 59 Ill. 170; Smith v. Bank, 32 Vt. 341. But see Blight v. Schenck, 10 Pa. St. 285; Wallace v. Harris, 32 Mich. 380.

[273] James v. Vanderheyden, 1 Paige (N. Y.) 385.

[274] Lindley v. Groff, 37 Minn. 338, 34 N. W. 26.

§ 267) REQUISITES OF DEEDS. 437

and his voluntary act. To this the officer makes a certificate. Provisions for acknowledgment are purely statutory, and do not exist at common law. In some states acknowledgment is required, in the absence of witnesses to the deed, to give it any validity, while in others acknowledgment is only for the purpose of admitting the deed to record.[275] In many states it is provided that a deed properly acknowledged may be read in evidence without further proof of the genuineness of its execution,[276] and this is true even though the deed has not been recorded.[277] Other courts hold to the contrary, however, but admit the unacknowledged deed as evidence against the grantor and his heirs.[278] In states where an unacknowledged deed cannot be recorded, if such an instrument is actually spread upon the records, it does not constitute notice,[279] though it may be actual notice to one who has examined the record.[280] No one has power to acknowledge a deed except the grantor, or one to whom he has given a power of attorney.[281] When husband and wife have joined in a conveyance of the wife's land, both must acknowledge the deed; and so when a wife joins in her husband's deed.[282] To release her dower she must acknowledge the deed, and in most states this acknowledgment must be separate and apart from the husband.[283] An acknowledgment may be made at any time before the deed is placed on record or used in evi-

[275] 1 Stim. Am. St. Law, art. 157. See Alt v. Stoker, 127 Mo. 466, 30 S. W. 132.

[276] 1 Stim. Am. St. Law, § 1572.

[277] Keichline v. Keichline, 54 Pa. St. 75.

[278] Jackson v. Shepard, 2 Johns. (N. Y.) 77; Brown v. Manter, 22 N. H. 468; Gibbs v. Swift, 12 Cush. (Mass.) 393. In some states the grantor can be compelled to acknowledge a deed executed and delivered. Sullivan v. Chambers, 18 R. I. 799, 31 Atl. 167.

[279] Blood v. Blood, 23 Pick. (Mass.) 80; Kerns v. Swope, 2 Watts (Pa.) 75; Dussaume v. Burnett, 5 Iowa, 95. Contra, Reed v. Kemp, 16 Ill. 445; Simpson v. Mundee, 3 Kan. 181.

[280] Bass v. Estill, 50 Miss. 300; Manaudas v. Mann, 14 Or. 450, 13 Pac. 449.

[281] 1 Devl. Deeds, § 468. For method of proving deed where grantor is dead or refuses to acknowledge it see 1 Stim. Am. St. Law, art. 159.

[282] Southerland v. Hunter, 93 N. C. 310; Ferguson v. Kingsland, Id. 337.

[283] 1 Dembitz, Land Tit. 379; Richmond v. Voorhees, 10 Wash. 316, 38 Pac. 1014; Chester v. Breitling (Tex. Civ. App.) 30 S. W. 464.

dence.[284] Certain officers are designated before whom acknowledgments may be taken; but if the person who takes the acknowledgment is a de facto officer the acknowledgment is sufficient.[285] An officer taking an acknowledgment must not, however, be a party to the deed,[286] though he may be a relative of one of the parties without invalidating the acknowledgment.[287] An acknowledgment must, in some states, show the place where it is taken,[288] and the certificate of acknowledgment should also show the official character of the officer taking it.[289] The certificate of acknowledgment must, in general, contain the name of the grantor,[290] and must state the facts which constitute the acknowledgment,[291] and a certificate that the deed was "acknowledged" is not sufficient.[292] The signing of the deed need not be in the presence of the officer who takes the acknowledgment. The officer is not allowed to impeach his certificate.[293] In some states the certificate of the officer is prima facie evidence only of the facts stated therein.[294] An officer taking an acknowledgment may correct the certificate at any time to conform to the actual facts of the acknowledgment.[295]

[284] Pierce v. Brown, 24 Vt. 165; Johnson v. McGehee, 1 Ala. 186. An acknowledgment bearing date earlier than the date of the deed is good. Gest v. Flock, 2 N. J. Eq. 108.

[285] Woodruff v. McHarry, 56 Ill. 218; Brown v. Lunt, 37 Me. 423.

[286] Groesbeck v. Seeley, 13 Mich. 329; Withers v. Baird, 7 Watts (Pa.) 227; Wilson v. Traer, 20 Iowa, 231.

[287] Lynch v. Livingston, 6 N. Y. 422; Kimball v. Johnson, 14 Wis. 674.

[288] Willard v. Cramer, 36 Iowa, 22; Hardin v. Osborne, 60 Ill. 93.

[289] Lake Erie & W. R. Co. v. Whitham, 155 Ill. 514, 40 N. E. 1014; Final v. Backus, 18 Mich. 218; Johnston's Lessee v. Haines, 2 Ohio, 55.

[290] Martind. Conv. (2d Ed.) § 259. But see Wilcoxon v. Osborn, 77 Mo. 621; Dail v. Moore, 51 Mo. 589.

[291] Carpenter v. Dexter, 8 Wall. 513; Calumet & C. C. & D. Co. v. Russell, 68 Ill. 426; Myers v. Boyd, 96 Pa. St. 427.

[292] Gill v. Fauntleroy's Heirs, 8 B. Mon. (Ky.) 177; Flanagan v. Young, 2 Har. & McH. (Md.) 38. But see McCormack v. James, 36 Fed. 14.

[293] Central Bank v. Copeland, 18 Md. 305; Allen v. Lenoir, 53 Miss. 321. And see Kranichfelt v. Slattery, 12 Misc. Rep. 96, 33 N. Y. Supp. 27.

[294] Jackson v. Schoonmaker, 4 Johns. (N. Y.) 161; Edgerton v. Jones, 10 Minn. 429 (Gil. 341); Lennon v. White (Minn.) 63 N. W. 620; Hutchison v. Rust, 2 Grat. (Va.) 394.

[295] Hanson v. Cochran, 9 Houst. 184, 31 Atl. 880; Jordan v. Corey, 2 Ind. 385. But see Newman v. Samuels, 17 Iowa, 528.

268. WITNESSES—In some states one or two disinterested witnesses to a deed are required by statute
  (a) For the validity of a deed, or,
  (b) In the absence of acknowledgment, to entitle it to record.

At common law no witnesses were necessary to the validity of the deed.[296] But now, by statute, in many states, they are required. In some states witnesses are necessary to the validity of a deed, even between the parties, while in others they are required only when there is no acknowledgment.[297] In some states only one witness is required, but in more two are necessary.[298] Some courts hold that deeds not witnessed as required by statute will support an action for specific performance.[299] The witnesses required for deeds are such as are competent to testify.[300] The witnesses must not be interested in the conveyance at the time they act as witnesses,[301] though an interest subsequently acquired will not disqualify them.[302] Where there are several grantors of a joint estate, they are not competent witnesses for each other.[303] The witnesses must sign at the grantor's request,[304] and are competent to testify as to his mental soundness at the time the deed is executed.[305]

269. REGISTRY—A deed must be registered or recorded in some public office provided by statute
  (a) To give it priority over other conveyances.
  (b) To give it validity, in some states.

[296] 2 Bl. Comm. 307.
[297] 1 Stim. Am. St. Law, §§ 1565, 1566. And see Price v. Haynes, 37 Mich. 487; Genter v. Morrison, 31 Barb. 155.
[298] Carson v. Thompson, 10 Wash. 295, 38 Pac. 1116.
[299] Day v. Adams, 42 Vt. 510.
[300] Frink v. Pond, 46 N. H. 125; Winsted Sav. Bank v. Spencer, 26 Conn. 195; Third Nat. Bank v. O'Brien, 94 Tenn. 38, 28 S. W. 293.
[301] Winsted Sav. Bank v. Spencer, 26 Conn. 195.
[302] Carter v. Corley, 23 Ala. 612.
[303] Townsend v. Downer, 27 Vt. 119.
[304] Pritchard v. Palmer, 88 Hun, 412, 34 N. Y. Supp. 787; Tate v. Lawrence, 11 Heisk. (Tenn.) 503.
[305] Brand v. Brand, 39 How. Prac. (N. Y.) 193. And see generally, as to statutes requiring attestation, 1 Dembitz, Land Tit. 348.

Recording laws, and their application to deeds and other conveyances, have already been discussed in connection with mortgages.[306]

SAME—COVENANTS FOR TITLE.

270. Covenants for title are contracts contained in a conveyance by which the grantor binds himself to the grantee as to certain facts in connection with the title to the land conveyed. The usual covenants are:

  (a) **Of seisin and right to convey** (p. 442).
  (b) **Against incumbrances** (p. 444).
  (c) **Of warranty and quiet enjoyment** (p. 446).
  (d) **For further assurance** (p. 449).

Express and Implied Covenants.

Covenants are contracts, and their form and requisites are governed by the law relating to that subject.[307] If the deed in which the covenant is contained is void, the covenant is void.[308] A covenant cannot enlarge the estate conveyed in the instrument which contains the covenant, but a covenant may, in some instances, operate in the same way as words of limitation.[309] Covenants in deeds are either express or implied. The word "give" in a common-law feoffment operated as a covenant of warranty during the grantor's life, but was not binding on his heirs.[310] It has already been seen[311] that implied covenants are raised by the use of the words "grant and demise" in a lease. So in the common-law exchange of lands there are implied covenants of warranty by each party to the conveyance.[312] Deeds operating under the statute of

[306] Ante, p. 218.
[307] Clark, Cont. 72.
[308] Scott v. Scott, 70 Pa. St. 248.
[309] Terrett v. Taylor, 9 Cranch, 53; Shaw v. Galbraith, 7 Pa. St. 111; Blanchard v. Brooks, 12 Pick. (Mass.) 47; Winborne v. Downing, 105 N. C. 20, 10 S. E. 888.
[310] 1 Dembitz, Land Tit. 434.
[311] Ante, p. 138.
[312] Goimes v. Redmon, 14 B. Mon. (Ky.) 234. But see Dean v. Shelly, 57 Pa. St. 427; Walker v. Renfro, 26 Tex. 142. As to implied warranty in partition, see ante, p. 346.

uses raise no implied covenants.[313] In some of our states implied covenants do not exist at all, while in others they are expressly provided for by statute; for instance, in several states it is provided that the words "grant, bargain, and sell" raise implied covenants of seisin, against incumbrances, of warranty, and for quiet enjoyment.[314] If express and implied covenants are both contained in the conveyance, the express covenants control.[315]

Real and Personal Covenants.

Covenants are also classified as real and personal.[316] What such covenants are in the case of leases has already been discussed,[317] and the same principles apply to covenants for title; that is, they are real, and run with the land, when they affect its value, and when their performance is made a charge upon the land.[318] Personal covenants are those which bind only the covenantor and his personal representatives.[319]

Independent and Dependent Covenants.

Dependent covenants are those which cannot be enforced without the performance by the covenantee of some condition precedent.[320] Independent covenants are those which one may enforce without first performing the obligations to which he is bound.[321]

---

[313] Allen v. Sayward, 5 Me. 227.

[314] 1 Stim. Am. St. Law, § 1501.

[315] Burr v. Stenton, 43 N. Y. 462; Vanderkarr v. Vanderkarr, 11 Johns. (N. Y.) 122. But see Funk v. Voneida, 11 Serg. & R. (Pa.) 109.

[316] See Clark, Cont. 545.

[317] Ante, p. 136.

[318] Suydam v. Jones, 10 Wend. (N. Y.) 180; Wead v. Larkin, 54 Ill. 489; First Nat. Bank v. Security Bank (Minn.) 63 N. W. 264; Thomas v. Bland, 91 Ky. 1, 14 S. W. 955; Bean v. Stoneman, 104 Cal. 49, 37 Pac. 777, and 38 Pac. 39; Allen v. Kennedy, 91 Mo. 324, 2 S. W. 142; Tillotson v. Prichard, 60 Vt. 94, 14 Atl. 302. Building restrictions run with the land. Muzzarelli v. Hulshizer, 163 Pa. St. 643, 30 Atl. 291.

[319] Cole v. Hughes, 54 N. Y. 444; Indianapolis Water Co. v. Nutte, 126 Ind. 373, 26 N. E. 72; Brewer v. Marshall, 18 N. J. Eq. 337; Lyford v. Railroad Co., 92 Cal. 93, 28 Pac. 103.

[320] Tompkins v. Elliot, 5 Wend. (N. Y.) 496; Cunningham v. Morrell, 10 Johns. (N. Y.) 203; Tileston v. Newell, 13 Mass. 410; McCrelish v. Churchman, 4 Rawle (Pa.) 26.

[321] Goodwin v. Holbrook, 4 Wend. (N. Y.) 377; Couch v. Ingersoll, 2 Pick. (Mass.) 300.

Wherever possible, courts will construe covenants to be dependent rather than independent, and will not permit a plaintiff to recover damages for the breach of a covenant without first showing performance on his part of all the obligations resting upon him.[322]

271. COVENANT OF SEISIN—A covenant of seisin is that the grantor has the very estate in quantity and in quality which he purports to convey.

272. WHEN BROKEN—As to when the covenant of seisin may be broken, there is a conflict.
 (a) In most states it is considered a covenant of lawful seisin, and can be broken only at the time of the conveyance.
 (b) In some states it is considered as a covenant of indefeasible seisin and can be broken at any time.

273. HOW BROKEN—The covenant of lawful seisin is broken when the grantor is not in lawful possession at the time of the conveyance. The covenant of indefeasible seisin is broken by acts which would be a breach of a covenant of warranty.

A covenant of seisin is an assurance by the grantor to the grantee that there is a right to convey the estate which is purported to be conveyed by the deed.[323] At common law one who had been disseised of his land had no right to convey it, though the one who had disseised him had.[324] In some of our states a disseisee now has power to convey.[325]

When Broken.

As to when the covenant of seisin is broken the cases are conflicting, most courts holding that it must be broken at the time the

[322] Mecum v. Railroad Co., 21 Ill. 533; Clopton v. Bolton, 23 Miss. 78.

[323] Pecare v. Chouteau's Adm'r, 13 Mo. 527; Howell v. Richards, 11 East, 642. For words raising a covenant of seisin, see Wetzel v. Richcreek (Ohio) 40 N. E. 1004.

[324] Thurman v. Cameron, 24 Wend. (N. Y.) 87; Loud v. Darling, 7 Allen (Mass.) 205.

[325] 1 Stim. Am. St. Law, § 1401.

deed is made if at all,[326] and others being to the effect that it may be broken at any time.[327] Under the former ruling the covenant is construed as a covenant of lawful seisin, while the other ruling would make it the same as one of indefeasible seisin, which would be practically the same as a covenant of warranty. The covenant may, of course, be expressly made one of lawful seisin or one of indefeasible seisin.[328] If the covenant of seisin is construed as for a lawful seisin only, it does not run with the land, and, if not broken when the conveyance is made, there can be no subsequent breach.[329]

How Broken.

The covenant for lawful seisin is satisfied if the grantor be in the possession of the land at the time of the conveyance, either himself or by another for him. Mere possession by the grantor under a claim of right is sufficient, even though his title is not good against all the world. All that is required under a covenant of lawful seisin is a seisin in fact.[330] A covenant of seisin is broken when the grantor does not have immediate possession of the land, as when his estate is in remainder,[331] when there is a deficiency in the amount of land conveyed,[332] or when the land described in the conveyance does not exist.[333] It is broken, also, if there are fixtures on the land which may be removed by a third person, who owns them.[334] If the grantor was not sole seised, but a joint owner was in posses-

---

[326] Abbott v. Allen, 14 Johns. (N. Y.) 248; McCarty v. Leggett, 3 Hill (N. Y.) 135; Wilson v. Cochran, 46 Pa. St. 229; Baker v. Hunt, 40 Ill. 265.

[327] Schofield v. Homestead Co., 32 Iowa, 317; Coleman v. Lyman, 42 Ind. 289; Backus' Adm'rs v. McCoy, 3 Ohio, 211. And see Dickson v. Desire's Adm'r, 23 Mo. 151, This is the English doctrine. Kingdon v. Nottle, 4 Maule & S. 53.

[328] Garfield v. Williams, 2 Vt. 327.

[329] Greenley v. Wilcocks, 2 Johns. (N. Y.) 1; Hamilton v. Wilson, 4 Johns. (N. Y.) 72; Bickford v. Page, 2 Mass. 455; Ogden v. Ball, 40 Minn. 94, 41 N. W. 453. But see Kimball v. Bryant, 25 Minn. 496.

[330] Follett v. Grant, 5 Allen (Mass.) 175; Raymond v. Raymond, 10 Cush. (Mass.) 134; Scott v. Twiss, 4 Neb. 133.

[331] Mills v. Catlin, 22 Vt. 106. See Wilder v. Ireland, 8 Jones (N. C.) 90.

[332] Martind. Conv. (2d. Ed.) § 165. But see McArthur v. Morris, 84 N. C. 405.

[333] Bacon v. Lincoln, 4 Cush. (Mass.) 212.

[334] Van Wagner v. Van Nostrand, 19 Iowa, 422.

sion with him, the covenant is broken,[335] as it is also by adverse possession by another.[336] But the covenant is not broken by the existence of a highway or other easement,[337] by a mortgage on the land,[338] nor by an outstanding right of dower.[339] An existing lease of the premises conveyed is no breach of the covenant of seisin if the lease is known to the grantee.[340] If the grantee is seised himself, he cannot claim a breach of the covenant of seisin.[341] For acts which are a breach of a covenant of indefeasible seisin, reference must be made to the covenant of warranty.* The covenant of right to convey is practically the same as the covenant of seisin.[342]

274. COVENANT AGAINST INCUMBRANCES—A covenant against incumbrances is that there are no outstanding rights in third persons, in the land conveyed.

275. HOW BROKEN—This covenant is broken by any right to or interest in the land which may subsist in third persons to the diminution of the value of the estate, but consistently with the passing of the fee.

This covenant is used to protect the grantee against incumbrances existing on land. The incumbrances which are covered by this covenant are of two kinds: Those which are permanent in their nature, such as easements, and those which may be removed, such as mortgages. The covenant against incumbrances is broken

---

[335] Downer's Adm'rs v. Smith, 38 Vt. 464; Sedgwick v. Hollenback, 7 Johns. (N. Y.) 376.

[336] Wetzel v. Richcreek (Ohio) 40 N. E. 1004.

[337] Whitbeck v. Cook, 15 Johns. (N. Y.) 483; Vaughn v. Stuzaker, 16 Ind. 338.

[338] Stanard v. Eldridge, 16 Johns. (N. Y.) 254; Reasoner v. Edmundson, 5 Ind. 393.

[339] Fitzhugh v. Croghan, 2 J. J. Marsh. (Ky.) 430; Tuite v. Miller, 10 Ohio, 383.

[340] Lindley v. Dakin, 13 Ind. 388.

[341] Fitch v. Baldwin, 17 Johns. (N. Y.) 161.

* Post, p. 447.

[342] Chapman v. Holmes' Ex'rs, 10 N. J. Law, 20.

§§ 274-275) COVENANT AGAINST INCUMBRANCES. 445

when the conveyance is made or not at all, because the incumbrances must exist then, if at all.[343] But incumbrances which do not detract from the value of the premises conveyed until they are enforced against it are held to run with the land, so that they may be sued on by the person who holds the land at the time the incumbrance is enforced.[344] When there are incumbrances of this kind on the land, they constitute a breach of the covenant from the time of conveyance,[345] though, if sued on before the incumbrance is enforced, only nominal damages can be recovered.[346]

How Broken.

The covenant against incumbrances is broken by an outstanding mortgage, unless the grantee is bound to pay it,[347] by a right of dower,[348] by a paramount title,[349] by an unexpired lease,[350] by an outstanding judgment,[351] or by unpaid taxes which constitute a lien on the land.[352] The existence of an easement is a breach of the covenant against incumbrances.[353] Even when the easement is known to the grantee at the time he takes the conveyance, most

[343] Clark v. Swift, 3 Metc. (Mass.) 390; Cathcart v. Bowman, 5 Pa. St. 317; Boyd v. Belmont, 58 How. Prac. (N. Y.) 513; Mitchell v. Warner, 5 Conn. 497. But see M'Crady's Ex'rs v. Brisbane, 1 Nott. & McC. (S. C.) 104. An implied covenant against incumbrances is broken immediately. Streeper v. Abeln, 59 Mo. App. 485.

[344] Richard v. Bent, 59 Ill. 43; Knadler v. Sharp, 36 Iowa, 236; Cole v. Kimball, 52 Vt. 639.

[345] Richard v. Bent, 59 Ill. 43.

[346] Bean v. Mayo, 5 Greenl. (Me.) 94.

[347] Or unless the mortgage is excepted from the operation of the covenant. Estabrook v. Smith, 6 Gray (Mass.) 572.

[348] Dower is an incumbrance, whether initiate or consummate. Bigelow v. Hubbard, 97 Mass. 195; Walker's Adm'r v. Deaver, 79 Mo. 664.

[349] Prescott v. Trueman, 4 Mass. 627.

[350] Clark v. Fisher, 54 Kan. 403, 38 Pac. 493.

[351] Jenkins v. Hopkins. 8 Pick. (Mass.) 346; Hall v. Dean, 13 Johns. (N. Y.) 105.

[352] Lafferty v. Milligan, 165 Pa. St. 534, 30 Atl. 1030; Hill v. Bacon, 110 Mass. 388; Mitchell v. Pillsbury, 5 Wis. 407; Campbell v. McClure, 45 Neb. 608, 63 N. W. 920; Long v. Moler, 5 Ohio St. 271. But not when they have not become a lien. Bradley v. Dike (N. J. Sup.) 32 Atl. 132.

[353] Schaeffler v. Michling, 13 Misc. Rep. 520, 34 N. Y. Supp. 693; Morgan v. Smith, 11 Ill. 194; Isele v. Bank, 135 Mass. 142. But see Dunklee v. Railroad Co., 4 Fost. (N. H.) 489.

cases hold that it is a breach of the covenant.[354] The covenant against incumbrances may also be broken by the premises conveyed being subject to covenants which run with the land,[355] and conditions which affect the use of the premises.[356]

276. COVENANT OF WARRANTY—A covenant of warranty is an assurance by the grantor of an estate that the grantee shall enjoy it without interruption by virtue of a paramount title.

277. HOW BROKEN—A covenant of warranty is broken by a lawful eviction from all or part of the premises.

278. SPECIAL WARRANTY—The covenant of warranty may be restricted to certain persons or claims.

In feudal law the covenant of warranty bound the warrantor in the covenant, on the breach of the covenant and eviction of the covenantee, to give the latter lands equal in value to those he had lost.[357] The modern covenant of warranty gives the grantee only a right of action to recover damages for the breach of the covenant.[358] The covenant of warranty runs with the land. It estops the warrantor, and those claiming under him, from setting up a subsequently acquired title against the grantee.[359] And some cases hold that if the grantor, after his conveyance, acquires a title paramount to

---

[354] Beach v. Miller, 51 Ill. 207; Barlow v. McKinley, 24 Iowa, 69; Yancey v. Tatlock (Iowa) 61 N. W. 997; Kellogg v. Malin, 62 Mo. 429. Contra, Patterson v. Arthurs. 9 Watts (Pa.) 152.

[355] Kellogg v. Robinson, 6 Vt. 276; Bronson v. Coffin, 108 Mass. 175.

[356] Kellogg v. Robinson, 6 Vt. 276. But a condition which may defeat the estate is not a breach. Estabrook v. Smith, 6 Gray (Mass.) 572.

[357] Dig. Hist. Real Prop. (4th Ed.) 249.

[358] Paxson v. Lefferts, 3 Rawle (Pa.) 67, note; Jones v. Franklin, 30 Ark. 631.

[359] Bates v. Norcross, 17 Pick. (Mass.) 14; White v. Patten, 24 Pick. (Mass.) 324; Jackson v. Stevens, 13 Johns. (N. Y.) 316; King v. Gilson, 32 Ill. 353; Terrett v. Taylor, 9 Cranch, 43, 53.

§§ 276-278)   COVENANT OF WARRANTY.   447

the one which he has transferred, it immediately inures to the benefit of the grantee.[360] Statutory provisions to this effect exist in some states.[361] The covenant of warranty prevents the heirs of the warrantor from setting up a paramount title to the lands conveyed if they have received assets from their ancestor, thus avoiding circuity of action; otherwise, if the heirs were permitted to recover from the grantee under their paramount title, the grantee could in turn sue them on the covenant of warranty, and enforce the damages out of the assets which they had received from the warrantor.[362]

How Broken.

The covenant of warranty is broken by an eviction by judgment of law from part or all of the premises.[363] A mere disturbance of the grantee will not constitute a breach of the covenant, for the disturbance, to be a breach, must be lawful.[364] The grantee, however, need not wait for an actual ouster under a judgment recovered against him, but may yield the possession to one having a paramount title without incurring the cost of a suit,[365] and he may even accept a title from such person without losing his right to rely on the covenant of warranty.[366] Though when he brings action on the covenant, he must show that the title to which he yielded was a valid one.[367] A mortgage enforced against the premises conveyed

[360] Knowles v. Kennedy, 82 Pa. St. 445; Crocker v. Pierce, 31 Me. 177.
[361] 1 Stim. Am. St. Law, § 1454 B.
[362] Bates v. Norcross, 17 Pick. (Mass.) 14; Cole v. Raymond, 9 Gray (Mass.) 217. But see Jones v. Franklin, 30 Ark. 631. When those who would be the grantor's heirs take by purchase, they are not bound. Whitesides v. Cooper, 115 N. C. 570, 20 S. E. 295.
[363] Norton v. Jackson, 5 Cal. 262; Hannah v. Henderson, 4 Ind. 174; Stewart v. Drake, 9 N. J. Law, 139. And see Lucy v. Levington, 2 Lev. 26.
[364] Gleason v. Smith, 41 Vt. 293.
[365] Hamilton v. Cutts, 4 Mass. 349; Claycomb v. Munger, 51 Ill. 376; Funk v. Creswell, 5 Iowa, 62.
[366] Eversole v. Early, 80 Iowa, 601, 44 N. W. 897; Hall v. Bray, 51 Mo. 288; Potwin v. Blasher, 9 Wash. 460, 37 Pac. 710; Dillahunty v. Railway Co., 59 Ark. 699, 27 S. W. 1002, and 28 S. W. 657. But see Huff v. Land Co. (Ky.) 30 S. W. 660.
[367] Somers v. Schmidt, 24 Wis. 417; Merritt v. Morse, 108 Mass. 276; Cheney v. Straube, 43 Neb. 879, 62 N. W. 234.

is a breach of the covenant of warranty,[368] as is the removal of fixtures by one having the right to do so.[369] The existence of a valid easement over the land conveyed is also a breach of the covenant.[370] But a taking of the land under the right of eminent domain does not constitute a breach.[371] The covenant for quiet enjoyment is the same as the covenant of warranty in all its practical effects.[372] It is an assurance to the grantee that his enjoyment of the land conveyed shall not be disturbed by lawful means,[373] but does not attempt to protect him against mere disturbances by trespassers.[374]

Special Warranty.

The covenant of warranty so far considered is one of general warranty, but the covenant may be limited in its operation to the claims of particular persons. A covenant of special warranty is many times inserted in quitclaim deeds, by which the granto. warrants the title against all persons claiming through him. Such a covenant of special warranty does not prevent the grantor from setting up a subsequently acquired title against the covenantee.[375] Another form of covenant of special warranty is where the grantor covenants that the title shall be good against all claims except a certain mortgage which exists upon the land.[376]

[368] Harlow v. Thomas, 15 Pick. (Mass.) 66; Tuft v. Adams, 8 Pick. (Mass.) 547; White v. Whitney, 3 Metc. (Mass.) 81; Cowdrey v. Coit, 44 N. Y. 382.
[369] West v. Stewart, 7 Pa. St. 122.
[370] Harlow v. Thomas, 15 Pick. (Mass.) 66; Russ v. Steele, 40 Vt. 310. But see Hymes v. Esty, 36 Hun (N. Y.) 147; Brown v. Young, 69 Iowa, 625, 29 N. W. 941.
[371] Peck v. Jones, 70 Pa. St. 83; Brimmer v. City of Boston, 102 Mass. 19.
[372] Bostwick v. Williams, 36 Ill. 65, 69; Emerson v. Proprietors of Land, 1 Mass. 464. But see Fowler v. Poling, 6 Barb. (N. Y.) 165.
[373] Sedgwick v. Hollenback, 7 Johns. (N. Y.) 376.
[374] Greenby v. Wilcocks, 2 Johns. (N. Y.) 1; Beebe v. Swartwout, 3 Gilman (Ill.) 180; Underwood v. Birchard, 47 Vt. 305.
[375] Jackson v. Winslow, 9 Cow. (N. Y.) 13; Trull v. Eastman, 3 Metc. (Mass.) 124; Western Min. & Manuf'g Co. v. Peytona Cannel Coal Co., 8 W. Va. 406; Buckner v. Street, 15 Fed. 365.
[376] Freeman v. Foster, 55 Me. 508.

Action for Breach.

At common law, after the breach of a covenant,[377] there could be no assignment of it.[378] This is still true, except in states where choses in action are assignable.[379] A covenant of warranty may be apportioned, as, when the land to which it is annexed is divided and held by a number of owners, the covenant attaches to each part, and each grantee may sue on the covenant.[380] When there have been several successive conveyances, each with covenants of warranty, and the last grantee is evicted, he may sue all of the warrantors, but can recover only from one.[381] When the grantor is sued on covenants of warranty, if the land has been warranted to him, he may vouch in his warrantor by giving him notice of the suit,[382] and by so doing he relieves himself of the necessity of proving in a subsequent suit against such warrantor that the action in which he was defeated was well founded.[383]

279. COVENANT FOR FURTHER ASSURANCE—A covenant for further assurance is an agreement by the grantor to do any other acts which may be necessary for perfecting the grantee's title.

The covenant for further assurance is used as a means of enforcing specific performance of a conveyance which has been made, and

---

[377] As to the measure of damages for breach of covenants, see Hale, Dam. 367.

[378] Lewes v. Ridge, Cro. Eliz. 863.

[379] Slater v. Rawson, 1 Metc. (Mass.) 450; Allen v. Kennedy, 91 Mo. 324, 2 S. W. 142.

[380] Dickinson v. Hoomes' Adm'r, 8 Grat. (Va.) 353. And see Kane v. Sanger, 14 Johns. (N. Y.) 89; Lane v. Woodruff (Kan. App.) 40 Pac. 1079.

[381] Withy v. Mumford, 5 Cow. (N. Y.) 137.

[382] Grant v. Hill (Tex. Civ. App.) 30 S. W. 952. The warrantor may be required to defend, though the claim set up is invalid. Meservey v. Snell (Iowa) 62 N. W. 767. An intermediate covenantee who has not been damnified cannot recover from prior covenantors. Booth v. Starr, 1 Conn. 244.

[383] Merritt v. Morse, 108 Mass. 276; Somers v. Schmidt, 24 Wis. 417; Paul v. Witman, 3 Watts & S. (Pa.) 409; McConnell v. Downs, 48 Ill. 271. The warrantee cannot recover from the warrantor when the former instigated a third person to claim title to the land. Hester v. Hunnicutt, 104 Ala. 282, 16 South. 162.

might prove defective in some respects. The covenant applies not only to the doing of further acts which may be necessary to protect the grantee's title, but applies also to the execution of additional instruments to give the grantee a perfect title of record, and to remove any clouds upon such title.[384] The covenant for further assurance is one which runs with the land,[385] and is broken by the failure of the covenantor to do the various acts necessary for perfecting the grantee's title when requested.[386]

ESTOPPEL.

280. Title by estoppel arises when the holder of the real title is prevented by law from asserting it in denial of his acts or representations, against one who has relied on them to his injury. The estoppel which gives such title is either

(a) **In pais** (p. 451), or

(b) **By deed** (p. 453).

Title by estoppel is that title which is created by presumption of law by an estoppel which prevents the actual owner of land from setting up his title against one who has acquired rights in the land in reliance upon some acts or representations of the owner, and would be injured by permitting the owner to say that those acts or representations were false.[387] When such presumptions arise, they are conclusive, and cannot be rebutted by the owner; though he may, of course, say that the necessary facts to constitute the estoppel do not exist.[388] The effect of an estoppel is to convey any title

---

[384] Lamb v. Burbank, 1 Sawy. 227, Fed. Cas. No. 8,012; Gwynn v. Thomas, 2 Gill & J. (Md.) 420; Warn v. Bickford, 7 Price, 550.

[385] Colby v. Osgood, 29 Barb. (N. Y.) 339; Middlemore v. Goodale, Cro. Car. 503.

[386] King v. Jones, 5 Taunt. 418. Cf. Kingdon v. Nottle, 1 Maule & S. 355.

[387] Bush v. Person, 18 How. 82.

[388] Welland Canal Co. v. Hathaway, 8 Wend. (N. Y.) 480; Hanrahan v. O'Reilly, 102 Mass. 204. Recitals do not estop a party from showing fraud. Hickman v. Stewart, 69 Tex. 255, 5 S. W. 833. An agreement to divide the proceeds of lands does not create an estoppel. Oliphant v. Burns, 146 N. Y. 218, 40 N. E. 980.

§ 280) ESTOPPEL. 451

subsequently acquired by the grantor to the one entitled to the estoppel,[389] and not merely to bind the title in the hands of the owner so that he cannot set it up. Some cases hold that the latter is the rule. But the weight of authority is that in estoppel the title inures to the benefit of the grantee or a person who has acquired rights in the land in reliance upon the facts which constitute the estoppel.[390] And in some states it is provided by statute that the title shall so inure.[391] The estoppel of a tenant to deny his landlord's title has been discussed in a former chapter.[392]

Estoppel in Pais.

When one claims title by an estoppel in pais, he must show that representations have been made to him for the purpose of influencing his conduct, that he has relied on those representations, and that he would be injured by permitting the other party to deny the truth of those representations.[393] A case of title by estoppel in pais may be illustrated by the instance of the owner of land inducing another to make improvements on the land under a mistaken belief of ownership. In a proper case the owner of the land might be held estopped to set up his title to the injury of the one who had been induced by him to make the improvements.[394] As to whether infants and married women may be bound by estoppel in pais, the cases

[389] The one claiming by estoppel cannot recover for the breach of a covenant in the deed to the former owner. Noke v. Awder, Cro. Eliz. 436. And see Andrew v. Pearce, 1 Bos. & P. (N. R.) 158.

[390] Doe v. Oliver, 10 Barn. & C. 181; Baxter v. Bradbury, 20 Me. 260; Somes v. Skinner, 3 Pick. (Mass.) 52; Walton v. Follansbee, 131 Ill. 147, 23 N. E. 332; Clark v. Baker, 14 Cal. 612; Ivy v. Yancey, 129 Mo. 501, 31 S. W. 937; Bush v. Marshall, 6 How. 284. And see Reese v. Smith, 12 Mo. 344. But the title does not inure to the grantee without his consent, so as to defeat his right to maintain an action on the covenants of the deed. Blanchard v. Ellis, 1 Gray (Mass.) 195.

[391] 1 Stim. Am. St. Law, § 1454 B.

[392] Ante, p. 143.

[393] Malloney v. Horan, 49 N. Y. 111; Brown v. Bowen, 30 N. Y. 519; Anderson v. Coburn, 27 Wis. 566; Little v. Giles, 25 Neb. 313, 41 N. W. 186; Hill v. Epley, 31 Pa. St. 334; Stuart v. Lowry, 42 Minn. 473, 44 N. W. 532; Parker v. Barker, 2 Metc. (Mass.) 423; Huntley v. Hole, 58 Conn. 445, 20 Atl. 469.

[394] Niven v. Belknap, 2 Johns. (N. Y.) 573; Wendell v. Van Rensselaer, 1 Johns. Ch. (N. Y.) 344; Des Moines & Ft. D. R Co. v. Lynd (Iowa) 62 N. W.

are conflicting. Some hold that they may be so bound if the one claiming title by estoppel can show fraudulent acts on the part of the infant or married woman without setting up any contract entered into by such person, because infants and married women would have no power to contract in relation to their lands, but could be bound by their fraudulent acts.[395] An estoppel in pais may arise either by positive acts or by the omission to do acts,—such as to give notice to one's title to land when required to do so. For instance, if one stands by and sees his land sold by another person without notifying the purchaser of his rights therein, he will be estopped from setting up his title against such purchaser.[396] If, however, the owner has his title on record, the record is notice to such purchaser, and no estoppel can arise.[397] The cases are conflicting as to whether fraud is a necessary element of estoppel in pais.[398] But there is substantial agreement that the effect must be the same as if a fraudulent intent existed.[399]

806; Phillips v. Clark, 4 Metc. (Ky.) 348; Muse v. Hotel Co., 68 Fed. 637; Union Pac. Ry. Co. v. U. S., 15 C. C. A. 123, 67 Fed. 975; Wehrmann v. Conklin, 155 U. S. 314, 15 Sup. Ct. 129. Where lots are sold as abutting on a street, the vendor is estopped to deny the dedication of the street by him. McLemore v. McNeley, 56 Mo. App. 556.

[395] For cases holding infants and married women estopped, see Blakeslee v. Sincepaugh, 71 Hun, 412, 24 N. Y. Supp. 947; Knight v. Thayer, 125 Mass. 25; Howell v. Hale, 5 Lea (Tenn.) 405; Appeal of Grim, 105 Pa. St. 375; Guertin v. Mombleau, 144 Ill. 32, 33 N. E. 49; Sandwich Manuf'g Co. v. Zellmer, 48 Minn. 408, 51 N. W. 379; Berry v. Seawall, 13 C. C. A. 101, 65 Fed. 742 (a parol partition). For cases holding infants and married women not estopped, see Innis v. Templeton, 95 Pa. St. 262; Spencer v. Carr, 45 N. Y. 406; McBeth v. Trabue, 69 Mo. 642; Hilburn v. Harris (Tex. Civ. App.) 29 S. W. 923. A married woman is not estopped by an invalid power of attorney. Brown v. Rouse, 104 Cal. 672. 38 Pac. 507.

[396] Cochran v. Harrow, 22 Ill. 345; Dickerson v. Colgrove, 100 U. S. 578; Wendell v. Van Rensselaer, 1 Johns. Ch. (N. Y.) 344; Bates v. Swiger (W. Va.) 21 S. E. 874; Mask v. Allen (Miss.) 17 South. 82; Swift v. Stovall (Ala.) 17 South. 186. But see Irwin v. Patchen, 164 Pa. St. 51, 30 Atl. 436.

[397] Lathrop v. Bank, 31 N. J. Eq. 273; Viele v. Judson, 82 N. Y. 32; Porter v. Wheeler (Ala.) 17 South. 221. But see Neal v. Gregory, 19 Fla. 356. The record of the forged deed raises no estoppel against the owner of the land. Meley v. Collins, 41 Cal. 663.

[398] That fraud is a necessary element of estoppel, see Henshaw v. Bissell,

[399] Maple v. Kussart, 53 Pa. St. 348; McNeil v. Jordan, 28 Kan. 7.

§ 280)　　　　　　　ESTOPPEL.　　　　　　　453

Same—Division Lines.

A large number of cases on estoppel in pais have arisen in connection with division lines and fences, and the holdings of the court are by no means uniform. If the parties, in locating the line, merely agree to put a fence or building on a certain line without any reference to where the actual boundary is, or if the fence or building was located otherwise than on the true line through mistake, no estoppel arises, and either party may claim to the true line when it is discovered.[400] On the other hand, if the true line is unknown through loss of monuments, and the parties agree upon a division line, either themselves or through arbitrators, the parties are estopped to claim that such line is not the true line.[401]

Estoppel by Deed.

No one can be estopped by deed who has not power to make a valid deed.[402] When title arises through estoppel by deed, the grantor is estopped to deny that he had the interest which he purports to convey by his deed.[403] When the deed is by indenture, both parties may be estopped to deny, unless one of them has been induced to execute the deed by fraud,[404] that the contract which arises from the conveyance is binding on them.[405] So, too, in a

18 Wall. 271; Davidson v. Young, 38 Ill. 145; Boggs v. Mining Co., 14 Cal. 279; Jewett v. Miller, 10 N. Y. 402; Andrews v. Lyons, 11 Allen (Mass.) 349. Contra, Maple v. Kussart, 53 Pa. St. 348.

[400] Proctor v. Machine Co., 137 Mass. 159; Proprietors of Liverpool Wharf v. Prescott, 7 Allen (Mass.) 494; Thayer v. Bacon, 3 Allen (Mass.) 163. But not after acquiescence for the period of the statute of limitations. Chew v. Morton, 10 Watts (Pa.) 321.

[401] Reed v. Farr, 35 N. Y. 113; Jackson v. Ogden, 7 Johns. (N. Y.) 238; Joyce v. Williams, 26 Mich. 332; Knowles v. Toothaker, 58 Me. 174.

[402] Bank of America v. Banks, 101 U. S. 240, 247; Jackson v. Vanderheyden, 17 Johns. (N. Y.) 167.

[403] Logan v. Eaton (N. H.) 31 Atl. 13; Bank of U. S. v. Benning, 4 Cranch, C. C. 81, Fed. Cas. No. 908; Carson v. Cochran, 52 Minn. 67, 53 N. W. 1130.

[404] Jackson v. Ayers, 14 Johns. (N. Y.) 224; Alderson v. Miller, 15 Grat. (Va.) 279.

[405] Fort v. Allen, 110 N. C. 183, 14 S. E. 685; Raby v. Reeves, 112 N. C. 688, 16 S. E. 760; Fitch v. Baldwin, 17 Johns. (N. Y.) 161. Acceptance of a devise may estop the devisee to set up a claim inconsistent with the will. Hyde v. Baldwin, 17 Pick. (Mass.) 303; Watson v. Watson, 128 Mass. 152.

deed poll, the grantee may, by his acceptance of the deed, be estopped to deny the contents of the deed.[406] A quitclaim deed estops the grantee as to the grantor's capacity.[407] The common-law conveyance by feoffment imposed an estoppel on the feoffor during his life, which prevented him from setting up a paramount title subsequently acquired.[408] But deeds of release and quitclaim place no estoppel on the grantor as to future-acquired interests,[409] though they do as to rights existing at the time of the conveyance.[410] Deeds operating under the statute of uses cause no estoppels as to either present or future titles, unless they contain covenants which so operate.[411] Estoppel by deed may arise through recitals contained therein, such as recitals as to the origin of the title,[412] or where the grantor recites that the land conveyed is bounded by a street.[413] A recital, however, to be effectual as an estoppel, must be definite.[414] Recitals in a will bind those claiming under the will as to particular facts stated therein.[415] Deeds containing covenants of warranty estop

[406] Comstock v. Smith, 26 Mich. 306; Chloupek v. Perotka, 89 Wis. 551, 62 N. W. 537. A compromise deed does not necessarily raise an estoppel. Strong v. Powell, 92 Ga. 591, 20 S. E. 6. A grantee may show that he was evicted under a title paramount to that of his grantor, and that he is holding as tenant under the owner of such paramount title. Moore v. Smead, 89 Wis. 558, 62 N. W. 426.

[407] A grantee under a quitclaim deed from a county is estopped, as against a former grantee of the county, to deny the county's power to convey. Roberts v. Railroad Co., 158 U. S. 1, 15 Sup. Ct. 756.

[408] 3 Washb. Real Prop. (5th Ed.) 103.

[409] Frost v. Society, 56 Mich. 62, 22 N. W. 189; Wight v. Shaw, 5 Cush. (Mass.) 56; Miller v. Ewing, 6 Cush. (Mass.) 34; Hanrick v. Patrick, 119 U. S. 156, 7 Sup. Ct. 147; Jourdain v. Fox (Wis.) 62 N. W. 936; Stephenson v. Boody, 132 Ind. 60, 38 N. E. 331; Brawford v. Wolfe, 103 Mo. 391, 15 S. W. 426; Kimmel v. Benna, 70 Mo. 52; Chauvin v. Wagner, 18 Mo. 531.

[410] Prewitt v. Ashford, 90 Ala. 294, 7 South. 831.

[411] Jackson v. Wright, 14 Johns. (N. Y.) 193.

[412] Stone v. Fitts, 38 S. C. 393, 17 S. E. 136; Mitchell v. Kinnard (Ky.) 29 S. W. 309. And see Lindauer v. Younglove, 47 Minn. 62, 49 N. W. 384; Goodwin v. Folsom (N. H.) 32 Atl. 159. But cf. Frick v. Fiscus, 164 Pa. St. 623, 30 Atl. 515.

[413] But it may be shown that such a recital was inserted by mistake. Long v. Cruger (Tex. Civ. App.) 28 S. W. 568.

[414] Onward Building Soc. v. Smithson [1893] 1 Ch. 1.

[415] Denu v. Cornell, 3 Johns. Cas. (N. Y.) 174; Katz v. Schnaier, 87 Hun,

§ 280)　　　　　　　　ESTOPPEL.　　　　　　　　455

the grantor from setting up a subsequently acquired title against his grantee.[416] When there is a conveyance by co-tenants of a joint estate, no estoppel is raised against any one tenant as to the shares of the others.[417] Many cases hold that a married woman may be estopped by her deed which is made effectual by her husband joining with her,[418] though other cases deny this to be the rule.[419] It would seem that a married woman should be estopped by her deed whenever statutes have provided that such deed shall be effectual to pass her title to the property. A wife is not estopped, however, by joining in her husband's conveyance to release her right of dower through any recitals or covenants in such deed. Nor is a husband estopped by joining in his wife's conveyance to release his right of curtesy.[420] Estoppels bind only parties and privies.[421] They cannot be set up against strangers [422] or by them.[423] All persons

343, 34 N. Y. Supp. 315. But see Hatch v. Ferguson, 15 C. C. A. 201, 68 Fed. 43.

[416] Wadhams v. Swan, 109 Ill. 46; Smith v. Williams, 44 Mich. 240, 6 N. W. 662; Thomas v. Stickle, 32 Iowa, 72. But see Younts v. Starnes, 42 S. C. 22, 19 S. E. 1011. Those claiming under the grantor are estopped. White v. Patten, 24 Pick. (Mass.) 324. And see ante, p. 446. An estoppel to set up an after-acquired title is created by a covenant for further assurance. Bennett v. Waller, 23 Ill. 183. But the heirs of the grantor are not estopped unless they have received assets from him, Chauvin v. Wagner, 18 Mo. 531; or when they claim by purchase, and not by descent, Trolan v. Rogers, 88 Hun, 422, 34 N. Y. Supp. 836.

[417] Weiser v. Weiser, 5 Watts (Pa.) 279; Walker v. Hall, 15 Ohio St. 355. But see Rountree v. Denson, 59 Wis. 522, 18 N. W. 518.

[418] Guertin v. Mombleau, 144 Ill. 32, 33 N. E. 49; Knight v. Thayer, 125 Mass. 25; Sandwich Manuf'g Co. v. Zellmer, 48 Minn. 408, 51 N. W. 379; Bailey v. Seymour, 42 S. C. 322, 20 S. E. 62. Her subsequent grantee may be estopped. Ramboz v. Stowell, 103 Cal. 588, 37 Pac. 519.

[419] Thompson v. Merrill, 58 Iowa, 419, 10 N. W. 796; Hempstead v. Easton, 33 Mo. 142; Jackson v. Vanderheyden, 17 Johns. (N. Y.) 167; and see Miller v. Miller, 140 Ind. 174, 39 N. E. 547.

[420] Raymond v. Holden, 2 Cush. (Mass.) 270; Strawn v. Strawn, 50 Ill. 33; O'Neil v. Vanderburg, 25 Iowa, 104.

[421] Campbell v. Hall, 16 N. Y. 575; Bates v. Norcross, 17 Pick. (Mass.) 14; Graves v. Colwell, 90 Ill. 612; Broadwell v. Merritt, 87 Mo. 95.

[422] Right v. Bucknell, 2 Barn. & Adol. 278; Jackson v. Bradford, 4 Wend. (N. Y.) 619.

[423] Sunderlin v. Struthers, 47 Pa. St. 411; Glasgow v. Baker, 72 Mo. 441.

claiming under one who is estopped are estopped also if they have notice of the facts constituting the estoppel.[424] The grantor, however, in a deed which would raise an estoppel against him, may acquire a new title against his grantee,[425] as under a tax sale for taxes levied after his conveyance.[426]

ADVERSE POSSESSION.

281. One who disseises the owner of land, and holds it adversely for the period prescribed by the statute of limitations, acquires title to the estate of the disseisee. Acquisition of title by adverse possession is subject to the following conditions:

(a) **The possession must be actual for part of the land at least** (p. 459).

(b) **It must be visible or notorious** (p. 462).

(c) **It must be hostile or adverse** (p. 463).

(d) **It must be exclusive** (p. 465).

(e) **It must be continuous by one person or by persons in privity** (p. 466).

(f) **Possession is adverse to all who have an immediate right to the possession and are not under disability** (p. 468).

(g) **Possession must be continued for the whole time required by the statute** (p. 469).

(h) **Abandonment by the disseisor after the full period has run does not divest his title** (p. 469).

One who has possession of land is entitled to hold such land against all persons except the rightful owner;[427] and, if there were

---

Heirs and assigns may claim an estoppel. Trull v. Eastman, 3 Metc. (Mass.) 121. A reversion may be created by estoppel. Sturgeon v. Wingfield, 15 Mees. & W. 224; Cuthbertson v. Irving, 4 Hurl. & N. 742. Cf. Beddoe v. Wadsworth, 21 Wend. (N. Y.) 120. Contra, Slater v. Rawson, 1 Metc. (Mass.) 450.

[424] Shay v. McNamara, 54 Cal. 169; Kimball v. Blaisdell, 5 N. H. 533; Doe v. Skirrow, 2 Nev. & P. 123.

[425] Ervin v. Morris, 26 Kan. 664.

[426] Hannah v. Collins, 94 Ind. 201.

[427] Hughes v. Graves, 39 Vt. 359.

no one entitled to the land, the first person taking possession thereof would become the owner, and his title would be said to arise by occupancy.[428] But as all public land in this country is owned by the United States or the states, no title can be acquired by occupancy now. When a man takes possession of land belonging to another he acquires rights therein which may ripen into a title either through the doctrine of estoppel, by which the true owner may be prevented from setting up his title against the one in possession, or through the statutes of limitations, which provide that, if one holds possession of land for the period provided by the statutes of the various states, the owner of the land shall have no power to dispossess him. There are two theories as to the manner in which statutes of limitation operate. One is that it merely destroys the remedy of the true owner, and thus cuts off his rights against the one in possession, who, as already stated, has title by that possession against all other persons, by the mere fact of having possession.[429] The other theory is that the statute of limitation operates to transfer the title of the real owner to the one in adverse possession of the land, and that the latter acquires a title which he can himself sue on.[430] All titles acquired by virtue of the statute of limitations are for the same estates as the one disseised owned. Though it is not presumed that one in possession claims any less estate than a fee simple,[431] it may be that a less estate will be gained, as in a case where a tenant for life is disseised, and statute of limitation has run against him. The disseisor has an estate only for the life of the person whom he has disseised, because the owners of the remainders dependent on that estate do not loose their right to recover the land until the expiration of the statutory period after their right to the possession of land accrues, which is not until the death of the life tenant.[432]

[428] 2 Bl. Comm. 258. As to occupancy of an estate per autre, see ante, p. 67.

[429] 2 Dembitz, Land Tit. 1345.

[430] Toll v. Wright, 37 Mich. 93; Farrar v. Heinrich, 86 Mo. 521; Stokes v. Berry, 2 Salk. 421. The disseisor may bring an action to quiet title. Independent Dist. of Oak Dale v. Fagen (Iowa) 63 N. W. 456.

[431] Some statutes provide that a fee simple shall be acquired. See East Tennessee Iron & Coal Co. v. Wiggin, 15 C. C. A. 510, 68 Fed. 446.

[432] Pluche v. Jones, 4 C. C. A. 622, 54 Fed. 860; Pinckney v. Burrage, 31

Seisin and Disseisin.

Seisin, as meaning possession of land, has already been discussed.[433] It is impossible for two persons, unless they are joint owners, to have lawful seisin of the same land at the same time. If two persons are thus in possession, the one who has title to the land will have the seisin also.[434] One who takes possession of land against the claims of the rightful owner is said to disseise the latter, and is called a disseisor. It is not necessary that such person be sui juris, for an infant may be a disseisor.[435] Before considering any details or elements of disseisin and adverse possession, it may be mentioned that one may be disseised by election; that is, he may treat certain acts of a trespasser as a disseisin, and proceed against him by the same remedies as are given one who is disseised of his land.[436] In order that a disseisin may be claimed in this way, the disseisee must actually abandon the possession.[437] A man may be seised of his land by reason of his being in actual possession or occupancy of it himself, or he may be seised through another, holding subordinate to him, as a landlord is seised though his tenant be in possession.[438] When the owner of lands has been disseised, his interest in the land has been reduced to a mere right of

---

N. J. Law, 21; Merritt v. Hughes, 36 W. Va. 357, 15 S. E. 56; Bagley v. Kennedy, 81 Ga. 721, 8 S. E. 742. So, where possession is taken as life tenant under a void will and title gained by lapse of time, the disseisor will have only a life estate as against the remainder-man in the will. Board v. Board, L. R. 9 Q. B. 48. But where husband and wife are disseised of the wife's lands, her right of entry accrues at once. Melvin v. Proprietors, 16 Pick. (Mass.) 161. Contra, Foster v. Marshall, 22 N. H. 491. If the estate in reversion or remainder is created after the disseisin, the reversioner or remainder-man is barred at the same time as the tenant of the particular estate. Doe v. Jones, 4 Term R. 308.

[433] Ante, p. 31.

[434] Hunnicutt v. Peyton, 102 U. S. 333; Farrar v. Heinrich, 86 Mo. 521.

[435] Lackman v. Wood, 25 Cal. 147.

[436] Busw. Lim. § 237, note; Blunden v. Baugh, Cro. Car. 302; Smith v. Burtis, 6 Johns. (N. Y.) 197, 215; Proprietors of Township No. 6 v. McFarland, 12 Mass. 325, 327; Prescott v. Nevers, 4 Mason, 327, 329, Fed. Cas. No. 11,390.

[437] Burns v. Lynde, 6 Allen (Mass.) 305, 312; Munroe v. Ward, 4 Allen (Mass.) 150.

[438] See ante, p. 285.

§ 281)　　　ADVERSE POSSESSION.　　　459

entry; that is, the owner must make an actual entry on the land in order to regain his seisin, but for this purpose a physical ouster of the disseisor is not essential.[439] It is simply necessary that the disseisee enter on the land with the intention of regaining his seisin, and do acts showing such intention.[440] At common law, if, before the right of entry is exercised, there be a descent cast,—that is, if the disseisor die, and his rights acquired by the disseisin are transferred to his heirs,—the disseisee's right of entry is changed to a mere right of action. This rule obtains, however, in only a few of our states.[441]

Possession must be Actual.

In order that title may be gained by adverse possession, it is necessary that there be an actual disseisin of the owner, and this can only be by the disseisor being in possession of the land in question.[442] No particular acts are necessary to show such possession, though some are of such a nature that they leave no doubt as to the character of the occupancy. Among these may be mentioned residence on the land,[443] the erection of buildings and other structures,[444] or the actual inclosure of the land with a fence.[445] None of these acts are absolutely necessary, and in some cases might be impossible, from the character of the property.[446] Adverse possession must be accompanied by an ouster of the real owner of the

[439] Shearman v. Irvine's Lessee, 4 Cranch, 367; Jackson v. Haviland, 13 Johns. (N. Y.) 229; Altemus v. Campbell, 9 Watts (Pa.) 28. But see Jackson v. Cairns, 20 Johns. (N. Y.) 301; Hall's Lessee v. Vandegrift, 3 Bin. (Pa.) 374.

[440] Altemus v. Campbell, 9 Watts (Pa.) 28.

[441] 3 Washb. Real Prop. (5th Ed.) 140.

[442] Ward v. Cochran, 150 U. S. 597, 14 Sup. Ct. 230; Ewing v. Elcorn, 40 Pa. St. 493.

[443] Hughs v. Pickering, 14 Pa. St. 297; Cunningham v. Brumback, 23 Ark. 336; Bell v. Denson, 56 Ala. 444. Cultivation is not always adverse possession. State v. Suttle, 115 N. C. 784, 20 S. E. 725.

[444] Ellicott v. Pearl, 10 Pet. 412; Goltermann v. Schiermeyer, 111 Mo. 404, 19 S. W. 484, and 20 S. W. 161; Moss v. Scott, 2 Dana (Ky.) 271; Hubbard v. Kiddo, 87 Ill. 578.

[445] Doolittle v. Tice, 41 Barb. (N. Y.) 181; Millar v. Humphries, 2 A. K. Marsh. (Ky.) 446. As to what is a sufficient inclosure, see Yates v. Van De Vogert, 56 N. Y. 526; Pope v. Hanmer, 74 N. Y. 240.

[446] People v. Van Rensselaer, 9 N. Y. 291; De Lancey v. Piepgras, 138 N.

land, though it is not necessary that it be by force. Cutting timber or grass on the land which is claimed to be held by adverse possession has been held insufficient to show disseisin.[447] And in all cases the disseisor must do the acts which constitute the disseisin with the intention to produce that effect.[448] A mere intention to disseise is not effectual unless accompanied by positive acts. For instance, the owner of the surface of land cannot disseise another who owns the mines under the soil by merely claiming such mines, but must work them, or do other acts indicative of ownership.[449] So, too, taking a deed to lands from one not the owner, and recording it, does not constitute a disseisin unless there is an entry under the deed.[450] Nor would an entry upon lands claimed under a deed be a disseisin if the entry was made by mistake, with no intention to disseise.[451] But an entry under a deed, though the deed be absolutely void, will be an ouster of the owner.[452]

Constructive Possession—Color of Title.

The possession which we have been discussing in the last section applies only to the tracts of land which are actually held by the dis-

Y. 26, 33 N. E. 822; Murphy v. Doyle, 37 Minn. 113, 33 N. W. 220; Webber v. Clarke, 74 Cal. 11, 15 Pac. 431; Hubbard v. Kiddo, 87 Ill. 578.

[447] Wiggins v. Kirby (Ala.) 17 South. 354; Mission of Immaculate Virgin v. Cronin, 143 N. Y. 524, 38 N. E. 964; Price v. Brown, 101 N. Y. 669, 5 N. E. 434. Adverse possession is not shown by building a shanty which is never occupied, Wickliffe v. Ensor, 9 B. Mon. (Ky.) 253; or by gathering seaweed, Trustees of East Hampton v. Kirk, 68 N. Y. 460; or by hauling sand at intervals for 20 years, Strange v. Spaulding (Ky.) 29 S. W. 137. But cutting timber in a well-settled district may be an actual disseisin. Murray v. Hudson, 65 Mich. 670, 32 N. W. 889; Horner v. Reuter, 152 Ill. 106, 38 N. E. 747; Scott v. Delany, 87 Ill. 146. And cutting hay for 20 years has been held sufficient. Sullivan v. Eddy, 154 Ill. 199, 40 N. E. 482. And see Whitaker v. Shooting Club, 102 Mich. 454, 60 N. W. 983.

[448] Jackson v. Huntington, 5 Pet. 402, 439; Ewing v. Burnet, 11 Pet. 41; Clarke v. McClure, 10 Grat. (Va.) 305.

[449] Algonquin Coal Co. v. Northern Coal & Iron Co., 162 Pa. St. 114, 29 Atl. 402.

[450] Trustees of Putnam Free School v. Fisher, 38 Me. 324.

[451] Skinner v. Crawford, 54 Iowa, 119, 6 N. W. 144. But see Rowland v. Williams, 23 Or. 515, 32 Pac. 402.

[452] Northrop v. Wright, 7 Hill (N. Y.) 476; North v. Hammer, 34 Wis. 425; McMillan v. Wehle, 55 Wis. 685, 13 N. W. 694; Moody v. Fleming, 4 Ga. 115.

§ 281) ADVERSE POSSESSION. 461

seisor, and occupied by him. But by the doctrine of constructive possession under color of title there may be a disseisin and adverse holding of more land than is actually occupied. This occurs when the disseisin is made under a deed or other instrument which purports to convey more land than is occupied by the disseisor. If the deed is recorded, or is otherwise brought to the notice of the owner, the disseisor is held to be in constructive possession of all the land purported to be conveyed by the instrument under which he claims.[453] Color of title is anything in writing which serves to define the extent of the disseisor's claim, or it is a writing which, upon its face, professes to pass title, but which in fact does not do it.[454] The instrument relied on to give color of title need not be valid. Color of title may be given by a deed,[455] an execution sale,[456] a decree of court,[457] and some cases hold that a quitclaim deed is sufficient,[458] though this is denied by others.[459] In order to acquire adverse title by constructive possession, claim of title must in all cases be brought to the notice of the owner of the land, either by actual knowledge or

[453] Jackson v. Vermilyea, 6 Cow. (N. Y.) 677; Peoria & P. U. Ry. Co. v. Tamplin, 156 Ill. 285, 40 N. E. 960; Cooper v. Cotton Mills Co., 94 Tenn. 588, 30 S. W. 353; Bon Air Coal, Land & Lumber Co. v. Parks, 94 Tenn. 263, 29 S. W. 130; Baker v. Swan's Lessee, 32 Md. 355; Whitehead v. Foley, 28 Tex. 1. But see, as to wild lands, Jackson v. Woodruff, 1 Cow. (N. Y.) 276.

[454] 2 Dembitz, Land Tit. 1414; 2 Pingree, Real Prop. § 1168; East Tennessee Iron & Coal Co. v. Wiggin, 15 C. C. A. 510, 68 Fed. 446; Bissing v. Smith, 85 Hun, 564, 33 N. Y. Supp. 123; Millett v. Lagomarsino, 107 Cal. 102, 40 Pac. 25; Studstill v. Willcox, 94 Ga. 690, 20 S. E. 120; Finley v. Hogan, 60 Ark. 499, 30 S. W. 1045. For facts insufficient to establish color of title, see Dubuque v. Coman, 64 Conn. 475, 30 Atl. 777.

[455] Welborn v. Anderson, 37 Miss. 155; Chickering v. Failes, 26 Ill. 508. But see Wright v. Tichenor, 104 Ind. 185, 3 N. E. 853. A defective tax deed gives color of title. Reusens v. Lawson, 91 Va. 226, 21 S. E. 347; Lennig's Ex'rs v. White (Va.) 20 S. E. 831. But see Nye v. Alfter, 127 Mo. 529, 30 S. W. 186.

[456] Falls of Neuse Manuf'g Co. v. Brooks, 106 N. C. 107, 11 S. E. 456; Kendrick v. Latham, 25 Fla. 819, 6 South. 871.

[457] Huls v. Buntin, 47 Ill. 396. That a void judgment is not sufficient under a short statute of limitations, see Latimer v. Logwood (Tex. Civ. App.) 27 S. W. 960.

[458] Minot v. Brooks, 16 N. H. 374; McDonough v. Jefferson Co., 79 Tex. 535, 15 S. W. 490.

[459] Swift v. Mulkey, 14 Or. 59, 12 Pac. 76.

through notice implied by law.[460] The doctrine of constructive possession does not apply to any land which is actually held by the owner.[461] When a deed conveys land to which the grantor has title, and also purports to convey land to which he has no title, if the grantee takes possession of the land rightfully conveyed, he is not in constructive possession of the other tract.[462] So, if two separate tracts of land are attempted to be conveyed by a void deed, and possession is taken of only one, adverse possession will not extend to the other tract under color of title.[463] The doctrine of color of title makes no difference as to the actual possession required for the part of the land as to which there is a disseisin in fact.[464]

Possession must be Visible or Notorious.

In order that title may be acquired by adverse possession, it is necessary that the acts of the disseisor be such that the owner will be given notice of the claim to his lands,[465] though it is not necessary that he have actual knowledge [466] of such claim, if the acts relied on by the disseisor are such as raise a presumption that the owner must have known of his claim.[467] Fencing or occupying the lands is sufficient,[468] though having them surveyed would not be.[469] Nor is a mere

[460] Potts v. Gilbert, 3 Wash. C. C. 475, Fed. Cas. No. 11,347; Ellicott v. Pearl, 10 Pet. 412; Ewing's Lessee v. Burnet, 11 Pet. 41; Jackson v. Woodruff, 1 Cow. (N. Y.) 276; Little v. Downing, 37 N. H. 355.

[461] St. Louis, A. & T. H. R. Co. v. Nugent, 152 Ill. 119, 39 N. E. 263; Word v. Box, 66 Tex. 596, 3 S. W. 93; Trimble v. Smith, 4 Bibb (Ky.) 257. And see Fox v. Hinton, Id. 559. When land is owned by several, possession of part under a deed to the whole does not disseise all. Turner v. Moore, 81 Tex. 206, 16 S. W. 929.

[462] Word v. Box, 66 Tex. 596, 3 S. W. 93; Bailey v. Carleton, 12 N. H. 9.

[463] Grimes v. Ragland, 28 Ga. 123; Morris v. McClary, 43 Minn. 346, 46 N. W. 238.

[464] Humes v. Bernstein, 72 Ala. 546.

[465] Wilson v. Henry, 35 Wis. 241; Ewing's Lessee v. Burnet, 11 Pet. 53; Florida S. R. Co. v. Loring, 2 C. C. A. 546, 51 Fed. 932; Huntington v. Allen, 44 Miss. 654; King v. Carmichael, 136 Ind. 20, 35 N. E. 509; Millett v. Lagomarsino (Cal.) 38 Pac. 308; Ponder v. Cheeves, 104 Ala. 307, 16 South. 145.

[466] Actual knowledge is always sufficient. Dausch v. Crane, 109 Mo. 323, 19 S. W. 61; Brown v. Cockerel, 33 Ala. 38.

[467] Musick v. Barney, 49 Mo. 458; Bailey v. Carleton, 12 N. H. 9.

[468] Cutter v. Cambridge, 6 Allen (Mass.) 20; Allen v. Allen, 58 Wis. 205, 16

[469] Thompson v. Burhans, 61 N. Y. 52; Beatty v. Mason, 30 Md. 409.

entry on the lands under a void deed sufficient unless it is brought to the notice of the owner by the deed being recorded, or in some other way.[470] If a tenant attorns to one claiming adversely and gives that as a reason for refusing to pay rent to the true owner, the latter has notice of the adverse claim.[471] In one case [472] it was said: "If the owner visit his land, the indications of adverse possession and claim should be so patent that he could not be deceived. In this case, if the owner should have visited this land, he might have seen wood cut and rails split and hauled off,—pretty good indications of trespass; but he would have seen no habitation, no inclosures, no fields; nothing, indeed, to advise him that an adverse claim was set up, that some one was disputing his title." The payment of taxes is not sufficient to constitute an adverse holding.[473]

Possession must be Hostile and Adverse.

It must also be shown that the possession of the disseisor is hostile and adverse to the true owner, and not subordinate to him.[474] There need not, however, be a distinct claim of right or title by the disseisor.[475] Whether or not the possession has been adverse is a question of fact in each case.[476] Where adjoining owners establish a fence between their lands for convenience, without reference to the true line, and possession is held by each up to the fence so established, such possession will not be treated as adverse, and no disseisin will occur, though the fence be not on the true line.[477] It is

N. W. 610. And see Leeper v. Baker, 68 Mo. 400. Living in a shanty on wild land while cutting timber has been held insufficient. McKinnon v. Meston (Mich.) 62 N. W. 1014.

[470] Bracken v. Jones, 63 Tex. 184.

[471] 2 Dembitz, Land Tit. 1391.

[472] Pike v. Robinson, 79 Mo. 615.

[473] Brown v. Rose, 48 Iowa, 231; Scott v. Mills, 49 Ark. 266, 4 S. W. 908.

[474] Chloupek v. Perotka, 89 Wis. 551, 62 N. W. 537; Cook v. Babcock, 11 Cush. (Mass.) 206; Jackson v. Berner, 48 Ill. 203; Sparrow v. Hovey, 44 Mich. 63, 6 N. W. 93; Washburn v. Cutter, 17 Minn. 361 (Gil. 355).

[475] Puckett v. McDaniel, 8 Tex. Civ. App. 630, 28 S. W. 360. But there must be, at least, a general claim of ownership. Kirkman v. Brown, 93 Tenn. 476, 27 S. W. 709; Wade v. Johnson, 94 Ga. 348, 21 S. E. 569.

[476] Cummings v. Wyman, 10 Mass. 465; Blackmore v. Gregg, 2 Watts & S. (Pa.) 182; Highstone v. Burdette, 54 Mich. 329, 20 N. W. 64. That adverse possession is a question of law, see Jackson v. Huntington, 5 Pet. 402.

[477] Bird v. Stark, 66 Mich. 654, 33 N. W. 754; Goltermann v. Schiermeyer,

held that if one in possession of land sues another for trespass, this is evidence of an adverse holding against the owner of the land.[478] So declarations by the disseisor that his holding is adverse to the owner are admissible.[479] When entry has been made under the owner, possession so acquired is not adverse.[480] For example, when an entry was made under a bond for a deed, no adverse possession would be acquired while the purchase price remains unpaid.[481] To make possession obtained under the owner adverse, there must be a subsequent disclaimer of the owner's title, and the disclaimer must be made known to the owner.[482] Whenever a person having a right to land enters, such entry is presumed to be under the existing right, and not as a disseisor.[483] But when one has entered under a conveyance of the fee by a life tenant, and continues in possession after the latter's death, his possession is adverse to the remainder-man.[484] We have already seen that possession by a co-tenant is not adverse to the other owners,[485] though it may be made so by an actual ouster of the co-tenants, and a denial of their title.[486] A deed by a joint owner of the whole of the premises to a stranger is not a disseisin unless there

111 Mo. 404, 19 S. W. 484, and 20 S. W. 161; Grube v. Wells, 34 Iowa, 148. But see Seymour v. Carli, 31 Minn. 81, 16 N. W. 495; Ramsey v. Glenny, 45 Minn. 401, 48 N. W. 322; Smith v. McKay, 30 Ohio St. 409; French v. Pearce, 8 Conn. 439.

[478] Hollister v. Young, 42 Vt. 403.

[479] But see Lynde v. Williams, 68 Mo. 360.

[480] Hoban v. Cable, 102 Mich. 206, 60 N. W. 466; Coleman v. Pickett, 82 Hun, 287, 31 N. Y. Supp. 480; Whiting v. Edmunds, 94 N. Y. 309; Campbell v. Shipley, 41 Md. 81; Abbey Homestead Ass'n v. Willard, 48 Cal. 614. But see Sands v. Hughes, 53 N. Y. 287.

[481] Tayloe v. Dugger, 66 Ala. 444; Knox v. Hook, 12 Mass. 329; Brown v. King, 5 Metc. (Mass.) 173; Harris v. Richey, 56 Pa. St. 395; Rigor v. Frye, 62 Ill. 507. But see Jackson v. Foster, 12 Johns. (N. Y.) 488.

[482] Hall v. Stevens, 9 Metc. (Mass.) 418; Long v. Mast 11 Pa. St. 189; Clarke v. McClure, 10 Grat. (Va.) 305; Allen v. Allen, 58 Wis. 202, 16 N. W. 610; Griswold v. Little, 13 Misc. Rep. 281, 34 N. Y. Supp. 703.

[483] Nichols v. Reynolds, 1 R. I. 30; Mhoon v. Cain, 77 Tex. 317, 14 S. W. 24.

[484] Christie v. Gage, 71 N. Y. 189; Doe v. Gregory, 2 Adol. & E. 14. But see Doe v. Hull, 2 Dowl. & R. 38.

[485] Ante, p. 340.

[486] Campau v. Dubois, 39 Mich. 274; Rickard v. Rickard, 13 Pick. (Mass.) 251; Jackson v. Tibbits, 9 Cow. (N. Y.) 246.

is an entry under the deed.[487] Possession in any case without claim of title does not give rise to any title in the occupant, though it be continued for the statutory period.[488] The taking of a deed by the disseisor from the disseisee before the bar of the statute of limitations is complete will interrupt its running.[489] One who takes possession of land for the purpose of becoming the owner by adverse holding is entitled to the statutory bar if his possession is continued the necessary number of years.[490]

Possession must be Exclusive.

So, also, possession under claim of adverse right must be exclusive, in order to ripen into a title.[491] This can never be the case when the possession is joined with that of the owner, for when two persons are thus in possession the seisin, as we have stated, belongs to the one who holds the title.[492] So, too, the doctrine of constructive possession under color of title does not apply if the lands which are so claimed are in the actual possession of the owner.[493] As has been stated, possession of a joint owner against his co-tenants must be exclusive and adverse to cut off their rights.[494]

---

[487] Jackson v. Smith, 13 Johns. (N. Y.) 411; King v. Carmichael, 136 Ind. 20, 35 N. E. 509.

[488] Gilchrist v. McLaughlin, 7 Ired. (N. C) 310; Brown v. Gay, 3 Greenl. (Me.) 126; Brown v. Cockerell, 33 Ala. 38; Grube v. Wells, 34 Iowa, 148; St. Louis University v. McCune, 28 Mo. 481; Winn v. Abeles, 35 Kan. 85, 10 Pac. 443. And see Crary v. Goodman, 22 N. Y. 170. But the title under which the land is claimed need not be even prima facie good. Sumner v. Stevens, 6 Metc. (Mass.) 337. But possession held under mistake may be adverse. Beckman v. Davidson, 162 Mass. 347, 39 N. E. 38; Wilson v. Hunter, 59 Ark. 626, 28 S. W. 419.

[489] A mere offer to purchase has been held to have this effect. Lovell v. Frost, 44 Cal. 471. But see Rowland v. Williams, 23 Or. 515, 32 Pac. 402. Agreeing to vacate for a valuable consideration stops the running of the statute. Eldridge v. Parish, 6 Tex. Civ. App. 35, 25 S. W. 49. And see Dietrick v. Noel, 42 Ohio St. 18.

[490] Craig v. Cartwright, 65 Tex. 413, 424. For exceptions, see 2 Dembitz, Land Tit. 1396. Possession need not be under color of title. Horner v. Reuter, 152 Ill. 106, 38 N. E. 747.

[491] Foulke v. Bond, 41 N. J. Law, 527.

[492] Farrar v. Heinrich, 86 Mo. 521; Hunnicutt v. Peyton, 102 U. S. 333.

[493] See ante, p. 460.

[494] Ante, p. 340.

REAL PROP.—30

Possession must be Continuous.

The rights gained by disseisin will in all cases be lost if the possession is interrupted or abandoned before the period prescribed by the statute of limitations has elapsed.[495] It is not necessary that during the whole time the disseisor be in actual occupancy of the land, or have his residence on it.[496] It is sufficient if the facts are such as to show actual possession in any way.[497] Where the disseisin has been by two or more persons jointly, the abandonment of possession by one causes his rights to pass to his co-disseisor.[498] When possession is interrupted, the running of the statute of limitations is stopped, and a subsequent return to possession will not avail. The running of the statute will only begin from the date of the return.[499] Acquirement of an adverse title is prevented if, before the statutory period has expired, the possession of the disseisor is interrupted by an entry by the owner.[500]

Same—Tacking.

By the doctrine of tacking it is held that possession during the whole period of limitation need not be by the same person, but the

[495] Yelverton v. Hillard, 38 Mich. 355; Sparrow v. Hovey, 44 Mich. 63, 6 N. W. 93; Brickett v. Spofford, 14 Gray (Mass.) 514; Bliss v. Johnson, 94 N. Y. 235; Moore v. Collishaw, 10 Pa. St. 224; Groft v. Weakland, 34 Pa. St. 308; Messer v. Reginnitter, 32 Iowa, 312. Possession once established will be presumed to have continued, in the absence of a contrary showing. Marston v. Rowe, 43 Ala. 271.

[496] Possession may be held for him by a tenant. Hunton v. Nichols, 55 Tex. 217. The fact that the buildings on the land are vacant from time to time for want of tenants will not necessarily interrupt the adverse holding. Downing v. Mayes, 153 Ill. 330, 38 N. E. 620; Costello v. Edson, 44 Minn. 135, 46 N. W. 299; Gary v. Woodham, 103 Ala. 421, 15 South. 840. Breaks in an inclosure which is relied on to establish adverse possession do not interrupt the running of the estate. Williams v. Rand (Tex. Civ. App.) 30 S. W. 509.

[497] Rieman v. Wagner, 74 Md. 478, 22 Atl. 72; Hughs v. Pickering, 14 Pa. St. 297.

[498] Congdon v. Morgan, 14 S. C. 587.

[499] Byrne v. Lowry, 19 Ga. 27; Susquehanna & W. V. R. & Coal Co. v. Quick, 68 Pa. St. 189; Core v. Faupell, 24 W. Va. 238; Overand v. Menczer, 83 Tex. 122, 18 S. W. 301.

[500] Brickett v. Spofford, 14 Gray (Mass.) 514; Burrows v. Gallup, 32 Conn. 493. But see Bowen v. Guild, 130 Mass. 121. Bringing an action is not necessary to stop the running of the statute. Shearer v. Middleton, 88 Mich. 621, 50 N. W. 737.

§ 281) ADVERSE POSSESSION. 467

land may be held by a number of persons if they are in privity,[501] and the length of their holdings added together to make up the statutory period.[502] In some cases, however, this doctrine is denied as to a vendee of the disseisor.[503] Where the rule obtains, its effect is to give a disseisor the right to convey the imperfect title which he has acquired by his disseisin and adverse holding.[504] Not only a grantee has a right to add his possession to that of his grantor in making up the statutory period, but an heir or a devisee may count the time during which the land was held by his ancestor or testator.[505] Possession held under a contract of sale may be added to that of the vendor.[506] In the same way the possession of several persons as tenants of the disseisor may be sufficient to give an adverse title.[507]

[501] Doswell v. De La Lanza, 20 How. 29, 32; Doe v. Brown, 4 Ind. 143; City and County of San Francisco v. Fulde, 37 Cal. 349; Crispen v. Hannavan, 50 Mo. 536; Weber v. Anderson, 73 Ill. 439; Allis v. Field, 89 Wis. 327, 62 N. W. 85; Smith v. Reich, 80 Hun, 287, 30 N. Y. Supp. 167; Hughs v. Pickering, 14 Pa. St. 297; Cooper v. Cotton-Mills Co., 94 Tenn. 588, 30 S. W. 353; Tucker v. Price (Ky.) 29 S. W. 857. A testator, a person to whom he has devised the land for life, and the remainder-man under his will, are in privity. Haynes v. Boardman, 119 Mass. 414. The existence of privity may be shown by parol evidence. Weber v. Anderson, 73 Ill. 439.

[502] McNeely v. Langan, 22 Ohio St. 32; Overfield v. Christie, 7 Serg. & R. (Pa.) 173; Smith v. Chapin, 31 Conn. 530; Shannon v. Kinny, 1 A. K. Marsh. (Ky.) 3; Davis v. McArthur, 78 N. C. 357; Scales v. Cockrill, 3 Head (Tenn.) 432.

[503] Beadle v. Hunter, 3 Strob. (S. C.) 331; King v. Smith, 1 Rice (S. C.) 10. As holding that the vendor must be in possession under color of title to make his deed effectual, see Nelson v. Trigg, 4 Lea (Tenn.) 701.

[504] Leonard v. Leonard. 7 Allen (Mass.) 277; City of St. Paul v. Chicago, M. & St. P. R. Co., 45 Minn. 387, 48 N. W. 17; Cooper v. Ord, 60 Mo. 420. But, where the conveyance is void on its face, there can be no tacking, Simpson v. Downing, 23 Wend. (N. Y.) 316; Potts v. Gilbert, 3 Wash. C. C. 475, Fed. Cas. No. 11,347; nor where the second claims adversely to the first, Jackson v. Leonard, 9 Cow. (N. Y.) 653.

[505] Williams v. McAliley, Cheeves (S. C.) 200; City of St. Paul v. Chicago, M. & St. P. R. Co., 45 Minn. 387, 48 N. W. 17. So a dowress may add her husband's possession to her own. Doe v. Carter, 9 Q. B. 863. Contra, Sawyer v. Kendall, 10 Cush. (Mass.) 241. And see Doe v. Barnard, 13 Q. B. 945.

[506] Brown v. Brown, 106 N. C. 451, 11 S. E. 647; Mabary v. Dollarhide, 98 Mo. 198, 11 S. W. 611.

[507] Fanning v. Willcox, 3 Day (Conn.) 258.

There must be no gap in any case between the holdings which are to be tacked.[508]

Against Whom Possession is Adverse.

Disseisin and adverse possession are effectual only against those who are entitled to the possession of land. For this reason the disseisin of the tenant of the particular estate is not a disseisin of the reversioner or remainder-man.[509] Where persons hold by the same title, a disseisin of one will act as a disseisin of the other. For instance, the disseisin of a tenant is a disseisin of his landlord, and the disseisin of a mortgagor or of a mortgagee is effectual against the other party.[510] So, too, a cestui que trust may be disseised by the ouster of his trustee; but possession by the trustee will not be adverse to the beneficiary without a disavowal by the trustee of the relationship.[511] Nor is possession by heirs adverse to the claims of the creditors of the testator.[512] In most states the statute of limitations does not begin to run against persons who are under disabilities, such as married women,[513] infants,[514] and insane persons,[515] until

---

[508] Louisville & N. R. Co. v. Philyaw, 88 Ala. 264, 6 South. 837; Warren v. Frederichs, 76 Tex. 647, 13 S. W. 643.

[509] Watkins v. Green, 101 Mich. 493, 60 N. W. 44; Doe v. Hull, 2 Dowl. & R. 38; Wells v. Prince, 9 Mass. 508. Cf. Taylor v. Horde, 1 Burrows, 60. The possession of the homestead, to which a dowress was entitled until her dower was assigned, by her assignee, is not adverse to the other heirs. Gosselin v. Smith, 154 Ill. 74, 39 N. E. 980; Fischer v. Silkmann, 125 Mo. 165, 28 S. W. 435.

[510] Poignard v. Smith, 8 Pick. (Mass.) 272.

[511] Jones v. Lemon, 26 W. Va. 629. That a cestui que trust does not hold adversely to the trustee, see Jeter v. Davis, 109 N. C. 458, 13 S. E. 908. A mortgagor does not hold adversely to the mortgagee, Ivy v. Yancey, 129 Mo. 501, 31 S. W. 937; nor a mortgagee to the mortgagor, Dunton v. McCook (Iowa) 61 N. W. 977.

[512] Rogers v. Johnson, 125 Mo. 202, 28 S. W. 635.

[513] State v. Trontman, 72 N. C. 551; Little v. Downing, 37 N. H. 355; Throckmorton v. Pence, 121 Mo. 50, 25 S. W. 843. But in many states married women are no longer regarded as under disability. See 2 Dembitz, Land Tit. 1358.

[514] Jackson v. Moore, 13 Johns. (N. Y.) 513; Swearingen v. Robertson, 39 Wis. 462. The infancy of one co-tenant will not prevent the statute running against the others. Peters v. Jones, 35 Iowa, 512.

[515] Edson v. Munsell, 10 Allen (Mass.) 557. To prevent the running of the

the disability is removed. But the disability must exist at the time the statute begins to run. Disability occurring after the statute begins to run will not suspend the operation of the statute.[516] It is usually provided that a short period shall be given to persons who have been under disability, for bringing their actions after the disability is removed.

Length of Possession Necessary.

The length of adverse possession necessary to give title varies greatly under the statutes of the several states. In a few states an absolute limit is fixed, beyond which mental unsoundness will not prevent the acquisition of title.[517] So a few states have an ultimate limit, beyond which neither exceptions nor disabilities can save the right of action.[518] In many of the states a possession based either on color of title, or upon a title which is defective only in some named particular, or on a mode of conveyance which it is the policy of the law to favor, is protected against the entry or suit of the dispossessed owner after a much shorter period than that which bars the right against a naked possession.[519]

Abandonment.

The loss of title by abandonment applies strictly and only to incorporeal hereditaments, and in that connection has already been treated of.[520] Title to corporeal property can be lost through abandonment only by means of estoppel or the statute of limitations. The imperfect title which a disseisor has before the expiration of the full statutory period is, of course, lost if he abandons possession before such time has expired.[521] But as to the effect of abandonment

---

statute, greater disability is necessary than to avoid a deed. Rugan v. Sabin, 3 C. C. A. 578, 53 Fed. 415; Asbury v. Fair, 111 N. C. 251, 16 S. E. 467.

[516] Bunce v. Wolcott, 2 Conn. 27; Fleming v. Griswold, 3 Hill (N. Y.) 85; Thorp v. Raymond, 16 How. 247; Cunningham v. Snow, 82 Mo. 587; Lynch v. Cannon, 7 Houst. 386, 32 Atl. 391; Asbury v. Fair, 111 N. C. 251, 16 S. E. 467. The rule is otherwise as to infant heirs in some states. Machir v. May, 4 Bibb. (Ky.) 43; Rose v. Daniel, 3 Brev. (S. C.) 438.

[517] 2 Dembitz, Land Tit. 1359.

[518] 2 Dembitz, Land Tit. 1369.

[519] Stoltz v. Doering, 112 Ill. 234; Burton v. Perry, 146 Ill. 71, 34 N. E. 60; Latta v. Clifford, 47 Fed. 614; Hunter v. Ayres, 15 B. Mon. (Ky.) 210.

[520] Ante, p. 357. But see Dikes v. Miller, 24 Tex. 417, 424.

[521] Dausch v. Crane, 109 Mo. 323, 19 S. W. 61.

of the possession of land to which title has been acquired by adverse possession under the statute of limitations the cases are conflicting. The courts which hold that title by adverse possession affects only the remedy of the real owner hold also that the rights so acquired may be lost by abandonment.[522] But in jurisdictions where the theory is that the statute of limitations transfers the title of the former owner to the disseisee, such a title cannot be lost by an abandonment of the premises after the full statutory period has expired.[523]

ACCRETION.

282. Where soil is gradually deposited on the shore of a body of water, the land so formed belongs to the riparian owner on whose property the deposit is formed. This is called accretion.

We have already seen that anything which becomes permanently attached to land becomes a part of the realty, such as buildings and fixtures put upon the land. This rule is extended to cases of what is called title by accretion. By this is meant that material washed up by the sea on the lands of adjoining owners and soil deposited by rivers, which becomes attached to the banks, becomes the property of the owner of the land on which it is deposited.[524] This process is called alluvion, and must be a gradual process, as distinct from a sudden change.[525] When alluvion takes place, and soil of one owner

[522] Doe v. Roe, 26 Ga. 582.

[523] Inhabitants of School Dist. No. 4 v. Benson, 31 Me. 381; Schall v. Railroad Co., 35 Pa. St. 191. A subsequent parol agreement will not divest the disseisor's title. Brown v. Cockerell, 33 Ala. 38. Nor does a re-entry by the disseisee after the bar is complete revest the title in him. Faloon v. Simshauser, 130 Ill. 649, 22 N. E. 835.

[524] Mulry v. Norton, 100 N. Y. 424, 3 N. E. 581; Camden & A. Land Co. v. Lippincott, 45 N. J. Law, 405. The fact that accretions are caused by obstructions placed in the river by third persons does not change the rule. Tatum v. City of St. Louis, 125 Mo. 647, 28 S. W. 1002. Bigelow v. Hoover, 85 Iowa, 161, 52 N. W. 124. Seaweed cast upon the beach belongs to the owner of the soil. Emans v. Turnbull, 2 Johns. (N. Y.) 314.

[525] Cook v. McClure, 58 N. Y. 437; County of St. Clair v. Lovingston, 23 Wall. 68; Trustees of Hopkins' Academy v. Dickinson, 9 Cush. (Mass.) 551.

is gradually worn away, and is deposited upon the land of another, the title is held to pass to the latter, because the soil so deposited cannot be identified by its former owner.[526] When, however, a sudden change transfers a considerable portion of soil from one owner and deposits it upon the land of another, title does not pass to the latter if the soil so transferred is removed within a reasonable time, and while it can be identified.[527] When islands are formed in nonnavigable rivers, if the land on each side is owned by different persons, the island, if wholly on one side of the channel, belongs to the owner on whose land it forms.[528] We have seen [529] that the boundary line of each riparian proprietor extends to the middle of the stream. If the island is formed in the middle of the channel, it belongs one-half to each.[530] Islands formed in navigable rivers or in the sea are the property of the state or of the United States, according to the ownership of the fee in the land under the water.[531] A person who owns a narrow strip along the bank or shore of a body of water becomes entitled to all deposits by alluvion.[532] The owner of land which is being washed away may protect his property by any means which will stop the action of the water, though he must not divert the current so as to

[526] Lovingston v. St. Clair Co., 64 Ill. 56; Miller v. Hepburn, 8 Bush. (Ky.) 326; Gifford v. Yarborough, 5 Bing. 163; Foster v. Wright, 4 C. P. Div. 438.

[527] Woodbury v. Short, 17 Vt. 387, 389. When a parcel of land is suddenly left bare by the sea or a navigable river, it belongs to the state. Halsey v. McCormick, 18 N. Y. 147; Attorney General v. Chambers, 4 De Gex & J. 55. See, also, Hodges v. Williams, 95 N. C. 331. And so land gradually covered by the sea belongs to the state. Emans v. Turnbull, 2 Johns. (N. Y.) 313, 322; In re Hull & S. Ry., 5 Mees. & W. 327.

[528] Ingraham v. Wilkinson, 4 Pick. (Mass.) 268; Minton v. Steele, 125 Mo. 181, 28 S. W. 746; McCullough v. Wall, 4 Rich. Law (S. C.) 68. When an island formed in midchannel is subsequently connected with the mainland by the water having receded, the title to the island is not changed. City of Victoria v. Schott (Tex. Civ. App.) 29 S. W. 681.

[529] Ante, p. 422.

[530] Inhabitants of Deerfield v. Arms, 17 Pick. (Mass.) 41. Trustees of Hopkins' Academy v. Dickinson, 9 Cush. (Mass.) 544; Johnston v. Jones, 1 Black, 209, 222.

[531] 3 Washb. Real Prop. (5th Ed.) 61; Cox v. Arnold, 129 Mo. 337, 31 S. W. 592; Cooley v. Golden, 117 Mo. 33, 23 S. W. 100; Heckman v. Swett, 99 Cal. 303, 33 Pac. 1099. And see ante, p. 5.

[532] Banks v. Ogden, 2 Wall. 57, 69; Saulet v. Shepherd, 4 Wall. 508; Bristol v. Carroll Co., 95 Ill. 84.

direct it against the land of another person, to the latter's injury.[533] When land is formed by the receding of a lake or pond, it belongs to the adjoining owners.[534] Property which has been acquired by accretion is transferred by a deed which conveys the land on which the deposit has been made.[535] A sudden change in the channel of a river does not change the boundary line of the riparian owners.[536]

DEVISE.

283. The title to real property may be transferred by devise subject to the following conditions:

(a) **The will must be properly executed by a competent testator** (p. 473).

(b) **It must contain words of conveyance, and a description of the property devised** (p. 473).

(c) **Any interest in real property may be devised, except, in some states, subsequently acquired interests** (p. 474).

(d) **The law of the place where the land is situated governs the devise** (p. 474).

(e) **The devisee takes the land as a purchaser immediately on the testator's death** (p. 475).

(f) **Devises are revoked if the testator's estate is divested after the execution of the will** (p. 476).

(g) **In some states, if a devisee dies before the testator, the devise lapses** (p. 477).

---

[533] Gerrish v. Clough, 48 N. H. 9; Menzies v. Breadalbane, 3 Bligh (N. S.) 414.

[534] Cook v. McClure, 58 N. Y. 437; Steers v. City of Brooklyn, 101 N. Y. 51, 4 N. E. 7; Eddy v. St. Mars, 53 Vt. 462; Bowman v. Sunnuchs, 42 Wis. 233; Olson v. Huntamer (S. D.) 61 N. W. 479. But not when drained by artificial means. Noyes v. Collins (Iowa) 61 N. W. 250.

[535] Chicago Dock & Canal Co. v. Kinzie, 93 Ill. 415; Camden & A. Land Co. v. Lippincott, 45 N. J. Law, 409. But see Terriere v. City of New Orleans, 35 La. Ann. 209.

[536] Buttenuth v. Bridge Co., 123 Ill. 535, 17 N. E. 439; Rees v. McDaniel, 115 Mo. 145, 21 S. W. 913; Nebraska v. Iowa, 143 U. S. 359, 12 Sup. Ct. 396; Id., 145 U. S. 519, 12 Sup. Ct. 976.

§ 283)   DEVISE.   473

Title by devise is that which is acquired by persons who are given land under a will. A will, as transferring land, differs from a deed principally in that it is an instrument operating after the death of its maker, while a deed operates inter vivos. The same instrument, however, may be construed either as a will or as a deed; the effort of the court construing such an instrument will be to carry out the intention of the maker.[537] But if it cannot take effect until after the latter's death, it will be deemed a will.[538] The competency of testators to make wills, and of devisees to take lands under them, was considered in discussing personal capacity.[539] For the history of wills, the formalities necessary for their valid execution, requirements of probate, and the method of construing them, reference must be made to works on the law of wills. It will be possible here merely to discuss a few points which bear particularly on real property.

Operative Words in Wills.

The words generally used in a will to dispose of real estate are "give and devise," but any other words which show the intention of the testator are sufficient.[540] The words of limitation which are necessary for the creation of the various interests in land by will have already been discussed in connection with the different estates.[541] A will must contain a sufficient description of the property intended to be devised to identify it,[542] though by construction, in order to carry out the intention of testator, terms used in wills in describing property are often given a broader meaning than they would be in other instruments.[543] For instance, the word

[537] Taylor v. Kelly, 31 Ala. 59; Robinson v. Schley, 6 Ga. 526.

[538] Turner v. Scott, 51 Pa. St. 126; Frederick's Appeal, 52 Pa. St. 338; Coffman v. Coffman, 85 Va. 459, 8 S. E. 672.

[539] Ante, p. 381.

[540] Jackson v. De Lancey, 11 Johns. (N. Y.) 365; Rossetter v. Simmons, 6 Serg. & R. (Pa.) 452. But see Stump v. Deneale, 2 Cranch, C. C. 640, Fed. Cas. No. 13,560.

[541] Ante, pp. 36, 48.

[542] Swift v. Lee, 65 Ill. 336; Kilburn v. Dodd (N. J. Ch.) 30 Atl. 868; McAleer v. Schneider, 2 App. D. C. 461; Asten v. Asten [1894] 3 Ch. 260. A mistake in the number of the township has been held not to vitiate. Priest v. Lackey, 140 Ind. 399, 39 N. E. 54.

[543] As to residuary devises, see Smith v. Saunders, 2 W. Bl. 736.

"house" has been held to be equivalent to "messuage," and to include not only the building itself, but the land appurtenant thereto within the curtilage, and other buildings upon the land.[544] So the word "barn" has been held to carry with it the land on which it stood.[545] And the term "homestead" would be sufficient in a devise to transfer the property occupied as such.[546] So, too, a devise of the income of land passes the land itself.[547]

What can be Devised.

The term "devise" applies only to real estate; when personal property is transferred by will the technical term proper is "bequeath." Any interest in real property may be devised, even possibilities, if the person who is to take is known.[548] So a right of entry may be given by will.[549] Property acquired after the execution of the will may pass in several states by that will if such appears to be the intention of the testator.[550] But in other states the common-law rule to the contrary has been followed.[551]

What Law Governs Devises.

Wills affecting real property are governed by the lex loci, not by the law of the place where the testator is domiciled at the execution of the will or at his death.[552] The same rule applies to

[544] Rogers v. Smith, 4 Pa. St. 93; Otis v. Smith, 9 Pick. (Mass.) 293. But see Elliot v. Carter, 12 Pick. (Mass.) 437; Leonard v. White, 7 Mass. 6.

[545] But not more than necessary for its complete enjoyment. Bennet v. Bittle, 4 Rawle (Pa.) 339.

[546] Ford v. Ford, 70 Wis. 19, 33 N. W. 188; Hopkins v. Grimes, 14 Iowa, 73.

[547] Reed v. Reed, 9 Mass. 372; Fox v. Phelps, 17 Wend. (N. Y.) 402.

[548] Pond v. Bird, 10 Paige (N. Y.) 140; Thompson's Lessee v. Hoop, 6 Ohio St. 480.

[549] 1 Redf. Wills, 392.

[550] Webb v. Archibald (Mo. Sup.) 28 S. W. 80; Briggs v. Briggs, 69 Iowa, 617, 29 N. W. 632; Morey v. Sohier, 63 N. H. 507, 3 Atl. 636. And see Stim. Am. St. Law, § 2634.

[551] Jackson v. Potter, 9 Johns. (N. Y.) 312; Girard v. Mayor, etc., 4 Rawle (Pa.) 323; Parker v. Cole, 2 J. J. Marsh. (Ky.) 503. For devises held insufficient to pass after acquired realty, see Price's Appeal, 169 Pa. St. 294, 32 Atl. 455; Webster v. Wiggin (R. I.) 31 Atl. 824; McAleer v. Schneider, 2 App. D. C. 461.

[552] White v. Howard, 46 N. Y. 159; Richards v. Miller, 62 Ill. 417; Kerr v. Moon, 9 Wheat. 565.

chattel interests in real property, although such interests are for most purposes treated as personal, and go to the personal representative on the death of the one intestate.[553] In many states a will executed according to the law of another state, where the testator is domiciled, is sufficient to pass real property within the state.[554] The validity of the will is not governed by the laws in force at the death of the testator, but by those which were in force when the will was made.[555] In many cases this is a rule prescribed by the statutes which make the change in the former law.[556]

Nature of Title by Devise.

One who takes land by devise takes it not as heir of the testator, but "by purchase."[557] A devise takes effect at once on the death of the testator, and therefore the devisee must be in esse, so as to be competent to take title.[558] One cannot be made to take land by devise against his will, though an acceptance is presumed, in the absence of a showing to the contrary.[559] Renunciation of title by devise can probably only be made by deed, because his title under the will vests at once on the death of the testator, and no entry by the devisee is necessary to perfect it.[560] A devisee of land takes it, of course, subject to all liens and incumbrances which

[553] Freke v. Carbery, L. R. 16 Eq. 461.

[554] 1 Stim. Am. St. Law, § 2656.

[555] Taylor v. Mitchell, 57 Pa. St. 209; Mullen v. M'Kelvy, 5 Watts (Pa.) 399; Mullock v. Souder, 5 Watts & S. (Pa.) 198. A will void at the time it is executed will not become effectual by a subsequent change in the law. Lane's Appeal, 57 Conn. 182, 17 Atl. 926.

[556] Lawrence v. Hebbard, 1 Bradf. Sur. (N. Y.) 252.

[557] Bear's Case, 1 Leon. 112; Scott v. Scott, Amb. 383. Cf. Davis v. Kirk, 2 Kay & J. 391. But not when land is devised to one to whom it would descend. Clerk v. Smith, 1 Salk. 241; Allen v. Heber, 1 W. Bl. 22; Hurst v. Winchelsea, Id. 187; Chaplin v. Leroux, 5 Maule & S. 14; Doe v. Timins, 1 Barn. & Ald. 530. But see Biederman v. Seymour, 3 Beav. 368. Contra, Ellis v. Page, 7 Cush. (Mass.) 161.

[558] Ex parte Fuller, 2 Story, 327, Fed. Cas. No. 5,147; Ives v. Allyn, 13 Vt. 629.

[559] Perry v. Hale, 44 N. H. 363.

[560] Webster v. Gilman. 1 Story, 499, Fed. Cas. No. 17,335; Graves v. Graves' Ex'r (Wis.) 63 N. W. 271. Ct. Hamilton v. Ritchie [1894] App. Cas. 310.

may exist on the land, and subject also to the right to the testator's creditors to enforce their claims against it.[561]

Revocation of Devises by Alteration of Estate.

With the general subject to the revocation of wills we have no concern here, but certain rules relative to the revocation of particular devises after they are made will be considered. If the testator, after the execution of his will, sells the land devised, such sale is a revocation of that devise.[562] A contract to sell, which is enforced by an action for specific performance after the testator's death, has the same effect.[563] If part only of the land is sold, it operates as a revocation pro tanto.[564] A mortgage, however, on land devised is not a revocation of the devise.[565] Nor is a partition of land held in joint ownership.[566] This effect is produced only when the estate of the testator is wholly divested. But the devisee would, of course, take only the equity of redemption where the land devised had been mortgaged.[567] If, after conveying land which has been devised, the testator subsequently buys back the same property, at common law the devise was not thereby made operative again,[568] but the rule is now otherwise in a number of states. In some states now, by statute, a change in the estate of the testator does not revoke a devise, unless the estate of the testator is wholly divested.[569] The deed which is to revoke a devise must be lawful and valid. If it is obtained by fraud, or at the time of its execution the grantor is incompetent, it does not af-

[561] Hattersley v. Bissett, 52 N. J. Eq. 693, 30 Atl. 86; Hyde v. Heller, 10 Wash. 586, 39 Pac. 249.

[562] Walton v. Walton, 7 Johns. Ch. (N. Y.) 258; Adams v. Winne, 7 Paige (N. Y.) 97; Bosley v. Wyatt, 14 How. 390.

[563] Brush v. Brush, 11 Ohio, 287; Wells v. Wells, 35 Miss. 638; Walton v. Walton, 7 Johns. Ch. (N. Y.) 258.

[564] 4 Kent, Comm. 528, 529.

[565] The devisee takes the land subject to the mortgage. Tucker v. Thurstan, 17 Ves. 131.

[566] Brydges v. Duchess of Chandos, 2 Ves. Jr. 417; Barton v. Croxall, Tam. 164. Nor is a lease a revocation. Hodgkinson v. Wood, Cro. Car. 23.

[567] See ante, p. 205.

[568] Marwood v. Turner, 3 P. Wms. 163; Goodtitle v. Otway, 2 H. Bl. 516; Cave v. Holford, 3 Ves. 650.

[569] 1 Stim. Am. St. Law, § 2810.

fect a previous devise.⁵⁷⁰ But an intention to revoke a devise by an alteration in the testator's estate may be shown by evidence in or out of the conveyance.⁵⁷¹ A general devise, as of "my land," is defeated if the testator parts with all his land, but revives when he acquires other land in states where after-acquired property passes by a general devise.⁵⁷²

Lapsed Devises.

By the rules of the common law, if a devisee dies before the testator, the devise lapses, and cannot be claimed by the devisee's heirs. It goes to the heir of the testator, and not to the residuary devisee.* This is, however, in some states now otherwise by statutory change, and the residuary devisee takes to the exclusion of the heir.† In many states also the statutes declare that, when a devise is to a child or a descendant of the testator, the devise shall not lapse if such descendant dies leaving issue who survive the testator, and in other states there is no lapse in any case.‡ Even at common law a devise of an estate to be held in joint tenancy does not lapse on the death of one of the joint tenants, even as to his share, because the rule of survivorship vests such share in the co-tenant.|| But if the estate was a tenancy in common, there would be a lapse of the share of any co-tenant on his death.** When a devise is to a class, as to "children" of the testator, there is no lapse,

---

⁵⁷⁰ Graham v. Burch, 47 Minn. 171, 49 N. W. 697; Rich v. Gilkey, 73 Me. 595; Hawes v. Wyatt, 3 Brown, Ch. 156.

⁵⁷¹ Hocker v. Gentry, 3 Metc. (Ky.) 463; Wickliffe's Ex'rs v. Preston, 4 Metc. (Ky.) 178.

⁵⁷² See McNaughton v. McNaughton, 34 N. Y. 201.

* Van Beuren v. Dash, 30 N. Y. 393; Moore v. Dimond, 5 R. I. 121. A devise to a charity will lapse if the institution ceases to exist before the testator's death. See Rymer v. Stanfield [1895] 1 Ch. 19; Merrill v. Hayden, 86 Me. 133, 29 Atl. 949.

† 1 Stim. Am. St. Law, § 2822. See St. Paul's Church v. Attorney General, 164 Mass. 188, 41 N. E. 231.

‡ 1 Stim. Am. St. Law, § 2823.

|| Dow v. Doyle, 103 Mass. 489; Jackson v. Roberts, 14 Gray (Mass.) 546; Putnam v. Putnam, 4 Bradf. Sur. (N. Y.) 308; Anderson v. Parsons, 4 Me. 486; Luke v. Marshall, 5 J. J. Marsh. (Ky.) 353.

** Horton v. Earle, 162 Mass. 448, 38 N. E. 1135; Morse v. Mason, 11 Allen (Mass.) 36; Van Beuren v. Dash, 30 N. Y. 393.

but the survivors take the share of the one deceased.[573] The lapse of a particular estate does not destroy remainders which depend thereon, if they can take effect at once; that is, at the death of the testator.[574]

DESCENT.

284. The title to the real property of an intestate descends to certain persons designated by law, called heirs. The acquisition of title by descent is governed by the following rules:

(a) **Only estates of inheritance go to the heirs** (p. 479).

(b) **Posthumous children may inherit** (p. 480).

(c) **In most states an illegitimate child inherits from its mother and from its father, when acknowledged or legitimized by marriage** (p. 480).

(d) **Advancements are deducted from the share of the person advanced** (p. 481).

(e) **By the common law, inheritance is governed by certain canons of descent which are in force in the United States in a more or less modified form** (p. 482).

(f) **If an intestate leaves no heirs, his lands escheat to the state** (p. 485).

Title by descent is a matter which is regulated in each state by the local statutes, and in no two states are the statutes of descent exactly the same. Titles arising by descent must be examined with reference to the law as it existed at the death of the owner. The statute of the several states governing descent are at the present time subject to such frequent changes that no attempt to give any detail as to the statutes is feasible.[575] Title by descent is, like

[573] Magaw v. Field, 48 N. Y. 668; Downing v. Marshall, 23 N. Y. 366; Schaffer v. Kettell, 14 Allen (Mass.) 528; Yeates v. Gill, 9 B. Mon. (Ky.) 203.

[574] Lawrence v. Hebbard, 1 Bradf. Sur. (N. Y.) 252; Goodall v. McLean, 2 Bradf. Sur. (N. Y.) 306.

[575] For an exhaustive discussion of statutes regulating descent, see 1 Demblitz, Land. Tit. c. 4.

§ 284)   DESCENT.   479

title by devise, governed by the lex loci;[576] that is, the law of the state in which the land is located determines the manner in which it shall descend to the heirs of its intestate owner. These statutes, though they differ in the minor details, are all founded on the English statute of descent, which was taken largely from the civil law. The owner of land may determine to whom it shall pass at his death by means of a will. If, however, he does not make a will, the law determines for him the division of his land among his heirs, or rather it selects those heirs. An ancestor is one from whom land descends, and an heir is one to whom land descends. It may be that an ancestor is really a descendant of the heir, as where a father inherits from a son.[577] Persons who take under a will are not heirs.[578]

What Descends to Heirs.

The word "descent" is applied only to real property. The personal property of one who has died intestate is said to be "distributed."[579] All the estates of inheritance of one who had died intestate descend to his heirs, unless disposed of during his life.[580] The heirs, of course, take no rights in life estates held by the ancestor unless they be estates per autre vie, so limited that the heirs take the remainder of such estates.[581] We have seen that chattels

[576] Darby's Lessee v. Mayer, 10 Wheat. 465; Williams v. Kimball, 35 Fla. 49, 16 South. 783.

[577] Prickett's Lessee v. Parker, 3 Ohio St. 394.

[578] In re Donahue's Estate, 36 Cal. 329. An heir apparent is one whose right of inheritance is indefeasible, provided he outlives the ancestor; for instance, under rules of primogeniture, the eldest son or his issue, who must be the heir to the father whenever he happens to die. An heir presumptive is one who, if the ancestor should die immediately, would, under present circumstances, be his heir, but whose right of inheritance may be defeated by the contingency of some nearer heir being born; for example, a brother or nephew, whose presumptive succession may be destroyed by the birth of a child. 2 Bl. Comm. 208. Heirs do not take as purchasers. Godolphin v. Abingdon, 2 Atk. 57.

[579] Lincoln v. Perry, 149 Mass. 368, 21 N. E. 671; In re Donahue's Estate, 36 Cal. 329; Swaine v. Burton, 15 Ves. 365. In some states the distinction between descent and distribution no longer exists. See 1 Dembitz, Land Tit. 204.

[580] See ante, 34.

[581] See ante, p. 67.

real do not descend to the heirs, but go to the personal representatives.[582] When the land of the decedent is subject to a right of curtesy, dower, or homestead, in states where these are only life interests, the land descends to the heir subject to these rights.[583] The heir takes the land subject also to any claims which the creditors of the intestate may have on it for the satisfaction of their demands.[584]

Posthumous Children.

Posthumous children are those who, at the death of their father, are en ventre sa mere, that is, those who are conceived but not born. By the early common law such children could not inherit,[585] but the disability does not exist in the United States,[586] though in some states it has been removed only as to children of the intestate, and does not apply to collateral heirs.[587] In a number of states it is provided by statute that the child must be born within ten months after the death of the intestate in order to inherit.[588] A disposition of the property before such a child is born will be binding on the child, and the title will not be avoided as to a purchaser, though the child can claim its share in the proceeds of the sale, as against the other heirs.[589]

Illegitimate Children.

Illegitimate children are those who are born out of lawful wedlock. At common law such a child is the heir of no one, and can have no heirs save those of his body.[590] Now, in most states, an

[582] Ante, p. 2.

[583] See ante, pp. 80, 102, 115.

[584] Belton v. Summer, 31 Fla. 139, 12 South. 371; Merrill v. Daffin, 24 Fla. 320, 4 South. 806; Bushby v. Dixon, 3 Barn. & C. 298; Stainback v. Harris, 115 N. C. 100, 20 S. E. 277.

[585] But it is changed now in England. Goodale v. Gawthorne, 2 Smale & G. 375; Richards v. Richards, Johns. Eng. Ch. 754.

[586] 1 Stim. Am. St. Law, §§ 2844, 3136.

[587] 1 Dembitz, Land Tit. 228.

[588] 1 Stim. Am. St. Law, § 3136.

[589] But see where the child is born before the sale. Massie v. Hiatt's Adm'r, 82 Ky. 314.

[590] Cooley v. Dewey, 4 Pick. (Mass.) 93; Bent's Adm'r v. St. Vram, 30 Mo. 268; Hicks v. Smith, 94 Ga. 809, 22 S. E. 153; Stover v. Boswell's Heir, 3 Dana (Ky.) 233. The issue of void marriages are in some states legitimate.

illegitimate child inherits from the mother equally with legitimate children,[591] and may take through the mother. In many states also illegitimate children inherit from the father if they have been acknowledged by him. In some they take from the father and mother when there are no other heirs; that is, they take only to prevent escheat. In a few states illegitimate children inherit from brothers and sisters, and in most states the mother inherits from an illegitimate child. In many states a subsequent marriage of the parents legitimizes the children, and makes them capable of inheriting, like children born in lawful wedlock.[592]

Advancements.

By the doctrine of advancements, when a lineal heir receives a gift or devise by way of portion or settlement in life, the amount so received is deducted from the share which that heir would otherwise receive from the ancestor.[593] This rule applies only when the advancement comes in the direct line, and not when it comes from a collateral; that is, it applies to children and grandchildren.[594] The advancement is valued at the time it is given.[595] If the value exceeds the share which the person advanced would otherwise receive as heir, he takes nothing as heir. If it is less than that, he receives

---

Green v. Green, 126 Mo. 17, 28 S. W. 752. As to the legitimacy of children born after separation of the parents, see McNeely v. McNeely, 47 La. Ann. 1321, 17 South. 928.

[591] See In re Waesch's Estate, 166 Pa. St. 204, 30 Atl. 1124.

[592] 1 Stim. Am. St. Law, §§ 3150-3155; Dembitz, Land Tit. 279. But see Hatch v. Ferguson, 15 C. C. A. 201, 68 Fed. 43. Some statutes provide that children born to persons living together as man and wife shall be legitimate. In re Matthias' Estate, 63 Fed. 523. As to evidence of legitimacy, see In re Pickens' Estate, 163 Pa. St. 14, 29 Atl. 875; Lavelle v. Corrignio, 86 Hun, 135, 33 N. Y. Supp. 376; Scanlon v. Walshe, 81 Md. 118, 31 Atl. 498; Jackson v. Jackson, 80 Md. 176, 30 Atl. 752.

[593] 1 Stim. Am. St. Law, §§ 3160-3168. Money expended in education is not an advancement. Brannock v. Hamilton, 9 Bush (Ky.) 446. But see Kent v. Hopkins, 86 Hun, 611, 33 N. Y. Supp. 767.

[594] Beebe v. Estabrook, 79 N. Y. 246; Simpson v. Simpson, 114 Ill. 603, 4 N. E. 137, and 7 N. E. 287; Parsons v. Parsons (Ohio Sup.) 40 N. E. 165. An advancement may exclude from participation in the real estate and not in the personalty. Palmer v. Culbertson, 143 N. Y. 213, 38 N. E. 199.

[595] Palmer v. Culbertson, 143 N. Y. 213, 38 N. E. 199; Moore v. Burrow, 89 Tenn. 101, 17 S. W. 1035.

enough of the estate to make up the difference. In some states, however, the advancement must be brought into hotchpot; that is, the one advanced must turn what he has received back into the corpus of the estate, so that the whole may be divided, otherwise he receives nothing in addition to the advancement.[596] In some states no gift is considered an advancement unless so expressed in the instrument of transfer, or acknowledged as such in writing by the person advanced.[597]

Canons of Descent.

At an early period in the history of the common law certain rules of inheritance, called the canons of descent, were formulated by Lord Chief Justice Hale, and, though these canons have been much changed as far as descent in this country is concerned, they are at the foundation of our laws of inheritance, and often have to be resorted to in construing statutory provisions. The canons are stated by Blackstone in the following form:

Same—Descending and Ascending Lines.

"The first rule is that inheritances shall lineally descend to the issue of the person who last died actually seised in infinitum, but shall never lineally ascend."[598] This rule has been changed in the United States, and persons in the ascending line, such as father and mother, are now permitted to inherit.[599]

Same—Preference of Males.

"A second general rule or canon is that the male issue shall be admitted before the female."[600] This canon has not been adopted in the United States,[601] except that in some states the paternal kin in the ascending line are preferred to the maternal kin in the same degree.[602]

---

[596] 1 Stim. Am. St. Law, § 3163 B, 2.

[597] 1 Stim. Am. St. Law, § 3162. And see Murphy v. Murphy (Iowa) 63 N. W. 697; Brunson v. Henry (Ind. Sup.) 39 N. E. 256.

[598] 2 Bl. Comm. 208.

[599] 1 Stim. Am. St. Law, §§ 3109, 3111.

[600] 2 Bl. Comm. 212.

[601] 1 Stim. Am. St. Law, § 3132.

[602] 1 Stim. Am. St. Law, §§ 3107, 3117, 3121.

Same—Primogeniture.

"A third rule or canon of descent is this: that where there are two or more males, in equal degree, the eldest only shall inherit; but the females all together."[603] This rule of primogeniture, as it is called, has been almost wholly abolished in the United States.[604] But in a few instances the statutes which have changed the common-law rules of descent do not apply to remote collaterals, and consequently the common-law rule of primogeniture is still in force. So, in some states, the rule still applies to the estate of a trustee, and in Maryland a right to "elect" in partition—that is, to have first choice among the several shares—is reserved to the eldest male.[605]

Same—Per Stirpes and Per Capita.

"A fourth rule or canon of descent is this: That the lineal descendants in infinitum of any person deceased shall represent their ancestor; that is, shall stand in the same place as the person himself would have done had he been living."[606] This is called taking per stirpes, and is not the rule in all the United States. In some states the heirs take per capita.[607] When the heirs take per capita, the descendants of the deceased heir take the same shares as those who stand in the same degree of relationship as the person deceased; that is, if there were two sons living, and three children of a deceased son, if they take per capita, each would have one-fifth of the intestate's real property. But if the inheritance was per stirpes, the sons would take one-third each, and the grandchildren would have each one-third of their father's third.

Same—Collateral Heirs and Ancestral Lands.

"A fifth rule is that, on failure of lineal descendants or issue of the person last seised, the inheritance shall descend to his collateral relation, being of the blood of the first purchaser, subject to the three preceding rules."[608] Lineal relations[609] are those in the

---

[603] 2 Bl. Comm. 214.
[604] 1 Stim. Am. St. Law, § 3132.
[605] 1 Dembitz, Land Tit. 225.
[606] 2 Bl. Comm. 216.
[607] 1 Stim. Am. St. Law, § 3137.
[608] 2 Bl. Comm. 220.

[609] Relationship is of two kinds,—by consanguinity and by affinity. The former is relationship by blood, as that of father and son. Relationship by affinity is that which arises by marriage, as husband and wife. By the common law, inheritance was only by consanguinity, never by affinity. But

ascending or descending line, such as father, mother, grandfather, grandmother, son, daughter, grandson, and granddaughter. Collateral relatives are those which are neither in the direct ascending or descending series. Examples of collateral relatives are uncles, aunts, nephews, and nieces.[610] The degrees of relationship are in most states calculated according to the civil-law rules;[611] that is, in ascertaining the degree of relationship between two persons you count up from the intestate to the common ancestor and then down to the collateral kinsman. In this way a father is related in the first degree, a brother or a grandfather in the second degree, an uncle or nephew in the third degree.[612] By the common-law rules the degrees of relationship are the same as by the civil law for all persons in the direct ascending or descending line. But for collateral kinsmen the degrees are calculated from the common ancestor to the more remote descendant. In this way brothers are related in the first degree, while a nephew and an uncle are related in the second degree, and cousins are the same.[613]

In many states a distinction is made in the descent of lands between, on the one hand, lands which the ancestor acquires by descent or by gift or devise from a person from whom the lands would have descended to him,[614] and, on the other hand, lands which the ancestor acquires by purchase, including devise or gift from a stranger. The lands embraced in the former class are called ancestral. In the states where this distinction is recognized, the inheritance of ancestral lands is restricted to those who are of the blood of the "first purchaser," as he is called; that is, to those who can trace a relationship by consanguinity to the one who acquired

in most of our states a husband or wife inherits all or part of the real estate of a decedent when there is no issue to take, in addition to curtesy or dower. 1 Stim. Am. St. Law, §§ 3109, 3123.

[610] 2 Bl. Comm. 202.

[611] 1 Stim. Am. St. Law, § 3139.

[612] McDowell v. Addams, 45 Pa. St. 430; Ryan v. Andrews, 21 Mich. 229; McCracken v. Rogers, 6 Wis. 278; Martindale v. Kendrick, 4 G. Greene (Iowa) 307.

[613] 2 Bl. Comm. 206.

[614] Oliver v. Vance, 34 Ark. 564; Galloway v. Robinson, 19 Ark. 396; Felton v. Billups, 2 Dev. & B. (N. C.) 308. Cf. Godbold v. Freestone, 3 Lev. 406.

the lands by purchase. In some of these states, persons who are not of the blood of the first purchaser cannot inherit at all; in others, they are merely postponed.[615]

Same—Whole and Half Blood.

"A sixth rule or canon * * * is that the collateral heir of the person last seised must be his next collateral kinsman of the whole blood."[616] By whole blood it is meant that the heir and the intestate are descendants from the same pair of ancestors. Relationship by the half blood would be when there was only one ancestor in common, as where the two persons were descendants of the same father, but of different mothers. The rule of the common law as given above has been changed in all states.[617] As to lands not deemed ancestral, the collaterals of the half blood are nowhere excluded altogether from the inheritance, though they are postponed or given lesser shares than the whole blood.[618] As to ancestral lands, they are in most cases where the distinction between ancestral and other lands prevails postponed to collaterals of the whole blood.[619]

Same—Preference of Males in Collateral Lines.

"The seventh and last rule or canon is that in collateral inheritances male stock shall be preferred to the female (that is, kindred derived from the blood of male ancestors, however remote, shall be admitted before those from the blood of the female, however near), unless where the lands have in fact descended from a female."[620] This rule has not been adopted in the United States. Where, as was seen in discussing the second canon, there is a postponement of the maternal to the paternal kin in the ascending line, the issue of such kin, who are collateral heirs of the intestate, take without any distinction between males and females.[621]

Escheat.

We have seen what provisions the law makes for the division of the lands of one who dies intestate, there being in most states rights of

[615] 1 Stim. Am. St. Law, § 3134.
[616] 2 Bl. Comm. 224. Cf. Doed v. Whichelo, 8 Term R. 211.
[617] 1 Stim. Am. St. Law, § 3133.
[618] Petty v. Maller, 15 B. Mon. (Ky.) 591; Milner v. Calvert, 1 Metc. (Ky.) 472; Marlow v. King, 17 Tex. 177; Hulme v. Montgomery, 31 Miss. 105.
[619] Den v. Jones, 8 N. J. Law, 340; Childress v. Cutter, 16 Mo. 24.
[620] 2 Bl. Comm. 234.
[621] 1 Stim. Am. St. Law, § 3121.

dower or curtesy in the surviving wife or husband, and the remainder going to the heirs of the owner; but, if no such heirs can be found, the land escheats to the state,[622] subject to the subsequent claims of heirs, if any are found. In some states there is no limitation on the time within which such claims may be brought forward, while in others various periods of limitation are prescribed.[623]

JUDICIAL PROCESS.

285. Title to real property may be acquired by virtue of judicial process,—
  (a) **By conveyances under licenses** (p. 486).
  (b) **By conveyances under decrees** (p. 488).
  (c) **By tax sales** (p. 490).
  (d) **By condemnation under the right of eminent domain** (p. 494).

There are many instances where the title to land is transferred by order of a court. Titles acquired in this way are often spoken of as titles by involuntary alienation. In some cases this is an accurate enough designation, but the mental attitude of the owner is immaterial. The validity of this sort of titles depends on whether the proper notices to the parties in interest have been given and the requirements of procedure complied with in other respects. In some cases of title by judicial process, the order of the court is in itself sufficient to transfer the title. In other cases a conveyance of some kind is ordered by the court to be executed by the person holding the title, or by some officer of the court.

SAME—CONVEYANCES UNDER LICENSES.

286. Licenses to convey lands are given by order of court in the following cases:
  (a) **To personal representatives to convey the land of decedents** (p. 487).

---

[622] 1 Stim. Am. St. Law, §§ 1151, 3125. This is not the feudal escheat, as to which see Johnson v. Norway, Winch, 37.

[623] 1 Stim. Am. St. Law, § 1154.

§ 286)   CONVEYANCES UNDER LICENSES.   487

(b) **To guardians to convey the land of persons under disability** (p. 487).
(c) **To tenants in possession to convey settled estates, in some states** (p. 488).

Conveyances by Personal Representatives.

In the administration of the estate of a decedent it often becomes necessary, because of the failure of the personal estate, to sell part of the real property to satisfy the claims of creditors and pay the expenses of administration, or to pay legacies which the testator has given. When executors are given a power to sell lands by the will which appoints them, the sale is, of course, according to the intention of the testator, and not under license of court.[624] Personal representatives may not dispose of realty without an order of the court.[625] Notice to persons interested or affected by the sale must be given before an order can be obtained.[626] And the other formalities prescribed by statute must be followed.[627]

Conveyances by Guardians.

In treating of personal capacity, it was seen that many persons could hold lands who had no power to convey them. But, as it is often necessary for the interests of such persons that some disposition be made of their lands, as that the lands of infants or insane persons be sold to provide for their support, their guardians are authorized, on presenting the matter to the court having jurisdiction, to make the necessary conveyances.[628] Certain formalities,

[624] White v. Moses. 21 Cal. 44; Payne v. Payne, 18 Cal. 291.

[625] See 2 Dembitz, Land Tit. 1114; First Nat. Bank v. Hanna, 12 Ind. App. 240, 39 N. E. 1054. And cf. Worthy v. Johnson, 8 Ga. 236; Campbell v. Knights, 26 Me. 224. The order to sell must describe the land. Borders v. Hodges, 154 Ill. 498, 39 N. E. 597; Melton v. Fitch, 125 Mo. 281, 28 S. W. 612.

[626] Rogers v. Johnson, 125 Mo. 202, 28 S. W. 635; Picard v. Montross (Miss.) 17 South. 375.

[627] See Durfee v. Joslyn, 101 Mich. 551, 60 N. W. 39; Melton v. Fitch, 125 Mo. 281, 28 S. W. 612; Rodgers v. Rodgers' Adm'r (Ky.) 31 S. W. 139.

[628] See 2 Dembitz, Land Tit. §§ 151, 152; Bellamy v. Thornton, 103 Ala. 404, 15 South. 831; Williams v. Pollard (Tex. Civ. App.) 28 S. W. 1020. An estate in remainder may be sold. Wallace v. Jones, 93 Ga. 419, 21 S. E. 89.

such as filing a bond,[629] giving notice,[630] and making a report,[631] are required.

Conveyances of Settled Estates.

Closely akin to sales of lands of persons under disability are sales of settled estates; that is, when the alienation of land in the ordinary ways is impossible because the whole ownership is divided between life tenants and remainder-men, some of whom may be unborn or unascertained, there are in some states statutes which permit the sale of such lands, and the investment of the proceeds in other realty under the same limitations. Such sales are often desirable when the lands are of no beneficial value to the life tenants, or are subject to incumbrances.[632] Sales of settled estates cannot be made unless there is a statute authorizing them.[633]

SAME—CONVEYANCES UNDER DECREES.

287. The principal cases in which the title to land is transferred under a decree of court are the following:

  (a) Partition proceedings (p. 488).
  (b) Decrees for specific performance (p. 488).
  (c) Sales on execution (p. 489).

Partition.

It has already been seen that partition is the method of dividing joint estates, so that they may be held in severalty, and that partition may be had against the will of the co-tenants. So, too, it has been seen that a sale will be ordered when the land cannot be divided.[634]

Specific Performance.

When an owner of land has made a binding contract to convey real property, and then refuses to execute a conveyance, a court

[629] McGale v. McGale, 18 R. I. 675, 29 Atl. 967.
[630] Garr v. Elble (Ky.) 29 S. W. 317.
[631] Swenson v. Seale (Tex. Civ. App.) 28 S. W. 143. The sale must be confirmed by the court. Lumpkins v. Johnson (Ark.) 32 S. W. 65.
[632] 2 Dembitz, Land Tit. § 156. And see Luttrell v. Wells (Ky.) 30 S. W. 10.
[633] Baker v. Baker, 1 Rich. Eq. (S. C.) 392.
[634] Ante, p. 346.

of equity will compel him to do so by a decree for specific performance.[635] So there may be a valid contract, founded on a sufficient consideration,[636] to give lands by will, and such a contract may be enforced by compelling the persons holding the title to the lands to convey to the one to whom they should have been devised.[637]

Sales on Execution.

At common law a man's lands were not liable to be sold for his debts,[638] but now, in all of our states, lands can be sold for debts. Before this can be done, however, a judgment must be obtained,[639] and a writ of execution must be issued. The sheriff thereupon makes the sale and executes the deed.[640] A certain period within which the debtor may redeem the land from the sale is usually provided.[641] The purchaser is said to take an estate on execution.[642] It has already been seen, in the discussion of estates, what interests in real property were subject to sale on execution.[643] A purchaser at an execution sale acquires the interest of the judgment debtor.[644]

[635] Engle v. White (Mich.) 62 N. W. 154; Roberts v. Cambridge, 164 Mass. 176, 41 N. E. 230; Prospect Park & C. I. R. Co. v. Coney Island & B. R. Co., 144 N. Y. 152, 39 N. E. 17; Haydon v. Haydon (Ky.) 27 S. W. 975; Wright v. Brown, 116 N. C. 26, 22 S. E. 313; Hoover v. Buck (Va.) 21 S. E. 474.

[636] Smith v. Pierce, 65 Vt. 200, 25 Atl. 1092; Fuchs v. Fuchs, 48 Mo. App. 18.

[637] Emery v. Darling, 50 Ohio St. 160, 33 N. E. 715.

[638] For an account of the remedies which were provided at different periods, see Digby, Hist. Real Prop. (4th Ed.) 279.

[639] In nearly all the states a judgment becomes a lien on the judgment debtor's real estate as soon as it is rendered or docketed. See 2 Dembitz, Land Tit. § 165.

[640] Finch v. Turner (Colo. Sup.) 40 Pac. 565. Higgins v. Bordages (Tex. Civ. App.) 28 S. W. 350; Diamond v. Turner, 11 Wash. 189, 39 Pac. 379.

[641] 2 Dembitz, Land Tit. 1300. And see McIlwain v. Karstens, 152 Ill. 135, 38 N. E. 555; Ritchie v. Ege, 58 Minn. 291, 59 N. W. 1020; Southern California Lumber Co. v. McDowell, 105 Cal. 99, 38 Pac. 627; Smith v. Bank, 102 Mich. 5, 60 N. W. 438.

[642] As to estates on execution, see 2 Washb. Real Prop. (5th Ed.) 31.

[643] Ante, pp. 39, 58, 149, 156, 205, 209, 274.

[644] Garrett v. Wagner, 125 Mo. 450, 28 S. W. 762; Bramlett v. Wettin, 71 Miss. 902, 15 South. 934; Butler v. Fitzgerald, 43 Neb. 192, 61 N. W. 640; Greenleaf v. Grounder, 86 Me. 298, 29 Atl. 1082.

Same—Effect of Reversal of Judgment.

Where land is sold as the result of an action, and the judgment is subsequently reversed, a third person, who has purchased the premises, will have a good title,[645] though, if one of the parties had been the purchaser, such would not have been the case.[646] When the purchaser is a third person, the defendant's remedy is in damages against the plaintiff.

SAME—TAX TITLES.

288. The title to land may be divested for failure to pay taxes. This may be
 (a) **By forfeiture to the state (p. 490).**
 (b) **By sale under a ministerial proceeding (p. 491).**
 (c) **By sale under a judgment obtained in a judicial proceeding. Such a proceeding is either**
  (1) **In personam against the person owing the tax, or**
  (2) **In rem against the land on which the tax is assessed (p. 492).**

289. The owner has a period of redemption before the tax deed is issued (p. 492).

290. The purchaser takes in some states only the tax debtor's interest in the land; in other states he takes the whole fee (p. 493).

Forfeiture.

In a few states it is provided in the statutes regulating the collection of taxes that land on which the taxes are in arrears may be forfeited to the state after certain notices have been given to the owner.[648] An opportunity is given the owner to redeem for a certain

---

[645] Whiting v. Bank, 13 Pet. 6; Feger v. Keefer, 6 Watts (Pa.) 297; Shultz v. Sanders, 38 N. J. Eq. 154, 293.

[646] Jackson v. Cadwell, 1 Cow. (N. Y.) 622. Reynolds v. Harris, 14 Cal. 677. The same is true of a purchase by the plaintiff's attorney. Hays v. Cassell, 70 Ill. 669; or by his wife, Ivie v. Stringfellow's Adm'r, 82 Ala. 545, 2 South. 22.

[648] Black, Tax Titles (2d Ed.) §§ 194, 197. See Lasher v. McCreery, 66 Fed. 834.

time after the forfeiture. If redemption is not made, the title becomes absolute in the state, and need not be followed by a sale of the land.[649] Statutes providing for a forfeiture for nonpayment of taxes are strictly construed.[650]

Ministerial Sale.

In most states summary methods of proceeding exist for the sale of lands for unpaid taxes which authorize the proper officers to advertise the land for sale and sell it after a certain period of delinquency. Such proceedings are constitutional, though no actual notice of the sale is brought home to the owner.[651] When a public officer sells lands for taxes, he has only a naked power; that is, one not coupled with an interest. Therefore his authority, which comes entirely from the statute, must be strictly followed.[652] In fact, the requirements have in some states been made so stringent as to make tax titles in all cases of very doubtful validity.[653] The modern tendency, however, is the other way, and a reasonable compliance with the statute is sufficient.[654] In all cases of sales of land for taxes by summary proceedings it should be remembered, however, that the proceeding is in itself ex parte, and no necessary steps must be omitted, or the title will fail. Therefore payment of the taxes takes away the power to sell,[655] and tender of payment has the same effect, if the payment or tender is made by one entitled to pay the taxes.[656] The following

[649] Garner v. Anderson, 27 La. Ann. 338; Morrison v. Larkin, 26 La. Ann. 699; Hall v. Hall, 23 La. Ann. 135.

[650] Bennett v. Hunter, 9 Wall. 326; Schenk v. Peay, 1 Dill. 267, Fed. Cas. No. 12,451.

[651] Kentucky Railroad Tax Cases, 115 U. S. 321, 6 Sup. Ct. 57.

[652] Cruger v. Dougherty, 43 N. Y. 107; Cahoon v. Coe, 57 N. H. 556; Millikan v. Patterson, 91 Ind. 515.

[653] Ferris v. Coover, 10 Cal. 589; Wilsons v. Doe, 7 Leigh (Va.) 22; Brown v. Veazie, 25 Me. 359.

[654] Jenkinson v. Auditor General (Mich.) 62 N. W. 163; Mosely v. Reily, 126 Mo. 124, 28 S. W. 895; Bedgood v. McLain, 94 Ga. 283, 21 S. E. 529; Stieff v. Hartwell, 35 Fla. 606, 17 South. 899; Henderson v. Ellerman, 47 La. Ann. 306, 16 South. 821.

[655] Reading v. Finney, 73 Pa. St. 467; Joslyn v. Rockwell, 128 N. Y. 334, 28 N. E. 604; Jackson v. Morse, 18 Johns. (N. Y.) 441; Rayner v. Lee, 20 Mich. 384; Sprague v. Coenon, 30 Wis. 209.

[656] Tacey v. Irwin, 18 Wall. 549; Schenk v. Peay, 1 Dill. 267, Fed. Cas. No. 12,451; Loomis v. Pingree, 43 Me. 299.

general rule is given by Mr. Black [657] for determining when there has been a sufficient compliance with the statute: "When the statute under which the land is sold for taxes directs an act to be done, or prescribes the form, time, and manner of doing an act, such an act must be done in the form, time, and manner prescribed, or the title is invalid, and in this respect the statute must be strictly, if not literally, complied with. But in determining what is required to be done, the statute must receive a reasonable construction; and when no particular form or manner of doing an act is prescribed, any mode which effects the object with reasonable certainty is sufficient. But special stress should always be laid upon those provisions which are designed for the protection of the taxpayer."

Judicial Sale.

In some states the method of selling land for taxes by summary proceedings is not employed, but the collector of taxes is required to bring an action in a court before any power is acquired to sell the land of the person owing the taxes.[658] These suits, as stated in the black letter, are of two kinds. If against the person who owes the taxes, jurisdiction of the person must be acquired. The judgment, when rendered, is a lien on his land, which may be enforced by execution. The other kinds of suits proceed against the land itself, as though the taxes were due from it, and notice of the proceeding to the owner of the land may be constructive only, as where it is by publication,[659] though such notice, when given, must contain a description of the land.[660] In this kind of suit the land is ordered to be sold, and the officer making the sale gives a certificate of purchase, which, after a period allowed for redemption, entitles the holder to a deed.

Redemption and Tax Deed.

After a sale of lands for taxes, the owner is given an opportunity to redeem before the title of the purchaser becomes absolute.[661]

[657] Tax Titles (2d Ed.) § 155.

[658] 2 Dembitz, Land Tit. 1334. As to who can sue, see San Diego Co. v. Southern Pac. R. Co., 108 Cal. 46, 40 Pac. 1052.

[659] Schmidt v. Niemeyer, 100 Mo. 207, 13 S. W. 405; Payne v. Lott, 90 Mo. 676, 3 S. W. 402. But see Martin v. Parsons, 49 Cal. 95.

[660] Smith v. Kipp, 49 Minn. 119, 51 N. W. 656; Vaughan v. Daniels, 98 Mo. 230, 11 S. W. 573; Milner v. Shipley, 94 Mo. 106, 7 S. W. 175.

[661] Black, Tax Titles (2d Ed.) c. 23. And see People v. Campbell, 143

§§ 288-290) TAX TITLES. 493

At the time of the sale the purchaser is given a certificate of purchase. The statutes usually provide that the rights of a purchaser under a certificate may be assigned.[662] Until the period of redemption expires, the owner is entitled to the possession of the land and to its profits.[663] In most states the holder of a certificate of purchase is entitled to a deed on the expiration of the period of redemption,[664] but in some states a foreclosure of the right of redemption is necessary.[665] The tax deed, when issued, must contain all the elements required by the statute, and show by its recitals a complete performance of all that is required by law, before a sale is lawful; such as authority,[666] assessment, and delinquency.[667] There must also be a description of the lands sold.[668] If any of these things are wanting, the deed cannot be reformed in equity.[669]

Estate Taken by Purchaser.

In many states a new title is created by a tax sale, and all contingent rights in the land are cut off, though, when this is the rule, a remainder-man, and others having contingent interests, are given

---

N. Y. 335, 38 N. E. 300; Douglass v. McKeever, 54 Kan. 767, 39 Pac. 703; Rich v. Braxton, 158 U. S. 375, 15 Sup. Ct. 1006; Stone v. Stone, 163 Mass. 474, 40 N. E. 897.

[662] An assignment in the absence of such a statutory authorization would probably be void. Billings v. McDermott, 15 Fla. 60; Sapp v. Morrill, 8 Kan. 677.

[663] Elliott v. Parker, 72 Iowa, 746, 32 N. W. 494; Mayo v. Woods, 31 Cal. 269.

[664] Wettig v. Bowman, 39 Ill. 416. Cf. Ives v. Lynn, 7 Conn. 505.

[665] Black, Tax Titles (2d Ed.) § 383; Alexander v. Thacker, 43 Neb. 494, 61 N. W. 738.

[666] Cogel v. Raph, 24 Minn. 194; Madland v. Benland, Id. 372; Atkison v. Improvement Co., 125 Mo. 565, 28 S. W. 861; Ward v. Montgomery, 57 Ind. 276.

[667] Gilfillan v. Chatterton, 38 Minn. 335, 37 N. W. 583; Hubbard v. Johnson, 9 Kan. 632.

[668] Campbell v. Packard, 61 Wis. 88, 20 N. W. 672; Ellsworth v. Nelson, 81 Iowa, 57, 46 N. W. 740. For descriptions held sufficient, see Sibley v. Smith, 2 Mich. 486; Taylor v. Wright, 121 Ill. 455, 13 N. E. 529; Harris v. Curran, 32 Kan. 580, 4 Pac. 1044; Levy v. Ladd, 35 Fla. 391, 17 South. 635.

[669] Altes v. Hinckler, 36 Ill. 265; Keepfer v. Force, 86 Ind. 81; Bowers v. Andrews, 52 Miss. 596. Contra, Hickman v. Kempner, 35 Ark. 505.

an opportunity to redeem from the sale.[670] If those having such interest do not redeem, they lose their rights. This extends even to the rights to dower [671] and homestead.[672] In other states the tax deed passes only the interest of the person assessed.[673] Even where this rule obtains, the rights of mortgagees will be lost if the land is sold for taxes,[674] and in the same way judgment liens and other rights growing out of and depending on the estate of the one owing the taxes are cut off.[675]

SAME—EMINENT DOMAIN.

291. Under the right of eminent domain, land belonging to private persons may be taken for public uses upon compensation being made. The right may be exercised

  (a) **By the United States or the states.**
  (b) **By private persons or corporations duly authorized.**

The taking of land under the right of eminent domain differs from taxation in that compensation is provided to the owner when his land is taken under the former. Land can be taken under this power only for public uses. This, however, is a question of constitutional law.[676] As to what constitutes a taking, and as to what will be an additional burden imposed on land taken under this power, as by putting a railway on lands previously taken for a highway, the same reference must be made. Power to condemn lands under the right of eminent

---

[670] Atkins v. Hinman, 7 Ill. 437; Kunes v. McCloskey, 115 Pa. St. 461, 9 Atl. 83; Langley v. Chapin, 134 Mass. 82; Jackson v. Babcock, 16 N. Y. 246.

[671] Black, Tax Titles, § 422. But that the wife must be made a party to a tax suit, see Blevins v. Smith, 104 Mo. 583, 16 S. W. 213.

[672] Shell v. Duncan, 31 S. C. 547, 10 S. E. 330.

[673] Cross v. Taylor (Ga.) 6 S. E. 179; Dyer v. Bank, 14 Ala. 622.

[674] Parker v. Baxter, 2 Gray (Mass.) 185; Becker v. Howard, 66 N. Y. 5; Fager v. Campbell, 5 Watts (Pa.) 287

[675] Jenkins v. Newman. 122 Ind. 99, 23 N. E. 683. But, if the land is redeemed by the owner, the judgment lien is not affected. Appeal of Singer (Pa. Sup.) 7 Atl. 800. The lien of prior taxes is also divested by a tax sale. Huzzard v. Trego, 35 Pa. St. 9; Law v. People, 116 Ill. 244, 4 N. E. 845.

[676] See Black, Const. Law, 355.

§ 291) EMINENT DOMAIN. 495

domain may be, and often is, delegated either to private persons or to corporations, though it is usually said that such persons or corporations must perform some public function.[677] The provisions in the federal and state constitutions prohibiting the taking of a person's property without due compensation cover cases of eminent domain.[678] Damages in such cases are in some states assessed by commissioners and in others by juries. It is generally provided that the compensation must be made before the land is actually taken. Any property is subject to the exercise of this right, even including franchises.[679] The United States may condemn lands belonging to a state as well as if owned by private persons.[680] But when the United States or a state take land under this right, they must make compensation, the same as other persons.[681]

[677] Beekman v. Railroad Co., 3 Paige (N. Y.) 45; Weir v. Railroad Co., 18 Minn. 155 (Gil. 139); In re Theresa Drainage Dist., 90 Wis. 301, 63 N. W. 288; Secombe v. Railroad Co., 23 Wall. 108; U. S. v. Certain Tract of Land, 67 Fed. 869; Jockheck v. Commissioners, 53 Kan. 780, 37 Pac. 621.

[678] Black, Const. Law, 366.

[679] Central Bridge Corp. v. Lowell, 4 Gray (Mass.) 474; Com. v. Canal Co., 66 Pa. St. 41; West River Bridge Co. v. Dix, 6 How. 507.

[680] Stockton v. Railroad Co., 32 Fed. 9. A state may condemn property of the United States. U. S. v. Railroad Bridge Co., 6 McLean, 517, Fed. Cas. No. 16,114; U. S. v. Chicago, 7 How. 185.

[681] For statutory provisions on eminent domain, see, in general, 1 Stim. Am. St. Law, §§ 1140–1144.

TABLE OF CASES CITED.

[THE FIGURES REFER TO PAGES.]

A

v. Cooper, 146.
Abbey v. Wheeler, 341.
Abbey Homestead Ass'n v. Willard, 464.
Abbiss v. Burney, 294, 323, 328.
Abbott v. Allen, 443.
    v. Berry, 346.
    v. Butler, 360.
    v. Essex Co., 326.
    v. Godfroy's Heirs, 191, 247.
    v. Kasson, 232.
    v. Powell, 204.
    v. Railway Co., 372.
    v. Upton, 209.
    v. Weekly, 354.
Abbott of Sherbourne's Case, 65.
Abercrombie v. Riddle, 60.
Absor v. French, 363.
Achorn v. Jackson, 418.
Acker v. Priest, 262.
Ackerman v. Shelp, 354, 355.
Ackerman's Adm'rs v. Vreeland's Ex'r, 305.
Ackland v. Lutley, 150.
Ackless v. Seekright, 306.
Ackroyd v. Smith, 355.
Acton v. Blundell, 371.
Adair v. Lott, 73, 75, 79.
Adams v. Adams, 79, 84, 165, 272.
    v. Beadle, 8.
    v. Buchanan, 193.
    v. Bucklin, 377.
    v. Corriston, 184, 195.
    v. Cuddy, 223.
    v. Freeman, 166.
    v. Guerard, 296.

Adams v. Hill, 85
    v. Jenkins, 118.
    v. Johnson, 191.
    v. Knowlton, 339.
    v. Lindell, 174.
    v. Logan, 75, 79.
    v. McKesson's Ex'x, 154.
    v. Medsker, 416.
    v. Niemann, 181.
    v. Parker, 210.
    v. Rivers, 362.
    v. Ross, 36, 297.
    v. Savage, 299.
    v. Sayre, 202.
    v. Terre-Tenants of Savage, 299.
    v. Walker, 371.
    v. Winne, 475.
Addison v. Hack, 167, 168, 358.
Aderhold v. Supply Co., 153.
Adlum v. Yard, 408.
Advance Coal Co. v. Miller, 12.
Aetna Fire Ins. Co. v. Tyler, 198.
Aetna Life Ins. Co. v. Corn, 232.
Agate v. Lowenbein, 65.
Agawam Canal Co. v. Edwards, 422.
Agricultural Bank of Mississippi v. Rice, 416.
Ahern v. McCarthy, 187.
Ahrend v. Odiorne, 192.
Aiken v. Benedict, 4.
    v. Railway Co., 232.
Aikin v. Railway Corp., 380.
Aiman v. Stout, 384.
Ainsworth v. Ritt, 153.
Alabama & G. Manuf'g Co. v. Robinson, 182.
Albany's Case, 322.
Albee v. Carpenter, 49.

CASES CITED.

[The figures refer to pages.]

Albert v. Burbank, 435.
Albright v. Albright, 434.
Alderson v. Caskey, 189.
   v. Miller, 453.
Alderson's Heirs v. Henderson, 98.
Aldine Manuf'g Co. v. Barnard, 18.
Aldrich v. Husband, 12.
Aldridge v. Dunn, 193.
Alexander v. Alexander, 82, 114, 319.
   v. Cunningham, 86.
   v. Ellison, 342.
   v. Fisher, 63.
   v. Jackson, 116.
   v. Pendleton, 213.
   v. Tams, 267.
   v. Thacker, 493.
   v. U. S., 4.
   v. Warrance, 74, 77.
   v. Welch, 204.
Alford v. Vickery, 162.
Algonquin Coal Co. v. Northern Coal & Iron Co., 460.
Alkire v. Kahle, 339.
Allan v. Gomme, 360.
Alleman v. Hawley, 342.
Allen v. Allen, 54, 462, 464.
   v. Bloomer, 57.
   v. Bryan, 145.
   v. Cadwell, 216.
   v. Cook, 123.
   v. De Groodt, 289.
   v. Elderkin, 196.
   v. Everly, 184.
   v. Hartnett, 109.
   v. Hawley, 116.
   v. Heber, 475.
   v. Hooper, 71.
   v. Hopper, 387.
   v. Howe, 172.
   v. Howley, 126.
   v. Keily, 165.
   v. Kennedy, 441, 449.
   v. Lenoir, 438.
   v. Loring, 193.
   v. McCoy, 87.
   v. Manasse, 114.
   v. Markle, 48.
   v. Pray, 109.
   v. Sayward, 441.
   v. Scott, 426.
   v. Trustees, 49, 302.
   v. Whitaker, 118.

Alley v. Bay, 119.
Allin v. Bunce, 48.
Allis v. Billings, 384.
   v. Field, 467.
Allore v. Jewell, 384.
Allyn v. Mather, 327.
Alston v. Grant, 142.
Alt v. Banholzer, 207.
   v. Stoker, 437.
Altemus v. Campbell, 459.
Altes v. Hinckler, 493.
Althof v. Conheim, 339.
Alwood v. Ruckman, 154, 155.
Ambler v. Woodbridge, 175.
Ambs v. Hill, 19.
   v. Railway Co., 417.
Amcotts v. Catherich, 84.
American Bank-Note Co. v. New York El. R. Co., 364.
American Button-Hole, Overseaming & Sewing-Mach. Co. v. Burlington Mut. Loan Ass'n, 201, 287.
American Emigrant Co. v. Clark, 416.
American Mortg. Co. v. Hill, 59.
   v. Hopper, 403.
American River Water Co. v. Amsden, 6.
Ames, Ex parte, 12.
   v. Cadogan, 317.
   v. Norman, 338, 343.
   v. Richardson, 198.
Amesbury v. Brown, 50.
Amick v. Brubaker, 159.
Amidon v. Harris, 355, 373.
Ammidown v. Ball, 426.
Amory v. Meredith, 316.
Amoskeag Manuf'g Co. v. Goodale, 356.
Amphlett v. Hibbard, 116, 120, 123, 247.
Amsden v. Atwood, 160.
Anderson v. Anderson, 145.
   v. Bank, 210.
   v. Baughman, 421.
   v. Cary, 395.
   v. Coburn, 451.
   v. Dugas, 223.
   v. Jackson, 326.
   v. Parsons, 477.
   v. Prindle, 158
   v. Roberts, 393.
   v. Smith, 180.

CASES CITED. 499

[The figures refer to pages.]

Anderson v. Spencer, 194.
Anding v. Davis, 238.
Andrae v. Haseltine, 367.
Andrew v. Pearce, 451.
Andrews v. Andrews, 108, 275.
   v. Bassett, 110.
   v. Button Co., 19.
   v. Emmot, 316.
   v. Hailes, 144.
   v. Lyons, 453.
   v. President, etc., 262.
   v. Senter, 175.
Andries v. Railway Co., 353.
Angell v. Rosenbury, 261, 262.
Angus v. Dalton, 353.
Anheuser-Busch Brewing Ass'n v. Peterson, 142.
Annable v. Patch, 301.
Ann Arbor Sav. Bank v. Webb, 231.
Anon., 5, 20, 45, 50, 65, 137, 252, 253, 260, 266, 315, 366, 368, 374, 375, 395.
Anon. v. Cooper, 146.
Anthony v. Anthony, 288.
   v. Railway Co., 142.
   v. Rice, 120, 124.
Antoni v. Belknap, 22.
Apple v. Apple, 84, 91.
Appleton v. Boyd, 336.
Appling v. Odom, 154.
Arcedeckne v. Kelk, 363.
Archer v. Bennett, 426.
Archer's Case, 294, 297, 303.
Ards v. Watkin, 148.
Arkwright v. Gell, 372.
Arlin v. Brown, 192.
Arment v. Hensel, 66.
Armour Pack. Co. v. Wolff, 196.
Arms v. Burt, 36.
Armstrong v. Abbott, 213, 215.
   v. Bicknell, 155.
   v. Dubois, 426.
   v. Michener, 38.
   v. Moore, 321.
   v. Mudd, 421.
   v. Wheeler, 149.
   v. Wilson, 80.
   v. Wolsey, 266.
Arnold v. Arnold, 343.
   v. Brown, 48.
   v. Elmore, 422, 423.
   v. Green, 203.
   v. Holbrook, 363.

Arnold v. Iron Works, 384.
   v. Mundy, 5.
   v. Patrick, 435.
   v. Ruggles, 25.
   v. Townsend, 384.
   v. Wainwright, 340.
Arnold's Heirs v. Arnold's Adm'r, 92.
Arnsby v. Woodward, 151.
Arp v. Jacobs, 114.
Arques v. Wasson, 185.
Asbury v. Fair, 469.
Ashcroft v. Railroad Co., 351, 417, 418.
Ashhurst v. Phonograph Co., 159.
Ashhurst's Appeal, 41.
Ashley v. Ashley, 287, 326.
   v. Warner, 178.
Ashton's Case, 108.
Ashville Division No. 15 v. Aston, 417.
Astbury, Ex parte, 13, 21.
Asten v. Asten, 473.
Astley v. Micklethwait, 293, 294.
Astor v. Miller, 148.
Astry v. Ballard, 64.
Atherton v. Pye, 287.
Atkins v. Bordman, 351, 353.
   v. Hinman, 494.
   v. Kron, 60.
   v. Sawyer, 209.
   v. Sleeper, 134.
Atkinson v. Atkinson, 114, 115.
   v. Baker, 68.
   v. Improvement Co., 493.
   v. Miller, 191.
   v. Walton, 182.
Atlantic Dock Co. v. Leavitt, 432.
Attersoll v. Stevens, 66, 145.
Attorney General v. Chambers, 5, 471.
   v. Gill, 329.
   v. Marlborough, 49.
   v. Merrimack Manuf'g Co., 170.
   v. Old South Soc., 275.
   v. Rector, etc., 276, 277.
   v. Wallace's Devisees, 275.
   v. Williams, 356.
Attwater v. Attwater, 395.
Atwater v. Bodfish, 360.
Atwood v. Atwood, 84, 101.
   v. Dolan, 72.
   v. Pulp Co., 195.
   v. Vincent, 192.
Auer v. Penn, 409.
Aughinbaugh v. Coppenheffer, 140.

[The figures refer to pages.]

Aultman & Co. v. Salinas, 123.
Aultman & Taylor Manuf'g Co. v. Richardson, 417.
Aurora Fire Ins. Co. v. Eddy, 198.
Austen v. Taylor, 258.
Austin v. Austin, 181.
    v. Cambridgeport Parish, 176.
    v. Pulschen, 214.
    v. Railroad Co., 65, 142, 365.
    v. Stanley, 121.
    v. Stevens, 61.
    v. Underwood, 126.
Auworth v. Johnson, 139.
Avelyn v. Ward, 302.
Averill v. Taylor, 132, 234.
Averitt v. Elliot, 250.
Avern v. Lloyd, 324.
Avery v. Clark, 193.
    v. Dougherty, 139.
    v. Payne, 344.
Axtell v. Warden, 127.
Aycock v. Railroad Co., 142.
Ayer v. Spring, 97.
Ayers v. Grill, 124.
    v. Hawks, 122.
    v. Staley, 200.
Aymar v. Bill, 210.
Ayres v. Draper, 162.
    v. Railroad Co., 363.
Ayton v. Ayton, 289.

B

Babb v. Perley, 70–72.
Babbitt v. Babbitt, 262.
    v. Day, 92, 93.
Babcock v. Collins, 416.
Bachelder v. Wakefield, 353.
Back v. Stacey, 363.
Backenstoss v. Stahler, 8.
Backus v. Burke, 249.
    v. Sternberg, 158.
Backus' Adm'rs v. McCoy, 443.
Bacon v. Bowdoin, 131.
    v. Cottrell, 202.
    v. Huntington, 170.
    v. Lincoln, 443.
    v. Smith, 304.
    v. Van Schoonhoven, 227.
Baggett v. Meux, 396.
Bagley v. Freeman, 149.

Bagley v Kennedy, 458.
    v. Morrill, 422.
Bagnell v. Broderick, 402, 403.
Bagott v. Orr, 5.
Baile v. Coleman, 297.
Bailey v. Carleton, 462.
    v. Duncan, 71.
    v. Gould, 210.
    v. Metcalf, 230.
    v. Seymour, 455.
    v. Sisson, 345.
    v. Stephens, 374.
Bain v. Brand, 20.
Bainbridge v. Sherlock, 370.
Bakeman v. Talbot, 356.
Baker v. Adams, 161.
    v. Atherton, 14.
    v. Baker, 191, 488.
    v. Bliss, 214.
    v. Bridge, 38.
    v. Collins, 246.
    v. Colony, 185, 191.
    v. Dening, 430.
    v. Frick, 356.
    v. Haskell, 434.
    v. Heiskell, 78.
    v. Hunt, 443.
    v. Leibert, 93.
    v. McIntirff, 143.
    v. Mather, 216.
    v. Mott, 171.
    v. Railway Co., 104.
    v. Swan's Lessee, 461.
    v. Terrell, 207.
    v. Thrasher, 190.
Bakewell v. Ogden, 317.
Baldwin v. Allison, 270.
    v. Breed, 20.
    v. Golde, 385.
    v. Hatchett, 212.
    v. Humphrey, 272.
    v. Sager, 215.
    v. Taylor, 167.
    v. Tuttle, 393.
Bales v. Perry, 315.
Balfour v. Russell, 152.
Ball v. Herbert, 370.
    v. Nye, 371.
    v. Setzer, 204.
Ballard v. Carter, 272.
    v. Dyson, 361.
    v. Johnson, 146.

CASES CITED. 501

[The figures refer to pages.]

Ballentine v. Poyner, 64.
Ballou v. Wood, 342.
Balston v. Bensted, 371.
Bamberger v. Geiser, 227.
Bancroft v. City of Cambridge, 31.
   v. Curtis, 386.
Bangor House Proprietary v. Brown, 362.
Bangs v. Smith, 316.
Banick v. Horner, 249.
Bank of America v. Banks, 453.
Bank of Healdsburg v. Bailhacke, 433.
Bank of Louisville v. Baumeister, 185.
Bank of New York v. Ballard's Assignee, 287.
Bank of Orleans v. Flagg, 217.
Bank of Oroville v. Lawrence, 225.
Bank of South Carolina v. Rose, 236.
Bank of State v. Forney, 395.
Bank of Suisun v. Stark, 171.
Bank of Ukiah v. Petaluma Sav. Bank, 226.
Bank of U. S. v. Benning, 453.
   v. Housman, 266.
Bank of Utica v. Finch, 229.
Bank of Versailles v. Guthrey, 113.
Banks v. Ogden, 471.
Banning v. Bradford, 248.
   v. Edes, 226.
Bannister v. Bannister, 110.
Bannon v. Angier, 357.
Barber v. Harris, 338.
   v. Root, 71.
   v. Stone, 152.
Barclay v. Picker, 153.
Bard v. Poole, 247.
Bare v. Bare, 110.
Barker v. Barker, 74, 77, 80.
   v. Keete, 266.
   v. Parker, 91.
Barkley v. Wilcox, 371, 372.
Barksdale v. Gamage, 54.
   v. Garrett, 111.
Barlow v. Dahm, 145.
   v. McKinley, 446.
   v. Salter, 327.
   v. Wainwright, 156.
Barnaby v. Barnaby, 382.
Barnard v. Cushman, 234.
   v. Godscall, 137.
Barnes v. Barnes, 168.

Barnes v. Burl, 418.
   v. Cunningham, 83.
   v. Dow, 396.
   v. Gay, 125.
   v. Lloyd, 357.
   v. Lynch, 343.
   v. Mott, 203.
   v. Sabron, 370.
Barnet v. Dougherty, 267.
Barnett v. Barnett, 420.
   v. Johnson, 3, 364.
   v. Nelson, 201.

Barnett's Appeal, 255, 272.
Barney v. Frowner, 97.
   v. Griffin, 394.
   v. Keith, 138.
   v. Keokuk, 5, 423.
   v. McCarty, 222.
Barnhart v. Lockwood, 152.
Barnitz's Lessee v. Casey, 306.
Barnstable Sav. Bank v. Barrett, 238.
Barnum v. Barnum, 60.
   v. Phenix, 211.
Barr v. Galloway, 75.
   v. Hatch, 318.
   v. Schroeder, 408.
   v. Vanalstine, 247.
Barrell v. Joy, 262.
Barrett v. Hinckley, 183, 196.
   v. Ice Co., 6.
   v. Trainor, 148.
Barrie v. Smith, 175.
Barron v. Barron, 72.
Barrows v. Barrows, 123.
Barry v. Exchange Co., 263, 389.
   v. Shelby, 58.
   v. Smith, 154.
Bartenbach, In re, 104.
Bartholomew v. West, 116.
Bartlet v. Harlow, 343.
   v. King, 276.
Bartlett v. Borden, 196.
   v. Drake, 430.
   v. Gouge, 89.
   v. Wade, 210, 228.
   v. Wood, 13.
Barton v. Briscoe, 396.
   v. Croxall, 476.
   v. Drake, 123.
Bascome v. Albertson, 277.

[The figures refer to pages.]

Bason v. Mining Co., 430.
Bass v. Edwards, 359.
   v. Estill, 219, 437.
   v. Power Co., 167.
   v. Wheless, 206.
Bassett v. Bradley, 208.
   v. Hawk, 432.
   v. Mason, 242.
   v. Messner, 118.
Batchelor v. Whitaker, 36.
Bateman v. Bluek, 363.
   v. Hotchkin, 66.
   v. Maddox, 159.
   v. Pool, 114.
Bates v. Bates, 322.
   v. Norcross, 446, 447, 455.
   v. Ruddick, 237.
   v. Schraeder, 80.
   v. Shraeder, 304.
   v. Swiger, 418, 452.
Battell v. Torrey, 383.
Batterman v. Albright, 8.
Battey v. Hopkins, 300.
Baugan v. Mann, 363.
Baum v. Gaffy, 181.
   v. Grigsby, 193.
Baumgartner v. Peterson, 226.
Baxter v. Bradbury, 451.
   v. Lansing, 151.
   v. Smith, 385.
Bayer v. Cockrill, 256.
Bayler v. Com., 305, 416.
Bayles v. Young, 213.
Bayley v. Bailey, 206.
   v. Greenleaf, 193.
Baylis v. Tyssen-Amhurst, 374.
Bayzer v. Mill Co., 6.
Beach v. Haynes, 37.
   v. Miller, 83, 446.
Beadle v. Hunter, 467.
Beal v. Car-Spring Co., 153.
   v. Harrington, 193.
   v. Warren, 393.
Beall v. Davenport, 144.
   v. Fox's Ex'rs, 277.
Beall's Lessee v. Holmes, 57.
Bealor v. Hahn, 81.
Bean v. Boothby, 232.
   v. Mayo, 445.
   v. Stoneman, 441.
Bear v. Snyder, 92.
   v. Stahl, 103.

Beard v. Nutthall, 108.
   v. Wescott, 324.
Beardslee v. Beardslee, 88.
Beardsley v. Bank, 15.
   v. Hilson, 434.
   v. Knight, 346.
Bear's Case, 475.
Beatie v. Butler, 217.
Beatty v. Clark, 318.
   v. Kurtz, 363.
   v. Mason, 462.
Beaty v. Bordwell, 342.
Beavan v. Speed, 122.
   v. Went, 388.
Beaver Brook Reservoir & Canal Co.
   v. St. Vrain Reservoir & Fish Co., 370.
Becker v. Howard, 494.
Becker's Estate, In re, 23.
Beckley v. Leffingwell, 287.
Beckman v. Davidson, 465.
Beekwith v. Rector, etc., 275.
Beddoe v. Wadsworth, 456.
Bedford v. Backhouse, 225.
   v. M'Elherron, 150.
   v. Terhune, 147.
Bedgood v. McLain, 491.
Beebe v. Estabrook, 481.
   v. Swartwout, 448.
Beecher v. Baldy, 122, 123.
Beekman v. Railroad Co., 495.
Beeman v. Beeman, 260.
   v. Cowser, 72.
Beers v. Beers, 65.
   v. St. John, 16.
   v. Strong, 101.
Beeson v. Burton, 55.
Beeszard v. Capel, 146.
Belden v. Carter, 434.
Bell v. Bruhn, 162.
   v. Denson, 459.
   v. Ellis' Heirs, 156.
   v. Evans, 225.
   v. Fleming's Ex'rs, 223.
   v. Mayor, etc., 60, 91, 201.
   v. Railroad Co., 375, 376.
   v. Scammon, 410.
   v. Twilight, 57, 59.
   v. Woodward, 232.
Bellamy v. Thornton, 487.
Bell Co. v. Alexander, 172.
Bellinger v. White, 127.

CASES CITED. 503

[The figures refer to pages.]

Bellows v. Sackett, 142.
Belser v. Youngblood, 146.
Belton v. Summer, 480.
Bemis v. Call, 232.
Benedict v. Morse, 163, 165.
Benesch v. Clark, 310, 322.
Benett v. Costar, 374.
Benjamin v. Heeney, 135.
Benner v. Evans, 96.
Bennet v. Bittle, 139, 141, 474.
Bennett v. Bates, 207.
    v. Bennett, 71.
    v. Chapin, 395.
    v. Child, 338.
    v. Conant, 243.
    v. Cook, 203.
    v. Harms, 103.
    v. Hibbert, 388.
    v. Hunter, 491.
    v. Keehn, 207.
    v. Morris, 294.
    v. Robinson, 156, 177, 178.
    v. Shipley, 192.
    v. Trustees of M. E. Church, 67.
    v. Waller, 455.
Bennock v. Whipple, 189.
Benson v. Corbin, 326.
Bent v. Coleman, 216.
    v. Weeks, 102.
Bente v. Lange, 119.
Bentley v. City of Atlanta, 142.
Benton Co. v. Czarlinsky, 195.
Bent's Adm'r v. St. Vram, 480.
Berger v. Hoerner, 19, 23.
Berkmeyer v. Kellerman, 270.
Bernier v. Bernier, 404.
Bernstein v. Humes, 209.
Berrien v. Conover, 111.
Berry v. Berry, 294.
    v. Dobson, 116.
    v. Insurance Co., 220.
    v. Norris, 264.
    v. Potter, 167.
    v. Seawall, 452.
    v. Snyder, 5.
    v. Wiedman, 268.
Bessell v. Landsberg, 161.
Besson v. Gribble, 84.
Bethlehem v. Annis, 181.
Bethune v. McDonald, 107.
Bevans v. Briscoe, 9, 143.

Bewick v. Fletcher, 13.
    v. Whitfield, 66.
Bexar Bldg. & Loan Ass'n v. Newman, 248.
Bibb v. Hunter, 263.
Bickford v. Page, 443.
Bickley v. Guest, 321.
Biddel v. Brizzolara, 208.
Bidwell v. Greenshield, 102.
Biederman v. Seymour, 475.
Big Black Creek Imp. Co. v. Kemmerer, 140.
Bigelow v. Hoover, 470.
    v. Hubbard, 445.
Biggerstaff v. Marston, 226.
Biggs v. Brown, 9.
Bigler v. Bank, 19.
Bigley v. Jones, 215.
Big Mountain Imp. Co.'s Appeal, 355.
Bilderback v. Boyce, 316.
Billings v. McDermott, 493.
    v. Marsh, 396.
    v. Taylor, 64, 88.
Billows v. Sackett, 372.
Bills v. Bills, 395.
Bingham's Appeal, 316.
Binney v. Proprietors, 368.
Bircher v. Parker, 23, 143.
Bird v. Higginson, 415.
    v. Keller, 238.
    v. Stark, 463.
Birmingham v. Rogers, 155.
Bishop v. Blair, 71.
    v. Boyle, 90.
    v. Howard, 130.
Bissell v. Grant, 355, 373.
    v. Railroad Co., 422.
Bissing v. Smith, 461.
Black v. Curran, 115.
    v. Lusk, 124.
    v. Mining Co., 88.
    v. Reno, 204, 210.
    v. Singley, 114.
    v. Zacharie, 2.
Blackburn v. Traffic Co., 121.
Blackman v. Hardware Co., 121.
Blackmon v. Blackmon, 108.
Blackmore v. Boardman, 135, 136.
    v. Gregg, 341, 463.
Blackstone Bank v. Davis, 40, 396.
Blackwell v. Broughton, 113.

[The figures refer to pages.]

Blades v. Blades, 223.
Blagge v. Miles, 316.
Blagrove v. Hancock, 328.
Blain v. Harrison, 95, 106.
Blair, Ex parte, 209.
— v. Carpenter, 240.
Blaisdell v. Railroad Co., 166, 167.
Blake v. Broughton, 230.
— v. Bumbury, 272.
— v. Dick, 139.
— v. Hawkins, 316.
— v. Ranous, 139.
Blakeney v. Ferguson, 89.
Blakeslee v. Sincepaugh, 452.
Blanchard v. Blanchard, 290, 312.
— v. Bowers, 12, 159.
— v. Bridges, 364.
— v. Brooks, 440.
— v. Ellis, 451.
— v. Moulton, 353.
— v. Porter, 5.
— v. Tyler, 428.
— v. Ware, 218.
Blanche v. Bradford, 146.
Blaney v. Rice, 424.
Blaney's Estate, In re, 110.
Blankenpickler v. Anderson's Heirs, 404.
Blantin v. Whitaker, 144.
Blass v. Terry, 241.
Blasson v. Blasson, 290.
Blatchford v. Newberry, 284.
Blatchley v. Osborn, 214.
Blauvelt, In re, 24.
Blazy v. McLean, 189.
Bleecker v. Hennion, 94.
— v. Smith, 151, 175.
Bless v. Jenkins, 149.
Blevins v. Smith, 494.
Bligh v. Brent, 25.
Blight v. Schenck, 435, 436.
Blim v. Wilson, 230.
Blinston v. Warburton, 38.
Bliss v. Johnson, 466.
— v. Misner, 14.
Block v. Latham, 146.
Blodget v. Brent, 84, 95.
Blodgett v. Hildreth, 266.
— v. Stone, 369.
Blodwell v. Edwards, 292.
Blomfield v. Eyre, 319.
Blood v. Blood, 84, 219, 437.

Bloodgood v. Ayres, 371.
Bloom v. Welsh, 7.
Bloomfield & R. N. Gaslight Co. v. Calkins, 362.
Blough v. Parry, 384.
Blove v. Sutton, 318.
Blue v. Blue, 116.
Blum v. Light, 125.
— v. Mitchell, 202.
Blumberg v. Birch, 241.
Blundell v. Catterall, 5.
Blunden v. Baugh, 458.
Blyth v. Dennett, 162.
Board v. Board, 458.
— v. Wilson, 194.
Board of Com'rs of Mahoning Co. v. Young, 172.
Board of Education of Normal School Dist. v. Trustees of First Baptist Church of Normal, 176.
Board of Education of State of Illinois v. Bakewell, 275.
Board of Education of Village of Van Wert v. Inhabitants of Village of Van Wert, 178.
Board of Sup'rs of Cass Co. v. Cowgill, 130.
Boatman v. Lasley, 355.
Boatwright v. Bookman, 374.
Bobb v. Wolff, 60.
Bodfish v. Bodfish, 353.
Bodwell v. Webster, 189.
Bodwell Granite Co. v. Lane, 181.
Bogan v. Mortgage Co., 404.
Bogardus v. Trinity Church, 389.
Bogert v. Bliss, 230.
— v. Bogert, 345.
— v. Striker, 229.
Boggs v. Mining Co., 453.
Bogk v. Gassert, 190.
Bogue v. Williams, 217.
Bohm v. Bohm, 265.
Bohon v. Bohon, 287.
Boland v. St. John's Schools, 351.
Boling v. Clark, 111.
Bolles v. Duff, 248.
— v. Munnerlyn, 319.
Bolling v. Bolling, 109.
— v. Carter, 218.
— v. Mayor, etc., of Petersburg, 178, 282.
— v. Teel, 344.

CASES CITED. 505

[The figures refer to pages.]

Bolman v. Lohman, 204.
Bolton v. Ballard, 91.
   v. Myers, 24.
Boltz v. Stoltz, 95.
Bombaugh v. Miller, 358.
Bon Air Coal, Land & Lumber Co. v. Parks, 461.
Bond v. Coke, 17.
Bone v. Tyrrell, 60.
Bonifaut v. Greenfield, 314.
Bonner, Petitioner, 345.
   v. Peterson, 99, 100, 104.
Bonomi v. Backhouse, 366.
Boocock v. Phipard, 188.
Boogs v. Mining Co., 7.
Bool v. Mix, 382, 383, 386.
Boone v. Chiles, 213, 275.
   v. Tipton, 175.
Boone's Representatives v. Boone, 109.
Booraem v. Wells, 317.
Boorum v. Tucker, 110.
Booth v. Goodwin, 119.
   v. Insurance Co., 208.
   v. Meyer, 173.
   v. Shepherd, 423.
   v. Starr, 449.
   v. Terrell, 282.
Boothby v. Vernon, 79.
Boothe v. Flest, 187.
Boothroyd v. Engles, 416.
Boqut v. Coburn, 234, 236.
Board v. Cudmore, 378.
Borders v. Hodges, 487.
Bordman v. Osborn, 145.
Borie v. Crissman, 60.
Borland v. Dean, 400.
   v. Marshall, 75.
Borst v. Boyd, 238.
   v. Corey, 241.
   v. Empie, 351.
Bosley v. Wyatt, 475.
Bostic v. Young, 222.
Boston v. Richardson, 422.
Boston & L. R. Corp. v. Salem & L. R. Co., 379.
Boston & P. R. Corp. v. New York & N. E. R. Co., 242.
Bostwick v. Leach, 10.
   v. Williams, 448.
Bosworth v. Sturtevant, 420.
Botsford v. Burr, 268.
   v. Morehouse, 434.

Botting v. Martin, 160.
Bottomley v. Fairfax, 89.
Bottomly v. Spencer, 108.
Boughton v. Boughton, 328.
Bouldin v. Miller, 396.
Bound Brook Mut. Fire Ins. Ass'n v. Nelson, 199.
Bouscaren v. Brown, 149.
Boutelle v. Bank, 38.
Bowditch v. Andrew, 271, 273.
Bowen v. Bowen, 174.
   v. Conner, 351.
   v. Guild, 466.
   v. Julius, 228.
   v. Prout, 402.
   v. Ratcliff, 181, 224.
Bowers v. Andrews, 493.
   v. Johnson, 210.
Bowlby v. Thunder, 262.
Bowles v. Poore, 68.
Bowles' Case, 62.
Bowling v. Cook, 220.
   v. Crook, 152.
Bowlsby v. Speer, 371, 372.
Bowman v. Farmer, 424.
   v. Faw, 193.
   v. Sunnuchs, 472.
Bowyer's Appeal, 123.
Boxheimer v. Gunn, 224.
Boyd v. Belmont, 445.
   v. Cudderback, 124.
   v. De La Montagnie, 393.
   v. Hunter, 92.
   v. Slayback, 433.
   v. Woolwine, 352, 360.
Boyer v. Williams, 22.
Boyers v. Newbanks, 100.
Boykin v. Ancrum, 67.
Boynton v. Pierce, 235.
   v. Rees, 213.
Bozeman v. Bishop, 57.
   v. Browning, 382.
Bracken v. Cooper, 341.
   v. Jones, 463.
   v. Miller, 213.
Brackett v. Goddard, 8, 9.
   v. Leighton, 87.
Braden v. Cannon, 48.
Bradford v. Griffin, 67.
   v. Randall, 429.
   v. State, 34.
   v. Trust Co., 121.

506   CASES CITED.

[The figures refer to pages.]

Bradish v. Gibbs, 318.
Bradley v. Bailey, 9.
   v. Dike, 445.
   v. Peixoto, 395.
   v Rice, 423.
   v. Snyder, 236, 246.
Bradley's Estate, In re, 60.
Bradner v. Faulkner, 8.
Bradshaw v. Eyre, 375.
Brady v. Nagle, 151.
Bragg v. Lyon, 345.
Brainard v. Cooper, 246, 247.
   v Hudson, 216.
Brainerd v. Brainerd, 187.
Brakken v. Railroad Co., 362.
Bramhall v. Ferris, 41.
Bramlett v. Wettin, 489.
Branch v. Makeig, 342.
Brand v. Brand, 439.
   v. Rhodes' Adm'r, 60.
Brandon v. Brown, 383.
   v. Dawson, 106, 107.
Brandt v. Brandt, 330.
   v. Mickle, 72.
Branham v. Mayor, 408.
Brannock v. Hamilton, 481.
Branson v. Yancy, 94.
Brant v. Iron Co., 310.
   v. Vincent, 159, 160.
Brantley v. Insurance Co., 432.
Brastow v. Ice Co., 6.
Bratt v. Bratt, 132.
Brattle Square Church v. Grant, 327, 329.
Bratton v. Clawson, 14.
   v. Massey, 256.
   v. Mitchell, 71.
Brawford v. Wolfe, 454.
Braxton v. Coleman, 98.
Bray v. Bree, 313.
Bream v. Dickerson, 137.
Breckenridge v. Ormsby, 384.
Breeding v. Davis, 82, 83.
Breese v. Bange, 220.
Bremer v. Dock Co., 234.
Brennan v. Wallace, 121.
   v. Whitaker, 15, 21.
Brent's Case, 255, 298.
Brettun v. Fox, 119.
Brewer v. Connell, 105.
   v. Hardy, 264, 411.
   v. Marshall, 441.

Brewer v. Staples, 207.
   v. Wall, 121.
Brewster v. Carnes, 226.
   v. Hill, 150.
Brickett v. Spofford, 466.
Bridge v. Ward, 396.
Bridges v. Linder, 190.
   v. Pleasants, 275.
   v. Purcell, 168.
Bridgewater v. Bolton, 38.
Briggs v. Briggs, 474.
   v. Hannowald, 245.
   v. Rice 189.
   v. Thompson, 217.
Brill v. Stiles, 403.
Brimmer v. City of Boston, 448.
Brinckerhoff v. Lansing, 213.
Bringloe v. Goodson, 321.
Brinkman v. Jones, 214, 216.
Brinkmeyer v. Helbling, 225.
Bristol v. Carroll Co., 471.
Bristol Hydraulic Co. v. Boyer, 369.
Bristow v. Boothby, 326.
Brittain v. McKay, 8.
Britton's Appeal, 223.
Broadbent v. Ramsbotham, 372.
Broadway Nat. Bank v. Adams, 396.
Broadwell v. Merritt, 455.
Brock v. Kellock, 74.
Brockway v. Wells, 191.
Brodbee v. Mayor, etc., of London, 368.
Brolasky v. Ferguson, 145.
Bronson v. Coffin, 368, 446.
Brook, Ex parte, 22.
Brooke v. Pearson, 396.
Brooke's Appeal, 221.
Brookfield v. Williams, 346.
Brooks v. Brooks, 61.
   v. Curtis, 367.
   v. Everett, 92.
   v. Galster, 9.
   v. Hyde, 156.
   v. McMeekin, 105.
   v. Rogers, 143, 152.
Brookville & Metamora Hydraulic Co. v. Butler, 6.
Broome v. Davis, 119, 125.
Brough v. Higgins, 61.
Broughton v. Langley, 253.
   v. Randall, 85.
Brown v. Adams, 96.
   v. Bank, 200.

CASES CITED.

[The figures refer to pages.]

Brown v. Bates, 336.
  v. Bowen, 451.
  v. Bragg, 134.
  v. Bronson, 99.
  v. Brown, 269, 427, 467.
  v. Budd, 193.
  v. Caldwell, 110, 382.
  v. Chadbourne, 6, 370.
  v. Cockerell, 462, 465, 470.
  v. Coon, 124.
  v. Cram, 183.
  v. Dean, 187.
  v. Dressler, 386.
  v. Fulkerson, 305.
  v. Gay, 465.
  v. Hospital, 48.
  v. Kayser, 161.
  v. King, 464.
  v. Kite, 141.
  v. Lawrence, 285.
  v. Lunt, 438.
  v. McKay, 182, 204.
  v. Mauter, 437.
  v. Peck, 173.
  v. Phillips, 309.
  v. Power Co., 19, 23.
  v. Raindle, 335.
  v. Richards, 87.
  v. Robins, 365.
  v. Rogers, 53.
  v. Rose, 463.
  v. Rouse, 452.
  v. Simpson, 219.
  v. Stackhouse, 146.
  v. Veazie, 491.
  v. Weaver, 49.
  v. Welch, 215.
  v. Williams, 90.
  v. Young, 448.
Browne v. Bockover, 67, 82.
  v. Potter, 105.
Browning v. Harris, 115.
Brown's Trust, In re, 319.
Brownsword v. Edwards, 301.
Bruce v. Bruce, 316.
  v. Nicholson, 80.
Brudnel's Case, 57.
Brummell v. Macpherson, 175.
Brundage v. Association, 196.
Brunker v. Cummins, 142.
Brunson v. Henry, 260, 482.
Brush v. Brush, 476.
  v. Ware, 403.

Bryan v. Bradley, 406.
  v. Knickerbocker, 397.
  v. Wash, 435.
Bryant v. Erskine, 181.
Brydges v. Duchess of Chandos, 476.
Brydon v. Campbell, 221.
Brymbo Water Co. v. Lesters Lime Co., 372.
Buchan v. Sumner, 339, 340.
Buchanan v. Buchanan, 109.
  v. Curtis, 362.
  v. Hamilton, 263.
  v. Monroe, 206.
Buchanan's Lessee v. Sheffer, 77.
Buck v. Conlogue, 121.
  v. Sanders, 212.
  v. Squiers, 422.
  v. Wroten, 72.
Buckeridge v. Ingram, 87.
Buckland v. Butterfield, 18.
Buckler v. Hardy, 284.
Buckley v. Duff, 394.
  v. Superior Court, 345.
Buckner v. Street, 448.
Buckworth v. Thirkell, 46, 73, 76, 77, 300.
Budd v. Brooke, 419.
  v. Hiler, 101.
Buffalo, N. Y. & E. R. Co. v. Stigeler, 424.
Buffum v. Hutchinson, 36.
Buford v. McKee, 260.
Bugbee, Appeal of, 214, 216.
Building & Loan Ass'n of Dakota v. Logan, 126.
Bull v. Bull, 261.
  v. Pritchard, 328.
  v. Shepard, 185.
Bullard v. Briggs, 427.
  v. Harrison, 359.
Bullock v. Grinstead, 134.
  v. Wilson, 5.
Bulwer v. Bulwer, 62.
Bunce v. Wolcott, 469.
Bunham v. Kidwell, 384.
Bunker v. Locke, 118.
  v. Paquette, 119.
Bunn v. Ahl, 392.
  v. Winthrop, 260.
Burbank v. Fay, 353.
  v. Roots, 207.
Burd v. Dandsdale, 80.
Burden v. Thayer, 148.

CASES CITED.

[The figures refer to pages.]

Burdeno v. Amperse, 387.
Burdet v. Hopegood, 283.
Burdick v. Jackson, 191.
Burge v. Smith, 107, 416.
Burgess v. Mawby, 50.
   v. Muldoon, 81.
   v. Wheate, 194, 252.
Burgher v. Henderson, 122.
Burke v. Roper, 276.
   v. Valentine, 82.
Burkhart v. Bucher, 49.
Burleigh v. Clough, 307, 313, 316.
   v. Coffin, 71.
Burn v. Phelps, 141.
Burnett v. Burnett, 54.
   v. Hoffman, 245.
   v. Pratt, 336.
   v. Strong, 172.
Burnham v. O'Grady, 153.
Burns v. Berry, 224.
   v. Bryant, 159.
   v. Cooper, 155.
   v. Lynde, 458.
   v. Thayer, 250.
   v. Thompson, 339.
Burnside v. Terry, 124.
   v. Twitchell, 14, 15, 21.
Burr v. Stenton, 441.
Burrall v. Bender, 91.
Burrell v. Burrell, 313.
Burris v. Page, 53.
Burrough v. Foster, 326.
Burroughs v. Saterlee, 371.
Burrows v. Gallup, 466.
   v. Hovland, 191, 222.
Burt v. Gamble, 182, 231, 240.
   v. Herron's Ex'rs, 262.
   v. Hurlburt, 71.
   v. Sheep Co., 111.
   v. Wilson, 266.
Burton v. Barclay, 148.
   v. Baxter, 247.
   v. Moffitt, 367.
   v. Perry, 469.
Bury v. Pope, 364.
Buschman v. Wilson, 153.
Busey v. Reese, 410.
Bush v. Bradley, 75.
   v. Cooper, 228.
   v. Lathrop, 211.
   v. Marshall, 451.
   v. Person, 450.
   v. Sherman, 249, 270.

Bushby v. Dixon, 480.
Bushey v. Santiff, 353, 360.
Bush's Appeal, 256, 261.
Buss v. Dyer, 352.
Butcher v. Butcher, 313.
Butler v. Cheatham, 84, 88, 92.
   v. Fitzgerald, 104, 489.
   v. Huestis, 296.
   v. Insurance Co., 268.
   v. Roys, 343.
   v. Thornburg, 85.
Butler's Estate, In re, 67.
Butt v. Gas Co., 364.
Buttenuth v. Bridge Co., 6, 472.
Butterfield v. Baker, 155.
   v. Beall, 72.
   v. Gilchrist, 370.
   v. Okie, 193.
   v. Reed, 357, 396.
   v. Wicks, 114.
Butterman v. Albright, 8.
Butterworth v. Crawford, 352.
Buttrick v. Holden, 214.
Buxton v. Inhabitants of Uxbridge, 48, 49.
Buzick v. Buzick, 84.
Buzzell v. Gallagher, 344.
Bybee v. Hageman, 420.
Byers v. Byers, 200.
   v. Engles, 216.
Byington v. Fountain, 231.
Byrne v. Lowry, 466.

C

Cabeen v. Mulligan, 121.
Cadawallader v. Lovece, 434.
Cadell v. Palmer, 133, 324.
Cadwalader v. Tindall, 146.
Cage v. Russel, 151.
Cahill v. Wilson, 118, 121.
Cahn v. Hewsey, 18, 66.
Cahoon v. Coe, 491.
Caiger v. Fee, 353.
Caillaret v. Bernard, 94.
Cain v. Cain, 110.
Caines v. Grant's Lessee, 269, 333.
Cairns v. Coleburn, 268.
Cake's Appeal, 226.
Calborne v. Wright, 149.
Calder v. Chapman, 222.

CASES CITED. 509

[The figures refer to pages.]

Caldwell v. Carrington's Heirs, 269.
   v. Fulton, 374.
   v. Jacob, 61.
   v. Neely, 341.
   v. Willis, 328.
Calhoun v. Curtis, 341.
Calkins v. Calkins, 238.
   v. Munsel, 234.
Callahan's Estate, In re, 291.
Callan v. McDaniel, 136.
Callard v. Callard, 262.
Callis v. Laugher, 363.
Calumet Iron & Steel Co. v. Lathrop, 21.
Calumet & C. C. & D'. Co. v. Russell, 438.
Calvert v. Aldrich, 342.
   v. Rice, 64.
Calvin's Case, 103.
Calvo v. Davies, 207, 208.
Calwell v. Warner, 234.
Cambreleng v. Graham, 230.
Cambridge Valley Bank v. Delano, 214, 216.
Camden & A. Land Co. v. Lippencott, 470, 472.
Cameron v. Railway Co., 340.
Camley v. Stanfield, 144.
Camp v. Cleary, 177, 396.
   v. Scott, 175.
   v. Smith, 404.
Campau v. Campau, 336.
   v. Dubois, 464.
   v. Michell, 160.
Campbell v. Adair, 118, 121.
   v. Ayers, 118.
   v. Beaumont, 395.
   v. Branch, 424.
   v. Campbell, 90, 93.
   v. Carson, 38.
   v. Dearborn, 188.
   v. Ellwanger, 234, 235.
   v. Freeman, 224.
   v. Hall, 455.
   v. Johnson, 420.
   v. Knights, 487.
   v. Kuhn, 384.
   v. Leach, 319.
   v. Lewis, 135, 148.
   v. McClure, 445.
   v. Mesier, 367.
   v. Murphy, 111.

Campbell v. Packard, 493.
   v. Potter, 121.
   v. Prestons, 271.
   v. Race, 363.
   v. Sandys, 54.
   v. Shipley, 464.
   v. Whitson, 392, 393.
Campbell's Case, 87.
Canby v. Porter, 80.
Canedy v. Marcy, 420.
Canfield v. Andrew, 369.
   v. Ford, 3.
Cannon v. Hare, 20, 102.
   v. McDaniel, 194.
   v. Villars, 360.
Canny v. Andrews, 357.
Capehart v. Foster, 17.
Capek v. Kropik, 115.
Capen v. Peckham, 10, 12.
Carbrey v. Willis, 352.
Cardross' Settlement, In re, 314.
Care v. Keller, 111.
Carger v. Fee, 134, 352.
Cargill v. Thompson, 136.
Carley v. Gitchell, 168.
Carll v. Butman, 89.
Carlton v. Buckner, 194.
   v. Jackson, 230.
Carmichael v. Carmichael, 111.
Carneal v. Banks, 388.
Carnegie Nat. Gas. Co. v. Philadelphia Co., 151.
Carney v. Mosher, 9, 143.
Caroon v. Cooper, 90.
Carpenter v. Carpenter, 184.
   v. Davis, 82.
   v. Dexter, 438.
   v. Insurance Co., 197, 198.
   v. Jones, 9, 157.
   v. Koons, 206.
   v. Marnell, 264.
   v. Mitchell, 194.
   v. Walker, 13.
   v. Westcott, 175.
Carper v. Crowl, 110.
   v. Munger, 209.
Carr v. Carr, 64, 188.
   v. Givens, 75, 79.
   v. Hobbs, 192.
   v. Lambert, 373.
   v. Rising, 121.
   v. Wallace, 376.

[The figures refer to pages.]

Carraher v. Bell, 152.
Carrel v. Read, 141.
Carrier v. Paper Co., 207.
Carriger's Estate, In re, 116.
Carrol v. City of East St. Louis, 389.
Carroll v. Ballance, 152, 183.
    v. Newton, 17.
    v. Renich, 259.
    v. Safford, 127.
Carruthers v. Caruthers, 107, 108.
Carson v. Blazer, 5.
    v. Carson, 313.
    v. Cochran, 240, 453.
    v. Fuhs, 78, 296.
    v. Murray, 106.
    v. Thompson, 439.
Carter v. Burr, 140.
    v. Champion, 219.
    v. Conner, 339.
    v. Corley, 439.
    v. Dale, 78.
    v. Goodin, 107.
    v. Insurance Co., 198.
    v. McDaniel, 92, 185.
    v. McMichael, 53.
    v. Thompson, 403.
    v. Warne, 149.
    v. Williams, 76.
    v. Wingard, 167.
Cartwright v. Wise, 268.
Caruthers v. Humphrey, 184, 228.
    v. Williams, 155.
Carver v. Smith, 338.
Carwardine v. Carwardine, 300.
Cary v. Warner, 67.
    v. White, 224.
Casborne v. Scarfe, 78.
Case v. Owen, 335.
    v. Peters, 189.
    v. Phelps, 394.
    v. Weber, 374.
Case Manuf'g Co. v. Garven, 15.
Case of Loringe's Ex'rs, 378.
Case of Mines, 7, 39.
Cass v. Martin, 91.
    v. Thompson, 106.
Casselman v. Packard, 122.
Cassilly v Rhodes, 10.
Casterton v. Sutherland, 313.
Castle v. Palmer, 123.
Castlemain v. Craven, 66.

Caswell v. Districh, 154, 155.
Cates v. Wadlington, 6.
Cathcart v. Bowman, 445.
Catlin v. Ware, 97, 416.
Cattlin v. Brown, 324, 325.
Caufman v. Sayre, 248.
C. Aultman & Co. v. Salinas, 123.
Cave v. Cave, 18, 20.
    v. Holford, 476.
Cedar Rapids & St. P. R. Co. v. Stewart, 431.
Central Bank v. Copeland, 80, 438.
Central Branch R. Co. v. Fritz, 23.
Central Bridge Corp. v. Lowell, 495.
Central Trust Co. of New York v. Bridges, 191.
    v. Kneeland, 185.
Central Trust & Safe Deposit Co. v. Cincinnati Grand Hotel Co., 21.
Cerf v. Ashley, 245.
Chadock v. Cowley, 326.
Chadwick v. Trower, 365.
Chaffe v. McIntosh, 339.
Chalfant v. Grant, 117.
Chalker v. Dickinson, 5.
Challefoux v. Ducharme, 340.
Chamberlain v. Bell, 221.
    v. Hutchinson, 317.
    v. Lyell, 123.
    v. Meeder, 228.
    v. Thompson, 183.
Chamberlayne v. Brockett, 329.
Chamberlin v. Donahue, 160.
Chambers v. Chambers, 289.
    v. Ross, 145.
    v. St. Louis, 275, 277.
Champlin v. Pendleton, 422.
Chancey v. Strong, 71.
Chandler v. Cheney, 338.
    v. Oldham, 143.
    v. Simmonds, 383.
    v. Von Roeder, 392.
Chapin v. Brown, 359, 363.
    v. Chapin, 78.
    v. Harris, 170, 177.
    v. Hill, 109.
    v. Shafer, 382.
Chaplin v. Chaplin, 50, 78, 89.
    v. Leroux, 475.
    v. Sawyer, 120.
    v. Simmon's Heirs, 94.
    v. U. S., 60.

CASES CITED.

[The figures refer to pages.]

Chapman v. Chapman, 104.
   v. Holmes' Ex'rs, 444.
   v. Pingree, 170.
   v. Porter, 200.
   v. Price, 78.
   v. Schroeder, 87, 111.
Charles v. Andrews, 108.
Charles River Bridge v. Warren Bridge, 421.
Charless v. Froebel, 149.
Chase v. Abbott, 246.
   v. Bank, 233.
   v. Box Co., 13.
   v. Hazelton, 63, 64, 304.
   v. McDonnell, 154.
   v. McLellan, 243.
   v. Peck, 233.
   v. Van Meter, 105, 232.
   v. Woodbury, 236.
Chasemore v. Richards, 371.
Chase's Case, 87, 99.
Chatfield v. Wilson, 371.
Chauncey v. Arnold, 428.
Chauvin v. Wagner, 454, 455.
Cheatham v. Jones, 116.
Cheeseborough v. Green, 366.
Cheever v. Pearson, 159.
Chenango Bridge Co. v. Paige, 380.
Chenery v. Stevens, 410, 411.
Cheney v. Straube, 447.
   v. Teese, 290.
Cherokee Nation v. Georgia, 400.
Cherrington v. Abney Mill, 364.
Cherry v. Arthur, 15.
   v. Greene, 310.
Chesley v. King, 371.
Chester v. Breitling, 437.
   v. Greer, 213.
Chew v. Chew, 86.
   v. Commissioners, 75, 78, 79.
   v. Farmers' Bank, 111.
   v. Hyman, 234.
   v. Morton, 453.
Chicago City Ry. Co. v. People, 379.
Chicago Dock Co. v. Kinzie, 106.
Chicago Dock & Canal Co. v. Kinzie, 472.
Chicago, D. & V. R. Co. v. Fosdick, 248.
Chicago, T. & M. C. Ry. Co. v. Titterington, 124.
Chicago & A. R. Co. v. Keegan, 144.

Chicago & C. Rolling-Mill Co. v. Scully, 233.
Chicago & G. W. Railroad Land Co. v. Peck, 245.
Chicago & N. W. Ry. v. Ft. Howard, 15.
Chicago & S. E. Ry. Co. v. Perkins, 160.
Chichester v. Bicherstaff, 23.
Chick v. Willetts, 184.
Chickering v. Failes, 461.
Chidley v. Churchwardens of West Ham, 16.
Child v. Baylie, 49, 327.
   v. Stair, 422.
Childers v. Bumgarner, 75.
   v. Lee, 156.
Childress v. Cutter, 485.
Childs v. Childs, 235.
   v. Clark, 148, 149.
   v. Railway Co., 64, 342.
   v. Smith, 101.
Chilton v. Corporation of London, 374.
Chirac v. Chirac, 388.
Chisholm v. Caines, 6.
   v. Georgia, 31.
Chiswell v. Morris, 100.
Chittenden v. Gossage, 181.
Chittock v. Chittock, 107.
Chloupek v. Perotka, 454, 463.
Choate v. Burnham, 418.
Choteau v. Jones, 213.
Chouteau v. Railway Co., 105.
Chouteau's Ex'r v. Burlando, 240.
Christian v. Dripps, 15.
Christie v. Gage, 464.
Christner v. Brown, 229.
Christopher v. Austin, 141.
   v. Christopher, 98.
Christ's Hospital v. Grainger, 329.
Christy v. Dyer, 119, 126.
   v. Pulliam, 315.
Chudleigh's Case, 252, 255, 298, 303.
Church v. Brown, 140.
   v. Bull, 109.
   v. Church, 106.
   v. Gilman, 435.
Churchill v. Hudson, 80.
   v. Hulbert, 168.
Cibel v. Hill's Case, 141.
Cincinnati, W. & Z. R. Co. v. Iliff, 436.
Cissna v. Haines, 229.

512

CASES CITED.

[The figures refer to pages.]

Citizens' Bank v. Knapp, 15.
Citizens' Nat. Bank v. Dayton, 247.
City Council of Augusta v. Burum, 168.
City of Alton v. Illinois Transp. Co., 421.
City of Chicago v. Garrity, 153.
   v. McGinn, 6.
   v. Witt, 214.
City of Denver v. Soloman, 142.
City of Ft. Scott v. Schulenberg, 240.
City of London v. Greyme, 65.
City of Peoria v. Simpson, 142.
City of Quincy v. Attorney General, 174.
City of St. Paul v. Chicago, M. & St. P. R. Co., 467.
City of San Antonio v. French, 158.
City of Stockton v. Weber, 171.
City of Victoria v. Schott, 471.
City Power Co. v. Fergus Falls Water Co., 141.
City and County of San Francisco v. Fulde, 467.
   v. Lawton, 412.
Claflin v. Claflin, 396.
   v. Railroad Co., 352.
   v. Van Wagoner, 314.
Clapp v. Bromagham, 340, 341.
   v. Ingraham, 320.
Clapper v. Kells, 135.
Clark v. Allen, 428.
   v. Baker, 35, 48, 451.
   v. Banks, 9.
   v. Bayley, 126.
   v. Clark, 78, 88.
   v. Cogge, 360.
   v. Condit, 189.
   v. Fisher, 445.
   v. Greenfield, 152.
   v. Gregory, 246.
   v. Harvey, 9.
   v. Henry, 186.
   v. Holland, 216.
   v. Jacobs, 194.
   v. Jones, 211.
   v. Owens, 57, 58.
   v. Powers, 420.
   v. Rainey, 341.
   v. Smith, 202.
   v. Swift, 445.
   v. Tainter, 315.
   v. Wheelock, 158.
   v. White, 379.

Clarke v. McClure, 460, 464.
   v. Saxton, 264.
   v. White, 223.
   v. Wright, 394.
Clarke's Lessee v. Courtney, 432.
Clarkson v. Clarkson, 53.
Clary v. Owen, 21.
Clavering v. Clavering, 64.
Clawson v. Primrose, 364.
Clay v. White, 76.
Claycomb v. Munger, 447.
Clayton v. Blakey, 132.
   v. Clayton, 38.
   v. Earl of Wilton, 394.
Clearwater v. Rose, 36.
Cleaver v. Burcky, 207.
Clemence v. Steere, 20, 63, 64.
Clements v. Landrum, 427.
Cleminger v. Gas Co., 152.
Clepper v. Livergood, 78.
Clerk v. Smith, 475.
Cleveland v. Martin, 229.
Cleveland Ins. Co. v. Reed, 240.
Clever's Estate, In re, 7.
Clifford v. Clifford, 318.
   v. Gresinger, 134.
Cliffton v. Anderson, 73.
Clifton v. Montague, 135.
Climie v. Wood, 21.
Clinton Nat. Bank v. Manwarring, 209.
Clopton v. Bolton, 442.
Clough v. Hosford, 156.
Clowes v. Dickenson, 237.
Clun v. Fisher, 60.
Clute v. Fisher, 423.
Coakley v. Chamberlain, 132.
   v. Perry, 105.
Coates v. Cheever, 64, 85, 88.
Cobb v. Davenport, 5.
   v. Lavalle, 145.
   v. Lucas, 417.
   v. Trammell, 269.
Cobbs v. Coleman, 113.
Cobel v. Cobel, 155.
Coburn, Ex parte, 166, 350.
   v. Herrington, 93, 99, 107.
   v. Stephens, 231.
Cocheco Manuf'g v. Whittier, 421.
Cochran v. Cochran, 60.
   v. Harrow, 452.
   v. O'Hern, 78.
   v. Pew, 151.
Cochrane v. Tuttle, 163.

[The figures refer to pages.]

Cocke's Ex'r v. Phillips, 91.
Cockrell v. Curtis, 114.
Cockrill v. Armstrong, 92, 93.
— v. Downey, 8.
Cockson v. Cock, 136.
Codman v. Evans, 362.
— v. Winslow, 25.
Cody v. Quarterman, 160.
Coe v. Hobby, 409.
— v. Manufacturing Co., 80.
— v. Railway Co., 15.
Coffin v. Loring, 181.
— v. Parker, 236.
Coffman v. Coffman, 473.
Cofran v. Shepard, 164.
Cogel v. Raph, 493.
Coggeshall v. Home for Friendless Children, 389.
Cogswell v. Cogswell, 60.
— v. Tibbetts, 103.
Cohen v. Kyler, 20.
Coker v. Whitlock, 195.
Colburn v. Morrill, 141.
Colby v. Duncan, 291.
— v. Osgood, 450.
— v. Poor, 243.
Colchester v. Roberts, 353.
Colclough v. Carpeles, 133.
Cole v. Bolard, 188.
— v. Bradbury, 372.
— v. Cole, 208.
— v. Gill, 119.
— v. Hughes, 367, 441.
— v. Kimball, 445.
— v. Lake Co., 36.
— v. Raymond, 447.
— v. Sewell, 299.
Coleman, In re, 397.
— v. Beach, 312.
— v. Coleman, 344, 347.
— v. Lyman, 443.
— v. Pickett, 464.
— v. Satterfield, 72.
— v. Van Rensselaer, 181.
Coles v. Coles, 91, 95.
Cole's Case, 138.
Collamer v. Langdon, 212.
Collamore v. Collamore, 53.
Collett v. Collett, 173.
Collier v. Jenks, 17.
— v. Pierce, 352.

Collins v. Canty, 162.
— v. Carlisle's Heirs, 261.
— v. Carman, 109.
— v. Corson, 267.
— v. Ewing, 380.
— v. Hasbrouck, 148.
— v. Hopkins, 315.
— v. Riley, 175.
— v. Warren, 94.
Collomb v. Caldwell, 394.
Colston v. McVay, 145.
Colton v. Colton, 262.
Colton v. Smith, 346.
Columbia Ins. Co. of Alexandria v. Lawrence, 198.
Colville v. Parker, 392.
Colwell v. Carper, 116.
Coman v. Thompson, 8.
Combs v. Jackson, 31.
Comer v. Chamberlain, 74, 82.
Commercial Bank v. Cunningham, 181.
— v. Hiller, 236.
— v. Weinberg, 182.
Commissioners of Burke Co. v. Catawaba Lumber Co., 370.
Commissioners of Canal Fund v. Kempshall, 5.
Commissioners of Charitable Donations & Bequests v. De Clifford, 329.
Commissioners of Homochitto River v. Withers, 6.
Commissioners of Knox Co. v. Nichols, 319.
Commissioners of Sewers v. Glasse, 374.
Commissioners of Sinking Fund v. Walker, 263.
Commonwealth v. Canal Co., 495.
— v. Chapin, 5.
— v. Dudley, 434.
— v. Duffield, 320.
— v. Inhabitants of Newbury, 362.
— v. Lay, 125.
— v. Low, 362.
— v. Rigney, 166.
— v. Robinson, 247.
— v. Roxbury, 400, 402.
— v. Tewksbury, 31, 39.
— v. Williams' Ex'rs, 312.
Compton v. Richards, 363.

REAL PROP.—33

CASES CITED.

[The figures refer to pages.]

Comstock v. Hitt, 207.
   v. Michael, 202.
   v. Sharp, 357.
   v. Smith, 454.
Conant v. Little, 96.
Concord Manuf'g Co. v. Robertson, 5.
Concord Union Mut. Fire Ins. Co. v. Woodbury, 199.
Conduitt v. Ross, 367.
Cone v. Insurance Co., 199.
Coney v. Sanders, 311.
Congdon v. Morgan, 466.
Conger v. Duryee, 152.
Congham v. King, 137.
Congregational Society of Dubuque v. Fleming, 12.
Congregational Society of Halifax v. Stark, 37.
Conklin v. Foster, 116.
Conlan v. Grace, 430, 433.
Conn v. Conn, 341.
Connah v. Hale, 146.
Connaughton v. Sands, 113.
Connecticut Mut. Life Ins. Co. v. Talbot, 227.
   v. Tyler, 208.
Connely v. Rue, 246.
Conner v. Jones, 162.
   v. Shepherd, 87.
Connery v. Brooke, 356.
Connolly v. Hammond, 250.
   v. Keating, 265.
Connor v. Bradley, 151.
Conover v. Insurance Co., 198.
   v. Wright, 111.
Conrad v. Mining Co., 16, 19.
Conrady v. Bywaters, 149.
Consolidated Coal Co. v. Peers, 149.
Consolidated Land & Irrigation Co. v. Hawley, 155.
Conway v. Carpenter, 152.
   v. Starkweather, 159.
   v. Taylor, 379.
Cook v. Babcock, 463.
   v. Brightly, 377, 378.
   v. Brown, 434.
   v. Cook, 101.
   v. Fisk, 98.
   v. Foster, 231.
   v. Gammon, 353.
   v. Hammond, 31, 280, 284, 306.
   v. Jones, 149.

Cook v. McClure, 470, 472.
   v. Norton, 163.
   v. Prindle, 185, 208.
   v. Transportation Co., 16, 65, 143.
   v. Webb, 94.
   v. Whiting, 13.
Cooke v. Bremond, 339.
   v. Dealey, 266.
   v. Husbands, 256.
Cooksey v. Bryan, 265.
Cooley v. Dewey, 480.
   v. Golden, 5, 471.
Coolidge v. Wells, 118.
Cooper v. Adams, 158.
   v. Basham, 121.
   v. Cooper, 114, 338.
   v. Cotton-Mills Co., 461, 467.
   v. Franklin, 261.
   v. Harvey, 21.
   v. Jackson, 433.
   v. Johnson, 16, 23.
   v. Macdonald, 82, 396.
   v. Merritt, 194.
   v. Newland, 245.
   v. Ord, 467.
   v. Page, 428.
   v. Smith, 380.
   v. Whitney, 89.
   v. Woolfitt, 8.
Coor v. Smith, 196.
Cope v. Cope, 205.
Copeland v. Stephens, 149.
Copp v. Swift, 12.
Corbett v. Laurens, 61.
   v. Woodward, 211.
Corbin v. Healy, 42, 48.
Corbit v. Smith, 383, 384.
Corby v. Corby, 57.
Cord v. Hirsch, 246.
Cordova v. Hood, 216.
Core v. Faupell, 466.
Corlies' Will, In re, 397.
Cornelius v. Den, 174.
Cornell v. Lamb, 31, 376.
Corning v. Burton, 207.
Cornish v. Gest, 345.
   v. Strutton, 65.
Corporation of Birmingham v. Allen, 365.
Corporation of London v. Riggs, 360.
Corriell v. Ham, 109, 110.
Corrigan v. City of Chicago, 154.

CASES CITED. 515

[The figures refer to pages.]

Corrothers v. Jolliffe, 346.
Cortelyou v. Van Brundt, 423.
Cortleyeu v. Hathaway, 242.
Corwithe v. Gritting, 345.
Cory v. Schuster, 121.
Cosner v. McCrum, 430.
Costello v. Edson, 466.
Cottingham v. Springer, 209.
Cottman v. Grace, 275.
Cotton v. Burkelman, 317.
Couch v. Ingersoll, 441.
Coudert v. Cohn, 159.
Coulter v. Holland, 98.
    v. Norton, 141.
    v. Trust Co., 432.
Countess of Shrewsbury's Case, 63.
Countryman v. Lighthill, 4.
County of St. Clair v. Lovingston, 470.
Cover v. Black, 225.
Covert v. Robinson, 49.
Cowdrey v. Coit, 448.
    v. Hitchcock, 114.
Cowell v. Daggett, 435.
    v. Hicks, 297.
    v. Lumley, 139.
    v. Springs Co., 40.
Cowen v. Rinaldo, 254.
Cowlam v. Slack, 374.
Cowles v. Balzer, 368.
    v. Marble, 235.
    v. Ricketts, 409.
Cowling v. Higginson, 361.
Cowman v. Hall, 89.
Cowx v. Foster, 316.
Cox v. Arnold, 471.
    v. Bent, 158.
    v. Forrest, 353.
    v. Freedley, 422.
    v. Garst, 89, 91.
    v. Glue, 375.
    v. Jagger, 95.
    v. Stafford, 113.
    v. Walker, 273.
    v. Wilder, 123.
Coxe v. State, 5.
Coyle v. Wilkins, 241.
Crabb v. Pratt, 84.
Craddock v. Edwards, 114.
Crafts v. Crafts, 85.
Craig v. Butler, 153.
    v. Cartwright, 465.

Craig v. Dale, 8.
    v. Leslie, 23, 24.
    v. Miller, 246.
    v. Railway Co., 362.
    v. Warner, 294.
    v. Wells, 417.
Craige v. Morris, 94.
Craige's Appeal, 291.
Crain v. McGoon, 228.
Cramer v. Hoose, 268.
Crane v. Bolles, 24.
    v. Brigham, 16.
    v. Caldwell, 193.
    v. Palmer, 90.
    v. Turner, 185.
    v. Waggoner, 117.
Cranson v. Cranson, 105.
Crary v. Goodman, 465.
Crawford v. Edwards, 206.
    v. Scoville, 385.
    v. Simon, 227, 239.
    v. Wearn, 174.
Crawl v. Harrington, 89, 106.
Creecy v. Pearce, 90.
Creek v. Waterworks Co., 370.
Creel v. Kirkham, 154.
Cregier, In re, 92.
Crerar v. Williams, 301.
Cresinger v. Welch, 382.
Cresson v. Stout, 19.
Crews' Adm'r v. Hatcher, 288, 289.
Crine v. Tifts, 7.
Crispen v. Hannavan, 467.
Criswell v. Grumbling, 59.
Critchfield v. Remaley, 161.
Crittenden v. Johnson, 89.
Crocker v. Pierce, 447.
    v. Society, 175.
Crockett v. Crockett, 63, 64.
    v. Maguire, 223.
    v. Railway Co., 168.
Crofts v. Middleton, 305.
Croker v. Trevithin, 395.
Crommelin v. Thiess, 147.
Cromwell v. Insurance Co., 198.
Cronkhite v. Cronkhite, 350, 351, 353.
Crook v. Hewitt, 143.
Crooker v. Jewell, 209.
Crosby v. Huston, 190.
    v. Loop, 148.
    v. Parker, 425.

CASES CITED.

[The figures refer to pages.]

Crosdale v. Lanigan, 168.
Cross v. Everts, 122, 123.
   v. Lewis, 352, 363.
   v. Taylor, 494.
   v. Upson, 159.
   v. Weare, 125.
Crouch v. Puryear, 64.
Crow v. Conant, 229.
   v. Wolbert, 359.
Crowell v. Currier, 208.
   v. Woodbury, 346.
Croxall v. Shererd, 256, 288, 291, 297.
Crozier v. Bray, 285.
Cruger v. Dougherty, 491.
   v. Jones, 273.
   v. McLaury, 378.
Crumlish v. Railroad Co., 227.
Cubbins v. Ayres, 19.
Cubitt v. Porter, 366.
Cullen v. Trust Co., 196, 204.
Cullum v. Erwin, 210.
Culver v. Harper, 90.
Cummings v. Glass, 434.
   v. Wyman, 340, 463.
Cumston v. Bartlett, 316.
Cunningham v. Brumback, 459.
   v. Freeborn, 427.
   v. Holton, 163.
   v. Moody, 78.
   v. Morrell, 441.
   v. Railroad Co., 250.
   v. Shannon, 110.
   v. Snow, 469.
   v. Webb, 426.
Cupples v. Galligan, 230.
Curling's Adm'rs v. Curling's Heirs, 277.
Curran v. Smith, 15.
Currie v. Donald, 432.
Currier v. Barker, 161.
   v. Earl, 156, 158.
   v. Gale, 228.
Curry v. Bott, 80.
Curtis v. Buckley, 191.
   v. Cockrell, 114.
   v. Galvin, 158.
   v. Gardner, 350.
   v. Hobart, 96, 99.
   v. Lukin, 331.
   v. Lyman, 222.
   v. Mundy, 214.
   v. Railroad Co., 372.

Curtis v. Root, 225.
Curtiss v. White, 137.
Cushing v. Blake, 78, 258, 259.
   v. Hurd, 209.
Cuthbertson v. Irving, 456.
Cutler v. Clemenston, 210, 244.
   v. James, 223.
   v. Smith, 166.
Cutter v. Cambridge, 462.
Cutts v. Com., 34.
   v. Manufacturing Co., 185.

D

Daggett v. Rankin, 191.
Dail v. Moore, 438.
Dailey v. Abbott, 200.
   v. Kastell, 216.
Daily v. State, 362.
Dalby v. Hirst, 140.
Dale's Case, 57.
Daley v. Quick, 142.
Dalton v. Angus, 353.
   v. Smith, 247.
   v. Webb, 125.
Daly v. Willis, 107.
Damm v. Damm, 236.
Dan v. Longstreet, 344.
Dana v. Bank, 263.
Daniel Bell, The, 6.
Daniel v. Coker, 200, 201.
   v. North, 353.
   v. Wilson, 206.
Daniels v. Bond, 157.
   v. Brown, 154.
   v. Daniels, 343.
   v. Eldredge, 326.
   v. Pond, 17, 18.
   v. Richardson, 71.
Danville Seminary v. Mott, 345.
Danziger v. Silberthau, 66.
Darby's Lessee v. Mayer, 479.
Darcus v. Crump, 301.
Dare v. Heathcote, 353.
Dareus v. Crump, 284.
Darlington v. Darlington, 24.
   v. Painter, 369.
Darst v. Murphy, 188.
Dart v. Dart, 415.
Dashiel v. Collier, 97.
Dates v. Winstanley, 237.

CASES CITED. 517

[The figures refer to pages.]

Datesman's Appeal, 61.
Daughaday v. Paine, 193.
Dausch v. Crane, 462, 469.
Davenport v. Alston, 120.
   v. Farrar, 89.
   v. Kirkland, 24, 327.
   v. Lampson, 361.
   v. Reg., 174.
   v. Shants, 15, 21.
Davidson v. Heydom, 334.
   v. Manufacturing Co., 143.
   v. Young, 453.
Davie v. Stevens, 38.
Davies, Ex parte, 327.
   v. Speed, 299.
Davies' Trusts, In re, 317.
Daviess v. Myers, 60.
Davis v. Andrews, 121.
   v. Bartholomew, 93.
   v. Bean, 202.
   v. Brandon, 429.
   v. Brocklebank, 9.
   v. Buffum, 22.
   v. Clark, 64.
   v Coburn, 275.
   v. Davis, 100, 433.
   v. Dendy, 202.
   v. Dickson, 303.
   v. Emery, 14.
   v. Eyton, 9.
   v. Gilliam, 63, 64, 72.
   v. Givens, 341.
   v. Hayden, 415.
   v. Hess, 425.
   v. Holmes, 248.
   v. Kelley, 121.
   v. Kirk, 475.
   v. Logan, 93.
   v. McArthur, 467.
   v. Mason, 75, 76, 77.
   v. Payne's Adm'r, 146.
   v. Pierce, 231.
   v. Power Co., 142.
   v. Spaulding, 371.
   v. State, 125.
   v. Stonestreet, 190.
   v. Thompson, 9, 157.
   v. Townsend, 67.
   v. Walker, 101.
   v. Wetherell, 91.
Davis' Adm'r v. Smith, 153.

Davis Sewing-Mach. Co. v. Barnard, 385.
Davison v. Stanley, 409.
   v. Whittlesby, 95.
Dawkins v. Penryhn, 395.
Dawley v. Ayers, 113, 121.
Dawson v. Clarke, 267.
   v. Danbury Bank, 217.
   v. Drake, 200.
   v. Parsons, 93.
Day v. Adams, 439.
   v. Clark, 213.
   v. Cochran, 74-76.
   v. Watson, 141.
Dayton v. Corser, 104.
   v. Dayton, 245.
   v. Newman, 433.
   v. Vandoozer, 8.
Deacons of Cong. Church in Auburn v. Walker, 421.
Dean v. Long, 216.
   v. McLean, 166.
   v. Mumford, 330.
   v. Shelly, 440.
Deane v. Hutchinson, 19.
Deans v. Pate, 105.
Dearing v. Thomas, 120.
Deaton v. Taylor, 152.
Deavitt v. Judevine, 237.
Debow v. Colfax, 9, 62.
Dech's Appeal, 342.
Decker v. Livingston, 71, 343.
De Cordova v. Hood, 193.
Deere v. Chapman, 116.
Deerfield v. Railroad Co., 362.
Deering v. Kerfoot's Ex'r, 93.
   v. Tucker, 33.
Deering & Co. v. Beard, 121.
De France v. Johnson, 84.
Defraunce v. Brooks, 37.
Degory v. Roe, 436.
Degraffenreid v. Scruggs, 13.
De Grey v. Richardson, 76, 79.
De Haro v. U. S., 167.
Dehoney v. Bell, 93.
Dei v. Habel, 114.
Dejarnatte v. Allen, 62, 72.
De Lancey v. Piepgras, 459.
   v. Stearns, 427.
Delaney v. Fox, 144, 145.
Delano v. Montague, 164.

[The figures refer to pages.]

Delaunay v. Burnett, 404.
Delaware, L. & W. R. Co. v. Sanderson, 4.
Demarest v. Willard, 135, 139.
Demby v. Parse, 20.
Demill v. Reid, 287, 289.
Deming v. Bullitt, 430.
— v. Comings, 243.
De Mott v. Hagerman, 154.
— v. Manufacturing Co., 204.
Den v. Adams, 164.
— v. Cooper, 273.
— v. Cox, 48.
— v. Demarest, 75.
— v. Drake, 161.
— v. Dubois, 49.
— v. Fogg, 48.
— v. Hance, 301.
— v. Howell, 158.
— v. Humphries, 9, 159.
— v. Hyatt, 49.
— v. Johnson, 106.
— v. Jones, 485.
— v. Kinney, 64.
— v. Lake, 48.
— v. Post, 141.
— v. Railroad Co., 176.
— v. Sauls, 81.
— v. Troutman, 272.
— v. Wanett, 76.
— v. Ward, 81.
Dendy v. Nicholl, 175.
Denfield, Petitioner, 173.
Denn v. Roake, 316.
Dennett v. Codman, 234.
— v. Dennett, 282, 294.
— v. Hopkinson, 8.
— v. Pass, 377.
Dennis v. McCagg, 271.
— v. Wilson, 354, 418.
Denton v. Nanny, 89, 90, 235.
Denton's Guardians v. Denton's Ex'rs, 80.
Denu v. Cornell, 454.
Denver, M. & A. Ry. Co. v. Lockwood, 420.
Department of Public Parks, In re, 3.
De Puy v. Strong, 343.
Derby v. Derby, 277.
Derrick v. Luddy, 144.
Derry Bank v. Webster, 434.
De Rush v. Brown, 89.

De Ruyter v. St. Peter's Church, 246.
Deshler v. Beery, 110.
Desilver's Estate, In re, 31.
Des Moines & Ft. D. R. Co. v. Lynd, 451.
Desnoyer v. Jordan, 70.
Despard v. Walbridge, 144.
Detmold, In re, 396.
Detroit Sav. Bank v. Trusdail, 204.
Detroit & B. Plank-Road Co. v. Detroit S. Ry. Co., 167.
De Uprey v. De Uprey, 345.
De Veaux v. Fosbender, 223.
Devereux v. McMahon, 430.
Devin v. Hendershott, 272.
— v. Hlmer, 428.
Devinney v. Reynolds, 432.
Dew v. Kuehn, 57.
Dewal v. Becker, 358.
Dewey v. Lambier, 343.
— v. Moyer, 265.
— v. Williams, 176.
Dewitt v. Eldred, 51.
— v. Harvey, 355.
— v. Pierson, 141.
— v. San Francisco, 333, 334.
De Wolf v. Johnson, 207.
— v. Murphy, 90.
Dexter v. Hall, 431.
— v. Harris, 222.
— v. Manley, 138.
Dey v. Dunham, 187, 214.
— v. Greenebaum, 149.
D'Eyncourt v. Gregory, 18, 20.
Deyo v. Bleakley, 134.
Diamond v. Turner, 489.
Dick v. Doughten, 105.
— v. Insurance Co., 199.
— v. Moon, 204.
Dickenson v. Wright, 394.
Dickerson v. Colgrove, 452.
— v. Cuthburt, 127.
Dickey v. Lyon, 217.
— v. M'Cullough, 175.
— v. Thompson, 237.
Dickinson v. Hoomes' Adm'r, 449.
Dickson v. Desire's Adm'r, 443.
Dietrick v. Noel, 465.
Dikes v. Miller, 469.
Dillahunty v. Railway Co., 447.
Dillaye v. Greenough, 266.
Dillard v. Dillard's Ex'rs, 387.

CASES CITED. 519

[The figures refer to pages.]

Dillman v. Bank, 120.
Dillon v. Dillon, 54.
    v. Reilly, 328.
Dilworth v. Gusky, 38.
Dinehart v. Wilson, 154.
Dingley v. Dingley, 288.
Dinwiddie v. Smith, 434.
Dircks v. Brant, 9.
Disher v. Disher, 60, 64.
Diver v. Diver, 338.
Dixon v. Buell, 147.
    v. Clow, 142.
    v. Dixon, 194.
    v. Hill, 215.
    v. Niccolls, 148, 154, 155.
    v. Stewart, 144.
D. M. Osborne & Co. v. Schoonmaker, 121.
Doane v. Badger, 356.
    v. Doane, 116.
Dobbin v. Rex, 346.
Dobson's Adm'r v. Butler's Adm'r, 114.
Dobson's Estate, 24.
Dockham v. Parker, 155.
Docktermann v. Elder, 93.
Dodd v. Acklom, 409.
    v. Adams, 394.
    v. Burchell, 360.
    v. Holme, 365.
    v. Witt, 422.
Dodge v. Davis, 66, 342.
    v. Evans, 192.
    v. Williams, 24.
Dodson v. Hay, 78.
Dodson's Appeal, 120.
Doe v. Abey, 333.
    v. Allen, 38, 152.
    v. Allsop, 222.
    v. Amey, 156.
    v. Barnard, 467.
    v. Bateman, 148.
    v. Bell, 132.
    v. Benjamin, 132.
    v. Bernard, 94.
    v. Bliss, 175.
    v. Britain, 322.
    v. Brown, 467.
    v. Carter, 467.
    v. Challis, 323.
    v. Chamberlaine, 156.
    v. Clarke, 290.

Doe v. Cole, 305, 407.
    v. Considine, 283, 285, 288, 292, 293.
    v. Cooper, 287, 297.
    v. Courtnay, 409.
    v. Cox, 156.
    v. Craig, 302.
    v. Craigen, 49.
    v. Crick, 162.
    v. Day, 133.
    v. Dorvell, 287.
    v. Dunbar, 162.
    v. Earl of Burlington, 65.
    v. Eyre, 302.
    v. Gatacre, 294.
    v. Glover, 395.
    v. Grady, 57.
    v. Gregory, 464.
    v. Harter, 39.
    v. Hawke, 396.
    v. Hazell, 161.
    v. Howell, 285, 294, 301.
    v. Hull, 163, 464, 468.
    v. Johnson, 152.
    v. Jones, 144, 175, 317, 458.
    v. Knight, 433.
    v. Ladd, 318.
    v. Lewis, 68.
    v. Luxton, 68.
    v. M'Kaeg, 158.
    v. McLoskey, 196.
    v. Manning, 392.
    v. Meux, 152.
    v. Miller, 152, 156.
    v. Moore, 289.
    v. Morphett, 162.
    v. Oliver, 451.
    v. Palmer, 162.
    v. Passingham, 256.
    v. Patten, 38.
    v. Pearson, 395.
    v. Peck, 135.
    v. Perryn, 288.
    v. Poole, 409.
    v. Porter, 160.
    v. Provoost, 288.
    v. Reed, 223, 408.
    v. Rees, 144, 152.
    v. Reynolds, 145.
    v. Richards, 38.
    v. Ries, 132.
    v. Roach, 285.

CASES CITED.

[The figures refer to pages.]

Doe v. Robertson, 388.
   v. Robinson, 68.
   v. Roe, 74, 306, 470.
   v. Rusham, 393.
   v. Scudamore, 79, 301.
   v. Seaton, 137.
   v. Selby, 285.
   v. Skirrow, 456.
   v. Smaridge, 159.
   v. Smeddle, 47.
   v. Smith, 162.
   v. Stratton, 132.
   v. Timins, 475.
   v. Tunnell, 184.
   v. Watts, 161.
   v. Webb, 287.
   v. Wells, 144.
   v. Williams, 162.
   v. Worsley, 287.
Doebler's Appeal, 40.
Doed v. Whichelo, 485.
Doescher v. Doescher, 181.
Dold v. Geiger's Adm'r, 71.
Dolde v. Vodicka, 421.
Dolittle v. Eddy, 166.
Dolph v. White, 137.
Dommett v. Bedford, 396.
Donahue's Estate, In re, 41, 479.
Donald v. Elliott, 66, 143.
Donalds v. Plumb, 273.
Dondero v. Vansickle, 346.
Dongrey v. Topping, 110.
Donlin v. Bradley, 238.
Donnelly v. Donnelly's Heirs, 84.
   v. Simonton, 229.
Donohue v. Chase, 200.
   v. McNichol, 171.
Donovan v. Donovan, 193.
Dooley v. Crist, 10.
   v. Potter, 202.
Doolittle v. Tice, 459.
Doremus v. Doremus, 107.
Doren v. Gillum, 284.
Dorkray v. Noble, 230, 231.
Dorr v. Dudderar, 195.
Dorrel v. Andrews, 141.
Dorsett v. Gray, 143.
Dorsey v. Hall, 184.
   v. Smith, 60.
Doswell v. De La Lanza, 467.
Doton v. Russell, 228.

Doty v. Hendrix, 109.
   v. Teller, 53.
Douglas v. Coonley, 357.
   v. West, 435.
Douglass v. Cline, 242.
   v. Dickson, 85.
   v. Durin, 212.
   v. McCrackin, 218.
   v. McKeever, 493.
   v. Wells, 208.
   v. Wiggins, 65.
Doupe v. Gerrin, 139.
Dow v. Doyle, 477.
   v. Whitney, 223.
Dowd v. Tucker, 271.
Dowling v. Hemings, 368.
Downard v. Groff, 10, 196.
Downer v. Miller, 204.
Downer's Adm'rs v. Smith, 444.
Downes v. Long, 288.
Downing v. Marshall, 478.
   v. Mayes, 466.
Downs v. Allen, 95.
Doyle v. Coburn, 114, 122.
   v. Lord, 364.
   v. Mellen, 195.
   v. Mullady, 51.
   v. Railway Co., 139.
Doyley v. Attorney General, 314.
D'Oyly v. Capp, 182.
Dozier v. Gregory, 65.
   v. Mitchell, 201.
Drake v. Drake, 313.
   v. Lacoe, 149, 151.
   v. Moore, 117.
   v. Paige, 185.
   v. Root, 119.
   v. Wells, 349, 407.
Drane v. Gregory's Heirs, 144.
Draper v. Draper, 180.
   v. Morris, 110.
Drda v. Schmidt, 148.
Dreutzer v. Bell, 393.
Drew v. Swift, 422.
Driscoll v. Marshall, 166.
Driver v. Edgar, 284.
Drost v. Hall, 99.
Droste v. Hall, 98.
Drown v. Smith, 63, 64.
Druid Park Heights Co. of Baltimore City v. Oettinger, 315.

CASES CITED.

[The figures refer to pages.]

Drury v. Bachelder, 121.
   v. Drury, 107.
   v. Foster, 428.
   v. Kent, 375.
Drybutter v. Bartholomew, 25.
Dubois v. Beaver, 4.
   v. Campau, 341.
   v. Kelly, 17, 22.
   v. Ray, 324.
Du Bois v. Ray, 324.
Dubs v. Dubs, 78.
Dubuque v. Coman, 461.
Dubuque Nat. Bank v. Weed, 186.
Dubuque & P. R. Co. v. Litchfield, 401.
Duclaud v. Rousseau, 184.
Ducote v. Rachal, 120.
Dudden v. Guardians of Poor of the Clutton Union, 371.
Dudley v. Bosworth, 268.
   v. Easton, 104.
   v. Foote, 14.
   v. Warde, 20.
Duer v. Boyd, 49.
Duffy v. Duffy, 109.
Dugdale, In re, 395.
Dugger v. Dugger, 78.
Duinneen v. Rich, 350.
Duke v. Brandt, 106.
   v. Bulme, 192.
   v. Compton, 148.
Duke of Cumberland v. Codrington, 205.
Duke of Devonshire v. Eglin, 168.
Duke of Norfolk's Case, 326.
Duke of Somerset v. Fogwell, 374, 415.
Dulanty v. Pynchon. 122.
Dumpor's Case, 175.
Dunagan v. Webster, 125.
Duncan v. City of Terre Haute, 105.
   v. Dick, 83.
   v. Drury, 231.
   v. Forrer, 343.
   v. Hodges, 428.
   v. Miller, 181.
   v. Rodecker, 357.
   v. Sylvester, 344, 345.
Duncklee v. Webber, 138.
Dungannon v. Smith, 324.
Dunham v. Kirkpatrick, 7.
   v. Provision Co., 182.
Dunklee v. Adams, 176.

Dunklee v. Railroad Co., 352, 445.
Dunlap v. Stetson, 423.
Dunman v. Railway Co., 22.
Dunn v. Flood, 327.
   v. Games, 417.
   v. Robbins, 135.
Dunn v. Sharpe, 182.
Dunn v. Zwilling, 263.
Dunning v. Bank, 209.
Dunphy v. Goodlander, 150.
Dunscomb v. Dunscomb, 78.
Dunseth v. Bank, 97.
Dunton v. McCook, 187, 468.
   v. Woodbury, 121.
Dunwoodie v. Reed, 302.
Durando v. Durando, 91, 92.
Durant v. Muller, 53.
Durel v. Boisblanc, 364.
Durette v. Briggs, 193.
Durfee v. Joslyn, 487.
Durham v. Angier, 111.
Durkee v. Felton, 102.
Dussaume v. Burnett, 437.
Dustin v. Cowdry, 165.
   v. Steele, 107.
Dutton v. Ives, 211, 232.
   v. McReynolds, 225.
   v. Warschauer, 184.
Duty v. Graham, 240.
Duval v. Becker, 195.
Dwight v. Eastman, 289.
D'Wolf v. Gardner, 322.
Dwyre v. Speer, 420.
Dye v. Mann, 123, 240.
Dyer v. Bank, 494.
   v. Clark, 93, 340.
   v. Sanford, 167, 357.
Dyer's Appeal, 262.
Dyett v. Pendleton, 138.
Dyke v. Rendall, 108.
Dyson v. Sheley, 119.

E

Eager v. Furnivall, 75.
Eagle v. Emmet, 99.
   v. Swayze, 139.
Eagle Fire Ins. Co. v. Cammet, 246.
Eales v. Drake, 317.
Earl v. De Hart, 368, 371.
Earle v. Fiske, 224.

[The figures refer to pages.]

Earle's Adm'rs v. Earle, 435.
Earl of Buckinghamshire v. Drury, 107.
Earnhart v. Earnhart, 297.
Eastman v. Batchelder, 181.
Easton v. Bank, 250.
East Tennessee Iron & Coal Co. v. Wiggin, 457, 461.
Eaton v. Eaton, 384.
 v. Simonds, 91, 202.
 v. Straw, 308.
 v. Winnie, 166.
Eberlein v. Abel, 162.
Ebert v. Wood, 344.
Eberts v. Fisher, 344.
Ecclesiastical Com'rs v. Kino, 364.
 v. O'Connor, 141.
Echols v. Cheney, 432.
Eckford v. Berry, 189.
Eckman v. Eckman, 410.
 v. Scott, 121.
Eddy v. St. Mars, 472.
Edesheimer v. Quackenbush, 138.
Edgar v. Jewell, 154.
Edgerton v. Jones, 438.
 v. McMullan, 357.
Edgerton v. Page, 141.
 v. Young, 231.
Edmands v. Insurance Co., 198.
Edminster v. Higgins, 192.
Edmondson v. Welsh, 85.
Edrington v. Harper, 71.
Edsell v. Buchanan, 238.
Edson v. Munsell, 468.
Edwards v. Banksmith, 218.
 v. Bibb, 86, 88.
 v. Hammond, 171.
 v. Thompson, 217.
 v. Trumbull, 192.
Edwardsville R. Co. v. Sawyer, 36.
Egbert v. Egbert, 114.
Ege v. Medlar, 78.
 v. Medlay, 77.
Egerton v. Brownlow, 299, 300.
 v. Massey, 294.
Egerton's Case, 262.
Eggert v. Beyer, 226.
Eggleston v. Bradford, 420.
Ehle v. Brown, 217, 225.
Ehrisman v. Sener, 59.
Eichengreen v. Appel, 163.
Ekin v. McCracken, 384.
Elam v. Parkhill, 20, 61.

Eldredge v. Torrestal, 91.
Eldridge v. Parish, 465.
Ellicott v. Mosier, 98, 100.
 v. Pearl, 459, 462.
 v. Welch, 90.
Elliot v. Carter, 474.
 v. Railway Co., 369.
 v. Smith, 61, 144, 145, 304.
Elliott v. Elliott, 327, 328.
 v. Parker, 493.
 v. Pearsoll, 51.
 v. Pray, 142.
 v. Sleeper, 416.
Ellis v. Alford, 386.
 v. Dittey, 75.
 v. Drake, 243.
 v. Leek, 248.
 v. Page, 475.
 v. Paige, 150, 157.
 v. White, 113.
Ellison v. Daniels, 196.
Ellsworth v. Cook, 75.
 v. Lockwood, 203.
 v. Nelson, 493.
 v. Railroad Co., 428.
Elmendorf v. Lockwood, 110.
Elmer v. Loper, 202.
Elmore v. Elmore, 119.
Elston v. Jasper, 131.
Elwes v. Maw, 17, 20.
Elwood v. Klock, 386.
Ely v. Dix, 322.
 v. Ely, 199, 229.
 v. Scofield, 226.
 v. Wilcox, 217, 220, 222.
Elyton Land Co. v. Denny, 111.
 v. South & North Alabama R. Co., 171.
Emans v. Turnbull, 470, 471.
Embrey v. Owen, 369, 370.
Emerson v. Atwater, 187.
 v. Cutler, 336.
 v. Mooney, 351.
 v. Proprietors of Land, 448.
Emerson's Homestead, In re, 116.
Emery v. Chase, 264.
 v. Darling, 489.
 v. Fowler, 425.
 v. Van Syckel, 41.
Emmons v. Scudder, 164.
Emson v. Polhemus, 344.
Engel v. Ayer, 36.

CASES CITED. 523

[The figures refer to pages.]

Engle v. Hall, 230.
v. White, 489.
Engleman Transp. Co. v. Longwell, 200.
English v. Young, 408.
Ennor v. Thompson, 188.
Ensminger v. People, 5, 370.
Enyard v. Nevins, 346.
Episcopal City Mission v. Appleton, 170.
Equitable Trust Co. v. Christ, 12.
Erb v. Brown, 358.
Erickson v. Willard, 261.
Erskine v. Davis, 417.
Ervin v. Morris, 456.
Erwin v. Olmsted, 340.
Eschmann v. Alt, 246.
Espley v. Wilkes, 361.
Estabrook v. Hapgood, 60.
v. Smith, 445, 446.
Ettlinger v. Carpet Co., 245.
Eulrich v. Richter, 369, 371.
Evans v. Brady, 36.
v. Calman, 118.
v. Evans, 77, 88.
v. Horan, 384.
v. Iglehart, 9.
v. Kimball, 231.
v. Kingsberry, 23, 24.
v. Lobdale, 80, 83.
v. McKanna, 153.
v. Walker, 323.
Evelyn v. Evelyn, 205.
Everly v. Harrison, 270.
Eversole v. Early, 447.
Everts v. Agnes, 215, 436.
Ewer v. Hobbs, 183.
Ewing v. Burnet, 460.
v. Elcorn, 459.
v. Shannahan, 36, 37.
Ewing's Lessee v. Burnet, 462.
Excelsior Fire Ins. Co. v. Royal Ins. Co., 199.
Exton v. Scott, 433.
Eyrick v. Hetrick, 396.
Eyster v. Hatheway, 126.

F

Fager v. Campbell, 494.
Fairbank v. Cudworth, 195.

Fairchild v. Chastelleux, 71.
v. Chaustelleux, 71.
v. Fairchild, 340.
v. Marshall, 109.
Faivre v. Daley, 122.
Falhers v. Corbret, 378.
Fallass v. Pierce, 213.
Falls v. Wright, 101.
Falls Manuf'g Co. v. Oconto River Imp. Co., 6.
Falls of Neuse Manuf'g Co. v. Brooks, 461.
Faloon v. Simshauser, 470.
Fanning v. Willcox, 467.
Farewell v. Dickenson, 378.
Farinholt v. Luckhard, 126.
Farley v. Craig, 377.
v. Parker, 384.
Farmer v. Farmer, 384.
v. Simpson, 125.
Farmers' Loan & Trust Co. v. Grape Creek Coal Co., 241.
v. Hendrickson, 14, 16.
v. St. Joseph & D. C. R. Co., 14.
Farmers' Nat. Bank v. Fletcher, 211.
Farmers' & Manufacturers' Bank v. Haight, 429.
Farmers' & Mechanics' Bank v. Gregory, 338.
Farmers' & Merchants' Nat. Bank v. Wallace, 338.
Farncombe's Trusts, In re, 312.
Farnum v. Metcalf, 234.
v. Platt, 361.
Farrar v. Bridges, 433.
v. Chauffetete, 12, 19.
v. Heinrich, 457, 458, 465.
v. Stackpole, 14.
Farrington v. Barr, 266.
Farris v. Farris, 269.
v. Houston, 200.
Farrow's Heirs v. Edmundson, 158.
Farwell v. Antis, 237.
Fash v. Blake, 428.
Fassett v. Smith, 214.
Faulkner v. Wynford, 313.
Faulkner's Adm'x v. Brockenbrough, 184.
Fauntleroy's Heirs v. Dunn, 408.
Faure v. Winans, 199.
Fay v. Brewer, 65.
v. Muzzey, 17.

524 CASES CITED.

[The figures refer to pages.]

Fay v. Taft, 255.
v. Valentine, 213.
Faylor v. Brice, 151.
Featherstonhaugh v. Fenwick, 270.
Feger v. Keefer, 490.
Felcher v. McMillan, 16.
Feldes v. Duncan, 121.
Felgner v. Hooper, 255.
Feliz v. Feliz, 341.
Felton v. Billups, 484.
v. Le Breton, 250.
v. West, 241.
Fennell v. Guffey, 149.
Fentiman v. Smith, 168.
Fenton v. Circuit Judge, 345.
v. Miller, 335.
v. Montgomery, 143.
v. Reed, 84.
Fergus v. Wilmarth, 198.
Ferguson v. Glassford, 227, 230.
v. Kingsland, 437.
v. Kumler, 122.
v. Thomason, 38.
v. Tweedy, 79.
Ferrall v. Kent, 154.
Ferrel v. Woodward, 380.
Ferrier v. Jay, 316.
Ferris v. Coover, 491.
v. Ferris, 109.
v. Quinby, 15.
Ferry v. Burnell, 95.
Festing v. Allen, 293.
Fetrow v. Merriwether, 410.
Fetters v. Humphreys, 354.
Fidelity Insurance, Trust & Safe-Deposit Co. v. Dietz, 290.
Fidler v. Lash, 317.
Fiedler v. Darrin, 188.
Field v. Barling, 3, 364.
v. Driving Co., 370.
v. Herrick, 131.
v. Howell, 133.
v. Mark, 359.
Fields v. Austin, 115.
v. Bush, 59.
v. Watson, 297.
Filbert v. Hoff, 341.
Fillebrown v. Hoar, 140.
Final v. Backus, 438.
Finch v. Turner, 489.
Findlay v. Smith, 63.

Finkelstein v. Herson, 161.
Finlay v. King, 172.
v. Mitchell, 172.
Finley v. Hogan, 461.
v. Simpson, 378, 432.
Firestone v. Firestone, 105.
First Nat. Bank v. Andrews, 210.
v. Bruce, 125.
v. Caldwell, 192.
v. Essex, 232.
v. Hanna, 487.
v. Salem Capital Flour-Mills Co., 194.
v. Security Bank, 441.
Fischer v. Silkmann, 468.
Fish v. Capwell, 167.
v. French, 211.
v. Glover, 208.
Fishback v. Lane, 123.
Fishburne v. Engledove, 145.
Fisher v. Cornell, 121.
v. Deering, 148.
v. Dixon, 20.
v. Edington, 294.
v. Fields, 261, 262.
v. Hall, 433, 435.
v. Lighthall, 139.
v. Milmine, 195.
v. Rochester, 423.
v. Saffer, 11.
v. Smith, 422.
v. Strickler, 410.
v. Taylor, 396.
Fisk v. Eastman, 92.
Fitch v. Baldwin, 444, 453.
v. McDowell, 211.
v. Pinckard, 209.
v. Rawling, 354.
v. Stallings, 202.
Fitzgerald v. Anderson, 23.
v. Libby, 223.
Fitzhugh v. Croghan, 444.
v. Foote, 96.
v. Smith, 191.
Fladung v. Rose, 337.
Flagg v. Bean, 80, 416.
v. Eames, 419.
v. Flagg, 197.
v. Geltmacher, 207.
v. Mann, 217.
v. Munn, 190.

CASES CITED. 525

[The figures refer to pages.]

Flanagan v. Young, 438.
Flanders v. Davis, 385.
   v. Lamphear, 181, 197.
Flannagan v. Philadelphia, 5.
Fleet v. Dorland, 60.
   v. Hegeman, 5.
Fleetwood v. Lord, 113.
Fleischman v. Toplitz, 153.
Fleming v. Griswold, 469.
   v. Townsend, 393.
Flentham v. Steward, 241.
Fletcher v. Ashburner, 23, 24.
   v. Bank, 125.
   v. Boom Co., 423.
   v. Carpenter, 210.
   v. Cary, 243.
   v. Fletcher, 48.
   v. Holmes, 184.
   v. Peck, 399.
Flickinger v. Shaw, 167.
Fliess v. Buckley, 209.
Flood v. Flood, 164.
Florida S. R. Co. v. Loring, 462.
Flournoy v. Flournoy, 72.
Flower v. Elwood, 229.
   v. Peck, 175.
Flowers v. Flowers, 106.
Fluke v. Fluke, 23.
Flynn v. Flynn, 428.
Fogarty v. Stack, 300.
Fogg v. Fogg, 120.
Folk v. Varn, 4344.
Follendore v. Thomas, 360.
Follett v. Grant, 443.
Folsom v. Carli, 123.
Folts v. Huntley, 140, 377.
Foltz v. Huntley, 377.
Fonda v. Sage, 176.
Fontaine v. Savings Inst., 85.
Foot v. Dickinson, 304.
   v. New Haven & Northampton Co. 166.
Foote v. City of Cincinnati, 153.
   v. Colvin, 270.
   v. Insurance Co., 198.
Forbes v. Balenseifer, 350.
   v. Dunham, 339.
   v. Smith, 78.
Force v. Dutcher, 432.
Ford v. Cobb, 13.
   v. Erskine, 101.
   v. Ford, 110, 301, 474.

Ford v. Garner's Adm'r, 32.
   v. Gregory's Heirs, 9, 428.
   v. Harris, 357, 359.
   v. Irwin, 188.
   v. Johnson, 47.
   v. Knapp, 345.
   v. Marcall, 217.
Fore v. Fore, 113, 114.
Forsythe v. Ballance, 403.
   v. Price, 8.
Fort v. Allen, 453.
Forth v. Chapman, 326.
   v. Duke of Norfolk, 274.
Ft. Plain Bridge Co. v. Smith, 363, 379, 380.
Fosdick v. Fosdick, 325.
   v. Gooding, 98.
Foss v. Crisp, 81.
Foster v. Browning, 350.
   v. Carson, 226.
   v. Dwinel, 89.
   v. Fowler, 379.
   v. Hickox, 247.
   v. Hilliard, 60.
   v. Joice, 36.
   v. Mansfield, 434, 436.
   v. Marshall, 73, 75, 80, 458.
   v. Robinson, 9.
   v. Van Reed, 199.
   v. Wright, 471.
Foster's Appeal, 226.
Fothergil v. Fothergil, 318.
Foulke v. Bond, 465.
Fowler v. Bott, 140.
   v. Fowler, 342.
   v. Poling, 448.
   v. Shearer, 106, 432.
Fowley v. Palmer, 199.
Fox v. Blossom, 237.
   v. Hinton, 462.
   v. Phelps, 474.
Fox's Case, 148.
Frafton v. Hawes, 427.
Francestown v. Deering, 268.
Francis v. Porter, 184, 240.
   v. Wells, 192.
Francis' Appeal, 359.
Frank v. Hicks, 185, 191.
Frankenthal v. Mayer, 195.
Franklin v. Osgood, 315.
   v. Talmadge, 417.
Franklin Ins. Co. v. Cousens, 359.

[The figures refer to pages.]

Fraser v. Trustees, 24.
Fratcher v. Smith, 145.
Frazer v. Hightower, 78.
Frazier v. Caruthers, 152.
Frederick's Appeal, 473.
Free v. Beatley, 93.
   v. Stuart, 23.
Freeman, In re, 80.
   v. Foster, 448.
   y. Hunnewell, 142.
   v. Pope, 393.
Freiberg v. Walzem, 125.
Freke v. Carbery, 475.
French v. French, 406.
   v. Fuller, 142.
   v. Kennedy, 203.
   v. Lord, 93, 104.
   v. Marstin, 360, 361.
   v. Pearce, 464.
   v. Peters, 96.
   v. Pratt, 96, 97.
   v. Richards, 140.
   v. Rollins, 59, 81.
   v. Row, 182.
   v. Turner, 211.
Frey v. Lowden, 357.
Frick v. Fiscus, 454.
Frick Co. v. Taylor, 269.
Friedland v. Myers, 135.
Friedlander v. Ryder, 22.
Friedley v. Hamilton, 187.
Friend v. Supply Co., 140.
Frink v. Le Roy, 238.
   v. Pond, 439.
Frisbee v. Frisbee, 238.
Fritz v. Tudor, 97.
Frogmorton v. Wharrey, 297.
Frohman v. Dickinson, 367.
Frommer v. Roessler, 140.
Frost, In re, 323.
   v. Bank, 230, 235.
   v. Beekman, 221.
   v. Cattle Co., 431.
   v. Iron Co., 150.
   v. Koon, 247.
   v. Rainbow, 118.
   v. Shaw, 207.
   v. Society, 412, 454.
Frothingham, In re, 57.
Frye v. President, etc., 225.
Fryer v. Rockefeller, 220.
Fuchs v. Fuchs, 489.

Fullam v. Stearns, 13.
Fuller, Ex parte, 475.
   v. Dauphin, 423.
   v. Griffith, 224.
   v. Montague, 345.
   v. Tabor, 21.
   v. Trust Co., 187.
Fulmer v. Williams, 370.
Funk v. Creswell, 411, 447.
   v. Eggleston, 39, 309, 316.
   v. Haldeman, 166.
   v. Vonelda, 441.
Furenes v. Michelson, 388.
Furguson v. Bond, 187, 434.
Furnish v. Rogers, 290.
Fusselman v. Worthington, 144, 158.
Fyffe v. Beers, 116, 121.

G

Gadberry v. Sheppard, 170.
Gaffield v. Hapgood, 18, 19.
Gaffney v. Hicks, 208.
Gage v. Gage, 268, 433.
   v. McDermid, 228.
   v. Sanborn, 412.
Gaines v. Gaines' Ex'r, 105.
   v. Mining Co., 64.
   v. Walker, 246.
Gainsford v. Dunn, 313.
Galbraith v. Gedge, 340.
   v. Reeves, 194.
Gale v. Nixon, 145.
   v. Ward, 19.
   v. Williamson, 427.
Gale's Ex'rs v. Morris, 191, 192.
Galford v. Gillett, 245.
Gallagher v. Shipley, 17.
Gallatin Co. v. Beattie, 184.
Galliers v. Moss, 255.
Galloway v. Findley, 404.
   v. Robinson, 484.
Galpin v. Abbott, 220.
Galt v. Galloway, 403, 404.
Galway v. Bryce, 397.
Gambette v. Brock, 117.
Games v. Stiles, 417.
Gamut v. Gregg, 248.
Gann v. Chester, 193.
Gannon v. Hargadon, 371.
Gano v. Aldridge, 421.

CASES CITED.

[The figures refer to pages.]

Ganson v. Baldwin, 159.
Garaly v. Dubose, 116.
Gardiner v. Derring, 64.
Gardner v. Astor, 273.
    v. Brown, 246.
    v. Finley, 14.
    v. Greene, 91, 92, 105.
    v. Hooper, 80.
    v. Keteltas, 133.
    v. Lansing, 247.
    v. Ogden, 270.
    v. Pace, 416.
    v. Webber, 181.
Garfield v. Williams, 443.
Garland v. Watson, 250.
Garner v. Anderson, 491.
Garnett v. City of Slater, 360.
Garnhart v. Finney, 152.
Garnsey v. Rogers, 208.
Garr v. Elble, 488.
Garrard v. Garrard, 108.
Garrett v. Clark, 56.
    v. Jones, 122.
    v. Moss, 386.
    v. Puckett, 216, 244.
    v. Wagner, 489.
Garrison v. Hayden, 221.
    v. Rudd, 355.
Garson v. Green, 193.
Garth v. Baldwin, 297.
Garwood v. Railroad Co., 369.
Gary v. Eastabrook, 120.
    v. Woodham, 466.
Garza v. Investment Co., 199.
Gashe v. Young, 267.
Gaskell v. Viquesney, 200.
Gass v. Wilhite, 277.
Gassett v. Grout, 393.
Gaston v. Wright, 73.
Gatenby v. Morgan, 302.
Gates v. Ege, 237.
    v. M'Daniel, 380.
    v. Sutherland, 187.
Gatewood v. Tomlinson, 85.
Gaunt v. Wainman, 87.
Gause v. Hale, 259.
    v. Wiley, 48.
Gavit's Adm'rs v. Chambers, 5, 423.
Gay v. Hamilton, 189.
Gayle v. Wilson, 207.
Gebhardt v. Reeves, 178.
Geer v. Hamblin, 92.

Geib v. Reynolds, 229.
Geiger v. Bolles, 432.
    v. Peterson, 210.
Gelston v. Thompson, 200.
Gelzer v. Gelzer, 108.
Gent v. Harrison, 62.
Genter v. Morrison, 439.
Gentry v. Wagstaff, 79.
George v. Andrews, 208.
    v. Bates, 420.
    v. Kent, 216.
    v. Putney, 144.
    v. Wood, 223.
Gerber v. Grabel, 364.
Gerdine v. Menage, 206, 207.
Germania Bldg. Ass'n v. Neill, 228.
German Sav. & Loan Soc. v. De Lashmutt, 384.
Gerrard v. Cooke, 361.
Gerrish v. Clough, 472.
    v. Shattuck, 356.
Gervoyes' Case, 108.
Gest v. Flock, 438.
    v. Packwood, 191.
Getzler v. Saroni, 123.
Gibbs v. Estey, 20.
    v. Johnson, 232.
    v. Swift, 437.
    v. Williams, 371.
Gilbert v. Peteler, 170.
Gibson v. Crehore, 91, 231, 247.
    v. Gibson, 107.
    v. Hough, 209.
    v. Hutchins, 187.
    v. Kelly, 6.
    v. Kirk, 378.
    v. Leonard, 166.
    v. McCormick, 205.
    v. Oliver, 151.
    v. Railway Co., 22.
    v. Sopher, 385.
Giddings v. Sears, 394.
    v. Smith, 49.
Giesen v. White, 288.
Gifford v. Corrigan, 208.
    v. McArthur, 370.
    v. Yarborough, 471.
Gilbert v. Bulkley, 135.
    v. Cowan, 124.
    v. Insurance Co., 436.
    v. Penn, 184.

[The figures refer to pages.]

Gilchrist v. Brown, 267.
   v. Gough, 224.
   v. McLaughlin, 465.
Gilfillan v. Chatterton, 493.
Gill v. Fauntleroy's Heirs, 438.
   v. Lyon, 237.
   v. Middleton, 139.
   v. Pinney's Adm'r, 220.
Gillespie v. Allison, 283.
   v. Miller, 286.
   v. Reed, 219.
   v. Worford, 81.
Gillett v. Balcom, 196.
Gillis v. Bailey, 175.
   v. Brown, 86.
   v. Chase, 369.
Gilman v. Hamilton, 275.
   v. Wills, 10, 196.
Gilmore v. Burch, 78.
   v. Driscoll, 365.
   v. Hamilton, 55.
   v. Severn, 289.
   v. Wilbur, 343.
Gilpin v. Hollingsworth, 337.
Gilson v. Gilson, 186.
Girard v. Mayor, etc., 474.
Girardin v. Lampe, 227.
Gladding v. Warner, 202.
Gladwyn v. Hitchman, 240.
Glascock v. Robards, 156.
Glasgow v. Baker, 455.
Glasgow College v. Attorney General, 276.
Gleason v. Kinney's Adm'r, 182, 235.
   v. Smith, 447.
Gledden v. Bennett, 20.
Glenn v. Clark, 85, 89.
   v. Glenn, 313.
Glidden v. Hunt, 213, 427.
   v. Strupler, 386.
Globe Ins. Co. v. Lansing, 242.
Glover v. Powell, 6.
Godall v. Mopley, 245.
Godbold v. Freestone, 484.
Goddard v. Chase, 19.
   v. Winchell, 7.
Godfrey v. Humphrey, 38.
Godman v. Simmons, 305.
Godolphin v. Abingdon, 479.
Godwin v. Collins, 192.
   v. King, 110.
Goedeke v. Baker, 143.

Goff v. Anderson, 74.
Golmes v. Redmon, 440.
Going v. Emery, 275.
Gold v. Ogden, 208.
Golden v. Hardesty, 433.
Goldsborough v. Martin, 328.
Goldsbrough v. Gable, 160.
Goldsmith v. Goldsmith, 269.
Goltermann v. Schiermeyer, 459, 463.
Gomber v. Hackett, 152.
Gomez v. Gomez, 133.
Gooch v. Atkins, 95.
   v. Botts, 202.
Gooch's Case, 392.
Goodale v. Gawthorne, 480.
Goodall v. McLean, 478.
Goodell v. Jackson, 400.
Goodenough v. Warren, 223.
Goodenow v. Allen, 159.
   v. Ewer, 248.
Goodnow v. Lumber Co., 383.
Goodrich v. Burbank, 355, 373.
   v. Jones, 14, 18.
Goodright v. Cordwent, 162.
   v. Davids, 175.
   v. Dunham, 287, 290.
   v. Morningstar, 42.
   v. Richardson, 134.
Goodrum v. Goodrum, 98, 109.
Goods of Merritt, In re, 317.
Goodspeed v. Fuller, 427.
Goodtitle v. Billington, 292.
   v. Otway, 476.
   v. Way, 131.
Goodwin v. Clark, 326.
   v. Folsom, 454.
   v. Gilbert, 378, 432.
   v. Goodwin, 87.
   v. Holbrook, 441.
   v. Richardson, 336.
   v. Thompson, 5.
Gordon v. Bank, 198.
   v. George, 136.
   v. Smith, 234.
Gore v. Gore, 299.
Goree v. Wadsworth, 431.
Gorham v. Electric Co., 426.
Goring's Ex'rs v. Shreve, 209.
Goss v. Froman, 103.
Gosselin v. Smith, 342, 468.
Gossett v. Drydale, 9, 143.
Gossin v. Brown, 204.

CASES CITED. 529

[The figures refer to pages.]

Gott v. Cook, 255.
Gouhenant v. Cockrell, 121.
Gould v. Lamb, 261, 262.
   v. Marsh, 211.
   v. Orphan Asylum, 24.
   v. School Dist., 147.
   v. Thompson, 156.
Gourley v. Woodbury, 288.
Gove v. Gove, 325.
Govin v. De Miranda, 260.
Gowan v. Fountain, 113.
Gowen v. Exchange Co., 166.
Gower v. Howe, 245.
   v. Quinlan, 340.
   v. Winchester, 247.
Grabenhorst v. Nicodemus, 141.
Grabfelder v. Gazetti, 132.
Grace, Ex parte, 270.
Graff v. Middleton, 223.
Graff's Estate, In re, 203.
Graham v. Anderson, 141.
   v. Burch, 477.
   v. Dempsey, 162.
   v. Dunigan, 102.
   v. Graham, 107.
   v. Houghtalin, 289.
   v. King, 315.
   v. Linden, 230.
   v. Van Wyck, 106.
Graham's Heirs v. Graham, 94.
Grainsford v. Dunn, 313.
Grandin v. Hernandez, 429.
Grand Island Sav. & Loan Ass'n v. Moore, 207, 241.
Grand Junction Canal Co. v. Shugar, 371.
Grandona v. Lovdal, 4.
Granger v. Brown, 162.
   v. Roll, 207.
Grannis v. Clark, 138.
Grant v. Bennett, 218.
   v. Chase, 351.
   v. Duane, 234.
   v. Hill, 449.
   v. Lynam, 316.
   v. Sutton, 84.
Grape Creek Coal Co. v. Farmers' Loan & Trust Co., 182, 185.
Grapengether v. Fejervary, 210.
Graves v. Berdan, 153.
   v. Colwell, 455.
   v. Dolphin, 397.

Graves v. Fligor, 105.
   v. Graves' Ex'r, 219, 475.
   v. Weld, 8.
Gray v. Blanchard, 170, 174.
   v. Cuthbertson, 137.
   v. Johnson, 143.
   v. McCune, 107.
   v. Mathis, 71.
   v. Packer, 57.
   v. Robinson, 154, 155.
   v. Shaw, 249.
   v. Waldron, 210.
   v. Worst, 143.
Graydon's Ex'rs v. Graydon, 173.
Great Falls Co. v. Worster, 197.
Greatrex v. Hayward, 372.
Green v. Armstrong, 8.
   v. Arnold, 346.
   v. Biddle, 21.
   v. Bridges, 176.
   v. Claiborne, 319.
   v. Cross, 238.
   v. Drinker, 220.
   v. Garrington, 222.
   v. Goff, 357.
   v. Green, 383, 481.
   v. Hall, 207, 241.
   v. Hewitt, 292.
   v. Liter, 75, 76.
   v. Marks, 123.
   v. Pettingill, 243.
   v. Phillips, 15.
   v. Putnam, 91.
   v. Root, 125.
   v. Rumph, 259.
   v. Sherrod, 187.
   v. Slayter, 216.
   v. Spicer, 397.
   v. Wilding, 383.
Greenbaum v. Austrian, 106.
Green Bay & M. Canal Co. v. Hewitt, 412.
   v. Kaukauna Water Power Co., 353, 369.
Greenby v. Wilcocks, 448.
Greene v. Reynolds, 88.
Greenleaf v. Grounder, 489.
Greenley v. Wilcocks, 443.
Greeno v. Munson, 144.
Greensburg Fuel Co. v. Irwin Nat. Gas Co., 228.
Green's Estate, In re, 38.

REAL PROP.—34

[The figures refer to pages.]

Greenwell v. Heritage, 204.
Greenwood v. Maddox, 113, 116, 126.
   v. Tyler, 419.
   v. Verdon, 326.
Greenwood's Appeal, 264.
Greer v. Haugabook, 379.
   v. Turner, 201.
Gregg v. Bostwick, 118, 119.
   v. Boyd, 9, 143.
   v. Patterson, 336.
   v. Railway Co., 21.
Gregory v. Oates, 121.
   v. Thomas, 229.
   v. Wilson, 151.
Gress Lumber Co. v. Coody, 420.
Grey v. McCune, 84.
   v. Mannock, 54.
Gridley v. Bingham, 393.
   v. Watson, 393.
Griffin v. Bixby, 4.
   v. Greutlen, 126.
   v. Griffin, 192.
   v. Marine Co., 249.
   v. Reece, 104.
   v. Sheffield, 164.
Griffith v. Schwenderman, 131.
Griggs v. Smith, 85.
Grim, Appeal of, 452.
Grimes v. Kimball, 230.
   v. Ragland, 462.
   v. Wilson, 94.
Grimes' Ex'rs v. Harmon, 277.
Grimshaw v. Belcher, 167.
Griswold v. Huffaker, 118.
   v. Johnson, 335.
   v. Little, 464.
Groesbeck v. Seeley, 438.
Groff v. Rohrer, 266.
Groft v. Weakland, 466.
Grogan v. Garrison, 108.
Grommes v. Trust Co., 149.
Groneweg v. Beck, 122.
Groome v. Almstead, 156.
   v. Ogden City Corp., 138.
Gropengether v. Fejervary, 192.
Grosholz v. Newman, 119, 122.
Grosvenor v. Bowen, 322.
Grouch v. Lumber Co., 270.
Groustra v. Bourges, 158.
Grout v. Townsend, 77, 81.
Grover v. Thatcher, 231.
   v. Wakeman, 394.

Grube v. Wells, 464, 465.
Gruenewald v. Schaales, 161.
Gruhn v. Richardson, 126.
Grussy v. Schneider, 230.
Grute v. Locroft, 71.
Grymes v. Boweren, 18.
Gudgen v. Besset, 434.
Guerin v. Moore, 98.
Guertin v. Mombleau, 452, 455.
Guest v. Farley, 256.
   v. Reynolds, 364.
Guffy v. Hukill, 175.
Guild v. Richards, 174.
Guion v. Anderson, 73, 74.
Gulf, C. & S. F. Ry. Co. v. Smith, 142.
Gully v. Ray, 89.
Gumbel v. Boyer, 211.
Gumbert's Appeal, 267.
Gunn v. Barry, 125.
Gunning v. Cusack, 356.
Guunison v. Twitchel, 84.
Gunson v. Healy, 360.
Gunyon's Estate, In re, 109.
Guthrie v. Gardner, 268.
   v. Jones, 16.
Gutman v. Buckler, 315.
Gwaltney v. Land Co., 370.
Gwynn v. Thomas, 450.
Gwynne v. City of Cincinnati, 105.

H

Haaven v. Hoaas, 268.
Hacker's Appeal, 316.
Hackett v. Marmet Co., 144.
   v. Reynolds, 192.
Hackwith v. Damron, 216.
Hadley v. Stewart, 202.
Haflick v. Stober, 20, 22.
Hagan v. Varney, 61.
Hagar v. Brainerd, 184.
   v. Wiswall, 346.
Hageman v. Hageman, 296.
Haggerty v. Hockenberry, 288.
Hagthorp v. Hook's Adm'rs, 201.
Haight v. Pearson, 269.
Haile v. Nichols, 206.
Haines v. Ellis, 82.
Hait v. Houle, 124.
Haldeman v. Bruckhart, 371.

CASES CITED.

[The figures refer to pages.]

Hale v. Hale, 317.
   v. James, 96, 98.
   v. Pew, 327.
   v. Plummer, 93.
Hales v. James, 96.
   v. Petit, 49.
Haley v. Colcord, 361.
Hall v. Bray, 447.
   v. Chaffee, 305.
   v. Crouse, 225.
   v. Dean, 445.
   v. Eaton, 424.
   v. Fields, 114, 115.
   v. Hall, 72, 491.
   v. Harris, 436.
   v. Lawrence, 375, 376.
   v. Nottingham, 354.
   v. Piddock, 345.
   v. Priest, 301.
   v. Savage, 107.
   v. Smith, 110.
   v. Stevens, 464.
   v. Thayer, 51.
   v. Vandegrift, 48.
   v. Wallace, 156.
Hallett v. Hallett, 87.
   v. Thompson, 41.
   v. Wylie, 140.
Hall's Lessee v. Vandegrift, 459.
Hallum v. Silliman, 317.
Halsey v. McCormick, 422, 471.
   v. Tate, 274, 275.
Halstead v. Lake Co., 388.
Hambrick v. Russell, 245.
   v. Security Co., 250.
Hamilton v. Buckwalter, 109.
   v. Cutts, 447.
   v. Denny, 341.
   v. Downer, 260.
   v. Elliott, 172, 174.
   v. Gilbert, 193.
   v. Pittock, 143.
   v. Ritchie, 475.
   v. Wentworth, 296.
   v. White, 356.
   v. Wilson, 443.
   v. Wright, 138.
Hamlin v. Hamlin, 89.
Hammerton v. Stead, 409.
Hammond v. Pennock, 265.
   v. Peyton, 194.
Hampton v. Holman, 327.

Hanchett v. Whitney, 162.
Hancock v. Beverly's Heirs, 224.
   v. Carlton, 175.
   v. Fleming, 232.
Handly's Lessee v. Anthony, 423.
Hanes v. Denby, 204.
Hanford v. Blessing, 190.
Hanks v. Enloe, 334.
Hanlon v. Doherty, 232.
Hannah v. Collins, 456.
   v. Henderson, 447.
   v. Swarner, 434.
Hannibal & St. J. R. Co. v. Green, 421.
Hanrahan v. O'Reilly, 450.
Hanrick v. Patrick, 454.
Hansard v. Hardy, 238.
Hansen v. Meyer, 136, 137.
Hanson v. Cochran, 438.
Hapgood v. Blood, 196.
   v. Houghton, 170.
Haralson v. Bridges, 71.
Harder v. Harder, 145.
Hardin v. Jordan, 423.
   v. Lawrence, 98.
   v. Osborne, 438.
Harding v. Allen, 223.
   v. Glyn, 313.
   v. Handy, 384.
   v. Manufacturing Co., 240.
Hare v. Stegall, 145.
Hargreaves, In re, 323.
   v. Menken, 241.
Harkness v. Sears, 17.
Harland v. Binks, 396.
Harlan's Heirs v. Seaton's Heirs, 224.
Harlow v. Thomas, 448.
Harmon v. Harmon, 392.
   v. Smith, 317.
Harper v. Edwards, 181.
   v. Ely, 200, 202, 250.
Harper's Appeal, 201.
Harral v. Leverty, 216.
Harries' Trust, In re, 317.
Harriman v. Gray, 107.
   v. Light Co., 180, 185.
Harris v. Carson, 9.
   v. Curran, 493.
   v. Frink, 8, 9, 157.
   v. Goslin, 143.
   v. Jex, 230.
   v. Knapp, 310.
   v. McElroy, 271.

CASES CITED.

[The figures refer to pages.]

Harris v. Richey, 464.
   v. Ryding, 366.
   v. Scovel, 10, 14.
   v. Sumner, 394.
Harrison v. Battle, 307.
   v. Boring, 349.
   v. Boyd, 94.
   v. Eldridge, 91.
   v. Foote, 171.
   v. Middleton, 158.
   v. Moore, 67.
   v. Ricks, 154.
   v. Simons, 416.
   v. Sterry, 41.
   v. Yerby, 210.
Hart v. Connor, 360.
   v. Dean, 32.
   v. Leete, 72.
   v. McCollum, 111.
   v. McGrew, 81.
   v. Randolph, 111.
Harter v. Twohig, 237.
Hartford Fire Ins. Co. v. Walsh, 198.
Hartley v. Harrison, 206, 207.
   v. Tatham, 207.
Hartley's Appeal, 189.
Hartman v. Fick, 357.
Harton v. Harton, 256.
Hartshorn v. Hubbard, 197.
Hartshorne v. Hartshorne, 90.
Hartwell v. Camman, 7.
   v. Kelly, 23.
   v. McDonald, 120.
Harvey v. Brisbin, 77, 317.
   v. Walters, 358, 372.
   v. Wickham, 75.
Harvill v. Holloway, 93.
Haskell v. Bissell, 220.
   v. Scott, 193.
Hasker v. Sutton, 285.
Haskins v. Tate, 58.
Hastings v. Clifford, 109.
   v. Dickinson, 107.
   v. Mace, 111.
   v. Stevens, 91.
Hasty v. Wheeler, 65.
Hatch v. Barr, 430.
   v. Ferguson, 455, 481.
   v. Haskins, 221.
   v. Hatch, 66, 429.
Hatcher v. Curtis, 321.

Hatfield v. Malcom, 246.
   v. Sneden, 77, 79.
Hathaway v. Insurance Co., 21.
   v. Payne, 434.
Hathon v. Lyon, 74.
Hattersley v. Bissett, 476.
Hauenstein v. Lynham, 388.
Haven v. Adams, 218.
   v. Foster, 205.
   v. Mehlgarten, 342.
Havens v. Electric Light Co., 19.
   v. Land Co., 305.
Haverstick v. Sipe, 364.
Haward v. Peavey, 288.
Hawes v. Wyatt, 477.
Hawkins v. Skeggs, 9.
   v. Skeggs' Adm'r, 62.
Hawksland v. Gatchel, 436.
Hawley v. Bradford, 90.
   v. Cramer, 270.
   v. James, 267.
   v. Northampton, 286, 302.
Haworth v. Taylor, 217, 221.
Hay v. Mayer, 77.
Hayden v. Merrill, 341.
   v. Paterson, 343.
   v. Smith, 229.
   v. Stoughton, 171.
Haydon v. Haydon, 489.
Hayes' Appeal, 345.
Hayes v. Di Vito, 361.
   v. Foorde, 297.
   v. Kershow, 260, 264.
   v. Mining Co., 16, 19.
   v. Railway Co., 171.
   v. Waldron, 369.
Hayner v. Smith, 138.
Haynes v. Boardman, 467.
   v. Investment Co., 151.
   v. King, 363.
   v. Powers, 101.
   v. Schaefer, 115.
Hays v. Cassell, 490.
Hayward v. Kinney, 59.
Haywood v. Building Soc., 351.
   v. Fulmer, 166.
   v. Rogers, 154.
Hazard v. Draper, 198.
   v. Robinson, 358.
Hazeltine v. Moore, 193.
Heald v. Heald, 324.

CASES CITED. 533

[The figures refer to pages.]

Healey v. Alston, 273.
   v. Worth, 219.
Heaney v. Heeney, 166.
Hearle v. Greenbank, 78.
Heasman v. Pearse, 324.
Heath v. Bishop, 397.
   v. Heath, 38.
   v. White, 74, 75.
Heaton v. Prather, 214, 221, 222.
Hebron Gravel Road Co. v. Harvey, 371.
Hecht v. Herrwagen, 153.
Heckman v. Swett, 5, 471.
Hedges v. Riker, 319.
Heelis v. Blain, 253.
Heermance v. Vernoy, 142.
Heffner v. Lewis, 11, 19.
Heibert v. Wren, 87.
Heidel v. Benedict, 118.
Heinouer v. Jones, 151.
Heintze v. Bentley, 139.
Heisen v. Heisen, 95, 99, 110.
Heister v. Madeira, 187.
Heister's Lessee v. Fortner, 219.
Heitkamp v. Granite Co., 195.
Helbreg v. Schumann, 189.
Hele v. Bond, 321.
Hellwig v. Bachman, 24.
Helm v. Boyd, 188.
   v. Gilroy, 21.
   v. Helm, 115.
   v. Webster, 178.
Helme v. Strater, 110.
Helmer v. Krolick, 211.
Helms v. Chadbourne, 214.
Hemenway v. Cutler, 21.
Hemphill v. Ross, 184.
Hempstead v. Easton, 455.
Henagan v. Harllee, 90.
Hender v. Rose, 109.
Henderson v. Baltimore, 428.
   v. Eason, 341.
   v. Ellerman, 491.
   v. Henderson, 297.
   v. Hunter, 177, 178.
   v. Truitt, 236.
   v. Vaulx, 322.
Hendrix v. McBeth, 88.
Hendrixson v. Cardwell, 9.
Hendy v. Dinkerhoff, 12.
Henegan v. Harllee, 90.
Henkel v. Bohnke, 204.

Henley v. Hotaling, 190.
Hennessy v. Patterson, 283.
Henning v. Burnet, 360.
Henry v. Simpson, 317.
   v. Tupper, 175.
Henry's Case, 20.
Henschel v. Mamero, 230.
Hensel v. Association, 126.
Hensey v. Hensey's Adm'r, 125.
Henshaw v. Bissell, 452.
   v. Wells, 184.
Herbemont's Ex'rs v. Thomas, 333.
Herber v. Thompson, 228.
Herbert v. Association, 204.
   v. Scofield, 192.
   v. Webster, 326.
Herdman v. Cooper, 117.
Herff v. Griggs, 206.
Herman v. Roberts, 357.
Herne v. Bembow, 63.
Herr v. Herr, 95.
Herrell v. Sizeland, 159.
Herrick v. Graves, 119, 121.
   v. Malin, 429.
Hersey v. Chapin, 158.
   v. Turbett, 218.
Hertell v. Van Buren, 314.
Hervey v. Hervey, 108.
Heslop v. Heslop, 103.
Hesnard v. Plunkett, 113, 127.
Hester v. Hunnicutt, 449.
Heth v. Cocke, 89, 91.
Hethrington v. Graham, 103.
Hetzel v. Barber, 322.
Hetzell v. Barber, 231.
Heuisler v. Nickum, 226.
Hewitt v. Rankin, 116, 117.
   v. Templeton, 123.
Hews v. Kenney, 267.
Hey v. Moorhouse, 145.
Heyward v. Judd, 248.
   v. Mining Co., 6.
Hiatt v. Parker, 181.
Hibberd v. Smith, 435.
Hicklin v. Marco, 201.
Hickman v. Irvine's Heirs, 87.
   v. Kempner, 493.
   v. Stewart, 450.
Hickox v. Railroad Co., 357.
Hicks v. Chapman, 131.
   v. Cochran, 337.
   v. Smith, 480.

[The figures refer to pages.]

Hiester v. Green, 192.
Higbie v. Westlake, 99.
Higginbottom v. Short, 346.
Higgins v. Bordages, 125, 489.
   v. Breen, 84.
   v. Higgins, 339.
   v. Kusterer, 7.
   v. West, 248.
Highstone v. Burdette, 463.
Highways Berridge v. Ward, 422.
Higinbotham v. Holme, 396.
   v. Stoddard, 424.
Hihn v. Peck, 342.
Hilburn v. Harris, 452.
Hildreth v. Conan, 158.
   v. Jones, 91.
Hiles v. Fisher, 338.
Hill v. Bacon, 288, 445.
   v. Barclay, 176.
   v. Crosby, 353.
   v. De Rochemont, 17.
   v. Epley, 451.
   v. Gibbs, 344.
   v. Gregory, 93.
   v. Hill, 15, 46, 48.
   v. Lord, 373.
   v. McNichol, 433.
   v. Meeker, 224.
   v. Murray, 214.
   v. Payson, 233.
   v. Railroad Co., 372.
   v. Robertson, 184.
   v. Roderick, 304.
   v. Sewald, 12.
   v. Townley, 247.
   v. Tupper, 355.
   v. Wentworth, 12.
Hillen v. Iselin, 329.
Hilliard v. Scoville, 345.
Hills v. Bishop, 4.
   v. Day, 346.
   v. Miller, 350, 355.
   v. Simonds, 325, 328.
Hill's Adm'rs v. Mitchell, 99.
Hilton v. Bank, 241.
Hinchliff v. Hinman, 433.
Hinchman v. Stiles, 91.
Hinde's Lessee v. Longworth, 393.
Hines v. Ament, 12.
Hinkley v. Black, 21.
   v. Wheelwright, 206.
Hinsdale v. Humphrey, 378.

Hirst's Estate, In re, 24.
Histe v. Buckley, 21.
Hitch v. Patten, 38.
Hitchcock v. Bank, 248.
Hitner v. Ege, 79.
Hitz v. Bank, 80, 83.
Hoban v. Cable, 420, 464.
Hobbs v. Harvey, 91.
   v. Trust Co., 185.
Hochenauer v. Hilderbrant, 135.
Hocker v. Gentry, 477.
Hocker's Appeal, 205.
Hodgdon v. Shannon, 181.
Hodge v. Amerman, 217.
Hodgen v. Guttery, 237.
Hodges v. Spicer, 57.
   v. Williams, 471.
Hodgkins v. Farrington, 168.
Hodgkinson, Petitioner, 345.
   v. Wood, 476.
Hodgson v. Halford, 172.
Hodson v. Treat, 206.
Hoeveler v. Fleming, 141.
Hoffar v. Dement, 337.
Hoffman v. Armstrong, 4.
   v. Clark, 164.
   v. Kuhn, 367.
   v. Stigers, 337, 338.
Hoff's Appeal, 204, 205.
Hofman v. Demple, 124.
Hogan v. Curtin, 173.
   v. Jaques, 266.
   v. Strayhorn, 266.
Hoge v. Hoge, 270.
Hogenson v. Railway Co., 372.
Hogg v. Water Co., 369.
Hogsett v. Ellis, 164.
Hoile v. Bailey, 188.
Hoitt v. Webb, 119, 122.
Holabird v. Burr, 201.
Holbird v. Anderson, 394.
Holbrook v. Chamberlain, 16.
   v. Dickenson, 224.
   v. Finney, 85, 89.
   v. Tirrell, 434.
Holden v. Boggess, 104.
   v. Pinney, 120.
   v. Wells, 48, 77.
Holder v. Coates, 4.
Hole v. Escott, 321.
Holford v. Hatch, 137.
Holladay v. Power Co., 166.

CASES CITED.

[The figures refer to pages.]

Holland v. Alcock, 276.
   v. Bank, 249.
   v. Hodgson, 21.
Holley v. Glover, 93.
Holliman v. Smith, 117.
Hollingsworth & Vose Co. v. Foxborough Water-Supply Dist., 371.
Hollister v. Shaw, 316.
   v. Young, 464.
Hollman v. Tigges, 317.
Holloman v. Holloman, 96.
Holly Manuf'g Co. v. New Chester Water Co., 12.
Holman v. Bailey, 228.
   v. Gill, 345.
Holmes v. Book, 90.
   v. Buckley, 351.
   v. Coghill, 320.
   v. Conway, 351.
   v. Godson, 395.
   v. Goring, 360.
   v. Penney, 396.
   v. Prescott, 293.
   v. Railway Co., 241.
   v. Seely, 359, 360.
   v. Tremper, 17.
Holton v. Guinn, 93.
   v. Kemp, 429.
Holtzapffel v. Baker, 140.
Homestead Ass'n v. Enslow, 124.
Honore's Ex'r v. Bakewell, 194.
Honywood v. Honywood, 66.
Hood v. Fahnestock, 217.
   v. Haden, 312, 315.
   v. Oglander, 395.
Hooker v. Hooker, 79.
Hooks v. Forst, 152, 153.
Hool v. Bell, 377.
Hooper v. Cummings, 170, 175.
   v. Henry, 232.
Hooton v. Holt, 140, 165.
Hoots v. Graham, 95.
Hoover v. Buck, 489.
Hopkins v. Garrard, 217.
   v. Glunt, 262.
   v. Grimes, 474.
   v. Hopkins, 255, 285.
   v. Railroad Co., 379.
   v. Smith, 172.
   v. Turnpike Co., 263.
Hopp v. Hopp, 434.
Hoppe v. Hoppe, 114, 115.

Hopper v. Calhoun, 207.
   v. Hopper, 100.
Hoppock v. Johnson, 215.
Horbach v. Hill, 190.
Hord v. James, 248.
Horn v. Bennett, 210.
   v. Keteltas, 188.
   v. Tufts, 116.
Hornbeck v. Westbrook, 418.
Horne v. Lyeth, 296.
Horner v. Leeds, 134, 144.
   v. Reuter, 460, 465.
   v. Watson, 371.
Horseley v. Moss, 155.
Horton v. Earle, 477.
Horwitz v. Norris, 313.
Hosford v. Ballard, 377.
   v. Johnson, 236.
Hoske v. Gentzlinger, 162.
Hoskins v. Rhodes, 155.
Hosli v. Yokel, 159.
Hoss v. Hoss, 173.
Houck v. Yates, 5.
Honell v. Barnes, 315.
Hough v. Brown, 153.
Houghton v. Hapgood, 78.
House v. Fowle, 104, 107.
   v. Jackson, 92.
Houston v. Newsome, 122.
   v. Smith, 84.
Houston & G. N. R. Co. v. Winter, 120.
Hovey v. Nellis, 67.
How v. Bank, 120.
Howard v. Merriam, 156, 157.
   v. Peace Soc., 277.
   v. Priest, 340.
   v. Shaw, 156, 220.
   v. Thornton, 315.
Howard Ins. Co. v. Halsey, 216.
Howard's Estate, In re, 171.
Howe, Ex parte, 191.
   v. Andrews, 6.
   v. Warren, 34.
Howell v. Hale, 452.
   v. Howell, 267.
   v. Jones, 117.
   v. Merrill, 424.
   v. Mills, 345.
   v. Rex, 361.
   v. Richards, 442.
   v. Schenck, 9.
   v. Tyler, 312.

[The figures refer to pages.]

Howlett v. Dilts, 84, 106.
Howze v. Barber, 38.
Hoxie v. Carr, 339.
Hoyle v. Railway Co., 15.
Hoyt v. Bradley, 181.
   v. Howe, 123.
   v Hoyt, 117.
   v. Swar, 386.
Hubbard v. Berry, 143.
   v. Elmer, 319.
   v. Hubbard, 174, 175.
   v. Johnson, 493.
   v. Kiddo, 459, 460.
   v. Shaw, 143, 202.
   v. Turner, 226.
Hubbell v. Canady, 125.
   v. Medbury, 270, 274.
   v. Moulson, 200.
Huckins v. Straw, 196.
Hudson v. Steere, 93.
Huebschmann v. McHenry, 21, 23.
Huey's Appeal, 123.
Huff v. Farwell, 237.
   v. Land Co., 447.
   v. McCauley, 349, 350, 407.
Huffell v. Armitstead, 163.
Huffmaster v. Ogden, 85.
Hughes v. Allen, 93.
   v. Edwards, 186, 241.
   v. Graves, 456.
   v. Johnson, 202.
   v. Nicklas, 296.
   v. Robotham, 281.
   v. Sayer, 326.
   v. Sheaff, 190.
   v. Windpfennig, 134.
Hughes' Minors' Appeal, 131.
Hughs v. Pickering, 459, 466, 467.
Hulbert v. Clark, 240.
Hulburt v. Emerson, 44.
Hulett v. Insurance Co., 224.
   v. Soullard, 191.
   v. Whipple, 193.
Hulick v. Scovil, 435.
Hull & S. Ry., In re, 471.
Hulme v. Montgomery, 485.
Huls v. Buntin, 461.
Humberston v. Humberston, 327.
Humble v. Glover, 378.
Humes v. Bernstein, 462.
Hummelman v. Mounts, 417.
Humphrey v. Phinney, 97.

Humphreys v. Blasingame, 353.
   v. McKissock, 426.
Humphries v. Brogden, 366.
Hunkins v. Hunkins, 106.
Hunnewell v. Bangs, 153.
Hunnicut v. Peyton, 458, 465.
Hunt v. Amidon, 135.
   v. Blackburn, 337.
   v. Comstock, 140.
   v. Danforth, 137.
   v. Hall, 304.
   v. Hunt, 195, 244, 273.
   v. Iron Co., 12.
   v. Johnson, 219.
   v. Mortgage Security Co., 210.
   v. Morton, 159.
   v. Mullanphy, 13.
   v. Nolen, 246.
   v. Peake, 365.
   v. Rousmanier's Adm'rs, 311.
   v. Stiles, 242.
   v. Thompson, 147.
   v. Waterman, 193.
   v. Watkins, 9, 60, 61.
   v. Wright, 327, 344.
Hunter v. Anderson, 24.
   v. Ayres, 469.
   v. Bryan, 57.
   v. Frost, 161.
   v. Le Conte, 145.
   v. Osterhoudt, 152.
   v. Stembridge, 261.
   v. Trustees of Sandy Hill, 363.
   v. Whitworth, 74.
Hunters v. Waite, 393.
Hunter's Adm'r v. Law, 115.
Huntington v. Allen, 462.
   v. Asher, 350, 374.
Huntley v. Hole, 451.
   v. Russell, 62, 65, 66.
Hunton v. Nichols, 466.
Hupp v. Hupp, 34.
Hurd v. Curtis, 137, 418.
   v. Cushing, 55.
   v. Darling, 154.
   v. Grant, 100.
   v. Shelton, 171.
Hurdman v. Railway Co., 372.
Hurlburt v. Firth, 358.
Hurley v. Estes, 184.
   v. Hamilton, 346.

[The figures refer to pages.]

Hurst v. Hurst, 396.
  v. Rodney, 135.
  v. Winchelsea, 475.
Hurto v Grant, 174.
Huston v. Clark, 15.
  v. Seeley, 95.
Hutchings v. Bank, 150.
  v. Huggins, 122.
Hutchings' Adm'r v. Bank, 78.
Hutchins v. Dixon, 80.
  v. Heywood, 274.
  v. Masterson, 12, 20.
Hutchinson v. Swartsweller, 229.
Hutchison v. Rust, 438.
Huth v. Dock Co., 383.
Hutton v. Bankard, 316.
Hutzler v. Phillips, 192.
Huxley v. Rice, 265.
Huyser v. Chase, 162.
Huzzard v. Trego, 494.
Huzzey v. Field, 380.
Hyatt v. Cochran, 221.
  v. Griffiths, 160.
Hyde v. Baldwin, 453.
  v. Heller, 476.
Hylton v. Brown, 21.
Hyman v. Devereux, 24.
  v. Kelly, 184.
  v. Read, 402.
Hymes v. Esty, 448.

I

Ibbs v. Richardson, 164.
Iglehart v. Bierce, 245.
Illinois Cent. R. Co. v. Illinois, 5.
  v. Indiana & I. C. R. Co., 418.
  v. McCullough, 217, 436.
Illinois Fire Ins. Co. v. Stanton, 197.
Imlay v. Huntington, 256.
Independent Dist. of Oak Dale v. Fagen, 457.
Indianapolis Manufacturing & Carpenters' Union v. Cleveland C. C. & I. Ry. Co., 147.
Indianapolis Water Co. v. Nutte, 441.
Ing v. Brown, 408.
Ingalls v. Atwood, 188.
Ingals v. Plamondon, 367.
Ingersoll v. Sergeant, 31, 376, 377.
Ingersoll's Estate, In re, 24.

Inglis v. Trustees, 276.
Ingraham v. Meade, 313.
  v. Wilkinson, 5, 471.
Ingram v. Little, 328.
  v. Morris, 90.
Inhabitants of Deerfield v. Arms, 471.
Inhabitants of First Parish in Sudbury v. Jones, 21.
Inhabitants of Plymouth v. Carver, 137.
Inhabitants of Rehoboth v. Hunt, 341.
Inhabitants of School Dist. No. 4 v. Benson, 470.
Inhabitants of West Roxbury v. Stoddard, 6.
Inhabitants of Windham v. Inhabitants of Portland, 95.
Inhabitants of Winthrop v. Fairbanks, 351.
Inhabitants of Worcester v. Green, 375.
Innes v. Sayer, 318.
Innis v. Templeton, 452.
Insurance Co. v. Stinson, 197.
International Bank of Chicago v. Wilshire, 233.
International Trust Co. v. Schumann, 138.
Interstate Bldg. & Loan Ass'n v. McCartha, 222.
Ipswich v. Browne, 379.
Ipswich Manuf'g Co. v. Story, 229.
Irish v. Sharp, 210.
Irvine v. Greever, 78.
  v. Irvine, 383.
  v. Marshall, 402.
  v. Newlin, 293.
  v. Tarbat, 403.
Irwin v. Covode, 64.
  v. Davidson, 201.
  v. Patchen, 452.
Irwin's Heirs v. Longworth, 419.
Isele v. Bank, 445.
Iselin v. Starin, 353.
Isham v. Morgan, 3.
Ive v. Sams, 400.
Ives v. Allyn, 475.
  v. Lynn, 493.
Ivie v. Stringfellow's Adm'r, 490.
Ivy v. Yancey, 195, 451, 468.
Izard v. Middleton, 54.

538   CASES CITED.

[The figures refer to pages.]

J

Jackman v. Arlington Mills, 369, 372.
Jackson v. Aldrich, 158.
   v. Alexander, 410.
   v. Allen, 123, 152, 175.
   v. Andrew, 63, 66.
   v. Andrews, 218.
   v. Aspell, 95.
   v. Austin, 226.
   v. Ayers, 453.
   v. Babcock, 167, 494.
   v. Baker, 162.
   v. Bard, 435.
   v. Berner, 463.
   v. Bradford, 455.
   v. Bradt, 160.
   v. Brownell, 154.
   v. Brownson, 63, 145.
   v. Bryan, 157, 161.
   v. Bull, 39.
   v. Cadwell, 490.
   v. Cairns, 459.
   v. Campbell, 430.
   v. Carpenter, 382.
   v. Cary, 256.
   v. Chamberlain, 225.
   v. Chase, 434.
   v. Chew, 302.
   v. Churchill, 100, 109.
   v. Clark, 421.
   v. Cleveland, 266.
   v. Crysler, 174.
   v. Delacroix, 132.
   v. Delancey, 272, 410, 473.
   v Dillon's Lessee, 411.
   v. Dubois, 225.
   v. Dunsbach, 299.
   v. Elston, 223.
   v. Embler, 57.
   v. Fish, 410.
   v. Ford, 226.
   v. Foster, 464.
   v. Harder, 344.
   v. Harrison, 151.
   v. Haviland, 459.
   v. Hayner, 429.
   v. Hodges, 82.
   v. Housel, 38.
   v. Hull, 241.
   v. Huntington, 460, 463.
   v. Ireland, 419.

Jackson v. Jackson, 83, 297, 318, 481.
   v. Johnson, 74, 75, 76, 303.
   v. Kip, 88.
   v. Lawrence, 187.
   v. Leek, 434.
   v. Leonard, 467.
   v. Ligon, 317.
   v. Loomis, 21.
   v. M'Chesney, 427.
   v. McKenney, 410.
   v. McLeod, 164, 165.
   v. Mancius, 57, 59.
   v. Matsdorf, 268.
   v. Merrill, 38.
   v. Moore, 468.
   v. Morse, 491.
   v. Myers, 256.
   v. Noble, 302.
   v. O'Donaghy, 95.
   v. Ogden, 453.
   v. Page, 223.
   v. Parkhurst, 150, 163, 165.
   v. Phillips, 275, 276, 277.
   v. Phipps, 434, 435.
   v. Potter, 474.
   v. Reeves, 424.
   v. Roberts, 477.
   v. Robins, 395.
   v. Schoonmaker, 281, 303, 438.
   v. Schutz, 152, 395.
   v. Sebring, 410.
   v. Sellick, 75, 76, 303.
   v. Sheldon, 151.
   v. Shepard, 437.
   v. Smith, 465.
   v. Stevens, 187, 446.
   v. Swart, 410.
   v. Thompson, 302.
   v. Tibbits, 464.
   v. Vanderheyden, 453, 455.
   v. Van Hoesen, 57.
   v. Van Valkenburgh, 214, 215.
   v. Van Zandt, 35.
   v. Vermilyea, 461.
   v. Vincent, 144.
   v. Von Zedlitz, 396.
   v. Walker, 274.
   v. Weaver, 234, 248.
   v. Wells, 57.
   v. Willard, 184, 212.
   v. Winslow, 448.
   v. Wood, 415.

CASES CITED.

[The figures refer to pages.]

Jackson v. Woodruff, 461, 462.
   v. Wright, 454.
Jacob v. Howard, 305.
Jacobs v. Rice, 80.
Jacques v. Short, 135.
Jaffe v. Harteau, 139.
Jamaica Pond Aqueduct Corp. v. Chandler, 350, 419.
James v. Cowing, 269.
   v. Dean, 157.
   v. Morey, 186, 220, 232, 273.
   v. Sammis, 362.
   v. Vanderheyden, 436.
Jameson v. Hayward, 67.
Jamison v. Perry, 195.
Janney v. Sprigg, 77.
Jarechi v. Society, 21.
Jarvais v. Moe, 119, 122.
Jarvis v. Dutcher, 192.
   v. Frink, 232.
   v. Hoffman, 127.
   v. Woodruff, 237.
Jauretche v. Proctor, 3 5.
Jee v. Audley, 323.
Jefferies v. Fort, 85.
Jefferis v. Land Co., 423.
Jeffersonville v. The John Shallcross, 379.
Jeffery v. Hursh, 186.
Jencks v. Alexander, 202.
   v. Smith, 8.
Jenkins v. Atkins, 431.
   v. Eldridge, 203.
   v. Fahey, 32, 345.
   v. Gerbing, 18, 19.
   v. Hopkins, 445.
   v. Hurt's Com'rs, 430.
   v. Jenkins, 297, 382.
   v. Jenkins' Heirs, 84.
   v. Keymes, 394.
   v. McCurdy, 10.
   v. Newman, 494.
   v. Wilkinson, 211.
Jenkinson v. Auditor General, 491.
Jenks v. Horton, 60.
   v. Pawlowski, 172.
Jenkyn v. Vaughan, 304.
Jenner v. Gurner, 172.
   v. Morgan, 60.
Jennings v. Conboy, 312.
   v. McComb, 156.
Jennings v. O'Brien, 170.

Jennison v. Hapgood, 90, 91.
Jenny v. Jenny, 106.
Jeremy v. Elwell, 6.
Jerome v. McCarter, 247.
Jervoise v. Duke of Northumberland, 258.
Jesser v. Gifford, 142.
Jesson v. Wright, 297.
Jesup v. Bank, 319.
Jeter v. Davis, 468.
Jevon v. Bush, 264.
Jewell v. Porter, 386.
   v. Warner, 49, 53.
Jewett v. Miller, 453.
   v. Tomlinson, 231, 247.
Jiggitts v. Jiggitts, 105.
Jockheck v. Commissioners, 495.
John and Cherry Sts., In re, 184.
John Morris Co. v. Southworth, 135.
Johnson v. Baker, 436.
   v. Bennett, 270.
   v. Branch, 435.
   v. Brown, 244.
   v. Cantrell, 90.
   v. Carter, 164.
   v. Cawthorn, 193.
   v. Clarke, 210.
   v. Cornett, 210.
   v. Cushing, 320.
   v. Doll, 159.
   v. Farley, 433, 435.
   v. Harmon, 236.
   v. Hart, 338.
   v. Hoffman, 154.
   v. Hosford, 202.
   v. Houston, 184.
   v. Jacob, 86.
   v. Johnson, 64, 249, 265.
   v. Jordan, 351, 352, 426.
   v. McGehee, 438.
   v. McIntosh, 31, 400.
   v. May, 378.
   v. Moore, 429.
   v. Mesher, 21.
   v. Muzzy, 378.
   v. Neil, 96.
   v. Norway, 486.
   v. Perley, 87.
   v. Plume, 85.
   v. Richardson, 4, 116.
   v. Skillman, 353.
   v. Smith, 60.

540 CASES CITED.

[The figures refer to pages.]

Johnson v. Stagg, 435.
   v. Touchet, 318.
   v. Van Velsor, 189.
   v. White, 195.
   v. Williams, 223.
   v. Zink, 204.
Johnson's Estate, In re, 109.
Johnson's Ex'r v. Wiseman's Ex'r, 18.
Johnson's Trusts, In re, 329.
Johnston v. Jones, 471.
   v. Turner, 119.
   v. Vandyke, 97.
   v. Zane, 41.
Johnston's Lessee v. Haines, 438.
Jones v. Adams, 351.
   v. Bank, 209.
   v. Bochove, 357.
   v. Brewer, 96, 100.
   v. Bull, 13.
   v. Butler, 383.
   v. Carter, 174.
   v. Chamberlin, 220.
   v. Crow, 352.
   v. Doe, 175.
   v. Durrer, 152, 154.
   v. Franklin, 446, 447.
   v. Gerock, 83.
   v. Gilbert, 115.
   v. Habersham, 329.
   v. Hollopeter, 96.
   v. Hughes, 88.
   v. Johnson, 6.
   v. Jones, 84, 98, 178, 334, 339.
   v. Kimble, 424.
   v. Lapham, 246.
   v. Lemon, 468.
   v. Millsaps, 139.
   v. Parker, 137.
   v. Pettibone, 423.
   v. Powell, 111.
   v. Pullen, 249.
   v. Railway Co., 172, 175.
   v. Ramsey, 12.
   v. Smith, 211.
   v. Swayze, 435.
   v. Swearingen, 284.
   v. Tainter, 226.
   v. Tapling, 358.
   v. Thomas, 196.
   v. Trust Co., 239.
   v. Van Bochove, 357.
   v. Wagner, 366.

Jones v. Walker, 175.
   v. Webb, 301.
   v. Webster, 185.
   v. Winwood, 317.
Jones' Ex'rs v. Jones, 24.
   v. Stills, 57.
Jorda' v. Adams, 297.
   v. Corey, 438.
   v. Godman, 124.
   v. Katz, 189.
   v. McClure, 36, 294.
   v. Roach, 53.
   v. Sayre, 184.
   v. Woodin, 397.
Joseph Smith Co. v. McGuinness, 191.
Josephthal v. Heyman, 215.
Joslin v. McLean, 153.
   v. Rhoades, 395.
   v. Wyman, 243.
Joslyn v. Parlin, 181.
   v. Rockwell, 491.
Josselyn v. Josselyn, 326.
Jossey v. White, 57.
Josslyn v. McCabe, 22.
Jourdain v. Fox, 188, 454.
Jourdan v. Haran, 93.
Joy v. Bank, 367.
Joyce v. Conlin, 356, 357.
   v. Williams, 453.
Joyner v. Farmer, 250.
Judd v. Seekins, 231.
Judge v. Insurance Co., 198.
   v. Reese, 189.
Judkins v. Woodman, 196.
Junction R. Co. v. Harris, 73.

K

Kabley v. Light Co., 166.
Kade v. Lauber, 84.
Kain v. Fisher, 101.
Kaine v. Weigley, 393.
Kaler v. Beaman, 356.
Kane v. Bloodgood, 274.
   v. Sanger, 449.
Kannady v. McCarron, 183.
Kansas City Land Co. v. Hill, 216, 289.
Kansas Inv. Co. v. Carter, 142.
Karchner v. Hoy, 171.
Karmuller v. Krotz, 360.

CASES CITED.

[The figures refer to pages.]

Kaster v. McWilliams, 119.
Kastor v. Newhouse, 139.
Katz v. Schnaier, 454.
Kay v. Oxley, 361.
   v. Railroad Co., 166.
   v. Whitaker, 246.
Kayser v. Maugham, 265.
Kean v. Tilford, 344.
Kearney v. Kearney, 57, 61.
Keates v. Lyon, 351.
Keating v. Condon, 24.
   v. Springer, 136.
Keating Implement Co. v. Marshall Electric Light & Power Co., 14.
Keats v. Hugo, 364.
Keeler v. Eastman, 63, 64.
   v. Keeler, 15.
Keepers, etc., of Harrow School v. Alderton, 63.
Keepfer v. Force, 493.
Keerl v. Fulton, 79.
Kelchline v. Kelchline, 437.
Keily v. Monck, 173.
Keith v. Horner, 192, 193.
Keithley v. Wood, 189.
Kelenk v. Town of Walnut Lake, 354.
Keller v. Ashford, 208.
Kellett v. Shepard, 92.
Kelley v. Ball, 110.
   v. Canary, 85.
Kellog v. Richardson, 393.
Kellogg v. Malin, 446.
   v. Robinson, 446.
Kelly v. Austin, 12.
   v. Baker, 122.
   v. Waite, 158.
Kelsey v. Durkee, 16.
Kemp v. Bradford, 288.
   v. Walker, 433.
Kendall v. Hathaway, 13.
   v. Lawrence, 217, 382.
   v. Mann, 267.
Kendrick v. Latham, 461.
Kenege v. Elliot, 376.
Kenicott v. Supervisors, 211.
Kennedy v. Borie, 206.
   v. Kennedy, 50, 265.
   v. McCartney's Heirs, 402.
   v. Moore, 231, 246.
   v. Northup, 224.
Kenner v. Contract Co., 174.

Kenny v. Udall, 72.
Kent v. Agard, 120.
   v. Gerhard, 192.
   v. Hartpoole, 79.
   v. Hopkins, 481.
   v. Judkins, 361.
   v. Riley, 393.
   v. Walte, 352.
Kentucky Railroad Tax Cases, 491.
Kenyon v. Kenyon, 86, 99.
   v. Lee, 305.
   v. Shreck, 247.
Kepple's Appeal, 395.
Kerley v. Kerley, 115.
Kern v. A. P. Hotaling, 230.
   v. Chalfant, 270.
Kerngood v. Davis, 195.
Kernochan v. Insurance Co., 199.
Kerns v. Swope, 214, 437.
Kerr v. Bell, 383.
   v. Day, 217.
   v. Freeman, 408.
   v. Kingsbury, 23.
   v. Kitchen, 216.
   v. Moon, 474.
   v. Shaw, 138.
Kerr's Trusts, In re, 319.
Kesner v. Trigg, 224.
Kessler v. Letts, 364.
Ketchum v. Corse, 330.
   v. Shaw, 90.
Kettleby v. Atwood, 23.
Kevern v. Williams, 327.
Kew v. Trainor, 136.
Keyport, etc., Steamboat Co. v. Farmers' Transp. Co., 6.
Keys v. Test, 427.
Keyser v. Mitchell, 41.
Key's Lessee v. Davis, 384.
Kidd v. Dennison, 63, 64.
   v. Lesler, 114.
Kiddall v. Trimble, 111.
Kieffer v. Imhoff, 358.
Kiene v. Gruehle, 57.
Kier v. Peterson, 7, 65.
Kiernan v. Terry, 144.
Kilburn v. Dodd, 473.
Kilpatrick v. Baltimore, 171.
Kimball v. Blaisdell, 456.
   v. Bryant, 443.
   v. Eaton, 429.

CASES CITED.

[The figures refer to pages.]

Kimball v. Johnson, 438.
   v. Rowland, 162.
   v. Semple, 420.
Kimmel v. Benna, 454.
Kincaid v. Howe, 417.
King v. Carmichael, 462, 465.
   v. Foscue, 62.
   v. Fowler, 9.
   v. Gilson, 446.
   v. Howland, 9.
   v. Jones, 148, 450.
   v. King, 90.
   v. Meighen, 238.
   v. Miller, 63.
   v. Ransom, 134.
   v. Reed, 346.
   v. Smith, 467.
   v. Stetson, 85.
   v. Whittle, 62.
   v. Wilcomb, 17.
Kingdom v. Nottle, 443, 450.
Kingman v. Harmon, 290.
Kingsbury v. Collins, 8, 160.
Kings Co. Fire Ins. Co. v. Stevens, 422.
Kingsley v. Ames, 163, 165.
   v. Holbrook, 8.
   v. Improvement Co., 360.
   v. Kingsley, 116.
   v. Purdom, 228.
   v. Smith, 75.
Kinna v. Smith, 209.
Kinney v. Ensign, 229.
   v. Slattery, 341.
Kinsell v. Billings, 20.
Kinsley v. Ames, 163, 165.
Kinsolving v. Pierce, 111.
Kintner v. Jones, 261.
   v. McRae, 105.
Kip v. Bank, 264.
Kircher v. Schalk, 184.
Kirchman v. Lapp, 18.
Kirk v. Dean, 106.
Kirkham v. Sharp, 361.
Kirkman v. Brown, 463.
Kirkpatrick v. Mathiot, 341.
Kirkwood v. Finegan, 364.
Kissam v. Barclay, 16.
   v. Dierkes, 321.
Kitchell v. Burgwin, 113, 118, 119, 121.
   v. Mudgett, 204, 216.
Kittle v. Van Dyck, 85, 245.

Kittredge v. Woods, 18.
Kleespies v. McKenzie, 159.
Klein v. McNamara, 188.
Kleppner v. Laverty, 296.
Kliene v. Gruehle, 57.
Kline v. Beebe, 75.
Klock v. Walter, 187.
Kloess v. Katt, 21.
Knadler v. Sharp, 445.
Knickerbacker v. Seymour, 86.
Knight v. Browne, 396.
   v. Elliott, 424.
   v. Land Ass'n, 403.
   v. Thayer, 452, 455.
Knolles' Case, 376.
Knowles v. Dodge, 320.
   v. Dow, 355.
   v. Kennedy, 447.
   v. Murphy, 144.
   v. Pierce, 146.
   v. Rablin, 236.
   v. Toothaker, 424, 453.
Knox v. Easton, 183, 206.
   v. Hook, 464.
   v. Knox, 261.
Koch v. Briggs, 238.
Koehler v. Brady, 152.
Koerper v. Railway Co., 220.
Kolasky v. Michels, 135.
Koon v. Tramel, 217, 224.
Koplitz v. Gustavus, 159.
Kortright v. Cady, 228.
Kottenbrock v. Cracraft, 80.
Kouvalinka v. Geibel, 301.
Kraemer v. Adelsberger, 190.
Kramer v. Bank, 240.
Kranichfelt v. Slattery, 438.
Kraut's Appeal, 360.
Kremer v. Railway Co., 167.
Kripp v. Curtis, 359.
Krouse v. Ross, 18.
Kruse v. Scripps, 206.
   v. Wilson, 421.
Kugel v. Painter, 136.
Kuhlman v. Hecht, 359.
Kuhn v. Kaler, 87.
Kunes v. McCloskey, 494.
Kurtz v. Hibner, 342.
Kuydendall v. Devecmon, 109.
Kyger v. Ryley, 184.
Kyle v. Kavanagh, 412.

[The figures refer to pages.]

L

Lacey v. Newcomb, 134.
Lackman v. Wood, 458.
Lacustrine Fertilizer Co. v. Lake Guano & Fertilizer Co., 7, 222.
Lacy v. Comstock, 418.
   v. Lockett, 125.
Ladd v Ladd, 314, 315.
   v. Wiggin, 209.
Lade v. Sheperd, 362.
Lafferty v. Milligan, 445.
Laflin v. Griffiths, 15.
Lahens v. Dupasseur, 273.
Laidley v. Aiken, 226.
Lake v. Doud, 191.
Lake Erie & W. R. Co. v. Kennedy, 168.
   v. Whitham, 328, 438.
Lake Superior Ship-Canal, Ry. & Iron Co. v. McCann, 12.
Lakin v. Dolly, 144.
Lamar v. Scott, 83, 100.
Lamb v. Burbank, 450.
   v. Crosland, 353.
   v. Foss, 197.
   v. Jeffrey, 235.
   v. Miller, 175.
   v. Pierce, 214.
   v. Shays, 123.
   v. Tucker, 207.
Lambert v. Kinnery, 123.
   v. Thwaites, 313.
Lamberton v. Stouffer, 155.
Lambertville Nat. Bank v. McCready Bag & Paper Co., 245.
Lamb's Estate, In re, 114.
Lamount v. Stimson, 214.
L'Amoureux v. Vandenburgh, 213.
Lampert v. Haydel, 41.
Lampet's Case, 286, 305.
Lampman v. Milks, 351.
Lamprey v. State, 423.
Lamson v. Drake, 234.
Lancashire v. Mason, 149.
Lancaster v. Dolan, 319.
Lancaster County Bank v. Stauffer, 80.
Lance's Appeal, 189.
Landers v. Beck, 188.
Landis' Appeal, 164.
Landon v. Platt, 13.

Lane v. Debenham, 315.
   v. Duchac, 222.
   v. King, 10.
   v. Logue, 224.
   v. Ludlow, 194.
   v. Nelson, 153.
   v. Shears, 188.
   v. Woodruff, 449.
   v. Young, 144.
Lane's Appeal, 475.
Lang v. Cadwell, 207.
   v. Cox, 19.
Langdon v. Ingram's Guardian, 40.
   v. Keith, 210.
Langley v. Baldwin, 296.
   v. Chapin, 494.
   v. Vaughn, 191.
Lanham v. Wilson, 53.
Lanpher v. Glenn, 133.
Lanphere v. Lowe, 13.
Lansing v. Goelet, 242.
   v. Van Alstyne, 140.
Lansing Iron & Engine Works v. Walker, 12.
Lantsbery v. Collier, 329.
Large's Case, 395.
Larned v. Donovan, 211, 220.
Larrowe v. Beam, 97.
Larsen v. Peterson, 354.
Lasala v. Halbrook, 365.
Lasher v. Lasher, 110.
   v. McCreery, 490.
Lashley v. Souder, 171.
Lass v. Sternberg, 250.
Lassell v Reed, 17, 18.
Lassells v. Cornwallis, 320.
Latham v. Atwood, 8.
   v. Henderson, 267, 268.
   v. Udell, 434.
Lathrop v. Bampton, 265.
   v. Bank, 389, 452.
   v. Clewis, 146.
Latimer v. Logwood, 461.
Latta v. Clifford, 469.
Laughlin v. Dock Co., 433.
Laughlin v. Braley, 185.
Laumer v. Francis, 355.
Lavelle v. Corrignio, 481.
Law v. People, 494.
Lawrence, In re, 104.
   v. Fletcher, 416.

[The figures refer to pages.]

Lawrence v. French, 141.
  v. Hammett, 145.
  v. Hebbard, 475, 478.
  v. Jenkins, 368.
  v. Springer, 168.
Lawson v. Hunt, 269.
  v. Morton, 98.
  v. Nicholson, 230.
Lawton v. Lawton, 17, 20.
  v. Salmon, 15, 20.
Laylin v. Knox, 203.
Layson v. Grange, 122.
Laytin, In re, 61.
Lazell v. Lazell, 121.
Leake v. Benson, 78.
  v. Robinson, 326.
Leaper v. Neagle, 57.
Leathers v. Gray, 296.
Leavell v. Lapowski, 122.
Leavitt v. Fletcher, 139.
  v. Lamprey, 107.
Leaycraft v. Hedden, 256.
Lechmere & Lloyd, In re, 289.
Lee v. Bumgardner, 4.
  v. Clark, 226.
  v. Gaskell, 10.
  v. Lake, 363.
  v. Lindell, 93.
  v. McLaughlin, 142.
  v. Miller, 119.
  v. Patten, 267.
  v. Simpson, 309, 316.
  v. Vincent, 315.
Leede's & Crompton's Case, 175.
Leeds v. Wakefield, 321.
Leeper v. Baker, 463.
Le Franc v. Richmond, 429.
Leggett v. Doremus, 307.
Legh v. Hewitt, 140.
Lehigh Coal & Nav. Co. v. Early, 175.
Lehman v. Nolting, 158.
Lehndorf v. Cope, 47, 59.
Leigh v. Dickeson, 342.
  v. Jack, 422.
Leishman v. White, 141.
Leiweke v. Jordan, 181.
Leland v. Gassett, 17.
Lemar v. Miles, 16.
Lemon v. Graham, 37.
Lenfers v. Henke, 88, 99.
Lennig's Ex'rs v. White, 461.

Lennon v. Porter, 243.
  v. White, 438.
Lennox v. Brower, 207.
Leonard v. Burr, 178, 282, 329.
  v. Clough, 20.
  v. Colcord, 361.
  v. Leonard, 361, 467.
  v. Morris, 241.
  v. White, 426, 474.
Lepage v. McNamara, 277.
Lerned v. Morrill, 422.
Lesley v. Randolph, 159, 160.
Lessard v. Stram, 372.
Lessee of Thompson's Heirs v. Green, 80.
Lester v. Garland, 396.
L'Etourneau v. Henquenet, 290.
Le Tourneau v. Smith, 159.
Lett v. Randall, 323.
Levet v. Needham, 266.
Levy v. Ladd, 493.
  v. Martin, 203.
Lewes v. Ridge, 449.
Lewis v. Baird, 220.
  v. Caperton's Ex'r, 193.
  v. Carstairs, 361.
  v. Coffee Co., 6.
  v. Jones, 18.
  v. Kirk, 211, 226.
  v. Klotz, 10.
  v. Lewellyn, 316.
  v. Lewis, 109.
  v. Lichty, 115.
  v. Lyman, 155.
  v. McNatt, 9.
  v. Nangle, 234.
  v. Payn, 141.
  v. Pier Co., 23.
  v. Rees, 261.
  v. Richey, 240.
  v. Sheldon, 145, 148.
  v. Smith, 109.
  v. Starke, 273.
  v. Stein, 369.
  v. Wilkins, 150.
Lewis' Appeal, 338.
Lewis' Lessee v. Beall, 411.
Leydecker v. Brintnall, 136.
Leyman v. Abeel, 375.
Liefe v. Saltingstone, 310.
Liford's Case, 49.

CASES CITED.

[The figures refer to pages.]

Ligare v. Semple, 103.
Liggins v. Inge, 358.
Liley v. Hey, 328.
Lillibridge v. Coal Co., 4.
Linahan v. Barr, 12.
Lincoln v. Perry, 479.
Lincoln Bldg. & Sav. Ass'n v. Hass, 185.
Lindauer v. Younglove, 454.
Lindeman v. Lindsey, 358.
Linden v. Graham, 102.
   v. Hepburn, 148.
Lindley v. Dakin, 444.
   v. Groff, 436.
Lindsay v. Garvin, 229.
Lindsley v. Brewing Co., 149.
Linn Co. Bank v. Hopkins, 118.
Lion v. Burtiss, 302.
Lippencott v. Allander, 379.
Liscomb v. Root, 340.
Lissa v. Posey, 193.
Litchfield v. Cudworth, 80.
Lithgow v. Kavenagh, 38.
Littell v. Jones, 125.
Little v. Bennett, 313.
   v. Downing, 462, 468.
   v. Giles, 451.
   v. Macadaras, 139.
   v. Palister, 142.
   v. Willford, 277.
Littlejohn v. Gordon, 241.
Little Rock Granite Co. v. Shall, 152.
Littleton v. Giddings, 214.
Livett v. Wilson, 352.
Livingston v. Bell, 394.
   v. Greene, 284.
   v. Ketcham, 375.
   v. Livingston, 264.
   v. Reynolds, 304.
   v. Tanner, 164, 165.
   v. Ten Broeck, 375.
Livingston's Ex'rs v. Livingston, 145.
Lloyd v. Carew, 323.
   v. Conover, 93.
   v. Hoo Sue, 235.
   v. Spillet, 253, 266.
Lobdell v. Hayes, 106.
Locke v. Caldwell, 240.
   v. Rowell, 59, 115, 118, 122.
Lockett v. Lockett, 38.
Lockhart v. Hardy, 205.
Lockman v. Reilly, 247.

Lockwood v. Benedict, 246.
Loddington v. Kime, 287, 290.
Loeb v. Drakeford, 431.
   v. Huddleston, 239.
Loftis v. Loftis, 126.
Lofton v. Murchison, 38.
Loftus' Case, 71.
Logan v. Bell, 309.
   v. Eaton, 453.
   v. Herron, 161.
   v. Phillips, 108.
Lomas v. Wright, 292, 302.
Lombard v. Culbertson, 222.
London, Paris & American Bank v. Smith, 245.
London & S. W. Ry. Co. v. Gomm, 327.
London & Westminster Loan & Discount Co. v. Drake, 22.
Lone Star Brewing Co. v. Felder, 126.
Long v. Beard, 380.
   v. Blackall, 323, 324.
   v. Cruger, 454.
   v. Dollarhide, 223.
   v. Fuller, 407.
   v. Long, 236.
   v. Mast, 464.
   v. Mellet, 235.
   v. Moler, 445.
   v. Wagoner, 420.
Longfellow v. McGregor, 211.
Longhead v. Phelps, 323.
Loomer v. Wheelwright, 232.
Loomis v. Brush, 387.
   v. Knox, 234.
   v. Pingree, 491.
   v. Wilbur, 61.
Loosemore v. Knapman, 204.
Lord v. Bunn, 397.
   v. Lord, 110.
   v. Morris, 240.
Lord Altham v. Earl of Anglesey, 253.
Lord Say & Seal's Case, 416.
Loring v. Bacon, 366.
   v. Eliot, 280.
   v. Taylor, 130.
Lorman v. Benson, 6.
Losey v. Bond, 386.
   v. Simpson, 223.
Lothrop v. Foster, 87.
   v. Thayer, 139.
Loubat v. Kipp, 435.

[The figures refer to pages.]

Loud v. Darling, 442.
Loughran v. Ross, 23.
Louisville & N. R. Co. v. Philyaw, 468.
Lounsberry v. Snyder, 138.
Lounsbury v. Norton, 237.
Love v. Wyndham, 327.
Lovejoy v. Lovett, 421.
Lovelace v. Hutchinson, 250.
Loveland v. Clark, 249.
Loveless v. Thomas, 121.
Lovell v. Frost, 465.
   v. Smith, 357.
Loverin v. Trust Co., 232.
Lovingston v. St. Clair Co., 471.
Low v. Burron, 68, 323, 324.
Lowe v. Miller, 154.
Lowell v. Robinson, 423.
Lowell South Congregational Meeting House v. Hilton, 135.
Lowery v. Rowland, 343.
Lowrie v. Ryland, 57.
Lowry v. Muldrow, 328.
Lowry's Lessee v. Steele, 76, 79.
Lowther v. Cavendish, 173.
Loy v. Insurance Co., 198.
Lucas v. Coulter, 139.
   v. Rickerich, 71.
Luce v. Carley, 422.
Luch's Appeal, 192.
Lucy v. Levington, 447.
Luddington v. Kime, 290.
Ludlow v. Railway Co., 175.
Lufkin v. Curtis, 107.
Luke v. Marshall, 477.
Lull v. Matthews, 184.
Lumpkin v. Wilson, 432.
Lumpkins v. Johnson, 488.
Lunt v. Brown, 145.
Luntz v. Greve, 78.
Lupton v. Lupton, 204.
Lushington v. Boldero, 62.
Lute v. Reilly, 120.
Lutkins v. Leigh, 205.
Luttrell v. Wells, 488.
Lutwich v. Milton, 254.
Lux v. Haggin, 423.
Lybe's Appeal, 371.
Lyford v. Railroad Co., 441.
Lykens Valley Coal Co. v. Dock, 7.
Lyle v. Ducomb, 181.
   v. Richards, 53.

Lyman v. Hale, 4.
Lynch v. Cannon, 469.
   v. Gas Co., 152.
   v. Livingston, 438.
   v. Pfeiffer, 232.
Lynde v. Williams, 464.
Lynn's Appeal, 63, 64.
Lyon v. McIlvaine, 231.
   v. Parker, 137.
   v. Reed, 409.
   v. Robbins, 234.
Lyons v. Bodenhamer, 216.
   v. Van Riper, 429.
Lytle v. Lytle, 37.
   v. Turner, 216.

M

Maatta v. Kippola, 116.
Mabary v. Dollarhide, 467.
Mabry v. Harp, 8.
   v. Harrison, 125.
Mabury v. Ferry Co., 379.
McAleer v. Schneider, 473, 474.
McAllister v. Devane, 358.
McAnally v. Heflin, 386.
McArthur v. Franklin, 84, 235.
   v. Morris, 443.
   v. Porter, 91.
   v. Robinson, 187, 234.
   v. Scott, 324.
McBee v. Sampson, 149.
McBeth v. Trabue, 452.
McBride's Estate, 82.
McBroom v. Thompson, 168.
McCabe v. Bellows, 91, 235.
   v. Mazzuchelli, 116.
   v. Swap, 90.
McCahill v. McCahill, 268.
McCall v. Walter, 16.
McCampbell v. Mason, 290.
McCarn v. Wilcox, 228.
McCartee v. Asylum, 389.
   v. Teller, 107, 108.
McCartney v. Osburn, 290.
McCarty v. Leggett, 443.
   v. Williams, 193.
McCauley v. Grimes, 85.
   v. Porter, 190.
McClanahan v. Porter, 97.

CASES CITED. 547

[The figures refer to pages.]

McClary v. Bixby, 116, 119.
   v. Stull, 384.
McClellan v. McClellan, 262, 263.
McClintock v. McClintock, 189.
M'Clung v. Ross, 340.
McClure v. Cook, 171.
   v. Fairchild, 104.
   v. Harris, 85, 90.
McClurg v. Price, 141.
McConihe v. Fales, 206.
McConn v. Delany, 425.
McConnell v. Blood, 15, 21.
   v. Downs, 449.
McCord v. Herrick, 367.
   v. High, 356, 357.
   v. Ochiltree, 277.
McCormick v. James, 438.
McCormic v. Leggett, 383.
McCormick v. Horan, 372.
   v. Knox, 202.
   v. Irwin, 203.
   v. Leonard, 214.
   v. Taylor, 100.
   v. Wilcox, 119.
McCormick Harvesting Mach. Co. v. Gates, 396.
McCorry v. King's Heirs, 59, 75.
McCosker v. Brady, 272.
McCoy v. Danley, 369.
McCracken v. Rogers, 484.
M'Crady's Ex'rs v. Brisbane, 445.
McCrea v. Marsh, 168.
   v. Purmort, 427.
McCready v. Virginia, 5.
McCreary v. Lewis, 110.
McCreery v. Davis, 111.
McCrelish v. Churchman, 441.
McCrory v. Little, 231, 232.
McCrosky v. Walker, 118.
McCulloch's Lessee v. Endaly, 224.
McCullough v. Allen, 109.
   v. Irvine, 65.
   v. Irvine's Ex'rs, 20, 64.
   v. Wall, 421, 471.
McCurdy v. Canning, 338, 343.
M'Cutchen v. Miller, 218.
McDaniel v. Grace, 76.
McDavid v. Wood, 12, 20.
McDermott v. French, 337.
   v. Railroad Co., 143.
McDodrill v. Lumber Co., 342.

McDonald v. Badger, 339.
   v. Black, 198.
   v. Clark, 122.
   v. Crandall, 115, 123, 124.
   v. Hannah, 95.
   v. Heylin, 60.
McDonogh's Ex'rs v. Murdock, 263.
McDonough v. Jefferson Co., 461.
   v. Starbird, 16.
McDowell v. Addams, 484.
McElroy v. McElroy, 259, 261.
McFadden v. Crawford, 12, 14.
   v. Ice Co., 6.
   v. Worthington, 225.
McFarland v. Birdsall, 394.
   v. Febiger's Heirs, 107.
McFarlane v. Williams, 131.
McFarlin v. Essex Co., 5.
   v. Leaman, 341.
McGahan v. Bank, 341.
McGale v. McGale, 231, 488.
McGee v. Hall, 287.
   v. McGee's Heirs, 106.
McGehee v McGehee, 97.
McGiven v. Wheelock, 232.
McGlynn v. Brock, 140.
McGowan v McGowan, 268.
McGowen v. Baldwin, 110.
McGown v. Yerks, 247.
MacGregor v. Gardner, 431.
McGuffey v. Finley, 244.
Machemer's Estate. In re, 24, 109.
Machir v. May, 469.
McIlvaine v. Smith, 41.
McIlwain v. Karstens, 489.
McInerney v. Beck, 412, 416.
McIntosh v. Ladd, 105.
McIntyre v. Clark, 59, 132.
   v. Costello, 84.
   v. McIntyre, 396.
McIver v. Estabrook, 23.
McJunkin v. Dupree, 17.
Mack v. Patchin, 138.
Mackay v. Douglas, 394.
McKeage v. Insurance Co., 21.
McKean & Elk Land Imp. Co. v. Mitchell, 220.
McKee v. Brown, 110.
   v. Cottle, 75.
   v. Marshall, 299.
   v. Perchment, 363.
   v. Wilcox, 116.

548 CASES CITED.

[The figures refer to pages.]

McKee's Lessee v. Pfout, 59, 81.
McKelway v. Seymour, 280.
McKenna v. Kirkwood, 211, 234.
McKenzie v. City of Lexington, 22.
   v. Hatton, 141.
Mackey v. Proctor, 79.
   v. Wallace, 120.
Mackey's Adm'r v. Coates, 273.
Mackie v. Cairns, 394.
McKim v. Mason, 15, 183.
McKinney v. Burns, 266.
   v. Settles, 417.
   v. Stacks, 57.
McKinnis v. Mortgage Co., 144.
McKinnon v. Meston, 463.
Mackintosh v. Trotter, 22.
McKissick v. Ashby, 144.
   v. Pickle, 176.
Macknet's Ex'rs v. Macknet, 284.
McKnight v. Ratcliff, 166.
Mackreth v. Symmons, 194.
McLane v. Paschal, 190.
McLaren v. Anderson, 125.
Maclary v. Turner, 143.
McLaughlin v. Johnson, 14.
   v. McLaughlin, 341.
   v. Nash, 20.
   v. Salley, 154.
   v. Shepherd, 189.
McLean v. Warehouse Co., 142.
Macleay, In re, 395.
McLellan v. Turner, 39.
   v. Whitney, 155.
McLemore v. McNeley, 452.
McLenan v. Sullivan, 267.
McLendon v. Horton, 59.
McLennan v. Grant, 144.
M'Loughlin v. Craig, 140.
McMahan v. Jacoway, 152.
   v. Kimball, 100.
   v. McMahan, 344.
McMahon v. Russell, 184.
   v. Williams, 354.
McManus v. Carmichael, 5, 6, 423.
   v. Shoe, etc., Co., 136.
McMasters v. Negley, 77.
M'Mechan v. Griffing, 217.
McMichael v. Craig, 59.
McMillan v. Parker, 117.
   v. Richards, 184.
   v. Warner, 121.
   v. Wehle, 460.
   v. William Deering & Co., 385.

McMonegle v. Wilson, 118.
McMurphy v. Minot, 140, 148.
McMurray v. Shuck, 113.
McMurtry v. Brown, 430.
McNair v. Picotte, 228.
McNaughton v. McNaughton, 477.
McNeeley v. Hart, 154.
McNeely v. Langan, 467.
   v. McNeely, 481.
McNeer v. McNeer, 83.
McNiece v. Eliason, 235.
McNeil v. Ames, 149.
   v. Call, 243.
   v. Jordan, 452.
McParland v. Larkin, 342.
McPherson v. Atlantic & P. R. Co., 139.
   v. Hayward, 238.
   v. Housel, 246.
   v. Rollins, 222.
McQuie v. Peay, 191.
McRae v. McRae, 105.
McRee v. Means, 261.
McRimmon v. Martin, 193.
McRoberts v. Washburne, 379.
McSorley v. Larissa, 210.
McTigue v. McTigue, 78.
Maddocks v. Jellison, 102.
Maddox v. Maddox's Adm'r, 173.
Madigan v. Burns, 174.
   v. McCarthy, 21.
Madland v. Benland, 493.
Magaw v. Field, 478.
Magee v. Magee, 126.
   v. Mellon, 110.
Magennis v. MacCullogh, 409.
Magie v. Reynolds, 207.
Magill v. Hinsdale, 144.
Magnusson v. Johnson, 189.
Magor v. Chadwick, 373.
Magruder v. Peter, 24.
Mahoney v. Young, 106.
Main v. Feathers, 135.
Maine v. Cumston, 367.
Major v. Bukley, 419.
   v. Watson, 424.
Makepeace v. Bancroft, 422.
   v. Worden, 362.
Malloney v. Horan, 106, 451.
Malone v. Kornrumpf, 121.
   v. McLaurin, 76, 79.
   v. Majors, 109.
   v. Roy, 195, 201.

[The figures refer to pages.]

Malony v. Horan, 123.
Manaudas v. Mann, 437.
Manchester v. Doddridge, 156, 157.
Mandelbaum v. McDonell, 395.
Manderson v. Lukens, 285, 301.
Mandlebaum v. McDonell, 314, 395.
Mangles v. Brewing Co., 244.
Manhattan Co. v. Evertson, 393.
Manhattan Trust Co. v. Sioux City & N. Ry. Co., 146.
Manly v. Pettee, 344.
Mann v. Corrington, 125.
 v. Jackson, 178.
 v. Mann, 195, 232.
 v. Pearson, 425.
Manning v. Laboree, 91, 92.
 v. Ogden, 18.
 v. Smith, 419.
Manning's Case, 79.
Mansfield v. McGinnis, 341.
 v. Mansfield, 431.
 v. Watson, 385.
Mantz v. Buchanan, 89, 90, 104.
Manwaring v. Tabor, 48.
Maple v. Kussart, 452, 453.
Maples v. Millon, 8.
Marco v. Hicklin, 233.
Mardes v. Meyers, 416.
Mardis v. Meyers, 421.
Marin v. Stearns, 409.
Marker v. Marker, 62.
Markland v. Crump, 135.
Marks v. Sewall, 346.
Marlow v. King, 485.
Marsellis v. Thalhimer, 74.
Marsh v. Austin, 212.
 v. Brace, 378.
 v. Lazenby, 113.
 v. McNider, 143.
 v. Renton, 276, 277.
Marshall v. Bacheldor, 126.
 v. Conrad, 388.
 v. Gingell, 294.
 v. Heard, 142.
 v. McPherson, 96.
 v. Palmer, 343.
 v. Roberts, 223.
Marsters v. Cling, 145.
Marston v. Rowe, 466.
Martin v. Ballou, 172.
 v. Cauble, 214.

Martin v. Cook, 418.
 v. Fridley, 236.
 v. Goble, 364.
 v. Houghton, 166.
 v. Hughes, 118.
 v. Jackson, 224.
 v. Maugham, 331.
 v. McReynolds, 245.
 v. Parsons, 492.
 v. Pine, 67.
 v. Price, 357.
 v. Roe, 23.
 v. Smith, 229, 333, 336.
 v. Stearns, 409.
 v. Tobin, 150, 281.
 v. Waddell, 5, 31.
 v. Waddell's Lessee, 399, 400, 402.
Martin Clothing Co. v. Henly, 122.
Martindale v. Kendrick, 484.
Martin's Heirs v. Martin, 106.
Martyn v. Clue, 136.
 v. Knowllys, 342.
Marvin v. Ledwith, 288.
 v. Mining Co., 366.
 v. Smith, 107.
 v. Vedder, 230.
Marwick v. Andrews, 176.
Marwood v. Turner, 476.
Maryland Mut. Ben. Soc. v. Clendinen, 316.
Mary Portington's Case, 51.
Masen v. Horton, 353.
Mask v. Allen, 452.
Mason v. Fenn, 143.
 v. Mason's Ex'rs, 273.
 v. White, 420.
Massey v. Hubbard, 216.
 v. Huntington, 260.
 v. Modawell, 24.
Massie v. Hiatt's Adm'r, 480.
Massot v. Moses, 374.
Masters v. Pollie, 4.
Masterson v. Munro, 421.
 v. Pullen, 24.
Masury v. Southworth, 137.
Mathews v. Duryee, 90.
Mathewson v. Smith, 90, 91.
Mathis v. Board of Assessors, 6.
 v. Hammond, 301.
 v. Stufflebeam, 267.
Matlock v. Lee, 101.

[The figures refer to pages.]

Matthews v. Hudson, 304.
   v. McPherson, 271, 272.
   v. Trust Co., 203.
   v. Ward, 31.
   v. Whitaker, 136.
Matthias' Estate, In re, 481.
Mattocks v. Stearns, 71, 81.
Matts v. Hawkins, 367.
Maul v. Rider, 214.
Maulding v. Scott, 286.
Maule v. Ashmead, 138.
   v. Weaver, 432.
Maundrell v. Maundrell, 311, 317, 322.
Maupin v. Emmons, 214.
Maurhoffer v. Mittnacht, 238.
Mautz v. Buchanan, 96.
Maxey v. O'Connor, 403.
Maxon v. Gray, 95.
Maxwell v. Newton, 250.
May v. Le Claire, 215.
   v. Oil Co., 152.
Mayburry v. Brien, 85, 89, 92, 93.
Mayfield v. Maasden, 120.
Mayham v. Coombs, 222.
Mayho v. Buckhurst, 137.
   v. Cotton, 118.
Maynard v. Esher, 364.
   v. Hunt, 230.
   v. Maynard, 434.
Mayo v. Newhoff, 366.
   v. Woods, 493.
Mayor of Kingston v. Horner, 352.
Mayor, etc., of Allegheny v. Ohio & P. R. Co., 401.
Mayor, etc., of Cartersville v. Lyon, 142.
Mayor, etc., of City of Mobile v. Eslava, 423.
Mayor, etc., of Congleton v. Pattison, 137.
Mayor, etc., of New Orleans v. U. S., 31.
Mayor, etc., of New York v. Brooklyn Fire Ins. Co., 136.
   v. Hamilton Fire Ins. Co., 136.
   v. Mabie, 138.
   v. Stuyvesant's Heirs, 324.
Mayor, etc., of Thetford v. Tyler, 156.
Maywood Co. v. Village of Maywood, 219.
Meacham v. Buntling, 81.
   v. Steele, 236.

Meader v Place, 114.
Mebane v. Mebane, 397.
Mechanics' & Traders' Fire Ins. Co. v. Scott, 140.
Mecum v. Railroad Co., 442.
Medary v. Cathers, 139.
Medley v Medley, 88, 306.
Meech v. Meech, 114.
Meehan v. Bank, 242.
   v. Forrester, 187.
   v. Williams, 217.
Meig's Appeal, 12.
Meley v. Collins, 452.
Mellon v. Reed, 344.
Mellon's Appeal, 224.
Melross v. Scott, 193.
Melton v. Fitch, 487.
Melvin v. Proprietors, 71, 73, 80, 458.
   v. Whiting, 352, 353, 355, 374.
Memphis & C. R. Co. v. Neighbors, 174.
Mendenhall v. Klinck, 166.
Menger v. Ward, 148.
Menzies v. Breadalbane, 472.
Meraman's Heirs v. Caldwell's Heirs, 80, 81, 303.
Mercer v. Selden, 75.
   v. Woodgate, 363.
Merchants' Nat. Bank v. Stanton, 21.
Merchants' & Farmers' Bank v. Hervey Plow Co., 224.
Mercier v. Railway Co., 37.
Meredith v. Joans, 262.
Meriwether v. Booker, 71.
   v. Howe, 71.
Merket v. Smith, 270.
Merreck v. Wallace, 221.
Merrill v. Brown, 255, 260.
   v. Bullock, 164.
   v. Daffin, 480.
   v. Elliott, 181.
   v. Emery, 109, 286.
   v. Hayden, 477.
   v. Hurley, 181.
   v. Luce, 220.
Merrills v. Swift, 435.
Merriman v. Moore, 207.
Merritt v. Bartholick, 210, 245.
   v. Clason, 427.
   v. Disney, 38.
   v. Hosmer, 236.
   v. Hughes, 458.
   v. Judd, 16, 23.

[The figures refer to pages.]

Merritt v. Loan Co., 272.
 v. Morse, 447, 449.
 v. Scott, 61.
 v. Simpson, 383.
Merritt's Lessee v. Horne, 75.
Mershon v. Castree, 196.
Meserve v. Meserve, 96, 99.
Meservey v. Snell, 449.
Messer v. Regiunitter, 466.
Messick v. Railway Co., 168.
Metcalf v. Smith, 121.
Methodist Church v. Remington, 389.
Methodist Episcopal Church v. Clark, 277.
Mettler v. Miller, 75.
Metz v. Todd, 229.
Metzger v. Huntington, 207.
Meyer v. Claus, 114.
 v. Henderson, 153.
Mhoon v. Cain, 464.
Michel v. O'Brien, 152.
Michigan Ins. Co. of Detroit v. Brown, 240, 246.
Michigan Mut. Life Ins. Co. v. Conant, 214.
 v. Cronk, 21.
Michigan Trust Co. v. Lansing Lumber Co., 196.
Mickles v. Dillaye, 201.
Middaugh v. Bachelder, 207.
Middlebrook v. Corwin, 17.
Middlemore v. Goodale, 450.
Middleton v. Findla, 416.
 v. Middleton, 205.
 v. Pritchard, 5.
Midgley v. Walker, 343.
Midland Ry. Co. v. State, 15.
Midland Terminal & Ferry Co. v. Wilson, 380.
Mildmay's Case, 50, 82, 266, 427.
Miles v. Barrows, 424.
 v. Miles, 64.
Milford Sav. Bank v. Ayers, 122.
Milhan v. Sharp, 379.
Millar v. Humphries, 459.
Millard v. Truax, 202.
Milledge v. Lamar, 88.
Miller v. Aldrich, 198.
 v. Baker, 8, 17.
 v. Beverly, 100.
 v. Bingham, 213.
 v. Bradford, 221.

Miller v. Clark, 249.
 v. Craig, 384.
 v. Curry, 201.
 v. Ewing, 454.
 v. Fletcher, 436.
 v. Hepburn, 471.
 v. Lapman, 358.
 v. Levi, 178.
 v. Lincoln, 201.
 v. Little, 127.
 v. Lullman, 434.
 v. Maguire, 140.
 v. Marckle, 114.
 v. Meers, 434.
 v. Miller, 81, 306, 346, 455.
 v. Plumb, 20.
 v. Prescott, 136, 152.
 v. Railway Co., 166.
 v. Richards, 360.
 v. Shackleford, 80, 143, 303.
 v. Shields, 64, 139.
 v. Thompson, 206, 246.
 v. Tipton, 184.
 v. Waddingham, 13, 21.
 v. Wilson, 84, 266.
Miller's Appeal, 120.
Millett v. Davey, 201.
 v. Lagomarsino, 461, 462.
Millikan v. Patterson, 491.
Milling v. Becker, 409.
Mills v. Catlin, 443.
 v. Franklin, 38.
 v. Gore, 433.
 v. Learn, 380.
 v. Railway Co., 171.
 v. Sampsel, 138.
 v. Seward, 297.
 v. Smith, 223.
 v. Van Voorhies, 91, 247.
Milner v. Clavert, 485.
 v. Shipley, 492.
Milnes v. Branch, 378.
Milton v. Turner, 221.
Mims v. Mims, 221.
Minard v. Burtis, 165.
Miner v. Beekman, 202.
 v. Gilmour, 369.
 v. Lorman, 342.
Mines, Case of, 7, 39.
Minneapolis Mill Co. v. Minneapolis & St. L. Ry. Co., 168.
 v. Tiffany, 31.

552 CASES CITED.

[The figures refer to pages.]

Minneapolis W. Ry. v. Minneapolis & St. L. Ry. Co., 167, 351.
Minnig v. Batdorff, 288.
Minot v. Brooks, 461.
— v. Taylor, 324.
Minshull v. Oakes, 136, 137.
Minter v. Crommelin, 403.
Minton v. Steele, 471.
Mission of Immaculate Virgin v. Cronin, 460.
Missouri, K. & T. Ry. Co. v. Fulmore, 142.
Missouri Pac. Ry. Co. v. Keys, 369.
Mitchell v. Billingsley, 22.
— v. Campbell, 38.
— v. Coombs, 229.
— v. Kinnard, 454.
— v. Pillsbury, 445.
— v. Ryan, 435.
— v. Simpson, 297.
— v. Starbuck, 344.
— v. Warner, 3, 445.
— v. Wilson, 419.
— v. Winslow, 185.
Mitchell's Lessee v. Ryan, 75.
Mittel v. Karl, 335.
Mizell v. Burnett, 171.
Model Lodging House Ass'n v. Boston, 232.
Moerlein v. Investment Co., 119.
Moffatt v. Smith, 148.
Moffat's Ex'rs v. Strong, 301, 302.
Moffitt v. Lytle, 356, 418.
Mohawk & H. R. Co. v. Clute, 25.
Mohr v. Tulip, 384.
Mollett v. Brayne, 415.
Monig's Adm'x v. Phillips, 143.
Monongahela Bridge Co. v. Kirk, 423.
Monroe v. Trenholm, 396.
Montag v. Linn, 429.
Montague v. Railroad, 200.
— v. Selb, 341.
Monteith v. Finkbeiner, 142.
Montello, The, 6.
Montgomery v. Beecher, 187.
— v. Chadwick, 201.
— v. Dorion, 388.
— v. Sturdivant, 419.
— v. Willis, 150, 160.
Moodie v Reid, 318.
Moody v. Fleming, 460.
— v. Harper, 111.

Moody v. King, 77, 86, 88.
— v. McClelland, 365.
— v. Mayor, etc., 142.
Mooers v. Bunker, 344.
Moomey v. Maas, 247.
Moor v. Parker, 296.
Moore, In re, 173, 242.
— v. Boyd, 158.
— v. Burrow, 481.
— v. Calvert, 79.
— v. Collishaw, 466.
— v. Crawford, 265.
— v. Dimond, 57, 316, 477.
— v. Esty, 85, 88.
— v. Frost, 111.
— v. Hazleton, 435.
— v. Horsley, 262.
— v. Hunter, 219.
— v. Jackson, 274.
— v. Kime, 228.
— v. Littel, 298.
— v. Mayor, etc., 84, 104.
— v. Miller, 133.
— v. Peacock, 115.
— v. Perry, 171.
— v. Pierson, 216.
— v. Rawson, 364.
— v. Reaves, 122.
— v. Rollins, 88.
— v. Simonson, 60.
— v. Smaw, 7.
— v. Smead, 121, 454.
— v. Smith, 16, 163.
— v. Starks, 246.
— v. Townshend, 63.
— v. Wade, 188.
— v. Walker, 206.
— v. Weber, 138.
— v. Wood, 143.
Moores v. Moores, 317.
Moore's Appeal, 207.
Moore's Heirs v. Moore's Devisees, 277.
Moran v. Hagerman, 190.
— v. Lezotte, 425.
Morecock v. Dickins, 225.
Morehead v. Watkyns, 161.
Morehouse v. Cotheal, 63.
Moreland v. Page, 424.
Morey v. Hoyt, 22.
— v. Sohier, 474.
Morgan v. Conn, 98.
— v. Fisher, 270.

CASES CITED.

[The figures refer to pages.]

Morgan v. Gronon, 329.
   v Hammett, 233.
   v. Hendrew, 97.
   v. Hudnell, 343.
   v. King, 6.
   v. Mason, 351.
   v. Milman, 318.
   v. Morgan, 48.
   v. Powers, 157.
   v. Reading, 6, 423.
   v. Smith, 445.
   v Stell, 431.
   v. Varick, 14.
Morice v. Bishop of Durham, 267.
Morley v. Pincombe, 146.
   v. Rodgers, 145.
Morling v. Brownson, 182.
Moroney's Appeal, 225.
Morrice's Case, 346.
Morrill v. Kilner, 394.
Morris v. Bolles, 330.
   v. Budlong, 201.
   v. Edgington, 360.
   v. Kettle, 141.
   v. McClary, 462.
   v. Nixon, 136.
   v. Ward, 123, 125.
Morris' Appeal, 15.
Morris Canal & Banking Co. v. Brown, 178.
Morrison v. Bean, 249.
   v. Berry, 13.
   v. Brand, 190.
   v. Brown, 219.
   v. Chadwick, 141.
   v. Funk, 225.
   v. Kelly, 217.
   v. Larkin, 491.
   v. Marquardt, 356.
   v. Morrison, 229, 429.
   v. Thistle, 72.
Morrow v. Jones, 187, 201.
Morse v. Aldrich, 136.
   v. Copeland, 166, 167, 358.
   v. Curtis, 213.
   v. Goddard, 138, 140, 145.
   v. Martin, 316.
   v. Mason, 477.
   v. Smith, 235.
   v. Whitcher, 197.
Mortimer v. O'Reagan, 148.

Morton v. Barrett, 255.
   v. Noble, 106.
   v. Palmer, 163.
Mosely v. Reily, 491.
Moser v. Lower, 154.
Moses v. Loomis, 152.
   v. Micou, 396.
Mosher v. Mosher, 87, 93.
Mosher v. Yost, 68.
Moshier v. Meek, 192, 193.
   v. Norton, 203.
   v. Reding, 133.
   v. Reynolds, 34.
Moss v. Anderson, 429.
   v. Gallimore, 132.
   v. Moss, 267.
   v. Scott, 459.
   v. Sheldon, 419.
   v. Warner, 121.
Motley v. Harris, 204.
Mott v. Hagerman, 154.
   v. Maris, 240.
   v. Palmer, 3, 12.
Moulton v. Robinson, 155.
Mounsey v. Ismay, 354.
Moursund v. Preiss, 122.
Movan v. Hays, 262.
Mowry v. Bradley, 93.
Moynihan v. Allyn, 142.
Mudd v. Mullican, 67.
Muehlberger v. Schilling, 192.
Muir v. Berkshire, 203.
Mulcahy v. Fenwick, 226.
Muldrow v. Robison, 221.
Mulford v. Brown, 230.
Mulholland's Estate, In re, 8.
Mullany v. Mullany, 82.
Mullen v. M'Kelvy, 475.
   v. Stricker, 364.
Muller v. Inderreiden, 123.
Mullins v. Looke, 113.
Mullock v. Souder, 475.
Mulry v. Norton, 470.
Mulvey v. Gibbons, 250.
Mumford v. Brown, 135.
   v. Whitney, 166.
Munday v. O'Neil, 143.
Munn v. Worrall, 418.
Munroe v. Ward, 458.
Munson v. Berdan, 316.
   v. Munson, 228.

554

CASES CITED.

[The figures refer to pages.]

Murdock v. Chapman, 185.
   v. Gifford, 13, 15, 20.
   v. Ratcliff, 150.
Murphy v. Barnard, 220, 226.
   v. Calley, 189.
   v. Copeland, 423.
   v. Crouch, 123.
   v. Doyle, 460.
   v. Farwell, 237.
   v. Murphy, 270, 482.
Murray v. Cherrington, 134, 159.
   v. Emmons, 131.
   v. Hall, 333.
   v. Hudson, 460.
   v. Jones, 302.
   v. Marshall, 208.
   v. Porter, 209.
   v. Sells, 117.
Murrell v. Mathews, 49.
Muse v. Hotel Co., 452.
Musgrave v. Sherwood, 163.
Musick v. Barney, 462.
Mussey v. Pierre, 81.
Mutton's Case, 299, 500.
Mutual Benefit Life Ins. Co. v. Brown, 430.
   v. Howell, 241.
Mutual Building & Loan Ass'n v. Wyeth, 238.
Mutual Life Ins. Co. of New York v. Dake, 221, 222.
   v. Everett, 318.
   v. Newell, 195.
   v. Shipman, 185.
Muzzarelli v. Hulshizer, 441.
Myers v. Boyd, 438.
   v. Evans, 123.
   v. Ford, 113, 120, 121.
   v. Wright, 245.
Myrover v. French, 435.

N

Naltner v. Tappey, 229.
Nannock v. Horton, 317.
Napier v. Howard, 301.
   v. Napier, 317.
Napper v. Sanders, 290, 292.
Nash v. Springstead, 145.
Nason v. Allen, 95.

National Bank v. North, 18.
National Oil-Refining Co. v. Bush, 164.
National Union Bank v. Segur, 137.
National Union Bldg. Ass'n v. Brewer, 153, 434.
Navassa Guano Co. v. Richardson, 184.
Nave v. Berry, 143.
Nazareth Literary & Benevolent Institute v. Lowe, 90.
Neal v. Bellamy, 154.
   v. Gregory, 452.
Neale v. Mackenzie, 141.
   v. Neale, 415.
   v Seeley, 372.
Nebraska v. Iowa, 472.
Needham v. Allison, 18.
Neel v. McElhenny, 274, 275.
   v. Neel, 64.
Neely v. Butler, 76.
Neilson v. Lagow, 261, 262, 264.
Neligh v. Michenor, 184.
Nelson v. Atkinson, 189.
   v. Brown, 109.
   v. Eachel, 152.
   v. Pinegar, 183.
   v. Pomeroy, 110.
   v. Russell, 284.
   v. Thompson, 153.
   v. Trigg, 467.
Nelson's Heirs v. Boyce, 225.
Neves v. Scott, 258, 259.
Nevil v. Saunders, 256.
Nevil's Case, 46.
Nevitt v. Bacon, 241.
New v. Potts, 312.
   v. Wheaton, 216, 217.
Newburgh & C. Turnpike Road Co. v. Miller, 379.
Newcomb v. Harvey, 378.
   v. Ramer, 155.
Newcomen v. Coulson, 360.
New England Jewelry Co. v. Merriam, 231.
New England Loan & Trust Co. v. Spitler, 384.
Newhall v. Bank, 90.
   v. Pierce, 217.
   v. Wheeler, 261, 262.
New Hampshire Land Co. v. Tilton, 422.
Newis v. Lark, 395.

[The figures refer to pages.]

Newkerk v. Newkerk, 38, 173.
Newman v. Anderton, 146.
 v. Chapman, 218.
 v. Newman, 109.
 v. Rutter, 144, 152.
 v. Samuels, 438.
New Orleans Canal & Banking Co. v. Hagan, 181.
Newstead v. Searles, 393.
Newton v. Cubitt, 380.
 v. Manwarring, 232.
New Vienna Bank v. Johnson, 191.
New York, C. & St. L. R. Co. v. Speelman, 369.
New York Real-Estate & Bldg. Imp. Co. v. Motley, 153.
New York Security & Trust Co. v. Saratoga Gas & Electric Light Co., 182.
New York & B. Bridge, In re, 104.
New York & N. E. R. Co. v. Board of Railroad Com'rs, 360.
New York & T. Land Co. v. Hyland, 341.
Nichol v. Levy, 171.
 v. Thomas, 131.
Nicholas v. Chamberlain, 352, 425.
Nichols v. Baxter, 198.
 v. Denny, 343.
 v. Eaton, 41, 397.
 v. Glover, 193.
 v. Hooper, 326.
 v. Levy, 41
 v. Luce, 351, 359, 360.
 v. Otto, 250.
 v. Reynolds, 464.
 v. Williams, 156.
Nicholson v. Bettle, 302.
 v. Drennan. 58.
 v. Walker, 212.
Nickells v. Atherstone, 409.
Nicklase v. Morrison, 66.
Nicoll v. Railroad Co., 176, 281, 282.
Nicolls v. Sheffield, 299, 326.
Nightingale v. Burrell, 48, 301.
 v. Hidden, 78.
Niles v. Nye, 91.
Nitzell v. Paschall, 358.
Niven v. Belknap, 451.
Noble v. Bosworth, 20.
 v. Hill, 341.
 v. Sylvester, 13.

Nocrosi v. Phillippi, 78.
Nodine v. Greenfield, 246.
Noel v. Henley, 321.
 v. Jevon, 89.
Noffts v. Koss, 91.
Noke v. Awder, 451.
Nokes v. Gibbon, 151.
 v. Smith, 41.
Nolan v. Grant, 217.
Noonan v. Albany, 372.
Norcross v. Griffiths, 5.
 v. James, 351.
Norman v. Wells, 136, 137.
Norman's Ex'x v. Cunningham, 78.
Norris v. Harrison, 60.
 v. Milner, 176.
 v. Morrill, 162.
 v. Teamsters' Co., 380.
 v. Woods, 319.
North v. Hammer, 460.
North v. Philbrook, 36, 310.
 v. Strafford, 145.
Northcut v. Whipp, 86, 88.
Northrop v. Wright, 460.
Northrup's Lessee v. Brehmer, 223.
Norton, Succession of, 114.
 v. Henry, 236.
 v. Jackson, 447.
 v. Norton, 261.
 v. Volentine, 372.
Norwich Fire Ins. Co. v. Boomer, 199.
Nottes' Appeal, 193.
Nowlin v. Whipple, 167.
Noyes v. Collins, 472.
 v. Hall, 246.
 v. Stone, 101.
Nudd v. Hobbs, 354, 362.
Null v. Howell, 92, 111.
 v. Jones, 241.
Nunnelly v. Iron Co., 351.
Nunu's Adm'rs v. Givhan's Adm'r, 71.
Nuttall v. Bracewell, 369.
Nutter v. Russell, 305.
Nycum v. McAllister, 127.
Nye v. Alfter, 461.
 v. Railroad Co., 104.

O

Oakford v. Robinson, 246.
Oakland Cemetery Co. v. Bancroft, 13.

CASES CITED.

[The figures refer to pages.]

Oakley v. Oakley, 94, 105.
Oatman v. Goodrich, 82.
Ober v. Brooks, 135.
Oberholtzer's Appeal, 220.
Obert v. Obert, 342.
O'Brien v. Barkley, 173.
— v. Kusterer, 16.
Obrien v. Obrien, 66.
Ocean Grove v. Asbury Park, 4.
O'Connor v. Kelly, 147.
Odell v. Buck, 383, 384.
— v. Odell, 329, 331.
Odessa Imp. & Irr. Co. v. Dawson, 171.
O'Donnell v. Hitchcock, 11, 13.
Offut v. Cooper, 207.
O'Gara v. Neylon, 111.
Ogburn's Estate, In re, 122.
Ogden v. Ball, 443.
— v. Chalfant, 242.
— v. Jennings, 426.
— v. Ogden, 78, 116.
— v. Stock, 21, 23.
Ogden's Appeal, 296.
Ogilvie v. Hill, 141.
Ogle v. Turpin, 226.
Ogontz Land & Imp. Co. v. Johnson, 172.
Ohio & M. R. Co. v. Weber, 3.
Oland's Case, 62.
Olcott v. Gabert, 37.
Oliphant v. Burns, 222, 450.
Oliver v. Cunningham, 208.
— v. Piatt, 269, 270, 275.
— v. Pitman, 359.
— v. Sanborn, 214.
— v. Vance, 484.
Olliffe v. Wells, 275.
Olney v. Hull, 291.
Olsen v. Webb, 142.
Olson v. Huntamer, 472.
— v. Merrill, 5.
Omaha & St. L. Ry. Co. v. Wabash, St. L. & P. Ry. Co., 185.
Omelvany v. Jaggers, 369.
Onderdonk v. Gray, 201.
Ondis v. Bates, 103.
Oneal v. Mead, 205.
O'Neil v. Vanderburg, 455.
O'Neill v. Clark, 208.
Ontario Bank v. Mumford, 264.
Ontario State Bank v. Gerry, 125.
Onward Building Soc. v. Smithson, 454.

Oregon Ry. & Nav. Co. v. Mosier, 21.
Orford v. Benton, 79.
Original Hartlepool Collieries Co. v. Gibb, 370.
Orland's Case, 9.
Orman v. Orman, 121.
Ormerod v. Mill Co., 369.
Orme's Case, 253.
Orr v. Shraft, 116, 117, 122.
Orrick v. Durham, 193.
Ortman v. Chute, 106.
Osborne v. Cabell, 208.
— v. Humphrey, 140.
— v. Ketcham, 182.
Osborne & Co. v. Schoonmaker, 121.
Osgood v. Franklin, 308, 311.
— v. Howard, 19.
— v. Osgood, 191.
Otis v. Browning, 428.
— v. McLellan, 324.
— v. Parshley, 92.
— v. Prince, 173.
— v. Smith, 474.
— v. Spencer, 214, 394.
— v. Thompson, 154.
Ott's Ex'x v. King, 191.
Ottumwa Lodge, etc., v. Lewis, 366.
Ottumwa Woolen Mill Co. v. Hawley, 12
Oulds v. Sansom, 387.
Overand v. Meuczer, 466.
Overdeer v. Lewis, 165.
Overfield v. Christie, 467.
Overman v. Sasser, 20.
Overman's Appeal, 396.
Overseers of Poor of City of Boston v. Sears, 37.
Overton v. Lacy, 333.
Owen v. Association, 182.
— v. Evans, 211.
— v. Field, 177, 358.
— v. Hyde, 64.
— v. Peacock, 111.
Owings v. Emery, 64.
Ownes v. Ownes, 260.
Oxley, Ex parte, 396.

P

Pacific Gas Imp. Co. v. Ellert, 5.
Pacific Nat. Bank v. Windram, 396.
Packard v. Ames, 170.

CASES CITED.   557

[The figures refer to pages.]

Packard v. Railway Co., 158.
   v. Ryder, 5.
Packer v. Wyndham, 71.
Paddock v. Potter, 185, 433.
Padelford v. Padelford, 61, 64.
Padgett v. Cleveland, 21.
Page v. Culver, 148.
   v. Waring, 217.
   v. Webster, 341.
Paice v. Archbishop of Canterbury, 266.
Paige v. Paige, 268, 340.
Paine v. French, 213.
   v. Lock Co., 146.
   v. Mason, 220.
   v. Woods, 423.
Paine's Case, 77.
Palmer v. Bank, 329.
   v. Culbertson, 481.
   v. Fletcher, 364.
   v. Forbes, 14.
   v. Hawes, 120, 122.
   v. Palmer, 213.
   v. Williams, 215, 427.
   v. Young, 341.
Palmeter v. Carey, 241.
Pancake v. Cauffman, 187, 189.
Pancoast v. Pancoast, 339.
Panton v. Holland, 365.
Papillon v. Voice, 297.
Paradine v. Jane, 141.
Pardee v. Lindley, 315.
   v. Treat, 208.
   v. Van Anken, 234.
Pardo v. Bittorf, 121.
Parfitt v. Hember, 327.
Park v. Baker, 16.
Parke v. Neely, 216.
Parkenham's Case, 137.
Parker v. Barker, 451.
   v. Baxter, 494.
   v. Beasley, 230.
   v. Carter, 75.
   v. Cole, 474.
   v. Constable, 157.
   v. Dean, 125.
   v. Foote, 364.
   v. Griswold, 142.
   v. Hayden, 110.
   v. Leach, 288.
   v. Lincoln, 182.
   v. Parker, 101, 285, 302.

Parker v. People, 374.
   v. Railroad Co., 185.
   v. Randolph, 210.
   v. Welsted, 360.
Parkes v. White, 321.
Parkhurst v. Hosford, 214.
Parkins v. Coxe, 64.
Parkist v. Alexander, 219.
Parkman v. Bowdoin, 49.
Parks v. Bishop, 361.
   v. City of Boston, 153.
   v. Newburyport, 372.
Parmenter v. Webber, 146.
Parret v. Shaubhut, 219.
Parrish v. Parrish, 93, 98, 99.
Parrott v. Barney, 139.
   v. Edmondson, 315.
Parsons v. Copeland, 15, 19.
   v. Freeman, 204.
   v. Johnson, 359.
   v. Parsons, 481.
   v. Welles, 233.
   v. Winslow, 61.
Partee v. Stewart, 117.
Parton v. Allison, 95, 99.
Partridge v. Cavender, 397.
   v. Dorsey, 49.
   v. Gilbert, 367, 368.
   v. Scott, 365.
Paske v. Haselfoot, 313.
Passumpsic Sav. Bank v. First Nat. Bank, 214.
Patch v. Keeler, 98.
Patrick v. Sherwood, 60.
Patridge v. Cavender, 397.
Patterson v. Arthurs, 446.
   v. Graham, 167.
   v. Park, 159.
   v. Patterson, 106.
   v. Trust Co., 185.
Pattison v. Shaw, 247.
Patton v. Eberhart, 206.
Patty v. Pease, 229.
Paul v. Carver, 422.
   v. Witman, 449.
Paxson v. Lefferts, 446.
Paxton v. Kennedy, 146.
Payne v. Atterbury, 194.
   v. Avery, 192.
   v. Becker, 95.
   v. Irvin, 142.
   v. James, 139.

CASES CITED.

[The figures refer to pages.]

Payne v. Lott, 492.
   v. Payne, 77, 78, 110, 487.
   v. Rogers, 142.
Pay's Case, 301.
Pea v. Pea, 20.
Peabody v. Hewett, 416.
   v. Minot, 343.
   v. Patten, 91.
Peacock v. Eastland, 256.
   v. Purvis, 8, 146.
Pearce v. Turner, 134.
Pearks v. Moseley, 325.
Pearsall v. Post, 354.
Pearson, In re, 396.
   v. Howey, 84.
   v. Pearson, 83.
Pease v. Egan, 203.
   v. Kelly, 192.
Peay v. Peay, 88.
Pecare v. Choteau's Adm'r, 442.
Pechaud v. Rinquet, 241.
Peck v. Conway, 351.
   v. Herrington, 372.
   v. Ingersoll, 149.
   v. Jones, 448.
   v. Ledwidge, 140.
   v. Lockwood, 376.
   v. Manufacturing Co., 139.
   v. Walton, 407.
Peckham v. Hadwen, 90, 92.
Peirce v. Goddard, 10, 23.
Pelan v. De Bevard, 116.
Pellizzarro v. Reppert, 109.
Pells v. Brown, 302.
Pelton v. Farmin, 248.
Pence v. Arbuckle, 128.
Pendill v. Maas, 143.
   v. Mining Co., 153.
Pendleton v. Dyett, 141.
   v. Vandevier, 59.
Peninsular Iron Co. v. Eells, 190.
Peninsular Stove Co. v. Roark, 125.
Penn v. Divellin, 145.
Penn v. Ott, 184
Penn v. Preston, 135.
Pennant's Case, 175.
Penniman v. Cole, 394.
   v. French, 3.
Pennington's Ex'rs v. Yell, 95.
Pennsylvania R. Co. v. Parke, 179.
Penny v. Corwithe, 428.
Pennybecker v. McDougal, 13.

Penry v. Richards, 421.
Pentland v. Keep, 353, 359.
People v. Appraisers, 5.
   v. Board of Education of Grand Rapids, 34.
   v. Campbell, 492.
   v. Canal Appraisers, 423.
   v. Conklin, 388.
   v. Darling, 159.
   v. Elk River Mill & Lumber Co., 6, 369.
   v. Ferry Co., 400.
   v. McClay, 113.
   v. Organ, 428.
   v. Platt, 5.
   v. Plumsted, 124.
   v. Robertson, 148.
   v. Tibbetts, 6.
   v. Van Rensselaer, 459.
   v. White, 178.
People's Bank v. Mitchell, 152.
People's Ice Co. v. The Excelsior, 6.
Peoria & P. U. Ry. Co. v. Tamplin, 461.
Pepper v. Pepper, 340.
   v. Thomas, 108.
Pepper's Will, 318.
Perkins v. Nichols, 267.
   v. Quigley, 118.
   v. Swank, 17.
Perley v. Chandler, 362.
Pernam v. Wead, 359, 425.
Perrin v. Blake, 296.
   v. Carey, 277.
   v. Garfield, 349, 353.
   v. Lepper, 148.
Perrine v. Cheeseman, 430.
Perrot v. Perrot, 66.
Perry v. Ashby, 127.
   v. Carr, 17, 157.
   v. Grant, 193.
   v. Hale, 475.
   v. Hamilton, 66.
   v. Kline, 49.
   v. Perryman, 108.
   v. Price, 406, 411.
   v. Ross, 124.
   v. Terrel, 9, 61.
Persons v. Persons, 268.
Peter v. Beverly, 308, 315.
   v. Kendal, 379.

CASES CITED. 559

[The figures refer to pages.]

Peters v. Bridge Co., 210.
   v. Jones, 468.
Peterson v. Clark, 304.
Petro v. Cassiday, 175.
Petry v. Ambrosher, 193.
Pettee v. Hawes, 418.
Pettibone v. Edwards, 245.
Pettingill v. Devin, 223.
   v. Hubbell, 245.
Petty v. Barrett, 118.
   v. Malier, 95, 485.
   v. Molier, 75.
Peugh v. Davis, 200, 206.
Pewaukee Milling Co. v. Howitt, 136.
Peyton v. Bury, 173.
   v. Jeffries, 98.
Pfanner v. Sturmer, 9.
Pfeiffer v. Brown, 372.
Pharis v. Leachman, 94.
Phelan v. Boyd, 21.
   v. Brady, 216.
   v. De Martin, 206.
   v. Fitzpatrick, 188, 235.
Phelan's Estate, In re, 121.
Phelps v. Chesson, 174.
   v. Fockler, 226.
   v. Nowlen, 371.
   v. Phelps, 89, 282, 284.
   v. Randolph, 142.
   v. Rooney, 122.
Phene v. Popplewell, 409.
Phene's Trusts, In re, 313.
Phifer v. Barnhart, 223.
Philadelphia v. Girard's Heirs, 328.
Philadelphia Trust, etc., Co. v. Lippincott, 315.
Philbrook v. Delano, 192, 266.
Philips v. Bank, 210, 211.
   v. Leavitt, 234.
Philleo v. Smalley, 122.
Phillips v. Brown, 309.
   v. Clark, 452.
   v. Costley, 216.
   v. Covert, 157.
   v. Ehrman, 142.
   v. Ferguson, 173.
   v. Green, 382.
   v. Harrow, 397.
   v. Library Co., 142.
   v. Roquemore, 225.
   v. Sherman, 404.
   v. Stauch, 123.
   v. Stevens, 153.

Phinizy v. Clark, 209.
Phipps v. Acton, 119.
   v. Ennismore, 396.
Pibus v. Mitford, 297.
Picard v. Montross, 487.
Pickard v. Collins, 142.
Picken v. Matthews, 325.
Pickens v. Webster, 7.
Pickens' Estate, In re, 481.
Pickens' Ex'rs v. Kniseley, 73.
Pickering v. Pickering, 342.
Pickwell v. Spencer, 38.
Pierce v. Brown, 438.
   v. Chace, 338.
   v. Drew, 362.
   v. Dyer, 366, 367.
   v. Goddard, 23.
   v. Hakes, 78.
   v. Indseth, 429.
Pierson v. Armstrong, 406.
   v. Lane, 53.
Pifer v. Ward, 90.
Piggot v. Mason, 135, 136.
   v. Penrice, 318.
Pike v. Gleason, 232.
   v. Robinson, 463.
Pike's Will, In re, 384.
Pile v. Pedrick, 367.
Pilkington v. Boughey, 267.
Pillars v. McConnell, 270.
Pillow v. Roberts, 429.
Pillsbury v. Mitchell, 135.
Pinchain v. Collard, 192.
Pinckney v. Burrage, 457.
Pine v. Leicester, 378.
Pinkerton v. Tumlin, 120.
Pinkum v. City of Eau Claire, 176.
Pinnington v. Galland, 360.
Pinnock v. Clough, 263.
Piper v. Johnston, 123.
Pit v. Chick, 374.
Pittman v. Sofley, 214.
Pitts v. Lancaster Mills, 369.
Pittsburg Consol. Coal Co. v. Greenlee, 149.
Pitzman v. Boyce, 168.
Pixley v. Clark, 371.
   v. Huggins, 225.
Pizzala v. Campbell, 94.
Planters' Bank v. Davis, 79.
Plate v. Koehler, 125.
Platner v. Sherwood, 85.
Plato v. Roe, 187.

CASES CITED.

[The figures refer to pages.]

Platt v. Squire, 213, 234.
Pleasant v. Benson, 162.
Plimpton v. Insurance Co., 198.
Ploen v. Staff, 135.
Pluche v. Jones, 457.
Plumer v. Guthrie, 188.
   v. Plumer, 17.
   v. Robertson, 217.
Plunket v. Holmes, 301.
Poe v. Paxton's Heirs, 193.
Pogue v. Clark, 244, 245.
Poignand v. Smith, 195, 468.
Poindexter v. Blackburn, 9, 62.
Pollard v. Barnes, 352.
   v. Cocke, 223.
   v. Hagan, 5.
   v. Merrill, 72.
   v. Shaaffer, 65.
   v. Shaffer, 139.
   v. Slaughter, 88.
Polley v. Johnson, 8.
Pollock v. Maison, 240.
   v. Speidel, 48, 49.
Polyblank v. Hawkins, 73.
Pomeroy v. Pomeroy, 105.
Pomfret v. Perring, 317.
   v. Ricroft, 356.
Pomroy v. Stevens, 216.
Pond v. Bird, 474.
   v. Eddy, 211.
Ponder v. Cheeves, 462.
Pool v. Blakie, 78, 82.
Poole v. Bentley, 131.
Poole's Case, 16.
Poor v. Horton, 84.
   v. McClure, 5.
Pope v. Hanmer, 459.
   v. Harkins, 143.
   v. Mead, 95.
   v. Pope, 215.
Poppers v. Meagher, 130, 150.
Popplewell v. Hodkinson, 371.
Porch v. Fries, 83.
Porter v. Bank, 72.
   v. Fox, 323.
   v. Greene, 224.
   v. Hill, 334, 343.
   v. Lazear, 104.
   v. Merrill, 163.
   v. Thomas, 316.
   v. Wheeler, 452.
Portington's Case, 51.

Posey v. Cook, 255.
Post v. Hover, 324.
   v. Kearney, 148.
   v. Pearsall, 350.
   v. Vetter, 135.
Postal Tel. Cable Co. v. W. U. Tel. Co., 136.
Posten v. Miller, 233, 235.
Postlethwaite v. Payne, 370.
Potter v. Couch, 311, 395.
   v. Cromwell, 10.
   v. McDowell, 393.
   v. Thornton, 389.
   v. Wheeler, 93.
Potts v. Davenport, 116, 119, 121.
   v. Gilbert, 462, 467.
   v. Plaisted, 230.
Potts' Appeal, 49.
Pottstown Gas Co. v. Murphy, 371.
Potwin v. Blasher, 447.
Poull v. Mockley, 355.
Powcey v. Bowen, 319.
Powell v. Bergner, 19.
   v. Gossom, 75, 76, 78.
   v. Manufacturing Co., 97, 107.
   v. Patison, 242.
   v. Rich, 8.
Powell's Trusts, In re, 329.
Powers v. Harlow, 360.
   v. Insurance Co., 198.
   v. Lumber Co., 234.
   v. McFarran, 224.
   v. Sample, 113.
Powles v. Jordan, 321.
Powley v. Walker, 140.
Prater v. Hoover, 79.
Pratt v. Colt, 274.
   v. Curtis, 393.
   v. Felton, 109.
   v. Leadbetter, 296.
   v. Levan, 149.
   v. Sweetser, 357.
Pratt's Lessee v. Flamer, 48.
Preiss v. Parker, 367.
Prentice v. Wilson, 156.
Preschbaker v. Feaman, 189.
Prescott v. Boucher, 146.
   v. Elm, 161.
   v. Nevers, 458.
   v. Trueman, 445.
   v. White, 143, 356, 369, 373.

CASES CITED. 561

[The figures refer to pages.]

President, etc., of City of Cincinnati v. White, 363.
President, etc., of Lincoln & K. Bank v. Drummond, 175.
P.esident, etc., of Newburgh & Cochecton Turnpike Road v. Miller, 380.
Preston v. Bowmar, 424.
    v. Carr, 306.
    v. Case, 211.
    v. Robinson, 336.
Prewit v. Wilson, 394.
Prewitt v. Ashford, 454.
Price v. Brown, 460.
    v. Cutts, 191.
    v. Hall, 293, 341.
    v. Haynes, 439.
    v. Hobbs, 84, 97.
    v. Jenkins, 394.
    v. Norwood, 175.
    v. Pickett, 9, 60, 62.
    v. Price's Heirs, 25.
    v. Railroad Co., 436.
    v. Wood, 182.
Price's Appeal, 474.
Prichard v. James, 53.
Prickett's Lessee v. Parker, 479.
Priddy v. Griffith, 88.
Priest v. Cummings, 103.
    v. Lackey, 473.
    v. Wheelock, 229.
Priestley v. Holgate, 173.
Prince v. Case, 167.
Prindle v. Anderson, 162.
Pringle v. Dunn, 213, 215, 219.
Pritchard v. Palmer, 439.
Probett v. Jenkinson, 421.
Proctor v. Bigelow, 111.
    v. Bishop of Bath & Wells, 325.
    v. Hodgson, 360.
    v. Machine Co., 453.
Prodgers v. Langham, 393.
Proffitt v. Henderson, 62.
Proprietors of Charles River Bridge v. Proprietors of Warren Bridge, 380, 402.
Proprietors of Church in Brattle Square v. Grant, 283, 284, 292, 325.
Proprietors of Enfield v. Permit, 37.
Proprietors of Liverpool Wharf v. Prescott, 453.
Proprietors of Mill Dam Foundry v. Hovey, 430.

REAL PROP.—36

Proprietors of Town of Shapleigh v. Pilsbury, 255.
Proprietors of Township No. 6 v. McFarland, 458.
Prospect Park & C. I. R. Co. v. Coney Island & B. R. Co., 489.
Prosser v. Wapello, 380.
Prout v. Roby, 72.
    v. Wiley, 383.
Pruitt v. Holland, 53.
Prutsman v. Baker, 433, 434.
Pry v. Pry, 219.
Puckett v. McDaniel, 340, 463.
Pugh v. Arton, 22.
    v. Bell, 106.
Pugsley v. Aikin, 160.
Pullen v. Pullen, 104.
    v. Rianhard, 255.
Pulling's Estate, In re, 105.
Purdy v. Huntington, 233.
Purefoy v. Rogers, 285.
Putnam v. Putnam, 477.
    v. Ritchie, 335.
Putney v. Dresser, 334.
Putzel v. Van Brunt, 420.
Pyer v. Carter, 352.
Pyle v. Pennock, 15.
Pynchon v. Stearns, 63.
Pyne v. Dor, 62.

Q

Queen's College v. Hallett, 145.
Quinby v. Paper Co., 13.
Quinnerly v. Quinnerly, 222.
Quinn's Estate, In re, 72.

R

Rabb v. Griffin, 75.
Raby v. Reeves, 453.
Race v. Ward, 373.
Ragor v. McKay, 145.
Ragsdale v. O Day, 85, 89.
Railroad Co. v. Carr, 369.
Ralls v. Hughes, 111.
Ralph, Ex parte, 326.
Ralston v. Ralston, 101.
Rambo v. Bell, 94.
Ramboz v. Stowell, 455.

[The figures refer to pages.]

Ramsey v. Glenny, 464.
   v. Merriam, 250.
Randall v. Josselyn, 301.
   v. McLaughlin, 352.
   v. Phillips, 269.
Randolph v. Doss, 85.
Rands v. Kendall, 84, 184.
Rank v. Hanna, 105.
Rankin v. Black, 336.
   v. Miller, 223.
Ranney v. Hardy, 217.
Ratcliffe v. Marrs, 419.
   v. Mason, 85, 93.
Rausch, In re, 107.
   v. Rausch, 397.
Rautenbusch v. Donaldson, 78.
Rawley v. Holland, 299.
Rawlings v. Adams, 73, 78, 105, 106.
   v. Lowndes, 85.
Rawlins v. Buttel, 103.
Rawson v. School Dist. 170.
Ray v. Alexander, 53.
   v. Johnson, 140.
   v. Pearce, 240.
   v. Pung, 105.
   v. Scripture, 244.
Raybold v. Raybold, 261.
Raymond v. Glover, 433.
   v. Hodgson, 148.
   v. Holden, 455.
   v. Palmer, 195.
   v. Raymond, 443.
   v. White, 19.
Rayner v. Lee, 95, 491.
Raynor v. Wilson, 434.
Razor v. Razor, 174.
Read v. Stedman, 280.
Reade v. Johnson, 378.
   v. Livingstone, 393.
Reading v. Finrey, 491.
Ready v. Kearsley, 261.
Reardon v. Murphy, 172.
Reasoner v. Edmundson, 444.
Reaume v. Chambers, 37, 75.
Reckhow v. Schanck, 163.
Rector v. Waugh, 37, 343.
Rector, etc., of King's Chapel v. Pelham, 176
Redden v. Miller, 215.
Rede v. Farr, 174.
Redlon v. Barker, 13.
Redwine v. Brown, 135.
Reece v. Miller, 5.

Reed v. Farr, 453.
   v. Inhabitants of Northfield, 362.
   v. Kemp, 219, 437.
   v. Kennedy, 92.
   v. Reed, 79, 202, 474.
   v. Shepley, 89.
   v. Whitney, 106.
Reeder v. Barr, 403.
   v. Purdy, 165.
   v. Sayre, 9.
Reed's Ex'rs v. Reed, 64.
Reel v. Elder, 103.
Rees v. Lowy, 153.
   v. McDaniel, 472.
Reese v. Kinkead, 192.
   v. Smith, 451.
   v. Waters, 81.
Reeve v. Long, 290.
Reeves v. McComeskey, 139, 153.
Reg. v. Inhabitants of Cluworth, 370.
   v. Pratt, 362.
Regan v. Light Co., 359.
Reichenbach v. Railway Co., 171.
Reichenbacker v. Pahmeyer, 142.
Reid v. Parsons, 151.
Reiff v. Horst, 107.
   v. Reiff, 9, 62.
Reigard v. McNeil, 188.
Reilly v Phillips, 249.
Reimer v. Stuber, 353.
Reinback v. Walter, 119.
Reinhart v. Lantz, 42.
Reinoehl v. Shirk, 48, 302.
Reitenbaugh v. Ludwick, 200.
Reitzel v. Eckard, 92.
Remington Paper Co. v. O'Dougherty, 239.
Rempt v. Geyer, 189.
Renals v. Cowlishaw, 351.
Rennie's Estate, In re, 61.
Rennyson's Appeal, 364.
Renoud v. Daskam, 135.
Renshaw v. Bean, 363.
Renwick v. Wheeler, 228.
Renziehausen v. Keyser, 261.
Rerick v. Kern, 168.
Retherick v. Chappel, 327.
Reusens v. Lawson, 461.
Rex v. Burchell, 395.
   v. Inhabitants of Aldborough, 147.
   v. Inhabitants of Leake, 362.
   v. Otley, 13.
Reyburn v. Wallace, 60.

CASES CITED. 563

[The figures refer to pages.]

Reynolds v. Black, 215.
   v. Crispin, 287.
   v. Harris, 490.
   v. Hull, 118.
   v. McCurry, 95.
   v. New York Security & Trust Co., 12.
   v. Reynolds, 92, 103.
   v. Webster, 225.
   v. Wilmeth, 342.
Rhea v. Meridith, 104.
Rhett v. Mason's Ex'r, 262.
Rhines v. Baird, 188.
Rhodes v. McCormack, 122, 366.
   v. McCormick, 120.
   v. Otis, 6, 168.
   v. Whitehead, 293.
   v. Williams, 117.
Ricard v. Williams, 352.
Rice v. Adams, 15.
   v. Nelson, 111.
   v. Railroad Co., 176.
   v. Railroad Corp., 171.
   v. Rice, 270.
Rich v. Bolton, 160.
   v. Braxton, 493.
   v. Cockell, 387.
   v. Gilkey, 477.
   v. Hobson, 154.
   v. Zeilsdorff, 418.
Richard v. Bent, 445.
   v. Hupp, 353, 357.
Richards v. Chace, 123.
   v. Miller, 474.
   v. Richards, 110, 171, 480.
   v. Rose, 365.
   v. Thompson, 247.
Richardson v. Copeland, 14.
   v. Gifford, 132.
   v. Harms, 99.
   v. Hockenhall, 231.
   v. Langridge, 159, 160.
   v. Noyes, 302.
   v. Pate, 386.
   v. Richardson, 302, 341.
   v. Sharpe, 317.
   v. Skolfield, 91, 105.
   v. Wheatland, 290, 291, 298.
   v. York, 57.
Richeson v. Crawford, 204.
Richmond v. Voorhees, 437.
Rickard v. Rickard, 345, 464.
Rickert v. Madeira, 212.

Ricketts v. Loftus, 313.
   v. Railroad Co., 309.
Rico Reduction & Mining Co. v. Musgrave, 342.
Riddell v. Riddell, 93.
Rider v. Bagley, 242.
Ridler, In re, 393.
Ridley, In re, 326.
Riehl v. Bingenheimer, 123.
Riehle v. Heulings, 357.
Rieman v. Wagner, 466.
Riggin v. Love, 419.
Riggs v. Sally, 42.
Right v. Bucknell, 455.
   v. Darby, 161.
Righter v. Forrester, 225, 297.
Rigler v. Cloud, 78.
Rigney v. Water Co., 369.
Rigor v. Frye, 464.
Riley v. Water Power Co., 7.
Riley's Adm'r v. Riley, 71.
Ring v. Burt, 123, 124.
   v. Hardwick, 325.
Ringgold v. Bryan, 216.
Ripley v. Waterworth, 68.
Risien v. Brown, 168.
Rising v. Stannard, 157.
Risk v. Hoffman, 207.
Ritchle v. Ege, 489.
   v. Railway Co., 171.
Ritger v. Parker, 358.
Rittgers v. Rittgers, 262.
River v. Withers, 6.
Rivers v. Adams, 374.
   v. Gooding, 110.
Roach v. Davidson, 94.
   v. Wadham, 312, 316.
Roan v. Holmes, 91.
Roane v. Baker, 225.
Robarts v. Haley, 268.
Robbins, In re, 422.
   v. Eaton, 382.
   v. Kinzie, 107.
   v. Robbins, 90, 104.
Roberts v. Cambridge, 489.
   v. Fleming, 202.
   v. Greer, 114.
   v. Halstead, 227.
   v. Jackson, 152, 435.
   v. Railroad Co., 454.
   v. Stevens, 396.
   v. Thorn, 341.
   v. Whiting, 59, 80.

[The figures refer to pages.]

Robertson v. Biddell, 144.
   v. Corsett, 16.
   v. Hay, 428.
   v. Norris, 71, 80.
   v. Stevens, 79.
   v. Wilson, 305.
   v. Wood, 274.
Robeson v. Pittenger, 364.
Robie v. Chapman, 78.
Robinson v. Baker, 115.
   v. Bates, 106.
   v. Beard, 134.
   v. Buck, 82.
   v. Ezzell, 7.
   v. Fife, 237, 238.
   v. Leach, 125.
   v. Litton, 304.
   v. Miller, 92, 94, 99.
   v. Mining Co., 144.
   v. Robinson, 57.
   v. Schley, 473.
   v. Swearingen, 121.
   v. Wood, 302.
Robinson Bank v. Miller, 206.
Robinson's Estate, In re, 53.
Robison v. Codman, 89, 334.
Rochford v. Hackman, 396.
Rochon v. Lecatt, 81.
Rockingham v. Penrice, 60.
Rockwell v. Hobby, 192.
Rodgers v. Burchard, 223, 224.
   v. Rodgers' Adm'r, 487.
   v. Wallace, 307.
Roe v. Archbishop of York, 409.
   v. Ashburner, 132.
   v. Galliers, 396.
   v. Grew, 297.
   v. Harrison, 152, 396.
   v. Jeffery, 327.
   v. Lees, 160.
   v. Tranmer, 254.
   v. Ward, 130.
Roet v. Somerville, 62.
Rogan v. Walker, 175, 186, 188, 267.
Rogers v. Brokaw, 12, 13, 21.
   v. Brown, 158.
   v. Cruger, 431.
   v. Donnellan, 267.
   v. Fire Co., 299, 411.
   v. Gillinger, 14.
   v. Grigg, 146.
   v. Herron, 235.

Rogers v. Hillhouse, 427.
   v. Humphreys, 132.
   v. Johnson, 468, 487.
   v. Jones, 216.
   v. Moore, 57, 59.
   v. Rawlings, 404.
   v. Rogers, 363.
   v. Smith, 474.
   v. Tucker, 226.
   v. Walker, 384.
Roggenkamp v. Roggenkamp, 269.
Rohn v. Harris, 289, 345.
Rolfe v. Harris, 151.
Roome v. Phillips, 289.
Rooney v. Crary, 200.
Roosevelt v. Bank, 230.
   v. Thurman, 395.
Roper v. Lloyd, 141.
Rose v. Chandler, 247.
   v. Daniel, 469.
   v. Davis, 144.
   v. Hawley, 174.
   v. Sanderson, 80.
   v. Watson, 194.
Roseboom v. Van Vechten, 55.
Rosenblat v. Perkins, 159.
Rosenthal v. Mayhugh, 110.
Roseville Alta Min. Co. v. Iowa Gulch Min. Co., 13.
Rosher, In re, 395.
Ross v. Adams, 407.
   v. Drake, 288.
   v. Dysart, 138.
   v. Gill, 131.
   v. Overton, 153.
   v. Porter, 121.
   v. Whitson, 192.
   v. Wilson, 93.
Rosse's Case, 67.
Rossetter v. Simmons, 473.
Rossiter v. Cossit, 90.
Rothschild v. Railway Co., 241.
Rothwell v. Dewees, 341.
Roundel v. Currer, 173.
Round Lake Ass'n v. Kellogg, 136.
Rountree v. Denson, 455.
Rous v. Jackson, 329.
Roush v. Miller, 85.
Routledge v. Dorril, 327, 329.
Rowbotham v. Wilson, 366.
Rowe v. Beckett, 412.
   v. Bridge Corp., 6.

CASES CITED.

[The figures refer to pages.]

Rowe v. Hamilton, 108.
   v. Nally, 357.
Rowell v. Jewett, 172, 201.
   v. Williams, 206.
Rowland v. Carroll, 98.
   v. Warren, 54, 179.
   v. Williams, 460, 465.
Roy v. Monroe, 23.
Royce v. Guggenheim, 141.
Royston v. Royston, 71.
Rozell v. Vansyckle, 265.
Rubens v. Prindle, 208.
Ruch v. Rock Island, 174.
Ruckman v. Astor, 200.
   v. Outwater, 17, 18.
Rudebaugh v. Rudebaugh, 288.
Rue v. Dole, 188, 190.
Rugan v. Sabin, 469.
Ruggles v. Lawson, 434, 436.
Rumfelt v. Clemens, 386.
Rumsey v. Railway Co., 5.
Runyan v. Stewart, 91.
Rupp v. Eberly, 301.
Rush v. Lewis, 314.
Rusk v. Fenton, 385.
Russ v. Perry, 110.
   v. Steele, 448.
   v. Stratton, 433.
Russel v. Gulwel, 135.
Russell, Ex parte, 394.
   v. Allard, 144.
   v. Bank, 64.
   v. Coffin, 412.
   v. Erwin's Adm'r, 144.
   v. Fabyan, 145, 163.
   v. Jackson, 267, 360.
   v. Petree, 214.
   v. Scott, 370.
   v. Southard, 186, 188.
   v. Woodward, 396.
Russell's Appeal, 219.
Rutherford v. Greene's Heirs, 37.
Ryan v. Adamson, 198.
   v. Andrews, 484.
   v. Brown, 6.
   v. Dox, 188, 271.
   v. Doyle, 269.
   v. Freeman, 74.
Ryder v. Rush, 214.
Ryerson v. Quackenbush, 148, 377.
Rymer v. Stanfield, 477.

S

Sacheverel v. Frogate, 376.
Sackett v. Mallory, 172.
   v. Sackett, 62.
Sadler v. Pratt, 319.
Saenger v. Nightingale, 244.
Safford v. Safford, 92.
Sager v. Tupper, 230, 235.
Saint v. Pilley, 22.
St. Amour v. Rivard, 327.
St. Clair v. Williams, 96.
St. Felix v. Rankin, 346.
St. John v. Conger, 220.
St. Louis, A. T. H. R. Co. v. Nugent, 462.
St. Louis Iron & Mach. Works v. Kimball, 219.
St. Louis University v. McCune, 465.
St. Paul's Church v. Attorney General, 477.
Salmon v. Bennett, 393.
   v. Hoffman, 192.
Salomon v. O'Donnell, 159.
Salter v. Boteler, 68.
   v. Sample, 23.
Saltmarsh v. Smith, 95.
Saltonstall v. Sanders, 276.
Saltoun v. Houstoun, 145.
Sammes' Case, 254, 334.
Sampson v. Cotton Mills, 10, 22.
   v. Easterby, 137.
   v. Henry, 165.
   v. Hoddinott, 369, 370.
Samson v. Rose, 9, 143.
Sanborn v. Adair, 223.
   v. Sanborn, 187.
   v. Woodman, 175.
Sand v. Hughes, 464.
Sanderlin v. Sanderlin's Adm'r, 113.
Sanders v. Cornish, 327.
   v. Ellington, 9.
   v. McMillian, 98.
   v. Partridge, 149.
   v. Wilson, 201.
Sandes' Case, 266.
Sandford v. McLean, 90, 104.
San Diego v. Southern Pac. R. Co., 492.
Sands v. Hughes, 464.
   v. Pfeiffer, 21, 23.

[The figures refer to pages.]

Sands Ale Brewing Co., In re, 198.
Sandwich v. Railway Co., 369.
Sandwich Manuf'g Co. v. Zellmer, 452, 455.
Sanford v. Goodell, 397.
   v. Harvey, 161.
   v. Hill, 236.
   v. Jackson, 110.
   v. Johnson, 159.
   v. Lackland, 397.
San Pedro & Cañon del Agua Co. v. U. S., 403.
Sapp v. Morrill, 493.
Sargeant v. Rowsey, 237.
Sargent v. Parsons, 341.
   v. Towne, 39.
   v. Wilson, 247.
Sarles v. Sarles, 63.
Sarsfield v. Nealey, 159.
Satchell v. Doram, 219.
Satterfield v. Malone, 215.
Saucer v. Keller, 167.
Saulet v. Shepherd, 471.
Saunders v. Blythe, 106.
   v. Railway Co., 5.
   v. Schmaelzle, 272.
   v. Vautier, 326.
Saundeys v. Oliff, 375.
Savage v. Burnham, 109.
   v. Lee, 255.
   v. Mason, 367.
Savile v. Blacket, 321.
Savings & Loan Soc. v. Burnett, 202, 224, 225.
Sawley v. Northampton, 285.
Sawyer v. Cubby, 323.
   v. Hanson, 130.
   v. Kendall, 467.
   v. Twiss, 18.
Say v. Stoddard, 157.
Sayer v. Sayer, 318.
   v. Tupper, 230.
Sayers v. Hoskinson, 64.
   v. Wall, 78.
Sayles v. Purifying Co., 13.
Sayre v. Townsend, 267, 268.
Scales v. Cockrill, 467.
Scammell v. Wilkinson, 387.
Scammon v. Campbell, 97.
Scanlan v. Cobb, 385.
   v. Wright, 386, 388.
Scanlon v. Walshe, 481.

Scarry v. Eldridge, 246.
Scatterwood v. Edge, 323.
Schaefer v. Schaefer, 57.
Schaeffler v. Michling, 445.
Schaffer v. Kettell, 478.
Schall v. Railroad Co., 470.
Schearff v. Dodge, 230.
Schedda v. Sawyer, 403.
Scheetz v. Fitzwater, 178, 282.
Schenck v. Ellingwood, 318.
Schenk v. Peay, 491.
Schenley v. Com., 353.
Schermerhon v. Miller, 73, 74, 80.
Schermerhorn v. Miller, 74.
   v. Negus, 395.
Schieffelin v. Carpenter, 409.
Schifferstein v. Allison, 240.
Schilling v. Holmes, 138.
   v. Rommger, 370.
Schintz v. McManamy, 428.
Schlesinger v. Railroad Co., 174.
Schley v. Lyon, 255.
Schmidt v. Niemeyer, 492.
   v. Quinn, 360.
Schmitt v. Schmitt, 430.
Schnebly v. Schnebly, 87, 96.
Schneider v. Hoffmann, 125.
Schnitzius v. Bailey, 357.
Schofield v. Homestead Co., 443.
School Committee v. Kesler, 429.
School Dist. v. Lindsay, 168.
   v. Trustees of First Baptist Church of Normal, 176.
Schorr v. Etling, 110.
Schroeder v. Bauer, 126.
Schulenberg v. Harriman, 176.
Schultz v. Schultz, 388.
Schultze v. Houfes, 215.
Schuster v. Schuster, 81.
Schutt v. Large, 213.
Schuyler v. Broughton, 339.
   v. Smith, 164.
Schuylkill Nav. Co. v. Stoever, 361.
Schwab Clothing Co. v. Claunch, 249, 389.
Schwatken v. Daudt, 109.
Schweiss v. Woodruff, 214.
Schweitzer v. Wagner, 89.
Schwinger v. Hickok, 241.
Scofield v. Alcott, 283.
   v. Olcott, 288.

CASES CITED. 567

[The figures refer to pages.]

Scott v. Beecher, 204.
   v. Brick Co., 136.
   v. Causey, 72.
   v. Delaney, 460.
   v. Guernsey, 82, 342.
   v. Henry, 234.
   v. Howard, 95.
   v. Lunt, 377.
   v. Magloughlin, 211.
   v. Mewhirter, 212.
   v. Mills, 463.
   v. Scott, 440, 475.
   v. State, 343.
   v. Twiss, 443.
   v. Webster, 195.
   v. West, 301.
Scott's Ex'r v. Scott, 409.
Scovill v. McMahon, 172.
Scripture v. Johnson, 236.
Scudmore v. Scudmore, 23.
Seabrook v. Mikell, 286.
Seager v. McCabe, 88.
Seaman v. Hax, 209.
Sears v. Cunningham, 262.
   v. Hanks, 123.
Sebald v. Mulholland, 367.
Sebastian v. Hill, 158.
Sebring v. Mersereau, 345.
Secard's Lessee v. Davis, 224.
Secheverel v. Dale, 49.
Seckel v. Engle, 336.
Secombe v. Railroad Co., 495.
Second Congregational Soc. v. First Congregational Soc., 277.
   v. Waring, 273.
Second Nat. Bank v. O. E. Merrill Co., 159.
Security Co. v. Cone, 288.
Security Loan & Trust Co. v. Willamette Steam Mills Lumbering & Manuf'g Co., 16.
Sedberry v. Verplanck, 138.
Sedgwick v. Hollenback, 138, 444, 448.
   v. Laflin, 36.
Seedhouse v. Broward, 21.
Seeger v. Leakin, 296.
   v. Pettit, 12.
Seekright v. Moore, 85.
Seeley v. Manning, 195.
Seibold v. Christman, 268.
Selden v. Canal Co., 166.
Sellers v. Sellers, 221.

Sentill v. Robeson, 78.
Sergeson v. Sealy, 318.
Serle v. St. Elvy, 205.
Sessions v. Kent, 203.
Sewall v. Wilmer, 308.
Sewell v. Holland, 216.
   v. Price's Adm'r, 188.
Sexton v. Carley, 144.
   v. Wheaton, 394.
Seymor's Case, 51.
Seymour v. Bull, 319.
   v. Carli, 464.
   v. Courtenay, 374.
   v. Freer, 274.
   v. Lewis, 352.
   v. Sanders, 126.
Shaeffer v. Weed, 90.
Shafer v. Wilson, 365.
Shaffer v. McCloskey, 231.
Shall v. Biscoe, 192.
Shalter's Appeal, 317.
Shand v. Hanley, 394.
Shanfelter v. Horner, 151.
Shank v. Dewitt, 312.
Shankland's Appeal, 272.
Shanks v. Lucas, 403.
Shannon v. Grindstaff, 148, 149.
   v. Hall, 221.
   v. Kinny, 467.
Shape v. Schaffner, 89.
Shapleigh v. Pilsbury, 290, 299.
Shapley v. Rangeley, 243.
Sharington v. Strotton, 266.
Sharon Iron Co. v. City of Erie, 175.
Sharp v. Johnston, 118.
   v. Ropes, 351.
Sharpe v. Kelley, 144.
Sharpsteen v. Tillou, 322.
Shattuck v. Gragg, 87, 96.
   v. Hastings, 170.
Shaughnessey v. Leary, 356.
Shaupe v. Shaupe, 95.
Shaw v. Carbrey, 14.
   v. Ford, 395.
   v. Galbraith, 440.
   v. Railroad Co., 248.
   v. Robinson, 297.
Shay v. McNamara, 456.
Sheafe v. Cushing, 57.
   v. O'Neil, 95, 388.
Sheaffer v. Sheaffer, 175.

[The figures refer to pages.]

Shearer v. Field, 235.
　v. Middleton, 466.
Shearman v. Hicks, 308.
　v. Irvine's Lessee, 459.
Shearman's Adm'r v. Hicks, 317.
Shee v. Hale, 396.
Sheets v. Joyner, 135.
　v. Selden, 139.
　v. Selden's Lessee, 134.
Sheetz v. Fitzwater, 179.
Sheffey v. Bank, 224.
Shelby v. Hearne, 139.
Shelden v. Erskine, 434.
Sheldon v. Patterson, 248.
Shell v. Duncan, 494.
　v. Kemmerer, 364.
Shelley's Case, 296.
Shelton v. Carroll, 95.
　v. Codman, 135.
　v. Ficklin, 15.
　v. Hadlock, 67.
　v. Homer, 314.
Shepard v. Rinks, 344.
　v. Shepard, 214, 386.
Shepherd v. Cassiday, 121.
　v. McEvers, 272.
　v. May, 228.
Sherard v. Sherard's Adm'r, 99.
Sherburne v. Jones, 9, 156, 157.
Sheriff v. Neal, 271.
Sherley v. Sherley, 262.
Sherman v. Ballou, 343.
　v. Dodge, 273.
　v. Newton, 109.
　v. Sherman, 228.
　v. Williams, 138.
Sherred v. Cisco, 367, 368.
Sherron v. Acton, 204.
Sherry v. Frecking, 4.
Sherwin v. Lasher, 140.
Sherwood v. Saxton, 190.
Shields v. Arndt, 369.
　v. Lozear, 228.
　v. Russell, 189.
　v. Schiff, 400.
Shiell v. Sloan, 90.
Shillaber v. Robinson, 190.
Shinkle's Assignees v. Bristow, 196.
Shipley v. Bunn, 382.
Shipp v. Snyder, 93.
Shirkey v. Hanna, 244, 245.
Shirley v. Crabb, 168.
　v. Shirley, 194.

Shively v. Bowlby, 5.
Shoecraft v. Bloxham, 191.
Shoemaker v. Commissioners, 263.
　v. Huffnagle, 49.
Shope v. Schaffner, 91.
Shores v. Carley, 79.
Short v. Caldwell, 226.
Shortall v. Hinckley, 80.
Shortridge v. Lamplugh, 266.
Shortz v. Unangst, 272.
Shotwell v. Mott, 275.
Shrunk v. Navigation Co., 5.
Shryock v. Waggoner, 264.
Shubert v. Winston, 118.
Shultz v. Sanders, 490.
Shumway v. Orchard, 241.
Shury v. Piggot, 370.
Sibley v. Ellis, 352.
　v. Holden, 422.
　v. Johnson, 107.
　v. Leffingwell, 214.
　v. Smith, 493.
Sidenberg v. Ely, 202.
Sidmouth v. Sidmouth, 268.
Sidney v. Sidney, 109.
Sigourney v. Larned, 220.
Silsby v. Bullock, 82.
Silverthorne v. McKinster, 314.
Simers v. Saltus, 145.
Simkin v. Ashurst, 163.
Simmons v. Ballard, 238.
Simons v. Bank, 225.
Simonton v. Gray, 91.
Simpkins v. Rogers, 22, 157.
Simpson v. Downing, 467.
　v. Leech, 93.
　v. Mundee, 192, 219, 437.
　v. Simpson, 481.
Simpson's Lessee v. Ammons, 335, 343.
Sims v. Hammond, 213.
Sinclair v. Armitage, 185, 191.
　v. Jackson, 319.
　v. Learned, 234.
　v. Slawson, 221.
Singer, Appeal of, 494.
Singleton v. Scott, 249, 315.
Singleton's Ex'r v. Singleton's Heirs, 97.
Sinnett v. Herbert, 329.
Sioux City & St. P. R. Co. v. Singer, 174.
Sir Edward Clere's Case, 317.

CASES CITED. 569

[The figures refer to pages.]

Skelliton v. Hay, 68.
Skelton v. Scott, 195.
Skinner v. Beatty, 125.
   v. Crawford, 460.
   v. Skinner, 130.
   v. Wilder, 4.
   v. Young, 235.
Skull v. Glenister, 361.
Slade v. Patten, 324, 325, 328.
Slater v. Rawson, 32, 449, 456.
Sleeper v. Laconia, 422.
Slegel v. Lauer, 170, 179, 281, 282.
Slingerland v. Sherer, 240.
Sloan v. Campbell, 194.
   v. Furniture Co., 417.
Slocum v. Clark, 146.
Small v. Small, 194.
Smalley v. Isaacson, 345.
Smart v. Waterhouse, 100.
   v. Whaley, 84.
Smiley v. Wright, 110.
Smith v. Adams, 371.
   v. Ashton, 318.
   v. Bank, 436, 489.
   v. Bell, 286, 301.
   v. Blake, 13.
   v. Brand, 248.
   v. Brannan, 176.
   v. Burtis, 458.
   v. Chapin, 467.
   v. Cranford, 309.
   v. Cremer, 189.
   v. Crosby, 190.
   v. Dayton, 146.
   v. Death, 321.
   v. Deschaumes, 116.
   v. Eustis, 89, 91.
   v. Floyd, 374, 375.
   v. Garey, 307.
   v. Gatewood, 374.
   v. Handy, 107.
   v. Haskins, 380.
   v. Hodsdon, 218.
   v. Horlock, 287.
   v. Hubert, 133.
   v. Hunter, 301.
   v. Jeffreys, 209.
   v. Jewett, 61, 64.
   v. Kearney, 318.
   v. Kemp, 374.
   v. Kimbell, 301.
   v. Kipp, 492.

Smith v. Lawrence, 406.
   v. Lee, 360.
   v. Levinus, 5.
   v. McCarty, 85.
   v. McKay, 464.
   v. Marrable, 139.
   v. Martin, 229.
   v. Mattingly, 66.
   v. Maxwell, 259.
   v. Miller, 124, 353.
   v. Morse, 319.
   v. Neilson, 219.
   v. O'Hara, 370.
   v. Packard, 244.
   v. Packhurst, 295.
   v. Parsons, 331.
   v. Pendergast, 153.
   v. Pierce, 489.
   v. Poyas, 61.
   v. Price, 8.
   v. Provin, 124.
   v. Raleigh, 141.
   v. Reich, 467.
   v. Rice, 181.
   v. Roberts, 232.
   v. Rumsey, 123.
   v. Russ, 370.
   v. Saunders, 473.
   v. Shuler, 196.
   v. Simons, 166.
   v. Smith, 82, 84, 93, 192, 268, 345.
   v. Snyder, 150.
   v. Stanley, 91.
   v. Starr, 211.
   v. Stewart, 145, 156.
   v. Stigleman, 141.
   v. Swan, 232.
   v. Thackerah, 365.
   v. Towers, 396.
   v. Townsend, 229, 329.
   v. Walser, 269.
   v. West, 291.
   v. Whitbeck, 151.
   v. Williams, 455.
   v. Yule, 216, 217.
Smith Paper Co. v. Servin, 15.
Smith's Appeal, 49, 50, 86, 322, 329.
Smith's Heirs v. Bank, 408.
   v. Smith, 99.
Smith's Lessee v. Folwell, 322.
Smithurst v. Edmunds, 185.
Smoot v. Lecatt, 81.

[The figures refer to pages.]

Smyles v. Hastings, 358.
Smyth v. Carter, 66.
Snavely v. Pickle, 203.
Snedeker v. Warring, 13, 21.
Sneed v. Sneed, 318.
Snell v. Levitt, 357.
Snell's Ex'rs v. Snell, 317.
Snow v. Boycott, 67.
 v. Parsons, 369.
 v. Pressey, 182.
 v. Pulitzer, 141.
 v. Stevens, 91.
Snyder v. People, 123.
 v. Snyder, 231.
 v. Sponable, 387.
Society for Promoting Theological Education v. Attorney General, 329.
Soffyns' Case, 133.
Sobier v. Eldredge, 61.
 v. Trinity Church, 170.
 v. Williams, 321.
Solicitors' Loan & Trust Co. v. Washington & I. Ry. Co., 237.
Sollers v. Sollers, 5.
Solomon v. Master, etc., of Mystery of Vintners, 365.
Somers v. Schmidt, 447, 449.
Somes v. Brewer, 213.
 v. Skinner, 244, 451.
Sommers v. Reynolds, 151.
Soper v. Guernsey, 181.
South v. South, 316.
Southampton v. Hertford, 331.
Southcote v. Stowell, 299.
Souther v. Pearson, 232.
Southerland v. Hunter, 437.
Southern v. Wollaston, 324.
Southern California Lumber Co. v. McDowell, 489.
Southern Life Ins. Co. v. Cole, 436.
Southern Marble Co. v. Darnell, 369.
Southern Pac. R. Co. v. Doyle, 190.
South Western Ry. v. Thomason, 25.
Souverbye v. Arden, 435.
Soverhill v. Suydam, 229.
Sowler v. Day, 215.
Spalding v. Hershfield, 109.
Spangler v. Stanler, 87, 88.
Sparhawk v. Wills, 201.
Sparkmau v. Roberts, 115.
Sparrow v. Hovey, 463, 466.
 v. Kingman, 105.

Spaulding v. Crane, 119.
 v. Hallenbeck, 171.
 v. Sones, 239.
Speck v. Riggin, 214.
Spencer v. Austin, 333, 335.
 v. Ayrault, 231.
 v. Carr, 452.
 v. Lewis, 62, 71.
 v. McGowen, 146.
 v. Slater, 392.
 v. Spencer, 208.
 v. Waterman, 206.
 v. Weston, 111.
Spencer's Case, 8, 136, 137.
Spensley v. Valentine, 354.
Sperry v. Sperry, 174.
Spinney v. Barbe, 18.
Sprague v. Baker, 135.
 v. Beamer, 232.
 v. Bond, 187.
 v. Cochran, 243.
 v. Coenon, 491.
 v. Woods, 412.
 v. Worcester, 369.
Spraker v. Van Alstyne, 39.
Spring v. Haines, 243.
 v. Russell, 6.
Springer v. Lehman, 196.
Springfield Fire & Marine Ins. Co. v. Allen, 198.
Sproul v. McCoy, 113.
Spruance v. Darlington, 109.
Spurgin v. Adamson, 235.
Squier v. Mayer, 20.
Squire v. Harder, 266.
Squires v. Summers, 434.
Stafford v. Lick, 431.
 v. Van Rensselaer, 192.
Stainback v. Harris, 480.
Stallard v. Cushing, 357.
Stanard v. Eldridge, 138, 444.
Standen v. Chrismas, 136.
 v. Standen, 317.
Standish v. Lawrence, 367.
Stanley v. Beatty, 210.
 v. Colt, 37, 170, 262, 272.
 v. Green, 420.
 v. Greenwood, 122.
Stansbury v. Hubner, 395.
Stansell v. Roberts, 226.
Stanwood v. Dunning, 85.

CASES CITED. 571

[The figures refer to pages.]

Staples v. Brown, 80.
   v. Emery, 17.
   v. Fenton, 217.
Star v. Ellis, 273.
   v. Rookesby, 368.
Stark v. Brown, 247.
   v. M'Gowen, 378.
   v. Olseu, 226.
Starr v. Jackson, 142.
   v. Leavitt, 343.
State v. Black River Phosphate Co., 6.
   v. Bradbury, 362.
   v. Brown, 280.
   v. Davis, 362.
   v. Eason, 6.
   v. Elliot, 18.
   v. Evans, 393.
   v. Gerard, 276.
   v. Gilmantou, 6.
   v. Jones, 154.
   v. Moore, 8.
   v. Pacific Guano Co., 5.
   v. Parrott, 363.
   v. Piper, 142.
   v. Pottmeyer, 4, 6.
   v. President, etc., of Bank of Maryland, 263.
   v. Ragland, 184.
   v. Stephenson, 8.
   v. Suttle, 459.
   v. Trask, 299.
   v. Trontman, 468.
   v. Votaw, 144.
State Bank v. Hinton, 89.
   v. Mathews, 210.
   v. Whittle, 393.
Steacy v. Rice, 255.
Steamboat Magnolia v. Marshall, 6.
Stearns v. Godfrey, 177, 178.
   v. Palmer, 273.
   v. Sampson, 165.
Stebbins v. Hall, 207.
   v. Merritt, 430.
Stedman v. Gassett, 144.
Steed v. Preece, 23.
Steel v. Board of Education, 105.
   v. Frick, 154.
Steele, In re, 61.
   v. Carroll, 89.
   v. La Frambois, 92.
Steere v. Steere, 262.
   v. Tiffany, 357.

Steers v. City of Brooklyn, 472.
Steffens v. Earl, 161.
Stehlin v. Stehlin, 110.
Stehman v. Stehman, 285.
Steib v. Whitehead, 396.
Steiger's Adm'r v. Hillen, 111.
Stein v. Stein, 99, 105.
   v. Sullivan, 220.
Steinmetz's Estate, In re, 387.
Stell v. Barham, 36.
Stephen v. Beall, 250.
Stephens v. Bridges, 152, 281.
   v. Evans' Adm'x, 323.
   v. Hussk, 433.
   v. Hume, 75.
   v. Insurance Co., 197.
   v. Rinehart, 434, 436.
   v. Stephens, 324.
Stephenson v. Boody, 454.
   v. Elliott, 207.
Sterling v. Penlington, 79.
   v. Warden, 166.
Stern v. Lee, 117.
   v. Thayer, 153.
Stevens v. Battell, 343.
   v. Campbell, 246.
   v. Cooper, 236.
   v. Ely, 267.
   v. Kelley, 6.
   v. Melcher, 60.
   v. Owen, 87, 107.
   v. Pantlind, 142, 153.
   v. Pierce, 139.
   v. Railway Co., 10, 15.
   v. Smith, 106.
   v. Town of Norfolk, 343.
   v. Winship, 59.
Steven's Estate, In re, 171.
Stevens' Heirs v. Stevens, 96, 99.
Stevenson v. Crapnell, 266, 436.
   v. Kaiser, 433.
   v. Lambard, 140, 148, 378.
   v. Lesley, 272.
Steward v. Harding, 162.
Stewart v. Bank, 345, 346.
   v. Barclay, 79.
   v. Brand, 121.
   v. Chadwick, 271.
   v. Clark, 56.
   v. Drake, 447.
   v. Gregg, 146.
   v. McMahan, 229.

[The figures refer to pages.]

Stewart v. McMartin, 95.
  v. McSweeney, 220.
  v. Neely, 305.
  v. Platt, 224.
  v. Ross, 82.
  v. Smith, 98.
  v. Stewart, 110, 342.
  v. Weed, 435.
  v. Wood, 194.
Stewart's Lessee v. Stewart, 94, 105.
Stickney v. Munroe, 142.
Stieff v. Hartwell, 491.
Stiles v. Probst, 428.
Stillman v. Flenniken, 20.
Stillman's Ex'rs v. Stillman, 204.
Stillwell v. Doughty, 59.
  v. Hamm, 233.
Stinchfield v. Milliken, 199.
Stinebaugh v. Wisdom, 75.
Stinson v. Ross, 196.
  v. Sumner, 106.
Stirbling v. Ross, 104.
Stivers v. Horne, 223.
Stockbridge Iron Co. v. Hudson Iron Co., 417.
Stockman v. Wallis, 242.
Stockport Waterworks Co. v. Potter, 369.
Stockton v. Martin, 49.
  v. Railroad Co., 495.
  v. Williams, 403.
Stockwell v. McHenry, 222.
  v. Sargent, 101.
Stoddard v. Forbes, 237.
  v. Gibbs, 79.
  v. Whiting, 188.
Stoever v. Stoever, 186.
Stokes v. Berry, 457.
  v. McAllister, 94.
  v. McKibbin, 78.
  v. Norwood, 109.
Stokoe v. Singers, 355, 364.
Stoltz v. Doering, 469.
Stone v. Darnell, 125.
  v. Ellis, 175.
  v. Fitts, 454.
  v. McMullen, 48.
  v. Stone, 493.
  v. Vandermark, 109.
Stookey v. Stookey, 97.
Storrs v. Benbow, 323, 328.
Story v. Springer, 188.

Stott v. Rutherford, 138.
Stoudinger v. Newark, 362.
Stoughton, Appeal of, 7.
  v. Leigh, 87, 88.
Stout v. Lye, 246.
  v. Merrill, 383.
Stover v. Boswell's Heir, 480.
  v. Eycleshimer, 415.
  v. Hazelbaker, 152.
  v. Jack, 6.
Stow v. Tifft, 85.
Stowe v. Banks, 189.
Stowell v. Waddingham, 66.
Strang v. Allen, 200, 237.
Strange v. Spaulding, 460.
Strattan v. Best, 334.
Strauss v. Abrahams, 392.
Straw v. Greene, 244.
Strawn v. Strawn, 455.
Streeper v. Abeln, 445.
Street v. Saunders, 101.
Strickland v. Parker, 12, 13.
Strobe v. Downer, 247.
Stroebe v. Fehl, 71, 72.
Strohm v. Good, 193.
Strong v. Clem, 95.
  v. Converse, 207.
  v. Doyle, 18.
  v. Insurance Co., 197.
  v. Lord, 340.
  v. Powell, 454.
  v. White, 3.
Strother v. Law, 315.
Stroud v. Lockart, 223.
  v. Rogers, 378.
Stroup v. Stroup, 89.
Strouse v. Cohen, 181.
Stuart v. Kissam, 72.
  v. Lowry, 451.
Stubblefield v. Boggs, 403.
  v. Menzies, 303.
Stubbs v. Parsons, 139.
Stuckey v. Keefe's Ex'rs, 338.
Studdard v. Wells, 171.
Studstill v. Willcox, 461.
Stull v. Graham, 87, 106.
Stults v. Sale, 114.
Stultz v. Dickey, 9.
Stump v. Deneale, 473.
  v. Findlay, 59.
Sturgeon v. Wingfield, 456.
Sturges v. Hart, 228.

[The figures refer to pages.]

Sturtevant v. Jaques, 267.
Stuyvesant v. Neil, 312.
Sudbury v. Jones, 21.
Suddarth v. Robertson, 144.
Suffield v. Brown, 351.
Sullivan v. Carberry, 23.
   v. Chambers, 255, 437.
   v. Eddy, 351, 433, 460.
   v. Jernigan, 370.
   v McLenans, 267.
   v. Mining Co., 371.
Sumerel v. Sumerel, 110.
Summers v. Babb, 95, 97, 101, 106.
   v. Bromley, 248.
Sumner v. Partridge, 74, 77.
   v. Skinner, 247.
   v. Stevens, 465.
Sunderlin v. Struthers, 455.
Supplee v. Timothy, 162.
Surplice v. Farnsworth, 135.
Susquehanna & W. V. R. & Coal Co.
   v. Quick, 466.
Sussex Co. Mut. Ins. Co. v. Woodruff, 199.
Sutherland v. Goodnow, 148.
   v. Rose, 233.
   v. Sutherland, 85.
Sutliff v. Forgey, 85, 95.
Sutphen v. Therkelson, 364.
Sutter v. Lackmann, 150.
Sutton v. Aiken, 256.
   v. Jervis, 216.
Suydam v. Dunton, 357.
   v. Jones, 135, 441.
Swain v. Mizner, 163.
Swaine v. Burton, 479.
   v. Perine, 60, 91.
Swan v. Busby, 144.
   v. Yaple, 210, 229.
Swatts v. Bowen, 232.
Swayne v. Chase, 117.
Sweaney v. Mallory, 110.
Swearingen v. Lahner, 182.
   v. Robertson, 468.
Sweet v. Myers, 18.
Sweetapple v. Bindon, 23, 78.
Sweetzer v. Atterbury, 187.
Swenson v. Plow Co., 245.
   v. Seale, 488.
Swetland v. Swetland, 187.
Swett v. Stark, 211, 245.

Swift v. Edson, 246.
   v. Lee, 473.
   v. Mulkey, 461.
   v. Stovall, 452.
   v. Thompson, 13.
Swihart v. Swihart, 109.
Swinburne v. Swinburne, 270.
Sykes v. Benton, 132.
   v. Sykes, 92.
Syler v. Eckhart, 415.
Sylvester v. Hall, 140.
Symmes v. Drew, 98.
Sym's Case, 71.
Synge v. Synge, 396.
Sypher v. McHenry, 270.

T

Tabele v. Tabele, 99.
Tabor v. Robinson, 16, 20.
Tacey v. Irwin, 491.
Taft v. Stetson, 12.
   v. Taft, 108, 261.
Tainter v. Clark, 272, 275, 315.
   v. Cole, 132.
Talamo v. Spitzmiller, 156.
Talbot v. Cruger, 23.
   v. Hill, 101.
   v. Tipper, 319.
Talbott v. Barber, 265.
Talley v. Thompson, 125.
Tallmadge v. Bank, 351.
Tallman v. Snow, 172, 174.
   v. Wood, 258, 259.
Taltarum's Case, 51.
Tameling v. Emigration Co., 403.
Taney v. Fahnley, 296.
Tanguay v. Felthousen, 207.
Tanner v. Hills, 154.
Tappan v. Deblois, 277.
Tarbell, In re, 240.
Tarbuck v. Tarbuck, 302.
Tarlotting v. Bokern, 156.
Tarrant v. Swain, 116.
Tasker v. Bartlett, 429.
Tate v. Goff, 115.
   v. Lawrence, 439.
   v. Tally, 49.
Tatem v. Chapliu, 136.
Tatton v. Mollineux, 327.

[The figures refer to pages.]

Tatum v. City of St. Louis, 470.
Tayloe v. Dugger, 464.
    v. Gould, 76, 79.
Taylor v. Benham, 272.
    v. Boulware, 118.
    v. Cooper, 145.
    v. Cox, 384.
    v. Eatman, 311.
    v. Hopper, 359, 363.
    v. Horde, 468.
    v. Kearn, 106.
    v. Kelly, 473.
    v. Lawrence, 111.
    v. McCrackin, 94.
    v. Mason, 172.
    v. Millard, 344, 351.
    v. Mitchell, 475.
    v. Murphy, 339.
    v. Page, 211.
    v. Porter, 31, 41, 234, 235.
    v. Smith, 78.
    v. Sutton, 170.
    v. Taylor, 48, 107, 268, 287, 302.
    v. Townsend, 14.
    v. Trust Co., 182.
    v. Vale, 377.
    v. Warnaky, 359.
    v. Whitehead, 361.
    v. Wright, 493.
Teaff v. Hewitt, 10, 11, 13.
Teague's Settlement, In re, 329.
Teape's Trusts, In re, 317.
Temple v. Scott, 290.
    v. Whittier, 232.
Templeman v. Biddle, 9.
Ten Eyck v. Craig, 206.
    v. Town of Warwick, 6.
Terhune v. Elberson, 8.
Terrell v. Reeves, 287, 327.
Terrett v. Taylor, 440, 446.
Terriere v. City of New Orleans, 472.
Thackara v. Mintzer, 396.
Tharp v. Brenneman, 432.
Tharpe v. Dunlap, 194.
Thayer v. Bacon, 453.
    v. Campbell, 210.
    v. McGee, 178.
    v. Mann, 240.
    v. Payne, 352, 356, 426.
    v. Thayer, 105.
    v. Torrey, 418.

Thayer v. Wellington, 263.
Thellusson v. Woodford, 323, 324, 330.
Theresa Drainage Dist., In re, 495.
Third Nat. Bank v. O'Brien, 439.
Thomas v. Bland, 441.
    v. Bridges, 193.
    v. Cook, 409.
    v. Crout, 19, 22.
    v. Hayward, 137.
    v. Hesse, 98.
    v. Howell, 172, 173.
    v. Inhabitants of Marshfield, 416.
    v. Jenks, 394.
    v. Linn, 211.
    v. Record, 174.
    v. Simpson, 95.
    v. Stickle, 455.
    v. Sylvester, 378.
    v. Thomas, 60, 341, 358.
    v. Wyatt, 417.
Thomas' Adm'r v. Von Kapff's Ex'rs, 135.
Thompson v. Barber, 343.
    v. Burhans, 462.
    v. Chandler, 234.
    v. Cochran, 90.
    v. Egbert, 109.
    v. Gregory, 417, 418.
    v. Hartline, 270.
    v. Hill, 290.
    v. Holladay, 182.
    v. Hoop, 286.
    v. Leach, 434.
    v. Lyon, 314.
    v. McCorkle, 105.
    v. Marley, 265.
    v. Marshall, 184.
    v. Merrill, 455.
    v. Morrow, 97.
    v. Murphy, 59.
    v. Railroad Co., 185.
    v. Rose, 137.
    v. Thompson, 106, 428.
    v. Vance, 86.
Thompson's Lessee v. Hoop, 474.
Thoms v. King, 104.
Thomson v. Ludington, 291.
    v. Peake, 38.
    v. Waterlow, 351.
Thomson-Houston Electric Co. v. Durant Land-Imp. Co., 135.

CASES CITED.

[The figures refer to pages.]

Thong v. Bedford, 297.
Thorington v. Thorington, 311.
Thorn v. Sutherland, 23.
— v. Woollcombe, 152.
Thornburg v. Wiggins, 338.
Thorndike v. Burrage, 143.
Thornton v. Burch, 9.
— v. Knox's Ex'r, 192.
— v. Thornton, 317, 334, 337, 338.
— v. Vaughan, 262.
Thornton's Ex'rs v. Krepps, 77.
Thoroughgood's Case, 406.
Thorp v. Raymond, 469.
Thorpe v. Goodall, 320.
Thresher v. Water Works, 13.
Throckmorton v. Pence, 468.
— v. Throckmorton, 267.
Thurber v. Martin, 370.
— v. Townsend, 82, 83.
Thurman v. Cameron, 442.
Thursby v. Plant, 378.
Thurston v. Dickinson, 61.
— v. Hancock, 365.
— v. Maddocks, 116.
— v. Prentiss, 240.
Thwayles v. Dye, 319.
Tibbals v. Iffland, 149.
— v. Jacobs, 393.
Tice v. Annin, 209.
Tidd v. Lister, 272.
Tifft v. Horton, 12, 13, 21.
Tilden v. Streeter, 189.
Tileston v. Newell, 441.
Tilford v. Fleming, 148.
Tilley v. King, 171.
Tillinghast v. Bradford, 397.
— v. Goggeshall, 78.
Tillotson v. Millard, 118, 122, 123.
— v. Prichard, 441.
Tillson v. Moulton, 187.
Tilton v. Hunter, 223.
Timmins v. Rowlinson, 162.
Tinicum Fishing Co. v. Carter, 373.
Tink v. Walker, 89.
Tinker v. Forbes, 351.
Tinney v. Tinney, 108.
Tipton v. Wortham, 250.
Tisdale v. Jones, 108.
Tisher v. Beckwith, 433.
Titcomb v. Vantyle, 383.
Titman v. Moore, 118, 119, 121.

Titus v. Mabee, 14.
— v. Neilson, 90.
— v. Warren, 125.
Titzell v. Cochran, 302.
Tobey v. Moore, 326.
— v. Reed, 196.
— v. Taunton, 359.
Tobias v. Ketchum, 110.
Toby v. Schultz, 145.
Tod v. Baylor, 98.
Todd v. Flight, 142.
— v. Jackson, 165.
— v. Johnson, 235.
— v. Nelson, 394.
— v. Outlaw, 225.
— v. Oviatt, 79.
— v. Sawyer, 396.
Toll v. Wright, 457.
Toll Bridge Co. v. Osborn, 25.
Tolle v. Alley, 221.
Tollet v. Tollet, 318.
Tomlin v. Railway Co., 5.
Tomlinson v. Insurance Co., 198.
Tompkins v. Elliot, 441.
— v. Fonda, 95.
Toms v. Williams, 261.
Tone v. Brace, 138.
Toney v. Goodley, 146.
Tooke v. Hardeman, 110.
Toole v. Dibrell, 125.
Toomer v. Randolph, 183.
Toomey v. McLean, 104.
Torrey v. Burnett, 23.
— v. Cook, 229, 241.
— v. Deavitt, 209.
— v. Minor, 110, 111.
Torriano v. Young, 139, 160.
Tottel v. Howell, 374, 415.
Totten v. Stuyvesant, 93.
Toupin v. Peabody, 134.
Tourville v. Pierson, 117, 118.
Tousley v. Tousley, 221.
Towanda Bridge Co., In re, 379.
Towle v. Ayer, 31.
Town v. Needham, 346.
Towne v. Bowers, 9.
— v. Fiske, 18, 21.
Town of Freedom v. Norris, 357.
Town of Old Town v. Dooley, 423.
Townsend v. Brown, 401.
— v. Downer, 439.

CASES CITED.

[The figures refer to pages.]

Townsend v. Hubbard, 432.
v. Townsend, 108.
v. Westacott, 394.
v. Wharf Co., 141.
Tracy v. Atherton, 353, 359.
v. Jenks, 221.
Trafton v. Hawes, 410, 412.
Transportation Co. v. Chicago, 365.
Trask v. Graham, 137.
v. Patterson, 72.
Traveller's Ins. Co. v. Patten, 246.
v. Yount, 420.
Travers v. Dorr, 208.
Trawick v. Harris, 114.
Trayser v. Trustees of Asbury University, 240.
Treary v. Cooke, 374.
Tress v. Savage, 158.
Trich's Ex'r v. Trich, 384.
Trimble v. Smith, 462.
Tripp v. Hasceig, 8.
Trolan v. Rogers, 455.
Trollope v. Linton, 319.
Tromans v. Mahlman, 118.
Troost v. Davis, 202.
Trotter v. Hughes, 207, 208.
v. Oswald, 327.
True v. Haley, 234.
v. Morrill, 118, 119.
Truett v. Funderburk, 85, 109.
Trull v. Bigelow, 213.
v. Eastman, 415, 448, 456.
v. Fuller, 15.
v. Granger, 133.
Trulock v. Donahue, 377.
Truman v. Weed, 218.
Trumbull v. Trumbull, 86.
Trusdell v. Lehman, 57.
Trustees of Amherst College v. Ritch, 271.
Trustees of Dartmouth College v. Clough, 149.
Trustees of East Hampton v. Kirk, 460.
Trustees of Hopkins' Academy v. Dickinson, 470, 471.
Trustees of Philadelphia Baptist Ass'n v. Hart's Ex'rs, 275, 277.
Trustees of Phillips Academy v. King, 263.
Trustees of Poor of Queen Anne's Co. v. Pratt, 104.

Trustees of Putnam Free School v. Fisher, 460.
Trustees of Schools v. Schroll, 5, 423.
v. Wright, 262.
Trustees of Western University v. Robinson, 376.
Trustees, etc., of Queen Anne's Co. v. Pratt, 90.
Tryon v. Munson, 184.
Tucker v. Byers, 156.
v. Eldred, 362.
v. Moreland, 382, 383.
v. Price, 467.
v. Thurstan, 476.
v. Tilton, 215.
Tudor Iron Works v. Hitt, 19.
Tuft v. Adams, 448.
Tuite v. Miller, 444.
Tulk v. Moxhay, 351.
Tullett v. Armstrong, 396.
Tumlinson v. Swinney, 120.
Tunison v. Chamblin, 394, 435.
Tunstall v. Christian, 365.
Turman v. White, 296.
Turner v. Bernheimer, 123.
v. Davis, 23, 24.
v. Doe, 158.
v. Flenniken, 237.
v. Kennedy, 23.
v. Lee, 377.
v. Moore, 462.
v. Rusk, 384.
v. Scheiber, 109.
v. Scott, 473.
v. Townsend, 139.
v. Watkins, 209.
v. Wright, 62.
Turner Coal Co. v. Glover, 195.
Turpin v. Ogle, 220.
Tusk v. Ridge, 181.
Tutter v. Fryer, 146.
Tuttle v. Bean, 162.
v. Brown, 231.
v. Turner, 435.
v. Willson, 111.
Tweddell v. Tweddell, 204.
Twynam v. Pickard, 137.
Twyne's Case, 393.
Tygret v. Potter, 189.
Tyler v. Hamilton, 245.
v. Hammond, 358.
v. Johnson, 126.

CASES CITED.

[The figures refer to pages.]

Tyler v. Moore, 419.
   v. Wheeler, 82.
   v. Wilkinson, 369.
Tyrrell's Case, 256.
Tyrringham's Case, 375.
Tyson v. Smith, 354.

U

Umbenhower v. Miller, 189.
Underhill v. Railroad Co., 170, 172, 176.
Underwood v. Birchard, 448.
   v. Carney, 351.
   v. Curtis, 24.
Unger v. Leiter, 90.
Union Depot Co. v. Chicago, K. & N. Ry. Co., 159.
Union Depot Street-Railway & Transfer Co. of Stillwater v. Brunswick, 423.
Union Mut. Life Ins. Co. v. Campbell, 433.
   v. Hanford, 208.
   v. Kirchoff, 236.
   v. Slee, 188, 210.
Union Pac. Ry. Co. v. U. S., 452.
United States v. Appleton, 364.
   v. Bostwick, 139.
   v. Certain Tract of Land, 495.
   v. Chicago, 495.
   v. Cook, 400.
   v. Duncan, 109.
   v. Fisher, 41.
   v. Iron Silver Min. Co., 403.
   v. Minor, 403.
   v. Nelson, 428.
   v. Railroad Bridge Co., 495.
   v. Sliney, 217.
   v. Steenerson, 403.
U. S. Bank v. Burson, 230.
United States Inv. Co. v. Phelps & Bigelow Windmill Co., 126.
United States Mortg. Co. v. Gross, 216.
Upchurch v. Anderson, 32.
Upington v. Corrigan, 171.
Upjohn v. Board, 371.
Upton v. Archer, 428.
Uridias v. Morrell, 163.
Usher v. Skate Co., 181.
Utermehle v. McGreal, 249.

V

Valentine v. Healey, 341, 342.
Vanarsdall v. Fauntleroy's Heirs, 75, 76, 79.
Vanatta v. Brewer, 177.
Van Beuren v. Dash, 477.
Vanhever v. Vanhever, 271.
Van Bibber v. Williamson, 61.
Van Brunt v. Schenck, 145.
Van Buren v. Olmstead, 189, 200.
Vance v. Vance, 107, 108.
Van Cleaf v. Burns, 104.
Vanderheyden v. Crandall, 295.
Vanderkarr v. Vanderkarr, 441.
Vanderplank v. King, 327.
Vanderpoel v. Van Allen, 13.
Van Deusen v. Sweet, 131, 384.
   v. Young, 304.
Van Doren v. Everitt, 9, 10, 131.
Van Duyne v. Thayre, 91.
Van Duzer v. Van Duzer, 80.
Vane v. Lord Barnard, 62.
Van Giesen v. White, 288.
Van Hoozer v. Cory, 185.
Van Horn v. Bell, 429.
Van Horne v. Campbell, 395.
   v. Crain, 148.
   v. Fonda, 341.
Van Keuren v. Corkins, 227.
Van Meter v. Thomas, 34.
Vann v. Marbury, 226.
Van Ness v. Pacard, 17, 22.
Van Note v. Downey, 71.
Van Ostrand v. Reed, 430.
Van Rensselaer v. Ball, 169, 176.
   v. Clark, 213.
   v. Dennison, 31, 169, 185.
   v. Hays, 31, 148, 376, 377.
   v. Poucher, 32.
   v. Radcliff, 375.
   v. Read, 376, 377.
   v. Smith, 31.
   v. Snyder, 151.
Vansant v. Allmon, 228.
Van Sickler v. Jacobs, 146.
Vanstory v. Thornton, 117.
Van Thorniley v. Peters, 225.
Van Vechten v. Terry, 246.
Van Vronker v. Eastman, 90, 202.
Van Wagner v. Van Nostrand, 443.
Van Wyck v. Seward, 393.

REAL PROP.—37

578

CASES CITED.

[The figures refer to pages.]

Varney v. Stevens, 60, 289.
Varnum v. Abbott, 343.
Varrell v. Wendell, 312. 313.
Vartie v. Underwood, 90.
Vasey v. Trustees, 124.
Vason v. Ball, 184.
Vaughan v. Daniels, 492.
   v. Greer, 224,
   v. Matlock, 135.
Vaughen v. Haldeman, 18.
Vaughn v. Stuzaker, 444.
   v. Tate, 424.
   v. Tracy, 214, 216.
Veal v. Fortson, 382.
Veazie v. Dwinel, 6.
Veghte v. Power Co., 168.
Venable v. Beauchamp, 347.
   v. Railway Co., 105, 110.
Ventress v. Collins, 116.
Verlander v. Harvey, 97.
Vermont v. Society for Propagation of Gospel, 176.
Verner v. Beltz, 195.
Vernon v. Smith, 135, 136.
   v. Wright, 38.
Vernon Irrigation Co. v. City of Los Angeles, 369, 370.
Vernon's Case, 108.
Verona Borough v. Allegheny Val. R. R., 354.
Verplanck v. Wright, 137.
Vest v. Michie, 213, 214.
Vickers v. Henry, 104.
   v. Leigh, 37.
Vidal v. Girard, 275.
   v. Girard's Ex'rs, 263.
Viele v. Judson, 452.
Villa v. Pico, 119.
Village of Brooklyn v. Smith, 4, 6.
Village of Dwight v. Hayes, 168.
Vincent v. Spooner, 108.
Vinson v. Gentry, 104.
Vlautin v. Bumpus, 339.
Voelckner v. Hudson, 94.
Volk v. Eldred, 6.
Voller v. Carter, 50.
Voorhees v. Burchard, 355.
   v. McGinnis, 11, 15, 20.
Voorhis v. Freeman, 14, 15.
   v. Westervelt, 225.
Vornberg v. Ewens, 115.
Voss v. King 144, 160.

Vreeland v. Jacobus, 90.
Vyvyan v. Arthur, 136.

W

Waddell v. Ratlew, 290.
Wade v. Brewing Co., 15.
   v. Deray, 421.
   v. Halligan, 138.
   v. Johnson, 463.
   v. Jones, 113.
   v. Malloy, 60.
Wadhams v. Swan, 455.
Wadleigh v. Janvrin, 13, 14.
Wadsworth v. Miller, 83.
   v. Wadsworth, 388.
   v. Williams, 393.
Waesch's Estate, In re, 481.
Waffle v. Railroad Co., 372.
Wager v. Wager, 419.
Wagner v. Hanna, 349.
Wahle v. Reinbach, 371.
Wainman v. Field, 325, 328.
Wainwright v. McCullough, 5.
Wait v. Belding, 38.
   v. Richardson, 342.
Wakefield v. Brown, 137.
Wakeman v. Banks, 197.
Waldo v. Cummings, 396.
Wales' Adm'r v. Bowdish's Ex'r, 320.
Walker v. Armstrong, 380.
   v. Board, 5.
   v. English, 239.
   v. Fitts, 154.
   v. Gergard, 361.
   v. Gilbert, 135.
   v. Githens, 153.
   v. Goodsill, 207, 232.
   v. Griswold, 91.
   v. Hall, 455.
   v. Long, 83.
   v. Mackie, 316.
   v. Mining Co., 189.
   v. Renfro, 440.
   v. Schreiber, 215.
   v. Schuyler, 97, 98.
   v. Sharpe, 162.
   v. Sherman, 15.
   v. Stetson, 367.
   v. Tucker, 140.
   v. Vincent, 395.

CASES CITED 579

[The figures refer to pages.]

Walker v. Walker, 433.
Walker's Adm'r v. Deaver, 445.
Walker's Case, 149.
Wall v. Byrne, 68.
  v. Hinds, 17, 18, 343.
Wallace v. Butts, 435.
  v. Fletcher, 353.
  v. Gooddall, 209.
  v. Hall's Heirs, 94.
  v. Harmstad, 31, 376, 428.
  v. Harris, 124, 436.
  v. Insurance Co., 123.
  v. Jones, 487.
  v. McKenzie, 213.
  v. Miller, 336.
  v. Presbyterian Church, 377.
Wallach v. Van Riswick, 400.
Waller v. Mardus, 95.
  v. Waller's Adm'r, 89, 104.
Wallis v. Harrison, 350.
  v. Wallis, 410.
Walls v. Baird, 229.
Walmsley v. Jowett, 321.
  v. Milne, 21.
Walsh v. Insurance Co., 200.
  v. Wallinger, 313.
Walters v. Association, 124.
  v. Hutchins' Adm'x, 143.
  v. People, 118, 119.
  v. Walters, 229.
Walton v. Cronly's Adm'r, 187.
  v. Follansbee, 451.
  v. Walton, 476.
  v. Wray, 16.
Walworth v. Jenness, 154.
Wamble v. Battle, 192.
Wansbrough v. Maton, 13.
Ward v. Amory, 297, 313.
  v. Cochran, 459.
  v. Green, 236.
  v. Huhn, 116.
  v. Montgomery, 493.
  v. Sheppard, 64.
  v. Thompson, 80.
  v. Ward, 357.
  v. Ward's Heirs, 342.
Warde v. Tuddingham, 266.
Warden v. Adams, 209.
  v. Jones, 394.
Ware v. Cann, 395.
  v. Richardson, 255, 256.
  v. Ware, 72.

Warford v. Noble, 104.
Waring v. Loder, 197, 198.
  v. Smyth, 429.
Waring's Ex'r v. Waring, 273.
Warland v. Colwell, 273.
Warn v. Bickford, 450.
Warner v. Bates, 261.
  v. Bennett, 170, 174, 176.
  v. Insurance Co., 316, 319.
  v. Southworth, 422.
  v. Tanner, 55.
  v. Van Alstyne, 90.
Warnock v. Campbell, 385.
Warren v. Brown, 363.
  v. Costello, 72.
  v. Fenn, 193.
  v. Frederichs, 468.
  v. Leland, 8.
  v. Lynch, 429, 430.
  v. Peterson, 121.
  v. President, etc., of Town of Jacksonville, 362.
  v. Tobey, 435.
  v. Warren, 109.
Washburn v. Burns, 338.
  v. Cutter, 463.
  v. Goodwin, 209.
  v. Merrills, 209.
Washington Bldg. & Loan Ass'n v. Beaghen, 204.
Washington Ice Co. v. Shortall, 6.
Wass v. Bucknam, 73, 75, 79, 80.
Waterbury v. Sturtevant, 393.
Waterman v. Soper, 4.
Waters v. Crabtree, 186.
  v. Lilley, 5, 373.
  v. Lumber Co., 356.
  v. Lyon, 296.
  v. Margerum, 51.
  v. Tazewell, 78.
Watkins v. Edwards, 217.
  v. Goodall, 142.
  v. Green, 60, 341, 468.
  v. Hill, 229.
  v. Holman, 41.
  v. Nash, 436.
  v. Spoull, 126.
  v. Thornton, 75, 79.
Watriss v. Bank, 23.
Watson v. Atkins, 139.
  v. Foxon, 287.
  v. Gray, 366.

[The figures refer to pages.]

Watson v. Hunkins, 148.
— v. Hunter, 145.
— v. O'Hern, 133.
— v. Peters, 422.
— v. Smith, 301.
— v. Spence, 246.
— v. Watson, 76, 80, 453.
Watson's Estate, In re, 86.
Wattengel v. Schultz, 198.
Watters v. Bredin, 170, 419.
— v. Jordan, 103.
Watts v. Ball, 78.
— v. Coffin, 375.
— v. Kelson, 351.
Wayman v. Jones, 207.
Wead v. Larkin, 441.
Wea Gas, Coal & Oil Co. v. Franklin Land Co., 123.
Weale v. Lower, 292.
Weare v. Johnson, 127.
Weatherhead v. Stoddard, 288.
Weaver v. Brown, 194.
— v. Crenshaw, 94.
— v. Fisher, 270.
— v. Gregg, 93.
— v. Sturtevant, 95.
Webb v. Archibald, 474.
— v. Bird, 352.
— v. Den, 417.
— v. Hayner, 118, 122, 124.
— v. Honnor, 317.
— v. Jiggs, 378.
— v. Mullins, 417.
— v. Rice, 187.
— v. Robinson, 193.
— v. Russel, 152.
— v. Townsend, 87.
— v. Trustees, 77.
Webber v. Boom Co., 423.
— v. Clarke, 460.
— v. Ramsey, 223.
Weber v. Anderson, 467.
— v. Huerstel, 182.
Webster v. Calden, 212.
— v. Cooper, 172, 295.
— v. Ellsworth, 79.
— v. Gilman, 67, 475.
— v. McCullough, 193.
— v. Morris, 261.
— v. Nichols, 147.
— v. Peet, 66.
— v. Trust Co., 122.

Webster v. Vandeventer, 343.
— v. Van Steenbergh, 213, 217.
— v. Webster, 61, 63.
— v. Wiggin, 474.
Webster's Trustee v. Webster, 38.
Wedekind v. Hallenberg, 288.
Wedge v. Moore, 89.
Weed v. Lindsay, 156.
Weed Sewing Mach. Co. v. Emerson, 211.
Weeks v. Thomas, 200.
Weeton v. Woodcock, 22.
Wehrmann v. Conklin, 452.
Weiner v. Heintz, 237.
Weir v. Mosher, 230.
— v. Railroad Co., 495.
— v. Smith, 316.
— v. Tate, 87, 89, 93.
Weise v. Smith, 6.
Weiser v. Weiser, 346, 455.
Weisinger v. Murphy, 80.
Welborn v. Anderson, 461.
Welch v. Adams, 144.
— v. Allen, 262.
— v. Anderson, 96, 109.
— v. Dutton, 412.
— v. Phillips, 183.
— v. Wilcox, 356.
Welch's Appeal, 345.
Welch's Heirs v. Chandler, 78.
Welcome v. Upton, 375.
Weld v. Traip, 133.
Welder v. McComb, 144.
Weldon v. Tollman, 228, 238.
Welland Canal Co. v. Hathaway, 450.
Weller v. Weller, 77, 88.
Welles v. Cowles, 25.
— v. Olcott, 48.
Wells v. Dillard, 418.
— v. Heath, 329.
— v. Hedenberg, 420.
— v. Ody, 363.
— v. Prince, 468.
— v. Ritter, 286.
— v. Thompson, 74, 76, 81.
— v. Tolman, 351, 356.
— v. Wells, 476.
Welsh v. Foster, 298.
— v. Solenberger, 80.
— v. Welsh, 392.
Wendell v. Crandall, 288.
— v. Van Rensselaer, 451, 452.

CASES CITED. 581

[The figures refer to pages.]

Wentworth v. Wentworth, 96.
West v. Bancroft, 362.
   v. Berney, 322.
   v. Stewart, 448.
   v. Ward, 116, 117.
   v. Williams, 306.
Westchester Fire Ins. Co. v. Foster, 198.
Westcott v. Campbell, 97.
   v. Delano, 8.
West Covington v. Freking, 423.
West Cumberland Iron & Steel Co. v. Kenyon, 371.
Western Boot & Shoe Co. v. Gannon, 131.
Western Maryland Railroad Land & Imp. Co. v. Goodwin, 249.
Western Massachusetts Ins. Co. v. Riker, 198.
Western Min. & Manuf'g Co. v. Peytona Cannel Coal Co., 418.
Western N. C. Ry. Co. v. Deal, 16, 19.
Western R. Corp. v. Babcock, 434.
Western Transp. Co. v. Lansing, 135.
Weston v. Sampson, 5.
   v. Weston, 18.
West Point Iron Co. v. Raymert, 418.
West River Bank v. Gale, 118.
West River Bridge Co. v. Dix, 379, 495.
West's Appeal, 230.
West Shore Mills Co. v. Edwards, 144.
Wettig v. Bowman, 493.
Wetz v. Beard, 119, 121.
Wetzel v. Richcreek, 442, 444.
Weynand v. Lutz, 351.
Whalen v. Cadman, 113.
Whaley v. Whaley, 267.
Wheat v. Morris, 343.
Wheatland v. Dodge, 48.
Wheatley v. Chrisman, 369.
Wheatley's Heirs v. Calhoun, 85.
Wheaton v. Andress, 57.
Wheeldon v. Burrows, 360.
Wheeler v. Gorham, 59.
   v. Hotchkiss, 81.
   v. Insurance Co., 198.
   v. Kirtland, 105.
   v. Morris, 91.
   v. Smith, 277.
   v. Walker, 170, 177.
Wheelwright v. Freeman, 244.
   v. Wheelwright, 434.

Whipple v. Fowler, 210.
Whitaker v. Brown, 417, 418.
   v. Miller, 217.
   v. Shooting Club, 460.
Whitbeck v. Cook, 444.
Whitby v. Duffy, 419.
   v. Mitchell, 327.
Whitcomb v. Taylor, 286.
White v. Arndt, 20, 22.
   v. Bass, 363.
   v. Bond, 234.
   v. Brown, 199.
   v. Clarke, 94.
   v. Cutler, 61, 87, 101.
   v. Davidson, 431.
   v. Denman, 220.
   v. Fitzgerald, 261.
   v. Foster, 214, 222.
   v. Godfrey, 422.
   v. Gouldin's Ex'rs, 72.
   v. Hampton, 231.
   v. Hicks, 316.
   v. Howard, 277, 474.
   v. Kinley, 125.
   v. Maynard, 163.
   v. Moses, 487.
   v. Patten, 446, 455.
   v. Railway Co., 168.
   v. Rittenmyer, 184.
   v. Story, 98.
   v. White, 103, 217.
   v. Whitney, 448.
   v. Williams, 193, 194, 424.
   v. Willis, 87.
Whiteaker v. Belt, 104, 111.
Whited v. Pearson, 110.
Whitehead v. Bennett, 16.
   v. Foley, 461.
   v. Hall, 235.
   v. Middleton, 91.
   v. Rennett, 325.
Whitelock v. Hutchinson, 373.
White's Adm'r v. White, 114.
White's Appeal, 12.
White's Bank of Buffalo v. Nichols, 422.
Whitesides v. Cooper, 287, 447.
Whitfield v. Bewit, 66.
Whiting v. Adams, 201.
   v. Bank, 490.
   v. Brastow, 13.
   v. Edmunds, 464.

582   CASES CITED

[The figures refer to pages.]

Whiting v. Gould, 262, 263, 267.
   v. Nichols, 111.
   v. Whiting, 262.
Whitley v. Gough, 409.
Whitlock's Case, 319.
Whitmarsh v. Cutting, 9.
   v. Walker, 8.
Whitmire v. Wright, 87.
Whitney v. Allaire, 133.
   v. Buckman, 184.
   v. McKinney, 244.
   v. Marshall, 85.
   v. Olney, 426.
   v. Parker, 346.
   v. Salter, 289.
Whittacre v. Fuller, 229.
Whittelsey v. Hughes, 249.
Whittlesey v. Fuller, 338.
Whyddon's Case, 436.
Whyte v. Mayor, etc., of Nashville, 101, 102.
Wickham v. Hawker, 373.
Wickliffe v. Ensor, 460.
Wickliffe's Ex'rs v. Preston, 477.
Wickman v. Robinson, 194.
Wiggenhorn v. Kountz, 5.
Wiggins v. Chance, 121.
   v. Kirby, 460.
   v. Lusk, 434.
   v. McCleary, 358.
Wight v. Leigh, 259.
   v. Shaw, 454.
Wightman v. Laborde, 103.
   v. Schleifer, 106.
Wilber v. Sisson, 154.
Wilburn v. Spofford, 321.
Wilcox v. Bates, 187, 188.
   v. Cate, 142.
   v. Hill, 214.
   v. Randall, 106, 407.
   v. Wheeler, 37.
   v. Wilcox, 110.
Wilcoxon v. Osborn, 438.
Wilde v. Cantillon, 165.
Wilder v. Haughey, 116.
   v. House, 165.
   v. Ireland, 443.
   v. Ranney, 314.
Wildey v. Bonney's Lessee, 344.
Wiles v. Wiles, 72.
Wiley v. Ewalt, 385.
   v. Sirdorus, 417.

Wilken v. Young, 338, 343.
Wilkes v. Holmes, 318.
   v. Leuson, 427.
   v. Lion, 285.
Wilkes-Barre v. Wyoming Historical & Geological Soc., 37.
Wilkins v. Jewett, 367.
Wilkinson v. Buist, 317.
   v. Duncan, 325, 328.
   v. Haygarth, 342.
   v. Parish, 93.
   v. Prond, 374.
   v. Scott, 427.
   v. Suplee, 351.
   v. Wilkinson, 64.
Wilks v. Back, 432.
Willard, In re, 234.
   v. Cramer, 438.
   v. Harvey, 230.
   v. Olcott, 175.
   v. Reas, 192.
   v. Rogers, 146.
   v. Warren, 145.
   v. Willard, 345.
   v. Worsham, .208.
Willcox v. Foster, 230.
Willets v. Burgess, 206.
Willey v. Laraway, 111.
William Deering & Co. v. Beard, 121.
Williams v. Angell, 294.
   v. Barber, 353.
   v. Barrett, 89.
   v. Chambers-Roy Co., 189.
   v. Clark, 356.
   v. Coade, 267.
   v. Deriar, 159.
   v. Dorris, 119.
   v. Downing, 407.
   v. Earle, 136.
   v. Evans, 272.
   v. Everham, 207.
   v. Follett, 241.
   v. Green, 436.
   v. Haddock, 24.
   v. Hall, 118, 425.
   v. Hayward, 377.
   v. Insurance Co., 199.
   v. James, 361.
   v. Jenkins, 117.
   v. Kerr, 247.
   v. Kimball, 479.
   v. McAliley, 467.

CASES CITED.

[The figures refer to pages.]

Williams v. McCarty, 193.
   v. Maftzger, 241.
   v. Mershon, 150.
   v. Moody, 207.
   v. Morland, 369.
   v. Pollard, 487.
   v. Railroad Co., 362.
   v. Rand, 466.
   v. Safford, 356, 361.
   v. Shelden, 340.
   v. Smith, 219.
   v. Starr, 123, 229, 429.
   v. Thurlow, 207.
   v. Vanderbilt, 152, 153.
   v. Vreeland, 271.
   v. Washington, 249.
   v. Wethered, 116.
   v. Whitaker, 114.
   v. Willis, 118.
   v. Woodard, 319.
   v. Woods, 90.
Williams' Appeal, 377.
Williams' Case, 78, 99.
Williamson v. Brown, 214.
   v. Hall, 424, 425.
   v. Jones, 4, 64.
   v. Railway Co., 15.
   v. Wachenheim, 393.
Williamston & T. Ry. Co. v. Battle, 168.
Williard v. Ware, 316.
Willingham v. Hardin, 223.
Willion v. Berkley, 46, 47.
Willis v. Bucher, 49.
   v. City of Perry, 371.
   v. Gay, 193.
   v. Henderson, 246.
   v. Martin, 309.
Willison v. Watkins, 158.
Willoughby v. Horridge, 380.
Wilson v. Beckwith, 426.
   v. Bigger, 385.
   v. Branch, 386.
   v. Cochran, 113, 443.
   v. Denig, 290.
   v. Dresser, 34.
   v. Duguid, 313.
   v. Edmonds, 61, 65.
   v. Forbes, 6.
   v. Goldstein, 151.
   v. Henry, 462.
   v. Hunter, 185, 214, 465.

Wilson v. Johnson, 420.
   v. McCullough, 215.
   v. Mackreth, 375.
   v. Martin, 163.
   v. Miller, 214.
   v. Oatman, 97.
   v. Parker, 61, 289.
   v. Patrick, 188.
   v. Piggott, 313.
   v. Proctor, 115.
   v. Traer, 438.
   v. Troup, 311, 319, 321.
   v. Welch, 5.
   v. White, 302.
   v. Wilson, 184.
   v. Wright, 185.
Wilsons v. Doe, 491.
Wilt v. Franklin, 435.
Wilton v. Mayberry, 204.
Wimbledon and Putney Commons Conservators v. Dixon, 360.
Wimer v. Simmons, 370.
Winans v. Peebles, 387.
Winborne v. Downing, 440.
Winchester v. Charter, 393.
Wineman v. Hughson, 148.
   v. Phillips, 149.
Winfield v. Henning, 351.
Wing v. Gray, 17.
Winkler v. Winkler's Ex'rs, 78.
Winn v. Ables, 465.
   v. Ingilby, 18.
   v. Strickland, 144.
Winne, In re, 74.
Winona & St. P. R. Co. v. St. Paul & S. C. R. Co., 273.
Winslow v. Insurance Co., 15, 21.
Winsor v. Mills, 395.
Winsted Sav. Bank v. Spencer, 439.
Winter v. Brockwell, 358.
Winterbottom v. Pattison, 433.
Wintermute v. Light, 8.
Winters v. Mining Co., 208, 242.
Winthrop v. Fairbanks, 418.
   v. Minot, 344.
Winton's Appeal, 248.
Wiscot's Case, 50, 334.
Wisdom v. Reeves, 429.
Wiseman v. Lucksinger, 166, 350, 351, 353.
Wissler v. Hershey, 360.
Wistar's Appeal, 346.

584   CASES CITED.

[The figures refer to pages.]

Witham v. Brooner, 255.
   v. Perkins, 74.
Withers v. Baird, 438.
   v. Jenkins, 75, 77–79.
   v. Yeadon, 313.
Withy v. Mumford, 449.
Witmark v. Railroad Co., 153.
Witt v. Rice, 204.
Witter v. Damitz, 362.
Wofford v. McKinna, 420.
Wolcott v. Sullivan, 135.
Wolf v. Fleischacker, 116.
   v. Guffey, 152.
   v. Holton, 143.
   v. Johnson, 144.
   v. Wolf, 344.
Wolfe v. Frost, 166, 349.
   v. Van Nostrand, 302.
Wood v. Appal, 423.
   v. Armour, 195.
   v. Bayard, 53.
   v. Beach, 410.
   v. Chambers, 393.
   v. Chapin, 410.
   v. Clark, 393.
   v. Fleet, 344.
   v. Fowler, 6, 423.
   v. Griffin, 143.
   v. Hawkins, 121.
   v. Hubbell, 133.
   v. Keyes, 98.
   v. Leadbitter, 168.
   v. Manley, 166, 167.
   v. Mann, 213.
   v. Manufacturing Co., 185.
   v. Morehouse, 247.
   v. Noack, 154.
   v. Phillips, 340.
   v. Reed, 353.
   v. Saunders, 356.
   v. Town of Edenton, 6.
   v. Trask, 184, 210.
   v. Trnax, 383.
   v. Wallace, 91.
   v. Waud, 369, 372.
   v. Whelen, 200.
   v. Wood, 301.
Woodbury v. Aikin, 238.
   v. Luddy, 121.
   v. Parshley, 168.
   v. Short, 471.
Woodham v. Bank, 21.

Woodhull v. Rosenthal, 147.
Woodman v. Pitman, 6.
Woodruff v. McHarry, 438.
   v. Mutschler, 227.
   v. Robb, 190.
Woods, In re, 330.
   v. Dille, 262.
   v. Hilderbrand, 184.
   v. Huntingford, 204.
   v. Shields, 248.
   v. Wallace, 91.
   v. Woods, 233.
Woodward v. Boro, 221.
   v. Dowse, 103.
   v. Phillips, 201.
   v. Pickett, 196.
Woodward-Holmes Co. v. Nudd, 93.
Woodworth v. Carman, 188.
   v. Paige, 106.
Wooldridge v. Lucas, 85.
Woolever v. Knapp, 341.
Wooliscroft v. Norton, 136.
Woolley v. Holt, 184.
Woolsey v. Donnelly, 161.
Wooten v. Bellinger, 192.
Worcester Nat. Bank v. Cheney, 233.
Word v. Box, 462.
Workman v. Greening, 187, 188.
   v. Mifflin, 153.
Worman v. Teagarden, 170.
Wormley v. Wormley, 269.
Worrell v. Forsyth, 108.
Worthington v. Gimson, 360.
Worthy v. Johnson, 487.
Wragg v. Comptroller General, 192.
Wren v. Bradley, 173.
Wright v. Brown, 489.
   v. Cartwright, 286.
   v. Ditzler, 120.
   v. Douglass, 261.
   v. Dunning, 119, 122.
   v. Gelvin, 85.
   v. Germain, 383.
   v. Henderson, 184.
   v. Herron, 49, 77.
   v. Jennings, 60.
   v. Lake, 196.
   v. Langley, 247.
   v. Macdonell, 23.
   v. Macdonnell, 143.
   v. Pearson, 258.
   v. Sperry, 195.

CASES CITED.

[The figures refer to pages.]

Wright v. Tallmadge, 309.
   v. Tichenor, 461.
   v. Trevezant, 132.
   v. Westheimer, 119.
   v. Wright, 38, 305, 312.
Wronkow v. Oakley, 107.
Wuestcott v. Seymour, 421.
Wunderle v. Wunderle, 388.
Wusthoff v. Dracourt, 57.
W. U. Tel. Co. v. Bullard, 166.
Wyatt v. Barwell, 218.
   v. Irrigation Co., 34.
   v. Smith, 80.
Wyatt's Estate, 60.
Wyman v. Brigden, 41.
   v. Brown, 255, 298, 299.
   v. Hooper, 210.
Wynkoop v. Burger, 360, 361.
   v. Cowing, 187.
Wynne v. Hudson, 121, 124.

Y

Yale v. Flanders, 430.
   v. Seely, 8.
Yancey v. Tatlock, 446.
Yard's Appeal, 328.
Yaryan v. Shriner, 192.
Yates v. Kinney, 154.
   v. Van De Vogert, 459.
Yearworth v. Pierce, 17.
Yeates v. Gill, 478.
Yeaton v. Roberts, 284.
Yellow River Imp. Co. v. Wood Co., 379.
Yelverton v. Hillard, 466.
Young, In re, 288.

Young v. ———, 370.
   v. Anon., 370.
   v. Boardman, 109.
   v. City of Boston, 163.
   v. Guy, 224.
   v. Langbein, 77.
   v. Miles' Ex'rs, 272.
   v. Miller, 244.
   v. Morehead, 92.
   v. Morgan, 203.
   v. Omohundro, 200.
   v. Ruth, 209.
   v. Spencer, 65.
   v. Tarbell, 91, 101.
   v. Thrasher, 93, 97.
   v. Young, 305.
Youngblood v. Eubank, 19.
   v. Vastine, 224.
Younge v. Guilbeau, 435.
Younghusband v. Gisborne, 397.
Youngman v. Railroad Co., 196, 218.
Younts v. Starnes, 455.
Youse v. Norcum, 386.

Z

Zabriskie v. Railroad Co., 273.
Zacharias v. Zacharias, 274.
Zackry v. Lockard, 83.
Zaegel v. Kuster, 234.
Zane v. Kennedy, 319.
Zebach v. Smith, 314.
Zimmerman v. Lebo, 109.
Zoller v. Ide, 430.
Zorntlein v. Bram, 338.
Zuver v. Lyons, 261.

INDEX.

[THE FIGURES REFER TO PAGES.]

A

ABANDONMENT,
    of homestead, 121.
    destruction of easements by, 357.
    of possession by joint disseisor, 466.
    of title by adverse possession, 469.

ACCEPTANCE,
    of deeds, 433.

ACCOUNTING.
    by mortgagee, 199.
        debits, 200.
        credits, 201.
        annual rests, 202.
    between co-tenants, 341.

ACCRETION,
    title by, 470.
        alluvion, 470.

ACCUMULATIONS,
    rule against, 330.
        application to charitable trusts, 276.

ACKNOWLEDGMENT,
    of deeds, 436.

ACTIONS,
    for breach of covenant of warranty, 449.
    real and personal, 1.
    affecting joint estates, 343.

ACTIVE TRUSTS,
    incidents of, 272.

ACTIVE USES,
    statute of uses does not operate on, 254.

588　　　　　　　　　　INDEX

[The figures refer to pages.]

ACTUAL NOTICE, 213.

ADAPTATION FOR USE,
 as test of character of fixture, 15.

ADVANCEMENTS, 481.

ADVERSE POSSESSION,
 by mortgagor against mortgagee, 195.
 against remainder-man, 464.
 by joint disseisors, 466.
 possession by trustee not, 274.
 abolished under system of registered titles, 414.
 title by, 456.
  requisites of, 456.
  seisin and disseisin, 458.
  effect of descent cast, 459.
  must be actual, 459.
  ouster necessary, 459.
  color of title, 460.
  disseisin, intention necessary, 460.
  must be visible or notorious, 460.
  what possession is adverse, 463.
  when possession up to division fence is adverse, 463.
  must be exclusive, 465.
  must be continuous, 466.
   tacking, 466.
  against whom possession is adverse, 468.
  length of possession necessary, 469.
  abandonment, 469.

ADVOWSONS, 349.

AFFINITY,
 relationship by, 483.

AFFIRMATIVE EASEMENTS, 354.

AFTER-ACQUIRED PROPERTY,
 may be mortgaged, 185.

AFTER-ACQUIRED TITLE,
 mortgagee may set up against his assignee, 211.

AGENTS,
 leases by, 131.

AGREEMENT TO MORTGAGE,
 treated as a mortgage, 191.

AGRICULTURAL FIXTURES, 17.

INDEX. 589

[The figures refer to pages.]

AIDS,
    incidents of tenure, 29.

ALIENAGE,
    as defeating dower, 103.

ALIENATION,
        see "Restraints on Alienation."
    history of right of, 390.
    power of, when acquired, 45.
    of fee simple, 39.
        voluntary and involuntary, 40.
    of life estates, 59.
    of estate during coverture, 72.
    of homestead, 122.
    of tenancies from year to year, 160.
    of future estates, 305.
    of franchises, 379.
    destruction of common appurtenant by, 375.
    by disseisor, 467.
    clauses forbidding, 394.
    clauses of forfeiture for, 394.

ALIENS,
    capacity of to hold and convey realty, 387.
    inheritance by, 388.
    naturalized citizens, 388.
    title of divested by office found, 388.

ALLODIAL,
    land declared to be, in many states, 31.

ALLUVION,
    title by, 470.

ALTERATION OF ESTATE,
    revocation of devise by, 476.

ALTERATIONS,
    in deeds, 428.

ALTERNATE REMAINDERS, 287.

AMBIGUITIES,
    latent, in description of property, 420.

ANCESTOR,
    defined, 479.

ANCESTRAL LANDS AND COLLATERAL HEIRS, 483.

[The figures refer to pages.]

ANCIENT DEMESNE,
  defined, 27.

ANNEXATION,
  as test of character of fixture, 13.
    constructive, 14.
    party making, 19.

ANNUAL CROPS,
  not real property, 7.
  what are, 8.
  are incorporeal hereditaments, 349.

ANNULMENT OF MARRIAGE,
  defeating dower, 104.

APPENDANT POWERS, 310.

APPENDANT EASEMENTS, 354.

APPOINTEES,
  of power defined, 307.
  classes of powers as to, 311.

APPOINTMENT,
  powers of, 309.

APPORTIONMENT,
  of rent, 377.
    in life estates, 60.
    in estates per autre vie, 68.
    in estates in dower, 102.

APPURTENANCES, 425.

APPURTENANT EASEMENTS, 354.

ASCENDING LINES,
  in title by descent, 482.

ASSIGNEE,
  of equity of redemption, rights of, 206.

ASSIGNMENT,
  of dower, 95.
    of common right, 96.
    against common right, 96.
    when value estimated, 97.
    method of division, 98.
    by whom, 99.
    recovery by action, 100.
  of lease, 148.
    liability of assignee, 149.

INDEX. 591

[The figures refer to pages.]

ASSIGNMENT—Continued,
    of equity of redemption, 205.
        by operation of law, 208.
    of mortgage, 209.
        by operation of law, 211.
    of mortgage debt, 210.
    of trustee's title, 273.
    a common-law conveyance, 409.

ASSUMED NAME,
    grantee in deed may be designated by, 416.

ATTACHMENT,
    mortgagee's interest before foreclosure not subject to, 212.

ATTORNEY,
    power of, to execute deed, 431.

AT WILL,
    see "Tenancies at Will," 155.

AUSTRALIAN SYSTEM,
    of registering titles, 413.

B

BANKRUPT AND INSOLVENT LAWS, 394.

BARGAIN AND SALE, 410.

BARRING ESTATE TAIL, 50.

BASE FEES, 178.

BENEFICIAL POWER, 320.

BENEFICIARY,
    defined, 260.
    in charitable trusts may be indefinite, 276.

BLANKS,
    filling, in deeds, 428.

BLOOD,
    see "Half Blood."

BOND FOR TITLE,
    may be mortgaged, 185.
    assignment of, may be a mortgage, 191

BOOM COMPANIES,
    rights of, 370.

BOUNDARIES,
    description in deeds, 419.

592 INDEX.

[The figures refer to pages.]

BREACH,
 of covenant of warranty, action for, 449.

BREACH OF CONDITIONS,
 termination of estates on condition, 175.

BRIDGES,
 franchises for, 380.

BUILDINGS,
 horizontal ownership of, 366.

C

CAESAREAN OPERATION, 74.

CANONS OF DESCENT, 482.

CAPACITY,
 personal, to hold and convey realty, 381.

CERTIFICATE,
 of acknowledgment, 438.
 and patent, 402.
 of purchase in tax titles, 493.

CESTUI QUE TRUST,
 defined, 260.
 rights of, 271.
 interest of, 273.
 is disseised by disseisin of trustee, 468.

CHARGES,
 on land under registered titles, 413.

CHARITABLE TRUSTS,
 defined, 274.
 distinguished from private, 274.
  beneficiary indefinite, 276.
  doctrine of cy-pres, 276.
  perpetuities and accumulations, 276.
 creation of, 275.
 objects of, 275.

CHARITIES,
 defined, 275.
 gifts to, application of rule against perpetuities, 329.

CHATTEL FIXTURES,
 defined, 10.

[The figures refer to pages.]

CHATTEL INTERESTS,
    estate tail in, 49.
    statute of uses does not operate on, 254.

CHATTELS REAL,
    defined, 24.

CHILDREN,
    illegitimate, 480.
    posthumous, 480.

CIVIL LAW,
    computation of relationship by, 484.

CLAIM OF TITLE,
    necessary in adverse possession, 465.

CLASS,
    limitations to, and rule against perpetuities, 328.

COLLATERAL HEIRS,
    defined, 484.
    and ancestral lands, 483.

COLLATERAL POWERS, 311.

COLOR OF TITLE, 460.

COMMON,
    tenancies in, 335.
    rights of defined, 373.
    of estovers, 373.
    of pasture, 373.
        appurtenant and appendant, 373.
    of piscary, 373.
    of turbary, 373.
    rights of, in United States, 375.

COMMON LAW,
    future estates at, 279.
    computation of relationship by, 484.
    conveyances, 405.
    powers, 308.
    theory of mortgage, 183.

COMMON RECOVERY, 50.
    conveyance by married woman by, 386.

COMMUNITY SYSTEM, 338.

COMPENSATION,
    for land taken under right of eminent domain, 495.

[The figures refer to pages.]

COMPULSORY PARTITION, 344.

CONDEMNATION OF LAND,
 under power of eminent domain, 494.

CONDITION,
 estates on, see "Estates on Condition."

CONDITIONAL FEES,
 what are, 45.

CONDITIONS,
 precedent and subsequent, 170.
 void, 172.
  effect, 173.
 breach of, in estates on condition, 175.
  relief against, 175.
 subject to rule against perpetuities, 326.
 against alienation, 395.
 of forfeiture for alienation, 395.

CONFIRMATION,
 a common-law conveyance, 408.

CONFISCATION AND ESCHEAT,
 acquisition of title by, 399.

CONGRESSIONAL SURVEY, 402.

CONQUEST,
 acquisition of title by, 399.

CONSANGUINITY,
 relationship by, 483.

CONSIDERATION,
 for deeds, 427.

CONSTRUCTION,
 of description in deed, 420.

CONSTRUCTIVE NOTICE,
 by possession, 216.
 by lis pendens, 218.
 by registration, 218.

CONSTRUCTIVE POSSESSION,
 seisin in law is, 32.
 in acquisition of title by adverse possession, 460.

CONSTRUCTIVE TRUSTS,
 see "Trusts."

CONTINGENCY,
 on which remainder may depend, 292.

[The figures refer to pages.]

CONTINGENT INTERESTS,
  rule against perpetuities applies to, 326.

CONTINGENT REMAINDERS,
  see "Remainders."

CONTINUOUS EASEMENTS, 354.

CONTINUOUS POSSESSION,
  in acquisition of title by adverse possession, 466.
  tacking, 466.

CONTRIBUTION,
  to redeem mortgage, 236.

CONVENTIONAL EASEMENTS, 354.

CONVENTIONAL LIFE ESTATES, 56.

CONVEYANCES,
  registration, see "Registration."
  priority of, 212.
    actual notice, 213.
    implied notice, 215.
    constructive notice, 216.
      possession, 216.
      recitals in title deeds, 216.
      lis pendens, 218.
      registration, 218.
  fraudulent 392.
  kinds of, 405.
  primary and secondary, 405.
  at common law, 405.
    feoffment, 405.
    gift, 406.
    grant, 407.
    lease, 407.
    exchange, 407.
    partition, 408.
    release, 408.
    confirmation, 408.
    surrender, 408.
    assignment, 409.
    defeasance, 409.
  under statute of uses, 409.
    covenant to stand seised, 410.
    bargain and sale, 410.
    lease and release, 411.

[The figures refer to pages.]

CONVEYANCES—Continued,
   modern statutory, 411.
      warranty and quitclaim deeds, 412.
   registered titles, 412.
      certificate of title, 413.
   under judicial process, 486.
      licenses, 486.
         by guardian, 487.
         by personal representatives, 487.
         of settled estates, 488.
      decrees, 488.
      tax titles, 490.
      eminent domain, 494.

COPARCENARY,
   estates in, 336.

COPARCENERS,
   lease by, 132.

COPYHOLD TENURE, 29.

CORNERS,
   when lost, how located, 424.

CORODIES, 349.

CORPORATION,
   capacity to hold and convey realty, 389.
   deeds by, how signed, 430.

CORPOREAL HEREDITAMENTS, 348.

CO-TENANTS,
   accounting between, 341.

COURSES AND DISTANCES,
   description by, 424.

COVENANT,
   to stand seised, 410.
   creation of easements by, 351.
   independent and dependent, 441.
   express, rights of landlord and tenant under, 134.
   implied, rights of landlord and tenant under, 138.
   real and personal, 441.
   personal, in leases, 136.
   running with the land, in leases, 136.
      not subject to rule against perpetuities, 326.
   of title, 440.
      express and implied, 440.

INDEX.

[The figures refer to pages.]

COVENANT—Continued,
    of seisin, 442.
        how broken, 442.
        when broken, 442.
    against incumbrances, defined, 444.
        how broken, 444.
    of warranty, defined, 446.
        how broken, 446.
        action for breach, 449.
        estoppel by, 454.
        special, 446.
    of quiet enjoyment, 448.
    for further assurance, 449.

COVERTURE,
  estate during, 70.
    power of husband over chattels real, 71.
    power of husband over real estate, 71.
    alienation of, 72.
    separate estate, 72.
    equitable doctrine, 72.
    statutory changes, 73.
    abolished, 73.

CREDITORS,
  whether constructive trust in favor of, 271.
  rights of, in powers, 320.
  restraints on alienation in favor of, 392.

CROSS REMAINDERS, 286.

CURTESY,
  defined, 73.
  requisites, 73.
    birth of issue, 74.
        Caesarean operation, 74.
        not necessary in Pennsylvania, 75.
    marriage, 74.
    seisin of wife, 75.
    death of wife, 76.
  initiate, 74.
  consummate, 76.
  in what estates, 76.
    estates of inheritance, 76.
    determinable estates, 77.
    equitable estates, 77.

598 INDEX.

[The figures refer to pages.]

CURTESY—Continued,
    estates in expectancy, 79.
    joint estates, 79.
  incidents, 79.
    alienation, 80.
    liability for debts, 80.
  how defeated, 81.
    alienage, 81.
    annulment of marriage, 81.
    conveyance by wife, 81.
    desertion, 81.
    devise, 81.
    forfeited by feoffment, 81.
  statutory changes, 82.

CY-PRES.
  application of doctrine of, to charitable trusts, 276.

D

DATE,
  whether requisite in deeds, 428.

DEATH OF HUSBAND,
  requisite of dower, 85.
  dower consummate by, 85.

DECREE,
  for deficiency in foreclosure, 241.
  of sale in foreclosure, 248.
  conveyance under, 488.

DE DONIS CONDITIONALIBUS,
  statute of, creating estates tail, 44, 46.

DEED,
  when required in creation of estates for years, 132.
  absolute may be a mortgage, 187.
  of trust may be a mortgage, 190.
  defined, 415.
  requisites of, 414.
    designation of grantee, 416.
    granting clause, 416.
    names of parties, 416.
    words of conveyance, 416.
    exceptions, 417.
    reservations, 418.

[The figures refer to pages.]

DEED—Continued,
    habendum, 418.
    description of property, 419.
        plats and maps, 421.
        monuments, 422.
        courses and distances, 424.
        quantity, 425.
        appurtenances, 425.
    execution of the writing, 426.
        what writing necessary, 427.
        consideration, 427.
        date, 428.
        alterations, 428.
        filling blanks, 428.
        reading, 429.
        sealing, 429.
        signing, 430.
            power of attorney, 431.
        indentures and deeds poll, 432.
    delivery and acceptance, 433.
        delivery in escrow, 435.
    acknowledgment, 436.
    registry, 439.
    witnesses, 439.
  estoppel by, 453.
  under tax titles, 492.
  poll and indenture, 432.

DEFEASANCE,
  a common-law conveyance, 409.

DEFICIENCY,
  decree for in foreclosure, 241.

DEFINITE FAILURE OF ISSUE, 326.

DEGREES OF RELATIONSHIP,
  how computed, 484.

DELIVERY,
  of deeds, 433.
    in escrow, 435.

DEMESNE,
  tenants in, 35.

DENYING LESSOR'S TITLE,
  lessee estopped, 143.

[The figures refer to pages.]

DEPENDENT COVENANTS,
    in deeds, 441.

DEPOSIT OF TITLE DEEDS,
    may be a mortgage, 192.

DESCENDING LINES,
    in title by descent, 482.

DESCENT,
    of future estates, 306.
    and purchase, 399.
    title by, 478.
    what descends to heirs, 479.
    illegitimate children, 480.
    posthumous children, 480.
    advancements, 481.
        hotchpot, 482.
    canons of, 482.
        descending and ascending lines, 482.
        preference of males, 482.
            in collateral lines, 485.
        collateral heirs and ancestral lands, 483.
        per stirpes and per capita, 483.
        primogeniture, 483.
        whole and half blood, 485.
    escheat, 485.

DESCENT CAST,
    what is, 459.
    effect of, on right of entry, 459.

DESCRIPTION OF PROPERTY,
    in deeds, 419.
    in wills, 473.

DESTRUCTION,
    of vested remainders, 289.
    of contingent remainders, 293.
        liability to, removed by statute, 293.
    of powers, 321.
    of easements, 357.
    of profits a prendre, 375.
    of premises, termination of estates for years by, 153.

DETERMINABLE ESTATES,
    curtesy in, 77.
    dower in, 88.

[The figures refer to pages.]

DETERMINABLE FEES, 178.

DEVICES,
    to bar dower, 105.

DEVISES,
    executory, see "Executory Devise."
    shifting, see "Shifting Devise."
    creation of fee simple by, 38.
    title by. 472.
        requisites of, 472.
        nature of, 475.
        operative words in wills, 473.
        what can be devised, 474.
        what law governs, 474.
        renunciation of, 475.
        revocation by alteration of estate, 476.
        lapsed devises, 477.

DISABILITY OF PERSONS,
    affecting title by adverse possession, 468.

DISCHARGE,
    of mortgage, 227.
        by payment, 227.
        by performance, 227.
        by tender, 230.
        by merger, 231.
        by redemption, 233.
        form of, 238.

DISCONTINUOUS EASEMENTS, 354.

DISCOVERY,
    acquisition of title by state by, 399.

DISSEISEE,
    leases by, 131.

DISSEISIN,
    by mortgagor, 195.
    equitable estates, lost by, 274.
    of joint owner, 340.
        what is, 464.
    leaves mere right of entry, 458.
    giving title by adverse possession, 458.

DISSEISOR,
    alienation by, 467.

[The figures refer to pages.]

DISTANCES,
>description by courses and, 424.

DISTRESS,
>for rent, 145.
>an incident of rent service, 376.

DIVISION LINES,
>estoppel in pais, 453.

DIVORCE,
>defeating dower, 104.

DOMESTIC FIXTURES, 18.

DOMINANT ESTATE, 350.

DONEE,
>of estate tail, 42.
>of power, 307.
>classes of powers as to, 310.

DONOR,
>of estate tail, 42.
>of power, 307.

DOWER,
>defined, 83.
>requisites, 83.
>>marriage, 84.
>>seisin of husband, 84.
>>>transitory, 84.
>>death of husband, 85.
>inchoate, 84.
>consummate, 85.
>in what estates, 86.
>>estates of inheritance, 86.
>>>in estate tail, 72.
>>>in rents, 87.
>>>lands capable of enjoyment, 87.
>>>inheritance by issue, 88.
>>determinable estates, 88.
>>equitable estates, 89.
>>>mortgages, 89.
>>estates in expectancy, 91.
>>>dower out of dower, 91.
>>joint estates, 92.
>>>partnership lands, 93.
>quarantine, 94.

[The figures refer to pages.]

DOWER—Continued,
  assignment, 95.
    of common right, 96.
    against common right, 96.
    when value estimated, 97.
    method of division, 98.
    by whom assigned, 99.
    recovery by action, 100.
  incidents, 101.
    emblements, 101.
    estovers, 101.
    repairs, 101.
    waste, 101.
    apportionment of rent, 102.
    improvements, 102.
    taxes, 102.
  how defeated, 102.
    alienage, 103.
    elopement and adultery, 103.
    annulment of marriage, 104.
    loss of husband's estate, 104.
    conveyance by husband, 105.
    devices to bar, 105.
    release by wife, 106.
    jointure, 107.
    widow's election, 109.
      testamentary provision, 109.
      statutory provision, 110.
    estoppel, 110.
    statute of limitations and laches, 111.
    waste, 111.
  statutory changes, 112.
  right of, not breach of covenant of seisin, 444.

DRUNKARDS,
  capacity to convey real property, 385.

E

EASEMENTS,
  defined, 349.
  essential qualities, 350.
  distinguished from licenses, 350.
  dominant estate, 350.
  servient estate, 350.

[The figures refer to pages.]

EASEMENTS—Continued,
    creation, 350.
        by grant, 350.
        by parol, 351.
        by covenants, 351.
        by prescription, 352.
    equitable, 351.
    classification, 354.
    appendant or appurtenant and in gross, 354.
    continuous and discontinuous, 354.
    natural and conventional, 354.
    negative and affirmative, 354.
    incidents, 355.
        obstruction, 356.
        repairs, 356.
        use of easements, 356.
    destruction, 357.
        by release, 357.
        by abandonment, 357.
        by license, 357.
        by misuser, 357.
        by merger, 357.
    specific, 359.
        rights of way, 359.
            repair of, 361.
        highways, 361.
            dedication, 362.
        light and air, 363.
        lateral and subjacent support, 365.
            horizontal, ownership of buildings, 366.
        party walls, 366.
        in water, 368.
            surface waters, 371.
            subterranean waters, 371.
            eaves' drip, 372.
            artificial water courses, 372.
    existence of, not breach of covenant of seisin, 444.
        as breach of covenant against incumbrances, 444.

EAVES' DRIP, 372.

EJECTMENT,
    termination of estate on condition by, 174.

[The figures refer to pages.]

ELECTION,
    testamentary provision in lieu of dower, 109.
    statutory provision in lieu of dower, 110.

ELOPEMENT,
    defeating dower, 103.

EMBLEMENTS,
    what are, 8.
    an incident of life estates, 61.
        of estate during coverture, 71.
        of dower, 101.
        of estates for years, 143.
        of tenancies at will, 156.
        of tenancies from year to year, 160.
    tenant at sufferance not entitled to, 164.
    mortgagor no right to, 196.
    right of tenant of mortgagor to, 196.

EMINENT DOMAIN,
    termination of estates for years by, 153.
    taking franchises under, 379.
    acquisition of title under, by state, 399.
    taking land under, not breach of covenant of warranty, 448.
    title by, 494.
    compensation for land taken under right of, 495.

ENTAIL,
    see "Estates Tail."
    barred by common recovery, 51.

ENTIRETY,
    estates in, 337.

ENTRY,
    right of, to defeat estate on condition, 174, 176.
    and possession, foreclosure by, 243.
    on public lands, 402.

EQUITABLE WASTE, 62.

EQUITABLE CONVERSION,
    defined, 23.

EQUITABLE EASEMENTS, 351.

EQUITABLE ESTATES, 251.
    curtesy in, 77.
    dower in, 89.
        mortgages, 89.

[The figures refer to pages.]

EQUITABLE ESTATES—Continued,
    homestead in, 116.
    use and trust defined, 252.
    statute of uses, 253.
        when statute does not operate, 254.
    classification of trusts, 257.
    executed and executory trusts, 258.
    express trusts, 258.
        creation, 260.
            limitation of trustee's estate, 261.
            precatory words, 261.
            statute of frauds, 262.
            parties, 263.
    implied trusts, 264.
        resulting trusts, 265.
            legal title only conveyed, 266.
            consideration paid by another, 267.
            failure of object of trust, 267.
            deed to wife or child, 268.
        constructive trusts, 269.
            fraud an essential element of, 269.
            devise procured by fraud, 270.
            in favor of creditors, 271.
    Incidents, 271.
        active trusts, 272.
        passive trusts, 271.
        interest of trustee, 272.
        interest to cestui que trust, 273.
        liability for owner's debts, 274.
        lost by disseisin, 274.
        possession by trustee not adverse, 274.
    subject to rule against perpetuities, 327.

EQUITABLE THEORY,
    of mortgage, 183.

EQUITABLE RIGHTS,
    may be mortgaged, 185.

EQUITY OF REDEMPTION,
    no mortgage without, 205.
    assignment of, 205.
        rights of assignee, 206.
        by operation of law, 208.

[The figures refer to pages.]

ESCAMBIUM,
    must be used in common-law exchange, 407.

ESCHEAT,
    an incident of tenure, 30.
    acquisition of title by, 399, 485.

ESCROW,
    delivery of deed in, 435.

ESTATES,
    defined, 33.
    classification of, 33.
    of freehold, 34.
    quantity of, 34.
        of inheritance, 35.
            dower in, 86.
            dower in rents, 87.
        in fee simple, 35.
        estates tail, 42.
        life estates, 55.
            restraints on alienation of, 395.
            per autre vie, 67.
                general occupancy, 68.
                incidents of, 68.
        conventional life estates, 56.
        legal life estate, estates by marriage, 69.
            during coverture, 70.
            curtesy, 73.
            dower, 83.
        less than freehold, 128.
    as to quality, 169.
        on condition, 169.
            mortgages, 169.
        on limitation, 177.
    as to time of enjoyment, 279.
        present and future, 279.
        in expectancy, dower in, 91.
    as to number of owners, 332.
        joint estates, 332.
    unknown forms cannot be created, 40.
    particular, 284.
    powers distinguished from, 308.

ESTATES FOR YEARS,
    defined, 128.

[The figures refer to pages.]

ESTATES FOR YEARS—Continued,
   history of, 129.
   creation, 130.
      contract or devise, 130.
      lease and agreement for lease, 130.
      who may create, 131.
      form, 132.
      commencement, 133.
      duration, 133.
      interesse termini, 133.
   rights and liabilities of landlord and tenant, see "Landlord and Tenant."
   transfer, 147.
      by lessor, 147.
      by lessee, 148.
      by operation of law, 149.
   termination, 150.
      lapse of time, 150.
      forfeiture, 150.
      merger, 152.
      surrender, 152.
      taking into power of eminent domain, 153.
      destruction of premises, 153.
   letting land on shares, 154.
   homestead in, 116.
   restraints on alienation of, 396.

ESTATES IN COPARCENARY,
   partition of, 344.

ESTATES IN ENTIRETY, 337.
   in the United States, 338.
   partition of, 344.

ESTATES IN EXPECTANCY,
   see "Future Estates."

ESTATES IN PARTNERSHIP, 339.

ESTATES ON CONDITION,
   distinguished from estates on limitation, 177.
   conditions precedent and subsequent, 170.
   void conditions, 172.
      effect of, 173.
   termination, 174.
   who can enforce a forfeiture, 176.

[The figures refer to pages.]

ESTATES ON LIMITATION,
    defined, 177.
    distinguished from estates on condition, 177.
    base or determinable fees, 178.

ESTATES TAIL,
    defined, 42.
    donor and donee, 42.
    classes of, 43.
        general tail, 43.
        special tail, 43.
        male, 44.
        female, 44.
    origin, 44.
    creation of, 47.
        words of limitation, 47.
        words of procreation, 47.
    in chattel interests, 49.
    incidents of, 49.
        tenant need not pay interest on incumbrances, 49.
        curtesy, 50.
        dower, 50.
        merger, 50.
    duration of, 50.
        barred by common recovery, 50.
            by fine, 51.
            by deed, 52.
    in United States, 52.
        abolished in some states, 53.
    tenant in tail after possibility of issue extinct, 52.
    in estates per autre vie, 54.
        quasi entail, 53.
    restraints on alienation of, 395.

ESTATE TAKEN BY PURCHASER,
    at tax sale, 493.

ESTOPPEL,
    dower defeated by, 110.
    to deny lessor's title, 143.
        tenant at sufferance, 164.
    title by, defined, 450.
        in pais, 451.
            division lines. 453.
        by deed, 453.

[The figures refer to pages.]

ESTOPPEL—Continued,
  by covenants of warranty, 454.
  by quitclaim deed, 454.
  by recitals, 454.
  in conveyance by joint tenants, 455.
  of married women, 455.

ESTOVERS,
  house bote, 61.
  fire bote, 61.
  hay bote, 61.
  plough bote, 61.
  incidents of life estates, 61.
    of dower, 101.
    of tenancies from year to year, 160.
  mortgagor entitled to, 195.
  common of, 373.

EVICTION,
  extinguishment of rent by, 378.

EXCEPTIONS,
  in deed, 417.

EXCESSIVE EXECUTION,
  of powers, 318.

EXCHANGE,
  a common-law conveyance, 407.

EXCLUSIVE FRANCHISES,
  may be protected as contracts, 379.

EXCLUSIVE POSSESSION,
  necessary in acquisition of title by adverse possession, 465.

EXCLUSIVE POWERS, 312.

EXECUTED TRUSTS, 258.

EXECUTION,
  interest of tenant at will cannot be sold on, 156.
  mortgagee's interest before foreclosure not subject to, 212.
  purchasers at, when protected under recording act, 225.
  of powers, 314.
    form of, 315.
    time of, 317.
    compelling, 318.
    defective, 318.
    excessive, 318.

[The figures refer to pages.]

EXECUTORS,
    leases by, 131.
EXECUTORY DEVISES,
    defined, 300.
    destruction of, 302.
    alienation, 305.
    descent of, 306.
EXECUTORY TRUSTS, 258.
EXEMPTIONS,
    see "Homestead."
EXPRESS COVENANTS,
    rights of landlord and tenant under, 134.
    in deeds, 440.
EXPRESS TRUSTS,
    see "Trusts."

F

FAILURE OF ISSUE,
    rule against perpetuities, 326.
FAILURE OF OBJECT,
    of resulting trust, 267.
FEDERAL HOMESTEAD ACT, 126.
FEE,
    defined, 35.
    under feudal system, 27.
FEE CONDITIONAL,
    at common law, 45.
    became estates tail, 45.
FEE FARM RENTS, 375.
FEE SIMPLE,
    defined, 35.
    creation, 36.
        by deed, 36.
            words of limitation, 36.
                in quitclaim deed, 37.
        by devise, 38.
        by joint tenant, 37.
    right of user, 39.
    alienation, 39.
        voluntary, 40.
        involuntary, 40.
        restraints on, 395.

[The figures refer to pages.]

FEE TAIL,
  see "Estates Tail."
FENCES,
  partition, 368.
    when possession up to is adverse, 403.
FEOFFMENT,
  defined, 405.
  tortious, operation of, 406.
FERRIES,
  rights to operate are franchises, 379.
  personal property in Iowa, 379.
FEUDAL SYSTEM, 26.
FEUD,
  defined, 27.
FICTITIOUS PERSON,
  deed to, void, 416.
FIEF,
  defined, 27.
FILLING BLANKS,
  in deeds, 428.
FINE,
  barring estate tail by, 51.
  conveyance of married woman by, 386.
FIRE BOTE,
  defined, 61.
FIRST PURCHASER,
  inheritance of ancestral lands by issue of, 484.
FISH,
  rights of common, 374.
FIXTURES,
  defined and classified, 10.
  real and chattel, 10.
  what are removable, 11.
  intention the test of character, 12.
  character determined by express contract, 12.
    by statutory regulation, 12.
    by annexation, 13.
      constructive annexation, 14.
    by adaptation for use of realty, 15.

INDEX. 613

[The figures refer to pages.]

FIXTURES—Continued,
 by nature, 16.
  trade fixtures, 16.
  agricultural fixtures, 17.
  domestic fixtures, 18.
 by party making annexation, 19.
 time of removal, 22.
 covered by mortgage of land, 185.
 removal of, breach of covenant of warranty, 448.

FORECLOSURE,
 see "Mortgage."

FORFEITURE.
 an incident of tenure, 30.
 re-entry for, 150.
 termination of estates for years by, 150.
 of estate on condition, waiver, 175
 who can enforce, in estates on condition, 176.
 of particular estate may destroy contingent remainder, 293.
 of franchises, 379.
 for alienation, clauses of, 394.
 of title for nonpayment of taxes, 490.

FOSSILS.
 are real property, 7.

FRANCHISES,
 defined, 378.
 are incorporeal hereditaments, 349.
 alienation, 379.
 forfeiture, 379.
 taken under right of eminent domain, 379.
 ferries, 379.
  personal property in Iowa, 379.
 for bridges on turnpike roads, 380

FRANKALMOIGNE,
 defined, 28.

FRAUD,
  see "Statute of Frauds."
 an essential element of constructive trusts, 269.

FRAUDULENT CONVEYANCE.
 restraints on alienation, 392.
 when conveyance of homestead is not, 393.
 test of, 393.
 marriage a valuable consideration, 393.

[The figures refer to pages.]

FREE ALMS,
　tenure by, 28.
FREE AND COMMON SOCAGE,
　tenure in, 28.
FREEHOLDS,
　defined, 34.
　when long terms of years are, 35.
　in futuro, 284.
　　estates for years may be created in futuro, 133.
FRUCTUS INDUSTRIALES,
　defined, 9.
FURTHER ASSURANCE,
　covenant for, 449.
FUTURE ACCESSIONS,
　covered by mortgage, 185.
FUTURE ADVANCES,
　mortgages for, 224.
FUTURE ESTATES,
　defined, 279.
　curtesy in, 79.
　dower in, 91.
　homestead in, 117.
　may be mortgaged, 184.
　at common law, 279.
　　reversions, 280.
　　possibility of reverter, 281.
　　remainders, 281.
　　　how created, 282.
　　　when they must take effect, 283.
　　　freehold in futuro, 284.
　　　the particular estate, 284.
　　　distinguished from shifting uses and devises, 285.
　　　cross, 286.
　　　successive, 286.
　　　alternate, 287.
　　　vested, 288.
　　　　remainders to a class, 288.
　　　　destruction of, 289.
　　　contingent, 289.
　　　　distinguished from vested, 290.
　　　　estates which will support, 291.

FUTURE ESTATES—Continued,
 New York Code definition of, 291.
 test of, 291.
 contingency on which remainder may depend, 292.
 destruction of, 293.
  by destruction of particular estate, 293.
  by expiration of particular estate, 293.
  by forfeiture of particular estate, 293.
  by merger of particular estate, 293.
  trustees to preserve, 293.
  liability to be destroyed removed by statute, 293.
rule in Shelley's Case, 295.
under statute of uses, 298.
 future uses, 298.
 springing uses, 299.
 shifting uses, 300.
under statute of wills, 300.
executory devises, devises presumed to be in præsenti, 301.
executory devises, destruction of, 301.
incidents of, 302.
 tenure, 303.
 waste, 304.
 alienation, 305.
 descent of, 306.

FUTURE USES,
 defined, 298.
 statute of uses does not operate on, 254.
 descent of, 306.

FUTURO,
 freehold in, 284.

G

GENERAL OCCUPANCY.
 of estates per autre vie, 68.

GENERAL POWERS, 312.

GERMAN GRUNDBUCH, 413.

GIFT,
 creation of estate tail is, 42.

GIFTS TO CHARITIES,
 application of rule against perpetuities, 329.

GLOUCESTER,
 statute of, 66.

[The figures refer to pages.]

GRAND SERJEANTY,
    defined, 28.
GRANT,
    creation of easements by, 350.
    from state to private persons, 401.
    a common-law conveyance, 407.
GRANT AND DEMISE,
    implied covenant by, 440.
GRANTEE,
    in deed, designation of, 416.
GRANTING CLAUSE,
    requisites of, in deeds. 417.
GRANTORS,
    of joint estates not competent witnesses for each other, 439.
GROSS,
    powers in, 310.
GRUNDBUCH,
    the German, 413.
GUARDIANS,
    leases by, 131.
    conveyances by, 487.

H

HABENDUM,
    in deeds, 418.
HALF BLOOD,
    descent to, 485.
HAY BOTE,
    defined, 61.
HEAD OF A FAMILY,
    who is, 113.
HEIRS,
    as word of limitation of fee simple, 37.
    who are, 479.
    collateral, defined, 484.
        and ancestral lands, 483.
    what descends to, 497.
HEREDITAMENTS,
    defined, 3.
    corporeal and incorporeal, 348.

[The figures refer to pages.]

HIGHWAYS,
    defined, 361.
    dedication of, 362.
    as boundaries, 422.

HOMESTEAD,
    defined, 112.
    origin, 112.
    head of a family, who is, 113.
    who entitled to, 113.
    duration of, 115.
    in what estates, 116.
    amount of exemption, 117.
    urban and rural, 117.
    how acquired, 118.
        occupancy, 118.
        recorded notice, 119.
        selection, 120.
    how lost, 120.
        abandonment, 121.
        alienation, 122.
        waiver, 122.
    privileged debts, 124.
        debts contracted before incumbrances, 124.
        debts contracted before passage of homestead law, 124.
        debts contracted before acquisition, 124.
        liabilities for tort, 124.
        liens for creation, improvements, and preservation, 124.
        public debts, 124.
    federal, 126.
    when conveyance of not fraudulent, 393.

HORIZONTAL DIVISION,
    of realty, 4.
    easements created by, 365.

HOSTILE POSSESSION,
    necessary in acquiring title by adverse possession, 463.

HOTCHPOT, 482.

HOUSE BOTE,
    defined, 61.

I

ICE,
    by whom owned, 6.

IDIOTS,
    capacity to hold and convey real property, 383.

[The figures refer to pages.]

IMMOVABLES,
    and movables, 3.

IMPLICATION,
    ways of necessity by, 359.

IMPLIED COVENANTS,
    rights of landlord and tenant under, 138.
    by lessor, 138.
    by lessee, 139.
    to pay rent, 140.
    in deeds, 440.

IMPLIED NOTICE, 215.

IMPLIED TRUSTS,
    see "Trusts."

IMPROVEMENTS,
    by life tenant, 61.
    by dowress, 102.
    covered by mortgage, 185.
    by mortgagor, 195.
    in partition of joint estates, 346.

INCLOSURE,
    as evidence of adverse possession, 459.

INCORPOREAL HEREDITAMENTS,
    defined, 348.
    kinds of, 348.
    easements, 349.
        distinguished from licenses, 350.
        dominant estate, 350.
        servient estate, 350.
        essential qualities, 350.
        creation, 350.
            by grant, 350.
            by covenants, 351.
            by parol, 351.
            by prescription, 352.
        classification, 354.
        appendant or appurtenant and in gross, 354.
        continuous and discontinuous, 354.
        natural and conventional, 354.
        negative and affirmative, 354.
        incidents, 355.
            use of easement, 356.

[The figures refer to pages.]

INCORPOREAL HEREDITAMENTS—Continued,
    repairs, 356.
    obstruction, 356.
    destruction, 357.
        by abandonment, 357.
        by license, 357.
        by merger, 357.
        by misuser, 357.
        by release, 357.
    specific easements, 359.
        rights of way, 359.
            repair of, 361.
        highways, 361.
        light and air, 363.
        lateral and subjacent support, 365.
            horizontal ownership of buildings, 366.
        party walls, 366.
        partition fences, 368.
        in water, 368.
            subterranean waters, 371.
            surface water, 371.
            eaves' drip, 372.
            artificial water courses, 372.
    profits a prendre, 373.
    rents, 375.
        effect by quia emptores, 376.
        charge and seck. 375.
        service, 375.
        application of merger, 378.
    franchises, 378.
        alienation, 379.
        forfeiture, 379.
        taking under eminent domain, 379.
        for ferries, 379.
        for bridges and turnpike roads, 380.

INCUMBRANCES,
    tenant in tail need not pay off, 49.
    interest on, payment by life tenant, 60.

INDEFEASIBLE SEISIN,
    covenant of, 443.

INDEMNITY FUND,
    under registered title, 414.

[The figures refer to pages.]

INDENTURES,
    and deeds poll, 432.

INDEPENDENT COVENANTS,
    in deeds, 441.

INFANTS.
    leases by, 131.
    power to hold and convey realty, 382.
    disseisin of, 468.

INFEUDATION,
    defined, 27.

INFORMAL MORTGAGE.
    may be effective in equity, 191.

INHERITANCE,
    estates of, defined, 35, 76.
    by aliens, 388.
    by naturalized citizens, 388.

INSANE PERSONS,
    capacity to hold and convey realty, 383.
    disseisin of, 468.

INSOLVENT LAWS, 394.

INSURANCE,
    on mortgaged premises, 197.

INTENTION TO DISSEISE,
    necessary for title by adverse possession, 460.

INTERESSE TERMINI, 133.

INTEREST,
    unity of, in joint tenancies, 333.

INTOXICATED PERSONS,
    leases by, 131.

IRRIGATION,
    rights to water, 370.

ISSUE.
    failure of, 326.

J

JOINT DISSEISOR,
    abandonment of possession by, 466.

JOINT ESTATES,
    curtesy in, 79.
    dower in, 92.
        partnership lands, 93.

[The figures refer to pages.]

JOINT ESTATES—Continued,
    letting land on shares may create, 154.
    defined, 332.
    joint tenancies, 333.
    tenancies in common, 335.
    estates in coparcenary, 336.
    estates in entirety, 337.
        in the United States, 338.
    community system, 338.
    estates in partnership, 339.
    incidents of, 340.
        possession and disseisin, 340.
        accounting between co-tenants, 341.
        repairs and waste, 342.
        actions affecting, 343.
        transfer of, 343.
    partition, 344.
        method of division, 345.
        question of title cannot be settled, 345.
        failure of title, 346.
        compulsory, warranty of title, 346.
        improvements, 346.
    grantors of, not competent witnesses for each other, to deed, 439.
    estoppel in conveyance of, 455.

JOINT MORTGAGES, 336.

JOINT OWNER,
    what is disseisin of, 464.

JOINT TENANCIES, 333.
    unities, 333.
    conveyances by one tenant, 334.
    partition of, 344.

JOINT TENANT,
    lease by, 132.

JOINTURE,
    legal and equitable, 107.

JUDGMENT,
    reversal of, effect on title, 490.

JUDGMENT CREDITORS,
    when protected under recording acts, 225.

JUDGMENT LIEN,
    as breach of covenant against incumbrances, 445.

[The figures refer to pages.]

JUDICIAL PROCESS,
    title by, 486.
    conveyances under licenses, 486.
        by personal representatives, 487.
        by guardians, 487.
        of settled estates, 488.
    conveyances under decrees, 488.
        specific performance, 488.
        partition, 488.
        sales on execution, 489.
            effect of reversal of judgment, 490.
    tax titles, 490.
        forfeiture, 490.
        ministerial sales, 491.
        judicial sale, 492.
        redemption, 492
        tax deed, 492.
        estate taken by purchaser, 493.
    eminent domain, 494.
        compensation for land taken under right of, 495.

K

KNIGHT'S SERVICE,
    tenure by, 27.

L

LACHES,
    defeating dower, 111.
LAKES,
    as boundaries, 423.
LAND,
    is real property, 3.
LANDLORD,
    defined, 128.
LANDLORD AND TENANT,
    rights and liabilities, 134.
        under express covenants, 134.
            covenants running with the land, 136.
            personal covenants, 136.
        under implied covenants, 138.
            covenants by the lessor, 138.
            covenants by the lessee, 139.
        rent, 140.

[The figures refer to pages.]

LANDLORD AND TENANT—Continued,
    independent of covenant, 141.
        landlord's right to protect reversion, 141.
        tenant's right to exclusive possession, 142.
        tenant estopped to deny landlord's title, 143.
        tenant's right to estovers, 143.
        tenant's right to emblements, 143.
        tenant's liability for waste, 143.
        distress for rent, 145.
    disseisin of tenant is disseisin of landlord, 468.

LANDS,
    tenements and hereditaments, 3.

LAND SYSTEM,
    public, 402.

LAPSED DEVISES, 479.

LAPSE OF TIME,
    termination of estates for years by, 150.

LATENT AMBIGUITIES,
    in description of property, 420.

LATERAL AND SUBJACENT SUPPORT, 365.

LAWFUL SEISIN,
    covenant of, 443.

LEASE,
    defined, 128.
    a common-law conveyance, 407.
    when writing necessity for, 407.
    under registered titles, 413.
    is a deed, 415.
    not breach of covenant of seisin, 444.
    as breach of covenant against incumbrances, 445.

LEASEHOLD,
    see "Estates for Years."

LEGAL CAPACITY,
    to hold and convey realty, 381.
    infants, 382.
    persons of unsound mind, 383.
    drunkards, 385.
    married women, 385.
        conveyance from husband, 386.
        separate examination, 386.
        wills of, 387.

[The figures refer to pages.]

LEGAL CAPACITY—Continued,
   aliens, 387.
      inheritance by, 388.
      office found, 388.
      inheritance by naturalized citizens, 388.
   corporations, 389.

LEGAL ESTATES, 251.

LEGAL LIFE ESTATES, 69.
   homestead has incidents of, 115.

LESSEE.
   defined, 128.
   implied covenants by, 139.
   transfer of estate by, 148.

LESSOR,
   ined, 128.
   implied covenants by, 138.
   transfer of estate by, 147.

LETTING LAND ON SHARES, 154.

LETTING OF LODGINGS,
   the relation established, 162.

LEX LOCI,
   governs title by devise, 474.

LIABILITY FOR TORT,
   homestead not exempt from, 124.

LICENSES.
   defined, 165.
   creation, 165.
   incidents of, 166.
   not assignable, 166.
   revocation, 167.
   distinguished from easements, 350.
   destruction of easements by, 357.
   conveyances under, 486.

LIEN,
   vendor's, an equitable mortgage, 192.
   vendee's, an equitable mortgage, 194.

LIEN THEORY,
   of mortgage, 183.

[The figures refer to pages.]

LIFE ESTATES,
    defined, 55.
    creation of, 55.
    kinds of, 55.
    per autre vie, 55.
    conventional, 56.
        creation, words of limitation, 57.
    legal, 69.
    incidents, 58.
        alienation, 59.
        interests on incumbrances, 60.
        apportionment of rent, 60.
        emblements, 61.
        estovers, 61.
        improvements, 61.
        repairs, 61.
        waste, 62.
        merger, 66.
    estate by curtesy has incidents of, 79.
    homestead in, 116.
    restraints on alienation of, 395.

LIGHT AND AIR,
    easement of, 363.

LIMITATION,
    estates on, see "Estates on Limitation."
    of trustee's estate, 261.
    in creation of fee simple, 36.
    technical words of, not required in creation of powers, 309.
    title by, 457.
    words of in wills, 473.

LINEAL RELATIONS,
    defined, 483.

LIS PENDENS,
    is constructive notice, 218.

LIVERY OF SEISIN, 406.

LOCATION,
    of rights of way, 360.

LODGINGS,
    see "Letting of Lodgings."

REAL PROP.—40

[The figures refer to pages.]

LOGGING,
  rights of boom companies, 370.
LOST CORNERS,
  how located, 424.
LUNATICS,
  leases by, 131.

M

MALES,
  preference of, in descent, 482.
  in collateral lines, 485.
MANURE,
  when realty, 17.
MAPS,
  in descriptions in deeds, 421.
MARRIAGE,
  an incident of feudal tenure, 29.
  a requisite of curtesy, 74.
  a requisite of dower, 84.
  is a valuable consideration, 393.
MARRIED WOMEN,
  leases by, 131.
  capacity to hold and convey real property, 385.
  conveyance from husband, 386.
  separate examination, 386.
  wills of, 387.
  acknowledgment by, 437.
  estoppel of, by conveyance, 455.
  disseisin of, 468.
MARRIED WOMEN'S ACTS, 73.
MARSHALING,
  of mortgage securities, 204.
MERGER,
  estate tail not subject to, 50.
  an incident of life estates, 66.
  termination of estates for years by, 152.
  discharge of mortgage by, 231.
  of particular estate may destroy contingent remainder, 293.
  destruction of easements by, 357.
  destruction of profits a prendre by, 375.
  application of, to rents, 378.

[The figures refer to pages.]

METALS,
    when real property, 7.
MILITARY TENURES,
    abolished, 29.
MILLS,
    water rights, 370.
MINERALS,
    when real property, 7.
MINES,
    when opening is waste, 64.
MINISTERIAL SALES,
    tax titles by, 491.
MISUSER,
    of easement, destruction by, 357.
MONOMANIA,
    as affecting capacity to convey realty, 384.
MONTH TO MONTH,
    tenancies for, see "Tenancies from Year to Year."
MONUMENTS,
    description by, in deeds, 422.
MORTGAGEE,
    rights and liabilities, see "Mortgages."
    purchase by, at foreclosure, 249.
MORTGAGES,
    registration of, see "Registration."
    dower in, 89.
    is an estate on condition, 169.
    defined, 180.
    the usual condition of defeasance, 181.
    parties to, 182.
    theories of, 182.
    nature, 183.
    what may be mortgaged, 184.
    form of, 186.
        deed absolute, 187.
        parol defeasance, 187.
        sale with agreement to reconvey, 189.
        deed of trust, 190.
        equitable mortgage, 190.
            agreement to mortgage, 191.
            informal mortgage may be effective in equity, 191.

628 INDEX.

[The figures refer to pages.]

MORTGAGES—Continued,
  vendor's lien, 192.
  vendee's lien, 194.
  deposit of title deeds, 192.
 rights and liabilities of mortgagor and mortgagee, 194.
  nature of mortgagor's estate, 195.
  possession of mortgaged premises, 196.
  insurance on mortgaged premises, 197.
  accounting by mortgagee, 199.
   debits, 200.
   credits, 201.
   annual rests, 202.
  marshaling, 204.
  subrogation, 203.
   relief of the real by the personal estate, 204.
 assignment of equity of redemption, 205.
  no mortgage without an equity of redemption, 205.
 assignment of, 209.
  by operation of law, 211.
 priority, 212.
  actual notice, 213.
  implied notice, 215.
  constructive notice, 215.
   possession, 216.
   recitals in title deeds, 216.
   lis pendens, 218.
   registration, 218.
 discharge of, 227.
  performance, 227.
  payment, 227.
  tender, 230.
  merger, 231.
  redemption, 233.
   who may redeem, 234.
   amount payable, 235.
   contribution to redeem, 236.
   redemption, when barred, 237.
  form of, 238.
 foreclosure, 239.
  when right accrues, 239.
  when right is barred, 240.
  personal remedies, 241.
  decree for deficiency, 241.

[The figures refer to pages.]

MORTGAGES—Continued,
 receivers, 241.
 kinds of, 242.
  by entry and possession, 243.
  by writ of entry, 244.
  in equity, 244.
   parties plaintiff, 244.
   parties defendant, 245.
 strict foreclosure, 248.
 decree of sale, 248.
 power of sale, 248.
 purchase by mortgagee, 249.
 when subject to rule against perpetuities, 328.
 joint, 336.
 under registered titles, 413.
 are deeds, 415.
 as breach of covenant against incumbrances, 444.
 not breach of covenant of seisin, 444.
 not revocation of devise, 476.

MORTGAGOR,
 rights and liabilities, see "Mortgages."
 lease by, 132.
 disseisin of mortgagee by, 195.

MORTMAIN,
 statutes of, 389.

MOVABLES AND IMMOVABLES, 3.

N

NAKED POWERS, 311.
 public officer selling for taxes has, 491.

NAME,
 assumed, grantee may be designated by, 416.

NATURAL EASEMENTS, 354.

NATURALIZED CITIZENS,
 inheritance by, 388.

NAVIGABLE RIVERS,
 ownership of bed, 5.
 as boundaries, 422.

NECESSITY,
 ways of, 359.

NEGATIVE EASEMENTS, 354.

630 INDEX.

[The figures refer to pages.]

NONEXCLUSIVE POWERS, 312.

NOTICE,
    acquisition of homestead by, 119.
    to terminate tenancy at will, 157.
    to terminate tenancy from year to year, 161.
    to terminate tenancy at sufferance, 165.
    priority of conveyances depends upon, 212.
    actual, 213.
    implied, 215.
    constructive, 216.
        possession, 216.
        recitals in title deeds, 216.
        lis pendens, 218.
        registration, 218.
            of what facts registration is, 222.
            to whom registration is, 222.

NOTORIOUS POSSESSION,
    necessary in acquiring title by adverse possession, 462.

NUISANCE,
    owner in fee simple must not maintain, 39.

NUMBER OF OWNERS,
    estates as to, 332.

O

OBSTRUCTION,
    of easements, 356.

OCCUPANCY,
    acquisition of homestead by, 118.
    title by, 457.

OCCUPANTS,
    general and special of estates per autre vie, 68.

OFFICE FOUND,
    divesting title of aliens, 388.

OFFICER,
    De facto, acknowledgment before, 438.

OFFICES,
    are incorporeal hereditaments, 349.

OPTION TO PURCHASE,
    may be mortgaged, 185.

OUSTER,
    necessary in acquisition of title by adverse possession, 459.

[The figures refer to pages.]

OWNERS,
number of estates as to, 332.

OWNERSHIP,
no absolute ownership of land under feudal system, 27.

P

PAIS,
estoppel in, 451.

PAROL,
easements cannot be created by, 351.

PAROL DEFEASANCE,
mortgage may have, 187.

PARTICULAR ESTATE,
preceding a remainder, 284.
destruction of, may destroy contingent remainder, 293.
expiration of, may destroy contingent remainder, 293.
forfeiture of, may destroy contingent remainder, 293.
merger of, may destroy contingent remainder, 293.

PARTIES,
to a mortgage, 182.
in creation of express trusts, 263.
names of, in deeds, 416.

PARTITION,
of joint estates, 344.
questions of title cannot be settled in, 345.
compulsory, warranty of title, 346.
failure of title in, 346.
improvements, 346.
horizontal, easements created by, 365.
a common-law conveyance, 408.
right of eldest male to elect, 483.
conveyance of title by, 488.

PARTITION FENCES, 368.

PARTNERSHIP,
realty, homestead in, 116.
dower in, 93.
estates in, 339.
partition, 344.

PASSIVE TRUSTS,
incidents of, 271.

[The figures refer to pages.]

PASTURE,
 common of, 373.
PATENT AND CERTIFICATE, 402.
PAYMENT,
 discharge of mortgage by, 227.
PENSIONS,
 incorporeal hereditaments, 349.
PER AUTRE VIE,
 defined, 55.
PER CAPITA,
 taking, in title by descent, 483.
PERFORMANCE,
 discharge of mortgage by, 227.
PER MY ET PER TOUT, 333.
PERPETUITIES,
 rule against, 322.
  not one of construction, 324.
  limits alienation of fee simple, 40.
  distinguished from restraints on alienation, 322.
  to what estates the rule applies, 323.
  gifts to charities, 329.
  effect of limitations too remote, 325.
  application to charitable trusts, 276.
  application to powers, 328.
  in United States, 330.
PERSONAL CAPACITY,
 to hold and convey realty, see "Legal Capacity."
 and restraints on alienation, 392.
PERSONAL COVENANTS,
 in leases, 136.
 in deeds, 441.
PERSONAL ESTATE,
 bound to relieve mortgaged realty, 204.
PERSONAL INTERESTS IN LAND, 24.
PERSONAL REMEDIES,
 in foreclosure, 241.
PERSONAL REPRESENTATIVES,
 conveyances of land by, 487.
PERSONS OF UNSOUND MIND,
 power to hold and convey realty, 383.

[The figures refer to pages.]

PER STIRPES,
  taking, in title by descent, 483.
PETTY SERJEANTY,
  defined, 28.
PISCARY,
  common of, 373.
PLATS AND MAPS,
  in descriptions in deeds, 421.
PLOUGH BOTE,
  defined, 61.
POSSESSION,
  see "Adverse Possession."
  lessee's exclusive right to, 142.
  of mortgaged premises, 196.
  is constructive notice, 216.
  by trustee not adverse, 274.
  unity of, in joint tenancies, 333.
  unity of, in tenancy in common, 335.
  constructive, 460.
  of joint estates, 340.
POSSIBILITY,
  may be devised, 474.
  of reverter, 281.
  on a possibility, 327.
  of issue extinct, tenant in tail after, 52.
POSTHUMOUS CHILDREN,
  descent to, 480.
POWER OF ATTORNEY,
  to execute a deed, 431.
POWER OF SALE,
  foreclosure by, 248.
POWERS,
  defined, 306.
  donor defined, 307.
  donee defined, 307.
  appointee defined, 307.
  distinguished from estates, 308.
  common-law powers, 308.
  creation, 309.
  revocation and appointment, 309.

[The figures refer to pages.]

POWERS—Continued,
    classes of, as to donee, 310.
        appendant and in gross, 310.
        collateral or naked powers. 311.
    classes of, as to appointees, 311.
        general powers, 312.
        special, 312.
            exclusive, 312.
            nonexclusive, 312.
    execution, 314.
        who may execute, 314.
        form of, 315.
        time of, 317.
        compelling, 318.
        defective, 318.
        excessive, 318.
    rights of creditors, 320.
        beneficial powers. 320.
    destruction, 321.
    application of rule against perpetuities to, 328.
    naked, public officer, selling for taxes has, 491.

PRECATORY WORDS,
    in creation of express trusts, 261.

PRECEDENT,
    see "Conditions Precedent and Subsequent."

PRE-EMPTION,
    of public lands, 404.
    laws repealed, 404.

PREFERENCE OF MALES,
    in title by descent, 482.
        in collateral lines, 485.

PRESCRIPTION,
    creation of easements by, 352.
        light and air, 363.

PRESENT ESTATES,
    and future, 279.

PRIMARY AND SECONDARY,
    conveyances, 405.

PRIMOGENITURE, 483.

PRIORITY,
    of mortgages and other conveyances, 212.

[The figures refer to pages.]

PRIVATE PERSONS,
acquisition of title by, see "Title."

PROCREATION,
words of, in creating estates tail, 47.

PROFITS A PRENDRE, 373.
commons, 373.
creation, 374.
destruction, 375.
alienation, 375.
merger, 375.

PROPERTY,
real and personal, 1.

PROTECTION,
of reversion by landlord, 141.

PUBLIC DEBTS,
homestead not exempt from, 124.

PUBLIC DOMAIN,
sale of, 402.

PUBLIC LANDS,
entry on, 402.
pre-emption, 404.

PUBLIC LAND SYSTEM, 402.

PUBLIC TRUSTS,
see "Charitable Trusts."

PURCHASE,
title by, 399.

PURCHASE MONEY MORTGAGE,
priority of, 225.

Q

QUALITY OF ESTATES, 169.

QUANTITY,
description by, 425.

QUANTITY OF ESTATES, 34.

QUARANTINE, 94.

QUARRIES,
when opening is waste, 64.

QUASI ENTAIL,
defined, 53.

[The figures refer to pages.]

QUIA EMPTORES,
    statute of, 30.
    application to rent service in fee, 376.

QUIET ENJOYMENT,
    covenant of, 448.

QUITCLAIM DEEDS, 412.
    technical words of limitation not necessary in, 37.
    covenant of special warranty in, 448.
    estoppel by, 454.
    whether color of title, 461.

R

RAILROAD CARS,
    whether real fixtures, 14, 16.

READING,
    of deeds, when requisite, 429.

REAL AND PERSONAL PROPERTY, 1.
    importance of distinction, 2.

REAL COVENANTS,
    in deeds, 441.

REAL FIXTURES,
    defined, 10.

REAL PROPERTY,
    equitable conversion, 23.
    corporate shares not, 24.
    long terms of years are, in some states, 24.

RECEIVERS,
    in foreclosure, 241.

RECITALS IN TITLE DEEDS,
    constructive notice, 216.
    estoppel by, 454.

RECOVERY,
    conveyance by married woman by, 386.

REDDENDUM,
    same as reservation, 418.

REDEMPTION,
    see "Equity of Redemption."
    discharge of mortgage by, 233.

[The figures refer to pages.]

REDEMPTION—Continued,
    of mortgage, who may redeem, 234.
        amount payable, 235.
        contribution, 236.
        when barred, 237.
    from tax sale, 492.

RE-ENTRY,
    for forfeiture, 150.

REGISTERED TITLES, 412.
    certificates of title, 413.
    transfers, 413.
    adverse possession abolished, 414.
    indemnity fund, 414.

REGISTRATION,
    constructive notice by, 218.
    what instruments recorded, 219.
    manner of recording, 220.
    of what facts record is notice, 222.
    to whom record is notice, 222.
    of deeds, 439.

RELATIONS,
    who are lineal, 483.

RELATIONSHIP,
    by consanguinity and affinity, 483.

RELEASE,
    of dower by wife, 106.
    destruction of easements by, 357.
    a common-law conveyance, 408.

RELIEF,
    an incident of feudal tenure, 29.

REMAINDER-MAN,
    adverse possession against, 464.

REMAINDERS,
    defined, 281.
    how created, 282.
    when they must take effect, 283.
    freehold in futuro, 284.
    the particular estate, 284.
    distinguished from shifting uses and devises, 285.
    cross, 286.
    successive, 286.

[The figures refer to pages.]

REMAINDERS—Continued,
    alternate, 287.
    vested, 288.
        destruction of, 289.
        not subject to rule against perpetuities, 326.
    contingent, 289.
        distinguished from vested, 290.
        estates which will support, 291.
        New York Code definition, 291.
        test of, 291.
        contingency on which remainder may depend, 292.
        destruction of, 293.
            by destruction of particular estate, 293.
            by expiration of particular estate, 293.
            by forfeiture of particular estate, 293.
            by merger of particular estate, 293.
            trustees to preserve, 293.
            liability to destruction removed by statute, 293.
        whether subject to rule against perpetuities, 326.
    tenure, 304.
    alienation, 305.
    descent of, 306.

REMEDIES,
    for waste, 66.

REMOTENESS,
    rule against, 322.

RENT,
    apportionment of, 60, 377.
        in estates per autre vie, 68.
        to dowress, 102.
    dower in, 87.
    implied covenant to pay, 140.
    distress for, 145.
    tenant at sufferance not liable for, 164.
    may be mortgaged, 185.
    charge and seck, 375.
    service, 375.
    distress, 376.
    effect of quia emptores, 376.
    estates in, 376.
    as an incorporeal hereditament, 375.
        creation, 377.

[The figures refer to pages.]

RENT—Continued,
 application of merger, 378.
 extinguished by eviction, 378.

RENUNCIATION,
 of title by devise, 475.

REPAIRS,
 of rights of way, 361.
 by life tenant, 61.
 when failing to make is waste, 65.
 by dowress, 101.
 duty of tenant from year to year to make, 160.
 of easements, 356.
 by joint tenants, 342.

REQUISITES OF DEEDS,
 see "Deeds."

RESERVATION,
 in deeds, 418.
  same as reddendum, 418.

RESTRAINTS ON ALIENATION, 390.
 history of right of alienation, 390.
 kinds of, 390.
 imposed by law, 390.
 by form of estate, 392.
 in favor of creditors, 392.
 personal capacity, 392.
 bankrupt and insolvent laws, 394.
 imposed in creation of estate, 394.
 separate estates of married women, 396.
 spendthrift trusts, 396.

RESULTING TRUSTS,
 see "Trusts."

RESULTING USES, 266.

REVERSAL OF JUDGMENT,
 effect of on title by sale on execution, 490.

REVERSION,
 landlord's right to protect, 141.
 defined, 280.
 tenure, 303.
 alienation of, 305.
 descent of, 306.
 not subject to rule against perpetuities, 326.

[The figures refer to pages.]

REVERTER,
> possibility of, 281.

REVOCATION,
> of license, 167.
> powers of, 309.

RIGHTS OF COMMON,
> see "Commons."

RIGHT OF ENTRY,
> to defeat estate on condition, 176.
> whether subject to rule against perpetuities, 327.
> by disseisee, 458.

RIGHT OF USER,
> of fee simple, 39.

RIGHT OF WAY, 359.
> by necessity, 360.
> use of, 360.
> location, 360.
> not a breach of covenant of seisin, 444.

RIPARIAN OWNER,
> easements of, 369.

RIVERS,
> as boundaries, 422.

ROYAL MINES,
> none in United States, 7.

RULE AGAINST ACCUMULATIONS,
> see "Accumulations."

RULE AGAINST PERPETUITIES,
> see "Perpetuities."

RULE IN SHELLEY'S CASE, 295.

RURAL,
> homestead, 117.

S

SALE,
> power of, see "Power of Sale."
> with agreement to reconvey may be a mortgage, 189.
> judicial, tax title by, 492.
> on execution, see "Execution."
>> title by, 489.
>>> effect of reversal of judgment, 490.

[The figures refer to pages.]

SCUTAGE,
    origin, 29.

SEAL,
    defined, 429.
    when necessary for deed, 429.

SECONDARY CONVEYANCES, 405.

SEISIN,
    defined, 31.
    in fact, 31, 406.
    in law, 31, 406.
    transitory as giving dower, 84.
    of future estates, 303.
    title by adverse possession, 458.
    of wife requisite of curtesy, 75.

SELECTION OF HOMESTEAD, 120.

SEPARATE ESTATE,
    of wife, 72.
    restraints on alienation of, 396.

SEPARATE EXAMINATION,
    of married woman, 386.

SEPARATE USE,
    statute of uses does not operate on estates for, 254.

SERIES,
    limitations to and rule against perpetuities, 328.

SERJEANTY,
    defined, 28.

SERVIENT ESTATE, 350.

SETTLED ESTATES,
    conveyances of, 488.

SEVERANCE,
    may make real fixtures personalty, 14.

SHELLEY'S CASE,
    rule in, 295.

SHIFTING DEVISE,
    distinguished from remainder, 285.

SHIFTING USES, 300.
    distinguished from remainder, 285.
    alienation, 305.

[The figures refer to pages.]

SIGNING,
> requisite of deeds, 430.

SOCAGE,
> tenure in, 28.

SPECIAL OCCUPANTS,
> of estates per autre vie, 68.

SPECIAL POWERS, 312.
> exclusive and nonexclusive, 312.

SPECIAL WARRANTY,
> covenant of, 446.

SPECIFIC EASEMENTS, 359.

SPECIFIC PERFORMANCE,
> conveyance of title by, 488.

SPENDTHRIFT TRUSTS, 396.
> may prevent involuntary alienation, 41.

SPRINGING USES, 299.
> alienation, 305.

STATE,
> acquisition of title by, 399.
>> discovery, conquest, and treaty, 399.
>> confiscation and escheat, 399.
>> transfer from individuals, 399.
>> power of eminent domain, 399.
>
> grant from, to private persons, 401.

STATUTE,
> de donis conditionalibus, 44, 46.
> of Gloucester, 66.
> of frauds, creation of estates for years, 132.
>> in creation of express trusts, 262.
>
> of limitations, barring dower, 111.
>> title by, 457.
>
> of mortmain, 389.
> of quia emptores, 30.
> of uses, 253.
>> when the statute does not operate, 254.
>> in the United States, 254.
>> future estates under, 298.
>> conveyance under, 409.
>
> of wills, future estates under, 300.

[The figures refer to pages.]

STATUTORY CONVEYANCE, 411.

STRICT FORECLOSURE, 248.

SUBINFEUDATION,
 prohibited by quia emptores, 30.

SUBJACENT SUPPORT, 365.

SUBLEASE,
 defined, 148.
 liability of subtenant, 149.

SUBROGATION,
 of insurer to rights of mortgagee, 199, 203.

SUBSEQUENT,
 see "Condition Precedent and Subsequent."

SUBTENANTS,
 under feudal system, 26.

SUBTENURE,
 what is, 27.

SUBTERRANEAN WATERS,
 easements in, 371.

SUCCESSIVE REMAINDERS, 286.

SUFFERANCE,
 see "Tenancy at Sufferance."

SUPPORT,
 lateral and subjacent, 365.

SURFACE WATERS,
 easements in, 371.

SURRENDER,
 termination of estates for years by, 152
 a common-law conveyance, 408.

SURVEY,
 the congressional, 402.

SURVIVORSHIP,
 doctrine of, in joint tenancies, 337.
  in estates in entirety, 338.

T

TACKING,
 of adverse possession, 466.

TALTARUM'S CASE,
 recognized common recoveries, 51.

[The figures refer to pages.]

TAX DEED, 492.

TAXES,
    fee simple liable for, 41.
    payment by dowress, 102.
    as breach of covenants against incumbrances, **445.**

TAX TITLES, 490.
    by forfeiture, 490.
    ministerial sales, 491.
    judicial sale, 492.
    redemption, 490, 492.
    tax deed, 492.
    estate taken by purchaser, 493

TENANCIES,
    at will defined, 155.
        incidents, 156.
        termination, 157.
    from year to year, 158.
        incidents, 160.
        termination, 161.
    at sufferance, 163.
        creation, 163.
        incidents, 164.
        termination, 165.
    in common defined, 335.
        unities necessary, 335.
        joint mortgages, 336.
        partition of, 344.
        creation, 158.

TENANT,
    see "Landlord and Tenant."
    under feudal system, 26.
    defined, 128.
    by curtesy, lease by, 132.
    in dower, lease by, 132.
    in common, lease by, 132.

TENDER,
    discharge of mortgage by, 230.

TENEMENTS, 3.

TENURE,
    defined, 26.
    kinds of, 27.

[The figures refer to pages.]

TENURE—Continued,
 by knight's service, 27.
 by serjeanty, 28.
 by grand serjeanty, 28.
 by petty serjeanty, 28.
 in frankalmoigne, 28.
 in socage, 28.
 villein, 28.
 incidents, 29.
  aids, 29.
  marriage, 29.
  relief, 29.
  wardship, 29.
  escheat and forfeiture, 30.
 services commuted for money payments, 29.
 military abolished, 29.
 statute of quia emptores, 30.
 in United States, 31.
 unknown forms cannot be created, 40.
 of future estates, 303.
 in capite, 27.
 in chief, 27.

TIME,
 unity of, in joint tenancies, 333.
 of enjoyment, estates as to, 279.
 of execution of power, 317.

TITHES, 349.

TITLE,
 defined, 399.
 unity of, in joint tenancies, 333.
 acquisition of, by state, 399.
  by confiscation and escheat, 399.
  by discovery, conquest, and treaty, 399.
  by transfer from individual, 399.
  under power of eminent domain, 399.
 descent and purchase, 399.
 acquisition by private persons, 401.
  by grant from state, 401.
   public land system, 402.
   certificate and patents, 402.
   pre-emption, 404.
   pre-emption laws repealed, 404.

[The figures refer to pages.]

TITLE—Continued,
  conveyance, 405.
  common-law conveyances, 405.
  registered, 412.
    certificates of, 413.
    transfers, 413.
    adverse possession abolished, 414.
    indemnity fund, 414.
  requisites of deeds, 414.
    property to be conveyed, 415.
    granting clause, 417.
    names of parties, 416.
    words of conveyance, 416.
    exceptions, 417.
    reservations, 418.
    habendum, 418.
    description of the property, 419.
      plats and maps, 421.
      monuments, 422.
      courses and distances, 424.
      quantity, 425.
      appurtenances, 425.
    execution of the writing, 426.
      consideration, 427.
      what writing necessary, 427.
      date, 428.
      alterations, 428.
      filling blanks, 428.
      reading, 429.
      sealing, 429.
      signing, 430.
      power of attorney, 431.
      indentures and deeds poll, 432.
    delivery and acceptance, 433.
      delivery in escrow, 435.
    acknowledgment, 436.
    witnesses, 439.
    registry, 439.
  covenants for, 440.
    express and implied, 440.
    real and personal, 440.
    independent and dependent, 441.
    of seisin, 442.

[The figures refer to pages.]

TITLE—Continued,
    when broken, 442.
    how broken, 442.
    against incumbrances, 444.
        how broken, 444.
    of warranty, 446.
        how broken, 446.
        action for breach, 449.
        special warranty, 446.
    for further assurance, 449.
  by estoppel, 450.
    division lines, 453.
  by adverse possession, 456.
    requisites of, 456.
    seisin and disseisin, 458.
    effect of descent cast, 459.
    must be actual, 459.
    ouster necessary, 459.
    constructive possession, 460.
    color of title, 460.
    intention to disseise necessary, 460.
    must be visible or notorious, 462.
    must be hostile and adverse, 463.
        when possession up to division fence is adverse, 463.
    must be exclusive, 465.
    must be continuous, 466.
        tacking, 466.
        joint disseisors, 466.
    against whom possession is adverse, 468.
    disabilities of persons, 468.
    abandonment, 469.
    length of possession necessary, 469.
  by occupancy, 457.
  by accretion, 470.
    alluvion, 470.
  by devise, 472.
    description of property, 473.
    operative words, 473.
    what can be devised, 474.
    what law governs, 474.
    nature of, 475.
    renunciation of, 475.

[The figures refer to pages.]

TITLE—Continued,
 revocation by alteration of estate, 476.
 lapsed devises, 477.
 by descent, 478.
  what descends, 479.
  posthumous children, 480.
  illegitimate children, 480.
  advancements, 481.
   hotchpot, 482.
  canons of descent, 482.
   descending and ascending lines, 482.
   preference of males, 482.
    in collateral lines, 485.
   collateral heirs and ancestral lands, 483.
   primogeniture, 483.
   whole and half blood, 485.
   escheat, 485.
 by judicial process, 486.
  conveyances under licenses, 486.
   by guardians, 487.
   by personal representatives, 487.
   of settled estates, 488.
   under decrees, 488.
   partition, 488.
   specific performance, 488.
   sales on execution, 489.
    effect of reversal of judgment, 490.
  tax titles, 490.
   forfeiture, 490.
   ministerial sale, 491.
   judicial sale, 492.
   tax deed, 492.
   redemption, 490, 492.
   estate taken by purchaser, 493.
  eminent domain, 494.
   compensation for land taken under right of, 495.
 procured by fraud raises constructive trust, 270.

TITLE DEEDS,
 mortgage by deposit of, 192.
 recitals in, constructive notice, 216.

TORRENS' TITLE SYSTEM, 412.

TRADE FIXTURES, 16.

[The figures refer to pages.]

TRANSFER,
    of estates for years, 147.
        by operation of law, 149.
    of joint estates, 343.
    of registered titles, 413.

TRANSITORY SEISIN,
    as giving dower, 84.

TREATY,
    acquisition of title by, 399.

TREES,
    when real property, 8.
    when fixtures, 21.
    when cutting is waste, 64.

TRUSTEE,
    defined, 260.
    leases by, 131.
    limitation of estate of, 261.
    rights and liabilities of, 271.
    interest of, 272.
    possession by, not adverse, 274.
    to preserve contingent remainders, 293.
    disseisin of, is disseisin of cestui que trust, 468.

TRUST,
    deed of, may be a mortgage, 190.
    defined, 252.
    classification of, 257.
    executed and executory, 258.
    express, 258.
        creation of, 260.
            precatory words, 261.
            statute of frauds, 262.
            parties, 263.
    implied, 264.
        resulting, 265.
            legal title only conveyed, 266.
            consideration paid by another, 267.
            failure of object of trust, 267.
            deed to wife or child, 268.
        constructive, 269.
            fraud an essential element of, 269.
            raised by titles procured by fraud, 270.
            creditors do not have, 271.

[The figures refer to pages.]

TRUST—Continued,
    charitable, defined, 274.
        objects of, 275.
        creation, 275.
        distinguished from private, 274.
            beneficiary indefinite, 276.
            doctrine of cy-pres, 276.
            perpetuities and accumulations, 276.
    when subject to rule against perpetuities, 328.
    spendthrift, 396.
    by operation of law, statute of uses does not operate on, 254.

TURBARY,
    common of, 373.

TURNPIKE ROADS,
    franchises for, 380.

TYRRELL'S CASE, 256.

U

UNITY,
    of interest in joint tenancy, 333.
    of possession in joint tenancies, 333.
        in tenancy in common, 335.
    of time in joint tenancies, 333.
    of title in joint tenancies, 333.

UNRECORDED CONVEYANCES,
    see "Registration."

UNSOUND MIND,
    persons of, power to hold and convey realty, 383.

URBAN HOMESTEAD, 117.

USE,
        see "Trust."
    defined, 252.
    origin, 252.
    upon a use, statute of uses does not operate on, 254.

V

VENDEE'S LIEN,
    an equitable mortgage, 194.

VENDOR'S LIEN,
    an equitable mortgage, 192.

VESTED INTERESTS,
    rule against perpetuities does not apply to, 326.

[The figures refer to pages.]

VESTED REMAINDERS,
see "Remainders."

VILLEINAGE, 28.

VILLEIN TENURE, 28.

VISIBLE POSSESSION,
necessary in acquiring title by adverse possession, 462.

VOID CONDITIONS, 172.

VOLUNTARY PARTITION, 344.

VOLUNTARY WASTE, 62.

VOUCHING TO WARRANTY,
in common recovery, 50.

W

WAIVER,
of homestead, 122.
of forfeiture of estate on conditions, 175.

WALLS,
see "Party Walls."

WARDSHIP,
an incident of tenure, 29.

WARRANTY,
doctrine of, in common recovery, 51.
assignment of mortgage does not create, 211.
covenant of, 446.
estoppel by, 454.

WARRANTY DEEDS, 422.

WASTE,
equitable, 62.
voluntary, 62.
tenant without impeachment for, 62.
husbandry, 63.
cutting trees, 64.
mines and quarries, 64.
buildings and fences, 65.
by strangers, liability of tenant for, 65.
as incident of estate during coverture, 71.
defeating dower, 111.
lessee liable for, 143.
tenant in tail not liable for, 49.
life tenant liable for, 62.

[The figures refer to pages.]

WASTE—Continued,
   an incident of tenancies at will, 156.
   by mortgagor, 195.
   protection of future estates, 304.
   by joint tenants, 342.
   remedies for, 66.
   double and treble damages for, 66.
WATER,
   when rights in are real property, 4.
   easements in, 368.
      subterranean, 371.
      surface, 371.
WATER COURSE,
   what is, 369.
   artificial, 372.
WAY,
   rights of, see "Rights of Way."
WEAKNESS OF MIND,
   as affecting capacity to hold and convey realty, 383.
WHOLE BLOOD,
   descent to, 485.
WILLS,
      see "Statute of Wills."
   of married women, 387.
   transfer of title by, 473.
WITNESSES,
   to deeds, 439.
WOMEN,
   see "Married Women."
WORDS OF LIMITATION,
   see "Limitation."
WRITING,
   what requisite in deeds, 426.
WRIT OF ENTRY,
   foreclosure by, 244.

Y

YEAR TO YEAR,
   see "Tenancy from Year to Year."

Lightning Source UK Ltd.
Milton Keynes UK
UKHW011822050220
358245UK00001B/77